Glebe Collegiate Institute. Children's writer; worked variously as a waiter, taxi driver, bricklayer, and jazz singer. Recipient: Canadian Library Association Book of the Year awards, 1983, for *Up to Low,* and 1989, for *Easy Avenue;* Vicky Metcalf Body of Work award, Canadian Authors Association; Mr. Christie Book of the Year award; three times runner up, Governor General's award, Canadian Authors Association. Address: 539 Rowanwood, Ottawa, ON K2A 3C9, Canada.

PUBLICATIONS FOR YOUNG ADULTS

Fiction

Hey, Dad! Toronto, Groundwood Books, 1978.
You Can Pick Me up at Peggy's Cove. Toronto, Groundwood Books, 1979.
Up to Low. Toronto, Groundwood Books, 1982.
Angel Square. Toronto, Groundwood Books, 1984.
Easy Avenue. Toronto, Groundwood Books, 1988.
Covered Bridge. Toronto, Groundwood Books, 1990.
Spud Sweetgrass. Toronto, Groundwood Books, 1992.

PUBLICATIONS FOR ADULTS

Other

Editor, *The Who's Who of Children's Literature.* London, Evelyn, 1968.
English and Englishness. London, and New York, Routledge, 1989.

*

Media Adaptations: *Angel Square* (film directed by Ann Wheeler).

Biography: Essay in *Something about the Author Autobiography Series,* Volume 16, Detroit, Gale, 1993.

Critical Study: Entry in *Children's Literature Review,* Volume 22, Detroit, Gale, 1991, pp. 27-34.

*   *   *

Brian Doyle's work presents universal themes of adolescence in deceptively light and refreshingly humorous stories. Deeply grounded in both place and character, Doyle's blunt though careful articulation of detail and event results in fast-moving and enjoyable narratives. While in several of his novels there is a clear focus on child-father relationships, other themes such as self-determination, independence, grief, responsibility, and love are also raised.

Doyle's work can be divided into three groups. His first two novels, *Hey, Dad!* (1978) and *You Can Pick Me up at Peggy's Cove* (1979), are first person accounts told by a sister and younger brother respectively and set in contemporary times. *Hey Dad!* tells the story of a family car trip across Canada from Ottawa to the west coast of Vancouver Island. Megan, the adolescent narrator, describes in hilarious detail the characters they meet, the mishaps they encounter, and her own diminishing resentment towards her rambunctious father as she learns how to talk with him. In *You Can Pick Me up at Peggy's Cove,* Megan's younger brother Ryan is sent to stay

with his aunt in Peggy's Cove, Nova Scotia, for the summer when their father temporarily "runs away" from the family. Colorful characters and a tentative exploration of Ryan's confusion at his father's abandonment carry this story through a somewhat tedious plot as Ryan falls in with a juvenile delinquent and tries to shock his father into coming back for him.

More successful and intriguing in their flirtation with fantastic characters and events, Doyle's next four novels all take place in Ottawa and the nearby Gatineau Hills at the end of, and shortly following World War II. In *Up to Low* (1982), he introduces Tommy, the narrator, and a crowd of other characters including the fanatically neat Aunt Dottie, Mean Hughie, his wife Poor Bridget, daughter Baby Bridget, and old Willie the Hummer. A trip with his father out to the backwoods of Low to open up the family cabin involves Tommy in a strange series of events with strong symbolic undertones. Mean Hughie dies and Tommy finds himself in a rowboat with his first love, Baby Bridget, transporting Hughie's coffin up the Gatineau River. Tommy is also the main protagonist in *Angel Square* (1984), a story which precludes *Up to Low* chronologically. In a wonderful evocation of Lowertown, one of Ottawa's working class neighborhoods, Tommy describes Angel Square as "a dangerous square as to cross four times a day" because of fights between the French Canadian "Pea Soups," the Jews, and the Catholic "Dogans." Not belonging to any of these groups, Tommy finds his identity in emulating "the Shadow," a radio mystery character. In this role, he sends notes to his love, Margot Lane, and investigates a neighborhood crime, only revealing his identity when he has established himself as a hero.

Doyle's light humor and intimate narrative style continue in a third series of two books, beginning with *Easy Avenue* (1988), the story of Hubbo O'Driscoll, a poor boy who moves away from Lowertown and starts hobnobbing with the rich. Colorfully named characters such as the wealthy golfer Mr. Donald D. DonaldmcDonald, Miss Collar-Cuff, the aristocratic old woman Hubbo reads to, and his first love, Fleurette Featherstone Fitchell, contribute to a thread of fantasy which weaves through this story and is further reinforced as an anonymous benefactor begins to send Hubbo monthly cheques. Hubbo's story continues in Doyle's next work, *Covered Bridge* (1990), but like *Up to Low,* this sequel moves into the rural setting of the lower Gatineau where the O'Driscoll family has relocated to a small farm. Hubbo takes a job as caretaker of the town's old covered bridge and in doing so embroils himself in a mystery involving a ghost, a lovelorn postman, a foolish priest, and a crazy goat. Lighter than his other stories, *Covered Bridge* presents a madcap ghost mystery for readers who like adventures.

In what is hopefully only the first of a third series of stories, Doyle's most recent book, *Spud Sweetgrass* (1992), brings together all of his strongest elements: a quick-moving plot, a strong sense of place, slightly fantastic characters, and an underlying foundation of deeper themes and moral conflicts. John or "Spud" Sweetgrass is still grieving for his trombone-playing father who died a few months before, and he is suspended from school for standing up to a bully teacher. Spud has a part-time job selling chips from a van in Chinatown and when he accidentally learns that oil from chip trucks all over the city is being dumped in the Ottawa River, he and his friends, Connie Pan and Dink the Thinker, organize themselves to solve this environmental crime. Multicultural elements are woven unobtrusively into the story as is Spud's growing awareness of the complexity of human nature.

Doyle's stories provide an atypically humorous and balanced view of adolescent adventures and coming of age experiences. His entertaining narratives capture the reader's attention while his intimate settings and strongly individualized characters beg sequels.

—Patricia Hill

———

DUANE, Diane. American. Born in New York, New York, 18 May 1952. Married Robert Peter Smyth in 1987. Novelist and television writer. Registered nurse, Pilgrim State Hospital, Brentwood, New York, 1974; psychiatric nurse, Payne Whitney Clinic, Cornell New York Hospital Medical Center, New York, 1974-76; assistant to writer, 1976-78; free-lance novelist and television writer, since 1978; staff writer, Filmation Studios, Reseda, California, 1983-84. Recipient: One of *School Library Journal's* Best Books, 1985, listed in *Voice of Youth Advocates'* Best Science Fiction and Fantasy titles for Young Adults, 1986, both for *Deep Wizardry;* listed in Best Science Fiction and Fantasy Titles for Young Adults, 1986, for *The Door into Shadow.* Agent: Donald A. Maass, 64 West 84th Street, Apartment 3-A, New York, NY 10024.

PUBLICATIONS FOR YOUNG ADULTS

Novels

The Door into Fire. New York, Dell, 1979; London, Magnum, 1981.
So You Want to be a Wizard. New York, Delacorte, 1983.
The Wounded Sky. New York, Pocket Books, 1983.
The Door into Shadow. New York, Bluejay, 1984.
My Enemy, My Ally. New York, Pocket Books, 1984.
Deep Wizardry. New York, Delacorte, 1985.
The Romulan Way, with Peter Morwood. New York, Pocket Books, 1987.
Spock's World. New York, Pocket Books, 1988.
Keeper of the City, with Peter Morwood. New York, Bantam, 1989.
Doctor's Orders. New York, Pocket Books, 1990.
High Wizardry. New York, Delacorte, 1990.
Support Your Local Wizard. New York, Guild American, 1990.
Space Cops: Mindblast, with Peter Morwood. New York, Avon, 1991.
Space Cops: Kill Station, with Peter Morwood. New York, Avon, 1992.
Space Cops: High Moon, with Peter Morwood. New York, Avon, 1992.
The Door into Sunset. New York, TOR, 1993.

Other

Contributor, *Sixteen: Short Stories by Outstanding Young Adult Writers,* edited by Donald R. Gallo. New York, Delacorte, 1984.
Contributor, *Dragons and Dreams: A Collection of New Fantasy and Science Fiction Stories,* edited by Jane Yolen and others. New York, Harper, 1986.
Story editor, "Dinosaucers" (sixty-four-episode, syndicated, animated television series), DIC Enterprises, 1986-87.
Contributor, *The Best of Star Trek,* D.C. Comics, 1991.

*   *   *

Diane Duane is not only highly talented but also unpredictable. She excels in three different genres and has also written TV scripts for *Star Trek: The Next Generation,* among others. The chronology of her writing shows an author switching genre and intended audience from one book to the next: between 1979 and 1985 she published two adult fantasies, two *Star Trek* novels, and the first two of her *Wizardry* children's fantasies. Then followed, to date, three more *Star Trek* novels (one in collaboration with her husband), another collaboration, third volumes in both the adult and children's fantasy series, and a fourth *Wizardry* book, *A Wizard Abroad.* She plans her work years ahead, particularly her fantasies. In 1979 *The Door into Fire* was published with a note that it was intended as the first of a quartet; so far two have come out. While in 1988, with the third Wizardry book not yet published, she announced plans for a fourth one—finally published in 1993!

The *Wizardry* series is a *tour de force* of "science fantasy." Although the wizards' power is magical, they go about their work scientifically by learning spells, by understanding the laws of nature, and also being knowledgeable about today's technological civilisation. Duane has also been compared to Madeleine L'Engle as her wizardry is infused with religion—a rather unorthodox Christianity. Religion is also bound up in her *Star Trek* and adult fantasy series. There are echoes of Tolkien and C. S. Lewis in her work: allusions deliberately positioned as homage to fantasists who, like Duane, concealed their Christianity beneath allegory or alternative mythology.

Wizardry, according to Duane, is not about selfish magic but about altruism: healing harms, helping the world run more smoothly, and occasionally saving the world from disaster. Wizardly science is acquired through ownership of the wizard's manual, a book which somehow gets into the hands of a person with magic potential, and which contains the awesome wizard's Oath. Once a wizard takes the Oath, s/he is faced with an ordeal. If passed, the manual is continually updated with fresh information and spells, plus a directory of other wizards with their status and power ranking. Wizards—both humans and intelligent animals—work under the authority of the Powers who created the universe (i.e. archangels, under Life [God]) and oppose the machinations of the Lone Power who invented Death at the dawn of time (i.e. Lucifer). This power confronts the thirteen-year-old heroine Nita and hero Kit in each volume.

In *So You Want to Be a Wizard,* Nita and Kit each come across a copy of the manual, say the Oath, become Novices, meet and become a team. Their initial dabbling in magic leads on to their ordeal, carried out in an alternative New York governed by the Lone Power. Their task is to recover a vital spellbook which he has stolen and hidden.

In *Deep Wizardry,* Kit and Nita, on a seaside holiday, encounter a whale who is also a wizard. Using wizardly speech—a special language—they discover that a group ritual is to be re-enacted in order to reduce environmental disasters affecting sea creatures, by generating a mass of good magic to hold down the Lone Power in its marine guise as the great Sea Serpent. If they fail, the eastern seaboard of the USA is likely to be flooded. Kit and Nita agree to shape-change into whales and join the ritual, and Nita volunteers to play the role of the sacrificed one, not realising that she will have to die as the food of the sinister Master-Shark. Luckily by another's substitution, Nita is freed of her fatal destiny.

High Wizardry is mainly the story of Nita's younger sister Dairine and her ordeal. Jealous of Nita's power, Dairine sneaks a look at her manual and rashly reads out the Oath. Next day, a new laptop computer arrives at home and Dairine discovers the wizard's manual stored in its memory, especially, as it will transpire, for her to use it. She begins a fantastic journey into space, at first thinking only of realising her fantasies of taking part in *Star Wars,* and then realising that there are actually real aliens, directed by the Lone Power, in chase of her. Little does she know that, as a computer expert, she has been chosen by the Powers to land on a silicon-based planet about to wake to sentience as a computer-style intelligence. The planet's mind then generates small silicon creatures which share its consciousness, and almost immediately the Lone Power arrives, having devised a way to tempt them to Fall. Homage to C.S. Lewis's *Perelandra (Voyage to Venus),* of course, but with a climax Lewis did not attempt, when the Lone Power is offered the chance to repent and return to Heaven...

A Wizard Abroad takes Nita and Kit to Ireland, in a tribute to Duane's new home. The plot recalls *Deep Wizardry* as wicked magic threatens the fabric of reality by bringing the past into the present, especially the violence of Irish legend. The Irish wizards decide to re-enact the Battle of Moytura, but first they must find the four treasures: the cup, sword, stone, and spear. The Lone Power returns in a grotesque guise as the Fomorian god Balor, and victory is barely won. This is a fresh treatment of the "Celtic fantasy" beloved of so many children's writers, and like the other *Wizardry* books it combines high poetic writing at the magical climaxes with down-to-earth American slang and cultural references. The latter will irritate fantasy purists, but one hopes it will help the average reader into the story.

Assessing Duane's adult works for YA reading, I look first at her *Star Trek* novels. These are not "tie-in" versions of the TV scripts, which were turned into prose fiction by James Blish years ago, or the six films. They are new novels linking the TV and film adventures. Over fifty *Star Trek* novels have been published by several authors in a continuing series. The authors must be consistent with the media presentations, with authorised nonfiction material such as *Mr. Scott's Guide to the Enterprise,* and with other novels in the series. Diane Duane was a *Star Trek* fan for years before she turned professional author. She has studied astronomy, astrophysics, and medicine, and thus can well cope with the jargon of science and pseudo-science which a *Star Trek* author must scatter through his/her books, even mapping a galactic voyage using real astronomical data. With her instinctive feel for the relationships between the core personalities of *Star Trek*—Kirk, Spock, McCoy, Scotty, Uhuru, Sulu and Chekov—she has produced outstanding genre fiction which the *Star Trek* fan may conjure up in the "mind's eye" as authentic adventures. Because they are not straightforward space war scenarios, they will extend young readers who can cope with their length and intellectual demands.

In *The Wounded Sky,* Kirk's ship, the *Enterprise,* is chosen to test a new space drive, taking it far further than the warp drive used in *Star Trek* for faster-than-light travel. They discover that this new drive is damaging the fabric of the universe, leading to a breach, and contact with a new universe whose Supreme Being is just awakening to consciousness. It is a highly metaphysical novel with clear allusions to C.S. Lewis's Ransom trilogy and Narnia books. *My Enemy, My Ally* and *The Romulan Way* are linked stories about the Romulan Empire, traditional enemies of the Federation whose background history is detailed by Duane. They are descended from tribes of Vulcans who rejected the way of logic and emigrated into space two thousand years before the *Star Trek* era. Duane packs a strong message for peace between races into these two stories of treachery, espionage, and space combat.

Doctors's Orders is an enjoyable novel about McCoy's first time in command of the *Enterprise.* Kirk beams down onto a new planet in the hope of negotiating a treaty with its three alien species so that they join the Federation (as opposed to siding with, or being exploited by, the Klingons). Then he disappears, and McCoy has to captain the ship as it suddenly comes under Klingon attack. Finally *Spock's World* is set on the planet Vulcan, where there is a campaign to take Vulcan out of the Federation, and Kirk and Spock are invited to speak at the public debate preceding the referendum. Chapters telling this story are interspersed with chapters about the history of Vulcan from the first awakening of hominid consciousness to the birth of Spock (who has a Vulcan father and Earthling mother). Again interplanetary politics is combined with philosophy: here, the history of how Vulcans coped with their inherently violent nature by developing an ethic of self-control.

In her *Door* adult fantasy series, Duane writes at full stretch without need to consider the restrictions of writing for juveniles or for *Star Trek* addicts who will pick on every minor deviation from the canon. The *Door* series is outstanding. Here is beauty, heroism, fear, magic, dragons, women warriors—and a wealth of fine writing. There is also an inherent eroticism, for these are genuine *adult* fantasies, though not as sexually explicit as those of Stephen Donaldson or Guy Kay. In this world ruled by the Goddess, lovemaking is good if done in love, friendship, or respect, and not unwillingly. Bisexuality is accepted, and the Goddess visits each individual once in his or her life in the form of a lover. Otherwise the ethic of the books is that of Good against Evil, with war as a necessity, sometimes a glorious endeavour, to bring about longed-for peace. I would suggest youngsters discover these books for themselves in the adult library or bookstore, rather than YA librarians shelving them alongside Duane's juveniles and *Star Trek* series.

—Jessica Yates

DUNCAN, Lois. Has also written as Lois Kerry. American. Born in Philadelphia, Pennsylvania, 28 April 1934. Educated at Duke University, Durham, North Carolina, 1952-53; University of New Mexico, Albuquerque, B.A. (cum laude) in English 1977 (Phi Beta Kappa). Married Donald Wayne Arquette in 1965, one daughter (deceased) and one son; three children from her first marriage. Writer; Lecturer in Journalism, University of New Mexico, 1971-82; contributing editor for *Woman's Day,* 1986-90; magazine photographer; lecturer at writers' conferences. Recipient: Three-time winner during high school years of *Seventeen* magazine's annual short story contest; Seventeenth Summer Literary award, Dodd, Mead & Co., 1957, for *Debutante Hill;* Best Novel award, National Press Women, 1966, for *Point of Violence;* Edgar Allan Poe award Runner-up, Mystery Writers of America, 1967, for *Ransom,* 1969, for *They Never Came Home,* 1985, for *The Third Eye,* 1986, for *Locked in Time,* and 1989, for *The Twisted Window;* Zia award, New Mexico Press Women, 1969, for *Major Andre: Brave Enemy;* grand prize winner, Writer's Digest Creative Writing Contest, 1970, for short story; Theta Sigma Phi Headliner award, 1971; American Library Association (ALA) Best Books for Young Adults citations, 1976, for *Summer of Fear,* 1978, for *Killing Mr. Griffin,* 1981, for *Stranger with My Face,* 1982, for *Chapters: My Growth as a Writer,* 1990, for *Don't Look Behind You,* and 1992, for *Who Killed My Daughter?; New York Times* Best Books for Children citations, 1981, for *Stranger with My Face,* and 1988, for *Killing Mr. Griffin;* Ethical Culture School Book award, Library of Congress' Best Books citation, and *English Teacher's Journal* and University of Iowa's Best Books of the Year for Young Adults citation, all 1981, and Best Novel award, National League of American Pen Women, 1982, all for *Stranger with My Face;* Notable Children's Trade Book in the Field of Social Studies, National Council for Social Studies and the Children's Book Council, 1982, for *Chapters: My Growth as a Writer;* Child Study Association of America's Children's Books of the Year citation, 1986, for *Locked in Time* and *The Third Eye;* Children's Book award, National League of American Pen Women, 1987, for *Horses of Dreamland.* Young Reader award, Essex-Hudson Regional Library Cooperative, 1989, for a body of work; Margaret A. Edwards award, for a distinguished body of work for Young Adults, from the Young Adult Services Committee of the School Library Journal, 1992. Duncan has also received numerous librarians', parents' and children's choice awards from the states of Alabama, Arizona, California, Colorado, Florida, Indiana, Iowa, Massachussetts, Nevada, New Mexico, Oklahoma, Tennessee, Texas, Utah, Virginia, South Carolina, and Vermont, as well as from groups in England. Agent: Claire Smith, Harold Ober Associates, 425 Madison Ave., New York, NY 10017 U.S.A.

PUBLICATIONS FOR YOUNG ADULTS

Novels

Debutante Hill. New York, Dodd Mead, 1958.
Love Song for Joyce (as Lois Kerry). New York, Funk and Wagnalls, 1958.
A Promise for Joyce (as Lois Kerry). New York, Funk and Wagnalls, 1959.
The Middle Sister. New York, Dodd Mead, 1960.
Game of Danger. New York, Dodd Mead, 1962.
Season of the Two-Heart. New York, Dodd Mead, 1964.
Ransom. New York, Doubleday, 1966; as *Five Were Missing,* New York, New American Library, 1972.
They Never Came Home. New York, Doubleday, 1969.
A Gift of Magic, illustrated by Arvis Stewart. Boston, Little Brown, 1971.
I Know What You Did Last Summer. Boston, Little Brown, 1973; London, Hamish Hamilton, 1982.
Down a Dark Hall. Boston, Little Brown, 1974.
Summer of Fear. Boston, Little Brown, 1976; London, Hamish Hamilton, 1981.
Killing Mr. Griffin. Boston, Little Brown, 1978; London, Hamish Hamilton, 1980.
Daughters of Eve. Boston, Little Brown, 1979.
Stranger with My Face. Boston, Little Brown, 1981; London, Hamish Hamilton, 1983.
The Third Eye. Boston, Little Brown, 1984; as *The Eyes of Karen Connors,* London, Hamish Hamilton, 1985.
Locked in Time. Boston, Little Brown, 1985; London, Hamish Hamilton, 1986.
The Twisted Window. New York, Delacorte Press, and London, Hamish Hamilton, 1987.

Don't Look behind You. New York, Delacorte Press, and London, Hamish Hamilton, 1989.

Nonfiction

Major Andre: Brave Enemy, illustrated by Tran Mawicke. New York, Putnam, 1969.
Peggy (on Margaret Arnold). Boston, Little Brown, 1970.

Other

Psychic Detectives in Action (cassette), RDA Enterprises, 1993.

PUBLICATIONS FOR CHILDREN

Fiction

The Littlest One in the Family, illustrated by Suzanne K. Larsen. New York, Dodd Mead, 1960.
Silly Mother, illustrated by Suzanne K. Larsen. New York, Dial Press, 1962.
Giving Away Suzanne, illustrated by Leonard Weisgard. New York, Dodd Mead, 1963.
Hotel for Dogs, illustrated by Leonard Shortall. Boston, Houghton Mifflin, 1971.
Wonder Kid Meets the Evil Lunch Snatcher, illustrated by Margaret Sanfilippo. Boston, Little Brown, 1988.

Poetry

From Spring to Spring: Poems and Photographs, photographs by the author. Philadelphia, Westminster Press, 1982.
The Terrible Tales of Happy Days School, illustrated by Friso Henstra. Boston, Little Brown, 1983.
Horses of Dreamland, illustrated by Donna Diamond. Boston, Little Brown, 1985; London, Hamish Hamilton, 1986.
The Birthday Moon, illustrated by Susan Davis. New York, Viking, 1989.
Songs from Dreamland, music by Robin Arquette, illustrated by Kay Chorao. New York, Knopf, 1989.

Nonfiction

The Circus Comes Home, photographs by Joseph Janney Steinmetz. New York, Delacorte, 1992.

PUBLICATIONS FOR ADULTS

Fiction

Point of Violence. New York, Doubleday, 1966; London, Hale, 1968.
When the Bough Breaks. New York, Doubleday, 1973.

Nonfiction

How to Write and Sell Your Personal Experiences. Cincinnati, Writer's Digest, 1979.
Chapters: My Growth as a Writer. Boston, Little Brown, 1982.

Who Killed My Daughter? The True Story of a Mother's Search for her Daughter's Murderer. New York, Delacorte Press, 1992.

Other

A Visit with Lois Duncan (videotape), RDA Enterprises, 1985.
Dream Songs from Yesterday (cassette), RDA Enterprises, 1987.
Our Beautiful Day (cassette), RDA Enterprises, 1988.
The Story of Christmas (cassette), RDA Enterprises, 1989.
Psychics in Action (series of cassettes), RDA Enterprises, 1992 and ongoing.

Contributor of over five hundred articles and stories to periodicals, including *Good Housekeeping, Redbook, McCall's, Woman's Day, The Writer, Reader's Digest, Ladies' Home Journal, Saturday Evening Post,* and *Writer's Digest.* Contributing editor, *Woman's Day.*

*

Media Adaptations: *Summer of Fear* (television movie, *Strangers in Our House*), NBC-TV, 1978; *Down a Dark Hall* (cassettes), Listening Library, 1985; *Killing Mr. Griffin* (cassettes), Listening Library, 1986, *Summer of Fear* (cassettes), Listening Library, 1986, and *Stranger with My Face* (cassettes), Listening Library, 1986; *Selling Personal Experiences to Magazines* (cassettes), RDA Enterprises, 1987, and *Songs from Dreamland* (cassettes), RDA Enterprises, 1987.

Biography: Essay in *Something about the Author Autobiography Series,* Volume 2, Detroit, Gale, 1986; essay in *Speaking for Ourselves: Autobiographical Sketches by Notable Authors of Books for Young Adults,* Volume 1, compiled and edited by Donald R. Gallo, National Council of Teachers of English, 1990.

Critical Study: Entry in *Contemporary Literary Criticism,* Volume 26, Detroit, Gale, 1983.

*   *   *

Lois Duncan began her writing career very early in life, shortly after she learned to print at age five or so. At age ten she submitted her first typed manuscript to *Ladies' Home Journal.* The editor did not publish it, but his kindly rejection letter encouraged her to keep trying. Some sage advice from a new neighbor, who turned out to be MacKinlay Kantor, led her to stop writing what he called romantic "trash" and write about what she knew. She did, and as a result sold her first short story to a teen magazine at age thirteen. A decade later Duncan's first novel, *Debutante Hill,* a piece of "sweet and sticky...pap," won a literary competition that awarded her one thousand dollars and a book contract from Dodd Mead.

The world of adolescent fiction by the mid-1960s was not a world of books like *Debutante Hill,* however. Fiction of this period was characterized by an often gritty realism; plots were no longer concerned solely with sports, dating, and horses. Their subject matter involved things happening in the real world—drugs, peer pressure, social and psychological problems, sex, divorce, etc. This new freedom to write more realistically for young readers appealed to Duncan, and her first novel written "under the new set of ground rules" was *Ransom,* a taut adventure story about a group of teenagers kidnapped by their school-bus driver. How different *Ransom*

was from Duncan's earlier teen novels is indicated by the fact that Dodd Mead refused to publish it because it "wasn't Duncan's style;" Doubleday then took it on, and it become a runner-up for the Edgar Allan Poe award. A second realistic teen novel, *They Never Came Home,* was also an Edgar runner-up, and Duncan was firmly set in the writing style that was to prove so successful for her over the next several decades.

The style Duncan uses is a simple one. She places an individual or a group of normal, believable young people in what appears to be a prosaic setting such as a suburban neighborhood or an American high school; on the surface everything is as it should be until Duncan introduces an element of surprise that gives the story an entirely new twist. In her novel *Down a Dark Hall,* for example, a young woman goes off to what appears to be a normal boarding school. It proves, however, to be run by a headmistress who is herself a medium, and the school is haunted by malevolent ghosts of artists and writers who invade the minds and bodies of the innocent students. *Summer of Fear* is about an average family in Albuquerque, New Mexico, who "inherit" a seventeen-year-old girl, Julia, from relatives who have died in a car crash. Rachael, the narrator, first suspects Julia of being strangely sinister, but when she finds out that Julia cannot be photographed, Rachael begins to realize that Julia is not merely different but is a witch, and an evil one at that. *Stranger with My Face* introduces astral projection when an evil young woman tries to take over the mind and body of her identical twin sister. *The Third Eye* tells the story of Karen, who must summon the courage to use her gift of extrasensory perception to stop the evil machinations of an older couple who kidnap babies to sell them on the baby market. One of Duncan's most exciting and sophisticated novels, *Locked in Time,* finds Nore spending the summer with her new step-relations and her father on her stepmother's Louisiana plantation. Strange events and unlikely occurrences lead her to believe her new relatives are "locked in time"—ageless—but her discovery of their secret reads for terrible danger for Nore. In each of these books, an element of the occult is an integral part of a fast-moving plot, but it is always believable because Duncan never carries her depiction of the supernatural into the sometimes goofy realms that some other authors do. Character and plot are always predominant; the books are first and foremost good mysteries made even more interesting for young readers by some aspect of the unusual.

Not all Duncan's novels depend on use of the supernatural, however. Some of her best works for young adults use the depths of human nature as an unexpected fillip that raises them above the level of the average teen novel. In *I Know What You Did Last Summer,* four teenage friends, riding in a car which is going too fast on a dark road, hit and kill a young boy on a bike. Barry, the driver, persuades the others that nothing will be gained by confessing what they have done, especially since they'd been coming from a party where they had smoked a little pot and drunk some beer. They all manage to put the incident out of their minds until a year later, when each receives a letter saying simply, "I know what you did last summer." A succession of letters follow, each more threatening than the last, until the young people realize that their very lives are in danger from a psychopath bent on revenge.

In *Killing Mr. Griffin,* a group of high-school students set out to scare a hated English teacher into being a little more reasonable by taking him to a remote spot in a woods, tying him to a tree, and leaving him overnight. It soon becomes apparent that Mark, the charismatic leader of the group, would like to go even further than frightening Mr. Griffin, but the rest refuse to go along with him.

The next morning when they go to release the teacher they find him dead; without his life-sustaining medication he has succumbed to a heart attack. This time Mark does prevail by convincing the others that nothing is to be gained by telling the truth about what has happened. It is only when Mark begins to pressure the group to kill again that they recognize him for the evil person he is, but by then it's almost too late.

One of Duncan's most chilling examples of the power of an evil person is in her portrayal of Irene Stark in *Daughters of Eve,* who uses the members of a high-school girls' service club as instruments of revenge on all men. Her pathological hatred results in tragic consequences for the naive young women she is ostensibly guiding as their advisor and mentor. In *The Twisted Window,* Tracy Lloyd, abandoned by her father after her mother's death, is drawn into helping a strange young man, Brad Johnson, rescue his baby sister, who was kidnapped by their stepfather and now living in the same town as Tracy. The plot backfires for Tracy, though, when she begins to realize that Brad is seriously disturbed and she finds herself and the child in terrible danger.

In each of these novels, it is a mark of Duncan's ability as a writer that the evils she describes are perfectly plausible and believable. As in her use of the occult, her use of warped human nature as a tool to move the plot along briskly never seems contrived or used solely for shock effect; it is integral to the story. In this respect, Duncan is strongly reminiscent of Robert Cormier in her no-holds-barred portraits of the consequences of human evil and perversity. For that very reason, Duncan's work is shocking to many adult critics who refuse to believe that so much evil exists, but a tragic incident in Duncan's own life belies their unbelief. In April 1989, Duncan's twenty-one-year-old daughter was shot down in cold blood by an as yet unidentified killer. For several years her grief over the murder left her unable to write another novel for young readers. During this period, however, she was at work on a new book, *Who Killed My Daughter? The True Story of a Mother's Search for Her Daughter's Murderer,* in which Duncan writes of the many suspicious aspects of the killing and the ineptitude of the crime's investigators; it is her hope that this book will help to bring to light the strange and terrible true story of why her child was murdered.

Young readers can only hope that Duncan will take fiction pen in hand again. Until then, however, they can enjoy the fast-moving plots, fine characterization, and excruciating suspense that characterize most of her earlier fiction and have made her one of the most popular writers for this age group on the contemporary scene.

—Audrey Eaglen

———

DUNLOP, Eileen (Rhona). British. Born in Alloa, Clackmannan, Scotland, 13 October 1938. Educated at Alloa Academy, 1943-56; Moray House College of Education, Edinburgh, 1956-59, diploma (honours) in primary education 1959. Married Antony Kamm in 1979. Teacher and writer. Assistant teacher, Eastfield Primary School, Penicuik, Midlothian, 1959-62, and Abercromby Primary School, Tullibody, Clackmannan, 1962-64; assistant headmistress, Sunnyside School, Alloa, 1964-79; headmistress of Preparatory School of Dollar Academy, Clackmannan, 1980-90. Recipient: Edgar Allan Poe award nomination, 1983, for *The Maze Stone;* Scottish Arts Council Book awards, 1983, for *The Maze Stone,* and 1986, for

Clementina; American Library Association Notable Book citation, and Carnegie Medal commendation, both 1987, for *The House on the Hill;* McVitie's Scottish Writer of the Year Prize for *Finn's Island,* 1991. Address: 46 Tarmangie Dr., Dollar, Clackmannan, FK14 7BP, Scotland.

Publications for Young Adults

Fiction

Robinsheugh, illustrated by Peter Farmer. London, Oxford University Press, 1975; as *Elizabeth Elizabeth,* New York, Holt Rinehart, 1976.
A Flute in Mayferry Street, illustrated by Phillida Gili. London, Oxford University Press, 1976; as *The House on Mayferry Street,* New York, Holt Rinehart, 1977.
Fox Farm. London, Oxford University Press, 1978; New York, Holt Rinehart, 1979.
The Maze Stone, illustrated by Martin White. Oxford, Oxford University Press, 1982; New York, Coward, McCann & Geohegan, 1983.
Clementina. Oxford, Oxford University Press, 1985; New York, Holiday House, 1987.
The House on the Hill. Oxford, Oxford University Press, and New York, Holiday House, 1987.
The Valley of Deer. Oxford, Oxford University Press, and New York, Holiday House, 1989.
The Chip Shop Ghost. London, Blackie & Son, 1991.
Finn's Island. London, Blackie & Son, 1991; New York, Holiday House, 1992.
Green Willow. New York, Holiday House, 1993.

Other (with Antony Kamm)

Edinburgh, illustrated by Helen Herbert. Cambridge University Press, 1982.
The Story of Glasgow, illustrated by Maureen and Gordon Gray. Glasgow, Drew Publishing, 1983.
Editor, with Antony Kamm, *A Book of Old Edinburgh.* Edinburgh, Macdonald Publishers, 1984.
Kings and Queens of Scotland, illustrated by Maureen and Gordon Gray. Glasgow, Drew Publishing, 1984.
Scottish Heroes and Heroines of Long Ago, illustrated by Maureen and Gordon Gray. Glasgow, Drew Publishing, 1984.
Editor, with Antony Kamm, *The Scottish Collection of Verse to 1800.* Glasgow, Drew Publishing, 1985.
Scottish Homes through the Ages, illustrated by John Harrold. Glasgow, Drew Publishing, 1985.
Editor, *Scottish Traditional Rhymes for Children.* Glasgow, Drew Publishing, 1985.
Tales of St. Columba. Chester Springs, Pennsylvania, Dufour Editions, 1992.

*

Biography: Essay in *Something about the Author Autobiography Series,* Volume 12, Detroit, Gale, 1991.

*   *   *

Three threads run through Eileen Dunlop's books for young adults: her love of her native Scotland (the setting of all her books), her interest in the links between past and present, and her use of the supernatural. These elements, combined with traditional romantic themes, make her books particularly appealing to young adults. Dunlop's skills as a storyteller have developed gradually throughout her career, though in her later novels she shows a greater ability to draw her reader into the story and is less inclined to overwhelm them with too much detail and explanation as in her earlier works.

Dunlop's first published book, *Robinsheugh,* is a time-travel story and a very dense and demanding read; only the fact that events are seen from the viewpoint of twelve-year-old Elizabeth Martin marks it as a book for young people. Elizabeth is spending the summer with her older, scholarly cousin Kate, who is carrying out research on the Melville family of Robinsheugh in the Scottish border country. An old mirror provides a link to the past and to a woman named Elizabeth who lived at Robinsheugh in the 1770s. The past becomes so real that present-day Elizabeth's relationship with Kate disintegrates into animosity.

Published the following year, *A Flute in Mayferry Street* is set in Edinburgh, where Colin Ramsay lives with his widowed mother and invalid sister, Marion. His ambition to play in the school orchestra seems futile because he does own a flute. The unravelling of a family mystery provides a solution; first a letter, then a photograph, and later a trunk containing a flute are found and Marion and Colin gradually piece together the story of their great-uncle Charles Ramsay and Alan Farquhar, who had been friends in the early part of the twentieth century.

After a gap of some years, during which Dunlop published *Fox Farm* for younger children, she produced *The Maze Stone,* in which the prose is more finely honed. The opening is dramatic, "On the twenty-fourth of June, in the year 1914, a young man went into a house, and never came out again." The date is significant; in the changes brought about by World War I, this mysterious happening is forgotten. Seventy years later, the area is vastly different around the Bieldlaw, and the hill which dominates the landscape is threatened through exploitation by a mining company. Central to the story are Fanny and Hester, stepsisters through the marriage of Fanny's father and Hester's mother. Alongside the re-enactment of the legend of the mortal who is enticed into fairyland is a very modern concern about the environment.

In *Clementina,* another modern institution, a time-share property, provides the setting for the story and a link with the past; changes in relationships are also important. Bridget Graham has persuaded her mother to spend a legacy on four weeks in a chalet in the newly developed Benalmond Forest Park. Bridget's best friend, Daisy, and the slightly older Clementina, an orphan from a children's home befriended by Mrs. Graham, are invited to join them for their holiday there. Clementina is, however, far from the stereotypical poor orphan; her strong personality, musical gifts, and her mysteri-

ous links with the Drummonds, whose family home is at the centre of the Park, make it a disturbing holiday for them all. The invasion of the present by the past is seen from the viewpoint of ordinary Daisy whose best-friend relationship with Bridget is ruined forever by the events of the summer.

Like *Clementina, The Valley of the Deer* is a powerful story about a girl growing up. It includes another dramatic opening: "For Anne Farrar, it all began on the night when her bedroom wall fell down." As a result of the collapsed bedroom wall, Anne finds an old family Bible and is fascinated by the entry for Alice Jardyne, born in 1701 and "blottit out of the Boke of Lyffe" in 1726. Anne wonders what Alice has done to deserve such a terrible epitaph. Sharing her parents' interest in the past, Anne begins to research Alice's story and thereby meets Polly Jardine, a young woman in a wheelchair and a contemporary representative of the Jardyne family.

Dunlop's books for young adults, set firmly in time and space, show young people maturing through experience; she always provides a clear viewpoint from which the reader can observe, but does not dictate the conclusions they should draw. She examines relationships, not only between siblings or friends or children and their parents, but between people of different ages. The reader feels that Dunlop's characters have a life outside of her books; Dunlop's books also have a satisfying pattern, whether it takes the form of past events repeated in the present or of some physical token, such as the pattern on the maze stone which manifests itself in various ways.

Since 1989 Dunlop, perhaps partly because of the declining British market for young adult novels of this quality, has published only stories for younger children and nonfiction. These stories have many of the qualities of her work for older children while her nonfiction is about Scotland, its past and its traditions.

—Sheila Ray

DWYER, Deanna. See KOONTZ, Dean R.

DWYER, K.R. See KOONTZ, Dean R.

E

EDGERTON, Clyde (Carlyle). American. Born in Durham, North Carolina, 20 May 1944. Educated at University of North Carolina at Chapel Hill, B.A. 1966, M.A.T. 1972, Ph.D. 1977. Served in U.S. Air Force, 1966-71, piloted reconnaissance and forward air control missions in Southeast Asia during Vietnam War; received Distinguished Flying Cross. Married Susan Ketchin in 1975; one daughter. English teacher, Southern High School, Durham, North Carolina, 1972-73; co-director, English Teaching Institute, Chapel Hill, North Carolina, 1976; associate professor, Campbell University, Buies Creek, North Carolina, 1977-81, assistant professor of education and psychology, 1981-85; associate professor of English and education, St. Andrews Presbyterian College, Laurinburg, North Carolina, 1985-89; writer. Visiting lecturer in English at North Carolina Central University, 1977; writer in residence at Agnes Scott College, 1990; creative writing instructor, Duke University, Durham, North Carolina, 1992; lecturer at conferences and workshops. Guest on television and radio programs, including *Today* and National Public Radio's *Sunday Weekend Edition, Morning Edition,* and *Good Evening with Noah Adams.* Musician; member of Tarwater Band. Recipient: *Publishers Weekly* named *The Floatplane Notebooks* one of the best books of 1988; Guggenheim fellow, 1989; Lyndhurst fellow, 1991. Agent: Liz Darhansoff, 1220 Park Avenue, New York, NY 10128. Address: c/o Dusty's Air Taxi, 714 Ninth Street, G-7, Durham, NC 27705, U.S.A.

Publications for Young Adults

Fiction

Raney. Chapel Hill, North Carolina, Algonquin Books, 1985.
Walking across Egypt. Chapel Hill, North Carolina, Algonquin Books, 1987.
Understanding the Floatplane. Chapel Hill, North Carolina, Mud Puppy Press, 1987.
The Floatplane Notebooks. Chapel Hill, North Carolina, Algonquin Books, 1988.
Cold Black Peas. Chapel Hill, North Carolina, Mud Puppy Press, 1990.
Killer Diller. Chapel Hill, North Carolina, Algonquin Books, 1991.
In Memory of Junior. Chapel Hill, North Carolina, Algonquin Books, 1992.

Recordings: *Walking across Egypt: Songs and Readings from the Books "Raney" and "Walking across Egypt,"* music performed by Edgerton and other members of the Tarwater Band, Flying Fish Records, 1987; *Clyde Edgerton Reads "The Floatplane Notebooks,"* Random House Audiobooks, 1989; *The "Killer Diller" Tapes,* Durham, North Carolina, Dusty's Air Taxi, 1991; *The Devil's Dream,* by Lee Smith and the Tarwater Band, Durham, North Carolina, Dusty's Air Taxi, 1993.

Other

Contributor, *Weymouth: An Anthology of Poetry,* edited by Sam Ragan. Laurinburg, North Carolina, St. Andrews Press, 1987.

Contributor, *Family Portraits: Remembrances by Twenty Distinguished Writers,* edited by Carolyn Anthony. New York, Doubleday, 1989.
Contributor, *New Stories from the South: The Year's Best, 1990,* edited by Shannon Ravenel. Chapel Hill, North Carolina, Algonquin Books, 1990.

*

Media Adaptations: *Walking across Egypt* (play, adapted by John Justice, produced 1989); *Raney* (play, adapted by John Justice, produced North Carolina 1990); *The Floatplane Notebooks* (play, adapted by Jason Moore and Paul Fitzgerald, produced Chicago 1992).

Critical Study: Entry in *Contemporary Literary Criticism,* Volume 39, Detroit, Gale, 1986.

Clyde Edgerton comments:

I recently received letters from two eleventh-grade classes in South Carolina. They had just read *The Floatplane Notebooks* and their letters were a response to my story. I was gratified that they found the story interesting and had raised important issues and questions related to the story. I am happy that young adults are able to bring their own lives and experiences to my writing and thus find pleasure and perhaps insights into their own relationships. So far, all my books have had young adults as main characters. I feel about these characters the same way I feel about young readers in general—their youth provides energy, enthusiasm, and fresh insights—and what writer doesn't need readers with these qualities?

*   *   *

Clyde Edgerton is a funny and a profound novelist. In the span of eight years he has published five rollicking stories of small town Southern life. His beat is the Piedmont area of North Carolina. His books are adult novels; individual imperfections and social problems are presented clearly and with humor, and there is no attempt to pass judgment on them. Young adults in their twenties are featured prominently, as are older adults in their seventies, and often the relationships between the two are central to the plot. Edgerton's characters have more faults than most, but they also have considerable virtues, and they are so likable that you want to invite them over for a cup of coffee, a piece of homemade apple pie, and a nice long chat.

Raney is the story of the first two years, two months, and two days in a modern marriage. Set in Listre, North Carolina, it begins just before the wedding, at the K and W Cafeteria, where Raney discovers that her mother-in-law-to-be is a vegetarian. She thought somehow that people were born vegetarians, and she is surprised that Mrs. Shepherd just changed over after some programs on simple living put on by the Episcopalians. Raney herself is Baptist. There are other things Raney learns about, and some adjustments she makes, to life with another family, another approach to class, religion and race, another way of doing the dishes and defining pornography. The need for adjustments continue until the end of the book, when Raney and Charles's first child is born. But throughout, love, and the joys and perplexities of living, are described in detail, with wit and wisdom.

In *Walking Across Egypt* we meet Mattie Rigsbee, a strong-willed senior citizen who at seventy-eight is slowing down, just a bit. Mattie still cooks three meals a day and her house in Listre always smells good from homemade biscuits, fried chicken, pound cake, and apple pie. When a stray dog comes into her yard, she knows she has as much business keeping him as she has Walking across Egypt, which is the title of her favorite hymn. But she warms him up some beef stew and he does not wish to leave. When Wesley Benfield enters her life, or rather when she enters Wesley's life with pieces of cake and pie, he is even less likely a companion than the stray dog. Wesley is a sixteen-year-old delinquent in the Young Men's Rehabilitation Center, there for stealing a car. But in the end Mattie keeps the dog and Wesley, and you can bet with her good spirit and her good cooking, they both will be better off. And maybe Mattie will be better off too. This book is about reaching out, about caring, and about the best southern cooking there is. Edgerton, also a folk musician, has thoughtfully supplied Mattie with the words and music to "Walking across Egypt." It is gratifying to have a new hymn to sing.

The Floatplane Notebooks chronicles the lives of five generations of the Copelands of Listre. There are a fair number of relatives to account for, so the author provides a genealogical chart in the beginning of the book. The time frame is 1956 to 1971, and the book is written from the perspectives of a number of younger family members, a single event being interpreted differently by different individuals. Building a floatplane is the hobby, obsession of the present head of the family, Albert. He writes frequently about its progress in his notebooks. If the plane should crash, he can look through the notebooks to determine why. The notebooks also contain the secrets of family yearning and love. The Copelands enjoy a family isolation until the Vietnam War, and the bonds of love and caring continue after that war, through tragedy and triumph.

In *Killer Diller*, Mattie Rigsbee, somewhat frailer, and Wesley Benfield, somewhat rehabilitated, return. And Edgerton gives us two more songs—"Sour Sweetheart Blues" and "When I Sleep in Class." Listre is a beehive of activity in this book because the Baptist college, Ballard University, has two new programs: Nutrition House, for overweight Christians, and Project Promise, for special education students of the county. Project Promise uses the residents of the rehabilitation halfway house adjacent to the Ballard campus to teach special ed students job-related skills of masonry and plumbing. Wesley is now a halfway house resident and project participant. He teaches bricklaying, while also writing songs for his Baptist band, preaching, and lusting for a certain girl in Nutrition House. Meanwhile Mattie becomes ill and after a hospital stay, ends up in the Shady Grove Nursing Home. Mattie hates the home because she can't cook there. It is Wesley, of course, who finds a way for her to escape to her home.

In *Memory of Junior* is about four generations of the Bales and McCord families. It has a genealogical chart in opening pages, and it too is written from the perspective of several family members and of other persons, a single event being interpreted differently by different individuals. Grove McCord was Albert Copeland's daddy's sister's boy. Grove was flying his own little plane before Albert started on his floatplane. The improbable plot of this novel focuses on three elderly people, contemplating their final resting places: Laura and Glen Bales and Grove McCord. The families end up with too many graves and too few tombstones. The importance of the grave site to family continuity has come up before in *The Floatplane Notebooks*. In this latter book the importance is explained simply by Uncle Grove, "You're history longer than you are fact." This book too is about day-to-day family life, described with kind-hearted humor.

Edgerton, like a number of Southern writers, credits his family with providing him with great family stories, told over and over, for as long as he could remember. His novels about family are full of likable, outrageous, and very human characters. They show love and tenderness, strong feelings of connection, despite death and divorce and desertion. The books are hilarious, touching, wonderful.

—Mary Lystad

***

EHRLICH, Amy. American. Born in New York City, 24 July 1942. Educated at Bennington College, Bennington, Vermont, 1960-62, 1963-65. Married Henry Ingraham in 1985; one son. Early jobs for short periods included teacher in day care center, fabric colorist, and hospital receptionist; roving editor, *Family Circle* magazine, New York, 1976-77; senior editor, Delacorte Press, New York, 1977-78; senior editor, Dial Books for Young Readers, New York, 1978-82, executive editor, 1982-84; vice president, editor-in-chief, Candlewick Press, Cambridge, Massachusetts, 1991—. Recipient: Best Book of the Year list, *School Library Journal*, 1972, *New York Times*, 1972, ALA Children's Books of Exceptional Interest citation, all for *Zeek Silver Moon*; Reviewer's Choice, *Booklist*, 1979, IRA-CBC Children's Choice, Child Study Association Children's Book of the Year, and *American Bookseller* Pick of the Lists citations, all for *Thumbelina*; IRA-CBC Children's Choice citation, for *The Everyday Train*; *American Bookseller* Pick of the Lists, Kansas State Reading Circle, Best Book of the Year list, *School Library Journal*, 1981, and Reviewer's Choice, *Booklist*, 1981, all for *Leo, Zack, and Emmie*; *Redbook* Children's Book of the Year citation, 1987, for *The Wild Swans*; *American Bookseller* Pick of the Lists and *Booklist* Reviewer's Choice citations, both for *The Snow Queen*. Child Study Association Children's Book of the Year, and Kansas State Reading Circle citations, all for *Cinderella*; *Booklist* Young Adult Reviewer's Choice and Best of the Decade citations, and Dorothy Canfield Fisher award, 1990, all for *Where It Stops, Nobody Knows*. Agent: F. Joseph Spieler, 154 West 57th Street, New York, NY 10019. Address: Box 73, RFD 3, St. Johnsbury, VT 05819, U.S.A.

PUBLICATIONS FOR YOUNG ADULTS

Fiction

Where It Stops, Nobody Knows. New York, Dial, 1988.
The Dark Card. New York, Viking, 1991.

PUBLICATIONS FOR CHILDREN

Zeek Silver Moon, illustrated by Robert Andrew Parker. New York, Dial, 1972.
Adapter, *Wounded Knee: An Indian History of the American West* (originally published as *Bury My Heart at Wounded Knee*), by Dee Brown. New York, Holt, 1974.
The Everyday Train, illustrated by Martha Alexander. New York, Dial, 1977.

Reteller, *Thumbelina,* by Hans Christian Andersen, illustrated by Susan Jeffers. New York, Dial, 1979.

Leo, Zack, and Emmie, illustrated by Steven Kellogg. New York, Dial, 1981.

Reteller, *The Wild Swans,* by Hans Christian Andersen, illustrated by Susan Jeffers. New York, Dial, 1981.

Annie and the Kidnappers, illustrated by Leonard Shortall. New York, Random House, 1982.

Annie Finds a Home, illustrated by Leonard Shortall. New York, Random House, 1982.

Adapter, *Annie: The Storybook Based on the Movie.* New York, Random House, 1982.

Reteller, *The Snow Queen,* by Hans Christen Andersen, illustrated by Susan Jeffers. New York, Dial, 1982.

Adapter, *Bunnies All Day Long,* illustrated by Marie H. Henry. New York, Dial, 1985.

Adapter, *Bunnies and Their Grandma,* illustrated by Marie H. Henry. New York, Dial, 1985.

Adapter, *Cinderella,* by Charles Perrault, illustrated by Susan Jeffers. New York, Dial, 1985.

Adapter, *The Ewoks and the Lost Children.* New York, Random House, 1985.

Editor and adapter, *The Random House Book of Fairy Tales,* illustrated by Diane Goode. New York, Random House, 1985.

Adapter, *Bunnies On Their Own,* illustrated by Marie H. Henry. New York, Dial, 1986.

Adapter, *Bunnies at Christmastime,* illustrated by Marie H. Henry. New York, Dial, 1986.

Buck-Buck the Chicken, illustrated by R.W. Alley. New York, Random House, 1987.

Leo, Zack, and Emmie Together Again, illustrated by Steven Kellogg. New York, Dial, 1987.

Emma's New Pony, photographs by Richard Brown. New York, Random House, 1988.

Adapter, *Pome and Peel: A Venetian Tale,* illustrated by Laszlo Gal. New York, Dial, 1989.

Adapter, *Rapunzel,* by the Brothers Grimm, illustrated by Kris Waldherr. New York, Dial, 1989.

The Story of Hanukkah, illustrated by Ori Sherman. New York, Dial, 1989.

Lucy's Winter Tale, illustrated by Troy Howell. New York, Dial, 1991.

Parents in the Pigpen: Pigs in the Tub, illustrated by Steven Kellogg. New York, Dial, 1993.

Maggie and Silky Joe, illustrated by Robert Blake. New York, Viking, 1994.

*

Amy Ehrlich comments:

Writing my two young adult novels meant a great deal to me. In them I wanted to tell truly gripping stories and to portray the pain and the searing discoveries of adolescence. This is a pivotal time in a human life and adults often flinch at remembering it. But I loved the intensity of recollection that came over me as I worked. The characters are made up and the stories of course are fiction, but I tried to tell the truth.

*   *   *

Amy Ehrlich's expansive involvement in children's and young adult literature includes both writing and editing. She earns acclaim for writing original picture books and early readers such as *The*

Everyday Train and *Leo, Zack, and Emmie Together Again.* Her interest in language and story infuses retellings of classic fairy tales such as Hans Christian Andersen's *Thumbelina* and the Grimm Brothers' *Hansel and Gretel.* In her two young adult novels, *Where It Stops, Nobody Knows,* and *The Dark Card,* Ehrlich turns to an older audience in an extended storytelling form in which she challenges these readers with intricate plots, psychologically complex characters, and enigmatic, provocative conclusions.

Both novels operate superficially as mysteries. Nina Lewis, the adolescent protagonist in *Where It Stops, Nobody Knows,* begins to question the reasons for her frequent relocations. Why must Joyce, her mother, always uproot them? Why is she so protective? Compelled by Nina, and equipped with the authorial tone of doubt and secrecy, readers face even more puzzles. What relationship do Joyce and Nina have? What motivates Joyce? Why does she fear stability and commitment? Will her undeniable love for Nina suffocate the girl?

In *The Dark Card,* seventeen-year-old Laura flirts with danger and Atlantic City's extravagance and exploitation. She leads a double life: in daylight, she's a blossoming adolescent innocently living in the family summer home; at night, she costumes herself in experience and enters the lurid surrealism of casinos. Ehrlich begs readers to question here, too. Will Laura pass the limits of safety? How far can the mature, gambler Ari be trusted? What happened to Laura's mother's bracelet?

Despite the complex plots, use of past tense, and dialogue written above the level of comprehension of the characters, Ehrlich masterfully involves the intelligent reader as observer and participant in the characters' lives. One cares about Nina and Joyce; about Laura, her boyfriend, her sister, and their father.

Both novels break the traditional expectations of fiction for young people. While Ehrlich invites readers to solve the enigmas, in fact, complete understanding may prove elusive and illusory. Disturbance, even profound disturbance, lies at the heart of these novels. Nina experiences frequent disruption with each new move; Joyce acts oddly at times. Instead of mourning her mother, Laura dresses in her clothes and acts dramatically unlike herself. Ehrlich crosses additional boundaries by writing of socially inappropriate and deviant behavior. The end of *Where It Stops, Nobody Knows* finds Joyce imprisoned for kidnapping. And in *The Dark Card,* Laura strips for Ari in a hotel room—a scene which shocks some readers with its explicitness—revealing this adolescent's profound psychological infirmity. Again, this ambitiousness to push the parameters of young-adult fiction testifies to Ehrlich's faith in her audience's intelligence and their ability to confront complexity.

These disturbances take on additional strength because Ehrlich contrasts them to the recognizable. Joyce may be troubled, but she loves Nina fully. And Nina exists completely within a realistic young-adult sphere. She wants to succeed in school; she wants to have friends; she experiences first love and boyfriends. Even the disquieting wrinkles of their mother-daughter relationship gain power because Ehrlich sets them against the normalcy of that relationship: Joyce makes the rules and Nina rebels; they understand each other and still struggle with each other. Similarly, Laura's double life pits the expected against the unexpected. Laura discovers the typical difficulties of her relationship with her mother when she begins to act outrageously outside that relationship. She can see the perverseness of her involvement with Ari because it deviates from her satisfying experiences with Billy.

In the characters of Nina and Laura, Ehrlich presents portraits of adolescents on the edge of womanhood. Unlike characters in much other fiction (e.g., Beverly Cleary's female protagonists), these young women strive for individuality against profoundly confused and confusing circumstances. Ehrlich uses a common experience of a girl's young adulthood—separation from mother—and explores it in hyperbolic ways. Joyce's love threatens to consume Nina. Nina dares to break out in little ways only because she finds safety in Joyce's protection. With detailed images of masks, makeup, and costuming, Laura almost totally fuses with her mother in order to separate from her. Female readers will recognize themselves similarly engaged. Ehrlich offers them confirmation and release.

Crossing yet another boundary, Ehrlich does not orchestrate that release for the reader. Secrecy dominates the novels to their very end. The characters hold secrets; the drive to discover their extent and the truth behind the secrets undeniably compels readers to keep turning the pages, but these novels conclude with only possible, not definite, resolution. The reader must bring her own experiences to articulate her individual conclusion—wherein lies Ehrlich's true impact as a writer.

—Cathryn M. Mercier

ELLEN, Jaye. See **NIXON, Joan Lowery.**

ELLIS, Sarah. Canadian. Born in Vancouver, British Columbia, Canada, 19 May 1952. Educated at University of British Columbia, B.A. 1973, M.L.S. 1975; Simmons College, Boston, M.A. 1980. Librarian, Toronto Public Library, c. 1975; children's librarian, Vancouver Public Library, Vancouver, British Columbia, 1976-81; children's librarian, North Vancouver District Library, North Vancouver, British Columbia, 1981—. Recipient: Sheila A. Egoff award, 1987, for *The Baby Project.* Address: 4432 Walden Street, Vancouver, British Columbia, V5V 3S3, Canada.

PUBLICATIONS FOR YOUNG ADULTS

Fiction

The Baby Project. Toronto, Ontario, Groundwood Books, 1986; as *A Family Project,* New York, Macmillan, 1988.
Next-Door Neighbours. Toronto, Ontario, Groundwood Books, 1989; as *Next-Door Neighbors,* New York, Macmillan, 1990.
Putting Up with Mitchell, illustrated by Barbara Wood. Brighouse Press, 1989.
Pick-Up Sticks. Toronto, Ontario, Groundwood Books, 1991; New York, Macmillan, 1992.

*   *   *

Sarah Ellis writes about ordinary people and their commonplace situations with a careful skill which illuminates and clarifies many of the basic themes and concerns of adolescence and family life. With a distinctive fidelity to a child-centered perspective, Ellis tells the stories of female protagonists who struggle with the daily issues of maturing as well as learning to face challenges of moving neighborhoods, dealing with new schools and friendships, and coping with death.

In *A Family Project,* winner of the Canadian Governor General's Award, eleven-year-old Jessica and her best friend, Margaret, change the subject of their animal project from platypuses to babies when Jessica's mother unexpectedly announces she is pregnant. Minute details of characterization and convincing dialogue sketch the members of Jessica's family, their renter downstairs, and Margaret and Jessica themselves. With humor and laughter communicated through subtle anecdotes, Ellis chronicles the family's adjustment to the pregnancy and eventual birth of Baby Lucie. When the tragedy of crib death suddenly takes Lucie away from them, Jessica has to fight to make sense of the "complicated hurt inside her."

Different themes are handled with the same sensitivity and humour in *Next-Door Neighbors,* a story of moving to a new neighborhood and trying to feel at home. Twelve-year-old Peggy struggles with shyness and has trouble fitting into her new school. She becomes further alienated from her classmates when she is caught lying to impress them. Peggy slowly develops an unlikely friendship with her two neighbors: George, whose family has immigrated from Eastern Europe, and Sing, the live-in gardener for the elderly lady next door. As she gets to know George and Sing, Peggy begins to recognize their unique talents and appreciate some of the cultural differences between them. She also learns to assert herself, and standing up to an adult for the first time, challenges the blatant racism of Sing's employer. Ellis weaves all of these issues into an entertaining and probing story of a young adolescent.

In her third novel, *Pick-Up Sticks,* Ellis moves away from traditional (though not typical) families, to the story of Polly, a thirteen-year-old who lives alone with her mother. Rather than focusing exclusively on this now commonplace family grouping, Ellis raises other issues connected to coming of age, financial security, and peer pressure. While her mother hunts for affordable housing, Polly lives with her wealthy uncle and aunt, an experience which calls into question all her previous longings for money and stability. Again, Ellis's characters are vividly and realistically drawn: Polly's scatterbrained, spontaneous mother, Stephanie, her overindulged cousin who turns to petty theft and vandalism for fun; Eric, the mentally handicapped neighbor, and Vanessa, Polly's best friend. A detectable maturing of perception and attitudes in the context of these relationships rounds out Polly's character and sustains the strong narrative drive.

Ellis's stories are all firmly rooted in place and supported by a wealth of realistic detail. Her themes though basic, elucidate concerns shared by her readers, while her self-possessed and hopeful protagonists lead the way into adolescence.

—Patricia Hill

ELLISON, Ralph (Waldo). American. Born in Oklahoma City, Oklahoma, 1 March 1914. Educated at a high school in Oklahoma City, and at Tuskegee Institute, Alabama, 1933-36. Served in the United States Merchant Marine, 1943-45. Married Fanny McConnell in 1946. Writer, since 1937; worked as a researcher and writer on Federal Writers' Project in New York City, 1938-42;

edited *Negro Quarterly,* 1942; lecture tour in Germany, 1954; lecturer at Salzburg Seminar, Austria, fall, 1954; U.S. Information Agency, tour of Italian cities, 1956; instructor in Russian and American literature, Bard College, Annandale-on-Hudson, New York, 1958-61; New York University, New York City, Albert Schweitzer Professor in Humanities, 1970-79; emeritus, since 1979. Chairman, Literary Grants Committee, American Academy, 1964-67; Alexander White Visiting Professor, University of Chicago, 1961; visiting professor of writing, Rutgers University, New Brunswick, New Jersey, 1962-64; visiting fellow in American studies, Yale University, New Haven, Connecticut, 1966. Gertrude Whittall Lecturer, Library of Congress, Washington, D.C., 1964; Ewing Lecturer, University of California, Los Angeles, 1964. Lecturer in American Negro culture, folklore, and creative writing at other colleges and universities throughout the United States, including Columbia University, Fisk University, Princeton University, Antioch University, and Bennington College; Carnegie Commission on Educational Television, 1966-67; honorary consultant in American letters, Library of Congress, Washington, D.C., 1966-72; Trustee, John F. Kennedy Center for the Performing Arts, Washington, D.C., Educational Broadcasting Corp., New School for Social Research, Bennington College, New York, Vermont, and Colonial Williamsburg Foundation; Member, National Council on the Arts, 1965-67. Recipient: Rosenwald grant, 1945; National Book award and National Newspaper Publishers' Russwurm award, both 1953, both for *Invisible Man;* Certificate of award, *Chicago Defender,* 1953; Rockefeller Foundation award, 1954; Prix de Rome fellowships, American Academy of Arts and Letters, 1955 and 1956; *Invisible Man* selected as the most distinguished postwar American novel and Ellison as the sixth most influential novelist by *New York Herald Tribune Book Week* poll of two hundred authors, editors, and critics, 1965; recipient of award honoring well-known Oklahomans in the arts from governor of Oklahoma, 1966; Medal of Freedom, 1969; Chevalier de l'Ordre des Arts et Lettres (France), 1970; Ralph Ellison Public Library, Oklahoma City, named in his honor, 1975; National Medal of Arts, 1985, for *Invisible Man* and for his teaching at numerous universities. Ph.D. in Humane Letters: Tuskegee Institute, 1963; Litt.D.: Rutgers University, 1966; University of Michigan, Ann Arbor, 1967; Williams College, Williamstown, Massachusetts, 1970; Long Island University, New York, 1971; College of William and Mary, Williamsburg, Virginia, 1972; Harvard University, Cambridge, Massachusetts, 1974; Wake Forest College, Winston-Salem, North Carolina, 1974; L.H.D.: Grinnell College, Iowa, 1967; Adelphi University, Garden City, New York, 1971; University of Maryland, College Park, 1974; Bard College, Annandale-on-Hudson, New York, 1978; Wesleyan University, Middletown, Connecticut, 1980; Brown University, Providence, Rhode Island, 1980. Commandant, Order of Arts and Letters (France), 1970. Member, American Academy, 1975; Coordinating Council of Literary Magazines-General Electric Foundation award, 1988. Agent: Owen Laster, William Morris Agency, 1350 Ave. of the Americas, New York, NY 10019. Address: 730 Riverside Dr., New York, NY 10031, U.S.A.

PUBLICATIONS

Novel

Invisible Man. New York, Random House, 1952; London, Gollancz, 1953.

Other

Contributor, *The Living Novel: A Symposium,* edited by Granville Hicks. London, Macmillan, 1957.
Shadow and Act (essays). New York, Random House, 1964; London, Secker & Warburg, 1967.
The Writer's Experience, with Karl Shapiro. Washington, D.C., Library of Congress, 1964.
Contributor, *Education of the Deprived and Segregated.* New York, Bank Street College of Education, 1965.
Contributor, *Who Speaks for the Negro?,* by Robert Penn Warren. New York, Random House, 1965.
The City in Crisis, with Whitney M. Young and Herbert Gnas. New York, Randolph Educational Fund, 1968.
Contributor, *To Heal and to Build: The Programs of Lyndon B. Johnson,* edited by James MacGregor Burns. New York, McGraw, 1968.
Contributor, *American Law: The Third Century, The Law Bicentennial Volume,* edited by Bernard Schwartz. Littleton, Colorado, F.B. Rothman for New York University School of Law, 1976.
Going to the Territory (essays). New York, Random House, 1986.

*

Media Adaptations: "Ralph Ellison: An Interview with the Author of Invisible Man" (sound recording), Center for Cassette Studies, 1974; "Is the Novel Dead?: Ellison, Styron and Baldwin on Contemporary Fiction," with William Styron and James Baldwin (sound recording), Center for Cassette Studies, 1974.

Biography: Entry in *Concise Dictionary of American Literary Biography: The New Consciousness, 1941-1948,* Detroit, Gale, 1987; *Contemporary Fiction in America and England, 1950-1970,* 1976; entry in *Dictionary of Literary Biography,* Volume 2: *American Novelists since World War II,* Detroit, Gale, 1978.

Bibliography: "A Bibliography of Ralph Ellison's Published Writings" by Bernard Benoit and Michel Fabre, in *Studies in Black Literature* (Fredericksburg, Virginia), Autumn 1971.

Critical Studies: *The Negro Novel in America,* revised edition, by Robert A. Bone, New Haven, Connecticut, Yale University Press, 1958; *Five Black Writers: Essays* by Donald B. Gibson, New York, University Press, 1970; *Twentieth-Century Interpretations of Invisible Man* edited by John M. Reilly, Englewood Cliffs, New Jersey, Prentice Hall, 1970; *The Merrill Studies in Invisible Man* edited by Ronald Gottesman, Columbus, Ohio, Merrill, 1971; entry in *Contemporary Literary Criticism,* Detroit, Gale, Volume 1, 1973, Volume 3, 1975, Volume 11, 1979; *Ralph Ellison: A Collection of Critical Essays* edited by John Hersey, Englewood Cliffs, New Jersey, Prentice Hall, 1973; article by Leonard J. Deutsch, in *American Novelists since World War II* edited by Jeffrey Heltermann and Richard Layman, Detroit, Gale, 1978; *Folklore and Myth in Ralph Ellison's Early Works* by Dorothea Fischer-Hornung, Stuttgart, Hochschul, 1979; *The Craft of Ralph Ellison* Cambridge, Massachusetts, Harvard University Press, 1980; *New Essays on Invisible Man* edited by Robert G. O'Meally, London, Cambridge University Press, 1988; *Ralph Ellison: The Genesis of an Artist* by Rudolf F. Dietze, Nuremberg, Carl, 1982; introduction by the author to thirtieth anniversary edition of *Invisible Man,* New York, Random House, 1982; *Speaking for You: The Vision of Ralph Ellison* edited by Kimberly W. Benston, Washington, D.C., Howard University Press, 1987; *Invisible Criticism: Ralph Ellison and the American Canon* by Alan Nadel, Iowa City, University of Iowa Press, 1988; *Creative Revolt: A Study of Wright, Ellison, and Dostoevsky* by Michael F. Lynch, New York, Lang, 1990.

*   *   *

Although Ralph Waldo Ellison did not write *Invisible Man* directly for young adults, it is assigned in schools and colleges across the United States and is one of the most widely read novels of the African American experience. It has attained the status of a literary classic, almost as well known as *Huckleberry Finn* and *Moby Dick,* though more often read than the latter. Ellison was virtually unknown as a writer when it was published, having only contributed to a number of magazines. He began working on the novel in 1945 and continued over the next seven years, a period of enormous change in the recognition of the role of African Americans in society. The armed forces and major sports were desegregated in this period, and the momentous, unanimous Supreme Court ruling of *Brown v. Board of Education* was soon to follow. *Invisible Man* became part of the growing civil rights movement of the postwar period and has informed all subsequent struggles for equal rights. It instantly made him one of the most celebrated authors in the world. He won the National Book Award with it, as well as several other awards, and though he has published little other than essays and a few short stories since, he remains among the most famous living writers.

Ellison grew up in Oklahoma City, which was, he thought, a fairly tolerant community, and though his time at the Tuskegee Institute and in New York after 1936 must have made him see the social situation differently, he insists he wrote *Invisible Man* thinking not of its brilliant sociological insights into injustice, but strictly of the art of writing. This concern with aesthetics derived at least partly from the strong influence of T. S. Eliot's *The Waste Land,* which Ellison was highly impressed with as a student at Tuskegee. He was also deeply interested in the works of Russian authors, about whom he has lectured and written, with the most obvious influence being Feodor Dostoyevsky's *Notes from the Underground* and its parallel "The Man Who Lived Underground" by Richard Wright, who exerted a great influence on Ellison during his New York stay. Ellison's invisible man also owes quite a bit to Joseph K. of Franz Kafka's *The Trial.*

The philosophical influences of transcendentalism and postwar French existentialism have also been argued, primarily because *Invisible Man* can be read as a novel of self-discovery as much, if not more than, a novel of racial identity. The narrator comes to recognize that if an individual accepts the role other members of society (black and white) impose upon him, he is doomed as a man, his invisibility made permanent. Interpreted in this way the novel is a universal statement about the human condition which is set in the black experience, but not limited to it. While this makes *Invisible Man* a novel for all people, it has caused criticism by commentators who feel Ellison played into the establishment's hands by putting the burden of equality upon the individual, without appreciating the onerous burden of societal pressure. It is for this reason, these critics argue, that the novel has been so blatantly praised and widely taught.

Despite Ellison's aesthetic intentions and the rich variety of literary allusions and references that *Invisible Man* contains, it is usually read for its illumination of the situation of the black man in America. In the paint company in which the narrator works, there is an old black man, deep in the bowels of the factory, who controls the machinery. Further, there is the imagery of the black additive which is mixed into white paint so that it will dry properly. Black people, Ellison is obviously saying, have made enormous contributions to white society which are absorbed and ignored, just like the additive. The races have a symbiotic relationship which white society refuses to acknowledge, imposing invisibility upon African Americans.

However, unlike many novels which are read for their social commentary, it is not a novel which could be described as realistic. The characters are fascinating, but represent an array of types rather than individuals. From Ras, a proselytizer for the back-to-Africa movement, to Bledsoe, the establishment black leader, the characters of the novel have a highly symbolic quality, and the words "dreamlike" and "surreal" are often used to describe it. As in Kafka, however, the distortions are all firmly within a particular milieu, which relates it more to the naturalistic novel of Emile Zola and Frank Norris. Ellison's scenes and settings are exaggerated, but still plainly recognizable as particular places in the black American's landscape, whether the southern Negro college or Harlem. Unlike Norris or Zola at their worst, however, Ellison never allows himself to become preachy, nor does he reduce his characters and events to simple allegory, though in most instances the characters seem to lack free will in the same way that Zola's and Norris's do. Determined by circumstances of birth and environment, they seem unable to escape. In a non-naturalistic revolt against determinism, however, the narrator himself, the invisible man, transcends his circumstances by stepping outside of normal human society in an act of will comparable to the absurd acts of the heroes of Jean-Paul Sartre and Albert Camus, and he becomes quite literally enlightened in his underground hiding place amongst his 1,369 lights operated on stolen power. Overt symbolism such as that of the light bulbs or the earlier image of the paint factory may be an important reason why *Invisible Man* appears on so many school reading lists, but it is also one reason it is so accessible to a large reading public, despite the sophisticated interlayering of literary techniques and allusions. Such a potent combination assures it a long life as a literary classic.

—J. Madison Davis

_____

EMERSON, Zack. See **WHITE, Ellen Emerson.**

_____

ENGDAHL, Sylvia Louise. American. Born in Los Angeles, California, 24 November 1933. Educated at Pomona College, Claremont, California, 1950; Reed College, Portland, Oregon, 1951; University of Oregon, Eugene, 1951-52, 1956-57; University of California, Santa Barbara, B.A. in education 1955; graduate work in anthropology, Portland State University, Oregon, 1978-80. Elementary school teacher, Portland, 1955-56; programmer, then computer systems specialist, SAGE Air Defense System, Lexington, Massachusetts, Madison, Wisconsin, Tacoma, Washington, and Santa Monica, California, 1957-67; full-time writer, 1968-80; self-employed developer and vendor of home computer software, 1981-84. Since 1985 member of online faculty, Connected Education Inc., New York. Recipient: Notable Book citation from American Library Association, Honor List citation from *Horn Book,* and Newbery Honor Book award, 1971, all for *Enchantress from the Stars;* Christopher Award, 1973, for *This Star Shall Abide;* Phoenix award, 1990, for *Enchantress from the Stars.* Address: 3088 Delta Pines Drive, Eugene, OR 97401, U.S.A.

PUBLICATIONS FOR YOUNG ADULTS

Fiction

Enchantress from the Stars, illustrated by Rodney Shackell. New York, Atheneum, 1970; London, Gollancz, 1974.
Journey between Worlds, illustrated by James and Ruth McCrea. New York, Atheneum, 1970.
The Far Side of Evil, illustrated by Richard Cuffari. New York, Atheneum, 1971; London, Gollancz, 1975.
This Star Shall Abide, illustrated by Richard Cuffari. New York, Atheneum, 1972; as *Heritage of the Star,* London, Gollancz, 1973.
Beyond the Tomorrow Mountains, illustrated by Richard Cuffari. New York, Atheneum, 1973.
The Doors of the Universe. New York, Atheneum, 1981.

Other

The Planet-Girded Suns: Man's View of Other Solar Systems, illustrated by Richard Cuffari. New York, Atheneum, 1974.
Editor, with Rick Roberson, *Universe Ahead: Stories of the Future,* illustrated by Richard Cuffari. New York, Atheneum, 1975.
Editor, *Anywhere, Anywhen: Stories of Tomorrow.* New York, Atheneum, 1976.
The Subnuclear Zoo: New Discoveries in High Energy Physics, with Rick Roberson. New York, Atheneum, 1977.
Tool for Tomorrow: New Knowledge about Genes, with Rick Roberson. New York, Atheneum, 1979.
Our World Is Earth (for children), illustrated by Don Sibley. New York, Atheneum, 1979.

*

Biography: Essay "An Observer of Planet Earth," in *Something about the Author Autobiography Series,* Volume 5, Detroit, Gale, 1988.

Critical Study: Entry in *Children's Literature Review,* Volume 2, Detroit, Gale, 1976.

Sylvia Louise Engdahl comments:
In many libraries my books fail to reach the audience for which they are most appropriate. Because of the success of *Enchantress from the Stars* they are usually shelved with children's books, although the other novels are enjoyed most by readers fourteen or older. Also, they are frequently shelved with science fiction, whereas they appeal more to a general audience than to science fiction fans. Both teenagers and adults who don't like other science fiction often like mine, while science fiction enthusiasts tend to dismiss mine as not being "far out" enough for their taste; this was one of my main reasons for choosing to publish in the young people's field rather than the science fiction genre.

*   *   *

One of Sylvia Louise Engdahl's primary strengths as a writer of science fiction for adolescents lies in her employment of this form to comment on personal and political questions both contemporary and timeless. While she is hardly unusual among science-fiction authors—from H.G. Wells onward—in using the future to illuminate the present, the restraints she places upon her didactic impulses and the sympathy she brings to her complex portraits of people and cultures, make her an interesting social observer.

Engdahl's novels vary in the challenge they offer readers. *Journey between Worlds,* for instance, straightforwardly describes its heroine's passage to adulthood as she moves from Earth to Mars, from fear of the unknown to acceptance of experience, and from her domineering Oregon fiancé to new love on Mars. Melinda's phobia about not being able to breathe when off her native planet is turned inside out as the narrative makes plain that real suffocation consists of denying growth—refusing to leave home. That Melinda's quest is predominantly framed in the terms of the teen romance, however, directs the story toward a different audience than that addressed by Engdahl's more characteristic works.

In *Enchantress from the Stars* (a 1971 Newbery Honor Book), Engdahl foregrounds concerns that extend throughout her works: the importance of empathy, intelligence, and moral courage; the individual's role in effecting change; and the need to approach problems on a symbolic as well as a literal level and to combine the mundane with the spiritual. *Enchantress* tells the story of a young anthropology student, Elana, who finds herself involved in the effort to save a feudal world from colonization by a technology-absorbed interstellar empire. While Elana is the primary narrator, we also share the viewpoints of representatives from the other cultures: Georyn, the woodcutter's son, and Jarel, the doctor.

This shifting narration underscores one of the novel's chief values, respect for others. Elana may belong to the most advanced culture—that which unites technological and mental powers—but her command of telepathy does not make her personally superior to Georyn or Jarel. The human element is always more important than material trappings; indeed, she and Georyn fall in love, although their separate responsibilities make continuing the romance impossible. While the three young people may "read" the situation differently (Georyn's narrative is cast in fairy-tale language, Jarel's in technological terms), we are constantly reminded that each viewpoint has its own truth.

The Anthropological Service to which Elana belongs is dedicated to preserving that truth, to studying cultures without changing them. Nonintervention, the service has learned, must take priority over the desire to help; like adolescents, cultures cannot grow if others do their thinking for them. To an idealist like Elana, this principle often appears harsh, as in *The Far Side of Evil* when she is sent to observe a planet apparently on the brink of nuclear annihilation. The emphasis is not on the Torisian Cold War but on Elana's progress toward self-knowledge, her friend Kari's progress toward courage, and her colleague Randil's progress toward responsibility. As in *Enchantress from the Stars,* the individual's spiritual quest mirrors that of the world: the totalitarians of Toris share Kari's lack of faith and Randil's unconscious arrogance, so that as each character evolves toward maturity, we are given hope that society may follow.

In addition to her novels, Engdahl has edited or coedited collections of science-fiction stories and written or collaborated on a number of nonfiction works on scientific subjects such as physics or genetics. The latter interest plays an important role in the tale unfolded in Engdahl's trilogy: *This Star Shall Abide, Beyond the Tomorrow Mountains,* and *The Doors of the Universe.* These novels take place on a metal-poor planet colonized generations previously by a group of scientists whose home sun had subsequently gone nova, presenting the colonists with the problem of surviving in a world whose biology is unfriendly and which cannot support the technology developed on the mother planet.

As is gradually revealed, the solution devised by the chief scientist among the initial group of settlers has required the establishment of a peculiar caste system that purports to be a theocracy but is in fact a meritocracy in which those demonstrating intelligence and independence of mind are chosen for the "priesthood"—actually, a secret cadre of scientists. What we learn about this world keeps pace with the discoveries made by the trilogy's protagonist, Noren. His rebellious questioning of his Stone Age society puts him at odds with his fellow villagers in the first volume, with a group of subhuman mutants in the second (descendants of people who have drunk untreated water), and in the third with those whose "heresies," like his own, have permitted their elevation to the rank of scientist. Similarly, he moves from self-discovery to romantic love to leadership of his world, a sequence of widening understanding that parallels the individual's attainment of maturity.

The trilogy is an extended meditation on the need for total commitment to an ideal, for willingness to challenge assumptions, and for change. Again the individual is paramount; Noren's intelligent iconoclasm finds a solution to his people's problem, while his own quest to learn to fit into his world parallels the colony's effort to become part of an alien environment. Likewise, these three novels consistently acknowledge the terrifying complexity of life—the awareness that what is necessary may not always be fair and that growth often involves hurt.

Engdahl's emphasis on being different, on the painfulness of responsibility, and on coming to terms with oneself and one's world accounts for much of her success as a writer for adolescents: the concerns she addresses on a symbolic level are indeed important. In their refusal to condescend to their readers, her novels practice the same respect for others that they preach. The consistently high quality of her prose and the unity of her moral vision make Engdahl's works exciting and deserving of addition to the canon of young-adult science fiction.

—Claudia Nelson

———

EYERLY, Jeannette Hyde. Has also written as Jeannette Griffith, a joint pseudonym with Valeria Winkler Griffith. American. Born in Topeka, Kansas, 7 June 1908. Educated at Drake University, 1926-29; University of Iowa, A.B. 1930. Married Frank Rinehart Eyerly in 1932; two daughters. Writer. Publicity director, Des Moines Public Library, 1930-32; creative writing teacher, Des Moines Adult Education Program, 1955-57. Des Moines Child Guidance Center, member of board of directors, 1949-54, president, 1953-54. St. Joseph Academy Guild, member of board of directors, 1954-57, president, 1957. Member of acquisition committee, Des Moines Art Center, 1960-63. Polk Mental Health Center, member of board of directors, 1968-78, president, 1977-78, 1982—. Iowa Commission for the Blind, member of board, 1977-80, chairman, 1978-79. Recipient: Susan Glaspell Award, 1965, for *Gretchen's Hill;* Christopher Award, 1970, for *Escape from Nowhere; Radigan Cares* selected as one of the Child Study Association's Books of the Year, 1970. Agent: Curtis Brown Ltd., 10 Astor Place, New York, NY 10003, U.S.A.

PUBLICATIONS FOR YOUNG ADULTS

Fiction

Dearest Kate, with Valeria Winkler Griffith, under joint pseudonym Jeannette Griffith. Philadelphia, Pennsylvania, Lippincott, 1961.
More Than a Summer Love. Philadelphia, Lippincott, 1962.
Drop-Out. Philadelphia, Lippincott, 1963.
The World of Ellen March. Philadelphia, Lippincott, 1964.
A Girl Like Me. Philadelphia, Lippincott, 1966.
The Girl Inside. Philadelphia, Lippincott, 1968.
Escape from Nowhere. Philadelphia, Lippincott, 1969.
Radigan Cares. Philadelphia, Lippincott, 1970.
The Phaedra Complex. Philadelphia, Lippincott, 1971.
Bonnie Jo, Go Home. Philadelphia, Lippincott, 1972.
Goodbye to Budapest: A Novel of Suspense. Philadelphia, Lippincott, 1974.
The Leonardo Touch. Philadelphia, Lippincott, 1976.
He's My Baby, Now. Philadelphia, Lippincott, 1977.
See Dave Run. Philadelphia, Lippincott, 1978.
If I Loved You Wednesday. Philadelphia, Lippincott, 1980.
Seth and Me and Rebel Make Three. Philadelphia, Lippincott, 1983.
Angel Baker, Thief. Philadelphia, Lippincott, 1984.
Someone to Love Me. Philadelphia, Lippincott, 1987.

PUBLICATIONS FOR CHILDREN

Fiction

Gretchen's Hill, illustrated by Burmah Burris. Philadelphia, Lippincott, 1965.
The Seeing Summer, illustrated by Emily McCully. Philadelphia, Lippincott, 1981.

PUBLICATIONS FOR ADULTS

Nonfiction

Writing Young Adult Novels, with Hadley Irwin. Cincinnati, Ohio, Writer's Digest, 1988.

*

Biography: Entry in *Fifth Book of Junior Authors and Illustrators,* New York, H.W. Wilson, 1983; essay in *Something about the Author Autobiography Series,* Volume 10, Detroit, Gale, 1990; essay in *Speaking for Ourselves, Too* compiled and edited by Donald R. Gallo, National Council of Teachers of English, 1993.

Jeannette Hyde Eyerly also wrote under the name of Jeannette Griffith. Her writing experience is extensive, beginning with magazine articles and a syndicated column then moving on to include short stories and novels in her repertoire. Her books have been adapted as educational resources both in the written format and in a television movie. Her insightful handling of the contemporary problems of youth has garnered her several prestigious literary awards.

Eyerly primarily relies on her life's encounters and experiences to generate ideas for her books and stories. An early book written for children, *Gretchen's Hill*, relates incidents from her childhood. As a mother of two daughters, she heard their complaints about the "gumdrop" teenage novels with patently happy endings and complete resolution of all conflicts. Her wisdom and experience led her to believe teenagers might prefer books which were somewhat closer to the truth. Her earliest book, *More Than a Summer Love*, dealt with the problems of teenagers in love. Several later books also addressed this theme. In *More Than a Summer Love*, this story of romance subtly enlightens teenagers on the "dangers" of becoming too seriously involved when they are too young to understand the future ramifications of their actions. Marriage is difficult enough without adding the concomitant obstacles faced by young people such as education and employment.

Beginning with *A Girl Like Me*, then *Bonnie Jo, Go Home, He's My Baby, Now*, and finally *Someone to Love Me*, Eyerly expands upon the "problems of teenage love" theme by dealing with the issue of teenage pregnancy. In *A Girl Like Me* she writes to teens in their own words as they communicate their fears to each other. She utilizes dialogue and vocabulary common to youth when they discuss issues in confidence. Though this book was written almost thirty years ago, teenage boys still try to persuade their girlfriends to "go all the way," and "you would if you loved me" is still a popular phrase. Teenage girls (and in some cases, younger now) can certainly relate to these sentiments. Though issues of birth control today may be clouded by the more pressing issue of sexually transmitted diseases, unwanted pregnancy is still a concern. Of course in some ways the stigma placed on the unmarried pregnant woman may be less today than it was years ago, the primary considerations remain the same as those which troubled Eyerly's characters. What does the girl do? What about school, her social life, her friends, her future? What about the boy? What about his plans? What about the baby? Are marriage and abortion options to consider? In *Bonnie Jo, Go Home*, Bonnie Jo decides to go to New York and seek an illegal (at that time) abortion. Without lecturing to readers, the book leaves teenagers with the frightening reality that there are consequences to their actions. Abortion, though legal in most areas now, is still not without a serious emotional, if not financial, price. This book allows the reader to go inside the characters' minds to experience their pain, their suffering, and their questioning of themselves and their actions. In *Someone to Love Me*, Patrice decides to keep her baby. This choice is also fraught with repercussions. When a young, unmarried girl becomes pregnant—whether through ignorance, foolishness, or both—her life must change in one way or another. If she decides to bear and keep her baby, she sacrifices her youth for motherhood. Eyerly researched her writing of this book in alternative high schools and groups for unwed teenage mothers. It was there she gained the understanding of the plights of these women she so skillfully conveys to her readers. Life is irrevocably changed when "children have children." She explicitly details her character's daily trials perhaps with the thought that she may one day save a reader from the same fate. Finally, *He's My Baby, Now* deals with the problem of teenage pregnancy by taking an unconventional tact. This book is told from the young unmarried father's perspective. In this story, the young man does not wish to have his child placed up for adoption and refuses to sign the legal papers. The teens are forced to realize that the product of their union is a living, breathing human being that requires love and care that will last a lifetime. Once again Eyerly shows the readers the consequences their lack of responsibility can have on their futures. Teenagers broaden their thinking when they realize the wide-ranging effects of an unexpected pregnancy on both the boy and the girl involved. The book was somewhat unique in its time in that it dealt with the feelings boys usually tried to hide. In writing the book from the boy's point of view, her message gained the wider audience to make it more educational, but in a palatable way. So great was the response to this book that it was eventually the basis for a special television program.

Eyerly also addressed other problems faced by youth. *Drop-Out*, another critically acclaimed book, led to many classroom discussions on the virtues of staying in school. Most teenagers can relate to the feelings of frustration and of wanting to "get out." Those without the experiences of the outside world may not know what's waiting for them unless they can see it through the eyes of the character. Another book which relates to escaping the everyday problems is *Seth and Me and Rebel Make Three*. This book is of a lighter fare than *See Dave Run*, which realistically portrays a teenage loner with real characters we might find in "Anytown, U.S.A." This story of a runaway boy who eventually takes his own life was written long before teenage suicide became the problem it is today. The author also looks at a teenager's attempted suicide due to her mental health in *The Girl Inside*.

Another award-winning book was *Escape from Nowhere*, which was frequently used in classrooms to discuss the issue of drug abuse. Eyerly's extensive research is evidenced by her exacting details and descriptions. The author also saw the problems of teenagers coming from broken homes. In *The World of Ellen March*, a teenager suffers through the divorce of her parents but eventually realizes life does go on and she will survive. Though divorce is more common today than it once was, children are no more ready to see it in their own homes.

We see many other sides to Eyerly. One book, *The Seeing Summer*, vividly describes the experience of blindness by capturing the friendship between a blind child and a sighted friend. This book was later adapted into a short classroom play used for instructing both sighted and blind students as well as teachers of the blind. Other books have students involved in politics as in *Radigan Cares*. Add intrigue and you have *Goodbye to Budapest: A Novel of Suspense* and *The Leonardo Touch*. It is no wonder that Eyerly eventually wrote (with Hadley Irwin) *Writing Young Adult Novels*, which was most favorably reviewed.

—Laurie Schwartz Guttenberg

F

FARLEY, Walter (Lorimer). American. Born in Syracuse, New York, 26 June 1915. Educated at Erasmus High School, Brooklyn, New York; Mercersburg Academy, Pennsylvania, 1931-35; Columbia University, New York, 1941. Served in the Fourth Armored Division, and as staff member of *Yank* magazine, United States Army, 1942-46. Married Rosemary Lutz in 1945; two daughters (one deceased) and two sons. Writer. Advertising copywriter, Batten Barton Durstine and Osborn, New York, 1941; Arabian horse breeder, Earlville, Pennsylvania, 1946-65. Consultant and promoter for films, "The Black Stallion" and "The Black Stallion Returns." Recipient: Pacific Northwest Library Association's Young Reader's Choice award, 1944, for *The Black Stallion,* and 1948, for *The Black Stallion Returns;* Boys Club Junior Book award, 1948, for *The Black Stallion Returns;* literary landmark established in Farley's honor by Venice Area Public Library, Venice, Florida. *Died 16 October 1989.*

PUBLICATIONS FOR YOUNG ADULTS

Fiction

The Black Stallion, illustrated by Keith Ward. New York, Random House, 1941; London, Lunn, 1947; abridged edition, as *The Black Stallion Picture Book,* Random House, 1979.
Larry and the Undersea Raider, illustrated by P.K. Jackson. New York, Random House, 1942; London, Muller, 1944.
The Black Stallion Returns, illustrated by Harold Eldridge. New York, Random House, 1945; London, Lunn, 1947.
Son of the Black Stallion, illustrated by Milton Menasco. New York, Random House, 1947; 2nd edition with drawings by Hofbauer, London, Collins, 1950.
The Island Stallion, illustrated by Keith Ward. New York, Random House, 1948; London, Hodder & Stoughton, 1973.
The Black Stallion and Satan, illustrated by Milton Menasco. New York, Random House, 1949; revised edition, London, Hodder & Stoughton, 1974.
The Blood Bay Colt, illustrated by Milton Menasco. New York, Random House, 1950; as *The Black Stallion's Blood Bay Colt,* New York, Random House, 1978.
The Island Stallion's Fury, illustrated by Harold Eldridge. New York, Random House, 1951; London, Knight, 1975.
The Black Stallion's Filly, illustrated by Milton Menasco. New York, Random House, 1952; London, Knight, 1979.
The Black Stallion Revolts, illustrated by Harold Eldridge. New York, Random House, 1953; London, Knight, 1978.
The Black Stallion's Sulky Colt, illustrated by Harold Eldridge. New York, Random House, 1954.
The Island Stallion Races, illustrated by Harold Eldridge. New York, Random House, 1955.
The Black Stallion's Courage, illustrated by Allen F. Brewer, Jr. New York, Random House, 1956; London, Knight, 1978.
The Black Stallion Mystery, illustrated by Mal Singer. New York, Random House, 1957; London, Hodder & Stoughton, 1973.
The Horse-Tamer, illustrated by James Schucker. New York, Random House, 1958.

The Black Stallion and Flame, illustrated by Harold Eldridge. New York, Random House, 1960; revised edition, London, Hodder & Stoughton, 1974.
The Black Stallion Challenged!, illustrated by Angie Draper. New York, Random House, 1964; as *The Black Stallion's Challenge,* London, Hodder & Stoughton, 1983.
The Great Dane, Thor, illustrated by Joseph Cellini. New York, Random House, 1966.
The Black Stallion's Ghost, illustrated by Angie Draper. New York, Random House, 1969.
The Black Stallion and the Girl, illustrated by Angie Draper. New York, Random House, 1971.
Walter Farley's Black Stallion Books (includes *The Black Stallion, The Black Stallion Returns, The Black Stallion and Satan,* and *The Black Stallion Mystery*). New York, Random House, 4 vols., 1979.
The Black Stallion Legend. New York, Random House, 1983.

Other

Man O'War, illustrated by Angie Draper. New York, Random House, 1962.
How to Stay Out of Trouble with Your Horse, photographs by Tim Farley. New York, Doubleday, 1981.

PUBLICATIONS FOR CHILDREN

Fiction

Big Black Horse, with Josette Frank (adaptation of *The Black Stallion*), illustrated by P.K. Jackson. New York, Random House, 1953.
Little Black, a Pony, illustrated by James Schucker. New York, Random House, 1961; London, Collins, 1963.
Little Black Goes to the Circus, illustrated by James Schucker. New York, Random House, 1963; London, Collins, 1965.
The Horse That Swam Away, illustrated by Leo Summers. New York, Random House, 1965.
The Little Black Pony Races, illustrated by James Schucker. New York, Random House, 1968.
The Black Stallion Picture Book, illustrated with photographs from the motion picture. New York, Random House, 1979.
The Black Stallion Returns: A Storybook Based on the Movie, edited by Stephanie Spinner. New York, Random House, 1982.
The Black Stallion: An Easy-to-Read Adaptation, illustrated by Sandy Rabinowitz. New York, Random House, 1986.
The Black Stallion Beginner Book. New York, Random House, 1987.

*

Media Adaptations: *The Black Stallion* (movie), United Artists, 1979; *The Black Stallion* (filmstrip with cassette), Media Basics, 1982; *The Black Stallion Returns* (movie), United Artists, 1983.

Biography: Entry in *Dictionary of Literary Biography,* Volume 22: *American Writers for Children, 1900-1960,* Detroit, Gale, 1983.

Manuscript Collections: Butler Library, Columbia University, New York; Venice Area Public Library, Venice, Florida.

Critical Study: Entry in *Contemporary Literary Criticism,* Volume 17, Detroit, Gale, 1981.

*   *   *

Animal stories for young adult readers frequently focus on the bonds of love and loyalty which develop between a character and an animal. Walter Farley's series of books describe the unbridled love between a boy, Alec Ramsey, and his horse, a wild Arabian stallion who appears in the first book of the series, *The Black Stallion.* Other books in the series feature a different racehorse, either a descendant or a rival of the Black.

The plots of Farley's books are fast-paced as the human protagonist, Alec Ramsey, recognizes the outstanding speed of each of his horses and then prepares it for racing. Conflict arises when some aspect of the horse's temperament threatens to undermine its success in the race. Resolution of the conflict is achieved through Alec's insights and loving, patient treatment of the horse. The climax of the story is usually the thrilling narration of the race itself. Victory is achieved despite obstacles, usually in a come-from-behind finish; the win can be attributed not only to the talent but also to the heart and courage of horse and rider.

Only in *Man O'War,* Farley's biography of the legendary race horse, does the pace of the story drag. It is a thoroughly researched piece; however, the facts weight the story and the author's attempts to introduce tension and conflict for each race seem contrived.

The development of character and setting take a back seat to plot in Farley's books. These are not coming-of-age stories; in fact, Alec's only growth is as a jockey. Introspection is infrequent and limited to concern about the horse's ability to race. The reader does not come to know Alec except as a horseman. As a student, he waits for the clock to signal dismissal so that he can be with his horse. When schoolmates come to see his horse and are frightened by its wild behavior, they leave and do not return. Alec doesn't miss them. His closest friend is Henry Daily, an older man who shares Alec's love and knowledge of horses and helps train them for racing. Daily is impressed by Alec's extraordinary ability to communicate with horses.

Alec's parents are also undeveloped characters. They do not share their son's passion for horses or feel comfortable about it for that matter. In *The Black Stallion* they are such background figures that they don't realize that their son is racing his horse in clandestine midnight training sessions at Belmont Park. Alec's father isn't informed that his son will compete in a nationally acclaimed challenge stakes until a week before the race and his mother is never told. Both parents do end up at the track to share in his triumph, however.

In *The Son of the Black Stallion,* Alec's father assumes a more prominent role, resisting, then finally supporting, his son's ambition to race the Black's fiery colt. Still, it is the trainer, Henry, who has the most influence on Alec.

In *The Black Stallion and Flame* an older Alec Ramsey is still racing partners with Henry Daily and his parents don't appear in the story. A disaster at sea occurs in this story as it did in *The Black Stallion.* This time Alec and his horse reach safety separately and Farley indulges in some anthropomorphism as he describes the Black's pleasure at running free on a desert island, competing with

another stallion for control of a herd of wild horses. Farley notes that the Black looked at the broodmares "lovingly" and that he preferred the dark brown mares.

Setting assumes some significance in *The Black Stallion Returns* because Alec visits the desert fortress of the Black's Arabian owner, who reclaims his horse and takes it home. Although Alec must relinquish his beloved Black, he is promised the first foal of the bloodline. In only a few other stories in this series does setting change from a horse barn and racetrack.

Travel by ship and airplane reveal the age of these tales. In addition, Farley's portrayal of females and ethnic groups is indicative of the era in which his books were written. His use of dialect is offensive by today's standards and so is his depiction of women as simple-minded homemakers (in *The Black Stallion*) or vacuous socialites (in *Man O'War*).

Despite these shortcomings young readers will vicariously thrill to Alec's ability to tame a wild stallion by virtue of the kindness and love which he transmits through a secret language of touches, whispers and whistles. Readers will identify with an average boy, who is the only person able to command the love and tame the savagery of that wildest of creatures—the wild stallion.

Farley's affection for horses is evident in his descriptions of sleek, muscular creatures that carry themselves with power, grace and dignity. All of the horses are lovingly portrayed: stallions; trotters; broodmares; colts; and even Napoleon, the cart horse who acts as the steadying influence for the high-strung stallions. Farley is the master of the horse story, and those who love horses or seek fast-paced adventure will treasure these books.

—Anne Drolett Creany

———

FARMER, Penelope (Jane). British. Born in Westerham, Kent, 14 June 1939. Educated at St. Anne's College, Oxford, Degree in History (with second-class honors) 1960; Bedford College, London, Diploma in Social Studies 1962; doctoral study at Keele University, since 1988. Married 1) Michael John Mockridge in 1962 (divorced, 1977), one daughter and one son; 2) Simon Shorvon in 1984. Writer. Teacher for London County Council Education Department, 1961-63, sociological researcher, 1985-90. Recipient: American Library Association notable book, 1962, and Carnegie Medal commendation, 1963, both for *The Summer Birds.* Agent: Deborah Owen, 78 Narrow St., London E14. Address: 30 Ravenscourt Rd., London W6 0UG, England.

PUBLICATIONS FOR YOUNG ADULTS

Novels

The China People, illustrated by Pearl Falconer. Stroudsburg, Pennsylvania, Hutchinson, 1960.
The Summer Birds, illustrated by James J. Spanfeller. New York, Harcourt, 1962.
The Magic Stone, illustrated by John Kaufmann. New York, Harcourt, 1964.

The Saturday Shillings, illustrated by Prudence Seward. London, Hamish Hamilton, 1965; as *Saturday by Seven,* New York, Penguin, 1978.

The Seagull, illustrated by Ian Ribbons. London, Hamish Hamilton, 1965; New York, Harcourt, 1966.

Emma in Winter, illustrated by James J. Spanfeller. New York, Harcourt, 1966.

Charlotte Sometimes, illustrated by Chris Connor. New York, Harcourt, 1969.

Dragonfly Summer, illustrated by Tessa Jordan. London, Hamish Hamilton, 1971; New York, Scholastic Book Services, 1974.

A Castle of Bone. New York, Atheneum, 1972.

William and Mary. New York, Atheneum, 1974.

Year King. New York, Atheneum, 1977.

Thicker Than Water. New York, Walker, 1989.

Stone Croc. New York, Walker, 1991.

Other

Editor, *Beginnings: Creation Myths of the World,* illustrated by Antonio Frasconi. London, Chatto & Windus, 1978; New York, Atheneum, 1979.

Translator, with Amos Oz. *Soumchi,* illustrated by William Papas. New York, Harper, 1980.

PUBLICATIONS FOR CHILDREN

Fiction

The Serpent's Teeth: The Story of Cadmus (picture book), illustrated by Chris Connor. London, Collins, 1971, New York, Harcourt, 1972.

Daedalus and Icarus (picture book), illustrated by Chris Connor. New York, Harcourt, 1971.

The Story of Persephone (picture book), illustrated by Graham McCallum. London, Collins, 1972; New York, Morrow, 1973.

August the Fourth, illustrated by Jael Jordon. London, Heinemann, 1975; East Orleans, Massachussetts, Parnassus, 1976.

Heracles (picture book), illustrated by Graham McCallum. London, Collins, 1975.

The Coal Train, illustrated by William Bird. London, Heinemann, 1977.

The Runaway Train, illustrated by William Bird. London, Heinemann, 1979.

PUBLICATIONS FOR ADULTS

Novels

Standing in the Shadow. London, Gollancz, 1984.

Eve: Her Story. London, Gollancz, 1985; San Francisco, Mercury House, 1988.

Away from Home: A Novel in Ten Episodes. London, Gollancz, 1987.

Glasshouses. London, Gollancz, 1988; North Pomfret, Vermont, Trafalgar Square, 1989.

Snakes & Ladders. London, Little, Brown, 1993.

*

Biography: Entry in *Fourth Book of Junior Authors and Illustrators,* New York, H.W. Wilson, 1978, pp. 124-126.

Critical Study: Entry in *Children's Literature Review,* Volume 8, Detroit, Gale, 1985; entry in *The Marble in the Water* by David Rees. Boston, The Horn Book Inc., 1980, pp. 1-13.

Penelope Farmer comments:

Adolescence is a very interesting age to me: there's so much raw power in kids of that age, before their instincts—sexual energies in particular—are understood and focussed. Some of the power, maybe, is dissipated now in the much greater sophistication of late twentieth-century teenagers. All the same I am interested in exploring the tensions, the aggressions, the passions, and the search for identity arising from the physical changes at puberty. And precisely because these emotions are so powerful, I have till now found it easier to do so, using mythological or supernatural themes. I feel strongly that fiction which attempts to corral all such feelings into stories of teenage romance—will she get the boy or won't she?—or which make the most controversial aspect a matter of how explicit you can make the details of the sexual act in a young adult novel diminish the characters it depicts and those for whom it is written. A lot of science fiction, on the other hand, gets it right—in that it confronts the young with real worlds, real issues of life and death, real levels of responsibility. Maybe that's where I will head next, therefore. Who knows!

*   *   *

Penelope Farmer's reputation as a children's writer has long rested securely on two books, *Charlotte Sometimes* and *A Castle of Bone,* published in 1969 and 1972. Farmer began to write while still at university, and *Charlotte Sometimes* was her seventh book. For all the grace and skill of her earlier books, *Charlotte Sometimes* was, however, breaking new ground, both for the author and in its genre. It is after all a "school story" opening with the first day at boarding school; and it must be the profoundest and most subversive such ever written, for the mechanism of the time slip is not really the little bed with wheels, but the disorientation, the displacement, the suppression of the self imposed by authoritarian contexts such as school. Changing places with Clare, who slept in the same bed forty years earlier, Charlotte loses a clear sense of who she is. Farmer's profound personal involvement in her work has often been remarked upon; the impression arises because the centre of awareness in the narration is interior to the central character, and the illumination offered by the fantasy is cast on the psyche, not primarily on the time or place or society portrayed by the story, in spite of the skill with which England in 1918 is evoked. Charlotte is simultaneously afraid of failing to achieve a return to her own time—failure to be herself—and afraid of being found out to be herself and not Clare, a most touching and realistic portrayal of the uncertainties of adolescence.

A Castle of Bone is still Farmer's masterpiece. Hugh's battered second-hand cupboard—it is never called a wardrobe—plays tricks, converting things put in it to earlier phases of themselves. It is in his room that he dreams, or perhaps hallucinates, moving across a mysterious landscape dominated by a castle, which both attracts and repels him. Hugh and his sister Jean, and his friend Penn, and Penn's sister Anna together play with the cupboard and struggle to understand it, experimenting till disaster strikes; Hugh travels the hallucinatory landscapes alone, not recognising what he sees there.

The Celtic tree alphabet controls the dreams and gradually unfolds a choice between life and death, or immortality, which the children must make. Most unusual for a work of fantasy, *A Castle of Bone* is both witty and funny. From a bolting pig nearly smashing banisters, to desperate attempts to stop a mother seeing her baby in case she recognises him, it is full of joyful relish for the funny side of the story.

It was nearly ten years before Farmer attempted such an ambitious work again, and then with *Year King* she tackled the edgy margins of psychology and fantasy to explore the nature of identity. Lan and Lew are identical twins, though not alike in character. The struggle between them, accompanied by terrifying telepathic episodes, is played out against the sensuous landscape of West Somerset and the ancient mythological patterning of the theme of the Year King. Farmer is herself a twin, and this book has passages of power and depth. But the freighting of her story with mythological material of huge import and the developing sexuality of her adolescent hero make this an unwieldy book, which Farmer has not entirely ordered and controlled, and it lacks the clarity and grace of which Farmer is capable.

The direction in which Farmer's talent was unfolding propelled her, after *Year King,* onto the adult list, to which she has made distinguished contributions. But she did not cease to write the shorter books for younger readers which she had been writing from the first alongside her books for older children. In this difficult field her command of simplicity and her power to suggest hidden meaning stand her in good stead, and her craftsmanship is immaculate.

In 1989 Farmer published *Thicker than Water,* a full-scale children's novel coming at a time when her public must have expected her to have moved permanently to the adult list. Once again twins are at the centre of the tale, which is a ghost story of sinister power. Becky doesn't know that her mother was a twin until her aunt dies and her mother takes in her sister's son—waiflike, sensitive Will. The pleasant country house in Derbyshire, with a worked out mine in the nearby field, is haunted for Will, though not for anyone else, by the voice of a child, crying and saying "Help me" and then, horribly, "Bury me." This complicates Will's already difficult choice between his family, till now unknown to him, and a foster home in London. In the end his attempts to save the ghost child, lost down the mine many years ago, nearly costs his own life. Against this dramatic story, the tug of resentment and love between the cousins is quietly explored and resolved. The use of alternating narration—Becky and Will taking turns in the first person—is effective, though Farmer's power to mimic a London voice is shaky here and there; but this is a genuinely frightening ghost story and a powerful one.

It is to be hoped that Farmer will not desert children's books, but continue to work in this genre, as well as in other literary forms. Her unique combination of reality and fantasy makes for challenging and rewarding reading.

—Jill Paton Walsh

FAST, Howard (Melvin). Also writes as E.V. Cunningham; Walter Ericson. American. Born in New York City, 11 November 1914. Educated at George Washington High School, New York, graduated 1931; National Academy of Design, New York. Served with the Office of War Information, 1942-43, and the Army Film Project, 1944. Married Bette Cohen in 1937; one daughter and one son. War correspondent in the Far East for *Esquire* and *Coronet* magazines, 1945. Taught at Indiana University, Bloomington, Summer 1947; imprisoned for contempt of Congress, 1947; owner, Blue Heron Press, New York, 1952-57. Since 1989 weekly columnist, New York *Observer.* Founder, World Peace Movement, and member, World Peace Council, 1950-55; currently, member of the Fellowship for Reconciliation. American-Labour Party candidate for Congress for the 23rd District of New York, 1952. Recipient: Bread Loaf Writers Conference award, 1933; Schomburg Race Relations award, 1944; Newspaper Guild award, 1947; Jewish Book Council of America award, 1948; Stalin (now Soviet) International Peace prize, 1954; Screenwriters award, 1960; National Association of Independent Schools, award, 1962; American Library Association Notable Book citation, 1972, for *The Hessian;* Emmy award, for television play, 1976.

PUBLICATIONS

Novels

Two Valleys. New York, Dial Press, 1933; London, Dickson, 1934.
Strange Yesterday. New York, Dodd Mead, 1934.
Place in the City. New York, Harcourt Brace, 1937.
Conceived in Liberty: A Novel of Valley Forge. New York, Simon and Schuster, and London, Joseph, 1939.
The Last Frontier. New York, Duell, 1941; London, Lane, 1948.
The Tall Hunter. New York, Harper, 1942.
The Unvanquished. New York, Duell, 1942; London, Lane, 1947.
Citizen Tom Paine. New York, Duell, 1943; London, Lane, 1946.
Freedom Road. New York, Duell, 1944; London, Lane, 1946.
The American: A Middle Western Legend. New York, Duell, 1946; London, Lane, 1949.
The Children. New York, Duell, 1947.
Clarkton. New York, Duell, 1947.
My Glorious Brothers. Boston, Little Brown, 1948; London, Lane, 1950.
The Proud and the Free. Boston, Little Brown, 1950; London, Lane, 1952.
Spartacus. Privately printed, 1951; London, Lane, 1952.
Silas Timberman. New York, Blue Heron Press, 1954; London, Lane, 1955.
The Story of Lola Gregg. New York, Blue Heron Press, 1956; London, Lane, 1957.
Moses, Prince of Egypt. New York, Crown, 1958; London, Methuen, 1959.
The Winston Affair. New York, Crown, 1959; London, Methuen, 1960.
The Golden River, in *The Howard Fast Reader.* New York, Crown, 1960.
Power. New York, Doubleday, 1962; London, Methuen, 1963.
Agrippa's Daughter. New York, Doubleday, 1964; London, Methuen, 1965.
Torquemada. New York, Doubleday, 1966; London, Methuen, 1967.
The Hunter and the Trap. New York, Dial Press, 1967.
The Crossing. New York, Morrow, 1971; London, Eyre Methuen, 1972.
The Hessian. New York, Morrow, 1972; London, Hodder and Stoughton, 1973.
The Immigrants. Boston, Houghton Mifflin, 1977; London, Hodder and Stoughton, 1978.

The Second Generation. Boston, Houghton Mifflin, and London, Hodder and Stoughton, 1978.
The Establishment. Boston, Houghton Mifflin, 1979; London, Hodder and Stoughton, 1980.
The Legacy. Boston, Houghton Mifflin, and London, Hodder and Stoughton, 1981.
Max. Boston, Houghton Mifflin, 1982; London, Hodder and Stoughton, 1983.
The Outsider. Boston, Houghton Mifflin, 1984; London, Hodder and Stoughton, 1985.
The Immigrant's Daughter. Boston, Houghton Mifflin, 1985; London, Hodder and Stoughton, 1986.
The Call of Fife and Drum: Three Novels of the Revolution. Seacaucus, New Jersey, Citadel Press, 1987.
The Dinner Party. Boston, Houghton Mifflin, and London, Hodder and Stoughton, 1987.
The Pledge. Boston, Houghton Mifflin, 1988; London, Hodder and Stoughton, 1989.
The Confession of Joe Cullen. Boston, Houghton Mifflin, 1989; London, Hodder and Stoughton, 1990.
The Trial of Abigail Goodman. New York, Crown, 1993.

Short Stories

Patrick Henry and the Frigate's Keel and Other Stories of a Young Nation. New York, Duell, 1945.
Departure and Other Stories. Boston, Little Brown, 1949.
The Last Supper and Other Stories. New York, Blue Heron Press, 1955; London, Lane, 1956.
The Edge of Tomorrow. New York, Bantam, 1961; London, Corgi, 1962.
The General Zapped an Angel. New York, Morrow, 1970.
A Touch of Infinity: Thirteen Stories of Fantasy and Science Fiction. New York, Morrow, 1973; London, Hodder and Stoughton, 1975.
Time and the Riddle: Thirty-One Zen Stories. Pasadena, California, Ward Ritchie Press, 1975.

Poetry

Never to Forget the Battle of the Warsaw Ghetto, with William Gropper. New York, Jewish Peoples Fraternal Order, 1946.
Korean Lullaby. New York, American Peace Crusade, n.d.

Plays

The Hammer (produced New York, 1950).
Thirty Pieces of Silver (produced Melbourne, 1951). New York, Blue Heron Press, and London, Lane, 1954.
George Washington and the Water Witch. London, Lane, 1956.
The Crossing (produced Dallas, 1962).
David and Paula (produced New York, 1982).
Citizen Tom Paine: A Play in Two Acts, adaptation of his own novel (produced Williamstown, Massachusetts, 1985). Boston, Houghton Mifflin, 1986.
The Novelist (produced Williamstown, Massachusetts, 1987).
The Second Coming (produced Greenwich, Connecticut, 1991).

Screenplays: *The Hill,* Doubleday, 1964; *Spartacus* (with Dalton Trumbo), 1965; *The Hessian,* 1971.

Television Plays: *What's a Nice Girl Like You...?,* 1971; *The Am-*

bassador (Benjamin Franklin series), 1974; *21 Hours at Munich,* with Edward Hume, 1976.

Nonfiction

Haym Salomon, Son of Liberty. New York, Messner, 1941.
Lord Baden-Powell of the Boy Scouts. New York, Messner, 1941.
Goethals and the Panama Canal. New York, Messner, 1942.
The Picture-Book History of the Jews, with Bette Fast. New York, Hebrew Publishing Company, 1942.
The Incredible Tito. New York, Magazine House, 1944.
Intellectuals in the Fight for Peace. New York, Masses and the Mainstream, 1949.
Literature and Reality. New York, International Publishers, 1950.
Tito and His People. Winnipeg, Contemporary Publishers, 1950.
Peekskill, U.S.A.: A Personal Experience. New York, Civil Rights Congress, and London, International Publishing Company, 1951.
Spain and Peace. New York, Joint Anti-Fascist Refugee Committee, 1952.
The Passion of Sacco and Vanzetti: A New England Legend. New York, Blue Heron Press, 1953; London, Lane, 1954.
The Naked God: The Writer and the Communist Party. New York, Praeger, 1957; London, Bodley Head, 1958.
The Howard Fast Reader. New York, Crown, 1960.
The Jews: Story of a People. New York, Dial Press, 1968; London, Cassell, 1970.
The Art of Zen Meditation. Culver City, California, Peace Press, 1977.
Being Red: A Memoir. Boston, Houghton Mifflin, 1990.
The Novelist: A Romantic Portrait of Jane Austen. New York, French, 1992.
War and Peace: Observations on Our Times. Armonk, New York, Sharpe, 1993.

Other

The Romance of a People (for children). New York, Hebrew Publishing, 1941.
Editor, *The Selected Works of Tom Paine.* New York, Modern Library, 1946; London, Lane, 1948.
Editor, *The Best Short Stories of Theodore Dreiser.* Cleveland, World, 1947.
Tony and the Wonderful Door (for children). New York, Blue Heron, 1952; as *The Magic Door,* Culver City, California, Peace Press, 1979.
April Morning (for children). New York, Crown, and London, Methuen, 1961.
Contributor, *The Human Almanac: People Through Time,* by Richard Burrill. Sierra Pacific Press, 1983.

Novels as E.V. Cunningham

Sylvia. New York, Doubleday, 1960; London, Deutsch, 1962.
Phyllis. New York, Doubleday, and London, Deutsch, 1962.
Alice. New York, Doubleday, 1963; London, Deutsch, 1965.
Lydia. New York, Doubleday, 1964; London, Deutsch, 1965.
Shirley. New York, Doubleday, and London, Deutsch, 1964.
Penelope. New York, Doubleday, 1965; London, Deutsch, 1966.
Helen. New York, Doubleday, 1966; London, Deutsch, 1967.
Margie. New York, Morrow, 1966; London, Deutsch, 1968.
Sally. New York, Morrow, and London, Deutsch, 1967.

Samantha. New York, Morrow, 1967; London, Deutsch, 1968; as *The Case of the Angry Actress,* New York, Dell, 1984.

Cynthia. New York, Morrow, 1968; London, Deutsch, 1969.

The Assassin Who Gave Up His Gun. New York, Morrow, 1969; London, Deutsch, 1970.

Millie. New York, Morrow, 1973; London, Deutsch, 1975.

The Case of the One-Penny Orange. New York, Holt Rinehart, 1977; London, Deutsch, 1978.

The Case of the Russian Diplomat. New York, Holt Rinehart, 1978; London, Deutsch, 1979.

The Case of the Poisoned Eclairs. New York, Holt Rinehart, 1979; London, Deutsch, 1980.

The Case of the Sliding Pool. New York, Delacorte Press, 1981; London, Gollancz, 1982.

The Case of the Kidnapped Angel. New York, Delacorte Press, 1982; London, Gollancz, 1983.

The Case of the Murdered Mackenzie. New York, Delacorte Press, 1984; London, Gollancz, 1985.

The Wabash Factor. New York, Delacorte Press, 1986; London, Gollancz, 1987.

Novels as Walter Ericson

Fallen Angel. Boston, Little Brown, 1951; as *The Darkness Within,* New York, Ace, 1953; as *Mirage* (as Howard Fast), New York, Fawcett, 1965.

*

Media Adaptations: *Man in the Middle* (film, based on *The Winston Affair),* 1964; *Mirage* (film), 1965; *Penelope* (film), 1966; *Jigsaw* (film, based on *Fallen Angel),* 1968; *Freedom Road* (film), 1980; *The Immigrants* (television miniseries), 1979.

Manuscript Collection: University of Pennsylvania, Philadelphia; University of Wisconsin, Madison.

Biography: Entry in *Dictionary of Literary Biography,* Volume 9, Detroit, Gale, 1981; essay in *Contemporary Authors Autobiography Series,* Volume 18, Detroit, Gale, 1993.

Critical Study: *History and Conscience: The Case of Howard Fast* by Hershel D. Meyer, Princeton, New Jersey, Anvil Atlas, 1958; *Counterpoint* by Roy Newquist, New York, Rand McNally, 1964; entry in *Contemporary Literary Criticism,* Volume 23, Detroit, Gale, 1983.

*   *   *

Howard Fast, who has written under the names E.V. Cunningham and Walter Ericson, is as multifaceted as he is multitalented. His writings are so diverse that the use of pseudonyms would be appropriate if they were indeed used to differentiate between the categories and periods of his works. This is, however, not the case. Fast used pseudonyms so that his work might be published during a time in which he was blacklisted by J. Edgar Hoover's FBI and the House Committee on Un-american Activities because of the alleged contents of his biographical novel *Citizen Tom Paine.*

Fast was active politically and even ran for Congress on the American Labor Party ticket. These activities, coupled with his interest in history, led him to serve as a war and foreign correspondent as well as to write factually based books. His early repertoire contains both historical works as well as novels that have their basis in historical fact. Some of these titles include (but are by no means limited to): *Conceived in Liberty: A Novel of Valley Forge; The Romance of a People; Lord Baden-Powell of the Boy Scouts; Haym Salomon, Son of Liberty; The Picture-Book History of the Jews; Goethals and the Panama Canal; Freedom Road;* and *Patrick Henry and the Frigate's Keel.*

At the time of his blacklisting, Fast had just finished writing the book that was eventually made into the award-winning film *Spartacus.* This novel, which also has its basis in history, is about the slave revolt against the Romans approximately seventy-five years before Christ. Spartacus was a slave whose thirst for freedom compelled him to lead the uprising. As in all of Fast's work, his vividly detailed descriptions of the characters and the events oblige the reader to form mental images as the stories unfold. Another book in this genre is *Moses, Prince of Egypt.*

A later historically based novel popular with young adults is *April Morning.* This story is set in Lexington, Massachusetts, during the American Revolution. A self-absorbed young boy is suddenly thrust into the responsibilities of manhood while the nation is fighting for its independence. The boy's maturation and desire to win the respect of his elders is dramatically represented by Fast's distinctive characterizations.

Under the name of E.V. Cunningham, the pseudonym he used in the United States during his blacklisting, Fast wrote many books in the suspense-murder-mystery genre. The first in this group, *Sylvia,* about a beautiful and mysterious woman, sparked an entire series of "mystery lady" books, including *Phyllis, Alice, Shirley, Lydia, Penelope,* etc., which in turn inspired a series of crime stories, including *The Case of the Kidnapped Angel* and *The Case of the Russian Diplomat.* The film *Mirage* was based upon a mystery written by Fast under the pseudonym of Walter Ericson.

The book *The Pledge* was based upon the author's own professional experiences and his tribulations during the McCarthy Era. Fast has also written nonfiction books on both the Jewish people and the Buddhist religion.

Young adults may be most familiar with Fast's intense character studies in the recent book *Max,* and in the series of novels beginning with *The Immigrants,* which was also made into a movie. This saga of the Lavette family, which courses through several decades, begins in *The Immigrants,* then continues with *Second Generation, The Establishment, The Legacy,* and *The Immigrant's Daughter.* These stories all vibrantly depict the emotionally charged scenes in which the characters find themselves. The appropriate political climate is also included to set the story in its proper framework. At first glance, these ponderous novels seem insurmountable to the average reader. Once begun, however, the "pages seem to fly," and readers are absorbed into Fast's telling of the tale. Even when the novel is finished, readers may be anxious to begin reading the next book in the series. It should be noted that although the books are written in time sequence, they "stand alone" and each may be read independently, though this is not preferable.

Fast has stated that he is "always delighted when any book of mine is read widely by young people." He feels the books they read "will endure." It is obvious that Fast's extensive literary talents most certainly will.

—Laurie Schwartz Guttenberg

FISK, Nicholas. Pseudonym for David Higginbottom. British. Born in London, 14 October 1923. Educated at Ardingly College, Sussex. Served in the Royal Air Force during World War II. Married Dorothy Antoinette Richold in 1949; twin daughters and two sons. Writer and illustrator. Has worked as an actor, journalist, musician, editor, publisher, and speaker to children and adults; former advertising creative director, head of creative groups, and consultant. Agent: Laura Cecil, 17 Alwyne Villas, Canonbury, London N1 2HG. Address: 59 Elstree Road, Bushey Heath, Hertfordshire WD2 3QX, England.

PUBLICATIONS FOR YOUNG ADULTS

Science Fiction

Space Hostages. London, Hamish Hamilton, 1967; New York, Macmillan, 1969.
Trillions. London, Hamish Hamilton, 1971; New York, Pantheon, 1973.
Grinny. London, Heinemann, 1973; Nashville, Nelson, 1974.
High Way Home. London, Hamish Hamilton, 1973.
Little Green Spacemen. London, Hamish Hamilton, 1974.
Time Trap. London, Gollancz, 1976.
Wheelie in the Stars. London, Gollancz, 1976.
Antigrav. London, Kestrel, 1978.
Escape from Splatterbang. London, Pelham, 1978; New York, Macmillan, 1979; as *Flamers,* London, Knight, 1979.
Monster Maker. London, Pelham, 1979; New York, Macmillan, 1980.
A Rag, A Bone, and a Hank of Hair. London, Kestrel, 1980; New York, Crown, 1982.
The Starstormer Saga (Starstormers, Sunburst, Catfang, Evil Eye, Volcano). London, Knight, 5 vols., 1980-83.
Robot Revolt. London, Pelham, 1981.
On the Flip Side. London, Kestrel, 1983.
You Remember Me! London, Kestrel, 1984; Boston, Hall, 1987.
Bonkers Clocks, illustrated by Colin West. London, Viking Kestrel, 1985.
Dark Sun, Bright Sun, illustrated by Brigid Marlin. London, Blackie, 1986.
Mindbenders. London, Viking Kestrel, 1987.
Backlash. London, Walker, 1988.
The Talking Car, illustrated by Ann John. London, Macmillan, 1988.
The Telly Is Watching You. London, Macdonald, 1989.
The Worm Charmers. London, Walker, 1989.
The Back-yard War. London, Macmillan, 1990.
The Model Village. London, Walker, 1990.
A Hole in the Head. London, Walker, 1991.
Pig Ignorant. London, Walker, 1991.

Fiction

The Bouncers. London, Hamish Hamilton, 1964.
The Fast Green Car. London, Hamish Hamilton, 1965.
There's Something on the Roof! London, Hamish Hamilton, 1966.
Emma Borrows a Cup of Sugar. London, Heinemann, 1973.
Der Ballon. Germany, Junior Press, 1974.
The Witches of Wimmering. London, Pelham, 1976.

Leadfoot. London, Pelham, 1980.
Snatched. London, Hodder & Stoughton, 1983.

Short Stories

Sweets from a Stranger and Other Science Fiction Stories. London, Kestrel, 1982.
Living Fire. London, Corgi, 1987.

Other

Look at Cars, illustrated by the author. London, Hamish Hamilton, 1959; revised edition, London, Panther, 1969.
Look at Newspapers, illustrated by Eric Thomas. London, Hamish Hamilton, 1962.
The Young Man's Guide to Advertising. London, Hamish Hamilton, 1963.
Making Music, illustrated by Donald Green. London, Joseph, 1966; Boston, Crescendo, 1969.
Lindbergh the Lone Flier, illustrated by Raymond Briggs. London, Hamish Hamilton, and New York, Coward McCann, 1968.
Richthofen the Red Baron, illustrated by Raymond Briggs. London, Hamish Hamilton, and New York, Coward McCann, 1968.

*

Illustrator: *A Fishy Tale* by Beryl Cooke, 1957; *Look at Aircraft* by Sir Philip Joubert de la Ferte, 1960; *The Bear Who Was Too Big* by Lettice Cooper, 1963; *Tea with Mr. Timothy* by Geoffrey Morgan, 1966; *Menuhin's House of Music* by Eric Fenby, 1969; *Skiffy* by William Mayne, 1972.

*   *   *

Nicholas Fisk's prodigious output of books for over thirty years, for children and young adults, has been characterised by a fierce narrative drive, a lucid and resonant style, an exceptionally free-ranging imagination which coheres round a number of urgent and consistent themes, a down-to-earth practicality which tempers the fantasy, and—above all—a respect for the enterprise and as yet untrammelled originality of the minds of the young. His major genre is science fiction: his stories range far in time and space—though *Grinny, Antigrav, Monster Maker, You Remember Me,* and *The Worm Charmers* are among his strongest novels and are set in recognisably contemporary surroundings. There is sometimes a return to a time of great personal significance for him—the 1940s. Not only is this period superbly evoked in his teenage memoir *Pig Ignorant,* but it is also reproduced movingly in what is probably his science fiction masterpiece, *A Rag, a Bone, and a Hank of Hair.*

The perennial science fiction device of outside threat based on an advanced technology becomes in Fisk's work a means of dramatising two of his most important themes: a technical expertise together with a trust in the clear thinking of children who are not yet forced into deadening adult moulds. Thus, in *Trillions,* Scott knows that the invading objects can be used creatively: the general's obsession with more and more force to get rid of them is a depressingly familiar adult reaction. In *Wheelie in the Stars,* a twentieth-century motorcycle alone saves an advanced but failed technology. In *Antigrav,* the young adults discover a red stone with the ability to defy gravity. They set up ingenious and crystal-clear experiments to both prove and illustrate the principle, and then fall foul of warring adults representing the futilities of the Cold War at its height. *Grinny* and *You Remember Me,* though separated by eleven years, form a sequence. Timothy and Beth, brother and sister, twice repel attempts by aliens to take over Earth. In each story, adults are manipulated with frightening ease but children see the truth and can counter it by commonsense, ingenuity, and bravery. There is no hint here of Eileen Colwell's devastating comment on Enid Blyton: "What chance has a gang of desperate criminals against three children and a dog?" The events, though fantastic, are entirely credible within the contract laid down between author and reader (in Fisk's own words: "One thumping lie only"). Their implications are thought through with disciplined exactitude.

Grinny has remained an unfailingly popular book. The family is visited unexpectedly by the self-proclaimed Great Aunt Emma (Grinny). Only Tim and Beth are not taken in. Discovering Grinny's true, nonhuman nature, elucidating "her" purpose and then finding a way of destroying her, forms a narrative of great power which remains compulsively readable. *You Remember Me* is just as compelling but is also a more reflective work. "Grinny" is replaced by Lisa Treadgold, the beautiful, idealistic leader of a growing mass movement, "The Rollers." Significantly, Timothy and Beth are now older. Timothy is nearer to adulthood: his mind is clouded, less proof against the wiles of the alien forces. Beth now bears the weight of the truth. There is another element in this more serious sequel. The Rollers, founded on "Rule of Law" and "Decency, Discipline, Dedication," have all the hallmarks of totalitarianism. There is undoubtedly a hint of political allegory in this compelling narrative. Beth's thwarting of Lisa is based on the same resourcefulness as the destruction of Grinny.

A similar seriousness underlies the magnificent *A Rag, a Bone, and a Hank of Hair.* In Fisk's dying future world, where youth is scarce and revered, genetic coding is used to prolong the species by producing the "Reborns," humans reconstituted from the ingredients listed in the book's title. Brin, a boy of startling intelligence, is set to live with three Reborns from the 1940s, as a sort of working trial. London Blitz conditions are reproduced: Brin finds himself identifying with his new companions. Their dirty, dangerous, emotional world contrasts with the anodyne luxury of his own. When they burst out of their bonds and create a new character by sheer force of imagination they must—with Brin—be destroyed. But they live on: their voices haunt their creators and the story becomes a defiant statement about human qualities and potentialities.

The pervasive themes of trust in the undistorted clarity of the young mind and the dangerous soullessness of alien technology (which seems equated with any human technology which is not based on craftsmanship) are shown in the collection of short stories *Sweets from a Stranger.* As a short-story writer, Fisk shows point and economy. The title story ironically rehearses the extraterrestrial menace of Grinny: "Mind Milk" (a truly virtuoso piece of plotting) shows this menace deliberately closing in on the minds of the young: "Space Invaders" and "Oddiputs" show the machines with minds and lives of their own.

A different version of the artefact with a life of its own is seen in *Monster Maker,* where Matt works with Chancey Balogh, builder of film monsters, and meets the reverberatingly sinister Ultragorgon. Among other virtues, this story celebrates careful craftsmanship and respect for a job well done—qualities which typify Fisk's own authorial achievement. Matt's ingenuity rivals that of his hero, Chancey Balogh—an ingenuity matched by the four Worm Charmers in the novel of that name, an urgent contemporary thriller about the discovery and foiling of a drug trafficker.

Nicholas Fisk is one of the few authors for young adults who approaches the unforced popularity of Blyton, Blume, or Dahl, who uses popular and accessible genres but who also possesses serious concern and a consistent world view to a profound degree.

—Dennis Hamley

————

FITCH, Clarke. See **SINCLAIR, Upton (Beall).**

————

FLEISCHMAN, Paul. American. Born in Monterey, California, 5 September 1952. Educated at University of California, Berkeley, 1970-72; University of New Mexico, Albuquerque, 1975-77, B.A. in university studies 1977. Married Becky Mojica in 1978; two sons. Has worked as janitor, bagel baker, bookstore clerk, and proofreader; author. Recipient: Silver Medal, Commonwealth Club of California, Golden Kite honor book, Society of Children's Book Writers, and *New York Times* outstanding book citation, all 1980, all for *The Half-a-Moon Inn;* Newbery honor book, American Library Association (ALA), 1983, for *Graven Images: Three Stories;* Golden Kite honor book, Society of Children's Book Writers, and Parents' Choice award, Parents' Choice Foundation, both 1983, both for *Path of the Pale Horse; Boston Globe-Horn Book* award honor book, best books for young adults nomination, ALA, both 1988, and Newbery Medal, ALA, 1989, all for *Joyful Noise: Poems for Two Voices; Boston Globe-Horn Book* award honor book, 1990, and ALA notable book, 1991, both for *Saturnalia;* ALA notable book and Golden Kite Honor Book, both 1991, both for *The Borning Room.* Address: 855 Marino Pines, Pacific Grove, CA 93950, U.S.A.

PUBLICATIONS FOR YOUNG ADULTS

Fiction

The Half-a-Moon Inn, illustrated by Kathy Jacobi. New York, Harper, 1980.
Graven Images: Three Stories, illustrated by Andrew Glass. New York, Harper, 1982.
Path of the Pale Horse. New York, Harper, 1983.
Phoebe Danger, Detective, in the Case of the Two-Minute Cough, illustrated by Margot Apple. Boston, Houghton Mifflin, 1983.
Coming-and-Going Men: Four Tales of Itinerants, illustrated by Randy Gaul. New York, Harper, 1985.
Rear-View Mirrors. New York, Harper, 1986.
Rondo in C, illustrated by Janet Wentworth. New York, Harper, 1988.
Saturnalia. New York, Harper, 1990.
The Borning Room. New York, HarperCollins, 1991.
Bull Run, woodcuts by David Frampton. New York, HarperCollins, 1993.
Dateline: Troy. Cambridge, Massachusetts, Candlewick Press, 1995.

Poetry

I Am Phoenix: Poems for Two Voices, illustrated by Ken Nutt. New
    York, Harper, 1985.
Joyful Noise: Poems for Two Voices, illustrated by Eric Beddows.
    New York, Harper, 1988.

Other

Townsend's Warbler. New York, HarperCollins, 1992.
Copier Creations. New York, HarperCollins, 1993.

PUBLICATIONS FOR CHILDREN

Fiction

The Birthday Tree, illustrated by Marcia Sewall. New York, Harper,
    1979.
The Animal Hedge (picture book), illustrated by Lydia Dabcovich.
    New York, Dutton, 1983.
Finzel the Farsighted, illustrated by Marcia Sewall. New York,
    Dutton, 1983.
Shadow Play (picture book), illustrated by Eric Beddows. New
    York, Harper, 1990.
Time Train, illustrated by Claire Ewart. New York, HarperCollins,
    1991.

*

Biography: Entry in *Fifth Book of Junior Authors and Illustrators,*
New York, H.W. Wilson, 1983; essay in *Speaking for Ourselves,
Too* compiled and edited by Donald R. Gallo, National Council of
Teachers of English, 1993.

Critical Study: Entry in *Children's Literature Review,* Volume 20,
Detroit, Gale, 1990.

*   *   *

Paul Fleischman's writing style is powerful, distinctive. His concise, yet lyrical use of language glides young readers through intriguing plots, appealing characters, unique content. In his poetry
and prose the author skillfully employs rhyme, alliteration, and
metaphor to evoke aural and visual imagery. Fleischman reports
that he tries to create an atmosphere in his writings, spending more
time tinkering with the harmony of the sounds than the sense of a
story. The writer gives credit to his father, author Sid Fleischman,
for his recognition of the importance of a story's sound "shape"
and for his love of research to uncover the past. His fascination
with "out-of-the-way corners of American history" is apparent in
his many stories that feature period settings and carefully compiled
historical facts.

Nowhere is Fleischman's mastery of language more evident than
in his poetry. *I Am Phoenix* and *Joyful Noise* are companion poetry
publications written to be read aloud, separately and simultaneously,
by two people. Composed in free verse, these imaginative musical
duets demonstrate the author's ingenious wordsmanship. *I Am Phoenix* includes fifteen verses on bird song and flight. His Newbery
Medal-winning *Joyful Noise* presents first-person profiles of four-

teen different insects. When read aloud as intended, the spoken
poems in *Joyful Noise* create the cadence of insect voices, producing
a rhythm reminiscent of the humming, buzzing, droning noises
made by crickets, honey bees, and cicadas.

The author's historical novels not only illustrate how skillfully
he crafts the sound "shape" of a story, but also the "sense," or plot,
of it. *Path of the Pale Horse, Saturnalia, The Borning Room,* and
Bull Run are four of Fleischman's young adult novels that portray
interesting aspects of Early American life. In addition to his figurative prose, each offers engaging characters, important themes, and
provocative plots.

Path of the Pale Horse takes place in Philadelphia during the
1793 yellow fever epidemic. Fourteen-year-old Lep is the protagonist, and Dr. Peale is his medical mentor. In this story of Lep's
search for his sister Clara, Fleischman subtly integrates the plot
with historical facts and makes the characters, especially Lep, come
to life.

Saturnalia is a satiric novel full of humor, atmosphere, and suspense. It is set in Puritan Boston in 1681 and focuses on the white
man's treatment of Indians and servants. The hero is a poor Indian
boy apprenticed to the town printer. The antagonist is a fanatical
tithingman whose job is to root out evil and blasphemy. The title
comes from the pagan Roman ritual of Saturnalia, a day in December when slaves and masters exchange roles.

The Borning Room is a convincing first-person narrative that
deftly weaves historical events—the Underground Railroad, the
Civil War, the suffragettes, and the rise of technology—into the
everyday life of one Ohio family. Georgina Lott, birthed in her
family's borning room, summarizes these important events to a
portrait painter who has been hired to sketch her picture before she
dies, in the same room. The borning room, a symbol in this story,
was common in the 1800s. It was usually located off the kitchen
and reserved for births, illnesses, and deaths.

In *Bull Run,* fictional characters give first-person accounts of the
first major battle of the Civil War. Through the sixteen individual
voices of men and women, blacks and whites, Northerners and
Southerners, Fleischman paints a vivid portrait of the bloodiest
U.S. war. The writer's character development is at its best here.
These people seem real, believable; they elicit sympathy and understanding from the reader.

Fleischman's short story collections present the same lyrical
prose, Early American settings, and mysterious atmospheres as his
novels. They are yet another vehicle for displaying his artistry in
the use of language, as well as his ability to create deceptively
simple tales that challenge the reader to discover hidden meaning.

Graven Images is an apt title for Fleischman's collection of three
stories that focus on a wooden sailor boy, a copper weathervane,
and a marble statue. In each of the tales, the graven image influences
the characters' actions and faith. "The Binnacle Boy" is a chilling
murder mystery involving a deaf serving girl, her fussy mistress,
and a sailing ship's dead crew. In the humorous "Saint Crispin's
Follower," the shoemaker's apprentice finds his own true love
through happenstance. "The Man of Influence" is a suspenseful
story of an arrogant stone carver and his ghost patron. Reviewers
praised Fleischman's powerful and mysterious narratives, claiming
that they held a timeless quality.

The stories in *Coming and Going Men* describe four travellers
passing through New Canaan, Vermont, in 1800. The travellers
each leave an impression but are also affected by the town. Cyrus
Snype (silhouette cutter), Mr. Hamby (ballad seller), Simeon and
Patrick Fyfe (exhibitors), and Jonathan Wardwell (peddler) are all

well-drawn and authentic. They transport young readers to previous times and give them new insights into the human condition.

Paul Fleischman is a master of his craft. His lyrical language and remarkable imagery enable him to create convincing characters and time periods. An added appeal of his work is that his protagonists often share young readers' powerful emotional needs, and therefore help them make discoveries about themselves. The success of his long list of young adult works shows that his attention to the sound and the sense of his writing—whether poetry, historical fiction, or short stories—is appreciated by his audience.

—Catherine Price

* * *

FLEMING, Ian (Lancaster). British. Born in London, 28 May 1908. Educated at Durnford School, Isle of Purbeck, Eton College; Royal Military Academy, Sandhurst; studied languages at the University of Munich and the University of Geneva. Served in the Royal Naval Volunteer Reserve, as personal assistant to the Director of Naval Intelligence, 1939-45: Lieutenant. Married Anne Geraldine Charteris in 1952; one son. Writer. Moscow correspondent, Reuters Ltd., London, 1929-33; associated with Cull & Co. (merchant bankers), London, 1933-35; stockbroker, Rowe & Pitman, London, 1935-39; Moscow correspondent, the *Times,* London, 1939; foreign manager, Kemsley (later Thomson) Newspapers, 1945-59; publisher, *Book Collector,* London, 1949-64. Order of the Dannebrog, 1945. Recipient: Young Readers' Choice award, 1967, for *Chitty Chitty Bang Bang. Died 12 August 1964.*

PUBLICATIONS FOR ADULTS AND YOUNG ADULTS

Fiction

Casino Royale. London, Cape, and New York, Macmillan, 1954; as *You Asked for It,* New York, Popular Library, 1955.
Live and Let Die. London, Cape, 1954; New York, Macmillan, 1955.
Moonraker. London, Cape, and New York, Macmillan, 1955; as *Too Hot to Handle,* New York, Permabooks, 1957.
Diamonds are Forever. London, Cape, and New York, Macmillan, 1956.
The Diamond Smugglers. London, Cape, 1957; New York, Macmillan, 1958.
From Russia, With Love. London, Cape, and New York, Macmillan, 1957.
Doctor No. London, Cape, and New York, Macmillan, 1958.
Goldfinger. London, Cape, and New York, Macmillan, 1959.
Thunderball. London, Cape, and New York, Viking, 1961.
The Spy Who Loved Me. London, Cape, and New York, Viking, 1962.
On Her Majesty's Secret Service. London, Cape, and New York, New American Library 1963.
You Only Live Twice. London, Cape, and New York, New American Library, 1964.
The Man with the Golden Gun. London, Cape, and New York, New American Library, 1965.

Octopussy, and The Living Daylights. London, Cape, and New York, New American Library, 1966.

Short Stories

For Your Eyes Only: Five Secret Exploits of James Bond. London, Cape, and New York, Viking, 1960.

Other

Thrilling Cities (thirteen essays). London, Cape, 1963; New York, New American Library, 1964.
Ian Fleming Introduces Jamaica, edited by Morris Cargill. London, Deutsch, 1965; New York, Hawthorn, 1966.

PUBLICATIONS FOR CHILDREN

Fiction

Chitty Chitty Bang Bang, illustrated by John Burningham. New York, Random, 1964.

*

Media Adaptations: Many of Fleming's James Bond books have been filmed, usually with Sean Connery, Roger Moore, or Timothy Dalton playing the lead; in addition, *Chitty Chitty Bang Bang* was adapted into a musical and into a film starring Dick Van Dyke.

Bibliography: *Ian Fleming: A Catalogue of a Collection: Preliminary to a Bibliography* by Iain Campbell, privately printed, 1978.

Critical Studies: *007 James Bond: A Report* by O.F. Snelling, London, Spearman, 1964, New York, New American Library, 1965; *The James Bond Dossier,* by Kingsley Amis, London, Cape, and New York, New American Library, 1965; *The Life of Ian Fleming,* London, Cape, and New York, McGraw Hill, 1966, *007 James Bond,* London, Sidgwick and Jackson, and New York, Morrow, 1973, and *James Bond: The Authorised Biography of 007,* London, Granada, 1985, New York, Grove Press, 1986, all by John Pearson; *The Bond Affair* by Oreste Del Buono and Umberto Eco, London, Macdonald, 1966; *Ian Fleming: The Spy Who Came in with the Gold* by Henry Zieger, New York, Duell, 1966; *You Only Live Once: Memories of Ian Fleming* by Ivar Bryce, London, Weidenfeld and Nicolson, 1975, Frederick, Maryland, University Publications of America, 1985; *The James Bond Films* by Steven Jay Rubin, London, Arlington, 1982; *Murder in the Millions: Erle Stanley Gardner, Mickey Spillane, Ian Fleming* by J. Kenneth Van Dover, New York, Ungar, 1984; *The James Bond Bedside Companion* by Raymond Benson, New York, Dodd Mead, 1984; *Secret Agents in Fiction: Ian Fleming, John Le Carré, and Len Deighton* by L.O. Saverberg, London, Macmillan, 1984; *James Bond: A Celebration* by Peter Haining, London, W.H. Allen, 1987; *Ian Fleming's James Bond* by John E. Gardner, New York, Avenel, 1987.

* * *

Best known for his James Bond thrillers, Ian Fleming's writing reflects both his time spent in the British Intelligence Service and his experience as a journalist. Plot-driven and with an emphasis on setting, the Bond adventure stories all follow a similar pattern: Bond encounters an easily defined enemy, and with the help of incredible gadgets, his unstoppable car, and his license to kill, he triumphs, conquering beautiful women along the way. Judging literature of past decades by modern standards poses innumerable problems, and seems somewhat unfair; but an intelligent young adult reader will move beyond Fleming's sometimes xenophobic and sexist undertones and enjoy the Bond novels for what they are—thrilling, outrageous, exciting spy stories. Unfortunately, many young people only know of the abundance of James Bond movies, and miss the insights into 007's character and the descriptions of setting and weaponry that the books offer.

The huge popularity of these novels defined the character of Bond as the quintessential spy. His enigmatic side, his physical endurance, and his abilities as a lover became standards by which to judge all superspies. To today's reader, or rereader, he seems almost a cliche. The dangerous and highly dramatic confrontations with foreign enemies seem dated in this post-Cold War age of corporate espionage and savings-and-loan debacles. Fleming's portrayal of women also poses some problems. Some are ruthless, sophisticated spies themselves, but all fall victim to Bond's endless charm and sex appeal—a chauvinistic ideal.

Fleming's success is not limited to his Bond novels. Younger readers continue to enjoy Fleming's timeless adventure story of the Pott family and their magical green car in *Chitty Chitty Bang Bang.* The delightfully improbable chain of events that begins with the purchase of the dilapidated buggy, which ultimately proves to have the capacity to speed, fly, swim, think, and, most importantly, feel, greatly appeal to young people. When Jeremy and Jemima are kidnapped, the young twins save themselves through quick thinking and resourcefulness. Young people feel empowered when children, of any age, triumph over adults.

While older readers may be reluctant to pick up a book about a magical car, even the most sophisticated reader will find this story captivating. This is Fleming's spoof on spy novels—perhaps on Bond himself—and shows his love of weaponry and the unexpected. Just when the Potts think their doom is sealed, Chitty Chitty Bang Bang proves to have another knob to pull or twist that saves the family. Commander Pott (retired) possesses extensive knowledge of explosive devices, and gangsters come complete with nicknames (Joe the Monster) and a big, black shiny car. The story moves quickly, and Fleming's chatty narrative voice, with its conspiratorial tone, involves the reader directly with the events. The open ending lets the reader's imagination take the Potts and their car wherever he or she desires. The movie adaptation of this book, like those of the Bond stories, is more familiar to most than the book, but, while amusing, it does not deliver the same rich detail the book provides.

Both the Bond books and *Chitty Chitty Bang Bang* quickly enthrall the reader with their action-oriented plots and amazing gadgets, and give the satisfaction of a good read.

—Karen E. Walsh

———

FOLEY, June. American. Born in Trenton, New Jersey, 6 June 1944. Educated at Montclair State College, Upper Montclair, New Jersey, B.A. in anthropology, 1974, teacher's certificate in social studies 1976; New York University, M.A. in English and American Literature, 1990, Ph.d. candidate, 1993—. Married Michael Lindenman in 1970 (divorced 1976); one son. Assistant editor, 1978-84, senior assistant editor, 1984-86, associate editor, 1986-88; senior editor, 1992—, *World Almanac,* New York; creative writing teacher, 1983—. Agent: Marilyn Marlow, Curtis Brown Ltd., 10 Astor Pl., New York, NY 10003 U.S.A.

PUBLICATIONS FOR YOUNG ADULTS

Novels

It's No Crush, I'm in Love! New York, Delacorte, 1982.
Love by Any Other Name. New York, Delacorte, 1983.
Falling in Love Is No Snap. New York, Delacorte, 1986.
Susanna Siegelbaum Gives up Guys. New York, Scholastic, 1991.

Other

Editor, with Mark Hoffman and Tom McGuire, *The World Almanac: The Complete 1868 Original and Selections from 25, 50, and 100 Years Ago.* New York, Pharos, 1992.

*

Media Adaptations: *It's No Crush, I'm in Love* (ABC Afterschool Special), ABC-TV, 1983.

*   *   *

June Foley writes about adolescence because she considers it to be one's most awkward yet exciting time of life. She enjoys writing about young love, and her *Falling in Love Is No Snap* about perky, likable Alexandra Susskind is a good example.

Foley's first novel, *It's No Crush, I'm in Love!,* is another example of her exemplary writing for young adults. She has written a humorous but touching story of Annie Cassidy, a fourteen-year-old who falls in love with her English teacher, David Angelucci. Annie's favorite book is *Pride and Prejudice,* and she imagines herself as the book's heroine, Elizabeth Bennet, and Mr. Angelucci as Elizabeth's love, Mr. Darcy. Annie has a communication problem with her mother whose life is filled with raising four girls by herself, Mr. Cassidy having died in a car accident some time ago. So Annie confides her feelings to her best friend, Susanna Siegelbaum, a fun-loving, outgoing girl who is just the opposite of Annie, but basically the same since both girls are oddballs. Susanna listens to Annie, doesn't really encourage her but supports her because Annie is finally overcoming her shyness and letting her feelings out. However, Annie's life changes when she becomes a writer for the school newspaper and meets Robby Pols, a fellow student and the editor-in-chief of the newspaper. Annie's rejection by Mr. Angelucci is painful, but Annie recovers, faces reality, learns that there are many kinds of love, and even finds a new warm and loving relationship with her mother, who is finally emerging from her cocoon. Foley's well-written story shows her understanding of young adults as they reach toward maturity, accompanied by the painful and frustrating emotions of adolescence.

Susanna Siegelbaum Gives Up Guys takes up where *It's No Crush, I'm In Love!* ends. This amusing story is about Susanna Siegelbaum and her promise to give up boys because she suddenly finds she has never really been part of any boy-girl couple. She has never known any boy well, and doesn't really stick with anyone long enough, anyway. So she decides to give up boys altogether, makes a bet with Annie Cassidy, her best friend, that she can do without boys, not even kiss or flirt with one for three months. However, Susanna also finds herself without a friend, because Annie has become engrossed in her boyfriend, Robby Pols, and doesn't spend time with Susanna anymore. When Susanna's parents become concerned because Susanna hasn't been going out, Susanna makes a deal with class clown Ben Green to pretend to be her new boyfriend. In return Susanna will tutor him in English and support him in the sports he participates in. The two learn to share thoughts and feelings and to boost each other's spirits when things get gloomy. However, when each criticizes the other for always wanting to be the center of attention and showing off, each decides to change and to grow up. Much to Susanna's astonishment, she discovers she really cares for Ben and he for her. Foley has written an appealing story about an enduring friendship between two girls who don't let boyfriends or personality differences come between them. Filled with sparkling dialogue, unpredictable characters, and topped by a surprise ending, the book keeps the reader laughing throughout.

Billie Quinn, just starting high school, has found she has matured physically, but not quite mentally and emotionally in *Love By Any Other Name*. Bubba Umlauf, a blond, handsome, number-one sports star of Central High, has two things on his self-centered mind—sports and making out with Billie Quinn. Billie loves the attention she receives from being Bubba's girl. She spends all her extra time with Bubba, neglecting her family and other responsibilities, barely getting by in school, and seems oblivious to anything but Bubba and her popularity. When Billie is paired with Cameron Ingersoll in her drama class, she is certain she is going to have a problem. Cameron is a tall, skinny boy Billie didn't even know existed, but Billie learns more from Cameron than how to act a part in a school play. She learns to grow up, to think for herself, to accept responsibilities, to become a supportive family member, and to realize there is more to life than being popular and dating a conceited high school jock. Foley has written a winner, portraying family problems along with peer pressures, sexual urges and how to handle them, and many other concerns that adolescents face. She has also written about a young girl who learns to care about the feelings of others and to stop thinking of herself all the time.

Although Foley hasn't written many books, each that she has written makes for good reading, with happy endings of young people conquering difficulties faced during the turbulent adolescent years, problems that young adults can easily identify with because they encounter them each and every day themselves.

—Carol Doxey

FORBES, Esther. American. Born in Westborough, Massachusetts, 28 June 1891. Educated at Bradford Junior College, graduated 1912; University of Wisconsin, Madison, 1916-18. Married Albert Learned Hoskins in 1926 (divorced 1933). Author of historical novels. Staff member, editor, Houghton Mifflin Co. (publishers), Boston, Massachusetts, 1920-26, 1942-46. Recipient: Pulitzer Prize (history), 1943, for *Paul Revere and the World He Lived In;* American Library Association Newbery Medal, 1944, for *Johnny Tremain: A Novel for Young and Old;* Metro-Goldwyn-Mayer Novel award, 1948. *Died 12 August 1967.*

PUBLICATIONS FOR YOUNG ADULTS

Fiction

Johnny Tremain: A Novel for Young and Old, illustrated by Lynd Ward. Boston, Houghton, 1943; London, Chatto & Windus, 1944.

Other

America's Paul Revere, illustrated by Lynd Ward. Boston, Houghton Mifflin, 1946.

PUBLICATIONS FOR ADULTS

Novels

O Genteel Lady! Boston, Houghton Mifflin, 1926; London, Heinemann, 1927.
Miss Marvel. Boston, Houghton Mifflin, 1935.
Paradise. New York, Harcourt Brace, and London, Chatto & Windus, 1937.
The General's Lady. New York, Harcourt, 1938; London, Chatto & Windus, 1939.
Paul Revere and the World He Lived In. Boston, Houghton Mifflin, 1942.
The Boston Book, with Arthur Griffin. Boston, Houghton Mifflin, 1947.
The Running of the Tide. Boston, Houghton Mifflin, 1948; London, Chatto & Windus, 1949.
Rainbow on the Road. Boston, Houghton Mifflin, 1954; London, Chatto & Windus, 1955.

Other

A Mirror for Witches in Which is Reflected the Life, Machinations, and Death of Famous Doll Bilby, Who, With a More than Feminine Perversity, Preferred a Demon to a Mortal Lover, woodcuts by Robert Gibbings. Boston, Houghton Mifflin, 1928.
Anne Douglas Sedgwick: An Interview. Boston, Houghton Mifflin, 1947.

*

Media Adaptations: *Johnny Tremain* (film), Walt Disney Productions, 1957; *Johnny Tremain* (cassette), Caedmon, 1974, and the Center for Literary Review, 1978; *Rainbow on the Road* adapted for Broadway as *Come Summer,* 1969; *A Mirror for Witches* adapted for Broadway as *Bilby's Doll,* 1976; *A Mirror for Witches* (ballet), Sadler Wells Company, London.

Biography: Essay in *Dictionary of Literary Biography,* Volume 22: *American Writers for Children: 1900-1960,* Detroit, Gale, 1983; essay in *Something about the Author Autobiography Series,* Volume

2, Detroit, Gale, 1986; essay in *Contemporary Authors Autobiography Series*, Volume 25, revised, Detroit, Gale, 1989.

Manuscript Collections: American Antiquarian Society, Worcester, Massachusetts; Clark University Library, Worcester, Massachusetts.

Critical Studies: Entry in *More Junior Authors,* edited by Muriel Fuller, New York, Wilson, 1963; *Esther Forbes* by Margaret Erskine, Worcester, Massachusetts, Worcester Bicentennial Committee, 1976; entry in *Contemporary Literary Criticism,* Volume 12, Detroit, Gale, 1980.

*   *   *

The reputation of Esther Forbes as a writer for children has been established by one book—*Johnny Tremain*. It is her only work of fiction for young adults. Young people who are interested in historical fiction, however, would enjoy her other works, particularly *Rainbow on the Road*.

Forbes had several unique advantages in writing *Johnny Tremain* which helped to make the book one of the most solid choices to win the Newbery Medal in the history of the award; they have also helped to make the book still worthwhile—even enabling it to survive the "trauma" of being required reading in many a school system.

The first advantage was her detailed knowledge of Paul Revere's world—its physical conditions, its contemporary events, its political figures and their influences. Information of all kinds, gathered in her exhaustive research for her earlier *Paul Revere and the World He Lived In* was so firm in her mind that complete scenes for *Johnny Tremain,* accurately detailed and furnished, could arise spontaneously. The creative process did not have to be interrupted and reaffirmed by research. The richness and liveliness added to the story by this ability are as rewarding as the plot and characters.

The second advantage derived also from her historical research: the curiosity and insight with which she considered people and the reasons for their behavior. She was always titillated by the quirk of thought or misunderstanding which could precipitate a historical incident. As she studied the Boston of the 1760s and 1770s, the role played by apprentices of all trades intrigued her—and she promised herself the indulgence of writing a piece of fiction about them in time.

When World War II brought the issue of freedom and fighting for it once more into daily consciousness, she found the crux for her story. She could reveal the universal and timeless problems of making difficult choices, believing in a cause, being responsible for one's actions, overcoming a handicap (Johnny's burned hand), and facing grief and loss (the death of Rab) by telling the story of Johnny Tremain, apprentice to a silversmith in Boston during the American Revolution. In her Newbery Medal acceptance speech, Forbes said, "I was anxious to show young readers something of the excitement of human nature, never static, always changing, often unpredictable, and endlessly fascinating." She might well have been defining the elements needed to produce a classic—which is what she did.

The text for *America's Paul Revere* is a distillation of the man and the most important facts of his life and times, prepared for younger readers as a counterpart for Lynd Ward's illustrations.

—Lee Kingman

FOX, Paula. American. Born in New York City, 22 April 1923; daughter of the writer Paul Hervey Fox. Educated at Columbia University, New York, 1955-58. Married 1) Richard Sigerson in 1948 (divorced 1954), two sons; 2) Martin Greenberg in 1962. She also has one daughter whose father is now deceased. Author. Has worked in numerous occupations, including model, saleswoman, public relations worker, machinist, staff member for the British publisher Victor Gollancz, reader for a film studio. News service correspondent, Paris and Warsaw, for the British wire service Telepress, late 1940s; English-as-a-second-language instructor at the Ethical Culture School, New York City; teacher for emotionally disturbed children, Dobbs Ferry, New York; from 1963 teacher of writing workshops and professor of literature, University of Pennsylvania, Philadelphia. Recipient: Finalist in National Book award children's book category, 1971, for *Blowfish Live in the Sea;* National Institute of Arts and Letters award, 1972; Guggenheim fellowship, 1972; National Endowment for the Arts grant, 1974; Newbery Medal, American Library Association, 1974, for *The Slave Dancer;* Hans Christian Andersen International Medal, 1978; National Book award nomination, 1979, for *The Little Swineherd and Other Tales;* one of *New York Times*'s Outstanding Books, 1980, and American Book award, for paperback fiction, 1983, for *A Place Apart;* Child Study Children's Book award from the Bank Street College of Education and one of *New York Times*'s Notable Books, both 1984, Christopher award and Newbery Honor Book, both 1985, and International Board on Books for Young People Honor List for Writing, 1986, all for *One-Eyed Cat;* Brandeis Fiction Citation, 1984; Rockefeller Foundation grant, 1984; one of the *New York Times*'s Notable Books, 1986, and one of the Child Study Association of America's Children's Books of the Year, 1987 *The Moonlight Man;* Silver Medallion, University of Southern Mississippi, 1987; *Boston Globe/Horn Book* award for fiction and Newbery Honor Book, 1989, for *The Village by the Sea.* Agent: Robert Lescher, 155 East 71st St., New York, NY 10021. Address: 306 Clinton Street Brooklyn, NY 11201, U.S.A.

PUBLICATIONS FOR YOUNG ADULTS

Fiction

A Likely Place, illustrated by Edward Ardizzone. New York, Macmillan, 1967; London, Macmillan, 1968.
Portrait of Ivan, illustrated by Saul Lambert. Englewood Cliffs, New Jersey, Bradbury Press, 1969; London, Macmillan, 1970.
Blowfish Live in the Sea. Englewood, New Jersey, Bradbury Press, 1970.
The Slave Dancer, illustrated by Eros Keith. Englewood, New Jersey, Bradbury Press, 1973; London, Macmillan, 1974.
A Place Apart. New York, Farrar Straus, 1980; London, Dent, 1981.
The Moonlight Man. New York, Bradbury Press, and London, Dent, 1986.
Lily and the Lost Boy. New York, Orchard Books, 1987; as *The Lost Boy,* London, Dent, 1988.
Western Wind. New York, Orchard Books, forthcoming.

PUBLICATIONS FOR CHILDREN

Fiction

Maurice's Room, illustrated by Ingrid Fetz. New York, Macmillan, 1966.

How Many Miles to Babylon?, illustrated by Paul Giovanopoulos. New York, David White, and London, Macmillan, 1967.

The Stone-Faced Boy, illustrated by Donald A. Mackay. Englewood Cliffs, New Jersey, Bradbury Press, 1968; London, Macmillan, 1969.

Dear Prosper, illustrated by Steve McLachlin. New York, David White, 1968.

The King's Falcon, illustrated by Eros Keith. Eaglewood Cliffs, New Jersey, Bradbury Press, 1969; London, Macmillan, 1970.

Hungry Fred, illustrated by Rosemary Wells. Englewood, New Jersey, Bradbury Press, 1969.

Good Ethan, illustrated by Arnold Lobel. Englewood, New Jersey, Bradbury Press, 1973.

The Little Swineherd and Other Tales (short stories), illustrated by Leonard Lubin. New York, Dutton, 1978; London, Dent, 1979.

One-Eyed Cat. New York, Bradbury Press, 1984; London, Dent, 1985.

The Village by the Sea. New York, Orchard Books, 1988.

In a Place of Danger. New York, Orchard Books, 1989.

Monkey Island. New York, Orchard Books, 1991.

Remembered by Florence Vecchi, retold by Fox, Amzat and His Brothers: Three Italian Tales (short stories), illustrated by Emily McCully. New York, Orchard Books, 1993.

PUBLICATIONS FOR ADULTS

Novels

Poor George. New York, Harcourt Brace, and London, Bodley Head, 1967.

Desperate Characters. New York, Harcourt Brace, and London, Macmillan, 1970; reprinted with an afterword by Irving Howe, Boston, Nonpareil, 1980.

The Western Coast. New York, Harcourt Brace, 1972; London, Macmillan, 1973.

The Widow's Children. New York, Dutton, 1976.

A Servant's Tale. Berkeley, California, North Point Press, 1984; London, Virago Press, 1986.

The God of Nightmares. Berkeley, California, North Point Press, 1990.

*

Media Adaptations: *Desperate Characters* (motion picture), Paramount, 1970; *One-Eyed Cat* (cassette and film with cassette), Random House.

Biography: Entry in *Dictionary of Literary Biography,* Volume 52: *American Writers for Children since 1960: Fiction,* Detroit, Gale, 1986; essay in *Speaking for Ourselves: Autobiographical Sketches by Notable Authors of Books for Young Adults,* Volume 1, compiled and edited by Donald R. Gallo, National Council of Teachers of English, 1990.

Critical Study: Entry in *Children's Literature Review,* Volume 1, Detroit, Gale, 1976; entry in *Contemporary Literary Criticism,* Volume 2, Detroit, Gale, 1974; Volume 8, 1978.

Paula Fox comments:

Why am I a writer? I can only answer that by saying that I tell stories; I am a storyteller and have been one for more than thirty years. When I finish one story, I watch the drift in my head and very soon am thinking of another story. All of one's experience shapes one's stories. Imagination is unifying, not separating. If I were to say that I wrote a book, for example *The Village by the Sea,* because a sand village I had built as a child had been knocked down, I would falsify terribly what is a complicated, intuitive process of imagination into which I am only afforded an occasional glimpse. I love writing—though it can be wearisome. I especially love writing for young people, although as I write, I do not think of ages, only of people.

*   *   *

Paula Fox is an author with tremendous versatility. Her works include picture and chapter books for the youngest readers, such as *Maurice's Room;* books for intermediate readers, like *How Many Miles to Babylon?, The Stone-Faced Boy,* and *Village by the Sea;* folktale retellings, including *Amzat and his Brothers: Three Italian Folktales;* and novels for adults, such as *Desperate Characters* and *A Servant's Tale.* Her realistic fiction for young adults complements this range with literary excellence. She received the Newbery Medal for *The Slave Dancer,* a Newbery Honor Award for *One-Eyed Cat,* and the prestigious Hans Christian Andersen Medal for her entire body of work for children and young adults.

Recurring aesthetic and ideological concerns pattern Fox's novels for young adults. In essays, lectures, and interviews, Fox reveals a prevailing respect for her audience. She addresses young readers frankly and helps them to understand the lives of other people. Isolation is a common theme of her work: characters often start out insecure and develop self-knowledge through their relationships with others. Her use of language—to establish mood, to evoke and extend images—speaks to her stylistic coherence and uniqueness. Using specific, telling details, she creates vivid settings with precision. However, the skillful vitality of her character portrayals also reveals an author plumbing the depths of human individuality. Her style, setting, plot, and character have a seamless unity.

The Slave Dancer stands as Fox's most externally directed novel. Beginning in the New Orleans of 1840, it traces with historical accuracy the slave trade. Thirteen-year-old Jessie Bollier is kidnapped and indentured to serve as fife player on the slave ship *Moonlight.* His first-person, retrospective narrative speaks intensely of the horrors and dehumanization he witnesses and in which he participates. His sensual descriptions of the city and the ship actualize the experience for readers. More than anything, his interactions with the ship's crew and his ability to see the ship's "cargo" as individual human beings structure Jessie's story. He moves beyond disdain for the intense personalities he meets to realize his own capacity for evil and eventually to demand accountability of himself.

Isolation plagues thirteen-year-old Victoria in *A Place Apart.* After her father's death, her comfort and security are gone. When she and her mother move to a small town, she experiences even deeper separation. Unlike Jessie, Victoria lives in a relatively understandable moral world. School and friends begin to fill her emptiness and Hugh, a new friend, helps her develop undiscovered attributes in herself. Her confidence grows and her isolation dissipates. However, Victoria learns that her strength always must stem from an inner force of stability. While Hugh, her friends, and her mother can appreciate who she is, only Victoria can create, sustain, or change that essence. She learns to maintain a tension between her need to be close to others and her need to have a private place.

In *One-Eyed Cat*, guilt consumes eleven-year-old Ned Wallis and forces him to stand alone after he shoots a forbidden air rifle. Thinking he maimed a one-eyed stray cat, Ned must find his way back to himself through forgiveness. He charts that course by slow, steady contact with others: his morally daunting minister father, his patient, ailing mother, and a supportive listener, elderly Mr. Scully. When he finally confesses and receives an equal confession from his mother in return, the family's recognition of each other's imperfections leads to reconciliation.

The essential bond between child and adult permeates all Fox's young adult novels in various combinations: child and mother, child and father, child and adult mentor. In *The Moonlight Man,* fifteen-year-old Catherine Ames yearns to establish a connection to her alcoholic father. Harry proves as unapproachable as Reverend Wallis, though his remoteness stems from physical distance and unreliability rather than high moral expectations. Like other Fox characters who must cope with human failings, Catherine must accommodate the facts of her father and discover a love strong enough to allow his weaknesses.

A quiet, emotionally withdrawn child also appears in *Lily and the Lost Boy*. Placed in contemporary times on the Greek island of Thasos, Lily feels abandoned when her older brother Paul turns to a mysterious boy for companionship. The island setting highlights Lily's sense of desertion, though it also provides a warm, inclusive community in which Lily gains perspective on her relationship with Paul. Like all Fox characters, her thoughtfulness and introspection enable her to perpetuate a friendship with Paul when his new comrade disappoints him.

Disappointment, abandonment, intergenerational bonds, and forgiveness unite in *Monkey Island*. Forsaken by his pregnant mother, Clay begins to live on the streets of New York City, a place in some ways as isolated as a Greek island. The eleven-year-old child discovers community with two homeless men he meets in the park. More important than the survival skills Calvin and Buddy teach him, Clay rediscovers his capacity to love and be loved. Fortified by them, Clay returns to his mother knowing he has discovered "a place beyond forgiveness," a nurturing place in its recognition of family as the fundamental link between imperfect human beings.

In every novel, Fox attributes significant capabilities to her readers. She pays tribute to their emotional, intellectual, and psychological abilities with layered, probing narratives, identifiable characters who achieve genuine illumination, and lucid, striking prose. Although critics occasionally label her work "depressing," most praise her integrity in writing honestly about relationships and emotional development. Her craft seems effortless; her vision essential and eloquent.

—Cathryn M. Mercier

FRANK, Anne(lies Marie). German. Born in Frankfort on the Main, Germany, 12 June 1929. *Died in Bergen-Belsen concentration camp in March 1945.*

PUBLICATIONS

Nonfiction

Het achterhuis (diary; foreword by Annie Romein-Verschoor). Amsterdam, Contact, 1947; as *Diary of a Young Girl,* translated from Dutch by B.M. Mooyaart-Doubleday, introduction by Eleanor Roosevelt, New York, Doubleday, 1952; with new preface by George Stevens, Pocket Books, 1958; as *Anne Frank: The Diary of a Young Girl,* Washington Square Press, 1963; as *The Diary of Anne Frank,* foreword by Storm Jameson, illustrated by Elisabeth Trimby, London, Heron Books, 1973; as *The Diary of Anne Frank: The Critical Edition,* edited by David Barnouw and Gerrold van der Stroom, translated by Arnold J. Pomerans and B.M. Mooyaart-Doubleday, introduction by Harry Paape, Gerrold van der Stroom, and David Barnouw, New York, Doubleday, 1989.
The Works of Anne Frank, introduction by Ann Birstein and Alfred Kazin. New York, Doubleday, 1959.
Tales From the House Behind: Fables, Personal Reminiscences, and Short Stories (translated from original Dutch manuscript, *Verhalen rondom het achterhuis* by H.H.B. Mosberg and Michel Mok). World's Work, 1962; revised edition, illustrated by Peter Spier, Pan Books, 1965.
Anne Frank's Tales From the Secret Annex (translated from original manuscript, *Verhaaltjes en gebeurtenissen uit het Achterhuis* by Ralph Manheim and Michel Mok). New York, Doubleday, 1983.

*

Media Adaptations: *Diary of Anne Frank* (play, adapted by Frances Goodrich and Albert Hackett, produced New York, 1955), New York, Random House, 1956; *The Diary of Anne Frank* (film), Twentieth Century-Fox, 1959; *The Diary of Anne Frank* (television movie), 1980; *The Diary of Anne Frank* (recording), Spoken Arts, 1974; *The Diary of Anne Frank* (recording), Caedmon, 1977.

Biography: *Anne Frank Remembered: The Story of the Woman Who Helped to Hide the Franks* by Miep Gies and Alison Leslie Gold, New York, Simon and Schuster, 1987; *Anne Frank* by Lina Tridenti, translated by Stephen Thorne, Morristown, New Jersey, Silver Burdett, 1985.

Critical Study: *Anne Frank: A Portrait in Courage* by Ernst Schnabel, translated from German by Richard and Clara Winston, Orlando, Florida, Harcourt Brace, 1958; as *Footsteps of Anne Frank,* Longmans, 1959; *A Tribute to Anne Frank* edited by Anna G. Steenmeijer, in collaboration with Otto Frank and Henri van Praag, New York, Doubleday, 1970.

*   *   *

By the end of the 1980s, 16 million copies of *The Diary of Anne Frank* had been sold worldwide; in 1992, forty years after its first publication in English, it was the twelfth most borrowed book in public libraries in the U.K. Besides being an extraordinary record of events which are rendered more immediate by the diary format and more dramatic by the unities of place and time imposed by the extraordinary circumstances, it reveals the uninhibited inner thoughts and feelings of an intelligent, articulate, self-critical young adult, and methodically and faithfully charts the development of her personality through various changes until she can say to her alter ego: "I know what I want, I have a goal, an opinion. I have a religion and love. Let me be myself and then I am satisfied. I know that I'm a woman, a woman with inward strength and plenty of courage" (11 April 1944). She has in the course of her unique exposition, as the poet and critic John Berryman pointed out, described "the conversion of a child into a person."

In 1933 Otto Frank, the second son in a banking family, emigrated from Germany to Holland, where he set up a business in Amsterdam, initially to sell pectin to housewives, but which diversified into chemical and pharmaceutical products, and herbs, particularly those used in the manufacture of sausages. He and his wife and two daughters lived in a modern apartment and had a wide circle of acquaintances, non-Jewish as well as Jewish, of whom many of the latter were members of the Liberal (i.e. Progressive) Jewish congregation. On 12 June 1942, the younger daughter, Anne, made the first entry in the diary she had been given for her birthday. On 9 July the family went into hiding in the "Secret Annexe" constructed by Otto Frank in the building which his firm occupied, where they were joined by another family and a dentist.

Anne kept her diary during their enforced incarceration. In March 1944, after listening to a radio broadcast about making a collection of diaries "after the war," she had the idea of writing a "romance" about their experiences. On 11 May she wrote: "My greatest wish is to become a journalist someday and later on a famous writer.... In any case, I want to publish a book entitled 'Het Achterhuis' after the war. Whether I shall succeed or not, I cannot say, but my diary will be a great help." On 20 May, in a passage not in the published *Diary,* she wrote; "At long last after a great deal of reflection I have started my 'Achterhuis,' in my head it is as good as finished...." She now began rewriting her original diary entries on loose sheets of paper. On 4 August armed German police, accompanied by Dutch Nazis in plainclothes, raided the building and arrested the occupants of the office and the Annexe, who were dispatched to concentration camps. Anne died of typhoid, a few days after her sister, in Bergen-Belsen, to which they had been transferred from Auschwitz.

Anne's diaries and other manuscripts (including some stories) were left on the floor of the Annexe in a briefcase, but they were tipped out by a policeman who had wanted a container for the money and jewelry he had ordered the families to hand over at gunpoint. Her writings were preserved under lock and key and given to Otto Frank when he returned after the war, the only one of the eight prisoners who survived. In a form transcribed by him from the loose sheets and diary entries, *The Diary of Anne Frank* was published in Holland in 1947, and in the U.K. and U.S. in 1952, the English translation incorporating several passages which had been bowdlerised by the Dutch publisher in deference to Catholic and Puritan sensibilities. Although written by a girl of fourteen, it approximates what Frank intended to offer for publication, rather than being simply a collection of diary entries for private consumption.

"I want to go on living after my death! And therefore I am grateful to God for giving me this gift, this possibility of developing myself and of writing, of expressing all that is in me" (4 April 1944). That, through her *Diary,* she has become for many the symbol of the six million Jews murdered by the Nazis is due to a combination of circumstances. The novelist and critic Frederic Raphael has suggested that the appalling nature of the Holocaust is such that language is incapable of describing it. Of those who survived, Elie Wiesel has stated: "If I moved away from the theme of

the Holocaust it was to protect it. I didn't want to abuse words; I didn't want to repeat words. I want to surround the subject with a fence of *kedusah,* of sacredness. To me the sanctuary of Jewish history is there; therefore I wrote other things in order not to write about that." The Italian novelist and poet Primo Levi was preoccupied with the predicament of those, such as himself, who "felt innocent, yes, but enrolled among the saved and therefore in permanent search of a justification in my own eyes and those of others. The worst survived—that is, the fittest; the best all died." Anne Frank was one of the best. It is the freshness as well as the innocence of her *Diary,* cut off at the point beyond which life was unbearable, that have ensured its appeal to many who cannot bring themselves to read about or even contemplate what happened thereafter.

In what she calls her "religion" lies a further key to the universal appeal of the *Diary.* The Franks were not Orthodox Jews; they were assimilated Jews of Progressive inclinations, as happy to celebrate Christmas with their Gentile friends as Chanukah with fellow Jews. Many young people today want to believe in God, without being shackled to a particular doctrine. Anne Frank, with her uncomplicated, universal brand of teenage theology, speaks for them, and to them.

—Antony Kamm

———

FREEDMAN, Russell (Bruce). American. Born in San Francisco, California, 11 October 1929. Educated at San Jose State College (now University), California, 1947-49; University of California, Berkeley, B.A. 1951. Served in the U.S. Army, Counter Intelligence Corps, 1951-53; served in infantry in Korea. Reporter and editor, Associated Press, San Francisco, California, 1953-56; publicity writer for television, J. Walter Thompson Co. (advertising agency), New York City, 1956-60; associate staff member of *Columbia Encyclopedia,* Columbia University Press, New York City, 1961-63; free-lance writer, particularly for juveniles, since 1961; editor, Crowell-Collier Educational Corp., New York City, 1964-65; writing workshop instructor, New School for Social Research, New York City, 1969-86. Recipient: Western Heritage award, National Cowboy Hall of Fame, 1984, for *Children of the Wild West;* Spur award Honor Book, Western Writers of America, 1985, and Jefferson Cup Honor Book, 1986, both for *Cowboys of the Wild West;* Jefferson Cup Honor Book, 1988, for *Indian Chiefs;* Golden Kite award Honor Book, Society of Children's Book Writers, 1987, American Library Association Newbery Medal and Jefferson Cup award, both 1988, International Board on Books for Young People (IBBY) Honor List choice, 1990, all for *Lincoln: A Photobiography;* Golden Kite award Honor Book, 1988, for *Buffalo Hunt;* Orbis Pictus award, 1990, for *Franklin Delano Roosevelt; Boston Globe*/Honor Book award (nonfiction), 1991, Newbery honor award, 1992, Golden Kite award for nonfiction, 1992, Jefferson Cup award, 1992, all for *The Wright Brothers: How They Invented the Airplane;* Golden Kite Honor for nonfiction, 1992, and Western Heritage award, 1993, for *An Indian Winter. Washington Post*/Children's Book Guild award for nonfiction, 1992; Knockerbocker award for Juvenile Literature, New York Library Association, 1993; Empire State award for Excellence in Literature for Young People, New York Library Association, 1993. Address: 280 Riverside Dr., New York, NY 10025, U.S.A.

PUBLICATIONS FOR YOUNG ADULTS

Nonfiction

Teenagers Who Made History, portraits by Arthur Shilstone. New York, Holiday House, 1961.
Two Thousand Years of Space Travel. New York, Holiday House, 1963.
Jules Verne: Portrait of a Prophet. New York, Holiday House, 1965.
Thomas Alva Edison. New York, Study-Master, 1966.
Scouting with Baden-Powell. New York, Holiday House, 1967.
How Animals Learn, with James E. Morriss. New York, Holiday House, 1969.
Animal Instincts, with James E. Morriss, illustrated by John Morris. New York, Holiday House, 1970.
Animal Architects. New York, Holiday House, 1971.
The Brains of Animals and Man, with James E. Morriss. New York, Holiday House, 1972.
The First Days of Life, illustrated by Joseph Cellini. New York, Holiday House, 1974.
Growing Up Wild: How Young Animals Survive, illustrated by Leslie Morrill. New York, Holiday House, 1975.
Animal Fathers, illustrated by Joseph Cellini. New York, Holiday House, 1976.
Animal Games, illustrated by St. Tamara. New York, Holiday House, 1976.
Hanging On: How Animals Carry Their Young. New York, Holiday House, 1977.
How Birds Fly, illustrated by Lorence F. Bjorklund. New York, Holiday House, 1977.
Getting Born, illustrated with photographs and drawings by Corbett Jones. New York, Holiday House, 1978.
How Animals Defend Their Young. New York, Dutton, 1978.
Immigrant Kids. New York, Dutton, 1980.
They Lived with the Dinosaurs. New York, Holiday House, 1980.
Tooth and Claw: A Look at Animal Weapons. New York, Holiday House, 1980.
Animal Superstars: Biggest, Strongest, Fastest, Smartest. Englewood Cliffs, New Jersey, Prentice Hall, 1981.
Farm Babies. New York, Holiday House, 1981.
When Winter Comes, illustrated by Pamela Johnson. New York, Dutton, 1981.
Can Bears Predict Earthquakes? Unsolved Mysteries of Animal Behavior. Englewood Cliffs, New Jersey, Prentice Hall, 1982.
Killer Fish. New York, Holiday House, 1982.
Killer Snakes. New York, Holiday House, 1982.
Children of the Wild West. New York, Clarion Books, 1983.
Dinosaurs and Their Young, illustrated by Leslie Morrill. New York, Holiday House, 1983.
Rattlesnakes, illustrated by the author. New York, Holiday House, 1984.
Cowboys of the Wild West. New York, Clarion Books, 1985.
Holiday House: The First Fifty Years (adult). New York, Holiday House, 1985.
Sharks, illustrated by the author. New York, Holiday House, 1985.

Indian Chiefs. New York, Holiday House, 1987.
Lincoln: A Photobiography. New York, Clarion Books, 1987.
Buffalo Hunt. New York, Holiday House, 1988.
Franklin Delano Roosevelt. New York, Clarion Books, 1990.
The Wright Brothers: How They Invented the Airplane, photographs by Orville and Wilbur Wright. New York, Holiday House, 1991.
An Indian Winter, paintings and drawings by Karl Bodmer. New York, Holiday House, 1992.
Eleanor Roosevelt: A Life of Discovery. New York, Clarion, 1993.

*

Media Adaptations: *Lincoln: A Photobiography* (filmstrip and video), McGraw-Hill Media, 1989.

Biography: Essay in *Authors and Artists for Young Adults,* Volume 4, Detroit, Gale, 1990; entry in *Sixth Book of Junior Authors and Illustrators,* New York, H.W. Wilson, 1989.

Critical Study: Entry in *Children's Literature Review,* Volume 20, Detroit, Gale, 1990, pp. 71-89.

*   *   *

When Russell Freedman was a boy, he and his family visited the Lincoln Memorial in Washington, D.C. There, his father counseled him to walk around the impressive statue, to observe Lincoln from different angles. The youthful Russell recalls that Lincoln looked somber and strong from one vantage point, more animated and soft from another. His father's advice, to examine a subject from a multiplicity of viewpoints, still serves as a benchmark for all of Russell Freedman's writings. His consistently inventive and multivalent interpretation of diverse subject matter elevates nonfiction for young adults to a new level of excellence.

His earliest book, *Teenagers Who Made History,* was motivated—as Freedman claims so much of his work has been—by chance. For this title, Freedman was inspired by an article he read in the *New York Times* about the Braille typewriter and its adolescent inventor. With his inquisitive journalistic mind, he wondered about other youth who had made striking contributions while still in their teens. A second title in the beginning of his career traced space travel over a two thousand year period. This definitive exploration was to intrigue and satisfy Freedman for a short time; he learned he was far less interested in such full treatment, that his attention lay in much more narrowly defining his focus. Still, the space travel book clearly led the way to his first biography detailing a single individual, that of Jules Verne. In both that biography and the one of Baden Powell, the founder of the boy scouts, Freedman was to reveal his consummate talents as a researcher and selector of material.

For the next fifteen years, Freedman confined his writings almost exclusively to the exploration of animal behavior. In these books for younger readers, he honed those skills that serve to distinguish his most memorable later work.

Another chance event marked a critical advance in his work. Attending a turn-of-the-century photography exhibit, Freedman was deeply moved by several photographs of immigrants whose faces spoke vividly and poignantly from the past. His *Immigrant Kids,* a perfect "picture book," integrates photographs and text with lucidity and grace. The success of that volume in which the photographs serve as powerful text, not as embellishment, convinced Freedman that evocative photography was underutilized as a potent means of communicating stories to young people, particularly young people engaged by the visual medium of television. With the same integrity and thoroughness that distinguishes his best writing, Freedman sought out those authentic pictures which would best reveal his subject. His commitment to choice photography as integral to the telling of story certainly applies to his companion books, *Children of the Wild West* and *Cowboys of the Wild West,* in which period photographs expose with striking authority the settlement of Western America. In both books, what emerges is Freedman's resolution to combat stereotype, to correct some egregious myths about our history and its people. Indeed, asked to comment on what characterizes his work, Freedman names his unrelenting desire for justice—justice for the Native American Indian, for immigrants, for cowboys, for all those too simply perceived as heroes and villains in history. In these particular books, and in *Indian Chiefs,* images seamlessly integrated with words help us to understand the violation which one group of people suffered at the hands of another. A haunting pair of photographs of Indian boys and girls, first in their native clothes on arrival at boarding school and then a year later, looking dazed and emotionless in their Americanized garb; a grim pile of buffalo hides, estimated at some forty thousand, purchased by the white man at the expense of the Indian who venerated the buffalo; and the prideful dignity revealed in the portrait photographs of Indian chiefs: these images impact the reader, commanding both attention and compassion for those against whom profound wrongs were committed.

Setting the historical record straight is representative of the best of Freedman's work. Not surprisingly, his first biography committed to amending the record of a legendary hero undertakes the man most venerated among Americans, the man about whom more has been written, perhaps, than any other American. In *Lincoln: A Photobiography,* Freedman hoped to uncover the man behind the myth. This Newbery award winning volume documents Freedman's meticulous research skills, his artful selective process as he sifts among inexhaustible material, and his brilliance in providing stunning images to deepen and broaden his portrayal. Few who read this remarkable portrait will forget the juxtaposition of five photographs which show the ravages of the presidency on the embattled and struggling Lincoln during his four years in office.

Freedman turned once again to an American president in *Franklin Delano Roosevelt,* a volume that further demonstrates the author's mastery in revealing not only the man in his complexity, but also the times which he shaped and which shaped him. Freedman's deft handling of the intensity and pain of the Civil War years of Lincoln is matched by his skillful treatment of the Roosevelt years, the times of the Depression through the Second World War. Without sentiment or bathos, Freedman looks honestly and directly at the man and his times. The portrait that emerges commands our respect for its passion and its intelligence: one never feels overloaded with facts, but gets a keen sense of balance and form in the composition and arrangement of information instead.

The Wright Brothers: How They Invented the Airplane once again shows Freedman as a creative artist, shaping his material for dramatic effect without ever compromising accuracy. From its effective opening sentence, "No one had ever seen what Amos Root [a curious beekeeper who travelled 200 miles to eyewitness the first airplane in controlled flight] saw on that September afternoon in 1904," to its poignant closing, detailing that a century later Neil Armstrong "stepped onto the lunar surface...carrying with him a piece of the original cotton wing covering from the Wright flyer," Freedman crafts a theater of genuine excitement. Original photo-

graphs by Wilbur and Orville Wright increase the tension. Nine internal pages of wordless photographs showing a glider in free flight remind one of the mounting exhilaration of Max cavorting with the wild things in the wordless pages of Maurice Sendak's classic.

Expert use of visuals finds Freedman turning occasionally away from photography when another art form would serve better. For *Buffalo Hunt* Freedman employs paintings of those artist adventurers who traveled West in the 1800s when Indians depended on the buffalo to fulfill all their material and spiritual needs. His *Indian Winter* records the adventures of German prince Alexander Phillip Maximilian among the Mandan Indians and utilizes the painting and drawings of Karl Bodmer, the Swiss painter who accompanied the prince on his travels. Freedman's text itself relies judiciously on the actual journal writings of the prince. His ability to use the words of others (often quotations serve to introduce his chapters) meshed with his own, foster his creation of all these tapestries of history which earn him a unique place in young adult literature.

—Susan P. Bloom

FRENCH, Paul. See **ASIMOV, Isaac.**

FRENCH, Simon. Australian. Born in Sydney, New South Wales, 26 November 1957. Educated at Mitchell College, Bathurst, New South Wales, 1976-79, diploma in teaching 1979. Has worked as library clerical assistant and fruitpicker; infants' teacher, Willow Tree, 1980, and St. Clair, 1981-84, both New South Wales; youth worker, 1984-87. Since 1988 teacher in New South Wales. Recipient: Special mention from the Australian Children's Book of the Year awards, 1976, for *Hey, Phantom Singlet;* commendations in Australian Children's Book of the Year competition, 1982, for *Cannily, Cannily;* Australian Children's Book of the Year award, 1987, for *All We Know.* Address: 24 Burdekin Road, Wilberforce, NSW 2756, Australia.

PUBLICATIONS FOR YOUNG ADULTS

Fiction

Hey, Phantom Singlet, illustrated by Alex Nicholas. Sydney and London, Angus & Robertson, 1975.
Cannily, Cannily. Sydney and London, Angus & Robertson, 1981.
All We Know. Sydney and London, Angus & Robertson, 1986.
Change the Locks. New York, Scholastic, 1993.

*   *   *

Hey, Phantom Singlet, Simon French's first novel, written while he was still at school and published when he was seventeen, contains many of the typical characteristics of the young adult novel, such as down-to-earth classroom dialogue. Math, a youth who suffers from growing pains and sees himself as an outsider, feels the need to establish a forceful presence by adopting bizarre gear—in this instance an orange singlet (vest) and a fur cap. Math is suffering because his father is in jail and his mother, married at seventeen, "sometimes felt that life had become too much for her."

In this, and each of his succeeding books, French is recording one step on a journey toward maturity. Because his novels are skillfully crafted and his prose finely honed, he is a writer both for those who are in the process of breaking free and stepping across the boundaries of childhood, and for adults, young or old, who have experienced the pain and the excitement of growing up.

French writes from his experience, as a schoolboy in Sydney in the 1960s, a teacher, a welfare worker with disturbed children, and as an astute and sympathetic observer of the human condition. In particular he is concerned with those who are "different"—the loners, the rejected, the emotionally deprived. All of these French dignifies as individuals to be valued and accepted for their own personal worth.

There is a growing maturity to his writing, both in subject matter and style. *Hey, Phantom Singlet* uses some now dated colloquialisms. Since then, while not eschewing idiom, French is careful to avoid that particular trap. So while he explores the contemporary scene and can be topical (as in raising the issue of competitive sport in *Cannily, Cannily)* he writes for all times and places. His young protagonists, their peers, their parents, and teachers are to be found the world over, not only in Australia.

Teachers have a high profile in his first three books. In *Hey, Phantom Singlet* and *Cannily, Cannily* they can be crass, authoritarian, and insensitive like Mad Dog Preston in the former, or bullies like Fuller, the sadistic football coach in *Cannily, Cannily.* But it is a sympathetic English teacher, Mr. Boon, who helps Math through his confusion and directs him forward to some degree of maturity. Mr. Boon is a forerunner to Mr. Clifton in *All We Know,* one of the most likeable teachers in contemporary fiction, who in his genuine concern for his students could well be a self-portrait of the author. In the same book, Arkie's mother and her stepfather, Michael, are both committed teachers and wise parents.

Parents, however, in French's books have shortcomings even when they are caring and understanding. Math's harassed mother is a shadow of Steven's mother in *Change the Locks.* Kath and Buckley, Trevor's parents in *Cannily, Cannily,* are concerned and loving but are itinerants whose casual life-style puts Trevor in jeopardy at a new school: his hair is all wrong, his patchwork shoulder bag brings ridicule. So he lies about his prowess as a footballer in a bid for acceptance. In *All We Know,* Arkie's friend Kylie is sad because her father only comes to take her out on weekends and her mother is constantly loading her with responsibility. Little Ian, in the same book, hangs around Arkie's house and often stays over because his mother is a drunk and his father is not around. Steven, in *Change the Locks,* takes responsibility for his irresponsible and disorganized mother who confesses that as a single teenage parent she was only "a kid with kids." But French does not cast stones. Like Arkie with her camera, he photographs life, but is selective enough to show its many facets. Math's life is influenced positively not only by Mr. Boon but by Steve Kerr, an artist who lives across the street. Trevor and his father, toward the end of *Cannily, Cannily* crack a wave together and an "inexplicable optimism" runs through the boy. Arkie, near the end of *All We Know* composes a letter to the dad whom she still misses and who is still very much a part of her inner life. Then at the close of the book she catches a glimpse of Ian, looking "forlorn and distant," part of a group of children in a state

institution. For French, time is a continuum and life is made up of pluses and minuses. This is most apparent in *Change the Locks* which embodies his recurring theme of "breaking free" and moving on. Steven, at his most troubled, has a school friend whose family provide him sanctuary.

French's novels are socially relevant without being tracts. His plots, in the first three books, particularly, are contemplative but not static. Although written in the third person the reader is told in the first two what Math and Trevor are thinking. In *All We Know,* Arkie's introspective mental monologue is printed in italics. We are privy to her obsession with detail, her examination of the minutiae of life. *Change the Locks* is in the first person but there are sentences and snippets in italics which bring the past into the present— a kind of subconscious thought-stream. Steven's preoccupation is with unrecalled past events which constantly haunt him. His mother's fecklessness is a burden, a situation similar to French's short story "Peace and Quiet." In *Change the Locks* there is a mystery and a solution, therefore more action and suspense than in the earlier works. It is a more robust book, more obviously concerned with social issues and personal problems, but it is never polemic or didactic. Again, it is a sympathetic unravelling of the threads of the characters' lives. Steven finally discovers the full story of his mother's teenage pregnancy and their life together in squalid city squats, and this in turn becomes a catharsis for both mother and son. There has been a "connection," and life can move forward as it always does in a Simon French novel.

The tolerance that French extends to his characters is not an easy acknowledgement that life is often difficult. Rather it is an optimistic statement of belief in the complexities of relationships and a sympathetic understanding of the ongoing struggle that is life.

—Maurice Saxby

FRITZ, Jean. Also writes as Ann Scott. American. Born in Hankow, China, 16 November 1915; lived in China until 1928. Educated at Wheaton College, Norton, Massachusetts, 1933-37 (associate editor, Wheaton *News*), A.B. 1937; Columbia University Teachers College, New York, 1938-39. Married Michael G. Fritz in 1941; one son and one daughter. Author of historical biographies and novels for young people. Research assistant, Silver Burdett, publishers, New York, 1937-41; researcher, Boy Scouts of America, New York, 1941; reviewer, San Francisco *Chronicle,* and Tacoma *Ledger-News-Tribune,* Washington, and free-lance writer, Macmillan and Prang publishers, 1940s-early 1950s; children's librarian, Dobbs Ferry Library, New York, 1955-57; founder and teacher, Jean Fritz Writers' Workshops, Katonah, New York, 1962-70; teacher, Board of Cooperative Educational Service, Westchester County, New York, 1971-73; faculty member, Appalachian State University, Boone, North Carolina, summers 1981-83. Book reviewer, *San Francisco Chronicle,* 1941-43, and *New York Times,* since 1970, and *Washington Post.* Lecturer. Recipient: Named *New York Times* outstanding book of the year, 1973, for *And Then What Happened, Paul Revere?,* 1974, for *Why Don't You Get a Horse, Sam Adams?,* 1975, for *Where Was Patrick Henry on the 29th of May?,* 1976, for *What's the Big Idea, Ben Franklin?,* 1981, for *Traitor: The Case of Benedict Arnold,* and 1982, for *Homesick: My Own Story;* named *Boston Globe-Horn Book* honor book, 1974, for *And Then What Hap-*

pened, *Paul Revere?*, 1976, for *Will You Sign Here, John Hancock?*, and 1980, for *Stonewall;* named outstanding Pennsylvania author, Pennsylvania School Library Association, 1978; Honor award for Nonfiction, Children's Book Guild, 1979, for the "body of her creative writing," and 1979; American Book award nomination, 1980, for *Where Do You Think You're Going, Christopher Columbus?*, and 1981, for *Traitor: The Case of Benedict Arnold;* LL.D., Washington and Jefferson College, 1982, Wheaton College, 1987; Child Study award and Christopher award, both 1982, Newbery Honor Book award, American Book award, and named *Boston Globe-Horn Book* honor book, all 1983, all for *Homesick: My Own Story; Boston Globe-Horn Book* Nonfiction award, 1984, and Knickerbocker award for Juvenile Literature, 1992, both for *The Double Life of Pocahontas;* Regina award, 1985; Laura Ingalls Wilder award, 1986; Orbis Pictus award, National Council of English Teachers, 1989, and Boston Globe/Horn Book award, 1990, both for *The Great Little Madison.* Agent: Gina MacCoby Literary Agency, 1123 Broadway, Suite 1010, New York, NY 10010. Address: 50 Bellewood Ave., Dobbs Ferry, NY 10522, U.S.A.

PUBLICATIONS FOR YOUNG ADULTS

Nonfiction

Stonewall, illustrated by Stephen Gammell. New York, Putnam, 1979.

Traitor: The Case of Benedict Arnold. New York, Putnam, 1981.

The Double Life of Pocahontas, illustrated by Ed Young. New York, Putnam, 1983.

Make Way for Sam Houston!, illustrated by Elise Primavera. New York, Putnam, 1986.

PUBLICATIONS FOR CHILDREN

Fiction

Bunny Hopwell's First Spring, illustrated by Rachel Dixon. New York, Wonder Books, 1954.

Fish Head, illustrated by Marc Simont. New York, Coward McCann, 1954; London, Faber, 1956.

Help Mr. Willy Nilly, illustrated by Jean Tamburine. New York, Treasure Books, 1954.

Hurrah for Jonathan!, illustrated by Violet La Mont. Racine, Wisconsin, Whitman, 1955.

121 Pudding Street, illustrated by Sofia. New York, Coward McCann, 1955.

The Late Spring, illustrated by Erik Blegvad. New York, Coward McCann, 1957.

The Cabin Faced West, illustrated by Feodor Rojankovsky. New York, Coward, 1958.

Champion Dog, Prince Tom, with Tom Clute, illustrated by Ernest Hart. New York, Coward McCann, 1958.

How to Read a Rabbit, illustrated by Leonard Shortall. New York, Coward McCann, 1959.

Brady, illustrated by Lynd Ward. New York, Coward McCann, 1960; London, Gollancz, 1966.

December Is for Christmas (as Ann Scott), illustrated by Alcy Kendrick. New York, Wonder Books, 1961.

Tap, Tap, Lion—1, 2, 3, illustrated by Leonard Shortall, New York, Coward McCann, 1962.

I, Adam, illustrated by Peter Burchard. New York, Coward McCann, 1963; London, Gollancz, 1965.

Magic to Burn, illustrated by Beth and Joe Krush. New York, Coward McCann, 1964.

Early Thunder, illustrated by Lynd Ward. New York, Coward McCann, 1967; London, Gollancz, 1969.

George Washington's Breakfast, illustrated by Paul Galdone. New York, Coward McCann, 1969.

The Secret Diary of Jeb and Abigail: Growing Up in America, 1776-1783, illustrated by Kenneth Bald and Neil Boyle. Pleasantville, New York, Reader's Digest Association, 1976.

Homesick: My Own Story, illustrated by Margot Tomes. New York, Putnam, 1982.

Other

Growing Up, illustrated by Elizabeth Webbe. Chicago, Rand McNally, 1956.

The Animals of Doctor Schweitzer, illustrated by Douglas Howland. New York, Coward McCann, 1958; Edinburgh, Oliver and Boyd, 1962.

San Francisco, illustrated by Emil Weiss. Chicago, Rand McNally, 1962.

Surprise Party (reader), illustrated by George Wiggins. New York, Initial Teaching Alphabet Publications, 1965.

The Train (reader), illustrated by Jean Simpson. New York, Grosset and Dunlap, 1965.

And Then What Happened, Paul Revere?, illustrated by Margot Tomes. New York, Coward McCann, 1973.

Why Don't You Get a Horse, Sam Adams?, illustrated by Trina Schart Hyman. New York, Coward McCann, 1974.

Where Was Patrick Henry on the 29th of May?, illustrated by Margot Tomes. New York, Coward McCann, 1975.

Who's That Stopping on Plymouth Rock?, illustrated by J. B. Handelsman. New York, Coward McCann, 1975.

What's the Big Idea, Ben Franklin?, illustrated by Margot Tomes. New York, Coward McCann, 1976.

Will You Sign Here, John Hancock?, illustrated by Trina Schart Hyman. New York, Coward McCann, 1976.

Can't You Make Them Behave, King George?, illustrated by Tomie dePaola. New York, Coward McCann, 1977.

Brendan the Navigator: A History Mystery about the Discovery of America, illustrated by Enrico Arno. New York, Coward McCann, 1979.

Where Do You Think You're Going, Christopher Columbus?, illustrated by Margot Tomes. New York, Putnam, 1980.

Back to Early Cape Cod. Philadelphia, Eastern Acorn Press, 1981.

The Man Who Loved Books, illustrated by Trina Schart Hyman. New York, Putnam, 1981.

The Good Giants and the Bad Pukwudgies (folktale), illustrated by Tomie dePaola. New York, Putnam, 1982.

China Homecoming, photographs by Mike Fritz. New York, Putnam, 1985.

Shh! We're Writing the Constitution. illustrated by Tomie dePaola. New York, Putnam, 1987.

China's Long March: 6000 Miles of Danger, illustrated by Yang Zhr Cheng. New York, Putnam, 1988.

The Great Little Madison. New York, Putnam, 1989.

Bully for You, Teddy Roosevelt!. New York, Putnam, 1991.

George Washington's Mother, illustrated by DyAnne DiSalvo-Ryan. New York, Grosset & Dunlap, 1992.
The Great Adventures of Christopher Columbus; a Pop-up Book, illustrated by Tomie dePaola. New York, Putnam, 1992.

PUBLICATIONS FOR ADULTS

Other

Cast for a Revolution: Some American Friends and Enemies, 1728-1814. Boston, Houghton Mifflin, 1972.
(Contributor) William Zinsser, editor, *Worlds of Childhood: The Art and Craft of Writing for Children.* Boston, Houghton Mifflin, 1990.

*

Manuscript Collection: Kerlan Collection, University of Minnesota, Minneapolis; Children's Literature Collection at the University of Oregon Library, Eugene; University of Southern Mississippi.

Biography: Entry in *Dictionary of Literary Biography,* Volume 52: *American Writers for Children since 1960: Fiction,* Detroit, Gale, 1986; essay in *Something About the Author Autobiography Series,* Volume 2, Detroit, Gale, 1986.

Critical Study: Entry in *Children's Literature Review,* Volume 2, Detroit, Gale 1976; Volume 14, 1988.

*   *   *

Jean Fritz is a literary craftsman who writes exceptional biographies for young adults. Noted for her meticulous research, she brings the facts to life with an abundance of humor and conversational style. She gives a concise historical interpretation of the times while imparting a sensitive glimpse into the character. Her research in American history satisfies her own curiosity about her roots, for Fritz, the daughter of missionaries, was reared in China until she was thirteen. As she herself explains, "Most of my childhood was spent...as far away as I could get [from America]—in China. Indeed, I think it is because I was so far away that I developed a homesickness that made me want to embrace not just a given part of America at a given time but the whole of it. No one is more patriotic than the one separated from his country; no one is as eager to find roots as the person who has been uprooted."

Fritz's historically correct biographies show her as a master writer and a creative researcher going beyond the facts to explain the real person. Following her award-winning American Revolutionary War biography series for children, she wrote *Traitor: The Case of Benedict Arnold* (1981) for young adults. Fritz skillfully intertwines the historical events of the American Revolution with Arnold's character and personality. Her eloquent style and compelling recreation of Arnold's twisted character widen one's understanding of his treasonable behavior. This anti-hero is portrayed as an unloved individual who is vain, jealous, and greedy. His seditious betrayal, acted out of self-pity rather than any noble principle, eventually causes his rejection by the very people he sought to serve. Fritz's extensive Revolutionary War research evidences itself in the authenticity of this biography.

The Double Life of Pocahontas (1983) imaginatively explores an earlier period of American history. Fritz develops a concise historical interpretation of a sensitive heroine. Pocahontas, the favorite daughter of an Algonquian Indian chief, befriends the English colonists in Jamestown. When she subsequently saves Captain John Smith from death at the hands of her father, she is considered Smith's sponsor into her tribe. Relations between the colonists and the Indians later deteriorate to the point where the colonists resort to kidnapping Pocahontas. Feeling rejected by her people, she marries colonist John Rolfe and moves to England. Fritz's poignant story recreates the troubled life of a young woman trapped between her Indian heritage and a strange English lifestyle. The extensive research by Fritz into a shadowy part of American history accurately depicts the double life of a remarkable Indian princess.

Stonewall (1979) is the life of the Civil War hero Thomas (Stonewall) Jackson. Fritz scrutinizes Stonewall's complex personality from his impoverished childhood to his idolized leadership role in the Confederate army. This eccentric, military genius is a curious mixture of toughness and humanity. Such a well-documented biography compassionately allows the reader to see Jackson's early years, particularly his inflexibility during his discouraging tenure as a teacher. In the end Jackson's love for God and country, together with his toughness and determination, make him the hero he was always afraid to be. Fritz thoughtfully and skillfully reveals the intricate no nonsense life of Jackson in her no nonsense style.

Another eccentric hero is the subject of *Make Way for Sam Houston* (1986). Sam Houston is realistically depicted with his hot temper and drunkenness contrasted against his charming, flamboyant, and patriotic lifestyle. Fritz gives a very human study of a shrewd leader and politician who became a United States congressman, governor of Tennessee, commander-in-chief of the Texas army, and eventually governor of Texas. Fritz's dependable research gives Houston credit for his devotion to the cause of Indian rights and the founding and preservation of Texas. Ingeniously she acquaints the readers with a remarkable Texas hero they will respect.

Fritz's books have consistently garnered numerous awards, prizes, and honors for more than forty years for their substantial and lasting contribution to literature. In addition to her biographies for young adults, Fritz has written critically acclaimed fiction and nonfiction for younger children. She has devoted her literary career to "surprising children into learning," a task she has done very well indeed for children and young adults.

—Linda Garrett

———

FURLONG, Monica (Mavis). English. Born in Harrow, Middlesex, England, 17 January 1930. Author; reporter for several London newspapers, 1956-68; producer, BBC, 1974-78; moderator of the Movement for the Ordination of Women, 1982 Agent: c/o Anthony Sheil Associates, 2/3 Morwell Street, London W.C.1, England.

PUBLICATIONS FOR YOUNG ADULTS

Fiction

The Cat's Eye. London, Weidenfeld and Nicholson, 1976.

Cousins. London, Weidenfield and Nicholson, 1983.
Wise Child. London, Gollancz, and New York, Knopf, 1987.
Juniper. New York, Random House, 1991.
A Year and a Day. London, Gollancz, 1990.

Poetry

God's a Good Man and Other Poems. London, Mowbray, 1974.

Nonfiction

Contributor, *Ourselves Your Servants: The Church's Ministry.* London, Advisory Council for the Church's Ministry, 1967.
Contemplating Now. London, Hodder and Stoughton, and Philadelphia, Pennsylvania, Westminster Press, 1971.
Travelling In. London, Hodder and Stoughton, 1971.
The End of Our Exploring. London, Hodder and Stoughton, 1973.
Puritan's Progress: A Study of John Bunyan. London, Hodder and Stoughton, and New York, Coward, 1975.
Burrswood, Focus of Healing. London, Hodder and Stoughton, 1978.
Editor, *The Trial of John Bunyan and the Persecution of the Puritans.* London, Folio Society, 1978.
Merton: A Biography. New York, Harper, 1980.
Christian Uncertainties. Cambridge, Massachusetts, Cowley, 1982.
Editor, *Feminine in the Church.* London, Society for Promoting Christian Knowledge, 1984.
Zen Effects: The Life of Alan Watts. Boston, Houghton Mifflin, 1986.
Therese of Lisieux. London, Virago, and New York, Pantheon, 1987.
Dangerous Delight: Women and Power in the Church. London, Society for Promoting Christian Knowledge, 1991.

*   *   *

Well-known as a broadcaster and writer for adults, Monica Furlong has produced one of the most complete historical/fantasy novels for young adults. *Wise Child* is set on the Isle of Mull in the seventh century, although its setting and period often appear to be timeless. Told through the voice of the wise child, the story describes the adoption and training of this young girl by Juniper, a white witch and pagan. The child's father is away on a long voyage when her mother uses her and scars her mentally before running away and deserting her. In the first of several of the book's set pieces, the child is auctioned off. Juniper, recognizing the wise child (whose name refers to her being "old beyond her years") as a healer in the making, casts the highest bid and takes her to her white house. There, life is often hard and the two work physically on the land. The child is torn between this torturing life and the glamorous world of her mother, who comes to reclaim her. However, after a trial for witchcraft following a severe winter for which Juniper is blamed by the villagers, the wise child discovers where her true loyalties lie.

Wise Child is a remarkable book in many ways, subtly drawn and told with a quiet urgency. While set firmly in the past, it manages to draw upon emotions with which many young adults can identify. The dismay felt by the wise child at her many problems is touchingly real, while the conflict produced due to her loyalty both to Juniper and her feckless mother is bound to provoke empathy.

Another of Furlong's books for young adults, *A Year and a Day,* continues the events in *Wise Child* and tells of the early life of Juniper. Known as Ninnoc to her family, she is the daughter of King Mark and niece of Mark's evil sister who is training her supposed son Gamal to take over the kingdom. Ninnoc is persuaded to live for a year and a day with her mysterious, shabby undemonstrative godmother, Euny, who oversees her initiation as a doran—a wise woman. Ninnoc rebels against her firm treatment at the hands of her godmother and the poverty-stricken life she is forced to lead and is seduced into the glamorous life of her aunt. However, Ninnoc's aunt's motives become all too obvious, resulting in a power struggle between the forces of good and evil.

A Year and a Day, while lacking the outstanding qualities of *Wise Child,* is a skillful piece of work. Hopefully Furlong will continue to write about these strong women and continue the sequence of novels set in this period.

—Keith Barker

G

GAINES, Ernest J(ames). American. Born in Oscar, Louisiana (some sources cite River Lake Plantation, near New Roads, Pointe Coupee Parish, Louisiana), 15 January 1933. Educated at Vallejo Junior College, California; San Francisco State College (now University), California, B.A. 1957; graduate study at Stanford University, California, 1958-59. Served in U.S. Army, 1953-55. Writer in residence, 1971, Denison University Granville, Ohio; writer in residence, 1981, Stanford University; visiting professor, 1983, writer in residence, 1986, Whittier College, California; professor of English and writer in residence, since 1983, University of Southwestern Louisiana. Recipient: Wallace Stegner Fellow, 1957, Stanford University; Joseph Henry Jackson Award, 1959, for "Comeback" (short story), from San Francisco Foundation; award from National Endowment for the Arts, 1967; Rockefeller grant, 1970; Guggenheim fellowship, 1971; award from Black Academy of Arts and Letters, 1972; fiction gold medal, 1972, for *The Autobiography of Miss Jane Pittman,* and 1984, for *A Gathering of Old Men,* from Commonwealth Club of California; award from Louisiana Library Association, 1972; honorary doctorate of letters from Denison University, 1980, Brown University, 1985, Bard College, 1985, and Louisiana State University, 1987; award for excellence of achievement in literature from San Francisco Arts Commission, 1983; D.H.L. from Whittier College, 1986; literary award from American Academy and Institute of Arts and Letters, 1987. Agent: JCA Literary Agency, Inc., 242 West 27th St., New York, NY 10001, U.S.A.

PUBLICATIONS FOR ADULTS AND YOUNG ADULTS

Fiction

Catherine Carmier. New York, Atheneum, 1964.
Of Love and Dust. New York, Dial, 1967.
Bloodline (short stories). New York, Dial, 1968.
The Autobiography of Miss Jane Pittman. New York, Dial, 1971.
In My Father's House. New York, Knopf, 1978.
A Gathering of Old Men. New York, Knopf, 1983.
A Lesson before Dying. New York, Knopf, 1993.

PUBLICATIONS FOR CHILDREN

Fiction

A Long Day in November (story originally published in author's collection *Bloodline*; illustrated by Don Bolognese). New York, Dial, 1971.

*

Media Adaptations: *The Autobiography of Miss Jane Pittman* (film), Columbia Broadcasting System (CBS-TV), 1974; *The Sky Is Gray* (film for public television), 1980; *A Gathering of Old Men* (film), CBS-TV, 1987.

Biography: *Porch Talk with Ernest Gaines: Conversations on the Writer's Craft,* edited by Marcia Gaudet and Carl Wooton, Baton Rouge, Louisiana State University Press, 1990. *Concise Dictionary of American Literary Biography: Broadening Views, 1968-1988,* Detroit, Gale, 1989; *Dictionary of Literary Biography,* Detroit, Gale, Volume 2: *American Novelists since World War II,* 1978, Volume 33: *Afro-American Fiction Writers after 1955,* 1984; *Dictionary of Literary Biography Yearbook: 1980,* Detroit, Gale, 1981.

Bibliography: *Contemporary Literary Criticism,* Detroit, Gale, Volume 3, 1975, Volume 11, 1979, Volume 18, 1981.

Manuscript Collection: Dupree Library, University of Southwestern Louisiana, Lafayette.

Critical Studies: *Interview with Black Writers,* edited by John O'Brien, Liveright, 1973; *The Way of the New World: The Black Novel in America,* by Addison Gayle, Jr., Doubleday, 1975; *The Black American Short Story in the Twentieth Century: A Collection of Critical Essays,* edited by Peter Bruck, B.R. Gruner (Amsterdam), 1977; *In the Singer's Temple: Prose Fictions of Barthelme, Gaines, Brautigan, Piercy, Kesey, and Kosinski,* by Jack Hicks, University of North Carolina Press, 1981.

*   *   *

Just as Isaac Bashevis Singer wrote about a European Jewish culture that had been destroyed before he began writing, so too has Ernest Gaines written about a culture that almost has been destroyed by economic and social changes in Louisiana. While *The Autobiography of Miss Jane Pittman* moves from the antebellum South to the beginning of the civil rights movement of the 1950s and 1960s, Gaines's other five novels and short stories (*A Long Day in November* is short enough to appear in the short story collection *Bloodline*) are mostly set between 1930 to 1970 on plantations with black and Cajun sharecroppers or in towns near such plantations. While whites are on top in this world, whites, Cajuns, and blacks are torn apart living under racist "rules." Many of the whites and Cajuns on which Gaines focuses, benefit from these rules, but love, usually of a black man or woman, makes these rules problematic even to them. For the black people in Gaines's works, a constant struggle exists between the demands of survival and the desire for dignity and self-respect.

Catherine Carmier explores the biases in the black community itself once white blood has been introduced into black families. Jackson, who is black, returns to his aunt who lives on a plantation. While trained to be a teacher or political leader, Jackson resists those roles that no longer seem appropriate to his identity, only to fall in love with Catherine Carmier, a Creole, whose father thinks his family a cut above blacks in the former slave quarters. As in so many of Gaines's novels, the dilemmas of the characters crystallize into a scene: in this case, it is a fight between Catherine's father and Jackson over Catherine's love and identity as a black person.

Set earlier than *Catherine Carmier, Of Love and Dust* occurs in 1948. The code of behavior for blacks is solidly in place, but interracial love upsets the fragile order. Bonbon, a Cajun overseer, uses the code in trying to break the spirit of Marcus, a young black man bonded to the plantation following his killing of another black man. Marcus to get even with Bonbon, tries to take Bonbon's black mistress away from him, but failing at that seduces Bonbon's white wife. The exploitation of both Bonbon and Marcus gives way to love, as Bonbon grows to love his black mistress and Marcus grows to love Bonbon's wife. While Bonbon kills Marcus, he does so more from the pressure of his Cajun background than from a desire for revenge. Though the black narrator, Jim, rejects Bonbon, Bonbon is a changed man who must leave the South—with his mistress and not his wife. Marcus grows from fool to hero in the eyes of the black people on the plantation, as they sense his quest for respect.

The Autobiography of Miss Jane Pittman, like Ellison's *Invisible Man,* is a fictive portrait of black people in America from the Civil War to the time of Martin Luther King, Jr. Gaines's ploy of having the work supposedly composed of tapes by a historian recording the words of Miss Jane Pittman, who is 108 or 109, as she and her friends look back at their lives allows this imaginative history to be created. Unlike Ellison's novel, in which the protagonist-narrator travels to college and then to New York, Miss Jane never leaves Louisiana. History is not simply given through Jane's life but through those who are important to her such as Ned whose maturity covers the turn of the century and Jimmy, who is a follower of King. The interracial love of earlier novels is present in a white and Creole liaison that ends in suicide as the "code" claims another victim.

In My Father's House, a novel set in 1970, also ends with a suicide, when the illegitimate son of a minister active in the civil rights movement takes his life. Before the minister, Phillip Martin, had become a responsible man following his conversion fifteen years earlier, he had left a woman he loved and his three children by her. Forced by a white power broker sheriff to trade a civil rights goal of equal pay for equal work for his incarcerated illegitimate son, Phillip chooses his son's freedom, but he loses everything he has worked for except his second legitimate family. The attempt by Phillip to achieve a unified character for the whole of his fragmented life is brave, however, and mirrors the growing pains of thousands of black Americans.

A Gathering of Old Men, like *The Autobiography of Miss Jane Pittman,* was made into a film. Just as the earlier novel had a great historical sweep because of Jane's age, so too is there a historical sweep to the later novel for a similar reason—the age of the nearly twenty old men who are in their seventies and eighties. They gather to provide protection to a revered friend by each claiming to have murdered the same Cajun. Mathu, their friend, is in turn shielding another man, only to find that unnecessary when Big Charlie admits to the murder and claims their respect. The character of the law and society are changing in this novel, as blacks, whites, and Cajuns cheer black and white running-backs for Louisiana State University's football team. As old black men, used to being humiliated, rise to claim their manhood, the code begins to be buried.

As in *Of Love and Dust* and *A Gathering of Old Men, A Lesson before Dying,* Gaines's latest novel, shows a black man achieving dignity and pride. Jefferson, a young black man reluctantly involved in the killing of a white man, is going to the electric chair. Tormenting him are the words of his defense attorney who calls Jefferson a hog. Grant Wiggins, a plantation school teacher who is college educated, is compelled by his own and Jefferson's relatives to educate Jefferson to self-respect before he dies. As the novel closes black and white witness Jefferson's transformation.

Gaines's novels and stories are dramatically powerful. Values always collide in powerful scenes featuring excellent dialogue. Gaines, distrustful of the symbol and the romance, writes gripping realistic narratives. Seldom in Gaines is there omniscience; his mostly first-person narrators establish authenticity through our reading of their tone of voice. While Gaines is not enamored of film or television, one can readily understand why his novels and stories attract producers, directors, and actors.

—Craig W. Barrow

GARD, Janice. See **LATHAM, Jean Lee.**

GARDAM, Jane (née Pearson). British. Born in Coatham, Yorkshire, 11 July 1928. Educated at Saltburn High School for Girls; Bedford College, London, 1946-49, B.A. (honours) 1949, graduate study, 1949-52. Married David Gardam in 1952; two sons and one daughter. Red Cross librarian, 1951; sub-editor, *Weldons Ladies Journal,* London, 1952-53; assistant literary editor, *Time and Tide,* London, 1952-54. Recipient: *A Long Way from Verona* received special mention from the Guardian award for children's fiction, and was selected an honor book by *Book World's* Spring Book Festival award, both 1972, and won the Phoenix award, 1991; *Boston Globe-Horn Book* honor book for text, 1974, for *The Summer after the Funeral;* David Higham Prize for fiction and Winifred Holtby Memorial prize for fiction, both 1977, both for *Black Faces, White Faces;* runner-up citation, Booker Prize, 1978, for *God on the Rocks;* Whitbread Literary award, 1981, for *The Hollow Land;* Carnegie Medal "highly recommended" award, for *The Hollow Land* and "commended" award, for *Bridget and William,* both 1983; Katherine Mansfield award, 1984, for *The Pangs of Love;* Whitbread Novel of the the Year award, for *The Queen of the Tambourine,* 1991. Fellow, Royal Society of Literature, 1976. Agent: Bruce Hunter, David Higham Associates, 5-8 Lower John Street, London, W1R 4HA. Lives at Haven House, Sandwich, Kent, England.

PUBLICATIONS FOR YOUNG ADULTS

Fiction

A Few Fair Days, illustrated by Peggy Fortnum. London, Hamish Hamilton, 1971; New York, Macmillan, 1972.

A Long Way from Verona. London, Hamish Hamilton, and New York, Macmillan, 1971.

The Summer after the Funeral. London, Hamish Hamilton, and New York, Macmillan, 1973.

Bilgewater. London, Hamish Hamilton, 1976; New York, Greenwillow, 1977.

The Hollow Land, illustrated by Janet Rawlins. London, MacRae, 1981; New York, Greenwillow, 1982.

Through the Dolls' House Door. London, MacRae, and New York, Greenwillow, 1987.

PUBLICATIONS FOR CHILDREN

Fiction

Bridget and William, illustrated by Janet Rawlins. London, MacRae, 1981.
Horse, illustrated by Janet Rawlins. London, MacRae 1982.
Kit, illustrated by William Geldart. London, MacRae, 1983.
Kit in Boots, illustrated by William Geldart. London, MacRae, 1986.
Swan, illustrated by John Dillow. London, MacRae, 1987.

PUBLICATIONS FOR ADULTS

Novels

Black Faces, White Faces. London, Hamish Hamilton, 1975; as *The Pineapple Bay Hotel,* New York, Morrow, 1976.
God on the Rocks. London, Hamish Hamilton, 1978; New York, Morrow, 1979.
Crusoe's Daughter. London, Hamish Hamilton, 1985; New York, Atheneum, 1986.

Short Stories

The Sidmouth Letters. London, Hamish Hamilton, and New York, Morrow, 1980.
The Pangs of Love and Other Stories. London, Hamish Hamilton, 1983.
Showing the Flag. London, Hamish Hamilton, 1989.
The Queen of the Tambourine. London, Sinclair-Stevenson, 1991.

*

Media Adaptations: Film, *God on the Rocks,* ITV, 1992.

Biography: Entry in *Dictionary of Literary Biography,* Volume 14, Detroit, Gale, 1983; Essay in *Something about the Author Autobiography Series,* Volume 9, Detroit, Gale, 1990.

Critical Study: Entry in *Children's Literature Review,* Volume 12, Detroit, Gale, 1987; Entry in *Contemporary Literary Criticism,* Volume 43, Detroit, Gale, 1987.

*   *   *

Jane Gardam's work as a whole is distinguished by a clearly delineated, often satiric representation of historical and cultural moments of English life and British educational, religious, and class institutions. Many of her characters are drawn from the milieu of Anglican church and school communities. The favoured chronology for her stories is the period during and immediately surrounding the Second World War. Gardam's concentration on a particular class, political, and professional group and its values accounts for the somewhat nostalgic feeling about much of her work. She offers us a perspective on changes in English culture, moments in time now lost. A sense of history, and of history within the lives of particular persons and groups, structures the progression of the narrative in works such as *The Hollow Land, Through the Dolls' House Door,* and *Crusoe's Daughter.*

A sense of place and period is also an important feature of Gardam's fiction. The landscape and customs of the north of England of her childhood form a backdrop to many stories. In addi-

tion, as the publisher's dustjackets of her books remind us, Gardam is a much-travelled writer. The depiction of the "English[wo]man abroad" is a facet of her adult fiction—influenced, no doubt, by the writings of Somerset Maugham, whose work she has admired.

One of the conventions of this tradition is the depiction of the eccentric or "larger than life" individual, and this is a trademark of Gardam's fiction. The dramatic representation of this category of character (usually female) often borders on the grotesque or the black comic.

Many of these eccentrics are genteel paupers of the superannuated middle classes, living as seedy, anachronistic reminders of a bygone age of privilege. Gardam reserves her harshest satire for the status-conscious backbiting and parsimony of the upper-middle classes, the last vestiges of a society upon the margins of which her young heroines and their families live.

Jane Gardam is not only a very English writer, she is also a very self-consciously literary one. Her works make constant allusion to classical myth and literature, English literature, and to art: Shakespeare, Brontë, Hardy, Joyce, Gauguin, Botticell—all these make themselves felt as influences in her texts. Often her protagonists identify with these intertextual literary models to structure their quest for self-definition. Athene Price, in *The Summer after the Funeral,* feels herself to be a tragic alter ego of Emily Brontë, while Folly Flint imaginatively defines herself as "Crusoe's Daughter." Allusive games, or games invoking the literary system, also abound. Proper names frequently have mythological or symbolic significance. The title story of *The Sidmouth Letters,* in which a collection of Jane Austen's letters to a lover are discovered, utilizes the mode of the fictional (literary) historical to satirize academic pretensions and obsessions.

Gardam is a writer for whom genre is flexible. Some of her works, such as *The Hollow Land; Black Faces, White Faces;* and *A Few Fair Days,* can be seen either as short stories or as episodic novels. Gardam favours the use of vignettes to capture moments in place and time, to covey the flavour of experience, placing them in an episodic narrative structure rather than relying on the primacy of complex traditional plotting. Her strength lies in the sense of balance between the comic impetus and the incisive scrutiny she brings to bear on matters of social hierarchy and the anxieties of the socio-sexual maturation process.

Gardam's status as a writer for young adults rests on three major texts, *A Long Way from Verona, The Summer after the Funeral,* and *Bilgewater,* to which can be linked her adult novel, *Crusoe's Daughter,* which shares the focus on the representation of adolescence and developing sexuality. She favours the first-person narrative in her dramatizations of the anxieties of the young female protagonist: a misfit saddled with a chaotic and eccentric family, anxiously aware of her existence on the margins of acceptable affluence and social respectability. The narratives enact the heroine's painful progress towards autonomy and identity against the odds of repressive religious or educational structures, and awkward social and economic horizons, which are often related to the equivocal status of her father.

The writer's novels have been described as "plotless," but they are not without a narrative trajectory, one which can be seen in the deliberate interruption or transgression of the romantic quest pattern. The protagonist's increasing disaffection with her father/family, leading to a literal or symbolic flight/separation, is linked to the increasing pressures of her own sexuality. Her search for autonomy is linked in her imagination to a romantic icon, a young male figure, often explicitly associated with a literary precursor in the romance mode. The novels exploit both romantic and antiromantic tendencies. However, the romance pattern is never successfully completed. The young male idol is discovered to have feet of clay: thus the heroine's existential quest is rerouted from its traditional trajectory towards a less ideal, though nevertheless autonomous conclusion.

The title of *A Long Way from Verona* announces the distance this text will place between itself and the conventions of Shakespearean love tragedy, while other references also signal the importance of *Romeo and Juliet* as a major intertext against which the failure of the ideal of romance in wartime in the north of England is to be read. At the same time, the dangers of impending sexual maturity for the young heroine, Jessica Vye, are suggested by Mrs. Looney Hopkins's description of her as "a little Juliet"—"younger than she are married mothers made." The world of Cleveland/Durham and the Tees District is, however, a long way from Juliet's Verona. It is a world where ideals are proved unreliable, where adolescent longing for the perfect beloved is revealed as wish-fulfillment fantasy, and where the dark side of sexuality, frightening but attractive, is revealed by the furtive admiration of the Italian POW Jessica meets in the Valley Gardens.

The novel is set in the district and period of Gardam's own adolescence, thinly disguised. The Vye family are forced to cope with the radical father's abrupt vocational change from a well-to-do schoolmaster's position to the lower hierarchy of the Anglican pastoral economy. Jessica's mother had functioned well enough as a comfortable professional's mate, with domestic help, but is completely ineffectual when confronted by the considerable domestic and parish duties of a poor curate's wife.

Though denigrated by her English mistress, Miss Dobbs, Jessica has literary ambitions and has been told by Arnold Hanger, a writer visiting her school, that she is "a writer beyond all possible doubt." The heroine is aware of the appeal of great art, and of herself as an artist. While her later discovery of Hanger's status as a third-rate practitioner deflates her pride and her romantic idea of attachment to art, her subsequent success in the poetry competition, judged by the highly reputable Walter de la Mare, affirms the validity of the claims of her story to be read as a portrait of the artist as a young woman.

Socially Jessica is seen as a misfit and a rebel at her school. She is an inappropriate Juliet with a fetish for Rupert Brooke, whose works are given to her by the (possibly lesbian) Miss Philemon, who is something of a mentor and a muse. Another of Gardam's eccentric marginalized spinster ladies, Miss Philemon not only gives Jessica a copy of *Romeo and Juliet,* she also shocks and titillates her with the implications of innocent sexual enjoyment and aesthetic pleasure suggested by the copy of Gauguin's painting of two naked Tahitians which hangs in her home.

The "Romeo" figure appears in the person of Christian Fanshawe, son of her father's old college friend. Jessica's first sight of the male Adonis strikes her like an epiphany: a revelation of the romantic ideal embodied, which has previously been represented in her imagination by the figure of Rupert Brooke. In Gardam's fiction, the presence of such perfect male beauty usually signals the circumvention of romantic aspirations. Like that of Jack Rose in *Bilgewater* and the "Heathcliff of the Summerhouse" in *The Summer after the Funeral,* Christian's promise of fulfillment is illusory. The reformminded Christian is interested in Jessica only because of her father's reputation as a Fabian commentator. His idea of a date is a visit to the slums, while the clammy misadventure of the hand-holding episode, signals the antiromantic embarrassments of adolescent

sexual forays. When Christian deserts Jessica during the bomb attack, leaving her to fend for herself and to make her own way home, the unreliability of the male hero figure and of patriarchal protection as a valid option is brought home remorselessly to the young female. Romantic idealization is forced to give way to self-sufficiency and painful autonomy.

For the beautiful Athene Price, the main protagonist of *The Summer after the Funeral,* the search for autonomy is impelled by sexual maturation and the necessity for escape from the post mortem influence of her father, an Anglican patriarch who "positively ate her up," attempting to possess her both intellectually and emotionally. Her quest for identity during the summer following his death takes the form of a journey in which she must negotiate a path between two stultifying possibilities. She must avoid the fate of the bitter and frustrated spinsters—Posie Dixon, Sybil Bowles, and Primrose Clark—while at the same time escaping seduction by older men who resemble her father in their desire to possess her: Basil, the fiftyish painter, and Henry Bell, the classicist schoolmaster.

Athene also represents her identity in terms of literary models. She identifies with Emily Brontë, resonating to the possibilities of tragic romantic passion and recoiling from the spectre of sterility represented by the life at the Haworth Parsonage under the structures of religious and patriarchal control, escape from which seems to be promised only by sexual initiation. Metaphors of natural fecundity are utilized to signal Athene's ripening into sexual anticipation: flowers (red hot pokers), the luxuriance of summer growth, fruit (the blood-red berries in Basil's pantry, which represent Athene's recoil from the grotesque suggestion of her own defloration). Her fear of the possibility of having been possessed by Basil while sleeping and her attraction to Henry Bell are staging posts in a quest whose perceived goal is the grand romantic potential signified by "the Heathcliff of the Summer-house," the dark "gypsy" lover of her imagination, who turns out to be, in actuality, the more prosaic Lucian, a Jewish school friend of her brother, Sebastian.

Bilgewater demonstrates its author's affection for the writing of James Joyce: its title announces to be as a *jeu d'esprit,* a parcel of nonsense. The playful human tendency towards corruption of language leads to the humiliating renaming of its heroine. Marigold Green, an unlikely flower, becomes "Bilgewater" (a corruption of "Bill's daughter"), a label which signals her frumpish lack of allure to the boys at the school at which her father teaches, and at which she is the only adolescent female interloper.

The first epigraph to the book—"Youth is a blunder"—points to the wryly, self-deprecating narrative stance, as the eighteen-year-old Marigold, now safely established in the intellectual haven of Cambridge with a reliable, if unexotic, partner, looks back to the mistakes and wrong-turnings of her earlier youth.

Bilgewater follows the "mythic" narrative model of *Ulysses,* structuring the quest upon the search of the child for its "true" parent. In Gardam's novel, the quest is not for the father, as it is in Joyce's work and in the classical Greek model of the Telemachus myth, but for the child's true mother. Marigold's father is a rather absent-minded scholar who has little regard for his daughter's existence, her needs as a female, and for her emerging sexuality. She seeks a sense of belonging and feminine identity through pursuit of the mystery surrounding the nature of her dead mother, Daisy. The name, Daisy Green, is the source of her daughter's romantic illusion about her mother's pastoral innocence and perfection. Flowers traditionally represent youth, purity, and beauty: a beauty without stain which is rendered sentimentally more desirable because of its inevitable transience. The sordid worldliness of the Rose family cast a sensual slur over the notion of the pure and perfect mother, and Bilgewater finds her true female parent in the practical school matron, Paula Rigg—with her reliable if rather unsentimental care for Bilgewater and her father—just as she will find her future partner in the reliable but unremarkable Boakes. Her developing sexuality leads her to veer between a schoolgirl idolization of Jack Rose, the most beautiful and popular boy in the school, and the ambiguously attractive Terrapin, a trickster figure who is more nearly her intellectual soul mate, but who offers a dangerous sexual intensity and an intermittent commitment. The whimsical, somewhat contrived ending of the narrative allows the heroine to find a "middle way" between these extremes. Her eventual husband is somewhat of a surprising choice, but less of a grotesque misalliance than those made by the other potential mates.

Crusoe's Daughter is another example of Gardam's literary self-reflexiveness. It deals with the nature of feminine isolation and with the nature of fictional narrative. Its feminist agenda is seen in its focus on the motif of the woman/everywoman, alone on an existential island which is at once austere and in touch with the landscape of abandonment. Polly Flint is stranded and imprisoned at six years of age, when she comes to live with her two maiden aunts in the yellow house, on the edge of a salt marsh somewhere on the Northumbrian coast. The story follows the changes in culture, landscape, industrial growth, times and manners, until Polly's death in 1985. Though she sees herself as "Crusoe's daughter," resolved to get on with the business of living in an unpromising environment for human fulfillment, she nevertheless dreams of rescue. The relationship with the dashing (Jewish) young man who engages her imagination as potential hero and rescuer never comes to fruition. He is finally returned to her an old and broken man, a victim of Hitler's concentration camps. Once more Gardam circumvents the romantic quest pattern, while dramatizing the pains and potential of adult female autonomy.

In addition to her works for young adults, Gardam has written fiction for younger readers and for adults.

—Leonie Margaret Rutherford

GARDEN, Nancy. American. Born in Boston, Massachusetts, 15 May 1938. Educated at Columbia University, New York, B.F.A. 1961, M.A. 1962. Contributing editor, *Junior Scholastic,* New York, 1969-70; *American Observer,* Washington, D.C., 1970-72; associate editor, Houghton Mifflin Co., New York, 1972, assistant editor, 1973, editor, 1974-76; teacher and free-lance writer, 1976—. Has also worked in the theatre as an actress and lighting designer, taught at various levels, and done free-lance editorial work for various publishers. Lecturer at schools and libraries to children on writing. Recipient: *Annie on My Mind* was selected to the 1982 *Booklist* Reviewer's Choice, the 1982 ALA Best Books, and the 1970-83 ALA Best of the Best lists; *Fours Crossing* was selected to the 1983-84 William Allen White award Master List. Lives in Carlisle, Massachusetts.

PUBLICATIONS FOR YOUNG ADULTS

Fiction

Berlin: City Split in Two. New York, Putnam, 1971.
What Happened in Marston, illustrated by Richard Cuffari. New York, Four Winds, 1971.
The Loners. New York, Viking, 1972.
Vampires. Philadelphia, Pennsylvania, Lippincott, 1973.
Werewolves. Philadelphia, Pennsylvania, Lippincott, 1973.
Witches. Philadelphia, Pennsylvania, Lippincott, 1975.
Devils and Demons. Philadelphia, Pennsylvania, Lippincott, 1976.
Fun with Forecasting Weather. Boston, Massachusetts, Houghton Mifflin, 1977.
Fours Crossing. New York, Farrar Straus, 1981.
The Kids' Code and Cipher Book. Hamden, Connecticut, Linnet, 1981.
Maria's Mountain. Boston, Massachusetts, Houghton Mifflin, 1981.
Annie on My Mind. New York, Farrar Straus, 1982.
Adaptor, *Favorite Tales from Grimm,* illustrated by Mercer Mayer. New York, Four Winds, 1982.
Watersmeet. New York, Farrar Straus, 1983.
Prisoner of Vampires, illustrated by Michele Chessare. New York, Farrar Straus, 1984.
Peace, O River. New York, Farrar Straus, 1986.
The Door Between. New York, Farrar Straus, 1987.
Mystery of the Night Raiders. New York, Farrar Straus, 1987.
Mystery of the Midnight Menace. Farrar Straus, 1988.
Mystery of the Secret Marks. New York, Farrar Straus, 1989.
Lark in the Morning. New York, Farrar Straus, 1991.
My Sister, the Vampire. New York, Knopf, 1992.

*

Biography: Essay in *Speaking for Ourselves, Too* compiled and edited by Donald R. Gallo, National Council of Teachers of English, 1993.

*   *   *

Much of the body of Nancy Garden's work demonstrates a tendency towards the intriguing and the fantastic. Her books for younger readers well illustrates this as they delve, within the genre of both fiction and nonfiction, into the supernatural and unexplained. Her nonfiction ties itself closely with her fiction as occult characters are featured in both. Garden's fantasy literature for young adults also explores the mystical realm. Her realistic fiction for older readers bravely departs from this trend to confront current issues with tact and sensitivity.

The "Fours Crossing" books create fantasy rooted in the city of Fours Crossing, a town steeped in history and mysticism. The series follows the adventures of Melissa and her friend Jed as they work against the evil will of a powerful hermit to maintain the balance of nature. A taste of one of Garden's works for younger readers, *The Kids' Code and Cipher Book,* pervades the series as mystical signs and symbols require decoding in order to overcome the evil. These well-constructed ciphers challenge the reader to participate in the adventure, creating an interactive reading experience. Though primarily plot-driven, intriguing fantasy elements make these books satisfying.

The internal struggles of Kate in *Peace, O River* make her one of Garden's most engaging young adult characters. Kate returns to her childhood home after a four-year absence to discover a feud raging between the two towns bordering the river. The feud manifests itself in Kate's high school as explosive gang violence. Kate struggles to unite the two towns in the face of a proposed local nuclear waste disposal site and in so doing learns about the nature of conflict and the price of peace. The cross-river relationships prove intriguing as does the character development of the protagonist. Occasionally approaching maudlin, the overall sentiment of the tale manages to convince and prove poignant.

Annie on My Mind depicts with clarity and sensitivity the first homosexual relationship of two young women. Garden takes no aspect of the relationship for granted—the reader participates in the wonder, the bliss, and the fear of the two characters coming to terms with their sexuality. This careful plotting combined with strong characterization allows for the development of a realistic dynamic between the couple, rendering the romance highly convincing. The romance turns bittersweet, though, when the couple must face the fear and hatred of a disapproving community. Garden's depiction of a homophobic society tends toward caricature as the antagonists are all extreme. A spectrum of opposition may have added balance to the conflict that reads as too black and white. The book remains highly valuable in its successful portrayal of teen romance.

Lark in the Morning presents a fresh presence in young adult fiction in its inclusion of a homosexual character whose struggle with sexuality is not central to the narrative. Seventeen-year-old Gillian reflects on the realization of her sexuality that took place the summer before, but focuses her attention on the two runaways she discovers hiding near her family's summer home. In an effort to respect the young siblings' fear of returning to their abusive parents, Gillian decides to help them on her own; a task that proves more than she bargained for. Garden deals with sexuality with tact, as Gillian's homosexuality is never treated as a random aspect of her character. Instead, her identity as a lesbian becomes relevant in a way that balances well with the plot's central issues.

Garden's success in the creation of dynamic and engaging works in the genres of both fantasy and realistic fiction demonstrates a breadth of ability. The topics explored in her writing show her making an important contribution to young adult libraries.

—Susan Rich

———

GARFIELD, Leon. British. Born in Brighton, Sussex, 14 July 1921. Educated at Brighton Grammar School in England. Served in the Royal Army Medical Corps, 1940-46: private; served in Belgium and Germany. Married Vivien Dolores Alcock in 1948; one daughter. Biochemical technician, Whittington Hospital, London, 1946-66; part-time biochemical technician in a hospital in London, 1966; since 1966 novelist. Recipient: Gold Medal, Boys' Clubs of America, 1966, for *Jack Holborn;* first *Guardian* award for children's fiction, 1967, for *Devil-in-the-Fog;* Arts Council of Great Britain award for the best book for older children, and American Library Association (ALA) Notable Book citation, both 1967, *Boston Globe-Horn Book* honor book citation, 1968, and Phoenix award, 1987, all for *Smith;* Carnegie Medal runner-up, 1967, for *Smith,* 1968, for

Black Jack, and 1970, for *The Drummer Boy; New York Times* Best Illustrated Book citation, 1968, for *Mister Corbett's Ghost;* Carnegie Medal for the most outstanding book of the year, and Kate Greenaway Medal commendation, both 1970, both for *The God beneath the Sea;* Kate Greenaway Medal commendation, and ALA Notable Book citation, both 1972, both for *The Ghost Downstairs;* Child Study Association of America's Children's Books of the Year citation, 1976, for *The House of Hanover: England in the Eighteenth Century;* Whitbread Literary award, 1980, for *John Diamond; Boston Globe-Horn Book* Fiction Honor citation, 1981, for *Footsteps;* Federation of Children's Book Groups award, 1981, for *Fair's Fair;* Hans Christian Andersen award nomination, 1981; Prix de la Fondation de France, 1984; Golden Cat award (Sweden), 1985; runner-up for Maschlev awards, 1985, for *Shakespeare Stories* and *The Wedding Ghost;* Children's Literature Association Phoenix award, 1987. Fellow, Royal Society of Literature, 1985. Agent: The Ellen Levine Literary Agency Inc., Suite 906, 370 Lexington Ave., New York, NY 10017. Address: 59 Wood Lane, Highgate, London N6, England.

PUBLICATIONS FOR YOUNG ADULTS

Fiction

Jack Holborn, illustrated by Antony Maitland. London, Constable, 1964; New York, Pantheon, 1965.
Devil-in-the-Fog, illustrated by Antony Maitland. London, Constable, and New York, Pantheon, 1966.
Smith, illustrated by Antony Maitland. London, Constable, and New York, Pantheon, 1967.
Black Jack, illustrated by Antony Maitland. London, Longman, 1968; New York, Pantheon, 1969.
Mr. Corbett's Ghost, illustrated by Alan E. Cober. New York, Pantheon, 1968.
The Boy and the Monkey, illustrated by Trevor Ridley. London, Heinemann, 1969; New York, Watts, 1970.
The Drummer Boy, illustrated by Antony Maitland. New York, Pantheon, 1969; London, Longman, 1970.
Mister Corbett's Ghost, and Other Stories, illustrated by Antony Maitland. London, Longman, 1969.
The Restless Ghost: Three Stories by Leon Garfield, illustrated by Saul Lambert. New York, Pantheon, 1969.
The Strange Affair of Adelaide Harris, illustrated by Fritz Wegner. London, Longman, and New York, Pantheon, 1971.
The Captain's Watch, illustrated by Trevor Ridley. London, Heinemann, 1972.
The Ghost Downstairs, illustrated by Antony Maitland. London, Longman, and New York, Pantheon, 1972.
Lucifer Wilkins, illustrated by Trevor Ridley. London, Heinemann, 1973.
The Sound of Coaches (with Edward Blishen), illustrated by John Lawrence. London, Kestrel, and New York, Viking Press, 1974.
The Prisoners of September. London, Kestrel, and New York, Viking Press, 1975.
The Pleasure Garden, illustrated by Fritz Wegner. London, Kestrel, and New York, Viking Press, 1976.
An Adelaide Ghost. London, Ward Lock, 1977.
The Confidence Man. London, Kestrel, 1978; New York, Viking Press, 1979.

Bostock and Harris; or, The Night of the Comet, illustrated by Martin Cottam. London, Kestrel, 1979; as *The Night of the Comet: A Comedy of Courtship Featuring Bostock and Harris,* New York, Delacorte Press, 1979.

John Diamond, illustrated by Antony Maitland. London, Kestrel, 1980; as *Footsteps,* New York, Delacorte Press, 1980.

Fair's Fair, illustrated by Margaret Chamberlain. London, Macdonald, 1981; American edition illustrated by S. D. Schindler, New York, Doubleday, 1983.

King Nimrod's Tower, illustrated by Michael Bragg. London, Constable, and New York, Lothrop, 1982.

The Writing on the Wall, illustrated by Michael Bragg. London, Methuen, 1982, New York, Lothrop, 1983.

Guilt and Gingerbread, illustrated by Fritz Wegner. London, Viking Kestrel, 1984.

The King in the Garden, illustrated by Michael Bragg. London, Methuen, 1984; New York, Lothrop, 1985.

The Wedding Ghost, illustrated by Charles Keeping. Oxford, Oxford University Press, 1985; New York, Oxford University Press, 1987.

The December Rose (novelization of his own television series). London, Viking Kestrel, 1986; New York, Viking Kestrel, 1987.

Blewcoat Boy. London, Gollancz, 1988; as *Young Nick and Jubilee,* illustrated by Ted Lewin, Delacorte Press, 1989.

The Empty Sleeve. London, Viking Kestrel, and New York, Delacorte Press, 1988.

Revolution! London, Collins, 1989.

"Apprentices" series:

The Cloak, illustrated by Faith Jaques. London, Heinemann, 1976.

The Lamplighter's Funeral, illustrated by Antony Maitland. London, Heinemann, 1976.

Mirror, Mirror, illustrated by Antony Maitland. London, Heinemann, 1976.

Moss and Blister, illustrated by Faith Jaques. London, Heinemann, 1976.

The Dumb Cake, illustrated by Faith Jaques. London, Heinemann, 1977.

The Fool, illustrated by Faith Jaques. London, Heinemann, 1977.

Labour in Vain, illustrated by Faith Jaques. London, Heinemann, 1977.

Rosy Starling, illustrated by Faith Jaques. London, Heinemann, 1977.

Tom Titmarsh's Devil, illustrated by Faith Jaques. London, Heinemann, 1977.

The Valentine, illustrated by Faith Jaques. London, Heinemann, 1977.

The Enemy, illustrated by Faith Jaques. London, Heinemann, 1978.

The Filthy Beast, illustrated by Faith Jaques. London, Heinemann, 1978.

The Apprentices. New York, Viking Press, 1978; London, Heinemann, 1982.

Other

The God beneath the Sea, with Edward Blishen, illustrated by Charles Keeping. London, Longman, 1970; American edition illustrated by Zevi Blum, New York, Pantheon, 1971.

Child O'War: The True Story of a Sailor Boy in Nelson's Navy, with David Proctor, illustrated by Antony Maitland. London, Collins, and New York, Holt Rinehart, 1972.

Editor, *Baker's Dozen: A Collection of Stories.* London, Ward Lock, 1973; as *Strange Fish and Other Stories,* New York, Lothrop, 1974.

The Golden Shadow, with Edward Blishen, illustrated by Charles Keeping. New York, Pantheon, 1973.

Editor, *The Book Lovers: A Sequence of Love-Scenes.* London, Ward Lock, 1976; New York, Avon, 1978.

The House of Hanover: England in the Eighteenth Century. London, Deutsch, and New York, Seabury Press, 1976.

Editor, *A Swag of Stories: Australian Stories,* illustrated by Caroline Harrison. London, Ward Lock, 1977.

Shakespeare Stories, illustrated by Michael Foreman. London, Gollancz, and New York, Schocken, 1985.

Tales from Shakespeare, illustrated by Michael Foreman. New York, Schocken, 1985.

Editor, *Hamlet,* illustrated by Natalia Orlova, Peter Kotov, and Natasha Demidova. New York, Knopf, 1993.

Editor, *Macbeth,* illustrated by Nikolai Serebriakov. New York, Knopf, 1993.

Editor, *A Midsummer Night's Dream,* illustrated by Elena Prorokova. New York, Knopf, 1993.

Editor, *Romeo and Juliet,* illustrated by Igor Makarov. New York, Knopf, 1993.

Editor, *The Tempest,* illustrated by Elena Livanova. New York, Knopf, 1993.

Editor, *Twelfth Night,* illustrated by Ksenia Prytkova. New York, Knopf, 1993.

PUBLICATIONS FOR ADULTS

Novels

The Mystery of Edwin Drood (completion of the novel by Charles Dickens). London, Deutsch, 1980; New York, Pantheon, 1981.

The House of Cards. London, Bodley Head, 1982; New York, St. Martin's Press, 1983.

Other

Editor, *Sketches from Bleak House,* with Mervyn Peake and Edward Blishen. London, Methuen, 1983.

*

Media Adaptations: *John Diamond* (film), BBC-TV, 1981; *Jack Holborn* (a Taurus Film), 1982; *The Ghost Downstairs* and *The Restless Ghost* (dramatized for TV), 1982 and 1983, respectively; *The December Rose* (six-part series), BBC-TV, 1986-87; *Mr. Corbett's Ghost* (film), 1987. Several of Garfield's other books have been dramatized for film and television. *Devil-in-the Fog, Smith* and *The Strange Affair of Adelaide Harris* (TV serials-British TV), and *Black Jack* (film), produced by Tony Garnett and directed by Ken Loach.

Biography: Essay in *Speaking for Ourselves, Too* compiled and edited by Donald R. Gallo, National Council of Teachers of English, 1993.

Critical Studies: Entry in *Children's Literature Review,* Volume 21. Detroit, Gale, 1990; entry in *Contemporary Literary Criticism,* Volume 12. Detroit, Gale, 1980.

*   *   *

Leon Garfield's novels vividly evoke another place and time, the England of the eighteenth century. Historical backgrounds and lifestyles are convincingly shown, but historical research never intrudes on the exciting plots of these fast-paced adventure stories, told in a strong narrative style.

The central characters are usually male adolescents who are at first naive children, taking others at face value and accepting whatever adults tell them. But as the heroes gain experience of the adult world and its changing values, they are forced to develop their own identities, deciding what to believe and whom to trust. In *Footsteps,* young William Jones sets out to right a wrong done by his dead father, so the father's troubled ghost will no longer walk at night. But people such as the law clerk Jenkins who seem eager to help turn out to be untrustworthy, while people he initially discounts, such as the unfriendly porter Seed, become his true friends. Deceptiveness of appearances and ambiguity between good and evil are refrains running through Garfield's works, encouraging the young adult reader to evaluate people as individuals, not as members of groups.

Travel is important in most of the novels, journeys which symbolize their young heroes' quests for identity and truth. *Jack Holborn* is a shipboard adventure. Stowaway Jack must decide whom, of several ambiguous men, including the paradoxical captain who turns out to be twins identical in appearance but differing in character, to believe. In *The Sound of Coaches* young Sam Chichester confronts problems of growing up, establishing an adult relationship with his adoptive father, and coming to terms with his disappointment on meeting the biological father he had romanticized. The passage of time and Sam's developing independence are symbolized by the constantly turning wheels of the London Chichester coach Sam drives in his disabled adoptive father's stead.

Garfield's novels show humans surviving however they must, sometimes forced by circumstances into undesired actions but capable of great generosity and even heroism. *The Sound of Coaches* illustrates the interdependence of human beings and their ability to bring happiness to each other, while *Black Jack* shows the power of love to transform an individual. In the latter, the title character is a criminal who evades the hangman's noose, captures young Tolly Dorking, and forces the boy to help him escape. Tolly grows fond of his captor and patiently urges him toward a better life.

Echoes of classic authors can be seen in Garfield's writing, not surprising since he learned to write fiction by studying such giants as Henry Fielding, Jonathan Swift, and Daniel Defoe, but he never merely copies any other writer. *Jack Holborn* has obvious parallels with Robert Louis Stevenson's *Treasure Island,* and several Garfield works recall those of Charles Dickens. *Smith,* like *Oliver Twist,* chronicles the adventures of a young pickpocket, while the French-Revolution story *The Prisoners of September* suggests *A Tale of Two Cities.* Like Dickens, Garfield writes of the plight of London's poor and satirizes institutions such as doctors and law courts. Also like Dickens, he often treats events melodramatically and invents eccentric characters. In *Black Jack* the people Tolly meets include a twelve-year-old blackmailer, a troop of traveling hucksters of "magi-

cal" elixir, and a "professional widow" who makes a living claiming and selling the corpses of hanged criminals.

Garfield writes in a highly readable, lively, and literate style. His plots are complex, his descriptions extravagant and filled with colorful imagery. Readers not only see and hear scenes but touch and smell them, whether it's the stench and filth of underworld London in *Smith* or the quiet damp of a mist-hung thicket in *Devil-in-the-Fog.* Settings vary from the chaotic, noisy, unspeakably awful, insane asylum where young Belle lives in *Black Jack,* to the London-rooftop "castle" the urchin Shot-in-the-Head builds of old clothing and stolen trinkets in *Footsteps.* Garfield is a master of the well-chosen detail and the apt figure of speech. Barnacle, the spunky chimney sweep of *The December Rose,* is described thus: "A boy, white as a chicken bone, stood outside St. Marylebone Public Baths, trying to hold up his trousers, which hung on him, loose as cobwebs." People of all walks of life are differentiated by their speech, as when the stableman in *Footsteps* tells William to "go dahn that way...then 'long Bishopsgit...and 'long past Bedlam 'orspittle."

Garfield's novels fall somewhere between literature for children and that for adults, being understandable to young people but with a mature point of view. He does not simplify or sweeten the world for adolescents; situations are often macabre, and his young heroes sometimes journey through dark and threatening passages before emerging into the light of self-knowledge and understanding of the adult world. But he writes with warmth, emphasis on moral choice, and tolerance for human frailty. Reading his works can prepare young readers for the complexity of feelings and masterful use of language found in writers such as Jane Austen, Fyodor Dostoevsky, and William Shakespeare.

—Elbert R. Hill

———

GARNER, Alan. British. Born in Congleton, Cheshire, England, 17 October 1934. Educated at Magdalen College, Oxford. Served two years in the Royal Artillery; became second lieutenant. Married Ann Cook, 1956 (marriage dissolved); married Griselda Greaves, 1972; children: (first marriage) one son, two daughters; (second marriage) one son, one daughter. Writer. Recipient: Carnegie Medal commendation, 1965, for *Elidor;* Carnegie Medal, 1967, and *Guardian* Award for children's fiction, 1968, both for *The Owl Service;* Lewis Carroll Shelf Award, 1970, for *The Weirdstone of Brisingamen;* selected as a highly commended author by the Hans Christian Andersen Awards committee of the International Board on Books for Young People, 1978; first prize, Chicago International Film Festival, 1981, for *Images;* Mother Goose Award, 1987, for *A Bag of Moonshine.* Address: "Toad Hall," Blackden-cum Goostrey, Cheshire CW4 8BY, England.

PUBLICATIONS FOR YOUNG ADULTS

Fiction

The Weirdstone of Brisingamen: A Tale of Alderley. London, Collins, 1960; as *The Weirdstone: A Tale of Alderley,* New York, F. Watts, 1961; revised edition, London, Penguin, 1963; New York, Walck, 1969.

The Moon of Gomrath (sequel to *The Weirdstone of Brisingamen*). London, Collins, 1963; New York, Walck, 1967.

Elidor, illustrated by Charles Keeping. London, Collins, 1965; New York, Walck, 1967.

The Old Man of Mow, illustrated with photographs by Roger Hill. London, Collins, 1966; New York, Doubleday, 1970.

The Owl Service. London, Collins, 1967; New York, Walck, 1968.

Red Shift. London, Collins, and New York, Macmillan, 1973.

The Breadhorse, illustrated by Albin Trowski. London, Collins, 1975.

Alan Garner's Fairy Tales of Gold (*The Golden Brothers, The Girl of the Golden Gate, The Three Golden Heads of the Well, The Princess and the Golden Mane*), illustrated by Michael Foreman. London, Collins, four volumes, 1979; one-volume edition, Collins, and New York, Philomel, 1980.

"The Stone Book" quartet (illustrated with etchings by Michael Foreman):

The Stone Book. London, Collins, 1976; New York, Collins & World, 1978.

Tom Fobble's Day. London, Collins, 1977; New York, Collins & World, 1979.

Granny Reardun. London, Collins, 1977; New York, Collins & World, 1978.

The Aimer Gate. London, Collins, 1978; New York, Collins & World, 1979.

The Stone Book Quartet (*The Stone Book, Granny Reardun, The Aimer Gate, Tom Fobble's Day*). London, Collins, 1983; New York, Dell, 1988.

Plays

Holly from the Bongs: A Nativity Play, music by William Mayne; photographs by Roger Hill (produced in Goostrey, Cheshire, 1965). London, Collins, 1966; revised version, music by Gordon Crosse (produced in London, 1974), published in *Labrys 7* (Frome, Somerset), 1981.

The Belly Bag, music by Richard Morris (produced in London, 1971).

Potter Thompson, music by Gordon Crosse (produced in London, 1975). London, Oxford University Press, 1975.

To Kill a King (televised, 1980). Published in *Labrys 7*, 1981.

The Green Mist (dance drama). Published in *Labrys 7*, 1981.

Additional Plays: *Lurga Lom*, 1980; *Sally Water*, 1982.

Screenplays: *Places and Things*, 1978; *Images*, 1981.

Radio Plays: *Have You Met Our Tame Author?*, 1962; *Elidor*, 1962; *The Weirdstone of Brisingamen*, 1963; *Thor and the Giants*, 1965, revised, 1979; *Idun and the Apples of Life*, 1965, revised as *Loki and the Storm Giant*, 1979; *Baldur the Bright*, 1965, revised, 1979; *The Stone Book, Granny Reardun, Tom Fobble's Day*, and *The Aimer Gate*, 1980.

Television Plays: *The Owl Service*, 1969; (with John Mackenzie) *Red Shift*, 1978; *Lamaload*, 1979; *To Kill a King*, (*Leap in the Dark* series), 1980; *The Keeper*, 1982.

Other

Editor, *The Hamish Hamilton Book of Goblins: An Anthology of Folklore*, illustrated by Krystyna Turska. London, Hamish Hamilton, 1969; as *A Cavalcade of Goblins*, New York, Walck, 1969; as *A Book of Goblins*, London, Penguin, 1972.

Compiler, *The Guizer: A Book of Fools*. London, Hamish Hamilton, 1975; New York, Greenwillow, 1976.

The Lad of the Gad (folktales). London, Collins, 1980; New York, Philomel, 1981.

Alan Garner's Book of British Fairy Tales (retellings), illustrated by Derek Collard. London, Collins, and New York, Delacorte, 1984.

Jack and the Beanstalk, illustrated by Julek Heller (for children; retelling). London, Collins, 1985, New York, Delacorte, 1992.

A Bag of Moonshine (folktales), illustrated by Patrick James Lynch. London, Collins, and New York, Delacorte, 1986.

*

Manuscript Collection: Brigham Young University, Provo, Utah.

Biography: Essay in *Speaking for Ourselves: Autobiographical Sketches by Notable Authors of Books for Young Adults*, Volume 1, compiled and edited by Donald R. Gallo, National Council of Teachers of English, 1990.

Critical Studies: *A Fine Anger: A Critical Introduction to the Work of Alan Garner* by Neil Philip, London, Collins, and New York, Philomel, 1981; "Alan Garner Issue" of *Labrys 7*, 1981; *Children's Literature Review*, Volume 20, Detroit, Gale, 1990, pp. 90-119.

*   *   *

Alan Garner is an outstanding writer for young adults, intensely individual, often demanding, repeatedly innovative. Books that seem simple and even naive on the surface, like the "Stone Book" quartet, can challenge adult readers by the resonance with which they explore universal themes within a brilliantly realised sense of time, place, and identity. Three novels (*Elidor, The Owl Service, Red Shift*), progressively more complex to read and morally demanding, transmute elements of myth and folklore into metaphors for significant experiences and relationships. They are particularly aimed at young adults and vividly realise the difficulties and pain of adolescence. Garner has said that, while writing primarily for himself, he finds readers from the ages of ten to eighteen "the most important of all, and...the best audience. Few adults read with a comparable involvement."

After his first two children's books, fantasies somewhat in the Tolkien mode, Garner pushed C.S. Lewis's rather timid conjunction of the everyday and fabulous (which he found "insufferable") to dramatically new limits in *Elidor*. Whereas for Lewis the contemporary world simply provided a prologue to the real, moralising story in Narnia, Garner achieves the infinitely trickier task of realising fantasy in a Manchester of slum clearance, home life, and television. Because the magic in the novel is only seen through children's eyes, *Elidor* can be read as their fantasy game. However, the everyday objects with which the children return—stone, railing, cracked cup—which they see as ritual treasures like lance and grail, also seem to have an unsettling power that interferes with the television, washing-machine, and father's electric razor.

In *The Owl Service,* three adolescents holidaying in a Welsh valley become possessed by the spirits of characters in a local myth and reenact elements of the tragedy. Garner has said that the Mabinogion story of Lleu Llaw Gyffes and the wife who was made for him out of flowers, who betrayed him and was herself turned into an owl, was animated for him by the discovery of a dinner service with a flower pattern that could be reassembled into the face of an owl. However, this myth is kept in the background, and the narrative concentrates on the bewildering emotions that take over Alison, her stepbrother Roger, and Gwyn, the cook's son: sexual tensions, class and national resentments, and the painful awareness of adult frailty. The novel is marked from the very beginning by a high proportion of dialogue, so that the characters reveal themselves and their attitudes by speech styles. There is a recurrent concern with what it means to "speak properly." The reader has to fill in the gaps in the talk and must also reconstruct what has gone before. Garner has said that his characters can be identified with their mythic equivalents in two distinct ways, and critics have varied in their evaluation of the ending. Most readers have admired the way in which Roger resists the dark feelings within him, forgives, and admits his responsibility, thus transforming the owls back into flowers. However, some feel that they have been tempted by the author to identify with Gwyn, that the conclusion is manipulated, and that in view of his character Roger's behaviour is implausible. Such disagreements may testify to the openness and intensity of the novel.

Perhaps a deliberately more problematic text, *Red Shift* requires more than a single reading. Some adolescent readers become frustrated by hunting for clues in the text and feel that they are missing the hidden key that will unlock it for them. The novel abandons many of the conventional devices of young adult fiction (chapter divisions, descriptions of characters, explanation of events) in favour of a multi-layered cinematic technique emphasising dialogue, abrupt cutting between scenes, and allusive references to other works. The narrative, although placed in a single locality in and around Mow Cop, switches between three different periods: the Roman occupation of Britain, the Civil War, and the present day. In each of these periods a similar narrative develops: a love triangle in which the sensitive man in a couple is threatened both by his own self-doubt and the intrusion of a stronger figure who eventually helps save the other two. The character sets are virtually interchangeable. The ultimate impression is one of timelessness: everything that has happened exists simultaneously in some eternal present.

Although his reputation as an author for adolescents rests at present chiefly on only three books, Garner is acknowledged as a seminal figure, whose works are quite unlike those of any other writer. His idiosyncratic power, his ability as a storyteller, his outstanding sense of place, and his meticulous craftsmanship assure him a leading place in any current account of literature for young adults.

—Robert Protherough

———

GARNETT, Eve. British. Born in Worcestershire. Educated at The Convent, Bideford, Devon; West Bank School, Devon; Alice Ottely School, Worcester; Chelsea Polytechnic School of Art, London; Royal Academy Schools, London (studentship; Creswick Prize

and Silver Medal). Artist: murals for Children's House, Bow, London; exhibitions at the Tate Gallery, 1939, Le Fevre Gallery, and New English Art Club, all London. Recipient: Library Association Carnegie Medal, 1938, for *The Family from One End Street and Some of Their Adventures;* Creswick Prize and Silver Medal. *Died in 1991.*

PUBLICATIONS FOR YOUNG ADULTS (ILLUSTRATED BY THE AUTHOR)

Fiction

"Is It Well with the Child?", illustrated by the author. London, Muller, 1938.
The Family from One End Street and Some of Their Adventures. London, Muller, 1937; New York, Vanguard Press, 1939.
In and Out and Roundabout: Stories of a Little Town. London, Muller, 1948.
Further Adventures of the Family from One End Street. London, Heinemann, and New York, Vanguard Press, 1956.
Holiday at the Dew Drop Inn: A One End Street Story. London, Heinemann, 1962; New York, Vanguard Press, 1963.
Lost and Found: Four Stories. London, Muller, 1974.

Other

Editor, *A Book of Seasons: An Anthology.* London, Oxford University Press, 1952; Boston, Bentley, 1953.
Contributor, *Chosen for Children.* British Library Association, 1952.
Contributor, *A Golden Land.* Constable, 1958.
Contributor, *Naughty Children.* Gollancz, 1962.
To Greenland's Icy Mountains: The Story of Hans Egede, Explorer, Coloniser, Missionary. London, Heinemann, and New York, Roy, 1968.
First Affections: Some Autobiographical Chapters of Early Childhood. London, Muller, 1982.

*

Illustrator: *The London Child* by Evelyn Sharp, 1927; *The Bad Barons of Crashbania* by Norman Hunter, 1932; *A Child's Garden of Verses* by Robert Louis Stevenson, 1948; *A Golden Land* edited by James Reeves, 1958.

*   *   *

Eve Garnett is both an author and artist, and her writing and illustrations are equally important in her books, stories, and poems. Each book that Garnett has written for young adults is enhanced by her peaceful, beautiful pencil illustrations. Garnett's writing and art can be described as nostalgic glimpses into simple times of the past when life was less complicated.

Garnett's writing typically focuses on common human experiences that occur within the context of the family. Her books, *The Family from One End Street, Further Adventures of the Family from One End Street,* and *Holiday at the Dew Drop Inn,* tell of the triumphs and trials of the Ruggles family; a large, poor family in England. In these books, each chapter is a complete episode that can be read like a short story.

Though her characters are often faced with what could be called trivial problems today, Garnett's ability to develop characters that the reader can easily identify with permits these problems to be presented as familiar, real-life situations. By focusing on the emotions and thoughts of the characters facing the problems, Garnett is able to create a connection between reader and character. Humor often plays an important role in how the characters deal with these problems. When the Ruggles children get the measles in *The Family from One End Street,* and Olav must give Fisker to the trader in "The Rusty-Eyed Seal," a happy ending occurs. Suitable, clever solutions to problems and happy endings characterize Garnett's fiction.

In *Is It Well with the Child?* she deals with the uncharacteristically serious issues of cruelty, poverty, and indifference toward children. Most of Garnett's verses and illustrations in this book are cheerful on the surface; upon closer look, however, they depict the pain and helplessness that some children are forced to experience in their lives.

In her fiction, Garnett develops her characters by describing their actions, words, thoughts, and by supplementing these with illustrations. In *Holiday at the Dew Drop Inn,* Lily Rose comes alive for the reader as Garnett eloquently tells of the thoughts, concerns, and fears of this adolescent as she realizes that she has just helped two prisoners escape. In *The Family from One End Street,* Garnett thoroughly develops the character of Kate so that the reader can empathize with Kate's concern over not having the appropriate clothes for entering the prestigious secondary school to which she has won a scholarship.

Garnett's main characters tend to be strong, resilient women and girls like Mrs. Ruggles, Lily Rose, and Kate. In addition, the most developed of her characters are young adults and children, such as Lily Rose and Kate in the three books dealing with the Ruggles family. Because Garnett tends to focus on and develop female characters more than male characters, her fiction may be more appealing to female readers. She also fully develops the characters in her nonfiction book *To Greenland's Icy Mountains* and goes beyond the traditional confines of nonfiction, including the feelings and thoughts that Hans Egede may have experienced during the events described therein.

Aware that many readers may not be familiar with the places and time periods she writes of, Garnett provides the necessary background information within the context of her stories. Garnett's settings, usually in England, often play important roles in her stories. The beach becomes a major character as it steals Kate's hat and disrupts a family gathering at the park in *The Family from One End Street.* The short story "Silver Treasure," about good fortune and hidden treasure, is appropriately set in Ireland. In "The Kind Visitor," the blueberry patch plays an important role in the loss and eventual return of My-Thomas. The two short stories mentioned above were originally intended for younger readers; however, they have many elements that may appeal to young adult readers.

A great respect for nature is evident in her poetry, fiction, and nonfiction. In the anthology *A Book of Seasons,* Garnett celebrates the quiet beauty of nature as it changes from season to season. Her books and short stories involve many situations and problems that occur in connection with nature. *Holiday at the Dew Drop Inn* describes the experiences of Kate, a town girl, as she learns about nature while spending the summer in the country. In her nonfiction

book *To Greenland's Icy Mountains,* nature is an important character that challenges Hans Egede throughout his life.

The use of old-fashioned words and colloquial expressions helps to set the mood and illustrates pictures of the characters and settings for the reader, though some of the language may be confusing to the young adult reader. In addition, some of the language used by Garnett now carries negative connotations that may interfere with the reader's understanding and appreciation of certain passages. For example, the phrase "ten little nigger boys" in *Further Adventures of the Family from One End Street,* refers to ten black piglets. In addition, many of her characters speak in dialects that may be unfamiliar to some readers.

Garnett's books, stories, poetry, and illustrations are all endearing and enduring. Garnett's works have delighted and entertained several generations of young readers. Because of her focus on the commonality of human emotions and experiences within the family, Garnett's works continue to appeal to today's young adult readers.

—Laurie Elish-Piper

GARRISON, Frederick. See **SINCLAIR, Upton (Beall).**

GEORGE, Jean Craighead. American. Born in Washington, D.C., 2 July 1919. Educated at Pennsylvania State University, State College, B.A. 1941; Louisiana State University, Baton Rouge, 1941-42, and University of Michigan, Ann Arbor. Married John Lothar George in 1944 (divorced 1963); one daughter and two sons. Reporter, International News Service, 1942-44, and Washington *Post* 1943-44, both in Washington, D.C., and United Features (Newspaper Enterprise Association), 1945-46; artist. *Pageant Magazine,* New York, 1945; continuing education teacher in Chappaqua, New York, 1960-68; staff writer 1969-74, and roving editor, 1974-82, *Reader's Digest,* Pleasantville, New York; author and illustrator of books and articles on natural history. Recipient: Aurianne award, American Library Association, 1956, for *Dipper of Copper Creek;* Newbery Medal honor book award and ALA notable book citation, both American Library Association, 1960, International Hans Christian Andersen award honor list, 1962, Lewis Carroll Shelf citation, 1965, and George G. Stone Center for Children's Books award, 1969, all for *My Side of the Mountain;* Woman of the Year, Pennsylvania State University, 1968; Claremont College award, 1969; Eva L. Gordon Award, American Nature Study Society, 1970; *Book World* First Prize, 1971, for *All upon a Stone;* Newbery Medal, National Book award finalist citation, German Youth Literature Prize from West German section of International Board on Books for Young People, and Silver Skate from Netherlands Children's Book Board, all 1973, and listing by Children's Literature Association as one of ten best American children's books in two hundred years, 1976, all for *Julie of the Wolves;* School Library Media Specialties of South Eastern New York award, 1981; Irvin Kerlan award, University of Minnesota, 1982; University of Southern Mississippi award, 1986; Grumman award, 1986; Washington Irving award,

Westchester Library Association, 1991; Knickerbocker for Juvenile Literature, School Library Media Section, New York Public Library Association. Agent: Curtis Brown Ltd., 10 Astor Place, New York, NY 10003. Address: 20 William St., Chappaqua, NY 10514, U.S.A.

PUBLICATIONS FOR YOUNG ADULTS

Novels (illustrated by the author)

Vulpes, the Red Fox (as Jean George), with John L. George. New York, Dutton, 1948.
Vison, the Mink (as Jean George), with John L. George. New York, Dutton, 1949.
Masked Prowler: The Story of a Raccoon (as Jean George), with John L. George. New York, Dutton, 1950.
Meph, the Pet Skunk (as Jean George), with John L. George. New York, Dutton, 1952.
Bubo, the Great Horned Owl (as Jean George), with John L. George. New York, Dutton, 1954.
Dipper of Copper Creek (as Jean George), with John L. George. New York, Dutton, 1956.
The Hole in the Tree (as Jean George). New York, Dutton, 1957.
Snow Tracks (as Jean George). New York, Dutton, 1958.
My Side of the Mountain (as Jean George). New York, Dutton, 1959; London, Bodley Head, 1962.
The Summer of the Falcon. New York, Crowell, 1962; London, Dent, 1964.
Gull Number 737. New York, Crowell, 1964.
Hold Zero! New York, Crowell, 1966.
Water Sky. New York, Harper, 1987.
On the Far Side of the Mountain. New York, Dutton, 1990.

Fiction

Tree House (play, music by Saul Aarons). Chappaqua, New York, 1962.
Coyote in Manhattan, illustrated by John Kaufmann. New York, Crowell, 1968.
All upon a Stone, illustrated by Don Bolognese. New York, Crowell, 1971.
Who Really Killed Cock Robin? An Ecological Mystery. New York, Dutton, 1971.
Julie of the Wolves, illustrated by John Schoenherr. New York, Harper, 1972.
All upon a Sidewalk, illustrated by Don Bolognese. New York, Dutton, 1974.
Hook a Fish, Catch a Mountain. New York, Dutton, 1975.
Going to the Sun. New York, Harper, 1976.
The Wentletrap Trap, illustrated by Symeon Shimin. New York, Dutton, 1978.
The Wounded Wolf, illustrated by John Schoenherr. New York, Harper, 1978.
River Rats, Inc. New York, Dutton, 1979.
The Cry of the Crow. New York, Harper, 1980.
The Grizzly Bear with the Golden Ears, illustrated by Tom Catania. New York, Harper, 1982.
The Talking Earth. New York, Harper, 1983.
Shark beneath the Reef. New York, Harper, 1989.

Missing Gator of Gumbo Limbo: An Ecological Mystery. New York, HarperCollins, 1992.
Famous Animals (stories), pictures by Christine Merrill. New York, HarperCollins, 1994.

"Thirteen Moons" nonfiction series:

The Moon of the Salamanders, illustrated by John Kaufmann. New York, Crowell, 1967, new edition illustrated by Marlene Werner, New York, HarperCollins, 1992.
The Moon of the Bears, illustrated by Mac Shepard. New York, Crowell, 1967, new edition illustrated by Ron Parker, New York, HarperCollins, 1993.
The Moon of the Owls, illustrated by Jean Zallinger. New York, Crowell, 1967, new edition illustrated by Wendell Minor, New York, HarperCollins, 1993.
The Moon of the Mountain Lions, illustrated by Winifred Lubell. New York, Crowell, 1968, new edition illustrated by Ron Parker, New York, HarperCollins, 1991.
The Moon of the Chickarees, illustrated by John Schoenherr. New York, Crowell, 1968, new edition illustrated by Don Rodell, New York, HarperCollins, 1992.
The Moon of the Fox Pups, illustrated by Kiyoaki Komoda. New York, Crowell, 1968, new edition illustrated by Norman Adams, New York, HarperCollins, 1992.
The Moon of the Wild Pigs, illustrated by Peter Parnall. New York, Crowell, 1968, new edition illustrated by Paul Mirocha, New York, HarperCollins, 1992.
The Moon of the Monarch Butterflies, illustrated by Murray Tinkelman. New York, Crowell, 1968, new edition illustrated by Kam Mak, New York, HarperCollins, 1993.
The Moon of the Alligators, illustrated by Adrina Zanazanian. New York, Crowell, 1969, new edition illustrated by Michael Rothman, New York, HarperCollins, 1991.
The Moon of the Gray Wolves, illustrated by Lorence Bjorklund. New York, Crowell, 1969, new edition illustrated by Sal Catalano, New York, HarperCollins, 1991.
The Moon of the Deer, illustrated by Jean Zallinger. New York, Crowell, 1969, new edition illustrated by Sal Catalano, New York, HarperCollins, 1992.
The Moon of the Moles, illustrated by Robert Levering. New York, Crowell, 1969, new edition illustrated by Michael Rothman, New York, HarperCollins, 1992.
The Moon of the Winter Bird, illustrated by Kazue Mizumura. New York, Crowell, 1969, new edition illustrated by Vincent Nasta, New York, HarperCollins, 1992.

"One Day" nonfiction series:

One Day in the Desert, illustrated by Fred Brenner. New York, Crowell, 1983.
One Day in the Alpine Tundra, illustrated by Walter Gaffney-Kessell. New York, Crowell, 1984.
One Day in the Prairie, illustrated by Bob Marstall. New York, Crowell, 1986.
One Day in the Woods, illustrated by Gary Allen. New York, Crowell, 1988.
One Day in the Tropical Rain Forest, illustrated by Gary Allen. New York, HarperCollins, 1990.
Dear Rebecca, Winter is Here, pictures by Loretta Krupinski. New York, HarperCollins, 1993.

The Fire Bug Connection: An Ecological Mystery. New York, HarperCollins, 1993.

Nonfiction

Spring Comes to the Ocean, illustrated by John Wilson. New York, Crowell, 1966.
Beastly Inventions: A Surprising Investigation into How Smart Animals Really Are, illustrated by the author. New York, McKay, 1970; as *Animals Can Do Anything,* London, Souvenir Press, 1972.
The Wild, Wild Cookbook: A Guide for Young Wild-Food Foragers, illustrated by Walter Kessell. New York, Crowell, 1982.
The First Thanksgiving, illustrated by Thomas Locker. New York, Philomel Books, 1993.
The Everglades, paintings by Wendell Minor. New York, HarperCollins, 1994.

PUBLICATIONS FOR ADULTS

Other

Everglades Wildguide, illustrated by Betty Fraser. Washington D.C., National Park Service, 1972.
New York in Maps 1972-73, with Toy Lasker. New York, New York Magazine, 1974.
New York in Flashmaps 1974-75, with Toy Lasker. Chappaqua, New York, Flashmaps, 1976.
The American Walk Book: An Illustrated Guide to the Country's Major Historic and Natural Walking Trails from New England to the Pacific Coast. New York, Dutton, 1978.
Journey Inward (autobiography). New York, Dutton, 1982.
Exploring the Out-of-Doors. Chicago, American Library Association, 1983.
How to Talk to Your Animals, illustrated by the author. San Diego, Harcourt Brace, 1985; London, Hodder and Stoughton, 1986.
How to Talk to Your Dog (originally published in *How to Talk to Your Animals*), illustrated by the author. New York, Warner, 1986.
How to Talk to Your Cat (originally published in *How to Talk to Your Animals*), illustrated by the author. New York, Warner, 1986.
Editor, *The Big Book for the Planet,* with Ann Durell and Katherine Paterson. New York, Dutton Children's Books, 1993.

Contributor to books, including *Marvels and Mysteries of Our Animal World,* Reader's Digest Association, 1964. Contributor of articles on natural history and children's literature to periodicals, including *Audubon, Horn Book, International Wildlife,* and *National Wildlife.* Consultant for science books.

*

Media Adaptations: *My Side of the Mountain* (film), starring Teddy Eccles and Theodore Bikel, Paramount, 1969; *Julie of the Wolves* (recording), read by Irene Worth, Caedmon, 1977; *One Day in the Woods* (musical video), with music by Fritz Kramer and Chris Kubie, Kunhardt Productions, 1989.

Biography: Entry in *Dictionary of Literary Biography,* Volume 52: *American Writers for Children since 1960: Fiction.* Detroit, Gale, 1986, pp. 168-74; essay in *Speaking for Ourselves: Autobiographi-* *cal Sketches by Notable Authors of Books for Young Adults,* Volume 1, compiled and edited by Donald R. Gallo, National Council of Teachers of English, 1990.

Manuscript Collection: Kerlan Collection, University of Minnesota, Minneapolis.

Critical Studies: Entry in *Children's Literature Review,* Volume 1, Detroit, Gale, 1976, pp. 89-94; entry in *Contemporary Literary Criticism,* Volume 35, Detroit, Gale, 1985, pp. 175-80.

Illustrator: *Hawks, Owls, and Wildlife,* by John J. Craighead and Frank C. Craighead, Jr., 1969.

Jean Craighead George comments:
    One day I built a pond and a waterfall in my backyard. The next day as I stood there admiring it a story began. A frog appeared on its shore. A dragonfly flew over it. I was delighted and so I watched for new life every day. In a short time the pond was occupied by diving beetles, mosquito larva, and salamanders. I had not put them there. They had heard the call of water through their miraculous senses and had come to my pond to give it meaning. I began to write.
    These are the everyday things that get me writing. Each morning is rich with new material. I go for a walk, climb a mountain, or sit with my grandchildren and the books come from the world around me through my head to my fingers. The only thing that I do that nonwriters do not is feel the fire of the material and write it down with love. And it is love.

*   *   *

    Jean Craighead George's fiction comes from a lifelong love of the outdoors and of writing. Both of her parents were naturalist-entomologists, and growing up she was surrounded by animals and spent much time exploring nature. Through her young adult novels about the natural environment, she teaches and informs, and shows young people that they can learn from nature and live comfortably in the natural environment. She writes only what she has seen or experienced, resulting in vivid descriptions, such as when fifteen-year-olds Joe and Crowbar run the Grand Canyon's Lava Fall rapids on their backs after abandoning their raft in *River Rats, Inc.* Perhaps best known for *My Side of the Mountain* and *Julie of the Wolves,* George is at her best putting adolescents in nature where they rely on their own ingenuity and learn to listen to and respect nature in order to survive.
    Ingenious survival techniques are abundant in George's books. Sam Gribley, thirteen-year-old narrator of *My Side of the Mountain,* whittles a fish hook out of a green twig, makes a tent and bed out of hemlock boughs, makes snowshoes out of ash saplings and deer hide, and burns out the inside of a living tree to make a home. In his sequel, *On the Far Side of the Mountain,* he makes a waterwheel-driven sawmill, and his sister, Alice, builds a plumping mill to grind acorns into flour, an idea from a book she has read. This, like much information passed on by George characters, is remembered from books those characters have read, sending a clear message of the importance of reading to readers. Another survival skill, garnered from books as well as from characters's own ingenuity, is the ability to trap or collect natural foods on which to live. Sam shows that an astute and resourceful nature observer can eat a balanced diet straight from nature. He explains how to make salt, recognize hawthorn

berries, smoke fish, and how to cook cattails, which he explains directly to the reader. "If you ever eat cattails, be sure to cook them well, otherwise the fibers are tough and they take more chewing to get the starchy food from them than they are worth." In *River Rats, Inc.,* Walter, the wild boy, survives on live lizards and other natural foods, as well as human garbage that he finds.

George illustrates the connection between nature and people when her characters learn to understand and heed nature's messages. By close observation of a wolf pack, thirteen-year-old Miyax, in *Julie of the Wolves,* learns to communicate with the wolves and is accepted by the pack. They supply her with food, give her comfort in companionship, and protect her from a bear and a lone wolf. Listening to nature is carried even further in *Who Really Killed Cock Robin?,* an ecological mystery solved by fourteen-year-old Tony Isidoro and friends as they carefully observe wildlife behavior and plant colonization to determine the origins and spread of various environmental pollutants. George explains the path of toxic chemicals up the food chain and its effects on both animals and humans. In *The Talking Earth,* thirteen-year-old Billie Wind, a Seminole Indian girl, is sent into the Everglades alone because she doesn't believe that nature talks to people. Through her experiences she learns to listen to the natural world and realizes that "all living things are a family, and one can not live without the other." The Eskimos of *Water Sky* survive on the ice during whaling season by watching the clouds and the wind, and are better able to predict whale behavior than are scientists who have modern equipment.

Another message which George presents is that of the wildness of nature and preservation of that wildness. Thirteen-year-old Mandy Tressel learns a hard lesson about wildlife in *The Cry of the Crow* when she raises an orphaned crow chick but refuses to let it return to the wild, and must kill it to protect her brother. In *Coyote in Manhattan,* characters are split between those who would kill the coyote in Central Park and those who would let it live wild. The wild side prevails when the coyote is set free outside the city.

George shows her respect for nature when she describes the ecology of wildlife in accurate and interesting detail. She immerses readers in the lemming cycle of the far north, nuthatch behavior in the Catskills, the food chain in the Everglades, and stream ecology in the Rocky Mountains, drawing rich descriptions of the natural balance of nature. However, she also points out where humans upset that balance. In *Hook a Fish, Catch a Mountain,* she details how timber clear-cutting destroys cutthroat trout fisheries, heating stream water, and silting natural pools.

Although some experiences are implausible, such as parents allowing thirteen-year-old Sam Gribley to live alone in the mountains for a year, Jean Craighead George writes reverently about the natural environment, conveying to readers its beauty and complexity. She places readers in the environment of her characters, teaching about the interaction of people and nature in engrossing tales, without being didactic. Tony Isidoro sums up the interrelationship between humans and nature in *Who Really Killed Cock Robin?* when he says "A team of people killed Cock Robin and a team of people solved the crime. And that's how it's going to be from now until the day we live in balance with all beasts and plants, and air and water." The necessity of teamwork between humans and nature to protect the environment is consistent in all of Jean Craighead George's young adult novels.

—Susanne L. Johnston

GERAS, Adèle (Daphne). British. Born in Jerusalem, Israel, 15 March 1944. Educated at St. Hilda's College, Oxford, 1963-66, B.A. (honors) in modern languages 1966. Married Norman Geras in 1967; two daughters. French teacher, Fairfield High School, Droylsden, Lancashire, 1968-71; writer, since 1976. Recipient: Taylor award (older children), 1991, for *My Grandmother's Stories.* Agent: Laura Cecil, 17 Alwyne Villas, London N1 2HG. Address: 10 Danesmoor Road, Manchester M20 9JS, England.

PUBLICATIONS FOR YOUNG ADULTS

Fiction

The Girls in the Velvet Frame. London, Hamish Hamilton, 1978; New York, Atheneum, 1979.
The Green behind the Glass. London, Hamish Hamilton, 1982; as *Snapshots of Paradise: Love Stories,* New York, Atheneum, 1984.
Other Echoes. New York, Atheneum, 1982.
Voyage. London, Hamish Hamilton, and New York, Atheneum, 1983.
Letters of Fire and Other Unsettling Stories. London, Hamish Hamilton, 1984.
Happy Endings. London, Hamish Hamilton, 1986; San Diego, Harcourt, 1991.
Daydreams on Video. London, Hodder & Stoughton, 1989.
The Tower Room. London, Hamish Hamilton, 1990; San Diego, Harcourt, 1992.
Pictures of the Night. San Diego, Harcourt, 1992; London, Hamish Hamilton, 1992.
Watching the Roses. San Diego, Harcourt, 1992; London, Hamish Hamilton, 1991.
Yesterday. London, Walker Books, 1992.

PUBLICATIONS FOR CHILDREN

Fiction

Tea at Mrs. Manderby's, illustrated by Doreen Caldwell. London, Hamish Hamilton, 1976.
Apricots at Midnight and Other Stories from a Patchwork Quilt, illustrated by Doreen Caldwell. London, Hamish Hamilton, 1977; New York, Atheneum, 1982.
Beyond the Cross Stitch Mountains, illustrated by Mary Wilson. London, Hamish Hamilton, 1977.
The Painted Garden, illustrated by Doreen Caldwell. London, Hamish Hamilton, 1979.
The Rug That Grew, illustrated by Priscilla Lamont. London, Hamish Hamilton, 1981.
A Thousand Yards of Sea, illustrated by Joanna Troughton. London, Hodder & Stoughton, 1981.
The Christmas Cat, illustrated by Doreen Caldwell. London, Hamish Hamilton, 1983.
Little Elephant's Moon, illustrated by Linda Birch. London, Hamish Hamilton, 1986.
Ritchie's Rabbit, illustrated by Vanessa Julian-Ottie. London, Hamish Hamilton, 1986; New York, Random House, 1987.
Finding Annabel, illustrated by Alan Marks. London, Hamish Hamilton, 1987.

Fishpie for Flamingoes, illustrated by Linda Birch. London, Hamish Hamilton, 1987.

The Fantora Family Files, illustrated by Tony Ross. London, Hamish Hamilton, 1988.

The Strange Bird, illustrated by Linda Birch. London, Hamish Hamilton, 1988.

The Coronation Picnic, illustrated by Frances Wilson. London, Hamish Hamilton, 1989.

Bunk Bed Night. London, Dent, 1990.

My Grandmother's Stories: A Collection of Jewish Folk Tales, illustrated by Jael Jordan. New York, Knopf, 1990; London, Heinemann, 1990.

Nina's Magic. London, Hamish Hamilton, 1990.

Pink Medicine. London, Dent, 1990.

A Magic Birthday. London, Simon & Schuster, 1992.

The Fantora Family Photographs, illustrated by Tony Ross. London, Hamish Hamilton, 1993.

Golden Windows and Other Stories of Jerusalem. New York, HarperCollins, 1993; London, Heinemann, forthcoming.

PUBLICATIONS FOR ADULTS

Poetry

Up on the Roof, with Pauline Stainer. Huddersfield, Smith Doorstep, 1987.

*

Theatrical Activities:

Actress: **Play**—in *Four Degrees Over* by David Wood and John Gould, London, 1966.

Adèle Geras comments:

Although my work is published on the children's lists (or the list for young adults), I would hope that it could be enjoyed by everyone. I don't believe in writing for children as being an easy option—indeed I'd even say that the younger the child is and the shorter a text is, the more difficult it is to get it *exactly* right! All that white space around a word means it *has* to be the right word. Also it is worth remembering that short texts for young children are read *aloud* maybe thousands of times, and therefore need to have the power and resonance of the best poetry. Try reading a paragraph of an adult novel (the *same* paragraph!) over and over again, and see how it stands up.

I like writing for young adults because they have all the best qualities of both adults and small children. That is, they are grown-up enough to understand most things, and still young enough to believe in *STORIES,* in the magic of a wonderful tale, in justice, in other worlds, in ghosts, in the possibility of a better life for everyone...in everything that's around...

*   *   *

Although she writes successfully for all ages, Adèle Geras is particularly outstanding as a writer for young adults, one of her finest achievements being the trilogy of "Egerton Hall" novels about girls growing up in the 1960s. She makes good use of her own experiences; she was born in Jerusalem, travelled around the world as a child, and then had an English, upper middle-class girlhood,

during which she progressed from Roedean, a leading girls' boarding school, to Oxford. Her travels, Jewish heritage, and school and university days are all reflected in her work although they seldom feature in the same book. Her well-crafted short stories, in particular, show her interest in traditional tales. Other important influences are the sea and the past, both of which pervade much of her writing.

An early short story, "A Thousand Yards of Sea" told in the style of a traditional tale, which linked the origins of taffeta material to the sea, appeared in *Cricket,* the American children's magazine in 1976, and was later extended and published as a picture book. Her first young adult novel *The Girls in the Velvet Frame* (1979) is set in Jerusalem in 1913; it revolves around the plan of five sisters to have their photograph taken as a present for their widowed mother. No word has come from their brother, Isaac, who has emigrated to the United States, and they decide that a copy of the photograph sent to the brother of their own rabbi, who is in New York, may help to find him.

There is much evocative detail in the descriptions of their home, the way in which clothes are passed down, the dressing up for special occasions, and above all the food. The sisters emerge from the pages of the book as very different personalities. Rifka the eldest, capable and responsible, starts work and begins to fall in love with David. Claudia is a feminist in the making, and through her eyes, the reader observes the preferential treatment given to males in this society. Although only eight, the imaginative and adventurous Naomi intends to go to America herself when she is sixteen; meanwhile, she weaves stories for the two youngest girls Dvora and Shoshie, who take great delight in feeding and playing with the rabbits belonging to the boy next door. The domestic detail and the characters are given shape by the framework of the story; it begins and ends with a photograph. First, a neighbor shows them the photograph of her daughter, and then she in turn is shown their photograph and hears of the letter which has come from Isaac. The large cast of characters, youthful and adult, enables Geras to paint a very clear picture of the pre-First World War Jewish community in Jerusalem.

Voyage (1983), in which the hardships facing Jewish immigrants to the United States in the early years of the twentieth century are described, lacks the strong focus of the earlier book. Events are seen mainly through the eyes of three unrelated girls: Mina, Golda, and Rachel. They are at different stages of growing up, but in order to give a realistic and wide-ranging picture of the people who might have sailed on a boat such as the S.S. *Danzig,* looking for a new and better life away from the persecution and hostility of central Europe, Geras has introduced other important characters, and the viewpoint is continually shifting. Golda's baby provides a unifying link between the many passengers, Jewish and non-Jewish, but the book is also held together by the images of the sea, described in all its manifestations at the end of each chapter. The book ends with the boat's arrival in a New York harbour and a final comment on the sea. "Blue enough," said Mina, looking into the distance where the water was the colour of a dark sapphire, "Not exactly what I expected, but blue enough."

The "Egerton Hall" trilogy, set in 1962, consists of *The Tower Room* (1990), *Watching the Roses* (1991), and *Pictures of the Night* (1992), which tell the stories of three friends, Megan, Alice, and Bella, who meet at Egerton Hall School and whose lives parallel those of three fairy tale heroines—Rapunzel, the Sleeping Beauty, and Snow White. The events in the books overlap to some extent as each girl tells her own tale, looking backwards to the events and influences which have shaped her life and attitudes. The fairy tale parallels become more apparent as the trilogy proceeds, gradually moving through the momentous year when the girls fall in love and face their emerging sexuality, creating a powerful tour de force, outstanding in young adult literature.

Geras's short stories have appeared in a variety of anthologies and magazines. Her skills in this field can be sampled in two collections, *The Green behind the Glass* (1982) and *Daydreams on Video* (1989). The theme of the first is love, but the manner of the telling varies considerably. "Bounce the Moon," for example, has powerful sea images which provide a counterpoint to the story of Miranda and her mother; "The Whole Truth," set in North Borneo, the scene of one of Geras's childhood homes, is a supernatural tale; and "Alice" foreshadows the fairy tale influences of the "Egerton Hall" trilogy. The title story in *Daydreams on Video* is set against the background of a pop music concert; "Vamp till ready or Zuleika Who?" in the same collection uses the author's experience of student drama activities at Oxford; and "Plain Miss," a romantic story about an older woman, also has links to the "Egerton Hall" books.

Storytelling of this quality retains the reader's attention, and it is not surprising that when Walker Books decided to initiate their series of "Teenage Memoirs" and invite young adult authors to write about their own teenage experiences, Adèle Geras was one of the first authors to do so. In *Yesterday* (1992), she describes her three years at Oxford and incidentally reveals some of the sources and influences which she later used in her novels and short stories.

—Sheila Ray

———

GIBSON, William (Ford). American. Born in Conway, South Carolina, 17 March 1948. Educated at University of British Columbia, B.A. 1977. Married Deborah Jean Thompson in 1972; one daughter and one son. Writer. Recipient: Nebula award nomination, c. 1983, for short story "Burning Chrome"; Hugo award, Philadelphia Science Fiction Society Philip K. Dick Memorial award for best U.S. original paperback, Nebula award, and Porgie award for best paperback original novel in science fiction from *West Coast Review of Books,* all 1985, and Australian National Science Fiction Convention Ditmar award, all for *Neuromancer;* Nebula award nomination and Hugo award nomination, both for *Count Zero.* Agent: Martha Millard Literary Agency, 204 Park Avenue, Madison, NJ 07940.

PUBLICATIONS FOR YOUNG ADULTS

Novels

Neuromancer. New York, Ace, 1984.
Count Zero. New York, Arbor House, 1986.
Mona Lisa Overdrive. New York, Bantam, 1988.
The Difference Engine, with Bruce Sterling. London, Gollancz, 1990; New York, Bantam, 1991.
Virtual Light. New York, Bantam/Spectra, 1993.

Other

Contributor, *Shadows 4.* New York, Doubleday, 1981.

Contributor, *Universe 11.* New York, Doubleday, 1981.
Contributor, *Nebula Award Stories 17.* New York, Holt Rinehart, 1983.
Contributor, with John Shirley, Bruce Sterling, and Michael Swanwick, *Burning Chrome.* New York, Arbor House, 1986.
Contributor, *Mirrorshades: The Cyberpunk Anthology.* New York, Arbor House, 1986.
Dream Jumbo (text to accompany performance art by Robert Longo), produced Los Angeles, 1989.

*

Media Adaptations: *Johnny Mnemonic* (film), in production.

Critical Study: Entry in *Contemporary Literary Criticism,* Detroit, Gale, Volume 39, 1986; Volume 63, 1991.

*   *   *

The youthful, speeding, slangy world invented by William Gibson in *Neuromancer*, *Count Zero*, and *Mona Lisa Overdrive* has an irresistible appeal for the young-adult audience. In a Bladerunner-style future, these toughs survive in a world barely recognizable to adults, but predicated on the kinds of changes that television and computer technology have made familiar to teenagers. At the same time, elements of current culture are incorporated into these novels in such a way that they lurk beneath the surface, haunting the characters in much the same way that events like Vietnam and Watergate haunt the edges of many young adults' consciousness.

Gibson's plots reflect a vision in which the future world moves in real space at speeds mirroring computer speeds; in which the depersonalization of the computer world is completed by the longing of artificial intelligences to become persons; in which incidents, persons, and places become so dependent on one another for meaning that meaning becomes a gestalt. Travel is almost constant in these novels; the characters are as restless as computer cursors. Large portions of all three novels could be interpreted as chase scenes—complex, involving, metaphoric chases, but chases nonetheless. The characters whisk themselves from one impersonal environment to another, as Case does in *Neuromancer;* those who linger long enough to leave their mark on a space are in danger, as Bobby discovers in *Count Zero.* Their lack of personal place may account for their need to provide themselves with constant points of reference. The reader shares this search for place through a constant stream of allusions to his (the reader's) world. Some provide simple coloring, such as the use of Rastafarian culture; others are critical moorings in the dizzy plot free-fall, such as references to the work of Joseph Cornell and the use of voodoo theology in *Count Zero.* In these plots, events may happen sequentially, but the reader and the characters experience them as one simultaneous rush. Only afterward are we and the characters able to sort out which events occurred concurrently and which were the result of cause and effect.

The characters who inhabit this literature are shaped by the same forces that shape today's youth. These speeding travelers are young and street-smart. Bobby Newmark, the cyberdeck cowboy of *Count Zero*, is typical. Bobby struggles to be tough and hip, to use the appropriate slang that will signal his belonging on the inner track. Like most of Gibson's human characters, he is engaged in an active pursuit of goals that he will understand only too late. Molly, the "hired gun" of *Neuromancer* and *Mona Lisa Overdrive,* is a slightly older and wiser version of this character; having protected herself as best she can with skills and weapons, she seeks further safety in studied ignorance. Desiring nothing, she hopes to become invulnerable. Typically, these tough punks are revealed to have both a moral sense and human feelings—if the reader can recognize them under the devil-may-care surface. Older characters, like Armitage in *Neuromancer* or the Finn in *Count Zero* are incomprehensible fanatics, some dangerous, some benign. Others, like Turner or Marly in *Count Zero* are destroyed by their essential humanity, never having learned to protect themselves. The artificial intelligences struggle to inherit this future earth from humanity, meek or otherwise.

This struggle is also a struggle to redefine the meaning of activity and passivity. Computers, having gained independence of thought, now seek to throw off their responsive role and take a directing part in humanity's future. This struggle and tension not only shapes the plots and characters, but also informs Gibson's prose style. Human characters express themselves in computer slang (even Bobby's nickname, Count Zero, is borrowed from "antique" computer jargon), and their conversations and thoughts are littered with words like "black ice" and "flat-lines," and imported Japanese terms. Contemplation is an activity for the artificial intelligences. Short, abrupt sentences convey the constant defensive responses of the human characters and move the plots along in a blinding rush of speed that gives the reader little more time for comprehension than the bewildered protagonists. Yet, young adults will recognize and embrace this slangy, confusing style, for it mirrors the reality of their own lives.

Gibson is not an author for the reluctant reader or for those who need their plots and prose straight up, but for the adventurous reader willing to be challenged by a not always pleasant view of humanity's future, a soul mate is waiting.

—Cathy Chauvette

———

GIOVANNI, Nikki (Yolande Cornelia Giovanni). American. Born in Nashville, Tennessee, 7 June 1943. Educated at Fisk University, Nashville, Tennessee, 1960-61, 1964-67, B.A. (honors) in history, 1967; University of Pennsylvania Social Work School, Philadelphia; Columbia University School of the Arts, New York. One son. Poet, writer, lecturer. Assistant Professor of Black Studies, Queens College of the City University of New York, Flushing, 1968; Associate Professor of English, Rutgers University, Livingston College, New Brunswick, New Jersey, 1968-72; visiting Professor of English at Ohio State University, 1984; Professor of Creative Writing at Mount St. Joseph on the Ohio, 1985; Editorial Consultant, *Encore* magazine, Albuquerque, New Mexico; Founder of publishing firm, Niktom Ltd., 1970. Co-chair of Literary Arts Festival for State of Tennessee Homecoming, 1986. Author of columns "One Woman's Voice," for Anderson-Moberg Syndicate of the *New York Times,* and "The Root of the Matter," in *Encore American and Worldwide News.* Editorial consultant, *Encore American and Worldwide News.* Recipient: Ford Foundation grant, 1967; National Endowment for the Arts grant, 1968; Harlem Cultural Council grant, 1969; named one of ten most admired black women by the

Amsterdam News, 1969; *Mademoiselle* award for outstanding achievement, 1971; Omega Psi Phi Fraternity award for outstanding contribution to arts and letters, 1971; Meritorious Plaque for Service, Cook County Jail, 1971; Prince Matchabelli Sun Shower award, 1971; life membership and scroll, National Council of Negro Women, 1972; National Association of Radio and Television Announcers award for best spoken word album, for *Truth Is on Its Way,* 1972; Woman of the Year Youth Leadership award, *Ladies' Home Journal,* 1972; Doctorate of Humanities, Wilberforce University, 1972; National Book award nomination for *Gemini,* 1973; American Library Association commendation for *My House,* 1973; Doctorate of Literature from University of Maryland, Princess Anne Campus, 1974, Ripon University, 1974, Smith College, 1975, and Mount St. Joseph on the Ohio, 1983; Cincinnati Chapter YWCA Woman of the Year, 1983; elected to Ohio Women's Hall of Fame, 1985; named Outstanding Woman of Tennessee, 1985. Keys to numerous cities, including Lincoln Heights, Ohio, Dallas, Texas, and Gary, Indiana, all 1972; New York, New York, 1975; Buffalo, New York, and Cincinnati, Ohio, both 1979; Savannah, Georgia, and Clarksdale, Mississippi, both 1981; Miami, Florida, 1982; New Orleans, Louisiana, Monroe, Louisiana, Fort Lauderdale, Florida, and Los Angeles, California, all 1984.

PUBLICATIONS FOR YOUNG ADULTS

Poetry

Black Feeling, Black Talk. Detroit, Broadside Press, 1968.
Black Judgement. Detroit, Broadside Press, 1968.
Black Feeling, Black Talk/Black Judgement. New York, Morrow, 1970.
Poem of Angela Yvonne Davis. New York, Afro Arts, 1970.
Re:Creation. Detroit, Broadside Press, 1970.
My House, with foreword by Ida Lewis. New York, Morrow, 1972.
The Women and the Men. New York, Morrow, 1975.
Cotton Candy on a Rainy Day, with introduction by Paula Giddings. New York, Morrow, 1978.
Those Who Ride the Night Winds. New York, Morrow, 1983.
Sacred Cows . . . and Other Edibles. New York, Morrow, 1988.

Recordings: *Truth Is on Its Way,* Right-On Records, 1971; *Like A Ripple on a Pond,* Niktom, 1973; *The Way I Feel,* Atlantic Records, 1974; *Legacies: The Poetry of Nikki Giovanni,* Folkways Records, 1976; *The Reason I Like Chocolate,* Folkways Records, 1976; *Cotton Candy on a Rainy Day,* Folkways Records, 1978.

PUBLICATIONS FOR CHILDREN

Poetry

Spin a Soft Black Song: Poems for Children, illustrated by Charles Bible. New York, Hill & Wang, 1971; reprinted with illustrations by George Martin, Westport, Connecticut, Lawrence Hill, 1985; revised edition, New York, Farrar, Straus, 1987.
Ego-Tripping and Other Poems for Young People, illustrated by George Ford. Westport, Connecticut, Lawrence Hill, 1973.
Vacation Time: Poems for Children, illustrated by Marisabina Russo. New York, Morrow, 1980.

PUBLICATIONS FOR ADULTS

Nonfiction

Gemini: An Extended Autobiographical Statement on My First Twenty-five Years of Being a Black Poet. Indianapolis, Bobbs-Merrill, 1971.

A Dialogue: James Baldwin and Nikki Giovanni, with James Baldwin. Philadelphia, Lippincott, 1973; London, Joseph, 1975.

A Poetic Equation: Conversations Between Nikki Giovanni and Margaret Walker, with Margaret Walker. Washington, D.C., Howard University Press, 1974.

Other

Editor, *Night Comes Softly: An Anthology of Black Female Voices.* Newark, New Jersey, Medic Press, 1970.

Editor, *Appalachian Elders: A Warm Hearth Sampler.* Blacksburg, Virginia, Pocahontas Press, 1991.

*

Media Adaptations: *Spirit to Spirit: The Poetry of Nikki Giovanni* (television film, featuring the poet reading from her published works), Public Broadcasting Corporation, 1986.

Biography: Entry in *Authors in the News,* Volume 1, Detroit, Gale, 1976; *Dictionary of Literary Biography,* Detroit, Gale, Volume 5: *American Poets since World War II,* 1980; Volume 41: *Afro-American Poets since 1955,* 1985; *Black Women Writers, 1950-1980: A Critical Evaluation* edited by Mari Evans, Doubleday, 1984; *Modern Black Poets: A Collection of Critical Essays* edited by Donald B. Gibson, Prentice-Hall, 1973; *Understanding the New Black Poetry: Black Speech and Black Music as Poetic References* by Stephen Henderson, Morrow, 1973; *Dynamite Voices I: Black Poets of the 1960s* by Don L. Lee, Broadside Press, 1971; *Beautiful, Also, Are the Souls of My Black Sisters: A History of the Black Woman in America* by Jeanne Noble, Prentice-Hall, 1978; *Black Women Writers at Work* by Claudia Tate, Crossroad Publishing, 1983.

Manuscript Collection: Mugar Memorial Library, Boston University, Massachusetts.

Critical Studies: Entry in *Children's Literature Review,* Volume 6, Detroit, Gale, 1984; entry in *Contemporary Literary Criticism,* Detroit, Gale, Volume 2, 1974, Volume 4, 1975, Volume 9, 1981.

*   *   *

Nikki Giovanni is not just a poet for blacks or for women. She is a poet and essayist for persons of all races, gender, and age. And she is a songstress for children. Her songs are of the spirit. They concentrate on blackness, womanhood, and also on living. They beat the drums of Martin Luther King, Jr., drums of triumph and of pain, drums of peace. They celebrate the mother who doesn't care if she owns the whole world; her universe is her little son. They tell what it's like to eat fresh corn and okra and greens in the South in the summertime.

All of Giovanni's works may be enjoyed by the young adult. Those found in the children's section of the library are among her more joyous and lyrical. Young adults will respond to her refer-ences of growing up, to her dreams of running faster than any gazelle, outswimming any fish, and beating a falcon up to the top of the mountain.

Spin a Soft Black Song includes a variety of poems—poems about love and friendship, hopes and dreams. In "Poem for Rodney," Rodney is always being asked what he is going to be when he grows up; he just thinks he'd like to grow up. In "Poem for Debbie," we meet a young girl who is tall and bold, with sneakers to make her run faster. In "If" a young man thinks about being Matthew Henson and exploring the North Pole or the man in Harriet Tubman's life who gives her support on her journeys south. The illustrations of children in this book are all of black children, and some of the words are descriptive of the children's blackness. But most of the emotions, happy and sad, apply to all young people.

Ego-Tripping and Other Poems for Young incorporate black history, past and current, more than the former book. "Poem for Black Boys" asks where are the heroes for black boys and suggests that they play run-away-slave or Mau Mau rather than cowboys and Indians. "Revolutionary Dreams" speaks of militant dreams of blacks taking over America, stopping the riots and negotiating the peace. "Revolutionary Music" digs Sly and the Family Stone and James Brown. Other poems are not about race. "Alone" is about loneliness and about communicating with others—universal concerns. Again, the illustrations are of black people, with the addition of one white cop.

Giovanni gained widespread popularity with two early works, *Black Feeling, Black Talk* and *Black Judgement,* because of their strident and often angry verse. She made her poems accessible to young people through public readings at colleges and through best-selling recordings accompanied by gospel music. In much of these works, Giovanni focuses on the individual's search for love and acceptance, reflecting what she considers a major struggle in the black community. "Nikki-Rosa," from *Black Judgement,* is often cited as her signature poem. It recounts her happy childhood, asserting that happiness depends on love rather than material possessions, that black love is black wealth.

The personal perspective of "Nikki-Rosa" is continued in her next work, *Re:Creation,* and in the essay collection, *Gemini: An Extended Autobiographical Statement on My First Twenty-five Years of Being a Black Poet.* These works, influenced by the birth of her son in 1969 and by her increasing affection for rhythm and blues, are less angry than her previous volumes. In them Giovanni views the black revolution more from a personal than a collective perspective and speaks to the need for change in order to address the possibilities of life. These works will have particular meaning to black youth, but they will also have meaning to all youth who are impatient for social change and who intend to devote energies to achieve it.

Those Who Ride the Night Winds is a collection of poems about people who have tried to affect change, who went against the status quo, who were willing to test their wings. Included are poems about Lorraine Hansberry, John Lennon, Billie Jean King, Charles White, Robert Kennedy, Rosa Parks. Lorraine Hansberry made it possible for all of us to look a little deeper. Robert Kennedy reminds us that trees should never be felled in the summer, before the promise is fulfilled.

Giovanni's poems are found in a number of popular anthologies, such as *Sing a Song of Popcorn: Every Child's Book of Poems* (selected by Beatrice Schenk de Regniers, et al., Scholastic Inc., New York, 1988) and *The Poetry of Black America: Anthology of the 20th Century* (edited by Arnold Adoff, Harper and Row, New

York, 1973). These poems deserve to be read; they will be enjoyed in whichever book cover they are found.

—Mary Lystad

*

GIPSON, Fred(erick Benjamin). American. Born in Mason, Texas, 7 February 1908. Educated at Mason High School, graduated 1926; University of Texas, Austin, 1933-37. Married Tommie Eloise Wynn in 1940 (divorced 1964); two sons. Farm and ranch hand, and clerk, 1926-33; reporter and columnist, Corpus Christi *Caller-Times,* San Angelo *Standard-Times,* and Paris *News,* all in Texas, 1938-40; associate editor, *True West* magazine, Austin, 1953-59; editorial director, *Frontier Times,* Bandera, Texas, 1958-59. President, Texas Institute of Letters, 1960. Recipient: McMurray Bookshop award, Dallas, Texas, 1949, for *Hound-Dog Man,* and 1950, for *Recollection Creek;* Cokesbury Book Store award, Dallas, Texas, for children's book by Texas writer on Texas subject, 1956, for *The Trail-Driving Rooster;* Newbery Medal runner-up, 1957, Maggie award for Western book, 1958, and William Allen White Children's Book award, 1959, all for *Old Yeller;* First Sequoyah award, Oklahoma, 1959; Northwest Pacific award, 1959; lifetime fellowship to Texas Institute of Letters, 1970. *Died 14 August 1973.*

PUBLICATIONS FOR YOUNG ADULTS

Fiction

Hound-Dog Man. New York, Harper, 1949.
The Home Place. New York, Harper, 1950; London, Joseph, 1951; abridged edition, as *Return of the Texan,* Edinburgh, Oliver and Boyd, 1962.
Recollection Creek. New York, Harper, 1955; revised edition, for children, 1959.
Old Yeller, illustrated by Carl Burger. New York, Harper, 1956; London, Hodder and Stoughton, 1957.
Savage Sam, illustrated by Carl Burger. New York, Harper, and London, Hodder and Stoughton, 1962.

Screenplays: *Old Yeller,* with William Tunberg, 1957; *Hound-Dog Man,* with Winston Miller, 1959; *Savage Sam,* with William Tunberg, 1962.

Television Play: *Brush Roper.*

Other

Fabulous Empire: Colonel Zack Miller's Story. Boston, Houghton Mifflin, 1946; as *Circles Round the Wagon,* London, Joseph, 1949.
Big Bend, with J. Oscar Langford. Austin, University of Texas Press, 1952.
Cowhand: The Story of a Working Cowboy. New York, Harper, 1953; London, Corgi, 1957.
The Cow Killers: With the Aftosa Commission in Mexico. Austin, University of Texas Press, 1956.

An Acceptance Speech. New York, Harper, 1960.
Fred Gipson before Old Yeller, edited by C. Richard King. Austin, Texas, Eakin Press, 1980.

PUBLICATIONS FOR CHILDREN

Fiction

The Trail-Driving Rooster. New York, Harper, 1955.
Little Arliss, illustrated by Ronald Himler. New York, Harper, 1978.
Curly and the Wild Boar, illustrated by Ronald Himler. New York, Harper, 1979.

*

Critical Studies: *Fred Gipson* by Sam H. Henderson, Austin, Texas, Steck Vaughn, 1967; *Fred Gipson, Texas Storyteller* by Mike Cox, Austin, Texas, Shoal Creek, 1980.

*   *   *

In an author's note to his biography *Cowhand,* Fred Gipson wrote, "I am, by profession and by nature, a collector and writer of tales, and for me, a good tale, well told, is enough." This is an outlook that throughout his writing makes itself as unmistakable and clear as any of the rosy, storm-signalling sunsets or ringing hound-dog calls he describes in his books about boyhood adventures in the wilds of late nineteenth and early twentieth century Texas. For Gipson, the achievement of literary significance was not the thing. It was the good tale he was after. Using plain-talking, shoot-howdy language that gets simply to the beauty, humor, longing, or pain of a matter, Gipson wrote about what he knew: hard work, hard play, the way old folks tell stories, and boys, dogs, and other creatures in their natural habitats. Through the telling of the specifics of these things—the chase and kill of a coon hunt, a faithful dog in a fight, losing oneself in a starry sky, bucking against a mother's wishes, bringing home meat for the family—Gipson gets at basic desires that have meaning for young readers, things like independence, adventure, companionship, connection with nature, receiving recognition for one's accomplishments.

Also elemental in Gipson's work is the boyhood passage from innocence to experience, described by the philosophical music maker Fiddling Tom in *Hound-Dog Man:* "There's a time when a boy can lay his belly on the ground and feel the heartbeats of the earth coming up to him through the grass roots. That's his time to prowl. That's his time to smell the par-fume of the wild flowers, to hear the wind singing wild in his ears, to hurt with the want of knowing what's on the yonder side of the next ridge."

Old Yeller, Gipson's best known and well loved book, a Newbery Honor book which has won a majority of awards for which young people do the voting, best exemplifies Gipson's boy into man theme. Because Old Yeller the dog meets an untimely death, the sentimentality that can come with adulthood crystallizes that climactic event in the mind so that many remember *Old Yeller* as a tearjerker of a dog story. But if it were only that, young people would not find the meaning and relevance in it that they do. The reasons they cite for liking this bare bones coming-of-age story have to do with interest in the hard details of daily survival on the 1860s Texas frontier, like carrying water in a cowhide pail, marking dangerous wild hogs, or sewing up a wound with horse hair, and the exciting adventures and newly tried independence of the main character, Travis. *Old Yeller* is not essentially about a dog that dies. It is about the young man he leaves behind. While Papa, along with most of the men in Salt Licks, is away driving a pooled herd of area cattle to Kansas markets, fourteen-year-old Travis gets a task enviable and romantic to most young readers: he is made man in charge until his father returns. Travis's companion through this trial is Old Yeller. The meat-stealing stray bravely proves his worth through fierce, life-threatening encounters and becomes a part of the family. As Travis's narrative unfolds, the early tone of little boy bravado and self-satisfied pride matures. Being man of the place entails more than the hard physical work of providing for and protecting the family. Travis learns about patience, discipline, restraint, and the unconditional caring required by family relationships.

Family and neighbor relationships are further tested in the sequel, *Savage Sam,* in which Travis, his feisty, comic-relief-providing younger brother Little Arliss, and a neighbor girl are captured by Apaches and carried away on a harrowing journey across the Texas plains. Other Gipson books with young adult themes are *Hound-Dog Man,* another coming-of-age/boy-dog companionship story about young Cotton who learns a number of life lessons when he and his friend Spud embark on a once-in-a-lifetime hunting trip with the good-hearted scoundrel Blackie Scantling; *Recollection Creek,* a humorous collection of episodes from an uproarious year in the life of the extended Creech family, as told by young Hopper Creech; and *Cowhand: The Story of a Working Cowboy,* a biography based on the life of west Texas cowboy Ed "Fat" Alford. *Little Arliss, Curly and the Wild Boar,* and *The Trail-Driving Rooster* are shorter, one-adventure tales for younger readers.

A Texan Mark Twain to some degree, Gipson, in writing so honestly and distinctly about an earlier time and a specific region, inevitably presents their inherent biases. His books are about a man's world, and unfortunately, his women characters, while clearly just as hard working, intelligent, and strong willed as his men, remain in the background, are often referred to as so-and-so's woman rather than by name, and are notable chiefly for their cooking abilities, for being pretty enough to frame for the mantel, or for their usefulness as a point of comparison for things weak, impractical, or confining. Ethnic slurs are also a part of his characters' vernacular. The collision of white and Native American cultures brought about by white man's westward expansion is an important underlying theme in *Savage Sam,* and the "Injun killing" in the book is a highly uncomfortable matter. This is offset only slightly by Travis's late realization that all creatures' lives are important and "...each of us would fight to keep them just as long as we could—and try to help those we loved to do the same." Through his well-told tales—tall ones and small ones—Gipson reminds us of society's slow, painful coming-of-age. Through the kinds of people we know—friends, enemies, family, and neighbors—he shows us, for better and for worse, what we have been. It is enough.

—Tracy J. Sukraw

———

GLENN, Mel. American. Born in Zurich, Switzerland, 10 May 1943. Educated at New York University, A.B. 1964; Yeshiva University, M.S. 1967. Married Elyse Friedman, 1970; two sons. Volunteer, 1964-66, Peace Corps, Sierra Leone, West Africa; teacher,

1967-70, Junior High School 240, Brooklyn, New York; English teacher, since 1970, Abraham Lincoln High School, Brooklyn; author, since 1980. Recipient: *Class Dismissed!: High School Poems,* selected one of the Best Books for Young Adults, 1982, American Library Association, and a Golden Kite Honor Book, 1982, Society of Children's Book Writers; Christopher Award, 1987, for *Class Dismissed II.* Address: 4288 Bedford Ave., Brooklyn, NY 11229, U.S.A.

PUBLICATIONS FOR YOUNG ADULTS

Fiction

One Order to Go. New York, Clarion, 1984.

Poetry

Class Dismissed!: High School Poems, illustrated with photographs by Michael J. Bernstein. New York, Clarion, 1982.
Class Dismissed II: More High School Poems, illustrated with photographs by Michael J. Bernstein. New York, Clarion, 1986.
Back to Class, illustrated with photographs by Michael J. Bernstein. New York, Clarion, 1988.
My Friend's Got This Problem, Mr. Candler, illustrated with photographs by Michael J. Bernstein. New York, Clarion, 1991.

PUBLICATIONS FOR CHILDREN

Fiction

Play-by-Play. Clarion, 1986.
Squeeze Play: A Baseball Story. Clarion, 1989.

Mel Glenn comments:

I write to remember. I write to open up the lines of communication, to explain my past to myself and others. On a certain level we are all emotionally fourteen. Good writing can put us in touch with who we were and who we are.

I write because I want to remember how it felt not making the basketball team, worrying about my future, agonizing over final exams. If because of what I have written some reader says "Oh, I've felt *exactly* like that" then I've succeeded in showing that we have all been touched by the same emotional brush.

*   *   *

Mel Glenn's poetry collections highlight the trials and tribulations, the angst and anxiety, and the joys and wonders of adolescence. His poems echo the voices of young adults who are struggling in two separate worlds: the world of adults and the world of children. They do not possess full membership in either; hence, the frustration which is adolescence. Glenn's poems seem to capture the essence of the adolescent: the emotions which sometimes seem to run out of control, the changing relationships with parents and other adults as the adolescent struggles for independence, the myriad of decisions which need to be made.

Glenn refers to *Class Dismissed!* as his literary firstborn. Subtitled *High School Poems,* this first collection was to establish the format for the books to follow. The poems, each titled with the name of a fictitious student, are accompanied by photographs (by Michael J. Bernstein) of actual students. The poems are short, one page. While the language is spare, the poems reveal much. Each takes on the persona of an individual student. "Benjamin Haywood," for example, exhibits an outward cool which belies the uncertainties he hides within. "Hildy Ross" lies to her teacher about the bruise on her cheek; she cannot confide in him about her father's abuse. These poems are vignettes, allowing readers a glimpse into the very center of an individual before snapping shut.

Class Dismissed II: More High School Poems deals with topics such as getting the keys to the car, picking out the correct college, and finding a job. The voices of each of the students resonate with candor. It is as if Glenn were eavesdropping inside the heads of adolescents; here are their thoughts and feelings without any of the artifice. Simile and metaphor are present. In "Robert Ashford," parents pore over college catalogs as if they were picking out a summer camp while Robert wonders if he will ever have some say on the subject of college. "Vinnie Robustelli" describes his new sports car in terms so seductive the reader is led to believe that he is describing his steady girlfriend. "Amanda Butler" laments that her mother's notes on the refrigerator are their only means of conversation; they leave her cold. "Paul Hewitt" asks his English teacher if he has any books that deal with real life because he never plans on going hunting for white whales or living in the Dust Bowl. This sly use of humor is also a hallmark of Glenn's work.

Perhaps Glenn's ironic sense of the absurd is best evidenced in *Back to Class*. What sets this book aside is the inclusion of poems about teachers who reveal a great deal about their personal and professional lives. Mr. Winograd who teaches first period English wonders why people are able to identify him as an English teacher so easily when he is *outside* of the school. Does he have a verb for a vein, a noun for a nose, a fragment for a forehead he wonders? Wouldn't it be "a novel experience" if someone mistook him for a baseball player instead? Mr. Pressman who teaches fine arts marvels at his best creation to date, his six-year-old son, who is just now trying his own hand at drawing. Accounting teacher Ted Sage wonders about his net worth after all the years he has spent working in a system which is educationally bankrupt. The inclusion of the teachers and their points of view strengthens the collection as they provide an opportunity for adolescents to draw parallels between themselves and adults.

My Friend's Got This Problem, Mr. Candler is the fourth collection of high school poems. Mr. Candler, a fictitious high school counselor, takes readers through a typical week in his office. Readers watch as students and parents share their joy and anguish with Mr. Candler. One of the overriding themes of this collection is that there are two sides to every story. Glenn reinforces this theme in several ways. First, he provides poems about one situation from two or more perspectives. Maureen and Hugh McDermott each took Mr. Pettis's history exam. Maureen shares her exhilaration at her 92 percent on the test; she respects Pettis even though he made her work so hard. On the other hand, her brother Hugh (his score was 29 percent) hates history and dislikes Pettis as well. Here is one of the hard truths about school and teaching. Perhaps even more moving are the accounts given by parents and their children when they call or visit Mr. Candler. Matthew Egan sees Mr. Candler because he is having difficulty dealing with the pressure his father applies for him to get better grades. Mr. Egan sees things a bit differently. He grew up in a household where he was beaten for not doing better in school. From his point of view, he only wants what is best for his son, just the way his father wanted what was best.

Another parent who refuses to give his name tells Candler that his daughter is lying when she talks about her abuse. He is just using discipline; Candler had better not interfere if he's smart.

Glenn's poems reach out to adolescents, even those who are not ordinarily readers of poetry. One of his greatest contributions to the field of young adult literature is that he has made poetry accessible to more readers, especially male readers. The honesty of the poems and the emotions Glenn conveys make for crisp reading. The simple language allows readers to clearly identify the themes of the works. Glenn does not avoid unpleasant topics; he addresses them head-on. The refreshing candor and range of personae are part of the reason for his continued popularity with adolescents and those who work with adolescents. Glenn's fictional students and teachers should help readers as they deal with their own personal dilemmas of adolescence. Each of his four collections has been named as a Best Book for Young Adults by the American Library Association.

—Teri S. Lesesne

GOLDING, William (Gerald). British. Born in St. Columb, Cornwall, 19 September 1911. Educated at Marlborough Grammar School; Brasenose College, Oxford, B.A. 1935, M.A. 1960. Served in the Royal Navy, 1940-45; became rocket ship commander. Married Ann Brookfield in 1939; one son and one daughter. Writer. Was a settlement house worker after graduating from Oxford University; writer, actor, and producer in small theatre companies, 1934-40, 1945-54; taught English and philosophy, 1939-40, schoolmaster, 1945-61, both at Bishop Wordsworth's School, Salisbury, Wiltshire; Visiting Professor and writer in residence, Hollins College, Virginia, 1961-62. Recipient: Commander, Order of the British Empire, 1965; James Tait Black Memorial Prize, 1980, for *Darkness Visible;* Booker McConnell Prize, 1981, for *Rites of Passage;* Nobel Prize for Literature, 1983, for body of work; D.Litt., University of Sussex, Brighton, 1970; University of Kent, Canterbury, 1974; University of Warwick, Coventry, 1981; Oxford University, 1983, the Sorbonne, Paris, 1983; LL.D.: University of Bristol, 1984. Honorary Fellow, Brasenose College, 1966. Fellow, 1955, and Companion of Literature, 1984, Royal Society of Literature. C.B.E. (Commander, Order of the British Empire), 1966. Knighted, 1988. *Died 19 June 1993.*

PUBLICATIONS

Fiction

Lord of the Flies. London, Faber, 1954; New York, Coward McCann, 1955.
The Inheritors. London, Faber, 1955; New York, Harcourt, 1962.
Pincher Martin. London, Faber, 1955; as *The Two Deaths of Christopher Martin,* New York, Harcourt, 1957.
Free Fall. London, Faber, 1959; New York, Harcourt, 1960.
The Spire. London, Faber, and New York, Harcourt, 1964.
The Pyramid. London, Faber, and New York, Harcourt, 1967.
Darkness Visible. London, Faber, and New York, Farrar, Straus, 1979.

Rites of Passage. London, Faber, and New York, Farrar, Straus, 1980.

The Paper Men. London, Faber, and New York, Farrar, Straus, 1984.

Close Quarters. London, Faber, and New York, Farrar, Straus, 1987.

Fire Down Below. London, Faber, and New York, Farrar, Straus, 1989.

Short Stories

The Scorpion God. London, Faber, 1971; New York, Harcourt, 1972.

Plays

The Brass Butterfly, adaptation of his story "Envoy Extraordinary" (produced London, 1958; New York, 1970). London, Faber, 1958; Chicago, Dramatic Publishing Company, n.d.

Radio Plays: *Miss Pulkinhorn,* 1960; *Break My Heart,* 1962.

Poetry

Poems. London, Macmillan, 1934; New York, Macmillan, 1935.

Other

Contributor, *Sometimes, Never.* New York, Ballantine, 1956.

The Hot Gates, and Other Occasional Pieces. London, Faber, and New York, Harcourt, 1965.

Talk: Conversations with William Golding, with Jack I. Biles. New York, Harcourt, 1970.

A Moving Target (essays). London, Faber, and New York, Farrar, Straus, 1982.

Nobel Lecture. Leamington Spa, Warwickshire, Sixth Chamber, 1984.

An Egyptian Journal. London, Faber, 1985.

*

Media Adaptations: *Pincher Martin* (radio play), British Broadcasting Corp., 1958; *Lord of the Flies* (film), Continental, 1963, and Castle Rock Entertainment, 1990.

Biography: Entry in *Dictionary of Literary Biography,* Volume 15: *British Novelists, 1930-1959,* Detroit, Gale, 1983; entry in *Dictionary of Literary Biography Yearbook: 1983,* Detroit, Gale, 1984.

Bibliography: *William Golding: A Bibliography* by R.A. Gekoski and David Hughes, London, Deutsch, 1990.

Critical Studies: *A Review of English Literature* by Peter Green, London, Longman, 1960; *The Modern Novel* by Walter Allen, New York, Dutton, 1964; *William Golding* by Samuel Hynes, New York, Columbia University Press, 1964; *The Art of William Golding* by Bernard S. Oldsey and Stanley Weintraub, New York, Harcourt, 1965; *William Golding: A Critical Study* by James R. Baker, New York, St. Martin's, 1965, and *Critical Essays on William Golding* edited by James R. Baker, Boston, Hall, 1988; *The Modern Confessional Novel* by Peter M. Axthelm, New Haven, Connecticut, Yale University Press, 1967; *William Golding* by Bernard F. Dick, New York, Twayne, 1967; *William Golding: A Critical Study* by Mark

Kinkead-Weekes and Ian Gregor, London, Faber, 1967, New York, Harcourt, 1968, revised edition, Faber, 1984; *The Tragic Past* by David Anderson, Louisville, Kentucky, John Knox Press, 1969; *William Golding* by Leighton Hodson, Edinburgh, Oliver and Boyd, 1969, New York, Putnam, 1971; *The Novels of William Golding* by Howard S. Babb, Columbus, Ohio State University Press, 1970; *Harvest of a Quiet Eve: The Novel of Compassion* by James Gindin, Bloomington, Indiana University Press, 1971; entry in *Contemporary Literary Criticism,* Detroit, Gale, Volume 1, 1973, Volume 2, 1974, Volume 3, 1975, Volume 8, 1978, Volume 10, 1979, Volume 18, 1981, Volume 27, 1984; *William Golding: The Dark Fields of Discovery* by Virginia Tiger, London, Calder & Boyars, and Atlantic Highlands, New Jersey, Humanities Press, 1974; *Number and Nightmare: Forms of Fantasy in Contemporary Fiction* by Jean E. Kennard, Hamden, Connecticut, Archon Books, 1975; *William Golding* by Stephen Medcalf, London, Longman, 1975; *William Golding: Some Critical Considerations* edited by Jack I. Biles and Robert O. Evans, Lexington, University Press of Kentucky, 1979; *Of Earth and Darkness: The Novels of William Golding* by Arnold Johnston, Columbia, University of Missouri Press, 1980; *A View from the Spire: William Golding's Later Novels* by Don Crompton, Oxford, Blackwell, 1985; *William Golding Novels: A Casebook 1954-1967* edited by Norman Page, London, Macmillan, 1985; *William Golding: The Man and His Books: A Tribute on His 75th Birthday* edited by John Carey, London, Faber, 1986, New York, Farrar, Straus, 1987; *William Golding: A Structural Reading of His Fiction* by Philip Redpath, London, Vision Press, 1986; *William Golding: A Study* by V.V. Subbarao, London, Oriental University Press, 1987; *The Novels of William Golding* by Stephen Body, Brighton, Sussex, Harvester Press, and New York, St. Martin's Press, 1988; *William Golding* by James Gindin, London, Macmillan, and New York, St. Martin's Press, 1988; *William Golding Revisited: A Collection of Original Essays* edited by B.L. Chakoo, New Delhi, Arnold, 1989; *The Modern Allegories of William Golding* by L.L. Dickson, Tampa, University of South Florida Press, 1990.

*   *   *

Because William Golding's *Lord of the Flies* and *The Inheritors* frequently appear in American high school English curricula, along with Knowles's *A Separate Peace* or Salinger's *Catcher in the Rye,* Golding is sometimes considered a young adult novelist or a science fiction writer. Neither of these genres really fits the majority of Golding's novels, however, which have more in common with the ethical romances of Hawthorne or Melville than Judy Blume's books. Even Goldings two early works suggest a greater complexity since in each the mythic archetypal qualities represent symbolic patterns outside their texts—typical of Golding—rather than within, as is frequently the case with adolescent novels. Also, unlike most young adult novels or science fiction, Golding's characters and narrative situations concretely portray spiritual and moral assumptions in conflict: Golding is a Christian novelist with an awareness of the spiritual and ethical dimension of cultural forces.

Lord of the Flies was Golding's first published novel after four previous attempts. Set in the near future during wartime, the adolescent boys on Golding's island revert to atavistic tribal and later savage impulses in the manner of Jack London. The values that the boys have been raised by, the rationality of preparing for rescue, providing for shelter, and caring for the very young are nothing compared to their desire to hunt, to rule autocratically, or to kill a scapegoat. Ralph's Apollonian rationality is only preserved from the Dionysian hunters by the ironic *deus ex machina* of a warship and a uniformed officer.

The Inheritors shows a similar clash in pre-history, in which a Neanderthal extended family is supplanted by a Cro-Magnon tribe. Golding, faithful to what was known about the Neanderthals when he composed the novel, portrays them initially as caring, compassionate, communal—Edenlike inhabitants of our genetic past. They are discovered by, and in turn learn from the Cro-Magnons who stalk them and are eventually led by example into selfishness and sin. Lok, the early Neanderthal point-of-view character, wills his own death in an effort to join the others of his group, as a new point-of-view character, Tuami, of the "new people" takes over, describing the bleak voyage as Eden is lost once again. *The Inheritors* demands more reader participation than *Lord of the Flies* does. Lok is an unreliable narrative agent, and so too is Tuami. The shift between point-of-view characters is a gap the reader must fill. As Golding's career progressed, he demanded more and more of readers to determine the meaning behind his novels.

In *Pincher Martin,* a novel of memories and dreams, Christopher Hadley Martin, winds up living a fantasy of survival after his ship is torpedoed. The novel, much like Ambrose Bierce's "Occurrence at Owl Creek Bridge," shows Christopher imagining his survival on a rock island in the middle of the ocean. Not until the novel's end is the reader certain that Christopher's story is a fantasy of survival by a man unable to accept his death. Christopher's disjointed memories and fantasies portray him as an adult version of Jack from *Lord of the Flies,* a man who must destroy those whose lives represent an altruism or goodness foreign to his nature. Christopher's hell is living in his own value system. He is the total opposite of Lok in *The Inheritors,* who accepts death and chooses it as a natural consequence of life.

Like *Pincher Martin, Free Fall* is a "memory" novel and has its artist-narrator, Sammy Mountjoy, examine episodes from his past to determine when he lost his freedom. The answer is not provided by his background in either the slums or a concentration camp, but his college seduction of a young girl, Beatrice, as he barters her sanity for his pleasure. Unlike Golding's previous novels, *Free Fall* utilizes sets of polarized characters demonstrating values throughout its episodes, although they are inadequately represented therein.

Set in the Middle Ages, *The Spire* is the story of Jocelyn, dean of a cathedral, whose goal is to erect a 400-foot spire on the cathedral before his death. The problem with this goal is that neither the foundation nor the ground on which the cathedral rests will support such a spire. Jocelyn, in pursuing his quest, the result of what he considers a divine vision, entails sacrifice and risk, and though the spire is erected for the greater glory of God, its construction causes sacrifice of others, treachery, and murder; it represents Jocelyn's vicarious sexuality and will as well as divine glory. With each step, the costs and sacrifices of building the spire mount, accentuating Jocelyn's blind willfulness in carrying out his priestly duties. The consequences of Jocelyn's choices are presented with the artistic economy of a Greek tragedy in this powerful novel.

The three episodes covering about thirty years in *The Pyramid* are tied together by Oliver, the narrator, and the stratified provincial town, appropriately named Stilbourne, in which his family lives. In its three sections *Pyramid* emphasizes social divisions in a story about sexual initiation and class and in two stories shows the inadequate call of art through characters in theatre and music. In *Pyramid* the narrative center does not hold, however. A similar problem occurs in a much more ambitious novel, *Darkness Visible,* also divided into three sections. The first part deals with Matty

Windrove, a child burned in the Blitz of World War II, whose parents are unknown; the second deals with Sophy Stanhope and her sister, raised by a father and a series of his mistresses; the third deals with the interaction of these characters, where Sophy as terrorist kills Matty. Matty and Sophy have a combined identity, one representing feeling and the other intellect. Neither is a successful human being because of this; each represents social forces of the 1960s and 1970s that Golding detests. Because of the symbolic and allegorical density of the novel, and because Matty at best attracts pity and Sophy disgust, even horror, *Darkness Visible* is a difficult novel to enter.

Golding's best novel since *The Spire, Rites of Passage* is composed of two narratives: the upper-class Edmund Talbot's journal addressed to his patron-godfather, and an extended letter by the Reverend James Colley to his sister. Both deal with life onboard the *Britannia,* bound for the Antipodes near the end of the Napoleonic era. The ship is a microcosm of shifting British society, which the snobbish Talbot explores from the top and Colley from the middle, looking up. The motive for the action is the discovery of the reasons for Colley's death, shame caused by others, and Colley's own nature.

The familiar dichotomies of Golding—Apollonian reasonableness and Dionysian feeling—are in part represented by the narrators and in the spiritual testing and measurement of person and class, in a time of real and metaphoric translation.

The Paper Men hopes to be a serious novel about writers and their critics, and art and its relation to life; however, none of the penetration or the humor of these authors results. The writer, Sir Wilfred Barclay, is somewhat limited, and the American would-be biographer, Rick L. Tucker, is caricature beyond belief. Better representation of both by Golding would have made for a dynamic novel, although the book has two memorable moments: Barclay's shooting of Tucker and Tucker's shooting of Barclay.

Surprising for a writer who loves the novel because no other medium exists in which readers may "live for so long and so intimately with a character" is that Golding should produce so few sympathetic characters. Perhaps the essential conflict in Golding is between scientific pessimism and what spiritual optimism science chooses to ignore.

—Craig W. Barrow

GORDIMER, Nadine. South African. Born in Springs, Transvaal, 20 November 1923. Educated at a convent school, and the University of the Witwatersrand, Johannesburg. Married 1) Gerald Gavronsky in 1949 (divorced, 1952), one daughter; 2) Reinhold H. Cassirer in 1954, one son. Writer. Ford Foundation visiting professor, under auspices of Institute of Contemporary Arts, Washington, D.C., 1961; lecturer, Hopwood awards, University of Michigan, Ann Arbor, 1970; writer in residence, American Academy in Rome, 1984; has also lectured and taught writing at Harvard (1969), Princeton (1969), Northwestern (1969), Columbia (1971), and Tulane universities; presenter, *Frontiers* television series, 1990. Recipient: W.H. Smith & Son Literary award, 1961, for short story collection *Friday's Footprint, and Other Stories;* Thomas Pringle award, 1969; James Tait Black Memorial Prize, 1972, for *A Guest of Honour;* Booker Prize for Fiction, National Book League, 1974, for *The Conservationist;* Grand Aigle d'Or (France), 1975; CNA award, 1975; Neil Gunn fellowship, Scottish Arts Council, 1981; Common Wealth award for Distinguished Service in Literature, 1981; Modern Language Association of America award, 1981; Premio Malaparte (Italy), 1985; Nelly Sachs Prize (Germany), 1985; Bennett award (U.S.A.), *Hudson Review,* 1986; Commandeur de l'Ordre des Arts et des Lettres (France), 1986; Royal Society of Literature Benson medal, 1990. D.Litt., University of Leuven, 1980, Smith College, City College of the City University of New York, and Mount Holyoke College, all 1985, and honorary degrees from Harvard University and Yale University, both 1987, and New School for Social Research, 1988; University of York, 1987; Cambridge University, 1992; Nobel Prize for literature, 1991. Honorary Member, American Academy of Art and Sciences, 1980, Honorary Fellow, Modern Language Association (U.S.A.), 1985. Agent: Russell & Volkening, Inc., 50 West 29th St., New York, NY 10001.

PUBLICATIONS

Novels

The Lying Days. London, Gollancz, and New York, Simon & Schuster, 1953.
A World of Strangers. London, Gollancz, and New York, Simon & Schuster, 1958.
Occasion for Loving. London, Gollancz, and New York, Viking, 1963.
The Late Bourgeois World. London, Gollancz, and New York, Viking, 1966.
A Guest of Honour. New York, Viking, 1970; London, Cape, 1971.
The Conservationist. London, Cape, 1974; New York, Viking, 1975.
Burger's Daughter. London, Cape, and New York, Viking, 1979.
July's People. New York, Viking, 1981.
A Sport of Nature. London, Cape, and New York, Knopf, 1987.
My Son's Story. London, Bloomsbury, and New York, Farrar, Straus, 1990.

Short Stories

Face to Face. Johannesburg, Silver Leaf Books, 1949.
The Soft Voice of the Serpent, and Other Stories. New York, Simon & Schuster, 1952; London, Gollancz, 1953.
Six Feet of the Country. London, Gollancz, and New York, Simon & Schuster, 1956.
Friday's Footprint, and Other Stories. London, Gollancz, and New York, Viking, 1960.
Not for Publication, and Other Stories. London, Gollancz, and New York, Viking, 1965.
Penguin Modern Stories 4, with others. London, Penguin, 1970.
Livingstone's Companions. New York, Viking, 1971; London, Cape, 1972.
Selected Stories. London, Cape, 1975; New York, Viking, 1976; as *No Place Like: Selected Stories,* London, Penguin, 1978.
Some Monday for Sure. London, Heinemann Educational, 1976.
A Soldier's Embrace. London, Cape, and New York, Viking, 1980.
Town and Country Lovers. Los Angeles, Sylvester & Orphanos, 1980.
Something Out There. London, Cape, and New York, Viking, 1984.
Crimes of Conscience. London, Heinemann, 1991.
Jump and Other Stories. New York, Farrar, Straus, 1991.

Why Haven't You Written?; Selected Stories, 1950-1972. New York, Penguin, 1992.

Other

Editor, with Lionel Abrahams, *South African Writing Today.* London, Penguin, 1967.
African Literature: The Lectures Given on This Theme at the University of Cape Town's Public Summer School, February, 1972. Cape Town, Board of Extra Mural Studies, University of Cape Town, 1972.
The Black Interpreters: Notes on African Writing. Johannesburg, Spro-Cas/Ravan, 1973.
On the Mines, photographs by David Goldblatt. Cape Town, Struik, 1973.
What Happened to Burger's Daughter; or, How South African Censorship Works, with others. Johannesburg, Taurus, 1980.
Lifetimes Under Apartheid, photographs by David Goldblatt. London, Cape, and New York, Knopf, 1986.
Reflections of South Africa, edited by Kirsten Egebjerg and Gillian Stead Eilersen. Herning, Denmark, Systime, 1986.
The Essential Gesture: Writing, Politics and Places, edited and introduced by Stephen Clingman. New York, Knopf, 1988.
Conversations with Nadine Gordimer, edited by Nancy Topping Bazin and Marilyn Dallman Seymour. Jackson, University Press of Mississippi, 1990.
Three in a Bed: Fiction, Morals, & Politics. Bennington, Vermont, Bennington College, 1991.

Television Plays and Documentaries: *A Terrible Chemistry,* (*Writers and Places* series), 1981 (UK); *Choosing for Justice: Allan Boesak,* with Hugo Cassirer, 1985 (USA and UK); *Country Lovers, A Chip of Glass Ruby, Praise,* and *Oral History* (all in *The Gordimer Stories* series), 1985 (USA); *Frontiers* series, 1990 (UK).

Contributor to *The Heinemann Book of Contemporary African Short Stories,* London, Heinemann Educational, 1992; *Best Short Stories of 1991, 1992, 1993,* and numerous other anthologies.

*

Theatrical Activities:
Director: **Television**—*Choosing for Justice: Allan Boesak,* with Hugo Cassirer, 1985.

Bibliography: *Nadine Gordimer, Novelist and Short Story Writer: A Bibliography of Her Works* by Racilia Jilian Nel, Johannesburg, University of the Witwatersrand, 1964.

Critical Studies: *Nadine Gordimer* by Robert F. Haugh, New York, Twayne, 1974; *Nadine Gordimer* by Michael Wade, London, Evans, 1978; *Nadine Gordimer* by Christopher Heywood, Windsor, Berkshire, Profile, 1983; *The Novels of Nadine Gordimer: Private Lives/Public Landscapes* by John Cooke, Baton Rouge, Louisiana State University Press, 1985; *The Novels of Nadine Gordimer: History from the Inside* by Stephen Clingman, London, Allen & Unwin, 1986; *Nadine Gordimer* by Judie Newman, London, Macmillan, 1988; entry in *Contemporary Literary Criticism,* Detroit, Gale, Volume 3, 1975, Volume 5, 1976, Volume 7, 1977, Volume 10, 1979, Volume 18, 1981, Volume 33, 1985, Volume 51, 1989; *Critical Essays on Nadine Gordimer* edited by Rowland Smith, Boston, Hall, 1990.

There is nothing easy about Nadine Gordimer's fiction. Her characters, themes, narrative strategies, and—for one who is not South African—even her vocabulary are complicated. The difficulty of her texts arises naturally from the shaky, troubled historical ground she visits again and again in her stories: "Apartheid...the dirtiest social swindle the world has ever known," as she states in *Burger's Daughter*.

Burger's Daughter, the Gordimer novel most concerned with the young-adult problem of establishing a consistent set of values, was published in 1979, just three years after the infamous Soweto Uprising, a benchmark in modern South African history. When some fifteen thousand black schoolchildren assembled in Soweto on June 16, 1976, to protest the enforced use of Afrikaans (the language of their oppressors) in their schools, they were met with brutal suppression. In the year-long hostilities that followed, hundreds of blacks were killed. Significantly, the original protest was directed not only at the ruling white class, but also at black parents who, it seemed to the children, had to some extent colluded in their own subordination by passively accepting their degraded roles. It was the height of the Black Consciousness movement when even the authenticity of white, liberal commitment to black equality—like Gordimer's—was being questioned. Apartheid, the policy undergirding white supremacy, was being turned on its head as militant blacks insisted on a new kind of separatism, one in which blacks were dominant.

The Black Consciousness movement and its culminating event, the Soweto Revolt, profoundly affected Gordimer. She found the generational aspects of the conflict—children turning on their parents—particularly upsetting. Also, the betrayal by the blacks of white liberals like herself who had spent their lives working for equity between the races disturbed her. Yet she could certainly grasp the arguments of the Black Consciousness activists and even see the need for their firm self-assertion. She was thus forced to examine her own conscience regarding the role whites should expect to play in liberating black South Africans and even in liberating themselves from the collective guilt of their race. *Burger's Daughter* is the site of that self-examination, for it centers on the conflicts, personal and historical, that arise from this period in the life of Gordimer and South Africa.

Focusing on the generational conflict between young Rosa Burger and her father, Lionel, the novel examines apartheid and its ideological opposite, Black Consciousness, through Rosa's developing personality. Daughter of a doctor whose dedication to the South African Communist Party lands him, time and again, in prison where he eventually dies while serving a life sentence, Rosa becomes, in effect, an extension of her father. As a child and adolescent, she is able to reach people and places that her father cannot in order to deliver Party messages. She furthermore is absorbed into the communal life chosen for her by both parents. Consequently, she becomes subject to the loss of privacy and individual attention that such communality entails.

For a time, Rosa "defects" from her father's influence. Ironically though, she flees to France and the Bohemian digs of her father's ex-wife, Katya. Thus she has escaped only to be united with another extension of her father—this time from his past. In France she experiences a community of a different sort, one committed to the trivialities of everyday life rather than the apocalyptic vision of Marxism. But she also encounters a lover, Bernard, the one person who (although married to another) declares, "You are the dearest thing in the world to me." Before Rosa and Bernard are able to carry out their plans for Rosa's permanent defection to Paris, Rosa en-

counters Baasie—a black, who, as a boy, was treated as a son by the Burgers and who was Rosa's closest childhood friend until she lost track of him after her father's death—and her past catches up with her, turns her around, and sends her back to South Africa where she lives out her own version of her father's social commitment.

From the opening of the novel outside the prison where Rosa's mother is incarcerated the reader assumes the posture of a surveillant, although at first it is not clear what we are watching for. The story progresses erratically, sometimes through the words of a government watchdog, other times by way of Rosa's private notes to a long-lost roommate/analyst, sometimes possibly via her father's biographer, eventually through her direct address to her dead father. Picking our way among these discordant voices, we come to realize that what we are seeking is an integrated Rosa, just as she is. We watch and listen to see if she will devote herself to her parents' dream of a future, integrated, socialized South Africa at the expense of her own private need for an intimate, exclusive relationship. Before the conclusion of the novel Rosa ends up in prison, but in the meantime she answers both the public and private demands of her nature.

Besides the various narrators or recorders Gordimer employs, her mode of providing background information is eccentric. She releases details into the plot piecemeal, almost surreptitiously, so that Rosa—and through Rosa, her father—comes to us in fragments. For example, we learn that Rosa's brother has died; only later do we realize that he has drowned; later still that he drowned in the family's private swimming pool.

This novel requires close, serious attention, but the rewards for the diligent reader are great. Not only does it absorb one in the most private aspects of Rosa Burger's life, it involves the reader in a twenty-five-year period of South African history. That history in many ways mirrors the history of Black civil rights in the United States, a period when our social consciences were stripped bare.

—Mary Lowe-Evans

————

GRAHAM, Lorenz (Bell). American. Born in New Orleans, Louisiana, 27 January 1902. Educated at the University of Washington, Seattle, 1921; University of California, Los Angeles, 1923-24; Virginia Union University, Richmond, 1934-36, B.A. 1936; Columbia University, New York; New York University. Married Ruth Morris in 1929; two daughters and two sons. Teacher, Monrovia College, Liberia, 1924-29, and Richmond Adult Schools, Virginia, 1930-33; educational adviser, Civilian Conservation Corps, Virginia and Pennsylvania, 1936-42; housing manager, Newport News Housing Authority, Virginia, 1942-46; real estate salesman and building contractor, Long Island, New York, 1946-49; social worker, Queens Federation of Churches, New York, 1948-56; probation officer, Los Angeles County, California, 1957-67; lecturer, California State University, Pomona, 1970-78. Recipient: Thomas Alva Edison Foundation special citation for *The Ten Commandments;* Charles W. Follett award, 1958, and Child Study Association of America award, 1959, both for *South Town;* Association for Study of Negro Life and History award, 1959; Los Angeles City Council award, 1966; Vassie D. Wright award, 1967; Southern California Council on Literature for Children and Young People award for significant contribution to the field of literature for young people, 1968; first prize from *Book World,* 1969, for *Whose Town?;* California Association of Teachers of English citation, 1973; Martin Luther King award from Southern California region of Christian Church, 1975; *Boston Globe-Horn Book* award, and Children's Book Showcase award, both 1976, both for *South Town.* D.H.L.: Virginia University, 1983. *Died 11 September 1989.*

PUBLICATIONS FOR YOUNG ADULTS

Fiction

South Town. Chicago, Follett, 1958.
North Town. New York, Crowell, 1965.
Whose Town? New York, Crowell, 1969.
Carolina Cracker. Boston, Houghton Mifflin, 1972.
Detention Center. Boston, Houghton Mifflin, 1972.
Stolen Car. Boston, Houghton Mifflin, 1972.
Runaway. Boston, Houghton Mifflin, 1972.
Return to South Town. New York, Crowell, 1976.

PUBLICATIONS FOR CHILDREN

Fiction

Tales of Momolu, illustrated by Letterio Calapai. New York, Reynal, 1946.
I, Momolu, illustrated by John Biggers. New York, Crowell, 1966.
Song of the Boat, illustrated by Leo and Diane Dillon. New York, Crowell, 1975.

Other

How God Fix Jonah, illustrated by Letterio Calapai. New York, Reynal, 1946.
The Story of Jesus, illustrated by William Walsh. New York, Gilberton, 1955.
The Ten Commandments, illustrated by Norman Nodel. New York, Gilberton, 1956.
John Brown's Raid: A Picture History. New York, Scholastic, 1972.
Directions 3-4, with John Durham and Elsa Graser. Boston, Houghton Mifflin, 2 vols., 1972.
John Brown: A Cry for Freedom. New York, Crowell, 1980.

*

Manuscript Collection: Kerlan Collection, University of Minnesota, Minneapolis; North Carolina Central University Library, Durham.

Biography: Entry in *Dictionary of Literary Biography,* Volume 76, Detroit, Gale, 1988; essay in *Something about the Author Autobiography Series,* Volume 5, Detroit, Gale, 1988.

Critical Study: Entry in *Children's Literature Review,* Volume 10, Detroit, Gale, 1985.

*   *   *

In his series of four novels that begins with *South Town,* Lorenz Graham has a message to give, more than a story to tell. It's a

message that encourages understanding and reconciliation between whites and blacks, rich and poor, powerful and weak. But the message needs a story—a vehicle to carry it and connect it, through the imagination, to the reader's life and actions. The danger of course is that the message drives the story rather than vice versa. Graham does not altogether escape that danger.

The story starts in *South Town* where we meet the Williams family, a model black family with their own piece of land and a lot of pride. David, sixteen, has ambitions to become a doctor plus a strong sense of mission to help those who can't help themselves and to right the wrongs of the South Town society. But David learns about the white power structure, personified by the Boyds, and how it intends to keep uppity blacks permanently subservient. David's father is forced to render equal work for unequal pay. When he protests, he is thrown in jail and nearly beaten to death. To make sure the Williams family gets the message, the whites, with the law's help, organize a night riders gang and terrorize those in the family home by threats and gunfire. Graham avoids a simple white versus black conflict, however. Several of the white community folk reject racism and stand with the Williams family against their own people, willing to risk both reputation and life. Yet, David's faith in white acceptance and racial equality is severely shaken. The family decides that the North may offer more opportunity for good employment, a better education, and a kinder acceptance within the human community. Reluctantly, feeling sad but hopeful, the Williams family leaves South Town and its nightmares behind.

We meet them again in *North Town.* The father has found a factory job, and David is enrolled at an integrated but mostly white North Town Central High where, like the character in Ralph Ellison's *Invisible Man,* he learns some painful lessons about his own invisibility. David's cynicism about race relations, justice, and his own prospects deepens. When he finds himself implicated in a stolen car incident, his future seems doomed. And when his father can no longer work because of a serious illness, David has to assume the role of breadwinner. Yet the bad times don't prevail. David is exonerated from guilt in the crime of his friends. He is able to stay in school even when he takes over his father's factory job. And he learns enough about football to have his own shining moment of game-winning heroics. Gradually David gains a sense of belonging to the human family, both black and white. Add to that Pa Williams's eventual recovery and the family's move out of the run-down ghetto that stigmatized them as inferior, and the wisdom of the migration north seems confirmed.

Though the plot, as in *South Town,* is not well integrated, the action line is stronger here and a range of characters again represents Graham's balanced emphasis, avoiding the danger of stereotyping and reducing the human relationships to simply a racial one. But he still too often presents his characters more as case studies than as dynamic individuals.

In *Whose Town?* that flaw is perpetuated. David, now eighteen and a senior, remains as principal character but now functions mostly as a passive victim and detached observer. It's the decade of the sixties with much racial unrest and violent eruptions into race riots. North Town is not exempt. David gets involved in an ugly racial incident, his friend is killed, and David spends a couple of nights in jail. What hurts especially is his discovery that most whites presume his guilt. His South Town bitterness resurfaces. He tries to find his way by listening to the voices of the radical black militants as well as to the more moderate voices of his father and his pastor. He vacillates. But the author's thematic intent manipulates both plot and character development. David graduates from high school, his conviction that "we're all Americans" shaken but not destroyed, and his professional aspirations still intact. Girlfriend Jeannette Lenoir answers the book title's question: "It's everybody's town."

Unfortunately, Lorenz Graham's literary inspiration and craft forsake him nearly altogether in *Return to South Town*. Apparently the author was eager to document the impact of the civil rights movement on the South during the sixties and seventies. Hence the plot becomes incidental and the characters function mostly as mouthpieces for the observations of the author.

David has completed his doctor's training and, true to his boyhood dreams, returns to South Town to establish himself as family physician. He is warmly welcomed by old friends but coldly rejected by Harold Boyd, the nemesis of his youth and now director of the Boyd Memorial Hospital. He finds that much has changed, except the human heart. But David distinguishes himself as hero at a serious accident scene and later at a fiery plane crash. And when, despite Harold Boyd's objections, the state ultimately grants him a license to practice medicine, David's noble dream comes true and his mission can begin, a mission in which Joyce Palmer, professor of sociology at the community college, is eager to join him. And as David's girlfriend did earlier, now it is Joyce, his future wife, who sums up the author's theme of the whole "Town" series: "I claim to be a human with problems living among a lot of other human beings who also have problems."

It is true that Lorenz Graham can hardly be acclaimed as a literary stylist or gifted writer. It is also true that in the nineties this series appears badly dated. Yet these books retain their value for they constitute an honest documentary of pre-to post-civil rights times, from the point of view of a struggling family whose humanity consistently strikes the reader more tellingly than the blackness of their skin.

—Henry J. Baron

GRANT, Cynthia D. American. Born in Brockton, Massachusetts, 23 November 1950. Married 1) Daniel Heatley, one son; 2) Erik Neel, one son. Writer, 1974—. Address: Box 95, Cloverdale, CA 95425, U.S.A.

PUBLICATIONS FOR YOUNG ADULTS

Fiction

Joshua Fortune. New York, Atheneum, 1980.
Summer Home. New York, Atheneum, 1981.
Big Time. New York, Atheneum, 1982.
Hard Love. New York, Atheneum, 1983.
Kumquat May, I'll Always Love You. New York, Atheneum, 1986.
Phoenix Rising, or, How to Survive Your Life. New York, Atheneum, 1989.
Keep Laughing. New York, Atheneum, 1991.
Shadow Man. New York, Atheneum, 1992.
Uncle Vampire. New York, Atheneum, 1993.

*

Cynthia D. Grant comments:

One reason I write for teenagers is because those years remain so vivid in my mind. Junior high and high school were difficult times. The kids were so mean to each other! If you stuck out in any way, by being especially smart, or handicapped, or saddled with a hideous home permanent, you were picked on until you bled to death of a thousand tiny cuts. Kids who were picked on took it out on smaller kids. Hurt people hurt people, and themselves. Is this a system?

In my writing I try to reach out to readers and let them know that they are not alone; that, unique as each of us is, we all feel lonely and scared and confused sometimes. And to say, in the words of an anonymous author: Be kind; everyone you meet is fighting a hard battle.

*   *   *

In five works of realistic fiction for young adults, Cynthia D. Grant demonstrates genuine insight to the young adult world. In *Joshua Fortune* she creates a title character on the verge of adolescence. In addition to the emotional, psychological, and physical changes shared by adolescents, Joshua also finds himself burdened by his name, resentful of his parents' sixties' attitudes, angry at his father's consistent absence, and struggling to accept the reality of his mother's impending marriage. Joshua's world lacks the stability he craves when his family moves to a new town. Grant allows Joshua his anger and frustration as understandable reactions to a befuddling, uncontrollable world; however, these negative emotions never overwhelm him. He vents, but he does not wallow. He lashes out, but he also releases compassion and understanding.

When his home life alienates him, he turns to his peers. Joshua finds himself surprisingly attracted to new friends in school. By observing other families, he realizes the solidity and love within his own family. His friends Alexa and Richard provide Joshua with the perspectives which often elude young adults. Alexa's quirkiness, her verbal banter, and her extravagant sense of humor pull Joshua out of himself. With her, he learns to laugh again. While Richard's own desperation seems familiar to Joshua, the two boys command a unique ability to understand each other implicitly.

Friendship is just what sixteen-year-old Dory lacks in *Big Time*. Like Joshua Fortune, Dory has a challenging younger sister. But unlike Joshua's appropriately named sister Sarah Sunshine, Dory's sister Missy offers no emotional relief. Her parents dwell on Missy, leaving Dory feeling excluded. The family's resources and aspirations center on nine-year-old Missy's potential to make it big in Hollywood. Behind the scenes, Dory knows her sister is difficult and excessively self-absorbed.

Although Dory cannot escape her family as they venture from Deadwood, Oklahoma, to Hollywood with a fast-talking, promise-making talent scout, she does learn about the idiosyncrasies of backstage life and personalities. She participates in this new arena with a healthy skepticism and a heavy dose of humor. As the lights fade in Missy's dream of stardom, Dory discovers her own resilience and individuality—she even gets asked to do a TV sitcom.

Dory's final words, that life may be strange but "it's always good for a few laughs," take on multifaceted intensity in Grant's two novels *Phoenix Rising, or, How to Survive Your Life* and *Keep Laughing*. In each of these novels, laughter operates as the freeing catalyst to emotional health. In them, Grant also exposes the imprisonment of laughter. After her sister has died from cancer, Jessie locks herself away from all she cares about and all who care about her. Her delightful, easy sense of humor no longer offers levity and perspective—it frightens her and burdens her. How can she laugh when Helen is dead? Will she ever deserve to be happy and light-hearted again?

And for the unfortunately named Shepherd Youngman, humiliation, rejection, and exclusion make up life's jokes. On the verge of his sixteenth birthday, Shep leaves the safety of home and his mother to travel with his comedian father, Joey. Armed with a comedy club and television deals, a swank apartment and financial comfort, Joey promises to give Shep the home and father he's put on hold for so long. Shep soon realizes the fragility of Joey's life and the hollowness of these promises. He hears himself used as material in Joey's act; he finds himself needing a father but being treated like a buddy, not a son. Like Joshua Fortune, Shep Youngman establishes a peaceful, if uneven, relationship with his father due to the loving, stable family created by his mother.

Grant's *Phoenix Rising* stands as an artistically ambitious undertaking in which she departs from a chronologically straightforward narrative to reveal the intricacies of Jessie and Helen's relationship with an equally complex way of storytelling. She alternates Jessie's ongoing grieving process in the past tense with parcels of Helen's journal. The past tense assures readers that Jessie will get well. This structure fortifies the novel by including Helen's living voice. Grant shapes Helen as a character through the journal, articulating her hopes, dreams, ambitions, disappointments, and frustrations. As readers come to know Helen, they mourn her loss with Jessie and her brother Lucas.

Shadow Man does not prove as gratifying in its structure. It, too, opens with the death of a character whose absence dominates the novel. As the many people who loved him learn of and react to eighteen-year-old Gabriel McCloud's death, he becomes the ultimate shadow man. However, unlike Helen, he never takes on any substance at all. Other people's responses to him never quite intersect; the reader learns the variety of Gabe's personality, but cannot unite them into a full character. As a result, one reads of others mourning him, but never personally participates in the grieving process.

In all her novels, Grant conveys an understanding of young adulthood as a time of challenge and growth. She displays and creates believable young adult characters. Her frequent use of dialogue as a crafting tool evokes a range of adolescent voices. In every novel, she places her young adult characters firmly within the spheres of family and friends. She presents the family as an essential, life-giving community. And, even when threatened by a negligent parent or untimely death, Grant's families always support the young adult. The truth of her families comes from their fragility which she dares to share with readers. Grant's characters, like most adolescents, may wish for the nuclear family, but they flourish in alternate forms; however shaken or wobbly, these families do not shatter—they remain the arena of sustenance and love. Absence—of a father, sister, a friend, or brother—demands attention in these novels. The characters recognize their loss and struggle to overcome it. The absence cannot be filled; the loss cannot be replaced. Yet, each character learns that, with the perspective afforded by laughter and the foundation established by family, they can be made whole again.

—Cathryn M. Mercier

GRAY, Elizabeth Janet. See **VINING, Elizabeth Gray.**

GREEN, Hannah. See **GREENBERG, Joanne (née Goldenberg).**

GREENBERG, Joanne (née Goldenberg). Also writes as Hannah Green. American. Born in Brooklyn, New York, 24 September 1932. Educated at American University, Washington D.C., B.A. Married Albert Greenberg in 1955; two sons. Writer; medical officer, Lookout Mountain Fire Department; certified emergency medical technician. Adjunct professor of anthropology, Colorado School of Mines, 1983—. Recipient: National Jewish Welfare Board Harry and Ethel Daroff Memorial Fiction award, 1963, and William and Janice Epstein Fiction award, 1964, both for *The King's Persons;* New York Association of the Deaf Marcus L. Kenner award, 1971; Christopher Book award, 1971, for *In This Sign;* Frieda Fromm-Reichman Memorial award, 1967, Western Maryland College, D.L., 1977, and Gallaudet College, D.H.L., 1979; Rocky Mountain Women's Institute award, 1983; J.H.L., University of Colorado, 1987; Denver Public Library Bookplate award, 1990; Colorado Author of the Year, 1991. Agent: Lois Wallace, Wallace Literary Agency, 1977 E. 70th Street, New York, NY 10021. Address: 29221 Rainbow Hill Road, Golden, CO 80401, U.S.A.

Publications for Young Adults

Fiction

The King's Persons. New York, Holt, 1963.
The Monday Voices. New York, Holt, 1965.
In This Sign. New York, Holt, 1968.
Founder's Praise. New York, Holt, 1976.
A Season of Delight. New York, Holt, 1981.
The Far Side of Victory. New York, Holt, 1983.
Simple Gifts. New York, Holt, 1986.
Age of Consent. New York, Holt, 1987.
Of Such Small Differences. New York, Holt, 1988.
No Reck'ning Made. New York, Holt, 1993.

Short Stories

Summering. New York, Holt, 1966.
Rites of Passage. New York, Holt, 1971.
High Crimes and Misdemeanors. New York, Holt, 1979.
With the Snow Queen and Other Stories. New York, Arcade, 1991.

Nonfiction as Hannah Green

I Never Promised You a Rose Garden. New York, Holt, 1964.

*

Media Adaptations: *I Never Promised You a Rose Garden* (film), New World Pictures, 1977.

Critical Study: Entry in *Contemporary Literary Criticism,* Detroit, Gale, Volume 7, 1977; Volume 30, 1984.

*   *   *

Joanne Greenberg, also known as Hannah Green, is a writer of versatility and verve. She is the writer with whom one can enjoy a rainy day at a vacation resort. Her style lends itself to the mature reader while simultaneously presenting themes suitable for all ages. Greenberg addresses the persistent doubts that plague all of us by relating stories of others in need. Though the scenarios in which her characters find themselves may be unfamiliar to the average reader, the emotions they feel while enmeshed in the plotlines are universal in appeal and scope. Her works include magazine publications, short stories, novels, and a movie adaptation of her book *I Never Promised You a Rose Garden.*

Greenberg wrote *I Never Promised You a Rose Garden* under the pseudonym of Hannah Green. In this book, she details the struggle of a sixteen-year-old girl fighting for her sanity. The descriptive and, at times, poetic use of language brings the reader inside the character's world of fantasy. The depiction of the brilliant psychiatrist grappling with the reality of her own life while immersed in the treatment of her patient is explicitly detailed and well written. One can sense the underlying common thread of the need for acceptance so familiar to all adolescents. We sense the character's desire for the unconditional love that all human beings need. We can see ourselves confronting the confusion of youth along with the feelings of isolation and rejection. Greenberg's personal encounter with mental problems was a basis for the character's ordeal with psychosis and schizophrenia. Her empathy for her character is clearly evident in the portrayal of the teen's pilgrimage through failure and success.

Another popular book deals once again with the theme of isolation—in the world of the deaf. The book *In This Sign* was heralded and awarded by those both within and outside of the deaf community. The themes of loneliness and of being different are dramatically brought to life by the experiences of Greenberg's characters. She is able to take the reader on a journey inside her characters' minds. She does not just bring their thoughts into the open, but she allows us to feel their emotions. She transforms the occurrences within the realm of her deaf character into common circumstances with which we can all identify. Readers can gain an affinity for the handicapped through edification and education which is expertly interwoven into the storyline.

In another book, *Of Such Small Differences,* Greenberg expands the reader's minds to encompass the daily trials and tribulations of a character who in this story is not only deaf, but also blind. Once again we see the universality of isolation. In this case it is related, as in the previous book, to a physical disability. The leading character's experiences and ensuing love affair are portrayed as one might relate a story told by one friend to another. The primary difficulties handled by the protagonist are those of anyone involved in a growing relationship. It is a love story. The physical disabilities are secondary in the development of the characters' union. We see the individuals expressing almost a degree of freedom in their solitude. Once again, the handicapping condition has been used to relate to the universality of the emotion. Everyone, especially adolescents, can relate to feeling as though they are different; when in fact, that is what makes us all the same. As indicated by Greenberg, we are "of such small differences."

In *Simple Gifts* we also see people somewhat out of sync with the world around them. Love, for these "misfits," comes after much

turmoil. Greenberg describes feelings we have all had through the eyes of her characters. We see the meanness as well as the kindness in the secrets of those in our lives. When we receive love, it usually comes as a surprise, when it is least expected.

One of Greenberg's sadder stories is described in *The Far Side of Victory.* This book examines such themes as crime and punishment of the human soul. Our guilt or innocence is primarily determined by our own abilities to cope with life's adversities. In our search for truth and meaning, we must experience love and loss.

In *Age of Consent,* Greenberg most strongly portrays the mysterious loner no one ever really knew. By examining a character's life following their untimely death at the hands of murderers, Greenberg cleverly intertwines the utilization of the technique of flashback combined with the present tense of the investigation. The investigators are forced to look at their own lives as the impact of both the life and death of the main character is revealed. Once again we see a study in solitude; of being alone while in the company of many. We are shown a character some may see as being unable to love, while others will recognize as being incapable of showing one's feelings. Adolescents may also relate to the character's being adopted in early childhood, complete with fragmented memories and mixed emotions. The character's involvement in nations of political unrest and abject poverty are as timely now as when the book was written.

Another book which also includes references to actual historical events is *Founder's Praise.* This book details the climb of a family through hard times in the history of the United States. Their belief in the goodness of people through religion and morality guides them into their future.

Greenberg has also written several collections of short stories. In one book, *Summering,* her tales again reflect the themes of love and misunderstanding, loneliness and friendship. We are subsequently captivated by her imaginative characterizations and narratives which uniquely embody her freshness and innovation. In another book of short stories, *With the Snow Queen and Other Stories,* she writes of people we know. We can relate to people with basic human needs, even in peculiar situations. In one story, she employs the unconventional tact of having a character break through the "third wall" to "speak" directly to the reader. Her range of unusual topics runs the gamut from time travel to the solemnity of the life of a monk. Another collection, *High Crimes and Misdemeanors,* utilizes much humor and fantasy. At the same time, Greenberg is still able to embroil the readers in the particulars of her characters which most closely link us all to the hopes, fears, and dreams of life. Additionally, this book also contains several stories which come from Greenberg's religious background.

Greenberg's popularity lies in both her creativity and her originality. Her ability to incorporate common themes into uncommon situations makes her a most readable author.

—Laurie Schwartz Guttenberg

———

GREENE, Bette. American. Born in Memphis, Tennessee, 28 June 1934. Educated at University of Alabama, 1952; Memphis State University, 1953-54; Alliance Française (Paris), 1954; Columbia University, 1955; Harvard University, 1972. Married Donald Sumner Greene in 1959; one daughter and one son. Reporter, Memphis

Hebrew Watchman, 1950, Memphis *Commercial Appeal,* 1950-52, and United Press International, Memphis bureau, 1953-54; public information officer, American Red Cross, Memphis, 1958-59, and Boston State Psychiatric Hospital, 1959-61. Recipient: *New York Times'* outstanding book award, Golden Kite award, Society of Children's Book Writers, and American Library Association (ALA) notable book citation, all 1973, and National Book award nomination for best children's book, 1974, all for *Summer of My German Soldier;* Children's Choice Book award, *New York Times'* outstanding book award, and ALA notable book citation, all 1974, and Newbery Honor Book award, 1975, all for *Philip Hall Likes Me. I Reckon Maybe; Parents' Choice* award, 1983, for *Them That Glitter and Them That Don't.* Agent: Alfred Lowman, Authors and Artists Group, 14 East 60th Street, New York, NY 10022. Address: 338 Clinton Road, Brookline, MA 02146, U.S.A.

PUBLICATIONS FOR YOUNG ADULTS

Fiction

Summer of My German Soldier. New York, Dial Press, 1973; London, Hamish Hamilton, 1974.
Philip Hall Likes Me. I Reckon Maybe, illustrated by Charles Lilly. New York, Dial Press, 1974; London, Hamish Hamilton, 1976.
Morning Is a Long Time Coming. New York, Dial Press, and London, Hamish Hamilton, 1978.
Get on out of Here, Philip Hall. New York, Dial Press, 1981; London, Hamish Hamilton, 1982.
Them That Glitter and Them That Don't. New York, Knopf, 1983.
I've Already Forgotten Your Name, Philip Hall! New York, Knopf, 1983.
The Drowning of Stephan Jones. New York, Bantam, 1991.

*

Media Adaptations: *Summer of My German Soldier* (television movie, starring Kristy McNichol, Bruce Davison, and Esther Rolle), National Broadcasting Company (NBC-TV), 1978; *Summer of My German Soldier* (audiocassette); *Philip Hall Likes Me. I Reckon Maybe* (audiocassette).

Biography: Essay in *Speaking for Ourselves: Autobiographical Sketches by Notable Authors of Books for Young Adults,* Volume 1, compiled and edited by Donald R. Gallo, National Council of Teachers of English, 1990; essay in *Authors and Artists for Young Adults,* Volume 7, Detroit, Gale, 1991; essay in *Something about the Author Autobiography Series,* Volume 16, Detroit, Gale, 1993.

Manuscript Collection: Kerlan Collection, University of Minnesota, Minneapolis.

Critical Studies: Entry in *Children's Literature Review,* Volume 2, Detroit, Gale, 1976; entry in *Contemporary Literary Criticism,* Volume 30, Detroit, Gale, 1984.

*   *   *

Celebrated for her emotionally powerful books and her strong characters, Bette Greene has left an indelible mark on twentieth-century young adult literature. A very intense woman who strongly

feels that children "are the most important part of our world," Greene devotes much of her writing to themes that deal with hypocrisy, prejudice, and the many forms of abuse—physical, emotional, and religious—that exist in society, and how they affect people, especially children and young adults. Hers is a strong voice that comes from the heart and dares to question what many don't want to think about.

People react so strongly to Greene's writing because she herself is intensely involved with her books. Her writing is steeped in human emotion and experience. "The best ideas," says Greene, "come from your response to living—to what makes you wake up in the morning wanting to break out into song and what makes you want to break out into tears." Anything else is "formula writing" which, according to Greene, is less difficult to write. "If you follow a template," explains Greene, "clearly writing and life are a lot easier for you. The really difficult thing about writing is the motivation of the characters, how people respond, what's going on inside—and that stuff is never formula." To Greene, writing is all about "trying to understand things which might not be really understandable—trying to understand this journey that we all take called life."

Greene's characters are born out of her life's experiences and are enhanced by what she sees in daily life. Seeing a parent yank a child's arm in a store can leave a lasting impression on her. "I hate violence towards children," she says. "I can write about those themes all day long because that is an issue that is very disturbing to me." When she wrote *Summer of My German Soldier,* probably Greene's best-known novel, she wrote it to try to understand abuse and life as she had partly experienced it. The childhood experiences of Greene's twelve-year-old character, Patty Bergen, are similar to those in Greene's own life. Like Patty, Greene grew up as a Jewish girl in a small town in Arkansas during World War II amidst the hatred and violence directed toward anyone who wasn't a white, Christian American. Patty offers a lot of insight into what it feels like to be mistreated, especially after she befriends a black woman and an escaped German prisoner and finds them kinder to her than her own parents. The sequel, *Morning Is a Long Time Coming,* continues with Patty's personal journey to find love and acceptance within herself and from others after graduation from high school.

Two of Greene's most popular books for younger readers may also be the funniest. *Philip Hall Likes Me. I Reckon Maybe* and *Get on out of Here, Philip Hall* are episodic novels about Beth Lambert, who likes a boy all of the time while he only likes her some of the time. Every year letters pour in to the author from young girls from around the globe who explain that the boys they know act an awful lot like Philip Hall.

Greene wrote her most recent novel, *The Drowning of Stephan Jones,* to try to understand what, to her, is "totally incomprehensible"—why people hate just because a person's sexuality is different from theirs. In this novel, Greene focuses on the treatment of homosexuals—the "designated victims" of our society. "Too much hate is coming from the pulpit," she says, "and people cannot separate the supposed sin from the sinner." These concerns are certainly evident in *The Drowning of Stephan Jones,* where a gay couple, Stephan Jones and Frank Montgomery, are the victims of hatred and harassment by people who believe that their violent actions are right and religious.

"People can easily identify and disapprove of political tyranny, but religious tyranny is much more difficult to pinpoint and discuss objectively." She recalls her own personal experience of what she considers religious abuse when she became a "born-again Christian" as a child. Greene said she spent six years trying to convert her Jewish parents to Christianity and cried because she actually believed that her parents' souls were going to hell. The irony is that the minister probably felt that he served Bette well, but Greene feels that, in her case, religion was carried too far—that "we each have a right to our own God."

Greene strongly feels that people need more moral courage—the courage to stand up to any form of violence, hatred, and abuse and say, "This [injustice] is wrong!" When people do not speak out, they are indirectly condoning the abuse by allowing it to continue. People often wait to see who will say something first because "people often find physical courage easier to come by than moral courage." In other words, people are more apt to physically risk their lives to save someone than publicly say something contrary to the "moral majority's" views on controversial religious issues.

Greene likens literature to "a mirror on the souls of readers" which has the potential of increasing people's "awareness, social skills, and compassion." Regarding her own writing, Greene says the biggest compliment people can give her after reading one of her books is that they feel and understand more about life than they did before the reading. Given the response to her writing, Greene often achieves that goal. While her novels generally deal with adolescent protagonists, Greene's audience is not limited to teenagers. She notes that in response to *The Drowning of Stephan Jones,* she received a letter which opened, "Thank you for opening the eyes of a sixty-two-year-old farm woman." Perhaps this wide range of readers exists because the issues that Greene deals with aren't limited by age, race, religion, or gender.

Greene can't imagine being anything but a writer. She loves what she does and would like to be remembered as having helped children. It is evident that Bette Greene has already exceeded that aspiration through her writing.

—Joan F. Kaywell and Heidi M. Quintana

* * *

GREENWALD, Sheila. American. Born in New York City, 26 May 1934. Educated at Sarah Lawrence College, Bronxville, New York, B.A. 1956. Married George Green in 1960; two sons. Writer and illustrator. Address: 175 Riverside Drive, New York, NY 10024, U.S.A.

PUBLICATIONS FOR YOUNG ADULTS

Fiction (illustrated by the author)

A Metropolitan Love Story. New York, Doubleday, 1962.
Willie Bryant and the Flying Otis. New York, Grosset, 1971.
The Hot Day. Indianapolis, Indiana, Bobbs Merrill, 1972.
Miss Amanda Snap. Indianapolis, Indiana, Bobbs Merrill, 1972.
Mat Pit and the Tunnel Tenants. Philadelphia, Pennsylvania, Lippincott, 1972.
The Secret Museum. Philadelphia, Pennsylvania, Lippincott, 1974.
The Secret in Miranda's Closet. Boston, Houghton Mifflin, 1977.
The Mariah Delany Lending Library Disaster. Boston, Houghton Mifflin, 1977.

The Atrocious Two. Boston, Houghton Mifflin, 1978.
All the Way to Wits' End. Boston, Little, Brown, 1979.
It All Began with Jane Eyre, or, the Secret Life of Franny Dillman. Boston, Little, Brown, 1980.
Give Us a Great Big Smile, Rosy Cole. New York, Atlantic Monthly Press, 1981.
Blissful Joy and the SATs: A Multiple-Choice Romance. New York, Atlantic Monthly Press, 1982.
Will the Real Gertrude Hollings Please Stand Up? New York, Atlantic Monthly Press, 1983.
Valentine Rosy. New York, Atlantic Monthly Press, 1984.
Rosy Cole's Great American Guilt Club. New York, Atlantic Monthly Press, 1985.
Alvin Webster's Sure Fire Plan for Success and How It Failed. Boston, Little, Brown, 1987.
Write On Rosy!: A Young Author in Crisis. Boston, Little, Brown, 1988.
Rosy's Romance. Boston, Little, Brown, 1989.
The Mariah Delany Author of the Month Club. Boston, Little, Brown, 1990.
Here's Hermione, A Rosy Cole Production. Boston, Little, Brown, 1991.
Rosy Cole Discovers America! Boston, Joy Street, 1992.
My Fabulous New Life. New York, Browndeer Press, 1993.
Rosy Cole! She Walks in Beauty. Boston, Little, Brown, forthcoming.

*

Illustrator: *Pocketful of Poems,* by Marie L. Allen, 1957; *The Pink Motel,* by Carol Ryrie Brink, 1959; *The Little Leftover Witch,* by Florence Laughlin, 1960; *Brave Betsy,* by Miriam Dreifus, 1961; *Come A-Witching,* by Grace V. Curl, 1964; *Amy and the Sorrel Summer,* by Laura H. Fisher, 1964; *The Remarkable Ramsey,* by Barbara Rinkoff, 1965; *The Boy Who Couldn't Make Up His Mind,* by Hila Colman, 1965; *Who'll Mind Henry?,* by Anne Mallet, 1965; *The Seventh Cousin,* by Florence Laughlin, 1966; *The Pretender Princess,* by Mary J. Roth, 1967; *When I Was Jersey,* by James Playsted Wood, 1967; *Jump the Rope Jingles,* by Emma V. Worstell, 1967; *The Mystery Cup,* by Jean Bothwell, 1968; *The New Boy on the Sidewalk,* by M. Jean Craig, 1968; *Veronica the Show Off,* by Nancy K. Robinson, 1982; *Henny Youngman's Book of Jokes,* by Henny Youngman, 1992.

Sheila Greenwald comments:

I can't remember a time when I wasn't drawing. Writing came later and was harder. In college I loved classics in creative writing, but was aware of the fact that at the time I didn't have much to write about. I began to illustrate books after college. Most of them were for children. By the time my own two sons started school, I had plenty of things I wanted to write about. My books are generated by issues involving values about which I either feel strongly or am unresolved. Sometimes the books help me to explore an issue, sometimes they are to expound on one. Humor helps both me and my characters achieve a necessary perspective.

* * *

Sheila Greenwald's sheer joy in her craft is evident in her many books for young people. Although she enjoys inventing characters and situations rather than recording actual events and emotions, Greenwald is not unsympathetic toward her characters. They must cope with difficult issues—such as divorce, anorexia, and mental illness—but Greenwald also injects a healthy dose of humor into her books, endowing her characters with the rare ability to laugh at themselves and their seemingly hopeless situations. The effortless quality of Greenwald's prose allows her characters to assume the guise of old friends. Greenwald also claims to be highly opinionated, and she admits that inventing stories allows her to showcase her beliefs.

One subject she obviously has strong feelings about is the annual rite of passage for high schoolers, the Scholastic Aptitude Test, which figures prominently in *Blissful Joy and the SATs: A Multiple-Choice Romance,* one of her most popular books. Greenwald's native New York is central to the story, though the setting is unobtrusive; Greenwald's familiarity with the city allows it to function as a backdrop against which the story develops. Blissful Joy Bowman prides herself on her good sense and responsibility. As the daughter of amicably divorced actors, Bliss has always played the parental role with her rather childlike parents. While they dart from one job to another, Bliss attends the proper school and achieves good grades to ensure herself a safe and secure future. Bliss is determined to have "a normal life." Bliss succeeds in keeping her life completely in order until the day she is befriended by Blackball, a stray dog, on the subway. This seemingly insignificant event sets into motion a chain of events over which she has no control. With the help of Blackball and the quirky group of people he introduces, Bliss learns that in the real world people do not always fit into her neatly assigned pigeonholes.

Greenwald creates an impressive array of characters in *Blissful Joy.* Many of the characters have amusing, even outrageously flamboyant names like Delphi Pilpel, the homely veterinarian. Yet, while these people are unique, they are also real and very human. Despite their familiar contemporary problems, Greenwald's characters are not stereotypes. Sibyl's anorexia and Louisa's mother's mental illness and desertion are not depicted in a heavy handed, moralistic manner, but with honesty and in keeping with their characters. The issues raised are well integrated within the context of the story. In the same fashion, Bliss's first experience with that which she and her fellow amateur psychologist and best friend, Jenny, call MPRWOS (Meaningful Peer Relationship With the Opposite Sex), is both touching and funny. Her relationships with Howard and Colin expose Bliss to the hurt and disappointment as well as to the fulfillment of a relationship. Greenwald provides a sensitive and witty account of the problems, real and imagined, of first love.

Another important theme in the book involves Bliss's feelings about her parents' divorce. Like many children of divorce, Bliss remains hopeful that her parents will reconcile. Although she is resigned to the reality of their relationship—thanks to numerous self-help books—Bliss still feels uneasy with her parents' romantic relationships with others. In the process of accepting her parents' weaknesses while appreciating their uniqueness, Bliss confronts her own prejudice and shallowness. When she adopts Blackball, Bliss begins to admit that she has ordinary emotions that she does not need to submerge. Bliss acknowledges that, while she should not allow her life to be run by her emotions, the capacity to feel is not a weakness. By giving of herself to relationships and to Blackball, whom she needs as much, if not more, than he needs her, Bliss becomes human. Allowing her parents the freedom to be themselves eventually leads to their increased responsibility for her and for themselves.

The concepts of reality and illusion also play a significant role in *Blissful Joy.* The Bowman adults treat their lives as theatrical roles; those roles parallel and intersect with the lives of those around them. For example, Colin, infatuated with Bliss, rehearses tender lines with her mother, and Bliss mistakenly thinks the two are involved. Mr. Bowman romances sensible Delphi under false pretenses (for the sake of Blackball), not realizing he is falling in love with her. Greenwald's expert use of irony and satire is one of the qualities that lifts this novel above other, more mundane "problem novels."

Sheila Greenwald writes seamlessly with a virtually invisible hand. She makes her points unobtrusively. It is through her characters' interaction that Greenwald conveys such messages as the importance of not stereotyping people, of accepting one's own and others' limitations, and above all, of maintaining a sense of humor. Clearly, Greenwald writes for her own enjoyment, but, fortunately for her readers, for theirs as well.

—Maryclare O'Donnell Himmel

————

GUY, Rosa (Cuthbert). American. Born in Trinidad, West Indies, 1 September 1925; moved to the United States, 1932. Educated at New York University. Married Warner Guy (deceased); one son. Worked with the American Negro Theatre, New York, mid-1940s. Since 1950 writer; founding president, Harlem Writer's Guild. Lecturer. Recipient: American Library Association "Best Book for Young Adults" citations, 1973, for *The Friends,* 1976, for *Ruby,* 1978, for *Edith Jackson,* 1979, for *The Disappearance,* and 1981, for *Mirror of Her Own;* "Children's Book of the Year" citations from Child Study Association, 1973, for *The Friends,* and 1986, for *Paris, Pee Wee, and Big Dog;* "Outstanding Book of the Year" citation from the *New York Times,* 1973, for *The Friends,* and 1979, for *The Disappearance; The Friends* was selected one of *School Library Journal*'s "Best of the Best" Books, 1979; *The Disappearance* and *Edith Jackson* were selected among the New York Public Library's Books for the Teen Age, 1980, 1981, and 1982; Coretta Scott King award, 1982, for *Mother Crocodile;* Parents' Choice award for Literature from the Parents' Choice Foundation, 1983, for *New Guys around the Block;* Other award, 1987, for *My Love, My Love; or, The Peasant Girl.* Agent: Ellen Levine Literary Agency, Inc., 432 Park Ave. S., Suite 1205, New York, NY 10016.

PUBLICATIONS FOR YOUNG ADULTS

Fiction

Bird at My Window. Philadelphia, Lippincott, and London, Souvenir Press, 1966.
The Friends. New York, Holt, Rinehart, 1973; London, Gollancz, 1974.
Ruby. New York, Viking Press, 1976; London, Gollancz, 1981.
Edith Jackson. New York, Viking Press, 1978; London, Gollancz, 1979.
The Disappearance. New York, Delacorte Press, 1979; London, Gollancz, 1980.
Mirror of Her Own. New York, Delacorte Press, 1981.

New Guys around the Block. New York, Delacorte Press, and London, Gollancz, 1983.

Paris, Pee Wee, and Big Dog, illustrated by Caroline Binch. New York, Delacorte Press, and London, Gollancz, 1984.

And I Heard a Bird Sing. New York, Delacorte Press, and London, Gollancz, 1987.

The Ups and Downs of Carl Davis III. New York, Delacorte Press, 1989.

Billy the Great, illustrated by Caroline Binch. New York, Doubleday, 1992.

The Music of Summer. New York, Delacorte Press, 1992.

Other

Translator, *Mother Crocodile: An Uncle Amadou Tale from Senegal,* illustrated by John Steptoe. New York, Delacorte Press, 1981.

PUBLICATIONS FOR ADULTS

Novels

A Measure of Time. New York, Holt, Rinehart, 1983; London, Virago Press, 1984.

My Love, My Love; or, The Peasant Girl. New York, Holt, Rinehart, 1985; London, Virago Press, 1987.

Play

Venetian Blinds (produced at Topical Theatre, New York, 1954).

Other

Editor, *Children of Longing.* New York, Holt, Rinehart, 1971.

Contributor to *Ten Times Black,* edited by Julian Mayfield, New York, Bantam, 1972; and to *Sixteen: Short Stories by Outstanding Writers for Young Adults,* edited by Donald R. Gallo, New York, Delacorte, 1984.

*

Media Adaptations: *The Friends* (documentary), Thames Television, 1984.

Biography: Entry in *Dictionary of Literary Biography* Volume 33: *Afro-American Fiction Writers after 1955.* Detroit, Gale, 1984; essay in *Speaking for Ourselves: Autobiographical Sketches by Notable Authors of Books for Young Adults,* Volume 1, compiled and edited by Donald R. Gallo, National Council of Teachers of English, 1990.

Critical Studies: Entry in *Children's Literature Review,* Volume 13, Detroit, Gale, 1987; entry in *Contemporary Literary Criticism,* Volume 26, Detroit, Gale, 1983.

*   *   *

In a voice full of probing and anguished sensitivity, Rosa Guy examines the intersection of race and class in twentieth-century urban America. The lives of the forgotten ones haunt her world,

taking and shaping for themselves identities which society would deny and destroy. The civilizing influence at the heart of her books is a call to compassion, a sustained imperative to care for one another, well and deeply and across all boundaries.

In her singular attention to the realities of inner-city adolescence, Rosa Guy claims a courageous place among contemporaries. Her stories demonstrate where and when the nation's vision fails its children, and the best of them illuminate the dark underside of the middle-class dream, laying bare the horrible irony of living with so little alongside those who seem to have so much. Poverty is the fault line shattering the lives of Guy's characters, turning friend against friend, neighbor against neighbor, brother against brother. While she tells the stories of those who survive, she never forgets and cannot condemn those who do not. A deep and empathic understanding of the forces which shape young lives informs Rosa Guy's work, shining like signal fire from the depths of her writer's soul.

Love is her fundamental concern. Her books beg the question of how love survives in the face of fear, poverty, betrayal, and hatred. *Edith Jackson* finds an answer in its heroine, an orphaned schoolgirl whose deep and responsible concern for siblings forms the story's moral compass. In a world where caring cannot logically endure, Edith roots like a sapling in cement, sprouting tough green shoots of growth.

Bird at My Window is another of Rosa Guy's sinewy, spiritual hymns to the lives of the ghetto born. Crushing poverty and prejudice strip Wade Williams of everything but his will to live, leaving him with little to live for in the end. The novel traces his descent into madness, borne of agonizing rejection by whites unwilling to tolerate the presence of a gifted black boy in their school. He is the brilliant fruit, ripened past season, falling heavy and far from the tree of life. He symbolizes all who live and die facelessly, their talents untapped, in the reaches of the inner city. If they are to survive, Rosa Guy's characters reach inside to that place where trust and love lie inviolate. Imamu Jones, the teenage hero of *The Disappearance, New Guys around the Block,* and *And I Heard a Bird Sing,* finds in himself the compassion to nurse an alcoholic mother, the courage to reveal the stunning blood-guilt of a murdering friend, and the strength to face down his own emerging adolescent fears. Because Imamu cares, he is horrified by the eruptions of violence which mark the passing of days in his neighborhood. Caring will disturb his dreams, cast long shadows on his waking hours, but sear pain and understanding permanently into his soul. Imamu will move out of the ghetto, but his destiny is bound to the lives of those who cannot.

Guy's stories invariably raise the disturbing question of race consciousness in America. Readers unfamiliar with her kind of relentless portrayal of inner-city devastation will find these books a harrowing surprise. A nightmarish sense of unreality pervades, in particular, the setting of *New Guys around the Block,* where homeless addicts live and raise children in burned out and deserted rubble-strewn buildings. In *Edith Jackson* a young orphaned woman is charged with the care of her siblings. Rosa Guy claims these young ones and celebrates survival in spite of all odds, claiming each success as her own, fixing our sights on the drama played out daily in the streets of the forgotten neighborhoods.

Into the same cloth as somber strains of death, loss, and betrayal, Guy deftly weaves the lighter elements of a comic touch, the poignant and aching excitement of a first love's stirring. The schoolboy hero of *The Ups and Downs of Carl Davis III* takes readers along for a magic carpet ride, inviting us to forget the tough streets he's left behind, while the adventurous *Paris, Pee Wee, and Big Dog* entertains mightily back in the big city. The laughter which Phyllisia and Edith share in *The Friends* echoes up and down the streets of New York City, pealing like bells, healing the loneliness of their separate lives. *Ruby*'s young lovers share the same secret; in one another's company they are safe, they are real, they know joy at last.

Guy's ear attends with delight to the snap and sensuousness of young adult dialogue, idiom, and inflection, whether the visceral jive of the street, the low, mourning cadence of disappointment, or the half-trembling voice of a teenager coming square up against life and authority. This is the sound of life happening all around, never stopping, always rushing on, and rushing in. Her heroes and heroines are compassionate, although they have seen much that is inhumane. They are doers and thinkers, feelers and believers. They are dreamers and lovers, sons and daughters, sisters and brothers. They are all of us.

—Laurie Ann Eno

H

HALAM, Ann. Pseudonym for Gwyneth A. Jones. British. Born in Manchester, Lancashire, 14 February 1952. Educated at the University of Sussex, Brighton, B.A. (honors) 1973. Married Peter Gwilliam in 1976; one son. Executive officer, Manpower Services Commission, Hove, Sussex, 1975-77; author of books for young people, since 1977. Recipient: First prize from *Manchester Evening News* children's story competition, 1967, for "The Christmas Church Mice"; runner-up for Guardian Children's Fiction award, 1981, for *Dear Hill.* Agent: Herta Ryder, c/o Toby Eady Associates, 7 Gledhow Gardens, London SW5 0BL. Address: 139 Ditchling Rise, Brighton, East Sussex BN1 4QQ, England.

PUBLICATIONS FOR YOUNG ADULTS

Fiction

The Alder Tree. London, Allen & Unwin, 1982.
King Death's Garden. London, Orchard, 1986.
The Daymaker. London, Orchard, 1987.
Transformations. London, Orchard, 1988.
The Skybreaker. London, Orchard, 1990.

Fiction as Gwyneth A. Jones

Water in the Air. London, Macmillan, and New York, Macmillan, 1977.
The Influence of Ironwood. London, Macmillan, 1978.
The Exchange. London, Macmillan, 1979.
The Hidden Ones. London, Women's Press, 1988.

PUBLICATIONS FOR CHILDREN

Fiction

Dear Hill. London, Macmillan, 1980.
Ally Ally, Aster. London, Allen & Unwin, 1981.

PUBLICATIONS FOR ADULTS

Novels as Gwyneth A. Jones

Divine Endurance. London, Allen & Unwin, 1984; New York, Arbor House, 1987.
Escape Plans. London, Allen & Unwin, 1986.
Kairos. London, Unwin Hyman, 1988.
White Queen. New York, Tor, 1993.

*　　*　　*

Gwyneth Jones did not intend to write under a pen name. Having published several critically acclaimed children's books, she wrote *Ally Ally, Aster* which was rejected by her publisher, and when another publisher accepted it she adopted a surname from her family tree. Her new publishers, Allen and Unwin, also encouraged her ambition to write adult SF for their own list, and so she decided to write all her children's books as "Ann Halam," and use her real name for her adult fiction. This essay will consider "Ann Halam's" books for twelve plus: *King Death's Garden,* the Daymaker trilogy, and her young adult novel *The Hidden Ones.* I shall not consider her four adult SF novels as YA reading, being complex in argument and exotic in their treatment of sexuality, written for experienced SF readers and not the kind of adult SF which bridges the gap to adult reading. (For a comparison, they are "harder" to read than Ursula Le Guin's adult SF such as *The Left Hand of Darkness.*)

King Death's Garden came after a gap of four years spent writing adult SF. Having changed children's publisher again, she revealed her identity, resolving the mystery of where the talented children's author Gwyneth Jones had gone! *King Death's Garden* is set in Brighton, where she lives, and a cemetery there. Maurice, a lonely asthmatic boy, is sent to stay with his great aunt who lives by the cemetery in the house left to her in the will of an eccentric scientist, to whom she was housekeeper. Maurice discovers traces of his research: gradually a sinister picture is built up, for this is neither fantasy nor science fiction, but a ghost story with a chilling climax. Maurice won't give up following the Professor's trail: he is too absorbed in the strange dreams which come to him whenever he goes to a special part of the cemetery, "King Death's Garden." The Professor found out how to raise the dead, first by calling up their memories and then, unavoidably, their bodies. Maurice is increasingly aware of being spied on—haunted—and one evening he lingers too late in the cemetery and is nearly trapped forever...an excellent evocation of the spirit of the M.R. James ghost stories, and a warning against letting one's obsessions take over.

Ann Halam's next work for young people was a major science fantasy trilogy, the "Inland" or "Daymaker" series. As with much children's SF, it is set in a future where twentieth-century civilisation has collapsed and humankind has revived a mediaeval way of life. About three centuries ahead of ours, this great disaster came about through the exhaustion of all modern ways of producing energy, particularly electricity. Instead, women have rediscovered magic, which keeps the desolation of the destroyed world at bay, and only works as long as people do not turn back to science. In *The Daymaker* our heroine Zanne is found to have strong magical powers, and so is sent to magic school to learn to use them for society's good, eventually to become a Covener, the head of a community who supervises the use of magic in that locality. This has obvious affinities with the education of the rebel Ged in *A Wizard of Earthsea,* including the acts of defiance which indicate that the hero/ine has a special destiny to fulfil.

Zanne is attracted by machines left over from the age of technology and tempted to make them work again (by magic instead of electricity). This results in the gradual drying-up of magic in her area: crops fail and a bridge repaired with magic starts to crack up. The village folk smash the machines, but Zanne still hasn't learned her lesson; she runs away to the "badlands" to find a rumoured Daymaker (i.e. electric power station) to set it going by magic. Just in time she learns that this would neutralise everyone else's magic powers, and her whole country of "Inland" would lose its fertility.

In *Transformations,* set four years later, Zanne is sent to the mountainous region of Minith to find and destroy another Daymaker. The puritanical sect of miners inhabiting the mountains refuses to help her: they would rather suffer blighted lives than reveal the truth to a stranger. This blight affects teenagers most, and we meet Sirato, a lonely girl whom Zanne befriends, and who dreams she is turning into a rat. In the first chilling climax, Zanne and Sirato watch how the teenagers are temporarily transformed into monsters by an evil power lurking in the old mines, and Zanne exercises magic to pull Sirato back from her shape-change. She explains to Sirato that: "The people of the past...were able to reach into the depth of being, where all the forms are destroyed and reborn and change into each other. They found there a power that belongs neither to them nor to us....They took that force and made it work for them, made it heat water and turn wheels. But when they'd taken what they wanted, what was left over was poison to them...they hid it away, buried it under a mountain..."

The reader must put a name to the evil (nuclear waste) which in Inland causes both magical transformations as well as lingering death. Even when Zanne explains it to the miners and offers her help, their fanaticism insists that they refuse and try to kill her: but all ends well.

In *The Skybreaker* Zanne has a companion, Holne of Minith, once one of the transformed teenagers, now training as a Covener. They travel by sea to Magia, where they have heard rumours of a "skybreaker." If Inland, Zanne's home, is our England, then Magia corresponds to the Netherlands and North Germany. Zanne finds a European city culture where magic is harnessed centrally by the constant repetition of formulae (recalling the mediaeval church) to maintain the network of waterways and hold back the sea. This production line has generated extra magic which the Great Mage, Lady Monkshood, has siphoned off, not to awake a "skybreaker" from the olden days but to manufacture a new one: to fly through space by magic. Zanne realises that the launch and flight of the rocket would destroy the magic networks of the whole world, while its very existence has already caused Holne to revert to his beast-shape.

The Daymaker trilogy is an outstanding achievement in the genre. Ann Halam's style rises to the challenge of describing the supernatural effects Zanne encounters; and each book can stand several re-readings, yielding different pleasures when the reader knows ahead of Zanne the identity of each mysterious menace. Then there is the riddle of guessing each location, though Gwyneth Jones has told me that "Inland" is not intended to be superimposed precisely on a map of England. Nevertheless, Zanne's home is somewhere in the West Midlands, the "Flying Road" camp might be Spaghetti Junction near Birmingham, and Minith is meant to be North Wales, where indeed there is a nuclear power station. The capital of Magia is The Hague, and the rocket-launching site Endemunde, where in the text "That lovely silver flame, *skybreaker*, had been born as an instrument of death," corresponds to Peenemünde, where the Nazis tested their V-rockets. This then accounts for Magia's totalitarianism and the dominance of the Great Mage.

The trilogy is also relevant to current socio-economic concerns. Ann Halam describes a world where the equality of the sexes, and sometimes the superiority of women, is natural (as are strong differences in skin colour); and a world where the results of the twentieth-century demand for electricity, disregarding consequent pollution, are dramatically brought home—and of course in the real world magic cannot come to our aid.

Finally *The Hidden Ones* is set in our world, now, and was published under her own name as a "feminist" young adult novel. Adele, a fifteen-year-old, has telekinetic powers: alienated from her family since her parents each remarried, she uses her powers mainly to get revenge on people she hates. Back with her father for one last chance at family life, she begins to receive supernatural messages from a secret grove in the woods, a store of rare earths threatened by miners, crying for help. This is a most detailed and sympathetic study of an alienated teenager within an original SF plot: not just SF by a woman, but feminist SF. Although Gwyneth Jones is now extremely popular with readers of adult SF, she will continue writing as "Ann Halam": each of her books is a little gem: no pot-boilers for her.

—Jessica Yates

HALL, Barbara. American. Born in Danville, Virginia, 17 July 1960. Educated at James Madison University, Harrisonburg, Virginia, B.A. 1982. Married Nick Harding in 1985; one daughter. Screenwriter for television, Los Angeles, California, since 1982; writer/developer, Castle Rock Entertainment; children's writer. Recipient: *Booklist* editors list citation, *School Library Journal*'s Ten Best of Books of 1990 citation, American Library Association Notable Book and Best Books of 1990 citations, all 1990, for *Dixie Storms;* ALA Best Books for Reluctant Readers citation, 1992, for *Fool's Hill;* Humanities award, 1992, for "Comfort and Joy," episode of *I'll Fly Away.* Agent: Cynthia Manson, 444 East 86th St., New York, NY 10028. Address: 10720 Le Conte Ave., Los Angeles, CA 90024, U.S.A.

PUBLICATIONS FOR YOUNG ADULTS

Fiction

Skeeball and the Secret of the Universe. New York, Richard Jackson/Orchard Books, 1987.
Dixie Storms. Orlando, Florida, Harcourt, 1990.
Fool's Hill. New York, Bantam, 1992.

Screenplays (television episodes)

Story editor, *Newhart.* CBS, 1982-83.
Executive story editor, *A Year in the Life.* NBC, 1986-87.
Producer, *Moonlighting.* ABC, 1989.
Producer, *Anything but Love.* ABC, 1990.
Co-executive producer, *I'll Fly Away.* NBC, 1992.
Creative consultant, *Northern Exposure.* CBS, 1993—.

Barbara Hall comments:

I've heard that a writer keeps writing about any part of his or her life which is unresolved. That certainly has something to do with why I write about adolescence. Every time I explore that age, I have the opportunity to go back and fix something that never got fixed, confront someone I never confronted, or reaffirm a desire or conviction that I possessed back then, and might be in danger of losing.

*   *   *

In Barbara Hall's first novel, *Skeeball and the Secret of the Universe*, Matty Collier, a rebel without a cause in his own right who idolizes James Dean and spends the summer before his final year of high school searching for "the Thing," thinks and talks a lot about teenage angst: "I was all the time praying to something that had no name, that had no real definition in my mind at all. More than anything else, I prayed to this feeling I had that there was some kind of great pattern, the one that kept things from falling apart, that rescued kids like me from working in a hot-dog joint." Who hasn't felt this way? In *Skeeball* and her two other novels, *Dixie Storms* and *Fool's Hill*, Hall presents common coming-of-age questions about self-identity, personal purpose, and interpersonal relationships through the stories of memorable, likeable characters like Matty. The constraints and standard peculiarities of small town or rural life influence these young people's quests; in fact, setting is a key component of their world views. Hall's novels are driven by character, action, and emotion in a scene-to-scene construction that makes the overall experience of them not unlike the experience of television drama.

As in teledramas, where stories are told largely through the things characters do and say rather than through significant exploration of the inner life a character might have but for which there is little or no visual evidence, Hall's novels present character and action as two sides of the same coin. Her characters are not without "mind life"; certainly each presents his or her own reasoned outlook and musings. But for the most part, Hall depends on plot action to motivate and reveal. The characters—genuine, strongly voiced, and often funny— begin with a premise of what they believe their lives should be like, which is then tested by reality. Matty, an only child who discovers he is the "accident" that caused his parents to marry as teenagers, bounces like one of his beloved skeeballs around his small, beach resort hometown with idealistic disdain for the inevitable responsibilities of adulthood. He believes that jobs, marriage, and families cause people to give up and glaze over before they have discovered and experienced that which gives their lives unique purpose. In *Dixie Storms*, Dutch Peyton is an empathetic mix of woman and child. Without a mother, Dutch lives on a Virginia farm with her hard-working father, a difficult adult brother whose wife has left him with their young son, and a nervous aunt. Dutch is responsible and practical to a fault, taking on the weight of household duties and looking after her wise-cracking, trouble-making nephew. But she is uncertain about matters of growing up and yearns for someone to show her the way. Finally, in *Fool's Hill*, Hall presents eager-to-please Libby, who from her vantage point in a small rural Virginia town, sees the world as being made up of the people who fall down (plain, awkward people like herself) and the people who laugh at them (perfect people like her older sister Gloria). With Gloria away in Chicago, which to Libby is as much an exotic idea as it is a place, she spends the summer trying to become a "laugher" and gets mixed up with the wrong crowd in the process.

What these characters have in common, and what makes them interesting and easy to identify with, is a quality of loneliness. They stand somewhat outside the circle of their peers and, to some extent, seem removed even from their own situations. As a result, they possess both a real longing to be a part of a meaningful whole and a special ability to comment on the adolescent condition. In each novel, Hall heightens plot tension by bringing in an outsider— a beautiful summer tourist, a worldly cousin, a pair of rough and tumble sisters willing to take a "faller" along for the ride. The technique provides contrast for her characters' positions and increases their sense of isolation. Hall links this character isolation

with small town settings, which are knowingly created and full of local sound and color. Sense of place is most convincing in *Dixie Storms*, where she fleshes out the relationship between modern farming families and their land. Using the theme of "The Country Mouse and the City Mouse," she brings in Dutch's city cousin Norma, who seems for a time to be everything Dutch wishes to become. Hall drops the fable's moralism, however, and gives it an original twist: even after Norma's superior facade crumbles, revealing undesirable superficial qualities, Dutch finds that it is still possible to like her.

Hall's novels appeal to emotions more often than to intellect. In each, she uses a teledrama-like method of setting up a scene where the balance of forces has been upset. There are no accidents or coincidences and few surprises. Secondary characters serve mainly to advance the main character's story to the climactic point where his or her false goal is revealed and new understanding is reached: Matty realizes that doing something important to him and doing it well is the "Thing"; Dutch learns to accept that people—herself included—can't always live up to her "hard hopes" of them; Libby finds, too, that there are no perfect people and that being herself takes courage but is right for the long run. Forces are brought back into balance. Hall's is an efficient method of storytelling and, on an emotional level, it satisfies.

—Tracy J. Sukraw

———

HALL, Lynn. American. Born in Lombard, Illinois, 9 November 1937. Educated at schools in Iowa. Married Dean W. Green in 1960 (divorced 1961). Secretary, Fort Worth, Texas, 1955-57; secretary and veterinarian's assistant in Des Moines, Iowa, 1957-66; copywriter, Ambro Advertising Agency, Des Moines 1966-68. Since 1969 full-time writer. Recipient: Book of the year selections from Child Study Association of America include *Ride a Wild Dream*, 1969, *Too Near the Sun*, 1970, *Gently Touch the Milkweed*, 1970, *To Catch a Tartar*, 1973, *Barry the Bravest St. Bernard*, 1973, *New Day for Dragon*, 1975, *Just One Friend*, 1985, and *Mrs. Portree's Pony*, 1987; Charles W. Follett award, 1971, for *A Horse Called Dragon*; Best Young Adult Books selections by American Library Association, 1972, for *Sticks and Stones*, 1980, for *The Leaving*, and 1984, for *Uphill All the Way*; Netherlands' Silver Quill award, 1976, for *Sticks and Stones*; Edgar Allan Poe award runner up from the Mystery Writers of America, 1980, for *The Whispered Horse*; *The Leaving* was selected as one of the best young adult books by American Library Association, 1980, received the *Boston Globe-Horn Book* award for fiction, 1981, and was selected as one of New York Public Library's books for teenagers, 1981 and 1982; Tennessee Children's Choice award from Tennessee Library Association, 1981, for *Shadows*; *The Horse Trader* was selected as one of New York Public Library's books for teenagers 1982; *Uphill All the Way* was selected as one of the best young adult books by American Library Association, 1984; *Tazo and Me* was selected an Outstanding Science Trade Book for Children by the National Science Teachers Association and the Children's Book Council, 1985; Golden Kite award Honor Book for Fiction from the Society of Children's Book Writers, 1986, for *The Solitary*; Children's Literature award from the Society of Midland Authors, 1987, for *Mrs. Portree's Pony*; Johnson Brigham award from the Iowa State Historical Society, 1989, for *The Secret Life of Dagmar Schultz*. Address: Touch-wood, Route 2, Elkader, IA 52043, U.S.A.

Fiction

The Shy Ones, illustrated by Greta Elgaard. Chicago, Follett, 1967.

Gently Touch the Milkweed, illustrated by Rod Ruth. Chicago, Follett, 1970.

Too Near the Sun, illustrated by Stefan Martin. Chicago, Follett, 1970.

A Horse Called Dragon, illustrated by Joseph Cellini. Chicago, Follett, 1971; as *Wild Mustang,* New York, Scholastic, 1976.

Dog Stories, illustrated by Joseph Cellini. Chicago, Follett, 1972.

The Siege of Silent Henry. Chicago, Follett, 1972.

Sticks and Stones, illustrated by Milton Glaser. Chicago, Follett, 1972.

Riff Remember. Chicago, Follett, 1973.

Troublemaker, illustrated by Joseph Cellini. Chicago, Follett, 1974.

New Day for Dragon, illustrated by Joseph Cellini. Chicago, Follett, 1975.

Flowers of Anger, illustrated by Joseph Cellini. Chicago, Follett, 1976.

Dragon Defiant, illustrated by Joseph Cellini. Chicago, Follett, 1977.

Shadows, illustrated by Joseph Cellini. Chicago, Follett, 1977.

Dog of the Bondi Castle, illustrated by Michael Mariano. Chicago, Follett, 1979.

The Whispered Horse. Chicago, Follett, 1979.

The Leaving, illustrated by Lloyd Bloom. New York, Scribner, 1980.

Danza!, illustrated by Sandra Rabinowitz. New York, Scribner, 1981.

Dragon's Delight. Chicago, Follett, 1981.

The Ghost of the Great River Inn, illustrated by Allen Davis. Chicago, Follett, 1981.

The Horse Trader, illustrated by Ted Lewin. New York, Scribner, 1981.

Half the Battle. New York, Scribner, 1982.

Tin Can Tucker, illustrated by Ruth Sanderson. New York, Scribner, 1982.

Denison's Daughter. New York, Scribner, 1983.

The Boy in the Off-White Hat. New York, Scribner, 1984.

Uphill All the Way. New York, Scribner, 1984.

The Giver. New York, Scribner, 1985; London, Macmillan, 1987.

Just One Friend. New York, Scribner, 1985.

The Something-Special Horse, illustrated by Sandy Rabinowitz. New York, Scribner, 1985.

Danger Dog. New York, Scribner, 1986.

If Winter Comes. New York, Scribner, 1986; London, Viking Kestrel, 1987.

Mrs. Portree's Pony. New York, Scribner, 1986.

The Solitary. New York, Scribner, 1986; London, Viking, 1988.

Flyaway. New York, Scribner, 1987.

In Trouble Again Zelda Hammersmith?, illustrated by Ray Cruz. San Diego, Harcourt Brace, 1987.

Letting Go. New York, Scribner, 1987.

Ride a Dark Horse. New York, Morrow, 1987.

Dagmar Schultz and the Powers of Darkness. New York, Scribner, 1988.

A Killing Freeze. New York, Morrow, 1988.

Murder at the Spaniel Show. New York, Scribner, 1988.

The Secret Life of Dagmar Schultz. New York, Scribner, 1988.

Zelda Strikes Again! San Diego, Harcourt Brace, 1988.

Dagmar Schultz and the Angel Edna. New York, Scribner, 1989.

Here Comes Zelda Claus and Other Holiday Disasters. San Diego, Harcourt Brace, 1989.

Where Have All the Tigers Gone? New York, Scribner, 1989.

Fair Maiden. New York, Scribner, 1990.

Halsey's Pride. New York, Scribner, 1990.

Murder in a Pig's Eye. San Diego, Harcourt Brace, 1990.

The Tormentors. San Diego, Harcourt Brace, 1990.

Dagmar Schultz and the Green-Eyed Monster. New York, Scribner, 1991.

Flying Changes. San Diego, Harcourt Brace, 1991.

The Soul of the Silver Dog. San Diego, Harcourt Brace, 1992.

Windsong. New York, Scribner, 1992.

Fiction

The Secret of Stonehouse, illustrated by Joseph Cellini. Chicago, Follett, 1968.

Ride a Wild Dream, illustrated by George Roth. Chicago, Follett, 1969.

The Famous Battle of Bravery Creek. Champaign, Illinois, Garrard, 1972.

Barry the Bravest St. Bernard, illustrated by Richard Amundsen. Champaign, Illinois, Garrard, 1973.

Flash Dog of Old Egypt, illustrated by Taylor Oughton. Champaign, Illinois, Garrard, 1973.

To Catch a Tartar, illustrated by Joseph Cellini. Chicago, Follett, 1973.

Bob Watchdog of the River, illustrated by Taylor Oughton. Champaign, Illinois, Garrard, 1974.

The Stray, illustrated by Joseph Cellini. Chicago, Follett, 1974.

Captain: Canada's Flying Pony, illustrated by Tran Mawicke. Champaign, Illinois, Garrard, 1976.

Owney the Traveling Dog, illustrated by Barbara Erikson. Champaign, Illinois, Garrard, 1977.

The Mystery of Pony Hollow, illustrated by Ruth Sanderson. Champaign, Illinois, Garrard, 1978.

The Mystery of the Lost and Found Hound, illustrated by Alan Daniel. Champaign, Illinois, Garrard, 1979.

The Mystery of the Schoolhouse Dog, illustrated by William Hutchinson. Champaign, Illinois, Garrard, 1979.

The Mystery of the Plum Park Pony, illustrated by Alan Daniel. Champaign, Illinois, Garrard, 1980.

The Mystery of the Stubborn Old Man, illustrated by Herman Vestal. Champaign, Illinois, Garrard, 1980.

The Disappearing Grandad, illustrated by William Jefferson. Chicago, Follett, 1981.

The Haunting of the Green Bird, illustrated by David Cunningham. Chicago, Follett, 1981.

The Mysterious Moortown Bridge, illustrated by Ruth Sanderson. Chicago, Follett, 1981.

The Mystery of the Caramel Cat, illustrated by Ruth Sanderson. Champaign, Illinois, Garrard, 1981.

Megan's Mare. New York, Scribner, 1983.
The Mystery of Pony Hollow Panda, illustrated by William Hutchinson. Champaign, Illinois, Garrard, 1983.

Nonfiction

Kids and Dog Shows. Chicago, Follett, 1975.
Careers for Dog Lovers. Chicago, Follett, 1978.
Tazo and Me, photographs by Jan Hall. New York, Scribner, 1985.

*

Biography: Essay in *Something about the Author Autobiography Series,* Volume 4, Detroit, Gale, 1987; essay in *Speaking for Ourselves: Autobiographical Sketches by Notable Authors of Books for Young Adults,* Volume 1, compiled and edited by Donald R. Gallo, National Council of Teachers of English, 1990.

Manuscript Collection: Kerlan Collection, University of Minnesota, Minneapolis.

*   *   *

A prolific author of books for young adults, Lynn Hall specializes in gentle and well-detailed stories about young people coming of age and their family relationships.

Hall shows her experience as a professional dog handler in the quietly written *The Shy Ones,* the story of Robin, a young girl so painfully shy she is without friends at school, a situation that worries her parents. Taming a lost, hurt, golden retriever leads Robin outside of her shyness: first she gets a job with the veterinarian who mends the dog, and then she unexpectedly finds a boyfriend while she is standing in front of the local drugstore teaching the dog not to fear people. When the dog turns out to be purebred and to have an owner, Robin conquers her fear, defies the dog's abusive owner, and shows the dog. Robin is a realistic character, and the reader is drawn to empathize with her struggle to accept both herself and her shyness while longing to be like the other teens around her. Her emergence from her shell is profoundly moving.

Flyaway is the story of seventeen-year-old Ariel, her younger sister, Robin, and their dysfunctional family. The father is a disguised dictator, perfect in the public eye but ruthless in his control of the family. Ariel's mother is so dominated that she betrays Ariel in her first bid for freedom. Ariel and Robin both hate their father but choose different ways to escape his control. Ariel works secretly, debating marriage and looking for a job. Robin, pushed to the breaking point, runs away with the father of her best friend and turns to prostitution. While well-written, *Flyaway* is not an easy book. The things that go unsaid by Hall are the more difficult for the unspoken understandings. Ariel is a determined character, but without the sharp edge of desperation that drives her sister to an even uglier life than the one with her family. When Ariel finally escapes her father's domination by selling the skis that previously had been her escape, relief is mixed with anxiety for the remaining child, alone and unsupported in the empty home.

In *Fair Maiden,* Hall uses a Renaissance fair as the setting for a teenager's first love, weaving the fantasy of the fair into Jenny's feelings for the man she hardly knows in real life but who, as John the Lutanist, is everything she dreamed. John has a history of falling in love with young girls, but Jenny is the first with whom he

is intimate, and instead of Jenny ending the relationship, John does, afraid of the reality of what they have done.

Hall again uses a dog theme in *Halsey's Pride,* in which thirteen-year-old March moves in with her father, a breeder of purebred collies, after her mother's new husband rejects her. March falls in love with her father's prized stud dog, Halsey's Pride, who returns March's love with the uncritical adoration March wants from her father. When Pride's puppies prove to have a genetic flaw, proving Pride is not as good as her father believes, March learns the hard lesson of acceptance that her father has failed to find.

A pony is the animal catalyst in *Mrs. Portree's Pony.* Addie Harvey finds herself an unwanted foster child until she comes upon a pony who belonged to the long-gone daughter of a local recluse. Addie and Mrs. Portree strike up a friendship, and the two find love and support in each other when Addie is eventually asked to leave her foster home.

Hall changes gears in *Murder in a Pig's Eye,* a mystery set in farm country in Wisconsin. Bodie Tureen and his sister, Gracie, stumble on a mystery in their small town and set out to solve it. Along the way, Bodie manages nearly to get arrested and cut in half by a chain saw, and gets covered in pig manure. While amusing, this book lacks the character involvement of Hall's more serious works. The delicate details of character so readily available in *Flyaway* or *The Shy Ones* is lacking, and Hall strives so hard for humor that the characters never seem to experience actual growth.

Most of Hall's books are quick reads, perfect for a reluctant reader. The characters' problems are easily empathized with and involving. Hall's works describing unusual careers, hobbies, or settings are meticulously researched and rich in detail, teaching while at the same time telling a story.

—Melanie Belviso

———

HAMILTON, Virginia (Esther). American. Born in Yellow Springs, Ohio, 12 March 1936. Educated at Antioch College, Yellow Springs, 1952-55, B.A. 1955; Ohio State University, Columbus, 1957-58; New School for Social Research, New York, 1958-60. Married Arnold Adoff in 1960; one daughter and one son. Whittall Lecturer, Library of Congress, Washington, D.C., 1975; Visiting Professor, Queens College, Flushing, New York, 1986-87. Recipient: American Library Association's list of notable children's books of 1967, Nancy Block Memorial award of the Downtown Community School awards Committee, New York, both for *Zeely;* Edgar Allan Poe award for best juvenile mystery, 1969, for *The House of Dies Drear;* Ohioana Literary award, 1969; John Newbery Honor Book award, 1971, for *The Planet of Junior Brown;* Lewis Carroll Shelf award, *Boston Globe-Horn Book* award, 1974, John Newbery Medal and National Book award, both 1975, and Gustav-Heinemann-Friedinspreis fur kinder und Lugendbucher (Dusseldorf, Germany), 1991, all for *M.C. Higgins, the Great;* John Newbery Honor Book award, Coretta Scott King award, *Boston Globe-Horn Book* award, and American Book award nomination, all 1983, all for *Sweet Whispers, Brother Rush;* *Horn Book* Fanfare award in fiction, 1985, for *A Little Love;* Coretta Scott King award, *New York Times* Best Illustrated Children's Book award, Children's Book Bulletin Other award, and *Horn Book* Honor List selection, all 1986, all for *The People Could Fly: American Black Folktales;*

Boston Globe-Horn Book award, 1988, and Coretta Scott King award, 1989, both for *Anthony Burns: The Defeat and Triumph of a Fugitive Slave;* John Newbery Honor Book award, 1988, for *In the Beginning: Creation Stories from around the World;* Jane Addams Children's Book award, 1990, for *Anthony Burns;* Honorary Doctor of Humane Letters, Bank St. College, 1990; Catholic Library Association Regina Medal, 1990; Coretta Scott King award, 1992, for *The Bells of Christmas;* Hans Christian Andersen award U.S. nominee, 1992, for body of work. Agent: Arnold Adoff Agency, Box 293, Yellow Springs, OH 45387, U.S.A.

PUBLICATIONS FOR YOUNG ADULTS

Fiction

Zeely, illustrated by Symeon Shimin. New York, Macmillan, 1967.
The House of Dies Drear, illustrated by Eros Keith. New York, Macmillan, 1968.
The Planet of Junior Brown. New York, Macmillan, 1971; London, Gollancz, 1987.
M.C. Higgins, the Great. New York, Macmillan, 1974; London, Hamish Hamilton, 1975; published with teacher's guide by Lou Stanek, Dell, 1976.
Arilla Sun Down. New York, Greenwillow, 1976; London, Hamish Hamilton, 1977.
Justice and Her Brothers. New York, Greenwillow, 1978; London, Hamish Hamilton, 1979.
Dustland. New York, Greenwillow, and London, MacRae, 1980.
The Gathering. New York, Greenwillow, and London, MacRae, 1981.
Sweet Whispers, Brother Rush. New York, Philomel, 1982; London, Walker, 1987.
The Magical Adventures of Pretty Pearl. New York, Harper, 1983.
Willie Bea and the Time the Martians Landed. New York, Greenwillow, 1983.
A Little Love. New York, Philomel, 1984; London, Gollancz, 1985.
The Mystery of Drear House: The Conclusion of the Dies Drear Chronicle. New York, Greenwillow, 1987.
A White Romance. New York, Philomel, 1987; London, Gollancz, 1988.
Cousins. New York, Philomel, 1990.

Other

W.E.B. Du Bois: A Biography. New York, Crowell, 1972.
Paul Robeson: The Life and Times of a Free Black Man. New York, Harper, 1974.
Editor, *The Writings of W.E.B. Du Bois.* New York, Crowell, 1975.
The People Could Fly: American Black Folktales, illustrated by Leo and Diane Dillon. New York, Knopf, 1985; London, Walker, 1986; published with cassette, 1987.
Anthony Burns: The Defeat and Triumph of a Fugitive Slave. New York, Knopf, 1988.
In the Beginning: Creation Stories from around the World, illustrated by Barry Moser. San Diego, Harcourt Brace, 1988.
The Dark Way: Stories from the Spirit World, illustrated by Lambert Davis. San Diego, Harcourt Brace, 1990.
Many Thousand Gone: African Americans from Slavery to Freedom, illustrated by Leo and Diane Dillon. New York, Knopf, 1992.

PUBLICATIONS FOR CHILDREN

The Time-Ago Tales of Jahdu, illustrated by Nonny Hogrogian. New York, Macmillan, 1969.
Time-Ago Lost: More Tales of Jahdu, illustrated by Ray Prather. New York, Macmillan, 1973.
Jahdu, illustrated by Jerry Pinkney. New York, Greenwillow, 1980.
Junius over Far. New York, Harper, 1985.
Bells of Christmas, illustrated by Lambert Davis. San Diego, Harcourt Brace, 1989.
The All Jahdu Storybook, illustrated by Barry Moser. San Diego, Harcourt Brace, 1991.
Drylongso, illustrated by Jerry Pinkney. San Diego, Harcourt Brace, 1992.

*

Media Adaptations: *The House of Dies Drear* (television series, "Wonderworks"), Public Broadcasting Service, 1984.

Biography: Entry in *Dictionary of Literary Biography,* Volume 52: *American Writers for Children since 1960: Fiction,* Detroit, Gale, 1986, pp. 174-184; entry in *Dictionary of Literary Biography,* Volume 33: *Afro-American Fiction Writers after 1955,* Detroit, Gale, 1984, pp. 107-110; essay in *Speaking for Ourselves: Autobiographical Sketches by Notable Authors of Books for Young Adults,* Volume 1, compiled and edited by Donald R. Gallo, National Council of Teachers of English, 1990.

Critical Studies: Entry in *Children's Literature Review,* Volume 1, Detroit, Gale, 1976, and Volume 11, 1986; entry in *Contemporary Literary Criticism,* Volume 26, Detroit, Gale, 1983.

*   *   *

Virginia Hamilton is a gifted writer, known for her versatility and command of the art of storytelling. Her works encompass every genre of prose and all of them reflect her experiences as an African American.

The characters in her realistic fiction books are vividly drawn. *The Planet of Junior Brown* revolves around three memorably unique outcasts. Mr. Pool is the teacher turned custodian who attempts to teach the boys in his underground hideaway in the school basement. Junior Brown is a huge, dreamy, musically talented boy who is psychologically fragile. Buddy Clark serves as his foil: he is rooted in the day-to-day business of survival—his own. The development of the boys is bittersweet; as Junior Brown becomes increasingly psychotic, Buddy Clark ceases to think only of his own well-being and takes responsibility for his friend and the other homeless boys in his neighborhood, as well.

In *M.C. Higgins, the Great,* the protagonist is another striking character who continuously seeks a way to convince his parents to leave their ancestral home, Sarah's Mountain, because he fears that the spoil heap, a residue of strip-mining, will one day smother them all. One avenue of escape is the possibility that his mother's beautiful voice will be discovered. The characters in both stories are survivors, concerned with the safety of those they love.

Other characters deal with personal issues. Geeder (in *Zeely*) is a dreamy, imaginative girl who concludes that the statuesque daughter of her uncle's tenant farmer, Zeely, must be a Watusi queen.

Zeely herself helps Geeder grow in awareness of her own identity and appreciation for her African American heritage.

In *Cousins,* Cammy must cope with grief and guilt when her outwardly perfect cousin drowns accidentally. Hamilton convincingly portrays all sides of a child who is, by turns, devoted to her invalid grandmother and teenage brother, jealous of her bulimic cousin's perfection, and insecure about her own inadequacies. Although the complexity of some of Hamilton's books is difficult for young readers, this book is among the most accessible.

Another fictional character with strong appeal for young readers is Thomas Small. Small overcomes his fear of bizarre events to uncover the mystery of Drear House, a former station on the Underground Railroad in *The House of Dies Drear.*

Hamilton's characters ring true for many reasons. The characters are prototypes for children who wrestle with similar issues of searching for identity and place in the family. They also come to life through Hamilton's skillful use of dialogue and, when appropriate, dialect. For example, in *Cousins,* Cammy's language usage, typical of her age-mates, is continually corrected by Gram who mutters about what schools must be teaching these days.

The historical characters in Hamilton's biographies and historical fiction do not come to life as vividly as her fictional characters. A meticulous researcher, Hamilton relates the lives and accomplishments of DuBois, Robeson, and Brown without bringing them to life as she does with her fictional protagonists. An exception is the book *Many Thousand Gone* which provides true accounts of slaves who fled to freedom. Perhaps the recording of a single heroic act provides more cohesion than attempting to describe famous people with multiple accomplishments.

Just as her characters are convincingly developed, Hamilton's settings are varied but realistic. Although most of Hamilton's books are set near her Yellow Springs, Ohio home each imparts its own unique, vividly described flavor to the reader. *The House of Dies Drear* is a fine example; the tranquil college town stands in contrast to the impressive, yet forbidding Drear House. Hamilton brings to life the drafty old house riddled with secret passages and the tensions of countless slaves who hovered in its chambers poised between capture and freedom. The reader's awe parallels the Small family's as the underground chamber is revealed, filled with antique treasures.

The sights and sounds of the nursing home where Cammy visits Gram are as poignantly real as the classroom where a shrine of sorts is created for her drowned cousin. Likewise, the home of M.C. Higgins conveys images of isolated mountain hollows. In addition to visualizing M.C. swaying atop the flagpole in front of his home, Hamilton also provides readers with the metaphor of a boy who attempts to rise above the environmental disaster he fears.

Hamilton's talents as a writer are not restricted to fiction and nonfiction. As a folklorist, Hamilton weds her scholarly research with her gift for telling tales. *In the Beginning* demonstrates both the uniqueness and the universality of various cultures' explanations of how this world came to be. *The People Could Fly* is a noteworthy chronicle of the tales African slaves brought to this land and the stories that evolved during their enslavement. Many of the stories focused on the people's overwhelming desire for freedom—none more poignantly than the title story. Some of the stories incorporate Gullah dialect. The author's notes about the dialect and origin of the stories are a welcome addition.

Hamilton's Jadhu stories are literary folktales—born of the folk tradition but a product of the author's rich imagination. Originally, these stories were told in the framework of a caregiver who told stories to a little boy. Recently, Hamilton has streamlined the stories to make them more accessible to a contemporary audience.

Both the fantasy *Sweet Whispers, Brother Rush* and the historical *Anthony Burns: The Defeat and Triumph of a Fugitive Slave* employ a similar story-within-a-story device. In the former story, a young girl slips through a time warp to learn about her past; in the latter, an imprisoned victim of the Fugitive Slave Act evades his captors by retreating to childhood memories. Both of these books (along with *The Planet of Junior Brown*) reveal Hamilton's penchant for the surreal which may limit their appeal to less mature or culturally aware readers.

Many themes, motifs, and symbols recur in Hamilton's work. The themes of self-understanding and the importance of family are evident in many of her books. However, family does not always fit the traditional "father knows best" mold. Mothers are frequently distant and fathers often absent (as in *The Planet of Junior Brown; Sweet Whispers, Brother Rush;* and *Cousins*). On the other hand, *Drylongso* and *The House of Dies Drear* depict a "traditional" family. As a motif, music resonates in Hamilton's books, revealing her own musical background. Many main characters are musical—Junior Brown is a pianist, as is Mac Darrow in *The House of Dies Drear;* Drylongso plays a harmonica; M.C.'s mother sings and Cammy plays the piano, and her cousin plays it better in *Cousins.*

Another motif is that of the traveler. From *Zeely,* in which Geeder tells about the night traveler, to *Drylongso,* in which a mysterious boy brings an end to the drought, travel (whether physical or psychic like Junior Brown's and Tree's in *Sweet Whispers, Brother Rush*) plays a prominent role. The ultimate traveler is the slave who travels to freedom. Readers can thank Virginia Hamilton for freeing their minds by passing along her stories.

—Anne Drolett Creany

HARNETT, Cynthia (Mary). British. Born in London, 22 June 1893. Educated at private schools: Chelsea School of Art, London; studied with the artist G. Vernon Stokes. Author and illustrator of children's books, 1930-49, and of historical novels for young people, since 1949. Served in the British Censorship during both world wars. Recipient: Library Association Carnegie Medal, 1951, for *The Wool-Pack;* Spring Book Festival, 1954, for *The Drawbridge Gate;* Carnegie (commended) 1959, for *The Load of the Unicorn;* Spring Book Festival, 1973, for *The Writing on the Hearth. Died 25 October 1981.*

PUBLICATIONS FOR YOUNG ADULTS

Fiction

Junk, the Puppy, with G. Vernon Stokes, illustrated by the authors. London, Blackie, 1937.
The Pennymakers, with G. Vernon Stokes, illustrated by the authors. London, Eyre & Spottiswoode, 1937.
Velvet Mask, illustrated by G. Vernon Stokes. London, Medici Society, 1937.
Banjo, the Puppy, with G. Vernon Stokes, illustrated by the authors. London, Blackie, 1938.

To Be a Farmer's Boy, with G. Vernon Stokes, illustrated by the authors. London, Blackie, 1940.

Mountaineers, with G. Vernon Stokes, illustrated by the authors. London, Collins, 1941.

Mudlarks, with G. Vernon Stokes, illustrated by the authors. London, Collins, 1941.

Ducks and Drakes, with G. Vernon Stokes, illustrated by the authors. London, Collins, 1942.

Bob-Tail Pup, with G. Vernon Stokes, illustrated by the authors. London, Collins, 1944.

Sand Hoppers, with G. Vernon Stokes, illustrated by the authors. London, Collins, 1946.

Two and a Bit, with G. Vernon Stokes, illustrated by the authors. London, Collins, 1948.

Follow My Leader, with G. Vernon Stokes, illustrated by the authors. London, Collins, 1949.

The Great House, illustrated by the author. London, Methuen, 1949; Cleveland, World, 1968.

Pets Limited, with G. Vernon Stokes, illustrated by the authors. London, Collins, 1950.

The Wool-Pack, illustrated by the author. London, Methuen, 1951; as *Nicholas and the Woolpack,* New York, Putnam, 1953; as *The Merchant's Mark,* Minneapolis, Lerner, 1984.

Ring Out, Bow Bells!, illustrated by the author. London, Methuen, 1953; as *The Drawbridge Gate,* New York, Putnam, 1954; as *The Sign of the Green Falcon,* Minneapolis, Lerner, 1984.

The Green Popinjay, illustrated by the author. Oxford, Blackwell, 1955.

Stars of Fortune, illustrated by the author. London, Methuen, and New York, Putnam, 1956.

The Load of Unicorn, illustrated by the author. London, Methuen, 1959; as *Caxton's Challenge,* Cleveland, World, 1960; as *The Cargo of Madalena,* Minneapolis, Lerner, 1984.

A Fifteenth Century Wool Merchant, illustrated by the author. London, Oxford University Press, 1962, and New York, Clarendon Press, 1962.

The Writing on the Hearth, illustrated by Gareth Floyd. London, Methuen, 1971; New York, Viking Press, 1973.

Other

Editor, *In Praise of Dogs: An Anthology in Prose and Verse,* illustrated by G. Vernon Stokes. London, Country Life, 1936.

David's New World: The Making of a Sportsman, with G. Vernon Stokes, illustrated by the authors. London, Country Life, 1937.

Getting to Know Dogs, illustrated by G. Vernon Stokes. London, Collins, 1947.

Monasteries and Monks, illustrated by Edward Osmond. London, Batsford, 1963; Cincinnati, Ohio, Soccer Associates, 1965.

*   *   *

Cynthia Harnett's historical novels combine meticulous research and believable characters. For each of these stories, from her first attempts in *The Great House* to her final work, *The Writing on the Hearth,* Harnett spent long periods of time getting all the details right. The result is always an accurate portrayal of the English past, populated by real and likeable characters to whom interesting things happen.

Before publishing the series of historical novels for which she is best known, Harnett had collaborated with her cousin G. Vernon

Stokes on text and illustrations for a number of books for somewhat younger children. Her background as an illustrator greatly influenced the historical novels, where her method of bringing the past to life is primarily visual. Unlike many earlier practitioners of the historical genre for young readers, Harnett, along with Rosemary Sutcliff, Geoffrey Trease, and Henry Treece, strove for accuracy. She was especially interested in presenting ordinary people of other times, not merely the aristocracy and royalty. Harnett, even more than the other pioneers in good juvenile historical fiction, strove to make her readers *see* what her characters would have seen. Thus the objects and practices of the wool trade, or of early printing, or of castle life, are so accurate and so easy to visualize that history teachers often use Harnett's books as background reading for the medieval period.

The Great House, Harnett's first venture into the juvenile historical field, concerns architecture at the end of the seventeenth century—a period when much rebuilding was under way and new architectural styles came into vogue. Her beautifully detailed line drawings are carried out with the same meticulous accuracy as the text. Though the plot is somewhat thin, the characters, Barbara and Geoffrey and their architect father, are plausible. Countryside and London city life contrast nicely. Though well received, *The Great House* has never been as successful as Harnett's fifteenth-century novels, which spanned a period of more than twenty years.

Nicholas and the Wool-Pack, the first historical novel to win the Carnegie Medal, focuses on the only son of a wool trading family in the Cotswolds. The plot concerns Nicholas's efforts to find out what the Lombards and his father's employee, Simon Leach, are plotting; in the end, somewhat predictably, Nicholas and his friends succeed in solving the puzzle and clearing his father of a serious charge of wrongdoing. Along the way, Nicholas grows from irresponsible boy to steady young man and acquires a fiancée who is also an equal and a friend. The charm of the book, though, lies not so much in its tidy and satisfying plot as in its loving evocation of the Cotswolds and the wool trade in the fifteenth century. Harnett makes this information simply fascinating, from details of manufacture to economic exchanges to subtle class distinctions and how they influenced trade.

Caxton's Challenge (British title *The Load of Unicorn*) carries out the same general scheme of a young man unravelling a plot against a businessman and his enterprise, but this time it is Caxton and printing rather than the Fetterlocks and wool shipping. Again the characters belong to the various strata of the middle class, and again the details of the printing trade are revealed in compelling detail: the machinery, the terminology, the texts, and even, surprisingly, the paper. For paper, something which modern readers regard as cheap and always available, is at the center of the plot in this exciting story. *Stars of Fortune* and *Ring Out, Bow Bells!* depart from the basic Harnett plot line as they are based on the lives of real people (George Washington's ancestors in the reign of Queen Mary and Dick Whittington about 1415, respectively).

In her last book, which required ten years of research, Harnett returned to the mid fifteenth century and to the themes and general plot line of her two most successful historical novels. *The Writing on the Hearth* presents Stephen, a schoolboy on the estate of William de la Pole, Earl of Suffolk. The setting shifts from the Chiltern Hills to the bustle of London, with some particularly exciting scenes set along the river. Unlike earlier books, this one shows a good deal about intrigues and rivalries among the aristocracy, with de la Pole's wife, Alice (granddaughter of the poet Chaucer) involved in the central secret. Glimpses of fifteenth century schoolroom education of several kinds, and the lure of Oxford, also offer more variety than is usual with Harnett. As Harnett was nearly eighty when *The Writing on the Hearth* appeared, she did not illustrate the book herself; the drawings are by Gareth Floyd and, though adequate, they are by no means the equal of Harnett's own sensitive and charming illustrations in her previous works. Even the cover painting by Trina Schart Hyman for the American edition does not equal the perfect match of text and picture that the author herself had achieved.

Harnett announced that *The Writing on the Hearth* would be her last book, and it was. Several of the historical novels were reissued in 1984, and *Nicholas and the Wool-Pack* has been reprinted many times in paperback.

—Caroline C. Hunt

———

HASKINS, James S. Also writes as Jim Haskins. American. Born in Montgomery, Alabama, 19 September 1941. Educated at Georgetown University, Washington, D.C., B.A. 1960; Alabama State University, Montgomery, B.S. 1962; University of New Mexico, Alburquerque, M.A. 1963; New School for Social Research, New York, 1965-67; Queens College of the City University of New York, 1967-68. Stock trader, Smith Barney & Co., New York City, 1963-65; teacher, New York City Board of Education, New York City, 1966-68; visiting lecturer, New School for Social Research, New York City, 1970-72; associate professor, Staten Island Community College of the City University of New York, Staten Island, NY, 1970-77; professor of English, University of Florida, Gainsville, since 1977. Reporter, New York *Daily News*, 1963-64. Visiting lecturer, Elisabeth Irwin High School, 1971-73; visiting professor, Indiana University/Purdue University, Indianapolis, 1973-76; visiting professor, College of New Rochelle, 1977. Director, Union Mutual Life, Health and Accident Insurance, 1970-73. Member of board of advisors, Psi Systems, 1971-72; member of board of directors, Speedwell Services for Children, 1974-76. Member of Manhattan Community Board No. 9, 1972-73, academic council for the State University of New York, 1972-74, New York Urban League Manhattan Advisory Board, 1973-75, and National Education Advisory Committee and vice-director of Southeast Region of Statue of Liberty, Ellis Island Foundation, 1986. Consultant, Education Development Center, since 1975, Department of Health, Education and Welfare, 1977-79, National Research Council, 1979-80, and Grolier, Inc., 1979-82. Member of National Education Advisory Committee, Commission on the Bicentennial of the Constitution. Recipient: Notable children's book in the field of social studies citations from *Social Education*, 1971, for *Revolutionaries: Agents of Change*, from *Social Studies*, 1972, for *Resistance: Profiles in Nonviolence* and *Profiles in Black Power*, and 1973, for *A Piece of the Power: Four Black Mayors*, from National Council for the Social Studies-Children's Book Council Book Review Committee, 1975, for *Fighting Shirley Chisholm*, and 1976, for *The Creoles of Color of New Orleans* and *The Picture Life of Malcolm X*, from Children's Book Council, 1978, for *The Life and Death of Martin Luther King, Jr.;* World Book Year Book literature for children citiation, 1973, for *From Lew Alcindor to Kareem Abdul Jabbar;* Books of the Year citations, Child Study Association of America, 1974, for *Adam Clayton Powell* and *Street Gangs;* Books

for Brotherhood bibliography citation, National Council of Christians and Jews book review committee, 1975, for *Adam Clayton Powell: Portrait of a Marching Black;* Spur award finalist, Western Writers of America, 1975, for *The Creoles of Color of New Orleans;* Eighth Annual Coretta Scott King award, and Books Chosen by Children citation, Children's Book Council, both 1977, both for *The Story of Stevie Wonder;* Woodson Outstanding Merit award, National Council for the Social Studies, 1980, for *James Van Der Zee: The Picture-Takin' Man;* American Society of Composers, Authors and Publishers-Deems Taylor award, 1980, for *Scott Joplin: The Man Who Made Ragtime;* Ambassador of Honor book, English-Speaking Union Books-Across-the-Sea, 1983, for *Bricktop;* Coretta Scott King honorable mention, 1984, for *Lena Horne;* American Library Association (ALA) Best Book for Young Adults citation, 1987, for *Black Music in America;* Alabama Library Association best juvenile work citation, 1987, for "Count Your Way" series; "Bicentennial Reading, Viewing, Listening for Young Americans" citations, ALA and National Endowment for the Humanities, for *Street Gangs: Yesterday and Today, Ralph Bunche: A Most Reluctant Hero,* and *A Piece of the Power: Four Black Mayors;* certificates of appreciation, Joseph P. Kennedy Foundation, for work with the Special Olympics program; Coretta Scott King Book award, 1990, for *A Black Dance in America: A History through Its People.* Address: 325 West End Ave., Apt. 7D, New York, NY 10013, U.S.A.

PUBLICATIONS FOR YOUNG ADULTS

Fiction

Resistance: Profiles in Nonviolence. New York, Doubleday, 1970.
Religions. Philadelphia, Lippincott, 1971.
Revolutionaries: Agents of Change. Philadelphia, Lippincott, 1971.
The War and the Protest: Vietnam. New York, Doubleday, 1971.
Jobs in Business and Office. New York, Lothrop, 1974.
Street Gangs: Yesterday and Today. Mamaroneck, New York, Hastings House, 1974.
Witchcraft, Mysticism and Magic in the Black World. New York, Doubleday, 1974.
The Consumer Movement. New York, F. Watts, 1975.
The Creoles of Color of New Orleans. New York, Crowell, 1975.
Who Are the Handicapped? New York, Doubleday, 1978.
The Quiet Revolution: The Struggle for the Rights of Disabled Americans, with J.M. Stifle. New York, Crowell, 1979.
The New Americans: Vietnamese Boat People. Hillside, New Jersey, Enslow, 1980.
Black Theatre in America. New York, Crowell, 1982.
The New Americans: Cuban Boat People. Hillside, New Jersey, Enslow, 1982.
The Guardian Angels. Hillside, New Jersey, Enslow, 1983.
Double Dutch, with David A. Walker. Hillside, New Jersey, Enslow, 1986.
Black Music in America: A History through Its People. New York, Crowell, 1987.
A Sixties Reader, with Kathleen Benson. New York, Viking, 1988.
The Autobiography of Rosa Parks, with Rosa Parks. New York, Dial, 1990.
Black Theater in America. New York, HarperCollins, 1991.
Religions of the World. New York, Hippocrene Books, 1991.

Biographies

From Lew Alcindor to Kareem Abdul Jabbar. New York, Lothrop, 1972.
A Piece of the Power: Four Black Mayors. New York, Dial, 1972.
Profiles in Black Power. New York, Doubleday, 1972.
Deep Like the Rivers: A Biography of Langston Hughes, 1902-1967. New York, Holt, 1973.
Adam Clayton Powell: Portrait of a Marching Black. New York, Dial, 1974.
Babe Ruth and Hank Aaron: The Home Run Kings. New York, Lothrop, 1974.
Fighting Shirley Chisholm. New York, Dial, 1975.
Dr. J: A Biography of Julius Irving. New York, Doubleday, 1975.
The Picture Life of Malcolm X. New York, F. Watts, 1975.
Always Movin' On: The Life of Langston Hughes. New York, F. Watts, 1976.
Pele: A Biography. New York, Doubleday, 1976.
The Story of Stevie Wonder. New York, Doubleday, 1976.
Barbara Jordan. New York, Dial, 1977.
The Life and Death of Martin Luther King, Jr. New York, Lothrop, 1977.
Bob McAdoo: Superstar. New York, Lothrop, 1978.
George McGinnis: Basketball Superstar. Mamaroneck, New York, Hastings, 1978.
Andrew Young: Man with a Mission. New York, Lothrop, 1979.
I'm Gonna Make You Love Me: The Story of Diana Ross. New York, Dial, 1980.
"Magic": A Biography of Earvin Johnson. Hillside, New Jersey, Enslow, 1981; as *Sports Great Magic Johnson,* 1992.
Katherine Dunham. New York, Coward-McCann, 1982.
Donna Summer. New York, Atlantic Monthly Press, 1983.
About Michael Jackson. Hillside, New Jersey, Enslow, 1985.
Diana Ross: Star Supreme. New York, Viking, 1985.
Corazon Aquino: Leader of the Philippines. Hillside, New Jersey, Enslow, 1988.
Leaders of the Middle East. Hillside, New Jersey, Enslow, 1988.
The Magic Johnson Story. Hillside, New Jersey, Enslow, 1988, as *Sports Great Magic Johnson,* Hillside, New Jersey, Enslow, 1989.
Shirley Temple Black: Actress to Ambassador, illustrations by Donna Ruff. New York, Puffin Books, 1988.
I Am Somebody! A Biography of Jesse Jackson. Hillside, New Jersey, Enslow, 1992.
The March on Washington. New York, HarperCollins, 1993.

Other as Jim Haskins

Jokes from Black Folks. New York, Doubleday, 1973.
Ralph Bunche: A Most Reluctant Hero. New York, Hawthorne, 1974.
Your Rights, Past and Present: A Guide for Young People. New York, Hawthorne, 1975.
The Long Struggle: The Story of American Labor. Louisville, Westminster, 1976.
Teen-Age Alcoholism. New York, Hawthorne, 1976.
Gambling—Who Really Wins? New York, F. Watts, 1978.
Real Estate Careers. New York, F. Watts, 1978.
James Van Der Zee: The Picture Takin' Man, illustrations by James Van Der Zee. New York, Dodd, Mead, 1979.
The Child Abuse Help Book, with Pat Connolly. Reading, Massachusetts, Addison Wesley, 1981.

Editor, *The Filipino Nation.* Three volumes, Danbury, Connecticut, Grolier International, 1982.
Sugar Ray Leonard. New York, Lothrop, 1982.
Werewolves. New York, Lothrop, 1982.
Donna Summer: An Unauthorized Biography, with J.M. Stifle. Boston, Little, Brown, 1983.
Space Challenge: The Story of Guion Bluford, an Authorized Biography, with Kathleen Benson. Minneapolis, Carolrhoda Books, 1984.
Break Dancing. Minneapolis, Lerner, 1985.
The Statue of Liberty: America's Proud Lady. Minneapolis, Lerner, 1986.
Count Your Way through China [*Japan, Russia, Arab World, Mexico* (illustrated by Helen Byers), *Canada* (illustrated by Steve Michaels), *Africa* (illustrated by Barbara Knutson), *Korea* (illustrated by Dennis Hockerman), *Israel* (illustrated by Rick Hanson), *India* (illustrated by Liz Brenner Dodson), *Italy* (illustrated by Beth Wright), *Germany* (illustrated by Helen Byers)]. Minneapolis, Carolrhoda Books, 12 vols., 1987-90.
Bill Cosby: America's Most Famous Father. New York, Walker, 1988.
Christopher Columbus: Admiral of the Ocean Sea. New York, Scholastic, 1991.
Scatman: An Authorized Biography of Scatman Crothers, with Helen Crothers. New York, Morrow, 1991.
Against All Opposition: Black Explorers in America. New York, Walker, 1992.
Amazing Grace: The Story behind the Song. Brookfield, Connecticut, Millbrook, 1992.
The Day Martin Luther King, Jr. Was Shot: A Photo History of the Civil Rights Movement. New York, Scholastic, 1992.
I Have A Dream: The Life & Words of Martin Luther King, Jr. Brookfield, Connecticut, Millbrook Press, 1992.
One More River to Cross: Twelve Black Americans. New York, Scholastic, 1992.
Get on Board: The Story of the Underground Railroad. New York, Scholastic, 1993.

PUBLICATIONS FOR ADULTS

Nonfiction as Jim Haskins

Diary of a Harlem Schoolteacher. Grove, 1969, 2nd edition, Briarcliff Manor, New York, Stein & Day, 1979.
Editor, *Black Manifesto for Education.* New York, Morrow, 1973.
The Psychology of Black Language, with Hugh F. Butts. New York, Barnes & Noble, 1973.
Snow Sculpture and Ice Carving. London, Macmillan, 1974.
The Cotton Club. Random House, 1977, 2nd edition, New York, New American Library, 1984.
The Great American Crazies, with Kathleen Benson and Ellen Inkelis. Ashland, Massachusetts, Condor, 1977.
The Stevie Wonder Scrapbook, with Kathleen Benson. New York, Grosset & Dunlap, 1978.
Voodoo and Hoodoo: Their Tradition and Craft as Revealed by Actual Practitioners. London, Briarcliff Manor, New York, Stein & Day, 1978.
Richard Pryor, a Man and His Madness: A Biography. Beaufort Books, New York, 1984.

Queen of the Blues: A Biography of Dinah Washington. New York, Morrow, 1987.

Outward Dreams: Black Inventors and Their Inventions. New York, Walker, 1991.

Other

Pinckney Benton Stewart Pitchback: A Biography. London, Macmillan, 1973.

A New Kind of Joy: The Story of the Special Olympics. New York, Doubleday, 1976.

Contributor, *Understanding Human Behavior in Health and Illness* by Emily Mumford. Baltimore, Williams & Wilkins, 1977.

Scott Joplin: The Man Who Made Ragtime, with Kathleen Benson. New York, Doubleday, 1978.

Contributor, *New York Kid's Catalog.* New York, Doubleday, 1979.

Contributor, *Notable American Women Supplement.* Cambridge, Massachusetts, Radcliffe College, 1979.

Lena: A Personal and Professional Biography of Lena Horne, with Kathleen Benson. New York, Stein & Day, 1984.

Nat King Cole, with Kathleen Benson. New York, Stein & Day, 1984.

Contributor, *Clearings in the Thicket: An Alabama Humanities Reader* by Jerry Brown. Kennebunkport, Maine, Mercer University Press, 1985.

Mabel Mercer: A Life. New York, Atheneum, 1988.

Mr. Bojangles: The Biography of Bill Robinson. New York, Morrow, 1988.

Winnie Mandela: Life of Struggle. New York, Putnam, 1988.

Hamp: An Autobiography (with discography), with Lionel Hampton. New York, Warner, 1989.

India Under Indira and Rajiv Gandhi. Hillside, New Jersey, Enslow, 1989.

Black Dance in America: A History through its People. New York, Crowell, 1990.

Lena: A Biography of Lena Horne, with Kathleen Benson. Lanham, Maryland, Scarborough House, 1990.

Editor, *Judaism.* New York, Hippocrene Books, 1991.

Editor, *The Catholic Church.* New York, Hippocrene Books, 1992.

The Methodists. New York, Hippocrene Books, 1992.

Thurgood Marshall: A Life for Justice. New York, Holt, 1992.

*

Media Adaptations: *Diary of a Harlem Schoolteacher* recorded by Recordings for the Blind; *The Cotton Club* inspired the 1984 film of the same name.

Biography: Entry in *Sixth Book of Junior Authors,* edited by Sally Holmes Holtze, New York, Wilson, 1989, pp. 115-17; essay in *Something about the Author Autobiography Series,* Volume 4, Detroit, Gale, 1987, pp. 197-209.

Critical Study: Entry in *Children's Literature Review,* Volume 3, Detroit, Gale, 1978, pp. 63-69.

*   *   *

James Haskins has written a prodigious number of nonfiction books, more than eighty to date. Haskins writes for adults, young adults, and children; his books are wide-ranging in their subject matter. One book, *The Cotton Club,* was made into a major movie. The majority of Haskins's books are for young adults, and through them he has tackled such topics as child abuse, street gangs, the war in Vietnam, the disabled, and Cuban boat people. Yet, for the most part, he has used his young adult books to explore the black experience in America. It is these books on the African American experience that represent Haskins's most important contribution to young adult nonfiction. They sensitively treat a multitude of diverse topics having to do with African American life and culture.

A great many of Haskins's books are biographies. He has written about athletes, entertainers, and high achievers in other fields. From Scott Joplin to Stevie Wonder, from Kareem Abdul Jabbar to Magic Johnson, from Ralph Bunche to Barbara Jordan, Haskins has not been content to record the "glitz and glitter," but has sought out the real person. In *The Life and Death of Martin Luther King, Jr.,* for example, Haskins writes about the man behind the image. He seeks to reveal King's feelings, his confusions, and his failings. In the process, Martin Luther King, Jr., is revealed, an extraordinary leader who is appealing and enormously strong emotionally, but a man with faults. In Haskins's hands, King becomes a real person, not a plaster saint.

The same can be said of *Scott Joplin: The Man Who Made Ragtime.* Written with Kathleen Benson, this book brings life and vitality to a man who died over seventy years ago. Haskins identifies Joplin as a major creator of a black musical form, but does more than merely chronicle the events of Joplin's life. Placing Joplin within a historical context, Haskins describes a man driven to make music, plagued by poverty and racism, but also a man who fought to make the larger white society accept ragtime.

Katherine Dunham introduced traditional West African and Afro-Caribbean dance to western audiences. In *Katherine Dunham,* Haskins tells how she did this. The problems she encountered were enormous, but Haskins manages to dig beneath the surface and never allows events to overwhelm his portrait of Dunham the person. He portrays her as a woman of deep convictions and strong emotions, who had to fight her middle-class family's disapproval to become a dancer and who had to endure life in a segregated America as well. Despite beauty and intelligence, Lena Horne had no easy time of it either. Written also with Kathleen Benson, *Lena: A Personal and Professional Biography of Lena Horne* tells the story of Horne's difficult childhood and her emergence from anger and repression into a black woman fully aware of her power and her own worth.

James Van Der Zee: The Picture Takin' Man is the life of the photographer who worked during the 1920s and 1930s taking pictures of the residents of Harlem. Little known and unappreciated until his enormous cache of pictures was made into an exhibition at the New York Metropolitan Museum of Art, he told his life story to Haskins. What emerges from the book through the use of those interview materials and a number of Van Der Zee's actual pictures is a wonderful portrait of a man who simply worked from day to day, trying to make a living at work he loved. Married twice and always on the edge of poverty, he made his living by taking pictures and did well for awhile. The Great Depression, changing lifestyles, and age finally caught up with him. He and his wife were evicted from their Harlem apartment when they were in their eighties because they were unable to pay the rent. What emerges from this book is a richly detailed view of one man's life, a view that also reflects black life in America in the last years of the nineteenth and the first half of the twentieth century. In addition to biography, Haskins has written books dealing with a number of different aspects of black life. All are characterized by an insider's detail and the use of little known or disregarded facts that take the reader behind the scenes. Haskins's most recent books, *The March on Washington* and *Get on Board: The Story of the Underground Railroad,* are two examples. Both books speak to the African American's quest for freedom, one in the antebellum South and the other in America in the 1960s.

Get on Board profiles the many personalities who worked on the Underground Railroad as conductors and stationmasters and the slaves who traveled the train's route. Haskins gives these people names and feelings. He recounts the well-known exploits of Harriet Tubman but includes the stories of others as well. Haskins emphasizes the efforts that slaves, ex-slaves, and free black men and women exerted on their own behalf, feeling that their contributions to their own freedom have too frequently been overlooked.

The March on Washington is filled with details, details that explain not only why the march was organized, but how. Bayard Rustin, the consummate civil rights organizer, emerges as the hero of this piece. In two short months, he was able to pull together all the thousands of pieces of organizational detail that enabled the march to succeed, from the provision of portable toilets to the provision of refreshments for 250,000 people. One also gets a glimpse of the many conflicts and tensions that existed among the leaders of the march, one such conflict nearly derailing the march minutes before it was to begin.

Black Music in America: A History through Its People is a collection of sketches of the many black Americans who have created and performed music, from opera to soul, from spirituals to blues and gospel. There are chapters on the music the slaves created and on the evolution of the blues. But perhaps the most fascinating chapters discuss the contributions to black music of more contemporary musicians. James Brown, Aretha Franklin, Michael Jackson, Wynton Marsalis, and Tina Turner are all here. *Black Theater in America* and *Black Dance in America: A History through Its People* similarly treat the contributions of African Americans to theater and dance by concentrating on personalities.

Departing from the arts, *The Creoles of Color of New Orleans* describes the rich history and culture of a New Orleans people of mixed African, French, and Spanish descent. On the other hand, the place of the supernatural in black America is traced in *Witchcraft, Mysticism and Magic in the Black World.* Haskins argues that African slaves brought their religious beliefs with them to this country and that these beliefs have survived in various ways. As a result, superstitions and mysticism are more accepted by blacks than by those in the larger society.

It is obvious that James Haskins is both a prolific and eclectic writer. Through his many books, he has been able to investigate and report on African American subject areas long ignored or undervalued by other writers. He has been able to a profile the lives of prominent African Americans in ways that highlight their uniqueness as human beings but still point to the additional burdens they incur by being black in America. He has been able to bring back from obscurity black people who have made enduring contributions to the arts, to sports, and to politics, showing them to be real people. He has written books on well-known and little-known events in black history and has been adept at taking an always unique insider's perspective. This is Haskins's great strength, to take little-known or seemingly unimportant facts about an event or a person and weave them into a fascinating whole, a whole that never fails to inform, educate, and entertain.

—Carol Jones Collins

HAUTZIG, Esther (née Rudomin). American. Born in Vilna, Poland (now Vilnius, Lithuania), 18 October 1930. Came to the United States in 1947, naturalized U.S. citizen in 1951. Educated at Hunter College (now Hunter College of the City University of New York), 1948-50. Married Walter Hautzig in 1950; one daughter and one son. Secretary, G.P. Putnam's Sons, New York City, 1951-52; publicity assistant, Children's Book Council, New York City, 1953; director of children's book promotion, 1954-59, consultant, 1961-68, Thomas Y. Crowell Co., New York City; free-lance children's book consultant, New York City, since 1959. Three-time speaker at the Summer Institutes of the Children's Literature Center, Simmons College, Boston, Massachusetts; lecturer and speaker on writing, reading and bookmaking at many schools, libraries, and professional association meetings, including the Westchester County Library Association, Annual Children's Book Meeting for the Association of New York City Children's Book Librarians, University of Minnesota book banquet, 1982, University of Arkansas/Little Rock Children's Book Author Festival, 1988, Central Missouri University in Warrensburg 23rd Annual Book Festival, 1991, and at many others. Support group member for the Division of Young Adult Services, and general volunteer, New York Public Library, New York City. Recipient: Shirley Kravitz award, Association of Jewish Libraries, 1968, Jane Addams Children's Book award, 1969, and Lewis Carroll Shelf Award, 1971, all for *The Endless Steppe,* which was named Book World Spring Book Festival honor book and *Boston Globe/Horn Book* honor book, both in 1968, was a National Book Award finalist in 1969, was named "Best Jewish Novel" by the Synagogue, School and Center Division of Jewish Libraries in 1970, and was named a Notable Book by the American Library Association; *A Gift for Mama* was an ALA Notable Children's Book; *The Seven Good Years and Other Stories* was a Parents' Choice Remarkable Book in the literature category. Agent: Schaffner Agency, 6625 Casas Adobes Rd., Tucson, AZ 85704. Address: 505 West End Ave., New York, NY 10024, U.S.A.

PUBLICATIONS FOR YOUNG ADULTS

The Endless Steppe: Growing up in Siberia (autobiography). New York, Crowell, 1968.

Other

Translator and adaptor, *The Case against the Wind and Other Stories* by I.L. Peretz, illustrated by Leon Shtainmets. New York, Macmillan, 1975.
Translator and adaptor, *The Seven Good Years and Other Stories* by I.L. Peretz. Philadelphia, Pennsylvania, Jewish Publication Society, 1984.
Remember Who You Are: Stories about Being Jewish (biographical sketches). New York, Crown, 1990.
On the Air: Behind the Scenes at a TV Newscast. New York, Macmillan, 1991.

PUBLICATIONS FOR CHILDREN

Fiction

A Gift for Mama, illustrated by Donna Diamond. New York, Viking, 1981.

"Four Languages" series (all contain text in English, Spanish, French, and Russian):

At Home: A Visit in Four Languages, illustrated by Aliki. New York, Macmillan, 1968.
In the Park: An Excursion in Four Languages, illustrated by Ezra Jack Keats. New York, Macmillan, 1968.
In School: Learning in Four Languages, illustrated by Nonny Hogrogian. New York, Macmillan, 1969.

Nonfiction

Let's Cook without Cooking: 55 Recipes without a Stove (as Esther Rudomin), illustrated by Lisl Weil. New York, Crowell, 1955.
Let's Make Presents: 100 Easy-to-Make Gifts under $1.00, illustrated by Ava Morgan. New York, Crowell, 1962.
Redecorating Your Room for Practically Nothing, illustrated by Sidonie Coryn. New York, Crowell, 1967.
Cool Cooking: 16 Recipes without a Stove, illustrated by Jan Pyk. New York, Lothrop, 1973.
Let's Make More Presents: Easy and Inexpensive Gifts for Every Occasion, illustrated by Ray Skibinski. New York, Macmillan, 1973.
Life with Working Parents: Practical Hints for Everyday Situations, illustrated by Roy Doty. New York, Macmillan, 1976.
Christmas Goodies, illustrated by Kelly Oechsli. New York, Happy House Books/Random House, 1981.
Holiday Treats. New York, Macmillan, 1983.
Make It Special. New York, Macmillan, 1986.
Riches. New York, HarperCollins, 1992.

*

Biography: Entry in *Third Book of Junior Authors,* Wilson, 1972; essay in *Something about the Author Autobiography Series,* Volume 15, Gale, 1993.

Critical Study: Entry in *Children's Literature Review,* Volume 22, Gale, 1991.

Esther Hautzig comments:

What I always wanted and loved to do was write. I did not expect to be an AUTHOR! Whether I write craft books, or cookbooks, or picture books or translations, they are all part of ME and I could not have written any of them without having lived in and written about Siberia, and Vilna, and translated from Yiddish. Everyone's story is unique. I urge young people to keep a journal and write down their story, whatever it may be. Wondrous things can happen each day, to be savored and shared with others.

*   *   *

Esther Hautzig is best known for her autobiographical account *The Endless Steppe: Growing Up in Siberia,* which is not only about her life in exile for the five years from age ten to fifteen, but is a magnificent survival story in both the physical and spiritual sense.

The story begins in Vilna, Poland, in 1941 when Hautzig and her parents and grandparents are transported by the invading Russians to Rubtsovsk, Siberia. The family run a prosperous jewelry store and are considered dangerous capitalists by the Russians. They are transported to Siberia in railway cattle cars, a journey which requires weeks. Hautzig's powers of detailed description are evident in the description of this harrowing journey and in the descriptions of the extremes of heat and cold, the hard work, the crowded living conditions, and the constant threat of starvation. There is also the grief for a grandfather reported dead in another labor camp and for the father ordered to work behind the Russian front lines in the war against the Germans.

In counterbalance against these constant deprivations are the optimism, the endurance, the persistence, and the sheer resilience of the female members of the Hautzig family—Esther, her mother, and her grandmother. This untiring effort to overcome obstacles is illustrated in Esther's learning Russian, developing a love for the Russian classics, and becoming editor of the school paper. Early in their stay in Siberia when the members of the family are working in a gypsum mine, the grandmother persistently manicures her nails at night—attempting to maintain something of the standard of her former life.

One of the most amusing incidents in the book occurs after Hautzig discovers her ability as a trader at the Sunday market. When an old peasant closely examines a book of Russian verse she is attempting to sell, she points out the virtues of the poems while he feels the thickness and quality of the paper. Upon her exclaiming that the paper makes no difference, he responds that different people see different things in books—this one, he contends, is not suitable as the pages are not right for rolling cigarettes. Hautzig is appalled at this and delighted that he did not buy the book.

Hautzig has given us not only a detailed, accurate, and poignant account of the Second World War with all its dangers and deprivations, but also the story of a young girl finding a best friend, going to a dance, having a boyfriend, in short, of a girl growing from childhood to maturity surrounded by love in the midst of hardship.

Although Hautzig finds at the end of the war that many of their family members and friends have been killed, miraculously she and her mother and grandmother are reunited with her father in Vilna, and she realizes Siberia will always hold a special place in her heart.

Hautzig has authored a number of craft books for young people growing out of her experience in Siberia making do with little or nothing. Out of her conviction of the importance of early language lessons, she pioneered a series of picture books in four languages. She has also translated from the Yiddish and has written a book for adults, *Remember Who You Are: Stories about Being Jewish,* which was recommended for young adults in *School Library Journal, The Book Report,* and *Books for the Teen Age, 1991,* by the New York Library. A collection of short sketches about various people she has known, it includes tales about some who perished and some who survived, some inspiring accounts and some funny. It acts as a fitting sequel and supplement to *The Endless Steppe.*

—Reba Pinney

————

HEAD, Ann. Pseudonym for Anne Christensen Morse. American. Born in Beaufort, South Carolina, 30 October 1915. Educated at Antioch College, student for three years. Married Stanley F. Morse, Jr. (second marriage), one daughter from each marriage. Free-lance fiction writer, 1943—. Agent: Constance Smith Associates, 119

West 57th St., New York, NY 10019. Address: 403 Church St., Beaufort, SC 29902, U.S.A.

PUBLICATIONS FOR YOUNG ADULTS

Fiction

Fair With Rain. New York, McGraw, 1957.
Always in August. New York, Doubleday, 1961.
Everybody Adored Cara. New York, Doubleday, 1963.
Mr. and Mrs. Bo Jo Jones. New York, Putnam, 1967.

Nonfiction

Good Dog! Educating the Family Pet. North Pomfret, Vermont, Trafalgar, 1988.

*   *   *

Ann Head's novels are engaging overall. She is skilled at supplying wonderful detail and interesting characters. The bulk of her work could be classified as enjoyable, light reading material, providing romance, suspense, mystery, and humor. *Always in August, Fair With Rain,* and *Everybody Adored Cara* are similar in style and contain engaging descriptions and scenery, while their characters explore different facets of human relationships, whether it be a cheating husband or the prospect of a son becoming engaged. Although adults will no doubt enjoy taking any of these books to the beach, young adults will most likely be uninterested in these novels. While young adults are fully capable of reading and understanding the matter of these novels, they will not be totally engaged in the stories. The narrators are all older, either mothers or married women, mostly interested in what revolves around their lives: their children, husbands, friends and themselves.

Head's only true young adult novel, *Mr. and Mrs. Bo Jo Jones,* should capture the attention of its intended audience. The story involves two teenagers whose relationship progresses to the point of parenthood. What follows is a tale of the tumultuous decision to have the baby, the upset parents of the teenagers, a breakup of the couple, and their eventual reuniting as the mother becomes Mrs. Bo Jo Jones and the family goes to college together. The story is gripping and the worn copies in libraries attest to its popularity.

The teenagers' choice, while a difficult one, ends well: they are back in love, still have their child, and are pursuing their education. Head has tied the novel up a little too neatly, giving a very idealistic portrayal of what very few teenage pregnancies result in. The title alone, a feminist's nightmare, gives way to fantasy and simplistic notions of teenage pregnancy. Although *Mr. and Mrs. Bo Jo Jones* seems dated, the story is enough to interest young adults.

—Kate Lentz

———

HEADLEY, Elizabeth. See **CAVANNA, Betty.**

———

HEINLEIN, Robert A(nson). American. Born in Butler, Missouri, 7 July 1907. Educated at Central High School, Kansas City, graduated 1924; University of Missouri, Columbia, 1924-25; United States Naval Academy, Annapolis, Maryland, B.S. 1929; University of California, Los Angeles, 1934-35. Served in the United States Navy, 1929 until retirement because of physical disability, 1934. Married 1) Leslyn McDonald (divorced 1947); 2) Virginia Doris Gerstenfeld in 1948. Owner, Shively and Sophie Lodes silver mines, Silver Plume, Colorado, 1934-35; worked in mining and real estate, 1936-39; Civilian Engineer, Philadelphia Navy Yard, 1942-45. Candidate for California State Assembly, 1938; Forrestal Lecturer, United States Naval Academy, 1973. Guest commentator during Apollo lunar landing, Columbia Broadcasting System, 1969. Recipient: Guest of Honor, World Science Fiction Convention, 1941, 1961, 1976; Hugo award, 1956, for *Double Star*, 1960, for *Starship Troopers*, 1962, for *Stranger in a Strange Land*, 1967, for *The Moon Is a Harsh Mistress*; Boys' Clubs of America Best Liked Book Award, 1959; Sequoyah Children's Book Award of Oklahoma, Oklahoma Library Association, 1961, for *Have Space Suit—Will Travel*; named best all-time author, *Locus* magazine readers' poll, 1973 and 1975; Grand Master Nebula award, 1974; Humanitarian of the Year award, National Rare Blood Club, 1974; American Association of Blood Banks Award, 1977; Council of Community Blood Centers Award, 1977; Inkpot award, 1977; L.H.D.: Eastern Michigan University, Ypsilanti, 1977; *Locus* award, 1985; Distinguished Public Service Medal, National Aeronautics and Space Administration (NASA), 1988 (posthumously awarded); the Rhysling Award of the Science Fiction Poetry Association is named after the character in Heinlein's story, "The Green Hills of Earth"; Tomorrow Starts Here award, Delta Vee Society; numerous other awards for his work with blood drives. *Died 8 May 1988.*

PUBLICATIONS FOR YOUNG ADULTS

Fiction

Rocket Ship Galileo, illustrated by Thomas Voter. New York, Scribner, 1947; London, New English Library, 1971.
Space Cadet, illustrated by Clifford Geary. New York, Scribner, 1948; London, Gollancz, 1966.
Red Planet, illustrated by Clifford Geary. New York, Scribner, 1949; London, Gollancz, 1962; expanded edition, New York, Del Rey, 1989.
Farmer in the Sky, illustrated by Clifford Geary. New York, Scribner, 1950; London, Gollancz, 1962.
Between Planets, illustrated by Clifford Geary. New York, Scribner, 1951; London, Gollancz, 1968.
The Rolling Stones, illustrated by Clifford Geary. New York, Scribner, 1952; as *Space Family Stone,* London, Gollancz, 1969.
Starman Jones, illustrated by Clifford Geary. New York, Scribner, 1953; London, Sidgwick and Jackson, 1954.
The Star Beast, illustrated by Clifford Geary. New York, Scribner, 1954; London, New English Library, 1971.
Tunnel in the Sky. New York, Scribner, 1955; London, Gollancz, 1965.
Time for the Stars. New York, Scribner, 1956; London, Gollancz, 1963.
Citizen of the Galaxy. New York, Scribner, 1957; London, Gollancz, 1963.

Have Space Suit—Will Travel. New York, Scribner, 1958; London, Gollancz, 1970.

Starship Troopers. New York, Putnam, 1959; London, New English Library, 1961.

Podkayne of Mars: Her Life and Times. New York, Putnam, 1963; London, New English Library, 1969.

PUBLICATIONS FOR ADULTS

Novels

Beyond This Horizon. Reading, Pennsylvania, Fantasy Press, 1948; London, Panther, 1967.

Sixth Column. New York, Gnome Press, 1949; as *The Day After Tomorrow,* New York, New American Library, 1951; London, Mayflower, 1962.

Waldo, and Magic Inc. New York, Doubleday, 1950; as *Waldo, Genius in Orbit,* New York, Avon, 1958.

The Puppet Masters. New York, Doubleday, 1951; London, Museum Press, 1953.

Double Star. New York, Doubleday, 1956; London, Joseph, 1958.

The Door into Summer. New York, Doubleday, 1957; London, Panther, 1960.

Methuselah's Children. New York, Gnome Press, 1958; London, Gollancz, 1963.

The Robert Heinlein Omnibus. London, Sidgwick and Jackson, 1958.

Stranger in a Strange Land. New York, Putnam, 1961; London, New English Library, 1965; revised and uncut edition with preface by wife, Virginia Heinlein, New York, Putnam, 1990.

Glory Road. New York, Putnam, 1963; London, New English Library, 1965.

Farnham's Freehold. New York, Putnam, 1964; London, Dobson, 1965.

Three by Heinlein (includes *The Puppet Masters, Waldo,* and *Magic, Inc.*), New York, Doubleday, 1965; as *A Heinlein Triad,* London, Gollancz, 1966.

A Robert Heinlein Omnibus. London, Sidgwick and Jackson, 1966.

The Moon Is a Harsh Mistress. New York, Putnam, 1966; London, Dobson, 1967.

I Will Fear No Evil. New York, Putnam, 1971; London, New English Library, 1972.

Time Enough for Love: The Lives of Lazarus Long. New York, Putnam, 1973; London, New English Library, 1974.

The Number of the Beast. New York, Fawcett; and London, New English Library, 1980.

Friday. New York, Holt Rinehart, and London, New English Library, 1982.

Job: A Comedy of Justice. New York, Ballantine, and London, New English Library, 1984.

The Cat Who Walks through Walls: A Comedy of Manners. New York, Putnam, 1985; London, New English Library, 1986.

To Sail Beyond the Sunset: The Life and Loves of Maureen Johnson, Being the Memoirs of a Somewhat Irregular Lady. New York, Putnam, and London, Joseph, 1987.

Short Stories

The Man Who Sold the Moon. Chicago, Shasta, 1950; London, Sidgwick and Jackson, 1953.

The Green Hills of Earth. Chicago, Shasta, 1951; London, Sidgwick and Jackson, 1954.

Universe. New York, Dell, 1951; as *Orphans of the Sky,* London, Gollancz, 1963; New York, Putnam, 1964.

Assignment in Eternity. Reading, Pennsylvania, Fantasy Press, 1953; London, Museum Press, 1955; abridged edition, as *Lost Legacy,* London, Digit, 1960.

Revolt in 2100. Chicago, Shasta, 1953; London, Digit, 1959.

The Menace from Earth. New York, Gnome Press, 1959; London, Dobson, 1966.

The Unpleasant Profession of Jonathan Hoag. New York, Gnome Press, 1959; London, Dobson, 1964; as *6 x H: Six Stories,* New York, Pyramid, 1962.

The Worlds of Robert A. Heinlein. New York, Ace, 1966; London, New English Library, 1970.

The Past through Tomorrow: Future History Stories. New York, Putnam, 1967; abridged edition, London, New English Library, 2 vols., 1977.

The Best of Robert Heinlein, 1939-1959, edited by Angus Wells. London, Sidgwick and Jackson, 2 vols., 1973.

Destination Moon. Boston, Gregg Press, 1979.

Expanded Universe: The New Worlds of Robert A. Heinlein. New York, Grosset and Dunlap, 1980.

Screenplays: *Destination Moon,* with Rip Van Ronkel and James O'Hanlon (based on *Rocket Ship Galileo;* produced by George Pal/Eagle Lion, 1950), edited by David G. Hartwell, Gregg Press, 1979; *Project Moonbase,* with Jack Seaman, Galaxy Pictures/Lippert Productions, 1953.

Television Plays: scripts for *Tom Corbett, Space Cadet* series, 1950s.

Other

The Discovery of the Future (address). Los Angeles, Novacious, 1941.

Of Worlds Beyond: The Science of Science Fiction, with others, edited by Lloyd Arthur Eshbach. Reading, Pennsylvania, Fantasy Press, 1947; London, Dobson, 1965.

Editor, *Tomorrow, the Stars: A Science Fiction Anthology.* New York, Doubleday, 1952.

Famous Science Fiction Stories, with others. New York, Random House, 1957.

The Science Fiction Novel: Imagination and Social Criticism, with others, edited by Basil Davenport. Chicago, Advent, 1959.

The Notebooks of Lazarus Long. New York, Putnam, 1978.

Author of preface, *High Frontier: A Strategy for National Survival,* by Daniel O. Graham. Chicago, Pinnacle Books, 1983.

Grumbles from the Grave (correspondences), edited by V. Heinlein. New York, Ballantine, 1989.

Robert A. Heinlein Requiem (collection of fiction and nonfiction), edited by Yoji Kondo. New York, Tor Books, 1992.

Tramp Royale (travel). New York, Putnam, 1992.

*

Media Adaptations: The television series *Tom Corbett: Space Cadet,* which aired from 1951-1956, was based on Heinlein's novel *Space Cadet;* television, radio, and film rights to many of Heinlein's works have been sold; a military simulation board game has been created based on *Starship Troopers.*

Biography: Entry in *Dictionary of Literary Biography* by Joseph Patrouch, Volume 8, Detroit, Gale, 1981.

Bibliography: *Robert A. Heinlein: A Bibliography* by Mark Owings, Baltimore, Croatan House, 1973.

Manuscript Collection: University of California Library, Santa Cruz.

Critical Study: *Seekers of Tomorrow* by Sam Moskowitz, Cleveland, World, 1966; *Heinlein in Dimension: A Critical Analysis* (includes bibliography) by Alexei Panshin, Chicago, Advent, 1968; entry in *Contemporary Literary Criticism,* Detroit, Gale, Volume 1, 1973, Volume 3, 1975, Volume 8, 1978, Volume 14, 1980, Volume 26, 1983, Volume 55, 1989; *Robert A. Heinlein, Stranger in His Own Land,* San Bernardino, California, Borgo Press, 1976, and *The Classic Years of Robert A. Heinlein,* Borgo Press, 1977, both by George Edgar Slusser; *Robert A. Heinlein* edited by Martin H. Greenberg and Joseph D. Olander, New York, Taplinger, and Edinburgh, Harris, 1978; *Robert A. Heinlein: America as Science Fiction* by H. Bruce Franklin, New York, Oxford University Press, 1980, Oxford, Oxford University Press, 1981; *Robert A. Heinlein* by Peter Nicholls, New York, Scribner, 1982; *Yesterday or Tomorrow? The Work of Robert A. Heinlein* by R. Reginald, San Bernardino, California, Borgo Press, 1984.

*   *   *

Known as the dean of science fiction, Robert A. Heinlein was a prolific writer of believable characters engaged in meaningful struggles even when placed in the most unbelievable situations. From Nazis plotting World War III on the moon to Venerian Dragons speaking Cockney English and debating issues of individual liberty, all are cast in what has long been recognized as a cogent vision of a future history that is rich in exploring the potential for individual achievement.

Although now seriously dated, Heinlein's 1947 *Rocket Ship Galileo* was among the first modern science fiction novels for young adults to be critically acclaimed, and its success led Heinlein to write a novel a year for the next thirteen years. The success of each lay primarily in Heinlein's combination of a straightforward narrative leading its protagonists to growth and maturity with detailed descriptions of very plausible future societies. In *Space Cadet,* Matt Dodson, initiated into the rules and regulations of the Space Patrol, struggles with learning how difficult it is to adjust to leaving home for the first time as well as coping with an entirely new set of demands and expectations as he helps police the Solar Federation of Earth, Mars, Venus, Luna, and Ganymede. Similarly, Rod Walker, in *Tunnel in the Sky,* is unexpectedly stranded on a primitive planet when a high school test in basic survival goes awry. Not only must Walker make sure that he and his classmates survive the dangers of their new world but also must find the maturity to place the group's needs above his own. Tom Bartlett, hero of *Time for the Stars,* helps explore the galaxy while maintaining a telepathic communications link first with his twin brother and then with successive generations of his family since he ages at a much slower rate than those on Earth. A convincing evocation of life on board a space ship, yet the novel's central conflict is Tom's internal battle with the psychological complexes that allowed his twin to dominate him throughout his life.

Not written as a series, twelve of the thirteen early novels do, nevertheless, present a consistent story about the conquest of space

without the didacticism or cynicism that so often weakens Heinlein's later works. In these future worlds hunger, war, political corruption, or oppression can all be overcome by eager, capable individuals who see science, technology, reason, and service to others as central to creating better worlds. Jim Marlowe of *Red Planet* runs away from his boarding school to warn fellow Martian colonists of the treachery planned by the Mars Company, a corporation modeled on the British East India Company. Jim's trip across the Martian deserts and the actions he takes to protect the colonists and native Martians test his maturing courage, tolerance, and altruism. *Between Planets,* a more complex novel with a plot and theme that Heinlein explores thoroughly in *The Moon Is a Harsh Mistress,* has as its hero Don Harvey, an unwitting courier for a secret group of Venusian freedom fighters who discovers that the fight for political freedom is a fight for individual liberty.

The last of the novels written specifically for young adults and winner of a Hugo Award, *Starship Troopers,* is profoundly different from all the others. Having an adult protagonist, it traces the making of a starship soldier. Set in a time of a vicious space war, it is a dark, disturbing novel which glorifies war and the fighting man with vivid, convincing detail. Nonetheless, its idealization of military leaders as concerned, paternalistic men coupled with its original yet plausible military equipment makes the novel highly popular.

While not written for young adults, *Double Star, Stranger in a Strange Land,* and *The Moon Is a Harsh Mistress,* all winners of Hugo Awards, are of particular appeal to older adolescents. Political and social revolution or intrigue are the central focus of each, and each contains a hero who must mature. In *Double Star,* Lorenzo Smythe, a down and out actor, substitutes for one of the Solar System's most powerful political figures when he is kidnapped. Carrying out the charade successfully, Lorenzo discovers the reality of power politics: No single person is ever in control, so he, a charlatan, along with a team of astute political advisors, is perfectly capable of exercising power effectively. In *Stranger in a Strange Land,* a work that has become something of a cult classic, Michael Valentine Smith, a human male raised from birth by a race of brilliantly advanced Martians, is returned in his twenties to what is, to him, an alien Earth. Because he is believed to hold legal rights to most of the wealth of Mars, the government tries unjustly to imprison him in a hospital. He escapes and ultimately forms a quasi-religious organization dedicated to teaching the Martian disciplines that have made Michael superior to most other human beings. Since these disciplines diverge radically from existing sexual and social mores, Michael is eventually killed by a rioting mob, leaving his disciples to continue his work. Younger readers are not likely to find this novel entertaining, however, since it not only is didactic but also is lacking in action and its pacing is slow. In contrast, *The Moon Is a Harsh Mistress* tells the engrossing tale of war between the Lunar Colony and Earth. A logical product of circumstance, the Lunar culture Heinlein develops is an intriguing mix of the familiar and the alien that nonetheless never fails to emphasize human values. Manuel Garcia O'Kelly, known as Mannie, a lunar-born computer expert, discovers that the moon's main computer has become a sentient being. Mannie and the computer, Mike, become friends as the two are drawn into a rebellion to free the moon from Earth's tyranny. One of Heinlein's most endearing characters, Mike learns friendship, love, and self-sacrifice as he helps his human friends achieve freedom.

A work quite unlike Heinlein's others is *Glory Road,* yet it remains one of his most well read by both adults and adolescents. A heroic fantasy, it sets Oscar Gordon, a former military advisor in Vietnam, on the road to adventure with a beautiful woman, Star, and a gnomish old man, Rufo, whom he meets in response to a help-wanted advertisement. Needed to help rescue the mysterious "Egg of the Phoenix," he joins the two armed only with a sword, and the three undergo a series of unlikely and extraordinary adventures that culminate in Oscar's discovery that Star is actually the Empress of Twenty Universes, Rufo her son, and the egg a sophisticated re-cording device necessary to her governing. What makes this novel transcend the ordinary is that Heinlein addresses what happens to a hero once the adventure has ended and the universe has been saved and, although fantastic in plot, once again Heinlein focuses on what he does best: individuals, their growth, and their relationships.

With characters who learn from both their mistakes and their successes, who build, use, and enjoy their technologies, who reach beyond today to redefine tomorrow, Robert A. Heinlein insists that religious hypocrisy, corporate avarice, and political chicanery exist only so long as good people tolerate them and that individuals dedicated to improving themselves and their worlds can make a difference in everything that they do. Thus, Heinlein's fictive world is a positive one, one where everything is possible.

—Marlene San Miguel Groner

HELLER, Joseph. American. Born in Brooklyn, New York, 1 May 1923. Educated at Abraham Lincoln High School, New York, graduated 1941; University of Southern California, Los Angeles, 1945-46; New York University, B.A. 1948 (Phi Beta Kappa); Columbia University, New York, M.A. 1949; Oxford University (Fulbright scholar), 1949-50. Served in the United States Army Air Force in World War II: Lieutenant. Married twice; 1) Shirley Held in 1945 (divorced); one daughter and one son. Instructor in English, Pennsylvania State University, University Park, 1950-52; advertising writer, *Time* magazine, New York City, 1952-56, and *Look* magazine, New York, 1956-58; promotion manager, *McCall's* magazine, New York, 1958-61; former teacher of fiction and dramatic writing at Yale University and University of Pennsylvania; City College of the City University of New York, New York City, Distinguished Professor of English, until 1975; full-time writer, since 1975. Has worked in the theater, movies, and television. Recipient: Fulbright scholar, 1949-50; National Institute of Arts and Letters grant in literature, 1963; American Academy grant, 1963; Prix Interallie (France) and Prix Médicis Etranger (France), both 1985, both for *God Knows.* Lives in East Hampton, Long Island, New York.

PUBLICATIONS

Novels

Contributor, *Nelson Algren's Own Book of Lonesome Monsters,* New York, Lancer, 1960; London, Panther, 1964.
Catch-22. New York, Simon & Schuster, 1961, critical edition, edited by Robert M. Scotto, Dell, 1973.
Something Happened. New York, Knopf, and London, Cape, 1974.
Good as Gold. New York, Simon & Schuster, and London, Cape, 1979.

God Knows. New York, Knopf, and London, Cape, 1984.
Picture This. New York, Putnam, and London, Macmillan, 1988.

Plays

We Bombed in New Haven (produced New Haven, Connecticut, 1967; New York, 1969; London, 1971). New York, Knopf, 1968; London, Cape, 1969.
Catch-22: A Dramatization, adaptation of his own novel. New York, Delacorte Press, and London, French, 1973.
Clevinger's Trial, adaptation of chapter 8 of his novel *Catch-22* (produced London, 1974). New York, French, 1973; London, French, 1974.

Screenplays: *Sex and the Single Girl,* with David R. Schwartz, 1964; *Casino Royale* (uncredited), 1967; *Dirty Dingus Magee,* with Tom and Frank Waldman, 1970.

Other

No Laughing Matter (autobiography), with Speed Vogal. New York, Putnam, and London, Cape, 1986.
Dear God: Children's Letters. New York, Doubleday, 1987.
Conversations with Joseph Heller, edited by Adam J. Sorkin. Jackson, University Press of Mississippi, 1993.

*

Media Adaptations: *Catch-22* (motion picture, directed by Mike Nichols, adapted by Buck Henry, and starring Alan Arkin as Yossarian), Paramount, 1970.

Biography: Entry in *Dictionary of Literary Biography,* Detroit, Gale, Volume 2: *American Novelists since World War II,* 1978, *Yearbook: 1980,* 1981, Volume 28: *Twentieth-Century American Jewish Fiction Writers,* 1984.

Bibliography: *Three Contemporary Novelists: An Annotated Bibliography* by Robert M. Scotto, New York, Garland, 1977; *Joseph Heller: A Reference Guide* by Brenda M. Keegan, Boston, Hall, 1978.

Critical Studies: "Joseph Heller's *Catch-22*" by Burr Dodd, in *Approaches to the Novel* edited by John Colmer, Edinburgh, Oliver and Boyd, 1967; "The Sanity of *Catch-22*" by Robert Protherough, in *Human World* (Swansea), May 1971; *A Catch-22 Casebook* edited by Frederick T. Kiley and Walter McDonald, New York, Crowell, 1973; entry in *Contemporary Literary Criticism,* Detroit, Gale, Volume 1, 1973, Volume 3, 1975, Volume 5, 1976, Volume 8, 1978, Volume 11, 1979, Volume 36, 1986; *Critical Essays on Catch-22,* Encino, California, Dickinson Seminar Series, 1974, and *Critical Essays on Joseph Heller,* Boston, Hall, 1984, both edited by James Nagel; "Something Happened: A New Direction" by George J. Searles, in *Critique* (Atlanta), vol. 18, no. 3, 1977; *From Here to Absurdity: The Moral Battlefields of Joseph Heller* by Stephen W. Potts, San Bernardino, California, Borgo Press, 1982; *Joseph Heller* by Robert Merrill, Boston, Twayne, 1987; *The Fiction of Joseph Heller: Against the Grain* by David Seed, London, Macmillan, 1989; *Understanding Joseph Heller* by Sanford Pinsker, Columbia, University of South Carolina Press, 1991.

Despite its World War II setting, Joseph Heller's *Catch-22* may well be the quintessential 1960s novel. Noisy, brash, anti-establishment, and profoundly moving, it captures the bureaucratic quagmire from which Captain John Yossarian seeks to escape. A bombardier, Yossarian is told that when he completes a certain number of missions, he can return home. The problem is that this number keeps increasing. Yossarian then adopts a more elemental mission, that of survival. He believes that if he can convince his superiors he is insane, he can be grounded. But there's a catch: Catch-22.

As Doc Daneeka patiently explains, government policy does indeed stipulate that an insane pilot must be relieved of duty: all the pilot has to do is officially declare his insanity. The "catch" is that if the pilot is rational enough to insist upon his insanity, he obviously must not be insane at all. Military doublespeak, with rules that seemingly address a problem and then tautologically shift around to deny their solution, implies more than linguistic chaos, according to Heller; it portends the death of civilization. Such language provides a screen from personal responsibility for the horror and meaninglessness of war, while paradoxically perpetuating that same barbarism.

Yossarian's choices are limited: like young Snowden, he can keep flying missions until he is killed; like Milo Minderbinder, he can gleefully learn to manipulate the system and gain enormous profit at the expense of his colleagues' lives; or like Orr, he may make a separate peace. His decision is a moral one, for he learns that mere survival is not enough. He cannot change the world, but he can make a statement of personal worth, since Snowden's death taught him that "The spirit gone, man is garbage."

Something Happened, published thirteen years after Heller's first novel, presents a comfortably hollow businessman who is Yossarian's antithesis. Bob Slocum, the book's protagonist and first-person narrator, has opted for being "garbage." He is somewhat likable, occasionally colorful, but nevertheless garbage, having lost his spirit long ago. That was the "something" that happened, and with this loss came the loss of his core identity (even his handwriting was stolen from someone else). In this novel, Heller continues to evaluate the question of life versus survival. Slocum does survive, but as a simpleton, the spiritual counterpart to his mentally retarded second son.

With *Good As Gold,* Heller initially seems to be scrutinizing the world of Washington in the same way he examined the military and the business community in his first two novels. It too is a bleak institution amazingly absurd and devoid of affirmation, a place where one is informed that he can do "Anything you want, as long as it's everything we tell you to say and do...." The single difference between this and the earlier novels is that Heller begins an exploration of his Jewish heritage. Bruce Gold, an English professor who has written a favorable review of the President's book, is rewarded with an invitation to join the White House staff. Although he cares nothing about politics, he would like to be the Secretary of State, specifically the first Jewish Secretary of State—not counting Henry Kissinger, whom he accuses of having sold out his Jewish roots in favor of praying with Richard Nixon and waging war upon oppressed people. Apart from government office, Gold is preoccupied with writing a book entitled *The Jewish Experience in America.* What is soon realized is that *Good As Gold* is Heller's book on the Jewish experience in America. More precisely, Heller's purpose is to satirize those individuals, Jews and Gentiles alike, who renounce their cultural and religious heritage in order to be assimilated into the power elite.

Heller enlarges his absurdist perspective in *God Knows,* espousing the theory that it's not just man's social institutions that defy purpose and meaning, the flaw is cosmic. The narrator of this unusual work is the Biblical King David, lying on his deathbed and anachronistically reviewing his life. His historical omniscience is amusingly evident in his criticism of Michelangelo's famous uncircumcised statue: "It may be a good piece of work, taken all in all, but it just isn't me." Linguistic anachronisms also abound in the frequent shifts from a King James diction to contemporary slang. Heller's point is that his David is not merely the Hebrew king; he is both an Everyman and a primordial hero. His dilemma is the universal one of loneliness and isolation, made particularly acute after a lifetime of stunning achievements.

Like *God Knows, Picture This* also contains meticulously researched history. One such topic is Rembrandt's "Aristotle Contemplating the Bust of Homer," while another is the world of Dutch mercantilism in the seventeenth century. And yet a third is Greek culture from the Age of Pericles through the fourth century B.C. Heller's actual concern, however, is ontological, the nature of reality itself. Thus, a painting of a model who is posing as a man who may never have contemplated a bust of Homer, achieves its own philosophical legitimacy completely separate from its historical coordinates. So too does the reader who contemplates a book about a painting about contemplating. With the question of the nature of reality, Heller masterfully continues the intellectual probing that he successfully began with *Catch-22.*

—Walker Rutledge

HENTOFF, Nat(han Irving). American. Born in Boston, Massachusetts, 10 June 1925. Educated at Northeastern University, Boston, B.A. (summa cum laude) 1945; Harvard University, Cambridge, Massachusetts, 1946; the Sorbonne, Paris (Fulbright fellow), 1950. Married 1) Miriam Sargent in 1950 (divorced 1950); 2) Trudi Bernstein in 1954 (divorced 1959), two daughters; 3) Margot Goodman in 1959, two sons. Writer, producer, and announcer, WMEX Radio, Boston, 1944-53; associate editor, *Downbeat* magazine, New York, 1953-57; co-founding editor, *Jazz Review,* 1959-60. Since 1958 staff writer and columnist, *Village Voice,* New York; since 1960 staff writer, the *New Yorker;* since 1984 columnist, Washington *Post.* Faculty member, New School for Social Research, New York, and New York University. Reviewer for several magazines, including *New York Herald Tribune Book Week, Peace News,* and *Reporter.* Lecturer at schools and colleges. Recipient: Children's Spring Book Festival award, *New York Herald Tribune,* and Nancy Bloch award, both 1965, both for *Jazz Country;* Woodward Park School award, 1966, for *Jazz Country;* Golden Archer award, 1980, for *This School Is Driving Me Crazy;* Hugh M. Hefner First Amendment award, Deadline Club, 1981, for *The First Freedom: The Tumultuous History of Free Speech in America;* Cranberry Award List, Acton Public Library, 1983, for *The Day They Came to Arrest the Book.* Address: 37 West 12th St., New York, NY 10011, U.S.A.

PUBLICATIONS FOR YOUNG ADULTS

Fiction

Jazz Country. New York, Harper, 1965.

Journey into Jazz, illustrated by David Stone Martin. New York, Coward McCann, 1968.

I'm Really Dragged but Nothing Gets Me Down. New York, Simon and Schuster, 1968.

In the Country of Ourselves. New York, Simon and Schuster, 1971.

This School Is Driving Me Crazy. New York, Delacorte, 1976; London, Angus and Robertson, 1977.

Does This School Have Capital Punishment? New York, Delacorte, 1981; London, Angus and Robertson, 1982.

The Day They Came to Arrest the Book. New York, Delacorte, 1982; London, Angus and Robertson, 1985.

Nonfiction

American Heroes: In and Out of School. New York, Delacorte, 1987.

PUBLICATIONS FOR ADULTS

Novels

Call the Keeper. New York, Viking Press, 1966; London, Secker and Warburg, 1967.

Onwards! New York, Simon and Schuster, 1968.

Blues for Charlie Darwin. New York, Morrow, 1982; London, Constable, 1983.

The Man from Internal Affairs. New York, Mysterious Press, 1985.

Other

Editor, with Nat Shapiro, *Hear Me Talking to Ya: The Story of Jazz by the Men Who Made It.* New York, Rinehart, and London, Davies, 1955.

Editor, with Nat Shapiro, *The Jazz Makers: Essays on the Greats of Jazz.* New York, Rinehart, 1957; London, Davies, 1958.

Editor, with Albert McCarthy, *Jazz: New Perspectives on the History of Jazz by Twelve of the World's Foremost Jazz Critics and Scholars.* New York, Rinehart, 1959; London, Cassell, 1960.

Jazz Street, photography by Dennis Stouk. London, Deutsch, 1960.

The Jazz Life. New York, Dial, 1961; London, Davies, 1962.

Peace Agitator: The Story of A.J. Muste. New York, Macmillan, 1963.

The New Equality. New York, Viking, 1964.

Our Children Are Dying. New York, Viking, 1966.

Editor, *The Essays of A. J. Muste.* Indianapolis, Bobbs Merrill, 1967.

A Doctor among the Addicts. Chicago, Rand McNally, 1968.

A Political Life: The Education of John V. Lindsay. New York, Knopf, 1969.

State Secrets: Police Surveillance in America, with Paul Cowan and Nick Egleson. New York, Holt, Rinehart, 1974.

Jazz Is. New York, Random House, 1976; London, W.H. Allen, 1978.

Does Anybody Give a Damn? On Education. New York, Knopf, 1977.

The First Freedom: The Tumultuous History of Free Speech in America. New York, Delacorte, 1980.

The 1984 Calendar: An American History, with Tim Keefe and Howard Levine. Lansing, Michigan, Point Blank Press, 1983.

Boston Boy (memoir). New York, Knopf, 1986.

John Cardinal O'Connor: At the Storm Center of a Changing American Catholic Church. New York, Scribner, 1988.

Free Speech for Me—But Not for Thee: How the American Left and Right Relentlessly Censor Each Other. New York, HarperCollins, 1992.

*

Biography: Entry in *Third Book of Junior Authors,* New York, H.W. Wilson, 1972, p. 124; essay in *Contemporary Authors Autobiography Series,* Volume 6, Detroit, Gale, 1988, pp. 165-74; essay in *Speaking for Ourselves: Autobiographical Sketches by Notable Authors of Books for Young Adults,* Volume 1, compiled and edited by Donald R. Gallo, National Council of Teachers of English, 1990.

Manuscript Collection: Boston University, Massachusetts.

Critical Study: Entry in *Children's Literature Review,* Volume 1, Detroit, Gale, 1976, pp. 107-109.

Nat Hentoff comments:

First, I tell stories, for otherwise there would be no readers. Second, I try through these stories, to show the reader people and ideas he or she may not have experienced. I want the readers to surprise themselves by their reactions.

*   *   *

The 1960s and 1970s were a time of cultural revolution in the United States. The seemingly idyllic "happy days" of the fifties ended suddenly with the deaths of John, Martin, and Bobby and with bloody civil rights marches, drugs, generation gaps, student demonstrations, and Vietnam. These years were also a time of the Beatles and Woodstock, lunar exploration, and the genesis of the information age. They began with the youngest American president in office and vanished as a vapor one thousand days later. This was a time when baby boomers—the largest group of youthful Americans of any generation—came of age. This was a time in which a writer such as Mark Twain would have reveled, a time for analytical literary skill, wit, humor, and even a touch of sarcasm. It was a time for Nathaniel Irving Hentoff.

Like Mark Twain, Nat Hentoff views life from both the perspective of one who has lived it and one who writes about it. His young adult fiction is the shadow image of his interests—jazz, education, journalism, and civil rights. The majority of book reviewers praise Hentoff's first novel for a young adult audience, *Jazz Country,* as his best. In one of his latest, *The Day They Came to Arrest the Book,* his unique style unites with that of the remarkable Mr. Twain. Both writers were zealots for freedom of the press and censorship issues. Under the setting of a school book review committee meeting, Hentoff skillfully recreates many of the adverse attitudes faced by *The Adventures of Huckleberry Finn* when that American classic was published over one hundred years ago.

Hentoff was raised and educated in the Boston area and moved to New York City as a young man. It is, therefore, not surprising that his characters are based in New York, or similar metropolitan environs, and frequently attend college in Massachusetts. We meet the majority of Hentoff's protagonists via third person narrative. However, Tom, the son of a corporate lawyer from New York, is discussed in the first person in *Jazz Country.* The author's youthful personal experiences with jazz greats such as Duke Ellington come across with the clarion tones of a trumpet solo. The language and dialect are "cool!" In fact, all of Hentoff's use of narrative in his novels evidences a knowledge of the thoughts and speech of contemporary teenagers.

Hentoff has been criticized for being a topically oriented writer. But if this is a weakness, it is also a strength. In a sense, he has chronicled a turbulent era in America for young adults. The sixties and seventies were a time for crusaders. Many of the teenagers in Hentoff's works are politically and socially conscious. Written at a time when the draft did not mean basketball players and money or beer and party times, *I'm Really Dragged but Nothing Gets Me Down* examines the threat of enforced military service that teenage males faced at the height of the Vietnam War, a concern which many adults—and even many of their peers—did not understand. Jeremy, a high school senior, is thrust into an exploration of conscience and differing views between his father and himself on the army and on life itself. *In the Country of Ourselves* continues the preceding theme of the alienation of youth and the questioning of authority. Revolutionaries and pacifists are skillfully portrayed. Conflict is conducted through dialogue rather than via violence.

While the sixties and seventies were times of turbulence, the winds of change for many teenagers had begun earlier as depicted by two young men, James Dean in the movie *Rebel without a Cause* and Elvis Presley. The appeal and persuasion of these two artists are frequently seen in the themes, plots, and even the characters of young adult novels. The protagonist in *Jazz Country* is a young white man who wants to learn jazz from black musicians just as Elvis drew his inspiration from black rhythm and blues artists. *I'm Really Dragged but Nothing Gets Me Down* and *In the Country of Ourselves* both deal with causes and with youth who are considered rebels in their time.

Even though concerned with serious topics, Hentoff also incorporates humor in his writings. Both *This School Is Driving Me Crazy* and its sequel *Does This School Have Capital Punishment?* examine themes of considerable importance to teenagers and to Mr. Hentoff—truth, friendship, education, relationships between fathers and sons, and jazz (although not necessarily in that order). We follow the antics and frustrations of Sam and his friends through puberty into adolescence. Hentoff started his literary career as a jazz critic, so it is not surprising that jazz is a major component of the school curriculum at Burr Academy.

Nat Hentoff has the ability to present social and political problems through fictional dialogue. His passion for the rights to free speech and expression are also documented in two works of young adult nonfiction, *The First Freedom: The Tumultuous History of Free Speech in America* and *American Heroes: In and Out of School*. The need that young Americans have to learn to think for themselves is the underlying philosophy of Hentoff's writing.

—Albert F. Spencer

HERALD, Kathleen. See **PEYTON, K.M.**

HERBERT, Frank (Patrick). American. Born in Tacoma, Washington, 8 October 1920. Educated at the University of Washington, Seattle, 1946-47. Married 1) Flora Parkinson in 1941 (divorced 1945), one daughter; 2) Beverly Ann Stuart in 1946, two sons; 3) Theresa. Reporter and editor for west coast newspapers; lecturer in general and interdisciplinary studies, University of Washington, 1970-72; social and ecological studies consultant, Lincoln Foundation and the countries of Vietnam and Pakistan, 1971. Director-photographer of television show, "The Tillers," 1973. Recipient: International Fantasy award, 1956, for *The Dragon in the Sea*; Nebula award, 1965, for *Dune*; Hugo award, 1966, for *Dune*; Prix Apollo, 1978; Doctor of Humanities, Seattle University, Washington, 1980. *Died 12 February 1986.*

PUBLICATIONS

Fiction

The Dragon in the Sea. Doubleday, 1956; London, Gollancz, 1960; as *21st Century Sub,* New York, Avon, 1956; as *Under Pressure,* New York, Ballantine, 1974.
Dune. Philadelphia, Chilton, 1965; London, Gollancz, 1966.
Destination: Void. New York, Berkley, 1966; London, Penguin, 1967.
The Eyes of Heisenberg. New York, 1966; London, Sphere, 1968.
The Green Brain. New York, Ace, 1966; London, New English Library, 1973.
The Heaven Makers. New York, Avon, 1968; London, New English Library, 1970.
The Santaroga Barrier. New York, Berkley, 1968; London, Rapp and Whiting, 1970.
Dune Messiah. New York, Putnam, 1969; London, Gollancz, 1971.
Whipping Star. New York, Putnam, 1970; London, New English Library, 1972; revised edition, New York, Berkley, 1977.
The God Makers. New York, Putnam, and London, New English Library, 1972.
Soul Catcher. New York, Putnam, 1972; London, New English Library, 1973.
Hellstrom's Hive. New York, Doubleday, 1973; London, New English Library, 1974; as *Project 40,* New York, Bantam, 1973.
Children of Dune. New York, Berkley, and London, Gollancz, 1976.
The Dosadi Experiment. New York, Putnam, 1977; London, Gollancz, 1978.
The Illustrated Dune. New York, Berkley, 1978; as *The Great Dune Trilogy* (includes *Dune, Dune Messiah,* and *Children of Dune*). London, Gollancz, 1979.
The Jesus Incident, with Bill Ransom. New York, Berkley, and London, Gollancz, 1979.
Direct Descent. New York, Ace, 1980; London, New English Library, 1982.
God Emperor of Dune. New York, Putnam, and London, Gollancz, 1981.
The White Plague. New York, Putnam, 1982; London, Gollancz, 1983.
The Lazarus Effect, with Bill Ransom. New York, Putnam, and London, Gollancz, 1983.
Heretics of Dune. New York, Putnam, and London, Gollancz, 1984.
Chapterhouse: Dune. New York, Putnam, and London, Gollancz, 1985.

Man of Two Worlds, with Brian Herbert. New York, Putnam, and London, Gollancz, 1986.

The Second Great Dune Trilogy (includes *God Emperor of Dune, Heretics of Dune,* and *Chapterhouse: Dune*). London, Gollancz, 1987.

Worlds beyond Dune: The Best of Frank Herbert (includes *The Jesus Incident, Whipping Star, Destination: Void, The God Makers,* and *The Dosadi Experiment*). New York, Berkley, 1987.

The Ascension Factor, with Bill Ransom. New York, Putnam, and London, Gollancz, 1988.

Songs of Muad'Dib: The Poetry of Frank Herbert, edited by Brian Herbert. New York, Ace, 1992.

Short Stories

Five Fates, with others. New York, Doubleday, 1970.

The Worlds of Frank Herbert. London, New English Library, 1970; New York, Ace, 1971.

The Book of Frank Herbert. New York, DAW, 1973; London, Panther, 1977.

The Best of Frank Herbert, edited by Angus Wells. London, Sidgwick and Jackson, 1975.

The Priests of Psi and Other Stories. London, Gollancz, 1980.

Eye, edited Byron Preiss. New York, Berkley, 1985; London, Gollancz, 1986.

Other

Editor, *New World or No World.* New York, Ace, 1970.

Threshold: The Blue Angels Experience. New York, Ballantine, 1973.

Editor, with others, *Tomorrow, and Tomorrow, and Tomorrow....* New York, Holt, Rinehart, 1974.

Without Me You're Nothing: The Essential Guide to Home Computers, with Max Barnard. New York, Simon and Schuster, and London, Gollancz, 1981; as *The Home Computer Handbook,* London, New English Library, 1985.

Editor, *Nebula Winners 15.* New York, Harper, 1981; London, W.H. Allen, 1982.

*

Media Adaptations: "Sandworms of Dune" (recording), Caedmon, 1978; "The Truths of Dune" (recording), Caedmon, 1979; "The Battles of Dune" (recording), Caedmon, 1979; *The Art of Dune* (book), New York, Berkley, 1984; *Dune* (film, screenplay by David Lynch), Universal, 1984; *The Dune Storybook* (book) by Joan Vinge, New York, Putnam, 1984; *Dune: The Making of Dune* (book), by Ed Naha, New York, Berkley, 1984; "The World of Dune" (teaching kit), Life-time Learning Systems, Inc., 1984.

Manuscript Collection: California State University Library, Fullerton.

Critical Study: *Herbert's Dune and Other Works* by Louis David Allen, Nebraska, Cliff's Notes, 1975; entry in *Contemporary Literary Criticism,* Detroit, Gale, Volume 12, 1980, Volume 23, 1983, Volume 35, 1985, Volume 44, 1987; essay in *Dictionary of Literary Biography,* Volume 8, Detroit, Gale, 1981; *Frank Herbert* by Timothy O'Reilly, New York, Ungar, 1981; *The Dune Encyclopedia* edited by Willis E. McNelly, New York, Putnam, and London, Corgi, 1984; *The Maker of Dune: Insights of a Master of Science*

Fiction edited by Timothy O'Reilly, New York, Berkeley, 1987; *The Notebooks of Frank Herbert's Dune* edited by Brian Herbert, New York, Perigree Books, 1988.

*   *   *

Frank Herbert was a prolific writer, mainly of science fiction, producing more than twenty novels and dozens of short stories in his fifty-year career. Nearly all of his novels and story collections are accessible to and appropriate for young adults even though they were written for an older audience and, therefore, occasionally contain depictions of violence and sexual behavior that may not be appropriate for younger readers. Most readers agree that the six novels in the Hugo and Nebula award-winning "Dune" series comprise Herbert's main achievement, while opinions vary about which of Herbert's other works are most worth reading.

Though the "Dune" series is appropriate for young adults, the opening novel, *Dune,* is fairly daunting. Herbert plunges the reader into an alien future centered around a complex interplanetary civilization. The social and political organization of this civilization is based on feudal models and seems strange at first because of the technologies and the socio-political consequences Herbert has imagined. The characters are driven by familiar human motives: love, power, and the need for self-knowledge. Duke Leto Atreides finds himself caught up in a subtle and highly complex power struggle that brings his family and forces to the planet Arrakis, or Dune, which is the source of "the spice," a kind of drug that releases the human mind into a hyper-perceptive state and lengthens the lifespan of its user. This drug is crucial to this civilization because it allows space travel between two points without moving while simultaneously allowing an accident-free course projection. The economic structure of this society is based on the "spice." Likewise, the spiritual organization of this civilization depends on this drug allowing women trained in its use, called Bene Gesserit, to share the literal memories of their foremothers. The vividness, completeness, and complexity of Herbert's universe are its most attractive features, but the fact that he opens the novel by dropping the reader into events already taking place makes the series difficult to begin. Readers must persist despite confusion for perhaps a quarter of the novel before gaining enough knowledge of Herbert's world to feel at home. A teacher might introduce students to this novel by viewing the David Lynch film adaptation.

Herbert encourages his readers to endure their confusion at the beginning of *Dune* by involving them quickly and deeply in the inner lives of the main characters, especially fifteen-year-old Paul, the Duke's son, and his mother, Jessica. All of the novels in the series focus on the relations between individuals in conflict over political power, so they are both political and personal. Herbert wants the reader to care for those characters who are trying to make and preserve affectionate relationships and who are trying to use political power for humane goals. He also reveals the inner lives of characters who live for personal power and those who have been forced or seduced into being the tools of power-seekers. The result is a combination of intense personal drama and political, economic, and military intrigue. This combination raises many questions and themes about the nature and limits of political power and about the qualities of a proper society.

Dune tells how the Atreides family is almost destroyed on the planet Arrakis. The Duke is killed, while Paul and his mother are lost and presumed dead in the desert that covers most of the planet. However, Paul and Jessica succeed in becoming leaders of the

Fremen, the powerful but reticent native population of the planet. Eventually, they are able to work with the ecology, wildlife, and people of Arrakis to defeat and replace the interplanetary emperor who has plotted their destruction all along.

The next three novels in the series span thousands of years, telling in the same compelling fashion the story of how humanity manages to spread itself among planets in such a way as to ensure the ultimate survival of the species, yet in each, stories of the personal struggle for love and the realization of humanity's best impulses are balanced with political and military adventure. In *Dune Messiah,* a central problem is Paul's wish to disengage from the restrictions of his being emperor in order to have an ordinary family life with his beloved Chani. This is complicated by a conspiracy to dethrone and kill him, by his loss of sight, and by his unique ability to infer and envision future events. In *Children of Dune,* Paul's son, Leto II, becomes the main character. He shares his father's power of prescience, but he sees a way to ensure increasing unpredictability in the behavior of human masses by fragmenting the species into widely separated groups inhabiting planets unknown to each other. This plan he calls "the golden path." *God Emperor of Dune* takes place 3500 years after *Children of Dune.* To achieve humanity's golden path, Leto has physically bonded with a sand-trout, and has become a sandworm, the animal responsible for producing the spice. This bonding has made him virtually invulnerable. He rules a boringly stable empire in which he secretly foments the rebellion that leads to the golden path. *Heretics of Dune* and *Chapter House: Dune* take up future human history thousands of years after the success of the golden path. These last two novels, in a series that would have included another had Herbert lived, develop a new and different story set in the universe of the first four.

None of Herbert's other works is so well-known as the "Dune" series. *The Dragon in the Sea, The Eyes of Heisenberg, The God Makers, The Green Brain, Hellstrom's Hive,* and *Whipping Star* are among the most popular, all having been translated into several European languages. Like the *Dune* series, these novels emphasize complex adventure plots with attention to cosmic questions about human nature and society.

—Terry Heller

——————

HERMES, Patricia. American. Born in Brooklyn, New York, 21 February 1936. Educated at St. John's University, Jamaica, New York, B.A. 1957. Married Matthew E. Hermes in 1957 (divorced 1984), four sons and one daughter. Teacher of English and social studies, Rollingcrest Junior High School, Takoma Park, Maryland, 1957-58; teacher of home-bound children, Delcastle Technical High School, Delcastle, Delaware, 1972-73; writer, 1977—; writer in residence, Norfolk Public School System, Norfolk, Virginia, 1981—; teacher of English and writing, Scared Heart University, Fairfield, Connecticut, 1986-87. Recipient: *A Solitary Secret* was named Best Book for young adults for 1985 by the American Library Association; several Children's Choice awards. Agent: Dorothy Markinko, McIntosh and Otis, Inc., 310 Madison Avenue, New York, NY 10017. Address: 1414 Melville Avenue, Fairfield, CT 06430, U.S.A.

PUBLICATIONS FOR YOUNG ADULTS

Fiction

What If They Knew. San Diego, California, Harcourt, 1980.
Nobody's Fault. San Diego, California, Harcourt, 1981.
You Shouldn't Have to Say Goodbye. San Diego, California, Harcourt, 1982.
Who Will Take Care of Me? San Diego, California, Harcourt, 1983.
Friends Are Like That. San Diego, California, Harcourt, 1984.
A Solitary Secret. San Diego, California, Harcourt, 1985.
Kevin Corbett Eats Flies, illustrated by Carol Newsom. San Diego, California, Harcourt, 1986.
A Place for Jeremy. San Diego, California, Harcourt, 1987.
A Time to Listen: Preventing Youth Suicide. San Diego, California, Harcourt, 1987.
Heads, I Win, illustrated by Carol Newsom. San Diego, California, Harcourt, 1988.
Be Still My Heart. New York, Putnam, 1989.
I Hate Being Gifted. New York, Putnam, 1990.
Mama, Let's Dance. Boston, Little Brown, 1991.
My Girl. New York, Simon and Schuster, 1991.
Take Care of My Girl. Boston, Little Brown, 1992.

*

Biography: Essay in *Speaking for Ourselves, Too* compiled and edited by Donald R. Gallo, National Council of Teachers of English, 1993.

*   *   *

The body of Patricia Hermes's work consists of realistic young adult fiction. Mainly contemporary, her novels focus on common adolescent concerns, including moving to a new town or making new friends, and more specific situations, such as incest or parental abandonment. Problem novels such as these tend to condescend to readers, focusing on a specific issue at the expense of plot and character development, and offering solutions where sometimes none can be reached. Hermes attempts to avoid these foibles by implementing a first-person narrative voice in the majority of her books. Allowing a character to tell his or her own story adds dimension and complexity to the character. A young reader recognizes the motivations of the characters because of their simultaneous experience of incidents. Tracy's shabby treatment of her lifelong friend Kelly in *Friends Are Like That* and her desire to be part of the popular crowd mirrors the experience of many young adults—her voice rings true.

Hermes's use of the first-person narrative unfortunately results in a lack of development of the other characters. Angela, the popular girl Tracy encounters, never goes beyond stereotype. The peripheral characters in most of Hermes's novels suffer from the same shallowness. The concentration on one individual interior voice also leads to weaker plots and settings.

The concentration on one young adult allows Hermes, in many of her works, to explore the idea of hidden shame. Most young people do not want to be different; conformity becomes almost an obsession. A step toward maturity comes with the realization that everyone has secrets, problems they will not tell even their "best friend." Hermes's writing becomes didactic in her desire to emphasize this point. *A Solitary Secret,* written in journal form, tells the story of a young, nameless incest victim. The novel is set during World War I, perhaps to remove the immediacy for a contemporary reader, and uses imagery to soften the horrifying abuse. A new girl, Sheila, moves to town, and the girls begin a game of sharing secrets. It quickly becomes obvious Sheila also has something to hide—a fatal illness. By creating such dramatic instances of secrecy, Hermes's writing becomes heavy-handed. This overkill also occurs in *You Shouldn't Have to Say Goodbye*. While dealing with her mother's cancer, Sarah also discovers that her best friend's mother suffers from agoraphobia. When tackling illness within a family—epilepsy, mental retardation, cancer, etc.—Hermes explores all the emotions of her character. The anger and selfish worry of a youngster sounds authentic. Death and illness force young people to grow up quickly. Sarah becomes frightened and angry when her mother teaches her how to do laundry because she knows what the lesson signifies.

Hermes also recognizes the pain of abandonment, either by death or by a parent leaving. In both *Take Care of My Girl* and *Mama, Let's Dance,* children are abandoned by a parent. When Brady attempts to find her father, she learns that he lives only about an hour from the house where she and her grandfather live. Acknowledging that her father does not want her, while painful, allows Brady to rework her definition of a family, and recognize her special relationship with her grandfather. When Mary Belle's mother abandons her three children, they attempt to survive on their own so that they will not be placed in separate foster homes. Both young girls gain a sense of worth and self-reliance from a painful lesson—that adults can, and do, fail.

Many of Hermes's protagonists also achieve self-reliance when their faith in God falters. Mary Belle wishes she could find peace in prayer like her brother Ariel, but she needs more tangible assurances. This doubt in the existence of a God who lets siblings and parents die will echo in the minds of some young readers, and Hermes does a commendable job of balancing lack of conviction with respect for religion.

Although many adults in these novels fail the children around them, some operate as saviors. The incest victim gives her journal to a kind neighbor who steers her toward help; Mary Belle's neighbors take her and her brother in once their secret is discovered. For younger readers, this assurance that adults can help provides security. Many problems like the ones Hermes's deals with in her novels cannot be solved by adolescents alone. The helping adult figure only becomes problematic when it offers a neat, clean resolution. The tidy endings seem preachy, and overly sentimental. Readers know that all situations do not resolve themselves easily, and may feel cheated by happy endings. Clean endings contrast with cluttered beginnings. Hermes sometimes tries to tackle too much, and she tends to concentrate on issues rather than characters. For example, in *Take Care of My Girl,* every page seems to contain some message about environmental responsibility.

What Hermes's novels may lack in literary value, they compensate for in their strong narrative voices and accurate portrayals of the pain of adolescence. Her dedication to young people also manifests itself in her nonfiction work, *A Time to Listen: Preventing Youth Suicide.* Indeed, many of her books of fiction occasionally read like self-help manuals, but will nonetheless reach young readers with their honesty and empathy.

—Karen Walsh

HERRIOT, James. Pseudonym for James Alfred Wight. English. Born in Sunderland, County Tyne and Werr, England, 3 October 1916. Educated at Glasgow Veterinary College, M.R.C.V.S. 1938. Served in Royal Air Force, 1943-45. Married Joan Catherine Danbury in 1941; one daughter and one son. General practitioner in veterinary medicine, Yorkshire, England, 1938—; writer, 1966—. Recipient: *All Things Bright and Beautiful* was chosen one of ALA's Best Young Adult Books, 1974, and *All Creatures Great and Small,* 1975; Officer of the British Empire, 1979; D.Litt., Watt University, Scotland, 1979; honorary D. Vsc., Liverpool University, 1984. Address: c/o Michael Joseph Limited, 27 Wrights Lane, London W8 5TZ, England.

PUBLICATIONS FOR ADULTS AND YOUNG ADULTS

Nonfiction

If Only They Could Talk. London, M. Joseph, 1970.
It Shouldn't Happen to a Vet. London, M. Joseph, 1972.
All Creatures Great and Small (includes *If Only They Could Talk* and *It Shouldn't Happen to a Vet*). New York, St. Martin's, 1972.
Let Sleeping Vets Lie. London, M. Joseph, 1973.
Vet in Harness. London, M. Joseph, 1974.
All Things Bright and Beautiful (includes *Let Sleeping Vets Lie* and *Vet in Harness*). New York, St. Martin's, 1974.
Vets Might Fly. London, M. Joseph, 1976.
Vet in a Spin. London, M. Joseph, 1977.
All Things Wise and Wonderful (includes *Vets Might Fly* and *Vet in a Spin*). New York, St. Martin's, 1977.
James Herriot's Yorkshire. New York, St. Martin's, 1979.
Animals Tame and Wild, with others. New York, Sterling, 1979; as *Animal Stories: Tame and Wild,* New York, Sterling, 1985.
The Lord God Made Them All. New York, St. Martin's, 1981.
The Best of James Herriot. New York, St. Martin's, 1983.
James Herriot's Dog Stories. New York, St. Martin's, 1986.
Every Living Thing. New York, St. Martin's, 1992.

PUBLICATIONS FOR CHILDREN

Fiction

Moses the Kitten, illustrated by Peter Barrett. New York, St. Martin's, 1984.
Only One Woof, illustrated by Peter Barrett. New York, St. Martin's, 1985.
The Christmas Day Kitten, illustrated by Ruth Brown. New York, St. Martin's, 1986.
Bonny's Big Day, illustrated by Ruth Brown. New York, St. Martin's, 1987.
Blossom Comes Home, illustrated by Ruth Brown. New York, St. Martin's, 1988.
The Market Square Dog, illustrated by Ruth Brown. New York, St. Martin's, 1989.
Oscar: Cat-About-Town, illustrated by Ruth Brown. New York, St. Martin's, 1990.
Smudge: The Little Lost Lamb, illustrated by Ruth Brown. New York, St. Martin's, 1991.
James Herriot's Treasury for Children, illustrated by Peter Barrett and Ruth Brown. New York, St. Martin's, 1992.

Media Adaptations: *All Creatures Great and Small* (film), EMI Productions, 1975; (television movie), NBC-TV, 1975; (television series), BBC, 1978; PBS-TV, 1979; (cassette), Listen for Pleasure, 1980; *All Things Bright and Beautiful* (film), BBC-TV, 1979; (cassette), Listen for Pleasure, 1980; *The Lord God Made Them All* (cassette), Listen for Pleasure, 1982; *All Things Wise and Wonderful* (cassette), Cassette Book; *Stories from the Herriot Collection* (cassette), Listen for Pleasure.

Biography: Essay in *Authors and Artists for Young Adults,* Volume 1, Detroit, Gale, 1989.

Critical Study: Entry in *Contemporary Literary Criticism,* Volume 12, Detroit, Gale, 1980.

*   *   *

Alf Wight may have been born in 1916 to be a veterinarian, but readers throughout the world can be grateful that in 1966 James Herriot the writer was born. The works of this gifted author have such a broad appeal that even the classification of children's works and adult publications is arbitrary. Each of his works appeals to the most fundamental values in the reader so that only the length, not the thematic sophistication, of such novels as *All Creatures Great and Small* would deter younger readers. And in all James Herriot's writing, the earthy portraits of both human and animal characters, combined with a delightful humor, attract an older reader.

Herriot's primary works are the five novels which detail his life as a veterinarian in the rural Yorkshire town of Darrowby where he and his partners Tristan and Sigfried Farnon treat the animals of the village folk and rugged farmers of the region. *All Creatures Great and Small* begins the reader's odyssey through the career of young James Herriot, and *Every Living Thing* brings this journey to a close (at least for the moment since Herriot fans no doubt hope for an additional volume in the future). Herriot's stories are not just about animals and the difficulties faced by a veterinarian in the rugged north country of England. In each novel, the reader meets extremely well-drawn characters: the peculiar senior partner in the veterinarian practice Sigfried, his reckless younger brother Tristan, the gentle Helen (later Herriot's wife), a range of elderly ladies with their beloved cats, and gruff farmers doubting the ability of a young veterinarian to heal their prized bulls, horses, and sheep. Combining this array of characters, Herriot builds a rich texture in his novels which makes them more than fine animal books; instead he creates a tapestry of human behavior as reflected by the relationships people have with the animals they rely on for both companionship and livelihood.

The simple didactic quality in Herriot's work emerges from the vignettes dealing with the life of a country veterinarian, many of which rely on an effective, understated humor. Memorable among these are the episodes involving the pampered Tricki Woo and his indulgent owner Mrs. Pumphrey, the scene when Herriot and Tristan mishandle an effort to milk a bull for the purposes of artificial insemination (with painful result), the episode when Herriot accidentally injects one of his helpers while attending to a large cow, and the many efforts made by Herriot to save an animal from the folk medicine diagnoses of various pretenders to medical skill. These episodes also give the reader a familiar look into the lifestyle of the Yorkshire farmer who scrapes out a living in a rugged country and the life of a small English village with its tiny shops and open air markets; they introduce the inspiring character of Granville Bennet whose skill in animal surgery is matched only by his Epicurean excesses and the knacker Jeff Mallock who picks up the remains of Herriot's unsuccessful efforts.

Herriot's descriptive skill is excellent. The reader is transported through his words to the snow-covered hillsides in the Yorkshire dales and the bustling streets and rowdy pubs on market day in the county's villages. And all this material—on the practice of veterinary medicine and the country lifestyle of Yorkshire—fuses well with the first person narratives of Herriot's life as he began a profession, courted and married Helen, served in the British Royal Air Force during World War II, raised his children, and, always, remained close to the animals he loves.

Herriot will not receive the critical accolades that his popularity would argue he deserves. But the very lack of a "literary" style is the most attractive feature of his work. He is a simple storyteller, somewhat in the vein of some of literary history's finest writers, such as Twain, Scott, and Poe. And if the literary scholars have not taken particular notice, readers throughout the world have, which for Herriot was no doubt the purpose for providing a glimpse into his life in the first place.

—Gerald W. Morton

———

HILL, Douglas (Arthur). Also writes as Martin Hillman. Canadian. Born in Brandon, Manitoba, Canada, 6 April 1935. Educated at schools in Prince Albert, Saskatchewan; University of Saskatchewan, Saskatoon, 1952-57, B.A. (honours) in English 1957; University of Toronto, 1957-59. Married Gail Robinson in 1958 (divorced 1978); one son. Series editor, Aldus Books, London, 1962-64. Since 1964 freelance writer. Literary editor, *Tribune,* London, 1971-84. Science fiction advisor, Rupert Hart-Davis, 1966-68, Mayflower Books, 1969-71, J.M. Dent and Sons, 1972-74, and Pan Books, 1974-80, all London. Recipient: Canada Council grant, 1966, 1969, 1970. Agent: Sheila Watson, Watson Little Ltd., 12 Egbert Street, London NW1 8LJ. Address: 3 Hillfield Ave., London N8 7DU, England.

PUBLICATIONS FOR YOUNG ADULTS

Fiction

Galactic Warlord. London, Gollancz, 1979; New York, Atheneum, 1980.
Deathwing over Veynaa. London, Gollancz, 1980; New York, Atheneum, 1981.
Day of the Starwind. London, Gollancz, 1980; New York, Atheneum, 1981.
Planet of the Warlord. London, Gollancz, 1981; New York, Atheneum, 1982.
Young Legionary: The Earlier Adventures of Keill Randor. London, Gollancz, 1982; New York, Atheneum, 1983.
The Huntsman. London, Heinemann, and New York, Atheneum, 1982.
Have Your Own Extraterrestrial Adventure. London, Sparrow, 1983.
Warriors of the Wasteland. London, Heinemann, and New York, Atheneum, 1983.

Alien Citadel. London, Heinemann, and New York, Atheneum, 1984.

Exiles of ColSec. London, Gollancz, and New York, Atheneum, 1984.

The Caves of Klydor. London, Gollancz, 1984; New York, Atheneum, 1985.

The Moon Monsters, illustrated by Jeremy Ford. London, Heinemann, 1984.

ColSec Rebellion. London, Gollancz, and New York, Atheneum, 1985.

How Jennifer (and Speckle) Saved the Earth, illustrated by André Amstutz. London, Heinemann, 1986.

Blade of the Poisoner. London, Gollancz, and New York, McElderry, 1987.

Master of Fiends. London, Gollancz, 1987; New York, McElderry, 1988.

Goblin Party, illustrated by Paul Demayer. London, Gollancz, 1988.

Penelope's Pendant, illustrated by Steve Johnson. London, Macmillan, and New York, Doubleday, 1990.

Unicorn Dream, London, Heinemann, 1992.

Trellie the Troog, London, BBC Radio and Longman, 1991.

The Voyage of Mudjack, London, Methuen, 1993.

Penelope's Protest, London, Pan, forthcoming.

World of the Stiks, London, Transworld, forthcoming.

Other

Coyote the Trickster: Legends of the North American Indians, with Gail Robinson, illustrated by Graham McCallum. London, Chatto and Windus, 1975; New York, Crane Russak, 1976.

The Exploits of Hercules, illustrated by Tom Barling. London, Pan, 1978.

Editor, *Alien Worlds.* London, Heinemann, 1981.

Editor, *Planetfall.* Oxford, Oxford University Press, 1986.

The Young Green Consumer Guide, with John Elkington, Joel Merkower, and Julia Hailes. London, Gollancz, 1990; as *Going Green: A Kid's Handbook to Saving the Planet,* New York, Viking, 1990.

PUBLICATIONS FOR ADULTS

Other

Contributor, *Poetmeat Anthology of British Poetry.* Blackburn, Lancashire, Screeches Publications, 1965.

The Supernatural, with Pat Williams. London, Aldus, 1965; New York, Hawthorn, 1966.

Editor, *The Peasants' Revolt: A Collection of Contemporary Documents.* London, Jackdaw, 1966.

Editor, *The Way of the Werewolf.* London, Panther, 1966.

Editor, *Window on the Future.* London, Hart Davis, 1966.

Editor, *The Devil His Due.* London, Hart Davis, 1967; New York, Avon, 1969.

The Opening of the Canadian West. London, Heinemann, and New York, Day, 1967.

Contributor, *Young British Poets.* Geneva, Poésie Vivante, 1967.

Magic and Superstition. London, Hamlyn, 1968.

John Keats. London, Morgan Grampian, 1968.

Contributor, *Poems from Poetry and Jazz in Concert.* London, Souvenir Press, 1969.

Regency London. London, Macdonald, 1969.

Fortune Telling. London, Hamlyn, 1970.

A Hundred Years of Georgian London. London, Macdonald, 1970; New York, Hastings House, 1971.

Return from the Dead. London, Macdonald, 1970; as *The History of Ghosts, Vampires, and Werewolves,* New York, Harrow, 1973.

Editor, *Warlocks and Warriors.* London, Mayflower, 1971.

The Scots to Canada. London, Gentry, 1972.

The Comet. London, Wildwood, 1973.

Witchcraft, Magic, and the Supernatural, with others. London, Octopus, 1974.

The English to New England. London, Gentry, and New York, Potter, 1975.

Editor, *Tribune 40.* London, Quartet, 1977.

Fortune Telling: A Guide to Reading the Future. London, Hamlyn, 1978.

Editor, *The Shape of Sex to Come.* London, Pan, 1978.

The Illustrated "Faerie Queene" (retelling). New York and London, Newsweek, 1980.

The Fraxilly Fracas. London, Gollancz, 1989.

The Colloghi Conspiracy. London, Gollancz, 1990.

The Lightless Dome. London, Pan, 1993.

The Leafless Forest. London, Pan, forthcoming.

Other as Martin Hillman

Bridging a Continent. London, Aldus, 1971; revised edition, London, Reader's Digest Association, 1978, 1979.

*

Biography: Essay in *Speaking for Ourselves, Too* compiled and edited by Donald R. Gallo, National Council of Teachers of English, 1993.

Douglas Hill comments:

Since no youthful reading habit comes into existence in a single, fully formed leap from (say) Ninja Turtles to the novels of Dickens, I think of myself as constructing some lower rungs on the ladder that is needed for that sort of ascent. At the same time, because I specialize in science fiction and fantasy, I like to think that I'm doing my bit towards maintaining the health of the imagination—which may be the only thing that distinguishes the human mind from another item of information technology.

*   *   *

Douglas Hill, a Canadian, came to London as a young man to further his writing career and was for years a journalist and author of popular nonfiction. A lifelong science-fiction fan, he was deploring the lack of SF for young readers in the hearing of a publisher, who took him at his word and challenged him to write some himself. Then began a period of intense midlife creativity, in which Hill produced thirteen science fiction/fantasy novels for ten- to fourteen-year-olds in nine years, plus some short fantasies for beginning readers. Now he is writing longer adult novels and, judging by the first two, they are accessible to teenage readers as well.

All Hill's YA novels are composed in the series format: first a quartet, with a prequel written afterwards, then two trilogies, and finally a two-parter. The "Last Legionary" quartet presents a tough fighting hero, a kind of space mercenary, but with a heart and conscience. Looking for a rationale for his hero's fighting superiority and relative invulnerability, Hill invented the planet Moros, where youngsters were trained in survival and combat skills in order to cope with their planet's hostile environment and native "monsters." Then adults from Moros would hire themselves out to other planets to help win wars, in conflicts chosen on a strictly ethical basis. When all living things on Moros are destroyed by radiation, Keill Randor, the only survivor, is recruited by a secret group of scientists to discover the cause, whom they have called the "Warlord," an evil genius bent on sowing dissent and eventually ruling the galaxy.

Because Keill is also dying of radiation, the scientists replace his bones "molecule by molecule" with "an organic alloy." This completely fantastic concept does however render plausible Keill's survival in his many hand-to-hand combats without even a broken bone. Eventually, by intelligence, strength, and guts, Keill slogs his way to the heart of the Warlord's empire, aided by a female telepathic alien who pilots his spaceship and warns him of danger. Hill's punchy, exaggerated style is best shown by quotation:

> The ship lurched sideways, metal screeching against stone like a death cry, and toppled with a slow finality into the yawning mouth of the pit that had opened beneath it.

> (From *Day of the Starwind*)

> OS-9 sprawled on the moss like a stringless puppet, his broken jaw askew and his head twisted in a manner that showed how cleanly his neck had been snapped.

> (From *Starwind*)

Hill had successfully identified a gap in the market. Juvenile SF was overliterary, full of "message" books about nuclear war and the destruction of civilisation. It needed an injection of traditional "space opera" to encourage the average reader, written in a professional "pulp" style. The time was right: the *Star Wars* craze had made reading SF fashionable among the young.

One could criticise the "Last Legionary" series for its overdetailed combat scenarios and lack of positive human female characters. Hill's following books remedied these faults. The "Huntsman" trilogy has a post-nuclear-war scenario. Earth has in fact suffered two disasters: centuries after the horror of nuclear war and radioactivity, Earth has been invaded by alien Slavers for its mining potential. Earthpeople are worked to death and regarded as barely sentient vermin. Set in Hill's native North America, the trilogy shows how two genetically altered humans bred in the Slavers' laboratories, the heroic Finn Ferral and the shaggy hair-covered beast-man Baer, team up to fight the Slavers. They journey to the Wastelands, the deserts of Central North America, where they join tribes of native Americans resisting the Slavers, and Finn meets his kidnapped foster-sister, now a woman-warrior. Success in the struggle against the Slavers restores humankind's pride, and eventually Planet Earth regains its freedom.

Hill's third trilogy returns to space opera with a theme from Heinlein: teenagers dispatched through space to colonise new planets. Sent as a punishment by ColSec—Colonization Section—five teenagers, three from street gangs and two minor offenders against the law, bond together on the planet Klydor, fight or make truce with aliens, defeat the ColSec inspectors, and lead a rebellion of the colonised planets to win self-government and the right to sell their products at market value. The teenagers include Cord, the hero, exceptionally strong, from the Scottish highlands; Samella, a girl who is a computer expert; and Heleth, a street-fighting girl.

Hill's fourth series switched to fantasy, using the Dungeons-and-Dragons formula of several questers, each possessing special powers, which Hill calls Talents. Four gifted people (two male, two female) are recruited by a good wizard to combat the forces of evil, presented here as hideous demons. Three have aided him before. The fourth is twelve-year-old Jarral, the young hero, who possesses the special Talent of being able to call up the forces of nature, for example earthquakes and thunderstorms. In this two-parter, Hill imports into young people's literature the conventions of sword-and-sorcery, that popular genre of adult fantasy born in the United States SF magazines decades before *The Lord of the Rings* was published, and offers a vigorous alternative to the literary fantasies of Lewis, Garner, and Cooper. And one of Hill's drawbacks, the way that his evil characters usually *look* ugly too, is irrelevant when the evil characters are demons or long-lived sorcerers who have worked evil for centuries.

Making the jump to adult SF, Hill wrote two comic space operas about Del Curb, an Intergalactic Courier, a fellow who thinks he's attractive to women. Accustomed to making sexist observations, he can't fool an intelligent woman, though he encounters a few females who make advances to *him,* some welcome, some not. Curb narrates himself, with throwaway lines like: "He seems crazy as a Phyquollian thorn-leaper" and "I felt as if I'd been kicked in the stomach by a Naspiddoric stone-tail." In this future, the galaxy is populated throughout, either by settlers from Earth or sentient aliens, and faster-than-light travel is essential. Earth itself was ruined by nuclear war centuries before, Curb tells us noncommittedly, and is now ruled by giant mutant cockroaches. Aided by his super-intelligent ship's computer-pilot, Curb's aim to make a profit from his shady deals is usually frustrated by pirates and criminal gangs, but in both books he wins out. Lacking explicit sex, these might go into YA SF collections, though not as good as Harry Harrison's humorous SF, their more accomplished model.

Douglas Hill writes more from the head (and the thesaurus) than the heart, but when both combine, as in the "Huntsman" and "Blade of the Poisoner" series, he deserves much praise for creating ethical fantasy which appeals to reluctant readers. The eagerness with which youngsters return a Douglas Hill book to demand the sequel justifies his midcareer change. Even as I write, his British publisher has announced *The World of the Stiks,* set on a distant planet.

—Jessica Yates

HILL, John. See **KOONTZ, Dean R.**

HILLERMAN, Tony. American. Born in Sacred Heart, Oklahoma, 27 May 1925. Raised among Pottawatomie and Seminole Indians; educated at Indian boarding school for eight years; Oklahoma State University, Stillwater; University of Oklahoma, Norman, B.A. in journalism 1948; University of New Mexico, Albuquerque, M.A. in English 1965. Served in the United States Army Infantry, 1943-45; Silver Star, Bronze Star, Purple Heart. Married Marie E. Unzner in 1948; three daughters and three sons. Reporter, *News Herald,* Borger, Texas, 1948; news editor, *Morning Press,* 1949, and city editor, *Constitution,* 1950, Lawton, Oklahoma; political reporter, United Press International, Oklahoma City, 1950-52; bureau manager, United Press, Santa Fe, New Mexico, 1952-54; political reporter, later executive editor, *New Mexican,* Santa Fe, 1954-62. Assistant to the President, 1963-66, 1976-81, Associate Professor, 1965-66, and Professor of Journalism and chair of Department, 1966-85, University of New Mexico; writer. Lecturer. Recipient: Shaffer award from the New Mexico Press Association, 1952, for reporting; Burrows award from the New Mexico Press Association, 1960, for editorial writing; *The Blessing Way* was selected one of American Library Association's Best Books for Young Adults, 1970, and *A Thief of Time,* 1988; Edgar Allan Poe award from the Mystery Writers of America, 1974, for *Dance Hall of the Dead;* Navajo Special Friend award, 1986, for "authentically depicting the strength and dignity of the Navajo culture in his books"; Western Writers of America Honor for Children's Literature, 1986, for *The Boy Who Made Dragonfly;* Grand Prix de Litterature Policiere (France), and Golden Spur award from the Western Writers of America for Best Novel of the Year, both 1987, both for *Skinwalkers.* D.H.L.: University of New Mexico. Agent: Curtis Brown Ltd., 575 Madison Ave., New York, NY 10022. Address: 1632 Francisca NW, Albuquerque, NM 87107, U.S.A.

PUBLICATIONS FOR ADULTS AND YOUNG ADULTS

Novels (series: Sergeant Jim Chee; Lieutenant Joe Leaphorn)

The Blessing Way (Leaphorn). New York, Harper, and London, Macmillan, 1970.
The Fly on the Wall. New York, Harper, 1971.
Dance Hall of the Dead. New York, Harper, 1973.
Listening Woman (Leaphorn). New York, Harper, 1978; London, Macmillan, 1979.
People of Darkness (Chee). New York, Harper, 1980; London, Gollancz, 1982.
The Dark Wind (Chee). New York, Harper, 1982; London, Gollancz, 1983.
The Ghostway (Chee). New York, Harper, and London, Gollancz, 1985.
Skinwalkers (Chee and Leaphorn). New York, Harper, 1987; London, Joseph, 1988.
A Thief of Time (Chee and Leaphorn). New York, Harper, 1988; London, Joseph, 1989.
The Joe Leaphorn Mysteries (omnibus). New York, Harper, 1989.
Talking God (Chee and Leaphorn). New York, Harper, 1989; London, Joseph, 1990.
Coyote Waits (Chee and Leaphorn). New York, Harper, 1990; London, Joseph, 1991.
Hillerman Country: A Journey through the Southwest with Tony Hillerman, photographs by Barney Hillerman. New York, HarperCollins, 1991.
Talking Mysteries: A Conversation with Tony Hillerman, illustrated by Ernest Franklin. Albuquerque, University of New Mexico Press, 1991.

Leaphorn and Chee: Three Classic Mysteries. New York, HarperCollins, 1992.

Other

The Great Taos Bank Robbery: And Other Indian Country Affairs. Albuquerque, University of New Mexico Press, 1973.
New Mexico, photographs by David Muench. Portland, Oregon, Belding, 1974.
Rio Grande, photographs by Robert Reynolds. Portland, Oregon, Belding, 1975.
Editor, *The Spell of New Mexico.* Albuquerque, University of New Mexico Press, 1976.
Indian Country: America's Sacred Land, photographs by Béla Kalman. Flagstaff, Arizona, Northland Press, 1987.
Editor, *The Best of the West: An Anthology of Classic Writing from the American West.* New York, HarperCollins, 1991.
Sacred Clowns. New York, HarperCollins, 1993.
New Mexico, Rio Grande, and Other Essays, photography by David Muench and Robert Reynolds. Portland, Oregon, Graphic Arts Center Press, 1992.
Tony Hillerman. Avenel, New Jersey, Outlet Book Company, 1992.

PUBLICATIONS FOR CHILDREN

Fiction

The Boy Who Made Dragonfly: A Zuni Myth, illustrated by Laszlo Kubinyi. New York, Harper, 1972; new edition, illustrated by Janet Grado, University of New Mexico Press, 1986.

*

Media Adaptations: *Dance Hall of the Dead* (cassette), Simon & Schuster, 1985; *A Thief of Time* (cassette), Caedmon, 1988; *Fly on the Wall* (cassette), Caedmon, 1989; *Talking God* (cassette), Caedmon, 1990.

Manuscript Collection: Zimmerman Library, University of New Mexico.

Critical Study: *Tony Hillerman: Blessing Way to Talking God,* by Louis A. Heib, n.p., Press of the Gigantic Hound, 1990.

*   *   *

Tony Hillerman writes mystery novels heavily salted with the myths and culture of the Navajo culture. *Newsweek* comments: "Hillerman consistently evokes nature and place.... He creates morality plays that are as subtly colored as their landscape." By exploring the places where the Navajo world abuts the white world, the author creates fascinating tales.

Hillerman concentrates on two major characters, both members of the Tribal Police: Joe Leaphorn, introduced in *The Blessing Way,* fiftyish, married to a traditional Navajo woman but insisting on rational explanations for the more primitive beliefs of his people; and Jim Chee, in his twenties, introduced in *The People of Darkness,* studying to be a yataalii, a shaman. In Hillerman's work it is the older man, rather than the younger, who is more skeptical, more inclined to question the cultural dictates of his people. Both men are steeped in their culture, but Leaphorn is less inclined to seek traditional measures to combat his ills. A Navajo ceremony, a Blessing Way, is needed after a person has been contaminated by the presence of a dead body. Chee undergoes this ritual several times in the course of the novels, Leaphorn only once. The shaman who holds the Way for Leaphorn is Jim Chee. Navajo beliefs about death and dying are very prevalent in Hillerman's novels, naturally enough, since most popular mysteries involve murder, and Hillerman's are no exception. The Navajo do not believe in an afterlife, merely in the presence of a ghost after death whose appearance contaminates a dwelling. Should a person die within a hogan, the home is abandoned, with a hole cut in the north wall to allow the ghost to escape.

The author addresses ecological and archeological concerns as well as cultural ones. Particularly in *A Thief of Time* and *Talking God*, Hillerman explores the dark underside of anthropologists' excavations in the southwest. Archeology for profit—disregarding the traditions of the descendants of the culture being explored—is the focus of *Talking God*. A member of the Smithsonian Institution is the focus of the inquiry. An Indian seeking to restore some of the bones in the museum's collections to their heirs, Henry Highhawk becomes a victim of the very forces he sought to enlist in his cause. Hillerman explores the morality of displaying Indian burials, by having his character, Highhawk, disinter the grandparents of a blue-blooded WASP who is Museum spokesperson. Highhawk sends her her grandparents' remains by UPS. His arrest for grave robbing (handled by Jim Chee) points up the difference between excavating ancient graves and opening modern ones. The title *A Thief of Time* refers to persons who steal artifacts from an archaeological site to sell for their own profit.

Hillerman's characters are given the opportunity to grow with each new adventure. Leaphorn's wife has died, and Chee has gone from an Anglo-Saxon, blue-eyed, blonde girlfriend to an uneasy relationship with a young Navajo woman who is a lawyer. The two men have gone from working separately to appearing together. Although they work for different offices of the Tribal Police, they make an effective team. By the finish of *Coyote Waits*, Joe Leaphorn is contemplating a trip to China with an Associate Professor of American Studies from Arizona State, Louisa Bourebonette, and Jim Chee ponders his relationship with the lawyer, Janet Pete. Leaphorn is also contemplating retirement; in fact his involvement in the case stems not from his role as a policeman, but from the fact that the accused criminal is a relative of Leaphorn's late wife.

The world of the modern Navajo provides the setting for the novels and plays almost as important a role as do the two protagonists. The vast arid land, populated by shepherds and horsemen, presents an entirely different aspect to the "detective" novel. Hillerman was an innovator in this respect, making the ethnic hero and setting popular with modern readers. In *Talking God*, for example, a great deal of the action fluctuates between cosmopolitan Washington, D.C. and the emptiness of the desert reservation. The crime was plotted in the city, but the wasteland of Arizona provides the perfect spot for the murderer to dispose of his target.

Leaphorn and Chee, as Tribal Police, are constantly running into conflicts of interest with the FBI and the Anglo police forces. Questions of jurisdiction often occupy the two men. Frequently, Leaphorn or Chee must figure out how to investigate a case that is not legitimately theirs without stepping on any other law enforcement officer's toes. The conflicts thus created add dimension to the characters and enhance the plot.

Tony Hillerman is a master of his craft. His work is well-constructed and well-plotted. The *Boston Globe* book review calls him "one of the finest and most original craftsmen at work in the genre today." He is that—and more.

—Louise J. Winters

HINTON, S(usan) E(loise). American. Born in Tulsa, Oklahoma, in 1950. Educated at the University of Tulsa, B.S. in education 1970. Married David E. Inhofe in 1970; one son. Writer of young adult novels since age sixteen. Consultant on film adaptations of her novels; minor acting roles in some film adaptations of her novels. Recipient: *New York Herald Tribune* best teenage books list, 1967; *Chicago Tribune Book World* Spring Book Festival Honor Book, 1967; American Library Association Best Young Adult Books, 1975, *Media and Methods* Maxi Award, 1975, American Library Association Newcott Caldeberry award, 1976, Massachusetts Children's Book Award, 1979, all for *The Outsiders*; ALA Best Books for Young Adults list, 1971, *Chicago Tribune Book World* Spring Book Festival Honor Book, 1971, and Massachusetts Children's Book Award, 1978, all for *That Was Then, This Is Now*; ALA Best Books for Young Adults list, 1975, *School Library Journal* Best Books of the Year list, 1975, and Land of Enchantment award, New Mexico Library Association, 1982, all for *Rumble Fish*; ALA Best Books for Young Adults List, 1979, *School Library Journal* Best Books of the Year list, 1979, New York Public Library Books for the Teen-Age, 1980, American Book Award nomination for children's paperback, 1981, Sue Hefly Honor Book, Louisiana Association of School Libraries, 1982, California Young Reader Medal nomination, California Reading Association, 1982, and Sue Hefly Award, 1983, all for *Tex*; Golden Archer Award, 1983; recipient of first ALA Young Adult Services Division/*School Library Journal* Author Award, 1988, for body of work. Address: c/o Press Relations, Dell Publishing Co., 666 Fifth Avenue, 10th fl., New York, NY 10103, U.S.A.

PUBLICATIONS FOR YOUNG ADULTS

Fiction

The Outsiders. New York, Viking Press, 1967; London, Gollancz, 1970.
That Was Then, This Is Now. New York, Viking Press, and London, Gollancz, 1971.
Rumble Fish. New York, Delacorte Press, 1975; London, Gollancz, 1976.
Tex. New York, Delacorte Press, 1979; London, Gollancz, 1980.
Taming the Star Runner. New York, Delacorte Press, 1988.

Screenplay: *Rumble Fish*, with Francis Ford Coppola, 1983.

*

Media Adaptations: *Rumble Fish* (recording), Viking, 1977; *The Outsiders* (filmstrip with cassette), Current Affairs and Mark Twain Media, 1978; *The Outsiders* (cassette), Random House, 1978; *That Was Then, This Is Now* (filmstrip with cassette), Current Affairs and Mark Twain Media, 1978; *Tex* (film), Walt Disney Productions, 1982; *The Outsiders* (film), Warner Brothers, 1983; *Rumble Fish* (film), Universal, 1983; *That Was Then, This Is Now* (film), Paramount, 1985; *The Outsiders* (television series), Fox, 1990.

Biography: Essay in *Authors and Artists for Young Adults,* Volume 2, Detroit, Gale, 1989; essay in *Speaking for Ourselves: Autobiographical Sketches by Notable Authors of Books for Young Adults,* Volume 1, compiled and edited by Donald R. Gallo, National Council of Teachers of English, 1990.

Critical Study: Entry in *Children's Literature Review,* Volume 3, Detroit, Gale, 1978, Volume 23, 1991; entry in *Contemporary Literary Criticism,* Volume 30, Detroit, Gale, 1984; *Presenting S. E. Hinton* by Jay Daly, Boston, Twayne, 1987; teacher's guides are available for *The Outsiders, That Was Then, This Is Now, Rumble Fish,* and *Tex,* all written by Lou Willett Staneck and published by Dell.

*   *   *

One of the most popular twentieth-century writers for young adults, S.E. Hinton has produced five novels about sensitive "greasers," "hoods," and abandoned teenagers which have become bestsellers, spawning four film adaptations and a television series. All of Hinton's novels are similar, both in their choice of characters and in their themes. Her characters are frequently larger than life, almost mythic, and are social outcasts, such as Dallas Winston of *The Outsiders* and Motorcycle Boy of *Rumble Fish.*

Hinton's books are usually narrated by macho, poor, and "cool" teenage boys who are also vulnerable and occasionally cry. They are often orphans, as in *The Outsiders,* or have been abandoned by their parents, as in *Tex.* Despite the fact that Hinton's protagonists often skip school and get into trouble with their teachers, they frequently enjoy reading and three of them, Ponyboy Curtis, Tex McCormick, and Travis Harris, are presented as potential poets or writers. Indeed, Hinton's characters make frequent allusions to their favorite books which include works as diverse as *Great Expectations, Gone with the Wind, Smokey the Cowhorse,* and the poems of Robert Frost. While Hinton's books often border on the melodramatic, they tackle issues important to many young adults, including prejudice and the struggle to maintain innocence and hope in an often corrupt world.

The Outsiders, written when Hinton was only sixteen, is narrated by Ponyboy Curtis who is supposedly writing his story as a term paper for his English class. He and his two older brothers have been orphaned and are part of a gang of what Ponyboy describes as "greasers." Throughout the book, Ponyboy and his friends are in conflict with the town's wealthy teenagers, known as "Socs." When Ponyboy's best friend, the innocent and abused Johnny Cade, kills a Soc in self-defense, he and Ponyboy flee the town and embark on an odyssey in which they learn that even Socs are human beings (after all, they see the same sunsets). Ponyboy also learns the importance of "staying gold" or maintaining some innocence, an idea expressed in his favorite poem.

The Outsiders has often been identified as one of the "groundbreaking" young adult books which helped usher in an era of realistic, and sometimes pessimistic, books about teenagers and their problems. While it has been criticized as cliched and somewhat melodramatic, *The Outsiders* provides a believable and likeable narrator who wrestles with the very real problems of prejudice and acceptance faced by many young adults. Despite the deaths of

Johnny Cade and the more dangerous Dallas Winston at the end of the novel, *The Outsiders* suggests that if anyone does stay gold, it will be dreamers like Ponyboy.

Hinton's next two novels, *That Was Then, This Is Now* and *Rumble Fish* are less optimistic. While Ponyboy Curtis and some of his friends reappear in *That Was Then, This Is Now,* it is not a direct sequel to *The Outsiders.* The novel is related by a boy named Byron who ultimately decides to turn in his foster brother and best friend, Mark, for dealing drugs when their young friend, M&M, has a bad LSD trip. There are no pat solutions in this novel; going to prison only hardens Mark further. At the end of the novel, Byron longs for the past when he did not have to make such difficult choices. Rusty James, the narrator of *Rumble Fish,* also loses his innocence and becomes as emotionless and hardened as his older brother, Motorcycle Boy, who, like Dallas Winston, meets a violent death. Like Hinton's first two novels, *Rumble Fish* takes place in a relatively short period of time, one which changes the main character forever.

Both of Hinton's most recent novels, *Tex* and *Taming the Star Runner,* feature protagonists with uncertain futures who must deal with family problems and first romances. Tex McCormick lives with his older brother, Mace, and keeps hoping that their father will return. His brother clearly wants to go on to college but has become Tex's surrogate father. Tex, who despite appearances is somewhat naive, is shocked when his brother sells their horses in order to survive. Eventually, Tex is able to help his brother let go and seek his dream. Along the way, Tex moves from innocence to experience, learning his true parentage and gaining a more realistic perspective of "Pop." As part of Tex's initiation into adulthood, he and Mace are abducted by an escaped convict (the now murderous Mark of *That Was Then, This Is Now,* who may be Tex's real brother) and Tex is shot by a drug dealer.

In *Taming the Star Runner,* Hinton provides a fictionalized version of her own success as a young adult writer. Sixteen-year-old Travis McCormick, like Hinton, has a novel accepted for publication, despite the fact that he is failing English. One part of the novel deals with Travis' growth as a writer and his interactions with his editor, Ms. Carmichael. *Taming the Star Runner,* however, is also a novel of maturation and loss. Travis has been forced to go live with his uncle because of an altercation with his abusive stepfather. As a newcomer to his high school, he is an outsider until he becomes involved with helping Casey Kencaide as she tries to tame her horse, Star Runner. Although the horse ultimately dies and Travis loses his intense feelings for Casey, the novel ends with Travis finally looking forward to life, having resolved some of his feelings about his family and personal situation.

While Hinton's earlier books contain references that might seem to date them, they are still popular, partly because the topics they explore continue to be important to young adults. All of Hinton's novels suggest how young adults are frequently shaped by their environment and are concerned with their struggles, only sometimes successful, to leave the past behind and face the future. Hinton has the great ability to create authentic characters who sound like real young adults and their journeys towards adulthood will likely remain popular with future readers, whether "Socs" or "greasers."

—Joel D. Chaston

HO, Minfong. Burmese. Born in Rangoon, Burma, 7 January 1951. Educated at Tunghai University, Taichung, 1967-69; Cornell University, Ithaca, New York, B.A. (honors) 1973. Married John Value Dennis, Jr., in 1976. Manual worker, Starlight Plywood Factory, Singapore, 1973; journalist, *Straits Times,* Singapore, 1973-75; lecturer in department of mass transportation, Chiengmai University, Chiengmai, Thailand, since 1976. Trade union representative, 1973-75. Recipient: First prize from Council of Interracial Books for Children, 1973, for *Sing to the Dawn.* Address: 7 Leedon Park, Singapore 10, Singapore.

PUBLICATIONS FOR YOUNG ADULTS

Fiction

Sing to the Dawn. New York, Lothrop, 1975.
Rice without Rain. New York, Lothrop, 1990.
The Clay Marble. New York, Farrar, 1991.

*   *   *

In Minfong Ho's most recent novel, *The Clay Marble* (1991), twelve-year-old Dara's most earnest wish is to return home to Cambodia, to repair their house, establish a family, and plant rice seed. During the relentless hardships that she endures, and despite all the horror that she sees, she keeps this hope alive. Finally, at the novel's conclusion, it is this hope which in fact maintains the integrity of the family, forcing Dara's brother to choose home over becoming a soldier.

This focus on home is dominant in the work of Minfong Ho. Having grown up in Singapore and Burma, she was later concerned that the books written especially for the young reader depicted Asia and Thailand as something out of *The King and I:* an unrealistic and anachronistic vision. When she came to Cornell University for her college education, she decided to write about the Asia that she knew, and she creates a world of great beauty and gentleness, with loving family relationships and ancient customs. But she also creates a world of poverty, drought, dreadful injustice, starvation, and death. Her protagonists are set between these two visions, but in that situation they discover their pride, integrity, and determination to love the land and overcome injustice.

Sing to the Dawn (1975), Ho's first and in some ways gentlest novel, tells of Dawan, a young girl who wins a scholarship to study in the city. Her teacher recognizes that she is a perceptive and sensitive student; she understands the injustice of the rent paid to the landlords: half of the rice harvest, leaving the farmers with little to eat. She also understands the responsibility of the scholarship; if Dawan is to study in the city, she must return and make life better for her village. But before Dawan can accept the scholarship, she must first overcome all of the prejudices built up by centuries of tradition; she is a girl, and consequently, it is presumed, she does not need an education.

Here is where Dawan's strength and determination develop, or, to use the major metaphor of the novel, where the lotus bud begins to open up and bloom. Blocked by what she sees as an almost irrational resistance by her father as well as the intransigence of the religious community, she forces her brother to recognize the injustice of making her refuse the scholarship. This is extraordinarily difficult for Kwai, for if she refuses the scholarship, he will receive it instead. Reluctantly, and with some bitterness, he becomes her

advocate, and the novel closes with Dawan on the bus, heading toward the city.

This is in a microcosm what all of Ho's work is about: a young girl overcoming established practices and finding her own way. At the same time, that protagonist is tied closely to a love for the land and for the culture. Dawan does not go off merely for herself; she goes for her village, as well as for her family. The result is a set of novels where Dawan, and later Dara and Jinda, come to understand something about themselves—how they are growing and developing—at the same time that they come to understand something about the needs of their culture. This dual growth makes each of the novels compelling; Ho has created real characters in real situations which may be unfamiliar to most Western readers.

In *The Clay Marble* and *Rice without Rain* (1990), Ho places her characters in situations more troublesome than those of *Sing to the Dawn.* Here the stakes are more than a scholarship; they are survival itself, both on the individual level and on the level of the culture. In *The Clay Marble,* the war between four or five factions in Cambodia has driven Dara and what remains of her family to the border refugee camps between Thailand and Cambodia. Despite the relative safety of the camp, there is still the danger of shelling and when that begins, Dara is separated from her family. To recover her family, she must display a courage and determination that she had not known she had.

In *Rice without Rain,* Jinda meets five university students who come to her village to learn what it is like to be a farmer in northern Thailand. When her father is arrested for leading the resistance against the highland rents, he is arrested and Jinda becomes part of the student movement that is urging reforms in the government. Her purpose is to free her father, but the other students' goals are more cloudy: they see him principally as a political symbol. But soon the struggle becomes more tangible as the peaceful rally is disrupted by government forces, and a massacre ensues—the massacre that occurred at Thammasart University in October, 1976. Jinda, fleeing, returns home and must then deal with the death of her father, as well as her disillusionment with the students.

The vividness of these novels comes from their portrayal of individual characters, not just economic and political realities. In *Rice without Rain,* Jinda is a young woman aware of her growing sexuality and her attraction to Ned, one of the university students. Her love for him is balanced against her perception that his cause is the foremost element in his life. She must deal with the realities of the drought, the injustice of the land rental, and the corruption of the government, but for her these are realities that affect everything about her life, from the land she works to the food she eats. Ned and the other students have, for much of the novel, an academic and social distance from that reality.

Dara and Dawan are much alike. Dawan, for perhaps the first time in her life, is confronted with the prejudice against women in society, and it is only through her own determination that she is able to win out against that prejudice. Dara is confronted by a mindless militarism that threatens to suck in her brother. Through the strength that she finds in her friendship with Jantu, she is able to combat that militarism with an assertion of the importance of family. This interaction of the individual with the large forces of her society and culture provides much of the conflict within the novels.

If there is one consistent center in the three novels, it is the family. *The Clay Marble* is, in fact, about the nature of the family. Dara has fled Cambodia with her brother and mother; she meets a friend with a sister and a grandfather. They recognize that they now have fragments of families, as do most of the refugees. The great task of the novel is to return home and forge new families, which in fact happens in the afterword of the novel. Like the rice harvest, the family is the thing most prized in each of the novels.

Again and again, the female protagonists of Ho's novels work out of the contexts of their families. Here is the repository of tradition. Here is the authority. Here is the group for which one works and which in turn gives one identity. To move outside of the family—like Dao who abandons the family to live in the city in *Rice without Rain*—is to risk ostracism and loss of identity, as well as culture. To stay within the family is to stay within the culture, and to find a kind of love and acceptance that gives strength even as it allows the individual to grow.

Ho's novels can be brutal, even as they can be sensitive. There is the image of the opening lotus blossom, but also the image of the corpse dangling from a limb. There is the image of a baby bathing in a river, but also an image of that same baby with a swollen stomach, dead. There's new love, and there is hideous murder. Ho does not hold back in presenting a land of stark contrasts. What enables the reader to leave the novels with a sense of hope is the strength of the central characters to endure the brutality and hardships, to overcome them, and to return stronger to the family to plant the rice fields, to marry, and to love.

—Gary D. Schmidt

HOBBS, Will. American. Stanford University, B.A. 1969, M.A. 1971. Married Jean Loftus in 1972. Reading and English teacher, Durango, Colorado, public schools, 1973-89; writer since 1990. Recipient: Notable Book, Children's Book Council, 1989, Best Book for Young Adults, American Library Association, 1989, and Teachers' Choice Award, International Reading Association, 1990, all for *Bearstone;* Best Book for Young Adults and Best Book for Reluctant Young Adult Readers, American Library Association, 1992, for *Downriver.* Address: c/o Atheneum Publishers, 866 Third Avenue, New York, NY 10022.

PUBLICATIONS FOR YOUNG ADULTS

Fiction

Changes in Latitudes. New York, Atheneum, 1988.
Bearstone. New York, Atheneum, 1989.
Downriver. New York, Atheneum, 1991.
The Big Wander. New York, Atheneum, 1992.
Beardance. New York, Atheneum, 1993.

*

Biography: Essay in *Speaking for Ourselves, Too* compiled and edited by Donald R. Gallo, National Council of Teachers of English, 1993.

*   *   *

Will Hobbs uses his personal outdoor experiences in Colorado, Mexico, and the canyon lands of the Southwest as the basis for the settings in his novels. For example, The Window and the Rio Grande Pyramid rock formations in *Bearstone* and *Bear Dance* are real places in the San Juan Mountains, and Hobbs has taken Colorado River raft trips in the Grand Canyon, as did the young people in *Downriver.*

Hobbs has also been influenced by his reading of natural history books and of early books written about the various areas. *Vagabond for Beauty* by Everett Bruce, written in the early 1930s, is one such book. In addition to providing unique settings for the action in his novels, Hobbs uses the environment as the background to voice his concern for nature. In his novels he interweaves human relationships and relationships with the natural world.

As a reading and English teacher of adolescents, Hobbs learned that young readers, as well as reluctant readers, were fascinated with adventure stories. His close association with adolescents assists him in providing accurate depictions of them in his novels. For instance, the character of Cloyd in *Bearstone* and *Bear Dance* developed from a composite of students he taught in his junior high reading class. As in many young adult novels, the adults are conveniently absent from the action, with only a few exceptions. Walter, the old rancher in *Bearstone* and *Bear Dance,* is based on a rancher friend of Hobbs's where he spent summers helping to bring in the hay crop. His characters are believable in their dialogue and their motivations.

Hobbs's first novel, *Changes in Latitudes,* involves the disintegration of the family structure and the parallel theme of the extinction of the sea turtle, viciously hunted for its oils. Told through the eyes of Travis, a "cool" sixteen-year-old teenager, the reader identifies with the pain of the father staying behind when the mother, Travis, and two other children (Jennifer, fourteen, and Teddy, nine) head for a holiday in Mexico. The mother, who is involved in an affair, allows the children to fend for themselves. Teddy's fascination with the sea turtles leads him to a friendship with a marine biologist and to adventure and tragedy. Guilt, a powerful emotion in the story, is experienced by several of the characters and provides a basis for significant discussion by readers of the novel.

Bearstone introduces a young Native American boy, Cloyd Atcitty, to a crusty old rancher/miner named Walter Landis. Walter is cautious about dealing with Cloyd, and neither of them is very communicative. When Cloyd is exploring the mountains near Walter's ranch, he finds Indian burial artifacts, including a turquoise stone in the shape of a bear. Cloyd thinks this will bring him luck, but he makes the mistake of telling one of Walter's visitors about seeing a grizzly bear in the mountains and that man goes out to kill the bear. When Walter is injured in a mine accident, Cloyd gets the visitor to pick Walter up in the helicopter which has come for the bear carcass. Cloyd has the opportunity to tell the game warden that the bear had been killed deliberately, but he decides not to out of his friendship for Walter. A rite of passage story, Cloyd learns to trust and love someone, in spite of his stubbornness. As a symbol of this love, he gives Walter the bear stone in the hospital.

In *Bear Dance,* a sequel to *Bearstone,* Cloyd wants to look in the mountains for the mother bear and her three cubs while Walter goes back to his neglected mine. Cloyd meets Ursa, a part-Indian woman, who is a professor at the University of Montana. She wants to find evidence of a grizzly, since that will permit the Wildlife division to reintroduce bears into Colorado. Cloyd saves the two surviving bear cubs and learns about the bear dance and bear dreams, both of which are important for his survival.

Downriver is told through the eyes of Jessie, a fifteen-year-old who is rebelling against her father, a professor at the university in

Boulder. Her mother has died, and Jessie is experimenting with the wrong crowd. Her father sends her on an outdoor experimental program where she is one of eight alienated young people. Rebellious, the kids decide to take their counselor Al's car and equipment and go down the Grand Canyon on their own. With no map but carrying the supplies Al had arranged for them, they board the boats and head down the treacherous river. They learn how to trust each other to succeed. In this survival story, the young people begin to understand peer pressure and other people's values. Young readers will be encouraged to look at their own motives and those of families and friends. The descriptions of the area and the excitement of running the rapids are evidence that the author has had those experiences himself.

The Big Wander is set in the desert canyon lands of Utah and Arizona where Clay Lancaster, fourteen, and his older brother Mike have gone in their creaky 148 Studebaker to search for their Uncle Clay. The time of the novel is 1962 and accurate references to songs, politics, and the Peace Corps could encourage dialogue with parents of young readers. The boys' mother is spending the summer with the Peace Corps in Guatemala, and the father has been killed in the Korean War. Departing for his summer job in Seattle, Mike is convinced Clay will be looked after by a family who run a trading post. But Clay is undaunted in his search for his uncle and, with a burro named Pal and his dog Curly for company, he gets involved with Indians who are trying to save wild mustangs and with a Mormon family who are ranchers. Their daughter Sarah provides a love interest for Clay. This exciting book is a journey of discovery, in which readers will learn along with Clay about wild creatures, wild places, and a diversity of life.

Will Hobbs has established himself as a careful researcher for books that have unique settings and determined young characters. His use of strong images, careful selection of words, and well-developed plots and characters have made his books popular with young adults, who have nominated his books in a number of states for reader awards. Teachers and librarians are cognizant of their appeal and have included his books on "Teachers' Choices" and "Best Young Adult" lists. Although a fairly new author for young adults, Will Hobbs is a popular speaker at meetings for teachers and librarians, as well as inspiring to student authors. Because his books deal with universal values and his characters are memorable, his reputation will deservedly grow in the years to come.

—Ruth K. J. Cline

HOLM, (Else) Anne (Lise). Danish. Born in Aal, Jutland, 10 September 1922. Married second husband, Johan Christian Holm in 1949; one child. Writer. Recipient: Gyldendal Prize for best Scandinavian children's book, 1963, American Library Association notable book citation, 1965, and Gold Medal, Boys' Club of America Junior Book award, all for *David*. Address: Strandvejen 661, Klampenborg, Denmark.

PUBLICATIONS FOR YOUNG ADULTS

Translated Fiction

David. Copenhagen, Gyldendal, 1963; as *North to Freedom,* translation from the Danish by L. W. Kingsland. New York, Harcourt, 1965; as *I Am David.* London, Methuen, 1965.

Peter. Copenhagen, Gyldendal, 1965; New York, Harcourt, 1968.
The Hostage, translation from the Danish by Patricia Crampton. London, Methuen, 1980.
The Sky Grew Red, translation from the Danish by Patricia Crampton. London, Methuen, 1991.

Untranslated Fiction

Dina fra Apotekergaarden. St. John's, Jespersen & Pio, 1956.
Familien i Apotekergaarden. St. John's, Jespersen & Pio, 1958.
Komtessen fra Baekkeholm. St. John's, Jespersen & Pio, 1959.
Adam og de voksne. Copenhagen, Gyldendal, 1967.

*

Media Adaptations: A British Broadcasting Corporation (BBC) television series was based on *David,* and the book has also been optioned for film.

Biography: Essay in *Something about the Author Autobiography Series,* Volume 7, Detroit, Gale, 1989, pp. 123-37.

* * *

Danish writer Anne Holm is best known for her young adult novel *David,* which has been translated into over twenty languages. In the United States it is known as *North to Freedom,* and in the United Kingdom as *I Am David.* This highly introspective story, called both a "journey of discovery" and an "allegory of freedom" by reviewer Alberta Eiseman, begins in a political internment camp in the Balkans where twelve-year-old David has lived since infancy. For some unknown reason one day, the camp commander arranges for him to escape and instructs him to travel south to Salonica, hide on a ship bound for Italy, and then go north to Denmark, where he will be safe. David, well aware of the evil of the camp, suspects that this escape will be an excuse to kill him. However, he decides that he prefers death to continued captivity and thus escapes.

He makes many discoveries on his harrowing flight, one being that he is strong and able to survive on little food. Then there is the matter of learning to deal with people. For a boy who has gone from childhood to a wary adulthood very quickly in a prison camp this is extremely difficult. Though David concludes that he can never be a normal boy, he maintains his integrity and gradually overcomes his fear of people, making good use of the languages he has learned in the camp—what *they* spoke, and French, German, Italian, and English. Finally, David comes to understand *them*—their treachery, brutality, and methods of operation. (Throughout the book the word Communist is never used and this adds to the pervading horror of this ever-present force which is referred to as *they* or *them.*)

Though she has been criticized for occasional factual inaccuracies in her novels, as in depicting "a carefree, peaceful Europe which did not exist during the years described," as Eiseman points out in *David,* Holm's novels are praised for their affirmations of life that will stimulate and challenge young adult readers.

—Reba Pinney

HOLMAN, Felice. American. Born in New York City, 24 October 1919. Educated at Syracuse University, New York, B.A. 1941. Married Herbert Valen in 1941; one daughter. Advertising copywriter, New York, 1944-50. Recipient: Austrian Book Prize, Lewis Carroll Shelf Award, Best Book for Young Adults award, and American Library Association Notable Book award, all 1978, for *Slake's Limbo;* American Library Association Notable Book award, 1979, for *The Murderer;* Best Book for Young Adults award, 1985, for *The Wild Children;* Child Study Committee Book Award, 1990, for *Secret City, U.S.A.* Address: c/o Scribner's, 866 Third Avenue, New York, NY 10022, U.S.A.

PUBLICATIONS FOR YOUNG ADULTS

Fiction

Slake's Limbo. New York, Scribner, 1974; London, Macmillan, 1980.
The Murderer. New York, Scribner, 1978.
The Wild Children. New York, Scribner, 1983.
Secret City, U.S.A. New York, Aladdin, 1990.

Poetry

At the Top of My Voice and Other Poems, illustrated by Edward Gorey. New York, Norton, 1970.
I Hear You Smiling and Other Poems, illustrated by Laszlo Kubinyi. New York, Scribner, 1973.
The Song in My Head and Other Poems, illustrated by James Spanfeller. New York, Scribner, 1985.

Other

The Drac: French Tales of Dragons and Demons, with Nanine Valen, illustrated by Stephen Walker. New York, Scribner, 1975.

PUBLICATIONS FOR CHILDREN

Fiction

Elizabeth, the Bird Watcher, illustrated by Erik Blegvad. New York, Macmillan, 1963.
Elizabeth the Treasure Hunter, illustrated by Erik Blegvad. New York, Macmillan, 1964.
Silently, the Cat, and Miss Theodosia, illustrated by Harvey Dinnerstein. New York, Macmillan, and London, Collier Macmillan, 1965.
The Witch on the Corner, illustrated by Arnold Lobel. New York, Norton, 1966; London, Lutterworth Press, 1967.
Victoria's Castle, illustrated by Lillian Hoban. New York, Norton, 1966.
Elizabeth and the Marsh Mystery, illustrated by Erik Blegvad. New York, Macmillan, 1966; London, Collier Macmillan, 1974.
Professor Diggins' Dragons, illustrated by Ib Ohlsson. New York, Macmillan, and London, Collier Macmillan, 1966.
The Cricket Winter, illustrated by Ralph Pinto. New York, Norton, 1967.
The Blackmail Machine, illustrated by Victoria de Larrea. New York, Macmillan, 1967; London, Collier Macmillan, 1968.

A Year to Grow, illustrated by Emily McCully. New York, Norton, 1968.
The Holiday Rat, and the Utmost Mouse, illustrated by Wallace Tripp. New York, Norton, 1969.
Solomon's Search, illustrated by Mischa Richter. New York, Grosset and Dunlap, 1970.
The Future of Hooper Toote, illustrated by Gahan Wilson. New York, Scribner, 1972.
The Escape of the Giant Hogstalk, illustrated by Ben Shecter. New York, Scribner, 1974; as *The Escape of the Giant Hogweed,* London, Abelard Schuman, 1978.
Terrible Jane, illustrated by Irene Trivas. New York, Scribner, 1987.

*

Biography: Essay in *Speaking for Ourselves, Too* compiled and edited by Donald R. Gallo, National Council of Teachers of English, 1993; essay in *Something about the Author Autobiography Series,* Volume 17, Detroit, Gale, 1994.

Manuscript Collection: Kerlan Collection, University of Minnesota, Minneapolis.

Felice Holman comments:
   In recent years I have been writing what have been called "survival stories" about children with unusual obstacles or difficult situations to cope with. The best known of these is *Slake's Limbo,* about a boy who lives for 121 days in a subway tunnel. Another is *The Wild Children* about the wandering gangs of children in Russia. The most recent is *Secret City, U.S.A.,* which tells about homeless kids who try to start a new city. In each of these books, I get drawn in while I am writing. I become very involved in the life of the characters I am writing about and I suffer a lot of wear and tear. In the end, though, I feel terrific: I get a great deal of satisfaction from the feeling that I may have done a little something. Writing for young adults (a whole new generation) keeps me hopeful that the things I worry about—things that make my characters have such a tough time—will be improved. It is those young adult readers who will be the ones who fix things.

*   *   *

   Though she has written stories and poems for young children *(At the Top of My Voice)* and co-authored a collection of mythic tales about dragons and supernatural beings *(The Drac),* Felice Holman is best known for her works of young adult literature. Here she has focused on characters that are, in some ways, completely foreign to most of her readers—a refugee in a subway station, a Russian child hiding from the government, a Jewish boy growing up in a Polish mining town. Yet all of these characters are familiar: each yearns for family and the peace to grow up and enjoy life, and each character struggles to find these in very different ways.
   Holman explores these needs in the context of their deprivation. These characters are frequently brought into situations which would have been difficult to imagine at the beginning of their respective novels. Each finds a darkness in the human soul that is terrible and frightening, yet at the same time finds, both within himself and in others, elements of unexpected grace. This grace, suggests Holman, is nurturing to the giver as well as its receiver. The result is a

compellingly hopeful vision. Having seen and been plunged down into the worst, the characters emerge to new hope, new life. At times this can be quite explicit, as when Slake emerges from his limbo in the subway and heads upward, both literally and metaphorically.

The Wild Children is arguably Holman's best-known work. Painstakingly researched, the novel focuses on the children abandoned during the early days of the Soviet Union, following one boy's sojourn among the wild children. Alex comes down from his hidden bedroom one morning to find that his entire family has been taken away. There is no place to turn—he fears the authorities, and others fear being connected to Alex. He turns to a beloved teacher who helps Alex get to his uncle in Moscow. But when he arrives there, he finds that his uncle has also disappeared. He is alone in Moscow, with no money, and no place to go.

In establishing this situation, Holman has deprived Alex not only of those things he must have to be happy—notably, a family—but also of those things he must have simply to survive. His situation is one of almost utter loss and loneliness. But this is where Holman allows grace to enter; he is taken up by one of the gangs of wild children who steal to survive. They lie and thieve, but they will not hurt, nor will they run drugs, as so many of the other gangs do. They do what must be done to survive. It is here that Alex finds what he has least expected and what he refuses at first to believe: a nurturing family. They feed him, shelter him, care for him when he is sick, and protect him from the situation in which he finds himself. Eventually they will help him to a new life outside of Russia, as he in turn helps most of them to join him.

The suggestion is very strong here that the family is crucial to the well-being of the adolescent, even if that family is not necessarily a biological one. No individual can truly live alone, and Alex knows that if he abandons the gang, he could not live long on the streets of Moscow.

This same theme is prominent in *Slake's Limbo,* where Slake, frustrated and wearied by the evils that encroach upon his life, escapes to a small room between two pillars down a subway tunnel. He is at first content with this life: structuring his days around the search for newspapers that he resells, taking the subway to all the many New York stations, finding treasures in trash cans to decorate his room, and making a true friend—a rat.

But he also finds that life cannot be lived alone—that is, if he hopes for a life with any meaning and joy. Soon he has regular customers for his newspapers, and is surprised to learn that they seem to care about him (one brings him a warm jacket). The waiters where he buys a daily sandwich begin to increase his order, though not its cost, seeing his need. And eventually, when he falls ill, he is brought to the hospital and a social worker by a subway engineer who finds him. He is in fact surrounded by a caring community. And though he will reject the formal help of the social worker, he will, at the novel's conclusion, emerge from the subway into the bright air, having learned an important truth—one that Alex would affirm as well.

Though the great power of Holman's narratives comes from the struggle of the protagonist to survive against very long odds, some comes from the vivid imagery she depicts: the abandoned cellar where Alex first meets the wild children, the overturned rocking chair that announces his family has been taken away, the rat peering into Slake's small room. Each image is arresting because of its moment in the plot, but also because of its thematic significance: the cellar is Alex's introduction to a new family, the rat a suggestion of mutual need.

Perhaps one of Holman's starkest images appears in *The Murderer,* where Hershey Marks is tied to a clothespole by some Polish kids, one of them Lorsh, whom Hershey had admired and tried to emulate. He is, as the narrator suggests, "mortified, disappointed, and scared." The disappointment is crucial here. Hershey is the only one of the Jewish children to attempt to make a connection with the Polish boys. He has wanted to be like Lorsh, to be accepted by him. But here Lorsh shows a kind of evil that is frightening in its carelessness and cruelty.

But here too grace interposes. Throughout the novel there has been a conflict between the miners, who are mostly Polish, and the merchants, who are predominantly Jewish. Set during the Depression, it is a time when most of the miners cannot pay their bills; they seem trapped forever by the need to use credit. At the end of the novel, Lorsh, who has just started to work in the mines, comes to Hershey's store and must ask for credit. Hershey's response is to give it immediately, but once Lorsh leaves, Hershey realizes that Lorsh is becoming trapped in the same cycle in which the others are trapped. Hershey wishes he could have given him the merchandise as a gift but it is too late. Hershey's response to his mock crucifixion on the clothespole is not rejection, but the yearning to respond with grace.

Hershey does not share the loss of a family with Alex and Slake, but like those two characters he yearns for a world in which he has a real place, where he is not constantly trying to survive. The dangers in his world come from a clash of cultures, and although those dangers are not as life-threatening as those which Alex faces, they are still dramatic parts of Hershey's life.

The needs that each of Holman's characters face are universal; she makes them vivid by placing her characters in a microcosm of the real world. All of her plots use confined settings: a room in a subway tunnel, a cellar, a small town surrounded by mountains. Within that microcosm, under the sharpened focus of fiction, Holman's characters play out elemental human needs. Their escape from those settings suggests not that those needs have been fulfilled, but instead their new awareness that those needs cannot be filled in isolation.

—Gary D. Schmidt

HOOVER, H(elen) M(ary). American. Born in Stark County, Ohio, 5 April 1935. Educated at Louisville High School; Mount Union College, Alliance, Ohio; Los Angeles County School of Nursing. Writer. Recipient: Children's Book of the Year, the Child Study Association of America, and one of the American Library Association's "Best Books for Young Adults," both 1974, for *The Lion's Cub;* one of the American Library Association's "Best Books for Young Adults," 1981, and received the Ohioana award, 1982, for *Another Heaven, Another Earth;* Central Missouri State College award for outstanding contribution to children's literature, 1984; Parents Choice Honor award, 1987, for *Orvis;* one of the American Library Association's "Best Books for Young Adults," named to Enoch Pratt Library's "Youth to Youth Books List," and received Parents Choice Honor award, all 1988, and also named to the Library of Congress best books for children list and a notable children's trade book by *Social Education,* both 1989, for *The Dawn Palace: The Story of Medea.*

PUBLICATIONS FOR YOUNG ADULTS

Science Fiction

Children of Morrow. New York, Four Winds Press, 1973; London, Methuen, 1975.
The Lion's Cub. New York, Four Winds Press, 1974.
Treasures of Morrow. New York, Four Winds Press, 1976.
The Rains of Eridan. New York, Viking, 1977; London, Methuen, 1978.
The Delikon. New York, Viking, 1977; London, Methuen, 1978.
The Lost Star. New York, Viking, 1979; London, Methuen, 1980.
The Return to Earth. New York, Viking, 1980; London, Methuen, 1981.
This Time of Darkness. New York, Viking, 1980; London, Methuen, 1982.
Another Heaven, Another Earth. New York, Viking, 1981; London, Methuen, 1983.
The Bell Tree. New York, Viking, 1982.
The Shepherd Moon: A Novel of the Future. New York, Viking, and London, Methuen, 1984.
Orvis. New York, Viking Kestrel, and London, Methuen, 1987.
The Dawn Palace: The Story of Medea. New York, Dutton, 1988.
Away Is a Strange Place to Be. New York, Dutton, 1990.
Only Child. New York, Dutton, 1992.

Other

Contributor, edited by Aileen Pace Nilsen and Kenneth L. Donelson, *Literature for Today's Young Adults.* Glenview, Illinois, Scott, Foresman, 1985.
Anatomy of Wonder: A Critical Guide to Science Fiction. New York, Bowker, 1987.
Contributor, *Innocence and Experience: Essays and Conversations on Children's Literature.* New York, Lothrop, 1987.
Contributor, *The Big Book for Our Planet,* New York, Dutton, forthcoming.

*

Biography: Essay in *Something about the Author Autobiography Series,* Volume 8, Detroit, Gale, 1989; essay in *Speaking for Ourselves: Autobiographical Sketches by Notable Authors of Books for Young Adults,* Volume 1, compiled and edited by Donald R. Gallo, National Council of Teachers of English, 1990.

Manuscript Collection: Kerlan Collection, University of Minnesota, Minneapolis.

*   *   *

One attribute of good science fiction is that it presents a good adventure tale while stimulating consideration of more serious matters relating to science, technology, and social science. H.M. Hoover's works are a reflection of this attribute. In *The Shepherd Moon,* privileged thirteen-year-old Merry discovers a being from one of Earth's artificial satellite moons, who is plotting to conquer the Earth until the plan is thwarted by Merry and her grandfather. The novel's underlying message is an exploration of the uses of power and privilege and the consequences of overcrowding on Earth, a dual thrust found in all of Hoover's science fiction.

Hoover's early books all feature a strong, young female protagonist. These characters are isolated in some way from their parents, and in most of the books are preoccupied with themselves until they establish a growing relationship with an elder mentor. In *The Delikon,* Varina, a Delikon and a three hundred and seven-year-old child, reveres Sidra, the t'kyna on a conquered Earth ruled by the Delikon. In *The Rains of Eridan,* Karen is orphaned in a mutiny and is befriended by Theo, a biologist. Together they unravel the many mysteries of the planet Eridan. Though there is a supportive adult, the youth is always the main focus and each character is fully realized. The youths of these novels all have qualities that make them special in some way, but each also behaves in the way a young adult would, with the attendant fears, hurts, and joys.

A frequent criticism of science fiction is that it consists of plot and no characterization. Hoover, however, presents the reader with a strong plot and her characters are as alive as the action. An exploration of emotions and interactions is an important element in each of her books, and there is always the development of some kind of caring relationship between characters. One could even say that Hoover writes love stories, when love is defined in terms of caring about another being. Lian, a teenage astrophysicist who is on the planet Balthor with her parents to study a supernova, is rescued from a crash by the leader of an archeological expedition. She finds satisfaction and possibly a new career when her trust and caring for supposedly native creatures called lumpies leads to the discovery that these beings are sentient travellers from another planet and that the site of the excavation is actually a starship. These travellers in *The Lost Star* evolve for the reader, through Lian's perspective, from endearing pets to intelligent beings.

Hoover's books are replete with imagery and her skill in crafting phrases and sentences that create vivid mental representations is marvelous. Her interest in nature is evident in the detailed descriptions of the landscapes of the worlds she has created, including Earth in future centuries. The reader never strains to enter these worlds because the land, with its flora and fauna, is so expressively presented. In *The Lost Star,* the exotic creatures on Balthor are seen through the eyes of humans on that planet. The description is so much a part of the action that it is not tedious.

Recently, Hoover has included male protagonists in her works. In *Away Is a Strange Place to Be,* Abby and Bryan have been kidnapped and transported to a developing world to aid in the construction of a space habitat. The conditions they live in are horrible and the resourceful Abby and spoiled Bryan finally work together to escape, and return to Earth. Not content with her own escape, Abby works to free the other children who are imprisoned in the habitat. As always, Hoover explores the ramifications of technology and its effects on human beings. Hoover takes the concept of an *Only Child* one step further when she introduces us to Cody, the only child living on a spaceship. In his first visit to the planet, Cody is kidnapped by aliens and discovers that they are sentient beings and that the code of colonization that decrees that a planet with intelligent life cannot be colonized has been breached. Hoover's handling of this moral question is deft.

The concept of myth is a feature in much of Hoover's science fiction. Because she is writing of a future time, Hoover enables the reader to see that much of the knowledge and many of the behaviors of the present will become myths centuries from now. The alert reader will make the connection to the myths shared today and realize that these myths were grounded in fact but have evolved into stories over time. This interest in myth has led Hoover into a new direction: a novel about Medea and the calamities that befell her.

Extensive research and an awareness of the cultural mores of the Greek world in the time of Medea led Hoover to present, in *The Dawn Palace,* an account that is atypically sympathetic to Medea. Using her talent for rich detail, Hoover allows the reader to be present in a world of long ago and to participate in the pain and frustration that Medea felt throughout her life. Young adults will relate to this finely crafted novel and will gain an appreciation for events in another time.

Whether travelling to the past or the future, Hoover carries her readers along by creating a vivid world that is immediately accessible, producing satisfying plots, and creating characters that readers care about.

—M. Jean Greenlaw

———

HOUSTON, James A(rchibald). Canadian. Born in Toronto, Ontario, 12 June 1921. Educated at John Wanless Primary School and Northern Vocational High School, both Toronto; Ontario College of Art, 1938-40, Ecole Grand Chaumière, Paris, 1947-48, Unichi-Hiratsuka, Tokyo, 1958-59, and Atelier 17, 1961. Served in the Toronto Scottish Regiment, 1940-45; became warrant officer. Married 1) Alma G. Bardon in 1950 (divorced 1966), two sons; 2) Alice Daggett Watson in 1967. Author and illustrator. Arctic adviser, Canadian Guild of Crafts, 1949-52; first civil administrator, Government of Canada, West Baffin, Eastern Arctic, Northwest Territories, 1952-62. Associate director of design, 1962-72, and since 1972 master designer, Steuben Glass, New York. Visiting lecturer at Wye Institute and Rhode Island School of Design. Chairman of board of directors of Canadian Arctic Producers, 1976-77, and American Indian Art Center; member of board of directors of Canadian Eskimo Arts Council; president of Indian and Eskimo Art of the Americas; vice-president of West Baffin Eskimo Cooperative and Eskimo Art, Inc. Member of primitive art committee of Metropolitan Museum of Art. Artist: individual shows—Canadian Guild of Crafts, 1953, 1955, 1957; Robertson Galleries, Ottawa, 1953; Calgary Galleries, 1966; Canadiana Galleries, Edmonton, 1977; Yaneff Gallery, Toronto, 1983, 1986; Steuben Glass, 1987; represented in collections of Glenbow-Alberta Museum of Art, Montreal Museum of Fine Arts, National Gallery of Art, Ottawa. Recipient: Canadian Library Association Book of the Year Medal, 1966, for *Tikta'liktak: An Eskimo Legend,* 1968, for *The White Archer: An Eskimo Legend,* 1980, for *River Runners: A Tale of Hardship and Bravery,* and runner-up, 1982, for *Long Claws: An Arctic Adventure;* American Indian and Eskimo Cultural Foundation award, 1966; American Library Association Notable Books awards, 1967, for *The White Archer,* 1968, for *Akavak,* and 1971, for *The White Dawn;* decorated officer of Order of Canada, 1972; Amelia Frances Howard-Gibbon award runner-up, 1973, for *Ghost Paddle;* Vicky Metcalf award, 1977; Inuit Kuavati award of merit, 1979; Vicky Metcalf Short Story award, 1980, for "Long Claws" in *The Winter Fun Book;* Canadian nominee, Hans Christian Andersen award, 1987; Citation of Merit award, Royal Canadian Academy of Art Citation of Merit award, 1987; Max and Gretta Ebel award, Canadian Society of Children's Authors, Illustrators, and Performers, 1989;

D.Litt.: Carleton University, Ottawa, 1972; D.H.L.: Rhode Island College, Providence, 1975; D.F.A.: Rhode Island School of Design, Providence, 1979; D.D.L., Dalhousie University, Halifax, Nova Scotia, 1987; Honorary Fellow, Ontario College of Art, and Fellow, Royal Society of Art, London, 1981. Address: 24 Main St., Stonington, CT 06378, U.S.A.

PUBLICATIONS FOR YOUNG ADULTS

Fiction (illustrated by the author)

Tikta'liktak: An Eskimo Legend. Toronto, Longman, and New York, Harcourt, 1965.
Eagle Mask: A West Coast Indian Tale. Toronto, Longman, and New York, Harcourt, 1966.
The White Archer: An Eskimo Legend. Toronto, Longman, and New York, Harcourt, 1967.
Akavak: An Eskimo Journey. Toronto, Longman, and New York, Harcourt, 1968.
Wolf Run: A Caribou Eskimo Tale. Toronto, Longman, and New York, Harcourt, 1971.
Ghost Paddle: A Northwest Coast Indian Tale. Toronto, Longman, and New York, Harcourt, 1972.
Editor, *Songs of the Dream People: Chants and Images from the Indians and Eskimos of North America.* Toronto, Longman, and New York, Atheneum, 1972.
Kiviok's Magic Journey: An Eskimo Legend. Toronto, Longman, and New York, Atheneum, 1973.
Frozen Fire: A Tale of Courage. Toronto, McClelland & Stewart, and New York, Atheneum, 1977; London, Penguin, 1979.
River Runners: A Tale of Hardship and Bravery. Toronto, McClelland & Stewart, and New York, Atheneum, 1979; London, Penguin, 1981.
Long Claws: An Arctic Adventure. Toronto, McClelland & Stewart, and New York, Atheneum, 1981.
Black Diamonds: A Search for Arctic Treasure. Toronto, McClelland & Stewart, and New York, Atheneum, 1982.
Ice Swords: An Undersea Adventure. Toronto, McClelland & Stewart, and New York, Atheneum, 1985.
The Falcon Bow: An Arctic Legend. Toronto, McClelland & Stewart, and New York, McElderry, 1986.
Whiteout. Toronto, Greey de Pencier, 1988.
Drifting Snow. Toronto, McClelland & Stewart, and New York, McElderry, 1992.

PUBLICATIONS FOR ADULTS

Novels (illustrated by the author)

The White Dawn: An Eskimo Saga. Toronto, Longman, New York, Harcourt, and London, Heinemann, 1971.
Ghost Fox. Toronto, McClelland & Stewart, New York, Harcourt, and London, Collins, 1977.
Spirit Wrestler. Toronto, McClelland & Stewart, New York, Harcourt, and London, Collins, 1980.
Eagle Song. Toronto, McClelland & Stewart, and New York, Harcourt, 1983.
Running West. Toronto, McClelland & Stewart, and New York, Crown, 1989.

Other

Canadian Eskimo Art. Ottawa, Queen's Printer, 1955.
Eskimo Graphic Art. Ottawa, Queen's Printer, 1960.
Eskimo Prints. Barre, Massachusetts, Barre Publishers, 1967.
America Was Beautiful, edited by Alice Watson. Barre, Massachusetts, Barre Publishers, 1970.
Ojibwa Summer, photographs by B. A. King. Barre, Massachusetts, Barre Publishers, 1972.

Screenplays: *The White Dawn,* 1973; *The Mask and the Drum,* 1975; *Kalvak,* 1976; *So Sings the Wolf,* 1976; *Art of the Arctic Whaleman,* 1978; *Legends of the Salmon People,* 1978; *Ghost Fox,* 1979; *Whiteout,* 1987.

*

Media Adaptations: *Ghost Fox* (eight cassettes), Crane Memorial Library, 1978.

Manuscript Collection: National Library of Canada, Ottawa.

Critical Study: Entry in *Children's Literature Review,* Volume 3, Detroit, Gale, 1978.

Illustrator: *Shoot to Live,* 1944; *Nuki* by Alma Houston, 1955; *Ayorama* by Raymond de Coccola and Paul King, 1956; *Tuktut/Caribou,* 1957; *The Unicorn Was There* by Elizabeth Pool, 1966; *The Private Journal of Captain G.F. Lyon of H.M.S. Hecla, During the Recent Voyage of Discovery under Captain Parry, 1821-1823* by George Francis Lyon, 1970; *The American Heritage Book of Fish Cookery* by Alice Watson Houston, 1980; *First Came the Indians* by Mary Jo Wheeler-Smith, 1982; *The Incredible Eskimo* by R. de Coccola and P. King, 1986; *Place Names of the Eastern Shore of Maryland* by J. Kenneth Keatley, 1987.

James Houston comments:

It is gratifying to me to write adventure stories for young adults. These stories are almost always based on true events. Beginning when I was young, I have had the good fortune to live for long periods of my life with Indian and Inuit/Eskimo people in the north. I choose to write about some of these first people in North America because of the unfamiliar way in which they have lived their lives and the many special skills they have developed.

To hold the attention of one's readers, I believe an author should try to tell a story that possesses truth and interesting characters, and is perhaps enhanced by an unusual environment. It should possess as well a driving sense of purpose and excitement.

*   *   *

James Houston has written several books for the junior high school audience; his adult novels are also of interest to young adults. His stories are set in Canada and the Arctic, showing a depth of understanding for the people there and their legends and customs. His characters include Inuit-Eskimos and also Indians of the Cree, Dene, Naskapi, Abnaki, and other tribes that once populated the northern part of the continent.

According to *Children's Literature Review* (Gale, 1978), Houston is a Canadian artist who lived for twelve years with the Eskimos of the Canadian Arctic. This "influenced both his fiction and the world of visual art. Houston uses his artistic talent to include sharp pen-and-ink drawings at the end of each chapter of the books for young teens. It was Houston who 'discovered' and promoted the sculpture of the Eskimos and introduced printmaking to them." Although Houston now spends much time in Canada, he lives in the United States, also.

Most of his books of interest to young adults are fiction. However, one book which he edited, *Songs of the Dream People,* is a collection of chants and poems for readers of all ages. The short selections in this book reflect the legends, feelings, cultures, and philosophies of the Native Americans of the far north. They represent the oral traditions of these people and are grouped by regions into four sections: Eskimo, Eastern, Central, and Northwest Coast Indians. Striking pen-and-ink drawings by Houston show weapons and other artifacts.

Many people feel that Houston's writings about Eskimo life and customs are what distinguishes him from other writers for young people, but some of his best books deal not with the Eskimo, but with Indians. *River Runners* is set among the Naskapi, a tribe living along the rivers of subarctic Quebec and northern Labrador. Several Indian tribes are brought into *Running West* and *Ghost Fox.*

It is interesting to note that although the settings are rugged and in places that are associated with men, several of Houston's protagonists are female, among them, Elizabeth of *Drifting Snow,* Sara, who was captured by hostile Indians in *Ghost Fox,* and Thana, also captured by hostile Indians in *Running West.* Thana proved to be a knowledgeable guide to the fur traders. *Running West, River Runners, Frozen Fire,* and *Drifting Snow* are based on true incidents.

Many of Houston's protagonists are in pairs: a native youth and a young friend new to the region. Survival is a theme that runs through much of his fiction, especially surviving the harsh environment of the Arctic winters in isolated locations where a person must depend on him or herself for everything: finding food, finding directions to travel, struggling against wild beasts and hostile people, and enduring chilling storms, all in places where there are few settlers and fewer signposts.

Running West is a powerful adult novel of survival in unexplored territory during the years 1715-1717. It's a love story of Thana, a Dene Indian, and William Stewart, a Scotsman who becomes indentured as a servant at the English fur trading fort in the Hudson Bay Territory. He is ordered to let Thana lead him and a company of traders to the tribe from which she was stolen by a band of very cruel Indians. In Dene country, Thana says, they will find furs of marten, fisher, otter, and ermine as well as the yellow pebbles (gold) which were used to make the handle of her special scraper, a tool for handling furs. This is all she has from her mother, an Indian who was murdered at the time Thana was stolen away.

The trip to Dene country is a perilous nine-moon trek filled with danger from enemy tribes, starvation, exhaustion, and fierce winter weather. Early on, most of her accompanying traders turn back. When the journey ends, Thana is pregnant with William's child. She and William become husband and wife when she weaves a wedding veil of beads and string and William asks her to remove it.

When William's navigational instruments are deliberately destroyed by an angry "carrier" or porter, William becomes frantic. However, Thana says that "Wolf Star" will guide them. Thana uses all her native skills to lead them and help them find food along the way. Starvation is a daily threat.

Thana's eagerness to learn the English or "Ballahouly" language adds humor to the narrative. Also amusing are her naive observations of the English customs. "All the Ballahouly ate in curious ways that always interested me. They used iron knives and scoops instead of fingers. The fat soup stirrer never once sat down with us. At home, our Dene women prepared all food. I would ask Williyumm why had they not brought any Ballahooly women with them? How did they get their babies?"

Alternating chapters narrated first by William and then by Thana carry the story from the perspective of each without slowing down the action. Thana's chapters show insight into the traditions and customs of the Indian people. Each "voice" describes the environment, some of which is rich with plants, fish, birds, and animal life. Much of it is desolate. *Running West* is recommended as historical fiction in *Best Books for Senior High Readers.*

Both *Running West* and *Ghost Fox* tell of the Indians' cruelty to a girl whose family and tribespeople are destroyed by other hostile tribes. Both are well written with insight into the culture of the people, plenty of action, and memorable characters. In *Ghost Fox,* Sara, the young Indian woman, eventually marries into the tribe who kidnapped her and finds a place there so that when she's given a chance to return to her people she does not want to do so.

Another adult novel recommended for teens is *Spirit Wrestler.* In this story, a friendless Eskimo boy is befriended by a female shaman. The boy named Shoona is introduced first as a dying man carried into the camp of the Northern Service Officer, the administrator of that vast barren arctic area of Canada known as Baffin Island, where Houston himself spent twelve years as an officer.

Houston's newest novel, *Drifting Snow,* is for children up through the junior-high age, but it is not as convincing in its depiction of people struggling to survive as some of his earlier books. It's the story of a young teenage girl's search for her biological parents among the Eskimos. The strength of this book is in the description of Eskimo life on a remote island where people cling to old customs and experience life-threatening travel on icy waters as their ancestors once did.

Three of Houston's junior novels, *Frozen Fire, River Runners: A Tale of Hardship and Bravery,* and *Ice Swords* are recommended by John T. Gillespie in his *Best Books for Junior High Readers. Frozen Fire* is the story of an Eskimo boy and his white friend who set out to find the Eskimo boy's father, who is a prospector who has disappeared. A sequel to this novel is *Black Diamonds.*

River Runners is an exciting contemporary novel about fifteen-year-old Andrew, a Scot, and his new friend Paskak, a Naskapi Indian youth. They meet at the far northern fur trading post of Fort Chimo. Paskak teaches Andrew, an apprentice fur trader, the Arctic survival skills of his native tribe. After a brief training period at the fort, the two boys set out on snowshoes, accompanied by Indian packmen and dog-drawn toboggans loaded with supplies, for a new fur trade outpost at Ghost Lake far into the interior of Quebec. Andrew struggles with every ounce of energy he can muster to keep up with the natives as they follow the frozen Kiksoak River south until they finally reach Ghost Lake. The packmen and their dogs return to Ft. Chimo and civilization. They leave the boys and scattered Naskapi Indian families searching against great odds for food and furs during the long hard winter in the frozen north.

Ice Swords is a third book in the series which starts with *Frozen Fire.* In this book the same boys, Matthew and his Inuit friend Kayak, are invited to spend the summer in the Arctic studying the migration of whales. They live and work with Dr. Lunan and his daughter Jill, who teaches the boys to deep-sea dive. This is an interesting story at first which turns into a scary adventure.

—Virginia L. Gleason

HOWKER, Janni. British. Born in Nicosia, Cyprus, 6 July 1957. Educated at Kendal High School, Westmorland; Lancaster University, Lancashire, B.A. (honours) in independent studies, 1980, M.A. in creative writing, 1984. Married Mick North in 1988 (second marriage). Writer; creator of writing workshops. Editor of the poetry magazine, *Brew,* for the Brewery Arts Centre in Kendal, England, 1978-79. Worked variously as assistant in hostel for the mentally ill, research assistant in sociology department at Lancaster University, examiner at Open University, census officer, park attendant, landlady, housemother for mentally handicapped children, tutor, and assistant on an archeological site. Recipient: International Reading Association children's book award and *Burnley Express* award, both 1985, for *Badger on the Barge,* which also was named Best Book of the Year by the American Library Association, 1984, shortlisted for the Carnegie Medal Award, 1984, commended by the Whitbread Literary Awards, 1985, and listed by *School Library Journal* as a "Best Book of 1985"; Tom-Gallon Trust Award, 1985, for short story "The Egg-Man"; Whitbread Literary Award, children's fiction category, *Young Observer* (now *Observer*) teenage fiction prize, and *Observer*-Rank Organisation prize, all 1985, and Silver Pencil award, 1987, all for *The Nature of the Beast,* which also was named an ALA Notable Book, 1985, highly commended by the Carnegie Medal Awards, 1985, and placed on *Horn Book's* honor list, 1986; *Boston Globe-Horn Book* fiction honor award and Somerset Maugham award, both 1987, for *Isaac Campion,* which also was highly commended by the Carnegie Medal Awards, 1986, and named Best Book of the Year by the ALA, a *New York Times* Notable Book, and a Best Book for Young Adults by *School Library Journal,* all 1987. Address: c/o Julia MacRae Books, 20 Vauxhall Bridge Road, London SW1V 2SA, England.

PUBLICATIONS FOR YOUNG ADULTS

Fiction

Badger on the Barge and Other Stories. London, MacRae, and New York, Greenwillow, 1984.
The Nature of the Beast. London, MacRae, and New York, Greenwillow, 1985.
Isaac Campion. London, MacRae, and New York, Greenwillow, 1986.

Screenplay: *The Nature of the Beast,* 1988.

Television Play: *Badger on the Barge,* from her own story, 1987.

*

Media Adaptations: *Badger on the Barge* (television movie), ITV, 1987; *The Nature of the Beast* (film), 4/British Screen, 1988.

Biography: Essay in *Something about the Author Autobiography Series* by Janni Howker, Volume 13, Detroit, Gale, 1992.

Critical Study: Entry in *Children's Literature Review,* Volume 14, Detroit, Gale, 1988.

*   *   *

Janni Howker was the most remarkable British writer of fiction for young people to emerge in the mid-1980s, a time when new talent was scarce. Her first book, *Badger on the Barge and Other Stories,* was highly acclaimed and won several awards; her second and third, *The Nature of the Beast* and *Isaac Campion,* swiftly consolidated her reputation. Though praise for these books was high, it was not excessive; they are of true quality.

Badger on the Barge is in no way apprentice work; the writer, though young and decidedly regional, was already very accomplished. The book consists of a group of five longish short stories, all of which are about relationships between young and old people. Helen in the title story befriends a crusty old woman who lives on a barge and is fighting for her independence; Liz in "The Topiary Garden" meets old Sally Beck who could only make a life for herself by pretending to be a boy. Jane in "The Egg-Man" glimpses the depth and vulnerability of love through a crazy old man's grief for a long-dead wife. Yet none of the stories are concerned only with the young-old relationship; each has also a subtheme, interwoven with the main one and resolved with it. They are ingeniously organized and limpidly written, and at the same time subtle and perceptive. The most poignant and atmospheric is "Jakey," in which an old boatman is about to die and his young friend Steven, dreaming, sees a dark shape following Jakey's boat: "a great grey shape, like a shark, swimming behind, slowly, secretly." It is Jakey's death.

In *The Nature of the Beast* Howker adapted her gift for the apt and sounding phrase to a first-person narration by a rough working-class boy. The setting is northern, on the edge of an industrial town; the Haverstock Beast—if it exists—prowls around, savaging farmers' stock and spreading fear among the people. Is the beast real or symbolic? The mill on which the town depended has closed; unemployment is also a beast that is ravaging the community. In the end it seems that a beast of anger and frustration is inside the boy himself: "I'm going to take over where the Beast left off," he says. Though there is warmth in the story, there is a chilling conclusion.

Isaac Campion has a similar setting to that of *The Nature of the Beast,* but it is set back in time to the limits of living memory, for Isaac is supposedly telling his story to the author, just before his death in 1984 at the age of ninety-six. The year is 1901. Isaac's older brother has been killed as the result of a foolish dare from the son of his father's hated enemy; Isaac must leave school to work without pay for Father, a horse dealer and a harsh, violent man. On impulse Isaac frustrates Father's plan to take a hideous revenge. Immediately afterwards the steamboat carrying a cargo of Irish mares for Father is thought to have sunk in a storm. Father comes home drunk, defeated, apparently ruined, yet hard and bitter still. Later the steamer is seen to be safe, riding at anchor; but Isaac has had enough, and will be off to America by the end of summer.

This is a brief, emotionally intense novel, full of the passionate power of hatred and the close but often suffocating or infuriating relationships between members of a family. There is compassion too for the horses that "dragged the whole weight of work behind them...until they were done for, and sent to the knacker's, or buried in a ditch." It gives a gritty, wholly convincing picture of a bleak world of hard-driven people. "I know I can endure it," thinks Isaac. "I was put on the earth to endure it. But there must be more to living a life than this." The book is not in the end pessimistic, however. In Isaac himself—poor, ordinary lad though he is—the human spirit shines. There's nothing shining about Father, but even in him there is something heroic: a fierce determination to fight, survive, and win in grim surroundings.

Howker's first three books suggest that hers is a major talent, but the second and third could be said to belong to general as much as to young people's fiction, and it remains to be seen whether she will stay within the bounds of the young adult's list.

—John Rowe Townsend

———

HOY, Linda. British. Born in Sheffield, 27 March 1946. Educated at Sheffield Polytechnic, Certificate of Education, 1973, B.Ed. (with honors), 1974. Divorced; three children. Worked as a shop assistant, barmaid, and civil servant; English teacher, Gosforth Comprehensive School, near Sheffield, England, 1974-83; lecturer, Sheffield City Polytechnic, 1986-1990. Agent: Gina Pollinger, 222 Old Brompton Rd., London SW5 OB2, England.

<small>PUBLICATIONS FOR YOUNG ADULTS</small>

Novels

Your Friend Rebecca. London, Bodley Head, 1981.
The Damned. London, Bodley Head, 1983.
Kiss File JC 100. London, Walker, 1988.
Haddock 'n' Chips. London, Walker, 1993.
United on Vacation. London, Walker, forthcoming.

Fiction

Nightmare Park. London, Collins, Armada, 1989.
Ring of Death. London, Collins, Armada, 1990.

Other

The Alternative Assembly Book (for teachers). Essex, Longman, 1985.
Emmeline Pankhurst. London, Hamish Hamilton, 1985.
Editor, *Poems for Peace.* Leichhardt, Australia, Pluto Press, 1986.
Emmeline Pankhurst. North Pomfret, Vermont, Trafalgar Square, n.d.

Television Play: *Emily,* TV South, 1985.

*   *   *

Linda Hoy is a Quaker committed to showing her young adult readers how to survive and keep the faith. Each of her books contains spiritual tools for readers to take with them as they try to construct their own lives. She explores the problems, rewards, and overall necessity of believing in something.

Her sole work of nonfiction, *Emmeline Pankhurst,* seems a natural biography for Hoy to write. Pankhurst, the founder of the militant women's suffrage movement, endured many hardships, including prison, for her belief. Hoy shows that although it wasn't an easy road for Pankhurst, it was a necessary one. It is because of the unfaltering faith of Pankhurst and others like her that women were granted the right to vote. Hoy avoids fictionalizing by allowing

Pankhurst's life to shine on its own, thus giving the reader a straightforward and naturally inspiring story.

Hoy's heavy hand proves problematic in her works of fiction. Her strengths and weaknesses are perhaps best exemplified in *Your Friend, Rebecca*. Rebecca is an instantly likable character with a wonderfully adolescent sense of humor. She calls her principal—Miss Hoggit—the Hog, burns cod fries, and ridicules teen fashion magazines. Because the story is told in the first person, we are privy to all private jokes and thoughts. Instead of letting Rebecca's engaging character flourish on its own, however, Hoy acts as a puppeteer, conveniently pulling the strings she finds appropriate to her ends.

Hoy loads the novel with overt references to *King Lear*. Each chapter begins with a quote from the play. When Rebecca's drama teacher, Mrs. Gloucester, tells Rebecca, who has not read the play, to play Cordelia and ad lib lines, she can't act, but says what she feels: "I have the feelings you'd expect a daughter to have for a father." When Rebecca is mad at Darren, whom she both has a crush on and must do the scene with, she plays Regan and tells him to get lost. Rebecca conveniently acts out all her frustrations through drama, letting all her pent-up emotions loose at just the right time in the play.

Drama class allows Rebecca to explore and release her true feelings. She becomes a new, improved person who goes to Quaker Meetings and starts liking her dad. Somewhere in the midst of her transformation, however, the real Rebecca becomes lost and Linda Hoy takes over. Hoy's descriptions, characters, and sharp sense of humor become overshadowed by the messages she unveils. Even in her novels that don't end happily, Hoy's voice, rather than that of her characters, is loudest. For example, in *Kiss File JC 110*, Julian's character is one the reader can easily relate to; however, from the start and throughout the story, Hoy's obvious symbolism and religious agenda prevail.

Hoy is at her best in the genre of nonfiction and, if she can find more characters from history that inspire her, perhaps that is where she will find her niche. Interestingly, her only book left in print in the United States is *Emmeline Pankhurst*. Although Hoy's message is important, it will most likely be lost on readers too old or too young to appreciate it. While older YA readers will most likely feel patronized by Hoy's loaded references, younger teen readers of Hoy's fiction may be able to enjoy her appealing characters, lively dialogue, and apt descriptions without feeling her authorial control.

—Kate Lentz

HUDSON, Jeffery. See **CRICHTON, Michael.**

HUGHES, Dean. American. Born in Ogden, Utah, 24 August 1943. Educated at Weber State College, Ogden, Utah, B.A. 1967; University of Washington, Seattle, M.A. 1968, Ph.D. 1972; postdoctoral study at Stanford University, Stanford, California, summer, 1975, and Yale University, New Haven, Connecticut, summer, 1978. Married Kathleen Hurst in 1966; one daughter and two sons. Asso-

ciate professor of English, Central Missouri State University, Warrensburg, 1972-80; part-time visiting professor, Brigham Young University, Provo, Utah, 1980-82; writer, part-time editor, and consultant, 1980-89. Guest author, speaker, and workshop leader at writing conferences. Recipient: National Endowment for the Humanities summer seminar stipend, 1975 and 1978; Outstanding Faculty Achievement award from Central Missouri State University, 1980; nominated for state awards in Tennessee, Missouri, Kansas, South Carolina, West Virginia, and Kentucky; Utah Children's Book award nominations for *Nutty for President, Switching Tracks, Nutty and the Case of the Ski-Slope Spy,* and *Family Pose; Honestly, Myron* was selected one of the "Best Books for Kids" by Children's Book Committee; *Family Pose* received an Editors' Choice award from *Booklist*. Address: 1466 West 1100 North, Provo, UT 84604, U.S.A.

PUBLICATIONS FOR YOUNG ADULTS

Fiction

Under the Same Stars. Salt Lake City, Utah, Deseret, 1979.
As Wide as the River. Salt Lake City, Utah, Deseret, 1980.
Nutty for President, illustrated by Blanche Sims. New York, Atheneum, 1981.
Hooper Haller. Salt Lake City, Utah, Deseret, 1981.
Facing the Enemy. Salt Lake City, Utah, Deseret, 1982.
Honestly, Myron, illustrated by Martha Weston. New York, Atheneum, 1982.
Switching Tracks. New York, Atheneum, 1982.
Jenny Haller. Salt Lake City, Utah, Deseret, 1983.
Millie Willenheimer and the Chestnut Corporation. New York, Atheneum, 1983.
Nutty and the Case of the Mastermind Thief. New York, Atheneum, 1985.
Nutty and the Case of the Ski-Slope Spy. New York, Atheneum, 1985.
Brothers. Salt Lake City, Utah, Deseret, 1986.
Nutty Can't Miss. New York, Atheneum, 1987.
Theo Zephyr. New York, Atheneum, 1987.
Cornbread and Prayer. Salt Lake City, Utah, Deseret, 1988.
Nutty Knows All. New York, Atheneum, 1988.
Family Pose. New York, Atheneum, 1989; as *Family Picture,* New York, Scholastic, 1990.
Jelly's Circus. New York, Aladdin, 1989.
Nutty the Movie Star. New York, Atheneum, 1989.
Big Base Hit, illustrated by Dennis Lyall. New York, Knopf, 1990.
Championship Game, illustrated by Dennis Lyall. New York, Knopf, 1990.
Line Drive, illustrated by Dennis Lyall. New York, Knopf, 1990.
Lucky Breaks Loose. Salt Lake City, Utah, Deseret, 1990.
Lucky's Crash Landing. Salt Lake City, Utah, Deseret, 1990.
Lucky's Gold Mine. Salt Lake City, Utah, Deseret, 1990.
Making the Team, illustrated by Dennis Lyall. New York, Knopf, 1990.
Pressure Play, illustrated by Dennis Lyall. New York, Knopf, 1990.
Rookie Star, illustrated by Dennis Lyall. New York, Knopf, 1990.
What a Catch!, illustrated by Dennis Lyall. New York, Knopf, 1990.
Winning Streak, illustrated by Dennis Lyall. New York, Knopf, 1990.

All Together Now, illustrated by Dennis Lyall. New York, Knopf, 1991.

Defense!, illustrated by Dennis Lyall. New York, Knopf, 1991.

Kickoff Time, illustrated by Dennis Lyall. New York, Knopf, 1991.

Lucky Fights Back. Salt Lake City, Utah, Deseret, 1991.

Lucky's Mud Festival. Salt Lake City, Utah, Deseret, 1991.

Play-Off, illustrated by Dennis Lyall. New York, Knopf, 1991.

Safe at First, illustrated by Dennis Lyall. New York, Knopf, 1991.

Stroke of Luck, illustrated by Dennis Lyall. New York, Knopf, 1991.

Superstar Team, Dennis Lyall. New York, Knopf, 1991.

Up to Bat, illustrated by Dennis Lyall. New York, Knopf, 1991.

Backup Goalie, illustrated by Dennis Lyall. New York, Knopf, 1992.

Lucky the Detective. Salt Lake City, Utah, Deseret, 1992.

Lucky's Tricks. Salt Lake City, Utah, Deseret, 1992.

Nothing but Net, illustrated by Dennis Lyall. New York, Knopf, 1992.

Point Guard, illustrated by Dennis Lyall. New York, Knopf, 1992.

Psyched!, illustrated by Dennis Lyall. New York, Knopf, 1992.

Total Soccer, illustrated by Dennis Lyall. New York, Knopf, 1992.

Victory Goal, illustrated by Dennis Lyall. New York, Knopf, 1992.

The End of the Race. New York, Atheneum, 1993.

Go to the Hoop!, illustrated by Dennis Lyall. New York, Knopf, 1993.

Nutty's Ghost. New York, Atheneum, 1993.

On the Line, illustrated by Dennis Lyall. New York, Knopf, 1993.

Quick Moves, illustrated by Dennis Lyall. New York, Knopf, 1993.

Shake Up, illustrated by Dennis Lyall. New York, Knopf, 1993.

Find the Power. New York, Random House, forthcoming.

Lucky in Love. Salt Lake City, Deseret, forthcoming.

Lucky's Cool Club. Salt Lake City, Deseret, forthcoming.

Quarterback Pass. New York, Random House, forthcoming.

Re-Elect Nutty! New York, Atheneum, forthcoming.

Other

Contributor, *Monsters, Ghoulies, and Creepy Creatures,* edited by Lee Bennett Hopkins. Morton Grove, Illinois, Whitman, 1977.

Contributor, *Merrily Comes Our Harvest In,* edited by Lee Bennett Hopkins. Orlando, Florida, Harcourt Brace, 1978.

Romance and Psychological Realism in William Godwin's Novels. Salem, New Hampshire, Arno, 1981.

The Mormon Church: A Basic History. Salt Lake City, Utah, Deseret, 1986.

Baseball Tips (nonfiction), with Tom Hughes, illustrated by Dennis Lyall. New York, Random House, 1993.

Publications for Adults

Fiction

Lullaby and Goodnight (as D.T. Hughes). New York, Pocket Books, 1992.

*

Dean Hughes comments:

I've always had a wide variety of interests. As a kid, I was as rough-and-tumble as the next boy, without the slightest fear of dirt. But my mom taught me to embroider, and I loved that too. Of course, I also love to read. In high school I played football, was on the debate team, and I wrote for the school literary magazine. And now, I write middle-grade humor; a sports series; historical fiction; mysteries; and serious, literary books for young adults. I have also published nonsense verse and an adult true-crime book.

I might be better off, commercially, to find a niche and stay with it. But I get so many ideas for stories for different ages and audiences, and I hate to limit myself to one kind of book. I happen to believe that an author can do excellent, important work in a book of humor, in a sports novel, or in a series book. I will admit, however, that my greatest love is to write serious fiction as I have done in books like *Family Pose* and *The End of the Race.*

*   *   *

Dean Hughes has written a wide variety of books for children and young adults. In most of his books, Hughes focuses on the day-to-day struggles of growing up. Occasionally, however, he addresses some of the larger issues that young people face, treating them with sensitivity and understanding. While he primarily concentrates on books for upper elementary and middle school students, his stories frequently span several grade levels by introducing characters of different ages.

The ability to create honest and believable characters—characters with whom young readers can empathize and relate—is Hughes' main strength as a writer. The interest generated by particular characters has led to several series for Hughes, including his "Lucky Ladd," books, his "Nutty" books, "The Angel Park All Stars" books, "The Angel Park Soccer" books, and his sports series. Although these books primarily feature grade-school children, interest in them often continues into the middle school, and they usually exemplify his themes of love, unity, and growing up.

Brothers (1986) brings together nine-year-old Dokey and his nineteen-year-old brother, Rob. While the book would not appeal to many high school students, it is certainly beyond the ability of most nine-year-olds. The adventure of hunting and the excitement of surviving in the snow makes it an interesting book for many students.

In the book, Rob is confronted with his own personal set of self-doubts, even though the story is told in third person from Dokey's point of view. Both boys struggle with their own conflicts as they attempt to reach out to one another through the differences created by time and age. Rob is struggling with his lifetime plan of spending two years doing missionary work and must also wrestle with the emotional conflicts brought about by his shaky relationship with his girlfriend. Dokey is simply trying to outgrow his nickname and redefine his position in his family. In this way, both brothers are struggling with growing up and this draws in readers of all ages who are faced with some of the same problems.

Many of his books, including *Brothers,* include references to Hughes' Mormon background without becoming overly didactic or preachy. His Mormon history trilogy, *Under the Same Stars* (1979), *As Wide as the River* (1980), and *Facing the Enemy* (1982) deals with the Mormon expulsion from Missouri and the ordeal of establishing a new colony as a part of the American westward expansion. It is a historical tale, an adventure story, a character study, and a religious history. The focus is not on the religion but on the characters. As in many of his books, he is able to involve readers of several ages by not stressing the age of the protagonist.

In the first book, the Williams' family has been called to be a part of the new settlement, and young Joseph has been told by the Prophet Joseph Smith that God has a special job for him. Joseph Williams is not an extraordinary boy—he gets into trouble, is willing to fight, and frequently resents his strict religious training. Although Joseph is only nine, his struggles and resentments can be appreciated by an audience which is much older and, in fact, should be older. Facing bigotry and hatred of those who do not want the Mormons to settle in Missouri, Joseph grows up much faster than his years might suggest.

In the last two parts of the trilogy, Joseph continues to grow, discovering that he must continue to struggle, sometimes with his own people. After facing the fact that the world can be wrong, he finally must face the knowledge that his own people may be wrong—a major obstacle in growing up for most young adults.

Two of Hughes' finest novels for the young adult audience never mention his interest in Mormon religion but are consistent in their repetition of his themes of love, family, and unity. One of his first young adult novels is *Switching Tracks* (1982). It is the story of a young boy who lives with guilt after his father's suicide, and an old man who is facing cancer and death. Although the resolution seems almost too simple in this realistic novel of facing mortality, Hughes' strength in developing believable and honest characters is at its pinnacle in this book. Mark's development as a troubled teenager fighting to protect his sanity, blocking all attempts by his mother to help him, and dealing with his horror of daring his father to kill himself is contrasted effectively with the characterization of Willard, a tired, old, railroad worker who knows he is dying. Neither man nor boy can cure the problems, but they find comfort in helping each other.

Family Pose (1989) is also about lonely people crossing barriers of age to find comfort. David is only eleven, but he is an orphan and a runaway. Paul is a forty-year-old alcoholic who works at a small hotel. As the story develops, so do the characters. Inside the hotel there are several workers; most of them are loners, most of them are very sad. In their effort to help David, they are brought together, and Paul and David both find a family to fill their lives.

Hooper Haller (1981) and *Jenny Haller* (1983), books in which the title characters are descendants of Joseph Williams from the Mormon trilogy, are directed at older readers. Both characters discover that the struggles to grow up do not end with high school graduation. Hooper goes directly to the major leagues after high school, while Jenny decides between law school and marriage.

Throughout his books Hughes concentrates on messages of unity, truth, and love, but the primary tie which pulls all of his works together is the note of hope on which they usually end. While it detracts from the realism in some cases, it also makes them very satisfying.

—Judith Gero John

HUGHES, (James Mercer) Langston. American. Born in Joplin, Montana, 1 February 1902. Educated at Columbia University, New York, 1921-22; Lincoln University, Jefferson City, Montana, A.B. 1929. Poet, novelist, short story writer, playwright, song lyricist, radio writer, translator, author of juvenile books, and lecturer. In early years worked as assistant cook, launderer, busboy, and at other odd jobs; worked as seaman on voyages to Africa and Europe.

Madrid correspondent for *Baltimore Afro-American,* 1937; visiting professor in creative writing, Atlanta University, Georgia, 1947; poet in residence, Laboratory School, University of Chicago, Illinois, 1949. Recipient: *Opportunity* magazine literary contest, first prize in poetry, 1925; Amy Spingarn Contest, *Crisis* magazine, poetry and essay prizes, 1925; Witter Bynner undergraduate poetry prize contests, first prize, 1926; *Palms* magazine Intercollegiate Poetry award, 1927; Harmon Gold Medal for Literature, 1931, for *Not without Laughter;* Rosenwald Fellowships, 1931, 1941; Guggenheim fellowship for creative work, 1935; Litt.D., Lincoln University, 1943, Howard University, 1960, Western Reserve University, 1964; National Institute and American Academy of Arts and Letters grant, 1947; Anisfeld-Wolfe award for best book on racial relations, 1954; Spingarn Medal, National Association for the Advancement of Colored People, 1960. *Died 22 May 1967.*

PUBLICATIONS FOR ADULTS AND YOUNG ADULTS

Poetry

The Weary Blues. New York, Knopf, 1926.
Fine Clothes to the Jew. New York, Knopf, 1927.
Dear Lovely Death. Amenia, New York, Troutbeck Press, 1931.
The Negro Mother and Other Dramatic Recitations. New York, Golden Stair Press, 1931.
Scottsboro Limited: Four Poems and a Play. New York, Golden Stair Press, 1932.
A New Song. New York, International Workers Order, 1938.
Shakespeare in Harlem, with Robert Glenn. New York, Knopf, 1942.
Freedom's Plow. New York, Musette Publishers, 1943.
Jim Crow's Last Stand. Negro Publication Society of America, 1943.
Lament for Dark Peoples and Other Poems. Azusa, California, Holland, 1944.
Fields of Wonder. New York, Knopf, 1947.
One-Way Ticket. New York, Knopf, 1949.
Montage of a Dream Deferred. New York, Holt, 1951.
Ask Your Mama: 12 Moods for Jazz. New York, Knopf, 1961.
The Panther and the Lash: Poems of Our Times. New York, Vintage, 1967.

Novels

Not without Laughter. New York, Knopf, 1930.
Tambourines to Glory. New York, John Day, 1958.

Short Stories

The Ways of White Folks. New York, Knopf, 1934.
Simple Speaks His Mind. New York, Simon & Schuster, 1950.
Laughing to Keep from Crying. New York, Holt, 1952.
Simple Takes a Wife. New York, Simon & Schuster, 1953.
Simple Stakes a Claim. New York, Rinehart, 1957.
Something in Common and Other Stories. New York, Hill & Wang, 1963.
Simple's Uncle Sam. New York, Hill & Wang, 1965.

Autobiography

The Big Sea. New York, Knopf, 1940.
I Wonder as I Wander. New York, Rinehart, 1956.

Nonfiction

A Negro Looks at Soviet Central Asia. Co-operative Publishing
Society of Foreign Workers in the U.S.S.R., 1934.
The Sweet Flypaper of Life, with Roy De Carava. New York, Simon
& Schuster, 1955.
A Pictorial History of the Negro in America, with Milton Meltzer.
New York, Crown, 1956; 4th edition published as *A Pictorial
History of Blackamericans,* 1973.
Fight for Freedom: The Story of the NAACP. New York, Norton,
1962.
*Black Magic: A Pictorial History of the Negro in American Enter-
tainment,* with Milton Meltzer. Englewood Cliffs, New Jersey,
Prentice-Hall, 1967.
Black Misery. Middlebury, Vermont, Paul S. Eriksson, 1969.

Editor

Four Lincoln University Poets. Jefferson City, Montana, Lincoln
University, 1930.
The Poetry of the Negro, 1746-1949, with Arna Bontemps. New
York, Doubleday, 1949; revised edition, as *The Poetry of the
Negro, 1746-1970,* 1970.
Lincoln University Poets, with Waring Cuney and Bruce M. Wright.
Fine Editions, 1954.
The Book of Negro Folklore, with Arna Bontemps. New York,
Dodd, 1958.
*An African Treasury: Articles, Essays, Stories, Poems by Black
Africans.* New York, Crown, 1960.
Poems from Black Africa. Bloomington, Indiana University Press,
1963.
New Negro Poets: U.S. Bloomington, Indiana University Press,
1964.
The Book of Negro Humor. New York, Dodd, 1966.
*The Best Short Stories by Negro Writers: An Anthology from 1899
to the Present.* Boston, Little, Brown, 1967.

Omnibus Volumes

Selected Poems. New York, Knopf, 1959.
The Best of Simple. New York, Hill & Wang, 1961.
Five Plays by Langston Hughes, edited by Webster Smalley.
Bloomington, Indiana University Press, 1963.
The Langston Hughes Reader. New York, Braziller, 1968.
Don't You Turn Back (poems), edited by Lee Bennett Hopkins.
New York, Knopf, 1969.
*Good Morning Revolution: The Uncollected Social Protest Writing
of Langston Hughes,* edited by Faith Berry. Brooklyn, New York,
Lawrence Hill, 1973.

Other

Translator, with Mercer Cook, *Masters of Dew,* by Jacques
Roumain. New York, Reynal & Hitchcock, 1947.
Translator, with Frederic Carruthers, *Cuba Libre,* by Nicolas
Guillen. Los Angeles, Anderson & Ritchie, 1948.
Translator, *Selected Poems of Gabriela Mistral.* Bloomington, Indi-
ana University Press, 1957.
Arna Bontemps-Langston Hughes Letters: 1925-1967, with Arna
Bontemps, edited by Charles H. Nichols, New York, Dodd, 1980.

Also author of numerous plays (most have been produced), includ-
ing *Little Ham,* 1935, *Mulatto,* 1935, *Emperor of Haiti,* 1936,
Troubled Island, 1936, *When the Jack Hollers,* 1936, *Front Porch,*
1937, *Joy to My Soul,* 1937, *Soul Gone Home,* 1937, *Little Eva's
End,* 1938, *Limitations of Life,* 1938, *The Em-Fuehrer Jones,* 1938,
Don't You Want to Be Free, 1938, *The Organizer,* 1939, *The Sun Do
Move,* 1942, *For This We Fight,* 1943, *The Barrier,* 1950, *The
Glory Round His Head,* 1953, *Simply Heavenly,* 1957, *Esther,* 1957,
The Ballad of the Brown King, 1960, *Black Nativity,* 1961, *Gospel
Glow,* 1962, *Jericho-Jim Crow,* 1963, *Tambourines to Glory,* 1963,
The Prodigal Son, 1965, *Soul Yesterday and Today, Angelo Herndon
Jones, Mother and Child, Trouble with the Angels,* and *Outshines
the Sun.*

Also author of screenplay, *Way Down South,* 1942. Author of libretto for operas, *The Barrier,* 1950, and *Troubled Island.* Lyricist
for *Just Around the Corner,* and for *Kurt Weill's Street Scene,* 1948.
Columnist for *Chicago Defender* and *New York Post.* Poetry, short
stories, criticism, and plays have been included in numerous anthologies.

PUBLICATIONS FOR CHILDREN

Popo and Fifina: Children of Haiti, with Arna Bontemps. London,
Macmillan, 1932.
The First Book of Negroes. New York, F. Watts, 1952.
Famous American Negroes. New York, Dodd, 1954.
The First Book of Rhythms. New York, F. Watts, 1954.
Famous Negro Music Makers. New York, Dodd, 1955.
The First Book of Jazz. New York, F. Watts, 1955.
The First Book of the West Indies. New York, F. Watts, 1956; as *The
First Book of the Caribbean,* London, E. Ward, 1965.
Famous Negro Heroes of America. New York, Dodd, 1958.
The First Book of Africa. New York, F. Watts, 1960.

*

Biography: Entries in *Dictionary of Literary Biography,* Detroit,
Gale, Volume 4: *American Writers in Paris, 1920-1939,* 1980; Vol-
ume 7: *Twentieth-Century American Dramatists,* 1981; Volume 48:
American Poets, 1880-1945, Second Series, 1986; Volume 51: *Afro-
American Writers from the Harlem Renaissance to 1940,* 1987;

Manuscript Collections: James Weldon Johnson Memorial Collection, Beinecke Library, Yale University, New Haven, Connecticut;
Schomburg Collection of the New York Public Library; Lincoln
University Library, Pennsylvania; Fisk University Library, Nashville, Tennessee.

Critical Studies: Entry in *Children's Literature Review,* Volume 17,
Detroit, Gale, 1989; entry in *Contemporary Literary Criticism,*
Detroit, Gale, Volume 1, 1973, Volume 5, 1976, Volume 10, 1979,
Volume 15, 1980, Volume 35, 1985, Volume 44, 1987.

*   *   *

During the Harlem Renaissance when the work of African-American writers was initially acknowledged as a significant feature of
American literature, Langston Hughes achieved a position of promi-

nence that eventually led to his recognition as "the Laureate of Black America." A wider historical perspective indicates that Hughes was an important contributor to an American poetic renaissance in which a singularly American voice—initially introduced by Walt Whitman—emerged as a distinct variant to the lingering strain of the British tradition still dominant in the United States. Hughes's poetry encompasses some of the experimentalism of such contemporaries as e. e. cummings and Marianne Moore, as well as the more immediately accessible lyricism of Carl Sandburg and the authenticity of community speech found in Robert Frost. He was driven by a desire to "explain and illuminate the Negro condition in America," and he was a pioneer in combining the rhythms of street speech, the blues, and the language of the black community with the formal patterns and structural conventions of the traditional English poetry he had mastered.

Hughes is not generally regarded as a poet whose work is specifically addressed to young adult readers and listeners, but in his attempt to address the concerns of African-Americans while exploring the universal questions of human existence, he has excluded no part of an audience with a degree of literacy and a grasp of the fundamentals of language. Almost all of his poetry is accessible and engaging because Hughes was influenced by such popular American poets as Sandburg, Vachel Lindsay, and Edgar Lee Masters who were interested in reaching a wide audience rather than a literary elite, but certain aspects of Hughes's poetry have a particular appeal for younger readers. The spirit of optimism and his faith in human beings pervades most of his work, but it is tempered by realistic assessment of the effects of racial hatred. There is a sense of a justifiable grievance in Hughes's writing, but it almost never shades into bitterness, so that the positive elements don't seem shallow or spurious. Instead, they reflect a determination to transcend the destructive and soul-crushing tendencies of poems written in rage and frustration.

With a title that echoes Sandburg, "I, too, sing America" is a call for inclusion, an anticipation of multicultural diversity that Hughes saw as one of the strengths of an American society that had tried to deny its rich ethnic mix. In spite of the history of racial terror and violence that Hughes knew from his own experience as well as from his reading, he saw himself in the spirit of Whitman as a poet who would not turn away from an idealistic vision of the promise of America. Hughes's self-description as "the darker brother" suggests the guilt haunting the American conscience but it is balanced by his belief in a true family that isn't riven by superficial differences but joined by the decency latent in most people. His appeal to this quality depends on his conviction that "They'll see / How beautiful I am / And be ashamed." His conclusion to the poem, "I, too, am America" is a testament of faith in his countrymen and women to recognize and appreciate the contributions of African-American citizens.

The poem "The Negro Speaks of Rivers" is a corollary in which Hughes suggests the richness of the historical legacy that African-Americans have brought to American society. Blending the history and heritage of black people who "bathed in the Euphrates when dawns were young," who "looked upon the Nile and raised the pyramids above it," with their lives in America where they "heard the singing of the Mississippi when Abe Lincoln / went down to New Orleans," Hughes opens a passage of centuries previously ignored by school texts. The concluding line, "My soul has grown deep like the rivers," is an attempt to project the elusive but powerful spirit of black culture that has enriched American lives into an image that can touch all Americans.

"Harlem" operates around the crucial question of "What happens to a dream deferred?" and offers the unsettling suggestion that it can "dry up / like a raisin in the sun," or that it can "explode" into violence. This prophetic poem, written in 1951, is not only a perceptive assessment of the psychological impact of racist policies, but a statement of the fragility of a young person's dreams. Characteristically, Hughes sees the counter-possibilities that can preserve the dream until it is realized, offering in "Dream Boogie" the awakening of the dream into the "good morning" of a "boogie-woogie rumble." Here, the irrepressible spirit of African-American vitality is projected in jazz rhythms—the sounds of survival—leading the poet to say, encouragingly: Sure, / I'm happy! / Take it away!/ He, pop! / Re-bop! / Mop! / Y-e-a-h!"

The energy, exuberance and playful sense of language illustrated here is one of the features that Hughes purposefully incorporated into his poetry as a literary equivalent of the verbal dexterity and intricate rhythmic structures of black music and colloquial speech. The poem "Children's Rhymes" skillfully weaves street chants and pointed commentary about how opportunity is often dependent on racial status: By what sends / the white kids / I ain't sent: / I know I can't / be President.

Hughes adjusts a familiar patriotic phrase by a sarcastic insertion—"Liberty And Justice— / Huh—For All."—before concluding the poem with the jump-rope chant: "Oop-pop-a-da! / Skee! Daddle-de-do! / Be-bop! / Salt'peanuts! / De-dop!"

A more meditative mood occurs in some of Hughes's reflective poems which focus on a young person near the beginning of life's journey. In "Mother to Son," the trials of the speaker ("Life for me ain't been no crystal stair") are acknowledged as basic, but the thrust of the poem is toward guidance and encouragement. The mother's example of perseverance ("I'se been a-climbin' on...And sometimes goin' in the dark / Where there ain't been no light") leads to an exhortation ("So boy, don't you turn back") stressing the necessity for endurance, exemplified by the older black woman who is still "climbin' on." The uncertainty and expectancy of a youth approaching adulthood is conveyed by Hughes's "Theme for English B," where he expresses the perennial doubt of an inquisitive young person who observes, "It's not easy to know what is true for you or me"—a universal exclamation—and proceeds with a series of meditative queries about life, skillfully joining youthful questions ("Me-who?") with the additional burden of racial consciousness. Even the poems like "Uncle Tom" or "Ballad of the Landlord" which are more caustic in their criticism of American society are cast in the mode of an observer commenting in sorrow rather than direct exhortations to action, and the lament "Song for a Dark Girl" places the horrifying image of a lynching in lyric form, which ameliorates the effect to some degree.

The same spirit of generosity and hope that informs Hughes's poetry is also present in his short fiction and in his two-volume autobiography. The occasionally anthologized story "On the Road" in which a black man is denied shelter at Christmastime and meets Christ on the highway combines Hughes's rueful humor and tempered judgement of the faults in American society, while the autobiography is generally a positive record of accomplishment and perseverance. In addition, Hughes invented a kind of voice-of-the-common-man he called Jesse B. Semple ("Just Be Simple") in 1943 who became very popular as a source of down-home wit and good sense in newspaper sketches Hughes eventually collected in four volumes. As in his poetry, these prose pieces are inspired by the same fundamental belief in the possibilities of American democracy that has made Hughes such an important and enduring figure in American literary history.

—Leon Lewis

———

HUGHES, Monica (Ince). Canadian. Born in Liverpool, England, 3 November 1925; daughter of the mathematician E.L. Ince; became Canadian citizen, 1957. Educated at the Convent of the Holy Child Jesus, Harrogate, Yorkshire, graduated 1942; Edinburgh University, 1942-43. Served in the Women's Royal Naval Service, 1943-46. Married Glen Hughes in 1957; two daughters and two sons. Dress designer, London, 1948-49, and Bulawayo, Rhodesia (now Zimbabwe), 1950; bank clerk Umtali, Rhodesia, 1951; laboratory technician, National Research Council, Ottawa, 1952-57. Since 1975 full-time writer; writer in residence at several universities, including University of Alberta, 1984-85. Recipient: Vicky Metcalf award from Canadian Authors Association, 1981, for body of work, 1983, for short story; Alberta Culture Juvenile Novel award, Bay's Beaver award, both 1981, for *Hunter in the Dark;* Canada Council prize for children's literature, 1982, a best book for young adults by the American Library Association and Young Adult Canadian Book award, both 1983; Canada Council prize for children's literature, 1981, for *The Guardian of Isis; The Keeper of the Isis Light* was named a best book for young adults by the American Library Association, 1981, and named to International Board on Books for Young People's honor list, 1982; Guardian award runner-up, 1983, for *Ring-Rise, Ring-Set;* Alberta R. Ross Annett award from Writers Guild of Alberta, 1983, 1984, 1986, 1992; Hans Christian Andersen award nomination, 1984. Agent: Pamela Paul Agency Inc., 253 High Park Avenue, Toronto, Ontario MGP 255. Address: 13816 110A Ave., Edmonton, Alberta T5M 2M9, Canada.

PUBLICATIONS FOR YOUNG ADULTS

Fiction

Gold-Fever Trail: A Klondike Adventure, illustrated by Patricia Peacock. Edmonton, Alberta, LeBel, 1974.
Crisis on Conshelf Ten. Toronto, Copp Clark, and London, Hamish Hamilton, 1975; New York, Atheneum, 1977.
Earthdark. London, Hamish Hamilton, 1977.
The Ghost Dance Caper. London; Hamish Hamilton, 1978.
The Tomorrow City. London, Hamish Hamilton, 1978.
Beyond the Dark River. London, Hamish Hamilton, 1979; New York, Atheneum, 1981.
The Beckoning Lights, illustrated by Richard A. Conroy. Edmonton, Alberta, LeBel, 1982, and New York, Watts, 1982.
Hunter in the Dark. Toronto, Clarke Irwin, 1982; New York, Atheneum, 1982.
Ring-Rise, Ring-Set. London, MacRae, and New York, Watts, 1982.
The Treasure of the Long Sault, illustrated by Richard A. Conroy. Edmonton, Alberta, LeBel, 1982.
My Name Is Paula Popowich!, illustrated by Leoung O'Young. Toronto, Lorimer, 1983.
Space Trap. Toronto, Groundwood, and London, MacRae, 1983; New York, Watts, 1984.

Devil on My Back. London, MacRae, 1984; New York, Atheneum, 1985.
Sandwriter. London, MacRae, 1984; New York, Holt, 1988.
Blaine's Way. Toronto, Irwin, 1986; London, Severn House, 1988.
The Dream Catcher. London, MacRae, 1986; New York, Atheneum, 1987.
Log Jam. Toronto, Irwin, 1987; as *Spirit River,* London, Methuen, 1988.
Little Fingerling: A Japanese Folk Tale, illustrated by Brenda Clark. Toronto, Kids Can Press, 1989.
The Promise. Toronto, Stoddart, and London, Methuen, 1989; New York, Simon & Schuster, 1992.
The Refuge. Toronto, Doubleday, 1989.
Invitation to the Game. Toronto, HarperCollins, 1990; New York, Simon & Schuster, 1990; London, Methuen, 1991.
The Crystal Drop. London, Methuen, 1992; New York, Simon & Schuster, 1993.
A Handful of Seeds. Toronto, Lester, 1993.
The Golden Aquarians. Toronto, HarperCollins, forthcoming.

"Isis" trilogy:

The Keeper of the Isis Light. London, Hamish Hamilton, 1980; New York, Atheneum, 1981.
The Guardian of Isis. London, Hamish Hamilton, 1981; New York, Atheneum, 1982.
The Isis Pedlar. London, Hamish Hamilton, 1982; New York, Atheneum, 1983.

Contributor

Magook. Toronto, McClelland & Stewart, 1977.
Out of Time. London, Bodley Head, 1984; New York, Harper, 1985.
Dragons and Dreams. New York, Harper, 1985.
The Windows of Dreams. London, Methuen, 1986.
Take Your Knee Off My Heart. London, Methuen, 1990.
Mother's Day. London, Methuen, 1992.

Short stories are included in *Owl's Fun Book for Spring, Summer and Fall,* Grey de Pencier, 1982; *Canadian Children's Annual,* Grolier, 1988; *Canadian Children's Treasury,* Key Porter, 1988.

*

Biography: Essay in *Something about the Author Autobiography Series,* Volume 11, Detroit, Gale, 1991; entry in *Sixth Book of Junior Authors and Illustrators,* New York, Wilson, 1989; essay in *Speaking for Ourselves, Too* compiled and edited by Donald R. Gallo, National Council of Teachers of English, 1993.

Manuscript Collection: University of Calgary, Alberta.

Critical Study: Entry in *Children's Literature Review,* Volume 9, Detroit, Gale, 1985, pp. 61-79.

Monica Hughes comments:
    I write in response to my excitement at the wonder of our world, and sometimes in response to my dismay at what we are doing to it. About two-thirds of my novels are in the science fiction genre, and which is often, like the myths of old, a metaphor for contrary ideas

that resonate with young people: independence and loneliness, adventure and responsibility, technology and the environment.

*   *   *

From her first young adult novel, *Gold-Fever Trail: A Klondike Adventure,* set during Canada's Gold Rush, Monica Hughes demonstrates the extensive research and careful attention to background detail that characterize her work; in fact, because of its authenticity, *Gold-Fever Trail* has been used as a supplemental history text in Alberta (Canada) schools. Hughes's recurring theme of self-reliance is central, as Harry and Sarah set out alone to find their father in the goldfields. Resourceful like all Hughes's protagonists, these motherless siblings find success far beyond their expectations.

In *The Ghost Dance Caper,* praised for its realistic description of the crime scene but criticized for its stereotypical Indian dialogue, Hughes depicts the search for individual identity, one of her favorite themes. Caught between the contempt of the "pureblood" Indians and the indifference of those who completely reject Indian ways, Tom, a young half-Blackfoot Indian, sets out to find his "spirit"—a task requiring access to a mystic "ghost bundle," available only through a museum burglary.

Identity is likewise the issue in *My Name Is Paula Popowich!,* as Paula Herman finds her paternal grandmother and discovers her half-Ukrainian heritage. Nearly twelve years old, Paula feels like a misfit in her mother's German-Canadian community; she even bleaches her hair to be blonde like everyone else. Gradually winning concessions from a mother embittered by the trials of single parenthood, Paula embraces her new identity.

Hughes sets several novels in the near future, describing technology that seems a plausible extension of what exists today. *Crisis on Conshelf Ten* and *Earthdark* relate adventures of young Kepler Masterman. Born on the Moon, he cannot adapt to the Earth's gravity; so his Earth visit is spent in an undersea colony which, like his lunar colony, is being exploited by the technocrats who initiated and support it. Hughes's concerns about the desirable limits of technology and the exploitation of underdeveloped countries can be seen as Kepler discovers that humans have been transformed into "gillmen," better adapted to working underwater. In *Earthdark* Kepler returns to the Moon colony with news of governmental reform. Inspired by the alienation, fear, and loneliness she felt upon first seeing the Canadian prairie landscape, Hughes creates a forbidding lunar landscape as backdrop for the power struggle in this colony.

Another power struggle figures in *Beyond the Dark River,* Hughes's account of Canadian life after a nuclear holocaust. Again drawing inspiration from the bleak Canadian prairies, Hughes describes a world, populated primarily by urban mutants, in which only isolated, self-sufficient groups like the German Hutterites and the Cree Indians are relatively unaffected. The Hutterites live simple, communal farm lives, but theirs is a closed society, characterized by bigotry. More admirable to Hughes is the natural wisdom seen in the lifestyle of the Cree, who follow ancient tribal customs. Like many of Hughes's youthful protagonists, fifteen-year-old Benjamin is dispatched on a mission, dangerous but vital to his community: the Hutterites, who have rejected all knowledge except the Bible, now need information from urban libraries. With the help of a young Cree who is training to become a medicine woman, Benjamin gains not only the scientific data, but also an appreciation of another culture and the independence to oppose his community's bigotry.

In an equally bleak picture of the near future, *Ring-Rise, Ring-Set,* technology again is both a necessity and an evil. Hughes's fears about environmental pollution have been fulfilled: Earth is surrounded by dust rings which block the sun's rays, threatening a new ice age. The conflict between developed and primitive societies recurs as the City People possess the technology to dissolve the rings, but the procedure would endanger the Ekoes, who live close to nature. Ultimately the Ekoes choose their values over physical survival, while the City People debate whether preserving their civilization is worth the cost.

Although Hughes's weakest novels *(The Beckoning Lights* and *Space Trap)* involve interplanetary travel and alien beings, she skillfully portrays the results of space colonization in the "Isis" trilogy. *The Keeper of the Isis Light,* the first of these and generally considered Hughes's masterpiece, is the story of sixteen-year-old Olwen Pendennis, who has grown up on the planet of Isis, attended only by Guardian, an anthropomorphic robot programmed by her dying parents to provide for her every need. Olwen experiences no loneliness until she is rejected by Mark London, a young settler newly arrived from Earth. Since the Isis environment has proven fatal to Olwen's parents, Guardian attempts—perhaps unwisely—to ensure her welfare by physical modifications that enable her to adapt to the planet's atmosphere: wider nostrils, larger lungs, and reptilian skin. Hughes suggests that Mark's rejection is based on ethnic prejudice; the colonists, and especially he, urge Olwen to have these modifications reversed. However, Olwen is secure in her own individuality; so she chooses isolation over conformity and retreats to the upland area of the planet, leaving the more hospitable valley for the settlers, who increasingly spurn her help.

The Guardian of Isis, the second "Isis" novel, is set approximately four generations later, when the colony has regressed to a primitive agricultural society bound by myths and taboos. Jody N'Kumo, an intelligent and inquisitive young misfit, challenges these taboos by reinventing simple mechanical devices and investigating supposedly supernatural occurrences. Alarmed by danger that, in typical Hughes fashion, only he sees, Jody challenges the taboos once too often, and the President (Mark London) exiles him to the Ugly One's realm. Though the colonists consider this a virtual death sentence, Jody finds that the Ugly One (Olwen) has been trying to warn of an impending flood. Again Hughes shows a self-absorbed adolescent required to become altruistic; and, as is usually the case, Jody is the only one able to act at the crucial moment. Neither Olwen nor Guardian can dive to the lakebottom and remove the obstruction; so Jody must use all his courage, endurance, and concentration to save his people.

In *The Isis Pedlar,* the final "Isis" novel and also the weakest and most controversial, David N'Kumo, the nephew of Jody, falls in love with the daughter of Michael Flynn, an unscrupulous itinerant pedlar. Using drugs and conjuring tricks, the outsider Flynn exploits the primitive Isis colonists, and to save him from their rebellion, Jody is forced finally to become the colony's leader. Perhaps because Flynn is a rather unlikable rogue, the emphasis upon his Irish nationality has brought charges of ethnic stereotyping.

Monica Hughes's novels are characterized by depth of characterization and plausibility of plot. Her protagonists are often literal or spiritual outsiders who must weigh the values of their societies. As her young adults struggle to become mature and responsible, they face universal young adult problems, but they also confront contemporary social and moral dilemmas for which Hughes offers some optimistic possibilities but no easy solutions.

—Charmaine Allmon Mosby

HUGHES, Ted (Edward James Hughes). British. Born in Mytholmroyd, Yorkshire, 17 August 1930. Educated at Mexborough Grammar School, Yorkshire; Pembroke College, Cambridge, 1951-54, B.A. in archaeology and anthropology 1954, M.A. 1959. Served in the Royal Air Force, 1948-50. Married 1) the poet Sylvia Plath in 1956 (died 1963), one daughter and one son; 2) Carol Orchard in 1970. Worked as a rose gardener, night watchman in a steelworks, zoo attendant, teacher, and reader for the Rank Organisation, in the 1950's; lived in the United States, 1957-59; taught at the University of Massachusetts, Amherst, 1957-58. Founding editor, with Daniel Weissbort, *Modern Poetry in Translation* magazine, London, 1964-71. Recipient: First Prize, Young Men's and Young Women's Hebrew Association Poetry Center contest, 1957, and first prize, Guinness Poetry Awards, 1958, both for *The Hawk in the Rain;* Guggenheim fellow, 1959-60; Somerset Maugham award, 1960, Hawthornden Prize, 1961, and Abraham Wonsell Foundation awards, 1964-69, all for *Lupercal;* City of Florence International Poetry prize, 1969, for *Wodwo;* Premio Internazionale Taormina Prize, 1972; Etna-Taormina prize, 1973; Queen's Medal for Poetry, 1974; *Season Songs* was a Children's Book Showcase Title, 1976; *Signal* Poetry award, 1979, for *Moon-Bells and Other Poems,* 1981, for *Under the North Star,* and 1983, for *The Rattle Bag: An Anthology of Poetry;* Royal Society of Literature Heinemann award, 1980, for *Moortown;* honorary doctorate, Exeter College, 1982, Open University, 1983, Bradford College, 1984, and Pembroke College, 1986; *The Iron Man: A Story in Five Nights* (new edition) was exhibited at the Bologna International Children's Book Fair, and received the Kurt Maschler Emil award from the National Book League, both 1985; *Guardian* award, 1985, for *What Is the Truth? A Farmyard Fable for the Young.* Honorary Fellow, Pembroke College, Cambridge, 1986. O.B.E. (Officer, Order of the British Empire), 1977. Poet Laureate, 1984. Agent: c/o Faber and Faber Ltd., 3 Queen's Square, London WC1N 3AU, England. Lives in North Tawton, Devon, England.

PUBLICATIONS FOR YOUNG ADULTS

Fiction

How the Whale Became and Other Stories, illustrated by George Adamson. London, Faber, 1963; illustrated by Rick Schreiter, New York, Atheneum, 1964.
The Iron Man: A Story in Five Nights, illustrated by George Adamson. London, Faber, 1968; as *The Iron Giant: A Story in Five Nights,* illustrated by Robert Nadler, New York, Harper, 1968.
Ffangs the Vampire Bat and the Kiss of Truth, illustrated by Chris Riddell. London, Faber, 1986.
Tales of the Early World, illustrated by Andrew Davidson. London, Faber, 1988.

Poetry

Meet My Folks!, illustrated by George Adamson. London, Faber, 1961; Indianapolis, Bobbs-Merrill, 1973; revised edition, Faber, 1987.
The Earth-Owl and Other Moon-People, illustrated by R.A. Brandt. London, Faber, 1963; New York, Atheneum, 1964; as *Moon-Whales and Other Moon Poems,* illustrated by Leonard Baskin, New York, Viking Press, 1976; revised edition, as *Moon-Whales,* London, Faber, 1988.

Nessie, the Mannerless Monster, illustrated by Gerald Rose. London, Faber, 1964; as *Nessie the Monster,* illustrated by Jan Pyk, Indianapolis, Bobbs-Merrill, 1974.
Five Autumn Songs for Children's Voices, illustrated by Phillida Gili. Crediton, Devon, Gilbertson, 1969.
Autumn Song, illustrated by Nina Carroll. Kettering, Northamptonshire, Steane, 1971.
Spring, Summer, Autumn, Winter. London, Rainbow Press, 1974; revised edition, as *Season Songs,* illustrated by Leonard Baskin, New York, Viking Press, 1975; London, Faber, 1976; revised edition, Faber, 1987.
Earth-Moon, illustrated by the author. London, Rainbow Press, 1976.
Moon-Bells and Other Poems. London, Chatto and Windus, 1978.
Under the North Star, illustrated by Leonard Baskin. London, Faber, and New York, Viking Press, 1981.
What Is the Truth? A Farmyard Fable for the Young, illustrated by R.J. Lloyd. London, Faber, and New York, Harper, 1984.
The Cat and the Cuckoo. Winchester, Wykeham Press, 1988.

Plays

The Coming of the Kings (broadcast 1964; produced London, 1972). Included in *The Coming of the Kings and Other Plays, 1970.*
The Tiger's Bones (broadcast 1965). Included in *The Coming of the Kings and Other Plays, 1970.*
Beauty and the Beast (broadcast 1965; produced London, 1971). Included in *The Coming of the Kings and Other Plays, 1970.*
The Price of a Bride (broadcast 1966). Excerpt published in *Here, Now and Beyond,* edited by Nancy Coniston Martin, London, Oxford University Press, 1968.
The Demon of Adachigahara, music by Gordon Crosse (cantata; produced Shrewsbury, 1968). London, Oxford University Press, 1969.
Sean, The Fool, The Devil and the Cats (broadcast 1968; produced London, 1971). Included in *The Coming of the Kings and Other Plays, 1970.*
The Coming of the Kings and Other Plays (includes *Beauty and the Beast; Sean, the Fool, The Devil and the Cats, The Coming of the Kings,* and *The Tiger's Bones*). London, Faber, 1970; augmented edition as, *The Tiger's Bones and Other Plays for Children* (includes *Orpheus*), illustrated by Alan E. Cober, New York, Viking Press, 1974.
The Iron Man (televised 1972). London, Faber, 1973.
Orpheus (broadcast 1971). Chicago, Dramatic Publishing Company, 1973. Included in *The Tiger's Bones and Other Plays for Children, 1974.*
The Pig Organ; or, Pork with Perfect Pitch, music by Richard Blackford (produced London, 1980).

Radio Plays: *The Coming of the Kings,* 1964; *The Tiger's Bones,* 1965; *Beauty and the Beast,* 1965; *The Price of a Bride,* 1966; *The Head of Gold,* 1967; *Sean, The Fool, The Devil and the Cats,* 1968; *Orpheus,* 1971.

Other

Poetry in the Making: An Anthology of Poems and Programmes from "Listening and Writing". London, Faber, 1967; abridged edition, as *Poetry Is,* New York, Doubleday, 1970.

Editor, with Seamus Heaney, *The Rattle Bag: An Anthology of Poetry.* London, Faber, 1982.

PUBLICATIONS FOR ADULTS

Poetry

The Hawk in the Rain. London, Faber, and New York, Harper, 1957.
Pike. Northampton, Massachusetts, Gehenna Press, 1959.
Lupercal. London, Faber, and New York, Harper, 1960.
Selected Poems, with Thom Gunn. London, Faber, 1962.
The Burning of the Brothel. London, Turret, 1966.
The Recklings. London, Turret, 1967.
Scapegoats and Rabies: A Poem in Five Parts. London, Poet and Printer, 1967.
Animal Poems. Crediton, Devon, Gilbertson, 1967.
Gravestones (6 broadsides), linocuts by Gavin Robbins. Exeter, Devon, Exeter College of Art, 1967; as *Poems,* 1 volume, 1968.
Poems: Ted Hughes, Fainlight, and Sillitoe. London, Rainbow Press, 1967.
I Said Goodbye to Earth. London, Turret, 1969.
A Crow Hymn. Frensham, Surrey, Sceptre Press, 1970.
The Martyrdom of Bishop Farrar. Crediton, Devon, Gilbertson, 1970.
A Few Crows. Exeter, Devon, Rougemont Press, 1970.
Four Crow Poems. Privately printed, 1970.
Crow: From the Life and Songs of the Crow. London, Faber, 1970; New York, Harper, 1971; revised edition, London, Faber, 1972.
Fighting for Jerusalem. Ashington, Northumberland, Mid-NAG, 1970.
Amulet. Privately printed, 1970.
Corgi Modern Poets in Focus I, with others, edited by Dannie Abse. London, Corgi, 1971.
Crow Wakes: Poems. Woodford Gree, Essex, Poet and Printer, 1971.
Poems, with Ruth Fainlight and Alan Sillitoe. London, Rainbow Press, 1971.
In the Little Girl's Angel Gaze. London, Steam Press, 1972.
Selected Poems, 1957-1967, illustrated by Leonard Baskin. London, Faber, 1972; New York, Harper, 1973.
Prometheus on His Crag: 21 Poems, illustrated by Leonard Baskin. London, Rainbow Press, 1973.
The Interrogator: A Titled Vulturess. London, Scolar Press, 1975.
Cave Birds. London, Scolar Press, 1975; revised edition, as *Cave Birds: An Alchemical Cave Drama,* illustrated by Leonard Baskin, London, Faber, 1978; New York, Viking Press, 1979.
The New World, music by Gordon Crosse. London, Oxford University Press, 1975.
Eclipse. Knotting, Bedfordshire, Sceptre Press, 1976.
Gaudete. London, Faber, and New York, Harper, 1977.
Chiasmadon. Baltimore, Seluzicki, 1977.
Sunstruck. Knotting, Bedfordshire, Sceptre Press, 1977.
Calder Valley Poems. London, Rainbow Press, 1978.
A Solstice. Knotting, Bedfordshire, Sceptre Press, 1978.
Orts. London, Rainbow Press, 1978.
Moortown Elegies. London, Rainbow Press, 1978.
Adam and the Sacred Nine. London, Rainbow Press, 1979.
All Around the Year, photographs by Michael Morpurgo. Murray, 1979.

Remains of Elmet: A Pennine Sequence, photographs by Fay Godwin. London, Rainbow Press, 1979; revised edition, London, Faber, and New York, Harper, 1979.
Night-Arrival of Sea-Trout, The Iron Wolf, Puma, Brooktrout, Pan, Woodpecker, Wolverine, Eagle, Mosquito, Tapir's Saga, Wolf-Watching, Mice Are Funny Little Creatures, Weasels at Work, Fly Inspects (broadsides). North Tawton, Devon, Morrigu Press, 1979-83.
Four Tales Told by an Idiot. Knotting, Bedfordshire, Sceptre Press, 1979.
In the Black Chapel (poster). London, Victoria and Albert Museum, 1979.
Moortown. London, Faber, 1979; New York, Harper, 1980.
Sky-Furnace, painting by Roger Vick. North Tawton, Devon, Caricia Fine Arts, 1981.
A Primer of Birds: Poems, illustrated by Leonard Baskin. Lurley, Devon, Gehenna Press, 1981.
Selected Poems: 1957-1981. London, Faber, 1982; as *New Selected Poems,* New York, Harper, 1982.
River, photographs by Peter Keen. London, Faber, 1983; New York, Harper, 1984.
Flowers and Insects: Some Birds and a Pair of Spiders, illustrated by Leonard Baskin. London, Faber, and New York, Knopf, 1986.
Wolfwatching. London, Faber, 1989.

Recordings: *Poets Reading 5,* Jupiter, 1962; *The Poet Speaks 5,* Argo, 1965; *Crow,* Claddagh, 1973; *The Poetry and Voice of Ted Hughes,* Caedmon, 1977; *Selections from Crow and Wodwo,* Caedmon, 1979.

Plays

The House of Aries (broadcast 1960). Published in *Audience,* (Cambridge, Massachusetts), Spring 1961.
The Calm (produced Boston, 1961).
The Wound (broadcast 1962). Included in *Wodwo,* 1967; revised version (produced London, 1972).
Epithalamium (produced London, 1963).
The House of Donkeys (broadcast 1965). Published in *Living Language,* Autumn 1974.
Seneca's Oedipus (produced London, 1968; Los Angeles, 1973; New York, 1977). London, Faber, 1969; New York, Doubleday, 1972.
Orghast (produced Persepolis, 1971). Excerpt published in *Performance* (New York), December 1971.
Eat Crow. London, Rainbow Press, 1971.
The Story of Vasco, music by Gordon Crosse, adaptation of a play by Georges Schehadé (produced London, 1974). London, Oxford University Press, 1974.

Radio Plays: *The House of Aries,* 1960; *A Houseful of Women,* 1961; *The Wound,* 1962; *Difficulties of a Bridegroom,* 1963; *Dogs,* 1964; *The House of Donkeys,* 1965.

Short Stories

The Threshold. London, Steam Press, 1979.

Other

Editor, with Patricia Beer and Vernon Scannell, *New Poems 1962.* London, Hutchinson, 1962.

Editor, *Here Today.* London, Hutchinson, 1963.

Editor, with Thom Gunn, *Five American Poets.* London, Faber, 1963.

Editor, *Selected Poems,* by Keith Douglas. London, Faber, 1964; New York, Chilmark Press, 1965.

Editor, with Olwyn Hughes, *Ariel,* by Sylvia Plath. London, Faber, 1965; New York, Harper, 1966.

Wodwo (miscellany). London, Faber, and New York, Harper, 1967.

Editor, *A Choice of Emily Dickinson's Verse.* London, Faber, 1968.

Translator, with Assia Gutmann, *Selected Poems,* by Yehuda Amichai. London, Cape Goliard Press, 1968; expanded edition, as *Poems,* New York, Harper, 1969; London, Penguin, 1971.

Editor, *Crossing the Water,* by Sylvia Plath. London, Faber, 1971; as *Crossing the Water: Transitional Poems,* New York, Harper, 1971.

Editor, *Winter Trees,* by Sylvia Plath. London, Faber, 1971; New York, Harper, 1972.

Editor, *With Fairest Flowers While Summer Lasts: Poems from Shakespeare.* New York, Doubleday, 1971; as *A Choice of Shakespeare's Verse,* London, Faber, 1971; introduction published as *Shakespeare's Poem,* London, Lexham Press, 1971.

Contributor, *Cricket's Choice.* Chicago, Open Court, 1974.

Editor, and translator with János Csokits, *Selected Poems,* by János Pilinszky. Manchester, Carcanet, 1976.

Editor, and Translator with Yehuda Amichai, *Amen,* by Yehuda Amichai. New York, Harper, 1977; London, Oxford University Press, 1978.

Translator, *Another Republic,* edited by Charles Simic and Mark Strand. New York, Ecco Press, 1977.

Editor, and author of introduction, *Johnny Panic and the Bible of Dreams, and Other Prose Writings,* by Sylvia Plath. London, Faber, 1977; augmented edition, London, Faber, and New York, Harper, 1979.

Henry Williamson: A Tribute. London, Rainbow Press, 1979.

Translator, with Yehuda Amichai, *Time,* by Yehuda Amichai. New York, Harper, and London, Oxford University Press, 1979.

Editor, *New Poetry 6.* London, Hutchinson, 1980.

Editor, *The Collected Poems of Sylvia Plath.* London, Faber, and New York, Harper, 1981.

Editor, with Seamus Heaney, *1980 Anthology: Arvon Foundation Poetry Competition.* Todmorden, Lancashire, Kilnhurst, 1982.

Editor, with Frances McCullough, *The Journals of Sylvia Plath.* New York, Dial Press, 1982.

Editor, *Sylvia Plath's Selected Poems.* London, Faber, 1985.

Translator, *The Early Books of Yehuda Amichai.* New York, Sheep Meadow Press, 1988.

Translator, with János Csokits, *The Desert of Love,* by János Pilinszky. London, Anvil Press Poetry, 1989.

Editor, *The Essential Shakespeare.* New York, Ecco Press, 1991.

Rain-charm for the Duchy and other Laureate Poems. London, Faber, 1992.

Shakespeare and the Goddess of Complete Being. New York, Farrar Straus, 1992.

*

Biography: Entry in *Dictionary of Literary Biography,* Volume 40, Detroit, Gale, 1985.

Bibliography: *Ted Hughes: A Bibliography 1946-1980* by Keith Sagar and Stephen Tabor, London, Mansell, 1983.

Critical Study: *Ted Hughes,* London, Longman, 1972, and *The Art of Ted Hughes,* London, Cambridge University Press, 1975, revised edition, 1978, both by Keith Sagar, and *The Achievement of Ted Hughes* edited by Keith Sagar, Manchester, Manchester University Press, and Athens, University of Georgia Press, 1983; "Dark Rainbow: Reflections on Ted Hughes," by John Adams, in *Signal,* May 1971, p. 65; entries in *Contemporary Literary Criticism,* Detroit, Gale, Volume 2, 1974; Volume 4, 1975; Volume 9, 1978; Volume 14, 1980; Volume 37, 1986; *Thom Gunn and Ted Hughes* by Alan Bold, Edinburgh, Oliver and Boyd, 1976; entry in *Children's Literature Review,* Volume 3, Detroit, Gale, 1978; *Sylvia Plath and Ted Hughes* by Margaret Dickie Uroff, Urbana, University of Illinois Press, 1979; *Ted Hughes: The Unaccommodated Universe, with Selected Critical Writings by Ted Hughes and Two Interviews* by Ekbert Faas, Santa Barbara, California, Black Sparrow Press, 1980; *Ted Hughes: A Critical Study* by Terry Gifford and Neil Roberts, London, Faber, 1981; *Myth in the Poetry of Ted Hughes: A Guide to the Poems* by Stuart Hirschberg, Portmarnock, County Dublin, Wolfhound Press, and Totowa, New Jersey, Barnes and Noble, 1981; *Ted Hughes* by Thomas West, London, Methuen, 1985; *Ted Hughes* by Dennis Walder, Milton Keynes, Buckinghamshire, Open University Press, 1987; *Ted Hughes as Shepherd of Being* by Craig Robinson, London, Macmillan, 1989.

*   *   *

Ted Hughes has written poetry, prose, and plays for young adults. The central themes in his works are life, death, and the power and mystery of the cosmos. Hughes's works have a sense of urgency as he tries to communicate his vision of the world to his young readers. Though full of humor, Hughes' writing typically reflects this deeper purpose, and he uses a variety of poetic and prose forms to match the diversity and richness he finds in nature. For example, his play *The Tiger's Bones* is a satire that warns about the dangers of the modern scientific mentality, and his book *Iron Giant: A Story in Five Nights* is a myth that deals with the issues of sacrifice and redemption. His collection of poems, *Season Songs,* encourages the reader to have an openness to nature and its processes.

Hughes believes, as he states in *Poetry in the Making,* that there is no ideal form of poetry or writing, and this is reflected in his varied pieces and styles of writing. His poetry ranges from free verse ("New Year Song") to highly structured forms and rhyme schemes ("The Loon" and "The Black Bear"). Hughes has used a wide variety of styles and formats for his writing, varying these at least as often as the themes about which he is writing.

Hughes's central focus is on nature, complete with the violence, destruction, purity, dignity, and harmony that make up the natural world. Hughes' books of poetry, *Under the North Star, The Cat and the Cuckoo, Moon-Whales and Other Moon Poems,* and *Season Songs,* all focus on various aspects of nature. In addition, his fable *What Is the Truth?* and his book *Tales of the Early World* also deal with the creation and existence of various creatures in nature. Within these natural settings, Hughes deals unblinkingly with death, violence, and destruction. He portrays these happenings in a realistic manner, and as a necessary and inevitable part of the cycle of life.

The cycles of nature form the theme of his popular and well-received collection of poetry *Season Songs.* The element of death is present as a part of the cycles of nature in all of these poems. This collection begins with "A March Calf" as it first experiences its mother and surroundings. But sentimentality has no place in this world. Hughes introduces the inevitability of death for the calf near the end of the poem by writing:

Hungry people are getting hungrier,
Butchers developing expertise and markets.

There is no sentiment again in the poem "There Came a Day," where Hughes pins autumn with these lines:

There came a day that caught the summer
Wrung its neck
Plucked it
And ate it.

Season Songs ends with "The Warm and the Cold," a poem full of opposites that focuses on the impending death and destruction that winter brings. The poem begins with the following description:

Freezing dusk is closing
Like the slow trap of steel
On trees and roads and hills and all
That can no longer feel.

The ineluctable intertwining of nature, mankind, fate and man's abuse of the earth are sharply present.

Animals are both metaphor and meaning when Hughes writes about them. In *Poetry in the Making,* Hughes devotes an entire chapter to the processes he goes through when writing his animal poems. He explains that his first animal poem, "Thought Fox," is based on real observations of and experiences with a fox that he recalled from his memory. He then thoroughly describes how he uses his five senses to capture the various aspects and dimensions of the animals so the reader can see, hear, smell, and actually experience the animal to the degree language permits.

Hughes is a highly imaginative writer, as one would expect from such an accomplished poet. Yet as he describes the grotesque, amazing creatures, plants, and events on the moon in his collection *Moon-Whales,* an element of comedy is often present in the poems. The majority of the poems in this collection focus on a specific animal or plant as it would be on the moon. "The Burrow Wolf" is a hideous, frightening creature at the beginning of the poem when Hughes tells the reader:

And the wolf's eyes start clean out of his head on eleven-inch stalks.

The comic element in these poems often takes on an ironic tone. "The Burrow Wolf" ends with these unexpected lines:

And he might lunatically mistake this wolf for his wife.
So the man in the moon ended his life.

In fact, there are so many horrible creatures and events on the moon that Hughes has written an entire poem entitled "Moon Horrors."

Hughes's passionate involvement in nature extends to include the celestial bodies, especially the Moon. Clearly, *Moon-Whales* is replete with cosmic references. In addition, cosmic imagery informs almost all of the poems in *Under the North Star.* In fact, Keith Cushman, in *The Achievement of Ted Hughes,* called this collection of poems Hughes' own "poetic constellation." The first poem in

Under the North Star is "The Loon," and it begins with these lines: "The Loon, the Loon / Hatched from the moon"—thus setting the tone and meaning from the beginning. "The Wolverine" describes the wolverine as he "Bobs up in the Northern Lights." Cosmic images are overt also throughout Hughes' prose works *Tales of the Early World* and *What Is the Truth?*

Ted Hughes has written a wide variety of finely illustrated, fiercely wrought, passionate poetry, prose, and plays for young adults. Hughes values the youth of the world too much to hide from them the bewildering and fantastic; his poet's eye and mind is everywhere probing the beauty and strangeness of nature in all its forms. His work cumulatively reveals his faith and respect in the abilities of children everywhere to make a sense of life. Hughes is quoted as saying, "Every new child is nature's chance to correct culture's error," and his books for young adults are implicit texts to help in this recovery.

—Nicholas Ranson

———

HUNT, Irene. American. Born in Newton, Illinois, 18 May 1907. Educated at the University of Illinois, Urbana, B.A. 1939; University of Minnesota, Minneapolis, M.A. 1946; University of Colorado, Boulder. French and English teacher, Oak Park public schools, Illinois, 1930-45; instructor in psychology, University of South Dakota, Vermillion, 1946-50; teacher, 1950-65, and director of language arts, 1965-69, Cicero public schools, Illinois. Recipient: Charles W. Follett award, 1964, Newbery Honor Book, 1965, Dorothy Canfield Fisher award, 1965, Clara Ingram Judson Memorial award, 1965, Lewis Carroll Shelf award, 1966, and ALA Notable Book citation, all for *Across Five Aprils;* Newbery Medal, 1967, and International Board on Books for Young People Honor List, 1970, both for *Up a Road Slowly;* Friends of Literature award, and Charles W. Follett award, both 1971, both for *No Promises in the Wind;* Omar's Book award, for *The Lottery Rose;* Parents' Choice award, 1985, for *The Everlasting Hills.* Address: 2591 Countryside Boulevard, Clearwater, FL 33519, U.S.A.

PUBLICATIONS FOR YOUNG ADULTS

Fiction

Across Five Aprils. Chicago, Follett, 1964; London, Bodley Head, 1965.
Up a Road Slowly. Chicago, Follett, 1966; London, Macdonald, 1967.
Trail of Apple Blossoms, illustrated by Don Bolognese. Chicago, Follett, 1968; London, Blackie, 1970.
No Promises in the Wind. Chicago, Follett, 1970.
The Lottery Rose. New York, Scribner, 1976.
William. New York, Scribner, 1977.
Claws of a Young Century. New York, Scribner, 1980.
The Everlasting Hills. New York, Scribner, 1985.

*

Media Adaptations: *No Promises in the Wind* has been optioned for production as a film.

Manuscript Collection: Kerlan Collection, University of Minnesota, Minneapolis.

Biography: Entry in *Dictionary of Literary Biography* by Philip A. Sadler, Volume 52, Detroit, Gale, 1986.

Critical Study: Entry in *Children's Literature Review,* Volume 1, Detroit, Gale, 1976.

*   *   *

Irene Hunt's novels are notable works for young people for their wide-ranging diversity. She demonstrates her virtuosity as a storyteller by never duplicating her use of characters, setting, and plot within the genre of historical fiction. In addition, all of Hunt's novels consistently demonstrate other important elements such as poetic yet simple language and a delicate appreciation of the natural world. Most outstanding of all, Hunt never fails to reveal to her reader the complexities and rewards of human relationships, especially within the context of the family.

In fact, family issues dominate Hunt's novels. Her characters struggle to construct stable family situations for themselves, sometimes in the absence of anything faintly resembling a nurturing family environment. Perhaps the death of Hunt's father and the consequent disruption of her childhood was a personal source for her novelistic explorations of family dynamics. In any case, she frequently juxtaposes the disrupted traditional family with its hopeful reconstruction. Of major importance to Hunt seems to be the overwhelming need young people have for stable role models; indeed, these individuals often assume the roles of surrogate parents to her main characters.

Hunt's first novel, the widely acclaimed *Across Five Aprils,* is a perfect illustration of her concern for the support which the family and the surrogate family can offer an adolescent. In it, she masterfully depicts the dissolution and reconstruction of the country during the Civil War and establishes the Creighton family as a microcosm of that internal conflict. Hunt's research of historical details is impeccable, and her use of her grandfather's memories of his childhood during the war gives the reader a sense of great intimacy with the lives of the characters. More importantly, Hunt's use of the Civil War and the corresponding tensions between North and South becomes a paradigm for the processes by which personal needs are met or left unfulfilled within the American family.

The Creightons are touched by the war even on their backwoods southern Illinois farm. Jethro Creighton, the youngest of his large family, sees the men he loves and admires leave one by one for wartime service. Their letters home gradually awaken in Jethro an awareness of the cruel and divisive nature of war. Once the pampered baby of the family, Jethro advances to adult status amid the disintegration of the family unit in which he had once felt security. Jethro's successful transition is made possible by the many father surrogates with whom he identifies: his sensitive brother Bill, his teacher Shadrach, astute and compassionate Ross Milton, the much-maligned Dave Burdow, and even President Abraham Lincoln, whose stern leadership tempered with mercy leaves an indelible mark on young Jethro.

Up a Road Slowly was Hunt's second novel and the one for which she received the Newbery Award. In it, Julie Trelling recounts her ten years with her aunt Cordelia, after the death of her mother and her father's inability to raise her on his own. Willful and adventurous, Julie clashes frequently with her aunt, a strict and

duty-bound woman who nonetheless exerts a loving and powerful influence over Julie. Julie's development is placed in meaningful counterpoint with the personality of her uncle Haskell, who has been rendered perpetually childlike as well as alcoholic by his permissive mother. As Julie overtakes and surpasses her uncle in maturity and self-acceptance, she finally realizes that she owes much to Aunt Cordelia, who has risen to her needs and provided the surrogate guidance that Julie's own parents could not.

In *Trail of Apple Blossoms* Hunt tells the story of folk-hero John Chapman (Johnny Appleseed), who befriended both native Americans and westward-looking settlers during the early 1800s. Chapman's efforts to plant apple trees throughout the Ohio Valley are familiar even to young children. To the well-known legends Hunt adds a fictional encounter with the Bryant family, whom Chapman befriends when he saves their small daughter's life. The lives of the Bryants and Johnny Appleseed cross several more times as if to remind Chapman of his purpose: to encourage families to further settlements of the new country, for in the family lies the country's strength.

The Depression era, a time when economic hardships placed unusual tensions on the American family, is the setting for *No Promises in the Wind.* For Josh Grondowski, the stresses of adolescence and the hopelessness of his family's poverty combine to make his relationship with his demanding father unendurable. Josh decides to run away, trusting his own strengths and abilities to make a new life for himself. He does not leave alone, however; with Josh is his younger brother Joey. As Josh fights not only for his survival but Joey's as well, he learns to understand his father's anger at his failures as a parent and as a person. Josh's growth to this level of empathy with his father is facilitated by the two people to whom he unconsciously looks as surrogate parents during his journey: Emily, who teaches Josh to look beyond superficialities to the nobility which lies within, and Lonnie, whose personal losses show Josh the value of his relationship, however troubled, with his father.

Hunt's last few novels continue to demonstrate her versatility. All, with one exception, abandon the genre of historical fiction while still maintaining her novelistic focus on family and surrogate family. In *The Lottery Rose,* Georgie Burgess's family life is a nightmare of abuse and neglect. Georgie's love for beauty survives his mistreatment and creates the avenue by which he is drawn back into a world of love and trust. The premise of *William* involves three orphaned black children who are cared for after their parents' deaths by a white, unwed, teenaged mother. Race, however, becomes a nonissue as Hunt again explores the loss of the traditional family structure and its replacement. *In Claws of a New Century* Hunt returns to historical fiction but with a feminist theme. Finally, *The Everlasting Hills* deals with the struggle of a neurologically impaired child to achieve selfhood. Family issues still remain at the forefront as twelve-year-old Jeremy Tydings learns that he is a product both of the family he has been given and of the family he has chosen.

Both modern parents and their children alike have the tendency to see the current shifts and changes in family dynamics as the unique products of their generation's cultural problems. Hunt's novels indicate otherwise; while the individual problems may be different, their influences on the family remain the same. Hunt's adolescent protagonists, regardless of the era in which they live, continually demonstrate the value of changed family relationships in contrast to the ones that have always been considered traditional. What remains important is not the normality or typicality of the family in which growth from adolescence to adulthood is achieved, but how the existing family structure supports and guides that transition.

—Patricia L. Bradley

————

HUNTER, Kristin (Elaine, née Eggleston). American. Born in Philadelphia, Pennsylvania, 12 September 1931. Educated at Charles Sumner School, Camden, and Magnolia Public School, both New Jersey; Haddon Heights High School, New Jersey, graduated 1947; University of Pennsylvania, 1947-51, B.S. in education 1951. Married 1) Joseph Hunter in 1952 (divorced 1962); 2) John I. Lattany in 1968. Columnist and feature writer, *Pittsburgh Courier,* 1946-52; teacher, Camden, New Jersey, 1951; copywriter, Lavenson Bureau of Advertising, Philadelphia, 1952-59, and Werman & Schorr, Inc., Philadelphia, 1962-63; research assistant, School of Social Work, University of Pennsylvania, 1961-62; information officer, City of Philadelphia, 1963-64, 1965-66; director of health services, Temple University, Philadelphia, 1971-72; director, Walt Whitman Poetry Center, Camden, 1978-79. Lecturer in Creative Writing, University of Pennsylvania, Philadelphia, 1972-79, Adjunct Associate Professor of English, 1981-83, Senior Lecturer in English, University of Pennsylvania, since 1983. Writer-in-residence, Emory University, Atlanta, 1979. Recipient: Fund for the Republic Prize, 1955, for television documentary, *Minority of One;* John Hay Whitney fellowship, 1959-60; Philadelphia Athenaeum award, 1964; Bread Loaf Writers Conference De Voto fellowship, 1965; National Council on Interracial Books for Children award, 1968, Mass Media Brotherhood award from National Conference of Christians and Jews, 1969, and Lewis Carroll Shelf award, 1971, all for *The Soul Brothers and Sister Lou;* Sigma Delta Chi reporting award, 1968; Spring Book Festival award, 1973, Christopher award, and National Book award finalist, both 1974, all for *Guests in the Promised Land;* Drexel Children's Literature Citation, 1981; New Jersey State Council on the Arts prose fellowship, 1981-82, 1985-86; Pennsylvania State Council on the Arts literature fellowship, 1983-84. Address: 721 Warwick Road, Magnolia, NJ 08049, U.S.A.

PUBLICATIONS FOR YOUNG ADULTS

Fiction

The Soul Brothers and Sister Lou. New York, Scribner, 1968; London, Macdonald, 1971.
Boss Cat, illustrated by Harold Franklin. New York, Scribner, 1971.
The Pool Table War. Boston, Houghton Mifflin, 1972.
Uncle Daniel and the Raccoon. Boston, Houghton Mifflin, 1972.
Guests in the Promised Land: Stories. New York, Scribner, 1973.
Lou in the Limelight. New York, Scribner, 1981.

PUBLICATIONS FOR ADULTS

Fiction

God Bless the Child. New York, Scribner, 1964; London, Muller, 1965.

The Landlord. New York, Scribner, 1966.
The Survivors. New York, Scribner, 1975.
The Lakestown Rebellion. New York, Scribner, 1978.

Other

Minority of One (documentary/television play, Columbia Broadcasting System, 1956).
The Double Edge (play, produced Philadelphia, 1965).
Contributor, *The Best Short Stories by Negro Writers* with Langston Hughes, editor. Boston, Little, Brown, 1967.

*

Media Adaptations: *The Landlord* (motion picture), United Artists, 1970.

Biography: Essay in *Something about the Author Autobiography Series,* Volume 10, Detroit, Gale, 1990; entry in *Dictionary of Literary Biography,* Volume 33: *Afro-American Fiction Writers after 1955,* Detroit, Gale, 1984.

Critical Study: Entry in *Children's Literature Review,* Volume 3, Detroit, Gale, 1978; entry in *Contemporary Literary Criticism,* Volume 35, Detroit, Gale, 1985.

*   *   *

Kristin Hunter, a pioneer in the field of young adult literature, began writing books about African-American teenagers in the mid-1960s. Her works deal with the black community as a self-contained entity and to a lesser extent with the impingement on that world by the larger, white-dominated society. The subtle caste distinctions of skin tone and hair color among people of color are mentioned frankly. Her characters are ordinary teenagers who learn to adjust their lives in response to a variety of circumstances.

The Soul Brothers and Sister Lou, published in 1968, is about Louretta Hawkins, a light-skinned African-American girl. She begins playing the piano with some friends who have formed a singing group. Blind Eddie Bell, a blues musician, teaches her how to compose music. When one member of the singing group is accidentally killed, another friend writes a poem about his death. Louella puts it to music; a music teacher contacts a recording company, and a single is cut. Thanks to a local disc jockey, "Lament for Jethro" becomes a big hit and life changes for the "Soul Brothers and Sister Lou." The black power movement is discussed sympathetically but is not offered as a solution to the problems of the ghetto. Although Jethro's accidental death is caused by a policeman, the antagonism towards authority figures already existed. Even though Louretta's family now has enough money to move out of the ghetto, discrimination prevents their relocation. In the end, the more things change, the more they remain the same.

The sequel, *Lou in the Limelight,* appeared in 1981. The title refers to the attempts by Marty Ross, the singing group's agent, to split the group apart. Lou and her friends resent this, but this becomes the least of their problems. Their first performances in New York lead to appearances in Las Vegas. The dangers of New York pale in comparison to the Mafia-sponsored threats in Nevada. Drugs and prostitution are only two of the problems facing them. After nearly being entrapped, the children testify for the government and help convict some of the criminals. Next, the Soul Brothers and Sister Lou go on a Southern tour to repay some of their debts. The drug problems catch up with Lou, though. After nearly dying from an unintentional overdose, she finds some unknown relatives. A newfound cousin adopts her and plans to send her to college. In this sequel, unfortunately, the action never stops. Little consideration is paid to the likelihood of all these terrible things happening to one group of musicians. The fairy-tale ending is probably the most unrealistic thing. It is an interesting story but lacking in credibility.

Guests in the Promised Land is a collection of short stories. The title story is about a young black boy who is treated to a day at an all-white country club. He oversteps the invisible bounds and gets kicked out. The problem was caused because he did not realize he was just a "guest in the Promised Land." Another story, "Two's Enough of a Crowd," deals with two young people who are misfits. When they find each other, they realize that they are not the only nonconformists. "Debut" is the story of a debutante who is trying to break into the society of light-skinned blacks. She finds out that in her own way she is more important than any of the flighty girls around her. A teenager's older brother comes home from prison in "Hero's Return," and dispels the myths about criminal life. The younger brother learns that education and honesty are more important than any short-lived benefits from crime. "The Scribe" is a thirteen-year-old boy who comes up with his own solution to the problem of illiteracy in his city. Six other stories cover such topics as integration and gang relations. The ideas in the stories are interesting: some themes are rendered very well. Unfortunately, many of the plots are trite and almost all the stories are dated.

Hunter's young adult fiction was undoubtedly fresh and original when it first appeared. With the exception of *The Soul Brothers and Sister Lou,* it has not stood the test of time. Even this novel is not really a classic, but it still is an entertaining book. Her real contribution has been to show that fiction for teenagers can be written about all types of people. Although most of her work deals with poor blacks, a good number of middle-class African Americans are also depicted. The ghetto society of the 1960s is accurately described, complete with slang and jive talk. Although certainly not intended that way, her fiction becomes historical. So, finally, these works become of interest to young people of today because they portray the way their parents lived.

—Sharon Clontz Bernstein

* * *

HUNTER, (Maureen) Mollie (née McVeigh). British. Born in Longniddry, East Lothian, 30 June 1922. Educated at Preston Lodge School, East Lothian. Volunteered services in a serviceman's canteen during World War II. Married Thomas "Michael" McIlwraith in 1940; two sons. Writer since 1953. May Hill Arbuthnot Lecturer in the United States in 1975, and in 1976 toured New Zealand and Australia lecturing under the joint auspices of the British Council, the International Reading Association and the education authorities for New Zealand and Australia; writer-in-residence, Dalhousie University, Halifax, Nova Scotia, 1980, 1981; organized and taught in writers' workshops for both adults and children; 29th Anne Carroll Moore Spring Lecturer, 1986; teacher of creative writing, Aberlour Summer School for Gifted Children, 1987, 1988. Recipient: Child Study Association of America's Children's Books of the

Year citations, 1968, for *The Ferlie,* 1970, for *The Walking Stones,* 1971, for *The Thirteenth Member,* both 1972, for *A Sound of Chariots* and *The Haunted Mountain,* 1974, for *The Stronghold,* 1975, for *A Stranger Came Ashore,* 1976, for *Talent Is Not Enough,* 1977, for *A Furl of Fairy Wind,* and 1987, for *Cat, Herself; Book World's* Children's Spring Book Festival honor book citation, 1970, for *The Lothian Run; New York Times* Outstanding Book of the Year citations, for *The Haunted Mountain* and *A Sound of Chariots,* both 1972, and *A Stranger Came Ashore,* 1975; Children's Book award from the Child Study Association of America, 1973, for *A Sound of Chariots;* Scottish Arts Council award, 1973, for *The Haunted Mountain;* Carnegie Medal for Children's Book of Outstanding Merit, British Library Association, 1974, and Silver Pencil award (Holland), 1975, both for *The Stronghold; A Stranger Came Ashore* was selected one of *School Library Journal's* Best Children's Books, 1975, and was a *Boston Globe-Horn Book* award Honor Book, 1976; *The Wicked One* was selected one of *School Library Journal's* Best Books for Spring and was selected a Scottish Arts Council award Book, both 1977; *You Never Knew Her as I Did!* was selected one of the New York Public Library's Books for the Teen Age, and a Notable Children's Trade Book in the Field of Social Studies by the National Council of Social Studies and the Children's Book Council, both 1982; *Cat, Herself* was chosen one of the American Library Association's Best Books for Young Adults, and one of *School Library Journal's* Best Books for Young Adults, both 1986; Phoenix award, Children's Literature Association, 1992, for *A Sound of Chariots.* Agent: McIntosh & Otis, Inc., 475 Fifth Ave., New York, NY 10017. Address: "The Shieling," Milton, by Drumnadrochit, Inverness-shire 1V3 6UA, Scotland.

PUBLICATIONS FOR YOUNG ADULTS

Fiction

Hi Johnny, illustrated by Drake Brookshaw. London, Evans, 1963; new edition illustrated by M. Christopherson, Byway Books, 1986.

Patrick Kentigern Keenan, illustrated by Charles Keeping. London, Blackie, 1963; as *The Smartest Man in Ireland,* New York, Funk and Wagnallis, 1965.

The Kelpie's Pearls, illustrated by Charles Keeping. London, Blackie, 1964; illustrated by Joseph Cellini, New York, Funk and Wagnalls, 1966.

The Spanish Letters, illustrated by Elizabeth Grant. London, Evans, 1964; New York, Funk and Wagnalls, 1967.

A Pistol in Greenyards, illustrated by Elizabeth Grant. London, Evans, 1965; New York, Funk and Wagnalls, 1968.

The Ghosts of Glencoe. London, Evans, 1966; New York, Funk and Wagnalls, 1969.

Thomas and the Warlock, illustrated by Charles Keeping. London, Blackie; illustrated by Joseph Cellini, New York, Funk and Wagnalls, 1967.

The Ferlie, illustrated by Michal Morse. London, Blackie, 1968; illustrated by Joseph Cellini, New York, Funk and Wagnalls, 1968; as *The Enchanted Whistle,* London, Methuen, 1985.

The Bodach, illustrated by Gareth Floyd. London, Blackie, 1970, as *The Walking Stones: A Story of Suspense,* illustrated by Trina Schart Hyman, New York, Harper, 1970.

The Lothian Run. New York, Funk and Wagnalls, 1970. London, Hamish Hamilton, 1971.

The Thirteenth Member: A Story of Suspense. New York, Harper, and London, Hamish Hamilton, 1971.

The Haunted Mountain: A Story of Suspense, illustrated by Trevor Ridley. London, Hamish Hamilton; illustrated by Lazslo Kubinyi, New York, Harper, 1972.

A Sound of Chariots. New York, Harper, 1972; London, Hamish Hamilton, 1973.

The Stronghold. New York, Harper, and London, Hamish Hamilton, 1974.

A Stranger Came Ashore: A Story of Suspense. London, Hamish Hamilton, and New York, Harper, 1975.

A Furl of Fairy Wind: Four Stories, illustrated by Stephen Gammell. New York, Harper, 1977.

The Wicked One: A Story of Suspense. London, Hamish Hamilton, and New York, Harper, 1977.

The Third Eye. London, Hamish Hamilton, and New York, Harper, 1979.

You Never Knew Her as I Did! London, Hamish Hamilton, and New York, Harper, 1981, as *Escape from Loch Leven,* Edinburgh, Canongate, 1987.

The Dragonfly Years. London, Hamish Hamilton, 1983; as *Hold on to Love,* New York, Harper, 1984.

The Knight of the Golden Plain, illustrated by Marc Simont. London, Hamish Hamilton, and New York, Harper, 1983.

I'll Go My Own Way. London, Hamish Hamilton, 1985; as *Cat, Herself,* New York, Harper, 1986.

The Three-Day Enchantment, illustrated by Marc Simont. New York, Harper, 1985.

The Brownie, illustrated by M. Christopherson. Byway Books, 1986.

The Enchanted Boy, illustrated by M. Christopherson. Byway Books, 1986.

A Furl of Fairy Wind, illustrated by M. Christopherson. Byway Books, 1986.

The Mermaid Summer. London, Hamish Hamilton, and New York, Harper, 1988.

Day of the Unicorn. New York, Harper, forthcoming.

Gilly Martin the Fox. New York, Hyperion Books, forthcoming.

Plays

A Love-Song for My Lady (produced Inverness, 1961). London, Evans, 1961.

Stay for an Answer (produced Inverness, 1962). London, French, 1962.

Nonfiction

Talent Is Not Enough: Mollie Hunter on Writing for Children. New York, Harper, 1976.

Flora MacDonald and Bonnie Prince Charlie. London, Methuen, 1987.

Other

The Pied Piper Syndrome (essays). New York, Harper, 1992.

*

Media Adaptations: *The Kelpie's Pearls* (BBC-Radio program series), *The Lothian Run* (BBC-Radio program series), and "The En-

chanted Whistle" (BBC-Radio program series); *The Ferlie* (radio, U.S., also on BBC-Radio); *A Stranger Came Ashore* has been read in serial form on Swedish radio, and also produced as a musical on a Swedish stage; the four stories in *A Furl of Fairy Wind* (cassette, U.K.); and *The Walking Stones,* and *The Wicked One,* both were featured in Yorkshire TV's "Book Tower" program.

Biography: Entry in *Third Book of Junior Authors,* New York, H.W. Wilson, 1972; essay in *Something about the Author Autobiography Series,* Volume 7, Detroit, Gale, 1989; essay in *Speaking for Ourselves, Too* compiled and edited by Donald R. Gallo, National Council of Teachers of English, 1993.

Manuscript Collection: National Library of Scotland.

Critical Study: Entry in *Contemporary Literary Criticism,* Volume 21, Detroit, Gale, 1982.

Mollie Hunter comments:

Being a Scot means, among other things, being heir to a distinctive literary tradition—much of which is concerned with the historical novel and with tales of the supernatural. In that same literary tradition, also, there has never been the clear-cut distinction between books for children and books for adults generally accepted in other cultures—a fact that suits very well with my own belief that a good book for children should simply be a good book per se.

I have always therefore used whatever gift I have by indulging my natural empathy with young people at the same time as I unleash the inborn impulse to tell a story—sometimes that of an adventure set at some particular period of my own country's history, sometimes that of some weird experience of the supernatural, and latterly in novels of the kind that could be expected to have particular appeal for teenage girl readers, since the changing face of publication has made this possible. Also, although Scotland is little known beyond its own geographical bounds, I have always tried in all such books to make its culture open and accessible to all young readers—thereby, I should say, giving myself as much pleasure as I hope will ultimately also be theirs.

*   *   *

Mollie Hunter, one of the most popular and influential contemporary Scottish writers of fiction for young adults, has written a number of award-winning books that have been almost universally praised for their suspenseful plots, evocation of Scottish settings, and effective use of folk customs, folktales, and historical references. Most of Hunter's books for young adults fall into three categories—literary folktales, historical novels, and realistic biographical fiction—and she has been praised for work in each of these genres.

Hunter's fantasies draw heavily on Scottish and Irish folklore and often involve characters who learn to control the supernatural and come to appreciate their own special gifts and talents. Often, they also involve conflicts between old beliefs and modern technology or the struggle between good and evil. Invariably, they validate the importance of storytelling and folk traditions.

In four of Hunter's fantasies, *The Smartest Man in Ireland, The Haunted Mountain, Thomas and the Warlock,* and *The Wicked One,* fathers and husbands come to value their wives' common sense or patience, eventually realizing that their families are more important than fairy gold. Several of Hunter's other fantasies feature characters with special gifts or talents who find themselves involved with supernatural creatures. In *The Kelpie's Pearls,* a seventy-two-year-old woman, Morag MacLeod, befriends a water sprite and learns that special gifts and talents are often misunderstood and unappreciated. Like many of Hunter's characters, the protagonist of *The Bodach* has "second sight" which he is supposed to use to enable thirteen ancient stones to walk about again as they have every hundred years.

Both *A Stranger Came Ashore* and *The Mermaid Summer* are about children who confront malevolent creatures from the sea. *A Stranger Came Ashore,* Hunter's best fantasy, is a deceptively simple work about a boy who suspects that a newcomer to his home in the Shetland Islands is a "selkie," a great seal who has taken the form of a human. The novel, which is filled with descriptions of traditional Shetland customs, is carefully ambiguous about the reality of the supernatural events it describes. In *The Mermaid Summer,* two children's love for their grandfather helps them defeat a proud mermaid.

Hunter's historical novels are noted for their extensive research and appealing teenage protagonists. Critic Peter Hollindale has suggested that in Hunter's historical novels, such as *Hi Johnny, The Spanish Letters,* and *The Lothian Run,* plot is more important than historical setting. *The Spanish Letters,* which involves a sixteenth-century plot against the Scottish king, is also one of several novels in which historical events are presented from the point of view of a teenage boy. Hunter also features characters who are at odds with society or who are torn by divided loyalties. Both *A Pistol in Greenyards* and *The Ghosts of Glencoe* recount fictionalized versions of massacres involving Scottish Highlanders, and are also told by teenage boys. In *The Thirteenth Member,* sixteen-year-old stablehand Adam Lawrie encounters a coven of witches which is being used to help depose King James VI, and explores the difficulty of knowing who to trust.

Two of Hunter's best historical novels are *The Stronghold* and *You Never Knew Her as I Did! The Stronghold* describes the attempts by the early inhabitants of the British Isles to protect themselves against Roman invaders. A lame boy, Coll, saves his people by creating a series of "strongholds." In *You Never Knew Her as I Did!,* young Will Douglas struggles with his desires to help the imprisoned Mary Queen of Scots and his loyalty to his family who are her jailers. In the course of the novel, Will learns the necessity of play-acting in order to survive.

In 1972, Hunter's *A Sound of Chariots* was published, one of her best and most moving books in which she provides an account of her childhood and her father's death. Her alter ego, Bridie McShane, eventually learns to openly grieve for her father and uses her feelings to write poetry, her one goal in life. In the sequel, *Hold on to Love,* Bridie continues her development as a writer and eventually marries a young man who encourages her and helps her deal with her continued sorrow over her father's death.

Besides these autobiographical works, Hunter has also written two other realistic books whose female protagonists face many of the same struggles as Bridie McShane and who also have the gift of second sight. In *The Third Eye,* a compelling look at Ballinford, West Lothian, during the early 1930s, Jinty Morrison learns to use her own "third eye" to better understand the world around her. The novel also explores the fine line between social classes. *Cat, Herself* focuses on Cat McPhie, a young "traveller" or "tinker," whose attitudes towards herself and her family change through the course of the novel. The novel also explores the persecution of those who are perceived as being different and the value of folk traditions.

Few writers for young adults have produced a body of work which encompasses so many genres and which appeals to such a wide audience. Mollie Hunter is as gifted a storyteller as the characters in her books. She invariably entertains her readers while helping them to gain what she calls the "third eye," the ability to clearly see the world. She also effectively introduces young adults to her own culture, educating them about Scotland both past and present.

—Joel D. Chaston

———

HURSTON, Zora Neale. American. Born in Eatonville, Florida, 7 January 1891(?). Educated at Howard University, Washington, D.C., 1923-24; Barnard College, New York, B.A. 1928; graduate study at Columbia University, New York. Married 1) Herbert Sheen in 1927 (divorced 1931); 2) Albert Price III in 1939 (divorced). Writer and folklorist. Collected folklore in the South, 1927-31; instructor in drama, Bethune-Cookman College, Daytona, Florida, 1933-34; collected folklore in Jamaica, Haiti, and Bermuda, 1937-38; collected folklore in Florida for the Works Progress Administration, 1938-39; staff writer, Paramount Studios, Hollywood, California, 1941; collected folklore in Honduras, 1946-48; worked as a maid in Florida, 1950; free-lance writer, 1950-56; librarian, Patrick Air Force Base, Florida, 1956-57; writer for *Fort Pierce Chronicle* and part-time teacher at Lincoln Park Academy, both in Fort Pierce, Florida, 1958-59; librarian at the Library of Congress, Washington, D.C.; professor of drama at North Carolina College for Negroes, Durham; assistant to writer Fannie Hurst. Recipient: Guggenheim fellowship, 1936 and 1938; Annisfield award, 1943, for *Dust Tracks on a Road.* D.Litt. *Died 28 January 1960.*

PUBLICATIONS

Fiction

Jonah's Gourd Vine. Philadelphia, Pennsylvania, Lippincott, 1934.
Mules and Men. Philadelphia, Pennsylvania, Lippincott, 1935.
Their Eyes Were Watching God. Philadelphia, Pennsylvania, Lippincott, 1937.
Moses, Man of the Mountain. Philadelphia, Pennsylvania, Lippincott, 1939.
Seraph on the Suwanee. New York, Scribner, 1948.
I Love Myself When I Am Laughing...And Then Again When I Am Looking Mean And Impressive, edited by Alice Walker. New York, Feminist Press, 1979.
The Sanctified Church. Berkeley, California, Turtle Island Foundation, 1983.
Spunk: The Selected Stories of Zora Neale Hurston. Berkeley, California, Turtle Island Foundation, 1985.
The Gilded Six-Bits. Minneapolis. Minnesota, Redpath Press, 1986.
The Complete Stories. New York, Harper, 1992.

Plays

Fast and Furious, with Clinton Fletcher and Time Moore; published in *Best Plays of 1931-32,* edited by Burns Mantle and Garrison Sherwood, 1931.

Mule Bone: A Comedy of Negro Life in Three Acts, with Langston Hughes. New York, Harper, 1931.

Stephen Kelen-d'Oxylion Presents Polk County: A Comedy of Negro Life on a Sawmill Camp with Authentic Negro Music, with Dorothy Waring, (produced New York, 1944).

Nonfiction

Tell My Horse. Philadelphia, Pennsylvania, Lippincott, 1938; as *Voodoo Gods: An Inquiry into Native Myths and Magic in Jamaica and Haiti,* Dent, 1939.

Dust Tracks on a Road. Philadelphia, Pennsylvania, Lippincott, 1942.

Contributor to various anthologies, including, *Black Writers in America, Story in America, American Negro Short Stories, The Best Short Stories by Negro Writers, From the Roots,* and *Anthology of American Negro Literature.*

*

Biography: Entry in *Dictionary of Literary Biography,* Detroit, Gale, Volume 51, 1987; Volume 86, 1989; *Zora Neale Hurston: A Literary Biography* by Robert E. Hemenway, Champaign, University of Illinois Press, 1977.

Critical Study: Entry in *Contemporary Literary Criticism,* Detroit, Gale, Volume 7, 1977; Volume 30, 1984; Volume 61, 1990.

*   *   *

Zora Neale Hurston was a novelist, anthropologist, and the most important collector of black folklore from the rural South. This collection of folklore was compiled into two books. She also wrote four novels, over fifty short stories and essays, and a prize-winning autobiography, and was twice the recipient of a Guggenheim award.

Although Hurston's work is primarily considered adult literature, some of her books are not only appropriate for a young adult audience, but necessary to provide an important voice, rich in a heritage too long disregarded. She is one of the major writers of the twentieth century to whom we should be grateful for capturing a uniquely imaginative and creative style of telling stories "before everybody forgets all of 'em."

Hurston was born on January 7, though there are vast discrepancies as to the exact year. According to a biography written by Robert E. Hemenway in 1977, research could not confirm Hurston's birth year: Hurston's brother claimed she was born in 1891, her gravestone reads 1901, and her second marriage certificate lists 1910.

Regardless of the year, the location of her birth and early childhood is a major factor in her subsequent work. Eatonville, Florida, was said to be the first all-black incorporated town. She grew up in a community of black people who, through self-governing, had tremendous confidence and a sense of wholeness that comes from a healthy environment—one free from persecution and violence. This was an unusual experience for the blacks of the early South.

The heart of the town was the general store owned by Joe Clarke. It was on the porch of this store where the tales were told and songs were sung. It was there that Hurston heard the "big old lies" that she later incorporated into her work. From the tales of Brer Rabbit

and "lying" sessions at the general store, to the confidence and strength instilled in Hurston by her parents and community; these experiences were woven into the fabric that gave us the celebration and joy, the lyrical prose of Zora Neale Hurston.

Mules and Men, Hurston's first book of folklore, was published in 1935. The product of extensive research in Florida and Louisiana, this was a popular and very important work of reference. She returned to her hometown of Eatonville to begin gathering information, choosing this as her starting point "because I knew that the town was full of material and that I could get it without hurt, harm or danger." She was happy to find the "same love of talk and song."

Now considered a classic of black literature, *Their Eyes Were Watching God* was met with great criticism when published in 1937, including that of her contemporary, the influential Richard Wright. Wright said the novel "carries no theme, no message, no thought." Other black writers of the Harlem Renaissance, a black literary movement of the 1920s, were writing serious novels of protest and social realism. While these writers were trying to distance themselves from their rural origins, Hurston was recreating the Southern blacks of her youth, dialect and all.

Their Eyes Were Watching God tells the story of Janie Crawford, a young woman who discovers that the black woman need not be "de mule uh de world" as was her grandmother's experience. Overcoming two oppressive marriages—the first arranged by her grandmother who has hoped for a better life for Janie; the second to a man with a vision and a promise, ultimately unkept, to always treat her like a lady—Janie marries a third man, Tea Cake, who treats her as an equal. It is through this loving relationship that she realizes all that life has to offer. Janie experiences a self-awakening and love of self she has not known before. While *Their Eyes Were Watching God* celebrates black culture and its oral tradition, more importantly it explores the pain of a young woman's search for her own identity in a racially oppressed culture, within a male-dominated world.

Her life forgotten, her books decades out of print, the work of Hurston has been resurrected thanks to the efforts of Alice Walker and Robert Hemenway. In an essay entitled "Looking for Zora," published in *Ms.* (1975), Alice Walker describes her August 1973 search through a neglected cemetery for the unmarked grave of Zora Neale Hurston. Upon what she thought was the approximate location, Walker placed a gravestone with an epitaph that reads:

Zora Neale Hurston
"A Genius of the South"
1901-1960
Novelist, Folklorist, Anthropologist

For her independent achievement of a college education against all odds, her courageous efforts in the pursuit for the preservation of black folklore, and for the accomplishment of having published more than any other black woman of her time—the life of Zora Neale Hurston proves to be as much an inspirational study as her art.

—Suzanne M. Valentic

———

HURWITZ, Johanna (née Frank). American. Born in New York City, 9 October 1937. Educated at Queens College, Flushing, New

York, 1955-58, B.A. in English 1958; Columbia University, New York, 1958-59, M.L.S. 1959. Married Uri Levi Hurwitz in 1962; one daughter and one son. Children's librarian, New York Public Library, 1959-64; lecturer in children's literature, Queens College, 1965-68; librarian, Calhoun School, 1968-75, and New Hyde Park school district, 1975-77, both New York. Since 1978 children's librarian, Great Neck Public Library, New York. Visiting story-teller, New York Public Library, 1964-67; teacher of writer's work-shops in children's literature, Hofstra University, Hempstead, New York, 1981, 1986. Recipient: *Parents' Choice* award, Parents' Choice Foundation, 1982, for *The Rabbi's Girls,* and 1984, for *The Hot and Cold Summer;* Texas Bluebonnet award and Wyoming Indian Paint-brush award, both 1987, both for *The Hot and Cold Summer;* Swed-ish Institute grant, 1988; Kentucky Bluegrass award, West Virginia Children's Book award, and Mississippi Children's Book award, all 1989, all for *Class Clown;* Florida Sunshine State award, 1990, and New Jersey Garden State award, 1991, both for *Teacher's Pet.* Address: 10 Spruce Place, Great Neck, NY 11021, U.S.A.

PUBLICATIONS FOR YOUNG ADULTS

Fiction

Busybody Nora, illustrated by Susan Jeschke. New York, Morrow, 1976.

Nora and Mrs. Mind-Your-Own-Business, illustrated by Susan Jeschke. New York, Morrow, 1977.

The Law of Gravity, illustrated by Ingrid Fetz. New York, Morrow, 1978.

Much Ado about Aldo, illustrated by John Wallner. New York, Morrow, 1978.

Aldo Applesauce, illustrated by John Wallner. New York, Morrow, 1979.

New Neighbors for Nora, illustrated by Susan Jeschke. New York, Morrow, 1979.

Once I Was a Plum Tree, illustrated by Ingrid Fetz. New York, Morrow, 1980.

Superduper Teddy, illustrated by Susan Jeschke. New York, Mor-row, 1980.

Aldo Ice Cream, illustrated by John Wallner. New York, Morrow, 1981.

Baseball Fever, illustrated by Ray Cruz. New York, Morrow, 1981.

The Rabbi's Girls, illustrated by Pamela Johnson. New York, Mor-row, 1982.

Tough-Luck Karen, illustrated by Diane deGroat. New York, Mor-row, 1982.

Rip-Roaring Russell, illustrated by Lillian Hoban. New York, Mor-row, 1983.

DeDe Takes Charge!, illustrated by Diane deGroat. New York, Morrow, 1984.

The Hot and Cold Summer, illustrated by Gail Owens. New York, Morrow, 1984.

The Adventures of Ali Baba Bernstein, illustrated by Gain Owens. New York, Morrow, 1985.

Russell Rides Again, illustrated by Lillian Hoban. New York, Mor-row, 1985.

Hurricane Elaine, illustrated by Diane deGroat. New York, Mor-row, 1986.

Yellow Blue Jay, illustrated by Donald Carrick. New York, Morrow, 1986.

Class Clown, illustrated by Sheila Hamanaka. New York, Morrow, 1987.

Russell Sprouts, illustrated by Lillian Hoban. New York, Morrow, 1987.

The Cold and Hot Winter, illustrated by Carolyn Ewing. New York, Morrow, 1988.

Teacher's Pet, illustrated by Sheila Hamanaka. New York, Morrow, 1988.

Hurray for Ali Baba Bernstein, illustrated by Gail Owens. New York, Morrow, 1989.

Russell and Elisa, illustrated by Lillian Hoban. New York, Mor-row, 1989.

Class President, illustrated by Sheila Hamanaka. New York, Mor-row, 1990.

Aldo Peanut Butter, illustrated by Diane deGroat. New York, Mor-row, 1990.

"E" Is for Elisa, illustrated by Lillian Hoban. New York, Morrow, 1991.

School's Out, illustrated by Sheila Hamanaka. New York, Morrow, 1991.

Ali Baba Bernstein: Lost and Found, illustrated by Karen Milone. New York, Morrow, 1992.

Roz and Ozzie, illustrated by Eileen McKeating, 1992.

New Shoes for Sylvia, illustrated by Jerry Pinkney. New York, Morrow, 1993.

The Up and Down Spring, illustrated by Gail Owens. New York, Morrow, 1993.

Other

Anne Frank: Life in Hiding, illustrated by Vera Rosenberry. Philadel-phia, Jewish Publication Society, 1988.

Astrid Lindgren: Storyteller to the World, illustrated by Michael Dooling. New York, Viking, 1989.

*

Manuscript Collection: Kerlan Collection, University of Minne-sota, Minneapolis.

*   *   *

Johanna Hurwitz has a special gift for knowing young adults intimately. She manages to tell her stories through the perspective of characters, whatever their ages, sharing their thoughts, emotions, and concerns. Prominent themes include growing up and friend-ship. In her novels for early adolescents these themes continue, yet the elements of responsibility and learning to like oneself are added. The tone is not at all philosophical, but friendly, like good friends confiding to each other, admitting mistakes, offering each other advice and consolation. Perhaps this is the reason she is so well-liked as an author and seems to hit the bull's eye every time in dealing with the concerns of eleven- through fifteen-year-olds.

In *Cold and Hot Winter* Derek is anxiously awaiting the arrival of his next-door neighbor's niece. Olivia had visited the previous sum-mer and her perkiness added some spice to Derek and his best friend's lives. Now, driving to the airport with his neighbors to pick up Olivia, he worries she has changed and won't like him, or that he won't like her. While he worries, the adults discuss the weather and express their desire for no more snow. "How silly grown-ups were, Derek thought. It was a cold day but that didn't bother him. Winter was supposed to be cold. And if they were lucky they would get a couple of good snow storms before the season ended."

Tough-Luck Karen describes the misfortunes of thirteen-year-old Karen Sossi. It seems everything goes wrong for her. She forgets her gym-locker key, accidently takes the beef intended for the family dinner in place of her school lunch, and struggles through her first baby-sitting job. Adolescence is difficult enough, but for Karen, her problems seem to be complicated further. Though she tells her mother she'll outgrow this phase in her life, Karen actually wonders if her luck will ever change. She thinks it has when she meets a new girl at school and invites her over. Unfortunately, Annette turns out to be allergic to the Sossi cats. "Karen stood about awkwardly. She didn't know if she should apologize or pretend that everything was normal. What was the etiquette for causing someone to have an allergic reaction? she wondered."

In *Hurricane Elaine* the speech and actions of both fifteen-year-old Elaine and her mother are realistic. Elaine is Karen Sossi's older sister. Their father refers to Elaine as a hurricane because she rushes into action without thinking through the consequences. Elaine is a very typical teenager. Her complaints about household rules and intolerance for her younger siblings is a characteristic with which many readers will relate: "Even if she doesn't want to make a call and she's not expecting one, my mother won't let me stay on the phone longer than five minutes." Then when Elaine gets a phone call from a boy in her class who wants to ask for a date, her mother clocks the call and shouts up the stairs, "Time's up."

Mrs. Sossi handles her adolescent charges with humorous firmness. When Elaine has a miserable day at school, she storms into the house, ignoring her mother's greeting, and takes her frustration out on the family cat. When Mrs. Sossi requests her help in the kitchen, Elaine shouts out "I'm busy" just as the phone rings. Mrs. Sossi explains to the caller that Elaine is very busy and can't be disturbed. When Elaine complains about this, Mrs. Sossi's response is very typical of that of parents of teenagers: "Why did you come home, if you won't greet anyone and won't answer me when I speak to you?"

Though struggling to grow up, learning to like oneself, and learning to be responsible are difficult for both her characters and real-life adolescents, Hurwitz adds humor that makes the ups and downs bearable. Readers may feel their own lives are quite boring, but if compared to Elaine, Karen, or Derek's life, many similarities would surface. Readers gain confidence that they too can face difficulties and are not alone in their struggles to gain self-confidence and to be taken seriously by the adults in their lives.

—Lisa A. Wroble

———

HUXLEY, Aldous (Leonard). British. Born in Godalming, Surrey, 26 July 1894. Educated at Hillside School, Godalming 1903-08; Eton College, 1908-13; Balliol College, Oxford, 1913-15, B.A. (honours) in English 1915. Married 1) Maria Nys in 1919 (died, 1955); 2) Laura Archera in 1956; one son. Worked in the War Office, 1917; taught at Eton College, 1918; member of the editorial staff of the *Athenaeum,* London, 1919-20; Drama Critic, *Westminster Gazette,* 1920-21; full-time writer from 1921; travelled and lived in France, Italy, and the United States, 1923-37; settled in California, 1937, and worked as a free-lance screenwriter. Recipient: Award of

Merit and Gold Medal, American Academy of Arts and Letters, 1959; D.Litt., University of California, 1959. Companion of Literature, Royal Society of Literature, 1962. *Died 22 November 1963.*

PUBLICATIONS

Novels

Crome Yellow. London, Chatto and Windus, 1921; New York, Doran, 1922.

Antic Hay. London, Chatto and Windus, and New York, Doran, 1923.

Those Barren Leaves. London, Chatto and Windus, and New York, Doran, 1925.

Point Counter Point. London, Chatto and Windus, and New York, Doubleday, 1928.

Brave New World. London, Chatto and Windus, and New York, Doubleday, 1932.

Eyeless in Gaza. London, Chatto and Windus, and New York, Harper, 1936.

After Many a Summer. London, Chatto and Windus, 1939; as *After Many a Summer Dies the Swan,* New York, Harper, 1939.

Time Must Have a Stop. New York, Harper, 1944; London, Chatto and Windus, 1945.

Ape and Essence. New York, Harper, 1948; London, Chatto and Windus, 1949.

The Genius and the Goddess. London, Chatto and Windus, and New York, Harper, 1955.

Antic Hay and The Gioconda Smile. London, Chatto and Windus, and New York, Harper, 1957.

Brave New World and Brave New World Revisited. London, Chatto and Windus, and New York, Harper. 1960.

Island. London, Chatto and Windus, and New York, Harper, 1962.

Short Stories

Limbo: Six Stories and a Play. London, Chatto and Windus, and New York, Doran, 1920.

Mortal Coils: Five Stories (includes play *Permutations among the Nightingales).* London, Chatto and Windus, and New York, Doran, 1922.

Little Mexican and Other Stories. London, Chatto and Windus, 1924; as *Young Archimedes and Other Stories,* New York, Doran, 1924.

Two or Three Graces and Other Stories. London, Chatto and Windus, and New York, Doran, 1926.

Brief Candles. London, Chatto and Windus, and New York, Doubleday, 1930; as *After the Fireworks,* New York, Avon, n.d.

The Gioconda Smile. London, Chatto and Windus, 1938.

Twice Seven: Fourteen Selected Stories. London, Reprint Society, 1944.

Collected Short Stories. London, Chatto and Windus, and New York, Harper, 1957.

The Crows of Pearblossom, illustrated by Barbara Cooney. London, Chatto and Windus, and New York, Random House, 1967.

Plays

Liluli, adaptation of a play by Romain Rolland, in *Nation* (London), 20 September-29 November 1919.

Albert, Prince Consort: A Biography Play for Which Mr. John Drinkwater's Historical Dramas Serve as a Model, in *Vanity Fair* (New York), March 1922.
The Ambassador of Capripedia, in *Vanity Fair* (New York), May 1922.
The Publisher, in *Vanity Fair* (New York), April 1923.
The Discovery, adaptation of the play by Frances Sheridan (produced London, 1924). London, Chatto and Windus, 1924; New York, Doran, 1925.
The World of Light: A Comedy in Three Acts (produced London, 1931). London, Chatto and Windus, and New York, Doubleday, 1931.
The Gioconda Smile, adaptation of his own story (produced London, 1948; New York, 1950). London, Chatto and Windus, 1948; as *Mortal Coils,* New York, Harper, 1948.
The Genius and the Goddess, with Ruth Wendell, adaptation of the novel by Huxley (produced New York, 1957).

Screenplays: *Pride and Prejudice,* with Jane Murfin, 1940; *Madame Curie,* 1943; *Jane Eyre,* with John Houseman and Robert Stevenson, 1944; *A Woman's Vengeance,* 1948.

Poetry

The Burning Wheel. Oxford, Blackwell, 1916.
Jonah. Oxford, Holywell Press, 1917.
The Defeat of Youth and Other Poems. Oxford, Blackwell, 1918.
Leda and Other Poems. London, Chatto and Windus, and New York, Doran, 1920.
Selected Poems. Oxford, Blackwell, and New York, Appleton, 1925.
Arabia Infelix and Other Poems. New York, Fountain Press, and London, Chatto and Windus, 1929.
Apennine. Gaylordsville, Connecticut, Slide Mountain Press, 1930.
The Cicadas and Other Poems. London, Chatto Doubleday, 1931.
Verses and a Comedy. London, Chatto and Windus, 1946.
The Collected Poetry of Aldous Huxley, edited by Donald Watt. London, Chatto and Windus, and New York, Harper, 1971.

Nonfiction

On the Margin: Notes and Essays. London, Chatto and Windus, and New York, Doran, 1923.
Along the Road: Notes and Essays of a Tourist. London, Chatto and Windus, and New York, Doran, 1925.
Jesting Pilate: The Diary of a Journey. London, Chatto and Windus, 1926; as *Jesting Pilate: An Intellectual Holiday,* New York, Doran, 1926.
Essays New and Old. London, Chatto and Windus, 1926; New York, Doran, 1927.
Proper Studies: The Proper Study of Mankind Is Man. London, Chatto and Windus, 1927; New York, Doubleday, 1928.
Do What You Will: Essays. London, Chatto and Windus, and New York, Doubleday, 1929.
Holy Face and Other Essays. London, The Fleuron, 1929.
Vulgarity in Literature: Digressions From a Theme. London, Chatto and Windus, 1930.
Music at Night and Other Essays. London, Chatto and Windus, and New York, Doubleday, 1931.
T.H. Huxley as a Man of Letters (lecture). London, Macmillan, 1932.

Beyond the Mexique Bay: A Traveller's Journal. London, Chatto and Windus, and New York, Harper, 1934.
1936...Peace? London, Friends Peace Committee, 1936.
The Olive Tree and Other Essays. London, Chatto and Windus, 1936; New York, Harper, 1937.
What Are You Going to Do About It? The Case for Constructive Peace. London, Chatto and Windus, 1936; New York, Harper, 1937.
An Encyclopedia of Pacifism. New York, Harper, 1937.
Ends and Means: An Inquiry into the Nature of Ideals and into the Methods Employed for Their Realization. London, Chatto and Windus, and New York, Harper, 1937.
The Most Agreeable Vice. Los Angeles, Ward Ritchie Press, 1938.
Words and Their Meanings. Los Angeles, Ward Ritchie Press, 1940.
Grey Eminence: A Study in Religion and Politics. London, Chatto and Windus, and New York, Harper, 1941.
The Art of Seeing. New York, Harper, 1942; London, Chatto and Windus, 1943.
The Perennial Philosophy. New York, Harper, 1945; London, Chatto and Windus, 1946.
Science, Liberty, and Peace. New York, Harper, 1946; London, Chatto and Windus, 1947.
Food and People, with John Russell. London, Bureau of Current Affairs, 1949.
Prisons, with the Carceri Etchings by G.B. Piranesi. London, Trianon Press, and Los Angeles, Zeitlin and Ver Brugge, 1949.
Themes and Variations. London, Chatto and Windus, and New York, Harper, 1950.
Joyce, the Artificer: Two Studies of Joyce's Methods, with Stuart Gilbert. London, Chiswick Press, 1952.
The Devils of Loudun. Chatto and Windus, and New York, Harper, 1952.
A Day in Windsor, with J.A. Kings. London, Britannicus Liber, 1953.
The Doors of Perception. London, Chatto and Windus, and New York, Harper, 1954.
The French of Paris, photographs by Sanford H. Roth. New York, Harper, 1954.
Adonis and the Alphabet, and Other Essays. London, Chatto and Windus, 1956; as *Tomorrow and Tomorrow and Tomorrow and Other Essays,* New York, Harper, 1956.
Heaven and Hell. London, Chatto and Windus, and New York, Harper, 1956.
A Writer's Prospect—III: Censorship and Spoken Literature. London, 1956.
Brave New World Revisited. New York, Harper, 1958; London, Chatto and Windus, 1959.
"Chemical Persuasion," in *Fantasy and Science Fiction* (New York), April 1959.
Collected Essays. London, Chatto and Windus, and New York, Harper, 1959.
On Art and Artists: Literature, Painting, Architecture, Music, edited by Morris Philipson. London, Chatto and Windus, and New York, Harper, 1960.
Selected Essays, edited by Harold Raymond. London, Chatto and Windus, 1961.
Literature and Science. London, Chatto and Windus, and New York, Harper, 1963.
The Politics of Ecology: The Question of Survival. Santa Barbara, California, Center for the Study of Democratic Institutions, 1963.
New Fashioned Christmas. Hart Press, 1968.

America and the Future. Austin, Texas, Jenkins, 1970.

Moksha: Writings on Psychedelics and the Visionary Experience 1931-1963, edited by Michael Horowitz and Cynthia Palmer. New York, Stonehill, 1977; London, Chatto and Windus, 1980.

The Basic Philosophy of Aldous Huxley. American Institute of Psychology, 1984.

Other

Editor, with W.R. Childe and T.W. Earp, *Oxford Poetry 1916.* Oxford, Blackwell, 1916.

Translator, *A Virgin Heart,* by Rémy de Gourmont. New York, Brown, 1921; London, Allen and Unwin, 1926.

Editor, *The Letters of D.H. Lawrence.* London, Heinemann, and New York, Viking Press, 1932.

Rotunda: A Selection From the Works of Aldous Huxley. London, Chatto and Windus, 1932.

Editor, *Text and Pretexts: An Anthology with Commentaries.* London, Chatto and Windus, 1932; New York, Harper, 1933.

Retrospect: An Omnibus of His Fiction and Non-Fiction Over Three Decades. New York, Doubleday, 1933.

Editor, *An Encyclopedia of Pacifism.* London, Chatto and Windus, and New York, Harper, 1937.

Stories, Essays, and Poems. London, Dent, 1937.

The World of Aldous Huxley: An Omnibus of His Fiction and Non-Fiction over Three Decades, edited by Charles J. Rolo. New York, Harper, 1947.

Contributor, *This I Believe.* New York, Simon and Schuster, 1952.

Great Short Works of Aldous Huxley, edited by Bernard Bergonzi. New York, Harper, 1969.

The Letters of Aldous Huxley, edited by Grover Smith. London, Chatto and Windus, 1969; New York, Harper, 1970.

Collected Works. London, Chatto and Windus, 1970.

Science, Liberty and Peace. London, Chatto and Windus, 1970.

The Human Situation: Lectures at Santa Barbara 1959, edited by Piero Ferrucci. New York, Harper, 1977; London, Chatto and Windus, 1978.

The Wisdom of the Ages. Found Class Reprints, 2 volumes, 1989.

Huxley and God: Essays on Mysticism, Religion, and Spirituality, edited by Jacqueline Bridgeman. San Francisco, Harper, 1991.

*

Media Adaptations: *Point Counter Point* (play), London, 1930; *Prelude to Fame* (film; based on "Young Archimedes"), Universal, 1950; *Brave New World* (television movie), NBC-TV, 1978; *Brave New World* (cassette; filmstrip with cassette), Current Affairs and Mark Twain Media, 1978.

Biography: *Aldous Huxley* by Jocelyn Brook, Longmans, Green, 1954; *The Huxleys* by Ronald W. Clark, New York, McGraw, 1968; *The Timeless Moment: A Personal View of Aldous Huxley* by Laura Huxley, New York, Farrar Straus, 1968, London, Chatto and Windus, 1969; *Aldous Huxley* by Harold H. Watts, New York, Twayne, 1969; *Aldous Huxley* by Keith M. May, London, Elek, 1972, New York, Harper, 1973; *Aldous Huxley: A Biography* by Sybille Bedford, London, Chatto and Windus-Collins, 2 volumes, 1973-74, New York, Knopf, 1 volume, 1974; *Huxley: A Biographical Introduction* by Peter Thody, New York, Scribner, 1973; entry in *Dictionary of Literary Biography,* Detroit, Gale, Volume 36, 1985; Volume 100,

1990; entry in *Concise Dictionary of British Literary Biography,* Volume 6, Detroit, Gale, 1991.

Bibliography: *Aldous Huxley: A Bibliography 1916-1959* by Claire John Eschelbach and Joyce Lee Shober, Berkeley, University of California Press, 1961; supplement by Thomas D. Clareson and Carolyn S. Andrews, in *Extrapolation 6* (Wooster, Ohio), 1964; *Aldous Huxley: An Annotated Bibliography of Criticism* by Eben E. Bass, New York, Garland, 1981.

Critical Study: *Aldous Huxley: A Literary Study* by John Atkins, London, Calder, and New York, Roy, 1956, revised edition, London, Calder, and Boyars, 1967, New York, Orion Press, 1968; *Aldous Huxley: A Memorial Volume* by Julian Huxley, New York, Harper, 1965; *Aldous Huxley: A Study of the Major Novels* by Peter Bowering, London, Athlone Press, 1968, New York, Oxford University Press, 1969; *Aldous Huxley: Satire and Structure* by Jerome Meckier, London, Chatto and Windus, and New York, Barnes and Noble, 1969; *Aldous Huxley: A Critical Study* by Laurence Brander, Lewisburg, Pennsylvania, Bucknell University Press, 1970; *Aldous Huxley and the Way to Reality* by Charles M. Holmes, Bloomington, Indiana University Press, 1970; *Aldous Huxley's Quest for Values* by Milton Birnbaum, Knoxville, University of Tennessee Press, 1971; *Aldous Huxley: A Satirist and Novelist* by Peter Firchow, St. Paul, University of Minnesota Press, 1972; *Dawn and the Darkest Hour: A Study of Aldous Huxley* by George Woodcock, London, Faber, and New York, Viking Press, 1972; entries in *Contemporary Literary Criticism,* Detroit, Gale, Volume 1, 1973; Volume 3, 1975; Volume 4, 1975; Volume 5, 1976; Volume 8, 1978; Volume 11, 1979; Volume 18, 1981; Volume 35, 1985; *Aldous Huxley: A Collection of Critical Essays* edited by Robert E. Kuehn, Englewood Cliffs, New Jersey, Prentice Hall, 1974; *Aldous Huxley: The Critical Heritage* edited by Donald Watt, London, Routledge, 1975; *Demon and Saint in the Novels of Aldous Huxley* by Lilly Zahmer, Bern, Schweizer Anglistische Arbeiten, 1975; *Aspects of Structure and Quest in Aldous Huxley's Major Novels* by Bharathi Krishnan, Uppsala, Sweden, University of Uppsala, 1977; *Aldous Huxley, Novelist* by Christopher S. Ferns, London, Athlone Press, 1980; *The Dark Historic Page: Social Satire and Historicism in the Novels of Aldous Huxley 1921-1939* by Robert S. Baker, Madison, University of Wisconsin Press, 1982.

*   *   *

As the grandson of eminent Victorian scientist Thomas Henry Huxley (a celebrated agnostic and popularizer of Darwinism), Aldous Huxley could have been expected to continue the family tradition as a rationalist and a skeptical advocate of empirical science. But Huxley was also descended from the famous Victorian schoolmaster Dr. Thomas Arnold, who was an ordained minister, an uncompromising moralist, and an exponent of the virtues of an education in the Greek and Roman classics, and it was this family tradition which Huxley ultimately embraced in his own idiosyncratic way. When failing eyesight in his adolescence became an obstacle to the study of science, Huxley, a lonely youth, turned to the study of literature. During his university years, unable to serve in the British army during World War I, he undertook a period of almost solitary study of English literature at Balliol College, Oxford. After an apprentice period as an undistinguished neo-romantic poet, he became an ironic novelist who will be long remembered as both a brilliant satirist of social behavior in the 1920s, and as a dedicated seeker of religious faith who rejected conventional religion, but chose the difficult path of private spiritual search and contemplative mysticism.

Huxley's early satirical fiction does not offer much of interest to young adult readers, although *Crome Yellow* presents a young poet's emotional confusion effectively, and *Antic Hay* treats London's social trends of the early twenties as the basis for grotesque comedy. A more probing effort to explore the disenchantment and amoral behavior of British intellectuals in the Jazz Age is *Point Counter Point;* but this fictional anatomy of modern disillusionment might have benefitted from a lighter tone and more of Huxley's humor. Instead, the influence of Fyodor Dostoyevsky and Huxley's contemporary, D.H. Lawrence, provide this novel with weighty themes.

As a prophetic critic of the twentieth-century obsession with science, technological development, and commercial and industrial advancement, Lawrence had become Huxley's mentor. An evangelist of sexual mysticism and a throwback to primitivist religious feeling, Lawrence was not only a great novelist, but a controversial social critic who continued to influence Huxley's thinking well after his death in 1930. Huxley resurrects Lawrence's passionate spirit in his next novel, his celebrated entry into the realm of speculative fiction. In *Brave New World,* Huxley produced a major dystopian novel which establishes a memorable opposition between behaviorist social programming, and a Lawrencian individualism, embodied in John, "the Savage," who serves as the novel's heroic and self-immolating protagonist.

Reared on a Pueblo reservation in northern New Mexico, and nurtured both by Native American mysticism and by his intense reading of the collected works of Shakespeare, John readily assaults the mindless pretenses of a supposed utopia, the programmed society described ironically by the title (a quotation taken from a romantic context in Shakespeare's *The Tempest*). This "brave new world," set six hundred years in the future from Huxley's time, is caustically attacked by "the Savage" in the ferocious tone exhibited by Lawrence in many of his expository essays, especially *Studies in Classic American Literature,* which Lawrence composed while living near Taos, New Mexico, not far from the Savage's own native grounds.

Armed with the humanist emotions in Shakespeare's verse, John levels scorching and withering criticism of a smug, self-satisfied world which has eliminated the nuclear and established social family order through the application of Henry Ford's mass production techniques to the nurturing of test-tube babies, who are given subliminal social training and educated to accept their pre-determined social roles through the methods of Watsonian behaviorism. As adults, the citizens of this false utopia are indoctrinated to the belief that they are happy, while their psychological frustrations are relieved by easily obtained sexual experience and mind-soothing drugs. But in the climactic debate of the novel, John, "the Savage," rejects the rhetoric justifying this behaviorist social tyranny. In response to the arguments of Mustapha Mond, the administrator of this future society, who echoes Dostoyevsky's Grand Inquisitor in claiming that human beings need to be protected from their own unhappiness, John asserts the classic humanist argument that human dignity requires "the right to be unhappy."

In *Brave New World,* Huxley produced an enduring novel in the science fiction genre, and one of the most brilliant satires in English literature. Although other intellectuals before Huxley—H.G. Wells, E.M. Forster, Yugeny Zamiatin, Karel Capek—had experimented with science fiction romances as a method of social criticism, Huxley's novel remains a seminal work and a remarkable achievement which influenced many later writers from George Orwell to Robert Silverberg.

After *Brave New World,* Huxley's fiction and nonfiction both became increasingly concerned with his interest in religious mysticism. Like Lawrence, Huxley left England to become a citizen of the world, settling ultimately in Southern California. The influence of Lawrence, however, was gradually replaced by that of Gerald Heard, a more conventional religious mystic. Although *Eyeless in Gaza* and *Time Must Have a Stop* are both concerned with religious quest, *After Many a Summer Dies the Swan,* which satirizes the popular culture of Southern California and a foolish attempt to gain physical immortality through technological innovation, displays some of Huxley's vintage comic irony.

Much of Huxley's later energy was devoted primarily to nonfiction, both in essays presenting social criticism, and in works like *The Perennial Philosophy,* which collects and comments on the texts that Huxley considered the vital essence of the world's mystical writings. *The Devils of Loudon,* a study of religious repression and sexual perversity, was adapted by John Whiting into a play and later transformed into an impressive film, *The Devils.*

In his final important novel, *Island,* Huxley presented a fictional counterpoint to *Brave New World* in a utopian novel which offered mystical experience stimulated by such drugs as mescaline and LSD as one of the goals of human experience. Unlike the drug called "soma" of *Brave New World,* which provides merely a temporary and pleasurable relief from social tension, the drug induced experience of *Island* reaches deeper levels of contemplation and vision. As a result, the novel had some influence on the cult of "mind expanding" drugs in the sixties; but this aspect of its teaching has not been appealing in the climate of the current reaction against drug usage.

Since *Island,* like many utopian novels, tends to substitute exposition for drama, it has never achieved the popularity of Huxley's other major venture into speculative fiction. But the novel remains important as a revelation of Huxley's intellectual development.

Although Huxley wanted to be remembered as a social novelist and essayist, he was aware that his extraordinary emotional detachment limited his ability to create sympathetic characters. In addition to his limitations as a fiction writer, many critics who admired his satire deplored his rejection of rationalism and his long devotion to the cause of mysticism. Yet Huxley's later work testifies to the seriousness of his religious quest. However, Huxley will probably owe his enduring reputation not to the writing describing his spiritual search but to his efforts as a satirist, and ultimately, perhaps, to the brilliant, imaginative satire in *Brave New World.*

—Edgar L. Chapman

I-J

IRWIN, Hadley. Joint pseudonym for Lee Hadley and Ann Irwin.
Lee Hadley: American. Born in Earlham, Iowa, 10 October 1934.
Educated at Drake University, Des Moines, Iowa, B.A. 1956; University of Wisconsin-Madison, M.A. 1961. Writer. Copywriter, Younkers of Des Moines (department store), 1955-58; high school English teacher, De Soto, Iowa, 1959-60; instructor in English, Ocean County Community College, Toms River, New Jersey, 1965-68; assistant then associate professor of English, Iowa State University, Ames, 1969—. **Ann Irwin:** American. Born in Peterson, Iowa, 8 October 1915. Educated at Morningside College, Sioux City, Iowa, B.A. 1937; University of Iowa, Iowa City, M.A. 1967. Married Keith C. Irwin, 1943; three daughters and one son. Writer. High school English teacher, Iowa, 1937-67; instructor in English, Buena Vista College, Storm Lake, Iowa, 1967-68; instructor in English, Midwestern College, Denison, Iowa, 1968-70; associate professor of English, Iowa State University, Ames, 1970-85. Recipients: Honor Book award, Jane Addams Peace Association, 1981, for *We Are Mesquakie, We Are One;* Society of Midland Authors award, 1982, for *Moon and Me;* Notable Children's Trade Book in the Field of Social Studies award from joint committee of the National Council on Social Studies and Children's Book Council and Best Young Adult Book award from American Library Association, both 1982, for *What about Grandma?,* and both 1985, for *Abby, My Love;* Children's Choice Book award, joint committee of Children's Book Council and International Reading Association, 1986, for *Abby, My Love.* Address: Department of English, Iowa State University, Ames, IA 50011, U.S.A.

PUBLICATIONS FOR YOUNG ADULTS

Fiction

The Lilith Summer. New York, Feminist Press, 1979.
We Are Mesquakie, We Are One. New York, Feminist Press, 1980.
Bring to a Boil and Separate. New York, Atheneum, 1980.
Moon and Me. New York, Atheneum, 1981.
What about Grandma? New York, Atheneum, 1982.
I Be Somebody. New York, Macmillan, 1984.
Abby, My Love. New York, Macmillan, 1985.
Kim/Kimi. New York, Macmillan, 1987.
So Long at the Fair. New York, Macmillan, 1988.
Can't Hear You Listening. New York, Macmillan, 1990.

Nonfiction

Writing Young Adult Novels. Cincinnati, Ohio, Writer's Digest Books, 1988.

Other (Ann Irwin)

Hawkeye Adventure, with Bernice Reida. Graphic Publishing, 1966.
Hawkeye Lore, with Bernice Reida. Graphic Publishing, 1968.
One Bite at a Time. New York, F. Watts, 1973.
Moon of the Red Strawberry, with Bernice Reida. Aurora, 1977.
Until We Reach the Valley, with Bernice Reida. New York, Avon, 1979.

Successful Treatment of Stuttering. Walker, 1980.

*

Media Adaptation: *The Lilith Summer* was released with a teaching guide by Aims, 1984.

Biography: Essay in *Speaking for Ourselves: Autobiographical Sketches by Notable Authors of Books for Young Adults,* Volume 1, compiled and edited by Donald R. Gallo, National Council of Teachers of English, 1990; essay in *Something about the Author Autobiography Series,* Volume 14, Detroit, Gale, 1992.

*   *   *

Hadley Irwin is the pen name for Lee Hadley and Ann Irwin. Together, as a "single identity," Hadley Irwin has authored a number of books for young adults. Like other works in this age class, her fiction addresses issues of concern to teenagers, including suicide, incest, and alcohol abuse. Particularly successful are *What about Grandma?, Abby, My Love,* and *Kim/Kimi.* These novels, as well as *So Long at the Fair* and *Can't Hear You Listening,* are not action-packed works that are sped through; rather, they're books a reader strolls with while contemplating a central problem and caring for various characters.

In *What about Grandma?,* sixteen-year-old Rhys and her mother find themselves looking after Grandma Wyn, who refuses to stay in a nursing home. The three women, initially "a pyramid of age locked into one house," gradually come to terms with the hurts and misunderstandings of the past, and find joy in their relationships.

In *Abby, My Love,* Irwin's focus is the sensitive issue of sexual abuse. The story is narrated by Chip, who reflects on his longtime friendship with Abby. For years, Chip had desired a closer relationship, but Abby would withdraw so that she simply couldn't be reached. When Abby finally turns to Chip in desperation, telling him that her father sexually abused her, Chip relies on his mother and her boyfriend for help. But as is often sadly true in such situations, Abby's mother is unable or unwilling to take any action to protect her daughter, so it is Chip's love and strength which ultimately prod Abby to seek the professional assistance she needs.

Kim/Kimi addresses the notion of identity, but with an important twist. Kim Andrews/Kimi Yoguchi is half Japanese. In response to her crisis of mixed racial identity, she travels to Sacramento to locate her Japanese family, armed only with an old photograph and her deceased father's name, Yoguchi. There Kimi learns about the parts of her heritage not covered in textbooks, including the forced internment of Japanese citizens in camps like Manzanar and Tule Lake during World War II. She is ultimately successful in her quest to locate her father's family, but the relationship established is very uncertain, although hopeful.

The conclusions of *So Long at the Fair* and *Can't Hear You Listening* are also fragile endings. Joel's slow and painful acceptance of his best friend Ashley's suicide is the subject of *So Long at the Fair.* After spending a week at the state fairgrounds, Joel is ready to begin his personal healing process. In *Can't Hear You Listening,* Tracy deals with her parents' separation, her mother's successful writing career, and the abuse of alcohol and drugs by her friend Stanley. While the family relationships have stabilized by the end of the novel, Stanley still has difficult times to face.

In addition to dramatizing teen concerns, several other recurring ideas emerge from Irwin's works. The first of these is the portrayal of the elderly as human beings with hopes, fears, loves, and problems. This is especially evident in *What about Grandma?* which features Grandma Wyn, her fun-loving and energetic neighbor Virene, the Reverend Baddeley, and others. Similarly, Mrs. Mueller in *Kim/Kimi,* while less fully developed as a character than Grandma Wyn, leads an interesting life and helps Kim in her search. Tracy's grandmother in *Can't Hear You Listening* abandons her role as a farm wife following her husband's death and transforms into a bridge-playing Arizona condo dweller, just to see if she still has the gumption to make such a change. In all these novels, the elderly are not only present, but portrayed realistically and humanly, an accomplishment of note in young adult fiction.

A second commonality in Irwin's novels is setting. Grandma Wyn's beloved Iowa lake could well be considered an additional character in *What about Grandma?* The lake brings back memories for all three women and serves as the backdrop for important conversations between the generations. Kim's quest to locate her Japanese family becomes more understandable given her upbringing in a small Iowa town. Abby's abuse within a middle-class family living in an Iowa town is all the more chilling for its occurrence in such a "safe" environment. And Joel's retreat from his comfortable and upscale home to the state fair is a believable escape. The choice of Iowa towns for the settings is a natural one, since both Irwin and Hadley are longtime residents. While the settings may appear somewhat idyllic to urban readers, their depiction is never negative or stereotypically provincial.

A third motif is the value of a strong parent-adolescent relationship. In *What about Grandma?* the relationship that slowly develops among the three women is what makes the work satisfying. This same type of generational trio appears in *Can't Hear You Listening* and again, these characters struggle to understand and respect one another. Similarly Chip's close relationship with his mother not only gives him the strength to help Abby, it also provides the support both Chip and his mother themselves require to cope with Abby's abuse.

A final thread running through Irwin's works is the self-worth that a number of characters find when they assume nurturing or teaching roles. Kimi's friend Ernie volunteers at a center for recent Asian immigrants, Joel coaches the Little League Baseball Bombers, and Ashley tutors at an alternative school. In fact, it is a newspaper article's focus on her, instead of her students, that precipitates Ashley's suicide.

Hadley Irwin's works sensitively and successfully portray adolescent concerns. There is occasional heavy-handedness ("Life is growth. To grow, you have to learn who you *were,* who you *are,* and what you *will become.*"), and several descriptions, while humorous, appear to be parodies of the romance novels Kim reads ("I had to admit he was kind of cute in a beefy way and had the biggest biceps of anyone on the team. His pectorals weren't bad, either"). But these faults are minor when considered in the greater context of the novels' characters and issues.

In the end, the great strength of Hadley Irwin's fiction can perhaps be reduced to a single concept: respect. In all her works, respect for others is a central theme, whether the respect is for the elderly, a parent, an adolescent, or persons different, younger, or less fortunate. This is indeed a valuable message for young adult readers.

—Bonnie O. Ericson

———

JACQUES, Brian. British. Born in Liverpool, 15 June 1939. Educated at a Roman Catholic school in Liverpool. Two sons. Seaman, 1954-57; railway fireman, 1957-60; longshoreman, 1960-65; long-distance truck driver, 1965-75; docks representative, 1975-80; freelance radio broadcaster, since 1980. Radio broadcasts for BBC-Radio Merseyside include the music programs "Jakestown" and "Saturday With Brian Jacques" and documentaries "We All Went Down the Docks," "Gangland Anthology," "The Eternal Christmas," "Centenary of Liverpool," "An Eyeful of Easter," "A Lifetime Habit," and "The Hollywood Musicals," a six-part series; broadcaster for BBC-Radio 1 and BBC-Radio 2; member of BBC Northwest Television Advisory Council. Presents humorous lectures at schools and universities. Patron of Royal Wavertree School for the Blind. Recipient: National Light Entertainment award for Radio from Sony Company, 1982, for BBC-Radio Merseyside's "Jakestown"; Rediffusion award for Best Light Entertainment Program on Local Radio, 1982, and Commendation, 1983, Parents' Choice Honor Book for Literature, 1987, and Children's Book of the Year award from Lancashire County Library, 1988, both for *Redwall;* W.A. Young Readers Book award, 1991, for *Mossflower.*

PUBLICATIONS FOR YOUNG ADULTS

Novels

Redwall, illustrated by Gary Chalk. New York, Philomel, 1987.
Mossflower, illustrated by Gary Chalk. New York, Philomel, 1988.
Mariel of Redwall, illustrated by Gary Chalk. New York, Philomel, 1991.
Mattimeo. New York, Avon, 1991.
Seven Strange & Ghostly Tales. New York, Philomel, 1991.
Salamandastron. New York, Philomel, 1992.

*   *   *

Brian Jacques has made the world of woodland and meadow his own. His books are populated with the creatures of the forest, and not a human among them. The heroes are the little folk, the "gentlebeasts" to use his own term: mice, voles, moles, squirrels, and badgers. Against these gentle creatures the author pits the predators: rats, foxes, wildcats. The animals are generally true to their natures, but a bit anthropomorphized.

The tales center themselves on a community consisting primarily of mice who live in the Abbey of Redwall. Although the mice seem organized on standard monastic lines, religion plays no part in the narratives. The Redwall community practices charity and love for all creatures, even those about whom it might be best to be a bit less charitable. Time and again Redwallers turn the other cheek only to find it slapped. In *Salamandastron,* for example, two renegade sea-rats (a loathsome variety of pirate) come to the Abbey for shelter. They steal the magical sword of Martin the Warrior and slink off into the night, leaving one of the brother mice dead. The theft is not their only legacy: one of them was carrying the germs of Dryditch Fever. Soon most of the Abbey residents are ill and dying.

Jacques has a standard approach to each of his works. Two problems are set: one for an individual or group of individuals, and a second for the entire Abbey. In *Salamandastron* a young badger and a young hare from the Mountain of Dragons have crept off with a smooth-talking weasel. They are met by Samkin Squirrel and Arula Mole from Redwall, who are trying to track the thieves who stole the sword. In the meantime Thugg, the otter, and Baby Dumble, the dormouse, have set out for the mountains of the north to find the Flowers of Icetor, the only cure for the fever. The narrative flows smoothly between the adventures of the various groups, eventually bringing all of them together.

Jacques gives his creatures individual "racial" characteristics by a unique use of language. Moles, for example, speak a dialect much like cockney English: "Ee be a gurt noisy trowt that un, eh?" The eagles and falcons of the northern mountains speak Scots: "We were searchin' for that young rip, mah son Rocangus, but six braw sojers like us wid be shamed if we couldnae give some crows a good tanning!" Less intelligent creatures, like the sparrows in *Redwall*, speak a variety of pidgin English: "Me hunt worms. Bring dandelions for Matthias. Mouse like eat flowers."

The tales are peppered with poetry and rhymes, often in the form of puzzles that the protagonists must solve to resolve their problem, like this piece from *Redwall:*

> Who says that I am dead
> Knows nought at all.
> I—am that is
> Two mice within Redwall.
> The Warrior sleeps
> 'Twixt Hall and Cavern Hole
> I—am that is
> Take on my mighty role.
> Look for the sword
> In moonlight streaming forth,
> At night, when day's first hour
> Reflects the North.
> From o'er the threshold
> Seek, and you will see;
> I—am that is
> My sword will wield for me.

The mouse Matthias and his abbot must decipher the rhyme to find the lost sword and reclaim the Abbey from the Sparrows that have infested its upper regions. Among the minor characters in *Mattimeo* is a poetical owl, Sir Harry the Muse, whose comments are always in rhymes:

> Dread words do not alarm me
> When food is on its way
> No parchment threat can harm me
> Lead on, lead on I say.

Jacques makes his tales palatable to the younger reader by sprinkling them with accounts of fabulous feasts. Any excuse to celebrate in Mossflower County means a lavish meal prepared by the cooks of Redwall: "Our Abbot...has declared that his first anniver-

sary shall be marked by a huge feast." "I never told him.... of the wonderful feast when the main gate was raised..." "The feast of The Autumn of the Warriors' Return began just after dawn." The hares and moles are particularly interested in eating until they are ready to burst. Good October ale, salads, jams, and jellies are the stuff upon which the Redwallers feed.

Jacques pictures a quiet simple time when virtue is always triumphant over evil. There is always a price, but it is paid with few recriminations.

—Louise J. Winters

———

JAMES, Mary. See **KERR, M.E.**

———

JANECZKO, Paul B(ryan). Also writes as P. Wolny. American. Born in Passaic, New Jersey, 27 July 1945. Educated at St. Francis College, Biddeford, Maine, A.B. 1967; John Carroll University, Cleveland, Ohio, M.A. 1970. Married Nadine Edris; one daughter. Poet and anthologist. High school English teacher in Parma, Ohio, 1968-72, and Topsfield, Massachusetts, 1972-77; guest editor of *Leaflet,* spring, 1977; Gray-New Gloucester High School, Gray, Maine, teacher of language arts, 1977-90; visiting writer, 1990—. Recipient: *Postcard Poems* was selected one of New York Public Library's Books for the Teen Age, 1980 and 1981, and *Don't Forget to Fly,* 1982; *Don't Forget to Fly,* 1981, *Poetspeak,* 1983, *Strings: A Gathering of Family Poems,* 1984, and *Pocket Poems: Selected for a Journey,* 1985, and *Going over to Your Place,* 1987, were selected by the American Library Association as Best Young Adult Books of the Year; *Don't Forget to Fly* was selected one of *School Library Journal's* Best Books, 1981, and *Poetspeak,* 1983; English-Speaking Union Books-across-the-Sea Ambassador of Honor Book award, 1984, for *Poetspeak; Pocket Poems* was chosen one of Child Study Association of America's Children's Books of the Year, 1985. Address: RR 1, Box 260, Marshall Pond Rd., Hebron, ME 04238, U.S.A.

PUBLICATIONS FOR YOUNG ADULTS

Fiction

Bridges to Cross, illustrated by Robert J. Blake. New York, Macmillan, 1986.

Nonfiction

Loads of Codes and Secret Ciphers. New York, Simon and Schuster, 1981.

Verse

Brickyard Summer, illustrated by Ken Rush. New York, Orchard, 1989.

Stardust Otel, illustrated by Dorothy Leech. New York, Orchard, 1993.

Editor

The Crystal Image. New York, Dell. 1977.
Postcard Poems. Scarsdale, New York, Bradbury, 1979.
It's Elementary. New York, Bantam, 1981.
Poetspeak: In Their Work, about Their Work. Scarsdale, New York, Bradbury, 1983.
This Delicious Day: 65 Poems. New York, Franklin Watts, 1987.
Going over to Your Place: Poems for Each Other. Scarsdale, New York, Bradbury, 1987.
The Music of What Happens: Poems That Tell Stories. New York, Franklin Watts, 1988.
The Place My Words Are Looking For: What Poets Say about and through Their Work. Scarsdale, New York, Bradbury, 1990.
Preposterous: Poems of Youth. New York, Orchard, 1991.
Looking for Your Name. New York, Orchard, 1993.

Other

Contributor, *Censorship: A Guide for Teachers, Librarians, and Others Concerned with Intellectual Freedom,* edited by Lou Willett Stanek. New York, Dell, 1976.
Contributor, *Children's Literature Review,* edited by Gerard J. Senick. Volume 3, Detroit, Gale, 1978.
Contributor, *Young Adult Literature in the Seventies,* edited by Jana Varlejs. Metuchen, New Jersey, Scarecrow, 1978.
Compiler, *Don't Forget to Fly: A Cycle of Modern Poems.* Scarsdale, New York, Bradbury, 1981.
Compiler, *Strings: A Gathering of Family Poems.* Scarsdale, New York, Bradbury, 1984.
Compiler, *Pocket Poems: Selected for a Journey.* Scarsdale, New York, Bradbury, 1985.

Author of "Back Pages," a review column in *Leaflet,* 1973-76. Author of numerous articles, stories, poems (under pseudonym P. Wolny), and reviews to newspapers, professional and popular magazines, including *Armchair Detective, New Hampshire Profiles, Modern Haiku, Dragonfly, Friend, Child Life,* and *Highlights for Children.*

*

Biography: Essay in *Authors and Artist for Young Adults,* Volume 9, Detroit, Gale, 1992.

Paul B. Janeczko comments:

I started writing when I was in the fifth or sixth grade. But, unlike many writers, I didn't begin with poems or short stories or "novels." No, I started by writing postcards to get free stuff. Stuff I didn't really need—e.g., a sample of tarnish remover, a moving kit, a stain removal chart—but had to have.

When I started teaching high school English nearly twenty-five years ago, I figured I could write a novel like the young adult novels I was teaching. I was wrong, so I started writing for teacher magazines and spent a lot of years developing my writing skills in that area.

Strictly speaking, my poems are not autobiographical. Oh, I borrow from people I've known and from experiences I've had, but

then my imagination kicks in and I create new people who have new experiences. I spend a great deal of time developing the characters in my books because I know if I can create interesting characters, they will, more than likely, do interesting things. And that's what readers are looking for.

*   *   *

It is difficult to imagine where, in the late 1970s, 1980s, and the beginning of the 1990s, young adults might have found exciting collections of contemporary poetry were it not for Paul Janeczko and his (by latest count) thirteen anthologies. Others have compiled a variety of thematic collections but Janeczko's ability to ferret out the unusual, the relevant, an amazing gift to students (as well as to teachers, librarians, families, and friends) who wish to be introduced to the latest in poetry.

Janeczko's instinct, both for the individual poem and the shape of a collection is that of a fine anthologist; poems with strong images stand by themselves, yet relate and dovetail into each other, one enriching the next, occurring in a progression which crescendos toward an end and still seems to circle back to the beginning. Thus, in *Preposterous,* the opening poem, Gary Hyland's "Zip on Good Advice," which begins with the line "What do parents know anyhow?" is a lead into "Dodo" by Henry Carlile, just as the last of the 108 selections, William Stafford's "Runaway Teen"—which ends with "It's hard being a person. / We all know that" recalls and echoes the first line of the Hyland.

Within the anthologies, many among the American Library Association's Best Books of the Year, Janeczko chooses the work of hundreds of contemporary poets. There is certainly William Stafford, X.J. Kennedy, Richard Eberhart, Donald Hall, and Randall Jarrell but there is also a wealth of lesser known poets Janeczko uses often—David Allan Evans, Jonathan Holden, Sheryl L. Helms, Mark Vinz, Ronald Wallace, Keith Wilson, and Paul Zimmer to name only a few. Each anthology bears its own special mark of distinction. *Pocket Poems: Selected for a Journey* is in a "pocket-size format for travelers and others on the move." *Strings: A Gathering of Family Poems* centers around the experiences of family life; *Going over to Your House: Poems for Each Other* is heralded by Peter Meinke's "The Heart's Location" wherein the narrator seeks "a poem full of ordinary words / about simple things / in the inconsolable rhythms of the heart." Janeczko's most recent, *Looking for Your Name* is an arresting collection of poems about life in America today, ranging in subject from acquired immunodeficiency syndrome (AIDS) to pacifism, violence, the nuclear freeze, unemployment, sports, love, peace, family, and offshore drilling.

Paul Janeczko's first book of his own poetry, *Brickyard Summer,* is rich with the people and places of a New England milltown; high school chums "hanging out in front of Manny's," the nuns who warn of the Seven Deadly Sins and lust, and the realisms of a dying cat, petty thievery, a first kiss. Friendship, comradery, and encounters with unusual adults also mark his second collection, *Stardust Otel,* 1993:

The H fell nearly 14 years ago:
the day I was born
Nick swung on it in joy
until it snapped off in his hands.
He never replaced it,
saying he liked to be reminded
of how he felt that day.

Janeczko remembers the small, telling details. There are "aunts smelling of rose water," Patrick who "spit into the pocket of his glove," Brady who chewed "Juicy Fruit" and Eduardo who "gave samba lessons / to ladies in a rented room / over Owen's Auto Parts." He writes of the elixir for Wayne's "damaged aura," the dare to meet at a cemetery and "press dry lips to the polished marble," and "girls in spike heels, / leopard pants snug / as a stamp on a first-class parcel," Charlie Hooper whose voice "was quiet but wild like pigeons taking flight" and Rusty who...

...mostly
works at the A&P
fielding questions
about chicken thighs,
Cornish hens,
and leg of lamb.

Certainly Janeczko is the poet of youth—casual, callow, alternately blustering and frightened—probing for life's discoveries; encountering its petty larcenies and pragmatism, its joys and pains, its important and abiding friendships, and often, moments of epiphany and serendipity. His nonfiction work *Loads of Codes and Secret Ciphers* seems almost as a footnote to the delicious puzzles and secrecy of youth, as does in a certain sense, *Bridges to Cross* a work of fiction in which the theme of hidden, untold secrets echoes with the quiet pain of salad days. Reading his poetry one not only realizes Janeczko's extreme sensitivity to the young but equally important encounters, head-on, a wry, delicious sense of humor which is all too rare in many poets who are apt to take themselves too seriously. For Janeczko life is not simple, but neither is it, as George Bernard Shaw took pains to tell us, wasted on the young. Janeczko's work makes this abundantly clear. Long may he continue as both anthologist and poet!

—Myra Cohn Livingston

JOHNSON, Annabel and Edgar. Have also written as A.E. Johnson. Americans. **Annabel Johnson (née Jones):** Born in Kansas City, Missouri, 18 June 1921. Educated at William and Mary College, Williamsburg, Virginia, 1939-40; Art Students' League, New York. Married Edgar Johnson in 1949. Worked in publishing houses, as a librarian, legal secretary, and in other secretarial posts prior to 1957; writer since 1957. **Edgar (Raymond) Johnson:** Born in Washoe, Montana, 24 October 1912. Educated at Billings Polytechnic Institute, Montana; Kansas City Art Institute, Montana; Alfred University, New York. Ceramic artist and head of the Ceramics Department, Kansas City Art Institute, 1948-49; model-maker, jeweler, and woodcarver with work exhibited in one-man show in New York City and included in Museum of Modern Art exhibition of American handcrafts; free-lance writer in collaboration with wife, Annabel Jones Johnson. Sometime restorer of antique musical instruments for Smithsonian Institution, Washington D.C. *Died 2 December 1990.* Recipients: Spring Book Festival award, 1959, for *The Black Symbol,* and 1960, for *Torrie;* Friends of American Writers award, 1962, for *The Secret Gift;* Golden Spur award, Western Writers of America, 1966, for *The Burning Glass;* William Allen White Children's Book award, 1967, for *The Grizzly.* Address: 2925 South Teller, Denver, CO 80227, U.S.A.

PUBLICATIONS FOR YOUNG ADULTS

Fiction

As a Speckled Bird (by Annabel Johnson alone). New York, Crowell, 1956; London, Hodder & Stoughton, 1958.
The Big Rock Candy. New York, Crowell, 1957.
The Black Symbol, illustrated by Brian Saunders. New York, Harper, 1959; Leicester, Brockhampton, 1960.
The Bearcat. New York, Harper, and London, Hamish Hamilton, 1960.
Torrie, illustrated by Pearl Falconer. New York, Harper, 1960; Leicester, Brockhampton, 1961.
Pickpocket Run. New York, Harper, 1961.
The Rescued Heart. New York, Harper, 1961.
The Secret Gift (as A.E. Johnson). New York, Doubleday, and London, Hodder & Stoughton, 1961.
Wilderness Bride. New York, Harper, 1962.
A Golden Touch. New York, Harper, 1963.
The Grizzly, illustrated by Gilbert Riswold. New York, Harper, 1964; Bath, Chivers, 1973.
A Peculiar Magic, illustrated by Lynd Ward. Boston, Houghton, 1965.
The Burning Glass. New York, Harper, 1966.
Count Me Gone. New York, Simon & Schuster, 1968.
A Blues I Can Whistle (as A.E. Johnson). New York, Four Winds, 1969.
The Last Knife. New York, Simon & Schuster, 1971.
Finders, Keepers. New York, Four Winds, 1981.
An Alien Music. New York, Four Winds, 1982.
The Danger Quotient. New York, Harper, 1984.
Prisoner of Psi. New York, Atheneum, 1985.
A Memory of Dragons. New York, Atheneum, 1986.
Gamebuster, illustrated by Stephen Marchesi. Bergenfield, New Jersey, Dutton, 1990.
I Am Leaper, illustrated by Stella Ormai. Portland, Oregon, Galley, 1990.
Niner. Browndeer Press, 1994.

*

Manuscript Collection: Kerlan Collection, University of Minnesota.

Biography: Entry in *Third Book of Junior Authors,* New York, H.W. Wilson, 1972.

*   *   *

Annabel and Edgar Johnson's historically located stories are distinguished by a highly economical use of detail which, without any evident labouring to do so, brings home to us just what life must have been like on the American frontier in the nineteenth century. Even more impressive is the unobtrusive but wholesomely insistent moral concern which is discreetly embodied in the narrative texture itself: as the story unfolds we find ourselves sharing the young protagonist's discovery of the realities of human nature in other people and in himself or herself. In *Torrie* the fourteen-year-old heroine is unwillingly uprooted from her comfortable home in St. Louis to undertake a 2000-mile trek by ox-drawn wagon to California. As the hardships of the journey unroll, only slowly does she learn to value the qualities of leadership now revealed in her insignificant-looking schoolmaster father, the staunchness and selflessness of her mother, the love of her parents for each other and for herself and her brother. It is not till the climax of the journey, when she accidentally learns that the true purpose of her parents in undertaking their migration has been concern for her own health, that the full extent of her misconception of herself and her parents is made clear to her. The rigours of the dangerous and eventful journey have brought a new stature as well as a new self-knowledge to each member of the family; and we leave them established in a cabin in California, with the prospect of a new pioneering farming life ahead of them, and a securely founded love burgeoning between Torrie and Jess, the family's young hired teamster.

Torrie has a strong emotional appeal for girls of any age above twelve, whereas *The Black Symbol* is rather more of a boys' book, though not exclusively so. The central character is Barney, who runs away from his uncle to search for his gold-miner father, and joins a travelling medicine show run by the smooth-talking Dr. Cathcart. Dr. Cathcart and his assistant Hoke Wilson clearly owe something to "The King" and "The Duke" in *Huckleberry Finn,* and the core of the book is Barney's gradual discovery of the cold-hearted sadistic ruthlessness of these two villains. The detailed trickery of the carnival is neatly worked into the plot, which involves two other members of the troupe, the frightened negro boy Billy, and the blind "Strong Man" Steve.

In their later fiction the Johnsons have moved increasingly towards the present day, and in their most recent novels into the future. In *Finders, Keepers* two independent-minded teenagers struggle desperately to survive in the aftermath of a catastrophic explosion at a nuclear power plant near Denver; there is a graphic and disturbing depiction of panic and savagery among the city dwellers who swarm westward into mountainous country to escape the radioactive fallout. In *An Alien Music* the ecological disaster is a manmade build-up of carbon dioxide in the atmosphere which heats the earth's surface to a point where it becomes uninhabitable. Jesse, a fifteen-year-old orphan girl with Indian blood, bluffs her way onto the NASA Sky-Lab which her brother has helped design to carry a select group of people to the planet Mars to form a human colony there. The excitements of the ensuing space voyage are exceptionally convincing, both in their technological aspects and in the treatment of human tensions within the crew. In particular Jesse's shifting and ambivalent relationship with the commander, Ben Hammond, brings into focus important questions concerning the nature of leadership, democracy, and self-discipline. *The Danger Quotient* starts in the year 2127 in an underground colony built as refuge from the nuclear holocaust, whence the young narrator journeys by means of a "time refractor" to Denver in 1981, 1945, and 1918 seeking insight into factors that could decide his own fate as well as that of his fellow-survivors. His contacts at these different dates with members of the same American family are interwoven with great ingenuity into a pattern adding an absorb-

ing human dimension to the temporal jigsaw puzzle. Each of these three novels is told in the first person, in the authentic-sounding idiom of an American teenager yet with a linguistic flair which is able to encompass subtle moral and social issues.

Prisoner of Psi achieves similar effects through a slightly more complex narrative structure in which segments of third-person narrative are intercut with excerpts from the diary kept by Tris, the psychically gifted son of a noted television psychic who has been kidnapped, in A.D. 2000, by a ruthless terrorist organisation. The gripping story of his eventual rescue makes skillful use of E.S.P. paraphernalia and at the same time explores subtly and sensitively (not for the first time in the Johnsons' fiction) the topic of misunderstanding and conflict between parent and child. *A Memory of Dragons* is set in an unspecified future of world conflict and shortages, with an impending secession from the United States by its western states actively on the cards. Sought as an ally by both sides on account of his flair for inventing high-tech gadgetry, Paul Killian's involvement is complicated by an inchoate burden of personal guilt which he is able to exorcise only after a series of time-travel excursions into an ancestor's experiences of the earlier American Civil War. As with its immediate predecessors, the intricate and absorbing narrative is conveyed through a series of brief, enticingly readable cameos which are brilliantly orchestrated into a complex yet coherent whole.

—Frank Whitehead

JONES, Allan Frewin. Also writes as Steven Saunders. British. Born in London, 30 April 1954. Educated at Lowden Road Primary School, London; The Strand Grammar School, London; mature student at Middlesex Polytechnic, 1981-83, received Diploma of Higher Education. Married Claudia Duwendag in 1991. Various clerical jobs, including Civil Service, Local Government, and a Trade Union. Active in local Group of Amnesty International. Recipient: Shortlisted for Children's Section of Whitbread Prize, 1991. Agent: Laurence Pollinger Ltd., 18 Maddox Street, Mayfair, London, W1R 0EU, England.

PUBLICATIONS FOR YOUNG ADULTS

Fiction

The Mole and Beverley Miller. London, Hodder and Stoughton, 1987.
The Cost of Going Free. London, Hodder and Stoughton, 1988.
Rabbit Back and Doubled. London, Hodder and Stoughton, 1989.
Bad Penny. London, Bodley Head, 1990.
Millions of Lisa. London, Hodder and Stoughton, 1990.
The Half-Good Samaritan. London, Hodder and Stoughton, 1991.
Tommy and the Sloth. London, Simon and Schuster, 1992.
Wishing Bird & Co. London, Simon and Schuster, 1993.

Fiction as Steven Saunders

Dark Secrets, Red Ink. London, Macdonald, 1988.
Kisschase. London, Macdonald, 1989.

Blind Ally. London, Macdonald, 1989.

*

Allan Frewin Jones comments:

I started writing books for a very simple reason: so that I could read them. I write about teenagers because I am fascinated by how young people cope for the first time with all the turmoil that life flings at them. It is a time of immense upheaval, conflict, pressure and passion—the perfect recipe for disasters and triumphs in the raw; unencumbered by hindsight or perspective. The only desire I have is that my writing should attempt to reflect my perception of reality. If I feel that I have managed that, I am marginally contented—until the next bunch of characters come along to keep me awake at night with their problems.

*   *   *

At a time when the teenage novel had revolved for years around sexual initiation and what happened afterwards: falling in love, out of love, pregnancy, abortion, keeping the baby... Allan Frewin Jones began to publish a fresh, comparatively innocent kind of teenage novel about first love, especially the "crush" period when one or both parties nurses unrequited love for the other. He charts the revelation which comes as a boy realises he is in love, his embarrassment about asking the girl out, his rapture when he learns that she loves him too. His characters may make love, but don't usually go all the way: in any case Frewin Jones is not an explicit writer, and in only one book does his heroine get pregnant (without full intercourse!). Within what is a shaped narrative he produces the effect of absolutely natural behaviour and dialogue. Teachers and parents looking for something to shock them will find it more in his characters' language, i.e. the swearwords and frank sex talk, than in their relatively modest sexual behaviour.

Frewin Jones is also an accurate observer of the class-based nuances of British society: the relatively secure, but hardly "posh" lower middle classes; society's young outcasts living in cardboard boxes in the subway; the working classes housed in high-rise flats plagued by criminals. He is also good on political trends and youngsters' disillusionment with their parents.

Frewin Jones's first book, *The Mole and Beverley Miller,* charts the impact on a shy boy of his and Beverley's mutual love, and of her bicycle accident and subsequent coma in hospital. The book is structured in two time streams, telling the story from their first meeting, and from her accident, in alternating units of one or two chapters each, a device which heightens our awareness of the Mole's suffering. Beverley's feminist grandmother is also a pleasantly original character.

In his second book, *The Cost of Going Free,* Sally, the daughter of a divorced mother, is attracted to a fairground worker. Her mother fears that her outright disapproval might bring about the outcome she least desires—pregnancy or elopement, perhaps. Horrible family rows ensue. Sally nearly loses her virginity at a party, but discovers that he doesn't care for her, and she and her mother are reconciled.

Frewin Jones found that he was writing more books than his publisher could handle, and so submitted three in quick succession elsewhere, taking the name of Steven Saunders for what turned out to be a rather racy trio of novels, with more candid sexuality and swearwords. *Dark Secrets, Red Ink* starts off as a comedy: Jax, daughter of a trade union official, has become an extreme left-wing activist, working for the newspaper *Red Ink,* but she has to choose between her politics and giving support to her newly pregnant sister while she decides what to do about the baby.

Blind Ally and *Kisschase* both describe a relationship between a boy from a conventional background and a girl who has gone "off the rails," recalling novels by Zindel such as *I Never Loved Your Mind.* Alasdair (Ally), sharing a holiday with his parents, meets a strange girl on the beach. They fall in love, but she has a weakness for drink and a criminal record. Ally wants to live with her and reform her, but the police catch up with her, and they are forever separated.

In *Kisschase,* Paul, an office worker, chats up Naomi, a student, in a snack bar at lunchtime. Their growing friendship is complicated by the girl's violent ex-boyfriend, who beats Paul up and vandalises Naomi's flat. Then her college project on London's homeless gets her into deep trouble with drug dealers and pimps. There could be a little more warning about forms of V.D. including AIDS. Paul's sexually experienced friend doesn't care about catching V.D. at all, though his viewpoint about girls is shown to be crude and far inferior to Paul's belief that sexual intercourse should be kept for a long-term relationship. Naomi then admits to Paul that although she has currently vowed celibacy, being weary of instant sex with every new boyfriend, she has had a number of sexual partners. However, committed relationships are shown to be superior to promiscuous ones, without preaching to the teenage reader.

Returning to his first publisher, Frewin Jones also returned to the innocent mode of his first two books. *Rabbit Back and Doubled* is one of his best. A boy and girl of sixteen and seventeen are starting an art course at school. The girl, Rachel Ronchetti, is known as Spag Bol for her Italian ancestry, but assumes it is because of her overweight appearance. She determines to be more positive about her appearance, goes for her young man, and gets him in the end. Unusually this story is told from both teenagers' viewpoints.

In *Millions of Lisa* we have the boy's side again. While Danny's girlfriend is away with her parents, his parents take in a lodger, Lisa, an attractive girl six years his senior. Soon Danny is completely overwhelmed by his feelings for both girls simultaneously; fortunately Lisa is mature enough to sort him out, though not before his girlfriend returns unexpectedly and finds him kissing Lisa!

Frewin Jones's last two teenage novels to date are both written from the girl's viewpoint, and take us into the sleazy world of council high-rise flats, filth and petty crime, recalling for me the clash between Rosa Guy's Harlem and the more respectable suburban culture to which characters like Edith Jackson and Imamu aspire. Frewin Jones is extremely accurate about poverty—material and spiritual—in today's Britain. Here indeed is an enviable body of work: eleven teenage novels, each with a distinct plot and three-dimensional characters (including the adults), published over only five years!

—Jessica Yates

———

JONES, Diana Wynne. British. Born in London, England, 16 August 1934. Educated at Friends' School, Saffron Walden, Essex, 1946-53; St. Anne's College, Oxford, 1953-56, B.A. 1956. Married John A. Burrow in 1956; three sons. Writer, since 1965. Recipient: Carnegie commendation, 1975, for *Dogsbody; Guardian* commendation, 1977, for *Power of Three;* Carnegie commendation, 1977, and *Guardian* award, 1978, for *Charmed Life;* Boston *Globe-Horn Book* Honor Book award, 1984, for *Archer's Goon; Horn Book* Honor List, 1984, for *Fire and Hemlock; Horn Book* Fanfare List, 1987, for *Howl's Moving Castle.* Agent: Laura Cecil, 17 Alwyne Villas, London N1 2HG. Address: 9, The Polygon, Clifton, Bristol BS8 4PW, England.

PUBLICATIONS FOR YOUNG ADULTS

Fiction

The Ogre Downstairs. London, Macmillan, 1974; New York, Dutton, 1975.
Dogsbody. London, Macmillan, 1975; New York, Greenwillow, 1977.
Eight Days of Luke. London, Macmillan, 1975; New York, Greenwillow, 1988.
Power of Three. London, Macmillan, 1976; New York, Greenwillow, 1977.
The Homeward Bounders. London, Macmillan, and New York, Greenwillow, 1981.
Archer's Goon. London, Methuen, and New York, Greenwillow, 1984.
Fire and Hemlock. New York, Greenwillow, 1984; London, Methuen, 1985.
Warlock at the Wheel and Other Stories. London, Macmillan, and New York, Greenwillow, 1984.
Howl's Moving Castle. London, Methuen, and New York, Greenwillow, 1986.
A Tale of Time City. New York, Greenwillow, and London, Methuen, 1987.
Black Maria. London, Methuen, 1991; as *Aunt Maria,* New York, Greenwillow, 1991.
Castle in the Air. New York, Greenwillow, 1991.
A Sudden Wild Magic. New York, Morrow, 1992.

"Chrestomanci" cycle:

Charmed Life. London, Macmillan, and New York, Greenwillow, 1977.
The Magicians of Caprona. London, Macmillan, and New York, Greenwillow, 1980.
Witch Week. London, Macmillan, and New York, Greenwillow, 1982.
The Lives of Christopher Chant. London, Methuen, and New York, Greenwillow, 1988.

"Dalemark" cycle:

Cart and Cwidder. London, Macmillan, 1975; New York, Atheneum, 1977.
Drowned Ammet. London, Macmillan, 1977; New York, Atheneum, 1978.
The Spellcoats. London, Macmillan, and New York, Atheneum, 1979.
The Crown of Dalemark. London, Mammoth, 1993.

Plays

The Batterpool Business (produced London at Arts Theatre, October, 1967).

The King's Things (produced London at Arts Theatre, February, 1969).
The Terrible Fisk Machine (produced London at Arts Theatre, January, 1970).

Other

The Skiver's Guide, illustrated by Chris Winn. London, Knight Books, 1984.
Editor, *Hidden Turnings: A Collection of Stories through Time and Space.* London, Methuen, 1989; New York, Greenwillow, 1990.

Contributor

The Cat-Flap and the Apple Pie. London, W. H. Allen, 1979.
Hecate's Cauldron. New York, DAW Books, 1981.
Hundreds and Hundreds. New York, Puffin, 1984.
Dragons and Dreams. New York, Harper, 1986.
Guardian Angels. New York, Viking Kestrel, 1987.

PUBLICATIONS FOR CHILDREN

Fiction

Wilkins' Tooth, illustrated by Julia Rodber. London, Macmillan, 1973; as *Witch's Business,* New York, Dutton, 1974.
Who Got Rid of Angus Flint?, illustrated by John Sewell. London, Evans, 1978.
The Four Grannies, illustrated by Thelma Lambert. London, Hamish Hamilton, 1980.
The Time of the Ghost. London, Macmillan, 1981.
Chair Person, illustrated by Glenys Ambrus. London, Hamish Hamilton, 1989.
Wild Robert, illustrated by Emma C. Clark. Boston, Hall, 1992.
Yes, Dear, illustrated by Graham Philpot. New York, Greenwillow, 1992.
Stopping for a Spell, illustrated by Joseph A. Smith. New York, Greenwillow, 1993.

Other

My Brother and I Like Cookies (cookie recipes), with Anna L. Carlson, illustrated by author. Lynnwood, Washington, Karwyn Enterprises, 1980.

PUBLICATION FOR ADULTS

Novel

Changeover. London, Macmillan, 1970.

*

Biography: Entry in *Fifth Book of Junior Authors,* New York, H.W. Wilson, 1983; essay in *Something about the Author Autobiography Series,* Volume 7, Detroit, Gale, 1989; essay in *Speaking for Ourselves, Too* compiled and edited by Donald R. Gallo, National Council of Teachers of English, 1993.

Critical Study: Entry in *Contemporary Literary Criticism,* Volume 26, Detroit, Gale, 1983.

Illustrator: *The Cookie Looker* by Anna L. Carlson, 1980.

* * *

Diana Wynne Jones did not set out to become a "YA author." The literary form she chose was the longer children's fantasy, as perfected by E. Nesbit in which children, often undergoing some family stress (e.g. separation from their parents, poverty, illness), encounter magic, which causes them further problems. The resolution of the magical problems also deals with the real-life crisis in *The Ogre Downstairs:* remarriage forces five step-siblings to share the same household, and their continual feuding is complicated by the gift of a magic chemistry set to each sibling group.

In *Eight Days of Luke,* David, the orphaned boy-hero, accidentally summons up the Norse god Loki and finds the other gods in hot pursuit, while Loki pleads for David's protection. A reader ignorant of Norse mythology will learn more by reading the book, which is also notable for its incomplete happy ending more suited to a YA novel than a children's book: David's wicked cousins revealed as criminals make their getaway, and he becomes the responsibility of his (good) cousin's wife, who will presumably divorce, maybe remarry.

Dogsbody also looks forward to a future after the book's conclusion. The child-heroine is not the leading character: the immortal Sirius, the Dog Star, is sent to Earth to search for a cosmic weapon and enchanted into a puppy's body. He is taken into a family of Earth children, becoming the special pet of Kathleen, treated as a "dogsbody" or Cinderella-type by her foster family. When Sirius discovers his own starry Companion betrayed him and caused his punishment on Earth, he realises he would now only choose Kathleen as his new Companion—and how can that be? After her earthly death?

With *Cart and Cwidder, Power of Three,* and *Charmed Life,* Diana Wynne Jones introduced a theme into her fantasies which has now become her trademark. The hero/ine of her books is likely to grow up among magical folk, often in an alternative world where history ran differently, or a secondary fantasy world, but this hero/ine feels inadequate because s/he does not appear to have magic powers. Using his/her own resources to cope with the problems magic is causing, at the climax a crisis reveals that our hero/ine does truly possess magic powers, sometimes superior to the others, and certainly unique. This plot twist also occurs in *The Magicians of Caprona, Archer's Goon, The Spellcoats,* and *Howl's Moving Castle,* and in a modified way *Aunt Maria* (British title, *Black Maria*) where the heroine rejects the power offered because it is tainted.

Charmed Life, which introduces the good enchanter Chrestomanci, has several sequels, as Wynne Jones became fond of her alternative fantasy world where magic is real, licensed and run by the government to make sure it is used for good. Various crooked sorcerers try to operate independently and even overthrow Chrestomanci. *The Magicians of Caprona* is set in an alternative Italy, using a Romeo-and-Juliet plot with a happy ending. *The Lives of Christopher Chant* is about Chrestomanci's childhood.

Nearly all Wynne Jones's books may be classified as domestic fantasy, as magic disrupts ordinary life, sometimes combined with high fantasy, as gods and goddesses become involved. Only a few belong to other supernatural genres: *Witch Week* and *The Time of the Ghost* are ghost-horror stories, with a twist: the witches in the former are children, desperately hiding their powers from a hostile State; the ghost in the latter is benign, but under the curse of a pagan goddess. Wynne Jones's two science fiction novels are based on the concept of alternative worlds (*The Homeward Bounders*) and the Time Patrol which prevents the bad guys changing history (*A Tale of Time City*).

Although most of her leading characters are too young for romance, Wynne Jones may nevertheless be claimed as a young adult author for her development of the "rite-of-passage" theme in a fantasy context. The youngster, aged between ten and thirteen, undergoes a crisis which results in the recognition of his/her powers, enhanced stature within the family, and feet set firmly on a career of using magic for good. It is also clear from the length of her books, their complex plots, and range of literary allusions to myths and other cultures that many youngsters will not be ready for them until they are teenagers. One must stress here how readable, funny, enjoyable, and "unputdownable" they are: they extend their readers, and the taste for her books is known to be addictive, for her adult fans as well as teenagers.

This is not all she offers young adult readers. In 1985 she began a series of romantic fantasies about a girl's (or boy's) first love, which is eventually requited. These are *Fire and Hemlock, Howl's Moving Castle,* and *Castle in the Air. Fire and Hemlock* is set in our world, now, and precisely charts the experience of the teenage "crush" on an older student or teacher. In real life, of course, the "crush" is best left unspoken and is generally unrequited, and even in this fantasy the girl cannot become an independent person until she turns her back on her dream lover. Maybe, after the book's ending, they reunite... The story describes a network of witchcraft centred on the court of the Faerie Queen, as in the "Tam Lin" ballad. Every nine years she takes a new lover, and the old lover is sacrificed to extend her consort's life, or her own life every eighty-one years. The Fairy Court schemes to prevent our heroine Polly saving Tom's life, and then to recruit her as the next female sacrifice: all is gradually revealed in this extraordinarily long, addictive read.

Howl's Moving Castle, of a more manageable length, is one of Wynne Jones's most perfect works. Attractive Sophie is cursed by the Witch of the Waste into the shape of an old woman, and bluffs her way into Wizard Howl's castle in search of a counter-spell. The wizard turns out to be youthful and immature; his fire demon promises to remove the spell if Sophie does him a good turn, but can't explain how she is to perform it. In the sequel, *Castle in the Air,* Wynne Jones creates a superb pastiche of the world of the Arabian Nights, and also provides a glimpse of Sophie's married life.

So far Wynne Jones has hardly written for adults, though she would say that most of her children's fantasies also function on an adult level; however, in publishing terms, she has written a few commissioned short stories and one adult fantasy. This, *A Sudden Wild Magic,* defies generic rules. It is for adults; the leading characters are all ages from late teenage upwards, and their partnerings are relevant to the plot; but sexual behaviour is not explicitly described, so it may be stocked in a young adult library. It has an extravagant plot and a typical surprise climax. The plot concerns dealings between our world and an alternate world which is plundering our scientific ideas, and is a fascinating mix of science fiction and sorcery which Wynne Jones's readers will eagerly devour.

Finally to Diana Wynne Jones's contribution to the "secondary world" aspect of high fantasy, the Dalemark Quartet. Dalemark resembles Scandinavia in its North, South Wales, and the Cotswolds in the South and, although it may be situated in our world, it has remained isolated. Magic is occasionally wielded by the Undying, by their favoured humans, or by renegade mages. As the epic opens, Dalemark has been divided for centuries into free North and authoritarian South, each split into several earldoms. The Southern earls are tyrants and their citizens dream of being liberated by the North. In the first book, *Cart and Cwidder,* a boy minstrel, Moril, is involved in smuggling a Northern earl's son from South to North; in the second, *Drowned Ammet,* a young spy, Mitt, narrowly escapes becoming an assassin, and flees North by sea. Both encounter or wield magic during their adventures. In the third, *The Spellcoats,* we go back to the founding of Dalemark when the chief God, the One, struggles to unite feuding tribes against the evil mage Kankredin, who wishes to enslave them and rule Dalemark forever. In the fourth book, *The Crown of Dalemark,* Moril and Mitt team up to look for the Crown and discover the person who will become the new king. In their quest they meet several Undying from *The Spellcoats.* Some useful points are made about political manipulation and the drive for power versus the impulse towards altruism: the good characters know that an uprising to liberate the South will result in many innocent deaths, but to do nothing leaves the Southerners prey to tyranny, while the Northern earls are corrupted by the need to employ spies and assassins. A vision of Dalemark 200 years after, in modern times, reveals a peaceful country which reveres the memory of the king who united it. Only recently completed, the Dalemark Quartet must stand as one of our author's greatest achievements.

—Jessica Yates

———

JORDAN, June. Pseudonym for June Meyer. American. Born in New York City, 9 July 1936. Educated at Midwood High School, Brooklyn, New York; Northfield School for Girls, Massachusetts, 1950-53; Barnard College, New York, 1953-55, 1956-57; University of Chicago, 1955-56. Married Michael Meyer in 1955 (divorced 1966), one son. Assistant to the producer of the film *The Cool World,* 1964; research associate, Mobilization for Youth Inc., New York, 1965-66; director, Voice of the Children, 1967-70; member of the English Department, City College, New York, 1967-70, 1972-75, and 1977-78, Connecticut College, New London, 1968, Sarah Lawrence College, Bronxville, New York, 1971-75, and Yale University, New Haven, Connecticut, 1974-75; Associate Professor, 1978-82, Professor of English, 1982-89, and director of the Poetry Center and the Creative Writing Program, 1986-89, State University of New York, Stony Brook. Chancellor's Lecturer, 1986, and since 1989 Professor of Afro-American studies and women's studies, University of California, Berkeley. Poet-in-residence, Teachers and Writers Collaborative, New York, 1966-68, MacAlester College, St. Paul, Minnesota, 1980, Loft Mentor Series, Minneapolis, 1983, and Walt Whitman Birthplace, Huntington, New York, 1988; Reid Lecturer, Barnard College, 1976; playwright-in-residence, New Dramatists, New York, 1987-88; Visiting Professor, Department of Afro-American Studies, University of Wisconsin, Madison, summer 1988. Political columnist, *The Progressive* magazine, since 1989, and *City Limits,* London, since 1990. Recipient: Rockefeller grant, 1969; American Academy in Rome Environmental Design prize, 1970; American Library Association Best Young Adult Book, 1970, for *Soulscript,* and 1971, for *His Own Where;*

Nancy Bloch Memorial award, 1971, for *The Voice of the Children;* National Book award finalist, and selected one of *New York Times'* Outstanding Young Adult Novels, both 1971, both for *His Own Where; New Life: New Room* was selected a Notable Children's Trade Book in the Field of Social Studies by the National Council for Social Studies and the Children's Book Council, and one of Child Study Association of America's Children's Books of the Year, both 1975; New York Council of the Humanities award, 1977; Creative Artists Public Service grant, 1978; Yaddo fellowship, 1979, 1980; *His Own Where* was selected one of New York Public Library's Books for the Teen Age, 1980; National Endowment for the Arts fellowship, 1982; National Association of Black Journalists award, 1984; New York Foundation for the Arts fellowship, 1985; Massachusetts Council on the Arts award, 1985, for essay "On the Difficult Miracle of Black Poetry, or Something Like a Sonnet for Phillis Wheatley"; MacDowell Colony fellowship, 1987; Nora Astorga Leadership award, 1989. Agent: Roberta Pryor, International Creative Management, 40 West 57th St., New York, NY 10019. Address: Department of Afro-American Studies, 3335 Dwinelle Hall, Berkeley, CA 94720, U.S.A.

PUBLICATIONS FOR YOUNG ADULTS

Fiction

His Own Where. New York, Crowell, 1971.
New Life: New Room, illustrated by Ray Cruz. New York, Crowell, 1975.
Kimako's Story, illustrated by Kay Burford. Boston, Houghton Mifflin, 1981.

Verse

Who Look at Me? New York, Crowell, 1969.

Other

Dry Victories. New York, Holt Rinehart, 1972.
Fannie Lou Hamer (biography), illustrated by Albert Williams. New York, Crowell, 1972.
Editor, with Terri Bush, *The Voice of the Children.* New York, Holt Rinehart, 1970.
Editor, *Soulscript: Afro-American Poetry.* New York, Doubleday, 1970.

PUBLICATIONS FOR ADULTS

Plays

In the Spirit of Sojourner Truth, (produced New York, 1979).
For the Arrow That Flies by Day, (produced New York, 1981).
Freedom Now Suite, music by Adrienne B. Torf (produced New York, 1984).
The Break, music by Adrienne B. Torf (produced New York, 1984).
The Music of Poetry and the Poetry of Music, music by Adrienne B. Torf (produced Washington, D.C., and New York, 1984).
Bang Bang Über Alles, music by Adrienne B. Torf, lyrics by Jordan (produced by Atlanta, 1986).

Verse

Some Changes. New York, Dutton, 1971.
Poem: On Moral Leadership as a Political Dilemma (Watergate, 1973). Detroit, Broadside Press, 1973.
New Days: Poems of Exile and Return. New York, Emerson Hall, 1973.
Okay Now. New York, Simon and Schuster, 1977.
Things That I Do in the Dark: Selected Poetry. New York, Random House, 1977; revised edition, Boston, Beacon Press, 1981.
Passion: New Poems, 1977-1980. Boston, Beacon Press, 1980.
Living Room. New York, Thunder's Mouth Press, 1985.
High Tide—Marea Alta. Willimantic, Connecticut, Curbstone Press, 1987.
Lyrical Campaigns: Selected Poems. London, Virago Press, 1989.
Naming Our Destiny: New and Selected Poems. New York, Thunder's Mouth Press, 1989.

Recordings: *Things That I Do in the Dark and Other Poems,* Spoken Arts, 1978; *For Somebody to Start Singing,* with Bernice Reagon, Black Box-Watershed, 1979.

Other

Civil Wars (essays). Boston, Beacon Press, 1981.
Bobo Goetz a Gun. Willimantic, Connecticut, Curbstone Press, 1985.
On Call: Political Essays 1981-1985. Boston, South End Press, 1985.
Moving Towards Home: Political Essays. London, Virago Press, 1989.
Technical Difficulties: African American Notes on the State of the Union. New York, Pantheon Books, 1992.

*

Biography: Entry in *Dictionary of Literary Biography,* Detroit, Gale, Volume 38, 1985; essay in *Authors and Artists for Young Adults,* Detroit, Gale, Volume 2, 1989.

Manuscript Collection: Radcliffe Schlesinger Archives, Harvard University, Cambridge, Massachusetts.

Critical Study: Entry in *Children's Literature Review,* Volume 10, Detroit, Gale, 1986.

Also author of *The Issue.* Author of column "The Black Poet Speaks of Poetry," *American Poetry Review,* 1974-77; contributing editor for *Chrysalis, First World,* and *Hoo Doo.* Contributor of stories and poems (prior to 1969 under name June Meyer) to national periodicals, including *Esquire, Nation, Evergreen, Partisan Review, Negro Digest, Harper's Bazaar, Library Journal, Encore, Freedomways, New Republic, Ms., American Dialog, New Black Poetry, Black World, Black Creation, Essence,* and to newspapers including *Village Voice, New York Times,* and *New York Times Magazine.*

*   *   *

June Jordan is a versatile writer known primarily as a poet who is also recognized as a political commentator. Her book *Civil Wars* was the first collection of political essays "to be published by a black woman in the United States." She has combined her artistic vision as a poet and her social commitment as an educator and activist in several books for young readers which concentrate on some of the circumstances facing African American children growing up on the streets of America's older cities. These works have been written with an attentive ear for the rhythms and vocabulary of black colloquial speech and join the social and cultural details of African American life with situations and problems common to young people anywhere. While these books are directed toward an audience approximately the age of their oldest characters, a sense of pervasive pressures accelerating the process of maturation makes them appropriate for young adult readers. *Kimako's Story* is narrated by a girl "seven going on eight" whose introduction to the exhilarating strangeness of street life in New York City carries her beyond the familiar concerns of someone her age, while *New Life: New Room* shows three children ages six through ten who must rearrange their already cramped living space to accommodate a new baby. Their ingenious, cooperative responses to the limits they face and the decisions they are forced to make indicate a maturity exceeding their relative youth.

Similarly, while her short novel *His Own Where* follows its sixteen-year-old protagonist Buddy Rivers for several months at a pivotal point in his life, Jordan's goals and strategies tend to restrict its potential audience to those young adults who are inquisitive, intellectually adventurous, and emotionally mature enough to appreciate an unconventional and distinctly original approach. Jordan has set the entire narrative focus within the mind of her protagonist and the novel advances as a series of image-impressions and thoughts akin to a Joycean stream-of-conscious projection of personality. In addition, she has chosen to use the narration as a demonstration of the linguistic vitality and literary possibilities of so-called "Black English," deftly fusing more conventional syntactic patterns with a carefully nuanced, creative and poetic "voice" that is effective in conveying Buddy's reactions and ideas. Although Buddy is often reflective and philosophical, the narration is almost entirely set in an ongoing present that infuses it with an energy and immediacy that enables Jordan to give Buddy a singularly individual style as well as a representative responsiveness to the emergence of Black Pride in the 1960s.

As the novel begins, Buddy's father is in critical condition in a hospital following a serious automobile accident. During his vigil at his father's bedside, Buddy meets Angela Figueroa, the daughter of a nurse on the hospital staff, and their relationship is dramatically intensified at an early stage when her father beats her in an alcoholic explosion of misguided disciplinary desperation. After Buddy takes her to the emergency room following her father's attack, they both realize that they are essentially removed from the protection and support of their families and that the various social services set up to provide some assistance are basically irrelevant. Instinctively, they move toward each other in an attempt to form a new family unit. They are teenagers on the threshold of adulthood forced to make choices without adequate preparation but aware that they are on a track toward a life of acquiescence, suppressed anger, and constant frustration interrupted by aimless outbursts of indulgence leading to incarceration, addiction, or death. Jordan has employed the traditional coming-of-age theme in a setting which demands an unusually rapid reaction to the changes brought on by physical maturity. One of the most appealing aspects of the two central characters is their understanding of the responsibilities of an adult's freedom to choose. Nonetheless, their choices are difficult and their time spent together is marked by uncertainty.

Jordan has made both Buddy and Angela sympathetic and engaging, writing with a straightforward candor that avoids condescension. As they struggle to find a place for themselves—the *Where* of the title—Jordan emphasizes their resilience, decency, and consideration for each other. The goal of their journey is a kind of private sanctuary (ironically located in a cemetery), a safe space both within and around them, and Jordan's social critique has made it clear that the various institutions supposed to provide guidance and assistance have failed due to the inherent hostility, indifference, and racism embedded in the authoritarian structures that reflect contemporary society. In their tentative steps toward selfhood and a measure of independence, Buddy and Angela are supported by their dreams of a community of fellowship, their vision of beauty amidst grime and decay, and their developing feelings for each other. Jordan does not underplay the force of their physical attraction, and their desire to conceive a child is acknowledged as an effort to fashion a new beginning but not endorsed as a wise choice. In her use of vivid poetic imagery, however, Jordan suggests that their mutual sensuality transcends the merely physical, expanding their sexual impulses into an emblem of a sustaining life force. Because she never avoids the most unsettling aspects of their life, her brief, intense glimpse at Buddy and Angela resonates with a kind of truth that an accomplished young adult can recognize and appreciate.

—Leon Lewis

JUDY, Stephen. See **TCHUDI, Stephen N.**

JUSTER, Norton. American. Born in Brooklyn, New York, 2 June 1929. Educated at the University of Pennsylvania, Philadelphia, B. Arch. 1952; University of Liverpool (Fulbright scholar), 1952-53. Served in the United States Naval Reserve Civil Engineer Corps, 1954-57. Married Jeanne Ray in 1964. Architect, Juster and Gugliotta, New York, 1960-68; adjunct professor in environmental design, Pratt Institute, New York, 1960-70. Since 1969 architect, Juster-Pope-Frazier Associates, Shelburne Falls, Massachusetts, and since 1992 Emeritus Professor of Design, Hampshire College, Amherst, Massachusetts. Recipient: Fulbright fellowship, 1952-53; Ford Foundation grant, 1960-61; National Academy of Arts and Sciences award for outstanding achievement, 1968-69; Guggenheim fellowship, 1970-71; George G. Stone Center for Children's Books Seventh Recognition of Merit, 1971. Agent: Sterling Lord Literistic, 1 Madison Avenue, New York, NY 10010. Address: 259 Lincoln Avenue, Amherst, MA 01002, U.S.A.

PUBLICATIONS FOR YOUNG ADULTS

Fiction

The Phantom Tollbooth, illustrated by Jules Feiffer. New York, Epstein and Carroll, 1961; London, Collins, 1962.

The Dot and the Line: A Romance in Lower Mathematics. New York, Random House, 1963; London, Nelson, 1964.
Alberic the Wise and Other Journeys, illustrated by Domenico Gnoli. New York, Pantheon, 1965; London, Nelson, 1966; reprinted as *Alberic the Wise,* illustrated by Leonard Baskinow, Saxonville, Massachusetts, Picture Book Studios, 1992.

Verse

Otter Nonsense, illustrated by Eric Carle. New York, Philomel, 1982; London, Faber, 1983.
As: A Surfeit of Similes, illustrated by David Small. New York, Morrow, 1989.

Other

Stark Naked: A Paranomastic Odyssey, illustrated by Arnold Roth. New York, Random House, 1969.
So Sweet to Labor: Rural Women in America 1865-1895. New York, Viking Press, 1979.

*

Media Adaptations: *The Dot and the Line* (film), MGM, 1965; *The Phantom Tollbooth* (film), MGM, 1970.

*   *   *

Norton Juster's *The Phantom Tollbooth* has proven to be timeless. Its survival on the shelves for over thirty years attests to its success. This fantasy novel presents a rare combination of a convincing, well-rounded secondary world with a rollicking use of wordplay that proves both entertaining and provocative. The Lands Beyond presents a unique world where nonsense is grounded in logic. The tale explores the fantasy quest of the young, disenchanted Milo who overcomes his discontent through his adventure in the fantasy realm. As is common to many young protagonists of this mode of fantasy, including Alice of *Alice in Wonderland,* and Dorothy of *The Wizard of Oz,* Milo is bored to distraction. Through a quest in the fantasy reality, Milo gains the survival tactics to find inspiration in his real world.

Milo proves himself ripe for adventure as he suffers from a consuming disinterest in all things. The crown of his apathy is his belief that the pursuit of knowledge presents the greatest waste of time of all. His summons into the fantasy realm occurs one typically dull day when a mysterious package containing a scaled-down genuine turnpike tollbooth appears in Milo's bedroom. As there seems to be nothing better to do, Milo assembles the package. He passes through the tollbooth in his small electric car and finds himself racing along a beautiful highway in the Lands Beyond.

Within the fantasy reality, Milo's experiences allow him to achieve insight and ability that will prove relevant in his real world. Milo meets his first challenge in the Doldrums where he must overcome the temptation of the Lethargarians—a species of apathetic creatures whose lifestyle is reminiscent of Milo's own. He manages to escape by utilizing his intellectual might. In so doing, Milo effectively leaves his old lifestyle behind and begins his journey towards learning the power of knowledge.

Milo is joined by a guide, a ticking watchdog named Tock. Together they journey to the city of Dictionopolis and learn that something is amiss in this kingdom founded on knowledge. Since the banishment of the princesses, Rhyme and Reason, wisdom has been robbed of its logic, and nonsense is sweeping the land. Milo takes on the task of rescuing the princesses. His quest takes him across the Lands Beyond towards the Mountains of Ignorance.

His journey allows him to collect the tools of knowledge that will allow him to battle the demons who rule in the realm of Ignorance. He receives from King Azaz, ruler of Dictionopolis, a box containing all the words the king knows. In the Forest of Sight, Milo learns that perception depends on point of view, and receives a telescope that will allow him to see things as they are. In the valley of sound, Milo receives from the Soundkeeper a collection of beautiful sounds. From the Mathemagician, ruler of Digitopolis, Milo receives a magic staff—a gleaming pencil with which to calculate. Thus equipped, Milo ventures into the Mountains of Ignorance in search of the Castle in the Air where the princesses are imprisoned.

In this realm where wisdom does not rule, Milo encounters and overcomes various demons who are the manifestations of ignorance. He overcomes the Everpresent Wordsnatcher, the Terrible Trivium, the Demon of Insincerity, the Gelatinous Giant, and the Senses Taker, all by employing the gifts of knowledge he had received throughout his journey. Upon finding the Princesses, Milo confides in them his new discovery—"there's so much to learn." He brings Rhyme and Reason back to the kingdom and returns to the city of Wisdom a hero.

Milo has also succeeded in returning rhyme and reason to his own existence, as is evident upon his return home. Now, even in absence of a quest that requires the use of his wit and intelligence, Milo's mind is open to the pursuit of knowledge. Milo realizes that there in his own room exists "all the puzzle and excitement of everything he didn't know." He brings into his reality the boon of his fantasy adventure—the appreciation of the pursuit of knowledge that will alleviate his life of his once profound boredom. Milo demonstrates his recovery from his affliction of apathy, when despite his desire to return to the Lands Beyond, he admits, "I really don't know when I'll have the time. There's just so much to do right here."

In conveying this theme with clarity, Juster employs in his narrative a brilliant use of language that renders concepts literal through wordplay. For example, Milo travels in a vehicle that runs only when all is quiet, for "it goes without saying." At a banquet in Dictionopolis, he regrets his dry pre-meal speech, for everyone there must eat their words. In Digitopolis, Milo only gets hungrier as he feasts on subtraction stew. Despite this nonsense that renders the obscure literal and the literal obscure, the theme of wisdom versus ignorance gives clear sense and logic to this fantasy realm where art and science become two distinct cities, and the senses translate into places on the map. In all cases, knowledge serves as power and ignorance proves debilitating. The entertaining and provoking presence of nonsense and wordplay harken back to Carroll's *Alice in Wonderland,* while the precision with which Juster creates a logical fantasy reality has more in common with the secondary world creators, Le Guin and Tolkien.

The narrative about a young protagonist presents the plot with clarity, rendering the novel accessible to younger readers. Yet, with age and repeated readings, the book reveals depth in its layers of meaning, creating a tale that promises to engage all ages. The same holds true for Juster's shorter works, directed more specifically to younger children, yet still satisfying for more advanced readers.

—Susan Rich

K

KAMM, Josephine. British. Born in London, 30 December 1905. Educated at Queen's College School, London, 1915-17; Parents' National Educational School, Burgess Hill, Sussex, 1917-23; Triangle Secretarial College, London, 1923. Married George Emile Kamm in 1929 (died); one son. Shorthand typist, British Commonwealth Union, London, 1924-26; assistant secretary, Empire Industries Association, London, 1926-29; shorthand typist, then senior information officer, Ministry of Information, London, 1939-46; senior information officer, Central Office of Information, London, 1946; writer. Member of National Council, 1957-69, and Executive Committee, 1963-69, National Book League; member of Executive Committee, London Centre of PEN International, 1965-69; member of Committee of Management, Fawcett Library, London, 1967-75; Society of Authors. Recipient: Jewish Book Council of America Isaac Siegel Memorial award, 1962, for *Return to Freedom. Died 31 August 1989.*

PUBLICATIONS FOR YOUNG ADULTS

Fiction

He Went with Captain Cook, illustrated by G.S. Ronalds. London, Harrap, 1952.
Janet Carr, Journalist. London, Lane, 1953; revised edition, Leicester, Brockhampton Press, 1972.
Student Almoner. London, Lane, 1955.
Out of Step, illustrated by Jillian Willett. Leicester, Brockhampton Press, 1962.
Return to Freedom, illustrated by William Stobbs. London and New York, Abelard Schuman, 1962.
Young Mother. Leicester, Brockhampton Press, and New York, Duell, 1965.
No Strangers Here. London, Constable, 1968.
First Job. Leicester, Brockhampton Press, 1969.
Where Do We Go from Here? Leicester, Brockhampton Press, 1972.
The Starting Point. Leicester, Brockhampton Press, 1975.
Runaways. London, Hodder & Stoughton, 1978.

Other

Abraham: A Biography, with Philip Cohen. London, Union of Liberal and Progressive Synagogues, 1948.
They Served the People (biographies). London, Lane, 1954.
Men Who Served Africa, illustrated by G.S. Ronalds. London, Harrap, 1957.
Leaders of the People. London and New York, Abelard Schuman, 1959.
The Story of Sir Moses Montefiore. London, Vallentine Mitchell, 1960.
The Story of Mrs. Pankhurst, illustrated by Faith Jaques. London, Methuen, 1961; as *The Story of Emmeline Pankhurst,* New York, Meredith Press, 1968.
Malaria Ross, illustrated by Anne Linton. London, Methuen, 1963; New York, Criterion, 1964.
Malaya and Singapore, illustrated by W.B. White and A.W. Gatnell. London, Longman, 1963.

A New Look at the Old Testament, illustrated by Gwyneth Cole. London, Gollancz, 1965; as *Kings, Prophets, and History,* New York, McGraw-Hill, 1966.
The Story of Fanny Burney, illustrated by Val Biro. London, Methuen, 1966; New York, Meredith Press, 1967.
The Hebrew People: A History of the Jews from Biblical Times to the Present Day. London, Gollancz, 1967; as *The Hebrew People: A History of the Jews,* New York, McGraw-Hill, 1968.
Joseph Paxton and the Crystal Palace, illustrated by Faith Jaques. London, Methuen, 1967.
Explorers into Africa. London, Gollancz, and New York, Crowell Collier, 1970.
Editor, *A Tale of Two Cities,* by Charles Dickens, illustrated by Barry Wilkinson. London, Collins, 1973.
The Slave Trade. London, Evans, 1980.

PUBLICATIONS FOR ADULTS

Novels

All Quiet at Home. London, Longman, 1936.
Disorderly Caravan. London, Harrap, 1938.
Nettles to My Head. London, Duckworth, 1939.
Peace, Perfect Peace. London, Duckworth, 1947.
Come, Draw This Curtain. London, Duckworth, 1948.

Other

Progress Toward Self-Government in the British Colonies. London, Fosh & Cross, 1945.
African Challenge: The Story of the British in Tropical Africa. London, Nelson, 1946.
Daughter of the Desert: The Story of Gertrude Bell. London, Lane, 1956; as *Gertrude Bell, Daughter of the Desert,* New York, Vanguard Press, 1956.
How Different from Us: A Biography of Miss Buss and Miss Beale. London, Bodley Head, 1958.
Hope Deferred: Girls' Education in English History. London, Methuen, 1965.
Rapiers and Battleaxes: The Women's Movement and Its Aftermath. London, Allen & Unwin, 1966.
Indicative Past: A Hundred Years of the Girls' Public Day School Trust. London, Allen & Unwin, 1971.
John Stuart Mill in Love. London, Gordon & Cremonesi, 1977.

*   *   *

When Josephine Kamm died in 1989, one of her obituarists, while acknowledging that in the 1960s she "pushed back the frontiers of teenage fiction" in Britain with her novels *Out of Step, Young Mother,* and *No Strangers Here,* also remarked that these books appear "squeaky clean and innocent" compared with present-day writing for young adults. This is true, if it means that Kamm examined teenage life within a context of social values which are less widely agreed upon today, but the comment also pinpoints the principal problem in evaluating Kamm's novels within this genre. It is the fate of any book which strives to deal with contemporary problems through a meticulous re-creation of life that, thirty years on, will have become literally a "period piece." It is therefore impossible to understand the impact of Kamm's work in the 1960s if one reads it as if it were written in and for the 1990s; *Out of Step* and *Young Mother,* along with the other books published between 1962 and 1978, are now best viewed historically, as a response to the challenge of writing for young adults at the time when the genre was in its infancy in America, and in Britain was virtually nonexistent.

Before embarking on the series of young adult novels for which she is probably best remembered Kamm had already written for adolescents as well as for adults. In the 1950s she published biographies intended for a young readership, reflecting her interest in Jewish affairs *(Leaders of the People; The Story of Sir Moses Montefiore)* and the British Commonwealth *(They Served the People; Men Who Served Africa).* The most ambitious of these is *Daughter of the Desert,* an account of the life of the British scholar and traveller Gertrude Bell. Although perhaps too respectful toward its subject for modern taste, the beginnings of the insight and scholarship which would mark Kamm's later biographies for adults are present. This prolific writer continued to publish books on these themes throughout the 1960s and 1970s. Her patient research is most evident in her one historical novel, *Return to Freedom,* an award-winning book, set in seventeenth-century London, which tells the story of Oliver Cromwell's attempts to revoke a 400-year-old edict prohibiting Jews from settling in England. Although the narrative is initially slowed down by more historical detail than present-day teenagers find palatable, the story is unusual and told with both skill and sympathy. The character of Cromwell, not superficially attractive, is particularly well-drawn.

In the 1950s, Kamm also wrote two "career novels," *Janet Carr, Journalist* and *Student Almoner,* titles in a series intended to give teenage girls insight into a variety of careers. Although the series is interesting historically, as one of the first attempts in Britain to cater to a specifically young adult readership, the characterisation of Janet Carr and Barbara Henderson, the trainee hospital social worker, inevitably suffers because Kamm's remit was to convey career information. These are not among her most successful novels, but they were important in Kamm's development as a young adult writer. They gave her the idea for other books in which, unconstrained by formulaic conventions, she could choose and develop her own themes.

It is difficult now to realise just how revolutionary Kamm's teenage novels seemed in Britain in the early 1960s; the wonder is not that, in accordance with the convention of the day, they were inexplicit, but that they were so frank. During the 1950s the book establishment had been edging towards the perception that teenagers, as a recently defined "group," might merit a literature of their own; Kamm's stories of young adults coping with single parenthood, mixed-race relationships, adoption, and early marriage established her as a pioneer in this genre. There are, perhaps, "stock situations," but the narratives are strong and there are no stock characters—although the need to explore problems in depth sometimes means that characters are less fully rounded than an adult reader might wish. Thus her most successful books are those with the fewest characters.

Young Mother, the most famous of Kamm's books and still in print in 1992, tells the story of schoolgirl Pat Henley's pregnancy with a brave honesty, remarkable when one reflects that Kamm was in her late fifties when she wrote it. The embarrassment and tedium of Pat's experience, and her doomed efforts to keep her child, are

well described; although changes in social attitudes have inevitably dated her stories, Kamm's nonjudgmental view of the young, her humanity and determination to eschew facile resolutions, give them lasting appeal.

Only those young in the 1960s can fully appreciate Kamm's evocation of that restless decade—the loving observation of London life, the self-importance and self-doubt of a young generation sensing emancipation, the determination of their parents to criticise what they could understand perfectly well. This atmosphere is caught most poignantly in *Out of Step,* the love story of Betty Fielding and her West Indian boyfriend, Bob Francis, which unfolds against a working-class background, at a time of low aspirations, full but undemanding employment, and cruel prejudice. British racism is indignantly exposed, and this excellent novel is read with an awareness that, although Kamm's work may be taking its place in history, many of the questions she raised then are yet to be answered.

—Eileen Dunlop

KEITH, Harold (Verne). American. Born in Lambert, Oklahoma Territory, 8 April 1903. Educated at Lambert High School, graduated 1921; Northwestern State College, Alva, Oklahoma (Scroll scholarship, 1922), 1921-24; University of Oklahoma, Norman, B.A. in history 1929, M.A., 1938, special courses in professional writing, 1953-56. Married Virginia Livingston in 1931; one son and one daughter. Elementary school teacher, Amorita Consolidated School System, Oklahoma, seventh-grade, 1922-23; sports correspondent, *Daily Oklahoman, Tulsa World, Kansas City Star,* and *Omaha World-Herald,* 1922-29; assistant to grain buyer, Red Star Milling Co., Hutchinson, Kansas, 1929-30; sports publicity director, University of Oklahoma, Norman, 1930-69. President, College Sports Information Directors, 1964-65. Set U.S. Masters national records for the two- and three-mile runs, 1973, and 10,000 meters run, 1974. Recipient: Helms Foundation Sports Publicist of the Year, 1950; American Library Association Newbery Medal for *Rifles for Watie,* 1958; Arch Ward Memorial Trophy for outstanding achievement in sports publicity, 1961; Charlie May Simon award for *The Runt of Rogers School;* Western Writers of America Spur award and Western Heritage award for *Susy's Scoundrel,* 1975; Western Heritage award for *The Obstinate Land,* 1979. Agent: Oscar Collier, Collier Associates, 280 Madison Avenue, New York, NY, 10016. Address: 2318 Ravenwood Lane, Hall Park, Route 4, Norman, OK 72071, U.S.A.

PUBLICATIONS FOR YOUNG ADULTS

Fiction

Shotgun Shaw: A Baseball Story, illustrated by Mabel Jones Woodbury. New York, Crowell, 1949.
A Pair of Captains, illustrated by Mabel Jones Woodbury. New York, Crowell, 1951.
Rifles for Watie. New York, Crowell, 1957.
Komantcia. New York, Crowell, 1965.

Brief Garland. New York, Crowell, 1971.
The Runt of Rogers School. Philadelphia, Lippincott, 1971.
The Bluejay Boarders, illustrated by Harold Berson. New York, Crowell, 1972.
Go Red, Go!, illustrated by Ned Glattauer. Nashville, Nelson, 1972.
Susy's Scoundrel, illustrated by John Schoenherr. New York, Crowell, 1974.
The Obstinate Land. New York, Crowell, 1977.
The Sound of Strings. Norman, Oklahoma, Levite of Apache Publishing, 1992.

Nonfiction

Boys' Life of Will Rogers, illustrated by Karl S. Woerner. New York, Crowell, 1937; as *Will Rogers, a Boy's Life: An Indian Territory Childhood,* Norman, Oklahoma, Levite of Apache Publishing, 1992.
Sports and Games. New York, Crowell, 1941; revised edition, 1960.

PUBLICATIONS FOR ADULTS

Nonfiction

Oklahoma Kickoff. Privately printed, 1948.
Forty-Seven Straight: The Wilkinson Era at Oklahoma. Norman, University of Oklahoma Press, 1984.

*

Biography: Entry in *Children and Books,* 3rd edition, edited by May Hill Arbuthnot, Glenview, Illinois, Scott, Foresman, 1964; *Books and the Teen-Age Reader* by G. Robert Carlson, New York, Harper, 1967; *Children's Literature in the Elementary School* edited by Charlotte S. Hack, New York, Holt, 1961; *Newbery and Caldecott Medal Books: 1956-1965* edited by Lee Kingman, Boston, Massachusetts, Horn Book, 1965.

Manuscript Collections: Northwestern State College Library, Alva, Oklahoma; University of Oklahoma Library, Norman.

*   *   *

Harold Vernon Keith's father was a grain buyer, so the family moved many times and Harold attended nine different schools. Perhaps this satisfied any wanderlust the young boy ever had, because for well over half a century he has been deeply rooted in the soil and history of Oklahoma, living in Norman for sixty-seven years and earning his state's Lifetime Achievement Book Award and membership in the Oklahoma Writer's Hall of Fame. Beginning writers are often advised to write what they know, and Keith thoroughly embraced the old principle, writing almost entirely for boys, about sports, and setting his stories in the heartland of America.

Sports has been his lifelong interest, both as observer and participant. He was sports editor of his high-school magazine and spent thirty-nine years as varsity publicist for the University of Oklahoma. His athletic career is incredible. He won the Penn Relays steeplechase as an undergraduate—despite having never run one before, the Oklahoma Athletic Union's cross-country race at age forty-two, and he set a U.S. Masters Association record for the three-mile run for men seventy and over. For much of his career, he

wrote almost entirely about sports in article and book form. One of his earliest books *Sports and Games* surveyed various recreational activities and sold well, becoming a Junior Literary Guild selection.

As a teacher for the Amorita school district he had close experience with the interests and dreams of children, and other than his publicity and a behind-the-scenes book about University of Oklahoma football, most of his writing has been for adolescent boys. *The Runt of Rogers School,* for instance, concerned boys of short stature attempting to compete in athletics. Of normal height himself, Keith talked with numerous short athletes to gain insight into the particular problems they might face. This concern with the reality of the characters and settings is one of the most important reasons Keith's writings stand out. His genuine interest in other people has allowed him to get close to his subjects and to use their experiences as the background of his fiction. This method of writing began with the work on his master's thesis, "Clem Rogers and His Influence on History," during which he made a large number of visits to eastern Oklahoma to interview people who had known the Rogers family. He then adapted his thesis into his first book, *Boy's Life of Will Rogers.*

His greatest fame was to come from his historical writings. Despite publishing regularly, he was dissatisfied with the level of his writing. He spent summers in the Professional Writing Program at the university, a course of study he still praises at every opportunity, saying he learned more in one class session than he had learned in years of trial and error. He had always considered plotting to be the easiest part of writing, whereas characters and the creation of scenes bedeviled him. As his characterization has always been one of his strong suits, one can assume the remark mainly illustrates his care in that area. The program emphasized the scene and sequel method, and combined with his research skills, historical interests, and insight into motivation, Keith soon reached the upper echelon of young adult authors.

In 1958, *Rifles for Watie* was awarded the thirty-seventh Newbery medal and its success illustrates how Keith's continuing attempts to improve his writing paid off. Young Jeff Bussey serves four years in the western Civil War, and becomes involved in finding out how General Stand Watie, who has been harrying Federal troops with Cherokee raiders, has gotten his rifles. This combination *Red Badge of Courage* and spy novel germinated through Keith's usual careful research. Not many veterans still lived from that war but Keith hunted up twenty-two of them, most nearly one hundred years old, and all Confederates. He immersed himself in the Western history materials of the university library, and while travelling with the football team visited historical societies and carefully read the diaries and letters of Union veterans. The result was highly praised for its vivid authenticity. One reviewer recommended it as supplemental historical reading for young adults, and the book is still used for that purpose. In 1992, for example, Keith was asked to speak to high schools students in several states about the book. What reviewers also highly praised, however, was his ability to convey all of this authenticity by means of a series of scenes which hurtled forward, never pausing in its action.

His *Komantcia,* a New York Times Best Book of 1965, was set among the Comanches. In his characteristic method he mined the collections at the university library and visited the tribe, who once ranged from Wyoming to Texas but had been forcibly resettled in Oklahoma. He even interviewed one of the wives of the Comanches' most famous chiefs, Quanah Parker. He gathered so much material, the publisher forced Keith to shorten the novel, and it was 1992 before *The Sound of Strings* was released as a sequel.

In the 1970s, Keith continued to win awards. *Susy's Scoundrel* won the Spur and Western Heritage Award. *The Obstinate Land* won a Western Heritage Award and was praised for being a convincing portrayal of a family striving to make a living in the harsh surroundings of the Cherokee Strip, an area in northern Oklahoma. Though his output was limited by his work as a publicist, Keith's careful attention to details and craftsmanship would probably have never allowed him to be a rapid writer. He approached writing doggedly, likening it to a long-distance run in which the competitor must keep moving even when exhausted. The high quality of his work and his amiable personality nonetheless has made him one of the most beloved writers in his home state and elsewhere.

—J. Madison Davis

————

KELL, Joseph. See **BURGESS, Anthony.**

————

KELLEHER, Victor (Michael Kitchener). British. Born in London, 19 July 1939. Educated at University of Natal, Pietermaritzburg, B.A. in English 1961; University of St. Andrews, Fife, Diploma in Education, 1963; University of the Witwatersrand, Johannesburg, B.A. (honors) 1969; University of South Africa, Pretoria, M.A. 1970, D.Litt. et Phil., 1973. Married Alison Lyle in 1962; one son and one daughter. Junior Lecturer in English, University of the Witwatersrand, 1969; Lecturer, 1970-71, Senior Lecturer in English, 1972-73, University of South Africa; Lecturer in English, Massey University, Palmerston North, New Zealand, 1973-76. Lecturer, 1976-79, Senior Lecturer, 1980-83, Associate Professor of English, 1984-87, University of New England, Armidale, New South Wales; writer. Recipient: Patricia Hackett Prize from *Westerly* magazine, 1978, for story "The Traveller"; senior writer's fellowship from the Literature Board of the Australia Council, 1982; West Australian Young Readers' Book award from the West Australian Library Association, 1982, for *Forbidden Paths of Thual;* West Australian Young Readers' Special award from the West Australian Library Association, 1983, for *The Hunting of Shadroth;* Australian Children's Book of the Year award from the Children's Book Council of Australia, 1983, for *Master of the Grove;* Australian Science Fiction Achievement award from the National Science Fiction Association, 1984, for *The Beast of Heaven;* Honour award from the Children's Book Council of Australia, 1987, for *Taronga;* Australian Children's Book Honor award, 1991, for *Brother Night.* Address: 149 Wigram Rd., Glebe, NSW 2037, Australia.

PUBLICATIONS FOR YOUNG ADULTS

Fiction

Forbidden Paths of Thual, illustrated by Antony Maitland. London, Viking Kestrel, and New York, Penguin Books, 1979.
The Hunting of Shadroth. London, Viking Kestrel, and New York, Penguin Books, 1981.

Master of the Grove. London, Viking Kestrel, and New York, Penguin Books, 1982.
The Green Piper. Melbourne, Viking Kestrel, and New York, Penguin Books, 1984; London, Viking Kestrel, 1985.
Papio: A Novel of Adventure. London, Viking Kestrel, and New York, Penguin Books, 1984.
Rescue! New York, Dial, 1985.
The Makers. New York, Penguin Books, 1986; Melbourne, Viking Kestrel, 1987.
Taronga. Melbourne, Viking Kestrel, and New York, Penguin Books, 1986; London, Hamish Hamilton, 1987.
Baily's Bones. Melbourne, Viking Kestrel, and New York, Dial, 1988.
Em's Story. St. Lucia, University of Queensland Press, 1988.
The Red King. New York, Dial, 1990.
Brother Night. New York, MacRae, 1991.
Voices from the River. St. Lucia, University of Queensland Press, 1991.
Del-Del, illustrated by Peter Clarke. New York, Walker, 1992.
Micky Darlin'. St. Lucia, University of Queensland Press, 1992.
To the Dark Tower. New York, MacRae, 1992.

PUBLICATIONS FOR ADULTS

Novels

Voices from the River. London, Heinemann, 1979.
The Beast of Heaven. St. Lucia, University of Queensland Press, 1984.
Wintering. St. Lucia, University of Queensland Press, 1990.

Short Stories

Africa and After. Brisbane, University of Queensland Press, 1983; as *The Traveller: Stories of Two Continents,* St. Lucia, University of Queensland Press, 1987.

* * *

Victor Kelleher is one of Australia's most outstanding writers of fantasy. Of his books for young people nine are fantasy novels, and seven of these have imaginary settings and involve quests. The adventure story *Papio,* a modern quest story, is the only novel without some supernatural element, whereas the effects of belief in the supernatural is a theme of the horror thriller *Del-Del.* Kelleher's writing for adults is more diverse in style and genre, but the intellectual and emotional challenges of his books are certainly not diminished for his younger readers.

The central precept of Victor Kelleher's writing is that things are not always what they seem. In all his novels the heroes struggle with hindrances to clear perception. His first three fantasy/quest adventures, *Forbidden Paths of Thual, The Hunting of Shadroth,* and *Master of the Grove,* involve young men setting out on dangerous although apparently straightforward missions. All find that the beliefs of their communities are based on false premises and each have to confront complex enemies, make difficult moral choices, and acknowledge the part chance plays in human lives. In the award-winning *Master of the Grove,* truth and falsehood are the heart of the novel. Derin, the hero, sets out on a quest accompanied by an old woman (Marna) and a raven to find his missing father. He doesn't know it, but Derin's mission is to unseat the evil Krob and restore peace to a war-torn land. But is witch Marna a friend or an enemy? He finds, right when he needs to know, that deception is his only protection from evil.

Concepts of truth, deception, and evil are related to control and power in the early novels and also in *The Makers, The Red King,* and *Brother Night*. All three are quest novels. *The Makers* is a disturbing book about a carefully controlled society which takes young children and trains them as warriors, telling them they have been made specifically for this purpose. There is a lighter touch in *The Red King* where Petie a magician, Timkin an acrobat, Crystal a monkey, and Bruno a bear seem an unlikely group to defeat the tyrant Red King who controls the forest kingdom. There is much trickery and confusion about good and evil as in *Master of the Grove*. Confusion also taunts the hero of Kelleher's most outstanding fantasy quest adventure to date, the richly symbolic *Brother Night*. The hero, Ramon, finds out that his mother is Pilar, the woman known by the village as the Moon Witch, and that he had a twin brother killed at birth because of his monstrous appearance. Ramon believes his father is the Sun Lord, Semlock, but why is Semlock trying to kill him? Ramon's giant and ugly brother, Lal, is not dead and together they set out for the Twin cities on tellingly different quests—Ramon to kill his father and compassionate, loving Lal to bury Pilar's bones.

Two novels, *Papio* and *Taronga,* look at animal-human relationships and *The Green Piper* is a horrific account of a strange plant-like creature with a hatred for flesh. Like the Pied Piper this creature attracts living things to it and destroys them. In *Papio* David and Jem save two baboons, Papio and Upi, from death at a laboratory but then need to stay with them once they're free, learning that freedom has a price. The setting of *Taronga* is postholocaust Sydney where all social systems have broken down, and desperate gangs roam the city and countryside. An orphaned boy, Ben, has a special ability to communicate with animals and influence their actions which he uses to good effect when stalked through Taronga Park Zoo by a tiger. Previously Ben had used his powers to lure animals to their death, providing food for survivors. There is a strong antiviolence stance, with an emphasis on how violence always escalates. The novel ends on an exciting and positive note with the zoo animals freed and Ben and an Aboriginal girl, Ellie, heading for the mountains to start a new life although neither know what this life might be like. As Ben says, "It's not only the animals that'll have to adapt. We'll have to as well. Anything can happen now. Anything."

The nature of truth is also a major theme in this author's contemporary adventures *Baily's Bones, Papio,* and the thriller *Del-Del*. In fast-moving, often violent narratives the faces of deception, be they superstition, nostalgia, or sentimentality, are revealed as dangerous shams and traps for soft thinkers. The intricacies of love and, of necessity, hate are an important part of *Brother Night* and this theme, too, is further explored in *Baily's Bones* and especially in *Del-Del*. The historical background to *Baily's Bones* is the massacre of a whole tribe of Aborigines in the mid-nineteenth century. A white man, escaped convict Frank Baily, sees it happen and swears revenge against the murderer, Walter Arnold. The hatred draws in others and in modern times Alex and Dee are involved when their "simple" brother Kenny, reminiscent of Lal, seems to be possessed by the spirit of Frank Baily. Supernatural possession is also the key to Kelleher's widely admired and controversial novel *Del-Del*. Sam, a year after the death of his much loved sister, starts to act in

a very peculiar manner and gradually his family come to believe he is possessed by a demon. Sam's mother resists this idea, but his grandmother urges them to use priests to rid Sam of the demon. The family starts to come apart, and Sam's behaviour gets worse but fortunately Beth, the eldest child, finds a solution. In this book about the power of grief Kelleher cleverly uses the form of the horror genre to point out the deceptiveness of superstition.

The dust-jacket notes for Kelleher's most recent book, *To the Dark Tower,* describe this novel as "challenging" and a reviewer more forthrightly said she found the book "a bit of a haul" whilst admiring the technical achievement. The hero, Tom, lives his waking life in the grimness of an industrial city, but in his dreams he is The Carrier bearing the mysterious Sleeper's spirit in the form of a beautiful child. Tom realises, just before his task is accomplished, that the Sleeper represents a grim past, worse by far than the difficult present. The dangers of yearning for a past golden age is a fine theme, but the road to the gripping conclusion is tediously repetitive. This is a very sophisticated fantasy quest book but the characterisation of Tom and his heroic companions is a disappointment compared to the riches of *Del-Del*.

—Kerry White

KENDALL, Carol (née Seeger). American. Born in Bucyrus, Ohio, 13 September 1917. Ohio University, Athens, A.B. 1939 (Phi Beta Kappa). Married Paul Murray Kendall in 1939 (died 1973); two daughters. Recipient: Ohioana Award and Newbery Medal Honor Book Award, American Library Association Honor Book, all for *The Gammage Cup,* 1960; Parents' Choice Award, 1982, and Mythopoeic Society Aslan Award, 1983, both for *The Firelings*. Address: 928 Holiday Dr., Lawrence, KS 66049, U.S.A.

PUBLICATIONS FOR YOUNG ADULTS

Fiction

The Other Side of the Tunnel, illustrated by Lilian Buchanan. London, Lane, 1956; New York, Abelard, 1957.
The Gammage Cup, illustrated by Erik Blegvad. New York, Harcourt, 1959; as *The Minnipins,* London, Dent, 1960.
The Big Splash, illustrated by Lilian Obligado. New York, Viking, 1960.
The Whisper of Glocken, illustrated by Imero Gobatto. New York, Harcourt, 1965; London, Bodley Head, 1967.
The Firelings. London, Bodley Head, 1981; New York, Atheneum, 1982.

Other

Sweet and Sour: Tales from China, with Yao-wen Li, illustrated by Shirley Felts. London, Bodley Head, 1978; New York, Houghton, 1979.
Reteller, *Haunting Tales from Japan*. Lawrence, Spencer Museum of Art, University of Kansas, 1985.

PUBLICATIONS FOR CHILDREN

The Wedding of the Rat Family (Chinese folktale; picture book),
    illustrated by James Watts. New York, Macmillan, 1988.

PUBLICATIONS FOR ADULTS

Novels

The Black Seven. New York, Harper, 1946; London, Lane, 1950.
The Baby-Snatcher. London, Lane, 1952.

*

Biography: Essay in *Something about the Author Autobiography
Series,* Volume 7, Detroit, Gale, 1989.

Manuscript Collection: Ohio University Library, Athens.

Carol Kendall comments:

People ask me "What made you decide to be a writer?" and laugh
knowingly when I answer "Six older brothers."

Those six brothers were as fine a set of boys and young men as
one could want, but they did talk a lot. By the time I made my
belated appearance into the family, they were so well gifted in the
flow of conversation that there were few pauses for the addition of
one small female voice. So I grew up listening. Family recollections
would indicate that I was just one sentence short of being completely mute—my single comment of record (at age four) was "Thank
goodness that noisy thing is gone." The noisy thing was my brother
Arden, whose goings and comings were as turbulent as a high wind
gusting through the house.

But then came school! I loved school. The teachers also talked a
lot, but they did it to me instead of to each other, and their words
were about reading and writing—worth all the missed conversations in the world. My voice could be heard at last! Before the year
was out, I started to write a "diary-book" with my new power. The
opening line was "I saw my first robin today." It was also the last
line, for clearly I had run out of words I knew how to write. The
rest of my thoughts would have to wait a spell.

I am still not adept at entering conversations when there are more
than three competing talkers, but I don't mind much because I
know I can put my own offerings into the computer and fish them
out when the time is ripe.

*   *   *

Carol Kendall is one of the twentieth century's most underrated
fantasy writers, possibly because she is not as prolific as many of
her contemporaries. Although she has written two run-of-the-mill
adventure stories and retold several Chinese folk tales, she is primarily known as the author of three fantasy novels: *The Gammage
Cup* (first published in 1959); its sequel, *The Whisper of Glocken*
(1965); and *The Firelings* (1981). These sparse publication dates
help to explain her relative obscurity. In 1960 *The Gammage Cup*
received recognition as a Newbery Honor book, but during the
following decade Lloyd Alexander remolded American fantasy into
a new genre with his Prydain books. As a result, gentler fantasies
like *The Gammage Cup* and its sequel fell out of favor. However,
Kendall's obscurity is not deserved. Her books weave important

social themes and moral concepts into well-paced fantasy adventures with a thread of subtle humor running throughout.

The Gammage Cup introduces a society of small hobbit-like
beings called Minnipins, who live along a river in the Land Between
the Mountains. According to their oral history, the Minnipins emigrated there in ancient times, led by the legendary hero Gammage,
to escape their enemies. Few Minnipins in the enlightened town of
Slipper-on-the-Water believe the legends; they prefer to believe the
stories about Fooley the Balloonist, who flew beyond the mountains and returned with several mysterious relics. Fooley's descendants have become the town leaders—the conservative, narrow-
minded Council of Periods. When the twelve Minnipin villages
hold a contest for the finest village, the Periods decide they must do
something about the five nonconformists in Slipper-on-the-Water.
The rest of the novel deals with the adventures of these five characters after they are banished from the village.

The novel abounds in subtle social satire. The Minnipins' misunderstanding of the Fooley artifacts sheds humorous light on the
nature of art and on social stratification, and their disdain for history and creativity provides a parody of contemporary American
society. The efforts of Walter the Earl to convince the Minnipins to
embrace their own glorious history rather than the false Fooley
history and the efforts of the other four nonconformists to establish lives of creative individualism highlight the natural enmity between society and the individual. Kendall does not favor one over
the other, however. The underlying theme of all her books is balance, so she attempts to balance the needs of an inherently conservative society with the needs of artistic individuals. Although the
Council of Periods is held up to ridicule, all the Minnipins rise to
heroism when their traditional enemies reappear, and the somewhat
chastened Periods remain in charge of the village at the end of the
book despite their lack of vision.

The sequel, *The Whisper of Glocken,* begins with the flooding of
the village of Water Gap. Five Minnipins from Water Gap are
reluctantly thrust into the role of heroes, sent beyond the mountains to determine the cause of the flood. Whereas *The Gammage
Cup* dealt with issues of conformity and individualism, the theme
of *The Whisper of Glocken* is the nature of heroism. Glocken, the
young bell ringer from Water Gap, has so thoroughly idealized the
Five Heroes of Slipper-on-the-Water that he is sorely disappointed
when he finally meets them. Glocken has dreamed of becoming a
hero himself, but he finds that the reality is not as glorious as his
dreams. His four Water Gap companions also learn valuable lessons
about themselves—lessons about mutual need and support. When
Glocken finally becomes a hero, he does not even recognize the
moment because he is intent on doing what must be done.

A third and more recent fantasy explores Kendall's most daring
theme to date: the nature of religious faith. *The Firelings* are a
cooperative society of small beings very like the Minnipins, but
living on the side of a volcano called "Belcher," which is their god.
On occasions the Firelings have pacified Belcher with a "Morsel,"
or human sacrifice. Now Belcher is acting up again, and the villagers
are discussing ways to pacify him. The adults cling to the old ways,
but the young people are free of these superstitions. Five young
firelings help a sixth escape his sacrificial fate, and they all desperately search for the legendary Way of the Goat that will lead their
people to safety. Kendall does not make religion a black and white
issue by pitting enlightened youngsters against superstitious elders; rather she seeks to create a balance between trust in tradition
and a legitimate questioning of authority. Although she seems to
cast MudLar, the hereditary religious leader and mystic, as a moun-

tebank who preys on the fears of his ignorant society, later events prove the hermit to be an intelligent man devoted to freeing his people from their own need of him. Many of the misunderstood religious beliefs of the firelings are the means by which they eventually escape the enslavement of the volcano. Mysticism also plays a role in the events of the novel. For example, there are tendrils of ESP between several of the younger firelings. This novel is darker and more ambitious than Kendall's earlier works. There are undercurrents of shame, guilt, madness, and drug addiction, although they barely disturb the surface of the fantasy adventure.

—Donna R. White

———

KERR, M.E. Pseudonym for Marijane (Agnes) Meaker; has also written as Ann Aldrich, Mary James, M. J. Meaker, Vin Packer. Born in Auburn, New York, 27 May 1927. Educated at the University of Missouri, Columbia, B.A. 1949. Assistant file clerk, E. P. Dutton, publisher, 1949-50; free-lance writer, since 1949. Volunteer writing teacher at Commercial Manhattan Central High, 1968. Founding member of the Ashawagh Writers' Workshop. Recipient: American Library Association (ALA) notable book, one of *School Library Journal's* best books of the year, both 1972, and winner of the *Media and Methods* Maxi awards, 1974, all for *Dinky Hocker Shoots Smack!*; *Book World's* Children's Spring Book Festival honor book, one of Child Study Association's Children's books of the year, and one of *New York Times'* outstanding books of the year, all 1973, all for *If I Love You, Am I Trapped Forever?*; one of *School Library Journal's* best books of the year, 1974, for *The Son of Someone Famous;* ALA notable book, one of ALA's best books for young adults, and one of *New York Times'* outstanding books of the year, all 1975, all for *Is That You, Miss Blue?;* one of *School Library Journal's* best books of the year, 1977, for *I'll Love You When You're More Like Me;* Christopher award, 1979, and The Christophers, *School Library Journal's* book of the year award, one of *New York Times'* outstanding books of the year, both 1978, and one of New York Public Library's best books for the teen age, 1980 and 1981, all for *Gentlehands;* Golden Kite award, Society of Children's Book Writers, one of *School Library Journal's* best books of the year, both 1981, and one of New York Public Library's books for the teen age, 1982, all for *Little Little;* one of *School Library Journal's* best books of the year, 1982, for *What I Really Think of You;* one of ALA best books for young adults, 1983, for *Me, Me, Me, Me, Me: Not a Novel;* one of ALA best books for young adults, 1985, for *I Stay Near You;* one of ALA recommended books for the reluctant young adult reader, 1986, and California Young Reader Medal, 1991, both for *Night Kites.* Margaret A. Edwards award, 1993, for body of work. Agent: Julia Fallowfield, McIntosh & Otis, Inc., 310 Madison Ave., New York, NY 10017. Address: 12 Deep Six Dr., East Hampton, NY 11937, U.S.A.

PUBLICATIONS FOR YOUNG ADULTS

Fiction

Dinky Hocker Shoots Smack! New York, Harper, 1972; London, Gollancz, 1973.

If I Love You, Am I Trapped Forever? New York, Harper, 1973; London, Pan, 1986.
The Son of Someone Famous. New York, Harper, 1974; London, Gollancz, 1975.
Is That You, Miss Blue? New York, Harper, 1975.
Love Is a Missing Person. New York, Harper, 1975.
I'll Love You When You're More Like Me. New York, Harper, 1977.
Gentlehands. New York, Harper, and London, Bodley Head, 1978.
Little Little. New York, Harper, 1981.
What I Really Think of You. New York, Harper, 1982.
Him She Loves? New York, Harper, 1984.
I Stay Near You. New York, Harper, 1985; London, Pan, 1986.
Night Kites. New York, Harper, 1986.
Fell. New York, Harper, 1987.
Fell Back. New York, Harper, 1989.
Shoebag (as Mary James). New York, Scholastic, 1990.
Fell Down. New York, Harper, 1991.
The Shuteyes (as Mary James). New York, Scholastic, 1993.
Linger, New York, Harper, 1993.

Other

Me, Me, Me, Me, Me: Not a Novel (autobiography). New York, Harper, 1983.
Contributor to *Sixteen: Short Stories by Outstanding Writers for Young Adults,* edited by Donald R. Gallo, Delacorte, 1984; *Connections,* edited by Donald R. Gallo, Delacorte, 1989; *Funny You Should Ask,* edited by David Gale, Delacorte, 1992.

PUBLICATIONS FOR ADULTS

Novels as Vin Packer

Dark Intruder. New York, Gold Medal Books, 1952; London, Miller, 1958.
Spring Fire. New York, Gold Medal Books, 1952; London, Consul, 1966.
Look Back to Love. New York, Gold Medal Books, 1953; London, Miller, 1958.
Come Destroy Me. New York, Gold Medal Books, 1954; London, Digit, 1958.
Whisper His Sin. New York, Gold Medal Books, 1954; London, Miller, 1959.
The Thrill Kids. New York, Gold Medal Books, 1955.
Dark Don't Catch Me. New York, Gold Medal Books, 1956.
The Young and Violent. New York, Gold Medal Books, 1956.
Three-Day Terror. New York, Gold Medal Books, 1957.
The Evil Friendship. New York, Gold Medal Books, 1958.
5:45 to Suburbia. New York, Gold Medal Books, 1958; London, Miller, 1959.
The Twisted Ones. New York, Gold Medal Books, and London, Miller, 1959.
Carol, in a Thousand Cities (as Ann Aldrich). New York, Gold Medal Books, 1960.
The Damnation of Adam Blessing. New York, Gold Medal Books, 1961; London, Muller, 1962.
The Girl on the Best Seller List. New York, Gold Medal Books, 1961; London, Muller, 1961.
Something in the Shadows. New York, Gold Medal Books, 1961; London, Muller, 1962.

Intimate Victims. New York, Gold Medal Books, 1962; London, Muller, 1963.

Alone at Night. New York, Gold Medal Books, 1963; London, Muller, 1964.

The Hare in March. New York, New American Library, 1967; London, Mayflower, 1968.

Hometown (as M.J. Meaker). New York, Doubleday, 1967.

Game of Survival (as Marijane Meaker). New York, New American Library, 1968.

Don't Rely on Gemini. New York, Delacorte Press, 1969; London, Macmillan, 1970.

Shockproof Sydney Skate (as Marijane Meaker). Boston, Little, Brown, 1972.

Other as Ann Aldrich

We Walk Alone. New York, Gold Medal Books, 1955.

We Too Must Love. New York, Gold Medal Books, 1958.

We Two Won't Last. New York, Gold Medal Books, 1963.

Sudden Endings (on suicide; as M. J. Meaker). New York, Doubleday, 1964; paperback edition published under pseudonym Vin Packer, New York, Fawcett, 1964.

Take a Lesbian to Lunch. New York, MacFadden, 1972.

*

Media Adaptations: *Dinky Hocker Shoots Smack!* (film and was a television afternoon special), Learning Corporation of America, 1978; *If I Love You Am I Trapped Forever?* (audio cassette), Random House, 1979.

Biography: Essay in *Something about the Author Autobiography Series,* Volume 1, Detroit, Gale, 1986; essay in *Speaking for Ourselves: Autobiographical Sketches by Notable Authors of Books for Young Adults,* Volume 1, compiled and edited by Donald R. Gallo, National Council of Teachers of English, 1990.

Critical Study: Entry in *Contemporary Literary Criticism,* Detroit, Gale, Volume 12, 1980, Volume 35, 1985; *Presenting M.E. Kerr* by Alleen Pace Nilsen, Twayne Publishers, 1986.

M.E. Kerr comments:

Although I had a long career writing suspense and regular novels for adults, my work aimed at young adults has given me the most pleasure and challenge. The teenage years fascinate me, for they are the beginning of the man and of the woman, and here we glimpse them unmasked and forming.

The too-tall nerd in the ill-fitting suit, hunched over in an attempt to hide himself, lopes into a future where he is the CEO of a major corporation...the brilliant beauty queen becomes a suburban wife/mother and a champion tennis player at the local country club...the big hero sports star is selling cars now...the one in the class that no one really remembers that well is a Nobel prize-winning scientist...the black sheep/cutup is a rock star, or a TV talk host or a children's writer—all of that sort of thing intrigues me.

Whole decades can be forgotten by people, but I know very few who forget what happened during those four vital years of high school.

*   *   *

Romance, humor, mystery, and a fascination with the underdog are the hallmarks of M.E Kerr's popular and highly respected writing for young adults. An expert manipulator of the conventions of the contemporary teen novel—troubled or vulnerable young protagonist, problematic parents, and an ironic stance towards reality—Kerr chronicles the self-absorption of adolescence with equal parts of sympathy and good-natured satire. Her sympathy with teen tunnel vision proceeds from the belief expressed in her 1993 autobiography, *Me Me Me Me Me: Not a Novel,* that "What's going on in the world is secondary to what's going on in high school, for in those vulnerable teen years high school *is* the world." At the same time, Kerr confesses that "whenever you find a little smart-mouth, tomboy kid in any of my books, you have found me from long ago...." (75). Humor helps the smart-mouth character cope with her situation while it suggests to the young reader that high school is not forever; it will be "the world" for just a few years. In Kerr's hands, being a teenager is significant, but more importantly, it is survivable.

Kerr's focus on high school or prep school as the world should not, however, be taken to mean that her characters never leave the halls of their respective schools. Kerr takes her characters to their favorite teen hang-outs, locales which reverberate with multiple associations in the context of the other novels. Eight of the books are set or partly set in Seaville, New York, a plush resort town modeled after East Hampton, Long Island where Kerr now lives. Three other novels take place either in Kerr's old hometown of Auburn, rechristened "Cayuta," or in La Belle, another one-factory town in upstate New York. If the setting is Seaville, Sweet Mouth is the place to go for a coke, The Surf Club is the place to dance, snobs belong to The Hadefield Club (a.k.a. The Hatefilled Club), and The Witherspoon Funeral Home is the last stop before burial for half the citizenry. A major character in one Seaville novel may reappear as a bit player in another. The three upstate New York novels are less identically referential but the institutions mentioned in their respective pages—a prison, an orphanage, and a high-priced recovery haven for alcoholics—evoke the same claustrophobia.

Despite Kerr's frequent returns to familiar locales, only the mystery/thriller novels featuring John Fell *(Fell, Fell Back,* and *Fell Down)* could be termed series novels. Fell's adventures start in Seaville, with most of the action then taking place at Fell's prep school in Cottersville, Pennsylvania. The other Seaville books and the novels set in upstate New York do lend themselves to being read differently, however, than they might be read if they did not overlap in some of their particulars. One clue to the reading they invite is suggested by the profession of a main character in *I'll Love You When You're More Like Me,* the second Seaville novel. Young Sabra St. Amour stars in a daytime soap opera named *"Hometown,"* and has a large and loyal following of teenage fans, as does M.E. Kerr. Each of her hometown locales provides a familiar and therefore inviting setting for her readers and allows her, life Fedora Foxe, the producer of *Hometown,* to introduce new plotlines and characters to retain fans' interest.

But just as the plotlines of soap operas are not so much new as they are "topical and updated," so too are Kerr's plots timely, and in some cases, eccentric refurbishings of standard soap opera fare. Romance shares top billing with domestic/familial ruptures, and there are plenty of dark family secrets and life-threatening or even fatal illnesses and accidents. The books featuring John Fell combine the romance plot with stock elements from the mystery and thriller genre: espionage, secret societies, conspiracy, and murder, with the answers to mysteries in earlier books revealed in their ever-more sensational sequels.

Kerr's characters are often familiar types as well, sometimes regrettably familiar in their perpetuation of negative images of young women. More important are the numerous well-realized characters who populate her books, many of whom make their appearances outside of Kerr's standard hometown locales and plots. Dinky Hocker, of *Dinky Hocker Shoots Smack,* lives in Brooklyn Heights with her sensitive cousin Natalia, lawyer father and do-gooder mother, Helen Hocker. Grossly overweight, Dinky drugs herself with food, not heroin; the book takes its title from the graffiti Dinky paints as a public act of revenge to embarrass her mother the night of a community awards banquet honoring Mrs. Hocker's volunteer work with recovering drug addicts. At home, Mrs. Hocker has mistaken manipulation for loving concern. Supposedly for Dinky's own good, Helen has cut her off from her politically conservative fellow weight watcher P. John, the one friend who supports Dinky's dieting but whom Mrs. Hocker views as being little better than a fat fascist. Although P. John plays second lead to Tucker Woolf, whose romance with Dinky's cousin Natalia occupies much of the book, P. John is a real scene stealer when he reappears near the end of the novel as a slimmed-down liberal who had shed prejudices along with pounds.

Even more arresting are the characters who come to life in *Is That You, Miss Blue?* Flanders Brown, uprooted by the break-up of her parents' marriage, has been sent to an Episcopalian boarding school in Virginia. On her own for the first time, she discovers who she is as she makes friends with several of the school's nonconformists and observes the self-serving exclusivity of many of her fellow students. The paradox of their exclusivity is their conformity to peer pressure and the standards set by class leaders such as sophisticated France Shipp. France helps engineer the dismissal of Miss Blue, an inspired science teacher whose equally inspired religious experiences strike the headmistress of this ostensibly religious school as incipient insanity. Flanders's attitude towards Miss Blue mirrors her own growing maturity as she moves from mocking Miss Blue to respect and empathy for her former teacher.

Kerr also takes up the subject of religious belief vs. religious hypocrisy in two later novels. *Little Little,* set in upstate New York, is narrated alternately by Little Little La Belle and Sydney Cinnamon, two young people whose friendship might become a romance once Little Little's fiance runs off with another woman. Knox Lionel, Little Little's sometime fiance, is better known as Little Lion, a popular evangelical preacher whose religion is pure show biz. All four characters (including the "other" woman) are dwarves, a fact which only heightens the novel's carnival atmosphere because here Kerr is too much the smart-mouth kid. The jokes and frenetic pace of the novel inadvertently work to deny Sydney and Little Little their humanity. Kerr is much more successful in persuading readers to see past labels and stereotypes in *What I Really Think of You.* This novel's two narrators, Opal Ringer and Jesse Pegler, learn to come to terms with their own spirituality and the social, economic, and religious complexities of being preacher's kids.

Preacher's kids are not the only Kerr adolescents whose fathers (or, as in the case of *Gentlehands,* grandfather) provoke identity crises. In *The Son of Someone Famous,* Adam Blessing finds himself more cursed than blessed by having a politically powerful father who is celebrated for his shuttle diplomacy. *Him She Loves* features a professional comedian who revives his career by ridiculing his daughter's boyfriend on national television, while *If I Love You, Am I Trapped Forever* portrays an absentee and alcoholic father who is still too much of a child himself to be a parent to his son. *Love Is A Missing Person* depicts a dad who favors one child over the other, with negative consequences for all involved. None of these dads is much of a role model, but that is just as well since the one father figure who invites emulation is the most problematic of all; he's the infamous "Gentlehands" of Auschwitz.

Given these troubled family histories, it is no wonder that the course of love does not run smoothly for the protagonists of most of the novels. Breaking up, rather than living happily ever after is the order of the day. For example, the three-generation saga *I Stay Near You* devotes the greater part of each of its interlocked narratives to detailing the unhappy consequences of the passionate emotions precipitated by a romantic misalliance in the summer of 1943. By the time the story reaches the present, love has become a ghost from summers past. *Night Kites,* another densely textured story, follows the romantic fortunes of its young male protagonist, but Erick Rudd's loving and losing Nicki Marr is less important than the fact that he loves and will soon lose his older brother. Pete has AIDS and has come home to spend his last months with his family. Kerr's presentation of Pete's story is multilayered, empathetic, and embedded within his family's reactions. Kerr provides no easy answers or consolations because there aren't any answers beyond a few all-important grace notes of understanding and love. And finally, no such grace notes characterize John Fell's experience. He discovers that his lover romanced him as part of a scheme to benefit the man she really loves.

Kerr's habitually ironic stance towards the possibilities of romance is modulated by the positive relationships the Peel brothers eventually enjoy with their respective girlfriends in Kerr's most recent novel, *Linger.* Those relationships are, however the result of putting aside their earlier fascination with Lynn Dunlinger, the beautiful daughter of a wealthy and influential restaurant owner. Bobby, the older brother, writes to Lynn from Saudia Arabia where he has been sent to fight in Operation Desert Storm. Back home, Bobby's younger brother Gary experiences his own crush on Lynn but realizes that she is completely absorbed by her love affair with their high school English teacher, a vocal opponent of Desert Storm. Although Lynn's romance ends in disillusionment, the Peel brothers' loss of illusions is accompanied by an energized political consciousness and a shedding of chauvinist responses to the young women who care deeply about them. Bobby's is the true baptism by fire—his tank was hit, injuring him and his friend Gus, and killing their buddy, Sugar—but Gary's love for his brother causes Gary to question his own habitually apolitical mind set. *Linger,* like so many of Kerr's books for young adults, entertains while at the same time prompting its readers to question their own habitual frames of thought.

—Janice M. Alberghene

KERRY, Lois. See **DUNCAN, Lois.**

KESEY, Ken (Elton). American. Born in La Junta, Colorado, 17 September 1935. Educated at high school in Springfield, Oregon; University of Oregon, Eugene, B.A. 1957; Stanford University, California (Woodrow Wilson fellow), 1958-59, graduate study, 1958-61, 1963. Married Faye Haxby in 1956; four children (one deceased). Multi-media artist and farmer. Night attendant in psychiatric Veterans Administration Hospital, Menlo Park, California, 1961; president, Intrepid Trips, Inc. (motion picture company), 1964. Since 1974 publisher, *Spit in the Ocean* magazine, Pleasant Hill, Oregon. Served prison term for marijuana possession, 1967. Recipient: Woodrow Wilson fellowship; Saxton Fund fellowship, 1959; Distinguished Service award, State of Oregon, 1978. Agent: Sterling Lord Literistic, Inc., 660 Madison Ave., New York, NY 10021. Address: 85829 Ridgeway Rd., Pleasant Hill, OR 97401, U.S.A.

PUBLICATIONS FOR ADULTS AND YOUNG ADULTS

Novels

One Flew over the Cuckoo's Nest. New York, Viking, 1962; London, Methuen, 1963.
Sometimes a Great Notion. New York, Viking, 1964; London, Methuen, 1966.
Demon Box. New York, Viking, and London, Methuen, 1986.
Caverns, with others. Viking, 1990.
The Further Inquiry. New York, Viking, 1990.
Sailor Song. New York, Viking, 1992.

Other

Contributor, *The Last Whole Earth Catalog: Access to Tools.* Portola Institute, 1971.
Editor and contributor, *The Last Supplement to the Whole Earth Catalog,* with Paul Krassner. Portola Institute, 1971.
Compiler and contributor, *Kesey's Garage Sale* (miscellany; includes screenplay *Over the Border*). New York, Viking, 1973.
Kesey. Eugene, Oregon, Northwest Review, 1977.

PUBLICATIONS FOR CHILDREN

Fiction

Little Tricker the Squirrel Meets Big Double the Bear, illustrated by Barry Moser. New York, Puffin, 1990.
The Sea Lion. New York, Viking, 1991.

*

Media Adaptations: *One Flew over the Cuckoo's Nest* was adapted for the stage by Dale Wasserman and produced on Broadway at the Cort Theatre on November 13, 1963, revived in 1971, and adapted for film by United Artists in 1975; *Sometimes a Great Notion* (film), Universal, 1972.

Manuscript Collection: University of Oregon, Eugene.

Biography: Entry in *Concise Dictionary of American Literary Biography, 1968-1988,* Detroit, Gale, 1989; entry in *Dictionary of Literary Biography,* Detroit, Gale, Volume 2: *American Novelists since World War II,* 1978; Volume 16: *The Beats: Literary Bohemians in Postwar America,* 1983.

Critical Studies: *The Electric Kool-Aid Test* by Tom Wolfe, New York, Farrar Straus, 1968, London, Weidenfeld & Nicolson, 1969; entries in *Contemporary Literary Criticism,* Detroit, Gale, Volume 1, 1973; Volume 3, 1975; Volume 6, 1976; Volume 11, 1979; Volume 46, 1987; *Ken Kesey* by Bruce Carnes, Boise, Idaho, Boise State College, 1974; "Ken Kesey Issue" of *Northwest Review* (Eugene, Oregon), vol. 16, nos. 1-2, 1977; *Ken Kesey* by Barry H. Leeds, New York, Ungar, 1981; *The Art of Grit: Ken Kesey's Fiction,* Columbia, University of Missouri Press, 1982, and *One Flew over the Cuckoo's Nest: Rising to Heroism,* Boston, Twayne, 1989, both by M. Gilbert Porter; *Ken Kesey* by Stephen L. Tanner, Boston, Twayne, 1983; *On the Bus: The Legendary Trip of Ken Kesey and the Merry Pranksters* by Ken Babbs, photographs by Rob Bivert, New York, Thunder's Mouth Press, 1989, London, Plexus, 1991.

*   *   *

Ken Kesey's appeal to young adults resides perhaps as much in the "text" of his personal life as that of his novels. As a precociously brilliant sixties' novelist, Kesey left for us his famous *One Flew over the Cuckoo's Nest* (1962) and the less well known *Sometimes a Great Notion* (1966). As a guru of the hallucinogenic drug culture of that time, he lived a wildly uninhibited and free-spirited life, not unlike the chief characters, McMurphy and Hank Stamper, in his novels. Although not about the drug culture, both works grew out of the sense of eroding individualism that permeated that era.

Told from the viewpoint of a huge Amerindian schizophrenic called Big Chief, *Cuckoo's Nest* depicts the plight of inmates in a mental ward presided over by a physically imposing matriarch named Big Nurse Ratched. Despite the "wretchedness" of their existence under the influence of what Big Chief calls "the Combine," most of these inmates ironically choose to remain in the degradation of harshly imposed routines rather than face the insecurities of the world outside the institution.

Kesey brilliantly fuses the thought and language of an authentically paranoid schizophrenic with a comic-book style narration in which the atmosphere seems "like a cartoon world, where the characters are flat and outlined in black, jerking through some kind of goofy story." Yet, for all its smart-aleck humor, the story is anything but wholly funny. Recognizing this tonal oppositeness, the young-adult reader is faced with an early example of the same dissonance found in films, where modern comic-book characters and settings often express serious social messages.

Big Chief perceives the hospital as a totally unnatural environment in which the essential spiritual bond between Indian and nature is blocked by a series of nightmarish, technological evil spirits. Into this inimical world steps McMurphy, dancing to the beat of a free-spirit drummer, an obvious perennial favorite character to many young adults who share that identity. Because of his obdurate dedication to free-willed, individual consent, McMurphy contends diametrically against the depersonalizing authority of Nurse Ratched, confounding her with his clever belligerence. He is her antithesis, the quintessential rebel against the unaccountable use of power. In effect, McMurphy becomes for Big Chief "a giant come out of the sky to save us from the Combine that was net-working the land with copper wire and crystal." This mythic allusion hyperbolically extends McMurphy's hero status into the neverending allegory where a youthful hero contends against an unloving and unjust monarch within a natural or social wasteland.

As in many such mythic allegories, however, the hero must be scapegoated in order to show the reader the brutality of oppressive authority and allow the reader to hold in reverence the indomitability of the hero's human spirit. Kesey has a treat for the young reader here in that he fashions this scapegoating both as externally imposed on and internally accepted by McMurphy. Externally imposed is McMurphy's lobotomy by order of Nurse Ratched as penance for his dissidence. Internally, though, McMurphy had already realized that his hero status was fated by its being an over-burdened projection of all the inmates' expectations. In brief, McMurphy had earlier given up taking heroic responsibility for those who would not be responsible for themselves. Thus neutralized by both parent-like authority and personal consent, McMurphy must be freed and his heroic boon carried on by Big Chief, whom he has freed to return to his homeland. The Indian smothers the former hero's helpless body in an act of humane dispatch. Though at first a difficult concept for some youth, this segment of the novel provides some serious contemplation about individual action and consequences.

A parallel theme links *Cuckoo's Nest* with Kesey's second novel, *Sometimes a Great Notion*, a story of rugged naturalism in a northwest logging town and of the conflict between two aspects of human nature. In this novel, Hank Stamper portrays a man of action and nature, the individualistic free spirit contending against intellectual authority. His nemesis is Draeger, a union official attempting to force local loggers into conformity. In a clear analogy, the young reader is revisiting McMurphy and Nurse Ratched in a different venue.

By contrast with Big Chief's isolation from nature, however, Hank's brother Lee has freely accepted a retreat into his intellect brought about by his attending an eastern university. Another interesting variation is found in Viv, Hank's wife, controlled and protected by Stamper, the later love object of Lee, who tries to reach out to what he wants her to be. Viv is the "viv-acious," life-loving, female counterpart of McMurphy, who cannot allow herself to become someone else's projected expectation of her. In these particular distinctions, *Great Notion* enlarges Kesey's message to contemporary young adults who are attempting to raise their intelligent identity and to find gender-free ways of empathy and relationship.

Kesey's works tell stories from varied viewpoints of traditionally overlooked characters, befitting the postmodern critical idea that all stories have multiple vantage points and are only the composite of all of them. For this and the unsentimentalized romanticism of his plots, Kesey remains good reading for young adults.

—Ron Evans

KINCAID, Jamaica. American. Born Elaine Potter Richardson in St. John's, Antigua, West Indies, 25 May 1949; immigrated to United States, naturalized U.S. citizen. Educated at Princess Margaret girls' school, Antigua; New School for Social Research, New York; Franconia College, New Hampshire. Married Allen Evan Shawn; one daughter and one son. Since 1974, contributor, and currently staff writer, the *New Yorker.* Recipient: American Academy Morton Dauwen Zabel award, 1984, for *At the Bottom of the River.* Address: The New Yorker, 25 West 43rd Street, New York, NY 10036, U.S.A.

PUBLICATIONS FOR YOUNG ADULTS

Novels

Annie John. New York, Farrar, Straus, and London, Pan, 1985.
Lucy. New York, Farrar, Straus, 1990; London, Cape, 1991.

Short Stories

At the Bottom of the River. New York, Farrar, Straus, 1983; London, Pan, 1984.
Annie, Gwen, Lily, Pam, and Tulip, illustrated by Eric Fischl. New York, Library Fellows of the Whitney Museum of American Art, 1986.

Other

A Small Place. New York, Farrar, Straus, and London, Virago Press, 1988.

*

Critical Study: Entry in *Contemporary Literary Criticism,* Volume 43, Detroit, Gale, 1987.

*   *   *

Best known for her works of fiction, Jamaica Kincaid, is a writer with a clear, illuminating vision of humanity, who scrutinizes the complex layers that exist in the mother and daughter relationship. Because Kincaid vividly remembers both the beauty and pain of childhood and adolescence, her female protagonists speak with a sense of powerful authenticity.

Utilizing prose that on occasion is reminiscent of poetry or the rhythm and repetition of folkloric chants, Kincaid's work has received wide critical acclaim. She writes as every woman's daughter who both loves and harshly judges every mother. At other times she writes as an outsider, observing American life. Even though she has lived in the United States more than half her life, Kincaid, who was born on the West Indian island of Antigua, views contemporary society with cool detachment. Of Americans, like the upper-middle class employers of her character Lucy, in the novel of the same name, Kincaid observes they make "no connections between their comforts and the decline of the world that lay before them."

Kincaid deals with such universal themes as coming-of-age and the necessity of separation from parents and establishing identity. The protagonists in *At the Bottom of the River, Annie John,* and *Lucy* experience the pain and pleasure of growing up as they strive to become women who are not shadows of their mothers but separate and distinct individuals.

In her nonfiction book, *A Small Place,* Kincaid continues these themes as she writes of her birthplace, the island country of Antigua, which has come of age and has had to establish independence after years of colonial British rule. Kincaid writes with anger about slavery, colonization, racism, and corruption. "Nothing can erase my rage—not an apology, not a large sum of money, not the death of the criminal—for this wrong can never be made right." *A Small Place* enables readers to look at Antigua and the greater issues Kincaid raises.

Kincaid's three novels, *At the Bottom of the River, Annie John,* and *Lucy,* if read together, act as companion pieces for one another. *Annie John* is the narrative of a young girl growing up and separating from her mother. The details of Annie's story seem to fill in some information not given by the young female narrator in the stories that comprise *At the Bottom of the River. Lucy* continues to explore the mother-daughter theme with a different protagonist, slightly older than the one in the other two books.

At the Bottom of the River consists of ten short stories. Some of the stories, like "Girl" and "The Letter from Home," are written in chant-like form, with folkloric repetition of certain refrains. "Girl," the first story in the collection, appears as one startlingly long, extended sentence, three pages in length, and consists of the orders a mother gives her daughter for how to live life. Suggestions for proper behavior in a wide variety of circumstances make up the story. Of primary importance to the mother is that everything be done her way, society's way, and done "not like the slut you are so bent on becoming."

In *Annie John,* Kincaid takes a long hard look at the end of childhood and the beginning of adolescence. At ten, Annie thought "only people I did not know died." Living near a cemetery for a summer, Annie learns that death comes even to children. After her mother prepares a young child for burial and her father makes the coffin, Annie begins to look at both parents, especially her mother, differently. The mother-daughter relationship begins to unravel, Annie's body changes as she begins puberty, and her life away from her parents becomes increasingly more important. Annie begins a secret life which includes lying, stealing, and the beginnings of sexual experimentation.

At the beginning of Kincaid's most recent novel, *Lucy,* the young female protagonist has just arrived in the United States from her Caribbean home. All appears new to the nineteen-year-old woman, from changing seasons and cold weather, to buildings with elevators. She says: "The undergarments that I wore were all new...and as I sat in the car, twisting this way and that...I was reminded of how uncomfortable new can make you feel."

In the United States to work as an au pair for an attractive, upper-middle class couple with four children, Lucy finds her homesickness to be surprising. She thought she could leave home completely behind like "an old garment" which she had outgrown. Readers sense the ambivalence and the strength Lucy possesses as she faces life. At the end of the novel, Lucy's future remains as uncertain as that of Annie John but both protagonists have stretched, expanded their vision, and gone beyond their mothers.

Lengthy sentences, unusual sentence structure, singular imagery, and vivid descriptions of sights, sounds, and smells characterize Kincaid's writing. Her young narrators comment with blunt honesty on what they see around them, without the societal constraints of their elders. For some readers, Kincaid's frankness about her protagonists' relationships with friends of the same sex as in *Annie John,* or with male lovers in *Lucy,* might be surprising. For others, these scenes will add to the complexity and authenticity of the novels.

Kincaid uses powerful symbolism, poetic language, and imagery. From a simple description of peals of laughter that "would fly up into the air wrapped around each other like a toffee twist" in *Lucy,* to the complicated transformation of mother and daughter into large reptiles in "My Mother," from *At the Bottom of the River,* Kincaid

takes great care in her use of language. Her books can be read, enjoyed, and interpreted on many levels. With a strong, distinctive voice and style, Kincaid appeals across generations and national boundaries.

Can a mother ever concede that her daughter will grow up to become the person she needs to be and not the person the mother wants her to be? Do the bonds between mothers and daughters endure despite years of separation, denial, and even death? These questions may not have a single answer. Neither do Kincaid's novels, but they raise important questions.

—Karen Ferris Morgan

KING, Stephen (Edwin). Also writes as Steve King; Richard Bachman; John Swithen. American. Born in Portland, Maine, 21 September 1947. Educated at University of Maine at Orono, B.Sc., 1970. Married Tabitha Jane Spruce; one daughter and two sons. Full-time writer. Worked as a janitor, a laborer in an industrial laundry, and in a knitting mill. English teacher, Hampden Academy, Hampden, Maine, 1971-73; writer in residence, University of Maine, Orono, 1978-79. Owner, Philtrum Press, a publishing house, and WZON-AM, a rock 'n' roll radio station, both in Bangor, Maine. Has made cameo appearances in films *Knightriders,* as Steven King, 1980, *Creepshow,* 1982, *Maximum Overdrive,* 1986, and *Pet Sematary,* 1989; has also appeared in American Express credit card television commercial. Served as judge for 1977 World Fantasy Awards, 1978. Participated in radio honor panel with George A. Romero, Peter Straub, and Ira Levin, moderated by Dick Cavett on WNET in New York, October 30-31, 1980. Recipient: *Carrie* named to *School Library Journal*'s Book List, 1975; World Fantasy award nominations, 1976, for *'Salem's Lot,* 1979, for *The Stand* and *Night Shift,* 1980, for *The Dead Zone,* 1981, for "The Mist," and 1983, for "The Breathing Method: A Winter's Tale" in *Different Seasons;* Hugo award nomination, and Nebula award nomination, both 1978, both for *The Shining;* Balrog awards, second place in best novel category for *The Stand,* and second place in best collection category for *Night Shift,* both 1979; *The Long Walk* was named to the American Library Association's list of best books for young adults, 1979; World Fantasy award, 1980, for contributions to the field, and 1982, for story "Do the Dead Sing?"; Career Alumni award, University of Maine at Orono, 1981; *Firestarter* was named to the American Library Association's list of best books for young adults, 1981; Nebula award nomination, 1981, for story "The Way Station"; special British Fantasy Society award for outstanding contribution to the genre, 1982, for *Cujo;* Hugo award, World Science Fiction Convention, 1982, for *Stephen King's Danse Macabre;* named *Us* Magazine Best Fiction Writer of the Year, 1982; Locus award for best collection, Locus Publications, 1986, for *Stephen King's Skeleton Crew.* Agent: Arthur Greene, 101 Park Avenue, New York, NY 10178. Address: P.O. Box 1186, Bangor, ME 04001, U.S.A.

PUBLICATIONS

Novels

Carrie: A Novel of a Girl with a Frightening Power. New York, Doubleday, and London, New English Library, 1974; as *Carrie,* New York, New American Library/Times Mirror, 1975.

'Salem's Lot. New York, Doubleday, 1975; London, New English
  Library, 1976.
The Shining. New York, Doubleday, and London, New English
  Library, 1977.
The Stand. New York, Doubleday, 1978; London, New English
  Library, 1979; revised edition with illustrations by Berni
  Wrightson, New York, Doubleday, and London, Hodder and
  Stoughton, 1990.
The Dead Zone. New York, Viking, and London, Macdonald and
  Jane's, 1979; as *The Dead Zone: Movie Tie-In,* New York, New
  American Library, 1980.
Firestarter. New York, Viking, and London, Futura, 1980.
Cujo. New York, Viking, 1981; London, Macdonald, 1982.
The Dark Tower: The Gunslinger, illustrated by Michael Whelan.
  Hampton Falls, New Hampshire, Grant, 1982; as *The Gunslinger,*
  New York, New American Library, 1988; London, Sphere, 1989.
Pet Sematary. New York, Doubleday, and London, Hodder and
  Stoughton, 1983.
Christine. New York, Viking, and London, Hodder and Stoughton,
  1983; with illustrated by Stephen Gervais in a limited edition,
  West Kingston, Rhode Island, Grant, 1983.
Cycle of the Werewolf, illustrations by Berni Wrightson. New York,
  New American Library, 1983; London, New English Library,
  1986.
The Talisman, with Peter Straub. New York, Viking Press/Putnam,
  and London, Viking, 1984.
The Eyes of the Dragon (for young adults), limited edition illus-
  trated by Kenneth R. Linkhauser. Bangor, Maine, Philtrum Press,
  1984; new edition illustrated by David Palladini, New York,
  Viking, 1987; London, Macdonald, 1988.
It. New York, Viking, and London, Hodder and Stoughton, 1986;
  first edition as *Es.* Munich, West Germany, Heyne, 1986.
Misery. New York, Viking, and London, Hodder and Stoughton,
  1987.
The Tommyknockers. New York, Putnam, 1987; London, Hodder
  and Stoughton, 1988.
The Dark Half. New York, Viking, 1989; London, Hodder and
  Stoughton, 1990.
The Drawing of Three, illustrated by Phil Hale. New York, New
  American Library, and London, Sphere, 1989.
Needful Things. Boston, G.K. Hall, 1991; London, Hodder and
  Stoughton, 1992.
The Waste Lands, illustrated by Ned Dameron. Hampton Falls,
  New Hampshire, Grant, 1991.
Dolores Claiborne. Boston, G.K. Hall, 1992.
Gerald's Game. New York, Viking, 1992; London, Hodder and
  Stoughton, 1993.
Nightmares and Dreamscapes. New York, Viking, 1993.

Novels as Richard Bachman

Rage. New York, New American Library/Signet, 1977.
The Long Walk. New York, New American Library/Signet, 1979.
Roadwork: A Novel of the First Energy Crisis. New York, New
  American Library/Signet, 1981.
The Running Man. New York, New American Library/Signet, 1982;
  London, New English Library, 1988.
Thinner. New York, New American Library, 1984; London, New
  English Library, 1987.

Short Stories

The Star Invaders (as Steve King). Durham, Maine, Triad, Inc., and
  Gaslight Books, 1964.
Night Shift. New York, Doubleday, and London, New English Li-
  brary, 1978; as *Night Shift: Excursions into Horror,* New York,
  New American Library/Signet, 1979.
Different Seasons. New York, Viking, and London, Futura, 1982.
The Breathing Method. Bath, Chivers Press, 1984.
*Rita Hayworth and Shawshank Redemption: A Story from "Differ-
  ent Seasons."* Thorndike, Maine, Thorndike Press, 1983.
Stephen King's Skeleton Crew, illustrated by J.K. Potter. New York,
  Viking, and London, Macdonald, 1985.
My Pretty Pony, illustrated by Barbara Kruger. New York, Knopf,
  1989.
Four Past Midnight. Boston, G.K. Hall, and London, Hodder and
  Stoughton, 1990.

Screenplays

Stephen King's Creep Show: A George A. Romero Film (adaptation
  of short stories "Father's Day," "Weeds," "The Crate," and
  "They're Creeping Up on You," released by Warner Brothers as
  Creepshow, 1982), illustrated by Berni Wrightson and Michele
  Wrightson. New York, New American Library, 1982.
Cat's Eye (adaptation of short stories "Quitters, Inc.," "The Ledge,"
  and "The General," MGM/UA, 1984).
Silver Bullet (adaptation of *Cycle of the Werewolf,* released by Para-
  mount Pictures/Dino de Laurentiis's North Carolina Film Corp.,
  1985).
Director, *Maximum Overdrive* (adaptation of short stories "The
  Mangler," "Trucks," and "The Lawnmower Man," released by
  Dino de Laurentiis' North Carolina Film Corp., 1986). New York,
  New American Library, 1986.
Pet Sematary (adaptation of novel, Laurel Production, 1989).

Also author of teleplay *Sorry, Right Number* for *Tales from the
Dark Side* series, and of screenplay *The Stand,* based on his novel
of same title. Author of unproduced versions of screenplays, in-
cluding *Children of the Corn, Cujo, The Dead Zone, The
Shotgunners, The Shining, Something Wicked This Way Comes,* and
Daylight Dead, (based on short stories "Strawberry Spring," "I
Know What You Need," and "Battleground").

Other

Contributor, *Frankenstein, Dracula, Dr. Jekyll and Mr. Hyde,* by
  Mary Shelley, Bram Stoker, and Robert Louis Stevenson. New
  York, New American Library/Signet, 1978.
Contributor, *Shadows,* edited by Charles L. Grant. New York,
  Doubleday, Volume 1, 1978; Volume 4, 1981.
Contributor, *The Year's Finest Fantasy,* edited by Terry Carr. New
  York, Putnam, 1978.
Another Quarter Mile: Poetry. Pittsburgh, Pennsylvania, Dorrance,
  1979.
Contributor, *Nightmares,* edited by Charles L. Grant. Playboy,
  1979.
Contributor, *More Tales of Unknown Horror,* edited by Peter
  Haining. London, New English Library, 1979.
Contributor, *Murderess Ink: The Better Half of the Mystery,* edited
  by Dilys Winn. East Brunswick, New Jersey, Bell, 1979.

Contributor, *New Tales of the Cthulhu Mythos,* edited by Ramsey Campbell. Sauk City, Wisconsin, Arkham House, 1980.

Contributor, *The Shapes of Midnight,* by Joseph Payne Brennan. New York, Berkley, 1980.

Contributor, *The 17th Fontana Book of Great Ghost Stories,* edited by R. Chetwynd-Hayes. Centerport, New York, Fontana, 1981.

Contributor, *The Arbor House Treasury of Horror and the Supernatural,* compiled by Bill Pronzini, Barry N. Malzberg, and Martin H. Greenberg. New York, Arbor House, 1981.

Contributor, *A Fantasy Reader: The Seventh World Fantasy Convention Program Book,* edited by Jeff Frane and Jack Rems. Seventh World Fantasy Convention, 1981.

Stephen King (includes *The Shining, 'Salem's Lot, Night Shift,* and *Carrie).* North Pomfret, Vermont, W.S. Heinemann/Octopus Books, 1981.

Stephen King's Danse Macabre. Everest House, 1981; London, Futura, 1982.

Contributor, *Tales from the Nightside,* by Charles L. Grant. Sauk City, Wisconsin, Arkham House, 1981.

Contributor, *When Michael Calls,* by John Farris. New York, Pocket Books, 1981.

Contributor, *New Terrors,* edited by Ramsey Campbell. New York, Pocket Books, 1982.

Contributor, *Terrors,* edited by Charles L. Grant. Playboy, 1982.

Contributor, *Death,* edited by Stuart David Schiff. Playboy, 1982.

Contributor, *The Do-It-Yourself Bestseller,* edited by Tom Silberkleit and Jerry Biederman. New York, Doubleday, Dolphin, 1982.

Contributor, *Fear Itself: The Horror Fiction of Stephen King,* edited by Tim Underwood and Chuck Miller. Lancaster, Pennsylvania, Underwood-Miller, 1982; London, Pan, 1991.

Contributor, *Mr. Monster's Movie Gold,* by Forrest J. Ackerman. Norfolk, Virginia, Donning, 1982.

The Plant. Bangor, Maine, Philtrum Press, Part I, 1982; Part II, 1983; Part III, 1985.

Contributor, *Stalking the Nightmare,* by Harlan Ellison. West Bloomfield, Michigan, Phantasia Press, 1982.

Contributor, *World Fantasy Convention '82,* edited by Kennedy Poyser. Eighth World Fantasy Convention, 1982.

Black Magic and Music: A Novelist's Perspective on Bangor. Bangor Historical Society, 1983.

Contributor, *Frankenstein, or The Modern Prometheus,* by Mary Wollstonecraft Shelley, illustrated by Berni Wrightson. New York, Dodd, 1983.

Contributor, *Grand Illusions,* by Tom Savini. Pittsburgh, Pennsylvania, Imagine, Inc., 1983; as *Bizarro,* Crown, 1983.

Contributor, *Satyricon II Program Book,* edited by Rusty Burke. Satyricon II/DeepSouthCon XXI, 1983.

Contributor, *Shadowings: The Reader's Guide to Horror Fiction, 1981-82,* edited by Douglas E. Winter. Mercer Island, Washington, Starmont House, 1983.

Contributor, *Tales by Moonlight,* edited by Jessica Amanda Salmonson. Chicago, Robert L. Garcia, 1983.

Contributor, *World Fantasy Convention 1983,* edited by Robert Weinberg. Weird Tales Ltd., 1983.

Contributor, *The Blackboard Jungle,* by Evan Hunter. New York, Arbor House, 1984.

Contributor, *The Writer's Handbook,* edited by Sylvia K. Burack. Boston, Writer, Inc., 1984.

Contributor, *The Year's Best Horror Stories, Series XII,* edited by Karl Edward Wagner. New York, DAW, 1984.

The Bachman Books: Four Early Novels (includes *Rage, The Long Walk, Roadwork,* and *The Running Man,* with introduction "Why I Was Richard Bachman"). New York, New American Library, 1985; London, Hodder and Stoughton, 1986.

Stephen King's Year of Fear 1986 Calendar. New York, New American Library, 1985.

Contributor, *Kingdom of Fear: The World of Stephen King,* edited by Tim Underwood and Chuck Miller. Lancaster, Pennsylvania, Underwood-Miller, 1986.

Contributor, *Now and On Earth,* by Jim Thompson. Belem, New Mexico, Dennis Macmillan, 1986.

Contributor, *The Dark Descent,* edited by David G. Hartwell. New York, Doherty Associates, 1987.

Contributor, *Masques II: All New Stories of Horror and the Supernatural,* edited by J.N. Williamson. Maclay and Associates, 1987.

Contributor, *The New Adventures of Sherlock Holmes: Original Stories by Eminent Mystery Writers,* edited by Martin Harry Greenberg and Carol-Lynn Roessel Waugh. New York, Carroll and Graf, 1987.

Contributor, *Stephen King Goes to Hollywood.* New York, New American Library, 1987.

Contributor, *Genuine Man,* by Don Robertson. Bangor, Maine, Philtrum Press, 1988.

Nightmares in the Sky: Gargoyles and Grotesques, photographs by f.Stop FitzGerald. London, Viking, 1988.

Contributor, *Prime Evil: New Stories by the Masters of Modern Horror,* edited by Douglas E. Winter. New York, New American Library, 1988; London, Bantam, 1989.

Contributor, *Dark Visions.* London, Gollancz, 1989.

Contributor, *Feast of Fear: Conversations with Stephen King,* edited by Tim Underwood and Chuck Miller. New York, Carroll and Graf, 1992.

Contributor, *Midnight Graffiti.* London, Svern Ho, 1993.

Also contributor of stories to numerous other anthologies, including "Squad D" to Harlan Ellison's *The Last Dangerous Visions.* Author of weekly column "King's Garbage Truck" for *Maine Campus* (February 20, 1969 through May 21, 1970), and of monthly book review column for *Adelina,* (June through November, 1980). Contributor of short fiction and poetry to numerous periodicals.

*

Media Adaptations: *Carrie* (film, directed by Brian De Palma), United Artists, 1976; (musical, adapted by Lawrence D. Cohen and Michael Gore), produced England, 1988; *'Salem's Lot* (television miniseries), Warner Brothers, 1979; *The Shining* (film, directed by Stanley Kubrick), Warner Brothers/Hawks Films, 1980; *Christine* (film), Columbia Pictures, 1983; *Cujo* (film), Warner Communications/Taft Entertainment, 1983; *The Dead Zone* (film, directed by David Cronenberg), Paramount Pictures, 1983; *Children of the Corn* (film), New World Pictures, 1984; *Firestarter* (film), Universal Pictures, 1984; *Rita Hayworth and Shawshank Redemption: Different Seasons I, The Body: Different Seasons II, Apt Pupil: Different Seasons III,* and *The Breathing Method: Different Seasons IV* (cassettes), Recorded Book, 1984; *The Word Processor* (television adaptation of *The Word Processor of the Gods* for *Tales from the Darkside* television show), Laurel Productions, 1984; *Night Shift* (cassette), Recorded Books, 1985; *Skeleton Crew* (cassette, including *The Ballad of the Flexible Bullet, Gramma,* and *The Mist),* Recorded Books, 1985; *Two Mini-Features from Stephen King's*

Nightshift Collection (videotape, includes *The Woman in the Room* and *The Boogeyman),* Granite Entertainment Group, 1985; *Gramma* (television episode of *The Twilight Zone),* CBS-TV, 1986; *The Mist* (radio dramatization), Boston; (cassette), Simon and Schuster Audioworks, 1986; (computer game), Mindscape, Inc.; *The Monkey, Mrs. Todd's Shortcut, The Reaper's Image,* and *Gramma* (cassettes), Warner Audio, 1986; *Stand by Me* (film, adaptation of novella *The Body),* Columbia Pictures, 1986; *Strawberry Spring, The Boogeyman, Graveyard Shift, The Man Who Loved Flowers, One for the Road, The Last Rung on the Ladder, I Know What You Need, Jerusalem's Lot,* and *I Am the Doorway* (cassettes), Walden, 1986; *Thinner* (cassette), Listen for Pleasure, 1986; *Creepshow 2* (film, including *The Raft, Old Chief Woodn'head* and *The Hitchhiker),* New World Pictures, 1987; *Graveyard Shift* (film), 1987; *The Running Man* (film), Taft Entertainment/Barish Productions, 1987; *The Gunslinger* and *The Drawing of Three* (cassettes), New York, New American Library, 1988; *Misery* (film), Castle Rock, 1990; *It* (television miniseries), ABC-TV, 1990; *The Lawnmower Man* (film), 1992; *Sometimes They Come Back* (television movie), 1992; *The Dark Half* (film, directed by George A. Romero), 1993; *The Tommyknockers* (television miniseries), 1993; *Sorry, Right Number* (television episode of *Tales from the Darkside); The Cat from Hell* (film, episode in four-segment film entitled *Tales from the Darkside— The Movie),* Laurel Productions, 1990; *Needful Things* (film), Castle Rock, 1993.

Several additional short stories have also been adapted for the screen. King's screenplay *The Stand* is in production as a television miniseries; *Battleground* has been optioned by Martin Poll Productions for NBC-TV; *The Long Walk* has been optioned for a film production; a film based upon a treatment by King of *Training Exercise* is scheduled for production by Dino De Laurentiis's North Carolina Film Corporation; *Apt Pupil: Summer of Corruption* is being developed for production by Richard Kobritz; *The Talisman* has been optioned for a television miniseries.

Biography: Entry in *Dictionary of Literary Biography Yearbook: 1980,* Detroit, Gale, 1981; essay in *Authors and Artists for Young Adults,* Volume 1, Detroit, Gale, 1989.

Bibliography: *The Annotated Guide to Stephen King: A Primary and Secondary Bibliography of the Works of America's Premier Horror Writer* by Michael R. Collings, Mercer Island, Washington, Starmont House, 1986.

Critical Study: Entry in *Contemporary Literary Criticism,* Volume 12, Detroit, Gale, 1980; Volume 26, 1983; Volume 37, 1985; *Stephen King: The Art of Darkness* by Douglas E. Winter, New York, New American Library, 1984; *Discovering Stephen King* edited by Darrell Schweitzer, Mercer Island, Washington, Starmont House, 1985; *The Many Facets of Stephen King* by Michael R. Collings, Mercer Island, Washington, Starmont House, 1985; *The Shorter Works of Stephen King* by Michael R. Collings and David Engebretson, Mercer Island, Washington, Starmont House, 1985; *Stephen King as Richard Bachman* by Michael R. Collings, Mercer Island, Washington, Starmont House, 1985; *The Films of Stephen King* by Michael R. Collings, Mercer Island, Washington, Starmont House, 1986; *Stephen King: At the Movies* by Jessie Horsting, New York, Signet/ Starlog, 1986; *The Stephen King Phenomenon* by Michael R. Collings, Mercer Island, Washington, Starmont House, 1987; *Bare Bones: Conversations on Terror with Stephen King* edited by Tim

Underwood and Chuck Miller, New York, McGraw-Hill, 1988; *The Stephen King Companion* edited by George Beahm, Kansas City, Missouri, Andrews and McMeel, 1989.

*   *   *

Called "a one-man entertainment industry" by critic Curt Suplee, Stephen King's tales of horror, science fiction, and fantasy have been public favorites since he published his first novel, *Carrie,* in 1974. In the six years that followed, he published *'Salem's Lot* (based on his short story "Jerusalem's Lot"), *The Shining, The Stand, The Dead Zone,* and *Firestarter;* had film versions of *Carrie* and *The Dead Zone* released; and had a television version of *'Salem's Lot* produced. By 1980, he had become the first writer to have three works listed simultaneously on the *New York Times'* best-seller list—*Firestarter, The Dead Zone,* and *The Shining.* To paraphrase his own words, Stephen King had become a "brand-name" author.

Young adults figure prominently in King's writing and make up a good portion of his readership. His novel *Carrie* centers around the peculiar life of sixteen-year-old Carrie White. Encompassing the problems of adolescence and peer pressure, the story opens in a high school gym class where, while showering, Carrie begins menstruating. She not only suffers the shock of this incident, having never been told about menstruation, but is humiliated by the other girls in her class, as they taunt her mercilessly. In addition to the constant harassment of her peers at school, Carrie must cope at home with the fanaticisms of her religious mother, in addition to controlling her own telekinetic powers. The story turns into a real bloodbath at a prom, but in spite of the horrors in plot that develop, *Carrie* has been compared to classic fairy tales like the Brothers Grimm's "Little Snow White" and "the Goose-Girl."

Though King writes primarily for adults, many of his works are accessible to a mature young adult audience; and his strong depictions of children, in novels like *Firestarter,* and *The Shining,* are strikingly realistic. The fact that his books are frequently banned from school libraries for their adult content doesn't faze the author at all since King feels teenagers will not be harmed by them, and they are more likely to go out of their way to seek out those titles to read anyway. In an interview for *High Times,* King explains: "We start kids off on things like 'Hansel and Gretel,' which features child abandonment, kidnapping, attempted murder, forcible detention, cannibalism, and finally murder by cremation. And the kids love it." Exposing children to tales of horror does not affect them adversely, he feels, for it's easier for children to suspend their beliefs when reading, whereas adults can clearly distinguish between what is real and what is not.

Some people think that King is not really a horror writer because horror fiction needs to be about the supernatural. *'Salem's Lot, Cycle of the Werewolf, Pet Sematary, It,* and other King novels contain these elements, but many of King's works are based on psychic phenomena, not supernatural monsters. In *Carrie,* Carrie uses telekinesis and pyrokinesis to gain revenge on her high school tormentors. Johnny Smith uses precognition in *Dead Zone* when he realizes that a presidential candidate is actually a potential dictator. Coincidences in *Apt Pupil* allow Todd Bowden to grow in evil from a bright thirteen-year-old fascinated by Nazi atrocities in the death camps to a seventeen-year-old murderer.

Carrie, Apt Pupil, and other novels by King could be classified as psychological thrillers, but to do so would ignore the fact that horror fiction's main purpose is to evoke uneasiness and fear in readers, and that King's novels repeatedly do so. King presents well-defined characters who are in surroundings like those his readers know. "The more frightened people become about the real world," said King in an interview, "the easier they are to scare." These familiar worlds in the novels are disrupted by dangers ranging from the slobbering werewolf in *Cycle of the Werewolf* to the monster which can take many forms in *It* to the homicidal car in *Christine* to a bizarre set of coincidences in *Apt Pupil*. By intruding into everyday life, rather than appearing in exotic settings and distant places, these dangers increase in shock value.

King evokes an even more complex set of reactions to these stories by his matter-of-fact telling and his tongue-in-cheek tone. In a passage in *Christine* he balances the horror by humorously describing a garage office as "Early American Carburetor." This casualness and humor disarms the reader, and makes the premise of a homicidal car in a familiar world more believable and unsettling than if the premise were presented by a more distant narrator using a less amiable tone. By repeatedly presenting the extraordinary and shocking in such a casual manner, Stephen King has established himself as the late twentieth century's master of colloquial horror.

Although it cannot be said that Stephen King's works are universally critically acclaimed, his works' overwhelming success with readers and moviegoers prove his enduring popularity and literary contribution.

—Harold Nelson

———

KLAUSE, Annette Curtis. American. Recipient: Best Book for Reluctant Readers, and Best Book for Young Adults, American Library Association, for *The Silver Kiss*.

PUBLICATIONS FOR YOUNG ADULTS

Fiction

The Silver Kiss. New York, Delacorte, 1990.
Alien Secrets. New York, Delacorte, 1993.

*

Biography: Essay in *Speaking for Ourselves, Too* compiled and edited by Donald R. Gallo, National Council of Teachers of English, 1993.

*   *   *

Rarely does a first novel generate such positive critical response as did Annette Curtis Klause's *The Silver Kiss*, a deceptively simple, yet seductive story that has been called the quintessential young adult novel. This hauntingly beautiful story combines modern realism and traditional vampire lore in a multifaceted tale. Zoë is attempting to deal with her mother's pending death from cancer, with her feelings of desertion by her father who is having his own problems coping, and with the fact that her best friend is moving away. She is fascinated and comforted by the mysterious, silver-haired Simon and is drawn into believing what she does not want to believe, that this handsome young man is a vampire on a mission to

avenge his own mother's death by killing his vampire brother, Christopher. Alternating chapters present Zoë's and Simon's perspectives on events and draw readers into their thoughts and feelings. Simon is a convincing character, a vampire with human emotions, yearning for affection in spite of his underlying anger and violence. There is a great deal of tension created by this clash of two worlds as well as restraint in dealing with both the tempting sexuality and violence. All of these layers of complexity are so skillfully crafted in language with such compelling simplicity that the book was named a Best Book for Reluctant Readers as well as a Best Book for Young Adults by the American Library Association.

Klause's second book, *Alien Secrets*, is a vivid science fiction adventure for younger adolescent readers that capitalizes on her ability to create multidimensional characters. Puck is a young heroine who makes mistakes but who continues to meet her commitments and accomplish her goals. Hush, a Shoowa, is an alien portrayed with humor, honor, dignity, and caring. Hush is tentative in reaching out, but, with Puck's help, learns the value of trust. This is a fast-moving mystery, a complex "whodunit" set in outer space that is not easy to solve. There are subtle clues, disguises, mistaken identities, and a search for a stolen object—in this case, the Soo, a religious symbol from Hush's homeland. There are also ghosts, the spirits of Hush's comrades killed by the evil Grakk who are trapped on the refitted spaceship on which they originally met their fate. Within the form of this mystery, Klause explores hyperspace and gives readers a sensitivity to the mathematical and scientific concepts involved. Especially appealing is her description of hyperspace from both an artistic and mathematical context. Klause seems to play with the imagery of the Soo and the hyperspace visualizations, implying an emotional and scientific relationship. It is no surprise that the ghosts who inhabit the spaceship, Cat's Cradle, are essential to plot movement. They are given peace by following the Soo, regained by Hush and Puck, to their home. Klause provides a crystalline image in the passages describing this: "Far above, ragged shreds tore off, sparkled for a moment, then turned to mist and disappeared, until the whole bolt of ghost cloth was unfurled and gone, back into the life force of its own world."

In both of these novels, Klause creates very appealing aliens who reach out to sensitive human characters in ways that benefit both. Her young protagonists are strong females who cope with realistic adolescent problems but still have the interest and the energy to help those outsiders rejected by others. Klause writes a good yarn, but she does much more than that; she has the ability to attract, fascinate, and thrill readers with exciting plots and memorable characters. The beauty of her language creates vivid images of those times and places where the real world touches the non-real, but very believable, world of magic and the imagination.

—Kay E. Vandergrift

———

KLEIN, Norma. American. Born in New York City, 13 May 1938. Educated at the Dalton School, New York, 1941-51; Elizabeth Irwin High School, 1952-56; Cornell University, Ithaca, New York, 1956-57; Barnard College, New York, 1957-60, B.A. (cum laude) in Russian 1960 (Phi Beta Kappa); Columbia University, New York, 1960-63, M.A. in Slavic languages 1963. Married Erwin Fleissner in

1963; two daughters. Author of novels, short stories, poetry, and children's fiction. Instructor of fiction at Yale and Wesleyan universities. Recipient: One of Child Study Association of America's Children's Books of the Year, 1973, *Girls Can Be Anything; Media & Methods* Maxi award for Paperbacks, 1975, and selected one of New York Public Library's Books for the Teen Age, 1980, both for *Sunshine;* one of *School Library Journal*'s Best Books of the Year, 1978, for *Love Is One of the Choices;* O. Henry award, 1983, for short story "The Wrong Man." *Died 25 April 1989.*

PUBLICATIONS FOR YOUNG ADULTS

Novel

Mom, the Wolf Man and Me. New York, Pantheon, 1972; London, Heinemann, 1986.
It's Not What You Expect. New York, Pantheon, 1973; London, Pan, 1986.
Coming to Life. New York, Simon & Schuster, 1974.
Confessions of an Only Child, illustrated by Richard Cuffari. New York, Pantheon, 1974.
Taking Sides. New York, Pantheon, 1974.
What It's All About. New York, Dial Press, 1975.
Girls Turn Wives. New York, Simon & Schuster, 1976.
Hiding. New York, Four Winds Press, 1976.
It's Okay If You Don't Love Me. New York, Dial, 1977.
Love Is One of the Choices. New York, Dial, 1978; London, Futura, 1981.
Tomboy. New York, Four Winds Press, 1978.
French Postcards (novelization of screenplay). New York, Fawcett, 1979; London, Coronet, 1980.
Breaking Up. New York, Pantheon, 1980; London, Pan, 1986.
A Honey of a Chimp. New York, Pantheon, 1980.
Robbie and the Leap Year Blues. New York, Dial, 1981.
Beginner's Love. New York, Dial, 1982; London, Pan, 1986.
The Queen of the What Ifs. New York, Fawcett, 1982.
Bizou. New York, Viking, 1983.
Angel Face. New York, Viking, 1984; London, Pan, 1987.
Snapshots. New York, Dial, 1984.
The Cheerleader. New York, Knopf, 1985.
Family Secrets. New York, Dial, 1985.
Give and Take. New York, Viking, 1985.
Going Backwards. New York, Scholastic, 1986; London, Pan, 1987.
My Life as a Body. New York, Knopf, 1987.
Older Men. New York, Dial, 1987; London, Women's Press, 1988.
No More Saturday Nights. New York, Knopf, 1988.
Now That I Know. New York, Bantam, 1988.
That's My Baby. New York, Viking, 1988.
Learning How to Fall. New York, Bantam. 1989.
Just Friends. New York, Knopf, 1990.

PUBLICATIONS FOR ADULTS

Novel

Give Me One Good Reason. New York, Putnam, 1973.
Sunshine (novelization of a TV play). New York, Holt Rinehart, 1975; London, Everest, 1976.

The Sunshine Years. New York, Dell, 1975; London, MacDonald, 1984.
Sunshine Christmas. Mount Kisco, New York, Futura, 1977.
Domestic Arrangements. New York, Evans, 1981; London, Futura, 1982.
Wives and Other Women. New York, St. Martin's, 1982; London, MacDonald, 1983.
The Swap. New York, St. Martin's, 1983.
Lovers. New York, Viking, 1984; London, Piatkus, 1986.
American Dreams. New York, Dutton, 1987.
The World as It Is. New York, Dutton, 1989.

Short Stories

Love and Other Euphemisms. New York, Putnam, 1972.
Sextet in A Minor: A Novella and Thirteen Short Stories. New York, St. Martin's, 1983.

PUBLICATIONS FOR CHILDREN

Fiction

Girls Can Be Anything, illustrated by Roy Doty. New York, Dutton, 1973.
Dinosaur's Housewarming Party, illustrated by James Marshall. New York, Crown, 1974.
If I Had It My Way, illustrated by Ray Cruz. New York, Pantheon, 1974.
Naomi in the Middle, illustrated by Leigh Grant. New York, Dial, 1974.
A Train for Jane (verse), illustrated by Miriam Schottland. Old Westbury, New York, Feminist Press, 1974.
Blue Trees, Red Sky, illustrated by Pat Grant Porter. New York, Pantheon, 1975.
Visiting Pamela, illustrated by Kay Chorao. New York, Dial, 1979.

Other

Baryshnikov's Nutcracker, photographs by Ken Regan, Christopher Little, and Martha Swope. New York, Putnam, 1983.
First Down & a Billion. New York, St. Martin's Press, 1987.

*

Media Adaptations: *Mom, the Wolf Man and Me* (cassette), Caedmon, 1977; *Mom, the Wolf Man and Me* (film), Time-Life Productions, 1979; *Confessions of an Only Child* (cassette), Caedmon, 1977.

Biography: Essay in *Authors and Artists for Young People,* Volume 2, Detroit, Gale, 1989, pp. 139-50; essay in *Speaking for Ourselves: Autobiographical Sketches by Notable Authors of Books for Young Adults,* Volume 1, compiled and edited by Donald R. Gallo, National Council of Teachers of English, 1990.

Critical Studies: *Children's Literature Review,* Volume 2, Detroit, Gale, 1976; entry in *Contemporary Literary Criticism,* Volume 30, Detroit, Gale, 1984.

*   *   *

When Norma Klein died from a heart infection at the age of fifty-one in 1989, she left the world of young adult literature a poorer place. Klein was a prolific American author who wrote for children, young adults, and adults. While all her books met with success, it was as a writer of children's and young adult fiction that Klein enjoyed the greatest recognition, becoming a superstar second only to Judy Blume when it came to having a large coterie of loyal young readers. Klein, like Blume, wrote with uncompromising frankness about issues that are of concern to contemporary youth: sex and sexism, single or gay parents, disintegrating families, pornography, feminism—all have been grist for Klein's mill. As a result, she shares another honor with Blume; Klein's books for young readers are second only to Blume's when it comes to censorship attempts in the United States, a fact of which Klein was quite proud.

In the 1970s, Klein wrote a number of children's books. These included *Girls Can Be Anything,* an expression of her strong feminist sentiments and a precursor of the firm feminist position that became clear in her later writings for older children and young adults. One of the books she wrote during this period was a taboo-breaking novel for its time for early adolescent readers, *Mom, the Wolf Man, and Me.* In it, Brett is the eleven-year-old daughter of an unmarried mother; their relationship is warm and mutually respectful. Her mother, to the consternation of many critics, relishes her life, and Brett suffers not at all from her highly unorthodox family situation. But into this tranquil situation comes a problem in the form of an unusual red-haired man with a wonderful Irish wolfhound called Norma. It becomes obvious early on that Brett's mother, Deborah, is not only interested in "The Wolf Man," as Brett has named him, but is considering marrying him. How Brett handles her jealousy and fears of the new relationship makes a warm, funny, and loving family story that many consider Klein's finest work, its controversial aspects notwithstanding.

Over the course of her career, Klein wrote over two dozen novels for teenage readers, almost all of which are still in print and read avidly by this age group. Klein said that her aim in writing young adult books was to present central characters who are "strong and interesting" in the face of the problems of growing up in American society; in this she succeeded admirably for the most part, as her legion of loyal young adult readers attests. *It's Not What You Expect* is a good example of how she managed to accomplish that aim. Fourteen-year-old twins Oliver and Carla decide to capitalize on Oliver's gourmet-cooking skills by opening a restaurant in a house the two are caring for over the summer and serve one dinner each evening at a reasonable price. They involve family and friends, and the restaurant is a success from the beginning, to the delight of everyone involved. Family problems arise, however: Dad, in a mid-life crisis, decides to leave and go to New York City to write a novel, picking up a new girlfriend in the process. Mom must cope with Dad's absence but also with the amorous advances of a neighbor, while older brother Tom's girlfriend is found to be pregnant. The twins offer Tom the restaurant's proceeds to pay for Sara Lee's abortion, but he angrily refuses. Carla, a strong young woman, is at first angry and hurt by all this, but eventually begins to realize that life just isn't always "what you expect," and grows as a result of her new understanding. The family is eventually reunited, but at some cost—and some acquired maturity—to all.

It's Okay If You Don't Love Me, another ground-breaking young adult book, is the story of Jody, an urbane, liberated Jewish young woman from a liberal, divorced New York family, who meets Lyle, a straightlaced midwestern Roman Catholic who has come to New York to live with his sister and her family. They fall in love despite their differences, and Jody attempts the difficult task of seducing Lyle. However, when Jody betrays Lyle with her former boyfriend Whitney, Lyle is alienated and deeply hurt. The clash of values arising from their differing backgrounds is not strong enough to keep Jody and Lyle apart forever, however, and eventually they are reconciled. What made *It's Okay* controversial to critics was its explicit and frank details about the young people's sexual activity; the book's publisher, in fact, went so far as to issue it as an adult book despite the fact that it was clearly written for teenagers, a not unusual occurrence with Klein's more explicit tales. In spite of this, the book remains one of Klein's most popular books among the young adult audience.

In the 1980s Klein began shifting from female protagonists' viewpoints in many of her young adult novels to young males' viewpoints. In *Snapshots,* for example, Sean and Marc, fine amateur photographers, take nude photographs of Marc's beautiful younger sister, not out of salaciousness but simply because Tiffany is an exquisite child who is a natural model. The boys get into trouble when the person developing the photos reports them to the district attorney, who accuses them of producing child pornography. In *Give and Take,* Spence, an eighteen-year-old naif, has to fend off the attentions of women who seek to seduce him. In *Beginner's Love,* the protagonist is Joel, a virgin who has his first affair, and *Angel Face* features Jason, who is not doing too well in either his school life or his love life, and whose family is falling apart. Klein has said that she writes from the boy's viewpoint because she wishes "there were more good novels about teenage boys, particularly about what boys feel about girls, their families, schools, the future."

Reviewers have occasionally faulted Klein for writing young adult books on "trendy" subjects; it can just as easily be argued that she wrote topical books, discussing in a way accessible to teenage readers, some of the issues of concern to kids today. Some of these topics she wrote of so well are Alzheimer's disease and its effects on a teenager and his family who take his grandmother into their home when she can no longer live alone *(Going Backwards);* a boy whose life is forever changed by a paralyzing accident but who still manages to reach out and help liberate a shy, insecure young woman who is his tutor *(My Life as a Body);* the effects of a mother's serious mental disease on a young woman and her father *(Older Men);* a thirteen-year-old's struggle to deal with not only her divorced parents but also her father's new life as a gay man *(Now That I Know);* an unmarried seventeen-year-old boy's successful fight to win custody of his infant son and parenthood's effects on his formerly carefree college life *(No More Saturday Nights);* and another seventeen-year-old boy, whose father is a recovering alcoholic and divorced from the boy's lesbian mother *(Learning How to Fall).* She wrote frankly, honestly, and usually with a leavening of humor to get the reader through the serious themes.

In all her books for young adults, Klein struck a note with her readers that few other authors for this age group do consistently. She wrote about the things that concern young people, both boys and girls: sexuality, sex roles and sexual behavior, love, peer relations, and family ties. Her portrayals of teenage angst always rang true, and like her friend Judy Blume, she respected and cared for her readers, who respond in kind to her books.

—Audrey Eaglen

KLEIN, Robin. Australian. Born in Kempsey, New South Wales, 28 February 1936. Educated at Kempsey Primary School, 1941-47, and Newcastle Girls High School, 1948-51, both New South Wales. Married Karl Klein in 1956 (divorced 1978); two sons and two daughters. Writer. Worked as a "tea lady" at a warehouse, and as a bookshop assistant, nurse, copper enamelist, and program aide at a school for disadvantaged children. Recipient: Special Mention from the Critici in Erba awards at the Bologna Children's Book Fair, 1979, for *The Giraffe in Pepperell Street;* Australian Junior Book of the Year award from the Children's Book Council of Australia, 1983, for *Thing;* Book of the Year award Highly Commended Citation from the Children's Book Council of Australia, 1984, for *Penny Pollard's Diary;* senior fellowship grant from the Arts Council of Australia Literature Board, 1985. Australian Human Rights award for Literature, 1989, and Australian Book of the Year award for older readers from the Children's Book Council of Australia, 1990, for *Came Back to Show You I Could Fly.* Dromkeen Medal, 1992. Agent: Curtis Brown, P.O. Box 19, Paddington, Sydney, NSW 2021. Address: Belgrave, VIC 3160, Australia.

PUBLICATIONS FOR YOUNG ADULTS

Fiction

Junk Castle, illustrated by Rolf Heimann. Melbourne, New York, and Oxford, Oxford University Press, 1983.
Penny Pollard's Diary, illustrated by Ann James. Melbourne and Oxford, Oxford University Press, 1983.
People Might Hear You, Melbourne and London, Penguin, 1983; New York, Viking Kestrel, 1987.
Penny Pollard's Letters, illustrated by Ann James. Melbourne and Oxford, Oxford University Press, 1984.
The Tomb Comb, illustrated by Heather Potter. Melbourne, Oxford University Press, 1984.
The Enemies, illustrated by Noela Young. North Ryde, New South Wales, Angus & Robertson, 1985; as *Enemies,* New York, Dutton, 1989.
Halfway Across the Galaxy and Turn Left. Melbourne and London, Viking Kestrel, 1985; New York, Viking, 1986.
Separate Places, illustrated by Anna Lacis. Kenthurst, New South Wales, Kangaroo Press, 1985.
Boss of the Pool, illustrated by H. Panagopoulos. Adelaide, Omnibus Books, 1986.
Games..., illustrated by Melissa Webb. Melbourne, Viking Kestrel, 1986.
Penny Pollard in Print, illustrated by James. Melbourne, Oxford University Press, 1986.
Get Lost, illustrated by June Joubert. Melbourne, Macmillan, 1987.
The Last Pirate, illustrated by Rick Armor. Melbourne, Rigby, 1987.
The Lonely Hearts Club, with Max Dunn. Melbourne, Oxford University Press, 1987; New York, Oxford University Press, 1988.
Parker-Hamilton, illustrated by Gaston Vanzet. Melbourne, Rigby, 1987.
Laurie Loved Me Best. Melbourne and London, Viking Kestrel, 1988.
Penny Pollard's Passport, illustrated by Ann James. Melbourne, Oxford University Press, 1988.
Against the Odds, illustrated by Bill Wood. Melbourne and London, Viking Kestrel, 1989.

Boris and Borsch. Sydney, Allen & Unwin, 1990.
Came Back to Show You I Could Fly. New York, Viking, 1990.
All in the Blue Unclouded Weather. New York, Viking, 1991.
Dresses of Red and Gold. Melbourne, Viking Kestrel, 1993.

PUBLICATIONS FOR CHILDREN

Fiction

Honoured Guest, illustrated by Margaret Power. Melbourne, Macmillan, 1979.
Sprung!, illustrated by Margaret Power. Willoughby, New South Wales, Rigby, 1982.
Thing, illustrated by Alison Lester. Melbourne and Oxford, Oxford University Press, 1982.
Oodoolay, illustrated by Vivienne Goodman. Flinders Park, South Australia, Era Publications, 1983.
Brock and the Dragon, illustrated by Rodney McRae. Rydalmere, New South Wales, Hodder & Stoughton, 1984.
Hating Alison Ashley, Melbourne and London, Penguin, 1984; New York, Penguin, 1985.
Ratbags and Rascals, illustrated by Alison Lester. Melbourne, Dent, 1984.
Thalia the Failure, illustrated by Rhyll Plant. Gosford, New South Wales, Ashton Scholastic, 1984.
Thingnapped!, illustrated by Alison Lester. Melbourne and Oxford, Oxford University Press, 1984.
The Princess Who Hated It, illustrated by Marie Smith. Adelaide, Omnibus Books, 1986.
Birk the Berserker, illustrated by Alison Lester. Adelaide, Omnibus Books, 1987.
I Shot an Arrow, illustrated by Geoff Hocking. Melbourne, Viking Kestrel, 1987.

Poetry

The Giraffe in Pepperell Street, illustrated by Gill Tomblin. Rydalmere, New South Wales, Hodder & Stoughton, 1978.
Snakes and Ladders: Poems about the Ups and Downs of Life, illustrated by Ann James. Melbourne, Dent, 1985.

Other

Annabel's Ghost (stories). Melbourne, Oxford University Press, 1985.
Christmas, illustrated by Kristen Hilliard. Sydney, Methuen, 1987.
Don't Tell Lucy, illustrated by Kristen Hilliard. Sydney, Methuen, 1987.
Robin Klein's Crookbook, illustrated by Kristen Hilliard. Sydney, Methuen, 1987.
Dear Robin...: Letters to Robin Klein. Sydney, Allen and Unwin, 1988.
Tearaways: Stories to Make You Think Twice. New York, Viking, 1991.

*

Critical Study: Entry in *Children's Literature Review,* Volume 21, Detroit, Gale, 1991.

*   *   *

Robin Klein is one of Australia's most prolific and versatile writers for young adults. Her work includes picture books, short stories, and fiction for both younger and older readers. Although the protagonists (who are mainly female) of Klein's young adult fiction range in age from around eleven to eighteen, the implied readership of her work seems to be a younger teenaged group. The author keeps sexual tension at a distance and the novels generally employ a child focalization, eschewing the dangerous complexities of developing adolescent sexuality. The anxieties of Klein's characters centre on peer-group exclusivity and family embarrassments: anxieties about being acceptable to the right "in-crowd" rather than to romantic soul mates.

Klein writes with humour and irony. Her characters frequently display a rueful or ironic mode of self-presentation. Their language is wry, witty, and knowing rather than sentimental—though lyric and nostalgic moments are to be found in the author's writing, particularly in her more recent autobiographically based novels, such as *All in the Blue Unclouded Weather* and *Dresses of Red and Gold*. Klein generally employs a collusive, even conspiratorial narrative stance. It is not her usual mode to challenge her audience's sense of reality, or its social and cultural assumptions. She writes at her reader's level, forging a comfortable alliance between "us" and "them." Her stories are full of characters one loves to hate: more fortunate classmates, glamorous older sisters (like Dovis, in *Halfway Across the Galaxy and Turn Left*), loutish boy-bullies, smart-alecky teachers, etc.; who conspire to humiliate the luckless and envious heroine.

Child characters in Klein's novels frequently suffer from an acute sense of responsibility towards the less-than-capable adults in their lives, are often represented as little old men and women, for whom the burden of holding things together in their dysfunctional families seems to weigh with a guilty imperative. For example, Patricia Miggs, the heroine of *Games...*, bears the burden of caring for her widowed, invalid, and morbidly possessive mother, and is consumed with guilt as she makes her escape to spend a weekend away with two treacherous girlfriends.

The comic version of this ultra-responsible character type is found in X, the young female "Family Organizer" in Klein's science fiction spoof, *Halfway Across the Galaxy and Turn Left*. Family roles are reversed in this alien ménage: X literally does have the burden of the family on her incompetent shoulders. In this story of a family of remarkable aliens, with an ordinary (if officious) daughter, Klein portrays a parodic inversion of the drama of the adolescent outcast who sees him/herself as an alien in a society into which other (more glamorous or fortunate) souls seem to fit easily.

Science fiction is not Klein's usual mode; her stories and novels more commonly inhabit the territory of social realism wherein she depicts an urban society, with its contemporary social problems: broken homes and single parents, working-class deprivation, middle-class emotional deprivation, drug-referral centers, peer-group "territories" which outsiders must avoid, homeless teenagers, and those who have homes which are not "homes."

More recently, however, Klein has turned to the past and her own life for inspiration. *All in the Blue Unclouded Weather* and *Dresses of Red and Gold* are set in "Wilgawa," a fictional town in rural Australia in the late 1940s. These novels are composed of vignettes from the lives of a family of working-class girls, with their youthful ambitions towards great and glamorous lives. The stories enact the girls' negotiation of hierarchies of class and adolescent social prestige, depicting their fascination for the attractions of wealth and elegance represented to them in magazines, and their embarrassment for their families and the makeshift gracelessness of their homes.

Klein's fictional world is one in which appearances deceive. Her characters are often afflicted with selective blindness, misinterpreting the evidence in front of them. The plots turn on the protagonist's reversal of her/his previous, mistaken opinions or expectations. The reader in *Hating Alison Ashley*, for example, is alerted quite early in the narrative to the possibility that Alison (Erica Yurken's rival and enemy) is really her secret ally. Long before Erica's eyes are opened, the reader is made privy to the knowledge that Alison has her own social discomforts and a deep need for intelligent female friendship. Similarly, while eleven-year-old Seymour, in *Came Back to Show You I Could Fly*, sees eighteen-year-old Angie as an elegant and exotic "flower" suffering from a mysterious "flu," the reader identifies her as a disorganized junkie, fired by imaginative but futile illusions and scarred by the rejection on the part of her well-to-do family.

Often Klein employs the device of the juxtaposition of narrative "voices," providing conflicting or revisionist focalizations. In *Laurie Loved Me Best*, the two friends, Andre and Julia, relate, by turns, their perceptions of events. The juxtaposed narrations reveal the flaws in each girl's representation of the other's home life; illusory utopias are revealed to be nothing of the sort.

In Klein's world, enemies turn out to be friends; longed-for social triumphs prove to be deliberately planned humiliations; rich little girls with "nice" families turn out to be "poor little rich girls," while poor and unfashionable homes turn out to have hidden "riches" of love and communality. Thus Klein's stories reveal a deep sense of class division. Her heroines are exposed as would-be social climbers, who are desperate to escape into an imagined world of wealth and glamour. They are conscious of their relative poverty and social deprivation and are anxious to be included into the cliques of rich and popular girls who seem to perpetually scorn and exclude them. These protagonists commonly find their redemption in a true friend—usually another unfashionable type—and in realizing that wealth is often merely a social facade. Moreover, wealth is usually equated with emotional poverty. Alison Ashley is a beautifully dressed, beautifully behaved interloper in the deprived world of Barringa East Primary School: she is also a lonely latchkey child whose high-powered executive mother has no time to give her the love she craves. Similarly, Angie's mother, in *Came Back to Show You I Could Fly*, has erased all evidence of her wayward daughter's presence from her former room in the spotless and elegant middle-class home, much as the family has apparently cut the disappointing teenage drug addict out of their elegant and well-regulated lives.

This plot tendency may display a predilection on Klein's part towards wish-fulfillment fantasy; the clichés, however, are not always acted out (Angie's parents do not, in the end, abandon her, while Seymour's domestic circumstances demonstrate that less-privileged homes may be as impoverished in love as rich ones). Fortunately, Klein's more mature writing demonstrates that she is flexible enough to show that these social and moral oppositions are never absolute.

—Leonie Margaret Rutherford

KNOWLES, John. American. Born in Fairmont, West Virginia, 16 September 1926. Educated at Phillips Exeter Academy, Exeter, New Hampshire, graduated 1945; Yale University, New Haven, Connecticut, B.A. 1949. Reporter, Hartford *Courant,* Connecticut, 1950-52; freelance writer, 1952-56; associate editor, *Holiday* magazine, Philadelphia, 1956-60. Writer-in-residence, University of North Carolina, Chapel Hill, 1963-64, and Princeton University, New Jersey, 1968-69. Recipient: Rosenthal Foundation award, William Faulkner Foundation award, both 1961, for *A Separate Peace;* National Association of Independent Schools award, 1961.

PUBLICATIONS FOR YOUNG ADULTS

Novels

A Separate Peace. London, Secker and Warburg, 1959; New York, Macmillan, 1960.
Morning in Antibes. New York, Macmillan, and London, Secker and Warburg, 1962.
Indian Summer. New York, Random House, and London, Secker and Warburg, 1966.
The Paragon. New York, Random House, 1971.
Spreading Fires. New York, Random House, 1974.
A Vein of Riches. Boston, Little Brown, 1978.
Peace Breaks Out. New York, Holt Rinehart, 1981.
A Stolen Past. New York, Holt Rinehart, 1983; London, Constable, 1984.
The Private Life of Axie Reed. New York, Dutton, 1986.

Short Stories

Phineas: Six Stories. New York, Random House, 1968.

Other

Double Vision: American Thoughts Abroad. New York, Macmillan, and London, Secker and Warburg, 1964.

*

Media Adaptations: *A Separate Peace* (film), Paramount, 1972.

Biography: Entry in *Dictionary of Literary Biography,* Volume 6, Detroit, Gale, 1980.

Manuscript Collection: Beinecke Library, Yale University, New Haven, Connecticut.

Critical Study: Entry in *Contemporary Literary Criticism,* Detroit, Gale, Volume 1, 1973; Volume 4, 1975; Volume 10, 1979.

*   *   *

John Knowles is best known for his first opus: *A Separate Peace.* The awards granted this work suggest one reason for its enormous popularity and persistence, especially in the academic milieu: it is a very useful text with which to teach students how a good book should be written.

Knowles's other novels have generally been judged by critics to display a pleasing style, a clear plot line, and a fine sense of place (perhaps a partial result of his work for *Holiday Magazine)*—but, *A Separate Peace* adds, in great measure, to these qualities three other elements of fiction that carry it beyond the other titles: a focused, useful point of view; a superb realization of character; and, a substantial, wholesome, and satisfying theme.

These attributes blend well in this minor classic. The first-person narrator, Gene Forrester (perhaps representing Knowles himself, at an earlier age), provides the point of view (the reader can know and feel only what the narrator observes and experiences), and this works to the novel's benefit, since the most important thrust in the text is Gene's feeling about, reaction to, and final understanding of the hero of the book: the delightful, admirable, charming Phineas ("Finny").

Making such a truly amiable figure believable is one of the great triumphs of *A Separate Peace.* Knowles accomplishes this by combining the characteristics of a superb athlete, an indifferent student, a wildly daring young man, and a profoundly extroverted character all in one. The setting is the Devon School (based on Phillips Exeter Academy, attended by Knowles) in the summer of 1942. Since the Second World War has begun for the United States, the world conflict becomes a sort of analogue for the conflicts in the novel.

The salient feature of Finny's character—and a thematic force in the book—is his refusal to accept conflict: "...there might be a flow of simple, unregulated friendliness between them, and such flows were one of Finny's reasons for living." This naturally charismatic boy (all but a few of the lads at the school are just a year or two too young to enlist in the military) is a credible counterpoise to the more introverted and intellectual Gene, who becomes his best friend and, indirectly, causes his death.

Since the events are told in retrospect, as Gene recalls them on a return visit to the school fifteen years later, the story gains substance from the more thoughtful recounting and interpreting of the plot and the people by an older person. Perhaps the most important interpretation is Gene's realization that Phineas was one of a kind: as he comments at the close of the book, regarding the difference between his friend and other people, "All of them, all except Phineas, constructed at infinite cost to themselves these Maginot Lines against this enemy they thought they saw across the frontier, this enemy who never attacked that way—if he ever attacked at all; if he was indeed the enemy."

Finny has shown his wonderful acceptance of people and his rejection of evil in his unwillingness to blame Gene for his disastrous fall from the tree, or for his friend's action when he does face the reality. In their last conversation, where Gene manages to convince Finny of his guilt, Finny interprets the motives in his typically generous way: "Something just seized you. It wasn't anything you really felt against me, it wasn't some kind of hate you've felt all along. It wasn't anything personal." To make such a saintly character believable is possibly one of the great accomplishments in modern literature. Nowhere can one find, also, such a lively and engaging picture of adolescence. How many readers would like to find a friend, as Gene does, of whom he or she could say, "Only Phineas was never afraid, only Phineas never hated anyone."

Knowles's other works are less known, though his third novel, *Indian Summer,* was a selection of the Literary Guild. The prime complaint among critics is that the characters in these later works are not developed as fully and vigorously as those in *A Separate Peace.* In *The Paragon,* the central character, Lou Colfax, emerges with considerable clarity; however, the other personages (such as Gordon Durand and the other moneyed people in the plot) seem stereotyped.

In *Peace Breaks Out,* Knowles wisely returns to the Devon School, this time with a World War II veteran who is an instructor at the academy. Since the instructor is an alumnus of Devon, much is familiar; the students now attending are not so, however. Hallam is a less appealing protagonist than either Phineas or Gene Forrester, and once more the scattered point of view distracts the reader's attention. The plot somewhat echoes that of *A Separate Peace,* but the ambiance is far more grim and even sinister, as Hallam comes to grips with the fact that the war is not really over; treachery, hatred, and cruelty still exist, even in this idyllic setting. At the close, he thinks of the monstrous boy Wexford that he has encountered here. "He is an incipient monster,...and I can't stop him. For the last dozen years we've seen in the world how monsters can come to the top and just what horrors they can achieve. And these monsters were once adolescents." He sees that monsters are forming even at Devon and that "people will have to try to cope with them, confront them, risk everything in defeating them, defeating them once again, for a time."

Clearly, this grimmer tone reveals adolescence—and, indeed, human nature—in a much darker fashion than *A Separate Peace.* However, the pervasiveness of war is keenly represented. While the personalities of the unappealing Wexford and Hochschwender are not fully outlined, their evil and misguided energy come to light, as in this observation by Hallam: "Nothing could be more vicious than a fight between boys, lacking any trace of the caginess or caution of men." While the events and the people in *Peace Breaks Out* fail to attain the force to be found in *A Separate Peace,* this tightly woven story seems to come closest to that high achievement. In any judgment of Knowles's work, one fact is certain: one would have to look far to find an author who can so ably set forth the feelings, thoughts, and actions of young men, especially in crisis situations.

—Fred McEwen

———

KNUDSON, R.R. Pseudonym for Rozanne Knudson. American. Born in Washington, D.C., 1 June 1932. Educated at Brigham Young University, Provo, Utah, B.A. 1954; University of Georgia, Athens, M.A. 1958; Stanford University, Stanford, California, Ph.D. 1967. English teacher in various public high schools in Florida, 1957-60; assistant professor of English, Purdue University, West Lafayette, Indiana, 1965-67; coeditor, *Quartet,* 1966-68; supervisor of English, Hicksville Schools, Long Island, New York, 1967-70; assistant professor, York College of the City University of New York, Jamaica, New York, 1970-71; full-time writer, 1972—; instructor in English, University of Lethbridge, Lethbridge, Alberta, summer, 1969; writer-in-residence, Kean College, 1986. Also, teacher of fiction writing, Rutgers University, New Brunswick, New Jersey. Recipient: Nominee for Maud Lovelace Book award, for *Zanboomer;* nominee for Dorothy Canfield Fisher Book award, for *Zanbanger.* Fellow at MacDowell Colony, Virginia Center for the Creative Arts, Ragdale, Dorland Mountain Colony, Cummington Community of the Arts, Villa Montalvo, and Gell House. Address: 73 The Boulevard, Sea Cliff, NY 11579, U.S.A.

PUBLICATIONS FOR YOUNG ADULTS

Fiction

Sports Poetry, with P.K. Ebert. New York, Dell, 1971.
Zanballer. New York, Delacorte, 1972.
Jesus Song. New York, Delacorte, 1973.
You Are the Rain. New York, Delacorte, 1974.
Fox Running. New York, Harper, 1975.
Zanbanger. New York, Harper, 1977.
Zanboomer. New York, Harper, 1978.
Rinehart Lifts. New York, Farrar Straus, 1980.
Just Another Love Story. New York, Farrar Straus, 1982.
Speed. New York, Dutton, 1983.
Zan Hagan's Marathon. New York, Farrar Straus, 1984.
Frankenstein's 10K. New York, Viking, 1986.
Rinehart Shouts. New York, Farrar Straus, 1987.
Editor with May Swenson, *American Sports Poems.* New York, Orchard Books/F. Watts, 1988.

Nonfiction

Selected Objectives for the English Language Arts, with Arnold Leslie Lazarus. Boston, Houghton Mifflin, 1967.
Books for You, with J.A. Wilson and others. New York, Washington Square Press, 1971.
Starbodies, with Franco Columbo. New York, Elesvier-Dutton, 1978.
Weight Training for Young Athletes, with Franco Columbo. Chicago, Illinois, Contemporary Books, 1979.
Muscles! New York, Avon, 1983.
Punch! New York, Avon, 1983.
Babe Didrikson: Athlete of the Century, illustrated by Ted Lewin. New York, Viking, 1985.
A Waterpower Workout, with Lynda Huey. New York, New American Library, 1986.
Martina Navratilova: Tennis Power, illustrated by George Angelini. New York, Viking, 1987.
Julie Brown: Racing against the World. New York, Viking, 1988.
Coaching Evelyn, with Pat Connolly. New York, Harper, 1990.
The Wonderful Pen of May Swenson. New York, Macmillan, 1993.

Other

Contributor, *The Scribner's Anthology for Young People.* New York, Scribner, 1976.

*

Manuscript Collection: Kerlan Collection, University of Minnesota.

R.R. Knudson comments:
I've written in silent rooms on Long Island and in Delaware, Virginia, Georgia, Florida, Arizona, California, and in New Hampshire. I've written only about my obsessions, and almost all of my characters are myself.

*   *   *

Most of R.R. Knudson's books deal with sports in one form or another, but they are so enjoyably written that even a nonparticipant can read them and be engrossed in the wants and needs of Knudson's characters. Her writing is clean and straightforward, lacking in lavish detail but filled with action and goals.

Her best known books are perhaps her series about the good-at-all-sports Suzanne Hagan, called "Zan" by her peers. Zan lives for sports of all kinds and is supported by her parents and best friend, the bookish Arthur Rinehart.

The first book in the series is *Zanballer* and is devoted to girls playing the man's sport of football. When the Robert E. Lee High School's gym is being refurbished, the girl's gym class is relegated to the home economics wing to learn to dance. Zan refuses to dance and begs to use the lacrosse field. Through Zan's begging and Rinehart's scheming, enough girls are coaxed from dancing to make a football team, and the coach takes notice. Once the girl's team, Catch-11, ties in a game with his junior varsity squad, even the reluctant principal bows to pressure from the press, and Catch-11, led by Zan, wins a special exhibition game played against the Richmond Redskins Junior Varsity.

Zanballer touches on some issues of concern to teenagers, especially girls, and reflects the growing willingness of schools to integrate girls into the previously all-male teams. Zan's fight against the principal, who tries through the entire series to force her into his idea of what a girl should be, is encouraging. That she wins in the end is even more so, since her victory is only achieved by being as good as the boys.

In *Zanbanger*, Zan and her friend E.J. are preparing for the girl's basketball season with delight. The gym floor is repaired, and the girl's team is ready to go—until Mrs. Butor, *Zanballer's* dance teacher is named as the coach. Mrs. Butor coaches polite, restrained play, and Zan is cut from the team for being "too aggressive." When Zan practices with the boys' team, she excels, and that gives her the idea to try out for boys' basketball. The principal forbids it, the community is outraged, and Zan goes to court to win the right to be allowed to play. Rinehart, acting as her lawyer, defends not only Zan's right to play with the boys, but the right of any girl who wants to, anywhere. Even though Zan's court battle is won, her troubles are only beginning since the boys' team is hostile toward both Zan and E.J. and refuses to help the two girls on the court. By the book's end, Zan and E.J. have won over the team, and the Generals have won the championship, once again beating the Redskins.

In *Zanboomer*, Zan, E.J., and Aileen, the prom queen turned player, reunite on the boys' baseball team. In a game with the Redskins, Zan is injured by Joe Donn Joiner, her enemy throughout the books. Shoulder separated, Zan can no longer play baseball, and in an attempt to keep her from eating her heart out over the loss of her team, Rinehart introduces her to long-distance running. Zan practices diligently, and by the end of the school year, she has once again defeated the Redskins, and Joe Donn Joiner's attempt to cheat Zan out of the race ends in failure.

Zan Hagan's Marathon puts Zan on the Olympic Team as a long-distance runner again, where instead of winning her race, she ties it, finally learning that winning is not all there is.

The first three books are written from Zan's point of view, with Rinehart getting a chapter for his opinions and view of what is happening to Zan. Each character is distinctly written, and Rinehart's scientific approach to sports is humorous and amusing. Knudson portrays the feelings of winning, losing, and almost being good enough with the intensity of a young person, and is careful not to bring adult responses to adolescent characters.

Another very noteworthy book is *Fox Running*, the story of Fox Running, a Mescalero Apache girl who runs away from her reservation after the death of her grandfather. Found by Kathy "Sudden" Hart, a former Olympic sprinter who has lost her nerve to race, and Sudden's coach, Fox's potential as a runner is discovered. Brought back to the University of Arizona, Fox proves to be useless to the coach since she is gun-shy and cannot bear the sound of the starter's pistol. Sudden will not give up on Fox, just as Fox refuses to allow Sudden to let her fears manipulate her future as a sprinter. Both learn from each other's pasts, and the book culminates triumphantly at the Olympics, where both Fox and Sudden win their races—Fox setting a new women's world record for the mile.

Fox Running is a gently told story of two hurt people, and how each finds the courage to go on. Fear of the past is the primary theme, with a secondary theme of perseverance. Both Sudden and Fox are well-drawn and distinct characters, people in their own right, and easy to care about. Knudson's secondary characters are also as clearly drawn, and memorable. All of R.R. Knudson's books are good, well-written sports stories, about believable, real people.

—Melanie Belviso

———

KOERTGE, Ron(ald). American. Born in Olney, Illinois, 22 April 1940. Educated at University of Illinois, Urbana, B.A. 1962; University of Arizona, Tucson, M.A. 1965. Married 1) Cheryl Vasconcellos; 2) Bianaca Richards. Professor of English, Pasadena City College, California, 1965—. Recipient: National Endowment for the Arts Fellowship, 1990; California Arts Council grant, 1993. Agent: William Reiss, Paul R. Reynolds, Inc., 12 East 41st Street, #1600, New York, NY 10017. Address: Department of English, Pasadena City College, 1560 Colorado Boulevard, Pasadena, CA 91106, U.S.A.

PUBLICATIONS FOR YOUNG ADULTS

Fiction

Where the Kissing Never Stops. New York, Atlantic Monthly, 1987.
The Arizona Kid. Boston, Joy Street, 1988.
The Boy in the Moon. Boston, Joy Street, 1990.
Mariposa Blues. Boston, Joy Street, 1991.
The Harmony Arms. Boston, Joy Street, 1992.

Poetry

Meat: Cherry's Market Diary. Mag Press, 1973.
The Father Poems. Fremont, Michigan, Sumac Press, 1974.
The Hired Nose. Mag Press, 1974.
My Summer Vacation. Venice Poetry Company, 1975.
Men under Fire. Fallon, Nevada, Duck Down Press, 1976.
Twelve Photographs of Yellowstone. San Francisco, California, Red Hill Press, 1976.
How to Live on Five Dollars a Day. Venice Poetry Company, 1976.
Cheap Thrills. Stockton, California, Wormwood Review Press, 1976.

Sex Object. Los Angeles, Little Caesar Press, 1979.
The Jockey Poems. Cape Elizabeth, Maine, Maelstrom Press, 1980.
Diary Cows. Los Angeles, Little Caeser Press, 1982.
Life on the Edge of the Continent: Selected Poems. Fayetteville, Arkansas, University of Arkansas Press, 1982.
High School Dirty Poems. Los Angeles, California, Red Wind, 1991.

PUBLICATIONS FOR ADULTS

Fiction

The Boogeyman. New York, Norton, 1980.

*

Biography: Entry in *Dictionary of Literary Biography,* Volume 105, Detroit, Gale, 1991; essay in *Speaking for Ourselves, Too* compiled and edited by Donald R. Gallo, National Council of Teachers of English, 1993.

Ron Koertge comments:
    I never intended to be a young adult writer, so it's a surprise to me and a lot more fun than if I'd become the sort of writer I'd planned. In a sense it was the failure to write a second novel after *The Boogeyman* that made it possible for me to succeed as a YA novelist. I like writing for kids, and as long as ideas for books keep showing up, I'll keep writing.

*   *   *

    With the publication of only five young adult novels, Ron Koertge has established himself as a talented and popular author of contemporary realistic fiction that aptly chronicles the male adolescent experience. Koertge's style is direct and natural; a remarkable ear for, and an emphasis on, dialogue serves to immediately engage the reader in the story. Enormously likeable, Koertge's fully-realized characters are convincingly honest, loyal to family and friends, and display a strong sense of integrity despite their teenage angst. One of Koertge's greatest gifts to his readers is his irresistibly witty sense of humor. While he frequently uses humor to reveal character, Koertge never downplays the seriousness of universal adolescent concerns. His books are both affecting and funny—a rare feat in a field deluged with issue-oriented books often overwhelmed by sentimentality or triteness.
    "God, I thought about sex a lot," says sixteen-year-old Walker in Koertge's first novel, *Where the Kissing Never Stops.* Walker's preoccupation with sex introduces a concern important to many of Koertge's characters. In a frank and funny exploration of sexuality, Walker struggles to nurture a romantic, fulfilling relationship with his girlfriend Rachel and to keep his mother's embarrassing occupation as a roadhouse stripper a secret from her. The consummation of Walker and Rachel's relationship is caring and respectful; Walker moves toward a mature acceptance of his mother's job when he realizes how happy it makes her. Dialogue about masturbation and body image is candid, but Koertge depicts Walker as both vulnerable and tender, much more than just a horny teenager out for some action.
    Sexuality also plays an important role in *The Arizona Kid.* The story's narrator—sixteen-year-old Billy, self-conscious about being too short, too pale, and too virginal—arrives in Tucson to spend the summer with his gay Uncle Wes. Billy faces a summer of change

and discovery as he experiences firsthand the colorful world of horse racing, falls head-over-heels in love, loses his virginity, and learns about his uncle's gay lifestyle. Billy's relationship with his feisty, understanding girlfriend Cara Mae boosts his shaky self-confidence; warm, witty, and generous Uncle Wes fosters Billy's growing sense of independence. Billy, at first uncertain how to behave in his uncle's company, quickly overcomes his discomfort as he and Wes develop a natural rapport and share frank, often funny discussions about romance, AIDS, and birth control. Koertge presents a range of sexuality with sensitivity and openness, but leavens serious themes with plentiful doses of humor. At summer's end a newly confident and assured Billy tells Uncle Wes that "I'm as tall as I am. It's okay."
    High school seniors Nick, Freida, and Kevin have been best friends forever, but suddenly things change dramatically in *The Boy in the Moon.* First Kevin turns into a bleached-blond muscle-head with whom the acne-riddled, insecure, self-effacing Nick has trouble relating. Then Nick finds himself romantically attracted to Freida. Nick and Freida's mutual attraction culminates in their first awkward but loving sexual experience. As Freida's caring and commitment help Nick overcome his insecurity and instill in him a sense of self-worth, Nick and Freida's support of Kevin help him deal with an abusive, alcoholic father. At summer's finish the trio part company, their friendship solidified and strengthened by their shared, transforming experiences.
    Mariposa Blues, set against the backdrop of a southern California racetrack, also chronicles a summer of change and confusion. After years of being considered a "chip off the old block," thirteen-year-old Grahame struggles to establish an identity separate from that of his father and finds himself engaged in constant confrontations with him. By summer's end, father and son move toward reconciliation and a fuller understanding of each other. Grahame's confusion and alienation from his father is portrayed in a vivid and credible manner, especially in the stormy confrontational scenes.
    The Harmony Arms focuses on some of Koertge's quirkiest characters to date. Fourteen-year-old Gabriel McKay's father Sumner, an eccentric who uses a ubiquitous handpuppet named Timmy the Otter as his mouthpiece and pretends his suitcase is a dog named Rover, causes Gabriel endless embarrassment. Then father and son move temporarily to Los Angeles, where Gabriel discovers his neighbors—a ninety-year-old vegetarian nudist; a mostly off-target psychic; an actress/animals-rights activist; and her daughter Tess, a fourteen-year-old aspiring filmmaker who carries a camcorder everywhere to film her life as it takes place—are just as offbeat as his father. As Gabriel and Tess develop a romantic friendship, they commiserate together over the mortifying and often unfathomable actions of their parents. Anything-goes LA helps to give Gabriel a new perspective on himself and his father; when Tess remarks about her mother that "you gotta throw away a lot of weird stuff, but what's left is pretty good," Gabriel comprehends that her comment holds true for Sumner as well. Infused with humor and snappy dialogue, Koertge's funniest novel yet offers the reader an oddball, unconventional, but enormously appealing coming-of-age story.
    Koertge's spirited, funny stories, uniquely attuned to contemporary adolescent concerns, offer their readers easy companionship while providing them with provocative explorations of sexuality and self-identity. As readers navigate the perilous realms of their own adolescence, they will surely want Koertge's books along to help ease their way.

—Carolyn Shute

KONIGSBURG, E(laine) L(obl). Born in New York City, 10 February 1930. Educated at Farrell High School, Pennsylvania; Carnegie Institute of Technology (now Carnegie-Mellon University), Pittsburgh, B.S. 1952; University of Pittsburgh, 1952-54. Married David Konigsburg in 1952; two sons and one daughter. Writer. Bookkeeper, Shenango Valley Provision Company, Sharon, Pennsylvania, 1947-48; science teacher, Bartram School, Jacksonville, Florida, 1954-55, 1960-62. Worked as manager of a dormitory laundry, playground instructor, waitress and library page while in college; research assistant in tissue culture lab and organic chemistry while in graduate school at the University of Pittsburgh. Recipient: Honor book in *Book Week* Children's Spring Book Festival, 1967, and as a Newbery Honor Book, 1968, for *Jennifer, Hecate, Macbeth, William McKinley, and Me, Elizabeth;* Newbery Medal, 1968, and William Allen White award, 1970, both for *From the Mixed-Up Files of Mrs. Basil E. Frankweiler;* Carnegie-Mellon Merit award, 1971; American Library Association notable children's book and National Book award nomination, both 1974, both for *A Proud Taste for Scarlet and Miniver;* American Library Association best book for young adults, for *The Second Mrs. Giaconda,* and *Father's Arcane Daughter;* American Library Association notable children's book and American Book award nomination, 1980, both for *Throwing Shadows; Jennifer, Hecate, Macbeth, William McKinley, and Me, Elizabeth, About the B'nai Bagels, A Proud Taste for Scarlet and Miniver,* and *Journey to an 800 Number* were all chosen Children's Books of the Year by the Child Study Association of America. Address: c/o Atheneum Publishers, 866 Third Ave., New York, NY 10022, U.S.A.

PUBLICATIONS FOR YOUNG ADULTS (ILLUSTRATED BY THE AUTHOR)

Fiction

From the Mixed-Up Files of Mrs. Basil E. Frankweiler. New York, Atheneum, 1967; London, Macmillan, 1969.
Jennifer, Hecate, Macbeth, William McKinley, and Me, Elizabeth. New York, Atheneum, 1967; as *Jennifer, Hecate, MacBeth, and Me,* London, Macmillan, 1968.
About the B'nai Bagels. New York, Atheneum, 1969.
(George). New York, Atheneum, 1970; as *Benjamin Dickenson Carr and His (George),* London, Penguin, 1974.
Altogether, One at a Time (stories), illustrated by Gail E. Haley, Mercer Meyer, Gary Parker, and Laurel Schindelman. New York, Atheneum, 1971; 2nd edition, London, Macmillan, 1989.
A Proud Taste for Scarlet and Miniver. New York, Atheneum, 1973; London, Macmillan, 1974.
The Dragon in the Ghetto Caper. New York, Atheneum, 1974; London, Macmillan, 1979.
Father's Arcane Daughter. New York, Atheneum, 1976; London, Macmillan, 1977.
Throwing Shadows (stories). New York, Atheneum, 1979.
Journey to an 800 Number. New York, Atheneum, 1982; as *Journey by First Class Camel,* London, Hamish Hamilton, 1983.
Up from Jericho Tel. New York, Atheneum, 1986.
Samuel Todd's Book of Great Colors. New York, Macmillan, 1990.
Samuel Todd's Book of Great Inventions. New York, Atheneum, 1991.
Amy Elizabeth Explores Bloomingdale's. New York, Atheneum, 1992.
T-Backs, T-Shirts, COAT and Suit. New York, Atheneum, 1993.

Other

Contributor, *Expectations 1980* (braille anthology). E. Falmouth, Massachusetts, Braille Institute, 1980.
The Mask beneath the Face; Reading about and with, Writing about and for Children. Washington, D.C., Library of Congress, 1990.

*

Media Adaptations: *From the Mixed-Up Files of Mrs. Basil E. Frankweiler* (record; cassette), Miller-Brody/Random House, 1969; *From the Mixed-Up Files of Mrs. Basil E. Frankweiler* (motion picture) starring Ingrid Bergman, Cinema 5, 1973, released under new title *The Hideaways,* Bing Crosby Productions, 1974; *Jennifer and Me* (television movie; based on *Jennifer, Hecate, Macbeth, William McKinley, and Me, Elizabeth*), NBC-TV, 1973; *The Second Mrs. Giaconda* (play), first produced in Jacksonville, Florida, 1976; *Jennifer, Hecate, Macbeth, William McKinley, and Me, Elizabeth* (cassette), Listening Library, 1986; *Caroline?* (based on *Father's Arcane Daughter*), Hallmark Hall of Fame Presentation, 1990.

Manuscript Collection: University of Pittsburgh, Pennsylvania.

Biography: Entry in *Third Book of Junior Authors,* New York, H.W. Wilson, 1972; essay in *Authors and Illustrators of Children's Books: Writings on Their Lives and Works,* New York, Bowker, 1972; entry in *Dictionary of Literary Biography,* Volume 52, Detroit, Gale, 1986; *E. L. Konigsburg* by Dorrel Thomas Hanks, Jr., New York, Twayne, 1992; essay in *Speaking for Ourselves, Too* compiled and edited by Donald R. Gallo, National Council of Teachers of English, 1993.

Critical Study: Entry in *Children's Literature Review,* Volume 1, Detroit, Gale, 1976; *Your Arcane Novelist: E. L. Konigsberg* by David Rees, Horn Book, 1978.

*　　*　　*

E. L. Konigsburg writes warm, funny books about young people who are searching for independence and adventure. Her style is crisp and clear, peppered with humorous details.

Her first book, *Jennifer, Hecate, Macbeth, William McKinley and Me, Elizabeth,* finds Elizabeth in a new apartment in suburban New York City. She always walks the back road to school alone and she feels very lonely. Enter Jennifer, a witch who also happens to go to William McKinley Elementary School and is also in the fifth grade. Jennifer allows Elizabeth to become her apprentice; Elizabeth has to learn, among other things, how to eat raw eggs and uncooked oatmeal, cast short spells, and get along with Jennifer. Over the school year the girls meet each Saturday at the library and go from there to the park, where they read books on witchcraft and hold special ceremonies. Hecate, the queen of the witches in *Macbeth,* is one of the witches that Jennifer looks to for instruction in the finer accomplishments of witchcraft. In the end, Jennifer and Elizabeth's best joint effort in witchcraft does not work, but by then the girls find that they don't have to be witches anymore, they can just be friends.

From the Mixed-Up Files of Mrs. Basil E. Frankweiler won the Newbery award in 1968 and later a William Allen White award. It was made into a major motion picture by Westfall Productions. This story is about Claudia Kincaid, who runs away from home to teach her parents a lesson in Claudia appreciation. She invites her young brother, Jamie, to go with her, to be a companion and to help finance the trip. They leave Greenwich, Connecticut for the Metropolitan Museum of Art, to live comfortably and interestingly. Claudia's choice of the Met as a getaway proves to be a good one. Thousands of school children visit the museum every day, so Claudia and Jamie walk unnoticed. The Met has a snack bar for sustenance and ample rest rooms. And there are rooms of fine French and English furniture from which to choose comfortable bedding. Claudia chooses a wonderful French bed dating from the sixteenth century. Once the fun of settling in is over though, Claudia is disappointed that she doesn't feel differently. Then she finds a statue at the museum so beautiful that she has to discover its maker. The former owner of the statue is Mrs. Basil E. Frankweiler, and with Mrs. Frankweiler's help, she learns about the statue and finds a way to go back home gracefully.

About the B'nai Bagels stars Mark Setzer, who is twelve years old and worries about his performance at his Bar Mitzvah. He also worries about his performance on the Little League baseball team, the B'nai B'rith (everyone calls it the B'nai Bagels). Mark has a special reason for concern with his baseball playing, because the manager of the team is his mother Bessie (everyone calls her Mother Bagel) and the coach of the team is his brother Spencer (everyone calls him Brother Bagel). In the end, the B'nai Bagels have a good season. Mark plays a good center field, and he and the manager and the coach gain a closer appreciation of one another.

Journey to an 800 Number is a beguiling story of love and friendship. Seventh grader Maximillian Stubbs is sent to stay with his father while his mother is on a first-class honeymoon cruise with a rich elderly man from Philadelphia. Max's father is a camel-keeper; his camel's name is Ahmed. Max does not like the fact that his father is a camel-keeper, he does not like Ahmed, and he does not appreciate sharing a less-than-first-class way of life in a trailer park in the southwest. During the month Max spends with his father, Ahmed gives rides in a shopping center, takes part in a travel agents' convention and a state fair, and performs in a Las Vegas night club act. Max makes friends with people who run a taco stand at the fair, summer ranch hands, and a young girl named Sabrina whose mother pretends a lot. Sabrina explains that in real life, "my mother is an eight hundred number." Her mother is one of a hundred people who sit in a room taking orders from about eighty mail catalogues. She is always a polite voice, never a face. By the end of this month, Max has learned some things about first-class, the art of pretending, kindness, and loyalty. This is a deeply moving book about survival and about connectedness.

Up from Jericho Tel is about two sixth-grade latchkey children who live with single parents in the Empire Estates Mobile Homes Park on Long Island. These children are different from the clones of Singer Grove Middle School who live in houses, have two parents, and whose mothers make cakes for PTA bake sales. Jeanmarie Troxell and Malcolm Soo are independent and ambitious—she to be a famous actress and he to be a famous scientist. And they are adventurous, adventurous enough to meet a quite dead actress named Tallulah, who allows them mysteries to solve and the ability, for short periods, to be invisible. Being invisible starts something inside them, and Jeanmarie and Malcolm learn things about their inner selves. The two do solve the mysteries and importantly, they gain confidence to become the famous people they wish to be.

Konigsburg's books are fresh and spirited, filled with delightful humor. Her plots are original and suspenseful, her characters are colorful and strong. The reader should look carefully at her sparse

illustrations (Konigsburg is also an artist), for they often reveal additional dimensions to the fine stories.

—Mary Lystad

———

KOONTZ, Dean R. Also writes as David Axton; Brian Coffey; Deanna Dwyer; K. R. Dwyer; John Hill; Leigh Nichols; Anthony North; Owen West. American. Born in Everett, Pennsylvania, 9 July 1945. Educated at Shippensburg State College, B.A. in English, 1966. Married Gerda Ann Cerra in 1966. Worked as teacher and counselor in Appalachian Poverty Program, Saxton, Pennsylvania, 1966-67; English teacher, Mechanicsburg school district, Pennsylvania, 1967-69. Since 1969, full-time writer. Recipient: Creative writing award, *Atlantic Monthly,* 1966, for "The Kittens"; Hugo award nomination, 1971, for *Beastchild.* D.Litt.: Shippensburg State College, 1989. Agent: Claire M. Smith, Harold Ober Associates, 425 Madison Avenue, New York, NY 10017. Lives in Orange, California, U.S.A.

PUBLICATIONS

Novels

Star Quest. New York, Ace, 1968.
The Fall of the Dream Machine. New York, Ace, 1969.
Fear That Man. New York, Ace, 1969.
Anti-Man. New York, Paperback Library, 1970.
Beastchild. New York, Lancer, 1970.
Dark of the Woods. New York, Ace, 1970.
The Dark Symphony. New York, Lancer, 1970.
Hell's Gate. New York, Lancer, 1970.
The Crimson Witch. New York, Curtis, 1971.
A Darkness in My Soul. New York, DAW, 1972; London, Dobson, 1979.
The Flesh in the Furnace. New York, Bantam, 1972.
Starblood. New York, Lancer, 1972.
Time Thieves. New York, Ace, 1972; London, Dobson, 1977.
Warlock. New York, Lancer, 1972.
A Werewolf among Us. New York, Ballantine, 1973.
Hanging On. New York, Evans, 1973; London, Barrie and Jenkins, 1974.
The Haunted Earth. New York, Lancer, 1973.
Demon Seed. New York, Bantam, 1973; London, Corgi, 1977.
After the Last Race. New York, Atheneum, 1974.
Nightmare Journey. New York, Berkley, 1975.
Night Chills. New York, Atheneum, 1976; London, W.H. Allen, 1977.
The Vision. New York, Putnam, 1977; London, Corgi, 1980.
Whispers. New York, Putnam, 1980; London, W.H. Allen, 1981.
Phantoms. New York, Putnam, and London, W.H. Allen, 1983.
Darkness Comes. London, W.H. Allen, 1984; as *Darkfall,* New York, Berkley, 1984.
Twilight Eyes. Plymouth, Michigan, Land of Enchantment, 1985.
Strangers. New York, Putnam, and London, W.H. Allen, 1986.
Watchers. New York, Putnam, and London, Headline, 1987.

Oddkins: A Fable for All Ages, illustrated by Phil Parks. New York, Warner, and London, Headline, 1988.
Lightning. New York, Putnam, and London, Headline, 1988.
Midnight. New York, Putnam, and London, Headline, 1989.
The Bad Place. New York, Putnam, and London, Headline, 1990.
Cold Fire. New York, Putnam, and London, Headline, 1991.
Dean R. Koontz: Three Complete Novels, The Servants of Twilight, Darkfall, Phantoms. Avenel, New Jersey, Outlet Book Company, 1991.
Dean R. Koontz: A New Collection. New York, Wings Books, 1992.
Hideaway. New York, Putnam, 1992.
Dragon Tears. New York, Putnam, 1993.

Novels as David Axton

Prison of Ice. Philadelphia, Lippincott, and London, W.H. Allen, 1976.
Stolen Thunder. New York, St. Martin's, 1993.

Novels as Brian Coffey

Blood Risk. Indianapolis, Bobbs Merrill, 1973; London, Barker, 1974.
Surrounded. Indianapolis, Bobbs Merrill, 1974; London, Barker, 1975.
The Wall of Masks. Indianapolis, Bobbs Merrill, 1975.
The Face of Fear. Indianapolis, Bobbs Merrill, 1977; as K. R. Dwyer, London, Davies, 1978.
The Voice of the Night. New York, Doubleday, 1980; London, Hale, 1981.

Novels as Deanna Dwyer

The Demon Child. New York, Lancer, 1971.
Legacy of Terror. New York, Lancer, 1971.
Children of the Storm. New York, Lancer, 1972.
The Dark of Summer. New York, Lancer, 1972.
Dance with the Devil. New York, Lancer, 1973.

Novels as K.R. Dwyer

Chase. New York, Random House, 1972; London, Barker, 1974.
Shattered. New York, Random House, 1973; London, Barker, 1974.
Dragonfly. New York, Random House, 1975; London, Davies, 1977.

Novels as Anthony North

Strike Deep. New York, Dial Press, 1974.

Novels as Aaron Wolfe

Invasion. Don Mills, Ontario, Laser Books, 1975.

Novels as John Hill

The Long Sleep. New York, Popular Library, 1975.

Novels as Leigh Nichols

The Key to Midnight. New York, Pocket Books, 1979; London, Magnum, 1980.
The Eyes of Darkness. New York, Pocket Books, 1981; London, Fontana, 1982.
The House of Thunder. New York, Pocket Books, 1982; London, Fontana, 1983.
Twilight. New York, Pocket Books, and London, Fontana, 1984; as Dean R. Koontz as *The Servants of Twilight,* New York, Berkley, 1988.
Shadowfires. New York, Avon, and London, Collins, 1987.

Novels as Owen West

The Funhouse (novelization of screenplay). New York, Jove, 1980; London, Sphere, 1981.
The Mask. New York, Jove, 1981; London, Coronet, 1983.

Novels as Richard Paige

The Door to December. New York, New American Library, 1985; as Leigh Nichols, London, Fontana, 1987.

Short Stories

Soft Come the Dragons. New York, Ace, 1970.

Other

The Pig Society, with Gerda Koontz. Los Angeles, Aware Press, 1970.
The Underground Lifestyles Handbook, with Gerda Koontz. Los Angeles, Aware Press, 1970.
Contributor, *Again, Dangerous Vision,* edited by Harlan Ellison. New York, Doubleday, 1972.
Contributor, *Infinity 3,* edited by Robert Haskins. New York, Lancer, 1972.
Contributor, *Infinity 4,* edited by Robert Haskins. New York, Lancer, 1972.
Contributor, *Androids, Time Machines, and Blue Giraffes,* edited by Roger Elwood and Vic Ghidalia. Follett, 1973.
Contributor, *Flame Tree Planet,* edited by Roger Elwood. St. Louis, Missouri, Concordia, 1973.
Contributor, *Future City,* edited by Roger Elwood. New York, Simon and Schuster, 1973.
Contributor, *Infinity 5,* edited by Robert Haskins. New York, Lancer, 1973.
Writing Popular Fiction. Cincinnati, Writer's Digest, 1973.
Contributor, *Children of Infinity,* edited by Roger Elwood. New York, Putnam, 1974.
Contributor, *Final Stage,* edited by Edward L. Ferman and Barry N. Malzberg. Charterhouse, 1974.
How to Write Best-selling Fiction. Cincinnati, Writer's Digest, and London, Poplar Press, 1981.
Contributor, *Night Visions Four.* Arlington Heights, Illinois, Dark Harvest, 1987.

Contributor, *Night Visions Six*. Arlington Heights, Illinois, Dark Harvest, 1988.

Stalkers: All New Tales of Terror and Suspense (stories), edited by Ed Gorman and Martin H. Greenberg, illustrated by Paul Sonju. Arlington Heights, Illinois, Dark Harvest, 1989.

Cold Terror: The Writings of Dean R. Koontz, edited by Bill Munster. Lancaster, Pennsylvania, Underwood Miller, 1990.

*

Media Adaptations: *Demon Seed* (film), MGM/UA, 1977; *Shattered* (film), Warner Bros., 1977; *Watchers* (film), Universal, 1988.

Biography: Essay in *Authors and Artists for Young Adults,* Volume 9, Detroit, Gale, 1992.

*   *   *

Many thriller or horror novelists achieve their success through strong plotting and description. Dean R. Koontz takes this genre a step further by pulling readers into his stories emotionally. His characters seem real, with fears and desires readers can relate to. He builds suspense not only through plot but through the use of foreshadowing. These hints about the possible outcome of the story plunge readers forward, as if they are detectives who must find out if their instincts prove true. Koontz also appeals to readers' senses with skillfully drawn metaphors and similes. But to prevent his work from becoming too overbearing, Koontz often includes elements of romance, humor, and spirituality in his books. As a result, Koontz engages readers with various interests, which has propelled many of his novels of dark suspense to the top of best-seller lists.

Koontz often elevates the theme of good versus evil, elements of which we all possess, through the use of unique metaphors. In *Visions,* for example, the sound of leathery wings fluttering against the air represents an evil lingering on the threshold of the occult. It recurs throughout the book, remaining mysterious, yet with each occurrence gaining strength and revealing more clues as to its origin. Like the clairvoyant whose visions it invades, the reader can almost recognize the object making the sound, yet fears identifying it.

In *The Voice of the Night,* evil is represented by a sound in the dark only shy, fearful Colin seems to hear. It murmurs and whispers, mixing with the natural night sounds. In the novel, fourteen-year-old Colin is befriended by Roy, his total opposite. Roy is strong, confident, and fearless, but Colin senses there is something else very different about Roy. Colin struggles with the gray areas between good and evil.

Koontz uses another metaphor, evil in the form of a dark secret, in *The Mask* and *The House of Thunder.* In each story, a secret from the past haunts the main character, threatening to push her over the edge of sanity. In *The House of Thunder,* Susan constantly relives the nightmare of witnessing her boyfriend's murder thirteen years before. Since she has never come to terms with the event, it remains her secret fear. This dark secret ripples through her mind, merging reality and delusion. It seems that the living dead have returned to take their vengeance on her, their accuser.

Koontz's use of simile and strong descriptive passages provide a further sensation that bonds readers to his stories and characters. His fascinating similes for fear invoke foreboding and often grip more than one of the senses. Koontz's novels are filled with the horrors our anxieties ignite: murder, death, phobias, the occult, insanity, the evils that lurk in the shadows of our rooms and our

minds. Yet a positive sense of hope also graces his pages. Though readers are distressed by the uncertainty, in the recesses of their minds they know good will prevail in the end. Perhaps this is what draws young adult readers to Koontz's novels. The uncertainty, the struggle to gain control of one's life is the very element young adult readers are struggling with in their own lives. They can identify with the characters, the action, and the themes. Like Colin in *The Voice of the Night,* young adults are coming to grips with the gray areas in life.

Though most of his books are read by adults or young adults, Koontz did write one book targeted to younger readers on the edge of adolescence. *The Oddkins,* labeled "a fable for all ages," adds the element of fantasy to the good versus evil theme. It speaks to the child within us all; the child who is reluctant to deal with the complexities of gray areas in life, and the child who wishes the world could again be simple black and white.

The Oddkins is about magical toys created for special children who need a friend to survive a crisis in their young lives. Though soft and stuffed, the Oddkins are alive and can speak to and comfort their child until that time when he no longer needs a secret friend. Then the Oddkins become merely stuffed toys and the child's memories of his secret friend fade into the innocence of childhood fantasy. When their creator dies, evil toys, created decades earlier to hurt children, emerge from the subcellar of his toy factory to spread harm and fear once more. The evil toys must be stopped, and a new toymaker must be found so the Oddkins can continue spreading hope.

Whether writing using a simple plot and clean-cut, black-and-white themes, or sketching a complex plot using numerous shades of gray, Koontz's strength emerges in his ability to involve readers in his stories emotionally. His sensory descriptions trap readers, further involving them in the outcome of the story. Koontz creates a unique juxtaposition in which readers are so caught up in the story that they must see it through to resolution, yet their fears and intuition warn them against turning the pages.

—Lisa A. Wroble

———

KRUMGOLD, Joseph (Quincy). American. Born in Jersey City, New Jersey, 9 April 1908. Educated at New York University, B.A. 1928. Married Helen Litwin in 1947; one son. Novelist and author of children's books. Publicity writer, Metro-Goldwyn-Mayer, New York City, 1928; screenwriter and producer for film companies, including Paramount, RKO, Columbia, and Republic, in New York, Hollywood, California, and Paris, France, 1929-40; producer and director, Film Associates, New York City, and Office of War Information, 1940-46; president in charge of production, Palestine Films, New York City and Jerusalem, Israel, 1946-52; Joseph Krumgold Productions (producer of motion pictures and television films), Hope, New Jersey, proprietor, 1952-60; writer, director, and producer for Columbia Broadcasting System, Inc., National Broadcasting Company, Inc., National Educational Television, and Westinghouse Television, New York, Rome, and Istanbul, 1960-70. Press agent. Member, Freling Huysen Township (New Jersey) school board. Recipient: American Library Association Newbery Medal, 1954, for *...And Now Miguel,* and 1960, for *Onion John;* Boys' Club of American Junior Book award, 1954, and Freedoms

Foundation award, 1973, both for *...And Now Miguel;* Robert Flaherty award honorable mention, 1954, for movie *...And Now Miguel;* Lewis Carroll Shelf award, 1960, for *Onion John; The Most Terrible Turk* was chosen as one of Child Study Association's Children's Books of the Year, 1969; first prizes for films and documentaries at Venice, Edinburgh, and Prague film festivals. *Died 10 July 1980.*

PUBLICATIONS FOR YOUNG ADULTS

Fiction

Sweeney's Adventure, illustrated by Tibor Gergely. New York, Random House, 1942.
...And Now Miguel, illustrated by Jean Charlot. New York, Crowell, 1953.
Onion John, illustrated by Symeon Shimin. New York, Crowell, 1959.
Henry 3, illustrated by Alvin Smith. New York, Atheneum, 1967.

Other

The Most Terrible Turk: A Story of Turkey, illustrated by Michael Hampshire. New York, Crowell, 1969.

PUBLICATIONS FOR ADULTS

Novel

Thanks to Murder. New York, Vanguard Press, and London, Gollancz, 1935.

Screenplays: *The Blackmailer,* with Lee Loeb and Harold Buchman, 1936; *Adventure in Manhattan,* with others, 1936; *Lady from Nowhere,* with Fred Niblo, Jr., Arthur Strawn, and Ben G. Kohn, 1936; *Lone Wolf Returns,* with Bruce Manning and Lionel Houser, 1936; *Jim Hanvey—Detective,* with Olive Cooper and Octavus Roy Cohn, 1937; *Join the Marines,* with Olive Cooper and Karl Brown, 1937; *Speed to Burn,* with others, 1938; *Lady Behave,* with Olive Cooper, 1938; *Main Street Lawyer,* 1939; *The Phantom Submarine,* 1940; *The Crooked Road,* with Garnett Weston, E.E. Paramore, and Richard Blake, 1940; *Seven Miles from Alcatraz,* 1942; *Hidden Hunger* (documentary), with Henwar Rodakiewicz, 1942; *Magic Town* with Robert Riskin, 1947; *Dream No More,* 1950; *...And Now Miguel,* 1953; *One Tenth of a Nation* (documentary), with Henwar Rodakiewicz, 1940; *Mr. Trull Finds Out* (documentary), 1941; *The Autobiography of a Jeep* (documentary), 1943.

Other

Where Do We Grow From Here: An Essay on Children's Literature. New York, Atheneum, 1968.
Editor, *The Oxford Furnace, 1741-1925.* Belvidere, New Jersey, Warren County Historical Society, 1976.

*

Media Adaptations: Audio cassette versions of Krumgold's work include *...And Now Miguel* (filmstrip with record or cassette), Miller-Brody, 1978; and *Onion John* (filmstrip with record or cassette, or record or cassette only), Miller-Brody, 1978.

Biography: Entry in *More Junior Authors,* edited by Muriel Fuller, New York, H.W. Wilson, 1963.

Critical Study: Entry in *Contemporary Literary Criticism,* Volume 12, Detroit, Gale, 1981.

*   *   *

In his two best books for young people, *...And Now Miguel* and *Onion John,* Joseph Krumgold succeeds in directing the genre of realistic fiction for a young audience to the same purpose of exposition and exploration that identifies the best novels for adults.

...And Now Miguel explores the developing awareness of a Mexican boy who lives on a sheep farm and, through Miguel's consciousness, gives us the texture and design of such a life. Krumgold was also a professional filmmaker and the subject of this widely acclaimed book evolved during a filmmaking trip when Krumgold had the opportunity to live among families like Miguel's. Working as a filmmaker yielded not only subject matter, but also particular techniques. While Krumgold's writing is not really "cinematic," he had an intensely visual sense for the telling detail which may well have evolved from his experience with the camera.

In some ways *Onion John* is a more unusual book, dealing, again through the consciousness of a young boy, with the way in which Onion John, an eccentric East European, part-hobo, part-wizard, interrelates with the highly conventional expectations of small-town Middle America. Onion John has lived happily for years in his tiny self-built house using candles as his only form of lighting and storing his vegetables in numerous bathtubs in his living room. The townspeople decide to build Onion John a "proper" house. No one realises that such a house embodies a mass of expectations about how everyday life is to be conducted and eventually Onion John, unable to accommodate himself to these narrow expectations, sadly takes to the road again. A story of this kind is unusual in a book for young people, and Krumgold sustains a moving narrative without dropping into sentimentality.

More alert readers are likely to find Krumgold's preoccupations excessively macho. He was, for example, almost exclusively concerned with father-son relationships and, rather laughably, in *Henry 3* manages to discover that flabby businessmen are really heroes under the skin when faced with a hurricane, while he turns their wives into caricatures of weakness and greed, hysterical over the loss of their furs. In this respect he can be viewed as the inheritor of such early writers of the boys' adventure tale as R.M. Ballantyne and G.A. Henty who, like Krumgold, celebrate a bonding of boys and men and an exclusion of females.

Krumgold's contribution rests less on such preoccupations than on his development of sophisticated narrative techniques. Few writers for children use the first person narrative with comparable conviction or have a comparable sense of how that form of narrative may be employed as a lens for exploring the world surrounding the "I."

—Gillian Thomas

L

LACKEY, Mercedes R. American. Born in Chicago, Illinois, 24 June 1950. Educated at Purdue University, West Lafayette, Indiana, B.S. 1972. Married 1) Anthony Lackey in 1972 (divorced 1990); 2) Larry Dixon in 1990. Artist's model in and near South Bend, Indiana, 1975-81; Associates Data Processing, South Bend, computer programmer, 1979-82; surveyor, layout designer, and analyst, CAIRS (survey and data processing firm), South Bend, 1981-82; computer programmer, American Airlines, Tulsa, Oklahoma, since 1982. Agent: Russell Galen, 331 Park Avenue South, Suite 1112, New York, NY 10016. Address: P.O. Box 8309, Tulsa, OK 74101-8309, U.S.A.

PUBLICATIONS FOR YOUNG ADULTS

Novels

Arrows of the Queen. New York, DAW Books, 1987.
Arrow's Flight. New York, DAW Books, 1987.
Arrow's Fall. New York, DAW Books, 1988.
Oathbound. New York, DAW Books, 1988.
Burning Water. New York, Tor Books, 1989.
Oathbreakers. New York, DAW Books, 1989.
Magic's Pawn. New York, DAW Books, 1989.
Reap the Whirlwind. Riverdale, New York, Baen, 1989.
A Knight of Ghosts & Shadows, with Ellen Guon. Riverdale, New York, Baen, 1990.
Magic's Promise. New York, DAW Books, 1990.
Magic's Price. New York, DAW Books, 1990.
By the Sword. New York, DAW Books, 1991.
The Elvenbane: An Epic High Fantasy of the Halfblood Chronicles, with Andre Norton. New York, T. Doherty, 1991.
Jinx High. New York, Tor, 1991.
Winds of Fate. New York, DAW Books, 1991.
Bardic Voices: The Lark & the Wren. Riverdale, New York, Baen, 1992.
Born to Run, with Larry Dixon. Riverdale, New York, Baen, 1992.
Children of the Night. New York, Tor Books, 1992.
Freedom Flight, with Ellen Guon. Riverdale, New York, Baen, 1992.
Summoned to Tourney, with Ellen Guon. Riverdale, New York, Baen, 1992.
Winds of Change. New York, DAW Books, 1992.
Winds of Fury. New York, DAW Books, 1992.
Fortress of Frost & Fire: The Bard's Tale II, with Ru Emerson. Riverdale, New York, Baen, 1993.
If I Pay Thee Not in Gold, with Piers Anthony. Riverdale, New York, Baen, 1993.
Rediscovery: A Novel of Darkover, with Marion Zimmer Bradley. New York, DAW Books, 1993.
The Ship Who Searched, with Anne McCaffrey. Riverdale, New York, Baen, 1993.
When the Bough Breaks, with Holly Lisle. Riverdale, New York, Baen, 1993.
Castle of Deception, with Josepha Sherman. Riverdale, New York, Baen, n.d.

*   *   *

Mercedes Lackey is one of the most prolific writers in the current science-fiction and fantasy field. Her popular fantasy novels set in the land of Valdemar and its surrounding countries are filled with magic, mystery, love, and laughter. She currently has twelve books set in this world of wonders.

Lackey has taken an historical perspective as the approach to her novels. This causes the reader to be in the unique position to know before reading a trilogy exactly how the story is going to end. An example is her second published series "The Last Herald Mage." The first few pages of *Arrows of the Queen* reveals the protagonist's fate quite clearly. Yet "The Last Herald Mage" series contains many of the writer's best character creations and is among the strongest of her work.

The author has populated her lands with a large variety of fascinating races both human and nonhuman. The magic-using, bird-loving Tayledras, for example, are contrasted with their cousins the plains-dwelling horse-breeders, the Shin'a'in. Both groups are strongly reminiscent of American Indians. Their histories are fascinatingly intertwined, each tribe having been assigned a specific task by the Goddess who is taskmistress to their people.

Lackey's strength is in her characters rather than her plots. The historical perspective allows her to reuse her characters; thus Talia, the protagonist of *Arrows of the Queen, Arrow's Flight,* and *Arrow's Fall* reappears in *By the Sword* as well as in the "Mage Winds" trilogy. In the latter works, however, Talia plays only a very minor role. Princess Elspeth, the heroine of the "Mage Winds" trilogy, is placed in the unique position of being an antagonist in *Arrows of the Queen,* while assuming the major role in the latter works.

The author's crowning triumph in characterization is the protagonist of "The Last Herald Mage," Vanyel Ashkevron. The young hero is foundering under the expections of his father and mother. Longing to be a Bard, he possesess only a trace of the "gift" of Bardic musical talent. He does not measure up to his father's image of the ideal son. Lord Ashkevron fears that the boy is at best effeminate, if not deliberately homosexual. Vanyel must grapple with his own uncertainty about his sexual orientation in addition to his other problems. When he is sent to the capital city of Haven to study, his life changes. Under the tutalege of his Aunt Savil, one of the most important and influential of the Herald Mages, the boy expands. He meets the love of his life and is trapped in an intolerable situation by the boy he loves. The result is the death of his lover, and the barriers in Vanyel's mind are torn open, making him the most powerful of all the Herald Mages. His reaction to his new powers and his attempts to learn to control them make the novels fascinating to read, even though a reader of the previous work knows that Vanyel is doomed.

The vast panorama of races and countries make Mercedes Lackey's novels well worth reading. Even her nonhuman characters become lifelike and realistic, while retaining enough mystery to be exotic. The gryphons of *Winds of Fate, Winds of Change,* and *Winds of Fury* are a prime example. Treyvan, the male, gives an entertaining account of how he met Darkwind, the Tayledras protagonist, when Darkwind was a child of eight. The boy was playing "monster" in the ruins outside his village when the Gryphon arrived. After watching curiously for a while, the bird-beast crept up behind the child and uttered a soft "Boo." The boy fled, screaming, leaving an apologetic gryphon to deal with the elders of his tribe.

Mercedes Lackey promises to keep readers enthralled with her tales of Valdemar for many years to come. She keeps her creative skills sharpened with a variety of other work, all characterized by the same attention to personality that is her hallmark. She continues to create creatures and people that delight, regardless of the setting in which she places them.

—Louise J. Winters

————

LANGE, John. See **CRICHTON, Michael.**

————

LANGTON, Jane (née Gillson). American. Born in Boston, Massachusetts, 30 December 1922. Educated at Wellesley College, Massachusetts, 1940-42; University of Michigan, Ann Arbor, 1942-45, B.S. (Phi Beta Kappa), 1944, M.A. 1945; Radcliffe College, Cambridge Massachusetts, 1945-46, 1947-48, M.A. 1948; Boston Museum School of Art, 1958-59. Married William Langton in 1943; three sons. Writer. Prepared art work and visual material for educational program in the natural sciences entitled *Discovery,* WGBH, Channel 2, Boston, 1955-56; taught children's literature, Graduate Center for the Study of Children's Literature, Simmons College, 1979-80, and suspense novel writing at the Radcliffe Seminars, 1981. Recipient: Mystery Writers of America Edgar award nomination, 1962, for *The Diamond in the Window;* American Library Association Newbery Honor Book award, 1980, for *The Fledgling;* Nero Wolfe award, for adult fiction, 1984, and Mystery Writers of America Edgar award nomination, 1985, for *Emily Dickinson Is Dead.* Address: 9 Baker Farm Rd., Lincoln, MA 01773, U.S.A.

PUBLICATIONS FOR YOUNG ADULTS

Fiction

The Majesty of Grace, illustrated by the author. New York, Harper, 1961; as *Her Majesty, Grace Jones,* 1974.
The Diamond in the Window, illustrated by Erik Blegvad. New York, Harper, 1962; London, Hamish Hamilton, 1969.
The Swing in the Summerhouse, illustrated by Erik Blegvad. New York, Harper, 1967; London, Hamish Hamilton, 1970.
The Astonishing Stereoscope, illustrated by Erik Blegvad. New York, Harper, 1971.
The Boyhood of Grace Jones, illustrated by Emily McCully. New York, Harper, 1972.
Paper Chains. New York, Harper, 1977.
The Fledgling. New York, Harper, 1980.
The Fragile Flag. New York, Harper, 1984.
The Hedgehog Boy, illustrated by Ilse Plume. New York, Harper, 1985.

PUBLICATIONS FOR ADULTS

Novels

The Transcendental Murder. New York, Harper, 1964.
Dark Nantucket Noon, illustrated by the author. New York, Harper, 1975.
The Memorial Hall Murder, illustrated by the author. New York, Harper, 1978.
Natural Enemy, illustrated by the author. New Haven, Connecticut, Ticknor & Fields, 1982.
Emily Dickinson Is Dead, illustrated by the author. New York, St. Martin's Press, 1984.
Good and Dead. New York, St. Martin's Press, 1986; London, Penguin, 1987.
Murder at the Gardner: A Novel of Suspense, illustrated by the author. New York, St. Martin's Press, 1988.
The Dante Game, illustrated by the author. New York, Viking, 1991.
God in Concord, illustrated by the author. New York, Viking, 1992.

*

Biography: Essay in *Something about the Author Autobiography Series,* Volume 5, Detroit, Gale, 1988.

Manuscript Collections: Kerlan Collection, University of Minnesota, Minneapolis; Boston University.

*   *   *

While Jane Langton is known as a writer of mysteries for adults which appeal to older teenagers, most of her works for young adults are aimed at readers aged ten to fourteen. Whether chronicling Grace Jones's bumpy journey into adolescence or the mystical adventures of the Hall family, Langton's works glow with a sense of history, place, and the value to be placed on the individual spirit.

The sense of history and place is strongest in Langton's fantasies set in Concord, Massachusetts, where eighteenth-century colonists fired the opening shots of the American Revolution and nineteenth-century transcendentalists rethought the goal of human endeavor. Concord's transcendentalist history bubbles like working yeast through *The Diamond in the Window, The Astonishing Stereoscope, The Swing in the Summerhouse,* and *The Fledgling; The Fragile Flag* carries the message out to the rest of the world. The five together tell the continuing story of the Hall family—Eddy and Eleanor, their uncle Freddy, and their stepcousin Georgie—in physical and metaphorical adventures that teach the children about themselves and the world. Particularly in the first work, Langton uses Concord and its past to great advantage, as in their magical dreams Eddie and Eleanor become toys Louisa May Alcott and her sisters loved and mice who share Henry David Thoreau's cabin beside Walden pond; their quest to free relatives who vanished years before ends as Concord celebrates the anniversary of the revolution's opening shots.

The works are, in effect, transcendentalist novels. The Hall family, unique and somewhat shabby, eschews monetary treasures for the greater riches of warm hearts and wide-ranging minds. The words of Thoreau and of Ralph Waldo Emerson echo through the novels in the conversations of Freddy, a great—if unhinged—transcendentalist scholar. In their dreams Eddy and Eleanor listen to Emerson's aeolian harp, hearing through it the sounds of the universe, and escape from inside a chambered nautilus only by "building more stately mansions" of intellect and soul; they learn the wonder of even the least significant creature by finding the representation of the universe in an atom in the cell of a kitten and evolve from fish to human to see truth-seeking humans as the pinnacle of natural progress. Georgie's friendship with a Canada goose emblematizes her stewardship of the earth, which she acts out by leading a children's crusade against nuclear holocaust.

A major theme of Langton's works is the value of the very individual human spirit. Grace Jones is one such spirit in *The Boyhood of Grace Jones,* set in the late 1930s. Suffused with the works of Arthur Ransome and reluctant to give up her individuality to become a painted doll giggling over boys and movie stars, Grace charts a choppy course through early adolescence, wearing her father's World War I middy over her clothes and imagining herself as adventure-seeking sailor "True Blue Tom." Grace's silent champion, as she swaggers through the halls of junior high school as if on the deck of a rolling ship, is handsome music teacher Mr. Chester who values her "vital spark." Though she gives up the middy and the mental image of Tom by the end of the book, the spark remains; Grace knows herself and has become infatuated with the power of words, with the "clashing together of the hot and the cold" inside her at the images in "Kubla Khan" and "The Rime of the Ancient Mariner" and with her own power to create those feelings with words.

Emphasis on the value of the individual is central to the fantasies. Many of Eddy and Eleanor's adventures teach them the value of their own individuality, and the Hall family adults guide them in working out their own identities; faced with Georgie's intensity, her parents quell their misgivings and help her start her antinuclear march to Washington, D.C. Langton constantly contrasts the impractical, individualistic, large-hearted Halls with their community. The Concord of the books—in the persons of Mr. Preek and Miss Prawn, the local banker and his secretary—is the one Thoreau fled: complacent, conforming, smug about its history, and barren of imagination. Preek and Prawn plot to eliminate the Halls' exotic Victorian house, planted among Concord's square white houses like a "tropical plant in a field of New England daisies" (*Diamond* 8), and Prawn is as proud of being descended from the man who jailed Thoreau for not paying his poll tax as she is of signing papers to commit the most individual man in Concord: Uncle Freddy.

Freddy is the ideal transcendentalist, Thoreau's "once-and-a-half-witted" man who is thought half-witted by his neighbors. Maddened in the first novel by the disappearance of his brother, sister, and best friend, Freddy acts out transcendentalist metaphors, becoming the poor but spiritual man in the hollow tree whom Thoreau would visit, blowing bubbles emblematic of Emerson's concentric circles that imprison the individual until a new idea breaks him free. Knocked back into reason by a bust of Louisa May Alcott—a delightful image, given Alcott's hardheaded stance against nonsense and fairy tales—Freddy remains the man who marches to his own drummer. Loving and lovable, rejoicer in nature and the spirit, he cares not what society thinks of him. Freddy lacks the dignity which Emerson may have felt essential, but his life is tinged by a rainbow as Thoreau wished his to be; Freddy literally slides down a rainbow and is left with a piece of it, symbolic of, in Thoreau's words, the "true harvest of [his] daily life."

Theme-rich as Langton's novels are, they also are rich in humor and in fascinating characters. The engaged reader glides happily through lucent prose in his layered novels. The setting of Langton's novels is precisely delineated from the beauties of Thoreau's Walden to the grimy landscape through which marches the Children's Crusade. Describing the bumpy course of young adolescence, Langton never forgets that each adolescence is unique. Eddy, Eleanor, Grace, and Georgie are three-dimensional individuals surrounded by secondary characters who come alive, from boisterous and irrepressible Oliver Winslow to practical and officious Frieda Caldwell. The result is that the reader comes away not just with messages, but with memories of lively, characters with all their humor and warts—individual spirits all.

—Pat Pflieger

———

LASKY, Kathryn. Also writes as Kathryn Lasky Knight. American. Born in Indianapolis, Indiana, 24 June 1944. Educated at University of Michigan, Ann Arbor, B.A. 1966; Wheelock College, Boston, Massachusetts, M.A. 1977. Married Christopher Knight in 1971; one daughter and one son. Writer. Recipient: *Boston Globe-Horn Book* award, 1981, for *The Weaver's Gift;* ALA notable book citations, 1981, for *The Night Journey* and *The Weaver's Gift,* 1984, for *Sugaring Time,* and 1985, for *Puppeteer;* National Jewish Book award, Jewish Welfare Board Book Council, and Sydney Taylor Book award, Association of Jewish Libraries, both 1982, both for *The Night Journey;* ALA best books for young adults citations, 1983, for *Beyond the Divide,* 1984, for *Prank,* and 1986, for *Pageant; New York Times* notable book citation, 1983, for *Beyond the Divide;* Newbery Honor Book, ALA, 1984, for *Sugaring Time; Washington Post*/Children's Book Guild Nonfiction award, 1986, for body of work; "Youth-to-Youth Books: A List for Imagination and Survival" citation, Pratt Library's Young Adult Advisory Board, 1988, for *The Bone Wars.* Agent: Jed Mattes, 200 West 72nd Street, Room 50, New York, NY 10023. Address: 7 Scott Street, Cambridge, MA 02138, U.S.A.

PUBLICATIONS FOR YOUNG ADULTS

Fiction

The Night Journey, illustrated by Trina Schart Hyman. New York, Warne, 1981.
Beyond the Divide. New York, Macmillan, 1983.
Prank. New York, Macmillan, 1984.
Home Free. New York, Four Winds Press, 1985.
Pageant. New York, Four Winds Press, 1986.
The Bone Wars. New York, Morrow, 1988.
Double Trouble Squared. San Diego, California, Harcourt, 1991.
Shadows in the Water. San Diego, California, Harcourt, 1992.
Voice in the Wind. San Diego, California, Harcourt, 1993.

PUBLICATIONS FOR CHILDREN

Fiction

Agatha's Alphabet, with Lucy Floyd, illustrated by Dora Leder. Chicago, Rand McNally, 1975.

I Have Four Names for My Grandfather, illustrated with photographs by Christopher Knight. Boston, Little Brown, 1976.

Tugboats Never Sleep, illustrated with photographs by Christopher Knight. Boston, Little Brown, 1977.

My Island Grandma, illustrated by Emily McCully. New York, Warne, 1979.

Jem's Island, illustrated by Ronald Himler. New York, Scribner, 1982.

Sea Swan, illustrated by Catherine Stock. New York, Macmillan, 1988.

Fourth of July Bear, illustrated by Helen Cogancherry. New York, Morrow, 1991.

I Have an Aunt on Marlborough Street, illustrated by Susan Guevara. New York, Macmillan, 1992.

The Tantrum, illustrated by Bobette McCarthy. New York, Macmillan, 1993.

Lunch Bunnies, illustrated by Marilyn Hafner. Boston, Joy Street, forthcoming.

Nonfiction

Tall Ships, illustrated with photographs by Christopher Knight. New York, Scribner, 1978.

Dollmaker: The Eyelight and the Shadow, illustrated with photographs by Christopher Knight. New York, Scribner, 1981.

The Weaver's Gift, illustrated with photographs by Christopher Knight. New York, Warne, 1981.

Sugaring Time, illustrated with photographs by Christopher Knight. New York, Macmillan, 1983.

A Baby for Max, illustrated with photographs by Christopher Knight. New York, Scribner, 1984.

Puppeteer, illustrated with photographs by Christopher Knight. New York, Macmillan, 1985.

Traces of Life: The Origins of Humankind, illustrated by Whitney Powell. New York, Morrow, 1989.

Dinosaur Dig, illustrated with photographs by Christopher Knight. New York, Morrow, 1990.

Surtsey: The Newest Place on Earth, illustrated with photographs by Christopher Knight. New York, Hyperion, 1992.

Think Like an Eagle: At Work with a Wildlife Photographer, illustrated with photographs by Christopher Knight and Jack Swedberg. Boston, Little Brown, 1992.

Monarchs, illustrated with photographs by Christopher Knight. San Diego, California, Harcourt, 1993.

Searching for Laura Ingalls: A Reader's Journey, with Meribah Knight, illustrated with photographs by Christopher Knight. New York, Macmillan, 1993.

Publications for Adults

Fiction as Kathryn Lasky Knight

Atlantic Circle, illustrated with photographs by Christopher Knight. New York, Norton, 1985.

Trace Elements. New York, Norton, 1986.

The Widow of Oz. New York, Norton, 1989.

Mortal Words. New York, Simon and Schuster, 1990.

Mumbo Jumbo. New York, Simon and Schuster, 1991.

Media Adaptations: *Sugaring Time* (filmstrip and cassette), Random House, 1986; (videocassette), 1988.

Biography: Essay in *Speaking for Ourselves: Autobiographical Sketches by Notable Authors of Books for Young Adults*, Volume 1, compiled and edited by Donald R. Gallo, National Council of Teachers of English, 1990.

Critical Study: Entry in *Children's Literature Review*, Volume 11, Detroit, Gale, 1986.

*   *   *

Kathryn Lasky is a versatile writer of books including fiction and nonfiction, picture books and novels for young adults. Her desire is that the readers will appreciate the world in which they live and come away with a sense of wonderment and joy. She also writes books under her married name of Kathryn Lasky Knight. As a very young girl, she was a voracious reader and "spinner of tales" who constantly wrote stories in secret and shared them with no one. She recalled, "I think I always felt that [writing] was my profession, announced or unannounced, paid or unpaid." Her mother noticed her creative expressions in talking and writing and encouraged her to be a writer.

Lasky's clear style, well-developed characterizations, and poetic imagery combine to produce books of facts that involve the reader. The books appeal to a wide audience, if they can get through her sometimes wordy texts. One of the themes in Kathryn Lasky's books has to do with Jewish culture. Writing directly from her own experiences, she explores the world with an artist's eye and imagination. *The Night Journey* (1981) is a true family story about her grandmother's escape from czarist Russia when Jews were being murdered or forced to serve in the army. Well written and exciting, switching from the present to past events adroitly, with memorable characters, the book won the National Jewish Book Award. Kathryn Lasky continues the Jewish autobiographical theme in *Pageant* (1986). Set at an exclusive girls' school in Indianapolis, it features Sarah Benjamin, who has hilarious adolescent problems while growing up, losing her sister to college, her best friend to a boy, and making decisions about what she really believes. For this work, Mrs. Lasky researched violins, plastic surgery, and ballet.

The Jewish theme is continued in *Prank* (1984). This book is set in Boston and opens with the desecration of a synagogue by the brother of the main character, Birdie. While trying to help her brother, Birdie researches the Nazi treatment of the Jews during World War II, and becomes increasingly aware of problems of anti-Semitism at home as well as of severe family problems. Though criticized for a weak plot, this book was distinguished for vital characterization and development of a topic not often addressed in young adult literature.

The theme of dinosaurs is explored with great enthusiasm by Kathryn Lasky. This interest started when she was in charge of the tape recorder on an archaeology dig with her photographer husband in Nevada. "I was so fascinated by what these guys were digging up that I forgot I was doing the sound. After that, I became an armchair archaeologist and read everything about it I could." *The Bone Wars* (1988) was a result of Lasky finding the story of Cope and Marsh, the real life archaeologists upon which the story is based. Set during the Sioux Indian Wars and the Battle of the Little Bighorn, this novel follows the adventures of a young man talented in discovering and uncovering the bones of dinosaurs. Based on true events leading to the establishment of dinosaur bones being placed in museums, this book is fascinating and fast-paced, informing the reader not only about fossils, geography, and geology, but also about the traditions and sacred heritage of some of our Native Americans.

Continuing with her research, Ms. Lasky found drawings by Whitney Powell, who is one of the first artists to illustrate early cave women. After taking a course in anthropology and studying in the bone labs at Harvard University for a year, Lasky wrote *Traces of Life: The Origins of Humankind* (1989) with illustrations by Whitney Powell. This book explains the history of research on hominids, evolution, and the scientists who had a part in that research.

The dinosaur theme harmonizes with another of her interests in the westward movement. *Beyond the Divide* (1983) tells the story of a young Amish girl, Meribah, who finds herself alone and starving in the wilderness of the Sierras. Assisted by Indians, she survives to become a strong woman and return to a valley found while on the wagon train. The novel is so realistic it would be easy to believe that *Beyond the Divide* is directly from a diary of a young girl going West.

Kathryn Lasky has made and continues to make an impact on young adult literature. Her well-researched books provide a thorough, accurate picture of whatever theme is being presented. Her use of lyrical language captures the moods as well as facts leaving the reader with "a sense of joy—indeed celebration" of the world in which they live.

—Linda Garrett

LATHAM, Jean Lee. Also writes as Janice Gard; Julian Lee. American. Born in Buckhannon, West Virginia, 19 April 1902. Educated at West Virginia Wesleyan College, Buckhannon, A.B. 1925; Ithaca Conservatory (now College), New York, B.O.E. 1928; Cornell University, Ithaca, New York, M.A. 1930; West Virginia Institute of Technology, Montgomery, 1942. Served as a trainer of inspectors, United States War Department Signal Corps, 1943-45: Silver Wreath, 1944. Teacher and professional speaker. Head of English department, Upshur County High School, West Virginia, 1926-28; substitute teacher of speech, West Virginia Wesleyan College, summer, 1927; teacher of English, history, and play production, Ithaca College, New York, 1928-29; editor-in-chief, Dramatic Publishing Co., Chicago, Illinois, 1930-36; freelance writer, 1936-41 and since 1945; trainer, U.S. War Department, Signal Corps Inspection Agency, 1943-45; director of workshops in juvenile writing, Indiana University Writers' Conference, Bloomington, 1959-60, and Writers' Conference in the Rocky Mountains, 1963. Recipient: American Library Association John Newbery Medal for most distinguished contribution to children's literature, 1956, for *Carry On, Mr. Bowditch;* D.Litt.: West Virginia Wesleyan College, 1956; Boys' Clubs of America Junior Book award, 1957, for *Trail Blazer of the Seas;* Dade County Women of the Year awards, Theta Sigma Phi, 1961, *Miami News,* 1962. Address: 12 Phoenetia Ave., Coral Gables, FL 33134, U.S.A.

PUBLICATIONS FOR YOUNG ADULTS

Fiction

Carry On, Mr. Bowditch, illustrated by John Cosgrave. Boston, Houghton Mifflin, 1955.
This Dear-Bought Land, illustrated by Jacob Landau. New York, Harper, 1957.
The Frightened Hero: A Story of the Siege of Latham House, illustrated by Barbara Latham. Philadelphia, Chilton, 1965.

Nonfiction

555 Pointers for Beginning Actors and Directors. Chicago, Dramatic Publishing, 1935.
The Story of Eli Whitney, illustrated by Fritz Kredel. New York, Aladdin, 1953.
Medals for Morse: Artist and Inventor, illustrated by Douglas Gorsline. New York, Aladdin, 1954.
Trail Blazer of the Seas, illustrated by Victor Mays. Boston, Houghton Mifflin, 1956.
On Stage, Mr. Jefferson!, illustrated by Edward Shenton. New York, Harper, 1958.
Young Man in a Hurry: The Story of Cyrus W. Field, illustrated by Victor Mays. New York, Harper, 1958.
Drake, the Man They Called a Pirate, illustrated by Frederick Chapman. New York, Harper, and London, Hamish Hamilton, 1960.
Samuel F.B. Morse: Artist-Inventor, illustrated by Jo Polseno. Champaign, Illinois, Garrard, 1961.
Translator, *Wa O' Ka,* by Pablo Ramirez, illustrated by Ramirez. Indianapolis, Bobbs Merrill, 1961.
Man of the Monitor: The Story of John Ericsson, illustrated by Leonard Everett Fisher. New York, Harper, 1962.
Eli Whitney: Great Inventor, illustrated by Louis F. Cary. Champaign, Illinois, Garrard, 1963.
The Chagres: Power of the Panama Canal. Champaign, Illinois, Garrard, 1964.
George W. Goethals: Panama Canal Engineer, illustrated by Hamilton Green. Champaign, Illinois, Garrard, 1965.
Retreat to Glory: The Story of Sam Houston. New York, Harper, 1965.
Sam Houston: Hero of Texas. Champaign, Illinois, Garrard, and London, Harper, 1965.
The Columbia: Powerhouse of North America. Champaign, Illinois, Garrard, 1967.
David Glasgow Farragut: Our First Admiral, illustrated by Paul Frame. Champaign, Illinois, Garrard, 1967.
Anchor's Aweigh: The Story of David Glasgow Farragut, illustrated by Eros Keith. New York, Harper, 1968.
Far Voyager: The Story of James Cook. New York, Harper, 1970.
Rachel Carson: Who Loved the Sea, illustrated by Victor Mays. Champaign, Illinois, Garrard, 1973.
Elizabeth Blackwell: Pioneer Woman Doctor, illustrated by Ethel Gold. Champaign, Illinois, Garrard, 1975.

Plays

The Alien Note. Chicago, Dramatic Publishing, 1930.
The Christmas Party, adaptation of the story by Zona Gale. Chicago, Dramatic Publishing, 1930.

Crinoline and Candlelight. Chicago, Dramatic Publishing, 1931.
The Giant and the Biscuits. Chicago, Dramatic Publishing, 1934.
The Prince and the Patters. Chicago, Dramatic Publishing, 1934.
Tommy Tomorrow. Chicago, Dramatic Publishing, 1935.
All on Account of Kelly. Chicago, Dramatic Publishing, 1937.
And Then What Happened? Chicago, Dramatic Publishing, 1937.
Mickey the Mighty. Chicago, Dramatic Publishing, 1937.
The Ghost of Rhodes Manor. New York, Dramatists Play Service, 1939.
Nine Radio Plays (includes *With Eyes Turned West, Mac and the Black Cat, Stew for Six, For Mister Jim, Debt of Honor, Cupid on the Cuff, Voices, The Way of Shawn,* and *Discipline by Dad*). Chicago, Dramatic Publishing, 1940.

Plays as Julian Lee

Another Washington. Chicago, Dramatic Publishing, 1931.
The Christmas Carol, adaptation of the story by Charles Dickens. Chicago, Dramatic Publishing, 1931.
A Fiancé for Fanny. Chicago, Dramatic Publishing, 1931.
I Will! I Won't! Chicago, Dramatic Publishing, 1931.
Keeping Kitty's Dates. Chicago, Dramatic Publishing, 1931.
Washington for All. Chicago, Dramatic Publishing, 1931.
Christmas for All. Chicago, Dramatic Publishing, 1932.
Thanksgiving for All, with Genevieve and Elwyn Swarthout, adaptation of *The Pompion Pie,* by Jane Tallman. Chicago, Dramatic Publishing, 1932.
The Children's Book, with Harriette Wilburr and Nellie Meader Linn. Chicago, Dramatic Publishing, 1933.
Just for Justin. Chicago, Dramatic Publishing, 1933.
Lincoln Yesterday and Today. Chicago, Dramatic Publishing, 1933.
Tiny Jim. Chicago, Dramatic Publishing, 1933.
He Landed from London. Chicago, Dramatic Publishing, 1935.
Christmas Programs for the Lower Grades, with Ann Clark. Chicago, Dramatic Publishing, 1937.
Thanksgiving Programs for the Lower Grades, with Ann Clark. Chicago, Dramatic Publishing, 1937.
Big Brother Barges In. Chicago, Dramatic Publishing, 1940.
The Ghost of Lone Cabin. Chicago, Dramatic Publishing, 1940.

PUBLICATIONS FOR CHILDREN

Fiction

The Cuckoo That Couldn't Count, with Bee Lewi, illustrated by Jacqueline Chwast. New York, Macmillan, 1961.
The Dog That Lost His Family, with Bee Lewi, illustrated by Karla Kuskin. New York, Macmillan, 1961.
When Homer Honked, with Bee Lewi, illustrated by Cyndy Szekeres. New York, Macmillan, 1961.
The Man Who Never Snoozed, with Bee Lewi, illustrated by Sheila Greenwald. New York, Macmillan, 1961.
What Tabbit the Rabbit Found, illustrated by Bill Dugan. Champaign, Illinois, Garrard, 1974.

Story Adaptations

Aladdin, illustrated by Pablo Ramirez. Indianapolis, Bobbs Merrill, 1961.

Ali Baba, illustrated by Pablo Ramirez. Indianapolis, Bobbs Merrill, 1961.
Hop O' My Thumb, illustrated by Arnalot. Indianapolis, Bobbs Merrill, 1961.
Jack the Giant Killer, illustrated by Pablo Ramirez. Indianapolis, Bobbs Merrill, 1961.
The Magic Fishbone, illustrated by Pablo Ramirez. Indianapolis, Bobbs Merrill, 1961.
Nutcracker, illustrated by Jose Correas. Indianapolis, Bobbs Merrill, 1961.
Puss in Boots, illustrated by Pablo Ramirez. Indianapolis, Bobbs Merrill, 1961.
The Brave Little Tailor, Hansel and Gretel, and *Jack and the Beanstalk,* illustrated by Pablo Ramirez and José Correas. Indianapolis, Bobbs Merrill, 1962.
The Ugly Duckling, Goldilocks and the Three Bears, and *The Little Red Hen,* illustrated by José Correas and Pablo Ramirez. Indianapolis, Bobbs Merrill, 1962.

Poetry

Who Lives Here?, illustrated by Benton Mahan. Champaign, Illinois, Garrard, 1974.

PUBLICATIONS FOR ADULTS

Plays

Thanks, Awfully! Chicago, Dramatic Publishing, 1929.
Christopher's Orphans. Chicago, Dramatic Publishing, 1931.
Lady to See You. Chicago, Dramatic Publishing, 1931.
A Sign unto You. Chicago, Dramatic Publishing, 1931.
The Blue Teapot. Chicago, Dramatic Publishing, 1932.
Broadway Bound. Chicago, Dramatic Publishing, 1933.
Master of Solitaire (produced in New York, 1936). Chicago, Dramatic Publishing, 1935.
The Bed of Petunias. Chicago, Dramatic Publishing, 1937.
Have a Heart! Chicago, Dramatic Publishing, 1937.
Here She Comes! Chicago, Dramatic Publishing, 1937.
Just the Girl for Jimmy. Chicago, Dramatic Publishing, 1937.
Smile for the Lady! Chicago, Dramatic Publishing, 1937.
Talk Is Cheap. Chicago, Dramatic Publishing, 1937.
Well Met by Moonlight. Chicago, Dramatic Publishing, 1937.
What Are You Going to Wear? Chicago, Dramatic Publishing, 1937.
They'll Never Look There! New York, Dramatists Play Service, 1939.
The Arms of the Law. Chicago, Dramatic Publishing, 1940.
Old Doc. Chicago, Dramatic Publishing, 1940.
Gray Bread. Evanston, Illinois, Row Peterson, 1941.
Minus a Million. New York, Dramatists Play Service, 1941.
People Don't Change. Chicago, Dramatic Publishing, 1941.
Señor Freedom. Evanston, Illinois, Row Peterson, 1941.
The House without a Key, adaptation of the novel by Earl Derr Biggers. Chicago. Dramatic Publishing, 1942.
The Nightmare. New York, Samuel French, 1943.

Radio Plays: for *First Nighter, Grand Central Station* and *Skippy Hollywood Theatre* programs, 1930-41.

Plays as Janice Gard

Lookin' Lovely. Chicago, Dramatic Publishing, 1930.
Listen to Leon. Chicago, Dramatic Publishing, 1931.
Depend on Me. Chicago, Dramatic Publishing, 1932.

*

Media Adaptations: *Old Doc* (television and presented on "Kraft Theatre" series), 1951.

Manuscript Collection: Kerlan Collection, University of Minnesota, Minneapolis.

Critical Study: Entry in *Contemporary Literary Criticism,* Volume 12, Detroit, Gale, 1980.

*   *   *

Jean Lee Latham is one of the most prolific biographers in children's and young adult literature, writing a series of substantial biographies for young adult readers whose length is astonishing, given the number of works she has published and the research that went into each. She was the first biographer to earn a Newbery Award, winning it in 1956 for *Carry on, Mr. Bowditch.* Her work spanned decades, but each biography is marked by one consistent factor: Latham's sense of story.

Latham's work is no longer as popular as it once was, both in public libraries and in critical circles. Following the work of writers like Jean Fritz and Milton Meltzer, biography for young readers began to become more rigorous in its application of scholarship. For Fritz, research is to mark every sentence; for Latham, research is only a foundation upon which one might build a large and wonderfully complex story.

The result is that Latham's work carries with it many techniques abhorred by biographers: fictionalized dialogue, fictionalized scenes and characters, interior thought which suggests motivations but which is not recorded in any historical document. In addition, Latham's characters each seem to have an annoyingly tidy life; each carries the seeds of his future in his childhood, and to anyone who might look hard enough, that future is evident. The result of these techniques is that Latham wrote what today would be called fictionalized biography, in which the central facts of the work are accurate, but much of the material built around those facts is conjecture or even pure fiction.

Latham's work focuses principally—though not exclusively—upon American male characters; her British characters, such as Sir Francis Drake, James Cook, and John Smith (of Jamestown fame) are explorers who never seem comfortable in England once their careers have begun. Latham treats these characters with remarkable consistency. Each, for example, begins as a young boy who shows little promise except to a single person—the Yankee peddler who senses Eli Whitney's technical skills, the teacher who perceives Matthew Maury's stubborn persistence, the tutor who recognizes the brilliant mind of Nathaniel Bowditch—but are unfortunately surrounded by other characters who do not see these qualities, and who in fact block the fulfillment of those qualities, with all good intentions.

However, each of the characters is also endowed with an extraordinary ability to persevere through and overcome the elements set in his path. And Latham gives each a phrase or symbol which is often repeated throughout the biography to stress that perseverance. "Carry on, Mr. Bowditch" is a line spoken by Bowditch's captain. Latham uses this phrase to suggest Bowditch's ability to overcome all difficulties—or, to put it in his own nautical terms, to not become becalmed. For James Cook, Latham suggests that he was determined to "keep on keeping on." At the end of *Medals for Morse,* when Samuel Morse is finally being cheered for inventing the telegraph, an admirer tells him that this is his hour of triumph. His reply is typical of a Latham character: "It's the only one that counts—the one when you finish what you set out to do."

This is biography cum fairy tale. A despised younger brother or son, faced with ridicule and abuse, finds the willing services of the larger-than-life character who perceives the son's true worth. After a time of difficulty and trial, the character's value is suddenly made dramatically manifest, and those who before had despised him cannot help but recognize his very special abilities. This is the pattern that Latham uses over and over again. James Cook, for example, the son of a common laborer, must prove his special abilities by serving aboard ships for twenty years before the navy grants him the commission which it gives to virtually any gentleman, whether or not it has been earned. But in the end, each one of these characters triumphs and overcomes poverty or accidents of birth or the ignorance and shortsightedness of those around him. The message in all of this is that by hard work and application, even a day laborer can become a captain. One needs only to exploit one's gifts and at the same time, suppress negative qualities. As in the fairy tale, goodness will win out.

This implicit didacticism in Latham's work is based on the proposition that a biography can in fact present models for behavior. In her work, Latham presents distinctly American role models in characters who are adventurous, eager, anxious to get ahead, technically competent, curious, and confident in their abilities as well as their natural goodness. The titles of Latham's biographies suggest these characteristics. Cyrus Field is the "Young Man in a Hurry." James Cook is the "Far Voyager." Matthew Maury is the "Trail Blazer of the Seas," etc.

The sense of a character functioning as role model appears vividly in Latham's biography of John Smith, *This Dear-Bought Land.* This story of the founding of Jamestown and the difficult years in which the settlers faced death by illness, starvation, Indian raids, and suicidal madness is quite different in technique from Latham's other works. She presents Smith only in his mature years, though he too follows the pattern of being despised until his true worth is demonstrated. But what is significantly different in this biography is the use of the character David Warren, a young boy, nobly born, who is despised by those around him for his weakness and dependence upon his noble birth, rather than his own qualities. When his father is killed, David goes to Jamestown in his place, and at first fears, and then admires John Smith for his stubborn insistence that the colony must survive, and for his willingness to make all contribute to the welfare of the colony, even the gentlemen who have come and wish to have others work for them. John Smith thusly becomes a strong model for David; Latham seems to conjecture a similar relationship between her characters and her readers.

Latham's characters were explorers like James Cook, inventors like Eli Whitney, men of political acumen like Sam Houston, and those who combined those characteristics, like Thomas Jefferson. Certainly she set out to present them as archetypal Americans. But she also set out to tell an entertaining and vivid story, one that would capture the attention of her young readers. If Latham's work is not so well regarded today because of the fictionalization that she uses, her sense of story in biography still merits some recognition. Though some of her characters led lives that lent themselves to drama, many did not. And yet Latham crafted those lives into stories by using the pattern of pain and frustration leading to fulfillment and accomplishment. The very qualities she wished to promote were the qualities that generated good stories. Her characters may not be the accurate representations of Jean Fritz or Milton Meltzer, but they are nonetheless real characters who struggle, who have doubts, who yearn for something, and who eventually achieve their goals.

—Gary D. Schmidt

———————

LAWRENCE, Louise. Pseudonym for Elizabeth Rhoda Holden. British. Born in Leatherhead, Surrey, 5 June 1943. Educated at Poplar Road Primary School, Leatherhead, 1948-54; Lydney Grammar School, Gloucestershire, 1955-60. Married twice; two daughters and one son. Assistant librarian, Gloucestershire Country Library, 1961-63, and at Forest of Dean branches, 1969-71; writer, since 1971. Agent: A.M. Heath, 79 St. Martin's Lane, London, WC2N 4AA. Address: 22 Church Road, Cinderford, Gloucestershire GL14 2EA, England.

PUBLICATIONS FOR YOUNG ADULTS

Fiction

Andra. London, Collins, 1971.
The Power of Stars. London, Collins, and New York, Harper, 1972.
The Wyndcliffe. London, Collins, 1974; New York, Harper, 1975.
Sing and Scatter Daisies. New York, Harper, 1977.
Star Lord. New York, Harper, 1978; London, Bodley Head, 1987.
Cat Call. New York, Harper, 1980.
The Earth Witch. New York, Harper, 1981; London, Collins, 1982.
Calling B for Butterfly. New York, Harper, 1982; London, Bodley Head, 1988.
The Dram Road. New York, Harper, 1983.
Children of the Dust. London, Bodley Head, and New York, Harper, 1985.
Moonwind. London, Bodley Head, and New York, Harper, 1986.
The Warriors of Taan. London, Bodley Head, 1986; New York, Harper, 1988.
Extinction Is Forever and Other Stories. New York, HarperCollins, 1990.
Ben-Harran's Castle. New York, Clarion Books, 1992.

*

Biography: Essay in *Speaking for Ourselves, Too* compiled and edited by Donald R. Gallo, National Council of Teachers of English, 1993.

*   *   *

The late 1960s and early 1970s saw a tremendous increase in young adult fantasy writing. Tolkien's impact had been digested;

authors were setting trilogies and longer sequences in fantasy worlds like Earthsea and Prydain; but more significant was Alan Garner's example: the Celtic or folklore fantasy set in the modern era. Of the many authors who made a science fiction/fantasy debut then, few have remained faithful either to the genre or the age group. Louise Lawrence, however, has persisted in her art, moving away from Garnerian fantasy towards pure science fiction, to the point where she should be recognised as Britain's senior woman practitioner of young adult science fiction. It has been a long and dogged journey, each accomplished novel giving no hint of the struggle to write it and to have it published.

In her first decade of writing, Louise Lawrence wrote in three genres: science fiction, fantasy, and horror (more specifically the "ghost story"). She began with *Andra*, set in the future when all humans live in underground cities because Earth's climate and orbit around the sun have been seriously damaged by war. The war continues: the Uralians intend to sabotage Sub-City One's plan to emigrate in spaceships to settle on an Earth-type planet. Andra, a girl whose brain transplant gives her memories of Earth before the disaster, becomes a rebel and inspires the young people. But—in a twist typical of Lawrence—there is no happy ending.

Next came *The Power of Stars,* blending science fiction and Garnerian fantasy. Bacteria from space infects a rabbit; the rabbit bites a girl; she becomes possessed by "the power of stars." Two teenage boys investigate the girl's strange behaviour. The clash between rich boy and poor local boy, the clipped dialogue, the sudden shifts of scene, and the Welsh border setting all recall Garner's *The Owl Service.*

Her third book was *The Wyndcliffe,* a ghost story about a girl haunted by the spirit of a dead Romantic poet, John Hollis. The sequel, *Sing and Scatter Daisies,* carried the story into the next generation, but British readers could not know this since the book was only published in the United States. Lawrence's British publisher turned down nearly everything she wrote while her American publisher continued to publish her writing. British audiences consequently missed her return to science fiction with *Star Lord,* and her powerful fantasy *Cat Call. The Earth Witch,* set in Wales, another Celtic fantasy in the Garnerian mode, was her last book for the British publisher Collins. It is about a teenager trapped in a love affair with the pagan Earth Witch. Collins then turned down her science fiction novel *Calling B for Butterfly* and her ghost story *The Dram Road,* in which a violent teenager is redeemed by an old man's love, the forces of nature, and a friendly village community, with the ghosts of the man's wife and son hovering in the background.

Lawrence continued her career in Britain with *Children of the Dust,* signalling a commitment to science fiction and a stronger emphasis on political and environmental issues. In the early 1980s the protest against nuclear weapons and the Cold War became an enormously popular movement in Western Europe. Inspired by the involvement of her own children in peace marches, Lawrence wrote about a nuclear attack on Britain, showing the effect it had on one family living near Bristol: those who went underground into the bunkers prepared for a nuclear war, and those who remained to try to survive the nuclear winter. Eventually in a fantastic conclusion, humankind evolves physically and mentally (with psychokinetic powers) to cope with nuclear radiation.

Lawrence's new British publisher, Bodley Head, encouraged more science fiction combining the rite-of-passage of a teenager with a political theme. Returning to her favourite Welsh background, she wrote *Moonwind,* about a boy from Wales awarded a holiday on the

Moon. There he encounters an alien spirit-woman stranded for 10,000 years by a fault in her starship. He helps to repair the smashed piece of equipment, and she offers a hint of escape from Earth's pollution by voyaging back to her beautiful home planet. But to do this, he would have to leave his physical body—die—and trust her assurance that his spirit would live on.

Next came *The Warriors of Taan*. Set on a planet colonized by Earthlings, it is still science fiction, but as the natives have a feudal culture, with women living separate from men and worshipping a Goddess, it is also something of a heroic, feminist fantasy. The sisterhood of Taan plots to take over the male culture and even tame the Earthlings.

Bodley Head also republished Lawrence's science fiction novels, some with revisions. *Star Lord,* about an alien starship crashing into a Welsh mountain, with hints that the mountain's power caused the crash (Celtic fantasy again), and *Calling B for Butterfly,* about six children surviving a starship disaster who are rescued by an alien force—but their fate is not to return to Earth, but to voyage on into space.

The characteristics of a mature Lawrence novel are now apparent: a setting in Wales or the Welsh borders, near Gloucestershire where she has lived for most of her life; a prophetic element, warning against pollution, nuclear war, and the overuse of technology, and hence a feminist outlook; the ethical dilemma of the central young adult character, posed directly to the reader; a downbeat ending, perhaps a temporary victory, or redemption through death. Finally a special way with words: poetic prose and the occasional "purple passage" describing the landscape, the forces of nature, the joy of music, or the incredible beauty of a nebula in deep space.

Having published a few short stories in a couple of anthologies, Lawrence's next project was a book of stories, entitled *Extinction Is Forever.* By the end of the book her talents and obsessions have been fully showcased. The title story is a chiller: nuclear war has nearly wiped out all life on earth; humans have mutated to become sea creatures; a time traveller discovers this, but the mutants destroy his time machine to stop him from returning to the past with this vital warning. Another story, "The Death Flower," suggests that only by destroying most of Earth's population—everyone with an aggressive streak—can the planet be saved. Human aggression is also the theme of her most recent novel, *Ben-Harran's Castle.*

The book depicts a universe where each planet is controlled by a mild, hypnotic system to control aggression, to keep them crime-free and ensure that wars never happen, apart from the planets in the galaxy where the Galactic Controller, Ben-Harran, has decreed that free will is God's will. But the High Council wants the population to stop destroying one another, and after another of Ben-Harran's planets has exploded in nuclear conflagration, the Council recalls him and puts him on trial. The book suggests that if planetary controls are imposed on Earth, humans would lose their artistic creativity and potential for spiritual development, for under these controls people are unaware of their souls and lose their awareness of God. The conflict is seen through the eyes of two teenagers, one from Earth, the other from a "controlled" planet, kidnapped by Ben-Harran to debate the issue with him and the Council. With this powerful metaphysical work Lawrence reaches the current height of her powers.

—Jessica Yates

———

LEE, (Nelle) Harper. American. Born in Monroeville, Alabama, 28 April 1926. Educated at Huntington College, Indiana, 1944-45; University of Alabama, Tuscaloosa, 1945-49; Oxford University, Wellington Square. Airline reservation clerk with Eastern Air Lines and British Overseas Airways, New York, during the 1950s; left to devote full time to writing. Member, National Council on Arts, 1966-72. Recipient: Pulitzer Prize, 1961, Alabama Library Association award, 1961, Brotherhood award of National Conference of Christians and Jews, 1961, *Bestsellers'* paperback of the year award, 1962, all for *To Kill a Mockingbird.* Agent: c/o McIntosh & Otis, Inc., 18 East 41st St., New York, NY 10017.

PUBLICATIONS

Novel

To Kill a Mockingbird. Philadelphia, Lippincott, 1960; London, Heinemann, 1960.

*

Media Adaptations: *To Kill a Mockingbird* (movie), Horton Foote, 1962. The book was adapted into a play by Christopher Sergel and produced in England in 1987.

Biography: Entry in *Dictionary of Literary Biography,* Volume 6: *American Novelists since World War II, Second Series,* Detroit, Gale, 1980.

Critical Study: Entry in *Contemporary Literary Criticism,* Volume 12, Detroit, Gale, 1980.

*   *   *

Harper Lee's only novel, *To Kill a Mockingbird,* won the 1961 Pulitzer Prize for Fiction and established her place in young adult literature. Universal themes of justice, compassion, racism, and family love enrich this drama set in Maycomb, Alabama (inspired by Lee's Monroeville, Alabama, home) in the 1930s. Transcending place and time, this modern American classic celebrates the courage of people who face adversity with dignity.

Narrator Jean Louise (Scout) Finch recollects three years of events leading to her brother Jem's accident: one arm was broken so badly that it healed shorter than the other. Scout obviously has emotional scars from this event twenty-five years ago. She begins the story when she was six, the summer their friend Dill encouraged them to make the reclusive Boo Radley emerge from his house. Neighborhood legend said this six-foot-six-inch terror dined on raw squirrels and stray cats, had rotten teeth, and drooled most of the time. After the novel's climactic scene on a frightening Halloween night, the children know more about the mysterious Boo who does indeed come out, yet their questions about the greater mystery of racism remain unanswered. The events following that summer of innocent play initiate the children into the darker experiences of social prejudice, cruelty, and fears. Scout and Jem witness the tragic consequences of persecuting people who are different, for Boo was very nice once they met him.

Not only are recluses such as Boo unfortunately branded as menacing threats to society, but blacks also suffer from social injustice. Some of the novel's most dramatic scenes occur in the courtroom as their father, Atticus Finch, a highly respected lawyer and citizen, defies townspeople's prejudice and heroically defends a black man falsely accused of raping a white woman. Before the trial, Atticus explains to Scout and Jem his belief in personal integrity: how people conduct themselves in trying times shows their true character. Atticus defends his unpopular decision to defend a black man accused of a heinous crime by telling his daughter that the only thing that does not abide by majority rule is a person's conscience.

In a Southern town dominated by whites, the ultimate crime is said to have been committed when Tom Robinson, a poor black laborer, is accused of raping Mayella Ewell, a poor white woman. Atticus proves that Tom is clearly innocent, and Bob Ewell, Mayella's father, is obviously guilty of beating her for making sexual advances toward Tom. However, as Atticus states, social injustice will prevail in a system ruled by white men convinced from childhood that "*all* Negroes lie, that *all* Negroes are basically immoral beings, that *all* Negro men are not to be trusted around our women...." His impassioned plea to let the court treat all races equally falls on the all-male, all-white jury's unsympathetic ears. Because "a court is only as sound as its jury, and a jury is only as sound as the men who make it up," Tom is murdered—the scapegoat of society's prejudice and violence.

By the same token, racism also destroys the lives of whites. Mayella, victimized by her father, helps crucify an innocent man to save herself. Although Bob Ewell may be a victim of the poverty, ignorance, and bigotry that create racism, he proves to be a truly malevolent character who warrants no sympathy for his fate. In addition to the destructive impact on the Ewells, Scout and Jem also suffer from Maycomb's racism by enduring the insults of both children and adults. After Jem confesses to vandalizing Mrs. Dubose's camellias (retaliating for her saying that Atticus was "no better than the niggers and trash he works for!"), Atticus explains that the sick old woman should not be held responsible for what she says; she is one more pitiable victim of society's bigotry. Jem is punished by having to read aloud two hours to the woman everyday after school and on Saturdays for a month; as a result, he gains greater insight into the woman he once despised. The lessons learned undoubtedly will strengthen his character as an adult.

All these experiences over the three-year period validate the truth of Atticus's remark that "it's a sin to kill a mockingbird." The analogy between the senseless slaughter of innocent songbirds and Tom's tragic death becomes clear to Scout. She suddenly understands that not protecting Boo Radley from being implicated in Bob Ewell's death would "be sort of like shootin' a mockingbird." Although Atticus fails to save Tom, he teaches his children about racial justice and human dignity. Harper Lee's *To Kill a Mockingbird* has remained popular with young adults because it dramatizes so well the best and worst in human nature.

—Laura M. Zaidman

———

LEE, Julian. See **LATHAM, Jean Lee.**

———

LEE, Mildred. American. Born in Blocton, Alabama, 19 February 1908. Educated at Cairo High School, Georgia; Bessie Tift College, Forsyth, Georgia, 1925-26; Troy Normal College, Alabama, 1927; Columbia University, New York, 1936; New York University; University of New Hampshire, Durham, 1944. Married 1) Edward Cannon Schimpff in 1929 (divorced), one daughter and one son; 2) James Henry Scudder in 1947, one daughter. Recipient: Child Study Association Children's Book Award, 1964, for *The Rock and the Willow;* Austrian National Award and Alabama Association Award, 1971, for *The Skating Rink.* Address: 1361 52 Avenue North, St. Petersburg, FL 33703, U.S.A.

PUBLICATIONS FOR YOUNG ADULTS

Fiction

The Rock and the Willow. New York, Lothrop, 1963; London, Oxford University Press, 1975.
Honor Sands. New York, Lothrop, 1966.
The Skating Rink. New York, Seabury Press, 1969; London, Abelard Schumann, 1972.
Fog. New York, Seabury Press, 1972.
Sycamore Year. New York, Lothrop, 1974.
The People Therein. New York, Clarion, 1980.

PUBLICATIONS FOR ADULTS

Fiction

The Invisible Sun. Philadelphia, Westminster Press, 1946.

*

Biography: Entry in *Third Book of Junior Authors,* New York, H.W. Wilson, 1972; essay in *Something about the Author Autobiography Series,* Volume 12, Detroit, Gale, 1991.

Manuscript Collection: University of Wyoming Library, Laramie; Kerlan Collection, University of Minnesota, Minneapolis.

Mildred Lee comments:

The Rock and the Willow was in a sense the beginning, though the desire and need to write goes back almost to the beginning of my life. There was nothing strange or even particularly serious about it to me. No more than the games and fantasies of my friends. I shared this characteristic of "making things up" with my younger siblings and, as I grew older, with those of my friends who were interested. Not many were; it was a very personal and private longing.

I was very greedy for life. Much as I wanted to write, it never occurred to me that I might sacrifice practically everything to achieve success. I wanted the same things other people had: marriage, a home, children. These I had and would not have missed the experience however much more time for writing I might have had had I made that choice. Still, when I neglected what I still call my Proper Work I carried a considerable burden of guilt. After I had had several short stories and a novel, *The Invisible Sun,* published I went through a staggeringly long barren time but I never gave up the idea of writing, not once.

It must have been some time in the 1950s when I began the novel I called "The Big Road" but later changed to *The Rock and the Willow.* I took an interminable time with it. The story was told from the viewpoint of the eldest daughter of a poor Alabama farm family. I had no thought in writing it of age or classification. The Singleton family were people. I lived close to them and they became very real to me. Somehow I managed eventually to finish it and send it forth to begin its many journeys—always round trips. I did not even know the term "Young Adult." I knew there were children's books and probably thought of them as juveniles—though no one could have derived more pleasure from the young people's books of my adolescence than I had.

I had copied a list of book publishers from a publication in the library and when *The Rock and the Willow* came back from one I sent it to another. Several times it had almost made it; I'd get a note instead of a rejection slip which softened the blow and some of the notes were downright encouraging. E.P. Dutton kept the manuscript for weeks and made the complaint that it was difficult to categorize it without, however, suggesting it be turned over to the young people's department (maybe they didn't have one then, I don't know).

I sent it to fifteen publishing houses and hope was ebbing if not nearly gone. I remember thinking, "It isn't going to be published." In my heart I knew it was a good book and told myself this, but it wasn't going to be published. Of course I'd had other books that had not been published but they had not hurt like this one that I knew was good. One blue Monday morning the phone rang and it was Beatrice Creighton, editor in chief of Lothrop, Lee and Shepard in New York, and she was saying "Miss Lee, we would *love* to publish your beautiful book..." I waited for the inevitable "but." It did not come. Instead she proffered an invitation to me to come to New York to discuss some possible slight changes in the book. I had not known that Lothrop was a publisher of books for young people only!

Through the haze of my delirious joy there was a recurring tinge of...what? Disappointment? Discontent? Dissatisfaction? I had intended my book for a general public's reading—not tucked into a pigeonhole. Well, it wasn't; I could not have asked for a more gracious, surprising, splendid reception than it got. Also it opened the door that must have been waiting for me. My only regret is that I have not a greater achievement—a longer list of books. Anything I have written that has been of help in the often difficult job of growing up cannot have been wasted.

*   *   *

Spanning two decades of her life, from her fifties to her seventies, Mildred Lee wrote six novels for young adults. In many ways, it seems remarkable that a woman at that age could have written so accurately and perceptively about the feelings and behavior of teenagers—both male and female, underprivileged and privileged, present-day and in the past.

All of Lee's main characters are adolescents who are introspective and sensitive, aware of their feelings of self-doubt and loneliness. In the course of the stories, all of them experience confusing and contradictory emotional, intellectual, and sexual awakenings. They survive death, loss, or abuse. All of them grow and are strengthened through these experiences, but their triumphs are never forced or flashy. Lee's style is quiet; her stories unfold naturally. Her closures are never final, pointing toward further pain, hope, and growth.

Two of Lee's main characters have physical disabilities—Tuck Faraday in *The Skating Rink* stutters and Ailanthus Farr in *The People Therein* limps—and Lee uses these handicaps to emphasize the sense of being different and the resulting alienation these characters feel. In some ways, their physical imperfections are metaphors for the limitations of all individuals, for even the more typical adolescents of her novels, such as *Fog, Sycamore Year,* and *Honor Sands,* seem very aware of circumstances, such as poverty, which they perceive as making them different or keeping them from realizing their potential.

All of Lee's novels are set in the southeastern United States, either in rural areas or small towns. Two, however, *The Rock and the Willow* and *The People Therein,* take place in the mountains of southern Appalachia and are strongly evocative of the beauty of the place and the values of the inhabitants. Earline "Enie" Singleton, the main character in *The Rock and the Willow,* grew up in Tired Creek, Alabama, in the 1930s, while *The People Therein,* which begins in 1910, is the story of Ailanthus "Lanthy" Farr who lived near Dewfall Gap, North Carolina. Although the novels are separated by two decades and several state borders, the sense of place and lifestyles of the families are similar. In both stories, Lee has presented young women who are strong and independent, hardworking and poor, women who love their families and homes but rebel against the rigid customs and beliefs of their parents and forge their own ways.

Through the encouragement and interest of a teacher, Enie discovers her passion for learning and writing, but her decision to go to college and become a teacher herself seems doomed due to lack of money, her mother's death, and her father's resistance. Although Enie remained skeptical whenever her mother would say, "God moves in mysterious ways His wonders to perform," in the end she comes to acknowledge the fact that things sometimes do work out in totally unanticipated ways.

Lee's novels definitely have an old-fashioned flavor about them, although the themes of alienation and developmental growth toward wholeness transcend time and place. Even those that are set in contemporary times depict a quieter and slower paced life, far removed from modern-day MTV (Music Television) and Nintendo. While her books predate these particular phenomena, she did write most of them during the sixties and seventies, certainly turbulent times for many young adults. That her books do not mirror contemporary historical events is certainly an intentional choice on her part. She seems content to focus on the smaller, more personal, and more universal issues of family relations and self-identity. Her novels have never appealed to all adolescents, but they have been and will continue to be satisfying and comforting reading experiences for more contemplative young adults.

—Linda J. Wilson

———

LEE, Tanith. British. Born in London, 19 September 1947. Educated at Prendergaste Grammar School; Catford Grammar School, London, and an art college. Librarian, writer. Recipient: August Derleth award, 1980; World Fantasy Convention award, 1983. Agent: c/o Macmillan London Ltd., 4 Little Essex Street, London WC2R 3LF, England.

PUBLICATIONS FOR YOUNG ADULTS

Fiction

The Dragon Hoard, illustrated by Graham Oakley. London, Macmillan, and New York, Farrar Straus, 1971.
Princess Hynchatti and Some Other Surprises, illustrated by Helen Craig. London, Macmillan, 1972; New York, Farrar Straus, 1973.
Companions on the Road. London, Macmillan, 1975.
The Winter Players. London, Macmillan, 1976.
Companions on the Road [and] *The Winter Players.* New York, St. Martin's Press, 1977.
East of Midnight. London, Macmillan, 1977; New York, St. Martin's Press, 1978.
The Castle of Dark. London, Macmillan, 1978.
Shon the Taken. London, Macmillan, 1979.
Prince on a White Horse. London, Macmillan, 1982.
Black Unicorn, illustrated by Heather Cooper. New York, Atheneum, 1991.
Dark Dance. New York, Dell, 1992.

PUBLICATIONS FOR CHILDREN

Fiction

Animal Castle, illustrated by Helen Craig. London, Macmillan, and New York, Farrar Straus, 1972.

PUBLICATIONS FOR ADULTS

Novels

The Birthgrave. New York, DAW, 1975; London, Futura, 1977.
Don't Bite the Sun. New York, DAW, 1976.
The Storm Land. New York, DAW, 1976; London, Futura, 1977.
Drinking Sapphire Wine. New York, DAW, 1977.
Volkhavaar. New York, DAW, 1977; London, Hamlyn, 1981.
Night's Master. New York, DAW, 1978; London, Hamlyn, 1981.
The Prince of Demons. DAW, 1978.
Quest for the White Witch. New York, DAW, 1978; London, Futura, 1979.
Vazkor, Son of Vazkor. New York, DAW, 1978; as *Shadowfire,* London, Futura, 1979.
Death's Master. New York, DAW, 1979; London, Hamlyn, 1982.
Drinking Sapphire Wine (includes *Don't Bite the Sun).* London, Hamlyn, 1979.
Electric Forest. New York, DAW, 1979.
Day by Night. New York, DAW, 1980.
Kill the Dead. New York, DAW, 1980.
Sabella; or, The Blood Stone. New York, DAW, 1980.
Delusion's Master. New York, DAW, 1981.
The Silver Metal Lover. New York, DAW, 1982; London, Unwin, 1986.
Anackire. New York, DAW, 1983; London, Futura, 1985.
Sung in Shadow. New York, DAW, 1983.
Days of Grass. New York, DAW, 1985.
Dark Castle, White Horse. New York, DAW, 1986.
Delirium's Mistress. New York, DAW, 1986.
Night's Sorceries. New York, DAW, 1987.

The White Serpent. New York, DAW, 1988.
Forests of the Night. London, Unwin Hyman, 1989.
A Heroine of the World. New York, DAW, 1989.

Short Stories

The Betrothed. Sidcup, Kent, Slughorn Press, 1968.
Cyrion. New York, DAW, 1982.
Red as Blood; or Tales from the Sisters Grimmer. New York, DAW, 1983.
The Beautiful Biting Machine. New Castle, Virginia, Cheap Street, 1984.
Tamastara; or, The Indian Nights. New York, DAW, 1984.
The Gorgon and Other Beastly Tales. New York, DAW, 1985.
Dreams of Dark and Light: The Great Short Fiction of Tanith Lee. Sauk City, Wisconsin, Arkham House, 1986.
The Book of the Beast. London, Unwin, 1988.
The Book of the Damned. London, Unwin, 1988.
Women as Demons: The Male Perception of Women through Space and Time. London, Women's Press, 1989.
The Book of the Dead. Woodstock, New York, Overlook Press, 1991.
The Book of the Mad. Woodstock, New York, Overlook Press, 1993.

Other

Unsilent Night (miscellany). Cambridge, Massachusetts, NESFA Press, 1981.

Radio Plays: *Bitter Gate,* 1977; *Red Wine,* 1977; *Death Is King,* 1979; *The Silver Sky,* 1980.

Television Plays: *Sarcophagus,* 1980, and *Sand,* 1981 (both *Blake's Seven* series).

*

Bibliography: by Mike Ashley, in *Fantasy Macabre 4* (London), 1983.

*   *   *

Tanith Lee is a prolific writer of adult and juvenile fantasy books. Since the early 1970s, she has generated more than twenty volumes filled with tales of witches, fairies, demons, and hidden realms. Lee creates highly descriptive prose and well-formed, engaging characters who usually happen upon some sort of magical adventure. She has often received praise for the originality of her work and her highly descriptive writing style.

The success of her first book for the young adult market, *The Dragon Hoard* was a harbinger of praise to come for following volumes. It tells the story of Prince Jasleth and his sister Princess Goodness who are bewitched by an evil fairy. Once they are freed from her spell, Jasleth sets off on a quest for the Dragon Hoard with Prince Fearless and his companions. In good fairy-tale fashion, all are married off in the end and live happily ever after. *Princess Hynchatti* followed this first success with ample acclaim of its own. This series of twelve short fantasies is geared toward the younger end of the young adult reading scale—appealing to those in the nine to twelve-year-old range. The tales are built around typical plots involving princes, princesses, witches, and fairies yet each contains a twist or two that adds freshness and originality to potentially hackneyed subject matter. The humor in these tales boarders on silliness, but this is an attractive feature to many young readers.

Companions on the Road did not fair as well as Lee's earlier works. Although the writing and characterization were viewed as adequate, general critical consensus held that both seemed forced. *Companions* also revealed Lee's dark side. Her next young adult work, *East of Midnight,* a tale of exchanged identity and its consequences, continued this darker mood. Once again, the work received mixed reviews although this book was regarded as more carefully crafted. Because it contained violent and terrifying episodes, reviewers classified it as a horror story rather than a fantasy.

The shift in Lee's writing style was indicative of her move to adult fantasy. From 1978 to 1991, her efforts were completely devoted to an adult audience. In 1991, however, she published another work for young adults, *Black Unicorn.* Her hiatus from the market produced a positive result. This adventurous tale relates the story of Taniquil (the daughter of a sorceress) and a beautiful black unicorn she brings to life. Though the work still reflects elements of Lee's darker side, the overall tone of the work is positive.

In this book, as in others, Lee addresses themes such as the search for identity, coping with inept or uncaring authority figures, abandonment, loneliness, and many other issues that face adolescent readers. Her characters are often young adults who, in the end, emerge victorious from struggles with these issues. In each of her novels, Lee constructs worlds in which these characters can call on magical powers to assist them in their struggles. One fresh aspect of Lee's work, however, is that her characters show vulnerability. They express feelings of self consciousness, inadequacy, fear, and being overwhelmed by circumstances. For example, when Taniquil is lost in the desert, Lee portrays her as a scared, vulnerable, and overwhelmed young girl who just hours earlier had informed her mother that she was ready to set out on her own. Fortunately, Lee is in control of the universe she has created and Taniquil is saved by the unicorn. In this as in every other conflict in Lee's work, the character emerges victorious yet transformed. This growth of the characters through conflict is an insightful and refreshing aspect of Lee's work. It places her stories in the realm of classic fairy tales which were intended to teach young readers about the difficulties they would find in life.

Lee's inability to maintain a consistent vision of her audience is the major drawback to her work. In her *Don't Bite the Sun,* her dialogue is too sophisticated for adolescents yet too self-conscious for adults. The same is true on occasion in *Black Unicorn.* The inconsistencies caused by this flaw can result in confusion that requires the reader to reread the confusing passage several times until they understand the meaning. This weakness, however, is overshadowed by the generally dynamic nature of her prose.

—Linda Ross

———

LEESON, Robert (Arthur). British. Born in Barnton, Cheshire, England, 31 March 1928. Educated at Sir John Deane's Grammar School (scholar), 1939-44; University of London, External B.A. (honors) 1972. Served in British Army in the Middle East, 1946-48. Married Gunvor Hagen in 1954; one son, one daughter. Journalist on local newspapers and magazines in England and Europe, 1944-56; reporter, 1956-58, parliamentary correspondent, 1958-61, feature writer, 1961-69, literary editor, 1961-80, children's editor, 1969-84, *Morning Star,* London, England; free-lance writer and editor, since 1969. Recipient: Eleanor Farjeon award, 1985. Address: 18 McKenzie Rd., Broxbourne, Hertfordshire, England.

PUBLICATIONS FOR YOUNG ADULTS

Fiction

The Last Genie. London, Collins, 1973.
The Third Class Genie. London, Collins, 1975.
Silver's Revenge. London, Collins, 1978; New York, Philomel, 1979.
It's My Life. London, Collins, 1980.
Candy for King. London, Collins, 1983.
Genie on the Loose. London, Collins, 1984.
Time Rope series (*Time Rope, Three against the World, At War with Tomorrow, The Metro Gangs Attack*). London, Longman, 4 vols., 1986.
Slambash Wangs of a Compo Gormer. London, Collins, 1987.
Jan Alone. London, Collins, 1989.
Coming Home. London, Collins, 1990.
Zarnia Experiment series (*Landing, Fire, Deadline, Danger Trail, Hide and Seek, Blast Off*). London, Reed Children's Book, 6 vols., 1993.

Historical Fiction

Bess, illustrated by Christine Nolan. London, Collins, 1975.
The White Horse. London, Collins, 1977.

Nonfiction

The Cimaroons. London, Collins, 1978.

PUBLICATIONS FOR CHILDREN

Fiction

The Demon Bike Rider, illustrated by Jim Russell. London, Collins, 1976.
Challenge in the Dark, illustrated by Jim Russell. London, Collins, 1978.
Harold and Bella, Jammy and Me. London, Collins, 1980.
The Reversible Giant, illustrated by Chris Smedley. London, A. & C. Black, 1986.
Wheel of Danger, illustrated by Anthony Kerins. London, Collins, 1986.
Never Kiss Frogs!, illustrated by David Simonds. London, Hamish Hamilton, 1988.
Hey Robin!, illustrated by Helen Leetham. London, A. & C. Black, 1989.
How Alice Saved Captain Miracle, illustrated by Gary Rees. London, Heinemann, 1989.
Burper, illustrated by Caroline Crossland. London, Heinemann, 1989.

Right Royal Kidnap, illustrated by Chris Smedley. London, A. & C. Black, 1990.

One Frog Too Many, illustrated by David Simonds. London, Hamish Hamilton, 1991.

Pancake Pickle, illustrated by Caroline Crossland. London, Hamish Hamilton, 1991.

April Fool at Hob Lane School, illustrated by Caroline Crossland. London, Hamish Hamilton, 1992.

No Sleep for Hob Lane, illustrated by Caroline Crossland. London, Hamish Hamilton, 1992.

Ghosts at Hob Lane, illustrated by Caroline Crossland. London, Hamish Hamilton, 1993.

Karlo's Tale, illustrated by Hilda Offen. London, Collins, 1993.

Smart Girls, illustrated by Axel Scheffler. London, Walker Books, 1993.

Tales of Robin Hood. London, Kingfisher Books, 1994.

Historical Fiction

Beyond the Dragon Prow, illustrated by Ian Ribbons. London, Collins, 1973.

'Maroon Boy, illustrated by Michael Jackson. London, Collins, 1974.

Nonfiction

Mum and Dad's Big Business, illustrated by Ken Sprague. Manchester, Cooperative Union, 1982.

The People's Dream, illustrated by Ken Sprague. Manchester, Cooperative Union, 1982.

Also wrote several books based on the British Broadcasting Corp. [BBC] television series *Grange Hill* published by Fontana Books, 1980-82, including: *Grange Hill Rules, O.K.?, Grange Hill Goes Wild, Grange Hill for Sale, Grange Hill Home and Away; Forty Days of Tucker J* (based on the BBC television series *Tucker's Luck* by Redmond), Fontana Books, 1983.

PUBLICATIONS FOR ADULTS AS R.A. LEESON

Other

United We Stand: An Illustrated Account of Trade Union Emblems. Bath, Adams & Dart, 1971.

Strike: A Live History, 1887-1971. London, Allen & Unwin, 1973.

Children's Books and Class Society: Past and Present, edited by Children's Rights Workshop. London, Writers and Readers Publishing Cooperative, 1977.

Travelling Brothers: The Six Centuries Road from Craft Fellowship to Trade Unionism. London, Allen & Unwin, 1978.

Reading and Righting: The Past, Present, and Future of Fiction for the Young. London, Collins, 1985.

*

Media Adaptations: *The Third-Class Genie* (play), London, BBC Schools Radio, 1986, and Leicester, England, 1987; *Slambash Wangs of a Compo Gormer,* London, BBC Schools Radio, 1989; *It's My Life,* Manchester, BBC Radio Five, 1992.

Robert Leeson comments:

Writing for Young Adults is writing for people crossing a frontier zone, badly mapped and studded with minefields. We made this frontier zone, we made these young people. We taught them to explore, to question, to find out, yet often we are alarmed at their loss of innocence.

The writer stands in a fortunate position in relation to many young people, who often cannot communicate with the adults closest to them, of being the friendly older person they may feel free to listen to. That means a great opportunity for the writer and a great responsibility.

*   *   *

Robert Leeson writes from a consistent and firmly held set of views on society and childhood which he sets out fully in *Reading and Righting.* Briefly, these are that books are a vital means of liberating and empowering humans—especially children and young adults—within a society which has been structured to deny a voice to a considerable proportion of its members. The paradox that the book, symbol of this restrictive culture, should be the desired agent of change accounts for the variety, energy, and sheer popularity of Leeson's work. His understanding and qualified acceptance of an existing literary tradition has led to a stream of historical, school, science fiction, humorous, and realistic novels which give central roles to characters previously denied recognition—whether because of gender, ethnic origin or social position—and at the same time redefine and revitalise conventional forms.

Thus his early historical trilogy *('Maroon Boy, Bess,* and *The White Horse)* presents a segment of history—concerning the Cimaroons—not encountered in any official view of the subject. *Silver's Revenge* provides a daring, subversive, wryly humorous sequel to Stevenson's *Treasure Island* and epitomises Leeson's affectionately critical attitude to the literary tradition (now reinforced by *Karlo's Tale,* his sequel to Browning's *The Pied Piper). Candy for King,* partly reflecting Leeson's own army experience, stands as a contemporary *Candide.* The "Time Rope" quartet *(Time Rope, Three against the World, At War with Tomorrow,* and *The Metro Gangs Attack)* using a science fiction convention, involves three young people from undervalued, disenfranchised backgrounds, and sustaining but unacknowledged roots at war within a future dystopia of disturbing logic and likelihood. The "Grange Hill" series of novels, based on a popular television series about an English comprehensive school, but always original works in themselves, moved the school story genre decisively into new territory. The final book in the series, *Forty Days of Tucker J,* took a character who, over his television school career and in Leeson's books, had achieved nationally recognised inimitability and was subjected searchingly to a contemporary world outside school. Leeson's acute ear for the language and lore of young adults shows itself to great advantage here, continuing the sensitivity to voice and register established in earlier books such as *The Demon Bike Rider, The Third Class Genie,* and continued in *Genie on the Loose.*

Leeson himself regards *Candy for King,* the "It's My Life" trilogy—*It's My Life, Jan Alone,* and *Coming Home*—the "Time Rope" quartet, and *Slambash Wangs of a Compo Gormer* as his major works for young adults.

Leeson's *Candy for King* portrays with all the relentless consistency of Voltaire a hero of complete innocence and absolute trust. Kitchener Candeford, anxious always to put into literal practice the great principles of "love, liberty, loyalty and leadership," goes through school, work, and into the army as an oblivious, gentle giant unwittingly leaving a trail of disaster behind him. An often anarchically funny novel, its wandering sequence unified by its extraordinary hero makes it a picaresque masterpiece. Candy himself remains unsullied but the story's undoubted message is that the world is not ready for his brand of nobility.

It's My Life appeared as a one-off novel. Jan Whitfield is sixteen, attending a comprehensive school in the north of England, attracted to Peter Carey at the same school, and living an apparently normal life with parents and brother. But her mother, without warning or seeming reason, walks out on the family. The story concerns Jan's attempts to come to terms with this. This quiet, perceptively written, entirely convincing novel quickly gained a large following both in schools and with independent readers. The appearance in 1989 of a sequel, *Jan Alone,* surprising after so long an interval, was in retrospect inevitable. The trilogy, completed in 1990 with *Coming Home,* stands as one of the great achievements in recent years in the realistic novel. Jan develops through the books to responsibility, adulthood, and understanding. The process is not easy: it involves self-knowledge of a high order. At the end of *It's My Life* the mother's disappearance was a given: its significance was that it "had everything to do with what was to happen to Jan." At the end of *Coming Home,* with the superbly realised episode of the mother's return ("why should I have to do the unforgivable to get away from the unbearable?") the situations of the two women are set in contrast and a whole, satisfying structure for the trilogy appears. There is an assertion of human continuity and also need for change: in Jan there is an acute dramatisation of the possibilities for young women in contemporary society. Leeson would not call this trilogy "feminist." However, there are several reasons for regarding it in this way. Jan's involvement in a male-dominated world is active: she makes her own luck against great odds.

A literal translation of *Slambash Wangs of a Compo Gormer* from the original Klaptonian would be "fighting fantasies of a complete idiot." This novel is an imaginative *tour-de-force,* funny, ingenious, with several contemporary targets neatly hit. Arnold's life in Denfield, with uncomprehending parents and inimical schoolfellows who regard him as a "wally" because he does not seem to inhabit their world, is relieved only by his private fantasy: the planet Klaptonia, where the Replic Dornal triumphs in one elemental, heroic adventure after another. Little does he know that his fantasy actually exists. There is trouble in Klaptonia, and Arnold and Replic Dornal are about to change places. Arnold's adventures on Klaptonia and Dornal's attempts to cope with life at Denfield Comprehensive School form an absorbing, resonant, highly comic narrative. There is a gallery of caricatured characters who have an uncomfortable ring of truth. Leeson provides a complete Klaptonian language which is a linguistic—as well as a comic—achievement in its own right. The whole novel stands as a remarkable feat of invention. Once again, established genres—science fiction, fantasy, and the school story—are reworked, affectionately mocked, and given new life.

Leeson's entire achievement—varied in tone, content, and genre: consistent in honesty, seriousness, and concern for giving voice to the usually unheard—stands as unique in contemporary literature for young adults.

—Dennis Hamley

———

LE GUIN, Ursula K(roeber). American. Born in Berkeley, California, 21 October 1929. Educated at Radcliffe College, Cambridge, Massachusetts, A.B. in French 1951 (Phi Beta Kappa); Columbia University, New York (Faculty fellow; Fulbright fellow, 1953), M.A. in romance languages 1952. Married Charles A. Le Guin in 1953; two daughters and one son. Instructor in French, Mercer University, Macon, Georgia, 1954, and University of Idaho, Moscow, 1956; department secretary, Emory University, Atlanta, 1955; taught writing workshops at Pacific University, Forest Grove, Oregon, 1971, University of Washington, Seattle, 1971-73, Portland State University, Oregon, 1974, 1977, 1979, in Melbourne, Australia, 1975, at the University of Reading, England, 1976, Indiana Writers Conference, Bloomington, 1978 and 1983, University of California, San Diego, 1979, Kenyon College, Tulane University, Bennington Writing Program, Beloit College, and Flight of the Mind. Creative consultant for Public Broadcasting Service, for television production of *The Lathe of Heaven,* 1979. Recipient: Fulbright fellowship, 1953; *Boston Globe-Horn Book* award, 1968, Lewis Carroll Shelf award, 1979, *Horn Book* honor list citation, and American Library Association Notable Book citation, all for *A Wizard of Earthsea;* Nebula Award nomination, novelette category, 1969, for "Nine Lives"; Nebula Award, Science Fiction Writers Association, and Hugo Award, International Science Fiction Association, both 1970, for *The Left Hand of Darkness;* Newbery Silver Medal Award, and National Book Award for Children's Literature finalist, both 1972, and American Library Association Notable Book citation, all for *The Tombs of Atuan;* Child Study Association of America's Children's Books of the Year citation, 1972, and National Book Award for Children's Books, 1973, both for *The Farthest Shore;* Hugo Award for best novella, 1973, for *The Word for World Is Forest;* Hugo Award nomination, Nebula Award nomination, and *Locus* Award, all 1973, all for *The Lathe of Heaven;* Hugo Award for best short story, 1974, for "The Ones Who Walk Away from Omelas"; American Library Association's Best Young Adult Books citation, 1974, for *The Dispossessed: An Ambiguous Utopia;* Nebula Award, and Jupiter Award, both 1975, for short story "The Day before the Revolution"; Nebula Award nomination and Jupiter Award, both 1976, for short story "The Diary of the Rose"; National Book Award finalist, American Library Association's Best Young Adult Books citation, Child Study Association of America's Children's Books of the Year citation, and *Horn Book* honor list citation, all 1976, and Prix Lectures-Jeunesse, 1987, all for *Very Far Away from Anywhere Else;* Gandalf Award nomination, 1978; Gandalf Award (Grand Master of Fantasy), 1979; Balrog Award nomination for best poet, 1979; University of Oregon Distinguished Service award, 1981; *Locus* Award, 1984, for *The Compass Rose;* American Book Award nomination, 1985, and Janet Heidinger Kafka Prize for Fiction, University of Rochester English Department and Writer's Workshop, 1986, both for *Always Coming Home.* Guest of Honor, World Science Fiction Convention, 1975; International Fantasy Award and Hugo Award, for *Buffalo Gals,* 1988; Nebula Award, for *Tehanu,* 1990; Pushcart Prize, for "Bill Weisler," 1991; Harold D. Vursell Award, American Academy & Institute of Arts & Letters, 1991; OILA Award for *Searoad,* 1992. D.Litt., Bucknell University, Lewisburg, Pennsylvania, 1978; Lawrence University, Appleton, Wisconsin, 1979; D.H.L.: Lewis and Clark College, Portland, 1983; Occidental College, Los Angeles, 1985; Emory University, Kenyon College, Portland State University. Agent: Virginia Kidd, P.O. Box 278, Milford, PA 18337, U.S.A.

PUBLICATIONS FOR YOUNG ADULTS

Novels

A Wizard of Earthsea, illustrated by Ruth Robbins. Berkeley, California, Parnassus Press, 1968; London, Gollancz, 1971.
The Tombs of Atuan, illustrated by Gall Garraty. New York, Atheneum, 1971; London, Gollancz, 1972.
The Farthest Shore, illustrated by Gail Garraty. New York, Atheneum, 1972; London, Gollancz, 1973.
Very Far Away from Anywhere Else. New York, Atheneum, 1976; as *A Very Long Way from Anywhere Else,* London, Gollancz, 1976.
Earthsea (includes *A Wizard of Earthsea, The Tombs of Atuan,* and *The Farthest Shore*). London, Gollancz, 1977; as *The Earthsea Trilogy,* London, Penguin, 1979.
The Beginning Place. New York, Harper, 1980; as *Threshold,* London, Gollancz, 1980.
Tehanu: The Last Book of Earthsea. New York, Atheneum, 1990.

PUBLICATIONS FOR CHILDREN

Fiction

Leese Webster, illustrated by James Brunsman. New York, Atheneum, 1979; London, Gollancz, 1981.
The Adventures of Cobbler's Rune, illustrated by Alicia Austin. New Castle, Virginia, Cheap Street, 1982.
Adventures in Kroy. New Castle, Virginia, Cheap Street, 1982.
Solomon Leviathan's Nine Hundred Thirty-first Trip around the World, illustrated by Alicia Austin. New Castle, Virginia, Cheap Street, 1983.
A Visit from Dr. Katz, illustrated by Ann Barrow. New York, Atheneum, 1988; as *Dr. Katz,* London, Collins, 1988.
Catwings, illustrated by S.D. Schindler. New York, Orchard, 1988.
Catwings Return, illustrated by S.D. Schindler. New York, Orchard, 1989.
Fire and Stone, illustrated by Laura Marshell. New York, Atheneum, 1989.
A Ride on the Red Mare's Back, illustrated by Julie Downing. New York, Orchard, 1992.
Fish Soup, illustrated by Patrick Wynne. New York, Atheneum, 1992.

PUBLICATIONS FOR ADULTS

Novels

Rocannon's World, with *The Kar-Chee Reign,* by Avram Davidson. New York, Ace, 1966; London, Tandem, 1972.
Planet of Exile, with *Mankind Under the Lease,* by Thomas M. Disch. New York, Ace, 1966; London, Tandem, 1972.
City of Illusions. New York, Ace, 1967; London, Gollancz, 1971.
The Left Hand of Darkness. New York, Ace, and London, Macdonald, 1969.
The Lathe of Heaven. New York, Scribner, 1971; London, Gollancz, 1972.
The Dispossessed: An Ambiguous Utopia. New York, Harper, and London, Gollancz, 1974.

The Word for World Is Forest. New York, Putnam, 1976; London, Gollancz, 1977.
Three Hainish Novels (includes *Rocannon's World, Planet of Exile,* and *City of Illusions*). New York, Doubleday, 1978.
Malafrena. New York, Putnam, 1979; London, Gollancz, 1980.
The Eye of the Heron and Other Stories. New York, Harper, and London, Gollancz, 1983.
Always Coming Home (includes cassette of *Music and Poetry of the Kesh*), illustrated by Margaret Chodos, diagrams by George Hersh. New York, Harper, 1985; London, Gollancz, 1986; without cassette, New York, Bantam, 1987.
Five Complete Novels. New York, Avenel, 1985.
The New Atlantis, with *The Return from Rainbow Bridge,* by Kim Stanley Robinson. New York, Tor, 1989.
Searoad: The Chronicles of Klatsand. New York, Harper Collins, 1991.

Short Stories

The Wind's Twelve Quarters. New York, Harper, 1975; London, Gollancz, 1976.
The Water Is Wide. Portland, Oregon, Pendragon Press, 1976.
Orsinian Tales. New York, Harper, 1976; London, Gollancz, 1977.
The Compass Rose. New York, Harper, 1982; London, Gollancz, 1983.
The Visionary: The Life Story of Flicker of the Serpentine, with *Wonders Hidden,* by Scott Russell Sanders. Santa Barbara, California, Capra Press, 1984.
Buffalo Gals and Other Animal Presences (includes verse). Santa Barbara, California, Capra Press, 1987; as *Buffalo Gals,* London, Gollancz, 1990.
The Ones Who Walk Away from Omelas. Mankato, Minnesota, Creative Education, 1992.

Poetry

Wild Angels. Santa Barbara, California, Capra Press, 1974.
Tillai and Tylissos, with Theodora K. Quinn. Red Bull Press, 1979.
Torrey Pines Reserve. Northridge, California, Lord John Press, 1980.
Gwilan's Harp. Northridge, California, Lord John Press, 1981.
Hard Words and Other Poems. New York, Harper, 1981.
In the Red Zone, with Hank Pander. Northridge, California, Lord John Press, 1983.
Wild Oats and Fireweed. New York, Harper, 1988.
No Boats. Ygor & Buntho, 1992.
Blue Moon over Thurman Street, photographed by Roger Dorband. NewSage, 1993.

Plays

No Use to Talk to Me, in *The Altered I: An Encounter with Science Fiction,* edited by Lee Harding. Melbourne, Nostrilia Press, 1976; New York, Berkley, 1980.
King Dog: A Screenplay, with *Dostoevsky: A Screenplay,* by Raymond Carver and Tess Gallagher. Santa Barbara, California, Capra Press, 1985.

Other

From Elfland to Poughkeepsie (lecture). Portland, Oregon, Pendragon Press, 1973.

Dreams Must Explain Themselves, illustrated by Tim Kirk. New York, Algol Press, 1975.

Editor, *Nebula Award Stories 11.* London, Gollancz, 1976; New York, Harper, 1977.

The Language of the Night: Essays on Fantasy and Science Fiction, edited by Susan Wood. New York, Putnam, 1979; revised edition, London, Women's Press, 1989.

Editor, with Virginia Kidd, *Interfaces: An Anthology of Speculative Fiction.* New York, Ace, 1980.

Editor, with Virginia Kidd, *Edges: Thirteen New Tales from the Borderlands of the Imagination.* New York, Pocket Books, 1980.

Contributor, *Burning with a Vision: Poetry of Science and the Fantastic,* by Thomas M. Disch. Philadelphia, Pennsylvania, Owlswick Press, 1984.

Uses of Music in Uttermost Parts, music by Elinor Armer (performed in part in San Francisco, California, 1986).

Dancing at the Edge of the World: Thoughts on Words, Women, Places. New York, Grove Press, and London, Gollancz, 1989.

Way of the Water's Going: Images of the Northern California Coastal Range, photographs by Ernest Waugh and Alan Nicholson. New York, Harper, 1989.

Contributor, *A Home-Concealed Woman: The Diaries of Magnolia Wynn Le Guin,* edited by Charles A. Le Guin. Athens, Georgia, University of Georgia Press, 1990.

Recordings: *The Lathe of Heaven,* Alternate World, 1976; *The Ones Who Walk Away from Omelas and Other Stories,* Alternate World, 1976; *Gwilan's Harp and Intercom,* Caedmon, 1977; *The Earthsea Trilogy,* Colophone, 1981; *Music and Poetry of the Kesh,* with Todd Barton, Valley Productions, 1985; *Rigel Nine: An Audio Opera,* with David Bedford, Charisma, 1985; *The Left Hand of Darkness,* Warner, 1985; *The Word for World Is Forest,* Book of the Road, 1986.

*

Media Adaptations: *The Word for World Is Forest* (recording), Book of the Road, 1968; *The Lathe of Heaven* (television broadcast), PBS-TV, 1979; *The Tombs of Atuan* (filmstrip with record or cassette), Newbery Award Records, 1980; *The Earthsea Trilogy* (recording), Colophone, 1981; *The Ones Who Walk Away from Omelas* (stage drama), performed at the Portland Civic Theatre, 1981.

Biography: Entry in *Dictionary of Literary Biography* by Brian Attebery, Volume 8, Detroit, Gale, Volume 8, 1981; *Ursula K. Le Guin* by Charlotte Spivack, Boston, Twayne, 1984; entry in *Dictionary of Literary Biography* by Andrew Gordon, Volume 52, Detroit, Gale, Volume 52, 1986; entry in *Concise Dictionary of American Literary Biography 1968-1988,* Detroit, Gale, 1989; essay in *Authors and Artists for Young Adults,* Volume 9, Detroit, Gale, 1992; essay in *Speaking for Ourselves, Too* compiled and edited by Donald R. Gallo, National Council of Teachers of English, 1993.

Bibliography: *Ursula K. Le Guin: A Primary and Secondary Bibliography* by Elizabeth Cummins Cogell, Boston, Hall, 1983.

Manuscript Collection: University of Oregon Library, Eugene.

Critical Study: *The Farthest Shores of Ursula K. Le Guin* by George Edgar Slusser, San Bernardino, California, Borgo Press, 1976; "Ursula Le Guin Issue" of *Science-Fiction Studies* (Terre Haute, Indiana), March 1976; Entry in *Children's Literature Review* Volume 3, Detroit Gale, 1978; Volume 28, 1992; Entry in *Contemporary Literary Criticism* Volume 8, Detroit, Gale, 1978; Volume 13, 1980; Volume 22, 1982; Volume 45, 1987; Volume 71, 1992; *Ursula Le Guin* by Joseph D. Olander and Martin H. Greenberg, New York, Taplinger, and Edinburgh, Harris, 1979; *Ursula K. Le Guin: Voyage to Inner Lands and to Outer Space* edited by Joseph W. De Bolt, Port Washington, New York, Kennikat Press, 1979; *Ursula K. Le Guin* by Barbara J. Bucknall, New York, Ungar, 1981; *Approaches to the Fiction of Ursula K. Le Guin* by James Bittner, Ann Arbor, Michigan, UMI Research Press, and Epping, Essex, Bowker, 1984; *Understanding Ursula K. Le Guin* by Elizabeth Cummins Cogell, Columbia, University of South Carolina Press, 1990.

*   *   *

Ursula Le Guin's immense reputation as a fantasy writer for children is founded essentially on the Earthsea trilogy—*A Wizard of Earthsea, The Tombs of Atuan,* and *The Farthest Shore.* Few writers have received more critical attention, and though this is partly due to her work as an adult science-fiction writer of great repute, it is mainly a well-justified tribute to the qualities of the Earthsea books.

The hero of all three books is Ged—a young magician in the first book, at the height of his powers in the second, and as the aging Archmage in the third. Misusing his powers in the first book *A Wizard of Earthsea,* he releases into the world a nameless shadow—an evil which he must then chase and battle with to the ends of the earth. When he finally finds and confronts it, it bears his own name. In the second volume, *The Tombs of Atuan,* searching for the missing half of a talismanic ring, he is captured and entombed in an underground labyrinth by the young priestess Tenar who is dedicated to death. His own fate and the fate of all the world depend on his being able to persuade her to choose life and reject the power of death. In the third volume, *The Farthest Shore,* he and his young companion, a future Great King, are pitched against an enemy whose evil-doing is sapping the power of all the magicians in the world, the power of hope and joy and ritual and craftsmanship among the people. To secure his own immortality the corrupt magician has made a hole in the barrier between life and death, and light and joy are flowing out through it.

No paraphrase of plot or setting can do justice to the profound originality of these books, which have been repeatedly imitated. In the first place, although there are wizards and dragons and other clear similarities to the medieval literary landscape used by Tolkien among many others, the setting, an elaborate huge archipelago of varied islands, is wholly invented and fully circumstantial. It is full of magic—magic used for high and commonplace purposes alike—but the magic is never arbitrary, and instead of convincing the reader that Earthsea is unlike the real world, it breathes a contagious sense that the real world, too, is full of wonders. More profound yet is the nature of the adventures that befall the characters. Imaginary the perils may be, as the magical defence for dealing with them are, but the adventures are real; they are the moral dangers and triumphs of the inner world seen with a fierce clarity. Far from being escapist, Le Guin's story turns the reader round to face him or herself. The language and imagery are extremely beautiful: "My name, and yours, and the true name of the sun, or a spring of water, or an unborn child are all syllables of the great word that is very slowly spoken by the shining of the stars...," but the moral vision of the work is challengingly bleak and austere. "You thought as a boy that a mage is one who can do anything. And the truth is that as a man's real power grows and his knowledge widens, ever the way he can follow grows narrower; until at last he chooses nothing, but does only and wholly what he *must* do..."

After an interval of seventeen years, in 1990, Le Guin published *Tehanu,* the fourth and last book of Earthsea. There was a book about young Ged, and a book about old Ged; now there is a book about young Tenar, and a book about Tenar as an old woman. We learn that Tenar left the Mage Ogion, and deliberately chose to live an obscure life as a farmer's wife. Now a widow, she is fostering a child who has been horribly scarred by acts of cruelty. Ged, no longer archmage, burnt out by the great crisis in The Farthest Shore, comes home to her, and in the world outside the High Magic, struggling with the humdrum difficulties of life and the danger to the child, the two of them at last consummate their love. *Tehanu* is a book of great depth and subtlety, deliberately confronting and altering the bedrock values of the old high fantasy on which the first three Earthsea books were based. It rejects the male-gendered tales of heroism, and in their place builds on women's experiences as the benchmarks of virtue, courage, love. The damaged child is at the centre of the book, and the triumph over evil is hers. Of course, the change of vision is the result of feminism, which has changed the weather in many minds since the early Earthsea books were written, and the author is very aware of that. But in two other ways *Tehanu* is unlike the earlier titles. Though it shares their dreamlike quality and many of their beauties, it is deeply self-conscious. Wrestling with the implied values in heroic narrative, it bring values above the subliminal, into view as a major part of the subject of the story. The thought process shaping the book is no longer innocent and implicit but urgently right-minded. The other great difference is that *Tehanu* can almost be defined as not being a book for young adults. The struggle between good and evil, as represented here, is not simple, though the powers of good and evil are more than ever frightening when evil is not a vast cosmic mysterious thing but something as familiar and realistic as the abuse of a child; but the child at the centre of the story is seen always through the eyes of the aging Tenar—in short the Earthsea sequence seems now to contain three young people's books and one adult novel. Le Guin has provided a powerful and in the strong sense self-critical commentary on the completed Earthsea sequence, and *Tehanu* in particular, in "Earthsea Revisioned."

The last thing one would have expected of the author of Earthsea was a realistic adolescent novel, such as *Very Far Away from Anywhere Else.* The two young protagonists, Natalie and Owen, are each highly individual—he wholly unable to be the car-loving, normal, tear-away son his parents yearn for, but instead desperate to study at a serious college; she a serious musician. Though he resists the pressure to conform to stereotype in other ways, Owen succumbs to it in his relationship with Natalie and nearly ruins everything with an unwelcome attempt to transform their friendship into a sexual one. Le Guin's admirers have objected to the didactic tone of this book, which is undoubtedly present as it is in so many other adolescent novels. But the rage which is palpable in the book—alongside a lot of human tenderness—is not really against the corrupting pressure on the young to advance too quickly into their sexual adulthood, rather it is against all the pressures by which individuals in their glorious oddity and variety are crushed into a few standard shapes by a society that hates nonconformity. With *The Beginning Place,* Le Guin twisted together the Earthsea strand and the realist strand in her imagination. A kind of place-slip happens when Hugh crosses a stream on the edge of the dismal modern city where he lives; he enters a wilderness of forest and stream and mountain. It is inhabited by another modern teenager, Irene, and by an ancient people living simple lives. Then there is a dragon that turns everything foul and that must be found and killed. Hugh plays Sigurd's part, and the two are released from the suffocating control of their parents to live in the real world and rent an apartment together. There are multiple resonances in this book—Oedipus and Sigurd among many others—and the position of the fantasy geography as a land of the inner world and of the mind is clearer than in Earthsea, though less compellingly beautiful.

In various miniature works for much younger readers, Le Guin shows a salty sense of humour that is barely apparent in the grander stories. It is less than ever possible to predict what she might do next, or put a limit on her possibilities. Hers is certainly one of the most powerful talents ever exercised in writing for the young.

—Jill Paton Walsh

———

L'ENGLE, Madeleine. American. Born in New York City, 29 November 1918. Educated at Smith College, A.B. (with honors) 1941; New School for Social Research, 1941-42; Columbia University, New York, 1960-61. Married Hugh Franklin in 1946 (died 1986); two daughters and one son. Worked in the theatre, New York, 1941-47; teacher with Committee for Refugee Education, during World War II; teacher, St. Hilda's and St. Hugh's School, Morningside Heights, New York, 1960-66; librarian, Cathedral of St. John the Divine, New York City, 1966—; member of the faculty, University of Indiana, Bloomington, summers, 1965-66, 1971; writer-in-residence, Ohio State University, Columbus, 1970, and University of Rochester, New York, 1972; since 1970 president, Crosswicks Ltd, New York; since 1976 lecturer, Wheaton College, Illinois; president, Authors Guild of America. Recipient: American Library Association Newbery Medal, Hans Christian Andersen Award runner-up, 1964, Sequoyah Children's Book Award from the Oklahoma State Department of Education, and Lewis Carroll Shelf Award, both 1965, all for *A Wrinkle in Time; Book World*'s Spring Book Festival Honor Book, and one of *School Library Journal*'s Best Books of the Year, both 1968, both for *The Young Unicorns;* Austrian State Literary Prize, 1969, for *The Moon by Night;* University of Southern Mississippi Silver Medallion, 1978, for "an outstanding contribution to the field of children's literature"; American Book Award for paperback fiction, 1980, for *A Swiftly Tilting Planet;* Smith Medal, 1980; Newbery Honor Book, 1981, for *A Ring of Endless Light;* Books for the Teen Ager selection, New York Public Library, 1981, for *A Ring of Endless Light,* and 1982, for *Camilla;* Sophie Award, 1984; Regina Medal from the Catholic Library Association, 1984; National Council of Teachers of English ALAN award, 1986. Agent: Robert Lescher, 155 East 71st St., New York, NY 10021. Address: Crosswicks, Goshen, CT 06756, U.S.A.

PUBLICATIONS FOR YOUNG ADULTS

Fiction

The Small Rain: A Novel (for adults). New York, Vanguard, 1945; abridged edition (for young adults) as *Prelude,* New York, Vanguard, 1968; London, Gollancz, 1972.

And Both Were Young. New York, Lothrop, 1949.
Camilla Dickinson. New York, Simon & Schuster, 1951, as *Camilla,* New York, Crowell, 1965.
Meet the Austins, illustrated by Gillian Willett. New York, Vanguard, 1960.
A Wrinkle in Time. New York, Farrar, Straus, 1962.
The Moon by Night. New York, Farrar, Straus, 1963.
The Arm of the Starfish. New York, Farrar, Straus, 1965.
The Young Unicorns. New York, Farrar, Straus, 1968.
Intergalactic P.S.3. New York, Children's Book Council, 1970.
A Wind in the Door. New York, Farrar, Straus, 1973.
Dragons in the Waters (sequel to *The Arm of the Starfish*). New York, Farrar, Straus, 1976.
A Swiftly Tilting Planet. New York, Farrar, Straus, 1978.
A Ring of Endless Light. New York, Farrar, Straus, 1980.
A House Like a Lotus. New York, Farrar, Straus, 1984.
Many Waters. New York, Farrar, Straus, 1986.
An Acceptable Time. New York, Farrar, Straus, 1988.

PUBLICATIONS FOR CHILDREN

Picture Books

The Twenty-four Days before Christmas: An Austin Family Story, illustrated by Inga. New York, Farrar, Straus, 1964.
Dance in the Desert, illustrated by Symeon Shimin. New York, Farrar, Straus, and London, Longman, 1969.
Everyday Prayers, illustrated by Lucille Butel. New York, Morehouse, 1974.
Prayers for Sunday, illustrated by Lizzie Napoli. New York, Morehouse, 1974.
Ladder of Angels: Scenes from the Bible Illustrated by the Children of the World. New York, Seabury, 1979.
The Anti-Muffins, illustrated by Gloria Ortiz. New York, Pilgrim Press, 1980.
The Sphinx at Dawn: Two Stories, illustrated by Vivian Berger. New York, Harper, 1982.
The Glorious Impossible, illustrated by Giotto. New York, Simon & Schuster, 1990.

Plays

18 Washington Square, South: A Comedy in One Act (first produced in Northhampton, Massachusetts, 1940). Boston, Baker, 1944.
How Now Brown Cow, with Robert Hartung (first produced in New York). 1949.
The Journey with Jonah, illustrated by Leonard Everett Fisher (produced in New York, 1970). New York, Farrar, Straus, 1967.

Poetry

Lines Scribbled on an Envelope and Other Poems. New York, Farrar, Straus, 1969.

PUBLICATIONS FOR ADULTS

Fiction

Ilsa. New York, Vanguard, 1946.
A Winter's Love. Philadelphia, Lippincott, 1957.
The Love Letters. New York, Farrar, Straus, 1966.

The Other Side of the Sun. New York, Farrar, Straus, 1971.
A Severed Wasp (sequel to *The Small Rain*). Farrar, Straus, 1982.
Certain Women. New York, Farrar, Straus, 1992.

Poetry

The Weather of the Heart. Wheaton, Illinois, Shaw, 1978.
Walking on Water: Reflections on Faith and Art. Wheaton, Illinois, Shaw, 1980.
A Cry like a Bell. Wheaton, Illinois, Shaw, 1987.

Nonfiction

A Circle of Quiet. New York, Farrar, Straus, 1972.
The Summer of the Great-Grandmother. New York, Farrar, Straus, 1974.
Editor with William B. Green, *Spirit and Light: Essays in Historical Theology.* New York, Seabury, 1976.
The Irrational Season. New York, Seabury, 1977.
And It Was Good: Reflections on Beginnings. Wheaton, Illinois, Shaw, 1983.
Dare to Be Creative. Washington, D.C., Library of Congress, 1984.
Trailing Clouds of Glory: Spiritual Values in Children's Books, with Avery Brooke. Philadelphia, Westminster, 1985.
A Stone for a Pillow: Journeys with Jacob. Wheaton, Illinois, Shaw, 1986.
Two Part Invention. New York, Farrar, Straus, 1988.
Sold Into Egypt: Joseph's Journey into Human Being. Wheaton, Illinois, Shaw, 1989.
A Rock That is Higher: Story as Truth. Wheaton, Illinois, Shaw, 1992.

*

Media Adaptations: *A Wrinkle in Time* was recorded by Newbery Award Records, 1972, and adapted as a filmstrip with cassette by Miller-Brody, 1974; *A Wind in the Door* was recorded and adapted as a filmstrip with cassette by Miller-Brody; *Camilla* was recorded as a cassette by Listening Library; *A Ring of Endless Light* was recorded and adapted as a filmstrip with cassette by Random House. *And Both Were Young, The Arm of the Starfish, Meet the Austins, The Moon by Night, A Wrinkle in Time,* and *The Young Unicorns* have been adapted into Braille; *The Arm of the Starfish, Camilla, Dragons in the Waters, A Wind in the Door,* and *A Wrinkle in Time* have been adapted into talking books; *The Summer of the Great-Grandmother* is also available on cassette.

Biography: Entry in *More Junior Authors,* New York, H.W. Wilson, 1963; essay in *Authors and Artists for Young Adults,* Volume 1, Detroit, Gale, 1989; essay in *Speaking for Ourselves: Autobiographical Sketches by Notable Authors of Books for Young Adults,* Volume 1, compiled and edited by Donald R. Gallo, National Council of Teachers of English, 1990; essay in *Something about the Author Autobiography Series,* Volume 15, Detroit, Gale, 1993.

Manuscript Collections: Wheaton College; Kerlan Collection, University of Minnesota, Minneapolis; de Grummond Collection, University of Southern Mississippi.

Critical Study: *Children's Literature Review,* Detroit, Gale, Volume 1, 1976, Volume 14, 1988. *Contemporary Literary Criticism,* Volume 12, Detroit, Gale, 1980.

The award-winning author of more than forty published books including plays, poems, essays, autobiographies, and novels, Madeline L'Engle is one of America's most popular writers of books for young adults. L'Engle's literate stories are ageless, weaving family life, values, science, history, and theology into complex, often suspenseful plots with life-affirming messages.

L'Engle's popularity mushroomed after winning the Newbery Medal in 1963 for *A Wrinkle in Time,* the first in her time-fantasy trilogy (including *A Wind in the Door* and *A Swiftly Tilting Planet).* L'Engle said winning the Newbery was especially rewarding because the book had been rejected by almost every publisher in New York because of its difficulty level and uncertainty about the audience.

L'Engle's books do offer young adults a reading challenge. She writes for intelligent readers, using carefully chosen vocabulary and literary allusions throughout her stories. She blends references to mythology and carefully researched details of history, science, architecture, and philosophy into her tales. The reader must accept references to the principles of physics, cellular biology, and extrasensory communication in the time-fantasy series. L'Engle tackles such concepts as human communication with dolphins, the future impacting the past, and regeneration in other novels.

Young adults rise to L'Engle's literary challenges because she creates recurring families and characters that readers befriend and care about, and fast-paced plots that engage readers in following several intertwining threads to satisfying conclusions. In *A Wrinkle in Time,* Meg Murray, the oldest child of the family featured in the time-fantasy series, must "tesser," travel through a wrinkle in time, to save her father and ultimately the world from the evil force IT. In the third book in the series, Meg's younger brother Charles Wallace travels back in time guided by a unicorn to inhabit the bodies of two brothers of ancient Welsh mythology in order to change the course of history. In *Many Waters,* Meg's other brothers, twins Sandy and Dennys, sketchily developed in the time-fantasy series, land in a world inhabited by seraphim, cherubim, fallen angels, and Japheth, Noah's father, where they must save themselves from the biblical Flood. In *The Arm of the Starfish,* Meg is a famous scientist married to Calvin O'Keefe of the time-fantasy series and is the mother of Polly O'Keefe, a secondary character in *Starfish* and a primary character in *An Acceptable Time,* in which she and Zachary, a young man she encountered in Greece in *A House like a Lotus,* find a door into another circle of time where a Druid priest saves Polly from becoming a human sacrifice after Zachary has betrayed her. The Austin family and their friends appear in *Meet the Austins, The Moon by Night,* and *The Young Unicorns.* Dr. Austin and his family play an important part in helping Dave of *The Young Unicorns* survive the violence and hatred of his former gang and begin a new life. Part of the great joy of reading L'Engle's books is the opportunities readers have to renew friendships and learn more about L'Engle's believable characters.

L'Engle writes about what is important to young adults. In an interview, L'Engle stressed the importance of teachers, librarians, and authors helping youngsters ask and search for answers to the big questions Why am I on the earth? Does my life matter? Does anybody care? Is there meaning to my existence? Am I really a human being? These questions are central to L'Engle's stories. The protagonists are intelligent, thoughtful, moral, and spiritual young people. Vicky Austin, in *A Ring of Endless Light,* deals bravely with the death of her beloved grandfather and family friend. Vicky's sensitivity and understanding of poetry allow her to communicate with the dolphins being studied by the scientists on her grandfather's

island. Her abilities to communicate with these beautiful creatures provide her the energy to understand and accept the naturalness of death. In *The Young Unicorns,* Dave befriends Emily, a young, blind girl, and it is her enhanced sense of hearing that saves their lives when trapped in the tunnels of the Cathedral Church of St. John the Divine. In *The Arm of the Starfish,* Adam risks his life to save his friend and the world, and in *A House like a Lotus,* Polly O'Keefe travels to Greece and Cyprus where she struggles to make sense of the confusing events of her life, learning about love, pain, and anger in the process.

The greatest pleasures in L'Engle's novels come from her commitment to sometimes frightening, always thought-provoking, optimistic situations and themes. L'Engle's stories emphasize mankind's oneness with everything in the universe, the idea that everything affects everything else. This idea of connectedness among peoples, even across universes and time, provides readers with a sense of belonging to something much larger than self. Christian allusions are prevalent in L'Engle's novels; however, even those readers who don't recognize these allusions sense the spiritualness of L'Engle's stories and are uplifted by the predominant message of her works: the power of love can cross all boundaries of time and space to transform and save mankind.

—Hollis Lowery-Moore

LESTER, Julius (Bernard). American. Born in St. Louis, Missouri, 27 January 1939. Educated at Fisk University, Nashville, Tennessee 1956-60, B.A. 1960. Married 1) Joan Steinau in 1962 (divorced 1970), one daughter and one son; 2) Alida Carolyn Fechner in 1979, one son and one stepdaughter. Musician and singer, recorded with Vanguard Records. Since 1971 Professor of Afro-American Studies; since 1982 Professor of Near Eastern and Judaic Studies, University of Massachusetts, Amherst. Associate editor, *Sing Out,* New York, 1964-69; contributing editor, *Broadside of New York,* 1964-70; director, Newport Folk Festival, Rhode Island, 1966-68; lecturer, New School for Social Research, New York, 1968-70; producer and host, WBAI radio, New York, 1968-75; host, *Free Time,* WNET-TV, New York, 1971-73; acting director and associate director of Institute for Advanced Studies in Humanities, 1982-84. Writer-in-residence, Vanderbilt University, 1985. Recipient: Newbery Honor Book citation, 1969, and Lewis Carroll Shelf Award, 1970, both for *To Be a Slave;* Lewis Carroll Shelf Award, 1972, and National Book Award finalist, 1973, both for *The Long Journey Home: Stories from Black History;* Lewis Carroll Shelf Award, 1973, for *The Knee-High Man and Other Tales;* honorable mention, Coretta Scott King Award, 1983, for *This Strange New Feeling,* and 1988, for *Tales of Uncle Remus: The Adventures of Brer Rabbit;* Distinguished Teacher's Award, 1983-84; Faculty Fellowship Award for Distinguished Research and Scholarship, 1985; National Professor of the Year Silver Medal Award, Council for Advancement and Support of Education, 1985; Massachusetts State Professor of the Year and Gold Medal Award for National Professor of the Year, both from Council for Advancement and Support of Education, both 1986; Distinguished Faculty Lecturer, 1986-87. Address: 600 Station Rd., Amherst, MA 01002, U.S.A.

PUBLICATIONS FOR YOUNG ADULTS

Fiction

The Long Journey Home: Stories from Black History. New York, Dial Press, 1972; London, Longman, 1973.
Two Love Stories. New York, Dial Press, 1972; London, Kestrel, 1974.
This Strange New Feeling (short stories). New York, Dial Press, 1982; as *A Taste of Freedom: Three Stories from Black History,* London, Longman, 1983.

Other (retellings)

Editor, with Mary Varela, *Our Folk Tales: High John, The Conqueror, and Other Afro-American Tales,* illustrated by Jennifer Lawson. Privately printed, 1967.
Editor, *To Be a Slave,* illustrated by Tom Feelings. New York, Dial Press, 1968; London, Longman, 1970.
Black Folktales, illustrated by Tom Feelings. New York, Baron, 1969.
The Knee-High Man and Other Tales, illustrated by Ralph Pinto. New York, Dial Press, 1972; London, Kestrel, 1974.
The Tales of Uncle Remus: The Adventures of Brer Rabbit, illustrated by Jerry Pinkney. New York, Dial Press, and London, Bodley Head, 1987.
More Tales of Uncle Remus: The Further Adventures of Brer Rabbit, illustrated by Jerry Pinkney. New York, Dial Press, 1988.
Further Tales of Uncle Remus: The Misadventures of Brer Rabbit, Brer Fox, Brer Wolf, the Doodang, and Other Creatures, illustrated by Jerry Pinkney. New York, Dial Press, 1990.
How Many Spots Does a Leopard Have? and Other Tales, illustrated by David Shannon. New York, Scholastic, 1990.

PUBLICATIONS FOR ADULTS

Novels

Do Lord Remember Me. New York, Holt Rinehart, 1985; London, Dent, 1987.

Poetry

The Mud of Vietnam: Photographs and Poems. New York, Folklore Press, 1967.
Who I Am, with David Gahr. New York, Dial Press, 1974.

Other

The 12-String Guitar as Played by Leadbelly: An Instructional Manual, with Pete Seeger. New York, Oak, 1965.
The Angry Children of Malcolm X. Nashville, Tennessee, Southern Student Organizing Committee, 1966.
Editor, with Mary Varela, *To Praise Our Bridges: An Autobiography,* by Fanny Lou Hamer. Jackson, Mississippi, KIPCO, 1967.
Look Out Whitey! Black Power's Gon' Get Your Mama! New York, Dial Press, 1968; London, Allison and Busby, 1970.
Editor, *Ain't No Ambulances for No Nigguhs Tonight,* by Stanley Couch. New York, Baron, 1969.
Search for the New Land: History as Subjective Experience. New York, Dial Press, 1969; London, Allison and Busby, 1971.

Revolutionary Notes. New York, Baron, 1969.
Editor, *The Seventh Son: The Thoughts and Writings of W.E.B. Du Bois.* New York, Random House, 2 vols., 1971.
Compiler, with Rae Pace Alexander, *Young and Black in America.* New York, Random House, 1971.
All Is Well: An Autobiography. New York, Morrow, 1976.
Lovesong: Becoming a Jew. New York, Holt Rinehart, 1988.
Falling Pieces of the Broken Sky. New York, Arcade, 1990.

*

Critical Study: Entry in *Children's Literature Review,* Volume 2, Detroit, Gale, 1976.

*   *   *

Julius Lester established his reputation by writing biographies of African Americans and by retelling collections of black folktales. The biographies include *The 12-String Guitar as Played by Leadbelly, To Be a Slave, Who I Am,* and *The Seventh Son: The Thought and Writings of W.E.B. Du Bois.* The folktales include *Black Folktales, The Knee-High Man and Other Tales* and *The Tales of Uncle Remus: The Adventures of Brer Rabbit.* Many of these books are collaborations. Lester worked with the singer Pete Seeger on *The 12-String Guitar as Played by Leadbelly,* with the artist Tom Feelings on several books, and with the photographer David Gahr on *Who I Am.*

Lester achieved his first critical success with *To Be a Slave,* published in 1968. The book was an ALA Notable Book and a Newbery Honor Book, and it received the Nancy Bloch Award. The book received this recognition during the decade in which the Civil Rights Movement was significant. Also, during this decade, historians including Jacqueline Bernard and Milton Meltzer had begun to consult original sources and, on the basis of these sources, to challenge accepted historical truths. In *To Be a Slave* Lester challenged the assumption prevalent at the time that African-American history is relatively unimportant in American history. He quotes an ex-slave as an epigraph for the book: "In all the books that you have studied you never have studied Negro history, have you?..." The book's success helped Lester establish himself as a major "social advocacy" historian.

Lester frames slaves' and ex-slaves' recorded statements with his own comments in the book. In one of his first comments, Lester writes:

> To be a slave. To know, despite the suffering and deprivation, that you were human, more human than he who said you were not human.
> To know joy, laughter, sorrow, and tears and yet be considered only the equal of a table. To be a slave was to be a human being under conditions in which that humanity was denied. They were not slaves. They were people. Their condition was slavery.

This passage is simultaneously passionate and thought-provoking. Lester begins the first paragraph with a sentence fragment to make his prose sound conversational, he repeats "human" three times in the second sentence to emphasize that the slaves were human beings and not inanimate objects like tables, and he lists the common human emotions the slaves felt to illustrate their membership in the human family. The passage is rich in feeling.

But Lester makes the passage intellectually rich as well by introducing two significant ethical ideas. First, he suggests that the institution of slavery debases slave and slave owner alike, and that by trying to limit their slaves' humanity the slave owners limited their own humanity. Second, he highlights the absurdity of considering slaves to be equal to inanimate objects like tables when slaves felt joy, laughter, sorrow, and tears. In his book Lester shows his thinking to be consistent with the Judeo-Christian tradition of finding meaning in suffering. The central idea uniting the slave reminiscences is that slavery is horrible and is wrong. Lester gives dignity and significance to these brief reminiscences by reinforcing and interpreting this idea in his comments. Ella Wilson's suffering would have been even more horrible if it would have gone unnoticed, if others could not have learned from it:

> My master used to throw me in a buck and whip me. He would put my hands together and tie them. Then he would strip me naked. Then he would squat me down. Then he would run a stick through behind my knees and in front of my elbows. My knee was up against my chest. My hands was tied together just in front of my shins. The stick between my arms and my knees held me in a squat. That what they call a buck. You couldn't stand up and you couldn't get your feet out. You couldn't do nothing but just squat there and take what he put on. You couldn't move no way at all. Just try to. You just fall over on one side and have to stay there till you were turned over by him. He would whip me on one side till that was sore and full of blood and then he would whip me on the other side till that was all tore up.... (Ella Wilson, Library of Congress)

The first chapter, titled "To Be a Slave," contains this and other brief reminiscences. The other seven chapters are equally loosely organized under general headings including "The Auction Block" and "The Plantation." *To Be a Slave* is similar to Lester's other books in this looseness of overall organization, power of particular passages, and reliance on Lester's voice to unify it.

Black Folktales, a collection he published in 1969, again contains stories loosely grouped under general headings. Lester writes in the Foreword:

> It is in stories like these that a child learns who his parents are and who he will become.... The stories in this book come from the black people of Africa and Afro-America.... These stories are told here not as they were told a hundred years ago, but as I tell them now. And I tell them now only because they have meaning now.

Lester has repeatedly proven through his biographies of famous and anonymous African Americans and his retellings of black folktales that African Americans' lives and stories have meaning long after the original living or telling.

—Harold Nelson

LEVENKRON, Steven. American. Born in New York City, 25 March 1941. Educated at Queens College of the City University of New York, B.A. 1963; Brooklyn of the City University of New

York, M.S. 1969. Married Abby Rosen in 1963; two daughters. Social studies teacher at secondary schools in New York, 1963-68; guidance counselor at secondary schools in New York, 1968-74; in part-time private practice of psychotherapy, 1972-74; visiting psychotherapist, Montefiore Hospital and Medical Center, Bronx, New York, 1975—; clinical consultant, Center for the Study of Anorexia, New York, 1981—. Recipient: Annual award from the National Association of Anorexia Nervosa and Associated Disorders, 1981, for bringing anorexia nervosa to public attention; *The Best Little Girl in the World* was named best book for young adults by the American Library Association, 1978-79. Agent: George Wieser, Wieser and Wieser, Inc., 79 Valley View, Chappaqua, NY 10514. Address: 16 East 79th Street, New York, NY 10021, U.S.A.

PUBLICATIONS FOR YOUNG ADULTS

Fiction

The Best Little Girl in the World. Chicago, Contemporary Books, 1978.

Nonfiction

Treating and Overcoming Anorexia Nervosa. New York, Scribner, 1982.
Obsessive-Compulsive Disorders: Treating and Understanding Crippling Habits. New York, Warner, 1991.

*   *   *

Given the fact that Levenkron is a psychologist and not a professional writer of literature for young adults, his one excursion into the world of the novel is quite impressive. *The Best Little Girl in the World* is the excruciatingly painful story of a teenage anoretic who nearly dies as a result of her illness. The book joins the Dietrich family—a typical white, middle-class family—just as fifteen-year-old Francesca's disease is beginning to climax. She clearly feels alienated from her family because her older brother and sister have seemingly gotten the lionshare of attention from their parents. Francesca was always "the good child" compared to her more confrontational sister Susanna and conceited but adored brother Gregg. Francesca's life has begun to revolve around the opinion of her ballet instructor—the sole adult in Francesca's life who seems to notice her. At the suggestion of the teacher, Francesca begins dieting with the hope that she will qualify for a position at a prestigious ballet camp. This suggestion, however, plays into Francesca's low self-esteem, and the girl becomes obsessed with the weight loss as a means of solving all of the unpleasant realities of her life.

The troubled youth even takes on a new identity, "Kessa" to cope with the pain of her circumstance. Levenkron describes with keen insight the thoughts and feelings of the slowly deteriorating Francesca as well as the experience of her concerned parents and physicians. As Francesca's disease progresses, her thinking becomes obscured partly because of malnutrition. Once her mother realizes her daughter is terribly ill, the rate of Francesca's deterioration increases. Eventually the girl is hospitalized. Her only hope comes from the relationship she has established with a psychologist who has just begun working with anoretic patients. As they realize the seriousness of Francesca's condition, the family is forced to deal with the dynamics within the unit that contributed to her illness. As it turns out, Francesca's behavior is motivated largely by a desire for attention. Since being the "good girl" obviously did not work, she turned to a negative, self-destructive behavior instead. In the end, a combination of a near-death experience, peer pressure, counseling, and family support make rehabilitation a feasible option for Francesca. When the novel closes, her prognosis is good.

The characters in this novel are somewhat flat and stereotypical. However, since the work is actually a modern Morality Play that presents a common dilemma and its successful resolution, the flatness of the characters enhances the work. Levenkron's glimpses into the depth of the secondary characters creates a bas relief against which the more fully formed Francesca is showcased. Throughout the book, Levenkron speaks primarily from Francesca's point of view. He provides his audience with a poignant image of a teenage girl in excruciating emotional, and eventually physical, pain. In so doing, he provides a vehicle of communication for those readers who experience this pain or know someone who does.

The Best Little Girl in the World is an excellent tool for counselors or lay people dealing with anorexia. Levenkron's clear depictions of each stage of the disease serve to warn would-be anoretics of the terrible consequences of their choices, while demonstrating that there are people who understand the fear and pain that lies at the root of their condition. It also dispels some of the fear of the unknown for those travelling this long, dark road. Perhaps most significantly, Levenkron provides a lively, easily accessible, and cogent argument against the societal values that contribute to this disease.

For those interested in a more technical discussion of anorexia and other obsessive/compulsive behaviors, Levenkron has written several nonfiction works on the subject. His accessible style is evident in these works as well.

—Linda Ross

LEVITIN, Sonia (née Wolff). Also writes as Sonia Wolff. American. Born in Berlin, Germany, 18 August 1934; brought to the United States, 1938. Educated at the University of California, Berkeley, 1952-54; University of Pennsylvania, Philadelphia, 1954-56, B.S. in education 1956; San Francisco State University, 1957-60. Married Lloyd Levitin in 1953; one son and one daughter. Elementary school teacher, Mill Valley, California, 1956-57; adult education teacher, Daly City, California, 1962-64, and Acalanes Adult Center, Lafayette, California, 1965-72; creative writing teacher, Palos Verdes Peninsula, California, 1973-76. Since 1978 teacher, Writers' Program, University of California at Los Angeles Extension. Since 1989 instructor in American Jewish literature, University of Judaism. Founder, STEP adult education corporation. Performed volunteer work, including publicity, for various charities and educational institutions. Recipient: *Journey to America* received the Charles and Bertie G. Schwartz award for juvenile fiction from the Jewish Book Council of America, 1971, and American Library Association Notable Book honors; *Roanoke: A Novel of the Lost Colony* was nominated for the Dorothy Canfield Fisher award, Georgia Children's Book award, and Mark Twain award; *Who Owns the Moon?* received American Library Association Notable Book honors; *The Mark of Conte* received the Southern Califor-

nia Council on Literature for Children and Young People award for fiction, 1976, and was nominated for California Young Reader Medal award in the junior high category, 1982; Golden Spur award from Western Writers of America, 1978, and Lewis Carroll Shelf award, both for *The No-Return Trail;* Southern California Council on Literature for Children and Young People award for a distinguished contribution to the field of children's literature, 1981; National Jewish Book award in children's literature, PEN Los Angeles award for young adult fiction, Association of Jewish Libraries Sydney Taylor award, Austrian Youth Prize, Catholic Children's Book Prize (Germany), Dorothy Canfield Fisher award nomination, Parent's Choice Honor Book citation, and American Library Association Best Book for Young Adults award, all 1988, all for *The Return;* Edgar Allen Poe award from Mystery Writers of America, Dorothy Canfield Fisher award nomination, and Nevada State award nomination, all 1989, all for *Incident at Loring Groves.* Agent: Toni Mendez, Inc., 141 East 56th St., New York, NY 10022, U.S.A.

PUBLICATIONS FOR YOUNG ADULTS

Fiction

Journey to America, illustrated by Charles Robinson. New York, Atheneum, 1970; London, Macmillan, 1987.

Rita the Weekend Rat, illustrated by Leonard Shortall. New York, Atheneum, 1971.

Roanoke: A Novel of the Lost Colony, illustrated by John Gretzer. New York, Atheneum, 1973.

Who Owns the Moon?, illustrated by John Larrecq. Berkeley, California, Parnassus, 1973.

Jason and the Money Tree, illustrated by Pat Grant Porter. New York, Harcourt Brace, 1974.

A Single Speckled Egg, illustrated by John Larrecq. Berkeley, California, Parnassus, 1975.

The Mark of Conte, illustrated by Bill Negron. New York, Atheneum, 1976.

Beyond Another Door. New York, Atheneum, 1977.

The No-Return Trail. New York, Harcourt Brace, 1978.

A Sound to Remember, illustrated by Gabriel Lisowski. New York, Harcourt Brace, 1979.

Nobody Stole the Pie, illustrated by Fernando Krahn. New York, Harcourt Brace, 1980.

The Fisherman and the Bird, illustrated by Francis Livingston. Boston, Houghton Mifflin, 1982.

All the Cats in the World, illustrated by Charles Robinson. New York, Harcourt Brace, 1982.

The Year of Sweet Senior Insanity. New York, Atheneum, 1982.

Smile Like a Plastic Daisy. New York, Atheneum, 1984.

A Season of Unicorns. New York, Atheneum, 1986.

The Return. New York, Atheneum, 1987.

Incident at Loring Groves. New York, Dial Press, 1988.

Silver Days. New York, Atheneum, 1989.

The Man Who Kept His Heart in a Bucket. New York, Dial Press, 1991.

Annie's Promise. New York, Macmillan, 1993.

The Golem and the Dragon Girl. New York, Dial Press, 1993.

Publications for Adults

Novels

Reigning Cats and Dogs, illustrated by Joan Berg Victor. New York,
Atheneum, 1978.
What They Did to Miss Lily (as Sonia Wolff). New York, Harper,
1981; London, New English Library, 1982.

*

Biography: Essay in *Something about the Author Autobiography
Series,* Volume 2, Detroit, Gale, 1986; essay in *Speaking for Ourselves, Too* compiled and edited by Donald R. Gallo, National Council of Teachers of English, 1993.

Critical Study: Entry in *Contemporary Literary Criticism,* Volume
17, Detroit, Gale, 1981.

Sonia Levitin comments:

Through my writing I try to create bridges—between childhood
and adulthood, between poeples of different beliefs and cultures.
My desire is to invite the reader to cross that bridge and to discover
not only the Other, but himself. Learning, knowing, and loving go
together. It is so with all things. So I try to make it easy for the
reader to know and learn while I entertain him, hoping that he will
also find new passions.

*   *   *

Versatility is a hallmark of Sonia Levitin's work. Her ability to
write historical as well as realistic fiction captures a wide range of
readers. She is an author who unfolds a story carefully and with
attention to the details that bring life and caring to characters.

Her trilogy, based on Levitin's own life, takes the reader through
the war years and offers rich insight into the survival of one family
in the midst of horrendous upheaval and personal tragedy. *Journey
to America,* is the story of the Platt family's escape from Nazi
Germany in 1938, told from the perspective of Lisa Platt. The
courage of each member of the family and their willingness to leave
everything held dear to seek freedom and safety capture the reader's
attention. Levitin uses Lisa's fears and language that binds the reader
to the story as the family arrive in Switzerland on their way to
America. *Silver Days* lacks the strength of the earlier work, but it is
still a fine portrayal of what it was like to come to America and
struggle through the early days of learning English and conforming
to different ways. Again, the story is told from Lisa's point of view
and explores the concept of adaptability, not only of Lisa but also
of the family itself. *Annie's Promise* brings the story of the Platt
family full circle. Annie is the youngest and this is clearly her story.
Her summer at "Quaker Pines," a Quaker-sponsored camp, is her
chance to test herself and determine who she will be as a young
woman. Although she fails in her antagonistic relationship with the
angry street kid, Nancy Rae, she learns a great deal from that hate-
ful encounter. Perhaps the most powerful scene in the book is
Annie's angry confrontation with her parents over their treatment
of Tally, her young black friend from camp. Annie screams: "You
are just like the Nazis. This is why there are wars!...Because people
hate for no reason—how could you?"

In *Beyond Another Door* Daria comes to grips with the frightening power of extrasensory perception. A nondescript object, a glass

dish won at a fair, acts as the catalyst to call her grandma's spirit
back to help her cope with this ability. Throughout the story her
mother is frightened and tries to push her away from anything that
encourages this talent. She won't speak of the problem or of the
grandmother's reputation as a gifted psychic. Most of Daria's friends
turn away from her in fear of weird happenings, but new ones like
Rob and Man believe in her. Levitin makes the distinction, so important to the story, of knowing something and causing it, which is
a burden that gifted people such as Daria carry. She makes a tremendous impact on the reader in having Daria say towards the end
of the story:"I can't just accept things without asking questions. It
wouldn't be logical. Some people go too far, believing everything
without even thinking." But it is also Daria's decision to commit
herself to her painting and at the same time to seek help from Rob's
father who is a psychologist studying psychic phenomenon that
brings the unfolding of this story to a fullness.

Levitin continues her interest in the preternatural with *The Golem
and the Dragon Girl* which, while it forces the reader to consider
cultural roots and heritage in a ghost-filled ancestral home, still
offers insights into the unstable world of adolescence. Jonathan and
Laurel each want to avoid moving from their homes and each becomes involved in a sharing of Jewish and Chinese cultures. Music
is one key in this novel that helps the reader focus on both the
protagonists' personal problems as well as the larger issues.

Levitin moves into historical fiction in *The No-Return Trail,* the
story, based on fact, of Nancy Kelsey, a seventeen-year-old wife
and mother and the first American woman to make the journey to
California in the Bidwell-Bartleson expedition of 1841. Nancy grows
and changes a great deal as she moves with the wagon train across
the land and struggles with her womanhood and her relationship to
her husband. In *Roanoke: A Novel of the Lost Colony,* sixteen-year-
old William Wythers joins emigrants bound for Virginia. Levitin
uses what little factual material is known about the colony at
Roanoke as the backdrop for William's growth into manhood.

A Season of Unicorns and *Incident at Loring Groves* offer insight
into adolescent concerns. Inky the protagonist of the first gathers
the strength to face her fears by changing herself, and Cassiday and
Ken risk peer pressure and their popularity to accept responsibility and report the murder of a classmate in the second story.

In *The Return* Desta, a young Ethiopian Jewish girl, struggles to
make the long journey to join "Operation Moses," the secret Exodus of Ethiopian Jews from the Sudan to Israel between 1984 and
1985. As in many of her books, prejudice, oppression, and racial
hatreds are explored. In this instance it is against the "Falasha," the
derogatory term other Ethiopians called the Ethiopian Jews. Having endured so much pain and suffering, it is Desta who releases
Dan from engagement bonds and leads in enunciating their common
need to study before they consider marriage. Told in the first person, this powerful and haunting story of thirst, starvation, and
death is grim in parts but lyrical in its portrayal of the power of the
human spirit—a power that permeates all of Levitin's work and
gives her stories their clarity and richness.

—Jane Anne Hannigan

———

LEVOY, Myron. American. Born in New York City, 30 January
1930. Educated at City College, New York, B.S. in chemical engineering 1952; Purdue University, West Lafayette, Indiana, M.S. in

chemical engineering 1953. Married Beatrice Fleischer in 1952; one daughter and one son. Has worked as a chemical engineer; now a full-time writer. Recipient: *Book World*'s Children's Spring Book Festival honor book, and one of Child Study Association of America's Children's Books of the Year, both 1972, and a Children's Book Showcase selection, 1973, all for *The Witch of Fourth Street, and Other Stories;* New Jersey Institute of Technology Authors award, 1973, for *Penny Tunes and Princesses; Boston Globe-Horn Book* award honor book for fiction, American Book award finalist, Woodward Park School Annual Book award, Jane Addams Children's Book award honor book, and New Jersey Institute of Technology Authors award, all 1978, Dutch Silver Pencil award, and Austrian State Prize for Children's Literature, both 1981, and Buxtehuder Bulle award, Buxtehuder, West Germany, and German State Prize for Children's Literature, both 1982, all for *Alan and Naomi; A Shadow Like a Leopard* was named one of American Library Association's Best Books for Young Adults, 1981, and received the Woodward Park School Annual Book award, and was one of New York Public Library's Books for the Teen Age, both 1982; *Pictures of Adam* was an ALA Best Book for Young Adults and an International Reading Association Young Adult Choice in 1986. Agent: Susan Cohen, Writers House Inc., 21 West 26th Street, New York, NY 10010.

PUBLICATIONS FOR YOUNG ADULTS

Fiction

Alan and Naomi. New York, Harper, 1977; London, Bodley Head, 1979.
A Shadow like a Leopard. New York, Harper, 1981.
Three Friends. New York, Harper, 1984.
Pictures of Adam. New York, Harper, 1986; London, Bodley Head, 1987.
Kelly 'n' Me. New York, Harper, 1992.

PUBLICATIONS FOR CHILDREN

Fiction

The Witch of Fourth Street and Other Stories, illustrated by Gabriel Lisowski. New York, Harper, 1972.
Penny Tunes and Princesses, illustrated by Ezra Jack Keats. New York, Harper, 1972.
The Hanukkah of Great-Uncle Otto, illustrated by Donna Ruff. Philadelphia, Pennsylvania, Jewish Publication Society, 1984.
The Magic Hat of Mortimer Wintergreen. New York, Harper, 1988; London, Macmillan, 1989.

PUBLICATIONS FOR ADULTS

Novels

A Necktie on Greenwich Village. New York, Vanguard Press, 1968.

Plays

The Penthouse Perspective (produced Northport, New York, 1967).
Eli and Emily (produced New York, 1969).

The Sun Is a Red Dwarf (produced New York, 1969).
Sweet Tom (produced New York, 1969).
Footsteps (produced New York, 1970). New York, Breakthrough Press, 1971.
Smudge (produced New York, 1971).

*

Media Adaptations: *The Witch of Fourth Street and Other Stories* (recording), Listening Library; *Alan and Naomi* (film), Levcadia Film Corporation and the Maltese Companies, Inc., 1992.

Biography: Essay in *Speaking for Ourselves: Autobiographical Sketches by Notable Authors of Books for Young Adults,* Volume 1, compiled and edited by Donald R. Gallo, National Council of Teachers of English, 1990.

Myron Levoy comments:

In my novels for young adults, I have a special interest in exploring the loner and outsider. From the ghetto boy who writes his own brand of poetry yet yearns for the security and camaraderie of the gang *(A Shadow like a Leopard)* to the wealthy girl who rejects her family's elitist values for her own compassionate view of life *(Kelly 'n' Me),* my teenagers must face a central decision of their lives: to conform or to be truly their own selves. I should add that I call them *my* teenagers because they are, in a sense, my children, or, indeed, me. Their stories are open-ended; as in most lives, their struggles are never fully resolved. It's my hope that from this, my readers can gain new insight into their own struggles and the courage to be truer to their own inner selves.

*   *   *

The consistent question that Myron Levoy poses in his novels for adolescent readers is this: What is it like to be on the outside of things? Again and again he creates characters who find themselves separated from what they perceive to be the normal experience of a North American adolescent. This difference may be generated by events from the past, by ethnicity, by social status, or by sexuality, but for the character the reason makes little difference; the enormity of the separation is what is paramount. It is that sense of difference which causes many of the plot situations in Levoy's novels. And it is a coming to grips with that sense of difference which leads to the novels' moving resolutions.

It would not have been easy to guess this direction in Levoy's work from his first fiction for young readers, *The Witch of Fourth Street and Other Stories* (1972). This set of stories focuses on a group of children living on the Lower East side of New York City, all of them coming from recently immigrated families. There are Italians, Jews, Greeks, Russians, and Irish, all united by their bonds of family love, their desire to make a new and better life, and their memories of the old country. Here are stories of fathers scrimping to buy their son an electric Lionel train and the joy that that train brings to the neighborhood children, street vendors and their aging horses, young girls coming to accept their parents' roles, matchstick bridges, children who find evil reminiscent of that left behind in the old country. And there is a story of a gentle falling into death, a moving back into memory until one is again in one's mothers arms. There is nothing like this in any of Levoy's later work.

And yet perhaps there is. Here is a group of children who are themselves apart. Their parents yearn to bring them into the mainstream American experience as they perceive it, yet they also yearn to remember the old country, to remember the past which gives the family its history, its meaning, and even its story. The children are caught in the tension, partly in one world partly in another, but not fully in either.

In some ways these stories about young protagonists set apart are not dissimilar to the story of Ramon Santiago in *A Shadow like a Leopard* (1981). In this novel, Ramon is getting sucked into a vision of being "macho" as his father and peers define it, so that he seems to be on the verge of losing his own chance to forge an identity. The one thing which is distinctly his—his writing—is something he hides from his father and friends. He robs an old woman, wanders the streets of New York City, and abandons school—such as it is—in search of something. His father in Attica, his mother in a hospital, Ramon seems to need the gang which beckons to him as a way of finding a place.

But Ramon finds, reluctantly, that he is different, not only from the mainstream culture that inhabits Fifth Avenue, but also from those around him. His writing is important to him, and he finds it to be cathartic. He has a vision which seems to generate metaphor easily: "a shadow like a leopard." Even his daydreams suggest his difference: he dreams of a nice white house and a sister and parents who all sit down with him at an evening meal, far away from the streets of New York City. Not until he meets Arnold Glasser does he come to recognize his own artistic tendencies and to value them, not see them as impediments to being macho. By the end of the novel he is able to affirm that he is who he is; his situation has not changed, but his acceptance of his differences has strengthened him to go beyond his situation: "Ramon Santiago! That's me!".

It is this affirmation—"That's me!"—that rings through all of Levoy's work; characters must work through their differences, understand the causes of their differences, and come to accept them. Thus, in *Three Friends* (1984) Karen and Joshua are able to affirm Lori, an artistic and sensitive girl confused about her sexuality, not by changing themselves and their relationship but by accepting Lori for who she is. In *Kelly 'n' Me* (1992) Anthony helps Kelly to both understand and accept who she is, going beyond the surfaces generated by money, social status, and dark secrets held closely. And in *Pictures of Adam* (1986) Lisa can take Adam down to a lake, both of them naked, and declare that they are who they are and everything else is irrelevant. The statement may not be completely true, but it is an affirmation of what comes first when one considers one's identity.

Levoy does not resolve his endings with complete ease. In *A Shadow like a Leopard,* Ramon still must deal with his father who tries to define his macho nature, Adam still dreams of killing his abusive father each night, and Kelly leaves Port Authority on a bus, searching for an identity that she may or may not find. But in no novel is the conclusion left so poignantly unresolved as in *Alan and Naomi* (1977), Levoy's most acclaimed book. Here Alan is persuaded by his parents to befriend a young war refugee, Naomi, who has seen her father beaten to death by the Gestapo. The sight has left her withdrawn and uncommunicative; she spends her days shredding tiny pieces of paper—representing the memory of the papers she and her father were shredding before the Nazis found them.

At first resentful of this duty and embarrassed by it, Alan visits Naomi only grudgingly. But as they begin to communicate through the use of puppets, Alan comes to truly see her as a friend and perhaps even more than that. Eventually he is able to speak directly with her, rather than through puppets, and he takes her to visit an airfield where they fly his toy plane. She returns to school. But when Alan and Naomi are attacked by a bully and Alan's face is bloodied, Naomi runs back home and hides in the coal, murmuring that the dead should be buried. She is more withdrawn than ever before, and must eventually be hospitalized. Not even Alan can reach her, and though Alan's father expresses some hope for her recovery, the novel ends with Alan's conviction that she will not recover. Some events in the past, Levoy suggests, cannot be resolved.

If Levoy's novels celebrate any one thing, they celebrate friendship. It is friendship, an intimate closeness with another, that Levoy uses to bring his characters to their resolutions. When Ramon first encounters Glasser, whom he has come to rob, he finds a man more alone, more outside than he is, an artist who sees his entire career as a failure and who is ready to die not because he is brave, but because he is tired and worn out. It takes Ramon to affirm Glasser, as it takes Glasser to affirm Ramon; each finds the validity of his artistic expression through the other. In *Pictures of Adam,* Lisa is beset with a family that seems to be breaking apart and a mother who seems to be becoming an alcoholic; though ostensibly she sets out to help Adam overcome his own horrific background—a father who beat him with a chain—as well as the fantasies he uses to shield himself from that horror, she too is affirmed by Adam's innocent love; she too does not need to be what others define her to be. Joshua and Karen help Lori cope with her sense of being outside of normal experience, but they too help each other to accept who they are. Their willingness to see themselves as "weirdos" sets up their later willingness to help each one be what he or she wants to be. Kelly learns to accept her past and to search for herself because of the unquestioning love of Anthony, who is himself struggling with an alcoholic mother whom he must learn to love.

If the friendships in Levoy's novels do not always lead to successful resolutions, as in *Alan and Naomi,* they nevertheless do point towards healing and growth. Adam and Lori will grow with Lisa's and Joshua's help; Kelly will be able to depend upon and remember Anthony's love; and Ramon will find new possibilities that he had never imagined under the guidance of Glasser. If the novels of Myron Levoy are filled with pain—and they are—then it is the pain of healing, the stretching of wounds to allow for growth.

—Gary D. Schmidt

LEWIS, C(live) S(taples). Also wrote as Clive Hamilton; N.W. Clerk. British. Born in Belfast, Northern Ireland, 29 November 1898. Educated at Wynyard House, Watford, Hertfordshire, 1908-10; Campbell College, Belfast, 1910; Cherbourg School, Malvern, Worcestershire, 1911-13, and Malvern College, 1913-14; privately, in Great Bookham, Surrey, 1914-17; University College, Oxford (scholar; Chancellor's English Essay prize, 1921), 1917, 1919-23, B.A. (honours) 1922. Served in the Somerset Light Infantry, 1917-19: First Lieutenant. Married Joy Davidman Gresham in 1956 (died 1960); two stepsons. Philosophy tutor, 1924, and lecturer in English, 1924, University College, Oxford; fellow and tutor in English, Magdalen College, Oxford, 1925-54; professor of medieval and renaissance English, Cambridge University, 1954-63. Lecturer, University College of North Wales, Bangor, 1941; Riddell Lecturer, University of Durham, 1943; Clark lecturer, Cambridge University, 1944. Recipient: Gollancz prize, 1937; Library Association Carnegie

Medal, 1957. D.D.: University of St. Andrews, Fife, 1946; Docteur-es-Lettres, Laval University, Quebec, 1952; D. Litt.: University of Manchester, 1959; Hon. Dr.: University of Dijon, 1962; University of Lyon, 1963. Honorary Fellow, Magdalen College, Oxford, 1955; University College, Oxford, 1958; Magdalene College, Cambridge, 1963. Fellow, Royal Society of Literature, 1948; Fellow, British Academy, 1955. *Died 22 November 1963.*

PUBLICATIONS FOR YOUNG ADULTS

"Chronicles of Narnia" series (illustrated by Pauline Baynes):

The Lion, The Witch, and the Wardrobe. London, Bles, and New York, Macmillan, 1950.
Prince Caspian: The Return to Narnia. London, Bles, and New York, Macmillan, 1951.
The Voyage of the "Dawn Treader." London, Bles, and New York, Macmillan, 1952.
The Silver Chair. London, Bles, and New York, Macmillan, 1953.
The Horse and His Boy. London, Bles, and New York, Macmillan, 1954.
The Magician's Nephew. London, Lane, and New York, Macmillan, 1955.
The Last Battle. London, Lane, and New York, Macmillan, 1956.

Other

Letters to Children, edited by Lyle W. Dorsett and Marjorie Lamp Mead. New York, Macmillan, and London, Collins, 1985.

PUBLICATIONS FOR ADULTS

Novels

Out of the Silent Planet. London, Lane, 1938; New York, Macmillan, 1943.
Perelandra. London, Lane, 1943; New York, Macmillan, 1944; as *Voyage to Venus,* London, Pan, 1953.
That Hideous Strength: A Modern Fairy-Tale for Grown-Ups. London, Lane, 1945; New York, Macmillan, 1946; abridged edition, as *The Tortured Planet,* New York, Avon, 1958.
Till We Have Faces: A Myth Retold. London, Bles, 1956; New York, Harcourt Brace, 1957.

Short Stories

Of Other Worlds: Essays and Stories, edited by Walter Hooper. London, Bles, 1966; New York, Harcourt Brace, 1967.
The Dark Tower and Other Stories, edited by Walter Hooper. London, Collins, and New York, Harcourt Brace, 1977.

Poetry

Spirits in Bondage: A Cycle of Lyrics (as Clive Hamilton). London, Heinemann, 1919.

Dymer (as Clive Hamilton). London, Dent, and New York, Dutton, 1926.
Poems, edited by Walter Hooper. London, Bles, 1964; New York, Harcourt Brace, 1965.
Narrative Poems, edited by Walter Hooper. London, Bles, 1969; New York, Harcourt Brace, 1972.

Other

The Pilgrim's Regress: An Allegorical Apology for Christianity, Reason, and Romanticism. London, Dent, 1933; New York, Sheed and Ward, 1935; revised edition, London, Bles, 1943; Sheed and Ward, 1944.
The Allegory of Love: A Study in Medieval Tradition. Oxford, Clarendon Press, and New York, Oxford University Press, 1936.
Rehabilitations and Other Essays. London and New York, Oxford University Press, 1939.
The Personal Heresy: A Controversy, with E.M.W. Tillyard. London and New York, Oxford University Press, 1939.
The Problem of Pain. London, Bles, 1940; New York, Macmillan, 1944.
The Weight of Glory. London, S.P.C.K., 1942.
The Screwtape Letters. London, Bles, 1942; New York, Macmillan, 1943; revised edition, as *The Screwtape Letters and Screwtape Proposes a Toast,* London, Bles, 1961; New York, Macmillan, 1962.
Broadcast Talks: Right and Wrong: A Clue to the Meaning of the Universe, and What Christians Believe. London, Bles, 1942; as *The Case for Christianity,* New York, Macmillan, 1943.
A Preface to "Paradise Lost" (lectures). London and New York, Oxford University Press, 1942; revised edition, 1960.
Christian Behaviour: A Further Series of Broadcast Talks. London, Bles, and New York, Macmillan, 1943.
The Abolition of Man; or, Reflections on Education with Special Reference to the Teaching of English in the Upper Forms of Schools. London, Oxford University Press, 1943; New York, Macmillan, 1947.
Beyond Personality: The Christian Idea of God. London, Bles, 1944; New York, Macmillan, 1945.
The Great Divorce: A Dream. London, Bles, and New York, Macmillan, 1946.
Miracles: A Preliminary Study. London, Bles, and New York, Macmillan, 1947.
Vivisection. London, Anti-Vivisection Society, and Boston, New England Anti-Vivisection Society, 1947.
Transposition and Other Addresses. London, Bles, 1949; as *The Weight of Glory and Other Addresses,* New York, Macmillan, 1949.
The Literary Impact of the Authorized Version (lecture). London, Athlone Press, 1950; Philadelphia, Fortress Press, 1963.
Mere Christianity. London, Bles, and New York, Macmillan, 1952.
Hero and Leander (lecture). London, Oxford University Press, 1952.
English Literature in the Sixteenth Century, Excluding Drama. Oxford, Clarendon Press, 1954.
De Descriptione Temporum (lecture). London, Cambridge University Press, 1955.
Surprised by Joy: The Shape of My Early Life. London, Bles, 1955; New York, Harcourt Brace, 1956.

Reflections on the Psalms. London, Bles, and New York, Harcourt Brace, 1958.

Shall We Lose God in Outer Space? London, S.P.C.K., 1959.

The Four Loves. London, Bles, and New York, Harcourt Brace, 1960.

The World's Last Night and Other Essays. New York, Harcourt Brace, 1960.

Studies in Words. London, Cambridge University Press, 1960; revised edition, 1967.

An Experiment in Criticism. London, Cambridge University Press, 1961.

A Grief Observed (as N.W. Clerk; autobiography). London, Faber, 1961; Greenwich, Connecticut, Seabury Press, 1963.

They Asked for a Paper: Papers and Addresses. London, Bles, 1962.

Beyond the Bright Blur (letters). New York, Harcourt Brace, 1963.

Letters to Malcolm, Chiefly on Prayer. London, Bles, and New York, Harcourt Brace, 1964.

The Discarded Image: An Introduction to Medieval and Renaissance Literature. London, Cambridge University Press, 1964.

Screwtape Proposes a Toast and Other Pieces. London, Fontana, 1965.

Letters, edited by W.H. Lewis. London, Bles, and New York, Harcourt Brace, 1966.

Studies in Medieval and Renaissance Literature, edited by Walter Hooper. London, Cambridge University Press, 1966.

Spenser's Images of Life, edited by Alastair Fowler. London, Cambridge University Press, 1967.

Christian Reflections, edited by Walter Hooper. London, Bles, and Grand Rapids, Michigan, Eerdmans, 1967.

Letters to an American Lady, edited by Clyde S. Kilby. Grand Rapids, Michigan, Eerdmans, 1967; London, Hodder and Stoughton, 1969.

Mark vs. Tristram: Correspondence Between C.S. Lewis and Owen Barfield, edited by Walter Hooper. Cambridge, Massachusetts, Lowell House Printers, 1967.

A Mind Awake: An Anthology of C.S. Lewis, edited by Clyde S. Kilby. London, Bles, 1968; New York, Harcourt Brace, 1969.

Selected Literary Essays, edited by Walter Hooper. London, Cambridge University Press, 1969.

God in the Dock: Essays on Theology and Ethics, edited by Walter Hooper. Grand Rapids, Michigan, Eerdmans, 1970; as *Undeceptions: Essays on Theology and Ethics,* London, Bles, 1971.

The Humanitarian Theory of Punishment. Abingdon, Berkshire, Marcham Books Press, 1972.

Fern-Seed and Elephants and Other Essays on Christianity, edited by Walter Hooper. London, Fontana, 1975.

The Joyful Christian: 127 Readings, edited by William Griffin. New York, Macmillan, 1977.

They Stand Together: The Letters of C.S. Lewis to Arthur Greeves 1914-1963, edited by Walter Hooper. London, Collins, and New York, Macmillan, 1979.

C.S. Lewis at the Breakfast Table and Other Reminiscences, edited by James T. Como. New York, Macmillan, 1979; London, Collins, 1980.

The Visionary Christian: 131 Readings, edited by Chad Walsh. New York, Macmillan, 1981.

On Stories and Other Essays on Literature, edited by Walter Hooper. New York, Harcourt Brace, 1982.

Of This and Other Worlds, edited by Walter Hooper. London, Collins, 1982.

The Cretaceous Perambulator, with Owen Barfield, edited by Walter Hooper. Oxford, C.S. Lewis Society, 1983.

The Business of Heaven: Daily Readings from C.S. Lewis, edited by Walter Hooper. London, Fount, and New York, Harcourt Brace, 1984.

Boxen: The Imaginary World of the Young C.S. Lewis, edited by Walter Hooper. London, Collins, and San Diego, Harcourt Brace, 1985.

Present Concerns, edited by Walter Hooper. London, Fount, and San Diego, Harcourt Brace, 1986.

Timeless at Heart: Essays on Theology, edited by Walter Hooper. London, Fount, 1987.

The Essential C.S. Lewis, edited by Lyle W. Dorsett. New York, Macmillan, 1988.

Letters: C.S. Lewis and D.G. Calabria, edited and translated by Martin Moynihan. London, Collins, 1989.

Editor, *George MacDonald: An Anthology.* London, Bles, 1946; New York, Macmillan, 1947.

Editor, *Arthurian Torso, Containing the Posthumous Fragment of "The Figure of Arthur,"* by Charles Williams. London, and New York, Oxford University Press, 1948.

*

Bibliography: "A Bibliography of the Writings of C.S. Lewis" by Walter Hooper, in *Light on C.S. Lewis* edited by Jocelyn Gibb, London, Bles, 1965; *C.S. Lewis: An Annotated Checklist of Writings about Him and His Works* by Joe R. Christopher and Joan K. Ostling, Kent, Ohio, Kent State University Press, 1974.

Manuscript Collections: Bodleian Library, Oxford; Wheaton College, Illinois.

Critical Studies (selection): *C.S. Lewis* by Roger Lancelyn Green, London, Bodley Head, and New York, Walck, 1963, revised edition, in *Three Bodley Head Monographs,* Bodley Head, 1969, *C.S. Lewis: A Biography* by Green and Walter Hooper, London, Collins, and New York, Harcourt Brace, 1974, revised edition, 1988, and *Past Watchful Dragons: The Narnian Chronicles of C.S. Lewis,* New York, Macmillan, 1979, and *Through Joy and Beyond: A Pictorial Biography of C.S. Lewis,* New York, Macmillan, 1982, both by Hooper; *Light on C.S. Lewis* edited by Jocelyn Gibb, London, Bles, 1965; *The Lion of Judah in Never-Never Land: The Theology of C.S. Lewis Expressed in His Fantasies for Children,* Grand Rapids, Michigan, Eerdmans, 1973, and *The C.S. Lewis Hoax,* Portland, Oregon, Multinomah, both by Kathryn Ann Lindskoog; *The Secret Country of C.S. Lewis* by Anne Arnott, London, Hodder and Stoughton, 1974, Grand Rapids, Michigan, Eerdmans, 1975; *The Longing for Form: Essays on the Fiction of C.S. Lewis* edited by Peter J. Schakel, Kent, Ohio, Kent State University Press, 1977, and *Reading with the Heart: The Way into Narnia* by Schakel, Grand Rapids, Michigan, Eerdmans, 1979; *The Inklings: C.S. Lewis, J.R.R. Tolkien, Charles Williams and Their Friends* by Humphrey Carpenter, London, Allen and Unwin, 1978, Boston, Houghton Mifflin, 1979; *The Literary Legacy of C.S. Lewis* by Chad Walsh, New York, Harcourt Brace, and London, Sheldon Press, 1979; *A Guide Through Narnia* by Martha C. Sammons, Wheaton, Illinois, Shaw, and London, Hodder and Stoughton, 1979; *Narnia Explored* by Paul A. Karkainen, Old Tappan, New Jersey, Revell, 1979; *Com-*

panion to Narnia by Paul F. Ford, New York, Harper, 1980; C.S. Lewis, Spinner of Tales: A Guide to His Fiction by Evan K. Gibson, Grand Rapids, Michigan, Christian University Press, 1980; C.S. Lewis by Margaret Patterson Hannay, New York, Ungar, 1981; C.S. Lewis: The Art of Enchantment by Donald E. Glover, Athens, Ohio University Press, 1981; C.S. Lewis by Brian Murphy, Mercer Island, Washington, Starmont House, 1983; The Politics of Fantasy: C.S. Lewis and J.R.R. Tolkien by Lee D. Rossi, New York and Epping, Essex, Bowker, 1984; Clive Staples Lewis: The Drama of a Life by William Griffin, New York, Harper, 1986; C.S. Lewis: His Literary Achievement by C.N. Manlove, London, Macmillan, 1987; C.S. Lewis by Joe R. Christopher, Boston, Twayne, 1987; C.S. Lewis, Man of Letters: A Reading of His Fiction by Thomas Howard, Worthing, Sussex, Churchman, 1987; Jack: C.S. Lewis and His Times by George Sayer, London, Macmillan, 1988; C.S. Lewis and His World by David Barratt, Grand Rapids, Michigan, Eerdmans, 1988.

*   *   *

In 1950, twenty-five years after accepting a post as an Oxford don, C.S. Lewis embarked on a project that was unusual for a man of his position: he published the first in a series of novels for children. The first book in the "Chronicles of Narnia," The Lion, the Witch, and the Wardrobe, introduces the Pevencie children, four English youngsters who have been sent to the countryside to stay with a wise old professor during the World War II bombing of London. During a game of hide-and-seek one stormy day, the youngest child, Lucy, hides in a wardrobe only to discover that it is really a doorway into the land of Narnia.

Thus begin the adventures of Peter, Susan, Edmund, and Lucy in a world inhabited by talking animals, mythical creatures, and a few humanlike beings. The children soon discover that something sinister has taken place in this newfound world: the evil White Witch has cast a spell on Narnia, condemning it to eternal winter. The only one who can break the power of the spell is Aslan, the great lion-king; and, since signs of spring have just begun to appear, the inhabitants of the land are sure "Aslan is on the move." The four Pevencie children and later a younger cousin and his friend become intricately involved in the future of Narnia as Lewis masterfully weaves an entire world from its creation to its close throughout the rest of the series (Prince Caspian, The Voyage of the "Dawn Treader," The Silver Chair, The Horse and His Boy, The Magician's Nephew, and The Last Battle).

Lewis crafted the books specifically for children, including, as he later said, "no love interest and no close psychology." The books encourage a child's imagination by presenting ideas that appeal to young people. Children are the main characters with adults rarely appearing. Narnia is a completely separate world from our own—one that can only be entered by children (we find out in The Magician's Nephew that the professor himself entered Narnia as a boy). Time in Narnia is totally unrelated to time in our world. One year in Narnia, for example, may be only a few minutes in England and vice versa. Above all of the events of Narnia presides the great king Aslan, the creator, savior, protector, and eventual finisher of Narnia.

Through his writings, Lewis fixes himself in opposition to a point of view that he considered "modern" and distressing, and in doing so, he forces his reader to come to terms with his view of truth. In her The Lion of Judah in Never-Never Land: The Theology of C.S. Lewis Expressed in His Fantasies for Children, Kathryn

Ann Lindskoog states: "In Lewis's opinion, the modern conception of progress, as popularly imagined, is simply a delusion supported by no evidence.... He calls the idea of the world slowly ripening to perfection a myth not a generalization from experience. He feels this myth distracts from our real duties and our real interests. [This] attitude is illustrated by the depressing picture of [the dying world of Charn] given in The Magician's Nephew."

Harkening back to a premodern era, Lewis's works, particularly his fiction, address such themes as betrayal and forgiveness, good and evil, the nature of life and death, courage, loyalty, tradition, and the existence of absolute truth and a fixed moral order. He consciously rejects such contemporary themes as the endless quest for fulfillment, relative truth, innovation as a positive force, individuality, and self-actualization. Thomas Howard maintains in his C.S. Lewis: Man of Letters that Lewis "wanted to lead his readers to a window, looking out from the dark and stuffy room of modernity, and to burst open the shutters and point us all to an enormous vista stretching away from the room in which we are shut." To Lewis, the noble ideas he espoused represented freedom rather than the imprisonment suggested by some of his critics.

Those who read Lewis's writings—especially the "Chronicles of Narnia"—generally embrace his ideas or reject them outright. Helen Gardner summarized critical response to Lewis: "He aroused warm affection, loyalty, and devotion.... [but] he also aroused strong antipathy, disapproval, and distaste among his colleagues and pupils, and among some readers. It was impossible to be indifferent to him." Most of Lewis's detractors objected to his fantasy writings on ideological not literary grounds. Some took issue with Lewis's ideas on conventional virtues and his use of violence in the "Chronicles of Narnia," viewing them as detrimental to children. Among those was Peter Hollindale who wrote in Use of English, "The structure of power in Narnia, with Aslan as its head, is enforced by battle, violence, retributive justice, pain and death. Anything which challenges the power is either evil or stupid, and frequently both."

Others who took issue with Lewis's writings, such as his friend and fellow Inkling J.R.R. Tolkien, objected to what they interpreted as an overuse of allegory. In response to this, Lewis insisted that Narnia was not an allegory of human experience. It was, he maintained, a story of what might happen if there were a place like Narnia and God wanted to relate to that world. Lewis argued that by looking at Narnia's experience, we might be able to examine our own situation apart from religious trappings that Lewis felt often interfere with an honest human relationship with God.

His supporters have seen his work as brilliant in both its literary and theological aspects. Chad Walsh observed in his The Literary Legacy of C.S. Lewis that "Lewis brought to traditional mythology as much as he took from it.... This absolute clarity of visual imagination is one of the main appeals of his more fantastic books. Anyone reading, say, The Lion, the Witch, and the Wardrobe is given so distinct a picture of Aslan's death that he could reproduce the scene on canvas with photographic detail." Walsh continues "Lewis is not the first writer to attempt serious fantasy, but he is one of the most powerful, haunting and successful. He makes this genre a means of dramatizing the human condition and posing the everlasting questions. He converts fantasy into a presentation of philosophic and theological insights."

Lewis, however, did not look to critics for success, his concern was a larger audience. It was with this audience that Lewis achieved his greatest influence as witnessed by the Times Literary Supplement critic who said "[for] the past thirty years of his life, no other

Christian writer in [England] had such an influence on the general reading public.... Each new book from his pen was awaited with an eagerness which showed that thousands of intelligent men and women had acquired a taste for his distinctive idiom and had come to rely on him as a source of moral and intellectual insight."

—Linda Ross

———

LEWIS, Elizabeth Foreman. American. Born in Baltimore, Maryland, 24 May 1892. Educated at Tome School, 1906-09; Maryland Institute of Fine Arts, 1909-10; Bryant and Stratton Secretarial School, Baltimore, Maryland 1916-17; Bible Seminary of New York, 1917. Married John Abraham Lewis in 1921 (died 1934); one son. Author of books for children. Associate mission treasurer, Women's Foreign Missionary Society, Shanghai, China, 1917-18; district supervisor of schools, Chunking, China, and teacher for schools in Nanking, China, 1918-21. Recipient: American Library Association Newbery Medal, 1933, for *Young Fu of the Upper Yangtze. Died 7 August 1958.*

PUBLICATIONS FOR YOUNG ADULTS

Fiction

Young Fu of the Upper Yangtze, illustrated by Kurt Wiese. Philadelphia, Winston, 1932; London, Harrap, 1934.
Ho-Ming, Girl of New China, illustrated by Kurt Wiese. Philadelphia, Winston, 1934; London, Harrap, 1935.
China Quest, illustrated by Kurt Wiese. Philadelphia, Winston, 1937; London, Harrap, 1938.
When the Typhoon Blows, illustrated by Kurt Wiese. Philadelphia, Winston, 1942; London, Harrap, 1944.
To Beat a Tiger, One Needs a Brother's Help, illustrated by John Huehnergarth. Philadelphia, Winston, 1956; London, Harrap, 1957.

PUBLICATIONS FOR ADULTS

Other

Portraits from a Chinese Scroll, illustrated by Virginia Hollinger Stout. Philadelphia, Winston, 1938; London, Harrap, 1939.
Test Tubes and Dragon Scales, with George C. Basil. Philadelphia, Winston, 1940.

*

Media Adaptations: *Young Fu of the Upper Yangtze* (recording and filmstrip).

Biography: Entry in *Junior Book of Authors,* second edition, Stanley J. Kunitz and Howard Haycraft, editors, New York, H.W. Wilson, 1951.

*   *   *

Elizabeth Foreman Lewis grew up amid a closely knit family whose love of church and of books influenced her choice of careers. As a young woman she studied religious education and literature and was active in church and settlement activities. In 1917 she was sent to China by the Methodist Women's Board. After her return to the United States, Lewis used her experiences in China as a background for her writings, both juvenile and adult. She saw opportunities in the first cultural revolution while portraying problems people have at times of social change. Her heroes and heroines have hope and determination; they make good use of opportunities for social and geographic mobility.

Lewis's most important novel for children is *Young Fu of the Upper Yangtze,* which won the Newbery Medal for 1933. This is the story of a thirteen-year-old Chinese country boy who is brought by his widowed mother to the bustling city of Chungking and apprenticed to a skilled coppersmith. As he delivers his master's wares Fu explores the large metropolis and finds everywhere the conflicts born of superstition and prejudice, of Civil War, of old and new ideas. Fu is not an idealized hero: he is brave and honest, but he also wastes his master's time and his own. The book contains many Confucian proverbs which are employed by adult characters to point out to Fu the folly of his ways: "Laziness never filled a rice bowl." "There is no merit worthy of boasting."

Others of Lewis's children's books are for older children. They too focus on individual response to social change. *Ho-Ming, Girl of New China* is the story of a young girl who must free herself from primitive beliefs before she can begin a new education in public-health nursing. As a girl not encouraged to think for herself, she must meet family resistance while retaining family loyalties. *To Beat a Tiger, One Needs a Brother's Help* is about young boys from different social backgrounds living in Shanghai. They witness disease, starvation, and violent death and become close friends as they pull together for survival during the Japanese invasion of China.

Lewis stated that by the time illness forced her to return to America, China and her people had become a major concern in her life. In time she had to write about them, she had to convince a few readers of the inherent greatness of the Chinese, who overcame mass torture and killing, poverty and disease, determined to structure a better world. Lewis's books were well received in America and in Europe. Indeed, through her sympathetic character portrayal, her swift plots, and her compelling prose, she has affected many young readers for several decades.

—Mary Lystad

———

LILLINGTON, Kenneth (James). British. Born in Catford, London, 7 September 1916. Educated at St. Dunstan's College, London, 1927-35; Wandsworth Training College, London, 1948-49. Served in the Royal Army Pay Corps, 1941-43; Royal Corps of Signals, 1943-46; became sergeant. Married Dulcie E. Lock in 1942; two daughters and two sons. Advertising copywriter, Temple Press, London, 1938-39; teacher, Walton-on-Thames School for Boys, Surrey, 1949-56; lecturer in French and English, Brooklands Technical College, Weybridge, Surrey, 1956-81; lecturer on modern literature, Workers' Educational Association, since 1950, on poetry for Poetry Society of London, 1950-57. Agent: c/o Faber and Faber, 3 Queen Square, London WC1N 3AU, England.

PUBLICATIONS FOR YOUNG ADULTS

Fiction

Soapy and the Pharoah's Curse, illustrated by Julia Faithful. London, Heinemann, 1957.
Conjurer's Alibi. London, Nelson, 1960.
The Secret Arrow, illustrated by Robert Hodgson. London, Nelson, 1960.
A Man Called Hughes, illustrated by D.L. Mays. London, Nelson, 1962.
Young Man of Morning. London, Faber, 1979.
What Beckoning Ghost? London, Faber, 1983.
Isabel's Double. London, Faber, 1984.
Selkie. London, Faber, 1985.
Full Moon. London, Faber, 1986.
An Ash-Blonde Witch. London, Faber, 1987.
Jonah's Mirror. London, Faber, 1988.
Josephine. London, Faber, 1989.
The Real Live Dinosaur and other Stories, illustrated by Gareth Floyd. London, Faber, 1990.
Give up the Ghost. London, Faber, 1991.
The Mad Detective. London, Faber, 1992.

Plays

Blue Murder, in *The Windmill Book of One-Act Plays,* edited by E.R. Wood. London, Heinemann, 1960.
My Proud Beauty, in *The Second Windmill Book of One-Act Plays,* edited by E.R. Wood. London, Heinemann, 1963.
The First Book of Classroom Plays (includes *The Case of the Golden Cockerel, Words Fail Me, The Cat Princess, Professor Tugnutt's Time Machine, The Perfect Customer, In Darkest Britain, The Christmas Spirit, The Stove, Skeleton Plays*). London, Hale, 1967.
The Fourth Windmill Book of One-Act Plays (includes *Make Your Play, Bring Out Your Dead, I'll Ring for More Toast, Is Horror Your Neighbour?, A Villa on Venus, You Never Heard Such Unearthly Laughter, The Cinderella Story*). London, Heinemann, 1967.
The Second Book of Classroom Plays (includes *The Blackfeet and the Cree, The Knocking on the Wall, The Picts Drop In, Professor Tugnutt's Truth Gas, For Crying Out Loud, The Boy Next Door, Robin Hood and the Jester, End of Part One*). London, Hale, 1968.
Cantaloup Crescent, in *The Fifth Windmill book of One-Act Plays,* edited by E.R. Wood. London, Heinemann, 1970.
Olaf and the Ogre, in *The Sixth Windmill Book of One-Act Plays,* edited by E.R. Wood. London, Heinemann, 1972.
The Seventh Windmill Book of One-Act Plays (includes *Mockery Hollow, The Avenging Phoenix, I Am a Dustbin, Postman's Knock, A Latin Lesson, The Devil's Grandson, The Adventures of Chastity Pewke, Come What May*). London, Heinemann, 1972.
There's an End of May, in *The Eighth Windmill Book of One-Act Plays,* edited by E.R. Wood. London, Heinemann, 1975.

Other (retellings)

A Christmas Carol. London, Faber Music, 1988.
The Mikado, music by Arthur Sullivan. London, Faber Music, 1988.

PUBLICATIONS FOR CHILDREN

Fiction

The Hallowe'en Cat, illustrated by Gareth Floyd. London, Faber, 1987.
Gabrielle, illustrated by Gareth Floyd. London, Faber, 1988.

PUBLICATIONS FOR ADULTS

Other

Editor, *Nine Lives: An Anthology of Poetry and Prose Concerning Cats.* London, Deutsch, 1977.
Editor, *For Better for Worse.* London, Angus & Robertson, 1979.
Read and Understand: Famous Stories, with Paul Snowden and Hiroshi Tsuchiya. Tokyo, Kirihara Shoten, 1988.

*   *   *

Kenneth Lillington's teenage novels contain a good helping of the supernatural and usually have a strong romantic element. Lillington's female characters are always intelligent and resourceful, not to mention forceful; his male characters are weaker, less decisive, and require support and leadership from the women they meet. Whether or not these are created with tongue-in-cheek humour, they make his books immensely attractive to teenage girls, who will find these inspiring role models. His books are always refreshing, bubbly, and intellectually quite demanding, but appeal to those who enjoy the lively exploration of ideas as much as the development of character and plot.

Whether the supernatural element is in the form of magic, ghosts, science fiction, or simply legend, the books are firmly rooted in reality. In *Selkie,* this encompasses the problems related to unemployment, growing up, changing relationships, class consciousness, and superstition. Catherine, the heroine, resents having to leave her boyfriend and move to Cornwall. She gets involved with Joe, a young labourer, and together they try to solve the mystery of the legend of the Selkie, or seal girl, that is at the centre of the book. Lillington captures the strong emotions of an adolescent girl trying to deal with her feelings about two boys from very different backgrounds. The book also presents a realistic portrait of the effects of unemployment on families that is relevant today as it was in 1935 when the book is set.

An Ash-Blonde Witch and *Jonah's Mirror* contain rather more of the supernatural than the natural. *An Ash-Blonde Witch* is set in the twenty-second century, when there are pockets of the world that have not changed, called Conservation Areas. When Sophie and her father are sent to study one of these areas—Urstwhile—the effect is like stepping back in time. The scientific skills of psychological healing and levitation that are commonplace in Sophie's world are taken to be magic by the people of Urstwhile and she is deemed a witch. On the other hand, emotions like love and jealousy are no longer felt outside of Urstwhile and Sophie's punishment for interfering in a Conservation Area is to suffer these emotions. The balance between science fiction and fairy-tale is nicely held and the ending, in which the witch Dorcas is transported out of the old-fashioned Urstwhile because her skills are thought to be valuable to the more advance society provides a humorous twist.

In *Jonah's Mirror* the two main characters, Jonah Sprockett, a millionaire and chairman of Sprockett Electricals, and his partner and fiancée Miss Wingbone, "arguably the cleverest woman in the world," are caught up in an elaborate fantasy. As a result of an experiment with a magic mirror, Jonah finds himself locked in the strange world of Sudonia which is inhabited by fairy-tale princesses, mythical beasts, and strange marauding knights, where he falls in love with the beautiful Princess Miranda. Jonah thinks he has spirited himself into a parallel universe, but Miss Wingbone's theory is that it is all a dream and therefore a figment of his imagination. This ingenious explanation is rather complex to follow at times, particularly when Miss Wingbone herself enters Sudonia, but it provides endless opportunities for some wonderful tongue-in-cheek humour.

What Beckoning Ghost?, *Full Moon*, *Isabel's Double* and *Give up the Ghost* all deal with ghosts or apparitions. *What Beckoning Ghost?* is a romance with a touch of the supernatural in which Emma finishes her O-levels and breaks up with her boyfriend. She is sent to stay with her godmother, where she meets a ghost and finds another boyfriend. In *Full Moon* Lillington creates an intricate web of relationships between twins, sisters, parent and child, boyfriend and girlfriend, old and young, living and dead, through which she explores the kind of tensions that exist in such very close relationships.

Isabel's Double is about the apparition of Isabel that has haunted her since childhood, which starts to haunt Mike who becomes her boyfriend. After some help from a psychiatrist, the "doppelganger" is finally conquered in a chilling climax involving psychic powers, spirits, and a painting of Isabel. *Give up the Ghost* begins, "Every night before going to bed, Mrs. Mason would drink a cup of Instant Postum and play a game of Scrabble with her husband, who had been dead for five years." Through her paranormal powers Mrs. Mason is introduced to the ghost of Fred Hopper and drawn into a wrangle with his sisters about his will, when he leaves all his money to a fellow gardener, Miss Grayling. The books dealing with ghosts and apparitions are perhaps more disturbing than Lillington's others, because it is not as easy to dismiss such psychic phenomena as pure fantasy.

The prevalence of romantic themes and strong female characters in Lillington's books makes them generally more appealing to teenage girls than to boys, but *Josephine* appeals to both groups. Set in the 1930s, it is the story of a young girl who is sent to a boys' boarding school where her uncle is the headmaster, when her own school is closed, where she affects the lives of all the boys she comes into contact with. The various under-plots—for example, the legend of the wolf-boy who has been seen around the school—fill the book with mystery and make this an immensely enjoyable read.

The Mad Detective is an engaging mixture of the Agatha Christie thriller and a comical farce. When two couples turn up in a hotel a murder is about to occur, according to clairvoyant Norman Norval. But what he can't determine is the victim. The intricate plot is peppered with highly original and amusing characters, and Lillington's dry wit and love of wordplay are given full rein here.

His characters are often working out their feelings for a boyfriend or girlfriend, which makes them particularly appealing to young adults at a time in their lives when they too may be experiencing similar anxieties.

—Fiona Lafferty

LINGARD, Joan (Amelia). British. Born in Edinburgh, Scotland, 1932. Educated at Bloomfield Collegiate School, Belfast; Moray House Training College, General Certificate of Education. Has three children. Schoolteacher, Midlothian, 1953-61. Full-time novelist and television scriptwriter. Since 1979 member of the Council, Scottish Arts Council. Recipient: Scottish Arts Council bursary, 1969; Buxtehude Bulle prize (West Germany), 1987. Agent: David Higham Associates, 5-8 Lower John Street, London W1R 4HA, England. Address: 72 Great King Street, Edinburgh EH3 6QU, Scotland.

PUBLICATIONS FOR YOUNG ADULTS

Fiction

The Twelfth Day of July. London, Hamish Hamilton, 1970; Nashville, Nelson, 1972.

Across the Barricades. London, Hamish Hamilton, 1972; Nashville, Nelson, 1973.

Into Exile. London, Hamish Hamilton, and Nashville, Nelson, 1973.

Frying as Usual, illustrated by Priscilla Clive. London, Hamish Hamilton, 1973.

The Clearance. London, Hamish Hamilton, and Nashville, Nelson, 1974.

A Proper Place. London, Hamish Hamilton, and Nashville, Nelson, 1975.

The Resettling. London, Hamish Hamilton, and Nashville, Nelson, 1975.

Hostages to Fortune. London, Hamish Hamilton, 1976; Nashville, Nelson, 1977.

The Pilgrimage. London, Hamish Hamilton, 1976; Nashville, Nelson, 1977.

The Reunion. London, Hamish Hamilton, 1977; Nashville, Nelson, 1978.

Snake among the Sunflowers. London, Hamish Hamilton, and Nashville, Nelson, 1977.

The Gooseberry. London, Hamish Hamilton, 1978; as *Odd Girl Out,* New York, Elsevier Nelson, 1979.

The File on Fraulein Berg. London, MacRae, and New York, Elsevier Nelson, 1980.

Strangers in the House. London, Hamish Hamilton, 1981; New York, Dutton, 1983.

The Winter Visitor. London, Hamish Hamilton, 1983.

The Freedom Machine. London, Hamish Hamilton, 1986.

The Guilty Party. London, Hamish Hamilton, 1987.

Rags and Riches. London, Hamish Hamilton, 1988.

Tug of War. New York, Dutton, 1990.

Between Two Worlds. New York, Dutton, 1991.

Hands Off Our School! London, Hamish Hamilton, 1992.

Night Fires. London, Hamish Hamilton, 1993.

Television Series: *Maggie,* 1981, 1982.

PUBLICATIONS FOR ADULTS

Novels

Liam's Daughter. London, Hodder and Stoughton, 1963.
The Prevailing Wind. London, Hodder and Stoughton, 1964.
The Tide Comes In. London, Hodder and Stoughton, 1966.

The Headmaster. London, Hodder and Stoughton, 1967.
A Sort of Freedom. London, Hodder and Stoughton, 1969.
The Lord on Our Side. London, Hodder and Stoughton, 1970.
The Second Flowering of Emily Mountjoy. Edinburgh, Harris, 1979;
   New York, St. Martin's Press, 1980.
Greenyards. London, Hamish Hamilton, and New York, Putnam,
   1981.
Sisters by Rite. London, Hamish Hamilton, and New York, St.
   Martin's Press, 1984.
Reasonable Doubts. London, Hamish Hamilton, 1986.
The Women's House. London, Hamish Hamilton, 1989.
After Colette. London, Sinclair, Stevenson, 1993.

Television Plays: *The Sandyford Place Mystery* and *A Kiss, A Fond
Embrace,* from the novel *Square Mile of Murder* by Jack House,
1980; *Her Mother's House,* 1982.

*

Media Adaptations: The "Maggie" books were adapted as a serial
for BBC television.

Biography: Essay in *Something about the Author Autobiography
Series* by Joan Lingard, Volume 5, Detroit, Gale, 1988.

*   *   *

Joan Lingard wrote six adult novels before she, on the suggestion
of a friend, embarked upon *The Twelfth Day of July.* Although its
main characters are still children, this famous book with the then
incipient Catholic-Protestant "Troubles" of Ulster as its background,
was the beginning of a distinguished career as a writer for young
adults. Since its publication in 1972, Joan Lingard has published
continuously for this age group, some "one-off" titles, others in
series—notably the "Kevin and Sadie" novels spearheaded by *The
Twelfth Day of July,* the "Maggie" books with their sprightly Glasgow
heroine and, most recently, books about the Latvian Petersons who
settle in Canada after World War II. Although she has continued to
write for adults, it is as a writer for teenagers that Joan Lingard has
established a well-deserved reputation, the reason for which is not
difficult to identify. She has a natural empathy with this reader-
group, understanding the hopes, aspirations, and emotional uncertainties of adolescents, yet paying her readers the compliment of
engaging them as adults on an intellectual level. There is not a scrap
of condescension in her uncompromising, humorous, and dramatic
narratives; she creates a world which young readers instantly
recognise as their own, and they pay her a compliment in return.
She is one of the few quality writers whose books teenagers, noto-
riously unbookish, eagerly buy for themselves.
   Joan Lingard's themes relate directly to the experience of her
readers. They are working-class life, the tensions of family living,
the destructive effect of social prejudice on family and community
relations, and the necessity, as young people approach adulthood,
to make decisions and take control of their own lives. These were
themes which Josephine Kamm pioneered in Britain in the 1960s;
Joan Lingard, a very different kind of writer, has carried them on
and developed them for a more disturbed and complex age.
   All of these themes make their first outing in the series of novels
featuring Kevin and Sadie, the young couple from opposite factions
in Ulster, a province torn apart by religious bigotry with its roots in

the distant past. Joan Lingard's objectivity, remarkable in a writer
who spent her formative years in Belfast, is explained in her 1986
essay published in *A Portrait of the Artist as a Young Girl.* There
she attributes her lack of sectarian prejudice to her upbringing by a
mother who was a Christian Scientist, adding that since she left
Belfast at the age of eighteen, she was not drawn emotionally into
the turmoil which has darkened Ulster life for more than twenty
years. Thus she has been able, uniquely, to combine the knowledge
of an insider with the observation of an outsider; one feels that this
informed detachment, allied to a warm concern for human beings,
has stood her in good stead when transferring her attention to other
conflicts and moral dilemmas. The extended story of Kevin and
Sadie, from their childhood in the now universally familiar back
streets of Belfast, through their struggle to find fulfillment in a
Belfast riven by virtual civil war to their flight to London, is told
with an appealing mixture of toughness, nonjudgemental realism
and tender understanding. Probably the best and most powerful of
these novels is *Across the Barricades* (awarded the German
Buxtehuder Bulle Prize for Children's Literature in 1987); the development of Kevin and Sadie's love against a bitter background of
family disapproval and civil disintegration is a moving variation on
a classic theme of young love under a comfortless star.
   Joan Lingard has stated that she began to write her "Maggie"
quartet as a respite from thinking about Ulster and its problems.
Certainly this series, which has been televised, is much lighter in
tone, although its concerns are perhaps closer to the experience of
most young readers. Told with humour and panache in the first
person, the series follows the doings of Maggie, a working-class girl
who wants to go to university and fulfil her potential in a way
closed to Sadie, fettered by the time of her birth and uncontrollable
circumstances. The career of Maggie, whose vigour and enterprise
enable her to establish her father in a plumbing business and re-
house her grandmother after a fire, is contrasted with the life of her
middle-class boyfriend, James. Glaswegian social divisions and,
paradoxically, cohesion are personified by James's mother and
Maggie's granny, two archetypal, vastly entertaining specimens of
Glasgow womanhood. Nowhere does Joan Lingard display her talent for seeing the world through young eyes more amusingly than in
these books.
   Joan Lingard's passionate belief in tolerance and social justice
runs through all her writing, and strikes a chord in the hearts and
minds of young people. In *The Guilty Party,* which recalls a famous
protest of women against nuclear missiles at Greenham Common in
the 1980s, Jodie, a teenage Belfast girl now living in an English
village, campaigns against the siting there of a nuclear power plant.
The story of a girl drawn from peaceful protest into a situation
calling for mature moral judgement is powerfully told. This gripping story, like the "Kevin and Sadie" and "Maggie" books, is
vividly contemporary, but Joan Lingard is also adept at making the
recent past—particularly the period around World War II—relevant to modern young people. This matters, as an understanding
of moral issues which seemed clear-cut in the earlier part of the
century becomes confused with the passage of time. In *The File on
Fraulein Berg,* set in wartime Belfast, three schoolgirls take their
teacher's name at face value and behave badly, failing to consider
that Fraulein Berg, a Jewish refugee, might herself be a victim of
Nazi persecution. The distinction between "Nazi" and "German,"
still often blurred after fifty years, is at the heart of this thought-
provoking and ultimately sombre book.
   More recently Joan Lingard, who is married to a Latvian-Cana-
dian, has embarked on a sequence of novels set in Europe and

Canada during and after World War II. *Tug of War* begins the story of the Petersons family, who have to flee their home in Latvia as the Russians advance, suffering the horrors of separation and being "displaced persons" in Europe after 1944. The disintegrating continent is poignantly evoked through images of rural life and family love, contrasted with the mechanised, destructive forces of bombers and submarines. In 1948, at the opening of *Between Two Worlds,* the reunited family arrives in Toronto where their struggle to survive continues in a scarcely less hostile environment. The tables are turned as the children have to support their parents, and the story tells of hardships surmounted and family affection firmly sealed. The dignified battle of the Petersons to preserve their identity as Latvians while achieving their aspiration to be good Canadians is unforgettable and very relevant to other, more recent attempts of minority groups to assimilate with larger societies. No novels could convey more truthfully to modern young people the trials and triumphs of the human spirit half a century ago.

—Eileen Dunlop

———

LIPSYTE, Robert (Michael). American. Born in New York City, 16 January 1938. Educated at Columbia University, New York, 1953-59, B.A. in English 1957, M.S. in journalism 1959. Served in the United States Army, 1961. Married Katherine L. Sulkes; one son and one daughter by a previous marriage. *New York Times,* copyboy, 1957-59, sports reporter, 1959-67, sports columnist, 1967-71 and 1991—; *New York Post,* columnist, 1977; Columbia Broadcasting Service, Inc. (CBS-TV), New York City, sports essayist for program *Sunday Morning,* 1982-86; National Broadcasting Company, Inc. (NBC-TV), New York City, correspondent, 1986-88; Public Broadcasting Service (PBS-TV), New York City, host of program *The Eleventh Hour,* 1989-90; writer. Has also worked as a journalism teacher and radio commentator. Recipient: Dutton Best Sports Stories award, E.P. Dutton, 1964, for "The Long Road to Broken Dreams," 1965, for "The Incredible Cassius," 1967, for "Where the Stars of Tomorrow Shine Tonight," 1971, for "Dempsey in the Window," and 1976, for "Pride of the Tiger"; Mike Berger award, Columbia University Graduate School of Journalism, 1966; Wel-Met Children's Book award, Child Study Children's Book Committee at Bank Street College of Education, 1967, for *The Contender; One Fat Summer* was named an outstanding children's book of the year by the *New York Times* and was selected as one of the American Library Association's best young adult books, both 1977; New Jersey Author citation, New Jersey Institute of Technology, 1978; Emmy award for on-camera achievement, Academy of Television Arts and Sciences, 1990, as host of the television program *The Eleventh Hour.* Agent: Theron Raines, Raines and Raines, 71 Park Avenue, Suite 4A, New York, NY 10016. Address: 126 E. 1657, New York, NY 10003, U.S.A.

PUBLICATIONS FOR YOUNG ADULTS

Fiction

The Contender. New York, Harper, 1967; London, Pan, 1969.
One Fat Summer. New York, Harper, 1977.

Summer Rules. New York, Harper, 1981.
Jock and Jill. New York, Harper, 1982.
The Summerboy. New York, Harper, 1982.
The Brave. New York, Harper, 1991.
The Chemo Kid. New York Harper, 1992.
The Chief. New York, Harper, 1993.

Other

Assignment: Sports. New York, Harper, 1970; revised edition, 1984.
Free to Be Muhammad Ali. New York, Harper, 1978.
Arnold Schwarzenegger: American Hercules. New York, Harper, 1993.
Jim Thorpe: 20th Century Jock. New York, Harper, 1993.

PUBLICATIONS FOR ADULTS

Novels

Something Going, with Steve Cady. New York, Dutton, 1973.
Liberty Two. New York, Simon and Schuster, 1974.

Other

Nigger, with Dick Gregory. New York, Dutton, 1964; London, Allen and Unwin, 1965.
The Masculine Mystique, illustrated by Tim Lewis. New York, New American Library, 1966.
Sportsworld: An American Dreamland. Chicago, Quadrangle, 1975.
Advisory editor, *Sports and Society,* edited by Gene Brown. New York, Arno Press, 1980.

Screenplays: *That's the Way of the World (Shining Star),* 1975; *The Act,* 1982.

Scriptwriter for *Saturday Night with Howard Cosell;* contributor to periodicals, including *TV Guide, Harper's Magazine, Nation, New York Times, New York Times Book Review,* and *Esquire.*

*

Biography: Essay in *Speaking for Ourselves: Autobiographical Sketches by Notable Authors of Books for Young Adults,* Volume 1, compiled and edited by Donald R. Gallo, National Council of Teachers of English, 1990; essay in *Authors and Artists for Young Adults,* Volume 7, Detroit, Gale, 1991.

Manuscript Collection: De Grummond Collection, University of Southern Mississippi; Kerlan Collection, University of Minnesota.

Critical Study: Entry in *Contemporary Literary Criticism,* Volume 21, Detroit, Gale, 1982; entry in *Children's Literature Review,* Volume 23, Detroit, Gale, 1991.

Robert Lipsyte comments:
    Boys don't read as much as we'd like them to, because (1) current books tend not to deal with the real problems and fears of boys, and (2) there is a tendency to treat boys as a group—which is

where males are at their absolute worst—instead of as individuals who have to be led into reading secretly and one at a time.

Boys need reassurance that their fears of violence and humiliation and competition are shared fears. Books can reassure them, but to be able to read a book—properly—you have to be able to sink into a scene, to absorb characters, to care, to empathize. You have to be willing to make yourself vulnerable to a book as surely as you need to make yourself vulnerable to a person. This is not easy for a male in this society to do, particularly an adolescent male who is unsure of his own identity, his sexuality, his future.

*   *   *

Robert Lipsyte, a widely read sports journalist, has made his mark on young adult literature with three breezily funny novels (One Fat Summer, Summer Rules, and The Summerboy) about teenager Bobby Marks, whose summers spent getting in and out of trouble while growing up in the fifties reflect some of the author's own experiences. Through the course of these first-person narratives, Bobby changes and grows—from a spoiled, 200-pound fourteen-year-old whom kids call The Crisco Kid "because he's fat in the can," through a summer as a sixteen-year-old camp counselor and would-be lover. Finally, in The Summerboy, Bobby shows his true character when he sacrifices his cherished summer job folding laundry to help his fellow employees get even with an unscrupulous and womanizing boss.

One of the ways that Lipsyte overcame his own early teen fat summers of overeating and over-reading was to dive into sports; his high school years were saturated with swimming, softball, track, and judo. When he graduated from college, he welded his compulsive interest in sports with his love for writing. He has utilized his journalistic skills to write two very successful nonfiction sports books for young adults—Free to Be Muhammad Ali, a biography of the famous boxer and Assignment: Sports, a collection of colorfully written articles on athletes and sports.

Even Lipsyte's romantic fantasy novel for younger readers, Jock and Jill, deals with sports. The story contains unlikely plot twists and turns, but Lipsyte's heroes—a suburban high school pitching star named Jack Ryder and Jillian, the unpredictably likeable and stubborn girl whose camera he smashes into while chasing a foul pop-up—are so believably portrayed that they convince even the more skeptical readers to accept the story's plot implausibities. Jillian involves Jack the Jock in a scheme to help poor and hungry New York City kids, and soon the Mayor and a Puerto Rican street gang get pulled into the story. Jack's reputation is threatened, and his baseball career is put in jeopardy. Although Jack falls down, he doesn't break his crown.

The Chemo Kid combines some of the romantic elements of Jock and Jill with a Bobby Marks-type teenager—a self-described "wimp" named Fred Bauer—who manages to acquire superhero powers. Bobby gains these powers of character through sheer will, while Fred acquires momentary physical super-strength as the unintended result of an experimental chemotherapy he has been taking to fight a virulent cancer. With the support of his environmental-activist girlfriend Mara (who resembles Jill in some respects), his two selfishly scheming buddies, and his newly made bizarre friends from the "cancer ward" of the hospital where Fred is being treated, Fred's wimpy life is transformed by his medically induced superpowers and he enters a sort of "twilight zone." He takes on his two classmate nemeses (a drug dealer and a brain-dead, bully football captain), a multitude of foolish adult authority figures (the mayor,

Fred's doctor, the football coach, the police, etc.), and a corporation that is polluting the city's water supply. The story's end parallels that of Jock and Jill: the hero again emerges a victor.

Lipsyte's best and most-read novel is probably his first published story, The Contender. It is about a young Harlem high school dropout named Alfred Brooks who fights against the pull of drugs and gangs, the guilt of abandoning his best friend caught by police in a robbery of a store where Alfred works, and against the pervasive despair he feels as a prisoner in a place with no future. One day, he wanders into Donatelli's gym and accepts the challenge that Donatelli throws at him: "Everyone wants to be a champion. That's not enough. You have to start by wanting to be a contender...It's the climbing that makes the man. Getting to the top is an extra reward." These words guide and strengthen Alfred in his darkest moments. He stands his ground not only against seasoned boxers but also against heavy peer pressure to rob the grocery store where he works. When Alfred faces the truth about himself—he's a good boxer but not a champion—he displays the grit of a contender: he stays three rounds in the ring with a champion fighter and win's Donatelli's respect and a new-found self-respect.

Lipsyte wrote The Contender in 1967, the same year that saw the publication of S.E. Hinton's groundbreaking realistic young adult novel The Outsiders and a year before the publication of The Pigman, Paul Zindel's trendsetting novel for teenagers. The Contender is also a trailblazer because it transformed the junior sports novel from an action-packed, predictable story of sports heroics into a realistic, coming-of-age story with sports serving as a metaphor for the real action in the novel: coping with life. Although today Lipsyte's first novel seems too dependent on plot coincidences and too filled with stereotyped secondary characters, The Contender set the stage for more sophisticated sports metaphor novels for teen readers, such as Bruce Brooks' The Moves Make the Man and Robert Lehrman's Juggling.

In the last three years, Lipsyte has written two sequels to The Contender. In The Brave, Alfred Brooks—now a police officer—interrogates Sonny Bear, a rebellious and confused runaway Moscondaga Nation Native American who has been arrested on a drug charge. Like Brooks twenty years before, Sonny is a promising young boxer who is faced with the conflict that Brooks also faced: the immediate but risky rewards of street life versus the discipline and training required to be a champion boxer. Brooks becomes Sonny's manager and helps guide him through this conflict. The Chief, published in 1993, continues Sonny's story. Brooks has become a paraplegic via a police shooting incident, although he is still Sonny's manager. The story is narrated by Marty Witherspoon, a young black college student and aspiring writer who is Sonny's close friend and publicist. Marty is responsible for getting Sonny back on track after the boxer loses his focus when he is cheated of a boxing victory. But when Sonny becomes involved in a plan to help heal deep wounds within the Moscondaga Nation as a result of their flirtation with gambling, Marty's counseling powers are sorely tested. As The Chief ends, there is no resolution to Sonny's boxing ambitions and his new interest in Moscondaga politics; readers also don't know what will become of Marty's writing ambitions and his romantic interest in Robin Bell, a gutsy young film producer.

"It's the climbing that makes the man...." Lipsyte is clearly not finished with Sonny and Marty because they still have more climbing to do.

—Jack Forman

LITTLE, (Flora) Jean. Canadian. Born in T'ai-nan, Formosa, now Taiwan, 2 January 1932. Educated at University of Toronto, B.A. 1955; attended Institute of Special Education, Salt Lake City; received teaching certificate from University of Utah. Teacher of children with motor handicaps, Canada; specialist teacher at Beechwood School for Crippled Children, Guelph, Ontario; children's writer. Visiting instructor at Institute of Special Education and Florida University, Tallahassee; summer camp director and leader of church youth groups. Recipient: Canadian Children's Book Award, joint award of American and Canadian branches of Little, Brown, 1961, for *Mine for Keeps;* Vicky Metcalf Award, Canadian Authors Association, 1974, for body of work inspirational to Canadian boys and girls; Governor General's Literary Award for Children's Literature, Canada Council, 1977, for *Listen for the Singing;* Children's Book Award, Canada Council, 1979; Children's Book of the Year Award, Canadian Library Association, and Ruth Schwartz Award, both 1985, for *Mama's Going to Buy You a Mockingbird; Boston Globe-Horn Book* Honor Award, 1988, for *Little by Little: A Writer's Education;* numerous Junior Literary Guild awards. Address: 198 Glasgow Street North, Guelph, ON N1H 4X2, Canada.

PUBLICATIONS FOR YOUNG ADULTS

Fiction

Spring Begins in March, illustrated by Lewis Parker, Boston, Little, Brown, 1966.
One to Grow On, illustrated by Jerry Lazare. Boston, Little, Brown, 1969.
Look through My Window, illustrated by Joan Sandin. New York, Harper, 1970.
Kate. New York, Harper, 1971.
Listen for the Singing. New York, Dutton, 1977.
Mama's Going to Buy You a Mockingbird. Markham, Ontario, Penguin, 1984; New York, Viking Kestrel, 1985.

Nonfiction

Little by Little: A Writer's Education. Markham, Ontario, and New York, Viking, 1987.
Stars Come out Within. New York, Penguin, 1990.

PUBLICATIONS FOR CHILDREN

Fiction

Mine for Keeps, illustrated by Lewis Parker. Boston, Little, Brown, 1962.
Home from Far, illustrated by Jerry Lazare. Boston, Little, Brown, 1965.
Take Wing, illustrated by Lazare. Boston, Little, Brown, 1968.
From Anna, illustrated by Sandin. New York, Harper, 1972.
Stand in the Wind, illustrated by Emily Arnold McCully. New York, Harper, 1975.
Lost and Found, illustrated by Leoung O'Young. Markham, Ontario, Penguin and New York, Viking, 1985.
Different Dragons, illustrated by Laura Fernandez. Markham, Ontario, Penguin, and New York and London, Viking Kestrel, 1986.

Once upon a Golden Apple. illustrated by Phoebe Gilman. New York, Viking, 1991.
Jess Was the Brave One, illustrated by Janet Wilson. New York, Viking, 1992.
Revenge of the Small Small, illustrated by Janet Wilson. New York, Viking, 1993.

Poetry

It's a Wonderful World. Privately printed, 1947.
When the Pie Was Opened. Boston, Little, Brown, 1968.
Hey World, Here I Am!, illustrated by Barbara DiLella. Toronto, Kids Can Press, 1986; illustrated by Sue Truesdell, New York, Harper, 1989.

*

Media Adaptations: *Hey World, Here I Am* and *Little by Little: A Writer's Education* are available on audiocassette; *Mama's Going to Buy You a Mockingbird* was adapted as a television movie.

Biography: Entry in *Fourth Book of Junior Authors and Illustrators,* New York, H.W. Wilson, 1978; essay in *Something about the Author Autobiography Series,* Volume 17, Detroit, Gale, 1994.

Manuscript Collection: Kerlan Collection, University of Minnesota, Minneapolis.

Critical Study: *Children's Literature Review,* Volume 4, Detroit, Gale, 1982.

*   *   *

Jean Little, a Canadian author, has eighteen books in print—two of which are autobiographical. Many of her novels are more appropriate for those within the younger age range of the young adult reader category. In 1961, she won the Canadian Children's Book Award for *Mine for Keeps,* a book for younger readers. However, her two books of memoirs, *Little by Little* and *Stars Come out Within* are appropriate for those at the older range of the young adult reader category.

In the two books of her memoirs, Little tells about growing up within a close and warm family, about becoming a writer, and about living with her own severe visual impairment. Little was born with very limited vision in both eyes and has had to adapt to this. As an adult, she became a teacher of children with handicaps before she became a published author. Her students encouraged her to write children's books in which a main character had a physically challenging condition. They wanted to read books about children similar to themselves. While reading these memoirs, the reader realizes not only the physical difficulties of having very limited sight, but also the emotional strain it places on a child and adolescent when this condition interferes with forming relationships with peers. Little's recollections of her own youth also help the reader gain insight into the feelings of those who are physically challenged.

Stars Come out Within, the second of her memoirs, continues with stories of her adult life by describing her experiences as a writer, her response to losing more of her vision, and finally, her reaction to becoming totally blind. She also recounts the joy of regaining independence through her Seeing Eye dog, Zephyr, and her talking computer, SAM.

Because Little has always been an avid reader, she creates main characters who enjoy reading. Throughout her own books, there are references to titles or other authors of children's books.

In Little's novels, the main character is usually a girl who differs from her peers, learns to accept this difference, and goes on to establish close relationships with others. The books are rich both in characterization and in examples about the importance of family and peer relationships. The contents, instead of dwelling on the limitations which may be imposed by being handicapped, focus on the inner struggles of the main characters as they adapt to the environment and form close relationships. The main characters struggle to solve personal problems, and through this, gain insight and strength.

In *Look through My Window,* Emily Blair, a lonely, only child, learns to live with other children when four young cousins come to stay with her family. At the same time, the family moves to a new house in a new town and she must adapt to this changing outside world as well. She finally realizes her dream of having a best friend, Kate. Both Emily and Kate are poets.

Kate, Emily Blair's best friend, has a book of her own, *Kate.* In it, Kate learns about the rift between her father and his family. There is also a rift between Kate and her best friend, Emily. Kate comes to appreciate her parents who had seemed "unusual" to her, to accept her Jewish background, and to recognize the importance of her friendship with Emily. *Spring Begins in March* is the story of Meg who is not doing well in school and who had to adjust to the fact that the promised room of her own will not happen because her grandmother must move in with the family. At first, Meg resents her grandmother. Having found and read her grandmother's diary, Meg learns there are common experiences between her grandmother's girlhood and her own. In the end, Meg comes to understand not only the difficulty the grandmother had of finding a place in their family but also what her grandmother offered to the family, especially to her.

One to Grow On is the story of twelve-year-old Jamie Chisholm who tells so many lies or exaggerations that her family does not always believe her. Tillie, Jamie's godmother, takes her on a vacation away from the rest of the family. During the time she spends with Tillie, Jamie gains insight into her own and a friends' behavior and through this learns her own strengths.

From Anna and *Listen for the Singing* are about Anna Solden, a visually-impaired immigrant from Germany to Canada. In *From Anna,* she struggles to become familiar with the ways of her new country. In the sequel, *Listen for the Singing,* set at the beginning of World War II, she leaves the security of a special class to attend a regular high school. Here, in addition to learning to make friends and to adjusting to the classroom, she experiences prejudice because of her family's German name. When her brother, Rudi, is blinded while in the navy, Anna helps him to accept this condition. Making friends, confronting the teacher who is prejudiced, and helping Rudi—all cause Anna to gain maturity and insight into herself.

Mama's Going to Buy You a Mockingbird is the story of a family coping with a father's illness and death as seen through the eyes of the twelve-year-old son Jeremy. As he comes to accept his father's death, Jeremy makes friends with Tess, a girl who is considered to be different from the other students in his class. They offer friendship and support to each other.

To avoid the pain of loss when he remembers his father, Jeremy tries to forget and never to talk about his father. However, the book ends with a Christmas scene in which Jeremy realizes the tenderness of the relationship between his parents and that his father's legacies to him are the happy memories.

Because the main characters struggle to overcome problems within themselves or have physically challenging handicaps, there may be a tendency to recommend certain titles for bibliotherapy. However, there is some criticism of Little's work for that use because the character's problems are solved quickly or limitations are too easily accepted. Little writes in the *Stars Come out Within* that in *Listen for the Singing,* Anna's brother adapts to his blindness very easily with Anna's help, in contrast to her own struggle to accept complete blindness.

—Etta Miller

LONDON, Jack (John Griffith London). American. Born in San Francisco, California, 12 January 1876. Educated at a grammar school in Oakland, California; Oakland High School, 1895-96; University of California, Berkeley, 1897-98. Married 1) Bessie Mae Maddern in 1900 (separated 1903; divorced 1905), two daughters; 2) Clara Charmain Kittredge in 1905; one daughter (died 1910). Novelist, short story writer, and political essayist. Worked at a succession of odd jobs, including salmon canner, oyster pirate, patrol agent of San Francisco shore police, seal fisher, jute millworker, coal shoveler, and laundry worker, 1889-90; oyster "pirate" then member of the California Fisheries Patrol, 1891-92; sailor on the *Sophie Sutherland,* sailing to Japan and Siberia, 1893; joined Coxey's Army (a band of jobless men who marched to Washington, D.C.), and tramped throughout the United States and Canada, 1893-96; arrested for vagrancy in Niagara Falls, New York and sentenced to one month in Erie County Penitentiary in New York; gold miner in the Yukon Territory, 1897-98; worked as a journalist and reported the Russo-Japanese War for the San Francisco *Examiner,* 1904; ran for mayor of Oakland, California, on the Socialist ticket, 1905; lecturer throughout the United States, 1905-06; attempted to sail round the world on a 45-foot yacht, 1907-09; reported the Mexican Revolution for *Collier's,* 1914. *Died 22 November 1916.*

PUBLICATIONS

Novels

The Cruise of the Dazzler. New York, Century, 1902; London, Hodder & Stoughton, 1906.
A Daughter of the Snows, illustrated by Frederick C. Yohn. Philadelphia, Lippincott, 1902; London, Isbister, 1904.
The Call of the Wild, illustrated by Philip Goodwin and Charles Livingston Bull. New York, Macmillan, and London, Heinemann, 1903.
The Kempton-Wace Letters (published anonymously), with Anna Strunsky. New York, Macmillan, and London, Isbister, 1903.
The Sea Wolf, illustrated by W.J. Aylward. New York, Macmillan, 1904, and London, Heinemann, 1904.
The Game, illustrated by Henry Hutt and T.C. Lawrence. New York, Macmillan, and London, Heinemann, 1905.

Before Adam. New York, Macmillan, 1906; London, Laurie, 1908.

White Fang. New York, Macmillan, 1906; London, Methuen, 1907.

The Iron Heel. New York, Macmillan, 1907; London, Everett, 1908.

Martin Eden. New York, Macmillan, 1909; London, Heinemann, 1910.

Burning Daylight. New York, Macmillan, 1910; London, Heinemann,, 1911.

Adventure. London, Nelson, and New York, Macmillan, 1911.

The Abysmal Brute. New York, Century, 1913; London, Newnes, 1914.

John Barleycorn, illustrated by H.T. Dunn. New York, Century, 1913; as *John Barleycorn; or, Alcoholic Memoirs,* London, Mills & Boon, 1914.

The Valley of the Moon. New York, Macmillan, and London, Mills & Boon, 1913.

Mutiny of the Elsinore. New York, Macmillan, 1914; London, Mills & Boon, 1915.

The Jacket. London, Mills & Boon, 1915; as *The Star Rover,* New York, Macmillan, 1915,

The Scarlet Plague, illustrated by Gordon Grant. New York, Macmillan, and London, Mills & Boon, 1915.

The Little Lady of the Big House. New York, Macmillan, and London, Mills & Boon, 1916.

Jerry of the Islands. New York, Macmillan, and London, Mills & Boon, 1917.

Michael, Brother of Jerry. New York, Macmillan, 1917; London, Mills & Boon, 1918.

Hearts of Three. London, Mills & Boon, 1918; New York, Macmillan, 1920.

The Assassination Bureau, Ltd., completed by Robert L. Fish. New York, McGraw, 1963; London, Deutsch, 1964.

Short Stories

The Son of the Wolf: Tales of the Far North. Boston, Houghton, 1900; London, Isbister, 1902; as *An Odyssey of the North,* London, Mills & Boon, 1915.

The God of His Fathers, and Other Stories. New York, McClure, 1901; as *The God of His Fathers: Tales of the Klondyke,* London, Isbister, 1902.

Children of the Frost, illustrated by Raphael M. Reay. New York, Macmillan, 1902.

The Faith of Men, and Other Stories. New York, Macmillan, and London, Heinemann, 1904.

Tales of the Fish Patrol, illustrated by George Varian. New York, Macmillan, 1905; London, Heinemann, 1906.

The Apostate (also as *The Apostate: A Parable of Child Labor*). Chicago, Kerr, 1906.

Moon-Face, and Other Stories. New York, Macmillan, and London, Heinemann, 1906.

Love of Life, and Other Stories. New York, Macmillan, 1906; London, Everett, 1908.

Lost Face. New York, Macmillan, 1910; London, Mills & Boon, 1915.

South Sea Tales. New York, Macmillan, 1911; London, Mills & Boon, 1912.

The Strength of the Strong (story). Chicago, Kerr, 1911.

When God Laughs, and Other Stories. New York, Macmillan, 1911; London, Mills & Boon, 1912.

The Dream of Debs. Chicago, Kerr, 1912(?).

The House of Pride and Other Tales of Hawaii. New York, Macmillan, 1912; London, Mills & Boon, 1914.

Smoke Bellew, illustrated by P.J. Monahan. New York, Century, 1912; as *Smoke and Shorty,* London, Mills & Boon, 1920.

A Son of the Sun, illustrated by A.O. Fischer and C.W. Ashley. New York, Doubleday, 1912; London, Mills & Boon, 1913; as *The Adventures of Captain Grief,* Cleveland, World, 1954.

The Night-Born.... New York, Century, 1913; London, Mills & Boon, 1916.

The Strength of the Strong (collection). New York, Macmillan, 1914; London, Mills & Boon, 1917.

The Turtles of Tasman. New York, Macmillan, 1916; London, Mills & Boon, 1917.

The Human Drift. New York, Macmillan, 1917; London, Mills & Boon, 1919.

The Red One. New York, Macmillan, 1918; London, Mills & Boon, 1919.

On the Makaloa Mat. New York, Macmillan, 1919; as *Island Tales,* London, Mills & Boon, 1920.

Dutch Courage, and Other Stories. New York, Macmillan, 1922; London, Mills & Boon, 1923.

Jack London's Tales of Adventure, edited by Irving Shepard. New York, Hanover House, 1956.

Short Stories, edited by Maxwell Geismar. New York, Hill & Wang, 1960.

Great Short Works of Jack London, edited by Earle Labor. New York, Harper, 1965.

Stories of Hawaii, edited by A. Grove Day. New York, Appleton-Century, 1965.

Goliah: A Utopian Essay. Berkeley, California, Thorp Springs Press, 1973.

Curious Fragments: Jack London's Tales of Fantasy Fiction, edited by Dale L. Walker. Port Washington, New York, Kennikat Press, 1975.

The Science Fiction of Jack London: An Anthology, edited by Richard Gid Powers. Boston, Gregg Press, 1975.

Jack London's Yukon Women. New York, Belmont, 1982.

Young Wolf: The Early Adventure Stories of Jack London, edited and introduced by Howard Lachtman. Santa Barbara, California, Capra, 1984.

In a Far Country: Jack London's Western Tales, edited by Dale L. Walker. New York, Jameson, 1986.

Plays

The Great Interrogation, with Lee Bascom (produced San Francisco, 1905).

Scorn of Women: In Three Acts. New York, Macmillan, 1906; London, Macmillan, 1907.

Theft: A Play in Four Acts. New York, and London, Macmillan, 1910.

The Acorn-Planter: A California Forest Play.... New York, Macmillan, and London, Mills & Boon, 1916.

Daughters of the Rich, edited by James E. Sisson. Oakland, California, Holmes, 1971.

Gold: A Play, with Herbert Heron, edited by James E. Sisson. Oakland, California, Holmes, 1972.

Other

The People of the Abyss. New York, Macmillan, and London, Isbister, 1903.

The Scab. Chicago, Kerr, 1904.

The Tramp. New York, Wilshire's Magazine, 1904.

Jack London: A Sketch of His Life and Work. London, Macmillan, 1905.

War of the Classes. New York, Macmillan, and London, Heinemann, 1905.

What Life Means to Me. Princeton, New Jersey, Intercollegiate Socialist Society, 1906.

The Road. New York, Macmillan, 1907; London, Mills & Boon, 1914.

Jack London: Who He Is and What He Has Done. New York, Macmillan, 1908(?).

Revolution. Chicago, Kerr, 1909.

Revolution, and Other Essays. New York, Macmillan, 1910; London, Mills & Boon, 1920.

The Cruise of the Snark. New York, Macmillan, and London, Mills & Boon, 1911.

London's Essays of Revolt, edited by Leonard D. Abbott. New York, Vanguard Press, 1926.

Jack London, American Rebel: A Collection of His Social Writings, Together With an Extensive Study of the Man and His Times, edited by Philip S. Foner. New York, Citadel Press, 1947.

The Fitzroy Editions of the Works of Jack London, edited by I.O. Evans. London, Arco, New York, Archer House, and Horizon Press, 18 vols., 1962-68.

The Bodley Head Jack London, edited by Arthur Calder-Marshall. London, Bodley Head, Volume 4 vols., 1963-66; as *The Pan Jack London,* London, Pan, 2 vols., 1966-68.

Letters from Jack London: Containing an Unpublished Correspondence Between London and Sinclair Lewis, edited by King Hendricks and Irving Shepard. New York, Odyssey Press, 1965; London, MacGibbon and Kee, 1966.

Reportage, the San Francisco Quake: Two Accounts, with Will Irwin. Perfection Form Co., 1968.

Jack London Reports: War Correspondence, Sports Articles, and Miscellaneous Writings, edited by King Hendricks and Irving Shepard. New York, Doubleday, 1970.

Jack London's Articles and Short Stories in The (Oakland) High School Aegis, edited by James E. Sisson, illustrated by Holly Janes. Cedar Springs, Michigan, London Collector, 1971.

Daddy Boy: A Series of Dedications to His First Wife by Jack London. Stockton, California, Holt-Atherton Pacifica Center for Western Studies, 1976.

Jack London on the Road: The Tramp Diary, and Other Hobo Writings, edited by Richard W. Etulain. Logan, Utah University Press, 1979.

No Mentor But Myself: A Collection of Articles, Essays, Reviews, and Letters on Writings and Writers, edited by Dale L. Walker. Port Washington, New York, Kennikat Press, 1979.

Revolution: Stories and Essays, edited by Robert Barltrop. London, Journeyman Press, 1979.

Sporting Blood: Selections From Jack London's Greatest Sports Writing, edited by Howard Lachtman. Novato, California, Presidio Press, 1981.

The Unabridged Jack London, edited by Lawrence Teacher and Richard E. Nicholls. Philadelphia, Running Press, 1981.

Novels and Stories and *Novels and Social Writings* (Library of America), edited by Donald Pizer. New York, Literary Classics of the United States, and London, Cambridge University Press, 2 vols., 1982-84.

Jack London's California: The Golden Poppy and Other Writings, edited by Sal Noto. New York, Beaufort, 1986.

Greater Nowheres: A Journey through the Australian Bush, with Dave Finkelstein. New York, Harper & Row, 1988.

*

Media Adaptations: *The Abysmal Brute* (film), Universal, 1923, later version released as *Conflict,* Universal, 1936; *Adventure* (film), Paramount, 1925; *The Call of the Wild* (film), United Artists, 1935; *White Fang* (film), Twentieth Century-Fox, 1936; *The Sea-Wolf* (film), Warner Brothers, 1941; *The Adventures of Martin Eden* (film based on *Martin Eden*), Columbia, 1942; *A Piece of Steak* and *To Kill a Man* (films), both Balboa Amusement Co., both 1913; *John Barleycorn* (film), Bosworth, Inc., 1914; *The Mutiny of the Elsinore* (film released under the title *The Mutiny),* Shurtleff, Inc., 1920; *The Star Rover* (film), Shurtleff, Inc., 1920; Burning Daylight, Rowland Distributors, 1928; *Smoke Bellew* (film), First Division, 1929; *Alaska* (film based on *Flush of Gold*), Monogram, 1944; *The Fighter* (film based on *The Mexican*), United Artists/Gottlieb, 1952; and *The Assassination Bureau Ltd.* (film), Paramount, 1969; *Jack London: The Sea Wolf* (recordings), read by Anthony Quayle, Caedmon, 1981; *To Build a Fire* (recordings), read by Robert Donly, Miller-Brody; *Jack London Cassette Library* (recordings), read by Jack Dahlby, Listening Library; *The Call of the Wild* (recordings), read by Arnold Moss, Miller-Brody; *The Iron Heel* (play), adapted by W.G. Henry, produced by the Karl Marx players in Oakland, California, 1911.

Biography: Entry in *Dictionary of Literary Biography,* Detroit, Gale, Volume 8: *Twentieth-Century American Science Fiction Writers,* 1981, Volume 12: *American Realists and Naturalists,* 1982, Volume 78, *American Short-Story Writers, 1880-1910,* 1989.

Bibliography: *Jack London: A Bibliography* by Hensley C. Woodbridge, John London, and George H. Tweney, Georgetown, California, Talisman Press, 1966; supplement by Woodbridge, Milwood, New York, Kraus, 1973; in *Bibliography of American Literature 5* by Jacob Blanck, New Haven, Connecticut, Yale University Press, 1969; *The Fiction of Jack London: A Chronological Bibliography* by Dale L. Walker and James E. Sisson, El Paso, University of Texas, 1972; *Jack London: A Reference Guide* by Joan R. Sherman, Boston, Hall, 1977.

Manuscript Collections: Huntington Library, San Marino, California; Merrill Library at Utah State University, Logan.

Critical Studies: *Jack London: A Biography,* by Richard O'Connor, Boston, Little, Brown, 1964, London, Gollancz, 1965; *The Alien Worlds of Jack London* by Dale L. Walker, Grand Rapids, Michigan, Wolf House, 1973; *Jack London* by Earle Labor, Boston, Twayne, 1974; *Jack London: The Man, the Writer, the Rebel,* by Robert Baltrop, London, Pluto, 1976; *Jack: A Biography of Jack London* by Andrew Sinclair, New York, Harper, 1977, London, Weidenfeld & Nicolson, 1978; *Jack London and the Klondike: The Genesis of an American Writer* by Franklin Walker, San Marino, California, Huntington Library Publications, 1978; *Jack London: Essays in Criticism* edited by Ray Wilson Ownbey, Layton, Utah, Peregrine Smith, 1978; *Jack London: An American Myth* by John Perry, Chicago, Nelson Hall, 1981; *Solitary Comrade: Jack London and His Work* by Joan D. Hedrick, Chapel Hill, University of

North Carolina Press, 1982; *The Novels of Jack London: A Reappraisal* by Charles N. Watson, Jr., Madison, University of Wisconsin Press, 1983; *Jack London* by Gordon Beauchamp, Mercer Island, Washington, Starmount House, 1984; *Jack London—An American Rebel?* by Carolyn Johnston, Westport, Connecticut, Greenwood Press, 1984; *The Tools of My Trade: The Annotated Books in Jack London's Library* by David Mike Hamilton, Seattle, University of Washington Press, 1986; *Jack London* by James Lundquist, New York, Ungar, 1987.

*   *   *

The works of Jack London, author of some twenty novels and novellas and over one hundred short stories, are marked by an enormous amount of preparation; he once asserted that he suffered a "lack of origination" and had to gather facts from sources such as newspaper accounts and his own voracious reading, much of it in his fifteen-thousand-volume personal library. A diligent, careful, and committed writer, London also relied on his own experiences for material, ranging from his travels in the United States, the Yukon, and the Pacific to his stint in jail for vagrancy to a boat trip halfway around the world. His works focus on a cluster of themes—what he liked to call his "philosophy of life"—which stress the survival of the fittest, especially in inhospitable environments, and the virtues of courage, strength, determination, and a healthy respect for the truth.

London stands in the lofty tradition of such giants as Robert Louis Stevenson, as an able storyteller; Joseph Conrad, with whom he shared a love and respect for the sea; and Rudyard Kipling, whose sense of conflict echoes throughout London's pages. Three types of conflict can often be identified in the works of London— Man versus Nature, Man versus Man, and Man versus Himself. These are clearly depicted in the representative novels *Call of the Wild, The Sea Wolf, Martin Eden, Adventure, Jerry of the Islands, Smoke Bellew,* and the classic short story "To Build a Fire."

"To Build a Fire" demonstrates the conflict of Man against Nature, in which Nature story, like *Call of the Wild* and *White Fang,* reveals London's sense of the awesome appearance of Nature, sometimes harsh but always impressive. A passage from *White Fang* illustrates the power of London's descriptive images of the northern regions of the United States that he knew so well: "Dark spruce forest frowned on either side of the frozen waterway. The trees had been stripped by the wind of their white covering of frost, and they seemed to lean to each other, black and ominous, in the fading light." It is a tribute to London's skill as a writer that as readers identify with and hope for the survival of the man in "To Build a Fire," they develop an increased appreciation and respect for the tremendous power of Nature.

While Nature is often a grim force in London's works, it plays no favorites, and those who measure up to its demands prevail, as does Buck, the canine hero of *Call of the Wild.* Buck seems almost like a human being, as readers have access to his thoughts and dreams. He overcomes terrible hardships and engages in fierce battles with both men and other animals, displaying a high level of courage and cunning, as when he attacks a bull moose in the forest: "Three hundred-weight more than a half a ton he weighed; he had lived a long, strong life, full of fight and struggle, and at the end he faced death at the teeth of a creature whose head did not reach beyond his great knuckled knees."

London's ability to humanize animals, to penetrate their minds and hearts, makes their struggles and triumphs more poignant and more accessible to the reader. This is best represented in *The Sea Wolf.* In this novel, the central character, Wolf Larsen is a powerful (in one scene, he crushes a raw potato with one hand), ruthless, and brutal sea captain. He readily permits the beating of a cabin boy, beats a sailor nearly to death, almost cripples two seal hunters for quarreling, and has the cook tossed overboard, where he loses part of his leg to a shark. Though Larsen is typically harsh and sometimes appears insane, London adds dimension to his character by making him an avid reader who can speak standard English when he chooses—for example, in the presence of "gentleman" Humphrey Van Weyden, who has the misfortune of finding himself on Larsen's aptly named ship, the *Ghost.*

In London's works, the internal conflict of Man against Himself is well developed in both men and animals, usually dogs. As Wolf Larsen in *The Sea Wolf* is made up of two selves at odds with one another, the noble dogs in *White Fang* and *Call of the Wild* also revolt against their roots. White Fang shifts from a life in the wild to one of domesticity, while Buck flees a tame existence in favor of the wilderness.

London's fiction is not without heroism and occasional self-sacrifice, as when his master saves the life of the dog Jerry in *Jerry of the Islands,* or when John Thornton saves Buck's life in *Call of the Wild,* or when White Fang saves his master's family from an intruder, at the near loss of his own life. If these narratives have a flaw, it is in the linearity of the plots; one adventure follows hard upon another, as seen in the progression of incidents in *Adventure,* and *Smoke Bellew.* However, the energy and movement of the story lines, the development of interesting and rounded characters, and the eloquence of a highly expressive style usually outweigh this deficiency.

Much of the appeal and popularity of London's fiction can be attributed to the universal themes made available to readers of all ages. The raging battles that exist between human and natural forces in these works erode the layers of civilization to reveal glimpses of the most primeval impulses inherent in men and their environments. London once complained that when he began writing, he had no one to give me tips, no one's experience to profit by." He was compelled to labor hard for his subject matter, his story lines, and his forceful style, the results of which are well worth the effort that went into them.

—Fred McEwen

———

LOWRY, Lois (née Hammersberg). American. Born in Honolulu, Hawaii, 20 March 1937. Educated at Brown University, Providence, Rhode Island, 1954-56; University of Southern Maine, Portland, B.A. in English 1972. Married Donald Lowry in 1956 (divorced 1977); two daughters and two sons. Free-lance writer and photographer, 1972—. Recipient: Children's Literature award, International Reading Association, 1978, for *A Summer to Die;* American Library Association Notable Book citation, 1980, for *Autumn Street;* American Book award nomination, 1983, for *Anastasia Again!; Boston Globe-Horn Book* award, Golden Kite award, and Child Study award, Children's Book Committee of Bank Street College, all 1987, all for *Rabble Starkey;* Christopher award, 1988; Newbery Medal, National Jewish Book award, and Sidney Taylor award, National Jewish Libraries, all 1990, all for *Number the Stars.*

Agent: Claire Smith, Harold Ober Associates, 40 East 49th Street, New York, NY 10017. Address: 8 Lexington Ave., Cambridge, MA 02138, U.S.A.

PUBLICATIONS FOR YOUNG ADULTS

Fiction

A Summer to Die, illustrated by Jenni Oliver. Boston, Houghton Mifflin, 1977; London, Kestrel, 1979.
Find a Stranger, Say Goodbye. Boston, Houghton Mifflin, 1978; London, Kestrel, 1980.
Anastasia Krupnik. Boston, Houghton Mifflin, 1979; London, Fontana, 1986.
Autumn Street. Boston, Houghton Mifflin, 1980; as *The Woods at the End of Autumn Street,* London, Dent, 1987.
Anastasia Again!, illustrated by Diane deGroat. Boston, Houghton Mifflin, 1981; London, Fontana, 1986.
Anastasia at Your Service, illustrated by Diane deGroat. Boston, Houghton Mifflin, 1982; London, Fontana, 1987.
The One Hundredth Thing About Caroline. Boston, Houghton Mifflin, 1983.
Taking Care of Terrific. Boston, Houghton Mifflin, 1983.
Anastasia, Ask Your Analyst. Boston, Houghton Mifflin, 1984.
Us and Uncle Fraud. Boston, Houghton Mifflin, 1984.
Anastasia on Her Own. Boston, Houghton Mifflin, 1985.
Switcharound. Boston, Houghton Mifflin, 1985.
Anastasia Has the Answers. Boston, Houghton Mifflin, 1986.
Anastasia's Chosen Career. Boston, Houghton Mifflin, 1987.
Rabble Starkey. Boston, Houghton Mifflin, 1987; as *The Road Ahead,* London, Dent, 1988.
Number the Stars. Boston, Houghton Mifflin, 1989.
Your Move J.P.! Boston, Houghton Mifflin, 1990.
Anastasia at This Address. Boston, Houghton Mifflin, 1991.
The Giver. Boston, Houghton Mifflin, 1993.

PUBLICATIONS FOR CHILDREN

All about Sam, illustrated by Diane deGroat. Boston, Houghton Mifflin, 1988.
Attaboy, Sam!, illustrated by Diane deGroat. Boston, Houghton Mifflin, 1992.

PUBLICATIONS FOR ADULTS

Other

Black American Literature (textbook). Portland, Maine, Weston Walsh, 1973.
Literature of the American Revolution (textbook). Portland, Maine, Weston Walsh, 1974.
Values and the Family. Portland, Maine, Weston Walsh, 1977.
Photographer, *Here in Kennebunkport,* text by Frederick H. Lewis. Brattleboro, Vermont, Durrell, 1978.

*

Biography: Essay in *Something about the Author Autobiography Series,* Volume 3, Detroit, Gale, 1986; entry in *Dictionary of Liter-* *ary Biography,* Volume 52, Detroit, Gale, 1987; essay in *Authors and Artists for Young Adults,* Volume 5, Detroit, Gale, 1990; essay in *Speaking for Ourselves, Too* compiled and edited by Donald R. Gallo, National Council of Teachers of English, 1993.

Manuscript Collection: Kerlan Collection, University of Minnesota, Minneapolis.

Critical Study: Entry in *Children's Literature Review,* Volume 6, Detroit, Gale, 1984.

*   *   *

Lois Lowry has admitted to being fascinated by life's beginnings, transitions, and endings. Her books, which depict teenagers coping with changes in their lives, reflect this fascination with the multifaceted dimensions of growing up. A Newbery Medalist, Lowry has been praised by critics for her ability to deal realistically with the concerns of young adults.

Ten of twenty-one novels published from 1979 to 1993 focus on Anastasia Krupnik and her family: father, Myron, a Harvard English professor; mother, Katherine, a free-lance artist; and brother, Sam. The books' superb characterization, realistic dialogue, clever humor, and relevant themes bring to mind Beverly Cleary's "Ramona" series. Lowry emphasizes strong family values that nurture children's self-esteem, and humor that helps them through the roller-coaster ride of everyday life's ups and downs. Anastasia struggles with all the typical concerns of adolescence: humiliation in school, sibling rivalry, crushes on classmates and teachers, indecision about religion, death of a grandparent, moving and making new friends, boredom, independence, money, peer pressure, and career decisions. As she matures from ten to thirteen, Anastasia faces many confusing changes, ranging from being upset about a wart to accepting her grandmother's death and her brother's birth. Sam, spotlighted in two books, adds another narrative voice to the Krupnik saga.

In her "Tate" series, Lowry has created equally endearing characters who enjoy close family ties. Caroline, eleven, her thirteen-year-old brother, J.P., and mother, Joanna Tate, affirm the single-parent family's ability to solve problems with humor and love. The title *The One Hundredth Thing about Caroline* is taken from Mrs. Tate's frequent praise of her children, such as finding 100 wonderful things to love about Caroline. The siblings explore the mysteries of their world, creating zany situations. In the sequel, *Switcharound,* Caroline and J.P. spend the summer with their father and stepmother, and their children: identical twins Holly and Ivy, and six-year-old son Poochie. Caroline and J.P. resolve their differences to survive their summer visit. In *Your Move, J.P.!,* first love creates havoc in J.P.'s life, but his sense of humor and creativity serve him well in getting out of embarrassing situations.

Contrasting with the lighthearted humor of her "Anastasia" and "Tate" books is the somber tone of Lowry's first novel, *A Summer to Die* (inspired by her own sister's death from cancer), in which the tragedy of a child's death strikes the Chalmers family. The father (like Dr. Krupnik) teaches college English and writes books, the mother (like Mrs. Krupnik) is warm and understanding, and the younger daughter Meg (like Anastasia) is precocious. Because Meg (thirteen) resents her popular older sister Molly, she feels tremendous guilt after Molly dies of leukemia. Her parents and friends ease her pain, and she realizes that eventually "the jagged edges of sadness are softened by memories."

Autumn Street offers another poignant vision of lost childhood. Elizabeth Lorimer and her mother live with her grandparents while her father serves in World War II. Many traumatic events mark the end of her innocence: her grandfather's stroke, two playmates' deaths, news of Nazi war atrocities, and her father's being maimed in the war. Looking back on these traumatic times, Elizabeth recalls aching memories of fear. In *Us and Uncle Fraud* a child's near-death experience ends the age of innocence for Louise Cunningham, eleven. Almost losing her older brother, Louise learns to appreciate her family, even Uncle Claude, whose dream-weaving fantasy world destroys her naive faith in all-powerful, ever-truthful adults. At the novel's end, Louise listens to "the regular sounds of family life and of the love that bound us together, despite our flaws."

Other Lowry novels focus on teenagers seeking their identity. In *Find a Stranger, Say Goodbye* Natalie Armstrong, seventeen, searches for her biological parents after she graduates from high school. Having learned the truth about her past, she discards her emotional baggage and packs for college with a freed spirit, ready to soar. *Taking Care of Terrific* portrays another confused teenager looking for her identity. Enid Crowley (she prefers "Cynthia" because she hates "Enid") babysits for Joshua (he prefers "Tom Terrific"). With some interesting adults, they explore the magical night world of Boston's Public Garden. When police arrest them for "borrowing" the swan boats, the consequences of parental neglect become clear. *Rabble Starkey* shows other harsh realities of life that tear at family unity. Years before the novel begins, love-struck Sweet Hosanna had left home at thirteen to marry a stranger; she returns home without a husband—but with baby Parable (Rabble). Surviving poverty and single parenting, Sweet Hosanna raises Rabble, twelve, while working as a housekeeper. As the novel ends, they move on to find a better future through a college education. Indeed, Lowry's parable of family love praises the indomitable human spirit.

In *Number the Stars* Lowry revisits the World War II era of *Autumn Street;* the setting is now Copenhagen's streets in 1943 during the Nazi Reign of Terror. The family of Annemarie Johansen saves her Jewish best friend Ellen Rosen and her family from the Holocaust. Winner of the 1990 Newbery Medal, *Number the Stars* pays tribute to the courage and decency of Danish Christians who risked their lives to save nearly all of Denmark's seven thousand Jews. In her acceptance speech, Lowry explains her repetition of the terrifying images of the Nazis' black boots: "those high shiny boots had trampled on several million childhoods and I am sorry I hadn't had several million more pages on which to mention that."

In *The Giver* Lowry explores new territory. This fantasy's seemingly perfect society (without pain, disorder, or overpopulation) is actually a frightening dystopia (without love, colors, or sense of the past). At twelve, Jonas becomes the next Receiver of Memory for this totalitarian community governed by order and uniformity. The way he resolves his moral dilemma affirms the courageous human spirit's power to prevail and find "places where families created and kept memories, where they celebrated love."

Lowry's many different books present the comic and tragic sides of young adulthood with a kaleidoscope of life's funny, bewildering, and frightening moments. With honesty and compassion, Lowry offers realistic situations that help young people survive the difficult transition from childhood to adulthood.

—Laura M. Zaidman

LUCAS, Victoria. See **PLATH, Sylvia.**

————

LYLE, Katie Letcher. American. Born in Peking, China, 12 May 1938. Educated at Hollins College, Virginia, B.A. 1959; Johns Hopkins University, Baltimore, Maryland, M.A. 1960; graduate study at Vanderbilt University, Nashville, Tennessee, 1961-62. Married Royster Lyle, Jr. in 1963; one daughter and one son. Teacher in Baltimore, Maryland, 1960-61, 1962-63; Southern Seminary Junior College, Buena Vista, Virginia, member of English faculty, 1963-87, chairman of English department, 1968-80, chairman of liberal arts division, 1971-73. Guest instructor, Washington and Lee University, 1987; Hollins College, writer in residence, 1989, guest instructor, 1989-93. Elderhostel instructor, Southern Seminary, Mary Baldwin College, and other places, 1984—. Has been a professional folksinger in Baltimore and Nashville. Recipient: Bread Loaf fellowship, 1973, 1974. Address: 110 West McDowell, Lexington, VA 24450, U.S.A.

PUBLICATIONS FOR YOUNG ADULTS

Fiction

I Will Go Barefoot All Summer for You. Philadelphia, Pennsylvania, Lippincott, 1973.
Fair Day, and Another Step Begun. Philadelphia, Pennsylvania, Lippincott, 1974.
The Golden Shores of Heaven. Philadelphia, Pennsylvania, Lippincott, 1976.
Scott's Marathon. New York, Coward, 1980.
Dark but Full of Diamonds. New York, Coward, 1981.
Finders Weepers. New York, Coward, 1982.

PUBLICATIONS FOR ADULTS

Nonfiction

Lyrics of Three Women, with Maude Rubin and May Miller. Baltimore, Linden Press, 1964.
On Teaching Creative Writing. National Defense Education Act, 1968.
Scalded to Death by the Steam: Authentic Stories of Railroad Disasters and the Ballads That Were Written about Them. Chapel Hill, North Carolina, Algonquin, 1983.
The Man Who Wanted Seven Wives. Chapel Hill, North Carolina, Algonquin, 1986.
The Big Berry Book. Minocqua, Wisconsin, Northword, 1994.

Other

Contributor, *Beyond the Square,* edited by Robert K. Rosenburg. Hollywood, California, Linden Press, 1972.

Also author of "Footsteps," a television series. Author of "A Foreign Flavor," a weekly column on food and humor, for *Roanoke Times,* 1970-74. Contributor to *A Guide to Chessie Trail,* 1988, and to *Virginia Wild Rivers Study,* edited by Paul Dulaney; of poems and short stories to *Shenandoah,* the *Virginia Quarterly Review,* and other literary magazines, and of articles and reviews to newspapers and magazines, including *Newsweek.*

*

Biography: Essay in *Speaking for Ourselves: Autobiographical Sketches by Notable Authors of Books for Young Adults,* Volume 1, compiled and edited by Donald R. Gallo, National Council of Teachers of English, 1990.

*   *   *

Katie Letcher Lyle is a writer whose prose has an exceptionally fine, often poetic quality and who is able to imagine believable and fascinating characters. Lyle likes to create young adult characters who are highly individual, have an unusual love of language, and are rooted in their Southern communities, which become more specific and well-realized with each book she writes (witness, for example, the movement from the generic Nashville setting in *The Golden Shores of Heaven* to the unspecified Southern state in *Dark but Full of Diamonds* to the highly particular southwestern Virginia setting of *Finders Weepers).* Lyle treats her characters' experiences of romance and sexuality with a mixture of sympathy, romanticism, and hardheaded insight.

One of the strengths of Lyle's writing is the self-possession of her young adult characters. Whether it is Scott Dabney in *Dark but Full of Diamonds* seeking to come to terms with his romantic feelings for his drama teacher who is also his father's fiancée, or Lee Eldridge in *Finders Weepers,* calmly arguing with a kidnapper who is trying to force her to show him where the hidden treasure she has found is located, Lyle's main characters are young people who certainly have struggles, doubts, and difficulties, but seem to possess, at some level, a remarkably strong and healthy sense of self. That strong sense of self is not unrelated to their sense of humor. It also may have something to do with their Southern sense of being rooted in a community, which includes but is not limited to an extended family. Lyle is at her best when she is demonstrating, as she often does, that her rural and Southern characters, anchored as they are in their small-town societies, are by no means necessarily provincial. Her principal characters are, in general, exceptionally smart, highly verbal, imaginative, and sane, even when they are doing crazy things. Her young adults face their share (or more) of teenage upheavals, but there is a hopefulness running like an indestructible ribbon through the fabric of Lyle's fiction.

Lyle's characters do much more than survive the angst of growing up. They invent ways to cope with disappointment and adversity, often through humorous fantasies or wild escapades. Jessie in *I Will Go Barefoot All Summer for You* makes a secret love vow to go barefoot for the boy she is in love with and, when she fails to keep her vow, decides to run away and live with him. Ellen Burd in *Fair Day, and Another Step Begun* virtually wills John Waters, the young man she loves, into loving her and acknowledging their unborn child, even though he has no inclination to do either. Ellen is stubborn and persistent, but she is also curiously sensible and free from self-pity. Her vision of what John will be to her and their child is strong enough to make his love become a reality—a romantic idea,

surely, but also powerfully attractive and perhaps not without wisdom. Mary Curlew in *The Golden Shores of Heaven* similarly has the single-minded determination to make her dream of becoming a country music singer in Nashville come true. Though Scott in *Dark but Full of Diamonds* fails in his desperate effort to win the love of the woman who loves his father, his love of theater, of assuming and creating dramatic roles, is the positive force in his life which enables him to begin healing himself. It is safe to say that though Lyle's main characters may suffer many doubts and anxieties, they do not doubt their self-worth. Not as superficial or alienated as Judy Blume's characters, they are on the whole wittier and wiser (or at least smarter). Although they may not be as profound or spiritually symbolic as some of Katherine Paterson's young people, they are as highly individuated as characters and at least equally complicated and genuine in their social relationships.

Lyle also brings to the young adult novel an intriguing mixture of romanticism and tough-mindedness. The romanticism is reflected in the sometimes extravagant (if not clichéd) premises of her novels: the quest for fame and fortune as a singer, for example, or a young man's hopeless love for an attractive older woman; or hidden treasure, surrounded by legend and folklore. The sources of Lyle's inspiration, on one level at least, often seem to lie close to myth, folklore, and sometimes even popular culture (with the exception of television which seems notably absent from or insignificant in the lives of her characters). The mythic or folkloric plot premises in Lyle's novels are given original and intriguing twists: Jessie in effect runs away from a home that doesn't exist in *I Will Go Barefoot All Summer for You;* Scott's oedipal attraction in *Dark but Full of Diamonds* does *not* result in the classical denouement; and Lee's real treasure in *Finders Weepers* is her relationship with the people of southwestern Virginia, particularly her grandmother, a possession threatened by her preoccupation with the hidden treasure. The tough-mindedness lies partly in the pervasive knowledge in Lyle's fiction that happiness does not result from easy gratifications but rather from lasting, genuine relationships and from satisfying pursuits of difficult-to-attain goals. And the psychological good sense of her fiction, of particular value to young people, is the persistent awareness that her characters reveal of the importance of being true to themselves. Her characters often realistically combine paradoxical qualities, as in Lee Eldridge's combination of sense and sensibility.

The strengths of Lyle's fiction, then, include strong, clear, often poetic prose writing, well-realized characters who are not represented in isolation but placed in believable social contexts, a vivid and affectionate sense of humor, and, a romantic imagination balanced by common sense about human nature. Lyle's novels for young adults received mixed reviews from critics when they first appeared, (partly because she has not been content to stick to formulas or repeat her successes, and has experimented with forms and themes (for example, mixing comic misadventures with serious flashbacks and dreams or blending romantic ballad and realistic contemporary novel), but she is an engaging, talented writer whose novels deserve a broader audience.

—J.D. Stahl

M

MacAVOY, R(oberta) A(nn). American. Born in Cleveland, Ohio, 13 December 1949. Educated at Case Western Reserve University, Cleveland, 1967-71, B.Sc. 1971. Married Ronald Allen Cain in 1978. Financial aid officer's assistant, Columbia College, New York, 1975-78; computer programmer, SRI International, Menlo Park, California, 1979-83. Since 1982, full-time writer. Recipient: John W. Campbell Best New Writer award, 1984. Agent: Richard Curtis Associates, 171 East 74th Street, New York, NY 10021. Address: Underhill at Nelson Farm, 1669 Nelson Road, House 6, Scotts Valley, CA 95066, U.S.A.

PUBLICATIONS FOR YOUNG ADULTS

Novels

Tea with the Black Dragon. New York and London, Bantam, 1983.
A Trio for Lute. New York, Doubleday, 1984.
Damiano. New York, Bantam, 1984; London, 1985.
Damiano's Lute. New York, Bantam, 1984; London, 1985.
Raphael. New York, Bantam, 1984; London, 1985.
The Book of Kells. New York, Bantam, 1985.
Twisting the Rope: Casadh and t'Sugain. New York, Bantam, 1986.
The Great Horse. New York, Bantam, 1987.
The Third Eagle: Lessons Along a Minor String. New York, Doubleday, 1989.
Lens of the World. New York, Morrow, 1990; London, Headline, 1991.
King of the Dead. New York, Morrow, and London, Headline, 1991.

*   *   *

In the work of R.A. MacAvoy, young adult readers will find familiar forms in the service of some of the themes they find most intriguing. MacAvoy explores the eternal questions of meaning, personal identity, and the "right" way of life through characters who embody and personalize these questions. These are books for the thoughtful reader, one who is willing to study character and enjoy the author's crafted prose.

The language employed in these novels is not difficult, but it is conscious. An appreciation for digression and simile will add to the reader's enjoyment. Sentences like, "I awoke before dawn for the whole week before Baron Howdl's next winnowing," from *Lens of the World*, will be much more effective for the reader who understands not only the meaning but the nuances of "winnowing." Similarly, "Less promptly, the bumblebees followed" (*Lens of the World*), will reveal itself only to the reader who has supplied both imagination and attention. The literalist will see only departing soldiers, while those who have missed previous references to the black-and-yellow uniforms will find themselves truly at sea. This poetic prose adds a dimension too often missing from works intended for the young adult audience.

MacAvoy frequently makes use of standard forms. *Tea with the Black Dragon* and *Twisting the Rope* are mysteries. It is a daring mystery reader, however, who will be willing to tolerate protagonists who are mystics and philosophers, one of whom also claims a previous life as a dragon. The "Damiano" trilogy follows the familiar fantasy format of coming-of-age quest, but again, the introspective character of the hero turns the form on its head. In *Lens of the World* and its sequel, *King of the Dead,* MacAvoy again uses a familiar form, the epistolary novel, to reveal her characters in ways that plot cannot.

Indeed, it is the similarities in her protagonists which are MacAvoy's most salient characteristic. They are inward-turning, self-questioning, thoughtful people. Not afraid of contemplation, they are most likely to respond to difficulties with thought rather than action. Life (and plot complications) may force them to act, but they will question those actions later. They are unable to see only one side of a question and, one and all, are seekers—of truth, peace, harmony, or inner balance. External warfare is often a metaphor for internal character struggles. The search for internal balance is played out in political complications, kidnappings, journeys into hostile territory. Mastery over one's self, whether as a musician, warrior, or lens grinder, yields mastery in the external world.

Zhurrie, in *Lens of the World,* is in many ways an ultimate creation in this embodiment of thematic development of character. His search for identity and belonging shape the plot. He is forced into action against his will when he hesitates to operate in a world he so imperfectly understands. Yet his self-comprehension informs all of his acts and his reports of them. Although Zhurrie's life is full of battles, travels, and invention, this is never his focus. He is always examining these experiences for reasons, causes, and meaning. It is when Zhurrie is uniquely qualified to interpret this reality that the full force of the thematic meaning is revealed to the reader. Because *Lens of the World* deals so successfully with many important themes of young adult literature, including coming-of-age, self-identity, relationships, and responsibility to the community, it deserves special mention. In it, young adult readers will find models and metaphors for many of their experiences.

—Cathy Chauvette

―――――

MAGORIAN, Michelle. British. Born in Portsmouth, England, 6 November 1947. Educated at Rose Bruford College of Speech and Drama, diploma, 1969; London University, certificate in film studies, 1984; Ecole Internationale de Mime, 1969-70. Married in 1987; one son. Writer and actress. Appeared in several television programs and the film *McVicar.* Has performed mime shows and was a member of a repertory theatre group. Recipient: Carnegie Medal commendation, 1981, for *Good Night, Mr. Tom;* International Reading Association Children's Book award, American Library Association Best Book for Young Adults, and British Guardian award for Children's Literature, all 1982, all for *Good Night, Mr. Tom;* West Australian Young Readers' Book award, Library Association of Australia, 1983, for *Good Night, Mr. Tom,* and 1987, for *Back Home;* American Library Association Best Book for Young Adults, for *Back Home,* 1984. Agent: Patricia White, Rogers, Coleridge & White, 20 Powis Mews, London W11 1JN, England. 803 Harrow Rd., Wembley, Middlesex HA0 2LP, England.

PUBLICATIONS FOR YOUNG ADULTS

Fiction

Good Night, Mr. Tom. London, Kestrel, and New York, Harper, 1981.
Back Home. New York, Harper, 1984; London, Kestrel, 1985.
Waiting for My Shorts to Dry (poetry), illustrated by Jean Baylis. London, Kestrel, 1989.
Who's Going to Take Care of Me?, illustrated by James Graham Hale. New York, HarperCollins, 1990.
A Little Love Song. New York, Methuen, 1991.
Orange Paw Marks (poetry), illustrated by Jean Baylis. London, Kestrel, 1991.
Not a Swan. New York, HarperCollins, 1992.
Jump! New York, Walker Books, in press.

*

Media Adaptations: *Back Home* (television film).

* * *

Although all of Michelle Magorian's young adult novels take place during World War II, their subjects would have been unmentionable in juvenile fiction of the 1940s: child abuse, illegitimacy, sexuality, gender roles, and class differences. Yet these are not harsh books, thanks to Magorian's engaging protagonists, her sensitive yet powerful writing style, and her emotional honesty. The war and its aftermath provide a setting of crisis and change in which believable characters and their struggles engage the reader's interest compellingly.

Magorian rose to fame with *Good Night, Mr. Tom,* the story of an abused London boy billeted on a gruff, elderly widower. It would seem unlikely that the well worn plot of a lonely child meeting an emotion-starved older person, to the lasting benefit of both, could excite readers and critics alike in the 1980s—but it did, moving many to tears. Showing the dark side of human nature, and of the war, *Good Night, Mr. Tom* succeeds by the power of its message: hope. Willie Beech, whose mother has sewn him into his clothes and packed a belt for his hosts to beat him with, is assigned to Tom Oakley simply because Tom lives near the church. That the transformation of Willie into a normal boy and Tom into a loving parent surrogate avoids sentimentality is almost miraculous. The narrative gradually reveals the extent of Willie's victimization at the hands of his mother, a religious fanatic; his bruises and his fear of everything and everyone are the outward signs of profound deprivation, for Willie has never eaten nourishing food, been allowed to play, or learned to read. As the nature of Willie's problems becomes clear, Tom experiences flashbacks to the terrible loss of his young wife and infant son. Magorian places her central fable in a meticulously detailed rural setting with other fully rounded characters: Carrie, who wins a scholarship but faces hostility from her working class family; Mrs. Hartridge, whose husband is missing in action; Zach (Will's best friend), a Jewish evacuee from a theatrical family. Finally, Magorian does not simply end the story with the transformation of Will and Tom; Will's return to London, his rescue by Tom, his prolonged recuperation, and the loss of Zach take up the second part of the book. The healing powers of the countryside are balanced by those of art, as Will learns to express himself in theatre and drawing.

Magorian's second young adult book, *Back Home,* also portrays complex characters from several generations. In addition to Rusty, who is returning from a wartime stay with American relatives, there are two compelling elderly women: the eccentric Beatie, who functions as a fairy godmother, and her malevolent counterpart, Rusty's grandmother. The transformation of Rusty from repressed child to happy young adolescent has already happened before the story begins; her attempts to fit into the conditions of postwar England are balanced by the freer ideals she has learned abroad.

Unlike *Good Night, Mr. Tom*'s focus on childhood and old age, *Back Home* also includes a searching examination of the generation between. Rusty's mother Peggy, sheltered and repressed, finds new strengths and abilities under wartime conditions. As Virginia has become Rusty overseas, so Margaret has turned into Peggy, skilled driver and mechanic, in Devon. Peggy's inarticulate love for Rusty, her unhappiness with her tyrannical mother-in-law and coldly conventional husband, and her eventual decision to make a new life are shown with understanding and skill.

Gender roles, barely mentioned in the earlier book, permeate *Back Home*. Rusty, with her androgynous name and skill in woodcutting and carpentry, has difficulty with British customs. Peggy, herself a mechanic, at first supports traditional gender roles for her children and only gradually comes to reject them after both Rusty and her younger brother Charlie run afoul of societal expectations. The scene in which Charlie is shorn of his thick hair, then caned by his father as Rusty tries to protect him, brings these questions into sharp focus.

Back Home examines issues of class and nationality in many ways, one of them education—as exemplified by the differences between Rusty's American school and the unspeakable Benwood House, a monument to institutional meanness unequalled since Jane Eyre's Lowood. In typical Magorian fashion, one of the most telling features of Benwood is its treatment of art and music as extras, and even at that, subjects to be learn by rote. By contrast, Rusty and Charlie's later school in Devon is run on progressive lines and vaguely resembles a West Country Summerhill. Particularly significant is the difference between the ostracism accorded to a scholarship student at Benwood and the unquestioned acceptance of Rusty's friend Beth at the Devon school, which she attends free because her parents work there. Also developed in detail is the question of sexual repression. The difference between Rusty's casual acceptance of male friends and the attitudes of most of the English characters is striking. Bertie's pleasure at seeing the children dance naked in the rain contrasts sharply with the grandmother's view that pregnancy must not be mentioned in front of children, especially at teatime. Rusty's classmates can be expelled for talking to any man, and one of them believes Rusty will have a baby because she spent the night talking to a boy.

After a hiatus of seven years, Magorian returned to World War II with *Not a Swan*. More lyrical than *Good Night, Mr. Tom,* more optimistic than *Back Home,* the story focuses for the first time on an adolescent main character, Rose, youngest of three sisters evacuated to Devon. The double plot balances Rose's maturation in wartime against her gradual discovery of the fate of Mad Hilda, whose cottage she and her sisters are living in. At sixteen, Rose has almost complete autonomy. For the first time, Magorian has a chance to develop her ideas about sexuality and repression with direct reference to the main character; for, after reading Hilda's journal and discovering the tragedy of her life after illegitimate pregnancy, Rose herself goes through sexual initiation and the growth of love in a very different fashion. Bridging the two stories is the saga of Dot, a young woman of a nearby home for pregnant evacuees, whose fiance has been killed. The graphically described birth of Dot's baby and the subsequent acceptance of Dot by her fiance's parents are high points. In all three of these plot strands, questions of love versus sex, true legitimacy versus respectability, and birth versus literal or metaphorical death are examined.

Women's roles, class distinctions, and the role of art come in for discussion once again in *Not a Swan*. The enforced seclusion of Mad Hilda by her wealthy family contrasts with the freedom enjoyed by Rose and her sisters and, indeed, by their absent mother, who is away entertaining the troops. The working-class characters, particularly Dot and her fiance's parents, have a conspicuously practical and unconventional response to crisis. Also as in *Good Night, Mr. Tom,* art has power to heal. Will draws; Rose, like Hilda before her, writes. The central position accorded to writing throughout the book makes the coincidence of Alec's identity seem not merely coincidental but inevitable.

—Caroline C. Hunt

MAHY, Margaret. New Zealander. Born in Whakatane, New Zealand, 21 March 1936. Educated at University of Auckland, B.A. 1957, Diploma of Librarianship 1958. Has two daughters. Writer. Petone Public Library, New Zealand, assistant librarian, 1958-59; School Library Service, Christchurch, New Zealand, librarian in charge, 1967-76; Canterbury Public Library, Christchurch, children's librarian, 1976-80. Writer in Residence, Canterbury University, 1984, and Western Australian College of Advanced Education, 1985. Recipient: Esther Glenn award, New Zealand Library Association, 1970, for *A Lion in the Meadow,* 1973, for *The First Margaret Mahy Story Book,* 1983, for *The Haunting;* New Zealand Literary Fund grant, 1975; *School Library Journal* Best Book citation, 1982, for *The Haunting;* Carnegie Medals, British Library Association, 1983, for *The Haunting,* 1985, for *The Changeover: A Supernatural Romance,* and 1987, for *Memory;* Notable Children's Book citation, 1984, Association for Library Service to Children, Children's Book of the Year citation, and Best Books for Young Adults award, American Library Association, all 1986, for *The Changeover;* Honor List citation, *Horn Book,* 1985, for *The Changeover,* and 1987, for *The Catalogue of the Universe; Observer* prize, 1987; Books of 1987 citation, ALA Young Adult Services Division, for *The Tricksters,* and 1989, for *Memory;* Society of School Libraries International Book award, and *Boston Globe/Horn Book* award, both 1988, for *Memory.* May Hill Arbuthnot Lecturer, ALSC, 1989. Agent: Vanessa Hamilton, The Summer House, Woodend, West Stoke Chichester, West Sussex PO18 9BP, England. Address: R.D.1, Lyttelton, New Zealand.

PUBLICATIONS FOR YOUNG ADULTS

Novels

The Haunting, illustrated by Bruce Hogarth. London, Dent, 1982; New York, Atheneum, 1983.
The Changeover: A Supernatural Romance. London, Dent, and New York, Atheneum, 1984.

The Catalogue of the Universe. London, Dent, 1985; New York, Atheneum, 1986.
Aliens in the Family. London, Methuen, and New York, Scholastic, 1986.
The Tricksters. London, Dent, 1986; New York, McElderry, 1987.
Memory. London, Dent, and New York, McElderry, 1987.

PUBLICATIONS FOR CHILDREN

Fiction

The Dragon of an Ordinary Family, illustrated by Helen Oxenbury. New York, Watts, and London, Heinemann, 1969.
A Lion in the Meadow, illustrated by Jenny Williams. New York, Watts, and London, Dent, 1969; augmented edition, as *A Lion in the Meadow and Five Other Favorites,* London, Dent, 1976.
Mrs. Discombobulous, illustrated by Jan Brychta. New York, Watts, and London, Dent, 1969.
Pillycock's Shop, illustrated by Carol Barker. New York, Watts, and London, Dobson, 1969.
The Procession, illustrated by Charles Mozley. New York, Watts, and London, Dent, 1969.
The Little Witch, illustrated by Charles Mozely. New York, Watts, and London, Dent, 1970.
Sailor Jack and the 20 Orphans, illustrated by Robert Bartelt. New York, Watts, and London, Dent, 1970.
The Boy with Two Shadows, illustrated by Jenny Williams. New York, Watts, and London, Dent, 1971.
The Princess and the Clown, illustrated by Carol Barker. New York, Watts, and London, Dobson, 1971.
The Man Whose Mother Was a Pirate, illustrated by Brian Froud. London, Dent, 1972; New York, Atheneum, 1973; revised edition illustrated by Margaret Chamberlain, New York, Viking, 1986.
The Railway Engine and the Hairy Brigands, illustrated by Brian Froud. London, Dent, 1973.
Clancy's Cabin, illustrated by Trevor Stubley. London, Dent, 1974.
The Rare Spotted Birthday Party, illustrated by Belinda Lyon. London, Watts, 1974.
Rooms to Rent, illustrated by Jenny Williams. New York, Watts, 1974; as *Rooms to Let,* London, Dent, 1975.
Stepmother, illustrated by Terry Burton. London, Watts, 1974.
The Witch in the Cherry Tree, illustrated by Jenny Williams. London, Dent, and New York, Parents' Magazine Press, 1974.
The Boy Who Was Followed Home, illustrated by Steven Kellogg. New York, Watts, 1975; London, Dent, 1977.
The Bus Under the Leaves, illustrated by Margery Gill. London, Dent, 1975.
The Great Millionaire Kidnap, illustrated by Jan Brychta. London, Dent, 1975.
Ultra-Violet Catastrophe! or, The Unexpected Walk with Great-Uncle Mangus Pringle, illustrated by Brian Froud. London, Dent, and New York, Parents' Magazine Press, 1975.
David's Witch Doctor, illustrated by Jim Russell. London, Watts, 1976.
Leaf Magic, illustrated by Jenny Williams. London, Dent, 1976; New York, Parents' Magazine Press, 1977.
The Wind Between the Stars, illustrated by Brian Froud. London, Dent, 1976.

Look under V, illustrated by Deidre Gardiner. Wellington, Department of Education School Publications Branch, 1977.

The Nonstop Nonsense Book, illustrated by Quentin Blake. London, Dent, 1977; New York, McElderry, 1989.

The Pirate Uncle, illustrated by Mary Dinsdale. London, Dent, 1977.

The Great Piratical Rumbustification, and The Librarian and the Robbers, illustrated by Quentin Blake. London, Dent, 1978; Boston, Godine, 1986.

Raging Robots and Unruly Uncles, illustrated by Peter Stevenson. London, Dent, 1981.

Cooking Pot, with Joy Cowley and June Melser, illustrated by Deidre Gardiner. Auckland, Shortland, 1982; Leeds, Arnold Wheaton, 1985.

The Crocodile's Christmas Sandals, illustrated by Deidre Gardiner. Wellington, Department of Education School Publications Branch, 1982; as *The Crocodile's Christmas Thongs,* Melbourne, Nelson, 1985.

Fast and Funny, with Joy Cowley and June Melser, illustrated by Lynette Vondruska. Auckland, Shortland, 1982; Leeds, Arnold Wheaton, 1985.

Roly-Poly, with Joy Cowley and June Melser, illustrated by Deidre Gardiner. Auckland, Shortland, 1982; Leeds, Arnold Wheaton, 1985.

Sing to the Moon, with Joy Cowley and June Melser, illustrated by Isabel Lowe. Auckland, Shortland, 1982; Leeds, Arnold Wheaton, 1985.

Tiddalik, with Joy Cowley and June Melser, illustrated by Philip Webb. Auckland, Shortland, 1982; Leeds, Arnold Wheaton, 1985.

The Bubbling Crocodile, illustrated by Deidre Gardiner. Wellington, Department of Education School Publications Branch, 1983.

A Crocodile in the Library, illustrated by Deidre Gardiner. Wellington, Department of Education School Publications Branch, 1983.

Mrs. Bubble's Baby. Wellington, Department of Education School Publications Branch, 1983.

The Pirates' Mixed-Up Voyage: Dark Doings in the Thousand Islands, illustrated by Margaret Chamberlain. London, Dent, 1983.

Shopping with a Crocodile. Wellington, Department of Education School Publications Branch, 1983.

The Birthday Burglar, and A Very Wicked Headmistress, illustrated by Margaret Chamberlain. London, Dent, 1984; Boston, Godine, 1988.

The Dragon's Birthday, illustrated by Philip Webb. Auckland, Shortland, 1984.

Fantail, Fantail, illustrated by Bruce Phillips. Wellington, Department of Education School Publications Branch, 1984.

Going to the Beach, illustrated by Dick Frizzell. Wellington, Department of Education School Publications Branch, 1984.

The Great Grumbler and the Wonder Tree, illustrated by Diane Perham. Wellington, Department of Education School Publications Branch, 1984.

The Spider in the Shower, illustrated by Rodney McRae. Auckland, Shortland, 1984.

Ups and Downs and Other Stories, illustrated by Philip Webb. Auckland, Shortland, 1984.

Wibble Wobble and Other Stories. Auckland, Shortland. 1984.

The Adventures of a Kite, illustrated by David Cowe. Auckland, Shortland, 1985; Leeds, Arnold Wheaton, 1986.

The Cake, illustrated by David Cowe. Auckland, Shortland, 1985; Leeds, Arnold Wheaton, 1986.

The Catten, illustrated by Jo Davies. Auckland, Shortland, 1985; Leeds, Arnold Wheaton, 1986.

Clever Hamburger, illustrated by Rodney McRae. Auckland, Shortland, 1985; Leeds, Arnold Wheaton, 1986.

A Crocodile in the Garden, illustrated by Deidre Gardiner. Wellington, Department of Education of Education School Publications Branch, 1985.

The Earthquake, illustrated by Dianne Perham. Auckland, Shortland, 1985; Leeds, Arnold Wheaton, 1986.

Horrakopotchin. Wellington, Department of Education School Publications Branch, 1985.

Jam: A True Story, illustrated by Helen Craig. London, Dent, 1985; Boston, Atlantic Monthly Press, 1986.

Out in the Big Wild World, illustrated by Rodney McRae. Auckland, Shortland, 1985.

Rain, illustrated by Elizabeth Fuller. Auckland, Shortland, 1985.

Sophie's Singing Mother, illustratied by Jo Davies. Auckland, Shortland, 1985; Leeds, Arnold Wheaton, 1986.

Arguments, illustrated by Kelvin Hawley. Auckland, Shortland, 1986.

Baby's Breakfast, illustrated by Madeline Beasley. Auckland, Heinemann, 1986.

Beautiful Pig. Auckland, Shortland, 1986; Leeds, Arnold Wheaton, 1987.

An Elephant in the House, illustrated by Elizabeth Fuller. Auckland, Shortland, 1986.

Feeling Funny, illustrated by Rodney McRae. Auckland, Heinemann, 1986.

The Fight on the Hill, illustrated by Jan van der Voo. Auckland, Shortland, 1986; Leeds, Arnold Wheaton, 1987.

The Funny Funny Clown Face, illustrated by Miranda Whitford. Auckland, Heinemann, 1986.

The Garden Party, illustrated by Rodney McRae. Auckland, Heinemann, 1986.

Grow Up Sally Sue. Auckland, Heinemann, 1986.

Jacko, The Junk Shop Man, illustrated by Jo Davies. Auckland, Shortland, 1986.

The King's Treasure. Auckland, Heinemann, 1986.

The Long Grass of Tumbledown Road. Auckland, Shortland, 1986; Leeds, Arnold Wheaton, 1987.

The Man Who Enjoyed Grumbling, illustrated by Wendy Hodder. Auckland, Heinemann, 1986.

Mr. Rooster's Dilemma, illustrated by Elizabeth Fuller. Auckland, Shortland, 1986; as *How Mr. Rooster Didn't Get Married,* Leeds, Arnold Wheaton, 1986.

Mr. Rumfitt, illustrated by Nick Price. Auckland, Heinemann, 1986.

The Mouse Wedding, illustrated by Elizabeth Fuller. Auckland, Shortland, 1986.

Muppy's Ball, illustrated by Jan van der Voo. Auckland, Heinemann, 1986.

My Wonderful Aunt, illustrated by Dierdre Gardiner. Auckland, Heinemann, 4 vols., 1986; revised edition, Chicago, Children's Press, 1988.

The New House Villain, illustrated by Elizabeth Fuller. Auckland, Heinemann, 1986.

A Pet to the Vet, illustrated by Philip Webb. Auckland, Heinemann, 1986.

The Pop Group, illustrated by Madeline Beasley. Auckland, Heinemann, 1986.

The Robber Pig and the Ginger Beer [Green Eggs], illustrated by Rodney McRae. Auckland, Shortland, 2 vols., 1986; Leeds, Arnold Wheaton, 2 vols., 1987.

Shuttle 4. Auckland, Heinemann, 1986.

Squeak in the Gate, illustrated by Jo Davies. Auckland, Shortland, 1986.

The Terrible Topsy-Turvy, Tissy-Tossy Tangle, illustrated by Vicki Smillie-McItoull. Auckland, Heinemann, 1986.

The Three Wishes, with others, illustrated by Rodney McRae and others. Auckland, Shortland, 1986.

Tinny Tiny Tinker, illustrated by David Cowe. Auckland, Shortland, 1986.

The Tree Doctor, illustrated by Wendy Hodder. Auckland, Heinemann, 1986.

Trouble on the Bus, illustrated by Wendy Hodder. Auckland, Heinemann, 1986.

The Trouble with Heathrow, illustrated by Rodney McRae. Auckland, Heinemann, 1986.

A Very Happy Birthday, illustrated by Elizabeth Fuller. Auckland, Shortland, and Leeds, Arnold Wheaton, 1986.

Tai Taylor and His Education, illustrated by Nick Price. Auckland, Heinemann, 1986-87.

Tai Taylor and the Sweet Annie, illustrated by Nick Price. Auckland, Heinemann, 1986-87.

Tai Taylor Goes to School, illustrated by Nick Price. Auckland, Heinemann, 1986-87.

Tai Taylor Is Born, illustrated by Nick Price. Auckland, Heinemann, 1986-87.

Elliott and the Cats Eating Out. Auckland, Heinemann, 1987.

The Girl Who Washed in Moonlight, illustrated by Robyn Belton. Auckland, Heinemann, 1987.

Guinea Pig Grass, illustrated by Kelvin Hawley. Auckland, Shortland, 1987.

The Haunting of Miss Cardamon, illustrated by Korky Paul. Auckland, Heinemann, 1987.

Iris La Bonga and the Helpful Taxi Driver, illustrated by Vicki Smillie-McItoull. Auckland, Heinemann, 1987.

The Mad Puppet, illustrated by Jon Davis. Auckland, Heinemann, 1987.

The Man Who Walked on His Hands, illustrated by Martin Bailey. Auckland, Shortland, 1987.

No Dinner for Sally, illustrated by John Tarlton. Auckland, Shortland, 1987.

As Luck Would Have It, illustrated by Deidre Gardiner. Auckland, Shortland, 1988.

A Not-So-Quiet Evening, illustrated by Glenda Jones. Auckland, Shortland, 1988.

Sarah, The Bear and the Kangaroo, illustrated by Elizabeth Fuller. Auckland, Shortland, 1988.

When the King Rides By. Glasgow, Thornes, 1988.

The Blood and Thunder Adventure on Hurricane Peak, illustrated by Wendy Smith. London, Dent, 1989.

The Great White Man-Eating Shark: A Cautionary Tale, illustrated by Jonathan Allen. New York, Dial, 1990.

Making Friends, illustrated by Wendy Smith. New York, McElderry, 1990.

Seven Chinese Brothers, illustrated by Jean and Mou-sien Tseng. New York, Scholastic, 1990.

Dangerous Spaces. New York, Viking, 1991.

Keeping House. New York, Macmillan, 1991.

Pumpkin Man and the Crafty Creeper. New York, Greenwillow, 1991.

The Queen's Goat, illustrated by Emma Chichester Clark. New York, Dial Press, 1991.

The Horrendous Hullabaloo, illustrated by Patricia MacCarthy. New York, Viking, 1992.

Underrunners. New York, Viking, 1992.

The Good Fortunes Gang, illustrated by Marion Young. New York, Delacorte, 1993.

Screenplays: Adaptor, *The Haunting of Barrey Palmer* (based on *The Haunting).* New Zealand, 1987.

Television Scripts: *A Land Called Happy Wooly Valley, Once upon a Story,* and *The Margaret Mahy Story Book Theatre.*

Poetry

Seventeen Kings and Forty Two Elephants, illustrated by Charles Mozley. London, Dent, 1972; revised edition edited by Phyllis J. Fogelman with illustrations by Patricia MacCarthy, New York, Dial Press, 1987.

The Tin Can Band and Other Poems, illustrated by Honey de Lacey. London, Dent, 1989.

Collections

The First Margaret Mahy Story Book: Stories and Poems, illustrated by Shirley Hughes. London, Dent, 1972.

The Second Margaret Mahy Story Book: Stories and Poems, illustrated by Shirley Hughes. London, Dent, 1973.

The Third Margaret Mahy Story Book: Stories and Poems, illustrated by Shirley Hughes. London, Dent, 1975.

The Great Chewing-Gum Rescue and Other Stories, illustrated by Jan Ormerod. London, Dent, 1982.

Leaf Magic and Five Other Favourites, illustrated by Margaret Chamberlain. London, Dent, 1984.

The Downhill Crocodile Whizz and Other Stories, illustrated by Ian Newsham. London, Dent, 1986.

Mahy Magic: A Collection of the Most Magical Stories from the Margaret Mahy Story Books, illustrated by Shirley Hughes. London, Dent, 3 vols., 1986.

The Horrible Story and Others, illustrated by Shirley Hughes. London, Dent, 1987.

The Door in the Air and Other Stories, illustrated by Diana Catchpole. London, Dent, 1988; New York, Delacorte, 1991.

Chocolate Porridge and Other Stories, illustrated by Shirley Hughes. London, Puffin, 1989.

Bubble Trouble and Other Poems and Stories, illustrated by Margaret Mahy. New York, Macmillan, 1992.

The Girl With the Green Ear: Stories About Magic in Nature, illustrated by Shirley Hughes. New York, Knopf, 1992.

A Tall Story and Other Tales, illustrated by Jan Nesbitt. New York, Macmillan, 1992.

Nonfiction

New Zealand: Yesterday and Today. London, Watts, 1975.

*

Media Adaptations: *The Haunting* (cassette), G.K. Hall, 1986; *The Chewing Gum Rescue and Other Stories* (cassette), G.K. Hall, 1988; *The Pirate's Mixed-Up Voyage* (cassette), G.K. Hall; *Nonstop Nonsense.* (cassette), G.K. Hall.

Biography: Essay in *Authors and Artists for Young Adults,* Volume 8, Detroit, Gale, 1992.

Manuscript Collection: J.M. Dent and Sons Ltd., London.

Critical Study: Entry in *Children's Literature Review,* Volume 7, Detroit, Gale, 1984.

* * *

The opening sentence of Margaret Mahy's *Aliens in the Family* gives as good a summary of the author's theory of fiction as is to be found in all the pages of criticism that have so far been written about this prolific and engaging writer of literature for children and young adults: "Even the most ordinary days can be full of secrets and mysteries...." Indeed, if one can take her fiction as an accurate measure, Mahy sees fantastic possibilities in almost all of life. The work of this librarian-turned-writer is often referred to as "Mahy Magic," an alliterative reference to the many fantastical elements that appear in much of her work for young adults. The appellation also does double duty in describing the artistic nature of her writing, for, indeed, there is a magical, a lyrical, a poetical quality to her work, which ranges from children's picture books to problem novels with threads of the supernatural expertly woven into the fabric of the story. The author's energy, zest, and imagination are evident from just a cursory glance at the catalogue of her published works: more than one hundred books with titles ranging from the fanciful (*An Elephant in the House, The Great Piratical Rumbustification*) to the alliterative (*Raging Robots and Unruly Uncles, Tinny Tiny Tinker*) to the provocative (*The Changeover: A Supernatural Romance, Catalogue of the Universe*).

Mahy's style in her young adult books is essentially to take a realistic theme within a family setting and to supercharge it with fantastical or supernatural elements; this she does expertly in *Aliens in the Family.* The story concerns a seemingly normal New Zealand family that is invaded by aliens, both literally and figuratively. As the story unfolds, we meet David Raven and his newly acquired family: Philippa, his wife; Dora and Lewis, his stepchildren. Then enters the figurative alien: Jake, his tomboyish daughter from a previous marriage whose rough exterior is decidedly at odds with Dora's fluffy, beauty-shop persona. The appearance of Bond, the real alien, interjects a supernatural dimension to the plot and gives the fractious Raven children something to focus on besides their own internecine conflicts. Bond, who is an information gatherer from another world, has traveled through space and back through time to absorb information about late twentieth-century culture in New Zealand. He is being pursued by dark and mysterious forces who want to gain access to Bond's database for their own nefarious purposes. In the process of helping Bond, the family, in fact, helps itself. There is something about this process that allows grace to flood into the family, so that the alien becomes not just a supernatural trick but a metaphor graphically portraying the movement of goodness in ordinary lives. In this sense, Mahy is not unlike the adult author Flannery O'Connor who distorted reality in another away—toward the grotesque—in an effort to get her readers to see more clearly the relationships between her characters and the forces (social, historical, religious) which propel them along to their destinies.

The alien in this case is typical of most of Mahy's supernatural characters in that rather than being threatening or frightening, he is appealing and engaging. In fact, most of her supernatural characters are ordinary persons who have supernatural characteristics added to their personalities. This was very much the case in *The Haunting,* Mahy's first young adult novel which earned her her first Carnegie medal. This story seems a simple fantasy at the outset, the tale of a young boy who has inherited a family tendency toward wizardry from a shadowy uncle no one has heard from for years but who was known to have the same magical powers the young boy seems to possess. However, in a masterful twist toward the end of the book, we discover that it is the boy's older sister who actually has the magical powers; she has used the powers to create for the boy the impression that he has magical abilities, thus drawing attention away from her own mysterious self. But the twisting is not over yet. We further discover that it is the grandmother, a fractious but seemingly harmless old lady, who is the most malevolent power holder in the family. Because it invests its female characters with so much power, the story has been applauded by many critics as being a feminist breakthrough in young adult fiction.

Like other literary stylists before her, Mahy makes frequent and effective use of the ironical device of juxtaposing opposites as a means of revealing the deeper truth inherent in both extremes, thereby casting a bright and incisive light on the beauty and ambiguity of the whole. This device is particularly evident in *Memory,* the story of a young man haunted by the death of his sister. His memory of the accidental death, which occurred when the two of them plus his sister's best friend were playing near a precipice, is in fragments as a result of the emotional trauma. For several years the event has haunted him to the point of alcoholism and, as the story opens, he is beginning a desperate search to piece the tragic event back together in an effort to purge his guilt. He finds unexpected help in the person of an elderly woman whose memory is being ravaged by Alzheimer's disease.

In *The Changeover: A Supernatural Romance,* which also won a Carnegie medal, Mahy tells the story of a fourteen-year-old girl with psychic powers. She has a romance with a boy some four years older than she, but the real story here is the heroine's decision to become a witch in order to protect her younger brother from school bullies. In *The Catalogue of the Universe* Mahy eschews the overtly fantastical to tell a story that is pretty fantastic on its nonsupernatural merits. Angela, the daughter of an unwed mother, is a ravishing eighteen-year-old whose best friend, Tycho, is very odd looking and self-conscious. Angela's mother neither wants nor needs a man in her life, but Angela is determined to learn more about her father. Tycho helps her and in the process Angela comes to realize that her feelings for him have gone beyond friendship.

As was previously noted, Mahy writes some books that are clearly aimed at children and others that are clearly aimed at young adults. Between these two extremes is a broad literary estuary where Mahy writes wildly fantastical, whimsical tales which can be appreciated by children, young adults, and adults. Representative of this category is *The Birthday Burglar and a Very Wicked Headmistress,* a slight novel in which Mahy creates an alliterative tour-de-force. Rendered with wit, whimsy, and extraordinary literary finesse, the story concerns a boy named Bassington who lives on Barleycorn Island where he is cared for by a butler named Baker. Bassington has everything he could possibly want except a birthday as his neglectful parents (a bank robber and a black sheep) failed to give him one. So Bassington—travelling by hot air balloon—begins stealing birthdays in a nearby town. The children whose birthdays are stolen are upset, but Bassington might have gotten away with the deed had he not stolen the birthday of ninety-nine-year-old Mrs. Herringbone. She had been anxiously awaiting her "Happy Hundredth Birthday" message from the Queen, but with no birthday to celebrate there will be no message. So Mrs. Herringbone rouses the children to action and plans are laid to thwart the birthday burglar. By the time the final chapter ("Bliss for Baker, Bright Beginnings for Bassington—Happy Birthday Everyone") is reached, the burglar is reformed, and everyone is having a rollicking good time, including the reader.

Mahy is obviously fascinated by the supernatural and the fantastic; however, she refrains from writing books that are fantasies in a vacuum. In her books for young adults, Mahy uses fantasy as a light to illuminate aspects of our so-called ordinary lives. The ordinary lives Mahy writes about are those with which children in the late twentieth century can readily identify: they are the lives of children who live in homes ranging from happy and whole to homes headed by divorced parents or parents who are single by choice. In her books for children at the lower end of the young adult age range, Mahy uses fantasy as a tool to explore the wildest possibilities of the human imagination. Mahy writes with power and intelligence; she invests her characters with dignity, wit, and enormous appeal, and, in the process, she gives her readers an often wild and exhilarating ride through her unpredictable universe.

—Bill Buchanan

———

MAJOR, Kevin (Gerald). Canadian. Born in Stephenville, Newfoundland, 12 September 1949. Educated at Memorial University of Newfoundland, St. John's, B.Sc. 1973. Married Anne Crawford in 1982; two sons. Teacher, Roberts Arm, Newfoundland, 1971-72, and Carbonear, Newfoundland, 1973; teacher of special education and biology, Eastport Central High School, Newfoundland, 1974-76; writer, since 1976. Substitute teacher, since 1976-88. Guest on television and radio programs. Recipient: Children's Literature Prize from Canada Council, and Ruth Schwartz Children's Book award from Ruth Schwartz Charitable Foundation and Ontario Arts Council, both 1978, for *Hold Fast;* Book-of-the-Year award from Canadian Association of Children's Librarians, 1979, for *Hold Fast; Hold Fast* was also named to the Hans Christian Andersen Honor List by the International Board on Books for Young People, and to the *School Library Journal* list of Best Books of the Year, both 1980; Canadian Young Adult Book award from the Young Adult Caucus of the Saskatchewan Library Association, and was named to the *School Library Journal* list of Best Books of the Year, both 1981, for *Far from Shore;* runner-up for Young Adult Canadian Book award, 1990, for *Blood Red Ochre;* Book-of-the Year award from Canadian Association of Children's Librarians, Ann Conner Brimer award, both 1992, both for *Eating Between the Lines,* Vicky Metcalf award for outstanding body of work for children in Canada, 1992. Agent: Stirling Lord Canada, 10 St. Mary St., Suite #510, Toronto, Ontario M5R 1K5. Address: 27 Poplar Avenue, St. John's, Newfoundland A1B 1C7, Canada.

PUBLICATIONS FOR YOUNG ADULTS

Fiction

Hold Fast. Toronto, Clarke, Irwin, 1978; New York, Delacorte, 1980.

Far from Shore. Toronto, Clarke, Irwin, 1980; New York, Delacorte, 1981.
Thirty-six Exposures. New York, Delacorte, 1984.
Dear Bruce Springsteen. Toronto, Doubleday, 1987; New York, Delacorte, 1987; London, Viking Kestrel, 1989.
Blood Red Ochre. Toronto, Doubleday, and New York, Delacorte, 1989.
Eating between the Lines. Toronto, Doubleday, 1991.
Diana: My Autobiography. Toronto, Doubleday, 1993.

Other

Editor and contributor of illustrations, *Doryloads: Newfoundland Writings and Art.* Portugal Cove, Newfoundland, Breawater Books, 1974.

PUBLICATIONS FOR ADULTS

Other

Terra Nova National Park: Human History Study, with James A. Tuck. Ottawa, Parks Canada, 1983.

*

Biography: Entry in *Dictionary of Literary Biography,* Volume 60: *Canadian Writers since 1960, Second Series,* Detroit, Gale, 1987; essay in *Speaking for Ourselves: Autobiographical Sketches by Notable Authors of Books for Young Adults,* Volume 1, compiled and edited by Donald R. Gallo, National Council of Teachers of English, 1990.

Critical Studies: Entry in *Children's Literature Review,* Volume 11, Detroit, Gale, 1986, pp. 123-133; entry in *Contemporary Literary Criticism,* Volume 26, Detroit, Gale, 1983.

Kevin Major comments:

I see my audience as both young people and adults. Each new book I like to be fresh in style and content—a challenge for me to write and offering something of the unexpected to the reader. I find it's the reinventing of myself as author that keeps me in front of the blank screen.

*   *   *

Kevin Major's first novel, *Hold Fast,* met immediate critical acclaim in Canada and received three national awards. Such a beginning could have lured the novice author into repeating a successful formula. Instead, Major has deliberately challenged himself by departing markedly from *Hold Fast's* style in each of his six subsequent novels. By doing this successfully, Major has established himself as one of Canada's premier writers for adolescents.

Hold Fast begins and ends with death. When fourteen-year-old Michael's parents are accidentally killed, Michael and his younger brother Brent are separated. Brent remains with Aunt Flo and Grandfather while Michael moves to the city to live with his aunt and uncle and their two teenage children, Curtis and Marie. Curtis and Michael, who initially share few common interests, gradually discover mutual concerns, including a growing dislike for Curtis's dictatorial father. Michael's environment becomes increasingly unbearable, reaching crisis proportions following a school incident in which Michael accidentally injures another student. Uncle Ted orders an expelled Michael to apologize to the victim. Unwilling to accept further injustices in this overly controlled house, Michael runs away to his old home and, surprisingly, is joined by Curtis. Death, which separated the brothers, reunites them: Grandfather's death allows Michael to remain with Aunt Flo and Brent. Curtis returns to his father with no guarantee that the message inherent in his running away has been heard.

Far from Shore follows Chris, fifteen, over an eleven-month period as his life and family disintegrate. Chris's father, unable to find work in Newfoundland, seeks employment in Alberta. Without his father's influence, Chris's behaviour deteriorates. He fails grade ten, and his increased drinking causes him to lose his old friends whom he replaces with an older, tougher crowd. Following one drunken spree, Chris is charged with vandalizing the local school. Given an opportunity to redeem himself as a summer camp counsellor, Chris displays poor judgment and almost kills a young camper. Sobered by the incident, Chris, at the book's conclusion, resumes his schooling while his father returns to seek work or to take the family to Alberta. The book's impact is enhanced by Major's multinarrator technique which involves five characters.

Each of the thirty-six chapters in *Thirty-six Exposures* serves as a snapshot revealing of seventeen-year-old Lorne, who is concluding grade twelve in Marten, Newfoundland. The final two months contain many endings and beginnings. When Lorne's friend Trevor is unjustly suspended from Mr. Ryan's history class, the normally shy Lorne leads a classroom strike and a school walkout until Trevor is reinstated. Beginnings include Lorne's not using his valedictory address as a vehicle of revenge against Mr. Ryan, and a romance with Elaine wherein sex and love become confused. Endings involve not only school and changed relationships with parents, but Trevor's accidental death. Not wanting to find himself saying at age sixty-five, "If only...," Lorne questions conforming to the pattern of further education, marriage, and local employment.

Dear Bruce Springsteen is the salutation of fifty-one letters that fourteen-year-old Terry Blanchard directs to the rock superstar over a seven-month period. While the letters treat many of Terry's egocentric problems—poor grades, girl anxieties, physique—the theme of a boy trying to "find" his father runs through the unanswered correspondence. Abandoned by his father some six months before, Terry lives in an apartment with his working mother and younger sister. Despite Terry's father's leaving to play in a country music band, Terry defends him against his mother's criticisms. Home tensions increase when Terry buys a guitar and his mother fears his father's "dreamer" pattern is being repeated. The longest letter, a nine-pager, describes Terry's physical journey to seek out his father and their discovery of each other.

Blood Red Ochre utilizes a pair of fifteen-year-old narrators who alternate chapters in relating two stories, one contemporary, the other historic, which merge at the book's conclusion via time fantasy elements. David, from present day Marten, Newfoundland, is coping with his discovery that the man he calls father is not his birth father; Dauoodaset, a nineteenth-century Beothuk, is struggling with fellow tribe members to survive a harsh winter in an area yet unsettled by whites whose diseases and guns have decimated Newfoundland's indigenous people. Each youth embarks on a journey, one to discover a father; the other to find food to provide a future for his starving people. Each meets disappointment. Uniting the two stories is Nancy/Shanawdithit. To David, Nancy is the school's new, mysterious dark complexioned girl, someone he finds

romantically interesting; to Dauoodaset, Shanawdithit is his future wife and mother to his children. In the book's penultimate chapter, Shanawdithit/Nancy becomes the narrator as David is swept into the past to be present when Dauoodaset is killed on Red Ochre Island by a white settler. Though David's story will hold readers' interest, the tragic tale of Dauoodaset's heroic struggle and Shanawdithit's inability to change the past will grab readers' emotions.

Eating between the Lines, Major's first venture into humour, won him his second Canadian Library Association Book of the Year award. Jackson, sixteen, faces a double-barrelled dose of romance problems. While his parents' marriage has lost its romance, Jackson cannot find any with Sara, the girl of his dreams and fantasies. Informed by his mother that she intends to leave her husband who is mired in a methodical, dull job, Jackson attempts to prevent his parents' separation while simultaneously trying to separate Sara from boyfriend Adam. Jackson unknowingly acquires the magical vehicle for achieving both ends when, as the "028th" customer of "Masterpizza," a restaurant run by an ex-librarian, he receives the grand opening prize, a pizza-shaped gold medal. Later, Jackson accidentally discovers that holding the medal in one hand while making contact with more gold completes a circuit that carries him into the setting and action of whatever he is reading. Jackson's visits into *The Odyssey, The Adventures of Huckleberry Finn, Romeo and Juliet,* plus his mother's journal, ultimately resolve everyone's problems in fun-filled ways.

Diana: My Autobiography, another humorous read, features Major's first female central character, his fictional about-to-enter-junior-high daughter who is obsessed with the Royal Family. Reading Andrew Morton's *Diana: Her True Story* gives Major's Diana the idea of writing her own autobiography. The preteen's overwritten version of her own "true" story is hilarious in its egocentrism. When an English boy, Willard Smith, and his family spend the summer in St. John's, Newfoundland, Diana's overactive imagination leads her to conclude that Will is really disguised royalty and that she, naturally, is to be his future bride. Each chapter consists of two parts: the first, in italics, is the autobiographical entry while the rest of the chapter, in ordinary type, chronicles Diana's everyday life as seen through her royal-coloured glasses.

—David Jenkinson

———

MARK, Jan(et Marjorie, née Brisland). British. Born in Welwyn, Hertfordshire, 22 June 1943. Educated at Ashford Grammar School, Kent, 1954-61; Canterbury College of Art, 1961-65, National Diploma in Design 1965. Married Neil Mark in 1969 (divorced 1989); one daughter and one son. Teacher, Southfields School, Gravesend, Kent, 1965-71. Writer-in-residence, Oxford Polytechnic, 1982-84. Recipient: Penguin/*Guardian* award, 1975, and Library Association Carnegie Medal, 1976, both for *Thunder and Lightnings; The Ennead* was named a Notable Children's Trade Book in the field of social studies by the National Council for Social Studies and the Children's Book Council, 1978; runner-up for Library Association Carnegie Medal, 1981, for *Nothing to Be Afraid Of;* co-winner of Young *Observer*/Rank Teenage Fiction Prize, 1982, for *Aquarius;*

Library Association Carnegie Medal, 1983, for *Handles;* Angel Literary award for fiction, 1983, for *Feet,* and 1987, for *Zeno Was Here;* British nominee for International Hans Christian Andersen Medal, 1984; runner-up for *Guardian* award for Children's Fiction, 1986, for *Trouble Halfway.* Agent: Murray Pollinger, 222 Old Brompton Road, London SW5 OBZ. Address: 98 Howard Street, Oxford OX4 3BG, England.

PUBLICATIONS FOR YOUNG ADULTS

Fiction

Thunder and Lightnings, illustrated by Jim Russell. London, Kestrel, 1976; New York, Crowell, 1979.
Under the Autumn Garden, illustrated by Colin Twinn. London, Kestrel, 1977; New York, Crowell, 1979.
The Ennead. London, Kestrel, and New York, Crowell, 1978.
Divide and Rule. London, Kestrel, 1979; New York, Crowell, 1980.
Aquarius. London, Kestrel, 1982; New York, Atheneum, 1984.
Handles. London, Kestrel, 1983; New York, Atheneum, 1985.
Trouble Half-Way, illustrated by David Parkins. London, Viking Kestrel, 1985; New York, Atheneum, 1986.
At the Sign of the Dog and Rocket. London, Longman, 1985.
Dream House. London, Viking Kestrel, 1987.
Man in Motion, illustrated by Jeff Cummins. London, Viking Kestrel, 1989.
The Hillingdon Fox. Turton and Chambers, 1991.
Great Frog and Mighty Moose. London, Walker, 1992.

Short Stories

Nothing to Be Afraid Of, illustrated by David Parkins. London, Kestrel, 1980; New York, Harper, 1981.
Hairs in the Palm of the Hand, illustrated by Jan Ormerod. London, Kestrel, 1981; as *Bold as Brass,* London, Hutchinson, 1984.
Feet and Other Stories, illustrated by Bert Kitchen. London, Kestrel, 1983.
Frankie's Hat, illustrated by Quentin Blake. London, Viking Kestrel, 1986.
Enough Is Too Much Already and Other Stories. London, Bodley Head, 1988.
A Can of Worms. London, Bodley Head, 1990.
In Black and White. London, Viking, 1991.
They Do Things Differently There. London, Bodley Head, forthcoming.

Plays

Izzy (televised 1983). London, Longman, 1985.
Interference (televised 1986). London, Longman, 1987.
Captain Courage and the Rose Street Gang, with Stephen Cockett. London, Collins, 1987.
Time and the Hour (two plays). London, Longman, 1990.

Other

Editor, *School Stories.* New York, Kingfisher, 1989.
Editor, *The Puffin Book of Song and Dance.* London, Viking, forthcoming.

PUBLICATIONS FOR CHILDREN

The Short Voyage of the Albert Ross, illustrated by Gavin Rowe. London, Granada, 1980.
The Long Distance Poet, illustrated by Steve Smallman. Cambridge, Dinosaur, 1982.
The Dead Letter Box, illustrated by Mary Rayner. London, Hamish Hamilton, 1982.
Fur, illustrated by Charlotte Voake. London, Walker, and New York, Harper, 1986.
Out of the Oven, illustrated by Antony Maitland. London, Viking Kestrel, 1986.
Fun (picture book), illustrated by Michael Foreman. London, Gollancz, 1987.
The Twig Thing, illustrated by Sally Holmes. London, Viking, 1988.
Strat and Chatto (picture book), illustrated by David Hughes. London, Walker, 1989.
Finders, Losers. New York, Orchard, 1990.
The Snow Maze, illustrated by Jan Ormerod. London, Walker, 1992.
All the Kings and Queens, illustrated by Lis Toft. London, Heinemann, 1993.
Fun with Mrs. Thumb (picture book), illustrated by Nicola Bayley. Cambridge, Massachusetts, Candlewick, 1993.
Carrot Tops and Cotton Tails (picture book), illustrated by Tony Ross. New York, Atheneum, 1993.

PUBLICATIONS FOR ADULTS

Novels

Two Stories, illustrated by Clive King. Oxford, Inky Parrot Press, 1984.
Zeno Was Here. London, Cape, and New York, Farrar Straus, 1987.

*

Media Adaptations: *The Dead Letter Box* (cassette), Puffin/Cover to Cover, 1987; *Frankie's Hat, Hairs on the Palm of the Hand,* and *Nothing to Be Afraid Of* (cassettes), Chivers Press, 1987, 1988, and 1989; *Izzy* (television movie), 1983; *Interference* (television movie), 1986; *Handles* (television movie), 1989.

Critical Study: Entry in *Children's Literature Review,* Volume 11, Detroit, Gale, 1986.

*   *   *

Jan Mark's novels and short stories for young adults are notable for unconventional themes and a variety of styles. A prolific author whose work ranges from picture books to adult novels, Mark's writings for young adults contain some of her best work.

The most controversial novels Mark has written comprise an informal trilogy. *The Ennead, Divide and Rule,* and *Aquarius* all consider issues of friendship and betrayal and offer a bleak perspective on how people manipulate each other.

Set in the future, *The Ennead* depicts a society where the primary motivation for action is self-preservation. The desolate planet Erato has solved its unemployment problem by banishing the unproductive. But the arrival of a sculptor unwilling to sacrifice her artistic integrity challenges the prevailing social controls and causes the adolescent protagonist Isaac to reconsider his values.

Divide and Rule explores the repressive aspects of institutional religion. Eighteen-year-old Hanno, a self-proclaimed unbeliever, is nevertheless selected to spend a year as the temple's ritual shepherd. Increasingly horrified by his discoveries about how religious leaders manipulate the gullible population, Hanno finds he cannot outwit those who consistently turn his words and actions against him.

In her third book for young adults, *Aquarius,* Mark deliberately set out to subvert the reader's identification with the main character, Viner. After establishing sympathy for him when he is forced to flee his rain-soaked country for a kingdom paralyzed by drought, Mark reveals Viner as a character with no moral scruples. Viner uses his powers to find water to secure a position of power and supplants the rain-king Morning Light. Unable to express his growing love for the king, he then tricks the king into returning to his water-soaked homeland.

The themes of these books seem to blur the boundaries between writing for young adults and adults. *At the Sign of the Dog and Rocket,* however is clearly written for young adults. It describes a series of misadventures when Lilian Goodwin has to manage the family pub with the help of a student teacher, Tom Collins, whom she had bedeviled when he taught her class. Their wariness and animosity develop into friendship as Tom demonstrates his ability with both customers and Lilian's disobedient younger siblings.

In other novels Mark has experimented with narrative style. *Man in Motion,* for example, records numerous telephone conversations that document the adjustments Lloyd must make following his move from a village to a large city school with a racially diverse population. Lloyd's diminishing conversations with his former friends reveal a divergence of interests and show how people can grow apart. Lloyd's insights into other cultures expand his awareness of different ways of life.

In *The Hillingdon Fox,* Mark includes journal entries of two brothers. In 1990, Hugh Marshall begins a diary on his seventeenth birthday, when Saddam Hussein invades Kuwait. Hugh's observations alternate with excerpts from the journal his older brother Gerald kept in 1982 during the Falklands' war, when Gerald had been eighteen. The commentary on the political situation intertwines with discussions of school and family, and the complex plot lines converge in Gerald's desperate attempts to enlist Hugh in recovering a time capsule that had been buried when Gerald was in school.

While Gerald and Hugh offer two perceptions of the same people at different time periods, *Finders, Losers* includes accounts by six young people whose lives intersect in various ways on a single day. All the characters are connected in some way to Shapton College, where much of the action occurs. However, each person can provide only one interpretation of events, and the reader must figure out how the lives of the people intersect.

In addition to her novels, Mark has written numerous short stories which reveal her facility with humor, her ability to create suspense, and her insights into human relationships. The collection *Enough Is Too Much Already* includes a series of stories told by three friends, Maurice, Nazzer, and Nina. Their re-creation of incidents at school and home contain both humorous anecdotes and wry commentary on their own lives, particularly their ability to draw on the inexhaustible supply of useless information they are amassing in preparation for re-sits of exams. The first and last

stories provide a frame of sorts since both deal with Maurice's failure to meet Nazzer and Nina at a disco as he had promised.

Most of Mark's collections are less interconnected, although the nine stories of *In Black and White* relate thematically since all deal with the supernatural. "Grow Your Own" describes a compost heap that slowly assumes a life of its own while "Birthday Girl" considers the mysterious yearly appearance of a young girl lying underwater in a bathtub. Mark's tales of ghosts and suspense appear in other collections of her own such as "Resurgam" in *A Can of Worms* as well as in anthologies of stories by many authors. For example, *Shades of Dark,* compiled by Aidan Chambers, contains Mark's "The Gnomon," a tale of revenge based on a betrayal of love.

Some of Mark's best short stories take place in school settings. The masterful "Time and the Hour" in *Hairs in the Palm of the Hand* reveals the useless waste of time that occurs during the school day and includes the surprising revelation for students that at least some teachers share their feelings. "The Choice Is Yours" in *Nothing to Be Afraid Of* describes how a student can be part of a senseless power struggle between adults. Play rehearsals provide the setting for "I Was Adored Once Too" in *Feet and Other Stories.* The poignant juxtaposition of lines from the play with contemporary experience reveals the pain of adolescents uncertain about establishing relationships.

Mark's characters gain insights about others in a variety of places besides school. Indeed, many of her stories involve young adults' acquisition of new perspectives about members of their own families. *You're Late, Dad,* an anthology edited by Tony Bradman, contains "Dan, Dan, the Scenery Man." Attending play practice at a community theater, June sees her reserved father as an indispensable part of the theater company. In fact, all the adults appear so far removed from their everyday occupations that June questions what their "real selves" are. "'Acting isn't just pretending, is it?'" she asks her father.

"Frankie's Hat" chronicles Frankie's seventeenth birthday, which is spent in the company of her younger sister Sonia. Freed from home responsibilities, Frankie quickly assumes the carefree behavior of her pre-marriage days only to revert to a more staid personality in the presence of her husband and baby son. The title story in *A Can of Worms* reveals to Dora her respectable grandmother's kleptomania while "Too Old to Rock and Roll" in the same collection explores how Greg's success in overcoming his widowed father's grief produces unexpected results.

Mark punctuates her stories with plot twists and pungent comments on wide-ranging matters from school bullies to slow-witted tourists to snobs preoccupied with social distinctions. Her high levels of invention and productivity assure her a place of continuing importance in contemporary fiction for young adults.

—Kathy Piehl

MARSDEN, John. Australian. Born in Melbourne, Victoria, Australia, 27 September 1950. Educated at Mitchell College, Bathurst, Australia, diploma in teaching, 1978; University of New England, Armidale, Australia, B.A. 1981. English teacher, Geelong Grammar School, Geelong, Victoria, Australia, 1982-90; writer, 1991—. Recipient: Children's Book of the Year award (Australia), 1988,

Premier's award (Victoria), 1988, Young Adult Book award (New South Wales), 1988, Christopher award, 1989, ALA Notable Book, 1989, all for *So Much to Tell You....* Address: Box 139, Newstead, Victoria 3462, Australia.

PUBLICATIONS FOR YOUNG ADULTS

Fiction

So Much to Tell You.... Montville, Queensland, Walter McVitty, 1988; Boston, Little, Brown, 1989.
The Journey. Pan Australia, 1988.
The Great Gatenby. Pan Australia, 1989.
Staying Alive in Year 5. Pan Australia, 1989.
Out of Time. Pan Australia, 1990.
Letters from the Inside. Pan Australia, 1991.
Take My Word for It. Pan Australia, 1992.
Everything I Know About Writing. Heinemann Australia, 1993.
Looking for Trouble. Pan Australia, 1993.
Tomorrow When the War Began. Pan Australia, 1993.

*

John Marsden comments:

My books vary a good deal. Most are contemporary, realistic novels dealing with average Australians—though they're often in extraordinary situations. I try to deal with universal experiences, universal feelings. I try to write with a light touch, so that the books are very readable, but there's usually something serious there for the reader to reflect on, too.

A teenager wrote to me recently saying: "When I read your books I feel that you're reading my mind." I certainly aim for authenticity, so I am pleased to get responses like that.

*   *   *

John Marsden's years of living and teaching in Australia's private schools have given him the capacity to breathe new life into the venerable form of the boarding school story, extending it to encompass much harsher institutions, and an unparalleled ability to render the language of young adult Australians of both sexes. He is acutely aware of their fears, needs, and aspirations, and understands their ambiguous status as people legally little more than children but physically and mentally little less than adults. Until recently Australian authors for young adults have depicted the relatively secure lives of children of the ordinary people highly valued in an aggressively egalitarian society. Marsden's characters, however, are often the daughters and sons of the wealthy; many of them are children of failed or faltering marriages; and some are members of families in which emotional and physical violence have caused enormous damage. Almost all are candid in discussing their sexuality and that of their peers. Marsden frequently requires his readers to piece together a story from hints and implications; he is drawn to the journal and the letter as ways of controlling the release of information while maintaining interest and suspense.

So Much to Tell You...., Marsden's first novel, is ostensibly the private journal of a fourteen-year-old girl who is an elective mute. Eventually the reader can piece together her story: her face has been scarred by acid intended for her mother, thrown by her father after an acrimonious divorce, and she has come to Warrington School as an alternative to entering a psychiatric institution. The device of the journal allows Marsden to reveal information with the tight control of a thriller-writer, and at the same time to describe the intense, shifting alliances of a girls' dormitory group from the viewpoint of a detached observer. Marina's withdrawal slowly alters to a limited trust, and her growing awareness of the loneliness and the difficulties of her peers enables her to understand that she has much in common with others—even with her father.

Underlying *The Journey* is Marsden's interest in rites of passage from adolescence to adulthood. The novel is set in a vaguely European, pre-industrial society which encourages adolescents of both sexes to leave home on a journey of self-discovery and return with seven stories that will, if accepted in their community, admit them to full adult status. Through experiences of sensual, sexual, and psychological awakening the aptly named Argus learns to see truths of value for all young adults: that the outlines of a fulfilling life for all human beings, even the apparently abnormal, are broadly similar, and that human beings and human problems are usually more complex than they at first appear. Despite the importance of its themes, the generality, occasional didacticism, and obvious symbolism of *The Journey* reduce its emotional impact.

The Great Gatenby returns to the world of the boarding school in the wise-cracking, self-opinionated, first-person narrative of Erle Gatenby, whose parents have made some sacrifices to send him to a private school where, they hope, he will find some sense of direction. He does, but not until he has gone through several scrapes with authority in a funny but fairly predictable narrative. Erle learns some self-discipline: he responds to good coaching, and makes something of his swimming prowess; he learns to see his teachers as people; he meets Melanie, and finds that falling in love with her brings him experiences he did not bargain for.

Technically more demanding, *Out of Time* presents brief descriptions of people who seem to have fallen out of existence: missing persons, orphans whose histories are unknown, children whose early deaths have left their siblings without memory of them. Across these meditative flashes Marsden lays a narrative that uses the well-worn device of a time-machine to enable a young adult narrator, psychologically devastated by blame for his sister's death, to return to the past to help others and, eventually, himself. James cannot change events, but he can bring together separated people and can assure himself of the accuracy of his own memory of his sister's last night alive.

In *Letters from the Inside* Marsden gives new life to the old form of the epistolary novel, exploiting his ear for the language of young Australians and the intimacy of personal letters in a story that questions the comfortable belief that Australian society is relatively free from violence. An advertisement for a pen-pal brings together what appear to be two young women from middle-class households until inconsistencies in one girl's letters provoke questions leading to an admission: Tracey is writing from a penal institution. More than that—she is a leader in its brutal world. Not all of the violence is "inside," however; Mandy's brother is obsessed with firearms and increasingly prone to attack his sister physically. Tracey's tough exterior begins to soften as she finds in Mandy an unsentimental but sympathetic friend whose optimism gives her a reason to rehabilitate herself. But Tracey's long acquaintance with violence also leads her to fear the outcome of Mandy's brother's worsening behaviour. The novel comes to a despairing and controversial end that is all the more chilling because it is implied rather than stated.

Take My Word for It returns to the scene of Marsden's first novel: it is the journal of Lisa, another of the girls in the Warrington dormitory. While Marsden effectively conveys Lisa's enjoyment of physical activity, especially of rowing, and provides a different view of Marina, he is breaking little new technical or thematic ground in this story.

—John Murray

MASON, Bobbie Ann. American. Born in Mayfield, Kentucky, 1 May 1940. Educated at the University of Kentucky, Lexington, 1958-62, B.A. 1962; State University of New York, Binghamton, M.A. 1966; University of Connecticut, Storrs, Ph.D. 1972. Married Roger B. Rawlings in 1969. Writer, Mayfield *Messenger,* Kentucy, 1960; contributor to magazines *Movie Stars, Movie Life,* and *T.V. Star Parade,* 1962-63, Ideal Publishers, New York; Assistant Professor of English, Mansfield State College, Pennsylvania, 1972-79. Recipient: National Book Critics Circle award nomination and American Book award nomination, both 1982, PEN-Faulkner award for fiction nomination and Ernest Hemingway Foundation award, both 1983, all for *Shiloh and Other Stories;* National Endowment for the Arts fellowship, 1983; Pennsylvania Arts Council grant, 1983, 1989; Guggenheim fellowship, 1984; American Academy and Institute for Arts and Letters award, 1984. Agent: Amanda Urban, International Creative Management, 40 West 57th Street, New York, NY 10019. Address: c/o HarperCollins, 10 East 53rd Street, New York, NY 10022, U.S.A.

PUBLICATIONS

Novels

In Country. New York, Harper, 1985; London, Chatto and Windus, 1986.
Spence + Lila. New York, Harper, 1988; London, Chatto and Windus, 1989.
Feather Crowns. New York, Harper, and London, Chatto and Windus, 1993.

Short Stories

Landscapes, with Martha Bennett. Monterey, Kentucky, Larkspur Press, 1984.
Shiloh and Other Stories. New York, Harper, 1982; London, Chatto and Windus, 1985.
Love Life: Stories. New York, Harper, and London, Chatto and Windus, 1989.

Other

The Girl Sleuth: A Feminist Guide to the Bobbsey Twins, Nancy Drew, and Their Sisters. New York, Feminist Press, 1975.
Nabokov's Garden: A Guide to Ada. Ann Arbor, Michigan, Ardis, 1976.

Also contributor of short stories to awards anthologies, including *Best American Short Stories,* 1981 and 1983, *The Pushcart Prize,* 1983, and *The O. Henry Awards,* 1986 and 1988.

Media Adaptations: *In Country* (film; directed by Norman Jewison), 1989.

Biography: Entry in *Dictionary of Literary Biography Yearbook: 1987,* Detroit, Gale, 1988.

Manuscript Collection: University of Kentucky, Lexington.

Critical Study: Entry in *Contemporary Literary Criticism,* Detroit, Gale, Volume 28, 1984, Volume 43, 1987.

*   *   *

Combining detailed description of everyday western Kentucky life with her characters' uneasy consideration of larger philosophical issues, Bobbie Ann Mason portrays people's search for individual identity in times of social and personal transition. Some, as in her story "Nancy Culpepper," turn to their ancestral past for clues, while others, like nine-year-old Peggy Jo of "Detroit Skyline, 1949" *(Shiloh and Other Stories)* lack the vocabulary to define their concerns for themselves, much less express their conflicts to others.

Mason's stories also emphasize the fragility of modern marriages. Mary Lou and Mack ("The Rookers") find communicating difficult after their youngest daughter leaves for college. Cleo ("Old Things") worries about her daughter's impending divorce. After "The Retreat," Georgeann ends her marriage as unemotionally as she decapitates a sick chicken. Norma Jean ("Shiloh") leaves Leroy when she realizes that the basis for their marriage is merely social conformity. Even Nancy ("Lying Doggo") briefly questions the security of her fifteen-year marriage.

Some of Mason's characters face an uncertain future without the support of tradition. There is no customary Christmas celebration to temper Carolyn's resentment of her constantly bickering family ("Drawing Names"), and her suspicions of her boyfriend's unreliability increase her sense of isolation. For others, however, traditions provide security. When Joe McClain ("Graveyard Day") fulfills his obligation to clean his family's burial plot, he wins the trust of Waldeen Murdock and her daughter, Holly. Tradition has likewise strengthened the Culpeppers' marriage *(Spence + Lila);* not even Lila's life-threatening illnesses can separate them permanently from each other or from their land. Likewise tradition has helped them cope with the divorce of one daughter and the somewhat unorthodox marriage of the other, just as they have adjusted to fast-food restaurants, discount stores, shopping malls, Top-40 radio stations, and the factory where their son now works.

Mason further treats the issues of individual identity and social change in her short-story collection *Love Life.* This volume too contains a coming-of-age story, "State Champions," the first-person narrator's nostalgic account of her schooldays, especially during the Cuba Cubs' remarkable season; however, generally the stories in this volume are darker in tone, and most involve some actual or impending loss. Joann ("Hunktown") must choose between her husband's ambition to be a musician in Nashville and her own desire to keep her job and live on her father's farm. Jeannette ("Big Bertha Stories") must commit her husband to a mental hospital because their son is terrorized by his father's stories, which confuse a strip-mining machine with the war machines in Vietnam. Mental instability also threatens Lynette Johnson ("Coyotes"), who wonders if someday she may repeat her mother's suicide attempt. In the title story, Opal has preserved her equilibrium by avoiding most emotional attachments, but she is distressed to see that same emotional pattern repeated in the life of the one person for whom she feels affection.

Not all losses have been openly acknowledged, though. In "Private Lies" Mickey becomes obsessed with finding the daughter given up for adoption eighteen years ago. After a clandestine affair, Barbara ("The Secret of the Pyramids") must deal secretly with her grief and guilt when her lover dies in a traffic accident. Ruth ("Bumblebees") refuses to grieve openly for her husband and daughter, killed in a car wreck. The alternating voices of mother and daughter ("Marita") also deny any loss as they react to Marita's pregnancy and subsequent abortion.

In Country, Mason's first novel, addresses the concerns of young adult readers, exploring questions of personal identity and family relationships. After high school graduation, seventeen-year-old Samantha ("Sam") Hughes attempts to make sense of her past so she can determine her future. Her mother, Irene—recently remarried and living in Lexington—wants Sam to enroll at the University of Kentucky in the fall, but Sam is contemptuous of her stepfather and resentful of what she considers her mother's abandonment. Thus, she insists she will live in Hopewell, commute to nearby Murray State University, and continue to assume responsibility for her mother's brother, Emmett, a psychologically disabled Vietnam veteran. Through Emmett, Sam meets other Vietnam veterans, and in each she searches for hints of her father's identity. She also examines her father's pictures and letters, but until she reads his long-ignored personal journal, Sam sees no link between her idealistic soldier father and the cynical veterans she knows.

Disillusioned by knowledge of her father, Sam further breaks with the past, initially deciding to deny her paternity by severing all ties with the Hughes family. Sam finds she cannot escape the past, however, until she can accept the flaws in both her biological father, Dwayne, and her surrogate father, Emmett. Understanding requires symbolic reenactment, and finally a healing pilgrimage to the Vietnam Memorial in Washington, D.C.

—Charmaine Allmon Mosby

MATHABANE, Mark. South African. Born in Alexandra, South Africa, 1960. Educated at Limestone College, 1978; St. Louis University, 1979; and Quincy College, 1981; Dowling College, B.A. 1983; Columbia University, 1984. Married Gail Ernsberger in 1987. Free-lance lecturer and writer, since 1985. Recipient: Christopher award, 1986, for *Kaffir Boy.* Agent: Fifi Oscard Agency, 19 West 44th Street, New York, NY 10036. Address: 341 Barrington Park Ln., Kernersville, NC 27284, U.S.A.

PUBLICATIONS FOR YOUNG ADULTS

Nonfiction

Kaffir Boy: The True Story of a Black Youth's Coming of Age in Apartheid South Africa. New York, Macmillan, 1986; as *Kaffir Boy: Growing out of Apartheid.* London, Bodley Head, 1987.
Kaffir Boy in America: An Encounter with Apartheid. New York, Scribner, 1989.

Love in Black and White: The Triumph of Love over Prejudice and Taboo, with Gail Mathabane. New York, HarperCollins, 1992.

*

Media Adaptations: *Kaffir Boy* (cassette), Dove Books on Tape, 1988.

*   *   *

South African writer Mark Mathabane's life is the subject of his writing. Though still in his early thirties, he has already written three volumes of autobiography: *Kaffir Boy, Kaffir Boy in America,* and *Love in Black and White* (co-authored with his wife, Gail Mathabane). Together the books document his unlikely and inspiring journey from hungry, hopeless, suicidal child to articulate, confident, successful adult. Each volume portrays a particular era in his life and is distinguished by unique experiences and feelings. Significant people and themes promote unity throughout the series. Foremost are Mathabane's family and American tennis stars Arthur Ashe and Stan Smith; Ashe provides inspiration by example, as tennis player and as human rights activist, while Smith and his wife provide financial and emotional support and a "home away from home" in the United States. These relationships reinforce two central themes: the importance of the family unit and the need to respect individuals regardless of race.

Although written for an adult audience, Mathabane's books nonetheless offer valuable historical and cultural information as well as inspiration to young adults. Determined and courageous, Mathabane has repeatedly refused to be intimidated when the odds are against him. From the anonymous squalor of his black South African childhood to his very public life as a best-selling author in America, Mathabane documents reality as he lives it.

In *Kaffir Boy in America,* Mathabane describes his "momentous discovery" of Richard Wright's *Black Boy,* which led him to become a writer: "I mentally replaced 'white south' with 'white South Africa' and 'nigger' with 'Kaffir' [Arabic for 'infidel'; a derogatory term for blacks] and was intrigued by how Richard Wright's feelings mirrored my own." Overwhelmed by the experience, Mathabane went on to read Malcolm X, Claude Brown, Maya Angelou, and every other black writer he could find.

Parallels with *Black Boy* are apparent in the title of *Kaffir Boy* and in many of its themes: the violence of life in the ghetto, fear and anger at whites, conflict between father and son, love of books, education as an escape, and the determination to succeed. The first and most emotionally powerful of Mathabane's books, *Kaffir Boy* portrays unflinchingly the brutality of his childhood in the black shantytown of Alexandra, just ten miles north of Johannesburg. A harrowing early scene finds five-year-old Johannes (he later changed his name to Mark), awakened in darkness from his "bed of cardboard, under the kitchen table." Soon, he is wetting his ragged shorts in terror as his mother, who lacks the "right" papers, flees a police raid, leaving him in charge of two younger siblings. Johannes's nightmare continues as the police reappear the following night, arresting and humiliating his father and other half-naked adults while their children watch in shame and fear. Later scenes depict more raids, murders, robberies, trips to the dump for food, childhood prostitution, and other events so painful that at age ten Johannes contemplates suicide. But his mother never gives up hope, and she inspires him as well. His grandmother, too, encourages Mathabane and brings him books from her white employers.

Despite his father's objections, much red tape, and enormous financial sacrifice, Mathabane's mother sends him to school, after a white nun helps obtain the right papers. He excels at school, and later at tennis, winning a scholarship to an American college. *Kaffir Boy* ends as he heads for the airport to "follow destiny" to America— the promised land.

Kaffir Boy in America documents Mathabane's gradual adjustment to life in a less idealized America. Equally direct but less powerful than *Kaffir Boy,* this volume is more exploratory than explosive. In it, Mathabane struggles to find himself and his place in the world. Caught between fears for his family in South Africa and the desire to succeed in America, Mathabane moves from college to college, attending four before deciding to stop fleeing and "confront [his] fate." He becomes a student leader, a speaker about South Africa, a graduate student, and ultimately a writer. Along the way, he considers both black and white racism and other social problems, offering fresh insights into an America he has come to know well. He also marries Gail Ernsberger, a white American writer, and brings his siblings to the United States to be educated when the success of *Kaffir Boy* makes this financially possible.

Love in Black and White continues the story of Mark and Gail Mathabane with warmth and candor. In alternating chapters, the authors describe the development of their relationship, sometimes recounting the same events from two perspectives. They address honestly their personal doubts and fears and the continuing societal reaction to them as a biracial couple. Mostly personal narrative, the book also includes some analysis of race relations and interracial marriage in the United States and South Africa. It ends on a note of hope for their biracial children and for the world.

Throughout his work, Mathabane offers young adults the opportunity to see victims of injustice overcome pain and regain their human dignity. He also invites readers to join the struggle for justice to which he has dedicated his life. In the concluding lines of *Love in Black and White,* the Mathabanes suggest that, "Racism is essentially a problem of the heart.... If in our hearts we truly accept one another as fellow human beings, many of our intractable problems would have solutions, and there would be no limit to the good we could do in making our world a better place for all." Using his own life as example, Mark Mathabane offers evidence and insight into major problems besetting today's world, but he also demonstrates an unwavering belief in the resilience of the human spirit. This is a message young adults cannot hear too often.

—Lois Rauch Gibson

———

MATHIS, Sharon Bell. American. Born in Atlantic City, New Jersey, 26 February 1937. Educated at Morgan State College (now Morgan State University), Baltimore, B.A. in sociology (magna cum laude) 1958; D. C. Teachers College; Catholic University of America, Washington, D.C., M.Sc. in library science 1975. Married Leroy Franklin Mathis in 1957 (divorced, 1979); three daughters. Interviewer, Children's Hospital of District of Columbia, 1958-59; teacher, Holy Redeemer Elementary School, Washington, D.C., 1959-65; special education teacher, Bertie Backus Junior High School, 1965-66, Charles Hart Junior High School, 1966-72, and Stuart Junior High School, 1972-75, all in Washington, D.C. Author of children's books; librarian, Benning Elementary School, Washington, D.C., librarian, 1975-76; library media specialist, Friendship Education Center (now called the Patricia Roberts Harris Edu-

cational Center), Washington, D.C., library media specialist, since 1976. Writer-in-residence, Howard University, Washington, D.C., 1972-74. Writer in charge of children's literature division, Washington, D.C., Black Writers Workshop, 1970-73. Member of board of advisers, Lawyers Committee of District of Columbia Commission on the Arts, 1972-73; member of Black Women's Community Development Foundation, 1973-74. Recipient: award for a children's book manuscript, Council on Interracial Books for Children, 1969, and chosen one of Child Study Association of America's Children's Books of the Year, 1971, both for *Sidewalk Story;* Bread Loaf Writers Conference Fellow, 1970; *Teacup Full of Roses* was chosen one of Child Study Association of America's Children's Books of the Year, one of *New York Times'* Best Books of the Year, and one of the American Library Association's (ALA) Best Young Adult Books, all 1972, and Coretta Scott King award, runner-up, 1973; Coretta Scott King award, 1974, for *Ray Charles; Listen for the Fig Tree* was selected one of ALA's Best Young Adult Books, 1974; *Boston Globe-Horn Book* Honor Book for Text, one of Child Study Association of America's Children's Books of the Year, Notable Children's Trade Book in the Field of Social Studies, National Council of Social Studies and the Children's Book Council, and one of the *New York Times'* Outstanding Books, all 1975, and Newbery Honor Book, 1976, all for *The Hundred Penny Box;* Arts and Humanities award, Club Twenty, 1975; District of Columbia Association of School Librarians award, 1976; Arts and Humanities award, Archdiocese of Washington, D.C., 1978; MacDowell fellowship, 1978; Wallace Johnson Memorial award, 1984, for "Outstanding Contributions to the Literary Arts"; Arts and Letters award, Boys and Girls Clubs of Greater Washington, 1984; Arts and Letters award, Delta Sigma Theta Sorority, 1985; Outstanding Writer award, Writing-to-Read Program, D.C. Public Schools, 1986. Agent: Marilyn Marlow, Curtis Brown Ltd., 10 Astor Place, New York, NY 10003. Address: P.O. Box 44714, Fort Washington, MD 20744, U.S.A.

PUBLICATIONS FOR YOUNG ADULTS

Fiction

Brooklyn Story, illustrated by Charles Bible. New York, Hill & Wang, 1970.
Teacup Full of Roses. New York, Viking, 1972.
Listen for the Fig Tree. New York, Viking, 1974.

Other

Ray Charles, illustrated by George Ford. New York, Crowell, 1973.
Cartwheels. New York, Scholastic, 1977.
Red Dog, Blue Fly: Football Poems. New York, Viking, 1991.

PUBLICATIONS FOR CHILDREN

Fiction

Sidewalk Story, illustrated by Leo Carty. New York, Viking, 1971.
The Hundred Penny Box, illustrated by Leo and Diane Dillon. New York, Viking, 1975.

Work included in anthology *Night Comes Softly: Anthology of Black Female Voices,* edited by Nikki Giovanni.

Media Adaptations: *Teacup Full of Roses* (record; cassette), Live Oak Media, 1977; *The Hundred Penny Box* (cassette; record; filmstrip), Random House.

Biography: Entry in *Dictionary of Literary Biography,* Volume 33: *Afro-American Fiction Writers after 1955,* Detroit, Gale, 1984; essay in *Something about the Author Autobiography Series,* Volume 3, Detroit, Gale, 1987; essay in *Speaking for Ourselves: Autobiographical Sketches by Notable Authors of Books for Young Adults,* Volume 1, compiled and edited by Donald R. Gallo, National Council of Teachers of English, 1990.

Critical Study: Entry in *Children's Literature Review,* Volume 3, Detroit, Gale, 1978.

*　　*　　*

Sharon Bell Mathis is a novelist, poet, and biographer. In her work she celebrates black children, teenagers, and black families. Her style is clear and crisp, and her message is one of strength, of triumph over adversity, of joy in living.

Although many of her books are for younger children, including her biography *Ray Charles* and her poetry, *Brooklyn Story* was to be "a high-interest, low-vocabulary novel for teenagers with reading deficiencies," written in the aftermath of the assassination of Martin Luther King, Jr., and dealing with responses to love and death. Published in 1970 after the success of her children's book *Sidewalk Story,* it led the way to other books for young adults.

Teacup Full of Roses, an ALA Notable Book, was praised by critics as a tribute not only to black youth, but to all youth of any race, and that the truths it related about a black world could be just as true for any other ethnic-American group. Seventeen-year-old Joe is the mainstay of a brilliant younger brother, an older brother on drugs, a disabled father, and a blindly devoted mother. How he deals with this responsibility is eloquently told, underscoring the values of hard work, education, and the hope for a better life, even as the story line leads to the inevitably tragic end.

In her second ALA Notable Book, *Listen for the Fig Tree,* Mathis portrays a blind teenager, Muffin, who must also contend with an alcoholic mother and the memory of her father's murder the Christmas before. Her determination to attend the Kwanza celebration, symbolizing black pride, is realized through the combination of her own prodigious efforts and the help of good neighbors, including one who is a homosexual.

Three girls in *Cartwheels* vie for the fifty-dollar prize in a gymnastic competition. The ensuing events reveal the aspirations and frustrations of each but conclude satisfactorily for all three, although only one wins the award.

Mathis is a black author who cares about black young people and the black community. She treats both with great dignity and good humor. She is a joyous writer, and her characters are spirited and competent.

—Mary Lystad

———

MAYNE, William (James Carter). Has also written as Martin Cobalt; Dynely James; Charles Molin. British. Born in Kingston upon Hull, Yorkshire, 16 March 1928. Educated at the Cathedral Choir School, Canterbury, 1937-42. Writer of children's books; lecturer, Deakin University, Geelong, Victoria, 1976, 1977; Fellow in Creative Writing, Rolle College, Exmouth, Devon, 1979-80. Recipient: Carnegie Medal from British Library Association for best children's book of year, 1957, for *A Grass Rope; Boston Globe-Horn Book* Honor award, 1989, for *Gideon Ahoy;* Phoenix award honor, 1991, for *A Game of Dark.* Agent: David Higham Associates Ltd., 5-8 Lower John St., Golden Square, London W1R 4HA, England.

PUBLICATIONS FOR YOUNG ADULTS

Novels

Follow the Footprints, illustrated by Shirley Hughes. London, Oxford University Press, 1953.
The World Upside Down, illustrated by Shirley Hughes. London, Oxford University Press, 1954.
A Swarm in May, illustrated by C. Walter Hodges. London, Oxford University Press, 1955; Indianapolis, Bobbs-Merrill, 1957.
Choristers' Cake, illustrated by C. Walter Hodges. London, Oxford University Press, 1956; Indianapolis, Bobbs-Merrill, 1958.
The Member of the Marsh, illustrated by Lynton Lamb. London, Oxford University Press, 1956.
The Blue Boat, illustrated by Geraldine Spence. London, Oxford University Press, 1957; New York, Dutton, 1960.
A Grass Rope, illustrated by Lynton Lamb. London, Oxford University Press, 1957; New York, Dutton, 1962.
The Long Night, illustrated by D.J. Watkins-Pitchford. London, Blackwell, 1957.
Underground Alley, illustrated by Marcia Lane Foster. London, Oxford University Press, 1958; New York, Dutton, 1961.
The Gobbling Billy (as Dynely James), with R.D. Caesar. London, Gollancz, and New York, Dutton, 1959; by William Mayne and Dick Caesar, Leicester, Brockhampton Press, 1969.
The Thumbstick, illustrated by Tessa Theobald. London, Oxford University Press, 1959.
Cathedral Wednesday, illustrated by C. Walter Hodges. London, Oxford University Press, 1960.
The Fishing Party, illustrated by Christopher Brooker. London, Hamish Hamilton, 1960.
The Rolling Season, illustrated by Christopher Brooker. London, Oxford University Press, 1960.
Thirteen O'Clock, illustrated by D.J. Watkins-Pitchford. Oxford, Blackwell, 1960.
The Changeling, illustrated by Victor Adams. London, Oxford University Press, 1961; New York, Dutton, 1963.
The Glass Ball, illustrated by Janet Duchesne. London, Hamish Hamilton, 1961; New York, Dutton, 1962.
Summer Visitors, illustrated by William Stobbs. London, Oxford University Press, 1961.
The Last Bus, illustrated by Margery Gill. London, Hamish Hamilton, 1962.
The Twelve Dancers, illustrated by Lynton Lamb. London, Hamish Hamilton, 1962.
The Man from the North Pole, illustrated by Prudence Seward. London, Hamish Hamilton, 1963.

On the Stepping Stones, illustrated by Prudence Seward. London, Hamish Hamilton, 1963.

A Parcel of Trees, illustrated by Margery Gill. London, Penguin, 1963.

Plot Night, illustrated by Janet Duchesne. London, Hamish Hamilton, 1963; New York, Dutton, 1968.

Words and Music, illustrated by Lynton Lamb. London, Hamish Hamilton, 1963.

A Day without Wind, illustrated by Margery Gill. London, Hamish Hamilton, and New York, Dutton, 1964.

Sand, illustrated by Margery Gill. London, Hamish Hamilton, 1964; New York, Dutton, 1965.

Water Boatman, illustrated by Anne Linton. London, Hamish Hamilton, 1964.

Whistling Rufus, illustrated by Raymond Briggs. London, Hamish Hamilton, 1964; New York, Dutton, 1965.

The Big Wheel and the Little Wheel, illustrated by Janet Duchesne. London, Hamish Hamilton, 1965.

Pig in the Middle, illustrated by Mary Russon. London, Hamish Hamilton, 1965; New York, Dutton, 1966.

Dormouse Tales (The Lost Thimble, The Steam Roller, The Picnic, The Football, The Tea Party) (as Charles Molin), illustrated by Leslie Wood. London, Hamish Hamilton, 5 vols., 1966.

Earthfasts. London, Hamish Hamilton, 1966; New York, Dutton, 1967.

The Old Zion, illustrated by Margery Gill. London, Hamish Hamilton, 1966; New York, Dutton, 1967.

Rooftops, illustrated by Mary Russon. London, Hamish Hamilton, 1966.

The Battlefield, illustrated by Mary Russon. London, Hamish Hamilton, and New York, Dutton, 1967.

The Big Egg, illustrated by Margery Gill. London, Hamish Hamilton, 1967.

The House on Fairmont, illustrated by Fritz Wegner. London, Hamish Hamilton, and New York, Dutton, 1968.

Over the Hills and Far Away. London, Hamish Hamilton, 1968; as *The Hill Road,* New York, Dutton, 1969.

The Toffee Join, illustrated by Shirley Hughes. London, Hamish Hamilton, 1968.

The Yellow Aeroplane, illustrated by Trevor Stubley. London, Hamish Hamilton, 1968; Nashville, Nelson, 1974.

Ravensgill. London, Hamish Hamilton, and New York, Dutton, 1970.

A Game of Dark. London, Hamish Hamilton, and New York, Dutton, 1971.

Royal Harry. London, Hamish Hamilton, 1971; New York, Dutton, 1972.

The Incline. London, Hamish Hamilton, and New York, Dutton, 1972.

Skiffy, illustrated by Nicholas Fisk. London, Hamish Hamilton, 1972.

The Swallows (as Martin Cobalt). London, Heinemann, 1972; as *Pool of Swallows,* Nashville, Nelson, 1974.

The Jersey Shore. London, Hamish Hamilton, and New York, Dutton, 1973.

A Year and a Day, illustrated by Krystyna Turska. London, Hamish Hamilton, and New York, Dutton, 1976.

It. London, Hamish Hamilton, 1977; New York, Greenwillow, 1978.

Max's Dream, illustrated by Laszlo Acs. London, Hamish Hamilton, and New York, Greenwillow Books, 1977.

Party Pants, illustrated by Joanna Stubbs. London, Knight, 1977.

While the Bells Ring, illustrated by Janet Rawlins. London, Hamish Hamilton, 1979.

The Mouse and the Egg, illustrated by Krystyna Turska. London, MacRae, 1980; New York, Greenwillow Books, 1981.

Salt River Times, illustrated by Elizabeth Honey. Melbourne, Nelson, and London, Hamish Hamilton, 1980; New York, Greenwillow Books, 1980.

The Patchwork Cat, illustrated by Nicola Bayley. London, Cape, and New York, Knopf, 1981.

All the King's Men. London, Cape, 1982; New York, Delacorte, 1988.

Skiffy and the Twin Planets. London, Hamish Hamilton, 1982.

Winter Quarters. London, Cape, 1982.

The Mouldy, illustrated by Nicola Bayley. London, Cape, and New York, Random House, 1983.

A Small Pudding for Wee Gowrie, illustrated by Martin Cottam. London, Macmillan, 1983.

Underground Creatures. London, Hamish Hamilton, 1983.

Drift. London, Cape, 1985; New York, Delacorte, 1986.

Animal Library (Come, Come to My Corner, Corbie, Tibber, Barnabas Walks, Lamb Shenkin, A House in Town, Leapfrog, Mousewing), illustrated by Kenneth Lilly, Peter Visscher, Martin Baynton, Jonathan Heale, Barbara Firth, and Sarah Fox-Davies. London, Walker, 8 vols., 1986-87; first 3 vols. published Englewood Cliffs, New Jersey, Prentice-Hall, 1987.

The Blemyahs, illustrated by Juan Wijngaard. London, Walker, 1987.

Gideon Ahoy! London, Viking Kestrel, 1987; New York, Delacorte, 1989.

Kelpie. London, Cape, 1987.

Tiger's Railway, illustrated by Juan Wijngaard. London, Walker, 1987.

The Farm that Ran Out of Names. London, Cape, 1989.

Antar and the Eagles. New York, Doubleday, 1990.

Low Tide. New York, Delacorte, 1993.

Other

Editor, with Eleanor Farjeon, *The Hamish Hamilton Book of Kings,* illustrated by Victor Ambrus. London, Hamish Hamilton, 1964; as *A Cavalcade of Kings,* New York, Walck, 1965.

Editor, with Eleanor Farjeon, *The Hamish Hamilton Book of Queens,* illustrated by Victor Ambrus. London, Hamish Hamilton, 1964; as *A Cavalcade Queens,* New York, Walck, 1965.

Editor (as Charles Molin), *Ghosts, Spooks, Spectres.* London, Hamish Hamilton, 1967; New York, David White, 1968.

Editor, *The Hamish Hamilton Book of Heroes,* illustrated by Krystyna Turska. London, Hamish Hamilton, 1967; as *William Mayne's Book of Heroes,* New York, Dutton, 1968.

Editor, *The Hamish Hamilton Book of Giants,* illustrated by Raymond Briggs. London, Hamish Hamilton, 1968; as *William Mayne's Book of Giants,* New York, Dutton, 1969.

Editor, *Ghosts.* London, Hamish Hamilton, and New York, Nelson, 1971.

Composer, music for *Holly from the Bongs,* by Alan Garner, 1965.

PUBLICATIONS FOR CHILDREN

Fiction

No More School, illustrated by Peter Warner. London, Hamish Hamilton, 1965.

Robin's Real Engine, illustrated by Mary Dinsdale. London, Hamish Hamilton, 1972.
Hob Stories (Red Book, Green Book, Yellow Book, Blue Book), illustrated by Patrick Benson. London, Walker, and New York, Philomel, 4 vols., 1984.

*

Biography: Essay in *Something about the Author Autobiography Series,* Volume 11, Detroit, Gale, 1991; entry in *Third Book of Junior Authors,* New York, H.W. Wilson, 1972.

Critical Study: Entry in *Contemporary Literary Criticism,* Volume 12, Detroit, Gale, 1979.

*   *   *

William Mayne has been extraordinarily prolific and has won many literary prizes; at the same time, he is an example of the kind of writer who is much admired by reviewers and librarians but ignored or even disliked by young adults. His work is difficult to tie-down, because he has written, using several pen names, for a range of age-groups in very different styles and genres. Early in his career Mayne was most at home with stories set in the Yorkshire Dales where he lives, effectively meshing realism and fantasy, but he has recently widened his settings to include America, New Zealand, and an anonymous Balkan country. He repeatedly writes of young people undertaking demanding tasks, and has written, particularly in the seventies and beyond, a number of unusual and challenging novels for young adults. The best of these are demanding and oblique, and can be read in more than one way.

Two of Mayne's earliest novels are powerful naturalistic stories set in a remote, rugged countryside marked with the decaying remains of nineteenth century industrialisation. One of Mayne's chief strengths has always been his ability to realise places, seasons, and weather vividly and to charge them with feeling. Both stories deal with passionate emotions: thwarted love, anger and jealousy, and tensions between the generations and between the sexes. In both, young people find that uncovering the truth is harder and more hazardous than it seems. In *Ravensgill* the young members of two village families try to probe the origins of a feud still bitterly kept alive by their grandparents. *The Incline* is set in a community whose livelihood is the slate quarry and where tensions arise when workers are laid off after an accident with the machinery.

Perhaps the greatest critical disagreement concerning Mayne has been prompted by *A Game of Dark,* a Freudian allegory about David Jackson, an introverted young man, overconscious of his own thoughts and feelings, grappling with the inability to love his dying father, who is emotionally and physically crippled. David's guilt and sexual fears are increased by his uneasy relationship with his mother, who is also his teacher at school. The fantasy world into which David retreats is a chivalric community threatened by a marauding worm. In this domain, the trendy vicar and father-substitute "becomes one" with the chivalric lord and features of the worm are associated with David's father. There is also an emotional complexity about the inglorious killing of the worm, symbolically linked as it is to David's father's death. In a strange way, David is left "consolate," but his sudden discovery that he is now able to love his father seems contrived rather than growing out of what has gone before.

A critically popular novel, *The Jersey Shore* essentially consists of two long journeys (each "lasted all night and all day") that frame the long central reminiscences of a grandfather talking to a small boy as they sit beside the sea in New Jersey. The novel can be read as a subtle exploration of memory and history, of family and race, in which Arthur is "growing his own history." Readers, like Arthur, have to piece together the real story from the dense cross-references and the insistent parallels between past and present. In the conclusion, a grown-up Arthur's return to the Norfolk from which his grandfather came repeats the pattern of love and freeing from slavery about which he has been learning.

There are weaknesses in parts of Mayne's extensive work. Some reviewers complain of the lack of narrative drive and coherence. Story lines can be contorted with contrived endings, and at times Mayne deliberately but implausibly withholds significant information, like the revelation that Grandma Florence in *The Jersey Shore* was black. At its best, Mayne's style is direct, using short sentences powerfully and conveying experiences or his characters' perceptions in clear images. At other times his writing can be mannered, whimsical, or oversophisticated, and the dialogue can seem not just quirky but unconvincing, like the pidgin put into the mouths of the Indian characters in *Drift* or the attempt at Welsh styles in *The Farm that Ran Out of Names.* Mayne expects his readers to construct knowledge and understanding from elliptical hints and vivid images. One repeated theme in his work is the need to find language with which to realise an undefined awareness, to cope with experience. In *A Game of Dark* Donald begins with "no throat to speak of and nothing to say." Rafe Considine in *Drift* discovers that he has "forgotten how to speak," and events force him to learn a new attitude to language. Most challengingly of all, *Gideon Ahoy!* centres on a deaf, brain-damaged teenager who cannot speak except in unintelligible sounds, but whose development is sensitively charted. In his best work, Mayne triumphantly solves the major technical problems he sets himself and thoroughly deserves his reputation.

—Robert Protherough

———

MAZER, Harry. American. Born in New York City, 31 May 1925. Educated at Union College, Schenectady, New York, B.A. 1948; Syracuse University, New York, M.A. 1960. Served in the U.S. Army Air Forces, 1943-45; became sergeant; received Purple Heart and Air Medal with four bronze oak leaf clusters. Married Norma Fox in 1950; three daughters and one son. New York Central, railroad brake man and switchtender, 1950-55; New York Construction, Syracuse, New York, sheet metal worker, 1957-59; Central Square School, Central Square, New York, teacher of English, 1959-60; Aerofin Corp., Syracuse, New York, welder, 1960-63; full-time writer, since 1963. Recipient: American Library Association (ALA) Best of the Best Books list, 1970-73, for *Snowbound;* Kirkus Choice list, 1974, for *The Dollar Man;* (with Norma Fox Mazer) ALA Best Books for Young Adults list, 1977, and International Reading Association-Children's Book Council Children's Choice, 1978, both for *The Solid Gold Kid;* ALA Best Books for Young Adults list, and Dorothy Canfield Fisher Children's Book award nomination, both 1979, both for *The War on Villa Street; New York Times* Best Books of the Year list, 1979, New York Public Library Books for the Teen

Age list, 1980, ALA Best Books for Young Adults list, 1981, and ALA Best of the Best Books list, 1970-83, all for *The Last Mission; Booklist* Contemporary Classics list, 1984, and German "Preis der Lesseratten," both for *Snowbound;* Arizona Young Readers award nomination, 1985, for *The Island Keeper;* ALA Best Books for Young Adults list, 1986, for *I Love You, Stupid!;* New York Library Books for the Teen Age list, 1986, and International Reading Association-Children's Book Council Young Adult Choice list, 1987, both for *Hey Kid! Does She Love Me?;* ALA Best Books for Young Adults list, 1987, Iowa Teen award Master list, 1988, and West Australian Young Reader's Book award, 1989, all for *When the Phone Rang;* ALA Best Books for Young Adults list, ALA Books for Young Adult Reluctant Readers list, 1988, and New York Public Library Books for the Teen Age list, 1988, all for *The Girl of His Dreams;* (with Norma Fox Mazer) New York Public Library Books for the Teen Age list, 1989, for *Heartbeat;* ALA Books for Young Adult Reluctant Readers list, 1989, for *City Light.* Agent: Marilyn Marlow, Curtis Brown Ltd., 10 Astor Pl., New York, NY 10003. Address: 330 3rd Ave., New York, NY 10010, U.S.A.

PUBLICATIONS FOR YOUNG ADULTS

Novels

Guy Lenny. New York, Delacorte, 1971.
Snow Bound. New York, Delacorte, 1973.
The Dollar Man. New York, Delacorte, 1974.
The Solid Gold Kid, with Norma Fox Mazer. New York, Delacorte, 1977.
The War on Villa Street. New York, Delacorte, 1978.
The Last Mission. New York, Delacorte, 1979.
The Island Keeper: A Tale of Courage and Survival. New York, Delacorte, 1981.
I Love You, Stupid! New York, Crowell Junior Books, 1981.
Hey Kid! Does She Love Me? New York, Crowell Junior Books, 1985.
When the Phone Rang. New York, Scholastic, Inc., 1985.
Cave under the City. New York, Crowell Junior Books, 1986.
The Girl of His Dreams. New York, Crowell Junior Books, 1987.
City Light. New York, Scholastic, Inc., 1988.
Heartbeat, with Norma Fox Mazer. New York, Bantam, 1989.
Someone's Mother Is Missing. New York, Delacorte, 1990.
Bright Days, Stupid Nights, with Norma Fox Mazer. New York, Bantam, 1992.

*

Media Adaptations: *Snowbound* ("After School Special") National Broadcasting Company, 1978; *Snowbound* (audiocassette), Listening Library, 1985; *The Last Mission* (audiocassette), Listening Library, 1985.

Biography: Essay in *Authors and Artists for Young Adults,* Volume 5, Detroit, Gale, 1990; essay in *Speaking for Ourselves: Autobiographical Sketches by Notable Authors of Books for Young Adults,* Volume 1, compiled and edited by Donald R. Gallo, National Council of Teachers of English, 1990; essay in *Something about the Author Autobiography Series,* Volume 11, Detroit, Gale, 1991.

Critical Study: Entry in *Children's Literature Review,* Volume 16, Detroit, Gale, 1989.

*   *   *

Harry Mazer writes fast-paced novels about young people coping with ordinary daily hassles and extraordinary life-threatening problems. Despite their predicaments, Mazer's protagonists usually emerge morally victorious as the following examples will show.

Snow Bound is a story of survival in a treacherous snowstorm, not unusual in upstate New York. Tony Laporte, age fifteen, leads an easy life because his parents want him to have all the things they didn't have. When his parents refuse to let him keep the stray dog he brings home with him, Tony decides to teach them a lesson by running off in his mother's old car. In the middle of a tremendous snowstorm, he picks up Cindy Reichart, who is hitchhiking home because she needs freedom after a weekend of being cooped up at her grandmother's house. Tony tries to impress Cindy by showing off his driving skills, only to end up wrecking the car in a desolate area far from the main highway. The two spend the first days bickering with each other and waiting to be rescued. When help doesn't come, they realize they must cooperate in order to survive. Snowbound, they are faced with starvation, frost bite, wild dogs, and broken limbs. In the process of finding a way out of the wilderness, they become caring and supportive of one another, developing a friendship likely to endure after their eleven-day ordeal.

The Dollar Man is about Marcus Rosenbloom, an overweight thirteen-year-old who dreams he is Marcus the Magnificent, the Great Invisible Man. In his invisible dream, Marcus is transformed from a fat, clumsy boy to a lean, athletic young man like his father, the father he has never seen except in dreams. Marcus lives with his feisty, unmarried, working mother on the east side of New York. When his mother refuses to tell him anything about his father, Marcus rejects her and hangs out with older boys who experiment with drugs and alcohol. He is expelled from school, charged with smoking marijuana on school grounds. It is his friends rather than he who were doing the smoking, but they neither own up to their offense nor stand up for him. Despondent, Marcus determines to find his father and live a new, better life with him. He finds his father, who is worth many dollars, and the confrontation between the two allows him to learn much about his father and about himself.

The War on Villa Street is about a boy growing up in New York City, with a passive mother and an alcoholic father. Willis Pierce and his family are always moving because of his father's alcoholic behavior, and Willis is always an outsider. On the street, in school, in the grocery store, he has to guard against a snub or negative remark. Willis sticks to himself, minds his own business—for him it's the only way—however, gradually, Willis's closed-off world falls apart. His father beats him up one Friday night in a fit of anger; the gang on Villa Street are out to get him. Willis challenges one of the gang members in a running race on Field Day, but his father, drunk and disorderly, comes to Field Day and Willis loses. Ashamed, Willis takes his father home where his father beats him. Willis turns on his father, punching him again and again, fighting for his life, then runs terrified from his apartment. Eventually he does return, finds a way to be free of his father, and to reach out to persons his own age for companionship and comfort.

Cave under the City is set during the 1930s in the heart of the Depression, and yet it seems a story of today when homelessness in many big cities is a major social problem. Tolley Holtz and his younger, dyslexic brother live with their parents in New York City. More and more people are out of work, and when their father can't find work anymore, he leaves for Baltimore to find a job. The mother becomes ill, collapses, and is taken by ambulance from work to a hospital. The hospital calls the apartment building to say that their mother wants the boys to go to their grandmother's, but Tolley and Bubber go, only to find their grandmother gravely ill. They return to their house, buy food on credit, try to survive. They also write their father to come home. When they decide to visit their mother at the hospital, the social service department steps in and tries to place the boys in a children's center, but Tolley resists, and the children run away. They live in an abandoned cellar with no lights, no windows, and call it a cave. They suffer hunger and starvation, wanting and smelling food, drinking lots of water. They steal food and milk, though they dislike doing so. Finally their father comes home and they go back to their apartment, back to school, and Tolley starts making money to repay the grocer.

Harry Mazer has also written books with his wife, Norma Fox Mazer. *The Solid Gold Kid,* one of their collaborations, is a striking thriller involving the kidnapping of a millionaire's son—swift-moving, vibrant, believable.

Mazer's forte is the emotional turmoil, the humor and pain of adolescent years. His characters are resilient and strong. His endings emphasize compassion, understanding, resourcefulness, and honesty.

—Mary Lystad

———

MAZER, Norma Fox. American. Born in New York City, 15 May 1931. Educated at Antioch College, Yellow Springs, Ohio, 1949-50; Syracuse University, New York, 1957-59. Married Harry Mazer in 1950; three daughters and one son. Writer, since 1964. Worked as a secretary at a radio station, punch press operator, waitress, and cashier. Recipient: National Book award nomination, 1973, for *A Figure of Speech;* Lewis Carroll Shelf award, University of Wisconsin, 1975, for *Saturday the Twelfth of October;* Christopher award, *New York Times* Outstanding Books of the Year list, *School Library Journal* Best Books of the Year list, American Library Association (ALA) Best Books for Young Adults list, ALA Notable Book, Lewis Carroll Shelf award, all 1976, all for *Dear Bill, Remember Me? and Other Stories;* (with Harry Mazer) ALA Best Books for Young Adults list, 1977, and Children's Book Council-International Reading Association Children's Choice, 1978, both for *The Solid Gold Kid;* ALA Best Books for Young Adults list, 1979, *School Library Journal* Best Books of the Year list, 1979, and ALA Best of the Best Books 1970-83 list, all for *Up in Seth's Room;* Austrian Children's Books list of honor, and German Children's Literature prize, both 1982, both for *Mrs. Fish, Ape, and Me, the Dump Queen;* Edgar award, Mystery Writers of America, 1982, and California Young Readers Medal, 1985, both for *Taking Terri Mueller;* ALA Best Books for Young Adults list, 1983, for *Someone to Love;* ALA Best Books for Young Adults list, *New York Times* Outstanding Books of the Year list, and New York Public Library Books for the Teenage list, all 1984, all for *Downtown;* Iowa Teen award, 1985-86, for *When We First Met;* Children's Book Council-International Reading Association Children's Choice, 1986, for *A, My Name Is Ami;* Newbery Honor

Book, *School Library Journal* Best Books of the Year list, ALA Notable Book, ALA Best Books for Young Adults list, Canadian Children's Books Council Choice, *Horn Book* Fanfare Book, and Association of Booksellers for Children Choice, all 1988, all for *After the Rain;* ALA Best Books for Young Adults list, 1989, Iowa Teen award, 1990, and New York Public Library Books for the Teenage list, all for *Silver;* (with Harry Mazer) Children's Book Council-International Reading Association Children's Choice, and New York Public Library Books for the Teen Age list, both 1989, both for *Heartbeat;* New York Public Library Books for the Teenage list, 1989 and 1990, both for *Waltzing on Water;* American Bookseller's Pick of the Lists, and New York Public Library Books for the Teenage list, both 1990, both for *Babyface.* Agent: Elaine Markson, 44 Greenwich Avenue, New York, NY 10012. Address: 330 3rd Ave., New York, NY 10010, U.S.A.

PUBLICATIONS FOR YOUNG ADULTS

Fiction

I, Trissy. New York, Delacorte, 1971.
A Figure of Speech. New York, Delacorte, 1973.
Saturday, the Twelfth of October. New York, Delacorte, 1975.
Dear Bill, Remember Me? and Other Stories. New York, Delacorte, 1976.
The Solid Gold Kid, with Harry Mazer. New York, Delacorte, 1977.
Up in Seth's Room. New York, Delacorte, 1979.
Mrs. Fish, Ape, and Me, the Dump Queen. New York, Dutton, 1980.
Taking Terri Mueller. New York, Avon, 1981; London, Methuen, 1988.
Summer Girls, Love Boys, and Other Short Stories. New York, Delacorte, 1982.
When We First Met. New York, Four Winds. 1982.
Someone to Love. New York, Delacorte, 1983.
Downtown. New York, Morrow, 1984.
Supergirl (novelization of screenplay). New York, Warner Books, and London, Severn House, 1984.
A, My Name Is Ami. New York, Scholastic, Inc., 1986; as *A for Ami,* London, Penguin, 1988.
Three Sisters. New York, Scholastic, Inc., 1986.
After the Rain. New York, Morrow, 1987; London, Macmillan, 1988.
B, My Name Is Bunny. New York, Scholastic, Inc., 1987; as *A Name Like Bunny.* London, Penguin, 1988.
Silver. New York, Morrow, 1988.
Heartbeat, with Harry Mazer. New York, Bantam, 1989.
Babyface. New York, Morrow, 1990.
C, My Name Is Cal. New York, Scholastic, Inc., 1990.
D, My Name Is Danita. New York, Scholastic, Inc., 1991.
E, My Name Is Emily. New York, Scholastic, Inc., 1991.
Out of Control. New York, Morrow, 1993.

Other

Editor, with Margery Lewis, *Waltzing on Water: Poetry by Women.* New York, Dell, 1989.

Contributor to *Sixteen: Short Stories by Outstanding Writers for Young Adults,* edited by Donald R. Gallo, New York, Delacorte, 1984; *Short Takes: A Short Story Collection for Young Readers,* edited by Elizabeth Segal, New York, Lothrop, 1986; and *Visions: Nineteen Short Stories by Outstanding Writers for Young Adults,* edited by Gallo, New York, Delacorte, 1987.

*

Media Adaptations: *When We First Met* (film), Home Box Office, 1984; *Taking Terri Mueller* (audiocassette), Listening Library, 1986; *Dear Bill Remember Me? and Other Stories* (audiocassette), Listening Library, 1987; *After the Rain* (audiocassette), Listening Library, 1988.

Biography: Essay in *Something about the Author Autobiography Series,* Volume 1, Detroit, Gale, 1986; essay in *Authors and Artists for Young Adults,* Volume 5, Detroit, Gale, 1990; entry in *Fifth Book of Junior Authors and Illustrators,* New York, H.W. Wilson, 1983.

Critical Study: Entry in *Contemporary Literary Criticism,* Volume 26, Detroit, Gale, 1983.

*   *   *

Norma Fox Mazer has written a number of highly acclaimed books for young adults. Her main characters are young people on the verge of adulthood, struggling with self-image and interest in the opposite sex. Some lead ordinary lives; some have to face enormous social problems, such as drunken driving, teenage sex, discrimination against the poor and handicapped, and care of the elderly. Mazer's characters are not all admirable, but they are believable and provide insight into why people behave the way they do. Because of her strong characterizations, Mazer is one of the most widely read writers for young adults today.

Up in Seth's Room is about an adolescent boy and girl who fall in love, with the boy demanding an active sexual relationship and the girl refusing because she wants to wait until she is older. Seth persists. "If at first you don't succeed...that's the male creed," he tells her. The girl, Finn, holds firm. And they find they can remain friends, good friends.

Mrs. Fish, Ape, and Me, the Dump Queen is about people who are on the fringe of society. Mrs. Fish is a middle-aged spinster and cleaning woman; Ape is an older bachelor who runs the town dump; and Me, the dump queen, is an orphan adolescent, ridiculed by her peers and desperate for affection. Eventually these three come together as a family unit; they are not your stereotypical family, but they are a functioning one, providing love and comfort to one another.

Taking Terri Mueller won the Edgar Allan Poe award for Best Juvenile Mystery in 1981. It is about a father who kidnaps his daughter in the aftermath of divorce. The father is afraid that he would never see his daughter again and that a stepfather would take his place in her affections. The father is forced to move a lot with his child—to big cities like New York and Chicago, to small towns such as Hap Falls and Amberville—to avoid being discovered. Father and daughter have a warm and caring relationship, but as the child becomes a teenager, she wonders about the mother she has been told died in a car accident when the daughter was four. What was her mother like? The father refuses to discuss her, and there are no pictures. Finally the child realizes that something in his story is wrong. She asks questions and she demands answers. As thirteen-year-old Terri struggles to find out about the mother she doesn't remember, and to figure out the father she has always loved, she

solves the mystery. But then she finds herself torn between father and mother. The child's bewilderment and anger are real, but her choices for the remainder of her life, though difficult, are now hers to make.

In *When We First Met,* Jenny Pennoyer falls in love with the son of the drunken driver who killed her older sister. Emotions of hatred, guilt, forgiveness, and caring are expressed. Relationships are complex, often explosive, and they ring true.

After the Rain is a stunning portrait of two human beings, a grandfather and a granddaughter, who begin to take walks together every afternoon when the grandfather's health is not such that he can safely go out alone anymore. For fifteen-year-old Rachel these after-school visits begin as a duty, but in time they become a source of comfort, growth, and strength.

Norma Fox Mazer has written several books with her husband, Harry Mazer. *Heartbeat* is about teenage friendship, romance, and death, bringing together the joys and sorrows, fun, and frustrations of growing up. This novel, too, is fast-paced, moving, and believable.

Mazer's descriptive ability is excellent. The reader is able to see vividly what her characters look like, what their physical environment consists of, and most importantly, how they feel about themselves and others. In addition to addressing their responses to social problems and adversity, Mazer tackles ordinary concerns of teenagers. What's life all about? Supposing I don't get married, then what do I do? Will I be able to earn my keep? What do I do besides work? Will I even grow up before the world blows up? And if so, do I want to? Do I want to be old? Why did that boy or girl walk past me in the hall without speaking today? What should I wear to school tomorrow? Mazer tackles these issues with concern, understanding, and humor.

—Mary Lystad

———

McCAFFREY, Anne (Inez). American. Born in Cambridge, Massachusetts, 1 April 1926. Educated at Stuart Hall, Staunton, Virginia; Montclair High School, New Jersey; Radcliffe College, Cambridge, Massachusetts, B.A. (cum laude) in Slavonic languages and literature 1947; studied meteorology at City of Dublin University; also studied voice for nine years. Married E. Wright Johnson in 1950 (divorced 1970); two sons and one daughter. Copywriter and layout designer, Liberty Music Shops, New York, 1948-50; copywriter, Helena Rubinstein, New York, 1950-52. Currently runs a thoroughbred horse stud farm in Ireland; since 1978, director, Dragonhold Ltd., and since 1979, director, Fin Film Productions. Has performed in and directed several operas and musical comedies in Wilmington and Greenville, Delaware. Secretary-Treasurer, Science Fiction Writers of America, 1968-70. Recipient: Hugo award for best novella, World Science Fiction Society, 1968, for "Weyr Search"; Nebula award for best novella, Science Fiction Writers of America, 1969, for "Dragonrider"; E.E. Smith award for fantasy, 1975; American Library Association notable book citations, 1976, for *Dragonsong,* and 1977, for *Dragonsinger; Horn Book* Fanfare Citation, 1977, for *Dragonsong;* Hugo award, Ditmar award, Gandalf award, and Eurocon/Streso award, all 1979, all for *The White Dragon;* Balrog citation, 1980, for *Dragondrums;* Golden Pen award, 1981; Science Fiction Book Club award, 1986, for

Killashandra, 1989, for *Dragonsdawn,* and 1990, for *The Renegades of Pern,* and *The Rowan.* Agent: Virginia Kidd, P.O. Box 278, Milford, PA 18337. Address: Dragonhold, Kilquade, Greystones, Ireland.

PUBLICATIONS FOR ADULTS AND YOUNG ADULTS

Novels

Restoree. New York, Ballantine, 1967; London, Rapp and Whiting, 1968.

Dragonflight. New York, Ballantine, 1968; London, Rapp and Whiting, 1969.

Decision at Doona. New York, Ballantine, 1969; London, Rapp and Whiting, 1970.

The Ship Who Sang. New York, Walker, 1969; London, Rapp and Whiting, 1971.

The Mark of Merlin. New York, Dell, 1971; London, Millington, 1979.

The Ring of Fear. New York, Dell, 1971; London, Millington, 1979.

Dragonquest: Being the Further Adventures of the Dragonriders of Pern. New York, Ballantine, 1971; London, Rapp and Whiting-Deutsch, 1973.

To Ride Pegasus. New York, Ballantine, 1973; London, Dent, 1974.

The Kilternan Legacy. New York, Dell, 1975; London, Millington, 1976.

Dragonsong. New York, Atheneum, and London, Sidgwick and Jackson, 1976.

Dragonsinger. New York, Atheneum, and London, Sidgwick and Jackson, 1977.

Dinosaur Planet. London, Futura, 1977; New York, Ballantine, 1978.

The Dragonriders of Pern. New York, Doubleday, 1978.

The White Dragon. New York, Ballantine, 1978; London, Sidgwick and Jackson, 1979.

Dragondrums. New York, Atheneum, and London, Sidgwick and Jackson, 1979.

The Harper Hall of Pern. New York, Doubleday, 1979.

Crystal Singer. New York, Ballantine, and London, Severn House, 1982.

The Coelura. Columbia, Pennsylvania, Underwood Miller, 1983; with *Nerilka's Story,* London, Bantam, 1987.

Moreta: Dragonlady of Pern. New York, Ballantine, and London, Severn House, 1983.

Dinosaur Planet Survivors. New York, Ballantine, and London, Futura, 1984.

Stitch in Snow. Columbia, Pennsylvania, Underwood Miller, 1984.

The Girl Who Heard Dragons. New Castle, Virginia, Cheap Street, 1985.

The Ireta Adventure (includes *Dinosaur Planet* and *Dinosaur Planet Survivors*). New York, Doubleday, 1985.

Killashandra. New York, Ballantine, 1985; London, Bantam, 1986.

Nerilka's Story. New York, Ballantine, 1986; with *The Coelura,* London, Bantam, 1987.

Habit Is an Old Horse. Seattle, Dryad Press, 1986.

The Year of the Lucy. New York, Tor, 1986; London, Corgi, 1987.

The Lady. New York, Ballantine, 1987; as *The Carradyne Touch,* London, Macdonald, 1988.

Dragonsdawn. New York, Del Rey, 1988; London, Bantam, 1989.

The Renegades of Pern. New York, Ballantine, 1989; London, Bantam, 1990.

The Death of Sleep, with Jody Lynn Nye. New York, Baen, 1990.

Pegasus in Flight. New York, Ballantine, and London, Bantam, 1990.

The Rowan. New York, Ace, and London, Bantam, 1990.

Sassinak, with Elizabeth Moon. New York, Baen, 1990.

Three Gothic Novels (includes *The Mark of Merlin, The Ring of Fear,* and *The Kilternan Legacy*). Columbia, Pennsylvania, Underwood Miller, 1990; as *Three Women,* New York, Tor, 1990.

All the Weyrs of Pern. New York, Ballantine, 1991.

Damia. New York, Putnam, 1991.

Generation Warriors, with Elizabeth Moon. New York, Baen, 1991.

Crisis on Doona, wth Jody Lynn Nye. New York, Ace, 1992.

Crystal Line. New York, Ballantine, 1992.

The Partnered Ship, with Margaret Ball. New York, Ace, 1992.

Powers That Be, with Elizabeth Ann Scarborough. New York, Ballantine, 1992.

The Ship Who Searched. New York, Simon and Schuster, 1992.

Damia's Children. New York, Putnam, 1993.

Short Stories

A Time When, Being a Tale of Young Lord Jaxom, His White Dragon, Ruth, and Various Fire-Lizards. Cambridge, Massachusetts, NESFA Press, 1975.

Get off the Unicorn. New York, Ballantine, 1977; London, Corgi, 1979.

The Worlds of Anne McCaffrey. London, Deutsch, 1981.

Other

Editor, *Alchemy and Academe: A Collection of Original Stories Concerning Themselves with Transmutations, Mental and Elemental, Alchemical and Academic.* New York, Doubleday, 1970.

Editor, *Cooking out of This World.* New York, Ballantine, 1973.

The People of Pern, with Robin Wood. Norfolk, Virginia, Donning, 1988.

The Dragonlover's Guide to Pern, with Jody Lynn Nye. New York, Ballantine, 1989.

Contributor to anthologies, including *Infinity One,* 1970, *Future Love,* 1977, and *Once Upon a Time,* 1991, and to magazines, including *Analog, Galaxy,* and *Magazine of Fantasy and Science Fiction.*

*

Media Adaptations: *Dragonsong* and *Dragonsinger* have been adapted as children's stage plays by Irene Elliott and produced in Baltimore, Maryland; the "Pern" books have also inspired a cassette of music, *Dragonsongs,* a board game, and two computer games. *The White Dragon, Moreta, Dragonlady of Pern, Nerilka's Story,* and *The Rowan* are all available on cassette.

Biography: Entry in *Dictionary of Literary Biography,* Volume 8, Detroit, Gale, 1981; essay in *Speaking for Ourselves: Autobiographical Sketches by Notable Authors of Books for Young Adults,* Volume 1, compiled and edited by Donald R. Gallo, National Council of Teachers of English, 1990; essay in *Authors and Artists for Young Adults,* Volume 6, Detroit, Gale, 1991; essay in *Something about the Author Autobiography Series,* Volume 11, Detroit, Gale, 1991.

Bibliography: *Leigh Brackett, Marion Zimmer Bradley, Anne McCaffrey: A Primary and Secondary Bibliography* by Rosemarie Arbur, Boston, Hall, 1982; *Anne McCaffrey: A Reader's Guide* by Mary T. Brizzi, Mercer Island, Washington, Starmont, 1986.

Manuscript Collection: Syracuse University, New York; Kerlan Collection, University of Minnesota, Minneapolis.

Critical Study: Entry in *Contemporary Literary Criticism,* Volume 17, Detroit, Gale, 1981.

*   *   *

Anne McCaffrey is a prolific writer in the field of young adult fiction. Her well-loved works include science fiction and fantasy, as well as adult romances.

Her most widely known books are the "Dragonriders of Pern" series, and the "Harper Hall" trilogy, both set on the planet of Pern. Pern is a male-dominated feudal society, menaced by the space-born Thread, a deadly spore that consumes all organic matter. The only thing standing between Thread and the people are the dragonriders, men bound for life to the telepathic, fire-breathing dragons.

The first two books in the "Dragonrider" trilogy, *Dragonflight* and *Dragonquest,* deal with the efforts and politics of Pern's protectors and people. In *Dragonflight,* Lessa, the heir to Ruatha Hold, watches as her parents are killed, and pursues their killer. Having succeeded, she searches for something to fill the void her victory has left, and becomes the female leader of Benden Weyr, the pre-eminent dragon home. *Dragonquest* shows the conflict between old ways and new, as the dragonriders, who Lessa has brought two hundred years forward into their future, try to force an evolved society back into the old mold. The third book in the trilogy, *The White Dragon,* showcases a minor character from the previous works, and follows the maturing and coming-of-age of Jaxom and his unusual white dragon, Ruth.

The dragon books tend to lean heavily on the theme of heroism, since the dragonriders are indeed Pern's heroes. McCaffrey tends to emphasize that the reason her characters cannot reach a goal is not a flaw in their personalities, but in their circumstances. With the dragons, McCaffrey speaks to teenagers who have ever longed for a friend who will instantly know their hurts and unhappiness, and always be there. McCaffrey depicts her dragons as large, gentle children, totally devoted to their riders, and the dragons bring both humor and life to the stories, as well as the necessary touch of the fantastic.

The "Harper Hall" trilogy is similar to the "Dragonriders" in that the first two books follow a theme, and the third explores a supporting character's life. *Dragonsong* and *Dragonsinger* tell the story of Menolly, a girl who wants to be a Harper more than anything in the world. Menolly achieves her goal, becoming Pern's first female Harper against all odds. *Dragondrums* tells the story of Menolly's best friend, Piemur, an apprentice who can't seem to find his place. Both Menolly and Piemur are engaging, generously drawn characters who evoke a genuine desire to read more about them. Unfortunately, in later books, McCaffrey uses them as background characters, and loses the depth of personality she achieved in the "Harper Hall" trilogy.

McCaffrey's later "Pern" books, among them *Moreta: Dragonlady of Pern, Nerilka's Story, Dragonsdawn, Renegades of Pern,* and *All the Weyrs of Pern,* seem rushed in both tone and style as compared to the first books. Characters who were rich in nuance become the cardboard versions of themselves, lacking the originality of detail that made them so well-loved in the first books. The later books are more devoted to science than to storytelling, and the lack of attention is felt.

Moreta and *Nerilka's Story* tell the story of a flu epidemic striking Pern. With the dragonriders ill, there is no one to repel the attacking Thread, and Pern's Healers race to discover the long-lost medical techniques that will combat the plague. *Moreta* has an unhappy ending, the heroine dying as she completes her task of vaccine delivery. *Nerilka's Story* was designed to be an ancillary tale, answering the questions left unresolved in *Moreta. Moreta*'s characters, while well-written, lack sympathy, and *Nerilka*'s are primarily stiff and dull.

The Rowan and *Damia* are books about a technological space-going society that relies on telekinetics and telepathies to support technology. These psychics are the defense of their solar system, as well as the freight-handling workhorses. *The Rowan* and *Damia* deal with a mother and daughter's search for love among equals, when they have none.

Occupying the same universe are McCaffrey's hugely popular "Ship Who Sang" series, including books co-written with Mercedes Lackey and Margaret Ball. The "Ship" books follow the lives of shell persons, crippled men and women who choose to give up their useless bodies and run ships and installations with their minds, and their "brawns," the mobile people chosen to aid them. The "Ship" protagonists are all female, and their brawns are all male. Eventually, like most of McCaffrey's works, there is a happy ending, in which brawn and shell person find love in spite of the physical barriers.

McCaffrey's writing on the whole is entertaining and crisp, with attention paid to the details of anything new to the reader. Her people tend to be superpersons in her early books, capable of anything through perseverance and natural gifts. In later books, she permits her characters to flesh out more and have flaws. In several of her books, difficult topics such as death and rape are glossed over, concealed by delicate wording, so only careful and aware reading indicates the underlying action. Many of her scientific conclusions have little base in current science, but in spite of her technical flaws, McCaffrey still writes compelling fantasy enjoyable for all ages.

—Melanie Belviso

———

McCAUGHREAN, Geraldine (née Jones). British. Born in Enfield, Middlesex, 6 June 1951. Educated at Enfield County Grammar School for Girls, 1963-69; Southgate Technical College, Middlesex, 1969-70; Christ Church College of Education, Canterbury, Kent, 1973-77, B.Ed. (honours) 1977. Married John McCaughrean in 1988. Secretary, Thames Television, London, 1970-73; secretary, 1977, and sub-editor, 1978-79 and 1983-88, Marshall Cavendish, publishers, London; editorial assistant, Rothmans, Ware, Hertfordshire, 1980-82; editor, Banbury *Focus,* Oxfordshire, 1982. Recipient: All-London Literary Competition, 1979, for short story "The Pike"; Whitbread award, 1987; Library Association Carnegie

Medal, and *Guardian* award, both 1989, both for *A Pack of Lies.*
Agent: Giles Gordon, Anthony Sheil Associates, 43 Doughty Street,
London WC1N 2LF. Address: 3 Melton Drive, Didcot, Oxfordshire
OX11 7JP, England.

PUBLICATIONS FOR YOUNG ADULTS

Fiction

A Little Lower Than the Angels. Oxford, Oxford University Press,
1987.
A Pack of Lies. Oxford, Oxford University Press, 1988; New York,
Oxford University Press, 1989.
Fires' Astonishment. London, Minerva, 1991.
Vainglory. London, Cape, 1991.
Gold Dust. Forthcoming.
Heart's Blood. Forthcoming.

Other (retellings)

1001 Arabian Nights, illustrated by Stephen Lavis. Oxford, Oxford
Unversity Press, 1982.
The Canterbury Tales, illustrated by Victor Ambrus. Oxford, Ox-
ford University Press, 1984; Chicago, Rand McNally, 1985.
Translator, *Who's That Knocking on My Door?,* by Michel Tilde.
Oxford, Oxford University Press, 1986.
The Story of Noah. Dorking, Surrey, Templar, 1987.
The Story of Christmas. Dorking, Surrey, Templar, 1988.
El Cid. Oxford, Oxford University Press, 1989.
Translator, *The Snow Country Prince.* New York, Knopf, 1991.
Translator, *The Cherry Tree,* illustrated by Geraldine McCaughrean.
New York, Knopf, 1992.
The Orchard Book of Greek Myths. New York, Orchard, 1992.
Editor, *Greek Myths.* New York, Macmillan, 1993.
Translator, *Over the Deep Blue Sea,* illustrated by Brian Wildsmith.
New York, Knopf, 1993.

PUBLICATIONS FOR CHILDREN

Other

Seaside Adventure, illustrated by Chrissie Wells. London, Hamlyn,
1986.
Tell the Time, with Chrissie Wells, illustrated by Wells. London,
Hamlyn, 1986.
My First Space Pop-up Book, illustrated by Mike Peterkin. New
York, Little Simon, 1989.
Saint George and the Dragon, illustrated by Nicki Palin. New
York, Doubleday, 1989.
My First Earth Pop-up Book, illustrated by Mike Peterkin. New
York, Little Simon, 1990.
Translator, *The Princess and the Moon,* by Daisaku Ikeda. Oxford,
Oxford University Press, and New York, Knopf, 1991.

PUBLICATIONS FOR ADULTS

Novel

The Maypole. London, Secker & Warburg, 1989.

Other (textbooks) as Geraldine Jones

Adventure in New York. London, Oxford University Press, 1979.
Raise the Titanic. Oxford, Oxford University Press, 1980.
Modesty Blaise. Oxford, Oxford University Press, 1981.

*　　*　　*

Geraldine McCaughrean is a writer impossible to categorise in
terms of "age suitability." While the universality of her novels for
the young, *A Little Lower Than the Angels* and *A Pack of Lies,*
brings to mind C. S. Lewis's dictum that a children's story enjoyed
only by children is a bad children's story, one notes too that her
adult work, especially the novel *Vainglory,* is accessible to teenagers with an interest in history and a zest for challenging prose.
Reading McCaughrean reinforces the belief that a good book is for
everyone capable of reading it, regardless of its intended primary
audience.

McCaughrean entered the field of books for young people as a
reteller of tales; her versions of *1001 Arabian Nights* and Chaucer's
The Canterbury Tales first marked her as an exciting new talent, a
writer capable of inspired storytelling. Although she has continued
to work in this field, one feels—since the publication of her novels—that McCaughrean's gift is to some degree wasted on the re-
creation of other writers' material; she has a rare power to evoke
wonderfully imagined worlds of her own.

A Little Lower Than the Angels, McCaughrean's first novel, was
published to immediate acclaim, winning the Whitbread Children's
Novel Award in 1987. Set in medieval England, it tells the story of
golden-haired Gabriel, a stonemason's apprentice who runs away
from his evil master and takes refuge with a troupe of travelling
players; the pageant cart on which they perform biblical plays is a
dominating presence in the story. On one level the book can be read
as an exciting adventure tale, recounting what happens to Gabriel
after he is wheedled into acting the part of an angel by the superficially beneficent playmaster, Garvey, in a wicked confidence trick.
Shunning the friendship of Lucie, who plays Lucifer and seems
devilish to innocent Gabriel, the boy comes very close to believing
that he has miraculous, angelic powers. His rude awakening begins
when his former master, the villainous mason, arrives and allies
himself with Garvey; it is completed when he is confronted by
dying plague victims, desperate for the miracle he cannot perform.
This brilliantly imagined, terrifying episode is the climax of the
story; thereafter Gabriel, facing the truth about Garvey, casts his
lot with Lucie and his daughter Izzie. The story moves towards a
warm, satisfying conclusion—and one of the most moving final
sentences in literature.

A short summary cannot do justice to the texture and variety of
this novel. As well as being a story full of action and dramatic
incident, it is an exploration of good and evil, reality and illusion,
truth and falsehood in relationships. The prose is ravishing, the
dialogue pithy and believable. Images burn themselves into the
reader's mind—the young Gabriel plunging on a rope through the
dusty air of the church, prefiguring other falls; the pageant cart with
its burden of truth and illusion, heaven and hell, lurching over the
rainswept moor; the peacock's feathers brightening the angel's wings.
Like all the best historical novels, *A Little Lower Than the Angels*
convinces by the sheer power of its writing; Geraldine McCaughrean
sustains a richly imagined, consistent world.

The same may be said of *Vainglory,* a long novel published for
adults, but well within the range of a historically-minded teenager.

Set in France during the fifteenth and sixteenth centuries and featuring both historical and fictional characters, it recounts the fortunes of the family de Gloriole, whose passion for their chateau, Gloriole-sur-Sablois in the Loire Valley, poisons their love for one another. Just as the pageant cart played a powerful symbolic role in *A Little Lower Than the Angels,* the chateau, ungrateful recipient of so much ostentatious devotion, haunts *Vainglory* and defines the book's moral thrust. The background is painted in loving, colourful detail, recalling the stylised art of Jean duc de Berry's *Très Riches Heures,* but the characters refuse to be confined in the landscape. Cruel, obsessed, and larger than life, they roam a world where terror and peril are incarnated in birds with curved beaks and creatures with sharp teeth. But the pervading motif of the book is fire, from the ominous pyre that consumed Jeanne d'Arc to a final conflagration brought about by the determination of the last de Gloriole to escape the thrall of the lovely, murderous chateau. *Vainglory* suspends our belief that the past is a foreign country; it is totally credible and underpinned by a deep moral sensibility.

It is proof of Geraldine McCaughrean's versatility that *A Pack of Lies,* winner of the *Guardian* Children's Fiction Award and the Carnegie Medal in 1988, is as different from the aforementioned books as can be imagined. Both a novel and a collection of short stories, *A Pack of Lies* concerns a mysterious young man, MCC Berkshire, who meets Ailsa Povey in a public library and arranges to work unpaid in her mother's unsuccessful antiques shop. There he displays his (and Geraldine McCaughrean's) brilliance as a storyteller, weaving tales around items of stock in which customers have shown—in the main, tepid—interest. So good are the stories that the enthralled customers invariably buy, to the embarrassment of Ailsa and Mrs. Povey, who regard MCC's stories as "a pack of lies." This gleeful, good-humoured tour de force may be read simply for fun: anyone can enjoy a spoof detective story, a "moral tale" in which a repellent Victorian schoolgirl gets a horrible comeuppance, a hilarious Gothic horror story featuring Baron Greefenbludd, the hunchbacked Fowlstrangler and the Reverend Lovegood Divine. But this is really a sophisticated book; the author moves confidently from one country, one period, and one genre to another, and only the well-read will experience the pleasure of its constant literary echoing. The problem posed by the conclusion is a tricky one; MCC Berkshire's "pack of lies" turns out to have been a pack of truth, and his disappearance from the shop forces the Poveys and the reader to consider the complex relationship between the teller of a story and the characters he creates.

Admirers of Geraldine McCaughrean's work will return to books they have already read, and find new riches in them. They will also be hungry for new stories. Taking another brave leap away from familiar ground, McCaughrean, in October 1993, will publish *Gold Dust,* a novel about two children caught up in a rush for gold in modern Brazil. Those who have enjoyed *Vainglory* will await eagerly the 1994 publication of *Heart's Blood,* a "prequel" set in twelfth-century France, the era of the crusaders and troubadours.

—Eileen Dunlop

———

McCULLERS, (Lula) Carson (Smith). American. Born in Columbus, Georgia, 19 February 1917. Educated at Columbia High School, graduated 1933; attended classes at Columbia University, New York, and New York University, 1935-36. Married 1) James Reeves McCullers, Jr., in 1937 (divorced, 1940); 2) remarried McCullers in 1945 (died, 1953). Writer. Recipient: Fiction fellowship, Houghton Mifflin, 1939; Bread Loaf Writers Conference fellowship, 1940; Guggenheim fellow, 1942, 1946; National Institute of Arts and Letters grant in literature, 1943; *Mademoiselle* award, 1948; New York Drama Critics Circle award, two Donaldson awards, and the Theatre Club, Inc. gold medal, all 1950, all for the stage adaptation of *The Member of the Wedding;* prize of the younger generation from German newspaper *Die Welt,* 1965, for *The Heart Is a Lonely Hunter;* University of Mississippi grant, 1966; Henry Bellamann award, 1967. Member, American Academy, 1952. *Died 29 September 1967.*

PUBLICATIONS

Novels

The Heart Is a Lonely Hunter. Boston, Houghton, 1940; London, Cresset Press, 1943.
Reflections in a Golden Eye. Boston, Houghton, 1941; London, Cresset Press, 1942.
The Member of the Wedding. Boston, Houghton, and London, Cresset Press, 1946.
The Ballad of the Sad Cafe: The Novels and Stories of Carson McCullers. Boston, Houghton, 1951; as *The Ballad of the Sad Cafe and Other Stories,* New York, Bantam, 1967; as *The Shorter Novels and Stories of Carson McCullers,* London, Barrie & Jenkins, 1972.
Clock without Hands. Boston, Houghton, and London, Cresset Press, 1961.

Short Stories

The Ballad of the Sad Cafe: The Novels and Stories of Carson McCullers. Boston, Houghton, 1951; London, Cresset Press, 1952; as *Collected Short Stories,* Houghton, 1961; as *The Shorter Novels and Stories of Carson McCullers,* London, Barrie & Jenkins, 1972.
Seven. New York, Bantam, 1954.

Plays

The Member of the Wedding, adaptation of her own novel (produced Philadelphia, 1949; New York, 1950; London, 1957). New York, New Directions, 1951.
The Square Root of Wonderful (produced Princeton, New Jersey, and New York, 1957; London, 1970). Boston, Houghton, 1958; London, Cresset Press, 1958.

Television Plays: *The Invisible Wall,* from her story, "The Sojourner," 1953; *The Sojourner,* from her own story, 1964.

Poetry

The Twisted Trinity, music by David Diamond. Philadelphia, Elkan Vogel, 1946.
Sweet as a Pickle and Clean as a Pig (for children). Boston, Houghton, 1964; London, Cape, 1965.

Other

The Mortgaged Heart: The Previously Uncollected Writings of Carson McCullers, edited by Margarita G. Smith. Boston, Houghton, 1971; London, Barrie & Jenkins, 1972.

*

Media Adaptations: *The Member of the Wedding* (film), Columbia, 1952; *Reflections in a Golden Eye* (film), Seven Arts, 1967; *The Heart Is a Lonely Hunter* (film), Warners-Seven Arts, 1968.

Biography: Entry in *Dictionary of Literary Biography,* Detroit, Gale, Volume 2: *American Novelists Since World War II,* 1978, Volume 7: *Twentieth-Century American Dramatists,* 1981.

Bibliography: *Katherine Anne Porter and Carson McCullers: A Reference Guide* by Robert F. Kiernan, Boston, Hall, 1976; *Carson McCullers: A Descriptive Listing and Annotated Bibliography of Criticism* by Adrian M. Shapiro, Jackson R. Bryer, and Kathleen Field, New York, Garland, 1980.

Manuscript Collection: Humanities Research Center, University of Texas, Austin.

Critical Studies: *Carson McCullers: Her Life and Work* by Oliver Evans, London, Owen, 1965, as *The Ballad of Carson McCullers,* New York, Coward McCann, 1966; *Carson McCullers* by Lawrence Graver, Minneapolis, University of Minnesota Press, 1969; *Carson McCullers* by Dale Edmonds, Austin, Texas, Steck Vaughn, 1969; *The Lonely Hunter: A Biography of Carson McCullers* by Virginia Spencer Carr, New York, Doubleday, 1975, London, Owen, 1977; *Carson McCullers* by Richard M. Cook, New York, Ungar, 1975; *Carson McCullers* by Margaret B. McDowell, Boston, Twayne, 1980; entry in *Contemporary Literary Criticism,* Detroit, Gale, Volume 1, 1973, Volume 4, 1975, Volume 10, 1979, Volume 12, 1980.

* * *

Although Carson McCullers did not consider herself a writer for young adults her fictions provide such notable adolescent heroines that they have become favorites of young readers and a staple of high school and college literature courses. Moreover, the writer, who published her first novel at twenty-three, infused her work with the emotional energy of her own troubled adolescence. In fact, gangling adolescent girls are just some of the misfit characters with whom McCullers peoples her works, making her pictures of kids and teens universally appealing to younger and older readers.

The gawky adolescent in her first novel, *The Heart Is a Lonely Hunter,* is Mick Kelley, whose nickname reveals her ambivalent sexual identity. The Kelley family operates a boarding house in the white working-class section of an unnamed Southern mill city, and the boarders form a group of lonely misfits who often puzzle and frighten the maturing young girl. Mick has matured beyond her twelve years because she is pressed into caring for her younger siblings by her busy, distracted mother. She finds some companionship with her weary, worked-out father, but in her awakening adolescence she adopts a surrogate father in the person of Mr. Singer, a deaf-mute boarder who repairs watches at a local jewelry store.

McCuller's original title for the novel was *The Mute,* since the ironically silent Singer becomes the central symbolic character around whom the other characters orbit. In addition to Mick, they include Biff Brannon, the owner of a nearby café and a childless widower who sees Mick as a surrogate daughter. The town's two intellectuals—Jake Blount, a white radical, and Dr. Copland, a black physician—also regard Singer with sympathy. Both of them believe the mute to be a Jew, which is not the case; in fact, Singer understands little of their intellectual ramblings, nor is he much more concerned with Biff or Mick. Actually he is devoted to another mute who has been institutionalized in a nearby mental hospital. When the friend dies suddenly, Singer commits suicide, leaving the others to puzzle out some meaning for their existence.

Although Mick is only one of the major characters in *The Heart Is a Lonely Hunter,* she remains the most fully developed and least symbolic, but also the most hopeful. With her interests in music and narrative as well as her desire to travel and create, Mick represents something of the author's own adolescence. Similar girls appear in many of McCullers's short fictions including many unpublished stories written before her successful first novel. Her first published story, "Wunderkind," concerns a young musician who is hailed as such by her overbearing mentor, another surrogate father who later abandons her to the confusions of adolescence. Later stories would see the reappearance of this adolescent character as well, often enough as a teenaged boy, though these stories seem less successful as serious literature.

However, the best example of the adolescent remains Frankie Addams, the protagonist of McCullers's novel *The Member of the Wedding.* Several characters in this novel are near analogues of those depicted in *The Heart Is a Lonely Hunter.* The most obvious pairing involves the female adolescents Frankie Addams and Mick Kelley, girls similar in age, appearance, and, to some extent, motivation. Frankie's father recalls Mick's in that both men are ineffective and estranged from their daughters; Frankie's mother is dead, while Mick's, busy caring for her small children and the boarders, was virtually nonexistent. Thus Frankie, like Mick, lacks a primary female role model. Both girls are alienated from other children by differences in age and interests, while they maintain a fitfully meaningful relationship with younger children, especially Mick with Bubber and Frankie with John Henry West. The relationship between Frankie and the family's cook, Berenice Sadie Brown, develops that of Mick and Portia in the earlier novel.

While McCullers used Mick Kelley as this type of symbolic adolescent in her first novel, in *The Member of the Wedding* she concentrates entirely on the adolescent and presents the story more completely and from the girl's point of view. Yet adolescence remains a metaphor and larger issues are present.

As the novel opens, Frankie feels that her recent and rapid growth spurt has made her a real freak, like the tall man in the carnival's Freak House. Frankie's physical maturation has made her unsure of her sexuality, so she is also fascinated by the Half-Man/Half-Woman in the Freak House. Her nickname again proves ambiguous in terms of gender, symbolizing as well her precarious state between childhood and adolescence. Her hair is cropped short, and her summer outfit consists of Boy Scout shorts and a BVD undershirt. In this transitional state, Frankie feels lost; she is not a "member" of anything in her own view.

Of course, she is still a member of her extended family, though she is an only child with a dead mother and a distant father. During the summer, she is part of a surrogate family consisting of Berenice, the family's black cook, and John Henry, her younger cousin. This mundane "family" is not romantic enough for her, however, and she wants to escape the Addams's kitchen to a more glamorous world of wartime adventure and romance. She believes her older brother who is stationed in Alaska has achieved this goal.

When her brother announces his marriage on an upcoming army leave, Frankie becomes fascinated with the idea that she will somehow be a "member of the wedding." Although she is included in the wedding party, the newly wedded couple have no intention of inviting her on their honeymoon. Frankie "throws a fit" of childish anger and later contemplates suicide. The novel's final section serves as a sort of coda, set some three months after the wedding. Frankie is leaving her situation at last; she and her father are moving to a new suburb, leaving behind Berenice, who is too old to move with them, and John Henry, who has died from meningitis in the interim. Her change is symbolized by her name—she prefers to be called Frances now—as well as by her new friendship with her suburban neighbor, Mary Littlejohn.

Critics have disagreed on how ironically McCullers intends her ending, but all agree that it rings true in both realistic and symbolic terms. The writer's fictions accurately depict the desires and disappointments of adolescence, and at the same time she portrays the young adult as an American "everyman" in the tradition of Huck Finn, bewildered by a world of dangerous choices and adult responsibilities. Adolescent characters populate McCullers's fiction from her first story to her final novel and although she did not create these characters for the pleasure of younger readers alone, these intriguing portraits have placed her fictions among the favorites of teenagers and their teachers alike.

—Joseph R. Millichap

McCULLOCH, John Tyler. See **BURROUGHS, Edgar Rice**

McGRAW, Eloise Jarvis. American. Born in Houston, Texas, 9 December 1915. Educated at Claussen High School, Oklahoma City, graduate 1932; Principia College, Elsah, Illinois, B.A. in art 1937; Oklahoma University, Norman, 1938; Colorado University, Boulder, 1939; Museum Art School, Portland, Oregon (now Pacific Northwest College of Art), Portland, Oregon, 1970-78. Married William Corbin McGraw in 1940; one son and one daughter. Instructor in portrait and figure painting, Oklahoma City University, Oklahoma City, 1943-44; writer since 1949; voluntarily corrected and graded English compositions for local district high school, 1961-62; teacher of adult education fiction writing classes, Lewis & Clark College, Portland, 1965-66, and Portland State University, summers, 1970-78; teacher at University of Oregon Haystack conference, manuscript clinic, summers, 1965-67. Has directed juvenile workshops in Portland, Oregon, Seattle, Washington, La Jolla, California, and elsewhere; speaks frequently on writing at schools and literary gatherings. Featured in writers' "Teleconferences," broadcast on educational channels. Recipient: *New York Herald-Tribune* Children's Book Festival named *Crown Fire* an honor book in 1951; *Moccasin Trail* named Newbery Honor Book, 1952; Lewis Carroll Shelf award, 1963; *The Golden Goblet* named Newbery Honor

Book, 1962; William Allen White award nominations, 1973, for *Master Cornhill* and 1983, for *The Money Room;* Mystery Writers of America Edgar Allan Poe award, for best juvenile mystery of the year, 1978, for *A Really Weird Summer;* Mark Twain award, Sequoyah award, and Bluebonnet award nominations, all 1983 for *The Money Room;* Western Writers Golden Spur award nomination, 1983-84, for *Hideaway;* L. Frank Baum Memorial award, with daughter Lauren Lynn McGraw, International Wizard of Oz Club, 1983, for contributions to the Oz saga; Evelyn Sibley Lampman award, Oregon Library Association, 1984, for "significant contribution to children's literature"; Iowa Children's Choice award and Tennessee Volunteer State Book award nominations, and West Virginia Children's Book award, all 1990-91 for *The Seventeenth Swap.* Agent: Curtis Brown Ltd., 10 Astor Pl., New York, NY 10003. Address: 1970 Indian Trail, Lake Oswego, OR 97034 U.S.A.

PUBLICATIONS FOR YOUNG ADULTS

Fiction

Sawdust in His Shoes. New York, Coward McCann, 1950.
Crown Fire. New York, Coward McCann, 1951.
Moccasin Trail. New York, Coward McCann, 1952.
Mara, Daughter of the Nile. New York, Coward McCann, 1953; London, Penguin, 1986.
The Golden Goblet. New York, Coward McCann, 1961; London, Methuen, 1964.
Merry Go Round in Oz, with Lauren Lynn McGraw, illustrated by Dick Martin. Chicago, Reilly & Lee, 1963.
Greensleeves. New York, Harcourt Brace, 1968.
Master Cornhill. New York, Atheneum, 1973; London, Penguin, 1987.
A Really Weird Summer. New York, Atheneum, 1977.
Joel and the Great Merlini, illustrated by Jim Arnosky. New York, Pantheon, 1979.
The Forbidden Fountain of Oz, with Lauren Lynn McGraw, illustrated by Dick Martin. N.p., International Wizard of Oz Club, 1980.
The Money Room. New York, Atheneum, 1981.
Hideaway. New York, Atheneum, 1983.
The Seventeenth Swap. New York, Atheneum, 1986; London, Viking Kestrel, 1988.
The Trouble with Jacob, illustrated by Jon Riley. New York, McElderry, and London, Viking Kestrel, 1988.
The Striped Ships. New York, Macmillan, 1991.
Tangled Webb. New York, McElderry, and Toronto, Maxwell Macmillan Canada, 1993.

Play

Steady, Stephanie. Chicago, Dramatic Publishing, 1961.

PUBLICATIONS FOR ADULTS

Novel

Pharaoh. New York, Coward McCann, 1958.

Other

Techniques of Fiction Writing. Boston, The Writer, 1959.

*

Media Adaptations: *Moccasin Trail* (sound recording and filmstrip), Newbery Award Records, 1973; *The Golden Goblet* (sound recording and filmstrip), Newbery Award Records, 1975.

Biography: Essay in *Something about the Author Autobiography Series,* Volume 6, Detroit, Gale.

Manuscript Collection: University of Oregon Library, Eugene.

*   *   *

With a forty-year writing career and some twenty juvenile titles to her credit, Eloise Jarvis McGraw is a widely respected author of young-adult fiction. As a rule, her novels are carefully and realistically plotted; invariably, a reader is made to care about her sharply drawn and appealing protagonists. At her best, McGraw demands much of the youthful readers she rigorously avoids talking down to, engaging in frequent wordplay, supporting her plots with understated foreshadowing and symbolism.

With the possible exception of McGraw's "Oz tales," her novels are concerned with adolescent loners—characters whose rebelliousness, prejudice, or scant assets block meaningful social interaction and who must learn to fit into their environments, to trust and appreciate other people. While the majority of her novels have male protagonists, four of her best works tell the stories of strong and highly individualized adolescent women: *Mara, Daughter of the Nile; Greensleeves; The Striped Ships;* and *Tangled Webb.*

McGraw's first novel, *Sawdust in His Shoes,* is a kind of *Toby Tyler* in reverse, the story of Joe Lang, a young bareback rider who temporarily leaves the circus and learns trust and lasting confidence from a family on a small farm. Contemporary adolescent readers would likely complain about the novel's occasionally cloying scenes and about its idealized portraits of family life. Nevertheless, the novel remains a moving and rather enchanting portrait of rural America in the early 1900s, as does a subsequent novel, *Crown Fire,* the tale of a quick-tempered young lumberjack/boxer who must learn self-control.

The most satisfying works from the first decade of McGraw's career are her historical novels. Three of these are set in ancient Egypt, providing a convincing glimpse of ancient Egyptian religion and culture: *Mara, Daughter of the Nile; Pharaoh,* sometimes considered an "adult" version of the history forming the basis of *Mara;* and *The Golden Goblet.* The best of these, *Mara,* combines a love story with political intrigue to underscore a young woman's gradual apprehension of her moral responsibility to herself and others. *Moccasin Trail,* set on the eighteenth-century American frontier, shows the struggles of a white youth raised by Indians to reintegrate himself in white society. It includes some of McGraw's finest scenes of daring adventure; its depiction of Indian society, while not always entirely accurate, is surprisingly objective. Nevertheless, the conclusion of the novel (wherein the protagonist throws off his Indian background) is abrupt and unconvincing.

Greensleeves marks a turning point in McGraw's career. Written in first person, set in contemporary America, and covering parts of two years in the life of its protagonist, the novel is the richest, the most immediate, the most "adult" of all McGraw's fiction. Employing as backdrop a mild mystery story where nothing is what it seems, *Greensleeves* is concerned with appearances vs. realities, especially those in the mind of its protagonist, Shannon Lightly. The reader immediately recognizes Shannon as a strong, intelligent, witty and very cosmopolitan eighteen-year-old; Shannon herself, however, is convinced she is gawky and socially inept. Ironically, it is only after she assumes the persona of a gum-popping, heavily mascaraed bimbo named Georgette that Shannon learns to live outside herself, gaining confidence in her ability to make and keep friends, to live a meaningful life. Eventually, she must face the question of her true identity, one apart from "Georgette" or the old Shannon. The delightful plot and characterizations make the novel immensely readable; its central issues—the ramifications of divorce, the changing nature of the modern family, the often agonizing process of self-discovery, the distinctions between sexual attraction and love—provide it with timeless viability.

With the exception of one of her most recent novels, *The Striped Ships,* and her "Oz" stories, McGraw's fiction following *Greensleeves* has been set in contemporary society and has dealt with contemporary issues, particularly the influences of parental separation or divorce on adolescent children. These later novels, beginning with *Master Cornhill,* are about half the length of McGraw's earlier works; their language is simpler; their protagonists are generally twelve or thirteen rather than sixteen or older. While long-time readers of McGraw may miss the relative complexity and stylistic richness of her earlier novels, it is important to recognize that her readership has shifted from older to younger adolescents, the majority of them pre-teens.

The best of these later "contemporary novels" is *A Really Weird Summer* which, despite its innocuous title, is a serious symbolic representation of the psychological impact of parental divorce, together with subsequent familial role shifting, on an oldest child. The novel's protagonist, unable to cope with the new dynamics of his family or the resulting responsibilities that seem to be falling upon him, creates his own "safe" reality in an imaginary world of increasingly vivid and "real" hallucinations. On the point of abandoning himself to his created world, he finally recognizes its danger and pulls back from it, acquiring a maturity that will see him through his real-life challenges.

Other later novels include *Hideaway,* a novel with two adolescent protagonists who help one another understand personal responsibility in the face of nonexistent or unsuitable parental role models; *The Seventeenth Swap,* an entertaining but thematically superficial tale of a boy who "swaps" his way to a gift for a handicapped friend; and *The Money Room* and *The Trouble with Jacob,* lighthearted mysteries concerned with sibling rivalry and the working out of personal identity in single-parent households. In *The Striped Ships,* McGraw returns to historical fiction, recounting the adventures of an eleven-year-old Norman British girl who is separated from her family. Though the novel is intended for a younger audience than McGraw's early novels, it convincingly echoes their contrasting themes of independence and socialization, of reaching outside oneself as the best way to self-discovery.

—Keith Lawrence

McINTYRE, Vonda N(eel). American. Born in Louisville, Kentucky, 28 August 1948. Educated at the University of Washington, Seattle, B.S. in biology 1970, graduate study in genetics, 1970-71. Writer, 1969—. Conference organizer, and riding and writing instructor. Recipient: Nebula award, 1973, for "Of Mist, and Grass, and Sand"; Hugo award and Nebula award, both 1978, both for *Dreamsnake.* Agent: Frances Collin, Literary Agent, 110 West 40th St., New York, NY 10018. Address: P.O. Box 31041, Seattle, WA 98103-1041, U.S.A.

PUBLICATIONS

Novels

The Exile Waiting. New York, Doubleday, 1975; London, Gollancz, 1976.
Dreamsnake. Boston, Houghton Mifflin, and London, Gollancz, 1978.
The Entropy Effect. New York, Pocket Books, and London, Macdonald, 1981.
Star Trek II: The Wrath of Khan (novelization of screenplay). New York, Pocket Books, and London, Futura, 1982.
Superluminal. Boston, Houghton Mifflin, 1983; London, Gollancz, 1984.
Star Trek III: The Search for Spock (novelization of screenplay). New York, Pocket Books, and London, Panther, 1984.
The Bride (novelization of screenplay). New York, Dell, 1985.
Barbary. Boston, Houghton Mifflin, 1986.
Enterprise: The First Adventure. New York, Pocket Books, 1986.
Star Trek IV: The Voyage Home (novelization of screenplay). New York, Pocket Books, 1986; London, Grafton, 1987.
Starfarers, illustrated by Byron Taylor. Norwalk, Connecticut, Easton Press, 1989.
Screwtop, with *The Girl Who Was Plugged In,* by James Tiptree, Jr. New York, Tor Books, 1989.
Transition. Norwalk, Connecticut, Easton Press, 1991.
Metaphase. New York, Bantam, 1992.
Nautilus. New York, Bantam, 1994.

Short Stories

Fireflood and Other Stories. Boston, Houghton Mifflin, 1979; London, Gollancz, 1980.
Contributor, *Lythande,* by Marion Zimmer Bradley (includes novelette "Looking for Satan"). London, Sphere, 1988.

Other

Editor, with Susan Janice Anderson, *Aurora: Beyond Equality.* New York, Fawcett, 1976.
Contributor, *The Crystal Ship: Three Original Novellas of Science Fiction,* edited by Robert Silverberg. Nashville, Tennessee, Nelson, 1976.
Contributor, *Interfaces,* edited by Ursula K. Le Guin and Virginia Kidd. New York, Ace, 1980.

Contributor to science fiction magazines, including *Analog: Science Fiction/Science Fact.* Currently working on novel entitled *Changeling.*

Critical Study: Entry in *Contemporary Literary Criticism,* Volume 18, Detroit, Gale, 1981.

Vonda N. McIntyre comments:

I don't label myself a young adult writer—only a writer. I've written one children's book, *Barbary,* and a novel, *Dreamsnake,* that earned some notice in young adult publications. But *Dreamsnake,* like *Superluminal* and the "Starfarers" quartet *(Starfarers, Transition, Metaphase,* and *Nautilus),* were written as novels for grown-ups. I don't myself believe that young readers would be hurt by reading anything I've ever written, including the scenes dealing directly with sexuality. But others would disagree, so you ought to be aware that you might take some heat, in our increasingly puritanical social climate, for mentioning books in which violence hurts, in which when people die, their deaths affect all the people around them for more than the forty-two minutes of the average TV episode, and in which people who love each other engage in sexual activity and enjoy it. (And in which people sometimes have sex just for fun and aren't punished for it afterwards.)

*   *   *

Nebula and Hugo award winner Vonda N. McIntyre, an astute storyteller who creates possible future worlds that often draw on her scientific background in genetics, is noted for her realistic characters who have believable flaws and strengths. Her short stories and novels most often center on the importance of being responsible for one's own choices and the realization of individual potential through commitment to oneself and others.

When McIntyre began publishing in the early 1970s, she was one of several new female science fiction writers with a strong feminist stance. McIntyre, however, avoids plots centered directly on the inequalities facing women in a society dominated by men. Her more subtle approach demands characters prove themselves in situations where being female is not the main issue—finding a way to live up to their fullest potential is. They may face challenging, repressive circumstances, but those circumstances grow from personal and social situations like those currently confronted in contemporary society. Instead of centering on gender issues, the focus is instead on the strength of mind and spirit necessary to move beyond inhibiting circumstances.

In her early work, McIntyre created young female protagonists who demonstrate the intelligence, ingenuity, and tenacity necessary to meet difficult goals. Characters like Mischa, the mutant telepath who must free herself from a dystopian city on a postholocaust world in McIntyre's first novel, *The Exile Waiting,* and Kylis, a spaceport "rat" serving time doing hard labor in a penal colony on another future world in *Screwtop,* survive on their intelligence and courage. Both learn the importance of commitment to other people—Mischa risks her life to save her tutor and Kylis passes up a chance for freedom because it requires she betray the men with whom she has partnered.

Snake is the healer serving her proving year in the Nebula-winning novelette "Of Mist, and Grass, and Sand" and *Dreamsnake,* the Nebula and Hugo award-winning novel developed from it. Snake becomes McIntyre's prototype female whose dedication to her personal goals in no way diminishes her concern for others. As a healer, Snake uses her knowledge of genetics and molecular biology to manipulate the biochemistry of the genetically altered snakes Mist and Sand so they create venoms which heal. Grass, a rare off-world dreamsnake, produces venom that allows the terminally ill to die peacefully. After a lapse in judgment which results in Grass's death, the grief-stricken Snake must face the realization that without the dreamsnake she cannot function as a healer. She recognizes her responsibility for her failure, but, in *Dreamsnake,* turns her regret and anger to strength as she faces the mental and physical challenges of a quest for a new dreamsnake.

In the course of Snake's journey, McIntyre introduces elements she develops in most all her subsequent writing: the importance of community and personal responsibility, conflicts about the use of technology, "partnerships" in which three or more adults form a relationship analogous to traditional marriages but free of the sex role stereotyping, the naturalness of the need for sexual expression, the importance of contraception (achieved in McIntyre's future worlds through biofeedback techniques taught to both males and females as children), and the necessity of moving beyond loss and grief in one's life.

Starfarers and its sequels, *Transition, Metaphase,* and *Nautilus,* extend these themes and explore the problems and consequences inherent in mixing science and technology with human needs and goals. Technophobia, the politics of research, the perversion of peaceful technology to destructive purposes, and conflicts between nationalistic factions combine and contrast with the joy of pure research, exploration, and discovery as the spaceship *Starfarer* transitions along cosmic strings between star systems on a search for intelligent alien life forms. Contact occurs in *Transition* and *Metaphase,* but "civilization" is closed to groups who practice war. Victoria MacKenzie, a brilliant mathematician, develops an equation that allows the Earth ship to travel the strings faster than civilization ships can. Civilization, it turns out, is old and existing on the technology of its creators. Victoria's algorithm offers significant progress and may be the "gift" required from new cultures. Humans, with their ingenuity, may be welcome after all.

Barbary, the only one of McIntyre's books written expressly for young readers, uses an alien contact event as a cover for a very human action. Barbary, a streetwise orphan being placed with a new family, uses the adults' distraction to sneak her pet cat Mickey aboard the ship taking her to her new home on the space research station *Einstein.* The clever ways she and her new sister deal with the problems of secretly caring for Mickey mark them as very young exemplars of McIntyre's strong females and fit them nicely into the tradition of the child in young adult literature who rebels against and subverts adult authority.

In 1982, McIntyre began writing novelizations of the Star Trek films. *Star Trek II: The Wrath of Khan, Star Trek III: The Search for Spock,* and *Star Trek IV: The Voyage Home* parallel the film plots, and *Enterprise: The First Adventure* provides backstory for the whole series by telling how Jim Kirk becomes captain and the crew becomes cohesive when their routine shakedown cruise encounters a new life form near Romulan space. Though the optimistic Star Trek view that science and technology clearly serve humankind's best interests and the fast-paced adventure remain intact, the deft, detailed characterization clearly stamps these books as McIntyre's work. She makes Spock's continuous struggle to control his human responses and Jim Kirk's insecurities sympathetic and realistic. In *Enterprise,* she introduces an element of jealousy in the ranks when one among the crew is promoted out of sequence to become the captain's yeoman. This quirk departs a bit from the usual Star Trek dictate that the crew never conflicts, but it certainly demonstrates a keen knowledge about how people actually relate to each other.

McIntyre shares with the Star Trek philosophy a basic optimism about the ultimate advantages of technology. Her worlds, however, are undercut by a dark element that suggests a cautionary approach. *Dreamsnake* and *The Exile Waiting* take place on a world recovering from the ruin of a nuclear war. In *Screwtop,* vastly superior people called "tetraparentals" are created by combining the genetic traits of four parents. They must spend their lives working on projects decided for them before they were born and are allowed no individuality. The novella "Aztecs" introduces a starship pilot who must have her heart replaced with pluseless electronic pumps so she can survive the faster-than-light-speed velocities required by interstellar travel. The technology allows the pilot to achieve her goals, but, because of some basic biomechanical incompatibility, it isolates her from normal humans. Ruin, enslavement, and alienation, then, can result as readily as the beneficent progress Star Trek promises.

—Linda G. Benson

———

McKILLIP, Patricia A(nne). American. Born in Salem, Oregon, 29 February 1948. Educated at San Jose State University, B.A. 1971, M.A. in English 1973. Writer. Recipient: World Fantasy award for best novel, 1975, for *The Forgotten Beasts of Eld;* Hugo award nomination, 1979, for *Harpist in the Wind.* Agent: Howard Morhaim Literary Agency, 174 Fifth Avenue, Room 709, New York, NY 10010. Address: 2661 California, No. 14, San Francisco, CA 94115, U.S.A.

PUBLICATIONS FOR YOUNG ADULTS

Fiction

The House on Parchment Street, illustrated by Charles Robinson. New York, Atheneum, 1973.
The Throme of the Erril of Sherill, illustrated by Julie Noonan. New York, Atheneum, 1973.
The Forgotten Beasts of Eld. New York, Atheneum, 1974; London, Futura, 1987.
The Night Gift, illustrated by Kathy McKillip. New York, Atheneum, 1976.
Harpist in the Wind. New York, Atheneum, and London, Sidgwick and Jackson, 1979.
Heir of Sea and Fire. New York, Atheneum, 1977; London, Sidgwick and Jackson, 1979.
The Riddle-Master of Hed. New York, Atheneum, 1976; London, Sidgwick and Jackson, 1979.
Riddle of Stars (includes *The Riddle-Master of Hed, Heir of Sea and Fire,* and *Harpist in the Wind*). New York, Doubleday, 1979; as *The Chronicles of Morgon, Prince of Hed,* London, Sidgwick and Jackson, 1981.
The Quest of the Riddlemaster. New York, Ballantine, 1980.
Moon-Flash. New York, Atheneum, 1984.
The Moon and the Face. New York, Atheneum, 1985.
The Changeling Sea. New York, Atheneum, 1988.
The Sorceress and the Cygnet. New York, Ace, 1991.
The Cygnet and the Firebird. New York, Ace, 1993.

PUBLICATIONS FOR ADULTS

Novels

Stepping from the Shadows. New York, Atheneum, 1982.
Fool's Run. New York, Warner, and London, Macdonald, 1987.

* * *

One of the best contemporary fantasy writers for young adults is Patricia McKillip. Her distinctive writing voice sets her books apart from more traditional fantasies. A mood of dreamy mysticism pervades most of her works, and her heroes and heroines are loners isolated from others by their own immense supernatural powers and/or by their search for some ultimate truth. Greed, the abuse of power, and the struggle between love and hate are all recurring themes for McKillip.

Two of McKillip's early works do not display the unique style that is the strength of her later novels. Her first book, *The House on Parchment Street,* is a standard ghost story inspired by McKillip's childhood in England. This book and *The Night Gift* (McKillip's only realistic novel, in which a group of young people try to make a hideaway for a teenager who has attempted suicide) are her only young adult works set in the real world.

McKillip found her voice in her second book, *The Throme of the Erril of Sherill,* a novelette in which a Cnite searches for a legendary song of unsurpassed beauty in order to win the hand of his beloved princess. This book set the tone for her future fantasies and introduced her favorite scenario: the king's greed creates the need for the quest and the power of love brings it to an end.

Following *The Throme of the Erril of Sherill* was *The Forgotten Beasts of Eld,* another fantasy of greed, power, hate, and love. The isolated sorceress of Eld Mountain finds her intellectual life interrupted by the arrival of a baby and a young lord. Her powers eventually become the focus of a war for control of the kingdom—a war reflected in her personal struggle between her strong mental powers and her awakening emotions. In a sense the book is a parable about the need for balance between pure reason and deep emotions.

A similar struggle is the basis for McKillip's well-known fantasy trilogy: *The Riddle-Master of Hed, Heir of Sea and Fire,* and *Harpist in the Wind.* Using the riddle concept she introduced in *The Forgotten Beasts of Eld,* McKillip creates a society in which asking and answering riddles represents the highest intellectual achievement. The trilogy follows the destiny of Morgon of Hed, a riddle master faced with the greatest riddle of all: his identity. Filled with prophecy, battles, sorcery, noble warriors, and ladies, the trilogy is an epic tale of one man's struggle between his need for the truth and his fear of it as he is pulled between his love and hatred for the mysterious harpist who directs his destiny.

McKillip turns her talents to science fiction in *Moon-Flash* and *The Moon and the Face,* in which she builds a living cultural museum on a planet that may or may not be Earth. The tribes who live on the planet are unaware of one another and of the advanced civilization that watches over them. In *Moon-Flash* a curious young girl from one of the tribes decides to follow a river to the world's end, where she and a friend discover the truth about their society. *The Moon and the Face* continues the story after the protagonists have uncovered the true nature of the annual moon-flash their people worship. Even in science fiction, McKillip maintains her mysticism: the primitive tribe has dreams about the more advanced civilization, even though they cannot interpret the dreams, and the young heroine can sense the stories behind alien artifacts by a mere touch.

Like *Moon-Flash,* McKillip's return to fantasy, *The Changeling Sea,* concerns one adolescent girl, Peri, a misfit in her society, who becomes involved in events beyond her understanding. To punish the sea for drowning her father, Peri hexes the sea, not realizing she actually has the power to do so. As the spells unravel, mythical sea creatures rise to the world of men and Peri becomes the unwitting catalyst in breaking the enchantments over two young princes. As in *Moon-Flash,* there is a touch of romance.

Because of their sexual content, McKillip's more recent books are more suited to an older audience. *Fool's Run* is a science fiction novel about a rock band that performs on a penal space station and gets involved in an escape. McKillip is at her most mystic in this novel, leaving the reader confused about what has actually happened in the story. The many characters are driven by hate, love, and a need for truth, but this is also a book about the power of music and of vision. *The Sorceress and the Cygnet* is similarly overladen with intuitive mysticism. In this fantasy, a young man from a gypsy-like tribe is coerced into freeing a group of mythical beings from their eternal prisons and helping them find a source of power protected by his distant relative. Again, the mystic element is so heavy that the reader is unsure of what transpires during the story's climax.

At her best McKillip is a powerful writer adept at juggling universal themes and subjects. No one is better at exploring the imperative of truth and its high personal cost.

—Donna R. White

McKINLEY, (Jennifer Carolyn) Robin. American. Born in Warren, Ohio, 16 November 1952. Educated at Dickinson College, Carlisle, Pennsylvania, 1970-72; Bowdoin College, Brunswick, Maine, B.A. (summa cum laude) in English 1975. Married Peter Dickinson in 1992. Editor and transcriber, Ward & Paul, Washington, D.C., 1972-73; research assistant, Research Associates, Brunswick, 1976-77; bookstore clerk, Maine, 1978; teacher and counselor in private secondary school, Natick, Massachusetts, 1978-79; editorial assistant, Little, Brown, Inc., Boston, Massachusetts, 1979-81; barn manager on horse farm, Holliston, Massachusetts, 1981-82; clerk, Books of Wonder, New York, 1983; freelance reader and editor, 1983-85. Recipient: one of the New York Public Library's Books for the Teen Age, 1980, 1981, and 1982, American Library Association Notable Book, and Horn Book Honor List, for *Beauty: A Retelling of the Story of Beauty and the Beast;* one of the American Library Association's Best Young Adult Books, 1982, and Newbery Honor Book, 1983, for *The Blue Sword;* Newbery Medal, 1985, and named a Notable Book by the Association for Library Service to Children of the American Library Association, for *The Hero and the Crown;* Best Anthology designation from World Fantasy awards, 1986, for *Imaginary Lands;* Horn Book Honor List, 1988, for *The Outlaws of Sherwood;* D.Let., Bowdoin College, 1986. Agent: Merrilee Heifetz, Writers House, Inc., 21 West 26th St., New York, NY 10010. Address: 33 Queensdale Rd., London W11 4SB, England.

PUBLICATIONS FOR YOUNG ADULTS

Fiction

The Door in the Hedge. New York, Greenwillow, 1981.
The Blue Sword. New York, Greenwillow, 1982; London, MacRae, 1983.
The Hero and the Crown. New York, Greenwillow, and London, MacRae, 1985.
The Outlaws of Sherwood. New York, Greenwillow, 1988.
Deerskin. New York, Putnam, 1993.
Kirith. New York, Greenwillow, in press.

Other

Beauty: A Retelling of the Story of Beauty and the Beast. New York, Harper, 1978; London, MacRae, 1983.
Contributor, Terri Windling and Mark Arnold, editors, *Elsewhere II.* New York, Ace Books, 1982.
Contributor, Terri Windling and Mark Arnold, editors, *Elsewhere III.* New York, Ace Books, 1984.
Editor, *Faery.* New York, Ace Books, 1985.
Editor, *Imaginary Lands.* New York, Greenwillow, 1985; London, MacRae, 1987.
Adapter, *Tales from the Jungle Book.* New York, Random House, 1985.
Adapter, *Black Beauty,* illustrated by Susan Jeffers. New York, Random House, 1986; London, Hamish Hamilton, 1987.
Adapter, *The Light Princess,* illustrated by Katie Thamer Treherne. San Diego, Harcourt, 1988.
The Little Mermaid. San Diego, Harcourt, 1989.

PUBLICATIONS FOR CHILDREN

Picture Books

My Father Is in the Navy. New York, Greenwillow, 1992.
Rowan. New York, Greenwillow, 1992.

*

Media Adaptations: *The Blue Sword* (cassette), Random House, 1984; *The Hero and the Crown* (cassette), Random House, 1986.

Critical Study: Entry in *Children's Literature Review,* Volume 10, Detroit, Gale, 1986.

Biography: Entry in *Dictionary of Literary Biography,* Volume 52: *American Writers for Children since 1960: Fiction,* Detroit, Gale, 1986; essay in *Speaking for Ourselves: Autobiographical Sketches by Notable Authors of Books for Young Adults,* Volume 1, compiled and edited by Donald R. Gallo, National Council of Teachers of English, 1990.

*   *   *

Robin McKinley, whose young-adult works include fairy tales, legends, and fantasies, creates female characters who are intelligent, loyal, and courageous—eager to cross the physical and psychological barriers that lie between them and the fulfillment of their desti-nies. In her acceptance speech for the Newbery Medal, which she received in 1985 for *The Hero and the Crown,* McKinley commented that she "can't remember a time when the stories I told myself weren't about shy, bumbling girls who turned out to be heroes." Such characters escape and defy the limiting spheres to which they seem confined, sometimes through extraordinary feats of prowess and endurance. As they become aware of their hidden strengths and potential, McKinley's inspirational young heroines mature, beginning to view the world around them with a "new clarity of perception."

In *Beauty,* a retelling of the "Beauty and the Beast" tale—McKinley keeps many of the traditional elements while bringing a freshness and intensity to the story, told from the viewpoint of Beauty, the youngest of three sisters, who is ever conscious of the inappropriateness of her chosen nickname. Beauty, who describes herself as "thin, awkward, and undersized," is nevertheless a courageous and determined heroine. During her enforced sojourn in the castle of the Beast, her image shifts from a tomboy to a beautiful, mature young woman able to wear the silver dress of a princess and to see, as she develops trust and sympathy for the Beast, with a "new depth or roundness." Beauty's love of books, her care and affection for her horse Greatheart, and the progression of her sisters' own romances are woven into the treatment of theme.

The seductive power of evil is broken by perceptive characters in McKinley's retellings of the fairy tales "The Frog Prince" and "The Twelve Dancing Princesses": in the first story, a princess fears rather than is dazzled by a necklace that "gleamed and seemed to shiver with life," and in the second, a soldier sees past the "grace and scintillation of gems and precious things beyond counting" to the deadness that lies across the underground "black lake," where the twelve princesses dance all night. As in *Beauty,* the protagonists in these stories possess the qualities of courage, clear-eyed intelligence, and a capacity for goodness and love, as McKinley retains the spirit of beauty and fairy tale in her imaginative retellings.

Adventure and romance abound in the fantasies *The Blue Sword* and *The Hero and The Crown* both of which are set in the imaginary kingdom of Damar and relate the story of a "damalur-sol," or "lady hero." In *The Blue Sword,* Harry Crewe is kidnapped from the outermost post of the Homelanders by Corlath, king of the hillfolk of Damar. Harry holds fast to her courage and gradually becomes aware of her inherited gift of "kelar"—the "gift of seeing." She is trained to ride and wield a sword in battle, earning a place as one of Corlath's elite riders. Possessing qualities similar to McKinley's other heroines, Harry is a vivacious, forthright, and determined leader in combat and diplomacy and a worthy inheritor of Gonturan, the legendary sword of the flame-haired Lady Aerin. Aerin, is the daughter of the king of Damar and "the witchwoman," who wins her title as "swordbearer" in her father's court by fighting the dragons that plague the kingdom. Almost destroyed by the great dragon Maur, Aerin travels to the valley of Luthe, an immortal "mage," who helps her physically and spiritually overcome the "dragon" of despair and acknowledge her inner strength and power. In a striking passage, Aerin meets Agsded—her uncle and the evil counterpart of herself—in an inner sanctuary and wrests from him the "hero's crown," which holds the strength of Damar. Triumphant in battle against the northerners who threaten Damar, Aerin returns to her home to claim her rightful position as queen.

Landscapes become integral elements in McKinley's work: in *The Blue Sword* and *The Hero and the Crown,* the harsh sand and gritty winds of the desert, and the Stone City and the Damarian Hills of the imaginary kingdom of Damar figure prominently. The haunting quality of landscape and its strong impetus to keep those who love it within its boundaries is felt by Maddie, a young woman who raises sheep in the "Hills" in "The Stone Fey," a short story found *Imaginary Lands,* a book of fantasy stories edited by McKinley. Like her landscapes, McKinley's narratives are richly descriptive. Whether she is describing the colorful, luxurious interior of a king's tent, a deathly combat against the scorching fire of a great dragon, or the warm breath and soft nose of a favorite horse, her attention to detail brings a vitality and vividness to her text.

In *The Outlaws of Sherwood,* McKinley's Robin Hood is an anxious, cautious, and somewhat enigmatic character, whose necessary escape after killing a fellow forester is seen by Lady Marian and the philosophizing much as an opportunity to establish a rebel Saxon band deep within Sherwood Forest. Lady Marian dons Robin Hood's mantle of decisive leadership, while other members of his band exude high spirit and a sense of adventure. Lady Cecily, disguised as a boy outlaw, is another of McKinley's courageous heroines, and her love for Little John adds a tender note. The tale contains both traditional and original elements, and life in Sherwood Forest for the "green young outlaws" is vividly presented in a version that McKinley hopes is "historically unembarrassing."

Written in a rich stylistic prose, McKinley's works range from retellings of fairy tales and legends to original renderings of fantasies and romances. A common thread tying her stories together is the memorable characters she creates whose external journeys and adventures are paralleled by their psychological growth and insistence on integrity at all costs. These stories invite young-adult readers not only to respond to inspirational role models who dare to "do things" but to venture, like McKinley's characters, beyond the borders of their own lands and across the boundaries of their own imaginations.

—Hilary S. Crew

McMILLAN, Terry. American. Born in 1951. Educated at University of California, Berkeley, B.A.; attended MFA Film Program at Columbia University, New York. Columnis, *New York Times;* book reviewer *New York Times Book Review, The Atlanta Constitution,* and the *Philadelphia Inquirer.* Visiting professor of creative writing, University of Wyoming, Laramie; associate professor of English, University of Arizona, Tucson; teacher of writer's workshop, Stanford University, Stanford, California. Recipient: New York Foundations for the Arts award for fiction, 1986; Before Columbus Foundation National Book award, 1987, for *Mama;* Women in Communication Matrix Award for Career Achievement in Books, 1993. Fellow, Yaddo Artist Colony, 1982, 1983, and 1985, MacDowell Colony, 1983; Doubleday literary fellowship, Columbia University, 1985; National Endowment for the Arts Fellowship and Rockland Center for the Arts Fellowship, both 1988; Tucson/Pima Arts Council Literary Arts Fellowship, 1990. Address: c/o Viking Penguin, 40 West 23rd Street, New York, NY 10010, U.S.A.

PUBLICATIONS

Fiction

Mama. Boston, Houghton Mifflin, and London, Cape, 1987.

Disappearing Acts. New York, Viking, 1989; London, Cape, 1990.
Editor, *Breaking Ice: An Anthology of Contemporary African-American Fiction.* New York, Viking, and London, Cape, 1990.
Waiting to Exhale. New York, Viking, 1992.

Nonfiction

Contributor, *Five for Five: The Films of Spike Lee.* New York, Stewart, Tabori and Chang, 1991.

*

Critical Study: Entry in *Contemporary Literary Criticism,* Volume 50, Detroit, Gale, 1988; Volume 61, 1990.

*   *   *

Terry McMillan is best known for her most recent novel, *Waiting to Exhale,* about four black professional women, their friendships, and their search for fulfilling relationships with men. Although this novel was a best-seller, its subject matter seems a bit adult for young adult readers (and its language a bit graphic). Still, given the dearth of contemporary novels, films, plays, etc., by and about professional black women, perhaps young adult readers, especially young women, would welcome a story of black upper-middle-class experience. In *Waiting to Exhale* they may find, at last, a novel about black women who are not stereotypes. These women pursue careers and relationships because they are educated, independent, and full of humor, self-awareness, and the desire to live fully.

The appeal of McMillan's work lies in her ability to create fresh, original black characters who lead intensely diverse lives. Although McMillan writes about the black community in general, she focuses particularly on the stories and struggles of young black women. McMillan's female characters are survivors—tough, hip, self-directed; with each novel, her female protagonists seem a bit stronger and a bit more focused.

McMillan's first novel, *Mama,* tells the story of the mother-daughter bond between Mildred, a hard talker, drinker, and fighter, and Freda, her oldest daughter, a thoughtful and conscientious young woman. The novel opens in 1964 in industrial Point Haven, Michigan, a fictional town that closely resembles Port Huron, Michigan, where McMillan grew up. Twenty-seven-year-old Mildred is in the midst of another brutal fight with her alcoholic husband, Crook, and thirteen-year-old Freda tries to shelter the younger children from their parents' violence. Throughout the first few chapters of the novel, Freda plays mother to Bootsey, Money, Angel, and Doll, as Mildred tries to find a steady job and a steady man. As the years go by, Mildred goes through jobs and men, struggling to help her children as they confront their own problems, such as drug addiction, unexpected pregnancy, and sexual assault. In particular, Mildred tries to maintain a close relationship with Freda, even after Freda moves to California for school and then to New York for work.

Mildred's fierce love for her children motivates her every move; she explains, "These is *my* kids...and this ain't half the shit they gon' see in this world, so they might as well find out from me now what's going on out there before some ignorant ass in the streets gives it to 'em wrong and then they'll really end up catching hell." Despite her mother's efforts and her own ambitions, Freda finds herself "catching hell" in the form of cocaine abuse, alcoholism, and bad relationships with men. But in the end, when Mildred is forty-eight, and Freda is thirty-four, both mother and daughter have sobered up and redirected their lives. They learn to heal each other: "Freda pressed her head into Mildred's bare shoulder.... Mildred's breasts felt full against her own, and Freda couldn't tell whose were whose. They held each other up.... It seemed as if they hugged each other for the past and for the future."

Another McMillan novel of interest to young adult readers (though again, the themes are definitely adult) is *Disappearing Acts,* the story of a love affair between Zora Banks, a teacher and singer, and Franklin Swift, a construction worker. At the beginning of the novel, both characters are wary of the opposite sex. Franklin, a divorced father of two, is cynical about his ability to sustain a relationship with a woman; he explains: "[Women] complicate shit.... All they do is throw me off track. It takes me too damn long to swing back." Zora, however, wants to be in a relationship but finds that her involvement with men keeps her from developing her talents as a teacher and singer. Like Franklin, Zora feels that romantic relationships complicate her life and ambitions, so she decides to avoid such entanglements, stating: "Instead of wasting my time wishing and hoping, sleeping with self-pity and falling in love over and over again with ghosts, I'm going to stop concentrating so hard on what's missing in my life and be grateful for what I've got. For instance, this organ inside my chest. God gave me a gift, and I'd be a fool not to use it."

Despite both characters' resistance, a passionate relationship develops between them. Each character alternates the role of narrator as the story of their relationship evolves through courtship, disagreements, moving in together, abortion, pregnancy and childbirth, and sex. But in dealing so explicitly with sexual issues, McMillan realistically addresses the challenges of contemporary relationships.

In fact, the novel is about love and commitment, and the characters' struggles to achieve both. Near the novel's end, Zora tells Franklin, "...understand this: I love you just as much now as I did three years ago. We've had some rough times, and maybe time might help us both; I don't know. But you see that little boy over there? He's ours. We made him. And if you ever get your divorce and you feel like you're ready, come get us." Franklin's choice, to live with Zora and his son as a family, reflects the theme running throughout all of McMillan's work, from *Mama* to *Waiting to Exhale:* emotional fulfillment and stability can be achieved through committed love relationships.

—Mary D. Esselman

MEAKER, M.J. See **KERR, M.E.**

MEANS, Florence Crannell. American. Born in Baldwinsville, New York, 15 May 1891. Educated at Henry Read School of Art, Denver, 1910-11; Kansas City Theological Seminary, 1912; Macpherson College, Kansas, summers 1922-29; University of Denver, 1923-24. Married Carleton Bell Means in 1912 (died 1973); one daughter. Lecturer, Writer's Conference in the Rocky Moun-

tains, Boulder, Colorado, 1947-48, and University of Denver Writers' Workshop, 1947-54. Recipient: Child Study Association annual award for character-building book, 1945, and Newbery Honor Book, 1946, for *The Moved-Outers;* Nancy Bloch Annual award for a book dealing with intercultural relations, 1957, for *Knock at the Door, Emmy;* Central Baptist Seminary churchmanship citation, 1962. *Died 19 November 1980.*

PUBLICATIONS FOR YOUNG ADULTS

Fiction

Rafael and Consuelo: Stories and Studies about Mexicans in the United States for Primary Children, with Harriet Fullen. New York, Friendship Press, 1929.
A Candle in the Mist, illustrated by Marguerite de Angeli. Boston, Houghton Mifflin, 1931.
Ranch and Ring, illustrated by Henry Peck. Boston, Houghton Mifflin, 1932.
Dusky Day, illustrated by Manning Lee. Boston, Houghton Mifflin, 1933.
A Bowlful of Stars, illustrated by Henry Pitz. Boston, Houghton Mifflin, 1934.
Rainbow Bridge, illustrated by Eleanor Lattimore. New York, Friendship Press, 1934.
Penny for Luck, illustrated by Paul Quinn. Boston, Houghton, 1935.
Tangled Waters, illustrated by Herbert Morton Stoops. Boston, Houghton Mifflin, 1935.
The Singing Wood, illustrated by Manning Lee. Boston, Houghton Mifflin, 1937.
Shuttered Windows, illustrated by Armstrong Sperry. Boston, Houghton Mifflin, 1938.
Adella Mary in Old New Mexico, illustrated by Herbert Morton. Boston, Houghton Mifflin, 1939.
Across the Fruited Plain, illustrated by Janet Smalley. New York, Friendship Press, 1940.
At the End of Nowhere, illustrated by David Hendrickson. Boston, Houghton Mifflin, 1940.
Children of the Promise, illustrated by Janet Smalley. New York, Friendship Press, 1941.
Whispering Girl, illustrated by Oscar Howard. Boston, Houghton Mifflin, 1941.
Shadow over Wide Rain, illustrated by Lorence Bjorklund. Boston, Houghton Mifflin, 1942.
Teresita of the Valley, illustrated by Nicholas Panesis. Boston, Houghton Mifflin, 1943.
Peter of the Mesa, illustrated by Janet Smalley. New York, Friendship Press, 1944.
Wither the Tribes Go Up. New York, Northern Baptist Convention, 1944.
The Moved-Outers, illustrated by Helen Blair. New York, Walker, 1945.
Great Day in the Morning, illustrated by Helen Blair. Boston, Houghton Mifflin, 1946.
Assorted Sisters, illustrated by Helen Blair. Boston, Houghton Mifflin, 1947.
The House under the Hill, illustrated by Helen Blair. Boston, Houghton Mifflin, 1949.
The Silver Fleece, with Carl Means, illustrated by Edwin Schmidt. Philadelphia, Winston, 1950.

Hetty of the Grande Deluxe, illustrated by Helen Blair. Boston, Houghton Mifflin, 1951.

Alicia, illustrated by William Barss. Boston, Houghton Mifflin, 1953.

The Rains Will Come, illustrated by Fred Kabotie. Boston, Houghton Mifflin, 1954.

Knock at the Door, Emmy, illustrated by Paul Lantz. Boston, Houghton Mifflin, 1956.

Reach for a Star. Boston, Houghton Mifflin, 1957.

Borrowed Brother, illustrated by Dorothy Bayley Morse. Boston, Houghton Mifflin, 1958.

Emmy and the Blue Door, illustrated by Frank Nichoas. Boston, Houghton Mifflin, 1959.

But I Am Sara. Boston, Houghton Mifflin, 1961.

That Girl Andy. Boston, Houghton Mifflin, 1962.

Tolliver. Boston, Houghton Mifflin, 1963.

It Takes All Kinds. Boston, Houghton Mifflin, 1964.

Us Maltbys. Boston, Houghton Mifflin, 1966.

Our Cup Is Broken. Boston, Houghton Mifflin, 1969.

Smith Valley. Boston, Houghton Mifflin, 1973.

PUBLICATIONS OF CHILDREN

Stories

All 'Round Me Shinin'. New York, Baptist Board of Education, c. 1940.

Frankie and Willie Go a Far Piece. New York, Baptist Board of Education, c. 1940.

Some California Poppies and How They Grew. New York, Baptist Board of Education, c. 1940.

Plays

The Black Tents: A Junior Play of Life among the Bedouins of Syria. New York, Friendship Press, 1926.

Tara Finds the Door to Happiness. New York, Friendship Press, 1926.

Pepita's Adventures in Friendship: A Play for Juniors about Mexicans in the United States. New York, Friendship Press, 1929.

Other

Children of the Great Spirit: A Course on the American Indian, with Frances Somers Riggs. New York, Friendship Press, 1932.

Carvers' George: A Biography of George Washington Carver, illustrated by Harve Stein. Boston, Houghton Mifflin, 1952.

PUBLICATIONS FOR ADULTS

Nonfiction

Sagebrush Surgeon (biography of Clarence G. Salsbury). New York, Friendship Press, 1955.

Sunlight on the Hopi Mesas: The Story of Abigail E. Johnson. Philadelphia, Judson Press, 1960.

Biography of Frederick Douglass. Imperial International, 1969.

*

Biography: Entry in *The Junior Book of Authors,* second edition, New York, H.W. Wilson, 1951.

Manuscript Collection: University of Colorado Library, Boulder.

*   *   *

As more children's book departments were established in American publishing companies during the 1930s, a new need also grew: books for "young adults." One of the first writers to fill this need was Florence Crannell Means. Moreover, she went far beyond the "career" type of story which soon became popular to tackle difficult real-life situations with characters presented in depth. She was one of the first to write sympathetically about minority groups, articulating their struggle for dignity, security, and education—or just plain survival.

Her first stories, such as *A Candle in the Mist,* were in the pioneer genre. But though her plots may have been built out of typical frontier activities, her characters are not stereotyped. They have individuality and strength.

It was probably natural to follow pioneer stories with Indian stories; but Means did not write typical Indian stories. A Baptist minister's daughter, she grew up in a household where people of many nationalities and races were welcomed wholeheartedly; thus she developed sympathy and insight into the problems of minorities, with a special interest in Indians of the southwest. Among others, she portrayed Navajos (*Tangled Waters*) and Hopis (*Whispering Girl*). She took time to observe people in their home territory before writing about them. She always put her characters first, bringing out their habits and problems as an integral part of their personalities and their stories.

This concern for human values accounts for the survivability of her stories. Although *Shuttered Windows* and *Great Day in the Morning* are now "period pieces" (blacks are called negroes, and their worlds are basically separate from whites), the books are still valid as to story and character, and valuable as social history. The same can be said of *The Moved-Outers* which deals with nisei (American-born children of Japanese parents) in internment camps on the West Coast during World War II. Reading this now, one wonders if the young people could really have been so mild and cooperative with officials; but they were patriotic, as well as heartbroken; it is still a moving story—and it stands as an obvious yardstick for the change to the cynical outspokenness of today's young people.

In later books, Means presented with great honesty the discouragement and bitterness of a twenty-year-old Hopi Indian girl (*Our Cup Is Broken*) and the unflattering selfishness in desperate times of some members of a young girl's family in Colorado in the early 1900s (*Smith Valley*). In other words, her multilayered stories of all kinds of people are not goody-goody, missionary-inspirational; they are honest, realistic, and, always, interesting and well-written.

—Lee Kingman

———

MEIGS, Cornelia Lynde. Also wrote as Adair Aldon. American. Born in Rock Island, Illinois, 6 December 1884. Educated at Bryn Mawr College, Pennsylvania, A.B. 1908. English teacher, St.

Katherine's School, Davenport, Iowa, 1912-13; Instructor, Professor of English, and Professor Emeritus, Bryn Mawr College, 1932-50; civilian employee, U.S. War Department, Washington, D.C., 1942-45; writing instructor, New School for Social Research, New York City, 1951. Recipient: Drama League prize, 1915, for *The Steadfast Princess;* American Library Association named *The Windy Hill* a Newbery honor book in 1922, *Clearing Weather* in 1929, and *Swift Rivers* in 1933; Newbery Medal, 1934, for *Invincible Louisa,* which was also named to the Lewis Carroll Shelf, 1963; Spring Book Festival middle honor, 1943, for *Mounted Messenger;* Little, Brown & Company prize for *The Trade Wind;* L.H.D., Plano University, Texas, 1967; Jane Addams award, 1971, for *Jane Addams: Pioneer for Social Justice. Died 8 October 1973.*

PUBLICATIONS FOR YOUNG ADULTS

Fiction

The Kingdom of the Winding Road, illustrated by Frances White. New York, Macmillan, 1915.
Master Simon's Garden. New York, Macmillan, 1916.
The Windy Hill. New York, Macmillan, 1921.
The New Moon, illustrated by Marguerite de Angeli. New York, Macmillan, 1924.
Rain on the Roof, illustrated by Edith Ballinger Price. New York, Macmillan, 1925.
As the Crow Flies. New York, Macmillan, 1927.
The Trade Wind, illustrated by Henry Pitz. Boston, Little Brown, 1927; London, Hodder and Stoughton, 1928.
Clearing Weather, illustrated by Frank Dobias. Boston, Little Brown, 1928.
The Wonderful Locomotive, illustrated by Berta and Elmer Hader. New York, Macmillan, 1928.
The Crooked Apple Tree, illustrated by Helen Mason Grose. Boston, Little Brown, 1929.
The Willow Whistle, illustrated by E. Boyd Smith. New York, Macmillan, 1931.
Swift Rivers, illustrated by Forrest Orr. Boston, Little Brown, 1932.
Wind in the Chimney, illustrated by Louise Mansfield. New York, Macmillan, 1934.
The Covered Bridge, illustrated by Marguerite de Angeli. New York, Macmillan, 1936.
Young Americans: How History Looked to Them While It Was in the Making. Boston, Ginn, 1936.
The Scarlet Oak, illustrated by Elizabeth Orton Jones. New York, Macmillan, 1938; Birmingham, Combridge, 1939.
Call of the Mountain, illustrated by James Daugherty. Boston, Little Brown, 1940.
Mother Makes Christmas, illustrated by Lois Lenski. New York, Grosset and Dunlap, 1940.
Vanished Island, illustrated by Dorothy Bayley. New York, Macmillan, 1941.
Mounted Messenger, illustrated by John Wonsetler. New York, Macmillan, 1943.
The Two Arrows. New York, Macmillan, 1949.
The Dutch Colt, illustrated by George and Doris Hauman. New York, Macmillan, 1952.
Fair Wind to Virginia, illustrated by John Wonsetler. New York, Macmillan, 1955.

Wild Geese Flying, illustrated by Charles Geer. New York, Macmillan, 1957.
Mystery at the Red House, illustrated by Robert Maclean. New York, Macmillan, 1961.

Fiction as Adair Aldon

The Island of Appledore, illustrated by W.B. King. New York, Macmillan, 1917.
The Pirate of Jasper Peak. New York, Macmillan, 1918.
The Pool of Stars. New York, Macmillan, 1919.
At the Sign of the Two Heroes, illustrated by S. Gordon Smyth. New York, Century, 1920.
The Hill of Adventure, illustrated by J. Clinton Shepherd. New York, Century, 1922.

Plays

The Steadfast Princess. New York, Macmillan, 1916.
Helga and the White Peacock. New York, Macmillan, 1922.

Other

Invincible Louisa: The Story of the Author of "Little Women." Boston, Little Brown, 1933; as *The Story of Louisa Alcott,* London, Harrap, 1935.
Editor, *Glimpses of Louisa: A Centennial Sampling of the Best Short Stories,* by Louisa May Alcott. Boston, Little Brown, 1968.
Jane Addams: Pioneer for Social Justice: A Biography. Boston, Little Brown, 1970.

PUBLICATIONS FOR ADULTS

Novel

Railroad West. Boston, Little Brown, 1937.

Other

The Violent Men: A Study of Human Relations in the First American Congress. New York, Macmillan, 1949.
Editor and part author, *A Critical History of Children's Literature.* New York, Macmillan, 1953, revised edition, 1969; London, Collier Macmillan, 1969.
What Makes a College?: A History of Bryn Mawr. New York, Macmillan, 1956.
Saint John's Church, Havre de Grace, Maryland, 1809-1959. Havre de Grace, Democratic Ledger, 1959.
The Great Design: Men and Events in the United Nations from 1945 to 1963. Boston, Little Brown, 1963.
Louisa May Alcott and the American Family Story. London, Bodley Head, 1970; New York, Walck, 1971.

*   *   *

Although Cornelia Meigs, who also wrote under the pseudonym of Adair Aldon, is best remembered for her Newbery Medal biography of Louisa May Alcott, *Invincible Louisa,* and for her comprehensive, astute *A Critical History of Children's Literature* (revised in 1969), she also made a significant contribution in several genres to children's literature with historical fiction, mysteries, and drama. Her particular interest in the development of the United States was reflected in many books; her experiences of storytelling within the family circle were a source of her sense of narrative flow; her empathy for children was echoed repeatedly in stories in which they are faced with obstacles and rise to conquer their problems.

Meigs's first book for young adults, *The Kingdom of the Winding Road,* was published in 1915 but is now out of print, as are many of her other titles. Her second book, *Master Simon's Garden,* received wider critical acclaim; it is a strikingly effective message about intolerance: in a rigidly Puritan Massachusetts town, Master Simon is reviled for wasting time and space on a beautiful garden—an expression of his love and tolerance—but his legacy is appreciated by future generations. Her interest in the past is also evident in *The Willow Whistle,* a tale of pioneer life in the midwest; in *Wind in the Chimney,* two English children are instrumental in helping their widowed mother keep her new home in America just after the American Revolution; and *The Covered Bridge,* set in Vermont in 1788, has a strong sense of local history and the New England countryside.

Meigs's play *The Steadfast Princess* won the Drama League Prize in 1915, and her dramatic flair is repeatedly clear in such mystery stories as *Mystery at the Red House,* which has a plot that is exciting despite the book's slow pace. In this book, as well as in *The Dutch Colt* and *Wild Geese Flying,* young protagonists rise to the occasion and solve problems in an exciting but believable manner.

While Meigs seldom created memorable characters or drew her characters in depth, her plots are absorbing, her historical backgrounds authoritative but unobtrusive, and her themes—especially in historical fiction—strong. She wrote with perspective and polish. If all her writing is not great, many of her books have elements of greatness. Reviewing another author's book, she wrote, "No book can be said to have even the elements of greatness unless it can stand the task of recollection," and many of Meigs's stories can indeed stand that task.

—Zena Sutherland

MELTZER, Milton. Born in Worcester, Massachusetts, 8 May 1915. Educated at Columbia University, New York, 1932-36. Served in the U.S. Army Air Force, 1942-46; became sergeant. Married Hilda Balinky in 1941; two daughters. Recipient: Staff writer, Federal Theatre Project of the Works Projects Administration, New York City, 1936-39; researcher and writer, Columbia Broadcasting System Inc. (CBS-Radio), New York City, 1946; Public Relations Staff of Henry A. Wallace for President, 1947-49; account executive, Medical and Pharmaceutical Information Bureau, New York City, 1950-55; assistant director of public relations, Pfizer Inc., New York City, 1955-60; editor, Science and Medicine Publishing Co. Inc., New York City, 1960-68; full-time writer of books, since 1968; historian; biographer. Consulting editor, Thomas Y. Crowell Co., 1962-74, Doubleday & Co. Inc., 1963-73, and Scholastic Book Services, 1968-72; adjunct professor, University of Massachusetts, Amherst, 1977-80; lecturer at universities in the United States and England and at professional meetings and seminars; writer of films and filmstrips. Recipient: Thomas Alva Edison Mass Media award for special excellence in portraying America's past, 1966, for *In*

Their Own Words: A History of the American Negro, Volume 2, *1865-1916;* Children's Literature award of the National Book award, finalist, 1969, for *Langston Hughes: A Biography,* 1975, for *Remember the Days: A Short History of the Jewish American* and *World of Our Fathers: The Jews of Eastern Europe,* and 1977, for *Never to Forget: The Jews of the Holocaust;* Christopher award, 1969, for *Brother, Can You Spare a Dime? The Great Depression, 1929-1933,* and 1980, for *All Times, All Peoples: A World History of Slavery; Slavery: From the Rise of Western Civilization to the Renaissance* was selected one of *School Library Journal*'s Best Books, 1971; Charles Tebeau award from the Florida Historical Society, 1973, for *Hunted Like a Wolf: The Story of the Seminole War;* Jane Addams Peace Association Children's Book award Honor Book, 1975, for *The Eye of Conscience: Photographers and Social Change; Boston Globe-Horn Book* Nonfiction Honor Book, 1976, for *Never to Forget: The Jews of the Holocaust,* and 1983, for *The Jewish Americans: A History in Their Own Words, 1650-1950;* Association of Jewish Libraries Book award, 1976, Jane Addams Peace Association Children's Book award, 1977, Charles and Bertie G. Schwartz award for Jewish Juvenile Literature from the National Jewish Book awards, 1978, Hans Christian Andersen Honor List, 1979, and selected by the American Library Association as a "Best of the Best Books 1970-1983," all for *Never to Forget: The Jews of the Holocaust; Dorothea Lange: A Photographer's Life* was selected one of the *New York Times*' Best Adult Books of the Year, 1978; Washington Children's Book Guild Honorable Mention, 1978 and 1979, and Nonfiction award, 1981, all for his total body of work; American Book award finalist, 1981, for *All Times, All Peoples: A World History of Slavery;* Carter G. Woodson Book award from the National Council for Social Studies, 1981, for *The Chinese Americans;* Jefferson Cup award from the Virginia State Library Association, 1983, for *The Jewish Americans: A History in Their Own Words, 1650-1950;* Children's Book award special citation from the Child Study Children's Book Committee, one of *School Library Journal*'s Best Books for Young Adults, both 1985, and Olive Branch award from the Writers' and Publishers' Alliance for Nuclear Disarmament, Jane Addams Peace Association Children's Book award, and New York University Center for War, Peace, and the News Media, all 1986, all for *Ain't Gonna Study War No More: The Story of America's Peace-Seekers;* John Brubaker Memorial award from the Catholic Library Association, 1986; Golden Kite award for nonfiction, Society of Children's Book Writers, 1987, for *Poverty in America;* Jane Addams Peace Association Children's Book award Honor Book, 1989, for *Rescue: The Story of How Gentiles Saved Jews in the Holocaust.* Many of Meltzer's books have been selected as Library of Congress' Best Children's Books of the Year, Notable Children's Trade Book in Social Studies from the National Council for Social Studies, and *New York Times* Outstanding Children's Books of the Year. Agent: Harold Ober Associates, 425 Madison Ave., New York, NY 10017. Address: 263 West End Ave., New York, NY 10023, U.S.A.

Publications for Young Adults

Nonfiction

In Their Own Words: A History of the American Negro. New York, Crowell, Volume 1, *1619-1865,* 1964; Volume 2, *1865-1916,* 1965; Volume 3, *1916-1966,* 1967; abridged edition, as *The Black Americans: A History in Their Own Words, 1619-1983,* New York, Crowell, 1984, New York, Trophy, 1987.

A Light in the Dark: The Life of Samuel Gridley Howe. New York, Crowell, 1964; Cleveland, Ohio, Modern Curriculum Press, 1991.

Tongue of the Flame: The Life of Lydia Maria Child. New York, Crowell, 1965.

Bread—and Roses: The Struggle of American Labor, 1865-1915. New York, Knopf, 1967, New York, Facts on File, 1991.

Thaddeus Stevens and the Fight for Negro Rights. New York, Crowell, 1967.

Langston Hughes: A Biography. New York, Crowell, 1968.

Brother, Can You Spare a Dime? The Great Depression, 1929-1933. New York, Knopf, 1969, New York, Facts on File, 1991.

Margaret Sanger: Pioneer of Birth Control, with Lawrence Lader. New York, Crowell, 1969.

Freedom Comes to Mississippi: The Story of Reconstruction. Chicago, Illinois, Follett, 1970.

Slavery: From the Rise of Western Civilization to the Renaissance. New York, Cowles, 1971; Volume 2, *Slavery: From the Renaissance to Today,* New York, Cowles, 1972; one-volume edition, as *Slavery: A World History,* New York, Da Capo, 1993.

To Change the World: A Picture History of Reconstruction. New York, Scholastic Book Services, 1971.

Hunted Like a Wolf: The Story of the Seminole War. New York, Farrar, Straus, 1972.

Underground Man (novel). Scarsdale, New York, Bradbury Press, 1972, New York, Harcourt, 1990.

The Right to Remain Silent. New York, Harcourt, 1972.

Bound for the Rio Grande: The Mexican Struggle, 1845-1850. New York, Knopf, 1974.

The Eye of Conscience: Photographers and Social Change, with Bernard Cole. Chicago, Illinois, Follett, 1974.

Remember the Days: A Short History of the Jewish American, illustrated by Harvey Dinnerstein. Garden City, Doubleday, 1974.

Taking Root: Jewish Immigrants in America. New York, Farrar, Straus, 1974.

World of Our Fathers: The Jews of Eastern Europe. New York, Farrar, Straus, 1974.

Never to Forget: The Jews of the Holocaust. New York, Harper, 1976, New York, Trophy, 1991.

Violins and Shovels: The WPA Arts Projects. New York, Delacorte, 1976.

The Human Rights Book. New York, Farrar, Straus, 1979.

All Times, All Peoples: A World History of Slavery, illustrated by Leonard Everett Fisher. New York, Harper, 1980.

The Chinese Americans. New York, Crowell, 1980.

The Hispanic Americans, photographs by Morrie Camhi and Catherine Noren. New York, Crowell, 1982.

The Jewish Americans: A History in Their Own Words, 1650-1950. New York, Crowell, 1982.

The Truth about the Ku Klux Klan. New York, F. Watts, 1982.

The Terrorists. New York, Harper, 1983.

A Book about Names: In which Custom, Tradition, Law, Myth, History, Folklore, Foolery, Legend, Fashion, Nonsense, Symbol, Taboo Help Explain How We Got Our Names and What They Mean, illustrated by Mischa Richter. New York, Crowell, 1984.

Ain't Gonna Study War No More: The Story of America's Peace-Seekers. New York, Harper, 1985.

Betty Friedan: A Voice for Women's Rights, illustrated by Stephen Marchesi. New York, Viking, 1985.

Dorothea Lange: Life through the Camera, illustrated by Donna Diamond and photographs by Dorothea Lange. New York, Viking, 1985.

The Jews in America: A Picture Album. Philadelphia, Pennsylvania, Jewish Publication Society, 1985.

Mark Twain: A Writer's Life. New York, F. Watts, 1985.

George Washington and the Birth of Our Nation. New York, F. Watts, 1986.

Poverty in America. New York, Morrow, 1986.

Winnie Mandela: The Soul of South Africa, illustrated by Stephen Marchesi. New York, Viking, 1986.

The American Revolutionaries: A History in Their Own Words, 1750-1800. New York, Crowell, 1987.

The Landscape of Memory. New York, Viking, 1987.

Mary McLeod Bethune: Voice of Black Hope, illustrated by Stephen Marchesi. New York, Viking, 1987.

Benjamin Franklin: The New American. New York, F. Watts, 1988.

Rescue: The Story of How Gentiles Saved Jews in the Holocaust. New York, Harper, 1988, New York, Trophy, 1991.

Starting from Home: A Writer's Beginnings. New York, Viking, 1988, New York, Puffin, 1991.

American Politics: How It Really Works, illustrated by David Small. New York, Morrow, 1989.

Voices from the Civil War: A Documentary History of the Great American Conflict. New York, Crowell, 1989.

The American Promise: Voices of a Changing Nation, 1945-Present. New York, Bantam, 1990.

The Bill of Rights: How We Got It and What It Means. New York, Harper, 1990.

Columbus and the World Around Him. New York, F. Watts, 1990.

Crime in America. New York, Morrow, 1990.

Thomas Jefferson: The Revolutionary Aristocrat. New York, F. Watts, 1991.

The Amazing Potato. New York, HarperCollins, 1992.

Lincoln: In His Own Words, illustrated by Stephen Alcorn. New York, Harcourt, 1993.

Andrew Jackson and His America. New York, F. Watts, 1993.

Gold. New York, HarperCollins, 1993.

PUBLICATIONS FOR ADULTS

Nonfiction

A Pictorial History of the Negro in America, with Langston Hughes. New York, Crown, 1956; 5th revised edition, with C. Eric Lincoln, as *A Pictorial History of Black Americans,* 1983; revised as *African American History: Four Centuries of Black Life,* New York, Scholastic Textbooks, 1990.

Mark Twain Himself. New York, Crowell, 1960.

Editor, *Milestones to American Liberty: The Foundations of the Republic.* New York, Crowell, 1961, revised edition, 1965.

Editor, with Walter Harding, *A Thoreau Profile.* New York, Crowell, 1962.

Editor, *Thoreau: People, Principles and Politics.* New York, Hill & Wang, 1963.

Time of Trial, Time of Hope: The Negro in America, 1919-1941 with August Meier, illustrated by Moneta Barnett. Garden City, New York, Doubleday, 1966, Cleveland, Ohio, Modern Curriculum Press, 1991.

Black Magic: A Pictorial History of the Negro in American Entertainment, with Langston Hughes. Englewood Cliffs, New Jersey, Prentice-Hall, 1967; as *Black Magic: A Pictorial History of the African-American in the Performing Arts,* New York, Da Capo Press, 1990.

Dorothea Lange: A Photographer's Life. New York, Farrar, Straus, 1978, reprinted, 1985.

Editor, with Patricia G. Holland and Francine Krasno, *The Collected Correspondence of Lydia Maria Child, 1817-1880: Guide and Index to the Microfiche Edition.* Kraus Microform, 1980.

Editor, with Patricia G. Holland, *Lydia Maria Child: Selected Letters, 1817-1880.* Amherst, University of Massachusetts Press, 1982.

Editor of "Women of America" series, New York, Crowell, 1962-74, "Zenith Books" series, Garden City, Doubleday, 1963-73, and "Firebird Books" series, New York, Scholastic Book Services, 1968-72. Also author of documentary films, including *History of the American Negro* (series of three half-hour films), Niagara Films, 1965; *Five,* Silvermine Films, 1971; *The Bread and Roses Strike: Lawrence, 1912* (filmstrip), District 1199 Cultural Center, 1980; *The Camera of My Family,* Anti-Defamation League, 1981; *American Family: The Merlins,* Anti-Defamation League, 1982. Member of U.S. editorial board of *Children's Literature in Education,* beginning in 1973, and of *Lion and the Unicorn,* beginning in 1980.

*

Biography: Essay in *Something about the Author Autobiography Series,* Volume 1, Detroit, Gale, 1986, pp. 203-221; entry in *Dictionary of Literary Biography,* Volume 61: *American Writers for Children since 1960: Poets, Illustrators, and Nonfiction Authors,* edited by Glenn E. Estes, Gale, 1987, pp. 214-223.

Critical Studies: Entry in *Children's Literature Review,* Volume 13, Detroit, Gale, 1987; entry in *Contemporary Literary Criticism,* Volume 26, Detroit, Gale, 1983.

Milton Meltzer comments:

What I hope my books do is to raise questions in the minds of young readers about the world they live in. Why do things come out this way? Do they have to be this way? Could they be changed? How do people go about changing their lives? Change is always taking place, whether we wish it or not. But shouldn't we, as thinking, feeling beings, grow conscious of it and try to shape change to more human ends? If my books raise the reader's consciousness of what freedom and equality and justice mean, then it will be one small step toward helping us all lead richer and more fulfilling lives.

*   *   *

Milton Meltzer is a man with a mission, the quintessential crusader. A perusal of the titles of his books, spanning close to forty years, gives evidence of the zealous dedication with which Meltzer documents the human struggle for justice and freedom, not only here and now in America, but everywhere throughout mankind's history. His strong belief that the function of literature is to disturb, not to ease or placate, explains what he writes: his books intentionally unsettle the reader and advocate change and action. Armed with the intelligence of a lifetime of reading and research, Meltzer lends his passionate voice to awaken young people especially, to the truths of history, truths not reflected in textbooks which gloss over or dismiss the difficult and the ugly. His social conscience demands that truth must embrace the vision of the underdog.

His first book, *A Pictorial History of the Negro in America,* a collaborative effort with Langston Hughes, traces the role of the African American in the history of this country. Meltzer expresses great pride in this book, not because it was his first, but because he thinks it has probably had the greatest influence of anything he has written. Leafing through the index at the back of the book reveals the names and topics of many subsequent volumes he has written, Meltzer himself acknowledged that "the material is rich enough to be mined for many other useful books."

A companion book, *Black Magic: A Pictorial History of the Negro in American Entertainment,* also written with Langston Hughes, catalogues names and events in the arts; yet its cumulative effect is a powerful and poetic evocation of the creativity in all phases of entertainment as African Americans struggle and rise triumphant against overwhelming odds. With the publication of these two volumes, Meltzer has become known as a graphic historian. Subsequent work relies heavily on visual material to deepen and enrich text. A much more recent book, *African American History: Four Centuries of Black Life,* a revision of *A Pictorial History of the Negro in America,* is directed to a largely young adult and more contemporary audience.

While the majority of Meltzer's earliest titles are aimed at an adult audience, his discovery of a young adult public thrills him: "They care more, respond more quickly, are more open to new ideas." He finds himself clearly excited about introducing young people to names like Lydia Maria Child, Margaret Sanger, Dorothea Lange, Thaddeus Stevens, and Samuel Gridley Howe, all of whom stand as subjects of his biographies, all of whom fought against injustice, oppression, and suppression. "My subjects choose action," Meltzer asserts. As biographer, Meltzer tackles such prominent Americans as George Washington and Thomas Jefferson. Here his emphasis is to present a balanced portrait whose selectivity reveals the fullness of the man, not just the mythology surrounding him. Turning from portraiture, Meltzer invests events with similar integrity; he wishes to present lesser known happenings about which the textbooks tell little, or tell it incorrectly—such titles include *Bound for the Rio Grande: The Mexican Struggle, 1845-1850, Hunted Like a Wolf: The Story of the Seminole War, Violins and Shovels: The WPA Arts Projects.*

Meltzer returns to the time of his own adolescence to record for a young adult audience what it was like growing up in the Depression. He was himself involved in the WPA Arts Project, as a writer in the press department, but the larger canvas of poverty and want, of a nation at risk, truly compels Meltzer. His thoughtful portrait *Brother, Can You Spare a Dime? The Great Depression, 1929-1933* draws liberally on eye-witness narratives of the Depression to recreate what happened. Here, as elsewhere, Meltzer reveals his consummate skill as a selector of convincing and illuminating material. Those whose voices he calls upon include such well known figures as John Steinbeck and Edmund Wilson, but the sounding of ordinary men and women presents parallel poignancy and power.

The technique of embedding his story with the kind of primary source material typically given to an older audience—diaries, letters, memoirs, speeches, news accounts—becomes Meltzer's signature. Over the years, he produced a number of books subtitled *A History in Their Own Words.* The first-person accounts of men, women, and children whose lives make up the underside of history elevates his books to a new plane of quality and authenticity, what he describes as a "giant step up and out of the textbook swamp." Over his illustrious career, Meltzer effectively uses this format to examine the lives of Jewish and Black Americans, of Hispanic and Chinese Americans. When a single issue rather than a people demand his focus, Meltzer's impeccable research unearths that information which will best convey his conviction. *The Right to Remain Silent, The Human Rights Book, Poverty in America,* and *Ain't Gonna Study War No More: The Story of America's Peace-Seekers* all make their case for the need for greater understanding and responsible, moral action.

In *Starting from Home: A Writer's Beginnings,* Meltzer turns to autobiography to reach back into his own early history to better understand himself and his roots. A child of immigrant parents caught in the Depression, Meltzer speaks of those people, those forces which empowered him. In school, an occasional teacher moved him outside of facts and memorization, and excited him with the world of ideas. Born with curiosity, an inveterate questioner, Meltzer needed only a spark to self-ignite. As an American, such a flame was inspired with his high school discovery of the antislavery poets. As a Jew, such a spark was inspired by a newspaper article citing the Nazi slogan "Jew perish!" Many of Meltzer's books deepen our understanding of both Black and Jewish history, two subjects which he returns to again and again.

With perhaps his most praised book, *Never to Forget: The Jews of the Holocaust,* winner of innumerable awards, Meltzer articulates passionately his conviction in the power and importance of nonfiction. Saddened and outraged both by high school textbooks whose treatment of Nazism is "brief, bland, superficial, and misleading" and whose treatment of the Holocaust is dismissive, Meltzer set out to write a book for Jew and non-Jew alike, whose presentation corrects such egregious errors. Searing first-person documents, many from children, complement Meltzer's unrelenting examination of the forces of hatred and destruction. Meltzer's artistry in communicating the unthinkable without resorting to other than the facts—and presenting those facts with such intelligence and sensitivity—respects the reader. This book cries out as a moral call to remembrance—and beyond, it is a moral call to action, lest history repeat itself.

Meltzer's partisan voice, heard on behalf of the disenfranchised and the neglected, speaks lucidly and fervently on behalf of nonfiction—he decries its status as the stepchild of literature for young people. His work serves as a model for the best of literature: his books consistently empower facts with enviable style and imagination.

—Susan P. Bloom

MERRIAM, Eve. American. Born in Philadelphia, Pennsylvania, 19 July 1916. Educated at Cornell University, Ithaca, New York; University of Pennsylvania, Philadelphia, A.B. 1937; University of Wisconsin, Madison; Columbia University, New York. Married Waldo Salt; two sons. Author, poet, playwright. Copywriter, 1939-42; radio writer, mainly of documentaries and scripts in verse for Columbia Broadcasting System and other networks, and conductor of weekly program on modern poetry for station WQXR, New York City, 1942-46; daily verse columnist, *PM,* New York City, 1945; feature editor, *Deb* magazine, New York, 1946; fashion copy editor, *Glamour* magazine, 1947-48; free-lance magazine and book writer, since 1949; taught courses in creative writing at City College of the City University of New York, 1965-69. Member of the field project staff, Bank Street College of Education, New York, 1958-60. Public lecturer, 1956-92. Recipient: Yale Younger Poets

Prize, 1945, for *Family Circle; Collier's* Star Fiction award for "Make Something Happen," 1949; William Newman Poetry award, 1957; grant to write poetic drama, Columbia Broadcasting System, 1959; *New York Times'* Best Illustrated award, 1970, for *Finding a Poem;* National Council of Teachers of English awards, 1970 and 1981, for excellence in poetry for children; Obie award, *Village Voice,* 1977, for play *The Club;* Parents' Choice award, 1985, for *Blackberry Ink; New York Times'* Best Illustrated award, 1987, for *Halloween ABC. Died 11 April 1992.*

PUBLICATIONS FOR YOUNG ADULTS

Poetry

Family Circle. New Haven, Connecticut, Yale University Press, 1946.
The Inner City Mother Goose, photographs by Lawrence Ratzkin. New York, Simon & Schuster, 1969.
Finding a Poem, illustrated by Seymour Chwast. New York, Atheneum, 1970.
The Nixon Poems. New York, Atheneum, 1970.
I Am a Man: Ode to Martin Luther King, Jr., illustrated by Suzanne Verrier. New York, Doubleday, 1971.
Out Loud, illustrated by Harriet Sherman. New York, Atheneum, 1973.
Rainbow Writing. New York, Atheneum, 1976.
A Word or Two with You: New Rhymes for Young Readers, illustrated by John Nez. New York, Atheneum, 1981.
If Only I Could Tell You: Poems for Young Lovers and Dreamers, illustrated by Donna Diamond. New York, Knopf, 1983.
Fresh Paint, illustrated by David Frampton. New York, Macmillan, 1986.

Fiction

The Wise Woman and Her Secret, illustrated by Linda Graves. New York, Simon & Schuster, 1991.

Other

The Real Book about Franklin D. Roosevelt, illustrated by Bette J. Davis. New York, Garden City, 1952; London, Dobson, 1961.
Editor, with Nancy Larrick, *Male and Female under Eighteen: Frank Comments from Young People about Their Sex Roles Today.* New York, Discus Books, 1973.
Ab to Zogg: A Lexicon for Science-Fiction and Fantasy Readers, illustrated by Al Lorenz. New York, Atheneum, 1977.

PUBLICATIONS FOR CHILDREN

Poetry

There Is No Rhyme for Silver, illustrated by Joseph Schindelman. New York, Atheneum, 1962.
Funny Town, illustrated by Evaline Ness. New York, Crowell Collier, 1963.
It Doesn't Always Have to Rhyme, illustrated by Malcolm Spooner. New York, Atheneum, 1964.

Don't Think about a White Bear, illustrated by Murray Tinkelman. New York, Putnam, 1965.

Catch a Little Rhyme, illustrated by Imero Gobbato. New York, Atheneum, 1966.

Independent Voices, illustrated by Arvis Stewart. New York, Atheneum, 1968.

The Birthday Cow, illustrated by Guy Michel. New York, Knopf, 1978.

Jamboree: Rhymes for All Times, illustrated by Walter Gaffney-Kessel. New York, Dell, 1984.

Blackberry Ink, illustrated by Hans Wilhelm. New York, Morrow, 1985.

A Book of Wishes for You. Norwalk, Connecticut, Gibson, 1985.

A Sky Full of Poems. New York, Dell, 1986.

Halloween ABC, illustrated by Lane Smith. New York, Macmillan, 1987.

You Be Good and I'll Be Night: Jump-on-the-Bed Poems, illustrated by Karen Schmidt. New York, Morrow, 1988.

Chortles: New and Selected Wordplay Poems, illustrated by Sheila Hamanaka. New York, Morrow, 1989.

A Poem for a Pickle, illustrated by Sheila Hamanaka. New York, Morrow, 1989.

Fiction

What Can You Do with a Pocket?, illustrated by Harriet Simon. New York, Knopf, 1964.

Do You Want to See Something?, illustrated by Abner Graboff. New York, Scholastic, 1965.

Small Fry, illustrated by Garry Mackenzie. New York, Knopf, 1965.

Miss Tibbett's Typewriter, illustrated by Rick Schreiter. New York, Knopf, 1966.

Andy All Year Round, illustrated by Margo Hoff. New York, Funk & Wagnalls, 1967.

Epaminondas, illustrated by Trina S. Hyman. New York, Follett, 1968, as *That Noodle-Head Epaminondas,* illustrated by Trina S. Hyman, New York, Scholastic, 1972.

Project One-Two-Three, illustrated by Harriet Sherman. New York, McGraw, 1971.

Boys and Girls, Girls and Boys, illustrated by Harriet Sherman. New York, Holt, 1972.

Unhurry Harry, illustrated by Gail Owens. New York, Four Winds, 1978.

Good Night to Annie, illustrated by John Wallner. New York, Four Winds. 1979.

The Christmas Box (picture book), illustrated by David Small. New York, Morrow, 1985.

The Birthday Door (picture book), illustrated by Peter J. Thornton. New York, Morrow, 1986.

Where Is Everybody? (picture book), illustrated by Diane de Groat. New York, Simon & Schuster, 1989.

Fighting Words (picture book), illustrated by David Small. New York, Morrow, 1991.

Other

The Real Book about Amazing Birds, illustrated by Paul Wenck. New York, Garden City, 1954; London, Dobson, 1960.

The Voice of Liberty: The Story of Emma Lazarus. New York, Farrar Straus, 1959.

A Gaggle of Geese, illustrated by Paul Galdone. New York, Knopf, 1960.

Mommies at Work, illustrated by Beni Montresor. New York, Knopf, 1961.

What's in the Middle of a Riddle?, illustrated by Murray Tinkelman. New York, Collier, 1963.

The Story of Benjamin Franklin, illustrated by Brinton Turkle. New York, Four Winds, 1965.

Translator, *Animal Tales,* by Hana Doskocilova, illustrated by Mirko Hanak. New York, Doubleday, 1971.

Translator, *Christmas,* by Dick Bruna, illustrated by Dick Bruna. New York, Doubleday, 1971.

Bam! Zam! Boom!: High Rise Going Up, illustrated by William Lightfoot. New York, Walker, 1972.

Daddies at Work, illustrated by Eugenie Fernadez. New York, Simon & Schuster, 1989.

PUBLICATIONS FOR ADULTS

Poetry

Tomorrow Morning. New York, Twayne, 1953.

The Double Bed: From the Feminine Side. New York, Cameron, 1958.

The Trouble with Love. New York, Macmillan, 1960.

Basics: An I-Can-Read-Book for Grownups. New York, Macmillan, 1962.

A Husband's Notes about Her: Fictions. New York, Macmillan, 1976.

Plays

Inner City, music by Helen Miller, adaptation of *The Inner City Mother Goose* by Eve Merriam (produced New York, 1971).

Out of Our Father's House, with Paula Wagner and Jack Hofsiss, music by Ruth Crawford Seeger and others, adaptation of the book *Growing Up Female in America* edited by Eve Merriam (produced New York, 1975). New York, French, 1975.

We the Women (television play), 1975.

The Club (produced New York, 1976; London, 1978). New York, French, 1976.

At Her Age. New York, French, 1979.

Dialogue for Lovers: Sonnets of Shakespeare Arranged for Dramatic Presentation (produced New York, 1980). New York, French, 1981.

And I Ain't Finished Yet (produced New York, 1981).

Plagues for Our Time, music by Tom O'Horgan (produced New York, 1983).

Woman Alive: Conversation Against Death (libretto), music by Patsy Rogers (also director; produced New York, 1983).

Street Dreams, music by Helen Miller (produced New York, 1984).

Other

Emma Lazarus: Woman with a Torch. New York, Citadel, 1956.

Figleaf: The Business of Being in Fashion. Philadelphia, Lippincott, 1960.

After Nora Slammed the Door: American Women in the 1960's: The Unfinished Revolution. Cleveland, World, 1964.

Equality, Identity, and Complementarity: Changing Perspectives of Man and Woman, with others, edited by Robert H. Amundson. Denver, Research Center on Women, 1968.
Man and Woman: The Human Condition. Denver, Research Center on Women, 1968.
Editor, *Growing Up Female in America: Ten Lives.* New York, Doubleday, 1971.

*

Media Adaptations: "Catch a Little Rhyme" (recording), 1976; "Out Loud" (recording), 1988.

Biography: Entry in *Dictionary of Literary Biography,* Volume 61: *American Writers for Children Since 1960: Poets, Illustrators, and Nonfiction Authors,* Detroit, Gale, 1987, pp. 224-233.

Manuscript Collections: Kerlan Collection, University of Minnesota, Minneapolis; de Grummond Collection, University of Southern Mississippi, Hattiesburg; Schlesinger Library, Radcliffe College, Cambridge, Massachusetts.

Critical Study: Entry in *Children's Literature Review,* Volume 14, Detroit, Gale, 1988, pp. 187-204.

*   *   *

Eve Merriam's versatility was astounding. A keen observer of contemporary life, she brought to her poetry, plays, and prose a fresh outlook on all phases of the modern world, its delights as well as absurdities. Agile and penetrating, she continually beguiled her poetry readers with a variety of rhythms, rhymes, word play, and inventive forms which had their roots in traditional prosody, yet breathed with a twentieth-century sophistication refreshing to read, delightful to hear. She was an outstanding performer whose training in the theatre enhanced all of her poetry readings.

Merriam's poetic themes ranged from the joy of words and word-play through a gamut of observations on contemporary life. Her concerns for humanity, the planet, ecology, the moot value of some phases of technology, science, and love often found a voice in the part played by poetry itself with its seemingly limitless possibilities for self-expression. What underlay all of her writing was the art of asking her readers to extend their horizons, develop their sensibilities, cultivate curiosity, and become aware of their potential both as individuals and members of a community. Artfully, she warned against mediocrity. "A cliché," she explained, "is what we all say when we're too lazy to find another way." A unique talent enabled her to avoid didacticism by playing a dual role as both poet and reader. Writing of *it* and *they,* she commented that *"They* just make it all up, / and *we* go along." By thus becoming part of the *we* she never pointed an accusing finger at her readers.

For those who enter into Merriam's work, there will be the love of words and sounds for their own sake as well as challenges to the intellect. In her poem "Having Words," she listed the things that the word *umbrage* is not, and advised her readers that "You'll have to find out for yourself what it is." She played with numbers, the alphabet, punctuation, the points of the compass, and a myriad of other objects and ideas, always asking the reader to join in the fun. As a playwright, she wrote for stage and television; as a nonfiction writer, she was engaged in work on such topics as fashion, American women in the 1960s, racial and gender equality, and biography.

In a playful mood, she wrote *Ab to Zogg, A Lexicon for Science-Fiction and Fantasy Readers,* 1977, introducing readers to creatures like XIVLCMXXXVILXVM ("Reincarnated Roman gladiator whose quarked tunic conceals deadly microwaves and whose name none dare pronounce aloud") and Hovvers ("Half souls who inhabit a zone midway between the mushroom caps and the sequoia tops...."). Such inventiveness was at the heart of one of her most beloved poems, "Mean Song," which begins "Snickles and podes, / Ribble and grodes: / That's what I wish you...."

She could be delightfully caustic, attacking television and its ridiculous commercials—the supermarket with its "banana detergent," "deodorant pie," plastic plants that "keep us germ-proof dirt-free," "artificial lawns with real crab grasses," and the "cult" of bargain sales. "You can take away my mother, / you can take away my sister, / but don't take away / my little transistor." Here, again, her pose is that of one with the reader. Often she used personification. All of the things of the day make us hurry and deprive us of time to speak. Yet, "slowly, says the darkness, / you can talk to me."

Eve Merriam wrote for all ages. Her *Inner City Mother Goose,* 1969, portrays the problems of city life: dirty streets, drugs, poverty programs, and political corruption, aspects of life certainly not for the nursery rhyme age for which she also wrote stories and verse. In a charming book for "young lovers and dreamers" *If Only I Could Tell You,* 1983, she, herself, becomes the lyric lover and dreamer: "At night / in the dark / thinking of you / the sky / becomes / so bright / I have to / put on / sunglasses." She wrote about people whose "independent voices" have wrought meaningful changes in the world. Many poems and some articles span all age categories; "Inside a Poem" and "What Can a Poem Do?" were first published as broadsides for the young, and later as adult articles in *The Writer* magazine.

Her poems on poetry are memorable. In "How to Eat a Poem" she advised the reader to "bite in." The poem is "ready and ripe now, whenever you are." In "Reply to the Question: *How Can You Become a Poet?*" she suggested that young writers observe the varying phases of a leaf in spring, summer and autumn, and then "in winter / when there is no leaf left / invent one."

A prodigious talent and recipient of the Yale Series of Younger Poets Award in 1945, the National Council of Teachers of English Excellence in Poetry Award in 1981, and an Obie Award in 1977, Eve Merriam will be remembered by those who have heard and watched as she read her work, conducted workshops for the young, or walked with her in Central Park or on the New York streets observing life at every level.

—Myra Cohn Livingston

————

MEYER, Carolyn (Mae). American. Born in Lewistown, Pennsylvania, 8 June 1935. Educated at Bucknell University, Lewisburg, Pennsylvania, B.A. (cum laude) 1957. Married 1) Joseph Smrcka in 1960 (divorced 1973); 2) E.A. Mares in 1987; three sons. Secretary, late 1950s; free-lance writer, 1963—. Institute of Children's Literature, instructor, 1973-79; Guest lecturer in children's literature. Gives talks and workshops in high schools and colleges. Presenter at history, library, literary, and reading conferences. Workshop leader for writing groups. Recipient: Notable Book citations from American Library Association, 1971, for *The Bread Book,* 1976, for *Amish People,* and 1978, for *C.C. Poindexter;* Best Book for Young Adults citations from American Library Association, 1985, for *The Mystery of the Ancient Maya,* 1987, for *Voices of South Africa* and *Denny's Tapes,* 1993, for *Where the Broken Heart Still Beats;* Author of the Year award from Pennsylvania School Librarians Association, 1990. Agent: Amy Berkower, Writers House Inc., 21 W. 26th St., New York, NY 10010. Address: 1120 N. Locust St., Denton, TX 76201, U.S.A.

PUBLICATIONS FOR YOUNG ADULTS

Fiction

C.C. Poindexter. New York, Antheneum, 1979.
Eulalia's Island. New York, Antheneum, 1982.
The Summer I Learned about Life. New York, Antheneum, 1983.
The Luck of Texas McCoy. New York, Antheneum, 1984.
Elliott and Win. New York, Antheneum, 1986.
Denny's Tapes. New York, McElderry, 1987.
Wild Rover. New York, McElderry, 1989.
Because of Lissa. New York, Bantam, 1990.
Killing the Kudu. New York, McElderry, 1990.
Japan—How Do Hands Make Peace? Earth Inspectors No. 10. New York, McGraw, 1990.
The Problem with Sidney. New York, Bantam, 1990.
Gillian's Choice. New York, Bantam, 1991.
The Two Faces of Adam. New York, Bantam, 1991.
Where the Broken Heart Still Beats: The Story of Cynthia Ann Parker. New York, Harcourt, 1992.
White Lilacs. New York, Harcourt, 1993.
Rio Grande Stories. New York, Harcourt, 1993.
Drummers of Jericho. New York, Harcourt, 1994.

Nonfiction

Miss Patch's Learn-to-Sew Book, illustrated by Mary Suzuki. New York, Harcourt, 1969.
Stitch by Stitch: Needlework for Beginners, illustrated by the author. New York, Harcourt, 1970.
The Bread Book: All about Bread and How to Make It, illustrated by Trina Schart Hyman. New York, Harcourt, 1971.
Yarn: The Things It Makes and How to Make Them, illustrated by Jennifer Perrott. New York, Harcourt, 1972.
Saw, Hammer, and Paint: Woodworking and Finishing for Beginners, illustrated by Toni Martignoni. New York, Morrow, 1973.
Christmas Crafts: Things to Make the 24 Days Before Christmas, illustrated by Anita Lobel. New York, Harper, 1974.
Milk, Butter, and Cheese: The Story of Dairy Products, illustrated by Giulio Maestro. New York, Morrow, 1974.
The Needlework Book of Bible Stories, illustrated by Janet McCaffery. New York, Harcourt, 1975.
People Who Make Things: How American Craftsmen Live and Work. New York, Antheneum, 1975.
Rock Tumbling: From Stones to Gems to Jewelry, photographs by Jerome Wexler. New York, Morrow, 1975.
Amish People: Plain Living in a Complex World, photographs by Michael Ramsey, Gerald Dodds, and the author. New York, Antheneum, 1976.

Coconut: The Tree of Life, illustrated by Lynne Cherry. New York, Morrow, 1976.
Lots and Lots of Candy, illustrated by Laura Jean Allen. New York, Harcourt, 1976.
Eskimos: Growing Up in a Changing Culture, photographs by John McDougal. New York, Antheneum, 1977.
Being Beautiful: The Story of Cosmetics from Ancient Art to Modern Science, illustrated by Marika. New York, Morrow, 1977.
Mask Magic, illustrated by Melanie Gaines Arwin. New York, Harcourt, 1978.
The Center: From a Troubled Past to a New Life. New York, Antheneum, 1980.
Rock Band: Big Men in a Great Big Town. New York, Antheneum, 1980.
The Mystery of the Ancient Maya, with Charles Gallenkamp. New York, Antheneum, 1985.
Voices of South Africa: Growing Up in a Troubled Land. New York, Harcourt, 1986.
Voices of Northern Ireland: Growing Up in a Troubled Land. New York, Harcourt, 1987.
A Voice from Japan: An Outsider Looks In. New York, Harcourt, 1988.

*

Biography: Essay in *Something about the Author Autobiography Series* Volume 9, Detroit, Gale, 1990; essay in *Speaking for Ourselves, Too* compiled and edited by Donald R. Gallo, National Council of Teachers of English, 1993.

Carolyn Meyer comments:

The two things I enjoy most are researching a subject, or maybe a cluster of subjects, and telling a story. The research part got me started in writing, nonfiction in the beginning. Then I discovered that the stories I most liked to tell were stories that required a lot of preliminary digging—sometimes in libraries, sometimes in conversations with all kinds of people. In the twenty-five years I've been writing for children and young adults, there has been a steady march toward more complex subjects, each book demanding more and more of me as researcher and storyteller. If readers share in even a part of what I have discovered in the process, I'm happy.

*   *   *

The young adult works of Carolyn Meyer come from her curiosity and her sense of place. She has been successful in writing both fiction and informational books, with selections in both forms being designated by the American Library Association as "Best Books for Young Adults." In her fiction, Meyer frequently imbues her characters with the social and personal problems they must face to attain maturity and self-acceptance. Characterization is a strong facet of her writing, and most are unconventional, creating the focus for the novel. The topics are timely, yet universal, and are stimulating to the teenage reader. Meyer does not duck controversial issues but rather presents them to the reader in a straight-forward manner with realistic dialogue. Because she is thorough in her research there is a verisimilitude that resonates for the reader.

An unconventional relationship and the consequences of stereotyping in society are the basis for the story of *Elliott and Win.* Win is a teenager, newly arrived in Santa Fe, whose only friend is Paul, a bully who dresses in battle gear. Win hasn't seen his father in seven years, so his mother enrolls him in a Big Brothers program, where he meets Elliott. Elliott is not what Win expected; he likes gourmet food and opera, and takes Win to kayak races and teaches him photography. Of course Paul is sure Elliott is gay and torments Win with these insinuations. Win struggles with his anger with Paul, his own uncertainties, and his adjustments to the new world that is being opened to him. An additional plot line is the relationship of Win and Heather, a girl beset with the problems of puberty and a bad reputation. The only incident that rings untrue is the revelation that Paul's father is gay, which seems a bit too coincidental.

Two other realistic fiction novels that present interesting premises are *Denny's Tapes* and *Killing the Kudu*. One month in the life of Dennis James Brown is recorded on tape as he flees his home in search of who he is to become. This device allows for the use of flashback as well as the dramatic presentation of the present. Denny reveals that he has been brought up white by his mother, but he has a black father he hasn't seen in years. Denny's mother has tried to protect him from cruelty, but his stepfather throws him out of the house with a racial epithet when he discovers Denny and his daughter embracing. Denny sets out to find three people: his black grandmother, his white grandmother, and his father. Through his search, he discovers much about his family, about black culture, and gains a direction for his life.

In *Killing the Kudu,* two cousins are emotionally separated by tragedy. When the boys were young, Scott accidently shot Alex, leaving him a paraplegic in a wheelchair. Now Alex is eighteen and comes to stay with his grandmother for part of the summer, where the boys are reunited. Meyer realistically portrays the tension of their relationship, including their rivalry for the affection of Claire, an Irish au pair with nurses' training, who has come to work for the summer. There are questions of the effects of paraplegia, including sexual capacity, as well as touching scenes of friendship. In time, Alex grows from a sheltered mama's boy to a young man determined to have a life of his own.

Meyer has recently begun writing historical fiction, and this is where she shines. Her sense of place is strong and she is able to give it free rein in novels that require greater development of setting. Couple this with her adept characterizations and the resulting stories thoroughly engage the reader. *Where the Broken Heart Still Beats: The Story of Cynthia Ann Parker* is a moving example of Meyer's gift of asking "what if." Many of the facts of Parker's life have been lost, but her legend lives on. Meyer has created a fictional cousin, whose diary conveys the reactions of the "civilized world" to Parker, who, in 1860, is returned to her family after twenty-five years of living with the Comanches. This alternates with chapters told from Naduah's (Parker's Comanche name) point of view. A tragic and poignant narrative of a clash of cultures, Meyer has combined excellent storytelling with information about the time and the Comanches to create a gripping book. The essence of the novel is revealed in the following quote: "But this woman who Grandfather insists is his brother's daughter does not look like one who has been rescued. She looks like one who is imprisoned."

In *White Lilacs,* Rose Lee is twelve the summer she learns her life will be changed forever; that the "white lilacs" her grandfather lovingly tends in his garden in Freedomtown will have to be transplanted along with all the lives of the blacks who live there. Freedomtown is a thriving black community within a small Texas town, but as the town has grown, the land has become more desirable and the whites want it for a city park. Because Rose Lee works for one of the prominent white families, these events are told through

her viewpoint. In the end, the only thing left of Freedomtown are the sketches made by Rose Lee. There are memorable characters, including Rose Lee's brother Henry, who refuses to accept inferior status, and visiting Aunt Susanna, inspired by the Langston Hughes poem, "When Sue Wears Red" that Meyer first included in *Denny's Tapes.* There can be no happy ending because the story adheres to its nonfiction roots, but there is fortitude and integrity in its telling.

Meyer's work for young adults always eschews the easy plotline and delves into the uncomfortable realities of our world. She is increasingly deft in her ability to tell her stories, and one awaits her new works with a sense of anticipation.

—M. Jean Greenlaw

MIKLOWITZ, Gloria D. American. Born in New York City, 18 May 1927. Educated at Hunter College (now Hunter College of the City University of New York), 1944-45; University of Michigan, Ann Arbor, B.A. 1948; New York University, 1948. Married Julius Miklowitz in 1948; two sons. Writer, since 1952. Scriptwriter, 1952-57; wrote documentary films for the U.S. Naval Ordinance Test Station, Pasadena, California; Pasadena City College, Pasadena, instructor, 1971-80; instructor for Writer's Digest School. Recipient: One of Child Study Association of America's Children's Books of the Year, 1969, for *The Zoo Was My World,* and 1975, for *Harry Truman;* Outstanding Science Book for Children from the National Council for Social Studies and the Children's Book Council, 1977, for *Earthquake!,* and 1978, for *Save That Raccoon!;* one of New York Public Library's Books for the Teen Age, 1980, for *Did You Hear What Happened to Andrea?,* 1981, for *The Love Bombers,* and 1982, for *The Young Tycoons;* Western Australia Young Reader Book award, 1984, for *Did You Hear What Happened to Andrea?;* Iowa Books for Young Adults Poll, 1984, for *Close to the Edge,* 1986, for *The War between the Classes,* 1989, for *After the Bomb,* and 1989, for *Good-Bye Tomorrow;* Humanitas Prize (awarded to scriptwriter) for humanitarian values, 1985, for "CBS Schoolbreak Special," "The Day the Senior Class Got Married;" Emmy (awarded to film producers) for Best Children's Special, 1986, for "CBS Schoolbreak Special," "The War Between the Classes"; Recommended Books for Reluctant Young Adult Readers for *Good-Bye Tomorrow* and *Secrets Not Meant to Be Kept,* both 1987; IRA Young Adult Choices, 1989, for *Secrets Not Meant to Be Kept.* Agent: Marilyn Marlow, Curtis Brown Ltd., 10 Astor Place, New York, NY 10003. Address: 5255 Vista Miguel Dr., La Canada, CA 91011, U.S.A.

PUBLICATIONS FOR YOUNG ADULTS

Fiction

Turning Off. New York, Putnam, 1973.
A Time to Hurt, A Time to Heal. New York, Tempo Books, 1974.
Paramedic Emergency. New York, Scholastic Book Services, 1977.
Runaway. New York, Tempo Books, 1977.
Unwed Mother. New York, Tempo Books, 1977.
Did You Hear What Happened to Andrea? New York, Delacorte, 1979.

The Love Bombers. New York, Delacorte, 1980.
Before Love. New York, Tempo Books, 1982.
Carrie Loves Superman. New York, Tempo Books, 1983.
Close to the Edge. New York, Delacorte, 1983.
The Day the Senior Class Got Married. New York, Delacorte, 1983.
After the Bomb. New York, Scholastic, 1985.
The War between the Classes. New York, Delacorte, 1985.
Love Story, Take Three. New York, Delacorte, 1986.
After the Bomb: Week One. New York, Scholastic, 1987.
Good-Bye Tomorrow. New York, Delacorte, 1987.
Secrets Not Meant to Be Kept. New York, Delacorte, 1987.
The Emerson High Vigilantes. New York, Delacorte, 1988.
Anything to Win. New York, Delacorte, 1989.
Suddenly Super Rich. New York, Bantam, 1989.
Standing Tall, Looking Good. New York, Delacorte, 1991.
Desperate Pursuit. New York, Bantam, 1992.
The Killing Boy. New York, Bantam, 1993.
Boiling Point. New York, Simon & Schuster, 1994.

Nonfiction

The Zoo Was My World, with Wesley A. Young. New York, Dutton, 1969.
Harry Truman, illustrated by Janet Scabrini. New York, Putnam, 1975.
Earthquake!, illustrated by Jaber William. New York, Messner, 1977.
Dr. Martin Luther King, Jr. New York, Tempo Books, 1977.
Nadia Comaneci. New York, Grosset & Dunlap, 1977.
Steve Cauthen. New York, Tempo Books, 1978.
Tracy Austin. New York, Tempo Books, 1978.
Natalie Dunn, Roller Skating Champion. New York, Tempo Books, 1979.
Roller Skating. New York, Tempo Books, 1979.
Movie Stunts and the People Who Do Them. New York, Harcourt, 1980.
The Young Tycoons. New York, Harcourt, 1981.

PUBLICATIONS FOR CHILDREN

Fiction

Barefoot Boy, illustrated by Jim Collins. Chicago, Follett, 1964.
The Zoo That Moved, illustrated by Don Madden. Chicago, Follett, 1968.
The Parade Starts at Noon, illustrated by Don Madden. New York, Putnam, 1969.
The Marshmallow Caper, illustrated by Cheryl Pelavin. New York, Putnam, 1971.
Sad Song, Happy Song, illustrated by Earl Thollander. New York, Putnam, 1973.
Ghastly Ghostly Riddles, with Peter Desberg, illustrated by Dave Ross. New York, Scholastic Book Services, 1977.
Save That Raccoon!, pictures by St. Tamara. New York, Harcourt, 1978.
Win, Lose, or Wear A Tie; Sports Riddles, with Peter Desberg, pictures by Dave Ross. New York, Random House, 1980.
Good Sport Jokes, with Peter Desberg, illustrated by Laurie Burruss. New York, Readers Digest Services, 1977.

Riddles for a Scary Night, with Peter Desberg, illustrated by Laurie Burruss. New York, Readers Digest Services, 1977.

*

Media Adaptations: "Andrea's Story: A Hitchhiking Tragedy" (television movie; based on *Did You Hear What Happened to Andrea?*), "Afterschool Special," ABC-TV, September, 1983; "The Day the Senior Class Got Married" (television movie), "Schoolbreak Special," CBS-TV, 1985; "The War Between the Classes" (television movie), "Schoolbreak Special," CBS-TV, 1986.

Biography: Essay in *Speaking for Ourselves: Autobiographical Sketches by Notable Authors of Books for Young Adults,* Volume 1, compiled and edited by Donald R. Gallo, National Council of Teachers of English, 1990; essay in *Authors and Artists for Young Adults,* Volume 6, Detroit, Gale, 1991; essay in *Something about the Author Autobiography Series,* Volume 17, Detroit, Gale, 1994.

Manuscript Collection: de Grummond Collection, University of Southern Mississippi.

Gloria D. Miklowitz comments:
    I feel a special kinship with young adults, maybe because my own teen years are still vivid. Today's young people, however, face much more difficult problems and issues than any previous generation. That's what I like to write about—kids trying to come to terms with life today, trying to find healthy options to what seem insurmountable problems.

*   *   *

Gloria Miklowitz's fiction for young adults deals with contemporary social issues and problems confronting adolescents. Her fiction explores topics such as rape, child abuse, AIDS, religious cults, nuclear bombs, and suicide. Miklowitz carefully researches each topic from different perspectives. Her message is clear, but not overly didactic and she attempts to show teenagers that they have alternative choices in life. Her books tend to evolve from problems and probe issues rather than spotlight individual characters.
    In *Did You Hear What Happened to Andrea?* Miklowitz deals with rape from the perspectives of a number of people. For research, she answered phones for a rape hotline center, and interviewed rape victims, families of victims, police, and doctors. Consequently, she depicts the reactions of Andrea, the rape victim; her boyfriend; her brother and sister; her removed parents; acquaintances and friends at school; the investigating policeman; and the rapist. Because the rape happened early in the book, after Andrea and her boyfriend recklessly hitchhiked, the remainder of the book deals with how characters emotionally handle the aftermath.
    Secrets Not Meant to Be Kept investigates a headline topic: child abuse in a day-care center. Adri, a teenager who has blotted out memory of her first six years of life and has trouble expressing affection, slowly remembers her experience as her three-year-old sister shows signs of abuse that she recognizes. Adri and her friend Ryan gather evidence about the abuse that shocks her parents and others in the community.
    The topic of AIDS or ARC (AIDS-related complex) is treated in *Good-bye Tomorrow.* The story is told through three people: Alex Weiss, a teenage swimmer who had a blood transfusion the year

before; Shannon, his girlfriend; and Christy, his younger sister. They relate their discovery or knowledge of Alex's ARC and the resulting reactions to and uncertainty of dealing with it. John, Alex's closest friend, provides a different perspective through the other three. Miklowitz's research on the topic and her open honesty are apparent in this novel.

In *The Love Bombers,* Miklowitz uses her reading, interviews, and time spent with the Moonies to create an inside view of a religious cult. The book centers around Jenna, who has gone to find her brother Jeremy, who has dropped out of college to join the cult. Jeremy's low self-esteem and his desire to win the approval he never felt he had at home make him a target of the cult. Jenna and her friend Rick experience how cult members bombard recruits with "love," constant supervision, exercise, and involvement so that they have no time to think for themselves. Although Jeremy remains with the cult, Jenna wonders if he will ever be able to leave and become independent.

The threat of nuclear war is the subject of *After the Bomb* and its sequel, *After the Bomb: Week One.* Miklowitz creates realistic descriptions of the desolate homes, land, and people after the Russians mistakenly release a bomb on Los Angeles. The novel forms the background for Philip Singer, a runner who is overshadowed by a handsome brother, to take leadership and overcome his sense of inadequacy as he rescues his mother, helps at the hospital, and aids in supplying water to the hospital. In the sequel Philip and Matt look for their father, who was working at the California Institute of Technology when the nuclear attack began.

The War between the Classes reveals prejudice and offers a classroom experiment as a means of enlightening people—one step in overcoming this social ill. The teacher uses the "Color Game," a social studies experience. Students are divided into four socio-economic groups, labeled by color codes, and follow strict behavior rules of intergroup actions. During the experiment, Amy (Emiko) Sumoto and Adam Tarcher, who are in love, and their classmates gain insight by tolerating and inflicting humiliations and abuses on each other. In this novel, Miklowitz confronts readers with questions of social class, ethnic prejudice, and sexism.

Miklowitz's carefully researched books for young adults illustrate the diversity of her curiosity and wide interests. They focus on the contemporary headline issues and problems young adults may face and provide ways to deal with these.

—Edna Earl Edwards

MILES, Betty. American. Born in Chicago, Illinois, 16 May 1928. Educated at Antioch College, B.A. 1950. Married Matthew B. Miles in 1949; two daughters, one son. Assistant kindergarten teacher at New Lincoln School, 1950-51; Bank Street College of Education, New York, instructor in children's language and literature, 1971-75; currently free-lance author. Frequent speaker to various parent, teacher, library, and classroom groups. Consultant to Beginner Books of Random House, National Coordinating Council on Drug Education, and "Sesame Street," Children's Television Workshop. Recipient: Distinguished Achievement award, Educational Press Association, 1973; Child Association Book of the Year award and Outstanding Science Books for Children award, both 1974, both for *Save the Earth! An Ecology Handbook for Kids;* Child Association

Book of the Year award, 1974; for *The Real Me;* Mark Twain award, 1984, and Georgia Children's Book award, 1986, both for *The Secret Life of the Underwear Champ.* Address: 94 Sparkill Ave., Tappan, NY 10983, U.S.A.

PUBLICATIONS FOR YOUNG ADULTS

Fiction

The Real Me. New York, Knopf, 1974.
All It Takes Is Practice. New York, Knopf, 1976.
Just the Beginning. New York, Knopf, 1976.
Looking On. New York, Knopf, 1978.
The Trouble with Thirteen. New York, Knopf, 1979.
Maudie and Me and the Dirty Book. New York, Knopf, 1980.
The Secret Life of the Underwear Champ, illustrated by Dan Jones. New York, Knopf, 1981.
I Would If I Could. New York, Knopf, 1982.
Sink or Swim. New York, Knopf, 1986.

Nonfiction

Save the Earth: An Ecology Handbook for Kids, illustrated by Claire A. Nivola and with photographs. New York, Knopf, 1974.
Save the Earth: An Action Handbook for Kids, illustrated by Nelle Davis. New York, Knopf, 1991.

PUBLICATIONS FOR CHILDREN

Picture books

A House for Everyone, illustrated by Jo Lowrey. New York, Knopf, 1958.
What Is the World? illustrated by Remy Charlip. New York, Knopf, 1958.
The Cooking Book, illustrated by Jo Lowrey. New York, Knopf, 1959.
Having a Friend, illustrated by Eric Blegvad. New York, Knopf, 1959.
A Day of Summer, illustrated by Remy Charlip. New York, Knopf, 1960.
A Day of Winter, illustrated by Remy Charlip. New York, Knopf, 1961.
Mr. Turtle's Mystery, illustrated by Margaret Tomes. New York, Knopf, 1961; London, Hamish Hamilton, 1961.
The Feast on Sullivan Street, illustrated by Kurt Werth. New York, Knopf, 1963.
Associate Editor, *The Bank Street Readers.* New York, Macmillan, 1965-69.
A Day of Autumn, illustrated by Marjorie Auerbach. New York, Knopf, 1967.
Joe Finds a Way, with Joan Blos; illustrated by Lee Ames. New York, Singer, 1967.
A Day of Spring, illustrated by Marjorie Auerbach. New York, Knopf, 1970.
Just Think, with Joan Blos; illustrated by Pat Grant Porter. New York, Knopf, 1971.
Around and Around—Love, illustrated with photographs. New York, Knopf, 1975.

How To Read: A Book for Beginners, illustrated by Sylvie Wickstrom. New York, Knopf, 1994.

*

Biography: Entry in *Fifth Book of Junior Authors and Illustrators,* New York, H.W. Wilson, 1983; essay in *Something about the Author Autobiography Series,* Volume 9, Detroit, Gale, 1990; essay in *Speaking for Ourselves, Too* compiled and edited by Donald R. Gallo, National Council of Teachers of English, 1993.

Betty Miles comments:

Reading is one way all of us—young adults and older ones, too— discover how other ordinary people learn to make choices, take stands and try to do what they think is right. I always hope that my books, along with all the others, will help to support and encourage young people as they are growing. I'm grateful for the dedicated parents, librarians, and teachers who—despite hard times and low budgets—work to bring books and young readers together.

*   *   *

It is apparent that Betty Miles writes about contemporary issues, making her a popular twentieth-century writer for young adults. She wrote *Save the Earth!* because she wanted people to care as she does about environmental problems. She also cares about young people and the problems they are faced with every day.

The Real Me is really about Betty Miles and the way she feels and thinks, but it is written about an adolescent girl, Barbara Fisher, fighting to end sex discrimination in PE classes in her school. Barbara wants to take tennis, but only boys are allowed to take that class, so Barbara pushes the school to allow girls to choose classes other than slimnastics, field hockey, modern dance, or acrobatics. Barbara also wants to be a paper carrier, but once again she faces sex discrimination because paper delivery is for boys only. Barbara's mother, a writer for the local newspaper, is fighting for women's rights, too, and the two females are all of a sudden treated like nuts. However, neither back down in what they believe. They find, to their delight and satisfaction, that they can and do help make changes in their community and make life more bearable for the female population in general. This is a comfortable story of a loving family that sticks together, works and plays together, and celebrates together the accomplishments of each member of the family. Young people will learn about justice and equality after reading this book and will see the importance of the women's liberation movement for everyone.

A real eye-opener, *Maudie and Me and the Dirty Book* portrays Kate Harris and Maudie Schmidt who volunteer for a special project in English class. The project involves working with first graders, helping them learn to read. Kate is not happy being paired with Maudie, because Maudie is not one of Kate's crowd and one who most kids tend to avoid. But the two girls go to the library where Kate, with the help of the librarian, innocently picks out a book about a dog that has puppies. She reads the book to the first graders, and an innocent discussion on sexual anatomy follows the reading. Later, Kate is shocked to find herself in the middle of a

protest at a town meeting where some of the narrow-minded citizens object to the book Kate read, saying it was smut. Kate bravely stands up in front of the crowded auditorium and voices her beliefs on the rights of kids to learn and to state that the book is not smut but is educational. Kate is warmly supported by her family and teacher, and a lasting friendship with Maudie develops. Both entertaining and enlightening, the story is humorous, educational, and well-written, subtly teaching a lesson in democracy.

A group of kids from New York City are chosen to spend two weeks with families in New Hampshire and are known as the Fresh Air kids in *Sink or Swim.* B.J. Johnson seems to be the only black kid in the New Hampshire town and finds himself with a white family, Jackie and Norm Roberts and their two children. B.J. is happy when everyone welcomes him and makes him feel right at home, but he has never been to the country and finds it a trifle frightening. Betty Miles has written an enjoyable story about new experiences, accepting and being accepted, and the joy with which B.J. greets each new day in the country. The reader can smell the chickens, the flowers and fresh air, and feel the fear as B.J. learns the hard way to swim to the raft at the swimming pond. The book is appealing with its undercurrent of inter-racial love and good feeling despite differences.

Cathy Myers is thirteen years old, her mother just became a cleaning lady, and Cathy is going to be suspended from school for leaving the school grounds to go to a local coffee shop in *Just the Beginning.* Besides that, George Waldman picks on Cathy constantly, even though she tries to avoid him. Cathy faces her suspension, learns to deal with her mother being a cleaning lady, and then has to face the trauma of George Waldman dying a violent death. Ms. Miles has written about growing up and facing responsibilities and of a teenager learning that life isn't always what we want it to be. Through Cathy's eyes we see the importance of family love and sharing, the pressure of trying to be like others, and the knowledge that one has to face growing up, regardless of obstacles. Although the pace is slow, the theme is clear.

The Trouble with Thirteen is full of changes. It is a story about two best friends, Annie Morrison and Rachel Weiss. Annie is very self-conscious about her changing body, her moods, and her feelings. She's not quite sure she's ready to grow up, but finds she really doesn't have any choice. Rachel's parents are getting a divorce and the family is moving to New York City, and Annie is devastated that Rachel is leaving her. Then the Morrison's dog dies in Annie's arms, and things seem too much for her to deal with all at once. Ms. Miles has written a perceptive story of a young girl coping reluctantly with changes in her life but accepting them because she has to. The story touches one's heart with the sadness of losing a beloved pet that dies and a beloved friend that moves away, but the story shows that young people can deal with these things and life does go on.

Rosalie Hudnecker in *Looking On* is a fourteen-year-old, tall, overweight junior high girl seeking love and happiness as does every young person. When a young married couple moves into a small trailer next door, Rosie sees a possible place to go to find a sense of belonging and sharing that she so desperately craves. She discovers she doesn't fit in with the Judsons because she has a life of her own to live. She goes on a diet, gets her hair cut, and becomes more involved with friends her own age. This is a quiet, slow-moving story of a girl growing up, determined to change herself for the better.

Whether the background issue is ecology or women's liberation, racial discrimination or censorship, Ms. Miles writes stories that appeal to youthful readers because ultimately her books are about changing and growing and helping young people to learn about themselves.

—Carol Doxey

———————

MILLER, Frances A. American. Born in New York City, 15 October 1937. Educated at Wellesley College, Wellesley, Massachusetts, B.A. 1959; California State University, Hayward, Teaching Credential, 1976; graduate study at San Jose State University, California. Married John David Miller; two daughters and two sons. Reading tutor and volunteer worker at public schools in Oakland and San Ramon, California, 1966-75; reading and English teacher at middle school in Hayward, California, 1976-77; member of executive board, Adult Literacy Program, Sydney, Australia, 1979-83; writer and public speaker, 1983—. Coordinator of "Aussie Books for Kids" exhibit, 1984-88. Recipient: ALA Best Book for Young Adults, California Young Reader Medal, both 1985, both for *The Truth Trap*. Address: Australian Connection, P.O. Box 341, Danville, CA 94526, U.S.A.

PUBLICATIONS FOR YOUNG ADULTS

Fiction

The Truth Trap. New York, Dutton, 1980.
Aren't You the One Who...? New York, Atheneum, 1983.
Losers and Winners. New York, Fawcett, 1986.
Cutting Loose. New York, Fawcett, 1991.

*   *   *

Frances A. Miller has written four novels which follow the same character through two-and-a-half years of living. *The Truth Trap* is the first in the series that follows Matt McKendrick on a quest beginning when he is fifteen-years-old. Until that time he had lived with a strong and loving family in a small town where they kept a cattle ranch. Suddenly everything changes for him when his parents are killed in an accident. Fearing that the authorities will take his younger sister away, Matt runs to Los Angeles believing he can take care of her if he finds work. Deaf since birth, his sister has a close relationship with Matt. While he is searching for a job she is murdered; Matt is accused of the crime, arrested, and although not found guilty, has his own recriminations to deal with. The policemen arresting Matt represent the two forces in society with which he will need to contend from then on: those who believe him, and those who don't. The officer who trusts Matt is the only real support he has, and Matt is eventually adopted by him.

Miller does a masterful job of climbing into her character and letting the reader hear his thoughts. Matt's inner voice is realistic, strong and relentless as it responds to the complexities of grief, anger and resentment, and most of all to the outrageous injustices inflicted on him. As *The Truth Trap* is essentially a story of survival, Matt is necessarily a self-absorbed character. In the next novel in the series, *Aren't You the One Who...?*, Matt begins to move forward in an attempt to establish relationships with the larger community, but the outside world is often hostile, and people

remember what he was accused of. Thus, the title is an appropriate question for Matt's conflict, since people are inclined to remember only the accusations, not the outcome of the case. Thus, Matt is believed to be guilty until he is able to prove that he is innocent and worthy of trust.

In this book, Matt becomes friends with the Schuylers, a family of four children who have lost their mother and are facing enormous adjustments and responsibilities of their own. In becoming friends with the Schuylers, Matt begins to take risks, to give to others, and to establish trust again. As he develops a greater acceptance for himself, he gains the courage to face the future and the challenges of going to high school. Unfortunately, school offers a new series of problems, including an insensitive running coach. Through dealing with this problem in his own way, Matt builds the confidence that he can continue to face the consequences of his decisions.

Losers and Winners takes the reader into Matt's senior year in high school and his competition for "Runner of the Year." The story further develops his relationship with the Schuylers as they continue to fill the empty spaces in his life. The fourth novel of the series, *Cutting Loose*, takes Matt home to Idaho where he and his friends work on a guest ranch. As it turns out, the guest ranch was once his family home, and Matt must now face the task of literally learning to let go of the past.

The plot in each of these novels is strong and appealing to young adult readers. Underlying the extraordinary events of the novels are numerous themes and messages. Although never didactic, Miller has strong convictions about her characters, young people and the relationships between them. She strives to create in Matt a character who in spite of atrocious odds is a winner, and who is able to grow, change, and learn. She provides a protagonist the reader cares about, because Matt is a problem solver who develops tenacity, possesses a strong sense of justice and fairness, and remains loyal and caring.

These stories can be read independently of each other, but following the growth of Matt is rewarding if the four are read in order. The thematic thread that connects them all is the fact that society often judges everything at face value rather than taking the time to learn and understand. Miller demonstrates her belief that all ages and stages of development are of value, and adults and young people need to share mutual respect. Making mistakes and taking risks are valued as agents of growth. The characters the reader does not care for are those who are unwilling to change, and who refuse to look beyond their preconceptions and stereotypical judgments.

As a parent of four children, a teacher of middle school students and an avid reader, Miller has accrued a storehouse of knowledge about young people. She gives voice to their strong emotions, and allows her characters a full range of feelings, reactions and reflections. Her dialogues ring true, and readers believe the words of her characters. Miller is exceptionally gifted in capturing the intensity of youth and the conflicts of the teenage years. She describes so well how quickly emotions can give way to other feelings; the ever changing emotional landscape of youth is what she knows best. Miller's words are clear, strong and succinct and she spends them generously on Matt's feelings; she provides enough knowledge about him to make the reader care about her character. Thus, Miller awards the reader with a sense of hope, and confirms the need to believe that anyone can overcome even the most difficult of circumstances.

—Caroline S. McKinney

———————

MILLER, Jim Wayne. American. Born in Leicester, North Carolina, 21 October 1936. Educated at Berea College, A.B. 1958; Vanderbilt University, Ph.D. 1965. Married Mary Ellen Yates in 1958; two sons and one daughter. German and English teacher, Fort Knox Dependent Schools, Fort Knox, Kentucky, 1958-60; assistant professor, 1963-66, associate professor, 1966-70, professor, since 1970, Western Kentucky University, Bowling Green. Affiliated with Poet-in-the-Schools Program, Virginia public schools, beginning 1977; poet-in-residence, Centre College of Kentucky, 1984. Staff member, Hindman Settlement School Writers Workshop, since 1978; fellow of the corporation of Yaddo, 1983-84. Invited reader, fiftieth anniversary meeting of South Atlantic Modern Language Association, 1978. Visiting professor, Appalachian Studies Workshop, Berea College, 1973-80, and James R. Stokely Institute for Liberal Arts Education, University of Tennessee, 1984-85. Chairman, Kentucky Humanities Council, Inc., 1973-74; board member, Appalachian Community Service Network. Consultant to poetry workshops in Kentucky, Virginia, North Carolina, Tennessee, Indiana, and West Virginia; consultant to Appalachian studies programs at colleges and universities throughout the Appalachian South; member of advisory board of "An Appalachian Experience," Children's Museum, Oak Ridge, Tennessee. Recipient: Alice Lloyd Memorial Prize for Appalachian Poetry from Alice Lloyd College, 1967, for poems in *Copperhead Cane;* Sigma Tau Delta Topaz award for Distinguished Service to the University, Western Kentucky University, 1969, Western Kentucky University faculty award for research and creativity, 1976; Thomas Wolfe Literary award, for *The Mountains Have Come Closer,* 1980; received honorary doctorate of letters, Berea College, 1981; Western Kentucky University faculty award for public service, 1982; Distinguished Alumnus award, Berea College Alumni Association, 1983; Appalachian Writers Association Book of the Year award, 1989, for *Newfound;* Zoe Kincaid Brockman Memorial award for Poetry, North Carolina Poetry Society, 1989; Appalachian Writers Association award for Outstanding Contributions to Appalachian Literature, 1990; Educational Service to Appalachia award, Carson-Newman College, Jefferson City, Tennessee, 1990; Laurel Leaves award, Appalachian Consortium of Colleges and Universities, 1991; literary awards for poetry, short stories, and translations from Kentucky Writers Guild, *Green River Review, Appalachian Harvest,* and *Kentucky Poetry Review.* Address: 1512 Eastland Dr., Bowling Green, KY 42104, U.S.A.

PUBLICATIONS

Poetry

Copperhead Cane. Nashville, Tennessee, Robert Moore Allen, 1964.
The More Things Change, the More They Stay the Same (ballads). Frankfort, Kentucky, Whippoorwill Press, 1971.
Dialogue with a Dead Man. Athens, Georgia, University of Georgia Press, 1974, reprinted Saginaw, Michigan, Green River Press, 1978.
The Mountains Have Come Closer. Boone, North Carolina, Appalachian Consortium, 1980, reprinted 1991.
Vein of Words. Big Timber, Montana, Seven Buffaloes Press, 1984.
Nostalgia for 70. Big Timber, Montana, Seven Buffaloes Press, 1986.
His First Best Country. Frankfort, Kentucky, Gnomon, 1987.
Brier, His Book. Frankfort, Kentucky, Gnomon, 1988.

Round and Round with Kahlil Gibran. Blacksburg, Virginia, Rowan Mountain, 1990.

Novel

Newfound. New York, Orchard, 1989, reprinted, 1991.

Other

Translator, *The Figure of Fulfillment,* by Emil Lerperger. University Center, Michigan, Green River, 1975.
Contributor, *Voices from the Mountains,* edited by Guy and Candie Carawan. New York, Knopf, 1975.
Contributor, *Voices from the Hills,* edited by Robert J. Higgs and Ambrose Manning. New York, F. Ungar, 1977.
Contributor, *A Geography of Poets,* edited by Edward Field. New York, Bantam, 1979.
Editor, *I Have a Place.* Pippa Passes, Kentucky, Appalachian Learning Laboratory, 1980.
Reading, Writing, Region: A Checklist and Purchase Guide for School and Community Libraries. Boone, North Carolina, Appalachian Consortium, 1984.
Contributor, *Strings: A Gathering of Family Poems,* edited by Paul B. Janeczko. Scarsdale, New York, 1984.
Contributor, *United States in Literature.* Glenview, Illinois, Scott, Foresman, 1984.
Contributor, *Geography and Literature: A Meeting of the Disciplines,* edited by Paul Simpson-Housley and William E. Mallory. Syracuse, New York, Syracuse University Press, 1986.
Contributor, *Going over to Your Place,* edited by Paul B. Janeczko. New York, Bradbury, 1987.
Editor, *A Jesse Stuart Reader.* Ashland, Kentucky, Jesse Stuart Foundation, 1988.
Editor, *A Ride with Huey the Engineer.* Ashland, Kentucky, Jesse Stuart Foundation, 1988.
Contributor, *The Music of What Happens: Poems That Tell Stories,* edited by Paul B. Janeczko. New York, Orchard Books, 1988.
Editor, *The Beatinest Boy.* Ashland, Kentucky, Jesse Stuart Foundation, 1989.
Contributor, *An Ear to the Ground: An Anthology of Contemporary American Poetry,* edited by Marie Harris and Kathleen Aguero. Athens, Georgia, University of Georgia Press, 1989.
The Examined Life: Family, Community, and Work in American Literature. Boone, North Carolina, Appalachian Consortium, 1989.
Editor, *The Rightful Owner.* Ashland, Kentucky, Jesse Stuart Foundation, 1989.
Contributor, *Our Words, Our Ways: Reading and Writing in North Carolina,* edited by Sally Buckner. Durham, North Carolina, Carolina Academic Press, 1991.
Contributor, *Preposterous: Poems of Youth,* edited by Paul B. Janeczko. New York, Orchard Books, 1991.
Contributor, *Perspectives* (grade 8 language arts anthology), edited by Ed Hannan and others. Toronto, Holt, 1991.
Contributor, *Men of Our Time: Male Poetry in Contemporary America,* edited by Fred Moramarco and Al Zolynas. Athens, Georgia, University of Georgia Press, 1992.
Editor, *Southern Mountain Speech.* Kentucky, Berea College Press, 1992.
Editor, *A Penny's Worth of Character,* by Jesse Stuart, illustrated by Rocky Zornes. Ashland, Kentucky, Jesse Stuart Foundation, 1993.

Jim Wayne Miller comments:

For me, writing has never been a matter of having something to say and then saying it. Rather, writing is an attempt to clarify concerns I have, questions I put to myself. Thinking of writing in this way, I've made experiments and probes, said a lot of things, and then decided which of those things I meant! Instead of knowing in advance what I want to say, I always have to discover my meaning in and through the process of writing.

But no matter how much or how little I write in the future, I know the quality I want the work to possess. Growing up in western North Carolina, I was often amused, along with other natives, at tourists who fished the trout streams. The pools, so perfectly clear, had a deceptive depth. Fishermen unacquainted with them, wearing hip waders, were forever stepping off into pools they judged to be knee-deep—and going in up to their waists or even their armpits, sometimes being floated right off their feet. I want to make my writing like those pools, so simple and clear its depth is deceptive. I want the writing to be transparent, so readers forget they are reading and are aware only that they are having an experience. They are suddenly plunged deeper than they expected and come up shivering.

*　　*　　*

Jim Wayne Miller, a professor of German at Western Kentucky University, has published essays, poetry, fiction, and drama, has translated the poetry of an Austrian poet, and has edited and introduced some of the works of Jesse Stuart. He is best known as an exceptionally gifted poet and as a wonderfully entertaining reader of his own poetry. His touching works about growing up in a rural area and about changing family relationships also appeal to young adult readers.

Central to his accomplishments is his emphasis on place. The specific place most often called up in his poetry is the southern Appalachian Mountains, particularly western North Carolina, where he was born. He dedicated his book *Dialogue with a Dead Man* to "the people of Appalachia wherever they are." Miller's poetic persona who embodies that culture is "the Brier." Much like a Kentucky hillbilly, the Brier has roots in rural, farming America. From the 1930s to 1960s, he may have gone north to places like Detroit, Chicago, and Cincinnati to make a living, but he never forgot his home nor the wisdom he gained from his ancestors. Nevertheless, the lore and ballads are in danger of being lost if someone does not commit them to paper. Even the places may no longer exist—as Miller expresses in his poem "Small Farms Disappearing in Tennessee" from *Brier, His Book.*

Fortunately, the Brier records in easily accessible language the essence of Appalachian culture. The first stanza of "Squirrel Stand," from *Dialogue with a Dead Man,* provides a good example:

Now burley's curing in the high-tiered barn
and yellow leaves ride out on slow black water.
Cold wind moving in the rows of corn
rattles the blades like an old man pulling fodder.
Down from the mountain pastures overnight,
cattle stand by the yellow salt block bawling.
Now it's September in the world; fine rain is falling.

From the perspective of his otherness, the Brier describes, sometimes satirically, what's wrong with modern man. In "Brier Sermon," from *The Mountains Have Come Closer,* the Brier berates his audience for forgetting about the past, about their innocent,

childlike selves, and for losing touch with nature. A clever reversal occurs in the self-mocking poem "The Brier Losing Touch with His Traditions," from the same collection. An "authentic mountain craftsman," the Brier goes north to be closer to his market. But his northern customers are dismayed to find that he uses electric power tools to make those authentic chairs, so he has to move back to Kentucky "to have some time for himself" and to keep his customers believing in his authenticity.

In addition to his emphasis on place, Miller believes that metaphor is the literal soul of poetry. In "From the Brier Glossary of Literary Terms," in *Brier, His Book,* he defines a poem as Thoreau might have: "A cold spring. Sweet water nobody knows is / there but you. You stand, looking down, and / see yourself outlined against the sky." And in "The Brier Plans a Mountain Vision Center," from the same collection, the Brier tells what poems do: unlike rose-colored glasses, they make "gentle contact with the mind's eye, / like a soft lens, lining up then with now, now with then, news with news that stays news, like front and / rear gun sights."

Miller "aims" various poems at death, for instance "Aunt Gladys's Home Movie No. 31, Albert's Funeral," from *Dialogue with a Dead Man.* This poem describes a family gathered after their uncle Albert's funeral to view a home movie eulogizing Albert and his love of flowers:

Our chairs drawn to one end of the living
room, we sit like faithful at a Sunday evening
service, viewing a miracle. Before our eyes
Albert stirs in the ticking coil of dark
film and comes riding a beam of light,
a smear of colors, finger painting—flowers.

Part of the attraction of the poem is its esoteric pattern: it is a sestina, an amazingly complex French lyric form.

A large number of Miller's poems focus on the concerns of middle-class Americans—the joys of raising children, the sound of a vacuum cleaner on Saturday morning, dreams, living and dying. The persona of a poem called "Skydivers," in *The Mountains Have Come Closer,* uses two apt metaphors to sum up the changing relationship between a parent and his family. Life, the poem suggests, is like riding a chair-lift in an amusement park. Everyone enjoys the ride and the thrills it provides, although each member of the family is ultimately separated from the others. As time passes, the metaphor changes. Now the family is skydiving, and the thrills are even greater, but so, finally, is the separation:

It is pleasant and so still but we are falling
farther and farther apart through private corridors
of air. The earth grows under us, and begins
to be patches of ground the size of our shadows.

The pleasure of skydiving, of living, is always modified by the persona's knowledge of the coming "shadows," or final separation places—their graves.

Provocative images, delightful, clarifying metaphors, gentle satire, insights into family living, and celebrations of his Appalachian past all mark Jim Wayne Miller as an accomplished writer. His poetry is well worth reading and comprehending.

—John Reiss

MITCHELL, Margaret (Munnerlyn). Also wrote as Peggy Mitchell, Margaret Mitchell Upshaw, Elizabeth Bennett. American. Born in Atlanta, Georgia, 8 November 1900. Educated at Washington Seminary, Atlanta, 1914-18; Smith College, Northampton, Massachusetts, 1918-19. Married 1) Berrien Kinnard Upshaw in 1922 (annulled 1924); 2) John Robert Marsh in 1925. Feature writer and reporter, Atlanta *Journal and Constitution* and *Sunday Journal Magazine,* 1922-26. Free-lance columnist, 1926; novelist, 1926-36; homemaker, 1936-49. Volunteer selling war bonds during World War II; volunteer for the American Red Cross in the 1940s. Recipient: Pulitzer Prize from Columbia University Graduate School of Journalism, 1937, for *Gone with the Wind;* Bohmenberger Memorial award, 1938; M.A.: Smith College, 1939; named honorary citizen of Vimoutiers, France, 1949, for helping the city obtain American aid after World War II. *Died 16 August 1949.*

PUBLICATIONS

Fiction

Gone with the Wind. New York and London, Macmillan, 1936.

Other

Margaret Mitchell's "Gone with the Wind" Letters, edited by Richard Harwell. New York, Macmillan, and London, Collier Macmillan, 1976.
Margaret Mitchell, A Dynamo Going to Waste: Letters to Allen Edee, 1919-1921, edited by Jane Bonner Peacock. Atlanta, Peachtree Publications, 1985.

*

Media Adaptation: *Gone with the Wind* (film, starring Clark Gable, Vivien Leigh, Leslie Howard, and Olivia De Havilland), Metro-Goldwyn-Mayer, 1939.

Biography: Entry in *Dictionary of Literary Biography,* Volume 9: *American Novelists, 1910-1945,* Detroit, Gale, 1981.

Manuscript Collections: University of Georgia, Athens; Atlanta Public Library.

Critical Studies: *Margaret Mitchell of Atlanta* by Finis Farr, New York, Morrow, 1965; *The Road to Tara: The Life of Margaret Mitchell* by Anne Edwards, New Haven, Connecticut, Ticknor and Fields, and London, Hodder & Stoughton, 1983; *Gone with the Wind as Book and Film* edited by Richard Harwell, Columbia, University of South Carolina Press, 1983.

* * *

Although Margaret Mitchell did not consider herself a writer for young adults, her single masterpiece, *Gone with the Wind,* and its blockbuster film version have been perennial favorites of American teenagers, to the point that both are often included in high school and college curriculums. The increased interest of recent years following the fiftieth anniversaries of both the novel (1986) and the film (1989), as well as the publication of an authorized sequel (1992) will surely extend the popularity of *Gone with the Wind* into

the next century. This popular phenomenon proves most interesting as Mitchell's masterwork seems a nineteenth-century book in subject, theme, and style—a twentieth-century reincarnation of the Victorian "triple-decker" romance. Thus the book's remarkable popularity is a combination of tradition and change much like the narrative it relates.

In critical terms, it is possible to read *Gone with the Wind* as a female development novel. At the novel's opening in 1861, Scarlett O'Hara is a sixteen-year-old coquette; when it concludes in 1873 she is a twenty-eight-year-old woman. In the twelve year span of the novel, she experiences Secession, Civil War, and Reconstruction, as well as romance, love, marriage, and motherhood. Scarlett lives through the adolescent trauma of American culture, which is matched by a traumatic personal history as much or more tumultuous. Energized by her own life, Mitchell created one of the most arresting tales of troubled adolescence in American literature and in so doing created a novel which will continue to captivate teenagers and fascinate their teachers well into the next century.

For younger readers, Scarlett O'Hara's development from teen-aged girl to mature woman proves as fascinating now as it did when the book was first published in 1936 or when the movie first appeared in 1939. The particular, indeed peculiar energy of the story proceeds from Mitchell's own girlhood, adolescence, and young adult life. During these years she heard the family legends of the Civil War era into which she projected her own development toward womanhood. The novel combines Mitchell's family and personal romances with historical facts to create powerful and popular fiction.

The popular image of Mitchell was as a Southern matron who turned to writing as her contemporaries might cultivate bridge, golf, or gardening. Although descended from old Georgia families and raised in comfortable circumstances, the future author was no simple Southern belle. Her mother's feminist leanings clashed with her father's conservatism, and a young Mitchell became a somewhat willful, rebellious tomboy, given to flights of imaginative fancy and a series of serious, debilitating accidents and illnesses. After the death of her first beloved on the Western Front and of her mother in the influenza epidemic, Mitchell became "a flapper," both living the wild times of the Jazz age and writing about them in nonfiction. Her first marriage was a disaster, climaxed by spousal rape and scandalous divorce, while her second marriage mirrored her dependent, and sometimes stressful relationships with her father and brother. The writer's social, psychological, and sexual ambiguities found expression in her greatest creation, Scarlett O'Hara, while other people in her life provided models for other characters in *Gone with the Wind.*

The critical history of *Gone with the Wind* is contradictory, as might be expected from the writer's conflicted biography. The reaction of reviewers and of general readers was quite positive in 1936, for no one would deny that the novel was a great "read." Even the initial response of the literary community seemed laudatory. Comparisons were made with the great novelists and novels of the nineteenth century—such as Thackeray and *Vanity Fair,* Tolstoy and *Anna Karenina,* and Flaubert and *Madame Bovary.* In terms of memorable characters, sweeping action, colorful settings, and grand themes the novel was a success. At the same time, qualifying statements about style, sentiment, racism, and melodrama raised legitimate questions about the book's literary status.

Unfortunately, the novel's existence as a cultural artifact subsumed its identity as a literary text and the immense power and popularity of the film version only complicated the situation. Book and film were conflated into a phenomenon of American and later international popular culture. Thus criticism was arrested at the levels of basic appreciation, often in the opposite poles of love and/ or hate, and evaluation, again often in bipolar terms of praise and/or scorn. On the popular level the novel was lauded and in the literary world it was defamed.

This critical neglect continued well into the 1960s when reconsiderations of American culture and society elicited new readings of classic texts. Mitchell and her novel were seen as important symbols of American cultural forces. A serious biography in 1965 sparked reconsideration simply by the assumption of Mitchell's importance as a writer. Other reevaluations followed which asserted the literary quality of the work, notably in feminist terms. The critical neglect of the novel thus was explained in terms of the largely male critical establishment, and Mitchell became the subject of articles and dissertations in the 1970s. Finally, in the 1980s, the half-century anniversaries of both novel and film provided new perspectives for critical focus in a number of important critical works, including a definitive biography.

—Joseph R. Millichap

———————

MOERI, Louise. American. Born in Klamath Falls, Oregon, 30 November 1924. Educated at Stockton Junior College, A.A. 1944; University of California, Berkeley, B.A. 1946. Married Edwin Albert Moeri in 1946; one daughter and two sons. Library assistant, Manteca Branch Library, Manteca, California, 1961-78; writer. Address: 18262 South Austin Road, Manteca, CA 95336, U.S.A.

PUBLICATIONS FOR YOUNG ADULTS

Fiction

The Girl Who Lived on the Ferris Wheel. New York, Dutton, 1979.
Save Queen of Sheba. New York, Dutton, 1981.
First the Egg. New York, Dutton, 1982.
Downwind. New York, Dutton, 1984.
Journey to the Treasure. New York, Scholastic, 1986.
Forty-third War. Boston, Houghton Mifflin, 1989.

PUBLICATIONS FOR CHILDREN

Fiction

Star Mother's Youngest Child, illustrated by Trina Schart Hyman. Boston, Houghton Mifflin, 1975.
A Horse for XYZ, illustrated by Gail Owens. New York, Dutton, 1977.
How the Rabbit Stole the Moon, illustrated by Marc Brown. Boston, Houghton Mifflin, 1977.
The Unicorn and the Plow, illustrated by Diane Goode. New York, Dutton, 1982.

*

Biography: Essay in *Something about the Author Autobiography Series,* Volume 10, Detroit, Gale, 1990; essay in *Speaking for Our-*selves, Too compiled and edited by Donald R. Gallo, National Council of Teachers of English, 1993.

Louise Moeri comments:

I consider writing to be one of the hardest jobs in the world, and if I weren't compelled to do it, I'd take up some other line of work. But the fact is, I was born to be a writer, as I feel most creative people are born to paint, compose, or whatever medium reaches out to them. Whatever your talents are, they are included in the package that you come into the world with, and it is up to you to look into that package and discover what it is you are meant to be. My particular obsession with words and sentences began very early in my life, and shows no sign of abatement as I now face my sixty-ninth birthday. Picking up a pencil or sitting down at my typewriter marks the beginning of just one more chapter in my struggle to put some piece of human life into printed words to make a difference in someone's understanding of the world around him. Creative people are like lenses—they reveal details and patterns in life that might otherwise be missed.

But as difficult, unrewarding, and unnoticed as it often is, there is nothing I can do that is as exiting as watching a story emerge from my pencil onto a piece of paper. Since I am not one of those masterful writers who knows exactly what is going to happen in the story from the first word, I am fascinated as each incident, each chapter appears. It is a wonder-filled experience as I live it along with the characters who tug at my sleeve and say—"Hey! Let me tell you what happened..." and no matter how hard it is, I'm going to go right on doing it.

*   *   *

When asked to recommend an author for a middle grade or junior high reader with a penchant for fast-paced adventure plots and hooks with page-turning appeal, Louise Moeri comes to mind. Moeri creates believable characters that foster empathy in readers. In contrast to many young adult novels with protagonists free of family responsibilities, Moeri's characters are children with adult challenges. Although Moeri's stories center on a variety of subject matter and themes, most of which are relevant and sometimes controversial, the novels are essentially about human nature and refrain from sensationalism.

The Girl Who Lived on the Ferris Wheel is described by the publisher as a psychological thriller. How will Clotilde (Til for short) continue to bear her mother's beatings? Won't her loving but unseeing father recognize Til's misery and danger? What will happen to Til's deeply disturbed mother? The suspense intensifies and the reader is breathless waiting to discover if Til escapes her mother's butcher knife. Divorce, child abuse, and mental illness are the topics of this novel, but the real story is eleven-year-old Til's struggle to survive in a world where the adults seem unable to help.

In *First the Egg* Sarah Webster and David Hanna become the unwilling parents of an egg. In order to complete their marriage and family class project, Sarah and David must protect and nurture the egg for an entire week; they can never leave it alone, and they must complete a baby book chronicling the egg baby's development. Sarah's responsibilities open her eyes to the disturbing patterns within her own family that she has previously ignored and helps her reach out to David who is headed for trouble. Natural language and everyday situations help the reader identify with Sarah. Moeri's realistic descriptions of Sarah's frustration with the silliness of the project when it is first assigned to actually "missing" the egg when the project is over enhances the credibility of the story. It is easy for readers to put themselves in Sarah's place.

Twelve-year-old King David and his six-year-old sister Queen of Sheba are the only survivors of a Sioux Indian attack on their Oregon Trail wagon train. David takes charge of his whiny, sulky sister and follows the trail of some wagons that may have gotten away, hoping to find his parents. Starving and exhausted David faces the temptations of abandoning the petulant Sheba. *True Queen of Sheba* is suspenseful and engaging. The reader respects David's responsibility and yearns for a happy ending even when the youngsters' plight seems hopeless.

In *Downwind* it is twelve-year-old Ephraim Dearborn who must act as an adult and take responsibility for his three younger siblings. Ephraim's family lives downwind of the local nuclear power plant and meltdown is imminent according to the local news. In panic, the Dearborn's attempt to escape, only to find chaos and traffic jams blocking the road to safety. Ephraim's mother breaks down and is unable to take care of the two children hurt in the scramble. *Downwind* is another page turner with an admirable young protagonist who rises to meet the challenges of an adult situation. Ephraim's world does not collapse, but he is changed forever.

Uno, Lolo, and Macio have managed to escape the soldiers—both the Revolutionaries and the Loyalists—who periodically round up all the boys in their Central American village and force them to become soldiers. War has always been a part of their lives, and the fathers and older men were taken long ago. No one in the villages goes untouched. Uno's sister is raped by the soldiers, and there is little food or money for the village families. During a surprise raid Uno, Lolo, and Macio are "recruited" at gunpoint to join the revolutionaries. Uno has never understood the reasons for fighting, but during eight days of training, patrol, and battles he sees villagers massacred by the government's Loyalist troops and becomes committed to the rebel cause. In *The Forty-third War,* Moeri once again uses realistic dialogue and emotion to create a novel which allows young adults to read with caring and belief the story of boys who must become men in order to survive.

In all of Moeri's thin, but powerful books, the protagonists not only survive but develop an understanding of the transience of life and the complexities of human nature. Cynical readers may scoff at the happy endings achieved in Moeri's chronicles of adverse conditions and unthinkable hardships, but the careful construction of credible characters and the tense plots ensure that most readers are cheering for these stalwart youngsters and will be dissatisfied with anything less than favorable resolutions. For the young adolescent the message is clear, life is often a struggle, but you, too, can overcome the hardships.

—Hollis Lowery-Moore

————

MOHR, Nicholasa. American. Born in New York City, 1 November 1938. Educated at Art Students' League, 1957-58; Taller de Grafica, Mexico City, 1956; New School for Social Research, New York, New York, 1959; Brooklyn Museum of Art School, 1965-67; Pratt Center for Contemporary Printmaking, 1967-70. Married Irwin Mohr in 1958 (deceased), two sons. Fine arts painter in New York, California, Mexico, and Puerto Rico, 1957-58; printmaker in New York, Mexico, and Puerto Rico, 1965—; teacher in art schools in New York, 1968-69. Art instructor, Art Center of Northern New Jersey, 1971-73; writer in residence, MacDowell Colony, Peterborough, New Hampshire, 1972, 1974, and 1976; artist in residence, New York City public schools, 1973-74; lecturer in Puerto Rican studies, State University of New York at Stony Brook, 1977; distinguished visiting professor at Queens College of the City University of New York, 1988-91; also visiting lecturer in creative writing for various educator, librarian, student, and community groups. Head creative writer and co-producer of videotape series *Aqui y Ahora.* Member of New Jersey State Council on the Arts; member of board of trustees, and consultant, of Young Filmmakers Foundation; consultant on bilingual media training for Young Filmmakers/Video Arts. Recipient: Outstanding book award in juvenile fiction, *New York Times,* 1973, Jane Addams Children's Book award, Jane Addams Peace Association, 1974, citation of merit for book jacket design, Society of Illustrators, 1974, and *School Library Journal*'s "Best of the Best 1966-78" citation, all for *Nilda;* outstanding book award in teenage fiction, *New York Times,* 1975, best book award, *School Library Journal,* 1975, and National Book award finalist for "most distinguished book in children's literature," 1976, all for *El Bronx Remembered;* best book award, *School Library Journal,* best book award in young adult literature, American Library Association, and Notable Trade Book award, joint committee of National Council for the Social Studies and Children's Book Council, all 1977, all for *In Nueva York;* Notable Trade Book award, joint committee of National Council for the Social Studies and Children's Book Council, 1980, and American Book award, Before Columbus Foundation, 1981, both for *Felita;* commendation from the Legislature of the State of New York, 1985, for *Rituals of Survival: A Woman's Portfolio;* honorary doctorate of letters, State University of New York at Albany, 1989. Address: 727 President St., Brooklyn, NY 11215, U.S.A.

PUBLICATIONS FOR YOUNG ADULTS

Novels

Nilda, illustrated by the author. New York, Harper, 1973; updated edition, Houston, Texas, Arte Publico, 1986.
Felita, illustrated by the author. New York, Dial Press, 1979.
Going Home. New York, Dial Press, 1986.
El Bronx Remembered: A Novella and Stories, illustrated by the author. New York, Harper, 1975; updated edition, Houston, Texas, Arte Publico, 1986.
All for the Better: A Story of el Barrio, illustrated by Rudy Gutierrez. Austin, Texas, Raintree, 1992.
Isabel's New Mom. New York, Macmillan, 1993.
Jaime and His Conch Shell. New York, Scholastic, 1994.
Old Letivia and the Mountain of Sorrows. New York, Viking, 1994.

Short Stories

In Nueva York. New York, Dial Press, 1977; updated edition, Houston, Texas, Arte Publico, 1988.

Radio Play: *Inside the Monster,* New York, Film Video Arts, 1981.

Television Play: *Aqui Y Ahora,* New York, Film Video Arts, 1975.

PUBLICATIONS FOR ADULTS

Fiction

Rituals of Survival: A Women's Portfolio. Houston, Texas, Arte Publico, 1985.

Nonfiction

In My Own Words. New York, Simon and Schuster, 1994.

Also author, with Ray Blanco, of *The Artist* (screenplay). Contributor of stories to textbooks and anthologies, including *The Ethnic American Woman: Problems, Protests, Lifestyles.* Contributor of short stories to *Children's Digest, Scholastic Magazine,* and *Nuestro.* Member of board of contributing editors, *Nuestro.*

*

Biography: Essay in *Something about the Author Autobiography Series,* Volume 8, Detroit, Gale, 1989; essay in *Speaking for Ourselves: Autobiographical Sketches by Notable Authors of Books for Young Adults,* Volume 1, compiled and edited by Donald R. Gallo, National Council of Teachers of English, 1990.

Critical Study: Entry in *Contemporary Literary Criticism,* Volume 12, Detroit, Gale, 1980; entry in *Children's Literature Review,* Volume 22, Detroit, Gale, 1991.

Illustrator: *Hispanic Temas* edited by Hilda Hidalgo and Joan McEniry, 1985.

* * *

Nicholasa Mohr, the first Puerto Rican woman born on the U.S. mainland to write about her ethnic roots in New York City's Lower East Side and the South Bronx, is an artist as well as an author of young adult novels. She attended art schools and worked as a freelance painter and graphic artist for years before she began writing novels and short stories for young adults. Therefore, it is not surprising that Mohr drew the colorful, eye-catching cover art for her first two books—*Nilda* and *El Bronx Remembered*—and the expressive character drawings in each book. Her writing, in fact, simulates her art—rich in descriptive and evocative detail, vivid in its realistic word-pictures depicting slices of life from her poverty-stricken El Barrio childhood.

Mohr's first novel, *Nilda,* describes four years in the life of a ten-year-old second-generation Puerto Rican girl living in New York City during World War II. From this story, one gets a clear sense of the hurt and humiliation suffered by migrating Puerto Ricans. Because of the Jones Act of 1917, Puerto Ricans born in Puerto Rico are automatically American citizens. As a result, their language and culture have been heavily influenced by American culture and the English language. Subsequently, when Nilda's parents move to the U.S. mainland during the 1920s, they are more open to social assimilation than immigrants from other countries because of this Americanization. But they and their children are greeted by racism, gang violence, drugs, job discrimination, and pervasive poverty and are made to feel unwelcome. Nilda is one of six children whose brave and strong mother holds together a large, extended family consisting of a physically sick father, a mentally ill aunt, a brother in prison, and his pregnant girlfriend. Nilda also has to contend with a school that questions her absence to mourn her father's death according to Puerto Rican custom, a policeman who brutalizes her neighbors and who denigrates her ethnic background, and a church that exploits the trust its Puerto Rican parishioners put in it. Permeating the novel are the twin themes of inner strength and ethnic survival; Nilda's mother's last words to her daughter are "You have something all yours...keep it." In the face of social adversity and family tragedy, Nilda draws on her self-esteem and sensitivity. She copes with her father's death by meditating on the beauty of spring, the season of new life. And when her mother dies, she consoles herself by recollecting special private moments in her mother's life.

This optimism during times of travail is further developed in Mohr's second book, *El Bronx Remembered*—a collection of short stories and a novella continuing Nilda's life. Set in the 1950s, the stories concern problems similar to those appearing in her first novel: broken families, out-of-wedlock pregnancies, unfulfilled gay relationships, gang violence, and school insensitivity to the needs of Puerto Rican students. These stories focus on the second generation of Puerto Ricans in New York City whose connection to their homeland is increasingly remote. More and more they form friendships with members of other ethnic groups, sharing their problems, hopes, and dreams. Mohr's characters in this melange of stories seem to draw strength from one another. Her main message is: Life goes on.

In her third book, *In Nueva York,* the characters are older and the time is later—the 1970s. But the social problems of New York's Puerto Rican communities persist and in some cases have worsened. Like its predecessor, this book is a collection of interconnected stories and survival is its main theme. Forty years before, Old Mary—a domestic servant in Puerto Rico—had given birth to William, a son fathered by her master. Now near the end of her unhappy and unfulfilled life, she has located William. The stories deal with Mary's shock and initial disappointment upon learning that her son is a dwarf and a variety of personal and family problems. Throughout these stories, a stray street cat appears, disappears and reappears, serving as the book's controlling metaphor of survival.

Felita and its sequel *Going Home* are novels written for older children about a nine-year-old girl whose family moves out of their predominantly Puerto Rican neighborhood in New York City to a middle-class, ethnically mixed area. But Felita and her family are singled out and harassed by prejudiced neighbors from the day of their move—and eventually they return to their old neighborhood.

Although Mohr's striking and memorable visual imagery and realistic writing lay bare the underside of life in New York's Puerto Rican communities from the 1940s to the 1980s, she introduces her readers to sympathetic, sensitive characters (many of whom are adults) who love deeply, help others, and are proud of their ethnic identity even when it comes under attack. Mohr would view the proverbial cup that is half-empty and half-full as being half-full...and getting fuller all the time.

—Jack Forman

———

MOMADAY, N(avarre) Scott. American. Born in Lawton, Oklahoma, 27 February 1934. Educated at the Augusta Military Academy, University of New Mexico, Albuquerque, A.B. 1958; Stanford

University, California (creative writing fellow, 1959), A.M. 1960, Ph.D. 1963. Married 1) Gaye Mangold in 1959 (divorced), three daughters; 2) Regina Heitzer in 1978, one daughter. Assistant Professor, University of California, Santa Barbara, 1963-65; Associate Professor of English, 1968-69, Associate Professor of English and Comparative Literature, 1969-73, University of California, Berkeley; Professor of English, Stanford University, 1973-82; Professor of English, University of Arizona, Tucson, since 1982. Professor, University of California Institute for the Humanities, 1970; Whittall Lecturer, Library of Congress, Washington, D.C., 1971; Visiting Professor, New Mexico State University, Las Cruces, 1972-73, State University of Moscow, Spring 1974, Columbia University, New York, 1979, and Princeton University, New Jersey, 1979; writer-in-residence, Southeastern University, Washington, D.C., 1985, and Aspen Writers' Conference, Colorado, 1986. Artist: has exhibited drawings and paintings. Since 1978 member of the Board of Trustees, Museum of the American Indian, Heye Foundation, New York City. Consultant, National Endowment for the Humanities and National Endowment for the Arts, since 1970. Recipient: Academy of American Poets prize, 1962, for poem "The Bear"; Guggenheim fellowship, 1966-67; Pulitzer Prize for fiction, 1969, for *House Made of Dawn;* National Institute of Arts and Letters grant, 1970; American Academy award, 1970; shared Western Heritage award with David Muench, 1974, for nonfiction book *Colorado, Summer/Fall/Winter/Spring;* Premio Letterario Internazionale Mondelo, Italy, 1979. Western Literature Association award, 1983. D.H.L.: Central Michigan University, Mt. Pleasant, 1970; University of Massachusetts, Amherst, 1975; Yale University, New Haven, Connecticut, 1980; Hobart and Williams Smith Colleges, Geneva, New York, 1980; College of Santa Fe, New Mexico, 1982; D.Litt.: Lawrence University, Appleton, Wisconsin, 1971; University of Wisconsin, Milwaukee, 1976; College of Ganado, 1979; D.F.A.: Morningside College, Sioux City, Iowa, 1980. Address: 1041 West Roller Coaster Rd., Tucson, AZ 85704, U.S.A.

PUBLICATIONS

Novels

House Made of Dawn. New York, Harper, 1968.
The Ancient Child. New York, Doubleday, 1989.

Poetry

Before an Old Painting of the Crucifixion, Carmel Mission, June 1960. San Francisco, Valenti Angelo, 1975.
Angle of Geese and Other Poems. Boston, David Godine, 1974.
The Gourd Dancer, illustrated by the author. New York, Harper, 1976.

Other

Editor, *The Complete Poems of Frederick Goddard Tuckerman.* New York, Oxford University Press, 1965.
The Journey of Tai-me (Kiowa Indian tales), etchings by Bruce S. McCurdy. Privately printed, 1967; revised edition, as *The Way to Rainy Mountain,* illustrated by father, Alfred Momaday, Albuquerque, University of New Mexico Press, 1969.
Colorado, Summer/Fall/Winter/Spring, illustrated with photographs by David Muench. Chicago, Rand McNally, 1973.

Editor, *American Indian Authors.* Boston, Houghton Mifflin, 1976.
The Names: A Memoir. New York, Harper, 1976.
Editor, *A Coyote in the Garden,* by Ann Painter. Lewiston, Idaho, Confluence, 1988.
In The Presence of the Sun: Stories and Poems, 1961-1991, illustrated by the author. New York, St. Martin's, 1992.
The Native Americans: Indian Country. Atlanta, Georgia, Turner Publishing, 1993.

Screenplay: *The Man Who Killed the Deer,* adaptation of a novel by Frank Waters.

*

Manuscript Collection: Bancroft Library, University of California, Berkeley.

Critical Studies: Entry in *Contemporary Literary Criticism,* Detroit, Gale, Volume 2, 1974, Volume 19, 1981; *Four American Indian Literary Masters* by Alan R. Velie, Norman, University of Oklahoma Press, 1982; *N. Scott Momaday: The Cultural and Literary Background* by Matthias Schubnell, Norman, University of Oklahoma Press, 1986; *Approaches to Teaching Momaday's The Way to Rainy Mountain* edited by Kenneth M. Roemer, New York, Modern Language Association of America, 1988; *Ancestral Voice: Conversations with N. Scott Momaday* by Charles L. Woodard, Lincoln, University of Nebraska Press, 1989.

*   *   *

In *The Way to Rainy Mountain,* arguably his most important work, Scott Momaday establishes the patterns of theme and technique which have characterized his novels, poems, and memoirs. An expansion of the Kiowa folktakes retold from *The Journey of Tai-me* is Momaday's attempt to develop a myth which incorporates individual lives as part of an overall ancestral past.

Each of the three sections ("The Setting Out," "The Going On," and "The Closing In") progresses from the most inclusive and remote to the most personal and recent: Momaday begins with Kiowa legends, followed by tribal history, then personal memoir. Using different typefaces to indicate the transitions, Momaday retells Kiowa origin myths, retraces the history of the tribe's three-century migration from Yellowstone to the Great Plains, and finally links these stories with personal memories and stories passed down by his paternal ancestors. Each layer of the narrative explains and so adds significance to those which precede it, as the psychic journey of Momaday the teller reenacts the wanderings of the Kiowa. Literally traveling to his grandmother's grave, he realizes that her lifespan encompassed the decline in tribal identity.

The Names: A Memoir continues the exploration of personal identity in the larger context of the family and the tribe. Again Momaday combines Kiowa tradition with genealogical exploration and almost idyllic memories, as he describes his boyhood among the Kiowas, who give names to every object in, and every characteristic of, their environment. Momaday's name, Tsoaitalee, is the Kiowa name for a spot important in tribal legends—a massive rock known in Anglo-American culture as the Devils Tower. Since the name was supposedly prophetic of an individual's character and fate, Momaday had been given a great honor and a profound responsibility.

This memoir emphasizes the importance of names, through those names tracing Momaday's Anglo-American heritage as well as the Kiowa. His mother's family included not only a Cherokee great-grandmother, but also a grandfather, Theodore Scott, who was a sheriff in Kentucky. In identifying with his Indian ancestors, however, Momaday is following the lead of his mother, who chose an Indian name, Indian dress, and an Indian school. Initially among the Kiowa, Momaday's paternal grandfather had only one name, Mammeday, but with the adoption of Christian names, the name John was added. Alfred, Scott's father, modified the family name to Momaday. The development of the family surname seems symbolic of the family's ability to remain Native Americans but to incorporate the best elements of the Anglo culture.

Momaday also treats the issue of cultural identity in his best known work, *House Made of Dawn,* winner of the 1969 Pulitzer prize for fiction. In this novel, praised for its mythic themes but criticized for its difficult narrative structure, a Native American veteran (interestingly, named Abel) cannot re-adapt to reservation life upon his return from World War II. After killing a man and serving a prison sentence, he is paroled to a halfway house in Los Angeles.

Unlike his roommate Ben, a narrative voice who appears to be a Momaday spokesman, Abel remains outside the Anglo-American culture; his attitude causes trouble on the job and with the police. Although the local groups he discovers do not practice the Native American ceremonies in their pure form, the sermons of medicine man/priest John Tosamah lead ultimately to Abel's return to the reservation and his dying grandfather. The novel's resolution is the ritual race at dawn, in which Abel's true opponents are evil and death. Thus, coinciding with his grandfather's death is Abel's symbolic rebirth into his culture.

Like his character Abel, Momaday finds strength and beauty in traditional Native American life, which he sees as an antidote to the prevailing modern mood of individual isolation. A part of their belief in the principle of harmony in the universe, the Kiowa's oral tradition links them to the land and establishes it as a spiritual entity, similar to themselves and worthy of reverence. The retelling of history and legends also taps into the tribal memory, providing a sense of personal and group identity.

Momaday's poems, which have received less attention than his prose, likewise recast traditional Kiowa legends in terms of family history. In *The Gourd Dancer* and *Angle of Geese and Other Poems,* Momaday draws upon "blood memories," becoming in effect the successor to ancient medicine men as he interprets for his contemporary audience the Native American consciousness.

In attempting to express his essentially intuitive perceptions about the Kiowa, however, Momaday is hampered by the limitations imposed in using the language of an alien culture. Nevertheless, Momaday, who does not speak Kiowa himself, understands how the language not only reflects but also influences the way a people think, and he believes that in relating these tales, he is offering hope and spiritual healing to modern American society.

This process of translating his ancient myths to benefit modern society is the subject of Momaday's second novel, *The Ancient Child,* which is primarily autobiographical. Using the myth associated with his own Kiowa name, Momaday portrays a Native American artist's efforts to maintain his culture and interpret it for the Anglo world. While the artist generally is an outsider in his society, the Native American can draw upon his advantage of an alternate world view found in tribal legends. Thus, like Momaday himself, the artist can use the traditional vehicles of dreams and visions to forge an identity which is at once personal and universal.

—Charmaine Allmon Mosby

* * *

MORRISON, Toni. American. Born Chloe Anthony Wofford, in Lorain, Ohio, 18 February 1931. Educated at Howard University, Washington, D.C., B.A. 1953; Cornell University, Ithaca, New York, M.A. 1955. Married Harold Morrison in 1958 (divorced 1964); two sons. Instructor in English, Texas Southern University, Houston, 1955-57, and Howard University, 1957-64; senior editor, Random House, New York, 1965-84; Associate Professor of English, State University of New York, Purchase, 1971-72; State University of New York at Albany, Visiting lecturer, Yale University, New Haven, Connecticut, 1976-77, Rutgers University, New Brunswick, New Jersey, 1983-84, and Bard College, Annandale-on-Hudson, New York, 1986-88. Schweitzer Professor of the Humanities, State University of New York, Albany, 1984-89; Regents' Lecturer, University of California, Berkeley, 1987; Santagata Lecturer, Bowdoin College, Brunswick, Maine, 1987. Since 1989, Robert F. Goheen Professor of the Humanities, Princeton University, New Jersey. Recipient: National Book award nomination and Ohioana Book award, both 1975, both for *Sula;* National Book Critics Circle award and American Academy and Institute of Arts and Letters award, both 1977, both for *Song of Solomon;* New York State Governor's Art award, 1986; National Book award nomination and National Book Critics Circle award nomination, both 1987, and Pulitzer Prize for fiction and Robert F. Kennedy award, both 1988, all for *Beloved;* Elizabeth Cady Stanton award from the National Organization of Women; Book of the Month Club award, 1986; Before Columbus Foundation award, 1988; Melcher award, 1988; Honorary degree: College of Saint Rose, Albany, 1987; Nobel Prize for literature, 1993. Agent: Lynn Nesbit, International Creative Management, 40 West 57th St., New York, NY 10019, U.S.A.

PUBLICATIONS

Novels

The Bluest Eye. New York, Holt, 1969; London, Chatto & Windus, 1980.
Sula. New York, Knopf, 1973; London, Allen Lane, 1974.
Song of Solomon. New York, Knopf, 1977; London, Chatto & Windus, 1978.
Tar Baby. New York, Knopf, and London, Chatto & Windus, 1981.
Beloved. New York, Knopf, and London, Chatto & Windus, 1987.
Jazz. New York, Knopf, 1992.

Play

Dreaming Emmett (produced Albany, New York, 1986).

Other

Editor, *The Black Book.* New York, Random House, 1974.

Editor, *Race-ing Justice, En-gendering Power: Essays on Anita Hill, Clarence Thomas, and the Construction of Social Reality.* New York, Pantheon, 1992.
Playing in the Dark: Whiteness and the Literary Imagination. Cambridge, Massachusetts, 1992.

*

Bibliography: *Toni Morrison: A Bibliography* by Mod Mekkawi, Howard University Library, 1986; *Toni Morrison: An Annotated Bibliography* by David L. Middleton, New York, Garland, 1987.

Critical Studies: Entry in *Contemporary Literary Criticism,* Detroit, Gale, Volume 4, 1975, Volume 10, 1979, Volume 22, 1982, Volume 55, 1989; entry in *Dictionary of Literary Biography,* Detroit, Gale, Volume 6: *American Novelists since World War II,* 1980, Volume 33: *Afro-American Fiction Writers after 1955,* 1984; entry in *Dictionary of Literary Biography Yearbook: 1981,* Detroit, Gale, 1982; *New Dimensions of Spirituality: A Biracial and Bicultural Reading of the Novels of Toni Morrison* by Karla F.C. Holloway, Westport, Connecticut, Greenwood Press, 1987; *The Crime of Innocence in the Fiction of Toni Morrison* by Terry Otten, Columbia, University of Missouri Press, 1989; *Toni Morrison* by Wilfred D. Samuels, Boston, Twayne, 1990.

*   *   *

Of the many adolescent readers captivated by the award-winning and very adult novels of Toni Morrison, the vast majority are high school females. And while Morrison is especially popular among young African Americans, her stories, characters, and themes are not bound by race or ethnicity. Young or old, Morrison's female readers are inclined to say similar things about the appeal of her works: they know real people *exactly* like the characters in her novels; her writings embrace contemporary life—the triumphs and failures, the hectic anxiety, the social strictures and pressures, the excitement, fears, and remorse; her writings present racial issues in ways that clarify and purge, in ways that lead to healing; she is not afraid to describe women and men as sexual beings; she knows precisely what it means to be a woman; and she helps illuminate the relative truth of the values which male society—and women themselves—have assigned to womanhood.

Adolescent readers point to yet another of Morrison's qualities they find important; she remembers what it means to be young. It is true that most of Morrison's protagonists are well beyond high school and in their twenties or thirties. Nevertheless, their concerns are those often associated with late adolescence: establishment of self-identity; formation of long-term social, familial, and professional goals; validation of a personal moral code; and creation of meaningful and enduring male-female and same-gender relationships.

The nightmare influences of democracy on the establishment of self-identity, where democracy can demand conformity to the frequently discriminatory ideals of the majority, is an important theme of Morrison's first novel, *The Bluest Eye.* This unforgettable parable of a young black woman who grows up believing that blonde hair and blue eyes would make her beautiful and bring social acceptance and familial harmony, is also concerned with the idea that "love is never any better than the lover." At the structural heart of the novel is an incestuous rape, at least partially the result of false ideals; for the novel's protagonist, the consequences of this love gone utterly wrong are self-rejection, despair, and finally madness.

Sula, very much a product of the early 1970s, was highly controversial when it first appeared—not only because of its authority-and-tradition-flouting protagonist and its unusual portraits of feminine bonding, but for its depictions of black males. There isn't a strong or admirable male character in the novel; instead, there are men with names like BoyBoy and Chicken Little. Leaving aside overly emotional responses to the novel, readers have come to see *Sula* as an exploration of traditional and contemporary values, an exploration ending in an implicit merging of the two worlds where some values on each side are preserved, and others discarded.

Morrison's third novel, *Song of Solomon,* has a male protagonist Macon (Milkman) Dead III; in part, perhaps, it is a response to critics of *Sula.* In simplest terms the novel recounts Milkman's search for his legacy (rumored to be a hidden cache of gold) in an effort to come into his own and escape the insignificance of his family. Eventually he comes to understand precisely who he is—not, ironically, through discovering his father's gold, but through learning his cultural history by uncovering his roots. In the end the novel is perhaps Morrison's most poetic, most complete exploration of the search for self; it suggests that the successful passage to adulthood ends in a merging of the intellectual, physical, spiritual, sexual, and cultural/historical selves.

In some respects, *Tar Baby* revisits the themes of *The Bluest Eye.* The story of a light-skinned African American woman who denies her blackness, *Tar Baby* is a moving analysis of the costs of self-denial, of seeing life in terms of duty and obligations rather than loyalty and love, of turning one's back on the sources of personal redemption. The deepest tragedy of the novel is that, in running from herself, the protagonist also maims or destroys the lives of those who know and care about her.

Beloved is Morrison's most ambitious, most highly imagined novel. Intentionally mimicking traditional slave narratives, *Beloved* is the nineteenth-century history of Sethe, an escaped slave who, while still in slavery, slashed the throat of her infant daughter in a "mercy killing." The ghost of her daughter haunts Sethe, eventually becoming flesh and confronting her as a twenty-year-old woman/child. The novel has a marvelous cast of characters and involved subplots; among its many themes are economic slavery, cultural and racial alienation, and the potentially oppressive, monstrous nature of traditional society.

Uncharacteristically lyrical in plot and structure, sharing more of the spirit of *Song of Solomon* than any other Morrison novel, *Jazz* tells of a middle-aged couple who are obsessed with the husband's dead lover: the husband, who kills his lover so she won't desert him, is overwhelmed by guilt and sorrow that nothing can dispel, not even his wife; the wife, cut off from her husband spiritually, attacks the dead lover in her coffin with a knife and then, in effect, makes her home and heart shrines to the dead woman's memory. The bulk of the novel tells how the couple eventually transcend the immediate past by returning to their historical pasts, learning where their lives began, how they evolved, and by whom they have been shaped. It is a story of profound emotions, simply and compassionately—even sweetly—told.

Morrison is also the author of *Playing in the Dark,* a critical history of African American writers, one which assesses black artistic accomplishment in a society whose tastes, methods, and impulses are all-too-obviously white.

—Keith Lawrence

MOWAT, Farley (McGill). Canadian. Born in Belleville, Ontario, 12 May 1921. Educated at public schools in Trenton, Belleville, Windsor, Richmond Hill, and Toronto, Ontario, and Saskatoon, Saskatchewan; University of Toronto, B.A. 1949. Served in the Canadian Army Infantry and Intelligence Corps, 1940-46: Captain. Married 1) Frances Thornhill in 1947, two sons; 2) Claire Angel Wheeler in 1965. Freelance writer. Recipient: President's Medal for best Canadian short story of 1952 from the University of Western Ontario, for "Eskimo Spring"; Anisfield-Wolfe award for contribution to interracial relations, 1954, for *People of the Deer;* Governor General's Medal for juvenile literature, 1957, for *Lost in the Barrens;* Book of the Year for Children award from the Canadian Association of Children's Librarians, and International Board on Books for Young People Honour List, Canada, both 1958, both for *Lost in the Barrens;* Canadian Women's Clubs award, 1958, for *The Dog Who Wouldn't Be;* Boys' Club Junior Book award from the Boys' Club of America, 1963, for *Owls in the Family;* National Association of Independent Schools award, 1963, for juvenile books; Hans Christian Andersen Honour List, 1965, for juvenile books; Canadian Centennial Medal, 1967; Leacock Medal from the Stephen Leacock Foundation, 1970, and L'Etoile de la Mer Honours List, 1972, for *The Boat Who Wouldn't Float;* Doctor of Literature, Laurentian University, 1970; Vicky Metcalf award from the Canadian Authors' Association, 1971, for his body of work; Curran award, 1977, for "contributions to understanding wolves"; Queen Elizabeth II Jubilee Medal, 1978; Knight of Mark Twain, 1980; New York Public Library's Books for the Teen Age, 1980, for *The Great Betrayal,* and 1981, for *And No Birds Sang;* Officer, Order of Canada, 1981. D.Litt.: Laurentian University, Sudbury, Ontario, 1970; University of Victoria, British Columbia, 1982; Lakehead University, Thunder Bay, Ontario, 1986; LL.D.: University of Toronto, 1973; University of Lethbridge, Alberta, 1973; University of Prince Edward Island, Charlottetown, 1979. Officer, Order of Canada, 1981. Agent: Herta Ryder, c/o Toby Eady Associates, 7 Gledhow Gardens, London SW5 0BL, England. Address: c/o McClelland and Stewart Ltd., 481 University Avenue, Suite 900, Toronto, ON M5G 2E9, Canada.

PUBLICATIONS FOR YOUNG ADULTS

Short Stories

The Snow Walker. Toronto, McClelland and Stewart, 1975; Boston, Little Brown, 1976; London, Heinemann, 1978.

Other

People of the Deer (on the Ihalmiut Eskimos). Boston, Little Brown, and London, Joseph, 1952; revised edition, Toronto, McClelland and Stewart, 1975.
The Regiment (on the Hastings and Prince Edward Regiment). Toronto, McClelland and Stewart, 1955.
The Dog Who Wouldn't Be. Boston, Little Brown, 1957; London, Joseph, 1958.
Editor, *Coppermine Journey: An Account of Great Adventure,* by Samuel Hearne. Toronto, McClelland and Stewart, and Boston, Little Brown, 1958.
The Grey Seas Under. Boston, Little Brown, 1958; London, Joseph, 1959.

The Desperate People (on the Ihalmiut Eskimos). Boston, Little Brown, 1959; London, Joseph, 1960; revised edition, Toronto, McClelland and Stewart, 1976.
Editor, *The Top of the World: Ordeal by Ice.* Toronto, McClelland and Stewart, 1960; Boston, Little Brown, and London, Joseph, 1961.
The Serpent's Coil (on salvaging ships). Toronto, McClelland and Stewart, 1961; Boston, Little Brown, and London, Joseph, 1962.
Never Cry Wolf. Toronto, McClelland and Stewart, and Boston, Little Brown, 1963; London, Secker and Warburg, 1964.
Westviking: The Ancient Norse in Greenland and North America. Boston, Little Brown, 1965; London, Secker and Warburg, 1966.
Canada North. Boston, Little Brown, 1967; revised edition, as *Canada North Now: The Great Betrayal,* Toronto, McClelland and Stewart, 1976; as *The Great Betrayal,* Little Brown, 1976.
Editor, *The Top of the World: The Polar Passion—The Quest for the North Pole, with Selections from Arctic Journals.* Toronto, McClelland and Stewart, 1967; Boston, Little Brown, 1968.
This Rock within the Sea: A Heritage Lost (on Newfoundland), photographs by John de Visser. Boston, Little Brown, 1968.
The Boat Who Wouldn't Float. Toronto, McClelland and Stewart, 1969; Boston, Little Brown, and London, Heinemann, 1970.
Sibir: My Discovery of Siberia. Toronto, McClelland and Stewart, 1970; as *The Siberians,* Boston, Little Brown, 1971; London, Heinemann, 1972.
A Whale for the Killing. Toronto, McClelland and Stewart, and Boston, Little Brown, 1972; London, Heinemann, 1973.
Editor, *The Top of the World: Tundra—Selections from the Great Accounts of Arctic Land Voyages.* Toronto, McClelland and Stewart, 1973.
Wake of the Great Sealers. Boston, Little Brown, 1973.
And No Birds Sang (war memoirs). Toronto, McClelland and Stewart, 1979; Boston, Little Brown, and London, Cassell, 1980.
The World of Farley Mowat: A Selection, edited by Peter Davison. Boston, Little Brown, 1980.
Sea of Slaughter. Toronto, McClelland and Stewart, and Boston, Atlantic Monthly Press, 1984; London, Bantam, 1986.
My Discovery of America. Toronto, McClelland and Stewart, and Boston, Atlantic Monthly Press, 1985.
Virunga: The Passion of Dian Fossey. Toronto, McClelland and Stewart, 1987; as *Woman in the Mists: The Story of Dian Fossey and the Mountain Gorillas of Africa,* New York, Warner, 1987; London, Macdonald, 1988.
The New Founde Land. Toronto, McClelland and Stewart, 1989.
Rescue the Earth. Toronto, McClelland and Stewart, 1990.
My Father's Son: Memories of War and Peace. Boston, Houghton Mifflin, 1992.

Television Scripts: *Sea Fare* (*Telescope* series), 1964; *Diary of a Boy on Vacation,* 1964; and others.

PUBLICATIONS FOR CHILDREN

Fiction

Lost in the Barrens, illustrated by Charles Geer. Boston, Little Brown, 1956; London, Macmillan, 1957.
The Black Joke, illustrated by D. Johnson. Toronto, McClelland and Stewart, 1962; Boston, Little Brown, 1963; London, Macmillan, 1964.

The Curse of the Viking Grave, illustrated by Charles Geer. Boston, Little Brown, 1966; London, Pan, 1979.

Other

Owls in the Family, illustrated by Robert Frankenberg. Boston, Little Brown, 1961; London, Macmillan, 1963.

Contributor to *Cricket's Choice,* Open Court, 1974, and to magazines, including *Saturday Evening Post, Argosy, Maclean's,* and *Cricket.*

*

Media Adaptations: *A Whale for the Killing* (film), ABC-TV, 1980; (cassette), Books on Tape; *Never Cry Wolf* (film), Disney, 1983; (cassette), Books on Tape, 1986; (cassette, voice by Mowat), Bantam, 1988; *Grey Seas Under* (cassette), Books on Tape, 1986; *The Snow Walker* (cassette), Books on Tape, 1986; *Lost in the Barrens* (cassette), Books on Tape; *People of the Deer* (cassette), Books on Tape.

Manuscript Collection: McMaster University, Hamilton, Ontario.

Biography: Entry in *Dictionary of Literary Biography,* Volume 68, Detroit, Gale, 1988; Essay in *Authors and Artists for Young Adults,* Volume 1, Detroit, Gale, 1989.

Critical Study: *Farley Mowat* by Alex Lucas, Toronto, McClelland and Stewart, 1976; Entry in *Children's Literature Review,* Volume 20, Detroit, Gale, 1990.

*   *   *

Sometimes referred to as "the Canadian Jack London," Farley Mowat nevertheless defies categorization or easy description. It is true that he shares with London a fascination for the Arctic. But while London saw only Arctic harshness and frigidity, turning the white land into a vast naturalistic metaphor, Mowat perceives delicately balanced ecosystems teeming with life, inspiration, and beauty. And unlike London, who is known primarily as a writer of fiction, Mowat's most respected works are nonfiction, the product of rich, varied and adventurous living. Mowat is also important for his political positions, especially his stance on the environment. He has become perhaps the most articulate spokesperson for Canada's Green Movement; his is one of the world's strongest voices demanding protection for wilderness lands and endangered wildlife.

Of the more than thirty books he has written or edited, Mowat has addressed only four to juvenile audiences. *Lost in the Barrens* is the story of two teenage males, a white and a Cree Indian, whose curiosity about legends of a "stone house" (which turns out to be a Viking tomb) causes them to become separated from their hunting party. Consequently, they are forced to spend much of one winter in the barrens of Canada's Keewatin District, preserved through their ingenuity and their cool-headed preparations for the winter snows. *Owls in the Family,* generally categorized as nonfiction and most often read by pre-teens, is an illustrated and greatly embellished version of the Wol and Weeps stories in *The Dog Who Wouldn't Be.* Mowat's other two juvenile novels, *The Black Joke* and *The Curse of the Viking Grave,* are out of print. *The Black Joke*

is the story of three adolescent males who steal back a sloop that whisky smugglers have, in effect, "stolen" from the father of one of the boys. But the plot is contrived, the characterizations and dialogue are weak, and the book never attracted a large audience. The sequel promised in the final lines of *Lost in the Barrens* was the ill-fated *The Curse of the Viking Grave,* a novel so poorly put together that Mowat himself is said to have condemned it.

Of Mowat's self-proclaimed juvenile novels only *Lost in the Barrens* is widely known to the many adolescents who have appropriated Mowat's popular "adult" books as their own, especially *The Dog Who Wouldn't Be* and *Never Cry Wolf.* A mildly fictionalized memoir of Mowat's childhood on the Canadian prairies near Saskatoon, *The Dog Who Wouldn't Be* recounts a boy's adventures with his dog, Mutt, and two owls, Wol and Weep. In the end, however, the book is as much about the boy's relationship with his family, especially his father, as it is about the boy and his pets. The book has the timeless appeal of James Herriot's works— and is much funnier. Some of the humor is derived from situations that make adult readers squeamish, but it is exactly right for adolescent males. What it says about father-son relationships affords it a human richness that few passages in Herriot achieve. But the Mowat work most popular among adolescents, males in particular, is *Never Cry Wolf.* Initially conceived by its author as a satire of bureaucracy, of governmental bungling and its impact on the environment, the book became instead, according to Mowat's preface, "a plea for understanding, and preservation, of an extraordinarily highly evolved and attractive animal." The account of the government-hired biologist whose fear of Arctic wolves is replaced by admiration, whose assignment to study the wolves gives way to a self-imposed mission to preserve them, is one of the finest contemporary statements on the human capacity to bond with other animals and thrive in the natural world, no matter how threatening either appears.

Other Mowat works enjoyed by adolescents twelve and older include *The Boat Who Wouldn't Float,* a Twain-inspired travelogue of Mowat's capricious voyage to sundry ports in the Maritime Provinces and eventually to Montreal, a voyage hazarded in a rebellious if not unseaworthy vessel named the *Happy Adventure; Siberia,* an appreciation of the environs, wildlife, and indigenous peoples of the regions often considered Russian wastelands; *A Whale for the Killing,* which recounts Mowat's efforts to save a fin whale trapped in a saltwater pond near Burgeo, Newfoundland, and which has been called the best animal story in Canadian literature; and *My Discovery of America,* a humorous account of a Canadian innocent dropping by America.

Mature adolescents also enjoy *People of the Deer,* Mowat's successful (and highly controversial) first book, and *The Desperate People,* its sequel, which together form an intensely detailed and moving portrait of the Barren Land Eskimos and suggest that the Canadian government and other white influences have resulted in the near-decimation of a once-proud tribe; *The Serpent's Coil,* which records Mowat's experiences on a small salvage boat operating out of the Halifax harbor; *The Snow Walker,* a collection of stories, memoirs and essays about Canada's Eskimos; *And No Birds Sang,* a narrative of Mowat's combat experiences in Italy and Sicily during World War II; *Sea of Slaughter,* an indictment of Canadian/U.S. fishing practices and environmental policies wreaking havoc on the sea life and coastline of Eastern Canada and New England; and *Woman in the Mists,* a biography of Dian Fossey. Mowat devotees may also read his ambitious history/appreciation of the Arctic known as "The Top of the World Trilogy," *Ordeal by Ice, The Polar Passion,* and *Tundra.* High school English teachers sometimes rely on

The World of Farley Mowat, a selection of his works, to introduce Mowat to their students.

—Keith Lawrence

———

MOYES, Patricia. British. Born in Bray, County Wicklow, Ireland, 19 January 1923. Educated at Overstone School, Northampton, 1934-39, Cambridge School Certificate, 1939. Served in the radar section of the British Women's Auxiliary Air Force, 1940-45; Flight Officer. Married 1) John Moyes in 1951 (divorced 1959); 2) John S. Haszard in 1962. Company secretary, Peter Ustinov Productions Ltd., London, 1945-53; assistant editor, *Vogue,* London, 1953-58; writer, since 1956. Recipient: Mystery Writers of America Edgar Allan Poe award, 1970, for *Many Deadly Returns.* Agent: Curtis Brown Ltd., 162-168 Regent Street, London WIR 5TB, England. Address: P.O. Box 1, Virgin Gorda, British Virgin Islands, West Indies.

PUBLICATIONS FOR YOUNG ADULTS

Novels (series: Henry and Emmy Tibbett in all books)

Dead Men Don't Ski. London, Collins, 1959; New York, Holt, 1960.
The Sunken Sailor. London, Collins, 1961; as *Down among the Dead Men,* New York, Holt, 1961.
Death on the Agenda. London, Collins, and New York, Holt, 1962.
Murder à la Mode. London, Collins, and New York, Holt, 1963.
Falling Star. London, Collins, and New York, Holt, 1964.
Johnny under Ground. London, Collins, 1965; New York, Holt, 1966.
Murder by 3's (omnibus volume). New York, Holt, 1965.
Murder Fantastical. London, Collins, and New York, Holt, 1967.
Death and the Dutch Uncle. London, Collins, and New York, Holt, 1968.
Who Saw Her Die? London, Collins, 1970; as *Many Deadly Returns,* New York, Holt, 1970.
Season of Snows and Sins. London, Collins, and New York, Holt, 1971.
The Curious Affair of the Third Dog. London, Collins, and New York, Holt, 1973.
Black Widower. London, Collins, and New York, Holt, 1975.
To Kill a Coconut. London, Collins, 1977; as *The Coconut Killings,* New York, Holt, 1977.
Who Is Simon Warwick? London, Collins, 1978; New York, Holt, 1979.
Angel Death. London, Collins, 1980; New York, Holt, 1981.
A Six-Letter Word for Death. London, Collins, and New York, Holt, 1983.
Night Ferry to Death. London, Collins, and New York, Holt, 1985.
Black Girl, White Girl. New York, Holt, 1989; London, Collins, 1990.
Twice in a Blue Moon. New York, Holt, 1993.

Plays

Time Remembered, adaptation of a play by Jean Anouilh (broadcast, 1954; produced London, 1954; New York, 1957). London, Methuen, 1955.

Screenplay: *School for Scoundrel,* with Peter Ustinov and Hal E. Chester, 1960.

Radio Play: *Time Remembered,* 1954.

Other

Helter-Skelter. New York, Holt, 1968; London Macdonald, 1969.
After All, They're Only Cats. New York, Curtis, 1973.
Contributor, *Techniques of Novel Writing.* Boston, The Writer, 1973.
How to Talk to Your Cat. London, Barker, and New York, Holt, 1978.

* * *

A leading contemporary practitioner of the classic British mystery, Patricia Moyes is known for carefully plotted puzzles which her sleuths solve through a combination of clues, intuition, persistence, logical thinking, physical courage, and calculated risk. To draw the reader into the detection game, Moyes provides an abundance of clues, several red herrings, and sometimes—as in *Who Is Simon Warwick?*—a final plot twist. Another device characteristic of Moyes is the epilogue which, like the denouement in plays, provides a final restoration of order in her fictional world.

Perhaps because of her experience in writing for movies and the stage, Moyes relies heavily upon dialogue. She has a good ear for everyday speech; her characters seem believable because they use diction and syntax appropriate to their age and social position. Even her favorite point of view, first person, becomes an extended dramatic monologue in her novels.

Also adding to the verisimilitude of Moyes' novels is her accurate depiction of the places and activities which provide a backdrop for the mystery. Because these situations reflect her own interests and experiences, Moyes can not only describe them in the manner of an expert, but also construct a mystery which seems to evolve logically from that background. For instance, her movie work is reflected in *Falling Star,* her days at *Vogue* in *Murder à la Mode,* her travels with her husband in *Night Ferry to Death,* her enthusiasm for crossword puzzles in *A Six-Letter Word for Death,* her love of skiing in *Dead Men Don't Ski,* and her passion for sailing in *Down among the Dead Men* and *Helter-Skelter.*

Moyes' best-known mysteries feature Chief Inspector Henry Tibbett and his wife Emmy. The obvious respect and affection between these two characters add a note of domesticity to these mysteries, and frequently the Tibbetts stumble upon a mystery during the course of their usual activities *(Night Ferry to Death)* or while vacationing with family *(The Curious Affair of the Third Dog)* or friends *(Down among the Dead Men).* Generally these friends are, like the Tibbetts, genteel and sophisticated; even criminal masterminds usually are superficially charming, though emotionally unbalanced to some degree. Lower-class characters are at best humorous eccentrics and many are at least technically guilty of violating the law.

Criminals typically underestimate the soft-spoken Henry, who usually downplays his reputation at Scotland Yard. He is particularly adept at recognizing hidden crimes, and his logical mind allows him to quickly deduce the identity of the perpetrators. Since he rarely takes another character completely into his confidence, neither the criminals nor his allies realize the extent of his knowledge until he can prove his case. Relying upon his instincts about individuals and their misdeeds, Henry shrewdly lays traps so that the culprits will reveal their own guilt. Often these stratagems are a calculated gamble which involve physical risk to Henry and sometimes to others.

While Henry usually solves the mystery and provides the final explanation, Emmy is his most valuable ally. She too is clever, courageous, and resourceful; and often her tact and sympathy are essential in gaining a significant bit of information. Emmy relies more on intuition, while Henry is more logical; thus, she provides the balance to make this a true partnership.

With their well-developed humor and relative lack of graphic violence, most of Moyes' mysteries are appropriate for readers of any age, but *Helter-Skelter* was written specifically for a young adult audience. Without sacrificing the intricate plotting and keen suspense of Moyes' other mysteries, it addresses a number of familiar teenage concerns, such as maturation, sibling rivalry, and conflict with parents and other authority figures.

Helter-Skelter takes on elements of the contemporary cloak-and-dagger novel when Felicity Bell, "Cat," realizes that a local murder is linked to a spy operation and enlists the help of several of her friends to solve the crime. Moyes provides abundant clues for any reader even slightly aware of the deep-seated conflict between the Irish and the English. Thus the reader can guess the murderer's identity long before Cat does, and suspense builds as the reader roots for Cat to solve the puzzle before it is too late. In her customary epilogue Moyes ties up some loose ends and prepares for a sequel—revealing that, after testifying at the murder trial, all the principle characters of the book are all well and good and ready for more adventures.

—Charmaine Allmon Mosby

MURPHY, Shirley Rousseau. American. Born in Oakland, California, 20 May 1928. Educated at the California School of Fine Arts (now San Francisco Art Institute), California, 1947-51, A.A. in fine art and commercial art 1951. Married Patrick J. Murphy in 1951. Packaging designer, Sam Kweller, Los Angeles, 1953-55; teacher of mosaics, San Bernardino Valley College, California, 1953-61; documents assistant, Canal Zone Library Museum, Panama, 1964-67. Painter and sculptor. Individual shows: Jack Carr Gallery, South Pasadena, California, 1957; San Bernardino Valley College, and Whittier Art Association, California, both 1958; Ojai Valley Art Center, California, and Ash Grove Gallery, Los Angeles, both 1959; Cherry Gallery, San Bernardino, and Light House Gallery, Hermosa Beach, California, both 1960; Richmond Museum, California, 1963. Since 1963 freelance writer. Recipient: Received eight awards for sculpture and four for painting at San Francisco Museum and other exhibitions, 1959-62; Dixie Council of Authors and Journalists' award, 1977, for *The Ring of Fire* and *Silver Woven in My Hair*, 1979, for *The Flight of the Fox*, 1981, for *Mrs. Tortino's*

Return to the Sun, 1986, for *Nightpool,* and 1988, for *The Ivory Lyre.* Address: 1977 Upper Grandview Rd., Jasper, GA 30143, U.S.A.

PUBLICATIONS FOR YOUNG ADULTS

Fiction

Carlos Charles, with Patrick J. Murphy. New York, Viking, 1971.
Poor Jenny, Bright as a Penny. New York, Viking, 1974.
The Grass Tower, illustrated by Charles Robinson. New York, Atheneum, 1976.
The Ring of Fire. New York, Atheneum, 1977.
Silver Woven in My Hair, illustrated by Alan Tiegreen. New York, Atheneum, 1977; London, Macdonald and Jane's, 1978.
The Wolf Bell. New York, Atheneum, 1979.
The Castle of Hape. New York, Atheneum, 1980.
Caves of Fire and Ice. New York, Atheneum, 1980.
The Joining of the Stone. New York, Atheneum, 1981.
Nightpool. New York, Harper, 1985.
The Ivory Lyre. New York, Harper, 1987.
The Dragonbards. New York, Harper, 1988.
Medallion of the Black Hound, with Welsh Suggs. New York, Harper, 1989.

Other

Contributor, *Anywhere, Anywhen,* edited by Sylvia Engdahl. New York, Atheneum, 1976.
The Catswold Portal, New York, Roc, 1992.

PUBLICATIONS FOR CHILDREN

Fiction

The Sand Ponies, illustrated by Erika Weihs. New York, Viking, 1967.
White Ghost Summer, illustrated by Barbara McGee. New York, Viking, 1967.
Elmo Doolan and the Search for the Golden Mouse, illustrated by Fritz Kredel. New York, Viking, 1970.
The Flight of the Fox, illustrated by Don Sibley. New York, Atheneum, 1978.
Soonie and the Dragon, illustrated by Susan Vaeth. New York, Atheneum, 1979.
The Song of the Christmas Mouse, illustrated by Donna Diamond. New York, Harper, 1990.

Picture Books

The Pig Who Could Conjure the Wind, illustrated by Mark Lefkowitz. New York, Atheneum, 1978.
Mrs. Tortino's Return to the Sun, with Patrick J. Murphy, illustrated by Susan Russo. New York, Lothrop, 1980.
Tattie's River Journey, illustrated by Tomie de Paola. New York, Dial Press, and London, Methuen, 1983.
Valentine for a Dragon, illustrated by Kay Chorao. New York, Atheneum, 1984.

Wind Child, illustrated by Leo and Diane Dillon. New York, Harper, 1995.

Other

Contributor, *The Unicorn Treasury,* edited by Bruce Coville. New York, Doubleday, 1988.
Herds of Thunder, Manes of Gold, edited by Bruce Coville. New York, Doubleday, 1989.

*

Media Adaptations: *Tattie's River Journey* (videotape), Listening Library, 1984.

Biography: Essay in *Speaking for Ourselves, Too* compiled and edited by Donald R. Gallo, Urbana, Illinois, National Council of Teachers of English, 1993.

Manuscript Collection: de Grummond Collection, University of Southern Mississippi, Hattiesburg.

Shirley Rousseau Murphy comments:

Adults read my younger books, and young readers enjoy my adult fantasy, age doesn't matter. What counts between writer and reader is, besides the real and involving quality of story, the inner view of the novel. It is the inner feelings of the reader that lead him to a particular writer, and it is the philosophy of the writer that makes his work unique. If a writer writes honestly, his beliefs will speak, and readers with similar beliefs will recognize a friend, and enjoy.

*　　*　　*

Shirley Murphy's young adult fiction runs the gamut: realistic family stories, problem novels, animal stories, modernized folk/ fairy tales, and original high fantasy. Strong, independent female heroines, varied plots and styles, and often complicated narratives distinguish her fiction. Her realistic novels use simple prose, but her fantasy novels of time travel, talking animals, telepathy among people and also between people and animals, flying horses, and fierce dragons matched to mystical bards can be quite mannered.

The only child of an artistic mother and a horsetrainer father, she learned to express her fantasies through art and literature and to exercise practical self-discipline. At age thirty-five, after a successful career as an artist she began to master writing distinctive books for children. Always testing her limits, at times she lets her plots become overly episodic and complicated and lets her shifting points of view get confusing. In some of her fantasy novels, the sustained telepathic dialogues of peoples and animals diminishes their individuality of characters. But her best books repay rereading and rethinking. All are filled with graphic details—often violent in the fantasy novels—and their plots conclude neatly.

White Ghost Summer (1967) and *The Sand Ponies* (1967), her first two books, are realistic family stories set on the coast of her California childhood. In *White Ghost Summer,* the mother, her four adolescent girls, and her preadolescent boy move from a city apartment to a commodious Victorian house near the Pacific Ocean, a city park, and a zoo. There eleven-year-old Melani, "Mel," from

whose point of view the story is told, glimpses a ghostly white horse early one morning in the fog and later discovers that this and two other horses hidden in a secret valley belong to a young man. She and her family help establish his legal claim. Her riding lessons at Mr. Blake's riding school nearby lead to prizes. But all is not perfect. The delinquent behavior of her brother, nine-year-old Spence, and some neighbor boys causes some difficulties. But at the end all is well, and the family is even reconciled with strict, disapproving Aunt Vivian.

Sand Ponies starts simply with the running away of two orphans—thirteen-year-old Karen and her twelve-year-old brother Tom—from their drunken guardians Aunt Hester and Uncle Tom and their dingy city apartment. But their journey by bus and on foot back to the California coast gets complicated by a mysterious tramp, actually a disguised policeman, who follows them, and by the children's accidentally learning that a group of men from the Black Turtle Inn are stealing and selling wild ponies. The children aid in the arrest. They are also taken in by the Tillman family who are remodeling a barn for a house. This leads to the romances of four adults. The point of view shifts widely including not only most of these characters, but also Karen and Tom's former horses who coincidentally find their way to Mr. Tillman's ranch, and even a watchful crow who sees part of the action of the story. Despite a nice simple style and tone, the plot is too episodic, coincidental, complex, and confusing.

The problem novels *Carlos Charles,* (1971) written with husband Patrick J. Murphy, and *Poor Jenny, Bright as a Penny* (1974) draw upon his experience as a career probation officer. The first is a sparse story of the arrest and rehabilitation of the twelve-year-old Carlos, a shoeshine boy of Jamaican-American birth, who lives on the streets of the Panama Canal Zone after his grandmother dies and his mother abandons him. Sergeant Romeros befriends Carlos and sees the boy placed on probation with a gruff boatbuilder, who gives him a home and a chance to learn a skill. As the story advances, Carlos meets Mexican-American geologist and pilot Vincente Baroja, who takes him flying and encourages him to go to school and seek a better life. Carlos helps bring a band of gunrunners to justice and rescues Vincente when his plane crashes in the jungle. A believable, honest book filled with action and moral choices, it gets realistic flavor from the many Spanish words—both translated and left in context—and from a spare style like Joseph Krumgold's *...and Now Miguel.*

Poor Jenny, Bright as a Penny is just as graphic about an American welfare family, which drifts from one dingy furnished apartment to another. It is told from the point of view of fifteen-year-old Jenny Middle, who wants to be a writer but has been forced to act as surrogate mother for her younger siblings since the death of her father three years ago when her irresponsible mother sold their home, wasted the money, and took Lud Merton as lover and drinking companion. Jenny struggles heroically to keep the family together despite their mother's neglect, frequent shifts from one school to another, and a life in cramped apartments and juvenile halls. This life leads Crystal, Jenny's older sister, into promiscuity, drug addiction, delinquency, and finally death. The mother cheats on welfare and later is imprisoned for fraudulent use of a credit card. As in *Carlos,* an interested police officer and his wife, a writer, rescue Jenny and her nine-year-old brother Bingo, giving them a home and later becoming their foster parents.

The Grass Tower (1976) marks a transition in Murphy's realistic novels. Its strong-minded Californian heroine is fifteen-year-old Bethany, a horse lover gifted with telepathic powers. As the complicated plot unravels, Bethany is first frightened and then fascinated as her strong telepathic powers, stimulated by the false storefront of the Church of Zagdeska. It leads her to discover who her real parents were, to communicate telepathically, and then be reunited with Ninea Ruiz.

As in *Poor Jenny*, two of Murphy's animal books concern research and writing. In the charming and educational *Elmo Doolan and the Search for the Golden Mouse* (1970), the entire Doolan mouse family researches the history of mice, using the resources of the public library where they live; they leave their manuscript on microfilm for the librarian to find, who types a copy and gets it published. The book includes the reference notes compiled by the Doolans. *The Flight of the Fox* (1978) details how after Rory a kangaroo rat becomes friends with twelve-year-old Charlie Gribble and Crispin his lemming, they learn from aircraft manuals how to repair a model airplane found in a town dump, so that Rory and Crispin can fly it and defeat the dastardly starlings who try to ruin the plane and soil the whole town.

The Song of the Christmas Mouse (1990) is partly realistic animal story and partly a sensitive family story. Rick, a single adolescent small town boy, discovers during Christmas vacation a strange silver-colored mouse living in the woodpile. From reading and his veterinarian father, he learns that its grey and white stripes are the result of crossbreeding of an escaped pet white mouse and a common wild one. When his pesky city cousin seven-year-old Hattie and her divorced mother arrive from the city, the two square off about the mouse as well as Rick's new Canadian Blazer sled, which Hattie steals and wrecks. When the mouse is discovered climbing the Christmas tree and singing "a long, trilling cry," the stage is set for reconciliation.

Murphy reworks traditional dragons tales in the three parts of *Soonie and the Dragon* (1979), which has the sixteen-year-old independent heroine Soonie, going out into the world, using her skills at dancing, singing, and storytelling to rescue three princesses, to find a mate for herself, and to claim from the king the reward for saving his three daughters. Likewise blond, blue-eyed, sixteen-year-old Thursey is too independent to wait for a fairy godmother in Murphy's reworking of the Cinderella story in *Silver Woven in My Hair* (1977). Significantly we first see her searching for her old white horse. Abused by her stepmother Augusta and stepsisters Delilah "fat as a young stoat" and Druscilla "thin as a saw blade," Thursey has been educated by the village monk Anwin. For her own instruction she has compiled books of the variants of the Cinderella story as well as writing her own stories. She first meets the prince, disguised as Gillie, a goatherd, whose stories inspire her to attend the ball, using the invitation gotten by Anwin. This reworking pushes literary parallels and erudition to extremes, but Thursey remains an admirable, independent, innkeeper's daughter.

The majority of Murphy's young adult novels are works of high fantasy, consisting of a quintet, a trilogy, and a single co-authored novel. *The Ring of Fire* (1977) begins the quintet about the conflict of the repressive state religion and culture of the land of Ere and invaders from Kubal with the telepathic, red-haired seers and Children of Ynell and the mysterious Luff Eresi and their winged horses. A map, an elaborate history, and a genealogy help to tie the five books together, along with a continuing quest to reunite the shards of a jade runestone. *The Ring of Fire* establishes the conflict and shows how the telepathic and visionary Children of Ynell are led by the girls Meahta and Zephy, the goatherd Thorn, and the magician Anchorstar in an escape from the corrupt village of Burdeeth and its Kubalese invaders to safety in Carriol.

The Wolf Bell (1979) set prior to *The Ring of Fire* traces the birth and boyhood of Ramad, a red-haired seer of Ynell, the legendary hero of the five books, and the love child of aristocratic, sensual, wilful thirteen-year-old Tayba who bares the child to spite her father and prevent an arranged marriage. Mother and child are taken in and educated by Gredillon, the witchlike bell woman, until they have to escape to Burgdeeth, where Tayba becomes the lover of Vinniver, its cruel ruler-seer, who institutes the land's false religion and oppressive culture. Ramad uses as weapons against enemies both his telepathic powers and Gredillon's wolf bell with a fragment of the runestone which calls both real and spirit wolves. He meets the slave Skeelie and her brother Jerthon, who is casting the bronze statue of the Luff Eresi beneath which the Children of Ynell are constructing the escape tunnel to be used in *The Ring of Fire*. Ramad gets the runestone but then lightning splits it into nine pieces.

In *The Castle of Hape* (1980), twelve years after Ramad's defeat of Vinniver, Seers of Carriol led by Ramad, Jerthon, and twenty-year-old Skeelie attack the evil forces led by the Pellian Seer BroogArl, whose chief weapon—the monster Hape—has the heads of a serpent, an eel, and a horned man (or cat). Ramad solicits aid from the Luff Eresi, who agree to institute a way to save future victims only if Ramad will be a willing sacrifice in Burgdeeth. One subplot deals with Ramad's search for Telien, a girl he has seen in a vision in *The Ring of Fire* as they travel through time. Another subplot concerns the romance triangle of Ram, Telien, and Skeelie. With the Hape, BroogArl, and the other Pellian Seers dead, Ramad is free to seek Telien through time with the aid of three starfire stones given by Anchorstar.

In *Caves of Fire and Ice* (1980), nine years in the future, Skeelie and a friendly wolf companion Tore, with whom she communicates telepathically, go on various quests. One is a journey to Gredillion's derelict bell house and a cell where an older Telien is captive having had a baby by a surviving Seer of the Castle of Hape. Evil characters continue to search for shards of the runestone as Ramad and Skeelie collect more fragments. Telien reappears possessed by a lustful wraith. When it is exorcised, she dies and Ram sets out for Carriol with Skeelie. *The Joining of the Stone* (1981), set twelve years after the death of Ramad, completes the quintet. Lobon, the grown son of Ramad and Skeelie, has taken on his dead father's quest to collect the remaining jade shards. Skeelie has married the Cutter of Stones, who shaped some of the shards. Zephy and Thorn, now the leaders of Carriol, organize a dive to get a shard from the sea to use against an evil trio: Kish, a woman; RilkenDal, an exile; and the dragon Dracvadrig. After an apocalyptic scene, Lobon kills Kish and restores the runestone except for a shard lost in *The Ring of Fire*. Lobon and Meahta fly off to the future. Skeelie and the Cutter of the Stones travel to the past. Time rolls back; continents reappear; and the inscription of the stone is restored. The novels of this series have much action. Inventive details about foods, herbs, and animals make this alternate world different but recognizable. Yet the shifts in time call for many recapitulations and explanations and the extended telepathic communications reduce the narrative largely to a mind trip.

The high fantasy trilogy about the land of Tirror with its singing dragons, visionary bards, and their defeat of the forces of evil—told in Attic style with touches of Old Norse and medieval romance—attempts less and succeeds better as a narrative. In *Nightpool* (1985), the sixteen-year-old hero and rightful heir to the kingdom of Auric, Tebriel, "Teb," is completing his education among the talking otters who saved him from being the usurper Sivich's bait for the sea monster Hydrus. Teb's charming life among the otters, especially their leader Thakkur, and his rescue by the talking foxes have both realistic and fantastic detail. The last flying dragon Dawncloud has five young, setting the stage for each bard to be united with a dragon. Teb gets Seastrider. Dawncloud searches other worlds for her bard, Meriden. In *The Ivory Lyre* (1987), Teb, disguised as a prince and with the young dragons changed to horses, visits the Kingdom of Dacia. Dacia is a land in collusion with the evil humans and un-men, agents of the evil forces that have come to the land through the Castle of Doors to kill all singing dragons and talking animals, especially in grotesque gladiatorial games. In Dacia, Teb meets Keri, daughter of the former horsemaster, makes contact with the resistance forces, and learns news of Camery, his sister left behind in Auric. Camery and Keri's father Colewolf get their singing dragons. Teb and Keri retrieve the ivory lyre of the dragon Bayzum from a sea cave below the castle of Dacia and defeat the evil forces as the people remember their heroic past and cast away their drugged mithnon liquor and the drug cadacus. Teb and Camery leave on their dragons through the Castle of Doors to search for Meriden.

After a lot of recapitulation, *The Dragonbards* (1988) completes the trilogy. Teb and four dragonbards find five more singing dragons in Yoorthed. He is caught trying to rescue two more bard children from the evil Quazelzeg's castle and must be rescued by Marshy and Keri. Though he feeds Sivich to the sharks, Teb's mind is enslaved by the dark forces and lets them through. After much self-struggle, Teb assumes his rightful role as dragonbard and King of Auric in the final battle where the Graven Light defeats Quazelzeg. At the end, men and talking animals and dragons are living in harmony as in the past.

Medallion of the Black Hound (1989), a fantasy adventure book co-authored with Welch Suggs the twelve-year-old son of a close friend, alternates between and compares the American present and a parallel but primitive Celtic one. David Shepherd, the twelve-year-old son of a history teacher and athletic coach, also the descendant of the eldest of three sons of the Celtic king Finn Mac Cumhal for whom three magical medallions were made, finds himself thrust back in time and space just after his father has given him the hound medallion before leaving to check on the raising of a twelfth Viking ship with its treasure cargo. David meets the girl Jendyfi in the Cymru forest, is introduced to evil ogres, droowgs, the zombie-like Degras, and the good beasts like the wyverlyn Haun. He has been called to use his medallion to help King Kastinoe, owner of another of the medallions, to defeat the evil Balcher, who has the third. After finding Siarl Kastinoe's missing son, killing the Chimotaur (a blend of Minotaur and Chimera), and calling up the avenging spirit hounds to defeat the enemy, David is suddenly transported back to the soccer field two weeks later.

This story's synthesis of action—a modern American family and an ancient Celtic society—is typical of Murphy's experimentation with language, integration of research materials, inventiveness of incidents, and vivid, morally distasteful monsters. Murphy's *Flight of the Fox* was a Literary Guild selection, and her novels have received five awards from the Council of Authors and Journalists.

—Hugh T. Keenan

MYERS, Walter Dean. Has also written as Walter M. Myers. American. Born in Martinsburg, West Virginia, 12 August 1937. Educated at Empire State College, New York, B.A. 1984. Served in the United States Army, 1955-58. Married Constance Brendel in 1973 (second marriage); one daughter and one son from first marriage. Employment supervisor, New York State Department of Labor, Brooklyn, 1966-69; senior editor, Bobbs Merrill, publishers, New York, 1970-77; part-time teacher of creative writing and black history, New York, 1974-75. Has also worked as a mail clerk, office messenger, and factory interviewer. Since 1977 freelance writer. Recipient: Council on Interracial Books for Children award, 1968, for the manuscript of *Where Does the Day Go?*; *The Dancers* was selected one of Child Study Association of America's children's books of the year, 1972; American Library Association notable book citation, 1975, for *Fast Sam, Cool Clyde, and Stuff*, 1978, for *It Ain't All for Nothin'*, 1979, for *The Young Landlords*, and 1988, for *Scorpions* and *Me, Mop, and the Moondance Kid*; Woodward Park School Annual Book award, 1976, for *Fast Sam, Cool Clyde, and Stuff*; American Library Association best books for young adults citation, 1978, for *It Ain't All for Nothin'*, 1979, for *The Young Landlords*, 1981, for *The Legend of Tarik*, 1982, for *Hoops*, and 1988, for *Fallen Angels* and *Scorpions*; Coretta Scott King award, 1980, for *The Young Landlords*, 1985, for *Motown and Didi*, and 1989, for *Fallen Angels*; National Endowment of the Arts grant, 1982, 1989; Notable Children's Trade Book in the Field of Social Studies from the National Council for Social Studies and the Children's Book Council, 1982, for *The Legend of Tarik*; Edgar Allan Poe award runner-up, 1982, for *Hoops*; Parents' Choice award from the Parents' Choice Foundation, 1982, for *Won't Know Till I Get There*, 1984, for *The Outside Shot*, and 1988, for *Fallen Angels*; New Jersey Institute of Technology Authors award, 1983, for *Tales of a Dead King*; *Adventure in Granada* was selected one of Child Study Association of America's children's books of the year, 1987; MacDowell fellowship, 1988; Newbery Honor Book, 1989, for *Scorpions*. Address: 2543 Kennedy Boulevard, Jersey City, NJ 07304, U.S.A.

PUBLICATIONS FOR YOUNG ADULTS

Fiction

Fast Sam, Cool Clyde, and Stuff. New York, Viking Press, 1975.
Brainstorm, photographs by Chuck Freedman. New York and London, Watts, 1977.
Mojo and the Russians. New York, Viking Press, 1977.
Victory for Jamie, illustrated by Norm Walker. New York, Scholastic, 1977.
It Ain't All for Nothin'. New York, Viking Press, 1978.
The Young Landlords. New York, Viking Press, 1979.
The Black Pearl and the Ghost; or, One Mystery after Another, illustrated by Robert Quackenbush. New York, Viking Press, 1980.
The Golden Serpent, illustrated by Alice and Martin Provensen. New York, Viking Press, 1980; London, MacRae, 1981.
Hoops. New York, Delacorte Press, 1981.
The Legend of Tarik. New York, Viking Press, 1981.
Won't Know Till I Get There. New York, Viking Press, 1982.
The Nicholas Factor. New York, Viking Press, 1983.
Tales of a Dead King. New York, Morrow, 1983.
Motown and Didi: A Love Story. New York, Viking Kestrel, 1984.

Mr. Monkey and the Gotcha Bird, illustrated by Leslie Morrill. New York, Delacorte Press, 1984.
The Outside Shot. New York, Delacorte Press, 1984.
Adventure in Granada. New York, Viking Kestrel, 1985.
The Hidden Shrine. New York, Viking Kestrel, 1985.
Duel in the Desert. New York, Viking Kestrel, 1986.
Ambush in the Amazon. New York, Penguin, 1986.
Crystal. New York, Viking Kestrel, 1987.
Shadow of the Red Moon. New York, Harper, 1987.
Sweet Illusions. New York, Teachers and Writers Collaborative, 1987.
Fallen Angels. New York, Scholastic, 1988.
Me, Mop, and the Moondance Kid, illustrated by Rodney Pate. New York, Delacorte Press, 1988.
Scorpions. New York, Harper, 1988.
The Mouse Rap. New York, Harper, 1990.
Somewhere in the Darkness. New York, Scholastic, 1992.
Mop, Moondance, and the Nagasaki Knights. New York, Delacorte Press, 1992.
The Righteous Revenge of Artemis Bonner. New York, Harper, 1992.
Young Martin's Promise, illustrated by Barbara H. Bond. Austin, Texas, Raintree, 1992.

PUBLICATIONS FOR CHILDREN

Where Does the Day Go? (as Walter M. Myers), illustrated by Leo Carty. New York, Parents' Magazine Press, 1969.
The Dancers, illustrated by Anne Rockwell. New York, Parents' Magazine Press, 1972.
The Dragon Takes a Wife, illustrated by Ann Grifalconi. Indianapolis, Bobbs Merrill, 1972.
Fly, Jimmy, Fly!, illustrated by Moneta Barnett. New York, Putnam, 1974.

Other

The World of Work: A Guide to Choosing a Career. Indianapolis, Bobbs Merrill, 1975.
Social Welfare: A First Book. New York, Watts, 1976.
Now Is Your Time!: The African-American Struggle for Freedom. New York, Harper, 1992.
A Place Called Heartbreak: A Story of Vietnam, illustrated by Frederick Porter. Austin, Texas, Raintree, 1992.
Malcolm X: By Any Means Necessary. New York, Scholastic, 1993.
Remember Us Well: An Album of Pictures and Verse. New York, Harper, 1993.

Editor of "18 Pine St." series of young adult novels, Bantam, 1992—. Contributor to *What We Must See: Young Black Storytellers.* Dodd, 1971, and *We Be Word Sorcerers: Twenty-five Stories by Black Americans.* Also contributor of articles and fiction to periodicals, including *Black Creation, Black World, Scholastic, McCall's, Espionage, Alfred Hitchcock Mystery Magazine, Essence, Ebony, Jr.!,* and *Boy's Life.*

*

Media Adaptations: *The Young Landlords* (film), Topol Productions.

Biography: Entry in *Dictionary of Literary Biography,* Volume 33, Detroit, Gale, 1984; essay in *Something About the Author Autobiography Series,* Volume 2, Detroit, Gale, 1986; essay in *Speaking for Ourselves: Autobiographical Sketches by Notable Authors of Books for Young Adults,* Volume 1, compiled and edited by Donald R. Gallo, National Council of Teachers of English, 1990.

Critical Study: Entry in *Children's Literature Review,* Volume 4, 1982, Volume 16, 1989, Detroit, Gale.

*   *   *

Harlem permeates Walter Dean Myers's novels for teenagers, even when a story is set in a place very remote from New York. In *Fallen Angels,* for example, Myers writes about the Vietnam War and a black seventeen-year-old recruit named Richie Perry who enlists because he can't afford college and he wants to get out of the crime-ridden Harlem neighborhood where he grew up. Although the agony and the tragedy of the war take place in the Vietnam hinterlands, Richie's thoughts are often of his family and friends who are still trying to cope with life in Harlem. One of the few in his unit to survive his tour of duty, Richie can't wait to return to the place from where he once fled.

The setting for *The Righteous Revenge of Artemis Bonner* takes place mostly in the Wild West during the 1880s, but the story ends with a sentiment for New York City that is similar to Richie's. Artemis is a fifteen-year-old New Yorker who treks from the East Coast to the western frontier in order to even the score with the killer of his uncle. There's also an exciting subplot about unearthing a family treasure hidden someplace in the West. Artemis and a half-Cherokee friend named Frolic eventually do return to New York City. "New York City," Artemis tells Frolic, "has more sights than all of Tombstone and San Francisco put together, plus it is a safe place to live."

Perhaps juxtaposing New York City favorably with the Vietnam War and the Wild West is faint praise, but Myers remembers from his own Harlem childhood many positive experiences (such as reading from the newspaper to his mother while she did housework and getting his first typewriter from his father). However, he doesn't tone down the dangerous and dead-end reality of Harlem—the deadly, violent gangs (such as he depicts in *Scorpions),* the families torn apart by crime and poverty (as in *Somewhere in the Darkness),* the drugs, school dropouts, and pervasive hopelessness. In *Motown and Didi,* one of the author's most adult-oriented novels, Myers creates two products of the Harlem tragedy: Didi, a girl stymied in her attempt to enter college because of a brother who eventually drugs himself to death and a mother who has a nervous breakdown; and Motown, a homeless, likeable loner. What these two young people do to survive demonstrates how Myers uses the harsh realities of Harlem to provide a proving ground in which his characters can mature. Didi and Motown employ their street smarts to overcome their environment while developing a capacity to love and creating an ethical code that emphasizes a commitment to help others.

In *Hoops,* seventeen-year-old Lonnie Jackson plays basketball to earn his ticket out of Harlem. His troubled but wise coach tells him, "You got to learn to use your talent and you got to cover yourself." When he and his coach are offered large sums of money to shave points off a game, Lonnie—who is used to depending solely on his considerable athletic skills to resolve problems—is forced to draw on his sense of right and wrong. The next year, to help pay off his college tuition debts, Lonnie helps an autistic child relate to the outside world (in a sequel entitled *The Outside Shot),* but he again has to fight off repeated bribes to fix basketball games.

Myers transforms the Harlem world of abandoned apartments into a business opportunity for the five bright, enterprising teenage heroes of *The Young Landlords,* and he provides four of them with the challenge of exonerating the fifth member of the group who has been accused of stealing. This scenario of Harlem neighborhood buddies extricating themselves from a crisis brought on by youthful irresponsibility and exuberance is repeated in three of his other novels—*Mojo and the Russians; Fast Sam, Cool Clyde, and Stuff;* and *Won't Know Till I Get There.* And in *The Mouse Rap,* Myers focuses on a Harlem fourteen-year-old half-pint boy who meets his father for the first time in eight years, gets wowed by a new girl from California, and involves his small circle of friends in a danger-ous search for lost treasure. There is a certain sameness to these lighthearted, humorous, and relatively innocent adventures, but they provide readers with evidence that kids are kids, even in Harlem.

The author's repertoire of stories also includes two science fic-tion and fantasy novels whose spiritual roots can be traced to Myers's Harlem experiences. *The Legend of Tarik* is ostensibly about a young knight in medieval North Africa who was orphaned early in life because of a genocidal attack on his people by a war-rior-tyrant named El Muerte (The Death). In this mixture of Don Quixote and The Lone Ranger, Tarik seems like a medieval Motown who—inspired by love for a woman and by vengeance for crimes against his loved ones—fights an uphill battle against Evil. Tarik does realize, though almost too late, the dehumanizing effect that even killing for "good" reasons can have. And, in a somewhat im-plausible and wooden novel called *The Nicholas Factor,* Myers tackles the issue of elitist, secret societies that depend on willing, unthinking followers—a characteristic common to both racist groups like the Ku Klux Klan and inner city youth gangs.

In 1992 and 1993, Myers wrote two nonfiction books on Afri-can-Americans for young adults. One is an episodic and personal-ized history of Black Americans entitled *Now Is Your Time: The African-American Struggle for Freedom,* which focuses on particu-lar events (such as John Brown's Raid and the Dred Scott Supreme Court decision) and on slices of life of both the famous and the ordinary that show the richness and variety of the African-Ameri-can experience and culture. The other is a respectful look at and accurate examination of the multi-faceted life of Malcolm X entitled *Malcolm X: By Any Means Necessary.* In his fiction for teenagers, Myers has always placed a premium on character development in his protagonists; likewise, in this biography he emphasizes the important changes of belief and action Malcolm made near the end of his short life—changes that were responsible for his long-lasting influence on the lives of black and white Americans.

In his prolific and entertaining fiction and instructive nonfiction focusing on black life in America, Myers has opened up a part of America that once was closed to young readers. He has at once illuminated the hopelessness of black urban life and pointed a way that it can be overcome. Just as importantly, he has helped narrow the gap between black and white youths.

—Jack Forman

N

NAIDOO, Beverley. British. Born in Johannesburg, South Africa, 21 May 1943. Educated at University of Witwatersrand, South Africa, B.A., 1963; University of York, B.A. (with honors) 1967; University of York, postgraduate certificate of education (PGCE) 1968; University of Southampton, Ph.D. 1991. Married Nandhagopaul Naidoo in 1969; two children. Kupugani Non-Profit Nutrition Corporation. Field worker, Johannesburg, South Africa; Primary and secondary teacher, London, 1969; writer, since 1985; researcher, 1988-91; currently Advisory Teacher for Cultural Diversity and English, Dorset, U.K. Recipient: Other award, *Children's Book Bulletin,* 1985; Children's Book award, Child Study Book Committee at Bank Street College of Education, 1986; one of Child Study Association for American's Children's Books of the Year, 1987, and Parents' Choice Honor Book for Paperback literature from the Parents' Choice Foundation, 1988, for *Journey to Jo'burg: A South African Story;* Notable Children's Trade Book in the Field of Social Studies, 1990, and Best Books for Young Adults list, American Library Association, 1991, all for *Chain of Fire.* Agent: Garty Carter, Roger Hancock Ltd., 4 Water Lane, London NW1 8NZ. Address: 13 Huntly Rd., Bournemouth, Dorset BH3 7HF, England.

PUBLICATIONS FOR YOUNG ADULTS

Fiction

Journey to Jo'burg: A South African Story, illustrated by Eric Velasquez. Harlow, Longman, 1985, Philadelphia, Lippincott, 1986.
Chain of Fire. New York, Collins, 1989.

Other

Editor, *Free as I Know.* London, Bell & Hyman, 1987.

PUBLICATIONS FOR CHILDREN

Fiction

Letang's New Friend [Trouble for Letang and Julie; Letang and Julie Save the Day], illustrated by Petra Röhr-Rouendaal. Harlow, Longman, 1994.

PUBLICATIONS FOR ADULTS

Other

Censoring Reality: An Examination of Books on South Africa. London, ILEA Centre for Anti-Racist Education and British Defence/Aid Fund for Southern Africa, 1985.
Through Whose Eyes? Exploring Racism: Reader, Text, and Context. Stoke on Trent, Trentham Books, 1992.

*

Biography: Essay in *Speaking for Ourselves, Too* compiled and edited by Donald R. Gallo, National Council of Teachers of English, 1993.

Beverley Naidoo comments:

Writing for me is a journey. It is a way of exploring the country of my childhood from the perspective of the child I was not. I was brought up with the usual ideas most white South Africans had at the time, completely taking for granted the services of our cook-cum-nanny, who was like a second mother to me, while her own children were prevented by apartheid laws from living with her. I still feel intensely angry about my "miseducation"—and how racism distorted my vision and segregated my experience from that of the majority of other young South Africans who were black. I was just very fortunate that after leaving school I met people who challenged my inability to see what was all around me.

South Africa is now in the process of great historical change but, as in the U.S., the rifts and scars of racism run deep. Writing allows me to use my imagination to challenge the segregation of experience caused through discrimination. While I am beginning to diversify, sometimes moving my focus away from South Africa, I want my writing always to be primarily a way of extending the limits of my own understanding. Hence the journey. Obviously I hope it is one my readers will find worth following.

*   *   *

In her juvenile novel *Journey to Jo'burg* (1986), Beverley Naidoo introduces the characters of Naledi, Tiro, and Dineo, as well as their grandmother, Nono, and their Mama. In this short story, Naledi and Tiro walk and ride to Johannesburg in order to find their mother and bring her back to their village to help nurse Dineo back to health. It is an important journey for Naledi, but not just in the sense that she expected: she also learns of the darkness of apartheid and comes to a new resolve to fight its influences.

By the time *Journey to Jo'burg* was published, Naidoo had already written *Censoring Reality* (about nonfiction books that discussed South Africa for young readers). Having grown up in South Africa, with a cook and nanny whose children lived hundreds of miles away, she had come to see the injustices of her situation as a white child versus that of black children. She began to write fiction quite consciously as a means of educating the world's children about apartheid.

In 1989, this purpose continued in *Chain of Fire,* a novel for adolescent readers and "dedicated to all those who have struggled to resist." It is a novel filled with pain, sorrow, anger, and frustration. But it is not mere propaganda; the story is never manipulated and distorted to gain a sympathetic response. It continues the story of Naledi, a strong, capable, and complex young woman, who comes to new awareness about justice and her own role in securing justice. It is a painful role she takes on.

The novel opens with the announcement that the South African government plans to evict all of the residents of Bophelong, including Naledi, Tiro, Dineo, and their grandmother, Nono, and to send them to what is termed a homeland but what is truly a barren desert. Abandoned by their chief, the residents are at a loss; there seems to be no way to fight the injustice. Encouraged by a growing relationship with Taola Dikobe, Naledi becomes a part of a student group that tries to fight back, organizing a large student march against the evictions. Pit against the students are the headmaster of their school, their village chief, informers and spies, black policemen pressured by the government, and all the forces of the government itself, replete with tanks and weapons.

The march is broken up but not before the children are filled with a firm resolve to stand against the government and its policy of apartheid. But despite their resistance, inexorably the government closes in. Arrests are made in the night, pensions are cut off, water is cut off, the school is closed down, the church is destroyed, Taola is beaten up, and finally his father, an outspoken opponent of the government, is assassinated. The government trucks come, and the families are removed to a deserted rocky place, there to live in tin huts.

Though *Journey to Jo'burg* concludes with the hopeful presence of Mama, Naledi's mother is not able to appear at the end of *Chain of Fire* to fix things. Taola and Naledi are separated, Naledi's friends are in prison, hospitals, or hiding, the community has indeed been removed, and Nono grows weaker with each day as though she has no more strength to deal with the government's atrocities. But in the same manner that Naledi came to understand the evil of apartheid in *Journey to Jo'burg,* she comes to understand in *Chain of Fire* the power of resistance; a powerful chain of resistance has been built between the hearts of those who would fight against the government, no matter what the government does. She realizes that she is not alone in the fight, that she is not an impotent victim.

The title of the novel is suggestive. The image of the chain recalls the sense of community that is so important in the novel. Bophelong is clearly a village where each family is closely linked to the others; it has been this way for generations. The community is weakened when links fall away: when Chief Sekete abandons them, when Rra Thopi informs against them. But the chain is not destroyed. Again and again Naledi discovers that the community must indeed stay together and must resist together. This fact remains true even when community is dispersed.

The image of fire is especially suggestive. This is in many ways a spiritual battle as much as it is a physical one; the government has all of the advantages in terms of brute force. But the battle is also one of a group of people refusing to have its spirit destroyed, refusing to be cowed and manipulated and abused. It is a battle for the soul of South Africa. And at the same, the fire suggests the depths of passion and commitment which those who resist must feel. Saul Dikobe is killed because he refuses to live as the government insists that he should live. "No! They are not going to make me run like a frightened dog.... Will they destroy me, my family, my people while I must sit quietly by and watch? Oh no!" This is the fire that fills the resistors.

If this novel was only about this struggle, seen from a distanced narrator, it would be a powerful indictment of the South African government. There is no happy ending to save the day, no resolution but the resolve to keep on fighting. But what makes this novel even more powerful is that it is consistently told from the point of view of Naledi. Naidoo does present other perspectives: the raging bitterness of Tiro, the despairing acceptance of Nono, the sheer terror of Dineo, the quiet courage and steel of Mama Dikobe. But the perspective that emerges most powerfully is that of Naledi.

It is significant that Naidoo does not make Naledi into a larger-than-life figure; she is in many ways quite ordinary, with ordinary concerns and interests—at first. When the government's announcement comes into her life, she must come to a difficult decision: should she work against the government despite her Nono's prohibitions? If such activities threaten her school career, should she still continue? She chooses to resist and to work for justice, despite the cost to herself and to her family. At first she simply deceives her grandmother, but when Nono finds out, she reprimands Naledi, who is more hurt by this than by the whips of government soldiers. But little by little she is drawn into the resistance, at first out of a sense of emergency when she must find Tiro, then because of her growing relationship with Tiro, and then because of the rightness of the cause. Elected a student leader, she is given responsibilities because of her commitment and willingness to do something about that commitment. Even her grandmother comes to accept Naledi's role, dangerous as it might be.

Thus, the ending of the novel is full of hope, despite the success of the government's plans and the destruction of Bophelong. "Naledi's heart burned. It was a fierce fire within her, as fierce as the sun bearing down on her now, forever welding new links in a chain.... Each day the chain was lengthening, strengthening. She was not alone. They were not alone." The novel concludes with Naledi moving towards a group to share this knowledge with them—a sign that her role has not diminished, that she will continue to resist and to help others resist. She is someone who has grown into this role, and her growth is an important part of the power of *Chain of Fire*.

—Gary D. Schmidt

———

NAMIOKA, Lensey. Chinese. Born 14 June 1929, in Beijing. Educated at Radcliffe College, Cambridge, Massachusetts, 1947-49; University of California, Berkeley, B.A., 1951, M.A., 1952. Married Isaac Namioka in 1957; two daughters. Instructor in mathematics, Wells College, Aurora, New York, 1957-58; instructor in mathematics, Cornell University, Ithaca, New York, 1958-61; broadcasting monitor, Japan Broadcasting Corp., 1969. Translator for American Mathematical Society, 1958-66. Agent: Ruth Cohen, Box 7626, Menlo Park, CA 94025. Address: 2047 23rd Ave. E., Seattle, WA 98112, U.S.A.

PUBLICATIONS FOR YOUNG ADULTS

Fiction

The Samurai and the Long-Nosed Devils. New York, McKay, 1976.
White Serpent Castle. New York, McKay, 1976.
Valley of Broken Cherry Trees. New York, Delacorte, 1980.
Village of the Vampire Cat. New York, Delacorte, 1981.
Who's Hu? New York, Vanguard, 1981.
Phantom of Tiger Mountain. New York, Vanguard, 1986.
Island of Ogres. New York, Harper, 1989.
The Coming of the Bear. New York, HarperCollins, 1992.
Yang the Youngest and his Terrible Ear, illustrated by Kees de Kiefte. Boston, Joy Street Books, 1992.

Other

Translator, *How to Order and Eat in Chinese,* by Buwei Y. Chao. New York, Vintage, 1974.

Japan: A Traveler's Companion. New York, Vanguard, 1979.
China: A Traveler's Companion. New York, Vanguard, 1985.

Contributor of plays to *Center Stage,* edited by Donald Gallo.

*

Lensey Namioka comments:

As a child, my greatest pleasure was reading. My aim is to write books that will give the same pleasure to young people today.

While my books contain messages—the need for understanding and tolerance—I also try to make them as entertaining as possible. If my readers agree with my message, then they deserve to have some fun. If they disagree, I'm certainly not going to convert them by being preachy and boring.

*   *   *

Lensey Namioka claims not to have had a young adult audience in mind when she wrote her first novel, *The Samurai and the Long-Nosed Devils,* in 1976. Perhaps her claim suggests why adolescent readers are inclined to criticize her style, plots, and characterizations—and why her primary audience is in the eleven through fifteen age range rather than among the older teens her publishers also target. Her male protagonists are not entirely believable, especially in terms of their sexuality: though in their late teens or early twenties, they are content to do no more than carry on mild flirtations with the women they admire from a safe distance. Dialogue in her historical novels is invariably forced, unconvincing, and idiomatically anachronistic. The plots of her least satisfying novels seem little more than thrown together admixtures of characters and situations; structural unity is further eroded by narrative digressions and the occasional failure to resolve a secondary or tertiary plot line. Finally, Namioka's historical novels often incorporate contrived "culture lessons," rather stiff doses of aesthetic medicine that, all too obviously, have been spooned into the text for the reader's good.

Interestingly, Namioka's claiming not to have written specifically to a young adult audience may also explain the loyalty of young readers who enjoy her novels. Excepting *The Coming of the Bear,* Namioka's historical fiction addresses its adolescent audience with respect, challenging their vocabulary skills and considering (however superficially) such issues as political corruption, racial prejudice, social and familial violence, and rape. And, at her best, Namioka tells engrossing tales of bravado and adventure in exotic settings. These qualities, in the view of her loyal readers, more than offset her stylistic or structural deficiencies.

Of Namioka's nine published novels to date, seven are historical novels read by teens ages fifteen and younger, especially males. Other than *Phantom of Tiger Mountain,* a "Robin Hood" tale of well-born outlaws who subvert untoward political forces in eleventh-century China, the historical novels are set in late sixteenth-century feudal Japan (about 1575-1600) and recount the continuing adventures of Konishi Zenta and Ishihara Matsuzo, two young and homeless *ronin.* The best of the Zenta/Matsuzo novels are *Valley of Broken Cherry Trees,* which establishes a believable bond between Zenta and a fourteen-year-old aristocrat who is utterly devoid of self-confidence and parental approval but who learns courage, pride, and self-acceptance from his association with the *ronin;* and *Island of Ogres,* which relegates Zenta and Matsuzo to its secondary plot lines, focusing on the coming-of-age (including the partially believ-

able romantic awakening) of a young swordsman who has nearly drowned his potential in alcohol.

Zenta/Matsuzo novels dealing with racial issues are *The Samurai and the Long-Nosed Devils,* concerned with relations between Portuguese missionaries and the Japanese of sixteenth-century Kyoto, and *The Coming of the Bear,* which recounts tensions between the Ainu of Hokkaido and the Japanese encroaching on their territory. Unfortunately, the first of these is guilty of reverse racism in its portrayal of what must be defined as the condescending acceptance of the Portuguese by "open-minded" Japanese; as previously suggested, the second is the least satisfying of all Namioka's novels, its subject matter trivialized by a hastily concocted plot, lifeless dialogue, and one-dimensional characterizations. *White Serpent Castle,* which anticipates a central tension of *Valley of Broken Cherry Trees* (the imminent disempowering of a warlord's rightful heir), is perhaps the most carefully plotted of Namioka's historical novels; *Village of the Vampire Cat,* the tale of a disguised warrior terrorizing a village through his brutal murders of young women, is the most "exciting"—and the most disturbingly sexist in its depictions of cruelty and violence.

Namioka has written two novels for preteens, *Who's Hu?* and *Yang the Youngest and his Terrible Ear.* In terms of stylistic consistency, these are Namioka's best works: the dialogue rings truer; the characters are more believable and individualistic; the plots seem less contrived. Despite expectations aroused by its title, *Yang the Youngest* is the story of a tone-deaf boy whose musician father forces him to study the violin. *Who's Hu?,* which one suspects is at least partially autobiographical, portrays the struggles of a young immigrant girl in the 1950s to surmount gender expectations and resolve questions of cultural identity.

Namioka has published plays for adolescents and her travel books for adults, *Japan: A Traveler's Companion* and *China: A Traveler's Companion,* are used and appreciated by English-speaking adolescents participating in study abroad programs in Asia.

—Keith Lawrence

———

NAYLOR, Phyllis Reynolds. Also writes as Phyllis Naylor. American. Born in Anderson, Indiana, 4 January 1933. Educated at Joliet Junior College, Illinois, 1951-53; American University, Washington, D.C., 1959-63, B.A. in psychology 1963. Married Rex V. Naylor in 1960 (second marriage); two sons. Clinical secretary, Billings Hospital, Chicago, 1953-56; elementary school teacher in Hazelcrest, Illinois, 1956; assistant executive secretary, Montgomery County Education Association, Rockville, Maryland, 1958-59; editorial assistant, National Education Association, *NEA Journal,* Washington, D.C., 1959-60. Full-time writer, since 1960. Active in civil rights and peace organizations. Recipient: Children's Books of the Year from Child Study Association of America, 1971, for *Wrestle the Mountain,* 1979, for *How Lazy Can You Get?,* and 1986, for *The Agony of Alice; Wrestle the Mountain* was a Junior Literary Guild selection, 1971; *To Walk the Sky Path* was a Weekly Reader Book Club selection, 1973; *Walking through the Dark* was a Junior Literary Guild selection, 1976; *Crazy Love: An Autobiographical Account of Marriage and Madness* was a Literary Guild selection, 1977; Golden Kite award for Nonfiction from Society of Children's Book Writers, 1978, and Children's Choice from International Reading Association and Children's Book Council, 1979, both for *How I Came to Be a Writer; How Lazy Can You Get?* was a Weekly Reader Book Club selection, 1979; Children's Choice, 1980, for *How Lazy Can You Get?,* and 1986, for *The Agony of Alice;* Best Book for Young Adults from Young Adult Services Division of American Library Association, and Notable Children's Book in the Field of Social Studies from National Council for Social Studies and Children's Book Council, both 1982, and South Carolina Young Adult Book award, 1985-86, all for *A String of Chances;* Child Study award from Bank Street of College of Education, 1983, for *The Solomon System;* Edgar Allan Poe award from Mystery Writers of America, 1985, for *Night Cry; The Agony of Alice* was an American Library Association (ALA) Notable book, 1985; Notable Children's Book in the Field of Social Studies, 1985, for *The Dark of the Tunnel,* 1985; *The Keeper* was a Junior Literary Guild selection, 1986; Best Book for Young Adults from Young Adult Services Division of the American Library Association, 1986, for *The Keeper,* and 1987, for *The Year of the Gopher;* Joan G. Sugarman award, 1987, for *Beetles, Lightly Toasted;* Creative Writing Fellowship Grant from National Endowment for the Arts, 1987; Society of School Librarians International Book award, 1988, for *Maudie in the Middle;* Best Young Adult Book of the Year from Michigan Library Association, 1988, for *The Year of the Gopher;* Christopher award from the Christophers, 1989, for *Keeping a Christmas Secret; Send No Blessings* was an ALA Notable Book for Young Adults, 1990; Hedda Seisler Mason award, 1991, for *Alice in Rapture, Sort of;* Newbery Medal, 1992, for *Shiloh; All But Alice* was an ALA Notable book, and a Recommended Book for Reluctant Readers, 1993; *Shiloh* was also an ALA Notable Book, and won the Pennsylvania Young Reader's Choice award, 1993; Dorothy Canfield Fisher award, 1993; Maine Student Book award, 1993; New Hampshire Great Stone Face award, 1993. Agent: John Hawkins & Associates, Inc., 71 West 23rd St., Suite 1600, New York, NY 10010. Address: 9910 Holmhurst Rd., Bethesda, MD 20817, U.S.A.

PUBLICATIONS FOR YOUNG ADULTS

Fiction

To Shake a Shadow, illustrated by Gloria Kamen. Nashville, Abingdon, 1967.
When Rivers Meet, illustrated by Allan Eitzen. New York, Friendship, 1968.
Making It Happen, illustrated by Joe De Velasco. Chicago, Follett, 1970.
No Easy Circle, illustrated by Lou Aronson. Chicago, Follett, 1972.
Walking through the Dark, illustrated by James and Ruth McCrea. New York, Atheneum, 1976.
Shadows on the Wall, illustrated by Ruth Sanderson. New York, Atheneum, 1980.
Faces in the Water, illustrated by Ruth Sanderson. New York, Atheneum, 1981.
Footprints at the Window, illustrated by Ruth Sanderson. New York, Atheneum, 1981.
A String of Chances, illustrated by Ruth Sanderson. New York, Atheneum, 1982.
The Solomon System, illustrated by Ronald Himler. New York, Atheneum, 1983.
Night Cry, illustrated by Ruth Sanderson. New York, Atheneum, 1984.

The Dark of the Tunnel, illustrated by Ronald Himler. New York, Atheneum, 1985.
The Keeper, illustrated by Ronald Himler. New York, Atheneum, 1986.
The Year of the Gopher, illustrated by John Steven Gurney. New York, Atheneum, 1987.
Send No Blessings. New York, Atheneum, 1990.
Alice in Between. New York, Atheneum, 1994.
The Fear Place. New York, Atheneum, 1994.

Nonfiction

How to Find Your Wonderful Someone, How to Keep Him/Her If You Do, How to Survive If You Don't. Philadelphia, Fortress, 1972.
An Amish Family, illustrated by George Armstrong. Chicago, O'Hara, 1974.

Short Stories

Grasshoppers in the Soup: Short Stories for Teen-agers, illustrated by Elsa Bailey. Philadelphia, Fortress, 1965.
Knee Deep in Ice Cream and Other Stories, illustrated by Johanna Sperl. Philadelphia, Fortress, 1967.
The Dark Side of the Moon, illustrated by Joseph Papin. Philadelphia, Fortress, 1969.
The Private I and Other Stories, illustrated by Elsa Bailey. Philadelphia, Fortress, 1969.
Ships in the Night, illustrated by Otto Reinhardt. Philadelphia, Fortress, 1970.
Change in the Wind. Minneapolis, Augsburg Press, 1980.
Never Born a Hero. Minneapolis, Augsburg Press, 1982.
A Triangle Has Four Sides. Minneapolis, Augsburg Press, 1984.

PUBLICATIONS FOR CHILDREN

Fiction

The Galloping Goat and Other Stories, illustrated by Robert Jefferson. Nashville, Abingdon, 1965.
Jennifer Jean, the Cross-Eyed Queen (as Phyllis Naylor), illustrated by Harold K. Lamson. Minneapolis, Lerner, 1967.
The New Schoolmaster (as Phyllis Naylor), illustrated by Mamoru Funai. Morristown, New Jersey, Silver Burdett, 1967.
A New Year's Surprise (as Phyllis Naylor), illustrated by Jack Endewett. Morristown, New Jersey, Silver Burdett, 1967.
What the Gulls Were Singing, illustrated by Jack Smith. Chicago, Follett, 1967.
Meet Murdock, illustrated by Gioia Fiammenghi. Chicago, Follett, 1969.
To Make a Wee Moon, illustrated by Beth and Joe Krush. Chicago, Follett, 1969.
Wrestle the Mountain, illustrated by Paul Giovanopoulos. Chicago, Follett, 1971.
To Walk the Sky Path, illustrated by Jack Endewett. Chicago, Follett, 1973.
Witch's Sister, illustrated by Gail Owens. New York, Atheneum, 1975.
Witch Water, illustrated by Gail Owens. New York, Atheneum, 1977; London, W.H. Allen, 1979.

The Witch Herself, illustrated by Gail Owens. New York, Atheneum, 1978; London, W.H. Allen, 1979.

How Lazy Can You Get?, illustrated by Alan Daniel. New York, Atheneum, 1979.

Eddie, Incorporated, illustrated by Blanche Sims. New York, Atheneum, 1980.

All Because I'm Older, illustrated by Leslie Morrill. New York, Atheneum, 1981.

The Boy with the Helium Head, illustrated by Kay Chorao. New York, Atheneum, 1982.

The Mad Gasser of Bessledorf Street, illustrated by Andrew Rhodes. New York, Atheneum, 1983.

Old Sadie and the Christmas Bear, illustrated by Patricia Montgomery Newton. New York, Atheneum, 1984.

The Agony of Alice, illustrated by Blanche Sims. New York, Atheneum, 1985.

The Bodies in the Bessledorf Hotel, illustrated by Gail Owens. New York, Atheneum, 1986.

The Baby, the Bed, and the Rose, illustrated by Mary Szilagyi. New York, Clarion, 1987.

Beetles, Lightly Toasted, illustrated by Melodye Rosales. New York, Atheneum, 1987.

Maudie in the Middle, with mother, Lura Schield Reynolds, illustrated by Judith Gwyn Brown. New York, Atheneum, 1988.

One of the Third Grade Thonkers, illustrated by Walter Gaffney Kessell. New York, Atheneum, 1988.

Alice in Rapture, Sort of, illustrated by Blanche Sims. New York, Atheneum, 1989.

Keeping a Christmas Secret, illustrated by Lena Shiffman. New York, Atheneum, 1989.

Bernie and the Bessledorf Ghost. New York, Atheneum, 1990.

The Witch's Eye, illustrated by Joe Burleson. New York, Delacorte, 1990.

King of the Playground, illustrated by Nola Langner Malone. New York, Atheneum, 1991.

Reluctantly Alice. New York, Atheneum, 1991.

Shiloh. New York, Atheneum, 1991.

Witch Weed, illustrated by Joe Burleson. New York, Delacorte, 1991.

All But Alice. New York, Atheneum, 1992.

Josie's Troubles, illustrated by Shelley Matheis. New York, Atheneum, 1992.

The Witch Returns, illustrated by Joe Burleson. New York, Delacorte, 1992.

Alice in April. New York, Atheneum, 1993.

The Boys Start the War. New York, Delacorte, 1993.

The Girls Get Even. New York, Delacorte, 1993.

The Face in the Bessledorf Funeral Parlor. New York, Atheneum, 1993.

The Grand Escape. New York, Atheneum, 1993.

Boys Against Girls. New York, Delacorte, 1994.

Nonfiction

Getting Along in Your Family, illustrated by Rick Cooley. Nashville, Abingdon, 1976.

How I Came to Be a Writer, illustrated by Lou Carbone. New York, Atheneum, 1978, revised edition, Aladdin Books, 1987.

Getting Along with Your Friends, illustrated by Rick Cooley. Nashville, Abingdon, 1980.

Getting Along with Your Teachers, illustrated by Rick Cooley. Nashville, Abingdon, 1981.

PUBLICATIONS FOR ADULTS

Novels as Phyllis Naylor

Revelations. New York, St. Martin's, 1979.
Unexpected Pleasures. New York, Putnam, 1986.

Other, as Phyllis Naylor

Crazy Love: An Autobiographical Account of Marriage and Madness. New York, Morrow, 1977.

In Small Doses (essays). New York, Atheneum, 1979.

The Craft of Writing the Novel (as Phyllis Reynolds Naylor). Boston, The Writer, 1989.

*

Media Adaptations: *The Keeper* ("Afterschool Special," "My Dad Can't Be Crazy, Can He?"), American Broadcasting Companies (ABC-TV), 1989; *Witch's Sister* (television special), Blue Marble Program.

Biography: Essay in *Something about the Author Autobiography Series,* Volume 10, Detroit, Gale, 1990.

Manuscript Collections: Kerlan Collection, University of Minnesota, Minneapolis; de Grummond Collection, University of Southern Mississippi, Hattiesburg.

Critical Study: Entry in *Children's Literature Review,* Volume 17, Detroit, Gale, 1989.

Phyllis Reynolds Naylor comments:

Readers frequently send suggestions to me for future books, and occasionally I receive something I can use. But if I spent the rest of my life working at the ideas I have already accumulated—summary plots of books-to-be—I still would not be able to finish them all. What happens, of course, is that while I am brushing my teeth some morning, I get an idea for a book that seems far superior to any of those currently occupying one of the ten notebooks on my shelf, and so there is a continual shifting in the hierarchy of what will be written next. I will do anything possible to save time in which to write. I shamelessly order meals to be delivered, pay for secretarial and cleaning help, and if I could allocate my three mile walk every morning to someone else, I would probably even pay for that. There aren't enough hours in the day or days in a year to ever give me time enough to do what I love best—write, write, write.

* * *

A versatile and prolific author of young-adult novels, Phyllis Reynolds Naylor's work is distinguished by her skill at diversity. From comedy to tragedy, from books for younger readers to older young adults, from rural settings to urban landscapes, from fantasy to realism, she reveals a fine sense of the unexpected difficulties and rewards of life through her authentically drawn characters. Some of her novels have strong autobiographical elements, but others—no less convincing—are not based on her own experiences.

One of her best novels is *A String of Chances,* in which sixteen-year-old Evie experiences a summer away from home, living with a cousin and the cousin's husband, who are expecting a baby. Evie has her first serious romance, gains insights into her family's patterns of behavior, and struggles with her long-standing dislike of a boy who is living at her parents' home for the summer. Evie's father is a country preacher, and she confronts her own religious doubts and questions, especially when the beloved baby Joshua suddenly dies. What might easily have become trite and stereotypical is not at all so: Evie's father is loving and genuine and has a sense of humor; the baby's death and the consequent grief of all involved are presented with truthfulness and depth; and Evie emerges stronger and wiser but without easy resolutions to her religious questions or to her difficulties in romance. The milieu of the small town is aptly brought to life, and even the minor characters are intriguing and vital.

In *The Year of the Gopher,* seventeen-year-old George Richards's well-to-do suburban Minneapolis family suffers from performance expectations that have ruled family behavior for three generations. George revolts against these expectations by refusing to go to an Ivy League college (as his lawyer father did) and chooses to find blue-collar work instead, at least for a year. Naylor draws the world of George's teenage peers with observant, accurate detail: George's first sexual relationship, his relationships with his siblings, and his maturing realizations about life all are presented without clichés or sensationalism.

Focusing directly on sibling relationships, *The Solomon System* is a story about loyal brothers Ted and Nory Solomon. Their closeness is threatened, however, by the tension between their parents, who are headed for divorce, and by the two brothers' growing apart in other ways. Naylor creates plausible and interesting characters in a Jewish family, sympathetically and sensitively portrayed.

Some of Naylor's novels can be described as problem novels, with a difficult social or psychological issue forming the central theme. *The Keeper* deals with the recognition and consequences of mental illness. This novel tells the terrifying story of Nick, whose father behaves more and more strangely, until Nick is forced to recognize that his father is mentally ill. *The Keeper* has its roots in Naylor's own experience: her first husband was seriously mentally ill. *Crazy Love* is her compelling account of her traumatic first marriage. Another novel dealing with problems is the Gothic *Night Cry,* in which Naylor explores the predicament of Ellen, who lives on a Mississippi farm and is often alone when her father, a traveling salesman, is away. Through her loneliness and involvement with a superstitious neighbor, she allows her fears to take on larger dimensions than they should.

Naylor treats her characters with an admirable mixture of sympathy and critical insight, gives them depth, individuality, and complexity, and has the power to make the reader care for them. Naylor earned the prestigious Newbery Medal for her moving novel *Shiloh,* the story of a West Virginia boy and his friendship with an abused dog. Naylor's portrayal of the boy's struggle to hide his involvement with the dog without being any more dishonest than necessary; his economically poor, but loyal family; and the West Virginia setting all contribute to this outstanding novel. Naylor created an especially popular character in Alice, whose humorous and touching misadventures began in *The Agony of Alice* and *Alice in Rapture, Sort of.* and continue in three further novels. Her mother dead, Alice lives with her father and brother, and yearns for a female role model—the one she has in mind is glamorous Miss Cole, not her own dumpy teacher Mrs. Plotkin.

Willing to present complex religious, ethical, and psychological issues in her fiction, Naylor does so without a hidden—or, for that matter, obvious—agenda, but with simple honesty and sensitivity.

—J.D. Stahl

———

NEEDLE, Jan. British. Born in Holybourne, 8 February 1943. Educated at Victoria University of Manchester, drama degree (with honors), 1971. *Portsmouth Evening News,* Portsmouth, England, reporter, 1960-64; reporter and sub-editor for *Daily Herald and Sun,* 1964-68; free-lance writer, since 1971. Agent: David Higham Associates, 5-8 Lower John Street, Golden Square London WIR 4HA, England.

PUBLICATIONS FOR YOUNG ADULTS

Fiction

Albeson and the Germans. Tubingen, Deutsch, 1977.
My Mate Shofiq. Tubingen, Deutsch, 1978.
A Sense of Shame and Other Stories. Tubingen, Deutsch, 1980.
Losers Weepers, illustrated by Jane Bottomley. New York, Methuen, 1981.
Another Fine Mess. Armada, 1982.
Piggy in the Middle. Tubingen, Deutsch, 1982.
Going Out. Tubingen, Deutsch, 1983.
A Pitiful Place and Other Stories. Tubingen, Deutsch, 1984.
Tucker's Luck. Tubingen, Deutsch, 1984.
Behind the Bike Sheds. New York, Methuen, 1985.
A Game of Soldiers. Tubingen, Deutsch, 1985.
Great Days at Grange Hill. Tubingen, Deutsch, 1985.
Tucker in Control. New York, Methuen, 1985.
Skeleton at School. New York, Heinemann, 1987.
Uncle in the Attic. New York, Heinemann, 1987.
Wagstaffe the Wind-Up Boy. Tubingen, Deutsch, 1987.

PUBLICATIONS FOR CHILDREN

Rottenteeth (picture book), illustrated by Roy Bentley. Tubingen, Deutsch, 1979.
The Bee Rustlers, illustrated by Paul Wright. New York, Collins, 1980.
The Size Spies, illustrated by Roy Bentley. Tubingen, Deutsch, 1980.

PUBLICATIONS FOR ADULTS

Novels

A Fine Boy for Killing. Tubingen, Deutsch, 1979.
Wild Wood, illustrated by William Rushton. Tubingen, Deutsch, 1981.

Other

Brecht (criticism), with Peter Thompson. Illinois, University of Chicago Press, 1981.
Rebels of Gas Street, with others. New York, Collins, 1986.

*   *   *

Jan Needle's diverse work for young adults represents the compromise which gifted modern writers must often make if they wish to win and entertain a large readership but also to make serious moral and political statements about issues which confront young citizens in our time. Needle is a conspicuously political writer, personally committed to what might be termed the "humanitarian left," and a number of his novels and stories are deeply concerned with questions of racial, class, and sexual identity, and with the moral dimension of nationality, patriotism, and war. In several of his books the immediate setting is contemporary Britain or places with which Britain is politically enmeshed *(A Game of Soldiers,* for example, is set in the Falkland Islands during the 1982 war with Argentina) but his themes are universal, and the common denominator of these stories is the writer's indignation at the folly and cruelty of people and societies who refuse to recognise their shared humanity.

Not all of Needle's work is as solemn as these themes make it sound. He is also a brilliant humorist and has produced a number of books which are sheer comic entertainment. Some of them, such as *The Size Spies,* are for pre-teenage children, but that book's appealing mode of zany and iconoclastic science fiction mixed with satire has also been adapted in some of Needle's recent work—*Wagstaffe the Wind-Up Boy* and *Wagstaffe and the Life of Crime*—in a form which also attracts older readers. These stories concern the adventures of a boy who, having been squashed flat by a truck on the motorway, is reconstructed as a machine. This is comedy of extravagant ruthlessness and hilarious bad taste which owes something to Roald Dahl and to comic book traditions but has a distinctive mockery of convention and satiric relish for absurdity which teenage readers enjoy.

More serious are Needle's novels on contemporary social issues. At their most accessible these are stories which originated in television scripts and were subsequently novelised. Books such as *Great Days at Grange Hill* are recast from Needle's scripts for a long-running television series about a state comprehensive school, for which many other writers have also written. Because an urban secondary school necessarily reflects many tensions which arise from class, race, and anti-social behaviour, the scripts and books gave Needle a chance to combine undemanding entertainment with social realism. *A Game of Soldiers,* which began life as a television serial, is a far more serious book, and reflects Needle's determination to exploit the available media which reach a mass young adult audience, and to use the screen as a way into the novel. Brief, vivid and moving, this tense, unsparing story describes the experience of three young Falklands children who find a severely wounded Argentinean boy-soldier and have to face the resulting crisis in their lives. The book's theme is, in Wilfred Owen's phrase, "war, and the pity of war."

Perhaps the most controversial of Needle's "documentary" novels is *Piggy in the Middle.* The protagonists in the book are all adults, mostly members of the police, and the book's theme is race prejudice in the police force. *Piggy in the Middle* is therefore a regional depiction of an almost universal problem which affects young adults deeply. By choosing as his key figure a young, inexperienced but intelligent and tolerant policewoman, Needle is able to demonstrate how sexual prejudices intertwine with racial ones, and to illustrate the problem when looking at frontline law enforcement of distinguishing between on the one hand understandable grievance and provocation and on the other naked and vindictive prejudice. Sandra, the young policewoman, is finally unable to reconcile her police role with her painfully acquired political insights, and has to resign. The book is utterly uncompromising in its implicit anti-racist stance, but it is educative rather than propagandist because Needle scrupulously shows us the faults and duplicities on both sides, the confusion of good and bad within the single individual—in short, the sheer complexity of urban social tensions. Needle can be an accusatory, unaccommodating writer, carefully sealing off the moral escape-routes which his readers might seek, but he articulates conflicting viewpoints and lets us see why anti-social forces, however mistaken, feel and act as they do. The anti-racist novel *My Mate Shofiq* and the stories in the collection *A Sense of Shame* (notably the fierce indictment of defective courtroom justice, "The Common Good") are other powerful explorations of prejudice in its many guises.

The peak of Needle's literary achievement to date, however, consists of two novels with less evident topicality and mass appeal but with much to offer to more advanced young adult readers. *Wild Wood* is a magnificent satiric reversal of Kenneth Grahame's *The Wind in the Willows,* presenting the misdoings of Toad and the unearned pleasure-filled lives of the River Bankers from the viewpoint of the impoverished proletarian weasels, stoats, and ferrets who inhabit the Wild Wood. Needle's version of the insurrection and takeover of Toad Hall (renamed "Brotherhood Hall" by its captors) is modelled like Orwell's *Animal Farm* on the Russian revolution, and it makes some shrewd political thrusts. But these are gently understated, and the book is a rich and spirited comedy, affectionately disrespectful to its great forerunner. Finest of all Needle's books is the superb historical novel *A Fine Boy For Killing,* set in the time of the Napoleonic War and depicting the brutality of press gangs and the intense suffering of life at sea under vicious captains, material hardships and a barbarous disciplinary regime. The book outshines such celebrated equivalent novels for adults as C. S. Forester's "Hornblower" series in its mingling of compulsive excitement with bleak realism and moral intelligence. *A Fine Boy For Killing* is a minor classic, and we must hope that Needle's populist fiction, however successful, will not impede him from giving his imagination such major expression in the future.

—Peter Hollindale

NEUFELD, John (Arthur). Has also written as Joan Lea. American. Born in Chicago, Illinois, 14 December 1938. Educated at Yale University, New Haven, Connecticut, B.A. 1960. Served in the United States Army; discharged honorably. Editor, teacher television scriptwriter, and author. Advertising copy writer, Harcourt, Brace, and World, New York City; publicist, Franklin Watts, Inc., McGraw-Hill, Holt, and Western Publishing. Recipient: Notable Book award, American Library Association, for both *Edgar Allan* and *Lisa, Bright and Dark.* Fellowship, Macdowell Colony, Peterborough, New Hampshire. Agent: Arthur Pine, 1780 Broadway, New York, NY 10019. Address: 1015 N. Kings Rd., Los Angeles, CA 90069, U.S.A.

PUBLICATIONS FOR YOUNG ADULTS

Fiction

Edgar Allan. New York, S. G. Phillips, 1968.
Lisa, Bright and Dark. New York, S. G. Phillips, 1969.
Touching. New York, S. G. Phillips, 1970.
Sleep Two, Three, Four! New York, Harper, 1971.
Freddy's Book. New York, Random House, 1973.
Sunday Father. New York, New American Library, 1975.
The Fun of It. New York, Putnam, 1977.
A Small Civil War. New York, Fawcett, 1982.
Sharelle. New York, New American Library, 1983.

Other

Lisa, Bright and Dark (teleplay; *Hallmark Hall of Fame* presentation). NBC-TV, 1973.

PUBLICATIONS FOR ADULTS

Fiction

For All the Wrong Reasons. New York, Norton, 1973.
Trading Up, (as Joan Lea). New York, Atheneum, 1975.
Family Fortunes. New York, Atheneum, 1988.

Also author of television scripts *Death Sentence,* and *You Lie So Deep My Love,* both ABC-TV.

*

Media Adaptations: *Edgar Allan, Freddy's Book, For All the Wrong Reasons, The Fun of It, A Small Civil War,* and *Sharelle* have all been optioned for television.

Biography: Essay in *Something about the Author Autobiography Series,* Volume 3, Detroit, Gale, 1986, pp. 175-87.

Manuscript Collection: Kerlan Collection, University of Minnesota.

John Neufeld comments:

As a child, I began to learn about life as an adult by reading fiction. I can't believe I was, or am, alone. The topics I select to address are those I feel strongly that young people should begin to consider as they mature...i.e., often my books center around problems or ideas or conflicts a young person has yet to meet. My hope is that, later, when they do meet these struggles, my work will have been of some help in making constructive, suitable decisions for themselves and for those around them. I'm also crazy about my

characters and their stories. One has to be in order to face the page day after day.

*   *   *

John Neufeld tackles sensitive issues—such as mental illness, physical handicaps, and racial prejudice—with tremendous insight that accurately and honestly addresses each issue's impact on society. He credits young adults with a perceptiveness and depth of character that contrasts sharply with the ineptitude of the adult world.

Attitudes toward mental illness are explored in *Lisa, Bright and Dark,* one of Neufeld's best-known works. When Lisa Shilling tells her parents she thinks she may be going crazy, they see it as a ploy for more attention. Her friends, however, become alarmed as Lisa's condition deteriorates and her behavior shows signs of being drastic cries for help from the adults in her life. Even after walking through a plate-glass window, however, her parents won't believe anything is seriously wrong. While they continue to try to get the adults to listen, her friends set up a "therapy session," in which Lisa receives some relief by talking about what is happening to her. Though the ending is too magically resolved, with one adult stepping in at the request of his daughter, who is trying to help Lisa, the book sufficiently deals with mental illness without belaboring the technical details.

Neufeld addresses racial prejudice in *Edgar Allan,* which is based on the true story of a white family that adopts a black boy in the late 1960s. The story is told honestly, in a straightforward style, from the perspective of twelve-year-old Michael Fickett. The son of a minister in a small, but privileged white suburb in California, Michael chronicles the events surrounding the adoption of three-year-old Edgar Allan which causes disunion within the family, antagonism from the community, and an ultimatum from the church board of directors.

Michael is analytical, slightly introverted, and open-minded and balances the account of Edgar Allan's stay with the Ficketts by adding insights into the reactions of the family members. The two younger children seem not to notice the color of Edgar Allan's skin; Michael is at first shocked but his older sister is absolutely furious and refuses to acknowledge the child's presence. This story is not simply about the taking in and the "giving back" of one black child, though. It is also about failure, decisions, and how all of these resulting issues affect and develop Michael's life.

Touching tells the story of a courageous sixteen-year-old girl with cerebral palsy and her refusal to be denied dignity or love. Twink's family realize the intelligence of their daughter and diligently search for a school that will meet her needs. Twink expresses a desire to write about her life, and in a desperate attempt to remain in control of the few faculties left to her, she agrees to undergo an experimental technique to control her arm spasms. Though her parents try to discourage her, she insists on going through with the experiment, for her sake as well as for the sake of others. Unfortunately the result leaves her blind, but her determination to write is not hindered despite the loss.

Neufeld succeeds in showing each teen's perspective in part by telling the story from mixed viewpoints. The narrative is told simply, yet it can be highly emotive. Twink's courage is admirable, but more importantly readers come to understand the needs and desires of the physically handicapped, and also learn to reevaluate attitudes about people they know little about.

John Neufeld creates teenage characters who are perceptive and make decisions to take action. They are willing to learn about and understand situations unfamiliar to them. Neufeld's reputation for portraying teens as more capable of facing complex problems than adults is an appealing affirmation for young adult readers.

—Lisa A. Wroble

———

NEVILLE, Emily Cheney. American. Born in Manchester, Connecticut, 28 December 1919. Educated at Oxford School, 1931-36; Bryn Mawr College, Pennsylvania, A.B. 1940; Albany Law School, New York, J.D. 1976; admitted to the New York bar, 1977. Married Glenn T. Neville in 1948 (died 1965); three daughters and two sons. Office worker 1940-41, and feature writer, 1941-44, New York *Daily Mirror.* Currently in private law practice. Recipient: American Library Association Newbery Medal, 1964, for *It's Like This, Cat;* Women's International League for Peace and Freedom Jane Addams award, 1966, for *Berries Goodman.* Address: Keene Valley, NY 12943, U.S.A.

PUBLICATIONS FOR YOUNG ADULTS

Fiction

It's Like This, Cat, illustrated by Emil Weiss. New York, Harper, 1963; London, Angus and Robertson, 1969.
Berries Goodman. New York, Harper, 1965; London, Angus and Robertson, 1970.
The Seventeenth-Street Gang, illustrated by Emily McCully. New York, Harper, 1966.
Traveler from a Small Kingdom, illustrated by George Mocniak. New York, Harper, 1968.
Fogarty, New York, Harper, 1969.
Garden of Broken Glass. New York, Delacorte Press, 1975.
The Bridge, illustrated by Ronald Himler. New York, Harper, 1988.
The China Year. New York, Harper, 1991.

*

Media Adaptations: *It's Like This, Cat* (recording), American School Publishers and (videotape), Newbery Productions.

Biography: Essay in *Something about the Author Autobiography Series* by Emily Cheney Neville, Volume 2, Detroit, Gale, 1986.

Manuscript Collection: Kerlan Collection, University of Minnesota, Minneapolis.

Critical Study: Entry in *Contemporary Literary Criticism,* Volume 12, Detroit, Gale, 1980.

*   *   *

Emily Cheney Neville writes primarily for young adults, though she has published one picture book. She is best known for her first book, *It's Like This, Cat,* a sensitive, funny story about Dave Mitchell, an ordinary teenage boy in an ordinary middle-class family in New York City.

Dave can't seem to do anything right as far as his father is concerned. He and his father argue a lot, and the arguments result in his mother having asthma attacks and Dave walking out of the house. His father says a dog can be educational for a boy, so Dave walks out and comes home with a cat. In the course of a summer, Dave and the cat have ordinary and not-so-ordinary adventures. They meet new people, and Dave, at age fourteen, finds the first girl that he feels comfortable with. Dave learns, through observing the relationship between his father and an older teenage male friend, that his father is not a bad guy after all. Seeing his family through the eyes of others, gives Dave understanding and compassion. A simple, straightforward story, *It's Like This, Cat* is memorable for its brilliant teenage dialogue, humor, and realism. New York City, with its dirt and its danger, its stray cats and stray people, is eloquently described.

Berries Goodman is about a nine-year-old boy who has a laid-back family and lives in an ethnically diverse big-city neighborhood. Berries accepts people as they are. After his family moves to the suburbs, with its "restricted communities," he is introduced to anti-Semitism. It puzzles and disturbs him since he values his best friend, a Jewish boy named Sidney Fine. The characters in this book are well delineated and the plot unfolds naturally. The first-person dialogue is as fresh and spirited as that of *It's Like This, Cat.* And the underlying subject of prejudice and its effects on children's lives is presented honestly and clearly.

Another fast-paced New York City story, *The Seventeenth-Street Gang* has believable characters too; the children talk as children and the adults talk as adults. The girls and boys of mixed ages are led by a strong-willed girl, Minnow. Minnow can be alternately charming and hostile; she is always resilient. The shifting power struggles within the gang are artfully described. The children's strategies for maintaining privacy and independence from adults are also well presented.

Neville's early childhood included a world of relatives, games and adventures with cousins, holidays celebrated with an extended family, and memories of a variety of family pets. *Travelers from a Small Kingdom* is an autobiographical account describing Neville's close-knit family living in a small town in the 1920s. This world may seem to some modern readers who are accustomed to a world of technology, speed, overcrowding, and violence, as uneventful and dull. But Neville makes her childhood and its setting real and satisfying.

Fogarty, like *It's Like This, Cat,* is strong in candor, pithy characterizations, and surprising situations. Dan Fogarty, twenty-three, a college graduate and law school drop-out, is first met loafing around in front of Malone's garage in Wilbur Flats. He describes himself as "the town flop"; his old school teacher, the preacher, and almost everyone around would like him to "be something." Next, Dan is seen in the East Village of New York City, sleeping with a young lady and facing an unsuccessful play production. *Fogarty* speaks of the emotional hold of a small town on even the most rebellious citizens, and describes a sensitive young man as he gets over an unhappy romance and deals with his artistic talents.

The China Year is the story of Henri, an eighth-grade New York City child who lives in a loft apartment with her painter mother and college professor father, and who summers in the Poconos. One day Henri is studying for finals, wondering about summer. The next day her father announces an exchange appointment for him to teach English literature in Beijing. Henri's China year is a year of school lessons by mail, no friends, no phone, no pizza, and throngs of people who do not speak her language. Henri explores Beijing on her bike, and at a busy corner meets Minyuan. Minyuan speaks English; he went to school in Philadelphia for a year while his mother taught Chinese at a college there. Minyuan offers to show Henri Tienanmen Square, "very important Chinese place." Later she wants to go to the Peking Hotel to use the bathroom and eat ice cream. He explains that ordinary Chinese people are not allowed in this elegant place. Through Minyuan and his family, Henri and her family get a close look at Chinese culture and its constrictions. Importantly, they make real Chinese friends. Because of Henri's mother's illness, the family leaves Beijing before the year is up, and before the Tienanmen Square massacre. Back in New York, Henri sees the TV footage of fighting and fears for Minyuan's safety. She sends him a letter, not mentioning the massacre but cautiously only writes of their friendship. She receives a letter back from him which is also only about their friendship. By describing cultural differences through day-to-day experiences of teenagers, Neville is able to give them intimacy and meaning. For those who do not have the unique opportunity of observing life in the Third World, this book may be a particularly enriching experience.

—Mary Lystad

—————

NICHOLS, Leigh. See **KOONTZ, Dean R.**

—————

NIXON, Joan Lowery. Has also written as Jaye Ellen. American. Born in Los Angeles, California, 3 February 1927. Educated at the University of Southern California, Los Angeles, 1944-47, B.A. in journalism 1947; California State College, 1948-49, elementary teaching certificate. Married Hershell H. Nixon in 1949; three daughters and one son. Writer. Elementary school teacher, Los Angeles, 1947-50; creative writing instructor, Midland College, Texas, 1971-73, and University of Houston, 1974-78; taught creative writing in numerous public schools in Texas. Member of the Board of Directors, Society of Children's Book Writers, Los Angeles, 1976-79. Recipient: Steck-Vaughn award, Texas Institute of Letters, 1975, for *The Alligator under the Bed;* Edgar Allan Poe award for best juvenile novel, Mystery Writers of America, 1980, for *The Kidnapping of Christina Lattimore,* 1981, for *The Seance,* and 1987, for *The Other Side of Dark;* Edgar Allan Poe award nominee, Mystery Writers of America, 1975, for *The Mysterious Red Tape Gang,* and 1985, for *The Ghosts of Now;* Outstanding Science Trade Book for children, National Science Teachers Association and Children's Book Council Joint Committee, 1979, for *Volcanoes: Nature's Fireworks,* 1980, for *Glaciers: Nature's Frozen Rivers,* and 1981, for *Earthquakes: Nature in Motion;* Crabbery award, Oxon Hill branch of Prince George's County (MD) Library, 1984, for *Magnolia's Mixed-Up Magic;* Young Hoosier award, 1988, for *A Deadly Game of Magic;* Golden Spur, Western Writers of America, 1988, for *A Family Apart,* and 1989, for *In the Face of Danger;* Young Hoosier award, 1989, for *The Dark and Deadly Pool;* Colorado Blue Spruce Young Adult award, 1988, Virginia Young Adult Silver Cup, 1989,

Oklahoma Sequoyah Young Adult Book award, 1989, Iowa Teen award, 1989, California Young Readers Medal, 1990, and Utah Young Adult award, 1991, all for *The Other Side of Dark;* California Young Readers Medal, 1990, for *The Stalker;* Virginia Young Reader's award, 1992, for *A Family Apart;* Nevada's Young Readers award, 1992, and Nebraska's Golden Sower award, 1993, both for *Whispers From the Dead;* Edgar Allan Poe award nominee, Mystery Writers of America, 1993, for *The Weekend Was Murder!* Agent: Amy Berkower, Writers House Inc., 21 West 26th St., New York, NY 10010. Address: 10215 Cedar Creek Dr., Houston, TX 77042, U.S.A.

PUBLICATIONS FOR YOUNG ADULTS

Fiction

The Kidnapping of Christina Lattimore. New York, Harcourt, 1979.
The Seance. New York, Harcourt, 1980; London, Granada, 1983.
The Spectre. New York, Delacorte, 1982; London, Granada, 1983.
The Trouble with Charlie (as Jaye Ellen). New York, Bantam, 1982.
Days of Fear, photographs by Joan Menschenfreund. New York, Dutton, 1983.
A Deadly Game of Magic. New York, Harcourt, 1983; London, Corgi, 1988.
The Ghosts of Now. Delacorte, 1984; London, Corgi, 1987.
The Stalker, illustrations by Wendy Popp. Delacorte, 1985.
The Other Side of Dark. New York, Delacorte, 1986; London, Hodder and Stoughton, 1988.
The Dark and Deadly Pool. New York, Delacorte, 1987.
A Family Apart. New York, Bantam, 1987.
Caught in the Act. New York, Bantam, 1988.
In the Face of Danger. New York, Bantam, 1988.
Secret, Silent Screams. New York, Delacorte, 1988.
The Island of Dangerous Dreams. New York, Dell, 1989.
A Place to Belong. New York, Bantam, 1989.
Star Baby. New York, Bantam, 1989.
Whispers from the Dead. New York, Delacorte, 1989.
Encore. New York, Bantam, 1990.
Overnight Sensation. New York, Bantam, 1990.
Candidate for Murder. New York, Delacorte, 1991.
High Trail to Danger. New York, Bantam, 1991.
A Deadly Promise. New York, Bantam, 1992.
Land of Hope. New York, Bantam, 1992.
The Weekend Was Murder! New York, Delacorte, 1992.
Land of Promise. New York, Bantam, 1993.
The Name of the Game was Murder. New York, Delacorte, 1993.
Land of Dreams. New York, Delacorte, 1994.
Shadowmaker. New York, Delacorte, 1994.

Other

Oil and Gas: From Fossils to Fuels, with Hershell H. Nixon, illustrated by Jean Day Zallinger. New York, Harcourt, 1977.
Volcanoes: Nature's Fireworks, with Hershell H. Nixon. New York, Dodd, 1978.
Glaciers: Nature's Frozen Rivers, with Hershell H. Nixon. New York, Dodd, 1980.
Earthquakes: Nature in Motion, with Hershell H. Nixon. New York, Dodd, 1981.

Land under the Sea, with Hershell H. Nixon. New York, Dodd, 1985.

PUBLICATIONS FOR CHILDREN

Fiction

The Mystery of Hurricane Castle, illustrated by Velma Ilsley. New York, Criterion, 1964.
The Mystery of the Grinning Idol, illustrated by Alvin Smith. New York, Criterion, 1965.
The Mystery of the Hidden Cockatoo, illustrated by Richard Lewis. New York, Criterion, 1966.
The Mystery of the Haunted Woods, illustrated by Theresa Brudi. New York, Criterion, 1967.
The Mystery of the Secret Stowaway, illustrated by Joan Drescher. New York, Criterion, 1968.
Delbert, the Plainclothes Detective, illustrated by Philip Smith. New York, Criterion, 1971.
The Mysterious Red Tape Gang, illustrated by Joan Sandin. New York, Putnam, 1974, in paperback as *The Adventures of the Red Tape Gang,* illustrated by Steven H. Stroud, Scholastic, 1983.
The Secret Box Mystery, illustrated by Leigh Grant. New York, Putnam, 1974.
The Mysterious Prowler, illustrated by Berthe Amoss. New York, Harcourt, 1976.
The Boy Who Could Find Anything, illustrated by Syd Hoff. New York, Harcourt, 1978.
Danger in Dinosaur Valley, illustrated by Marc Simont. New York, Putnam, 1978.
Muffie Mouse and the Busy Birthday, illustrated by Geoffrey Hayes. New York, Seabury, 1978, as *Muffy and the Birthday Party,* New York, Scholastic, 1979.
Bigfoot Makes a Movie, illustrated by Syd Hoff. New York, Putnam. 1979.
Casey and the Great Idea, illustrated by Amy Rowen. New York, Dutton, 1980.
Gloria Chipmunk, Star!, illustrated by Diane Dawson. Boston, Houghton, 1980.
If You Say So, Claude, illustrated by Lorinda Bryan Cauley. New York, Warne, 1980.
The New Year's [Halloween, Valentine, Happy Birthday, April Fool, Thanksgiving, Easter, Christmas Eve] Mystery, illustrated by Jim Cummins. Chicago, Whitman, 8 vols., 1979-81.
Kidnapped on Astarr, illustrated by Paul Frame. Champaign, Illinois, Garrard, 1981.
Mysterious Queen of Magic, illustrated by Paul Frame. Champaign, Illinois, Garrard, 1981.
Mystery Dolls from Planet Urd, illustrated by Paul Frame. Champaign, Illinois, Garrard, 1981.
The Spotlight Gang and the Backstage Ghost. Tarrytown, New York, Harlequin, 1981.
The Gift, illustrated by Andrew Glass. New York, Macmillan, 1983.
Magnolia's Mixed-Up Magic, illustrated by Linda Bucholtz-Ross. New York, Putnam, 1983.
The House on Hackman's Hill. New York, Scholastic Inc., 1985.
Maggie, Too, illustrations by Darrel Millsap. San Diego, Harcourt, 1985.
And Maggie Makes Three. San Diego, Harcourt, 1986.

Beats Me, Claude, illustrated by Tracey Campbell Pearson. New York, and London, Viking, 1986.
Fat Chance, Claude, illustrated by Tracey Campbell Pearson. New York, Viking Kestrel, 1987.
Haunted Island. New York, Scholastic Inc., 1987.
Maggie Forevermore. San Diego, Harcourt, 1987.
You Bet Your Britches, Claude, illustrated by Tracey Campbell Pearson. New York, Viking, 1989.
The Haunted House on Honeycutt Street. New York, Dell, 1991.
Honeycutt Street Celebrities. New York, Dell, 1991.
Mystery Box. New York, Dell, 1991.
Watch Out for Dinosaurs. New York, Dell, 1991.
That's the Spirit, Claude. New York, Viking, 1992.

Picture Books

The Alligator under the Bed, illustrated by Jan Hughes. New York, Putnam, 1974.
The Butterfly Tree, illustrated by James McIlrath. Huntington, Indiana, Our Sunday Visitor, 1979.
Will You Give Me a Dream?, illustrated by Bruce Degen. New York, Four Winds Press, 1994.
When I Am Eight, illustrated by Dick Gackenbach. New York, Dial, 1994.

Other

Five Loaves and Two Fishes: Feeding of Five Thousand for Beginning Readers; John 6:1-15 for Children, illustrated by Aline Cunningham. St. Louis, Concordia, 1976.
Who Is My Neighbor?: The Good Samaritan for Beginning Readers; Luke 10:29-37 for Children, illustrated by Aline Cunningham. St. Louis, Concordia, 1976.
The Son Who Came Home Again: The Prodigal Son for Beginning Readers; Luke 15:11-32 for Children, illustrated by Aline Cunningham. St. Louis, Concordia, 1977.
When God Listens, illustrated by James McIlrath. Huntington, Indiana, Our Sunday Visitor, 1978.
When God Speaks, illustrated by James McIlrath. Huntington, Indiana, Our Sunday Visitor, 1978.
Before You Were Born, illustrated by James McIlrath. Huntington, Indiana, Our Sunday Visitor, 1980.
If You Were a Writer, illustrated by Bruce Degen. New York, Four Winds Press, 1988.

PUBLICATIONS FOR ADULTS

Other

People and Me (textbook), with others. New York, Benefic, 1975.
This I Can Be (textbook), with others. New York, Benefic, 1975.
Writing Mysteries for Young People. Boston, The Writer, 1977.
The Grandmother's Book. Nashville, Abingdon Press, 1979.

*

Biography: Essay in *Something about the Author Autobiography Series,* Volume 9, Detroit, Gale, 1990; essay in *Speaking for Ourselves: Autobiographical Sketches by Notable Authors of Books for*

Young Adults, Volume 1, compiled and edited by Donald R. Gallo, National Council of Teachers of English, 1990.

Joan Lowery Nixon comments:

From the time I was very young I wanted to be a writer. In fact, I *knew* I would be a writer. I wrote nearly every day—diary entries, stories, poems—and I used to read, read, read. I began writing short nonfiction articles for magazines while I was still in high school, and at the University of Southern California I majored in journalism. It was later, while I was a busy mother of four young children that I wrote my first book for children and loved the experience. My memories of childhood and teenaged years are vivid, and I write for young people of today through my emotions. While today's problems are different from problems of my generation, the emotions involving fear, uncertainty, joy, sorrow, excitement, the desire to love and be loved remain the same. I was always the optimist, strengthened by hope, and I try to pass along this same hope to my readers.

*   *   *

Joan Lowery Nixon is a prolific writer of books for children at elementary, junior high, and high school levels. She is best known for her fast-paced, ingenious mystery stories and is a three-time winner of the Mystery Writers of America Edgar Allan Poe Award.

Her mysteries for older children are psychological thrillers, involving complicated characterizations and plots that demand the reader's participation in solving the crime. In *The Kidnapping of Christina Lattimore,* Christina and a young reporter set out to prove Christina's innocence when her kidnappers claim that she was an accomplice to their crime. In *The Seance,* what begins as a game, with Lauren and five other girls gathered in a candlelight circle, develops into murder of the participants.

The Spectre is about nine-year-old Julie, an abused child, and the friend she makes in the hospital, seventeen-year-old Dina, a victim of Hodgkins disease. Julie and Dina share feelings of fear and despair, but eventually their support of each other allows them to feel hopeful towards the future.

A Deadly Game of Magic tells about Lisa and her friends caught in a violent storm. The storm leaves them stranded by an old deserted house, strewn with odd tricks and gadgets, the paraphernalia for a practiced magician. Lisa has always dreamed of being a magician; now her life depends on it.

Nixon also writes funny, rollicking books about people, their predicaments, and their relationships. *Beats Me, Claude* is about a happy couple who live quietly in a cabin in the rolling hills of Texas. Shirley attempts to make an apple pie for Claude and ends up using the pie both to capture escaped criminals and to cajole Claude into adopting two deserving orphans.

In quite a different vein, Nixon has written a series of historical novels, *The Orphan Train Quartet.* During the period from 1854 to 1929, the Children's Aid Society sent more than 100,000 children on orphan trains from the slums of New York City to new homes in the West. This out-placing was judged successful and other child welfare groups, such as the New York Foundling Hospital, followed its example. *The Orphan Train Quartet* was inspired by true stories of these children. It follows the six Kelly children, whose poverty-stricken widowed mother sends them West from New York in 1856 because she feels she cannot adequately care for them. The children go to various homes around St. Joseph, Missouri. The books are: *A Family Apart, Caught in the Act, In the Face of Danger,* and *A Place to Belong.*

In *A Place to Belong,* Danny and Peg Kelly feel lucky to be adopted by Alfrid and Olga Swenson. But when Olga dies unexpectedly they fear for their future. Danny comes up with a solution: Alfrid should marry their own mother. This does not come to pass, but another satisfactory solution is found. The book takes place just before the outbreak of the Civil War and critical aspects of a family's history are juxtaposed with those of American history. *The Orphan Train Quartet* offers readers a glimpse of other times in America where young people faced different kinds of family and community crises, as well as similar needs for self-esteem, love, and adventure.

More recently Nixon has written a trilogy, *Hollywood Daughters,* telling the stories of three generations of mothers and daughters who dream and struggle within the glamorous world of Hollywood. *Star Baby, Overnight Sensation,* and *Encore* describe fifty years of Hollywood history, as played out within one family. Gladys Baynes is a beautiful and ambitious woman who does not succeed in a career as a serious actress; she hopes though to achieve success vicariously through her daughter, Abby Grant. Abby subsequently becomes a superstar TV comic. Now comes Abby's daughter, Cassie Martin, who is interested in becoming a serious still photographer. Cassie falls in love with Marc and agrees to play the leading role in his first film. She is sensational. The plots of these three books are fast-paced, filled with grueling hours of studio work and glittering Beverly Hills play. The reader is pulled from Gladys to Abby to Cassie, and finally to Cassie's children.

Nixon's skillful writing and boundless imagination make young readers want to read on, to find out what surprises wait on the next page and discover if their solutions to her never-ending puzzles are the correct ones. She is also a writer of warmth, understanding young people's serious concerns about self and life, as well as their need for excitement and fun.

—Mary Lystad

———————

NORTH, Andrew. See **NORTON, Andre.**

———————

NORTH, Anthony. See **KOONTZ, Dean R.**

———————

NORTH, Sterling. American. Born near Edgerton, Wisconsin, 4 November 1906. Educated at the University of Chicago, A.B. 1929. Married Gladys Buchanan in 1927; one son and one daughter. Reporter, 1929-31, and literary editor, 1932-43, Chicago *Daily News;* literary editor, New York *Post,* 1943-49, and New York *World Telegram and Sun,* 1949-56; founding editor, North Star Books, Houghton Mifflin, publishers, Boston, 1957-64. Recipient: Witter Bynner Poetry award; *Poetry* magazine's Young Poet's Prize; *New*

York Herald Tribune's Spring Book Festival honor book, 1956, for *Abe Lincoln: Log Cabin to White House;* Dutton Animal Book award, New Jersey Institute of Technology Authors award, both 1963, Newbery Honor Book, 1964, Lewis Carroll Shelf award, 1964, Dorothy Canfield Fisher Children's Book award, 1965, Aurianne award, 1965, William Allen White Children's Book award, 1966, Pacific Northwest Library Association Young Readers' Choice award, 1966, Sequoyah Children's Book award, 1966, ALA Notable Book citation, and *Horn Book* honor citation, all for *Rascal: A Memoir of a Better Era;* New Jersey Institute of Technology Authors award, 1965, for *Little Rascal;* New Jersey Institute of Technology Children's Book Writer of the Year award, 1966; Dutton Animal Book award, 1969, for *The Wolfling. Died 21 December 1974.*

PUBLICATIONS FOR YOUNG ADULTS

Fiction

So Dear to My Heart. New York, Doubleday, 1947; London, Odhams Press, 1949.
Rascal: A Memoir of a Better Era, illustrated by John Schoenherr. New York, Dutton, 1963; as *Rascal: The True Story of a Pet Raccoon,* London, Hodder and Stoughton, 1963; abridged edition, as *Little Rascal,* New York, Dutton, 1965; Leicester, Brockhampton Press, 1966.

PUBLICATIONS FOR CHILDREN

The Five Little Bears, illustrated by Clarence Biers and Hazel Frazee. Chicago, Rand McNally, 1935; London, Shaw, 1940.
The Zipper ABC Book, illustrated by Keith Ward. Chicago, Rand McNally, 1937.
Greased Lightning, illustrated by Kurt Wiese. Philadelphia, Winston, 1940.
Midnight and Jeremiah, illustrated by Kurt Wiese. Philadelphia, Winston, 1943.
The Birthday of Little Jesus, illustrated by Valenti Angelo. New York, Grosset and Dunlap, 1952; Manchester, World Distributors, 1953.
Son of the Lamp-Maker: The Story of a Boy Who Knew Jesus, illustrated by Manning Lee. Chicago, Rand McNally, 1956.
The Wolfling, illustrated by John Schoenherr. New York, Dutton, 1969; London, Heinemann, 1970.

Other

Abe Lincoln: Log Cabin to White House, illustrated by Lee Ames. New York, Random House, 1956.
George Washington, Frontier Colonel, illustrated by Lee Ames. New York, Random House, 1957.
Young Thomas Edison, illustrated by William Barss. Boston, Houghton Mifflin, 1958.
Thoreau of Walden Pond, illustrated by Harve Stein. Boston, Houghton Mifflin, 1959.
Captured by the Mohawks and Other Adventures of Radisson, illustrated by Victor Mays. Boston, Houghton Mifflin, 1960.
Mark Twain and the River, illustrated by Victor Mays. Boston, Houghton Mifflin, 1961.

The First Steamboat on the Mississippi, illustrated by Victor Mays. Boston, Houghton Mifflin, 1962.

PUBLICATIONS FOR ADULTS

Novels

Midsummer Madness. New York, Grosset and Dunlap, 1933.
Tiger. Chicago, Reilly and Lee, 1933.
Plowing on Sunday. New York, Macmillan, 1934.
Night Outlasts the Whippoorwill. New York, Macmillan, 1936; London, Cobden Sanderson, 1937.
Seven Against the Years. New York, Macmillan, 1939.
Reunion on the Wabash. New York, Doubleday, 1952.

Poetry

Poems. Chicago, University of Chicago Press, 1925.

Other

The Pedro Gorino: The Adventures of a Negro Sea-Captain in Africa, with Harry Dean. Boston, Houghton Mifflin, 1929; as *Umbala,* London, Harrap, 1929.
The Writings of Mazo De La Roche. Boston, Little Brown, n.d.
Editor, with Carl Kroch, *So Red the Nose; or, Breath in the Afternoon: Literary Cocktails* (recipes). New York, Farrar and Rinehart, 1935.
Being a Literary Map of These United States Depicting a Renaissance No Less Astonishing Than That of Periclean Athens or Elizabethan London, with Gladys North, map by Frederic J. Donseif. New York, Putnam, 1942.
Editor, with C.B. Boutell, *Speak of the Devil: An Anthology of the Appearances of the Devil in the Literature of the Western World.* New York, Doubleday, 1945.
Hurry Spring! New York, Dutton, 1966.
Raccoons Are the Brightest People. New York, Dutton, 1966; as *The Raccoons of My Life,* London, Hodder and Stoughton, 1967.

*

Media Adaptations: *So Dear to My Heart* (film), RKO, 1948; *Rascal: A Memoir of a Better Era* (film), Disney Studios, 1969; (record/ cassette), Miller-Brody, 1979.

Manuscript Collection: Boston University Library.

*   *   *

Although Sterling North wrote a considerable body of literature, mostly for young readers, he is primarily known for two of his works, *So Dear to My Heart* (1947) and *Rascal: A Memoir of a Better Era* (1963), with the raccoon Rascal being the most memorable of this gifted writer's creations. So clearly is North in his element when writing stories which bring the essential truths we learn from nature into a context which young readers understand, that even his well-written biographies about notable Americans have been largely ignored. In these, as well as his better known works, however, Sterling North displays such a command of literary technique and a clarity of theme that his writing appeals to a diverse audience, from young readers to adults.

Rascal: A Memoir of a Better Era is somewhat presented as an autobiography, although the techniques of fiction-writing are well in command. The time is the World War I era, the setting rural Wisconsin, and the conflict that of a maturing boy who has lost his mother and is being raised by a gentle but somewhat preoccupied father. Told from the child's perspective, the story allows the reader to see the difficulties and joys of such a life, the loneliness of a child left much on his own and the freedom of this lifestyle which allows him to bring into his home a raccoon kit who, like the child, is prepared to test life's possibilities, to experience its joys, and to deal with its sorrows. For North, however, the parallels go further; in one poignant passage the child narrator refers to his decision to put away his traps, and to forgo the income derived from the suffering of animals. As he says, if nations could bring the killing in Europe to an end, he could sign—and keep—a pact with the animals who, like his pet raccoon, sought only to live out their lives in natural, secure surroundings. The parallel is profound and only heightens the reader's awareness that the maturing child will keep his oath; nations will not.

Such depth of theme strikes the older reader immediately and emerges from the rich texture of this novel. For the younger reader, the adventures of the child and his pet raccoon are perhaps more fulfilling. In these adventures, however, lie the simpler truths of life. From the moment the narrator takes on the time-consuming responsibility of raising the raccoon kit, the reader sees a bond develop which reveals that the child's maturing process is intact. The raccoon's explorations of the world are those of the engrossed narrator who shares in the adventures of his pet, marveling at the animal's refined instincts and delighting at its lessons, such as learning to overcome a raccoon's instinct to wash its food, rather than losing a second sugar cube to this natural behavior.

The impending crisis of the novel arrives when Rascal passes his companion in the maturing process, and the call of nature—of a mate—overcomes the ties of a yearlong friendship. Even in that crisis, however, a fundamental truth about life emerges, and the narrator takes a further step, releasing his pet despite the overwhelming sense of loss that doing so gives him.

North tries in his biographies of Abraham Lincoln, Thomas Edison, and other notables to point up the same basic moral truths which give *Rascal* and *So Dear to My Heart* their thematic quality. The young reader will find in these works a celebration of curiosity, determination, and gentleness as well as sound history. These basic qualities—a respect for fact and accuracy and a deep appreciation for the struggles of youth—make Sterling North's works especially worthwhile reading for any generation of young people and proper reminders of essential values for adults.

—Gerald W. Morton

NORTON, Andre. Pseudonym for Alice Mary Norton; also writes as Andrew North; Allen Weston. American. Born in Cleveland, Ohio, 17 February 1912. Educated at Western Reserve University, Cleveland, 1930-32. Children's librarian, Cleveland Public Library, 1932-50; special librarian, Library of Congress, Washington, D.C., during World War II; editor, Gnome Press, New York, 1950-58. Recipient: Award from Dutch government, 1946, for *The Sword Is Drawn;* Ohioana Library Juvenile award honor book, 1950, for

Sword in Sheath; Boys Club of America Medal, 1951, for *Bullard of the Space Patrol,* and Certificate of Merit, 1965, for *Night of Masks;* Hugo award nominations, 1962, for *Star Hunter,* 1964, for *Witch World,* and 1968, for *Wizard's World;* Headliner award, Theta Sigma Phi, 1963; Invisible Little Man award for sustained excellence in science fiction, 1963; Phoenix award, 1975; Gandalf Master of Fantasy award, 1977, for lifetime achievement in fantasy; Andre Norton award, Women Writers of Science Fiction, 1978; Balrog Fantasy award, 1979; Ohioana award, 1980, for body of work; Ohio Women's Hall of Fame, 1981; Fritz Leiber award for work in the field of fantasy, 1983; Lensman award, 1983 and 1987; Nebula Grand Master award for lifetime achievement, 1984; Jules Verne award for work in the field of Science Fiction, 1984; Daedalus award, 1986; Guest of honor, World Science Fiction Earescon, 1989. Agent: Russell Galen, Scovil-Chichak-Qalen Agency. Address: 1600 Spruce Avenue, Winter Park, FL 32789, U.S.A.

PUBLICATIONS FOR YOUNG ADULTS

Fiction

The Prince Commands, illustrated by Kate Seredy. New York, Appleton Century, 1934.

Ralestone Luck, illustrated by James Reid. New York, Appleton Century, 1938.

Follow the Drum. New York, Penn, 1942.

The Sword Is Drawn, illustrated by Duncan Coburn. Boston, Houghton Mifflin, 1944; London, Oxford University Press, 1946.

Scarface, illustrated by Lorence Bjorklund. New York, Harcourt Brace, 1948; London, Methuen, 1950.

Sword in Sheath, illustrated by Lorence Bjorklund. New York, Harcourt Brace, 1949; as *Island of the Lost,* London, Staples Press, 1953.

Star Man's Son, 2250 A.D., illustrated by Nicolas Mordvinoff. New York, Harcourt Brace, 1952; London, Staples Press, 1953; as *Daybreak, 2250 A.D.,* New York, Ace, 1954.

Star Rangers. New York, Harcourt Brace, 1953; London, Gollancz, 1968; as *The Last Planet,* New York, Ace, 1955.

At Swords' Point. New York, Harcourt Brace, 1954.

The Stars Are Ours! Cleveland, World, 1954.

Yankee Privateer, illustrated by Leonard Vosburgh. Cleveland, World, 1955.

Star Guard. New York, Harcourt Brace, 1955; London, Gollancz, 1969.

The Crossroads of Time. New York, Ace, 1956; London, Gollancz, 1967.

Stand to Horse. New York, Harcourt Brace, 1956.

Sea Siege. New York, Harcourt Brace, 1957.

Star Born. Cleveland, World, 1957; London, Gollancz, 1973.

Star Gate. New York, Harcourt Brace, 1958; London, Gollancz, 1970.

The Time Traders. Cleveland, World, 1958.

The Beast Master. New York, Harcourt Brace, 1959; London, Gollancz, 1966.

Galactic Derelict. Cleveland, World, 1959.

Storm over Warlock. Cleveland, World, 1960.

The Sioux Spaceman. New York, Ace, 1960; London, Hale, 1976.

Shadow Hawk. New York, Harcourt Brace, 1960; London, Gollancz, 1971.

Ride Proud, Rebel! Cleveland, World, 1961.
Catseye. New York, Harcourt Brace, 1961; London, Gollancz, 1962.
The Defiant Agents. Cleveland, World, 1962.
Lord of Thunder. New York, Harcourt Brace, 1962; London, Gollancz, 1966.
Rebel Spurs. Cleveland, World, 1962.
Key Out of Time. Cleveland, World, 1963.
Judgment on Janus. New York, Harcourt Brace, 1963; London, Gollancz, 1964.
Ordeal in Otherwhere. Cleveland, World, 1964.
Night of Masks. New York, Harcourt Brace, 1964; London, Gollancz, 1965.
The X Factor. New York, Harcourt Brace, 1965; London, Gollancz, 1967.
Quest Crosstime. New York, Viking Press, 1965; as *Crosstime Agent,* London, Gollancz, 1975.
Steel Magic, illustrated by Robin Jacques. Cleveland, World, 1965; London, Hamish Hamilton, 1967; as *Gray Magic,* New York, Scholastic, 1967.
Moon of Three Rings. New York, Viking Press, 1966; London, Longman, 1969.
Victory on Janus. New York, Harcourt Brace, 1966; London, Gollancz, 1967.
Octagon Magic, illustrated by Mac Conner. Cleveland, World, 1967; London, Hamish Hamilton, 1968.
Operation Time Search. New York, Harcourt Brace, 1967.
Dark Piper. New York, Harcourt Brace, 1968; London, Gollancz, 1969.
Fur Magic, illustrated by John Kaufmann. Cleveland, World, 1968; London, Hamish Hamilton, 1969.
The Zero Stone. New York, Viking Press, 1968; London, Gollancz, 1974.
Postmarked the Stars. New York, Harcourt Brace, 1969; London, Gollancz, 1971.
Uncharted Stars. New York, Viking Press, 1969; London, Gollancz, 1974.
Dread Companion. New York, Harcourt Brace, 1970; London, Gollancz, 1972.
Ice Crown. New York, Viking Press, 1970; London, Longman, 1971.
Android at Arms. New York, Harcourt Brace, 1971; London, Gollancz, 1972.
Exiles of the Stars. New York, Viking Press, 1971; London, Longman, 1972.
The Crystal Gryphon. New York, Atheneum, 1972; London, Gollancz, 1973.
Dragon Magic, illustrated by Robin Jacques. New York, Crowell, 1972.
Breed to Come. New York, Viking Press, 1972; London, Longman, 1973.
Forerunner Foray. New York, Viking Press, 1973; London, Longman, 1974.
Here Abide Monsters. New York, Atheneum, 1973.
The Jargoon Pard. New York, Atheneum, 1974; London, Gollancz, 1975.
Lavender-Green Magic, illustrated by Judith Gwyn Brown. New York, Crowell, 1974.
Iron Cage. New York, Viking Press, 1974; London, Kestrel, 1975.
Outside, illustrated by Bernard Colonna. New York, Walker, 1975; London, Blackie, 1976.
The Day of the Ness, with Michael Gilbert, illustrated by Gilbert. New York, Walker, 1975.

Knave of Dreams. New York, Viking Press, 1975; London, Kestrel, 1976.
No Night Without Stars. New York, Atheneum, 1975; London, Gollancz, 1976.
Red Hart Magic, illustrated by Donna Diamond. New York, Crowell, 1976; London, Hamish Hamilton, 1977.
Wraiths of Time. New York, Atheneum, 1976; London, Gollancz, 1977.
Star Ka'at, with Dorothy Madlee, illustrated by Bernard Colonna. New York, Walker, 1976; London, Blackie, 1977.
The Opal-Eyed Fan. New York, Dutton, 1977.
Trey of Swords (short stories). New York, Grosset and Dunlap, 1977; London, Star, 1979.
Star Ka'at World, with Dorothy Madlee, illustrated by Jean Jenkins. New York, Walker, 1978.
Quag Keep. New York, Atheneum, 1978.
Seven Spells to Sunday, with Phyllis Miller. New York, Atheneum, 1979.
Star Ka'ats and the Plant People, with Dorothy Madlee, illustrated by Jean Jenkins. New York, Walker, 1979.
Voorloper, illustrated by Alicia Austin. New York, Ace, 1980.
Star Ka'ats and the Winged Warriors, with Dorothy Madlee, illustrated by Jean Jenkins. New York, Walker, 1981.
Gryphon in Glory. New York, Atheneum, 1981.
Ten Mile Treasure. New York, Pocket Books, 1981.
House of Shadows, with Phyllis Miller. New York, Atheneum, 1984.
Ride the Green Dragon, with Phyllis Miller. New York, Atheneum, 1985.

Fiction as Andrew North

Sargasso of Space. New York, Gnome Press, 1955; as Andre Norton, London, Gollancz, 1970.
Plague Ship. New York, Gnome Press, 1956; as Andre Norton, London, Gollancz, 1971.
Voodoo Planet. New York, Ace, 1959.

Other

Rogue Reynard, illustrated by Laura Bannon. Boston, Houghton Mifflin, 1947.
Huon of the Horn, illustrated by Joe Krush. New York, Harcourt Brace, 1951.
Bertie and May, with Bertha Stenn Norton, illustrated by Fermin Rocker. New York, World, 1969; London, Hamish Hamilton, 1971.
Editor, with Ernestine Donaldy, *Gates to Tomorrow: An Introduction to Science Fiction.* New York, Atheneum, 1973.
Editor, *Small Shadows Creep: Ghost Children.* New York, Dutton, 1974; London Chatto and Windus, 1976.

Novels

Murder for Sale (as Allen Weston, with Grace Hogarth). London, Hammond, 1954; as *Sneeze on Sunday,* by Andre Norton and Grace Allen Hogarth, New York, Tor, 1992.

Secret of the Lost Race. New York, Ace, 1959; as *Wolfshead,* London, Hale, 1977.

Star Hunter. New York, Ace, 1961.

Eye of the Monster. New York, Ace, 1962.

Witch World. New York, Ace, 1963; London, Tandem, 1970.

Web of the Witch World. New York, Ace, 1964; London, Tandem, 1970.

Three Against the Witch World. New York, Ace, 1965; London, Tandem, 1970.

Year of the Unicorn. New York, Ace, 1965; London, Tandem, 1970.

Warlock of the Witch World. New York, Ace, 1967; London, Tandem, 1970.

Sorceress of the Witch World. New York, Ace, 1968; London, Tandem, 1970.

Merlin's Mirror. New York, DAW, 1975; London, Sidgwick and Jackson, 1976.

The White Jade Fox. New York, Dutton, 1975; London, W.H. Allen, 1976.

Velvet Shadows. New York, Fawcett, 1977.

Yurth Burden. New York, DAW, 1978.

Zarsthor's Bane. New York, Ace, 1978; London, Dobson, 1981.

Snow Shadow. New York, Fawcett, 1979.

Iron Butterflies. New York, Fawcett, 1980.

Horn Crown. New York, DAW, 1981.

Forerunner. New York, Tor, 1981.

Moon Called. New York, Simon and Schuster, 1982.

Caroline, with Enid Cushing. New York, Pinnacle, 1982.

Ware Hawk. New York, Atheneum, 1983.

Wheel of Stars. New York, Simon and Schuster, 1983.

Stand and Deliver. New York, Dell, 1984.

Gryphon's Eyrie, with A.C. Crispin. New York, Tor, 1984.

Were-Wrath. New Castle, Virginia, Cheap Street, 1984.

Forerunner: The Second Venture. New York, Tor, 1985.

Flight in Yiktor. New York, Tor, 1986; London, Methuen, 1988.

The Gate of the Cat. New York, Ace, 1987.

Imperial Lady: A Fantasy of Han China, with Susan Shwartz. New York, Tor, 1989.

Black Trillium, with Marion Zimmer Bradley and Julian May. New York, Doubleday, 1990; London, Grafton, 1991.

Dare to Go A-Hunting. New York, Tor, 1990.

The Jekyll Legacy, with Robert Bloch. New York, Tor, 1990.

The Elvenbane. New York, Tor, 1991.

Storms of Victory, with Pauline Griffin. New York, Tor, 1991.

Flight of Vengeance, with P.M. Griffin and Mary H. Schaub. New York, Tor, 1992.

Mark of the Cat. New York, Ace, 1992.

Songsmith, with A.C. Crispin. New York, Tor, 1992.

Golden Trillium. New York, Bantam, 1993.

Redline the Stars, with P.M. Griffin. New York, Tor, 1993.

Short Stories

High Sorcery. New York, Ace, 1970.

Garan the Eternal. Alhambra, California, Fantasy, 1972.

Spell of the Witch World. New York, DAW, 1972; London, Prior, 1977.

The Many Worlds of Andre Norton, edited by Roger Elwood. Radnor, Pennsylvania, Chilton, 1974; as *The Book of Andre Norton,* New York, DAW, 1975.

Perilous Dreams. New York, DAW, 1976.

Lore of the Witch World. New York, DAW, 1980.

Serpent's Tooth. Winter Park, Florida, Andre Norton Ltd., 1987.

Moon Mirror. New York, Tor, 1988.

Wizards' Worlds, edited by Ingrid Zierhut. New York, Tor, 1989.

Other

Editor, *Bullard of the Space Patrol,* by Malcolm Jameson. Cleveland, World, 1951.

Editor, *Space Service.* Cleveland, World, 1953.

Editor, *Space Pioneers.* Cleveland, World, 1954.

Contributor, *Best Science Fiction Stories and Novels, 1955,* edited by T.E. Dikty. Hollywood, Florida, Frederick Fell, 1955.

Editor, *Space Police.* Cleveland, World, 1956.

Contributor, *Swordsmen in the Sky,* edited by Donald A. Wollheim. New York, Ace, 1964.

Contributor, *The Time Curve,* edited by Roger Elwood and Sam Moskowitz. Portland, Maine, Tower, 1968.

Contributor, *Alien Earth and Other Stories,* edited by Roger Elwood and Sam Moskowitz. Macfadden-Bartell, 1969.

Contributor, *Many Worlds of Science-Fiction,* edited by Ben Bova. New York, Dutton, 1971.

Contributor, *Zoo 2000: Twelve Stories of Science-Fiction and Fantasy Beasts,* edited by Jane Yolen. Seabury, 1973.

Contributor, *In Saving Worlds: A Collection of Original Science-Fiction Stories,* edited by Roger Elwood and Virginia Kidd. New York, Doubleday, 1973.

Contributor, *Science-Fiction Adventures from Way Out,* edited by Roger Elwood. Racine, Wisconsin, Western Publishing, 1973.

Contributor, *Flashing Swords! #2,* edited by Lin Carter. New York, Doubleday, 1973.

Contributor, *The Long Night of Waiting by Andre Norton and Other Stories,* edited by Roger Elwood. Santa Fe, New Mexico, Aurora, 1974.

Contributor, *The Gifts of Asti and Other Stories,* edited by Roger Elwood. Crystal Lake, Illinois, Follett, 1975.

Editor, *Baleful Beasts and Eerie Creatures.* Chicago, Rand McNally, 1976.

Contributor, *The DAW Science-Fiction Reader,* edited by Donald A. Wollheim. New York, DAW, 1976.

Contributor, *Flashing Swords! #3: Warriors and Wizards,* edited by Lin Carter. New York, Dell, 1976.

Contributor, *Sisters of Sorcery: Two Centuries of Witchcraft Stories by the Gentle Sex,* edited by Seon Manley and Gogo Lewis. New York, Lothrop, 1976.

Contributor, *Swords Against Darkness II,* edited by Andrew J. Offrett. New York, Zebra, 1977.

Contributor, *Phantasmagoria: Tales of Fantasy and the Supernatural,* edited by Jane Mobley. Homer, Arkansas, Anchor Books, 1977.

Editor, with Robert Adams, *Magic in Ithkar.* New York, Tor, 2 vols., 1985.

Editor, *Tales of Witch World.* New York, Tor, 2 vols., 1987-88.

Editor, *Four from the Witch World.* New York, Tor, 1989.

Editor, with Martin H. Greenberg, *Catfantastic.* New York, DAW, 1989.

Editor, with Ingrid Zierhut, *Grand Master's Choices.* Cambridge, Massachusetts, NESFA, 1989.

Editor, with Martin H. Greenberg, *Catfantastic II.* New York, DAW, 1991.

Contributor of stories to *Fantasy Book* and *Fantastic Universe* (as Andrew North), *Magazine of Fantasy and Science-Fiction, Phantom Magazine, Golden Magazine for Boys and Girls, Worlds of If, Spaceway Science-Fiction,* and *The World of Fantasy.*

*

Media Adaptations: *The Beastmaster* (film), MGM/UA, 1982; *Witch World* (recording); Norton has also authorized numerous *Witch World* items, such as maps, acrylic sculptures, and stationery.

Biography: Entry in *Dictionary of Literary Biography,* Volume 8, Detroit, Gale, 1981; Volume 52, 1986.

Bibliography: *Andre Norton: A Primary and Secondary Bibliography* by Roger C. Schlobin, Boston, Hall, 1980.

Manuscript Collection: Andre Norton Ltd., Winter Park, Florida; George Arents Research Library, Syracuse University, New York.

Critical Study: Entry in *Contemporary Literary Criticism,* Volume 12, Detroit, Gale, 1980.

*   *   *

One of America's more prolific young adult writers, Andre Norton also ranks as one of the earliest, having started her career in 1934—long before publishers singled out young adults as a specialized market in the 1960s. During her most productive years (1954-85) she averaged three books a year, and most of her books remain in print. Although she has written a number of historical adventures and gothics for adolescents (*Scarface, Ride Proud, Rebel!, The White Jade Fox, The Opal-Eyed Fan,* to name a few), Norton is best known for her science fiction, or as some critics prefer to call it, "science fantasy." In these books she has created a complex universe in which elements of science fiction interact with the kind of supernatural events usually found in fantasy.

Norton's first science fiction book for young adults, *Star Man's Son, 2250 A.D.,* introduces many of the themes that pervade her created universe. On a planet decimated by nuclear war, the descendants of the survivors attempt to make a new life for themselves and avoid the mistakes of the Old Ones. Fors, a young mutant cast out by his tribe, is caught in the middle of a brewing conflict between two other tribes, while the Beast Things from the destroyed cities prey on all the humans. His telepathic cat and a young black warrior from another tribe are his only friends as he seeks his destiny in a ravaged world.

Like Fors, most of Norton's heroes (and her few heroines) are outcasts in their society. Sometimes they are isolated by physical deformities, sometimes by unusual mental powers. Often they are part or wholly of alien blood. Usually orphaned, these heroes strike out on their own across a hostile, alien landscape, pursuing a personal quest even as they are pursued by enemies. Their journey brings them self-knowledge and self-acceptance and generally ends with group acceptance into their true society, which is not always their original one. Sometimes the society in which the hero finds a place for himself is itself isolated in space or time. In *Operation Time Search,* for instance, the hero remains trapped in the past, and the heroine of *Ice Crown* is quite content to be stranded forever on a planet whose medieval culture cuts it off from interstellar contact.

Some of the recurring elements in these novels are survivalism, underground labyrinths, time travel, parallel universes, supernatural powers, mutants, telepathic animals, and ethnic heroes. The animals are usually feline, but Norton has also used telepathic wolverines and dolphins as well as created a number of alien animal species with telepathic powers. Other supernatural powers appear in her protagonists and in alien communities, such as the Wyverns of *Storm Over Warlock.*

The universe Norton has created is a macrocosm of Earth (or "Terra," as she calls the home planet). It contains postwar ghettoes like the Dipple, which appears in several books as the original community from which the hero sets out, and which is a stronghold of the Thieves' Guild, the organized criminals of the future. Keeping an eye on the Guild and its operations is the Patrol, an intergalactic police corps that often appears in the nick of time to rescue the hero. The Free Traders are the licensed merchants who carry goods from planet to planet, and Survey is an elite corps of scientific explorers who map the universe. One recurring theme is the existence of the Forerunners, a mysterious race of star travellers who lived eons before the Terrans and who have left incomprehensible and often powerful artifacts behind on a number of planets. A search for Forerunner treasure provides the plot for a number of Norton's books.

Many of the novels are linked in some way, although few of the links are strong enough to create a series. For example, two of the characters from *Moon of Three Rings* and *Flight in Yiktor* also appear in *Dare to Go A-Hunting,* but each story is independent and the books can be read in any order. A minor character in *Forerunner Foray* is the son of the hero of *Storm Over Warlock.* An early series about Time Agents includes *The Time Traders, Galactic Derelict, The Defiant Agents,* and *Key Out of Time;* although they contain overlapping characters, these books too can be read out of sequence. The "Witch World" series, written for adults, is also of interest to adolescent readers. This series includes *Witch World, Web of the Witch World, Three Against the Witch World, Year of the Unicorn, Warlock of the Witch World,* and *Sorceress of the Witch World.* Although the "Witch World" series is fantasy rather than science fiction and does not seem to be set in the same universe as Norton's science fiction books, many familiar themes and elements appear in the series.

Most of Norton's more recent titles have been co-authored by writers such as Dorothy Madlee, Phyllis Miller, Mercedes Lackey, Susan Shwartz, and P. M. Griffin. These books continue Norton's science fantasy tradition.

—Donna R. White

———

NÖSTLINGER, Christine. Austrian. Born in Vienna, Austria, 13 October 1936. Educated at art school in Vienna, Austria. Married in 1959; two daughters. Journalist for a Vienna daily newspaper; writer. Recipient: Friedrich-Boedecker Prize, 1972, for contribution to children's literature; Buxtehuder Bulle award, 1973, for *Fly Away Home;* German Youth Literature Prize, 1973, for *The Cucumber King;* Oesterreichischer Staatspreis fuer Kinder-und Jugendliteratur, 1975, for *Achtung! Vranek sieht ganz harmlos aus,* 1979, for *Guardian Ghost,* and 1987, for *A Dog's Life; The Cucumber King* was selected for the International Board on Books for Young People

(IBBY) honor list in the translator's category, 1978; Mildred L. Batchelder award, 1979, for *Konrad;* Kinder-und Jugendbuchpreis der Stadt Wien, 1980, for *Dschi Dsche-i Dschunior;* *Luke and Angela* was selected as an American Library Association Notable Book, 1981; Hans Christian Andersen Medal from the IBBY, 1984, for body of work; Children's Book award, City of Vienna, 1987, for *Der geheime Grossvater;* Fourteenth Children's Book Prize of Zurich, 1991, for *Der Zwerg in Kopf.*

PUBLICATIONS FOR YOUNG ADULTS

Novels (with translations from the German by Anthea Bell)

Marrying Off Mother. London, Andersen Press, 1978, Orlando, Florida, Harcourt, 1982; as *Ein Mann fuer Mama,* Hamburg, Germany, F. Oetinger, 1972.

Fly Away Home. New York, F. Watts, 1975; as *Maikaefer, flieg! Mein Vater, das Kriegsende, Cohn und ich,* Weinheim, Germany, Beltz & Gelberg, 1973.

Girl Missing. New York, F. Watts, 1976; as *Ilse Janda, 14,* Hamburg, Germany, F. Oetinger, 1974.

Four Days in the Life of Lisa. New York, Abelard-Schuman, 1977; as *Studentplan,* Weinheim, Germany, Beltz & Gelberg, 1975.

Die unteren sieben Achtel des Eisbergs. Weinheim, Germany, Beltz & Gelberg, 1978.

Luke and Angela. London, Andersen Press, 1979; Orlando, Florida, Harcourt, 1981; as *Luki-live,* Hamburg, Germany, F. Oetinger, 1978.

Pfui Spinne! Weinheim, Germany, Beltz & Gelberg, 1980.

Zwei Wochen im Mai: Mein Vater, der Rudi, der Hansi und ich. Weinheim, Germany, Beltz & Gelberg, 1981.

But Jasper Came Instead. London, Andersen Press, 1983; as *Das Austauschkind,* Germany, 1982.

PUBLICATIONS FOR CHILDREN

Fiction (with translations from the German by Anthea Bell)

Fiery Frederica, illustrated by David McKee. New York, Abelard-Schuman, 1975; as *Die feuerrote Friedrike,* Vienna, Austria, Jugend & Volk, 1970.

The Disappearing Cellar: A Tale Told by Pia Maria Tiralla, a Viennese Nanny, illustrated by Heidi Rempen. New York, Abelard-Schuman, 1975; as *Die Kinder aus dem Kinderkeller: Aufgeschrieben von Pia Maria Tiralla,* Weinheim, Germany, Beltz & Gelberg, 1971.

Mr. Bat's Great Invention, illustrated by F. J. Tripp. London, Andersen Press (London), 1978; as *Mr. Bats Meisterstueck; oder, Die total verjuengte Oma.* Hamburg, Germany, F. Oetinger, 1971.

The Cucumber King: A Story With a Beginning, a Middle, and an End, in Which Wolfgang Hogelmann Tells the Whole Truth, illustrated by Werner Maurer. New York, Abelard-Schuman, 1975; as *Wir pfeifen auf den Gurkenkoenig,* Weinheim, Germany, Beltz & Gelberg, 1972.

Der kleine Herr greift ein, illustrated by Rolf Rettich. Hamburg, Germany, F. Oetinger, 1973.

Sim Sala Bim, illustrated by Wolfgang Zoehrer. Vienna, Austria, Jugend & Volk, 1973.

Achtung! Vranek sieht ganz harmlos aus (title means "Careful! Vranek Seems to Be Totally Harmless"). Vienna, Austria, Jugend & Volk, 1974.

Gugerells Hund, with Hans Arnold. Bethesda, Maryland, Betz, 1974.

Iba de guanz oaman Kinda (poem), woodcut illustrated by Thomas Bewick. Vienna, Austria, Jugend & Volk, 1974.

Das Leben der Tomanis, illustrated by Helme Heine. Cologne, Germany, G. Middelhauve, 1974-76.

Conrad: The Factory Made Boy, illustrated by Frantz Wittkamp. London, Andersen Press, 1976; as *Konrad,* illustrated by Carol Nicklaus, New York, F. Watts, 1977; as *Konrad; oder, Das Kind aus der Konservenbuechse,* Hamburg, Germany, F. Oetinger, 1975.

Der kleine Jo (title means "Little Jo"), illustrated by Bettina Anrich-Woelfel. Lucerne, Switzerland, H. Schroedel, 1976.

Das will Jenny haben, illustrated by Anrich-Woelfel. H. Lucerne, Switzerland, Schroedel, 1977.

Lollipop, illustrated by Angelika Kaufmann. London, Andersen Press, 1982; as *Lollipop,* Weinheim, Germany, Beltz & Gelberg, 1977.

Pit und Anja entdecken das Jahr: Der Fruehling kommt (title means "Pit and Anja Discover the Year: Spring Comes"), illustrated by Bernadette Parmentier. Lucerne, Switzerland, H. Schroedel, 1978.

Pit und Anja entdecken das Jahr: Im Sommer (title means "Pit and Anja Discover the Year: In the Summer"), illustrated by Bernadette Parmentier. Lucerne, Switzerland, H. Schroedel, 1978.

Guardian Ghost. London, Andersen Press, 1986; as *Rosa Reidl, Schutzgespenst,* Vienna, Austria, Jugend & Volk, 1979.

Dschi Dsche-i Dschunior. Vienna, Austria, Jugend & Volk, 1980.

Einer, illustrated by Janosch. Weinheim, Germany, Beltz & Gelberg, 1980.

Brainbox Sorts It Out. London, Andersen Press, 1985; as *Brainbox Cracks the Case,* New York, Bergh, 1986; as *Der Denker greift ein,* Vienna, Austria, Jugend & Volk, 1981.

Gretchen Sackmeier. Hamburg, Germany, F. Oetinger, 1981.

Rosalinde hat Gedanken im Kopf (title means "Rosalinde Has Thoughts in Her Head"). Hamburg, Germany, F. Oetinger, 1981.

Anatol und die Wurschtelfrau. Vienna, Austria, Jugend & Volk, 1983.

Gretchen hat Haenschen-Kummer: Eine Familiengeschichte. Hamburg, Germany, F. Oetinger, 1983.

Jokel, Jula, und Jericho, two volumes, illustrated by Edith Schindler. Weinheim, Germany, Beltz & Gelberg, 1983.

Der geheime Grossvater (title means "The Secret Grandfather"), illustrated by Christine Noestlinger, Jr. Vienna, Austria, Jugend & Volk, 1986.

A Dog's Life, illustrated by Jutta Bauer. London, Andersen Press, 1990 as *Der Hund kommt!,* Weinheim, Germany, Beltz & Gelberg, 1987.

*

Critical Study: Entry in *Children's Literature Review,* Volume 11, Detroit, Gale, 1987, pp. 179-189.

*   *   *

Christine Nöstlinger is probably Austria's most renowned writer of books for young people. Winner of the international Hans Christian Andersen award, her books have been translated into a variety of languages and have proven to be popular wherever they are read.

This is not surprising as the themes she writes about are universal and her strong, often anti-authoritarian characters are likely to appeal to young people all over the world.

Her young adult books with a contemporary setting stand comparison with those of Judy Blume and Paula Danziger. In *Marrying Off Mother,* Sue and Julia face a situation with which many young people have to contend: their parents' separation. The girls are sent to live in their grandmother's house, an all-female establishment. Their grandmother is a tyrant, while one of their aunts is neurotically houseproud and the other scatterbrained. Sue and Julia decide that if they cannot get their parents together again (and they do try strenuously to do so), they will have to find a suitable spare male to marry their mother. The events which occur when they try to put this plan into operation often end in farce of the broadest type. The theme of this book is similar to many "problem" novels produced for young adults. However, it is told in such a light way that any moralising is conveyed far more subtly than is usual with this kind of book. Young adult readers in a similar situation to the heroines could both sympathise with and laugh gently at Sue and Julia's reactions.

In *Luke and Angela,* the hero returns from a summer school in England with some highly original ideas—such as wearing pyjamas to school. However, Luke's behaviour tests his relationship with Angela, who has previously been his closest friend; and the book, through its use of comedy, raises many issues about friendship. Another interesting feature about this book, and others written by Nöstlinger, is its strong anti-authoritarian streak, particularly in Luke's clashes with his Latin teacher. In English-speaking countries, young adult novels, particularly in recent years, have sidestepped this subject, perhaps to avoid the wrath of parents. Nöstlinger is most firmly on the side of her adolescent hero as he struggles to take an individual stance.

Another book likely to be of interest to young people deals with exchange visits. In *But Jasper Came Instead* the Mittermeier family is expecting an English boy, Tom, to come on a visit to Vienna. However, Jasper, Tom's younger brother, appears instead and this truculent English boy, who appears to have an aversion to washing, is something of a shock to the staid and conventional Mittermeier parents. It is their daughter Billie who discovers the insecurity which lies at the heart of Jasper's behaviour problems as well as finding strength within herself to stand up to her parents. As with the previous books discussed, the story is told with such a light touch that any didacticism on the author's part is easily subsumed in the narrative.

Fly Away Home is partly autobiographical, tells of the World War II years in Vienna, and was published at a time when writers in other parts of the world (such as Nina Bawden in Great Britain and Esther Hautzig in America) were recounting their war lives through the use of fiction. One thing in common with all these authors is the emotion of the characters. It is the minutiae which count in Christel's life as the Nazis retreat from Vienna and the Russians advance near the end of the war. Christel's father has deserted from the army and has to go into hiding. This situation is made all the more precarious when a group of Russian soldiers commandeers the country villa in which the family is living. Christel makes friends with Cohn, the gentle cook whose behaviour is totally different from the other brutish soldiers. The style of *Fly Away Home* varies from Nöstlinger's normal narrative structure and its short, staccato sentences mirror the urgency of the family's situation almost as in a newsreel.

Young adult readers will gain much from the work of Christine Nöstlinger. The emotions her characters demonstrate are universal and sympathetic to any adolescent, whatever their background. The style of writing is sufficiently central European, and her unique handling of anti-authoritarian situations will undoubtedly be attractive to young adults struggling with these feelings themselves.

—Keith Barker

O

O'BRIEN, Robert C. Pseudonym for Robert Leslie Conly. American. Born in Brooklyn, New York, 11 January 1918. Educated at schools in Amityville, Long Island, New York; Williams College, Williamstown, Massachusetts, 1935-37; Juilliard School of Music, New York, Columbia University, New York; University of Rochester, New York, B.A. in English 1940. Married Sally McCaslin in 1943; one son and three daughters. Author and editor. Worked in an advertising agency, 1940; researcher and writer, *Newsweek* magazine, New York, 1941-44; rewrite man, *Times-Herald,* 1944-46, and *Pathfinder* magazine, 1946-51, both Washington, D.C.; staff member, rising to senior assistant editor, *National Geographic* magazine, Washington, D.C., 1951-73. Recipient: "Children's Books of the Year" citation, Child Study Association of America, 1971, Lewis Carroll Shelf award, 1972, Newbery Medal, American Library Association (ALA), 1972, runner-up for National Book award, 1972, "Honor Book" citation, *Boston Globe*-Horn Book, 1972, Mark Twain award, 1973, Young Readers' Choice award, Pacific Northwest Library Association, 1974, and William Allan White Children's Book award, 1974, all for *Mrs. Frisby and the Rats of NIMH;* "Best Young Adult Books" citation, ALA, 1972, for *A Report from Group 17;* "Children's Books of the Year" citation, Child Study Association of America, 1975, "Best Young Adults Books" citation, ALA, 1975, Jane Addams Children's Book award, 1976, best juvenile novel, Mystery Writers of the America, 1977, "Books for the Teen Age" citations, New York Public Library, 1980, 1981, and 1982, and "Honor Book" citation, *Boston Globe-Horn Book,* all for *Z for Zachariah. Died 5 March 1973.*

PUBLICATIONS FOR YOUNG ADULTS

Fiction

The Silver Crown, illustrated by Dale Payson. New York, Atheneum, 1968; London, Gollancz, 1973.
Mrs. Frisby and the Rats of NIMH, illustrated by Zena Bernstein. New York, Atheneum, 1971; London, Gollancz, 1972.
Z for Zachariah. New York, Atheneum, 1975; London, Gollancz, 1975.

PUBLICATIONS FOR ADULTS

Novel

A Report from Group 17. New York, Atheneum, 1972; London, Gollancz, 1973.

*

Manuscript Collection: Kerlan Collection, University of Minnesota, Minneapolis.

Media Adaptations: *Mrs. Frisby and the Rats of NIMH* (record and cassette), Newbery Award Records, 1972; *Mrs. Frisby and the Rats of NIMH* (filmstrip with cassette), Miller-Brody, 1973; *The Secret of NIMH* (motion picture; based on *Mrs. Frisby and the Rats*

of NIMH), Metro-Goldwyn-Mayer/United Artists, 1982; *Mrs. Frisby and the Rats of NIMH, A Report from Group 17,* and *Z for Zachariah* are all available as "talking books."

*   *   *

Robert Leslie Conly, using the pseudonym Robert C. O'Brien, began his writing career for young adults in his late forties, after spending most of his professional life as a journalist and editor. Although he wrote only four young adult novels before his death at age fifty-six, his reputation remains as a significant writer of science fiction and fantasy, especially for his multiple award winning *Mrs. Frisby and the Rats of NIMH.* All of his novels have an adventure/survival core with three of them directly exploring the nature of evil in man and man's obsession for violence, destruction, control, and power. However, O'Brien's most creative and provocative work emerges with the NIMH title as he speculates on the possibility of new life forms created by man on Earth, and the irony that these new life forms would have more humane sensibilities than their human counterpart.

O'Brien's initial novel *The Silver Crown* blends adventure and survival in a present day American setting with historical allusions linked to malevolent power, strangely derived from the fifth century and St. Jerome. A group or sect, who align themselves to the influence of St. Jerome, perpetrates destructive acts on contemporary society—first with arson and muggings, then with race riots with the eventual goal to gain control over everybody's minds. The silver crown, the talisman in the possession of a young girl named Ellen, can either be used for good or evil according to the mind of its possessor. The crown becomes the object the sect pursues along with Ellen, and this becomes the primary action in this lively, albeit predictable plot.

With the publication of his second work *Mrs. Frisby and the Rats of NIMH,* O'Brien established himself as a skillful and significant writer blending elements of traditional animal fantasy with science fiction. A group of super intelligent rats are developed by rearranging their DNA at the NIMH (National Institute of Mental Health) laboratory. Although the rats are not changed physically, they keep their growing intellectual capacities such as learning to read and to reason from Dr. Schultz and his colleagues. When the rats learn to unlock their cages by reading the instructions for unlatching the doors, their escape from the lab is imminent. Once escaping they must confront more complex issues such as their new identity: "We don't know where to go, because we don't know who we are." As they accept their identity as a new life-form they know they cannot return to being rats living off garbage. At the same time they don't want to depend on humans so they devise "the Plan" which is "to live without stealing" and to grow their own food in their new civilization in a remote forest preserve away from human detection. Human response may be one of fear and loathing which is implied when the scientists from NIMH try to exterminate the rats before they are completely prepared to initiate "the Plan." Compassion, courage, and ingenuity form the moral personality of the rats from NIMH as they help other animals such as the mother mouse Mrs. Frisby in saving the life of one of her children. This novel is saturated with delightful surprises and wonders and probably inspired former Disney animator Don Bluth to create the feature length animated film "The Secret of NIMH" in the early eighties.

In his third novel, *A Report from Group 17*, O'Brien recycles and blends narrative elements from his earlier novels into a cold war atmosphere of political intrigue between the United States and Russia. The evil conspiracy to take over the world in *The Silver Crown* is transposed to the Russians in *A Report from Group 17* as they attempt to contaminate the water supply of Washington, D.C. with mutagens that will eventually render a population indifferent to being taken over by a foreign power. This variation of germ warfare which gradually introduces its effects through the genes of succeeding generations is used by O'Brien in a similar way as that used by the scientist in the NIMH novel. In fact, the name of the former Nazi scientist now working for Russia who coordinates this plan is Schultz, the same name of the scientist at NIMH, although, the character is much more malevolent in *A Report from Group 17*. The plot remains fairly taut since O'Brien once again uses a young female adolescent in peril, this time named Allie Adams, who is captured by the evil scientist Schultz and kept partially sedated with Pentothal and curare. Overall the novel belongs to the cold war spy thriller genre.

O'Brien's last novel *Z for Zachariah*, set in the eastern United States, discloses a world where super powers have exchanged nuclear attacks and only two characters have survived the aftermath. Sixteen-year-old Ann Burden is confronted by the menacing adult John Loomis who, as he wanders about in the life suit he has claimed by killing others, discovers her protected valley that was spared the desolation of the rest of the continent. Through Ann Burden's journals, O'Brien creates macabre and terrifying experiences as Loomis asserts himself initially through sexual innuendos, and ultimately through outright attempts for domination. What shines through this narrative is Ann's resiliency, decency, and humanity in this solid, well-paced, science fiction thriller. Although O'Brien's young adult novel legacy is brief, they are worthy of attention since they confront relevant issues that will be with us well into the twenty-first century.

—Richard D. Seiter

O'DELL, Scott. American. Born in Los Angeles, California, 23 May 1898. Educated at Occidental College, Los Angeles, 1919; University of Wisconsin, Madison, 1920; Stanford University, California, 1920-21; University of Rome, 1925. Served in the United States Air Force during World War II. Writer, 1934-89. Formerly worked as a technical director for Paramount and as a cameraman for Metro-Goldwyn-Mayer, 1920s; book editor of a Los Angeles newspaper, 1940's. Established Scott O'Dell award for historical fiction, 1981. Also grew citrus fruit and taught a mail-order course in photoplay writing. Recipient: Rupert Hughes award, 1960, John Newbery Medal, American Library Association (ALA), Lewis Carroll Shelf award, and Southern California Council on Literature for Children and Young People Notable Book award, all 1961, Hans Christian Andersen award of Merit, International Board on Books for Young People, 1962, William Allen White award, and German Juvenile International award, both 1963, Nene award, Hawaii Library Association, 1964, OMAR award, 1985, and ALA Notable Book Citation, all for *Island of the Blue Dolphins;* Newbery Honor

Book, 1967, German Juvenile International award, 1968, and *Horn Book* honor citation, all for *The King's Fifth;* Newbery Honor Book, 1968, ALA Notable Book citation, and *Horn Book* honor citation, all for *The Black Pearl;* Newbery Honor Book, 1971, ALA Notable Book citation, and *Horn Book* honor citation, all for *Sing Down the Moon;* Hans Christian Andersen Medal for lifetime achievement, 1972. "Children's Books of the Year" citations, Child Study Association of America, 1970, for *Sing Down the Moon,* 1972, for *The Treasure of Topo-el-Bampo,* 1974, for *Child of Fire,* 1975, for *The Hawk That Dare Not Hunt by Day,* 1976, for *Zia* and *The 290,* and 1987, for *Streams to the River, River to the Sea: A Novel of Sacagawea;* Freedoms Foundation award, 1973, for *Sing Down the Moon; New York Times* Outstanding Book citation, 1974, and ALA Notable Book citation, both for *Child of Fire;* University of Southern Mississippi Medallion, 1976; ALA Notable Book citation, for *Zia;* Regina Medal, Catholic Library Association, 1978, for body of work; *Focal* award, Los Angeles Public Library, 1981, for "excellence in creative work that enriches a child's understanding of California"; Parents Choice award for Literature, Parents Choice Foundation, 1984, for *Alexandra,* and 1986, for *Streams to the River, River to the Sea;* Scott O'Dell award for Historical Fiction, 1986, for *Streams to the River, River to the Sea;* School Library Media Specialist of Southeastern New York award for contribution to children's literature, 1989; Northern Westchester Center for the Arts award, 1989. *Died 15 October 1989.*

PUBLICATIONS FOR YOUNG ADULTS

Fiction

Island of the Blue Dolphins. Boston, Houghton, 1960; London, Constable, 1961.
The King's Fifth, illustrated by Samuel Bryant. Boston, Houghton, 1966; London, Constable, 1967.
The Black Pearl, illustrated by Milton Johnson. Boston, Houghton, 1967; London, Longman, 1968.
The Dark Canoe, illustrated by Milton Johnson. Boston, Houghton, 1968; London, Longman, 1969.
Journey to Jericho, illustrated by Leonard Weisgard. Boston, Houghton, 1969.
Sing Down the Moon. Boston, Houghton, 1970; London, Hamish Hamilton, 1972.
The Treasure of Topo-el-Bampo, illustrated by Lynd Ward. Boston, Houghton, 1972.
Child of Fire. Boston, Houghton, 1974.
The Hawk That Dare Not Hunt by Day. Boston, Houghton, 1975.
The 290. Boston, Houghton, 1976; London, Oxford University Press, 1977.
Zia, illustrated by Ted Lewin. Boston, Houghton, 1976; London, Oxford University Press, 1977.
Carlota. Boston, Houghton, 1977; as *The Daughter of Don Saturnino,* London, Oxford University Press, 1979.
Kathleen, Please Come Home. Boston, Houghton, 1978.
The Captive. Boston, Houghton, 1979.
Sarah Bishop. Boston, Houghton, 1980.
The Feathered Serpent. Boston, Houghton, 1981.
The Spanish Smile. Boston, Houghton, 1982.
The Amethyst Ring. Boston, Houghton, 1983.
The Castle in the Sea. Boston, Houghton, 1983.
Alexandra. Boston, Houghton, 1984.

The Road to Damietta. Boston, Houghton, 1985.
Streams to the River, River to the Sea: A Novel of Sacagawea. Boston, Houghton, 1986.
The Serpent Never Sleeps: A Novel of Jamestown and Pocahontas, illustrated by Ted Lewin. Boston, Houghton, 1987.
Black Star, Bright Dawn. Boston, Houghton, 1988.
My Name Is Not Angelica. Boston, Houghton, 1989.
Thunder Rolling in the Mountains, with Elizabeth Hall. Boston, Houghton, 1992.

Other

The Cruise of the Arctic Star, illustrated by Samuel Bryant. Boston, Houghton, 1973.

PUBLICATIONS FOR ADULTS

Novels

Woman of Spain: A Story of Old California. Boston, Houghton, 1934.
Hill of the Hawk. Indianapolis, Bobbs-Merrill, 1947; London, Corgi, 1955.
The Sea Is Red. New York, Holt, 1958.

Other

Representative Photoplays Analyzed: Modern Authorship. Hollywood, Palmer Institute of Authorship, 1924.
Man Alone, with William Doyle. Indianapolis, Bobbs-Merrill, 1953; as *Lifer,* London, Longman, 1954.
Country of the Sun, Southern California: An Informal History and Guide. New York, Crowell, 1957.
The Psychology of Children's Art, with Rhoda Kellogg. San Diego, California, Communications Research Machines, 1967.

*

Media Adaptations: *Island of the Blue Dolphins* (film), Universal, 1964; *The Black Pearl* (film), Diamond Films, 1976; *Island of the Blue Dolphins* (filmstrip/cassette set), Pied Piper Productions, 1965; *Island of the Blue Dolphins* (filmstrip), Teaching Films, 1965; *The Black Pearl, Sing Down the Moon, The King's Fifth, Child of Fire,* and *Zia* (record/cassette/filmstrip sets), Miller-Brody, 1974-77; *Child of Fire* (filmstrip/cassette sets), Random House, 1979; *Zia,* (filmstrip/cassette sets), Random House, 1982; *Island of the Blue Dolphins, The Black Pearl, The Dark Canoe,* and *The King's Fifth* (all available in Braille); *Island of the Blue Dolphins, The King's Fifth, Child of Fire, The Cruise of the Arctic Star, Sing Down the Moon,* and *Zia* (all available as talking books).

Biography: Entry in *Dictionary of Literary Biography,* Volume 52: *American Writers for Children since 1960: Fiction,* Detroit, Gale, 1986; essay in *Authors and Artists for Young Adults,* Volume 3, Detroit, Gale, 1990; essay in *Speaking for Ourselves: Autobiographical Sketches by Notable Authors of Books for Young Adults,* Volume 1, compiled and edited by Donald R. Gallo, National Council of Teachers of English, 1990.

Manuscript Collection: University of Oregon Library, Eugene.

Critical Studies: Entry in *Children's Literature Review,* Detroit, Gale, Volume 1, 1976, Volume 16, 1989; entry in *Contemporary Literary Criticism,* Volume 30, Detroit, Gale, 1984.

*   *   *

Scott O'Dell is a magnificent storyteller. For thirty years, he has woven wondrous tales of human struggle for independence and connectedness. His adolescent heroines and heroes are courageous and strong, and they enrich the world around them. His settings are usually historical, with rich and carefully researched details. O'Dell was raised in California, and most of his novels are set on the West Coast or in the southwestern United States.

His first and most acclaimed book, *Island of the Blue Dolphins,* is set on a remote island in the Pacific, off the coast of California, which was first settled by Indians about 2000 B.C. When the Indians left and sailed to the east in 1835, one twelve-year-old girl was left behind. This is Karana's story; she lives for eighteen years in isolation on the Island of the Blue Dolphins. Year after year she watches the seasons pass and waits for a ship to take her away too. She keeps herself alive by building shelters, making weapons, scavenging for food, and fighting her enemies—wild dogs. This is a story not only of unusual survival, but also of natural beauty and personal discovery. When she is found, Karana is wearing a necklace of black stones, an otter cape, and a cormorant skirt. The girl whose story O'Dell tells actually lived upon the island during this period and is known historically as the Lost Woman of San Nicolas. She is buried on a hill near the Santa Barbara Mission, where she was befriended when brought to California. *Island of the Blue Dolphins* won many awards, among which was the John Newbery Medal.

O'Dell's Seven Serpents Trilogy looks at the Spanish colonization of the Southwest and the conflicts between explorers and native peoples. Consisting of *The Captive, The Feathered Serpent,* and *The Amethyst Ring,* the trilogy focuses on the story of a young New World missionary in conflict with his compatriots' cruel treatment of Mayan Indians.

Another of O'Dell's highly acclaimed historical novels is *The King's Fifth,* a dramatic account of the steel-helmeted conquistadors of Spain, who strike out into unknown territories—what is now the state of Arizona—to find gold. Their greed causes them to sacrifice blood, honor, life itself, for a lake of gold. The story is passionate, setting white men against red men, Spaniard against Spaniard. No characters are all good or all bad, they are deeply complex, committed, and human.

The sequel to *Island of the Blue Dolphins, Zia* is an excellent novel in its own right, its narrator, fourteen-year-old Zia, lives in a California Mission and wants to rescue her Aunt Karana, left behind on the Island nearly twenty years ago. Though longing to see and help her aunt, Zia fears that Karana might not wish to live at the Mission, might miss the freedom of her own place far away from the white people who tell Indians what to do. Zia and Karana are united and Zia's fears are realized. Karana cannot sleep in a dormitorio. She runs away to the beach, becomes ill, and dies there. Zia feels she dies because she misses her island home.

Alexandra is about a modern girl living in a Florida village. Like O'Dell's historical heroines, Alexandra is strong, courageous, and determined. Under the guidance of her grandfather Stefanos, who in his day was a renowned fisherman, she learns the dangerous craft of the sponge diver. In addition to learning the ways of watermen, she learns about those who use the waters for drug trafficking. She has to decide whether to remain silent or to implicate her close friends.

My Name Is Not Angelica is a stunning novel, set on the Island of St. John in the Atlantic Ocean, at the time of the African slave revolt of 1733-34. Sixteen-year-old Raisha is kidnapped and sold by a West African king to Danish planters on St. John. Raisha becomes a house servant, and the planter's wife calls her "Angelica" because she has the smile of an angel from Heaven. But even as a sheltered house servant, Raisha is caught up in the terrible suffering of other slaves. Many of these slaves at the time of the revolt lose all hope and leap over a cliff to death in the sea. Raisha's husband holds out his strong hand to her so they may leap together. This surprising ending is a compelling portrayal of the human spirit as well as an effective indictment of slavery.

O'Dell is a master of historical fiction. His sense of time and place, and his understanding of human beings and human societies, are truly remarkable. His works will surely be enjoyed by many generations to come.

—Mary Lystad

OKIMOTO, Jean Davies. American. Born 14 December 1942. Attended DePauw University, 1960-63, and University of Washington, Seattle, 1971-72; Antioch College, M.A. 1977. Married 1) Peter C. Kirkman, 1961 (divorced, 1971), two daughters; Joseph T. Okimoto, 1973, two sons. High school teacher of remedial reading in Seattle, Washington, 1972-73; University of Washington, Seattle, editorial consultant in child psychiatry, 1973-74; Mount Baker Youth Service Bureau, Seattle, assistant to director, 1974-75; private practice of psychotherapy in Seattle, 1975—. Seattle Public Schools, volunteer tutor, 1969; Franklin Area School Council, chairman, 1970; Mount Baker Youth Service Bureau, chairman, 1973. Creator and chairperson of Mayor's Reading Awards. Agent: Ruth Cohen, P.O. Box 7626, Menlo Park, CA 94025. Address: 2700 East Madison, Seattle, WA 98112. Washington State Governor's Writers' Award, 1982, for *It's Just Too Much;* American Library Association Best Book for Young Adults and International Reading Association Choice Book, both 1987, both for *Jason's Women.*

PUBLICATIONS FOR YOUNG ADULTS

Fiction

My Mother Is Not Married to My Father. New York, Putnam, 1979.
It's Just Too Much. New York, Putnam, 1980.
Norman Schnurman, Average Person. New York, Putnam, 1982.
Who Did It, Jenny Lake? New York, Putnam, 1983.
Jason's Women. New York, Atlantic Monthly Press, 1986.
Boomerang Kids. New York, Little, Brown, 1987.
Blumpoe the Grumpoe Meets Arnold the Cat. New York, Little, Brown, 1990.
Molly by Any Other Name. New York, Scholastic, 1990.
Take a Chance, Gramps! New York, Little, Brown, 1990.

Contributor of short stories to books, including *Visions,* edited by Don Gallo, Delacorte, 1988; and *Connections,* edited by Gallo, Delacorte, 1989; contributor of play to *Hum It Again, Jeremy* (one-act play), published in *Center Stage,* edited by Gallo, Harper, 1990.

*

Biography: Essay in *Speaking for Ourselves, Too* compiled and edited by Donald R. Gallo, National Council of Teachers of English, 1993.

*   *   *

Writing as a psychotherapist as well as a twice-married mother of a blended family, Jean Davies Okimoto brings both theoretical and practical knowledge to the body of literature she has created for young adults. Most of her novels are so-called problem novels and deal with many of the real situations which teens today encounter in their domestic and school environments, including the trauma of divorce, conflict with step siblings, fear of failure, and loss of friends.

Okimoto brings a light, easy style to her books. This, coupled with the fact that most of her books are around one hundred pages in length, makes them very approachable reading material for virtually all intermediate and middle school children. Okimoto's basic approach in her problem fiction is to set up an emotional, adjustment, or some other sort of problem or set of problems in the first chapter and then to take the characters through to the resolution of those difficulties. Occasionally, Okimoto has a tendency to allow her fiction to become subservient to her psychotherapeutic interests; consequently, at times one gets the feeling that the story has been created as a means of showcasing a problem, and then the story begins to sound like a case study. Fortunately, the author keeps a fairly tight rein on these tendencies, and the majority of her fiction avoids the case-study pitfalls.

In her first novel, *My Mother Is Not Married to My Father,* Okimoto begins setting the problem up in the first sentence of the first chapter: "I knew something was wrong." In the ninety-odd pages which follow the opening, Okimoto gets the parents divorced, has the protagonist (eleven-year-old Cynthia) resolve her fears that the divorce was all her fault, pairs the father off with a new girlfriend, and ends with the mother (a self-employed potter) announcing her engagement to a seemingly ideal mate, an earth-sensitive medical doctor.

In *It's Just Too Much,* a sequel to *My Mother Is Not Married to My Father,* Okimoto has Cynthia resolving her adjustment problems to blended-family living, particularly her resentment of what she perceives to be the favored treatment received by her two stepsiblings, who visit on weekends. To this domestic mix is added Cynthia's embarrassment over being a no-bra adolescent in a school full of girls who are wearing bras.

In one of her more ambitious undertakings, *Take A Chance, Gramps!,* Okimoto attempts—with varying degrees of success—to link the adjustment problems of adolescence with the adjustment problems of aging. Janie, the protagonist, has always relied on her best friend Alicia in all social situations, and when she learns that Alicia is moving to another town on the eve of her first day in junior high school, she feels helpless and dejected. These feelings are veritable mirror images of the feelings her grandfather has been having since the death of his wife. "Gramps" now lives with Janie and her family but has become a virtual recluse, and everything he says is garbled beyond recognition as a result of his not wearing his false teeth. The book explores the relationship between these two characters and shows how they are able to help each other overcome their fears and begin enjoying life. At her mother's encouragement, Janie talks Gramps into taking an outing downtown where they happen upon a senior citizens' dance; it is, they learn, a weekly affair. Gramps is taken by the vision of all these older people having fun but is embarrassed because he does not have his teeth in. So he and Janie plan a return trip, complete with teeth. One thing leads to another, and the two finally meet and develop romantic interests in an elderly woman and her grandson who comes regularly to the dances. In the meantime, Gramps has told Janie that if she wants to develop friends on her own at school without Alicia, she has to extend herself. So she devises a plan whereby she forces herself to say "Hi" to every third person she meets in the hall. Sure enough, it works. Before the first term is over Janie has become popular enough to be elected to the student council.

In her more recent problem novels (*Jason's Women* and *Molly by Any Other Name*), Okimoto addresses the adjustment difficulties faced by Asian Americans and weaves in a variety of other problems not related to Asian culture, such as adoption and death.

The concerns which Okimoto identifies in her novels are real enough; however, her determination to sew everything up neatly and produce a happy ending results in her plots becoming fairly predictable, even if they are well-rendered and enjoyable. The result is a diminution of the tension that is needed to drive a strong piece of fiction. To her credit, Okimoto does present viable solutions to many problems teens are likely to encounter during the arduous process of growing up. Many adolescents experiencing adjustment problems will find welcome solace in the pages of Okimoto's fiction.

Perhaps Okimoto's finest piece of writing is not a problem-novel per se, but a humorous slice-of-life novel (*Norman Schnurman, Average Person*) which details the exploits of a sixth-grade boy who is trying to find his own identity within the towering shadow of his father, the former star running back of the University of Washington's football team. The book's protagonist, Norman Schnurman, is more interested in scavenging in junk stores than in playing football. On one of his junk store outings, he finds a bare-chested Hawaiian hula-doll lamp with light bulbs for breasts. He and his best friend, P.W., devise an after-school peep show featuring the doll, a poster of a girl in a wet tee shirt, and various other artifacts. The humor which ensues from this situation is good-natured and infectious; it is representative of the consistently high quality of writing to be found in the rest of the book. The character development in this novel is perhaps the strongest in her writing to date, with the relationship between Norman and P.W. being particularly well realized.

In 1983 Okimoto stepped out of her problem-novel persona entirely to write a young-adult mystery/romance, *Who Did It, Jenny Lake?* The plot of the mystery is well crafted, and there are enough red herrings to keep even a die-hard Agatha Christie fan jumping to wrong conclusions in an effort to figure out whodunit. However, for the romance part of the book, the author seems to have resorted to the Sweet Valley High school of fiction writing wherein every girl is as cute as a button and every guy is a bronze god. It is rather as if Barbie and Ken have gone sleuthing.

Okimoto's problem novels should be high on anyone's list who is counseling middle schoolers through adjustment problems related to relationships in the home or school setting. The books are generally well written, and, because of their sympathetic and insightful treatment of adolescent problems, they are excellent bibliotherapeutic tools. The books which are not aimed quite so obviously at psychotherapeutic problem solving are more interesting as pieces of literature and will have broader appeal among young adult readers.

—Bill Buchanan

ONEAL, Zibby (Elizabeth Oneal, née Bisgard). American. Born in Omaha, Nebraska, 17 March 1934. Educated at Stanford University, 1952-55; University of Michigan, B.A. 1970. Married Robert Moore Oneal in 1955; one daughter and one son. Lecturer in English, University of Michigan, Ann Arbor, 1976-85. Member of board of trustees, Greenhills School, Ann Arbor, 1975-79. Recipient: Friends of American Writers award, 1972, for *War Work;* "Notable Book" citations and "Best Books for Young Adults" citations, American Library Association, 1980, for *The Language of Goldfish,* 1982, for *A Formal Feeling,* and 1985, for *In Summer Light;* "Best Books of the Year" citation, *New York Times,* 1982, and Christopher award, 1983, both for *A Formal Feeling; Horn Book* Honor Book, and *Boston Globe/Horn Book* award, both 1986, both for *In Summer Light.* Agent: Marilyn Marlow, Curtis Brown Ltd., 575 Madison Ave., New York, NY 10022. Address: 501 Onondaga St., Ann Arbor, MI 48104, U.S.A.

PUBLICATIONS FOR YOUNG ADULTS

Fiction

War Work, illustrated by George Porter. New York, Viking, 1971.
The Language of Goldfish. New York, Viking, 1980; London, Gollancz, 1987.
A Formal Feeling. New York, Viking, 1982; London, Gollancz, 1983.
In Summer Light. New York, Viking, 1985.

Other

Grandma Moses: Painter of Rural America, illustrated by Donna Ruff. New York, Viking, 1986.

PUBLICATIONS FOR CHILDREN

Fiction

The Improbable Adventures of Marvelous O'Hara Soapstone, illustrated by Paul Galdone. New York, Viking, 1972.
Turtle and Snail, illustrated by Margot Tomes. Philadelphia, Lippincott, 1979.
Maude and Walter, illustrated by Maxie Chambliss. New York, Lippincott, 1985.
A Long Way to Go, illustrated by Michael Dooling. New York, Viking, 1990.

*

Biography: Entry in *Sixth Book of Junior Authors and Illustrators,* edited by Sally Holmes Holtze, New York, H.W. Wilson, 1989; essay in *Speaking for Ourselves: Autobiographical Sketches by Notable Authors of Books for Young Adults,* Volume 1, compiled and edited by Donald R. Gallo, National Council of Teachers of English, 1990.

Manuscript Collection: Kerlan Collection, University of Minnesota, Minneapolis.

Critical Study: Entry in *Children's Literature Review,* Volume 13, Detroit, Gale, 1987; entry in *Contemporary Literary Criticism,* Volume 30, Detroit, Gale, 1984.

*   *   *

Zibby Oneal is most noted for her three young adult novels, *The Language of Goldfish, A Formal Feeling,* and *In Summer Light.* Though each book is a distinct entity, there are common threads throughout. There is a female protagonist in each book whose struggle to find out who she is and what her place in the world will be is the focus of the book. Art also plays a major role in two of the books, and images of color, line, and shape abound in all three of these novels. Though there is the expected misconnection between the protagonist and the adults in her life, each has a supportive sibling who ameliorates the sense of isolation. Oneal also makes use of flashback, which allows the reader to gain a context for the protagonists' ordeals. Each book is one of intense conflict, though there is a coolness of style that permeates them; the reader watches as if at a play, and ultimately applauds the resolution.

For Carrie, in *The Language of Goldfish,* growing up is very hard and she fights the changes that are happening to her body and to her emotions; she can't seem to fit in anywhere. Carrie and her sister had enjoyed a secret language that they used with a goldfish in the pond in their yard, which becomes a symbol of the aspects of childhood that Carrie wants to remain the same. She wants nothing to change, while her sister Moira is eagerly accepting maturity and considers their secret language to be a thing of the past. This powerful internal struggle causes Carrie anxiety attacks and she attempts suicide. *The Language of Goldfish* reflects the trauma of growing up that many young adults face. The feeling of being on the outside, of having no one to talk to who understands the sense of isolation and fear, is paramount in the book. The use of rich metaphor in descriptive passages and short sentences in dialogue heightens the sensation of personal isolation within a vibrant world. The only device that doesn't work is the image of the island in the middle of the pond. It plays a central role as the metaphor for Carrie's anguish, yet the image keeps slipping and is never fully recognized.

Emily Dickinson wrote "After great pain, a formal feeling comes," which functions as the metaphor for Oneal's second novel. Anne is home from boarding school and is still trying to come to terms with the sudden death of her mother the year before, and the unexpected remarriage of her father. She runs compulsively in an attempt to forget, and as the book progresses it becomes obvious that she has repressed a great many incidents of her relationship with her mother as well as the attendant emotions. Oneal maintains a formal feeling in images such as Anne perceiving everyone as being on the other side of a glass pane, and in the repetition of the feeling that to lose control is the worst thing possible. Oneal makes excellent use of detail and creates suspense by using small incidents to build to the climax. This is a powerful novel that probes human emotions with insight and an elegant style.

A modern rendition of the fairy tale of Sleeping Beauty, *In Summer Light* is the story of Kate, a young woman forced by a bout of mono to spend her summer at her parents' island home, where a conflict with her artist father and her lack of understanding of her mother fosters a feeling of oppression. Kate finally wins release when a visiting graduate student, there to catalog her father's work, encourages her to resume her painting. Oneal once again uses the elements of conflict with a parent, a sense of separateness, the need to be liked, and the need to please. She has also made use of the image of an island, and color flows throughout the story. There is a warmth to this book that is reflected in the hot summer setting as well as in the relationships of the characters.

Oneal has carved a niche for herself in young adult literature. Though her books are about the travails of adolescents, they are written with elegance and style and transcend the popular offerings that come with monotonous regularity from so many authors within this genre.

—M. Jean Greenlaw

———

O'NEILL, Judith (Beatrice). Australian. Born in Melbourne, Victoria, 30 June 1930. Educated at Mildura High School, Victoria, 1942-47; University of Melbourne (Derham prize, 1950; Rotary Foundation fellowship, 1952), 1948-52, B.A. (honors) in English 1951, M.A. in English 1952; University of London (Story-Miller prize, 1953), 1952-53, postgraduate certificate in education 1953. Married John Cochrane O'Neill in 1954; three daughters. Tutor in English, University of Melbourne, 1954-56 and 1960-62; tutor, Open University, Cambridge, England, 1971-72; English teacher, St. Mary's School, Cambridge, 1973-82; free-lance writer, since 1982. Recipient: Third prize, Rigby Anniversary Literary Contest (Australia), 1982, for *Jess and the River Kids;* shortlisted for Australian Children's Book Council award, 1989, for *Deepwater;* shortlisted for Carnegie award and *Guardian* Children's Fiction award, 1993, for *So Far from Skye.* Agent: A.P. Watt Ltd., 20 John Street, London WC1N 2DL, England. Address: 9 Lonsdale Terrace, Edinburgh EH3 9HN, Scotland.

PUBLICATIONS FOR YOUNG ADULTS

Fiction

Jess and the River Kids. London, Hamish Hamilton, 1984.
Stringybark Summer, illustrated by Valerie Littlewood. London, Hamish Hamilton, 1985.
Deepwater. London, Hamish Hamilton, 1987.
The Message. London, Hamish Hamilton, 1989.
So Far from Skye, London, Hamish Hamilton, 1992.

Other

Martin Luther. London, Cambridge University Press, 1975; Minneapolis, Lerner, 1979.

Transported to Van Diemen's Land: The Story of Two Convicts. London, and New York, Cambridge University Press, 1977.

Critical Studies

Editor, *Critics on Keats.* London, Allen & Unwin, 1967; Coral Gables, Florida, University of Miami Press, 1968.
Editor, *Critics on Charlotte and Emily Brontë.* London, Allen & Unwin, and Carol Gables, Florida, University of Miami Press, 1968.
Editor, *Critics on Pope.* London, Allen & Unwin, and Carol Gables, Florida, University of Miami Press, 1968.
Editor, *Critics on Jane Austen.* London, Allen & Unwin, and Carol Gables, Florida, University of Miami Press, 1969.
Editor, *Critics on Blake.* London, Allen & Unwin, and Carol Gables, Florida, University of Miami Press, 1970.
Editor, *Critics on Marlowe.* London, Allen & Unwin, and Carol Gables, Florida, University of Miami Press, 1970.

*

Judith O'Neill comments:
I am an Australian, but for thirty years I have lived in Britain. My stories are all set in Australia and all in the past, drawing on my own childhood and on the childhoods of my parents, grandparents, and great-grandparent. My books are enjoyed by imaginative and thoughtful boys and girls of eleven and older, and also by adults. Though the stories are set in the past, the themes are perennial ones—love and loss, imagination and discovery, family conflicts and their resolution, prejudice, and self-knowledge.

*   *   *

Judith O'Neill's family history is particularly relevant to her writing. Her great-great grandparents were among the crofters who emigrated from the Isle of Skye in Scotland to Victoria, Australia, in the "famine clearances" of 1852. O'Neill was born and brought up in Australia and she uses her own experiences and those of her ancestors for much of the background of her novels, which are vivid portrayals of life in Australia.

The novels are all set in the past, and although the setting is always important, historical details are so deftly woven into the whole, they can seem incidental to the story from time to time. O'Neill writes with strong feeling about her subjects making her books quite compelling. She brings the past alive and makes the reader feel as if he or she is learning something about life in another country, and another time. The stories all deal with family relationships, friendships, and the domestic details that are part of every-day life, which makes them particularly accessible to young adults. They chronicle the type of adventures and dramas that adolescents identify with and enjoy vicariously, and they end happily in the safety and warmth of loving families.

Two of O'Neill's earlier novels, *Stringybark Summer* and *Jess and the River Kids,* are aimed at younger adolescents. They are both straightforward adventure stories peopled with close-knit, happy, hard-working families, who live tough lives in the outback. *Stringybark Summer,* set in turn-of-the-century Australia, is the story of Sophie, the only daughter of a farming couple, who is sent to stay with her aunt's family miles away on a sawmill, while her mother is having another baby. She goes reluctantly but ends up enjoying herself as she joins a large, rather chaotic family and their

work. The children, Sophie's cousins, run free, watching the logging, helping with the horses, and generally being part of the community. Various episodes, such as getting a sick baby to the doctor in the middle of a stormy night, or saving a horse that has been bitten by a snake, will have readers captivated throughout this realistic portrayal of life in Australia. Progress is at the forefront of the novel, too, when the steam train is brought in to replace the horses, with disastrous consequences. Sophie learns a lot about herself and understands why her father has been so sullen and depressed; her older brother was killed at the age of six months when he was kicked by a horse accidentally. Sophie returns home to see her new baby brother and finds her father a changed man, enthusiastically looking forward to the future.

Jess and the River Kids, is set during the World War II, although this impinges little on the events of the story. The real story centres around Jess and the two boys she meets by the river. The boys' father, a gold prospector, and mother are away at the time, and they live in a houseboat, next to a deaf old lady, Lizzie. The three spend a fairly ordinary summer playing games, camping out, and listening to Lizzie's tales of her past, until their boat is broken into and a golden nugget brooch is stolen. In the process Lizzie's houseboat is set alight and cast off into the river and the children must rescue her from the burning boat.

The Message, features Don, whose father is off fighting in New Guinea, and who feels ignored and unappreciated at home. He runs away and finds himself in a strange town with no money, where he is befriended by Sal and Gray, who take him back to their community, Arcady. Don gradually realises there is something strange about the group. They keep talking about the good Waves that they believe control events, bringing people to them and making things happen, and they believe that the radio news bulletin contains a special message just for them. But the whole thing is beginning to go sour; several of the group's leading members have left, or leave shortly after Don arrives, and the community that was founded on truth and trust is being destroyed by suspicion and deceit. They have been remarkably adept in illegally printing petrol coupons, thinking they were helping the war effort. Don manages to escape as the police find out about the forgery and is reunited with his family, having learnt a few lessons about himself and life in the process. This is an extremely thought-provoking book, which raises some interesting questions about the problems of such alternative religious cults founded on the strong beliefs of one charismatic leader.

In *Deepwater,* O'Neill uses World War I as an integral part of the story. The families who live in the small farming community of Deepwater in the Australian bush are all touched by the outbreak of war. One by one the eldest sons go off to fight, while at home the farmers are facing the worst drought in years, which is threatening to ruin many of them. When Charlotte's elder brother enlists she has to give up the idea of going away to high school and do her brother's share of the farmwork. Then a woman teacher comes to the school and takes a very jingoistic stance on the war. An anti-German feeling develops against the Henschke family causing bitterness, distress, and chaos in what was a close community. Even with this sort of subject O'Neill manages to make "good" prevail in the form of Charlotte and her family who are determined that the community must survive. Ideas of what nationalism and patriotism actually mean are played out and the final ghastly tragedy of Gallipoli touches everyone.

O'Neill's most important book to date, *So Far from Skye,* tells her own family history and incorporates a little known story. It is the account of the crofting families who were forcibly rounded up and sent to Australia after the famines in the Highlands of Scotland in 1852. Bewildered, half-starved, badly clothed and dirty, many speaking only the Gaelic, they were transported on ships to begin new lives working for Australian farmers. Hundreds died on the long voyage, but for those who survived it was a complete change of lifestyle, from the harsh weather and subsistence on the tiny island of Skye to the blistering heat, strange animals, the struggle with a new language, and the vast distances of the Australian outback. This is a very moving account of the long, painful journey from one culture to another. Plenty of adventure on the voyage makes for exciting reading.

In all her novels, O'Neill captures the feelings, fears and hopes of the people. Their overwhelming spirit and bravery shine through and their strong faith in God and an intense commitment to family and friends enable them to weather the fiercest storms and come through together, ready to make the best of what life has to offer them.

—Fiona Lafferty

———

ORGEL, Doris (née Adelberg). Also writes as Doris Adelberg. American. Born in Vienna, Austria, 15 August 1929; emigrated to the United States, 1940. Educated at Radcliffe College, Cambridge, Massachusetts. 1946-48; Barnard College, New York, B.A. (cum laude) 1950 (Phi Beta Kappa). Married Shelley Orgel in 1949; two sons and one daughter. Author and translator of children's books. Worked for magazine and book publishers, 1950-55; taught writing workshops, Bridgeport University and Fairfield University, both Connecticut; frequent contributor, *Cricket Magazine;* children's book reviewer, *New York Times.* Recipient: Lewis Carroll Shelf award, 1960, for translation of *Dwarf-Long-Nose; Sarah's Room* was named one of *New York Times* best 100 books, 1963; *Book World* Children's Spring Festival First Prize in picture book division, 1972, for *Little John;* American Library Association Notable Book award, for *A Certain Magic; New York Times* Best Illustrated Book award, for *Merry, Merry Fibruary;* Child Study Association award, Golden Kite Honor Book award, American Library Association Notable Book award, all 1978, and Association of Jewish Libraries award, 1979, all for *The Devil in Vienna.* Agent: Writers House Inc., 21 West 26th Street, New York, NY 10010. Lives in New York, NY.

PUBLICATIONS FOR YOUNG ADULTS

Fiction

The Mulberry Music, illustrated by Dale Payson. New York, Harper, 1971.
A Certain Magic. New York, Dial Press, 1976.
The Devil in Vienna. New York, Dial Press, 1978; London, Simon and Schuster, 1989.
Risking Love. New York, Dial Press, 1985.

PUBLICATIONS FOR CHILDREN

Fiction

Sarah's Room, illustrated by Maurice Sendak. New York, Harper, 1963; London, Bodley Head, 1972.
Cindy's Snowdrops, illustrated by Ati Forberg. New York, Knopf, 1966; London, Hamish Hamilton, 1967.
Cindy's Sad and Happy Tree, illustrated by Ati Forberg. New York, Knopf, 1967.
In a Forgotten Place, illustrated by James McMullan. New York, Knopf, 1967.
Whose Turtle?, illustrated by Martha Alexander. Cleveland, World, 1968.
On the Sand Dune, illustrated by Leonard Weisgard. New York, Harper, 1968.
Merry, Rose, and Christmas-Tree June, illustrated by Edward Gorey. New York, Knopf, 1969.
Next Door to Xanadu, illustrated by Dale Payson. New York, Harper, 1969; as *Next-Door Neighbors,* 1979.
Phoebe and the Prince, illustrated by Erik Blegvad. New York, Putnam, 1969.
The Uproar, illustrated by Anita Lobel. New York, McGraw Hill, 1970.
Bartholomew, We Love You!, illustrated by Pat Grant Porter. New York, Knopf, 1973.
My War with Mrs. Galloway, illustrated by Carol Newsom. New York, Viking Kestrel, 1985.
Whiskers Once and Always, illustrated by Carol Newsom. New York, Viking Kestrel, 1986.
Midnight Soup and a Witch's Hat, illustrated by Carol Newsom. New York, Viking Kestrel, 1987.
Crack in the Heart. New York, Fawcett, 1989.
Starring Becky Suslow, illustrated by Carol Newsom. New York, Viking Kestrel, 1989.
Nobodies and Somebodies. New York, Viking Press, 1991.
The Mouse Who Wanted to Marry, illustrated by Holly Hannon. New York, Bantam, 1993.

Poetry

Grandma's Holidays (as Doris Adelberg), illustrated by Paul Kennedy. New York, Dial Press, 1963.
Lizzie's Twins (as Doris Adelberg), illustrated by N.M. Bodecker. New York, Dial Press, 1964.
The Good-byes of Magnus Marmalade, illustrated by Erik Blegvad. New York, Putnam, 1966.
Merry, Merry Fibruary, illustrated by Arnold Lobel. New York, Parents' Magazine Press, 1977.

Other (retellings)

Translator, *Dwarf-Long-Nose,* by Wilhelm Hauff, illustrated by Maurice Sendak. New York, Random House, 1960; London, Bodley Head, 1979.
The Tale of Gockel, Hinkel, and Gackeliah, illustrated by Maurice Sendak. New York, Random House, 1961.
Schoolmaster Whackwell's Wonderful Sons: A Fairy Tale, illustrated by Maurice Sendak. New York, Random House, 1962.
The Heart of Stone: A Fairy Tale, illustrated by David Levine. New York, Macmillan, and London, Collier Macmillan, 1964.

The Story of Lohengrin, The Knight of the Swan, illustrated by Herbert Danska. New York, Putnam, 1966.

A Monkey's Uncle, illustrated by Mitchell Miller. New York, Farrar Straus, 1969.

Translator, *The Enchanted Drum,* by Walter Grieder, illustrated by Walter Grieder. New York, Parents' Magazine Press, 1969.

Translator, *The Grandma in the Apple Tree,* by Mira Lobe, illustrated by Judith Gwyn Brown. New York, McGraw Hill, 1970.

Baron Munchausen: Fifteen Truly Tall Tales, illustrated by Willi Baum. Reading, Massachusetts, Addison Wesley, 1971.

The Child from Far Away, illustrated by Michael Eagle. Reading, Massachusetts, Addison Wesley, 1971.

Little John, illustrated by Anita Lobel. New York, Farrar Straus, 1972.

Godfather Cat and Mousie, illustrated by Ann Schweninger. New York, Macmillan, 1986.

Next Time I Will: An Old English Tale, illustrated by Betsy Day. New York, Bantam, 1993.

The Flower of Sheba, with Ellen Schecter, illustrated by Laura Kelly. New York, Bantam, 1994.

*

Manuscript Collection: Kerlan Collection, University of Minnesota, Minneapolis.

Doris Orgel comments:

As the field of children's books becomes increasingly mass-market-driven, gimmicky and reductive, I feel grateful that it remains possible to write out of inwardness and singularity, and still hope to stir responses in individual children.

*   *   *

Doris Orgel's writing for young adults encompasses two very different historical and social settings: Austria in the 1930s, and the United States in the 1980s, but her work is more united thematically than one might imagine at first glance, namely by her characters' coming to terms with loss, fear, and painful love. Through her fiction, Orgel has made a major contribution to understanding the destructive effects of anti-Semitism and fascism in Europe in this century. Her realistic works set in America also add to her list of valuable contemporary novels for young adults.

Born Doris Adelberg in Vienna, Austria, in 1929, she emigrated to the United States in 1940, barely escaping the Nazi threat. In her novel *A Certain Magic,* Orgel addresses the legacy of mid-twentieth-century events in Europe. Through the symbols of a magical emerald and a special doll, the device of a wartime journal kept by the refugee girl Gertrude Ehrenteil, and the affectionate, inquisitive friendship of eleven-year-old Jenny for her Aunt Trudl (the Gertrude of the journal), Orgel recreates, in an interesting synthesis, a contemporary American young person's realization of what Hitler's threat was like to an Austrian child in 1938. The distance between Jenny's comparatively innocent life and Trudl's dislocated, threatened existence is bridged with honesty and imagination.

In the award-winning *The Devil in Vienna* Orgel transforms her own experience into powerful fiction most directly and completely. In this novel, told partially through letters between Inge Dornenwald, who is Jewish, and Lieselotte Vessely, who is Catholic, the period of the Austrian *Anschluss* is vividly recreated, not only in its political but also in its cultural and mundane personal details. The friendship of Inge and Lieselotte undergoes severe testing, but it endures. It is a dramatic and moving story, complex, realistic, and suspenseful. The novel effectively shows the links between personal and political values under the pressures of a totalitarian movement. *The Devil in Vienna* is a major achievement and a book of considerable significance for young people seeking to understand what happened in Europe under Hitler's rule. It has been published in many languages in Europe and has been made into a television movie titled *A Friendship in Vienna.*

Orgel has also written young adult novels set in the contemporary American milieu. In her acclaimed novel *Risking Love,* Dinah Moskowitz, Barnard student, tells the story of her self-discovery and evolution through therapy. Her humor and defensiveness, her experience of sexuality and romance, her fear—rooted in her parents' divorce—that love is not lasting, and the exploratory digressions of psychotherapy are absorbingly created.

Less highly praised by critics, *Crack in the Heart* is the story of seventeen-year-old Zanna, who moves to New York City with her mother after Zanna's father dies. Isolated at the privileged girls' school where her mother works, Zanna meets a college student named Jeff who is creative, musical, and charismatic, but also involved in drugs. Though Zanna experiments with drugs, she does not get hooked. The deeper theme of her life is coming to terms with the loss of her father.

Orgel is a skillful writer who has bridged her European origins and American experience with insight and imagination, creating a legacy of historical awareness, humor, and shared humanity through her fiction.

—J.D. Stahl

———

ORLEV, Uri. Polish. Born in Warsaw, 24 February 1931. Served in the Israeli Army, 1949-51. Recipient: Awards from Israeli Broadcast Authorities, 1966, for "The Great Game," 1970, for "Dancing Lesson," and 1975, for "The Beast of Darkness," and Television Prize, 1979, for youth program "Who Will Ring First?"; prize from Youth Alia, 1966, for *The Last Summer Vacation;* Prime Minister Prize (Israel), 1972, and 1989, for body of work; Ze-ev Prize from Israel Ministry of Education and Culture, 1977, International Board on Books for Young People (IBBY) Honor List (Israel), 1979, both for *The Beast of Darkness;* Haifa University Prize for Young Readers, 1981; IBBY Honor List (Israel), 1982, *Horn Book* Books of 1984 honor list citation, 1984, and Sydney Taylor Book award from the Association of Jewish Libraries, Mildred L. Batchelder award for Translation, Edgar Allan Poe award runnerup from the Mystery Writers of America, and Jane Addams Children's Book award Honor Book from the Jane Addams Peace Association, all 1985, Silver Pencil Prize for best book translated to Dutch, 1986, and Honor award from the Ministry of Youth, Family, Women and Health of the Federal Republic of Germany and West Berlin, 1987, and first recipient of Janusz Korczak Literary Prize (Poland), 1990, all for *The Island on Bird Street;* Television Prize from Broadcast Authorities for television script, 1990; Mildred L. Batchelder award (foreign language book translated into English, 1992, to Houghton Mifflin, for *The Man from the Other Side,* translated by Hillel Halkin. Address: Yemin Moshe, 4 Ha-berakhah, Jerusalem, Israel.

PUBLICATIONS FOR YOUNG ADULTS

Novels, translated into English

The Lead Soldiers. Tel Aviv, Sifriat-Poalim, 1956; translated from the original Hebrew by Hillel Halkin, Battle Ground, Washington, P. Owen, 1979.
The Island on Bird Street, translated from the original Hebrew by Hillel Halkin. Boston, Massachusetts, Houghton, 1984.
The Man from the Other Side, translated from original Hebrew by Hillel Halkin. Boston, Massachusetts, Houghton, 1991.
Lydia, Queen of Palestine, translated from original Hebrew by Hillel Halkin. Boston, Massachusetts, Houghton, 1993.

Fiction

The Beast of Darkness. Tel Aviv, Am Oved, 1976.
The Big-Little Girl. Jerusalem, Keter, 1977.
The Driving-Mad Girls. Jerusalem, Keter, 1977.
Noon Thoughts. Tel Aviv, Sifriat-Poalim, 1978.
It's Hard to Be a Lion. Tel Aviv, Am Oved, 1979.
The Lion Shirt. Givatayim, Massada, 1979.
Siamina. Tel Aviv, Am Oved, 1979.
The Good Luck Passy. Tel Aviv, Am Oved, 1980.
Granny Knits. Givatayim, Massada, 1980.
Mr. Mayer, Let Us Sing. Givatayim, Massada, 1980.
The Island on Bird Street. Jerusalem, Keter, 1981.
Wings Turn. Givatayim, Massada, 1981.
Big Brother. Jerusalem, Keter, 1983.
The Dragon's Crown. Jerusalem, Keter, 1985.
Journey to Age Four. Tel Aviv, Am Oved, 1985.
Shampoo on Tuesdays. Jerusalem, Keter, 1986.
The Wrong Side of the Bed. Jerusalem, Keter, 1986.
The Man from the Other Side. Jerusalem, Keter, 1988.
The Lady with the Hat. Jerusalem, Keter, 1990.
Lydia, Queen of Palestine. Jerusalem, Keter, 1991.

PUBLICATIONS FOR ADULTS

Fiction

The Lead Soldiers. Sifriat Poalim, 1956; Jerusalem, Keter, 1989.
Till Tomorrow. Tel Aviv, Am Oved, 1958.
The Last Summer Vacation. Daga, 1966.

Translator from Polish to Hebrew

In the Desert and Jungle, by Henryk Sienkiewicz. Paris, Y. Marcus, 1970.
King Matthew I, by Janusz Korczak. Jerusalem, Keter, 1979.
The Stories of Bruno Schulz. Tel Aviv, Schocken, 1979.
Eden, by Stanislaw Lem. Givatayim, Massada, 1980.
The Invincible, by Stanislaw Lem. Tel Aviv, Schocken, 1981.
Pirx the Pilot, by Stanislaw Lem. Tel Aviv, Schocken, 1981.
The Little Jack's Bankruptcy, by Janusz Korczak. Hakibutz Hameuchad, 1985.
The Devil of the Junior Year, by Kornel Makuszinski. Tel Aviv, Zmora-Bitan, 1990.

*

Uri Orlev comments:

When I was eleven I wanted to be a poet, and I did indeed begin to write poems. At the time, I was living in Poland, and therefore the poems were not written in Hebrew. I still have the notebook I wrote in; I find dates like January 20th, 1944, or May 13th, 1945, and on the cover, in large letters, the word "Perhaps." Only my brother understood the meaning of "Perhaps"—it was what we said constantly to each other: "Perhaps we'll be saved." This was during World War II—and the Holocaust.

A woman once asked me about one of my books on the subject: "Did writing this book enable you to 'finish' with the Holocaust?" I replied that I cannot "finish" with it because I went through it as a child. What other people call the Holocaust was, for me, my childhood. Like any childhood, there were many beautiful and exciting things in it, and, in my case, many painful and frightening things.

When I came to Israel after the war, I learned a new language and lost the language of my childhood. And when I tried to write poetry I found that I was no longer able to. So I began to write stories, and later, books for adults. Not until I was forty-five did I write my first book for young people, *The Beast of Darkness.*

I once asked some school children whether they thought the Beast of Darkness was real or imaginary. One child replied, "It's partly imaginary, partly not, because you can create such a beast only in your imagination, but you can rely on it as though it were real." And that is what I do when I write. I invent things and then I find that they are real and that I can rely on them and live with them.

*   *   *

To read the novels of Uri Orlev is in some ways to read the story of Orlev's life. Like many of his characters he was born in Warsaw, Poland, and he spent his childhood in part behind the Ghetto walls, and then in hiding beyond them. His father was captured by the Russians, his mother murdered by the Nazis. He was loved and protected by his aunt, with whom he was sent to Bergen-Belsen, where he and his brother were among the few that survived. After the war he and his brother emigrated to what was then Palestine, where he lived on a kibbutz in Galilee.

Parts of this story—particularly the years in the Warsaw Ghetto—are in all of Orlev's work. Fathers are consistently absent; mothers are brave and loving but often separated by circumstances from their children; children themselves must struggle to survive. This struggle is particularly prominent in Orlev's work; he consistently depicts the struggle of the human soul towards love, family, joy, and childhood, and away from the horror represented by the faceless Nazis that bring death and terror.

Though Orlev is prolific and is much published in Israel, only a handful of his works have been published in North America, all of which have been translated by Hillel Halkin. The first of these was *The Lead Soldiers,* the most clearly autobiographical of all of his novels. "The hero of this story, which is more than half true, is a small boy who hadn't seen very much of anything in life, which may be why he wasn't afraid to see more," Orlev suggests in the prologue. The union between author, narrator, and character is very strong here. This novel in fact deals with the period in Orlev's life when he moved from the suburbs of Warsaw to the Ghetto, and from there to Bergen-Belsen.

The point of view of the novel is significant, for unlike many novels which deal with the Holocaust, this one focuses on the child's point of view. It is written in an impressionistic style, where scenes shift quickly from one moment to another, each representing a moment which would imprint itself upon a small child's memory: hiding in a bin to escape those searching for him, finding a box of photographs—all that is left of a family—and flinging them out the window, being hit and arrested by a man in a grey suit, and being held against a wall with your brother knowing that you were about to be shot. Each scene is a vivid image of life from a child's point of view in the Ghetto.

The child protagonist, Yurik, tries to make sense of what is happening to his family, but ultimately he cannot; instead, he turns to his imagination to bring order to the things he sees happening around him. Yurik and his brother bring their lead soldiers to play at war every place they go, endowing them with heroic names along the way. All the while they seem to be watched by Orlev the narrator, who even enters into the story at times to interact with the children. Only when they are safely out of Poland and in a kibbutz in Palestine is the narrator able to leave the children, able to leave himself: "My story is finished and a new story, it would seem, is about to begin."

The Island on Bird Street is more straightforward in its narrative approaches, but it too deals with the experience of Jews in Poland; here the experience is much more focused, for the setting remains the Warsaw Ghetto. Where the father had been gone in *The Lead Soldiers,* here the mother has been taken away in the beginning of the novel. Alex is in hiding with his father, one of those left behind after deportations from the Ghetto in order to work in the factories. When they are discovered and marched off, together with others, Alex's father and Boruch, another worker in the factory, help Alex to escape; Boruch is killed protecting Alex, and his father assumes when he hears shots that Alex too is dead.

The rest of the novel is a vivid description of Alex's life spent in hiding in the Ghetto. He refuses to leave the ruined house to which he has escaped, believing his father will come back; as the months go by, however, and his father does not return, Alex begins to lose this dream. Nevertheless, Orlev is once again concerned with the story of survival. Against all hope Alex is able to find food, protect himself against a soldier, rig a clever hiding place, and even to occasionally escape from the Ghetto and meet a girl over on the Polish side of the wall. He refuses all chances of escaping the Ghetto entirely, for he is waiting for his father. In the end Alex's struggle to survive is successful, and his father does indeed return.

The power of this novel does not lie merely in its dramatic adventures and escapes, nor in its ability to depict life in the Ghetto—though both of these are important elements of the novel. Instead, the power of the book comes through Alex's unwavering hope, his sense that he will do whatever it takes to survive and wait for his father. All those he meets seem marked by desperation, as though they hide out with no real hope. But Alex hides out with hope, and that hope consequently gives him purpose.

The Man from the Other Side also depicts life in the Warsaw Ghetto, though here the story is not Orlev's, but that of his friend Marek, whom Orlev names as the protagonist. Marek's stepfather smuggles food to the Jews in the Ghetto by carrying it through the sewer system, and eventually Marek begins to help him. He seems to feel little sympathy for those on the other side of the wall, but this changes when his mother tells him that his father, who was killed under torture (another absent father), was Jewish. Marek suddenly feels a kinship with those in the Ghetto, and this leads

him to help hide Pan Jozek until the uprising in the Ghetto. Then he helps him return to the Ghetto to participate in the revolt, and Marek, who is trapped there with him, sees firsthand what has been happening all this time on the other side of the wall.

Each of these three novels uses a child protagonist to mediate the experience of the war. Each of the children are aware of what is happening to a limited extent; not until real separation comes upon them do they realize the enormity of the war. They deal with the horrors of the war through the imagination (like Yurik), or through finding someone to care for (like Alex and Marek), or through focusing on their family's life. But for each, the war forces itself upon them completely, utterly, and terrifyingly.

Like *The Island on Bird Street* and *The Man from the Other Side, Lydia, Queen of Palestine* uses a first-person narrator to show how a young child deals with the events of the war, this time in Romania. More than any other narrator, Lydia is unaware of what the war means. She does not seem to understand why she and her mother are growing poorer, why she is no longer allowed to attend the public school, or why the Iron Guard is dangerous. She too is faced with the prospect of surviving the war—this she does when her mother puts her on a train to Turkey and then to Palestine—but she must also survive the breakup of her family, as her father divorces her mother and heads off to Palestine on his own. This betrayal overshadows all else that has gone on before.

Much of the story is about Lydia's escape to Palestine and her life on a kibbutz, learning to adjust to an entirely new way of thinking. The caring community that surrounds her is in stark contrast to that of Bucharest. It takes some time before Lydia is able to accept this new community. Her defense against her losses lies in her imagination—she dreams of marrying the prince of Romania and becoming the queen of Palestine—and in her strong character, which is manipulative, assertive, and dominant. These are not qualities particularly useful on a kibbutz, but they are ones useful in surviving.

In each of these novels the war is always in the foreground. There are scenes of betrayal and loss of hope—the man who throws himself and his two children off a burning roof, the family that sits down at a beautiful meal to take poison and end their plight, the dying grandmother waiting to hear news of her granddaughter's escape, the two boys taken from a train leading to freedom and brought back to who knows what. But overpowering these are the stories of Yurik and Alex and Marek and Lydia who find the means to live and to remember and, perhaps like Orlev himself, to tell a story so their ordeals might not be forgotten.

—Gary D. Schmidt

———

ORWELL, George. Pseudonym for Eric (Arthur) Blair. British. Born of English parents in Motihari, Bengal (now Bihar), India, 25 June 1903; brought to England, 1904. Educated at a convent school, Henley-on-Thames, Oxfordshire; St. Cyprian's, Eastbourne, Sussex, 1911-16; Wellington School, 1917; Eton College, (King's Scholar), 1917-21. Served in the United Marxist Workers' Party militia in Catalonia, 1937; served on Aragon front during Spanish Civil War; became lieutenant. Wounded in action; served in the Home Guard, Local Defence Volunteers, 1940-43; served in England during World War II; became sergeant. Married 1) Eileen

O'Shaughnessy in 1936 (died 1945), one adopted son; 2) Sonia Brownell in 1949. Writer. Police officer for Indian Imperial Police in Burma at Police Training School, Rangoon, 1922-23, assistant superintendent of police at Myaungmya, 1923, Twante, 1924, Syriam, 1925, Insein, 1925-26, Moulmein, 1926, and Katha, 1927 (resigned 1927); dishwasher in Paris, France, 1929; teacher, The Hawthorns (private school), Hayes, Middlesex, England, 1932-33; teacher, Frays College (private school), Uxbridge, England, 1933; clerk, Booklovers' Corner (used book store), London, England, 1934-36; shopkeeper in Wallingford, Herfordshire, England, beginning in 1936; began as assistant, became producer of educational radio programs, British Broadcasting Corp. (BBC), London, 1941-43; literary editor, 1943-45, author of "As I Please" column, 1943-47, *Tribune,* London; correspondent in France, Germany, and England, 1945, *Observer,* London. *Died 21 January 1950.*

PUBLICATIONS

Novels

Burmese Days. New York, Harper, 1934; London, Gollancz, 1935.
A Clergyman's Daughter. London, Gollancz, 1935, New York, Harper, 1936.
Keep the Aspidistra Flying. London, Gollancz, 1936; New York, Harcourt, 1956.
Coming Up for Air. London, Gollancz, 1939; New York, Harcourt, 1950.
Animal Farm: A Fairy Story. London, Secker & Warburg, 1945, New York, Harcourt, 1946.
1984. London, Secker & Warburg, and New York, Harcourt, 1949; edited by Bernard Crick, Oxford, Oxford University Press, 1984.

Other

Down and Out in Paris and London. London, Gollancz, and New York, Harper, 1933.
The Road to Wigan Pier. London, Gollancz, 1937; New York, Harcourt, 1958.
Homage to Catalonia. London, Secker & Warburg, 1938; New York, Harcourt, 1952.
Inside the Whale, and Other Essays. London, Gollancz, 1940.
The Lion and the Unicorn: Socialism and the English Genius. London, Secker & Warburg, 1941; New York, AMS Press, 1976.
Editor, *Talking to India: A Selection of English Language Broadcasts to India.* London, Allen & Unwin, 1943.
Critical Essays. London, Secker & Warburg, 1946; as *Dickens, Dali, and Others: Studies in Popular Culture,* New York, Reynal, 1946.
James Burnham and the Managerial Revolution. London, Socialist Book Centre, 1946.
The English People. London, Collins, 1947; New York, Haskell House, 1974.
Editor, *British Pamphleteers 1: From the Sixteenth Century to the French Revolution.* London, Wingate, 1948.
Shooting an Elephant, and Other Essays. London, Secker & Warburg, and New York, Harcourt, 1950.
Such, Such Were the Joys. New York, Harcourt, 1953; as *England Your England, and Other Essays,* London, Secker & Warburg, 1953.
A Collection of Essays. New York, Doubleday, 1954.

The Orwell Reader, edited by Richard H. Rovere. New York, Harcourt, 1956.
Selected Essays. London, Penguin, 1957; as *Inside the Whale and Other Essays,* 1975.
Selected Writings, edited by George Bott. London, Heinemann, 1958.
Collected Essays. London, Secker & Warburg, 1961.
Decline of English Murder and Other Essays. London, Penguin, 1965.
The Collected Essays, Journalism, and Letters of George Orwell, 4 vols., edited by wife, Sonia Orwell, and Ian Angus. London, Secker & Warburg, and New York, Harcourt, 1968.
The Complete Works. New York, Harcourt, 17 vols., 1984.
The War Broadcasts and *The War Commentaries,* edited by W.J. West. London, British Broadcasting Corp. Publications-Duckworth, 2 vols., 1985; as *George Orwell: The Lost Writings,* New York, Avon, 1988.

Radio Plays: *The Voyage of the Beagle,* from work by Darwin, 1946; *Animal Farm,* from his own novel, 1947.

*

Media Adaptations: *Animal Farm* (animated film), 1955; *Animal Farm* (play by Nelson Slade Bond), Samuel French, 1964; *1984* (films), 1956 and 1984; *1984* (play), Dramatic Publishing, 1963.

Biography: Entry in *Dictionary of Literary Biography,* Volume 15: *British Novelists, 1930-1959,* Detroit, Gale, 1983.

Manuscript Collection: University College, London.

Critical Studies (selection): *George Orwell* by Tom Hopkinson, London, Longman, 1953, revised edition, 1962; *George Orwell: A Literary Study* by John Atkins, London, Calder & Boyars, 1954, New York, Ungar, 1955, revised edition, London, Calder & Boyars, 1971; *A Study of George Orwell, The Man and His Works* by Christopher Hollis, London, Hollis & Carter, and Chicago, Regnery, 1956; *The Crystal Spirit: A Study of George Orwell* by George Woodcock, Boston, Little Brown, 1966, London, Cape, 1967; *The Making of George Orwell: A Study in Literary History* by Keith Alldritt, London, Arnold, and New York, St. Martin's Press, 1969; *Orwell's Fiction* by Robert A. Lee, Notre Dame, Indiana, University of Notre Dame Press, 1969; *The World of George Orwell* edited by Miriam Gross, London, Weidenfeld and Nicolson, 1971, New York, Simon & Schuster, 1972; *Orwell* by Raymond Williams, London, Fontana, and New York, Viking Press, 1971, and *George Orwell: A Collection of Critical Essays* edited by Williams, Englewood Cliffs, New Jersey, Prentice Hall, 1974; *The Unknown Orwell* by Peter Stansky and William Abrahams, London, Constable, and New York, Knopf, 1972, *Orwell: The Transformation* by Stansky, London, Constable, 1979, New York, Knopf, 1980, and *On Nineteen Eighty-Four* edited by Stansky, New York, Freeman, 1984; *A Reader's Guide to George Orwell,* London, Thames & Hudson, 1975, Totowa, New Jersey, Rowman & Littlefield, 1977, and *George Orwell: The Critical Heritage,* London, Routledge, 1975, both edited by Jeffrey Meyers; *George Orwell and the Origins of 1984* by William Steinhoff, Ann Arbor, University of Michigan Press, 1975, as *The Road to 1984,* London, Weidenfeld & Nicolson, 1975; *The Road to Miniluv: George Orwell, The State and God* by Christopher Small, London, Gollancz, 1975, Pittsburgh, University of Pittsburgh Press, 1976; *Primal Dream and*

Primal Scream: Orwell's Development as a Psychological Novelist by Richard I. Smyer, Columbia, University of Missouri Press, 1979; *George Orwell: A Life* by Bernard Crick, London, Secker & Warburg, 1980, Boston, Little Brown, 1981, revised edition, Secker & Warburg, 1981, and *Orwell Remembered* by Crick and Audrey Coppard, London, BBC, and New York, Facts on File, 1984; *Approaching 1984* by Donald McCormick, Newton Abbot, Devon, David and Charles, 1980; *George Orwell: The Road to 1984* by Peter Lewis, London, Heinemann, 1981; *George Orwell: A Personal Memoir* by T.R. Fyvel, London, Weidenfeld & Nicolson, 1982; *A George Orwell Companion* by J.R. Hammond, London, Macmillan, and New York, St. Martin's Press, 1982; *George Orwell's Guide through Hell: A Psychological Study of 1984* by Robert Plank, San Bernardino, California, Borgo Press, 1984; *Orwell: The Road to Airstrip One* by Ian Slater, New York, Norton, 1985; *George Orwell and the Problem of Authentic Existence* by Michael Carter, London, and Dover, New Hampshire, Croom Helm, 1985; *Critical Essays on George Orwell* edited by Bernard Oldsey, Boston, Hall, 1986; *Reflections on America, 1984: An Orwell Symposium* edited by Robert Mulvihill, Athens, University of Georgia Press, 1986; *George Orwell: The Age's Adversary*, New York, Macmillan, 1986, and *Nineteen Eighty-four: Past, Present, and Future*, Boston, Twayne, 1989, both by Patrick Reilly; *A Preface to Orwell* by David Wykes, London, and New York, Longman, 1987; *The Diminished Self: Orwell and the Loss of Freedom* by Mark Connelly, Pittsburgh Pennsylvania, Duquesne University Press, 1987; *George Orwell* edited by Courtney T. Wemyss and Alexej Ugrinsky, New York, Greenwood 1987; *George Orwell* by Averil Gardner, Boston, Twayne, 1987; *George Orwell: A Reassessment* edited by Peter Buitenhuis and I.B. Nadel, New York, Macmillan, 1988; *Orwell and the Politics of Despair: A Critical Study of the Writings of George Orwell* by Alok Rai, Cambridge, Cambridge University Press, 1988; *George Orwell* by Alok Rai, Cambridge, Cambridge University Press, 1988; *George Orwell* by Nigel Flynn, Hove, Wayland, 1989, Vero Beach, Florida, Rourke, 1990; *The Politics of Literary Reputation: The Making and Claiming of "St. George Orwell"* by John Rodden, Oxford, Oxford University Press, 1990.

*   *   *

Only George Orwell's last two novels have been much read by young adults, and these were, of course, the two that enjoyed the greatest fame and largest sales: *Animal Farm* and *1984*. Together they gave Orwell an international reputation. When concentrating on these works, it can't be ignored that some young readers have also enjoyed the earlier books, such as the nostalgic *Coming Up for Air;* the various documentaries and the vivid prose sketches, like "Shooting an Elephant"; and the autobiographical account of his schooldays, *Such, Such Were the Joys.*

Animal Farm is a brief, simple fable about the animals of Manor Farm who unite in rebellion against the cruelties and exploitation of the farmer, Mr. Jones, drive out him and his men, and set about running the farm themselves. Inspired by the example of Boxer, the hard-working horse, they survive difficulties and make the experiment in equality and cooperation prosper. However, as the years pass, the pigs, cleverest of the animals, gradually assume more and more power as a new elite under their leader Napoleon. The revolutionary ideals of equality are replaced by a new hierarchy, and the slogan "All animals are equal" is extended by the clause, often quoted since, "but some animals are more equal than others." At the end, the farm reverts to its original title, Napoleon restores relation-

ships with the human farmers, and when the other creatures peep in the farmhouse windows they "looked from pig to man...but already it was impossible to say which was which." It is a pessimistic ending for a fable, and the nearest we get to a moral is the opinion of the choreic donkey, Benjamin, that "life would go on as it had always gone on—that is, badly." Particularly at its time of publication *Animal Farm* was seen by many readers as an anti-Communist tract, in which Snowball represented Trotsky and Napoleon was Stalin. Certainly this satirical fable about the nature of totalitarian societies was rooted in Orwell's experiences in Spain and his awareness of Bolshevik methods, but it can be read too simply as an allegory of the Russian revolution. Squealer represents any propagandist and, significantly, the book has been banned in countries of very different political persuasions. In *Animal Farm,* Orwell simplified the style he had used in earlier novels, writing in direct, concrete terms, largely avoiding metaphor, and using the vigorous language of speech. He himself said that it was the first book in which he had consciously tried "to fuse political purpose and artistic purpose in one whole."

Four years later came *1984* and the title has become a symbolic shorthand sign for totalitarian oppression. Written by a dying man and based on the work of the Russian author Zamyatin, it is a chilling picture of how the power of the state could come to dominate the lives of individuals through cultural conditioning. Perhaps the most powerful science fiction novel of this century, this apocalyptic Swiftian satire shows with grim conviction how Winston's individual personality is wiped out and how he is recreated in the Party's image, until he does not just obey but even loves Big Brother. There is an intense personal feeling throughout the novel and some critics have related Winston Smith's sufferings to those Orwell underwent at preparatory school, about which he wrote so passionately just before *1984*. Orwell said that the book was written with the explicit intention "to alter other people's idea of the kind of society they should strive after."

1984 is a dystopia, a negative utopia, in which a single, self-perpetuating elite has replaced all earlier forms of social and political hierarchy, ruling over a submissive slave class and maintaining a convenient warring balance between the three power blocks into which the world is divided. The monstrous O'Brien expresses the gospel of eternal power that Hitler had preached in extreme form. The opening is superbly economical. After the arresting first sentence ("It was a bright cold day in April, and the clocks were striking thirteen") Orwell swiftly sketches in all the major themes of the book in scenes based on the shabby, rationed London of the post-war years but transmuted into a Kafkaesque nightmare in which War is Peace, Freedom is Slavery, Ignorance is Strength. Orwell's mistrust of empty political slogans is even more graphically conveyed in the linguistic destructiveness of the Ministry of Truth than in the changing proclamations of *Animal Farm.* One central theme is the idea that the destruction of language underlies all other destructive social changes, and that the real purpose of Newspeak was "to make all other modes of thought impossible," to cancel the past. Winston's doomed love for Julia, expressed in terms of fleeting memories, eventually exposes the fallacy of her belief that "they can't get inside you."

Apart from arguments about the quality of his writing, there has been much debate about Orwell's last two major books. Are they simply negative, lacking any positive view? Is he a propagandist rather than a true novelist? Is his pessimism about the future justified or is he simply uttering a warning? Does he show a lack of belief in the qualities and the resistance of ordinary people, the proles? However we answer these questions, it is undeniable that his books have sharpened our awareness of the issues and that many of his words and ideas (Big Brother, more equal than others, double think) have become part of the way in which we ourselves think today.

—Robert Protherough

————

P

———

PARK, (Rosina) Ruth (Lucia). Australian. Born in Auckland, New Zealand. Educated at St. Benedict's College; University of Auckland; New Zealand University. Married the writer D'Arcy Niland in 1942 (died 1967); five children. Proofreader and editor of children's page, Auckland *Star;* editor of children's page, *Zealandia,* Auckland; welfare worker in Auckland; reporter, *Sydney Mirror,* Australia, since 1941; scriptwriter, Twentieth Century-Fox, London, England; free-lance writer and journalist. Recipient: *Sydney Morning Herald* prize, 1948, for *The Harp in the South;* runner-up in Australian Book of the Year award, 1975, for *Callie's Castle;* Miles Franklin award, for novel, 1978; Australian Children's Book Council Book of the Year award, 1981, *Boston Globe-Horn Book* award, 1982, runner-up, Guardian, 1982, IBBY honour list (author), 1982, and Parents' Choice, 1982, all for *Playing Beatie Bow;* Premier's award, 1981; Young Australian's Best Book award for picture story book, 1986, for *When the Wind Changed.* Agent: Curtis Brown, P.O. Box 19, Paddington, NSW 2021, Australia.

PUBLICATIONS FOR YOUNG ADULTS

Fiction

The Hole in the Hill, illustrated by Jennifer Murray. Sydney, Ure Smith, 1961; London, Macmillan, 1962; as *Secret of the Maori Cave,* New York, Doubleday, 1964.
The Ship's Cat, illustrated by Richard Kennedy. London, Macmillan, and New York, St. Martin's Press, 1961.
The Road to Christmas, illustrated by Noela Young. London, Macmillan, and New York, St. Martin's Press, 1962.
The Road under the Sea, illustrated by Jennifer Murray. Sydney; Ure Smith, 1962; London, Macmillan, 1963; New York, Doubleday, 1966.
The Shaky Island, illustrated by Iris Millington. London, Constable, and New York, McKay, 1962.
Uncle Matt's Mountain, illustrated by Laurence Broderick. London, Macmillan, and New York, St. Martin's Press, 1962.
Airlift for Grandee, illustrated by Sheila Hawkins. London, Macmillan, and New York, St. Martin's Press, 1964.
Ring for the Sorcerer, illustrated by William Stobbs. Sydney, Horwitz Martin, 1967.
The Sixpenny Island, illustrated by David Cox. Syndey, Ure Smith, and London, Macmillan, 1968; as *Ten-Cent Island,* illustrated by Robert Frankenberg, New York, Doubleday, 1968.
Nuki and the Sea Serpent: A Maori Story, illustrated by Zelma Blakely. London, Longman, 1969.
The Runaway Bus, illustrated by Peter Tierney. Sydney, Hodder & Stoughton, 1969.
Callie's Castle, illustrated by Kilmeny Niland. Sydney and London, Angus & Robertson, 1974.

The Gigantic Balloon, illustrated by Kilmeny and Deborah Niland. Sydney, Collins, 1975; London, Collins, and New York, Parents' Magazine Press, 1976.
Come Danger, Come Darkness. Sydney and London, Hodder & Stoughton, 1978.
Playing Beatie Bow. Melbourne, Nelson, 1980; London, Kestrel, 1981; New York, Atheneum, 1982.
When the Wind Changed, illustrated by Deborah Niland. Sydney, Collins, 1980; New York, Coward McCann, 1981.
The Big Brass Key, illustrated by Noela Young. Sydney, Hodder & Stoughton, 1983.
My Sister Sif. Ringwood, Victoria, Viking Kestrel, 1986; London, Viking Kestrel, 1987; New York, Viking, 1991.
Callie's Family, illustrated by Kilmeny Niland. Sydney, Angus & Robertson, 1988; Lodnon, Angus & Robertson, 1989.
James, illustrated by Deborah Niland. Ringwood, Victoria, Viking O'Neil, 1988.
Things in Corners (short stories). Ringwood, Victoria, and New York, Viking, 1989.
A Fence around the Cuckoo. Ringwood, Victoria, Viking, 1992.

PUBLICATIONS FOR CHILDREN

Fiction

The Muddle-Headed Wombat, illustrated by Noela Young. Sydney, Educational Press, 1962; London, Angus & Robertson, 1963.
The Muddle-Headed Wombat on Holiday, illustrated by Noela Young. Sydney, Educational Press, and London, Angus and Robertson, 1964.
The Muddle-Headed Wombat in the Treetops, illustrated by Noela Young. Sydney, Educational Press, and London, Angus & Robertson, 1965.
The Muddle-Headed Wombat at School, illustrated by Noela Young. Sydney, Educational Press, and London, Angus & Robertson, 1966.
The Muddle-Headed Wombat in the Snow, illustrated by Noela Young. Sydney, Educational Press, and London, Angus & Robertson, 1966.
The Muddle-Headed Wombat on a Rainy Day, illustrated by Noela Young. Sydney, Educational Press, 1969; London, Angus & Robertson, 1970.
The Muddle-Headed Wombat in the Springtime, illustrated by Noela Young. Sydney, Educational Press, and London, Angus & Robertson, 1970.
The Muddle-Headed Wombat on the River, illustrated by Noela Young. Sydney, Educational Press, and London, Angus & Robertson, 1971.
The Muddle-Headed Wombat and the Bush Band, illustrated by Noela Young. Sydney, Angus & Robertson, 1973.
The Muddle-Headed Wombat and the Invention, illustrated by Noela Young. London, Angus & Robertson, 1975.
The Muddle-Headed Wombat on Clean-Up Day, illustrated by Noela Young. Sydney and London, Angus & Robertson, 1976.

The Adventures of the Muddle-Headed Wombat, illustrated by Noela Young. Sydney, Angus & Robertson, 1979; London, Angus & Robertson, 1980.
The Muddle-Headed Wombat Is Very Bad, illustrated by Noela Young. Sydney, Angus & Robertson, 1981.
The Muddle-Headed Wombat Stays at Home, illustrated by Noela Young. Sydney, Angus & Robertson, 1982.

Plays

The Uninvited Guest. Sydney and London, Angus & Robertson, 1948.
Radio Plays: *The Muddle-Headed Wombat* series.

Poetry

Roger Bandy, illustrated by Deborah and Kilmeny Niland. Adelaide, Rigby, 1977.

Other

Merchant Campbell, illustrated by Edwina Bell. Sydney, Collins, 1976.

PUBLICATIONS FOR ADULTS

Novels

The Harp in the South. Sydney, Angus & Robertson, London, Jospeh, and Boston, Houghton Mifflin, 1948.
Poor Man's Orange. Sydney, Angus & Robertson, 1949; London, Joseph, 1950; as *12 1/2 Plymouth Street,* Boston, Houghton Mifflin, 1951.
The Witch's Thorn. Sydney, Angus & Robertson, 1951; London, Joseph, and Boston, Houghton Mifflin, 1952.
A Power of Roses. Sydney, Angus & Robertson, and London, Joseph, 1953.
Pink Flannel. Sydney, Angus & Robertson, 1955; as *Dear Hearts and Gentle People,* Ringwood, Victoria, Penguin, 1981.
One-a-Pecker, Two-a-pecker. Sydney, Angus & Robertson, 1957; London, Joseph, 1958; as *Frost and the Fire,* Boston, Houghton Mifflin, 1958; London, Pan, 1962.
The Good-Looking Women. Sydney, Angus & Robertson, 1961; London, Joseph, 1962.
Serpent's Delight. New York, Doubleday, 1962.
Swords and Crowns and Rings. Melbourne, Nelson, 1977; London, Joseph, and New York, St. Martin's Press, 1978.
Missus. Melbourne, Nelson, and London, Joseph, 1985; New York, St. Martin's Press, 1987.

Plays

The Harp in the South, with Leslie Rees, adaptation of the novel by Park (broadcast 1949). Montmorency, Victoria, Yackandandah, 1987.

Radio Play: *The Harp in the South,* with Leslie Rees, 1949.

Television Play: *No Decision,* with D'Arcy Niland, 1964.

Other

The Drums Go Bang (autobiographical), with D'Arcy Niland. Sydney, Angus & Roberston, 1956.
Tales of the South. London, Macmillan, 1961.
The Companion Guide to Sydney. Sydney and London, Collins, 1973; New York, Scribner, 1976.
Flights of Angels. Melbourne, Nelson, 1981.
Norfolk Island and Lord Howe Island. Dover Heights, New South Wales, Serendip, 1982.
The Sydney We Love, with Cedric Emanuel. Melbourne, Nelson, 1983.
The Tasmania We Love. with Cedric Emmanuel. Melbourne, Nelson, 1987.

*   *   *

For a writer to be immensely popular and still receive critical acclaim is a difficult feat in Australia, where commercial success is sometimes viewed with suspicion, but Ruth Park is an exception. Her compelling narratives are so seductive they make readers gallop to the conclusion. With the exception of the family stories *Callie's Castle* and its sequel, her other writing is not easily pigeonholed, being variously a combination of history, fantasy, romance, and adventure. *My Sister Sif,* for example, is set in the future, features merpeople and underwater cities, has an ecological theme and a subplot about the sacrifices one makes for love.

Already famous for her adult novels and the "Muddle-Headed Wombat" series for children, Park achieved the special distinction of producing a classic in young adult fiction with the publication of *Playing Beatie Bow,* a time-slip novel set in The Rocks, an old harbourside Sydney suburb. *Playing Beatie Bow* is about the growing up of fourteen-year-old Abigail Kirk. When she was ten Abigail's father had left his wife and daughter for another woman but now wants the family back together again. Abigail is outraged that her mother could consider it, "He whistles and back she goes like a well-trained dog." In a mood of resentment and twisted pride Abigail, through the agency of a spooky children's game, Beatie Bow, finds herself in the hard, dangerous world of nineteenth-century Sydney. Here she sees life from a different perspective and experiences love. The extraordinarily vivid re-creation of colonial Sydney in this book is arguably the high-point of Park's writing.

Confronting change in oneself and those around you is the emotional core of Ruth Park's writing for young adult readers. The young heroines and heroes are usually puzzled and angered by adult perspectives on love or other relationships and through unsettling experiences of their own become more knowledgeable and therefore accepting of human foibles. In the short story "Where Freedom Is" from *Things in Corners* the troubled hero Gideon reflects, "It came to him then that when you're a small kid you don't realise much. You just are. But the time comes when you know what you're feeling, you can describe it, or take steps to change things." Facing hidden things is the major theme of the five stories in this fine collection of spooky tales. In the title story, illness prompts Theo to partly recall suppressed childhood memories of life with his mother before he was adopted. These memories take on the form of a frightening creature that inhabits lifts (elevators). That this is not a sombre tale of psychological disfunction but rather a wise, moving, and funny story says much for Park's storytelling ability.

Callie, the heroine of *Callie's Castle* and *Callie's Family,* needs solitude before she can understand why her once trouble-free life now seems tainted. She has fought with her best friend, is irritable with her mother, hates her once loved teacher, and is plagued by her younger siblings. Then Grandpa Cameron comes back into Callie's life and sees that she needs a place to herself, and so she gets the beautiful cupola—a feature of the family's new house—and gains a new perspective on change and relationships. Similarly Riko in *My Sister Sif* faces changes in the people she loves best. Riko and her sister, Sif, are part merpeople, part "landcrabs." Sif longs for the sea, but Riko is torn between two lifestyles. Linked to this is a strong message about environmental damage in the ocean.

Thirteen-year-old Otter Cannon, in the historical adventure novel *Come Danger, Come Darkness,* fights difficulties in others rather than within himself. He knows what he wants to be, a surgeon. However the Cannons are always soldiers and strict Uncle Daniel, Commandant of the penal colony Norfolk Island, is determined Otter will follow the family line. But apart from this battle, Otter is also planning the escape of a convict, Corny Stack, a childhood friend and retainer from the family estate in Ireland.

Park's first novel for older children, *The Hole in the Hill,* is an exciting adventure tale about two Australian children, Brownie and Dunk, who discover some extraordinary caves, the source of the terrifying noise heard on their dead uncle's New Zealand farm. The caves prove to be a special place for the Maoris. Although a particularly fine book of its type, it lacks the emotional depth of her more recent work. The fact that Park's first novel, *The Harp in the South,* has now been republished in a condensed version for younger readers, points to a change in what is thought acceptable adolescent reading and to the attraction of her adult novels for this readership.

—Kerry White

PATERSON, Katherine (Womeldorf). American. Born in Qing Jiang, China, 31 October 1932; came to the United States, 1940. Educated at King College, Bristol, Tennessee, 1950-54, A.B. (summa cum laude) 1954; Presbyterian School of Christian Education, Richmond, Virginia, 1955-57, M.A. 1957; Kobe School of Japanese Language, Japan, 1957-60; Union Theological Seminary, New York, 1961-62, M.R.E. 1962. Married John Barstow Paterson in 1962; two sons and two adopted daughters. Public school teacher, Lovettsville, Virginia, 1954-55; missionary, Presbyterian Church Board of World Missions, Nashville, Tennessee, and in Shikoku Island, Japan, 1957-62; teacher of Sacred Studies and English, Pennington School for Boys, Pennington, New Jersey, 1963-65; writer. Recipient: American Library Association (ALA) Notable Children's Book award, 1974, for *Of Nightingales That Weep;* ALA Notable Children's Book award, 1976, National Book award for Children's Literature, 1977, runner-up for Edgar Allan Poe award (juvenile division) from Mystery Writers of America, 1977, and American Book award nomination, children's fiction paperback, 1982, all for *The Master Puppeteer;* ALA Notable Children's Book award, 1977, John Newbery Medal, 1978, Lewis Carroll Shelf award, 1978, and Division II runner-up, Michigan Young Reader's award, 1980, all for *Bridge to Terabithia;* Lit.D., King College, 1978; ALA Notable Children's Book award, 1978, National Book award for

Children's Literature, 1979, Christopher award (ages 9-12), 1979, Newbery Honor Book, 1979, CRABbery (Children Raving About Books) Honor Book, 1979, American Book award nominee, children's paperback, 1980, William Allen White Children's Book award, 1981, Garden State Children's Book award, younger division, New Jersey Library Association, 1981, Georgia Children's Book award, 1981, Iowa Children's Choice award, 1981, Massachusetts Children's Book award (elementary), 1981, all for *The Great Gilly Hopkins;* D.H.L.: Otterbein College, Westerville, Ohio, 1980; U.S. nominee, Hans Christian Andersen award, 1980; *New York Times* Outstanding Book List, 1980, Newbery Medal, 1981, CRABbery Honor Book, 1981, American Book award nominee, children's hardcover, 1981, children's paperback, 1982, and Hans Christian Andersen award nominee, 1990, all for *Jacob Have I Loved; The Crane Wife* was named to the *New York Times* Outstanding Books and Best Illustrated Books lists, both 1981; Saint Mary-of-the-Woods College, Indiana, 1981; University of Maryland College Park, 1982; Washington and Lee University, Lexington, Virginia, 1982; Parent's Choice award, Parent's Choice Foundation, 1983, for *Rebels of the Heavenly Kingdom;* Irvin Kerlan award, 1983, "in recognition of singular attainments in the creation of children's literature"; University of Southern Mississippi School of Library Service Silver Medallion, 1983, for outstanding contributions to the field of children's literature; *New York Times* notable book citation and "Parent's Choice" citation, both 1985, for *Come Sing, Jimmy Jo;* nominee, Laura Ingalls Wilder award, 1986; Winchester, Virginia, 1986; Regina Medal award, Catholic Library Association, 1988, for demonstrating "the timeless standards and ideals for the writing of good literature for children"; *Boston Globe-Horn Book* award, 1991, for *The Tale of the Mandarin Ducks.* Agent: c/o E.P. Dutton, 2 Park Avenue, New York, NY 10016, U.S.A. Lives in Norfolk, Virginia.

PUBLICATIONS FOR YOUNG ADULTS

Fiction

The Sign of the Chrysanthemum, illustrated by Peter Landa. New York, Crowell Junior Books, 1973; London, Kestrel, 1975.
Of Nightingales That Weep, illustrated by Haru Wells. New York, Crowell Junior Books, 1974; London, Kestrel, 1976.
The Master Puppeteer, illustrated by Haru Wells. New York, Crowell Junior Books, 1976.
Bridge to Terabithia, illustrated by Donna Diamond. New York, Crowell Junior Books, 1977; London, Gollancz, 1978.
The Great Gilly Hopkins. New York, Crowell Junior Books, 1978; London, Gollancz, 1979.
Jacob Have I Loved. New York, Crowell Junior Books, 1980; London, Gollancz, 1981.
Rebels of the Heavenly Kingdom. New York, Lodestar, 1983.
Come Sing, Jimmy Jo. New York, Lodestar, 1985; London, Gollancz, 1986.
Park's Quest. New York, Lodestar, 1988; London, Gollancz, 1989.
Lyddie. New York, Dutton, 1991.

Other

Who Am I?, illustrated by David Stone. Richmond, CLC Press, 1966.
Justice for All People. New York, Friendship, 1973.

To Make Men Free: Learning Center Box. Richmond, John Knox, 1973.

Translator, *The Crane Wife,* by Sumiko Yagawa, illustrated by Suekichi Akaba. New York, Morrow, 1981.

Consider the Lilies: Flowers of the Bible, with husband, John Paterson, illustrated by Anne Ophelia Dowden. New York, Crowell Junior Books, 1986.

Translator, *Tongue-Cut Sparrow* (Japanese folktale), retold by Momoko Ishii, illustrated by Suekichi Akaba. New York, Lodestar, 1987.

PUBLICATIONS FOR CHILDREN

Fiction

Angels and Other Strangers: Family Christmas Stories. New York, Crowell Junior Books, 1979; as *Star of Night: Stories for Christmas,* London, Gollancz, 1980.

The Smallest Cow in the World, illustrated by Jane Clark Brown. Burlington, Vermont Migrant Education Program, 1988.

The Tale of the Mandarin Ducks, illustrated by Leo and Diane Dillon. New York, Dutton, 1990.

The King's Equal, illustrated by Vladimir Vagin. New York, HarperCollins, 1992.

Editor, with Ann Durell and Jean Craighead George, *The Big Book for the Planet.* New York, Dutton, 1993.

PUBLICATIONS FOR ADULTS

Other

Gates of Excellence: On Reading and Writing Books for Children. New York, Elsevier Nelson, 1981.

The Spying Heart: More Thoughts on Reading and Writing Books for Children. New York, Lodestar, 1989.

*

Media Adaptations: "Bridge to Terabithia" (listening record or cassette; filmstrip with cassette), Miller-Brody, 1978, (filmstrip), Random House/Miller-Brody, 1980, (film), PBS-TV, 1985; *The Great Gilly Hopkins* (film), Hanna-Barbera, 1980, (listening record or cassette; filmstrip with cassette), Random House; "Angels and Other Strangers" (cassette), Random House; "Jacob Have I Loved" (listening cassette; filmstrip with cassette), Random House, 1982, (film) PBS-TV, 1990; "Getting Hooked on Books: Challenges" (filmstrip with cassette, with teacher's guide, contains "The Great Gilly Hopkins"), Guidance Associates, 1986.

Biography: Entry in *Fifth Book of Junior Authors and Illustrators,* Bronx, New York, Wilson, 1983; entry in *Dictionary of Literary Biography,* Volume 52: *American Writers for Children since 1960: Fiction,* Detroit, Gale, 1986, pp. 296-314; essay in *Authors and Artists for Young Adults,* Volume 1, Detroit, Gale, 1989; essay in *Speaking for Ourselves: Autobiographical Sketches by Notable Authors of Books for Young Adults,* Volume 1, compiled and edited by Donald R. Gallo, National Council of Teachers of English, 1990.

Manuscript Collection: Kerlan Collection, University of Minnesota, Minneapolis.

Critical Studies: Entry in *Children's Literature Review,* Volume 7, Detroit, Gale, 1984; entry in *Contemporary Literary Criticism,* Detroit, Gale, Volume 12, 1980; Volume 30, 1984.

Katherine Paterson comments:

I write as a way to struggle with the questions that life throws at me. I write for the young because we seem to be wrestling with the same questions.

*   *   *

In her own work on writing, *Gates of Excellence: On Reading and Writing Books for Children,* Paterson stresses the importance of writers "telling a story." And that, Katherine Paterson herself does very well. She did not set out to become a writer and was not particularly encouraged as a writer by her early teachers. Although she began writing seriously in 1964, she did not publish her first novel until 1973. In spite of her protest about not being a natural storyteller, she indeed is. Her books and speeches are laden with anecdotes about herself, family, and friends. Paterson's use of metaphors from country cooking, popular culture, nature, and the Bible brings life and poetic imagery to her characters and settings. Although she was born in China and spent her early childhood there, Paterson comes out of the southern tradition of writing. In a talk she gave at Simmons College, Paterson attributed three dominant influences to her development as a writer—her birth in China and later missionary years in Japan, her growing up in the American South, and her strong Biblical heritage.

Her fiction defies categorization as either intended for children or young adults. Her love and concern for children is demonstrated in her own life. She and her husband adopted one child and have taken in foster children. Paterson's passion for children is also evident in her speeches to various groups around the country.

Drawing on her knowledge of Japanese history and culture, Paterson's first three young adult novels are set in feudal Japan. *The Sign of the Chrysanthemum* takes place in twelfth-century Japan. Muna is a young orphan who sets out to find his samurai father and thus his identity. *Of Nightingales That Weep* and *The Master Puppeteer* are also set in medieval Japan. These novels are highly regarded for their accurate depiction of Japanese history and culture, particularly the features of the puppet theater in the latter. *The Master Puppeteer* received the Edgar Allan Poe Special Award from the Mystery Writers of American and the National Book Award in 1982. The sense of place and time is aptly conveyed by Paterson in all three novels, evident through her use of significant authentic details to set scene and atmosphere. Both *The Master Puppeteer* and *Of Nightingales that Weep* have also been praised by critics for their skillfully constructed plots, supported by strong characterizations.

Bridge to Terabithia, her fourth novel, is a shift from the historical fiction genre to a contemporary setting. It is the story of two fifth graders who become best friends and is based in part on the experience of Paterson's younger son whose best friend dies. Jesse and Leslie, the two main characters from very different backgrounds, spend much of their time together creating a fantasy world, Terabithia. The strength of *Bridge to Terabithia* lies in the convincing portrayal of the unusual relationship between Jesse and Leslie. But the novel presents an unromantic, realistic, and moving reaction to personal tragedy, demonstrating Paterson's skill in dealing with one of the most difficult topics in young adult literature — death. Jess and Leslie are effectively developed as characters that young readers might well recognize as classmates who sit next to them or ride on the same school bus. After the crushing blow of Leslie's death, rather than lingering on the lost friendship, Paterson allows Jesse to move toward maturity as he passes Terabithia on to his younger sister, May Belle. *Bridge to Terabithia* brought Paterson the literary and critical recognition that her earlier historical novels had not been able to do.

In 1978, *The Great Gilly Hopkins* was published, based on Paterson's personal experience as a foster mother, marking Paterson's entrance into the young adult social problem novel. Gilly, an eleven-year-old, like many of Paterson's earlier characters is in search of a parent, a common theme in her novels. Gilly has learned to survive the many foster homes in which she has been placed. She fights against any sign of love or care by lying and swearing, her defense from being emotionally hurt. Some critics felt the novel did not measure up to Paterson's previous *Bridge to Terabithia*. While the emotional impact of the novel is a very different one, Gilly does pull at the emotional strings of the reader. In spite of the critics' claims of shortcomings, the novel gained the attention of numerous awards and was named a Newbery Award Honor Book and earned Paterson a second National Book Award.

Jacob Have I Loved is set on the imaginary Chesapeake Island of Rass. The title of the novel refers to the Biblical story of the twins Jacob and Esau and is a story of the bitter jealousy of twin sisters, Louise and Caroline. The setting of the novel on an isolated Chesapeake Island contributes to and intensifies the theme of sibling rivalry between the twins. Unlike Paterson's earlier novels, it is written from the first person point of view, through Sarah Louise "Wheeze's" eyes. Some critics took Paterson to task on the first-person narrative suggesting that the first-person narrative loses some of its momentum as the main characters mature into adulthood. The voices of other reviewers and critics clearly praised the depth of characterization and the vitality and freshness in the writing style. *Jacob Have I Loved* garnered a second Newbery award for Paterson in 1980.

Returning to her historical fiction writing roots, Paterson in 1983 wrote *Rebels of the Heavenly Kingdom,* set in mid-nineteenth-century China. It is the story of Wang Lee who becomes an impassioned warrior of the Heavenly Kingdon, killing wantonly and bloodily, convinced that the cause of the kingdom is greater than individual human life. Paterson again faithfully demonstrates her knowledge of Oriental culture and history.

Paterson returns to the theme of the "quest for parents" in *Come Sing, Jimmy Jo* and *Park's Quest. Come Sing, Jimmy Jo* follows the musical achievements of shy, gifted mountain boy James Johnson, who later becomes "Jimmy Jo" in the world of country music. The novel did not receive the critical acclaim of Paterson's earlier works. *Park's Quest,* on the other hand, received wide acclaim with some reviewers calling it her best work. Park is the son of a pilot killed during the Vietnam war and his quest is to find out the kind of man his father was. The novel has been praised for its realistic portrayal of characters and sensitive treatment of a touchy event in our country's history.

Paterson's latest novel for young adults is *Lyddie,* a historical novel set in New England. The novel received glowing critical acclaim. Its riveting plot, engaging characters, and a New England setting make it a true grit story. The strength of the novel rests with its superb characterization. The spirited portrayal of Lyddie Worten serves as a model of hope for teenage readers.

Paterson's contribution to the field of young adult literature has been immeasurable. She not only knows how to "tell a good story" but does it in way that is challenging to her young adult audience. Paterson does not write about the trite; instead, she zeroes in on events and characters that ring true to life. She does not always choose to write about people and events that are uplifting, and the "happy ending" resolution so typical of many young adult novels cannot be applied to hers. It is this honesty that has gained her not only critical acclaim but the devoted following of young adult readers today.

—Donald J. Kenney

PATON WALSH, Jill. British. Born in London, England, 29 April 1937. Educated at St. Michael's Convent, North Finchley, London, 1943-55; St. Anne's College, Oxford, 1955-59, Dip. Ed. 1959, M.A. (honours) in English. Married Antony Edmund Paton Walsh in 1961; one son and two daughters. English teacher, Enfield Girls Grammar School, Middlesex, 1959-62; writer, since 1962. Whittall Lecturer, Library of Congress, Washington, D.C., 1978. Visiting Faculty Member, Center for the Study of Children's Literature, Simmons College, Boston, 1978-86. Founder, with John Rowe Townsend, *q.v.,* Green Bay Publishers, 1986. Recipient: *Book World* Festival award, 1970, for *Fireweed;* Whitbread Prize (shared with Russell Hoban), 1974, for *The Emperor's Winding Sheet; Boston Globe-Horn Book* award, 1976, for *Unleaving;* Arts Council Creative Writing Fellowship, 1976-77, and 1977-78; Universe Prize, 1984, for *A Parcel of Patterns;* Smarties Prize Grand Prix, 1985, for *Gaffer Samson's Luck.* Address: 72 Water Lane, Histon, Cambridge CB4 4LR, England.

PUBLICATIONS FOR YOUNG ADULTS

Fiction

Hengest's Tale, illustrated by Janet Margrie. London, Macmillan, and New York, St. Martin's Press, 1966.
The Dolphin Crossing. London, Macmillan, and New York, St. Martin's Press, 1967.
Fireweed. London, Macmillan, 1969; New York, Farrar Straus, 1970.
Goldengrove. London, Macmillan, and New York, Farrar Straus, 1972.
The Dawnstone, illustrated by Mary Dinsdale. London, Hamish Hamilton, 1973.
Toolmaker, illustrated by Jeroo Roy. London, Heinemann, 1973; New York, Seabury Press, 1974.
The Emperor's Winding Sheet. London, Macmillan, and New York, Farrar Straus, 1974.
The Butty Boy, illustrated by Juliette Palmer. London, Macmillan, 1975; as *The Huffler,* New York, Farrar Straus, 1975.
Unleaving. London, Macmillan, and New York, Farrar Straus, 1976.
Children of the Fox. New York, Farrar Straus, 1978.
Crossing to Salamis, illustrated by David Smee. London, Heinemann, 1977.

The Walls of Athens, illustrated by David Smee. London, Heinemann, 1977.

Persian Gold, illustrated by David Smee. London, Heinemann, 1978.

A Chance Child. London, Macmillan, and New York, Farrar Straus, 1978.

The Green Book, illustrated by Joanna Stubbs. London, Macmillan, 1981; illustrated by Lloyd Bloom, New York, Farrar Straus, 1982; as *Shine,* London, Macdonald, 1988.

Babylon, illustrated by Jenny Northway. London, Deutsch, 1982.

A Parcel of Patterns. London, Kestrel, and New York, Farrar Straus, 1983.

Gaffer Samson's Luck, illustrated by Brock Cole. New York, Farrar Straus, 1984; London, Viking Kestrel, 1985.

Torch. London, Viking Kestral, 1987; New York, Farrar Straus, 1988.

Grace. London, Viking, 1991; New York, Farrar, Straus, 1992.

Other

Wordhoard: Anglo-Saxon Stories, with Kevin Crossley-Holland. London, Macmillan, and New York, Farrar Straus, 1969.

The Island Sunrise: Prehistoric Britain. London, Deutsch, 1975; as *The Island Sunrise: Prehistoric Culture in the British Isles,* New York, Seabury Press, 1976.

PUBLICATIONS FOR CHILDREN

Fiction

Lost and Found, illustrated by Mary Rayner. London, Deutsch, 1984.

Birdy and the Ghosties, illustrated by Alan Marks. London, Macdonald, 1989.

When Grandma Came, illustrated by Sophie Williams. New York, Viking, 1992.

PUBLICATIONS FOR ADULTS

Novels

Farewell, Great King. London, Macmillan, and New York, Coward McCann, 1972.

Lapsing. London, Weidenfeld & Nicolson, 1986; New York, St. Martin's, 1987.

A School for Lovers. London, Weidenfeld & Nicolson, 1989.

Short Stories

Five Tides. Cambridge, Green Bay, 1986.

*

Biography: Essay in *Something about the Author Autobiography Series,* Volume 3, Detroit, Gale, 1987; essay in *Speaking for Ourselves: Autobiographical Sketches by Notable Authors of Books for Young Adults,* Volume 1, compiled and edited by Donald R. Gallo, National Council of Teachers of English, 1990.

Manuscript Collection: Kerlan Collection, University of Minnesota, Minneapolis.

Critical Studies: Entry in *Children's Literature Review,* Volume 2, Detroit, Gale, 1976; entry in *Contemporary Literary Criticism,* Volume 35, Detroit, Gale, 1985.

*   *   *

Throughout a long and prolific career, Jill Paton Walsh has presented young-adult readers with a great range and variety of novels. Although different in setting, genre, and style, they share an underlying seriousness and introduce young people to thought-provoking and often uncomfortable issues. Through strong and fully explored central characters, Paton Walsh draws young readers into a sensitive exploration of the difficulties of finding their own identities and making decisions for themselves. The most immediately attractive features of these novels, however, are their absorbing plots and believable settings.

Her two early novels, *Fireweed* and *Dolphin Crossing,* both set during the Second World War, explore the possibilities and dangers of a world in which young people are set free from the support or constraint of adults. Her characters experience dangers and insecurities as well as the pleasure of new friendships and love.

In *Goldengrove,* Paton Walsh again sensitively and poignantly explores love between young people. Dramatic wartime action is replaced by an account of the apparently uneventful days of a late summer holiday told through a series of vivid, impressionistic scenes. On the verge of adulthood, Madge eagerly anticipates her annual holiday reunion in her grandmother's Cornwall house with Paul, the younger boy she knows as her cousin. When this September holiday disappoints their expectations, only the watching grandmother and the reader realize how Madge's growing up is unbalancing their relationship. The novel charts the changing feelings of the young people through the events of their visit until the climax, in which two revelations shatter Madge's expectations of the future and her faith in adults. In keeping with the title, the novel is poetic in the vivid evocation of its scenes, in its structure, and in its haunting use of images, in particular the "golden" leaves which have fallen by the end of the novel.

In a later book, *Unleaving,* the author returns to a slightly older Madge. The challenging structure of the novel intercuts scenes from her summer before university with others centering around an unnamed "Gran." At the conclusion, the reader learns that Gran is the older Madge at last coming to an understanding of her own life. Through this extended portrait of Madge, Paton Walsh is able to show the development of a sensitive and intelligent girl into a young woman and also to suggest how "growing up" continues through old age.

All of Paton Walsh's historical novels have foundations in painstaking research. *The Emperor's Winding Sheet,* set in Constantinople in the last days of the Byzantine Empire, gives an unflinching account of the siege and sacking of the city by the Turks. The events are seen through the eyes of Piers, an English youth who is found and adopted as mascot and servant by the new emperor, Constantine. Often reluctant and resentful, Piers watches as the siege tightens around the city, but he learns to recognize Constantine's unsparing service to his people as bravery, and his resentment is transformed to loyalty. Although the novel is slow to start, weighed down by the apparent need to inform the reader about the historical and religious background, the scenes of action are convincingly portrayed, and the impressionable boy's viewpoint becomes a poignant way of conveying the brutality of war.

A Parcel of Patterns draws from records of the lives and deaths of the inhabitants of the Derbyshire village of Eyam, recounting the effects of the plague brought to the community in 1665. Under the guidance of the vicar, the villagers cut themselves off from the surrounding community to stop the further spread of infection. The narrator, Mal, is a young woman whose own life is cruelly disrupted by the plague, and the reader is drawn to her as a warm and intelligent girl of strength and independence. As a positive and thought-provoking ending, Mal is encouraged to "charm" away her grief through writing her account of the plague, and it is a measure of Paton Walsh's writing that the archaic style she adopts for Mal's narration seems unforced and in character with her directness. Through her eyes we are introduced to a group of varied and memorable characters. Although Parson Momphesson could, like Emperor Constantine, be seen as the hero of the novel for his selfless dedication to the people of the village and Marshall Howe as the villain in his brutal disrespect for others' feelings, Paton Walsh avoids such easy distinctions. Under the pressure of suffering, all are seen to be at different times both weak and strong.

Torch takes the reader on a journey through struggling countries in a post-holocaust world, and in an extended parable offers some bleak truths about human nature and society while suggesting that there is hope in the tested unselfishness of young people. Cal and Dio, two young people living in a future Greece, inherit the responsibility of guarding a torch which the reader recognizes as the Olympic flame. It has survived through "Ago," the time "when the mechanical birds carried people over mountains," but has been unused for many generations since. Dio believes it is his mission to take the torch "To the Games. Wherever they are," and joined by a small group of friends, he and Cal begin a journey which takes them to Games organized in countries around the Mediterranean and eventually to England. It is through this story that Paton Walsh is able to show a world in which the Olympic values have been destroyed and replaced by cruelties and greeds. When the disillusioned young people eventually reach the "Island," they set up a community by themselves, and when they race each other for joy, the torch breaks into flame. Although the novel develops all the young people's characters, it is action and ideas which seem to interest the author most, and it is primarily these which carry the reader along.

Jill Paton Walsh cannot be categorized. Although she clearly draws inspiration from well-researched historical periods, she is equally interested in the contemporary world and in ideas of a possible future. In her very different novels, she shows her understanding of her young readers' interests and concerns but pays them the tribute of neither patronizing nor sparing them.

—Judith Atkinson

PAULSEN, Gary. Also writes as Paul Garrisen. American. Born in Minneapolis, Minnesota, 17 May 1939. Educated at Bemidji State University, Minnesota, 1957-58; University of Colorado, Boulder, 1976. Served in the United States Army (sergeant), 1959-62. Married Ruth Ellen Wright in 1971 (third marriage), one son; one son and one daughter from previous marriage. Has worked as a teacher, electronics field engineer, editor, actor, director, farmer, rancher, truck driver, trapper, professional archer, migrant farm worker, singer, satellite tracker, musher, sculptor, and sailor. Recipient: Central Missouri award for Children's Literature, 1976; *The Green Recruit* was chosen one of New York Public Library's Books for the Teen Age, 1980, 1981 and 1982, and *Sailing: From Jibs to Jibbing,* 1982; *Tiltawhirl John, The Foxman, The Night the White Deer Died, Popcorn Days and Buttermilk Nights,* and *Dancing Carl,* all American Library Association's Best Young Adult Books, 1983; ALA Best Book list, *Tracker,* 1984; Society of Midland Authors award, 1985, for *Tracker. Dogsong,* Parents' Choice award for Literature, Parents' Choice Foundation, 1985; ALA Notable Children's Book, 1986; and selected one of ALA Best Books for Young Adults, 1986. Newbery Honor Book, 1986, for *Dogsong,* 1988, for *Hatchet,* and 1990, for *The Winter Room; Dogsong* was chosen one of Child Study Association of America's Children's Books of the Year, 1986; ALA Notable Children's Book, 1988, for *Hatchet. The Crossing* and *The Island* were selected one of ALA Best Books for Young Adults, 1989; *The Voyage of the Frog,* one of ALA Best Books for Young Adults, and ALA Notable Children's Book, both 1990; *Canyons,* one of ALA Best Books for Young Adults, 1990; *The Winter Room,* Newbery Honor Book, 1990; *The Boy Who Owned the School* and *Woodsong,* selected as ALA Best Books for Young Adult, 1991; *Woodsong,* ALA Notable Children's Book, 1991; *The Haymeadow,* Spur award, Western Writers of America, 1993. Agent: Jennifer Flannery, 34-40 28th Street #6, New York, NY 11106-3516, U.S.A. Lives in Tularosa, New Mexico.

PUBLICATIONS FOR YOUNG ADULTS

Fiction

Mr. Tucket, illustrated by Noel Sickles. New York, Funk and Wagnalls, 1969.
The C.B. Radio Caper, illustrated by John Asquith. Milwaukee, Raintree, 1977.
The Curse of the Cobra, illustrated by John Asquith. Milwaukee, Raintree, 1977.
The Foxman. Nashville, Nelson, 1977.
The Golden Stick, illustrated by Jerry Scott. Milwaukee, Raintree, 1977.
Tiltawhirl John. Nashville, Nelson, 1977.
Winterkill. Nashville, Nelson, and London, Abelard, 1977.
The Green Recruit, with Ray Peekner. Independence, Missouri, Independence Press, 1978.
Hope and a Hatchet. Nashville, Nelson, 1978.
The Night the White Deer Died. Nashville, Nelson, 1978.
The Spitball Gang. New York, Elsevier, 1980.
Dancing Carl. Scarsdale, New York, Bradbury Press, 1983.
Popcorn Days and Buttermilk Nights. New York, Dutton, 1983.
Tracker. New York, Bradbury Press, 1984.
Dogsong. New York, Bradbury Press, 1985.
Sentries. New York, Bradbury Press, 1986.
The Crossing. New York, Orchard, 1987.
Hatchett. New York, Bradbury Press, 1987; as *Hatchet,* London, Macmillan, 1989.
The Island. New York, Orchard, 1988.
Hatchet Rack Trim. New York, Puffin, 1989.
The Voyage of the Frog. New York, Orchard, 1989.
The Winter Room. New York, Orchard, 1989.
The Boy Who Owned the School. New York, Orchard, 1990.
Canyons. New York, Delacorte, 1990.

Woodsong, illustrated by Ruth Wright Paulsen. New York, Bradbury Press, 1990.

The Cookcamp. New York, Orchard, 1991.

The Monument. New York, Delacorte, 1991.

The River. New York, Doubleday, 1991.

A Christmas Sonata, illustrated by Leslie Bowman. New York, Delacorte, 1992.

Clabbered Dirt, Sweet Grass, illustrated by Ruth Wright Paulsen. Orlando, Florida, Harcourt, 1992.

Culpepper's Cannon. New York, Dell, 1992.

Dogteam, illustrated by Ruth Wright Paulsen. New York, Delacorte, 1992.

Dunc and the Flaming Ghost. New York, Dell, 1992.

Dunc Breaks the Record. New York, Dell, 1992.

Dunc's Doll. New York, Dell, 1992.

Dunc Gets Tweaked. New York, Dell, 1992.

Dunc's Halloween. New York, Dell, 1992.

The Haymeadow. New York, Doubleday, 1992.

Nightjohn. New York, Delacorte, 1993.

Amos Gets Famous. New York, Dell, 1993.

Dunc and Amos Hit the Big Top. New York, Dell, 1993.

Dunc and the Scam Artist. New York, Dell, 1993.

Dunc's Dump. New York, Dell, 1993.

Dunc and Amos and the Red Tattoos. New York, Dell, 1993.

Harris and Me. Orlando, Florida, Harcourt, 1993.

Dunc's Undercover Christmas. New York, Dell, 1993.

Sisters/Hermanas. Orlando, Florida, Harcourt, 1993.

Wild Culpepper Cruise. New York, Dell, 1993.

Dunc and the Haunted House. New York, Dell, 1993.

Cowpokes and Desperados. New York, Dell, forthcoming.

Prince Amos. New York, Dell, forthcoming.

Coach Amos. New York, Dell, forthcoming.

The Case of the Falling Star. New York, Dell, forthcoming.

Dunc Meets the Slasher. New York, Dell, forthcoming.

Other

Dribbling, Shooting, and Scoring Sometimes, photographs by Heinz Kluetmeier. Milwaukee, Raintree, 1976.

The Grass Eaters: Real Animals, illustrated by Kathy Goff, photographs by Wilford Miller. Milwaukee, Raintree, 1976.

Martin Luther King: The Man Who Climbed the Mountain, with Dan Theis. Milwaukee, Raintree, 1976.

The Small Ones, illustrated by Kathy Goff, photographs by Wilford Miller. Milwaukee, Raintree, 1976.

Careers in an Airport, photographs by Robert Nye. Milwaukee, Raintree, 1977.

Hitting, Pitching, and Running Maybe, photographs by Heinz Kluetmeier. Milwaukee, Raintree, 1977.

Riding, Roping, and Bulldogging—Almost, photographs by Heinz Kluetmeier. Milwaukee, Raintree, 1977.

Tackling, Running, and Kicking—Now and Again, photographs by Heinz Kluetmeier. Milwaukee, Raintree, 1977.

Forehanding and Backhanding—If You're Lucky, photographs by Heinz Kluetmeier. Chicago, Children's Press, 1978; revised edition, with Roger Barrett, as *Tennis,* Milwaukee and London, Macdonald, 1980.

Hiking and Backpacking, with John Morris, illustrated by Ruth Wright Paulsen. New York, Messner, 1978.

Running, Jumping, and Throwing—If You Can, photographs by Heinz Kluetmeier. Chicago, Children's Press, 1978; revised edition, with Roger Barrett, as *Athletics,* Milwaukee and London, Macdonald, 1980.

Canoeing, Kayaking, and Rafting, with John Morris, illustrated by John Peterson and Jack Storholm. New York, Messner, 1979.

Downhill, Hotdogging and Cross-Country—If the Snow Isn't Sticky, photographs by Heinz Kluetmeier and Willis Wood. Milwaukee, Raintree, 1979; revised edition, with Roger Barrett, as *Skiing,* Milwaukee and London, Macdonald, 1980.

Facing Off, Checking and Goaltending—Perhaps, photographs by Heinz Kluetmeier and Melchior DiGiacomo. Milwaukee, Raintree, 1979; revised edition, with Roger Barrett, as *Ice Hockey,* Milwaukee and London, Macdonald, 1980.

Going Very Fast in a Circle—If You Don't Run Out of Gas, photographs by Heinz Kluetmeier and Bob D'Olivo. Milwaukee, Raintree, 1979; revised edition, with Roger Barrett, as *Motor Racing,* Milwaukee and London, Macdonald, 1980.

Launching, Floating High and Landing—If Your Pilot Light Doesn't Go Out, photographs by Heinz Kluetmeier. Milwaukee, Raintree, 1979.

Pummeling, Falling and Getting Up—Sometimes, photographs by Heinz Kluetmeier and Joe DiMaggio. Milwaukee, Raintree, 1979.

Track, Enduro and Motocross—Unless You Fall Over, photographs by Heinz Kluetmeier. Milwaukee, Raintree, 1979; revised edition, with Roger Barrett, as *Motor-cycling,* Milwaukee and London, Macdonald, 1980.

TV and Movie Animals, with Art Browne, Jr. New York, Messner, 1980.

Sailing: From Jibs to Jibing, illustrated by Ruth Wright Paulsen. New York, Messner, 1981.

Full of Hot Air: Launching, Floating High, and Landing, photos by Ann Heltshe. New York, Delacorte, 1993.

PUBLICATIONS FOR ADULTS

Novels

The Death Specialists. New York, Major, 1976.

The Implosion Effect. New York, Major, 1976.

C.B. Jockey. New York, Major, 1977.

The Sweeper. New York, Raven, 1980.

Meteorite-Track 291. New York, Pinnacle, 1981.

Survival Guide. New York, Pinnacle, 1981.

Compkill. New York, Pinnacle, 1981.

Clutterkill. New York, Raven, 1981.

The Meatgrinder. New York, Raven, 1984.

Murphy. New York, Walker, and London, Hale, 1987.

Murphy's Gold. New York, Walker, 1988.

Night Rituals. New York, Fine, 1989.

The Madonna Stories. Minneapolis, Van Bliet, 1989.

Murphy's Herd. New York, Walker, 1989.

Dirk's Run (as Paul Garrisen). New York, HarperWesterns, 1990.

Dirk's Revenge (as Paul Garrisen). New York, HarperWesterns, 1990.

Kill Fee. New York, Fine, 1990.

Murphy's War. New York, Walker, 1990.

The Case of the Dirty Bird. New York, Dell, 1992.

Murphy's Stand. New York, Walker, 1993.

Winterdance: The Fine Madness of Running the Iditarod. Orlando, Florida, Harcourt, forthcoming.

Plays

Communications (produced New Mexico, 1974).
Together-Apart (produced in Denver, 1976).

Screenplays: *A Cry in the Wind* (adaptation of *Hatchet*), Concorde-New Horizons, 1990.

Other

The Special War, with Raymond Friday Locke. Los Angeles, Sirkay, 1966.
Some Birds Don't Fly. Chicago, Rand McNally, 1968.
The Building a New, Buying an Old, Remodeling a Used, Comprehensive Home and Shelter How-to-Do-It Book. Englewood Cliffs, New Jersey, Prentice Hall, 1976.
Farm: A History and Celebration of the American Farmer. Englewood Cliffs, New Jersey, Prentice Hall, 1977.
Successful Home Repair. Farmington, Michigan, Structures, 1978.
Money-Saving Home Repair Guide. Milwaukee, Ideals, 1981.
Beat the System: A Survival Guide. New York, Pinnacle, 1983.
Eastern Sun, Winter Moon: An Autobiographical Odyssey. Orlando, Florida, Harcourt, 1993.

*

Media Adaptations: *Dogsong* (filmstrip with cassette), Random House/Miller-Brody, 1986; *Hatchet* (filmstrip with cassette), Random House, 1988; *A Cry in the Wind* (film adaptation of *Hatchet*), Concorde-New Horizons, 1990.

Biography: Essay in *Authors and Artists for Young Adults,* Volume 2, Detroit, Gale, 1989; essay in *Speaking for Ourselves: Autobiographical Sketches by Notable Authors of Books for Young Adults,* Volume 1, compiled and edited by Donald R. Gallo, National Council of Teachers of English, 1990.

Critical Study: Entry in *Children's Literature Review,* Volume 19, Detroit, Gale, 1990.

Gary Paulsen comments:

I was a miserable student. I flunked the ninth grade and finally graduated from high school with probably a D- average. I had a miserable home life, and I would sell newspapers to the drunks at the local bars to make a little money. One night I went into a library to get warm and the librarian asked me if I wanted a library card. Then she started giving me books—Westerns and science fiction and every once in a while she'd slip in a Melville. It saved me, it really did. And now I tell kids to read like a wolf eats.

*   *   *

Gary Paulsen's young adult novels are largely rites-of-passage stories in which protagonists struggle to come to terms with themselves and the trials they face. Their call to adventure, to use Joseph Campbell's term in his monomyth of the hero's journey, may be quite literal, as with Russel in *Dogsong,* John in *Tracker,* and Brian in *Hatchett* and *River,* who emerge from their wilderness experiences with new knowledge of self and their world. Or the transition may be more introspective, as with Wil in *The Island,* Janet in *The Night the White Deer Died,* and Brennan in *Canyons,* who come to terms with self through reflection rather than through an emphasis on physical action. His characters are believable, and their circumstances are unique, not given to formulas that characterize much contemporary young adult fiction. One recent exception to the latter is his *The Boy Who Owned the School,* a light romantic exercise playing on the insecurities of a teenage boy living in the shadow of his older beauty-queen sister. Even here, however, the lean Paulsen style of short sentences and fragments prevails, but in substance it is not the vintage work that has earned him Newbery Honor Book recognition for *The Winter Room, Hatchett,* and *Dogsong.*

Paulsen's writing reflects his close association with nature and the knowledge that can be gained through observing and respecting the natural order. In *Woodsong,* his nonfiction account of his preparation for and running of the Iditarod—a grueling thousand-mile, dogsled race in Alaska—he demonstrated the necessary interdependence he and his dogs shared in their race ordeal. He also told of his desire to kill a bear rummaging in the trash near his home, but reason prevailed over anger and Paulsen credited the bear with teaching him the importance of sharing the woods with its creatures. Also in *Woodsong* he explored the mysteries of the woods, just as Wil explores the mysteries of the island and learns to express himself through writing and painting.

In *The Night the White Deer Died* and *Canyons* there are elements of the mystical, reminiscent of the mysterious person that Paulsen encountered on several timely occasions in *Woodsong.* In *White Deer* Janet's dream of the young Indian warrior and the white deer foreshadows her experience with Billy Honcho, an old alcoholic Indian whose dissipation masks the inner strength and beauty that Janet comes to love and whose death she comes to accept. In *Canyons* Brennan's dreamlike awakening in a small cave leads to his finding the skull of Coyote Runs, thus linking Brennan to an Apache boy who had been executed on that spot more than a hundred years before while on his way to manhood. Accepting the challenge of returning Coyote Runs' skull to the ancient medicine place becomes Brennan's ritual passage to knowledge and adulthood. Similarly, John Borne in *Tracker* comes to terms with the approaching death of his grandfather as he tracks a doe for two days in the wilderness, and his new appreciation for life causes him not to kill the deer. Paulsen conveys to his readers in these books the intricate connections between life and death and the value of understanding fragile relationships across generations and across cultures.

Whether set in the Canadian wilderness, Minnesota, Wisconsin, Kansas, New Mexico, or Texas, Paulsen's stories always convey a strong sense of place and a compelling awareness of the interrelatedness of people and nature. The son of a career soldier and a former soldier himself, Paulsen has used war associations in several books. Carl Wenstrom, the eccentric veteran of *Dancing Carl,* harbors devastating memories of his war experiences, as does the old recluse of *The Foxman,* who had been gassed and disfigured in World War I but still retains his humanity as he befriends a teenager who discovers his simple shack. The relationship in *The Crossing* between Sergeant Robert Locke, an alcoholic veteran of Vietnam, and Manny Bustros, a Mexican street child, is an unlikely one, yet they become linked in a way that has special consequences for both of them. In *The Monument* the desire of the people of Bolton, Kansas, to honor their war dead by erecting their own Vietnam memorial leads to their commissioning an artist from outside the community. The story unfolds from the perspective of Rocky

Turner, a young, racially mixed girl with a physical handicap, who, like Wil Neuton, discovers that she has an artistic gift. The monument project causes the people of Bolton to look at themselves in unexpected ways. Stories of war experiences are also significant plot elements in *Sentries*, a none too subtle reminder of the devastation of war.

To say that writing is a passion for Paulsen is an understatement. While he had tried many other jobs, he learned that writing was the only thing that mattered. The seeds for his career as an author had undoubtedly been sown early in his life. In *Eastern Sun, Winter Moon: An Autobiographical Odyssey,* Paulsen recounted his early years with his mother in Chicago during World War II while his father served on Patton's staff in Europe, and then the two years they spent with his father in the Philippines after the war. This vivid reconstruction reveals aspects of Paulsen's formative years which are reflected in various works. Never having developed a close relationship with his father in these early years, Paulsen often writes young adult novels in which the father is absent. In some books (such as *Tiltawhirl John, The Crossing,* and *Tracker*) the father is deceased; in others the parents are divorced (e.g., *Hatchett* and *The Night the White Deer Died*), the father has deserted the family (*Canyons*), or he is away in the military (*The Cookcamp*). In *The Island* Wil Neuton's parents are present, but with the tension brought on by the family's move to northern Wisconsin, Wil retreats to the island. In the end Wil and his father seem ready to begin to build a close relationship, just as Paulsen was able in later years to grow closer to his father.

In *Eastern Sun, Winter Moon* Paulsen described his close relationship with his mother, yet he also resented her various romantic interludes with other men. In *Hatchett* Brian's mother gives him the tool that becomes symbolic of his survival in the wilderness, but Brian also carries the burden of "the Secret," his knowledge that his mother was seeing another man before the divorce. The unnamed protagonist in *The Cookcamp* who has been staying with his grandmother in northern Minnesota returns to his mother in Chicago, but he resents his mother's boyfriend. For readers who want to know more about Paulsen, his autobiographical odyssey suggests an interesting matrix of situations that find fictional expression in his creative process.

As a man of multiple experiences and a close observer of the emotional and psychological dimensions of complex relationships, Gary Paulsen is a gifted and versatile storyteller. His young adult readers have come to expect new twists and turns with each story. Paulsen's greatest challenge is to maintain this expectation, which, after all, is not too much to ask of a talented writer. Paulsen's record is in his favor.

—Hugh Agee

PEARSON, Kit. Born in Edmonton, Alberta, 30 April 1947. Educated at a boarding school in Vancouver, Canada. Worked as a children's librarian, teacher, and reviewer of juvenile literature. Recipient: Canadian Library Association's Book of the Year for Children award, 1988, for *A Handful of Time;* Canadian Library Association Book of the Year for Children award, 1990, inaugural Mr. Christie Book award, and runner-up Ruth Schwartz award, all for *The Sky Is Falling.* Address: 2195 West 15th Ave., Vancouver, BC V6K 2Y4, Canada.

PUBLICATIONS FOR YOUNG ADULTS

Novels

The Daring Game. Markham, Toronto, Viking Kestrel, and New York, Viking Kestrel, 1986.
A Handful of Time. Markham, Toronto, Viking Kestrel, and New York, Viking Kestrel, 1987.
The Sky Is Falling. Markham, Toronto, Viking Kestrel, and New York, Viking Kestrel, 1987.
Looking at the Moon. Toronto and New York, Viking, 1991.

Other

Editor, *The Singing Basket.* Willowdale, Ontario, Firefly Books, 1991.

*   *   *

Kit Pearson is a writer with a long memory—one which stretches back to enable her to recreate with absolute conviction the intense feelings of longing, frustration, and occasional bliss which overpower all of us in youth but tend to fade in later life. The young girls who are the central characters in all her novels are wholly believable in their hesitations, insecurities, and aspirations; they grow and change in the course of the novels as each comes to some new point of understanding and acceptance of her place in the world through the action which has occurred. That action, like Pearson's writing as a whole, is quiet and undramatic but deeply grounded in felt experience. The novels conform to no particular fashion or current theory about what young women ought to feel or do but rise from honest recollection and observation, as well as a strong feeling for young people.

Although the tone and the fundamental concerns of each of her novels are somewhat similar, Pearson has written in the three quite different genres of the boarding school story, the time-slip fantasy, and the historical novel. In her first novel, *The Daring Game,* which was based to some extent upon her own experiences of being a boarder at a private girls' school in Vancouver, Pearson established her capacity for an intensely realistic evocation of the thoughts and feelings of her young protagonist and for writing convincingly about relationships between girls. Although the novel is episodic in structure, depicting both the pleasures and tensions of boarding-school life, a crisis builds as the shy eleven-year-old Eliza is increasingly drawn into friendship with the rebellious Helen, whose unhappy home life is reflected in her defiant and provocative attitude towards the school. Sympathizing with Helen and concerned for what will become of her if she is expelled, Eliza eventually has to make a choice between loyalty to the values of the school and loyalty to her friend. The ethical dilemma posed, and Eliza's eventual choice, give the novel a dimension beyond the usual "larks and scrapes" recounted in the genre. None of Pearson's subsequent novels present their protagonists with quite such an awkward decision, but at the climax of each of them some sort of choice or decision needs to be made which marks a significant point of emotional growth.

The relationships among the school girls in *The Daring Game* are created with a remarkably observant and unsentimental eye and ear; once established, however, they do not remain static as often happens in genre fiction where certain characters play the same roles continuously. Rather, Pearson shows the relationships within this little world as always in flux, with alliances forming and reforming in response to the pressures of school life and to the changing moods and preoccupations of the adolescent girls themselves. In Pearson's other novels, however, adults play a more significant role than do the teachers and house-mothers of *The Daring Game,* who are inevitably seen by the girls as alien authority figures to be appeased or outwitted.

A real mother cannot be so easily dealt with, and Pearson's second novel, *A Handful of Time,* concerns twelve-year-old Patricia's troubled feelings about her own mother. Slipping back and forth between her own time, where she is spending a lonely summer with unfriendly cousins at their lakeside cottage and the time of her mother's own girlhood spent at the same cottage, Patricia becomes an invisible but fascinated observer of crucial scenes from her mother's past life. She sees Ruth, her mother, treated differently from the boys of the family and denied the privileges they take for granted. She discovers how Ruth's mother, deprived of emotional fulfillment herself, slights her daughter's desire to be given the same educational opportunities as the boys in the family and wants her daughter to fit into a traditional feminine mold which Ruth rejects. Embittered by her own struggle to achieve and succeed on her own terms, Ruth has in turn neglected Patricia's emotional needs and tries to force her into a mold for which she is unsuited. Pearson has been criticized for having this daughter of the upwardly mobile Ruth say "softly" while discussing her own career plans that "maybe I'll be a mother." In the context of the novel, however, this comment should be seen as marking Patricia's emotional growth away from the unhappiness and resentment which has blighted the relationships of three generations of women in her family. As Patricia learns to feel compassion rather than bitterness towards the emotional limitations of her own mother and grandmother, her interest in becoming a mother herself is a measure of the new security and capacity to love which she has found within herself. Through the three generations of women in this novel, Pearson shows the necessity for women, like men, to be free to find the balance between satisfaction in their work and emotional fulfillment. In her expression of interest in someday becoming a mother, Patricia is not denying but finding something of her full capacity as a human being.

The family, whether its members are present or absent, is shown to be of great importance in the lives of all of Pearson's protagonists; the experience of living away from home, however, is used to lead each of them to a greater self-reliance and self-acceptance. Norah, in the two published volumes of Pearson's projected trilogy set during World War II, and her younger brother Gavin, who is to be the protagonist of the third volume, are sent for safety to Canada from their English home and experience many problems adjusting to this displacement and to the domineering Mrs. Ogilvie who becomes their substitute parent. While both Eliza and Patricia were shown in the relatively confined worlds of boarding school and summer cottage, *The Sky Is Falling* has a larger canvas, showing Norah in England, in Canada, in relationships with her peers in and outside school, and with a number of adults as well as Mrs. Ogilvie. In the sequel, *Looking at the Moon,* Pearson returns to a single setting as she depicts a month spent by an older Norah at the Ogilvie's family cottage north of Toronto. Winner of a number of awards, *The Sky Is Falling* is a sensitive and absorbing account of Norah's transition between two very different lives. Norah is a sturdy, fiercely independent girl, who is completely at ease collecting newly-fallen shrapnel with her English schoolmates but unhappy in Mrs. Ogilvie's wealthy and strictly regulated home. Pearson's delicate but effective handling of symbol and her readiness to refer to other works of children's literature are both notable

in this novel: Norah hears the folktale about Alenoushka's journey with her little brother, and the story becomes a metaphor for her own travails and for her eventual recognition of her bond with Gavin. The discovery of Arthur Ransome's novels is another important solace for Norah as she works through the difficult process of adjustment to life in Canada and with Mrs. Ogilvie. That adjustment takes on new dimensions in *Looking at the Moon* as the now thirteen-year-old Norah encounters the physical and emotional changes of adolescence, which are aggravated by the War and her long displacement from home. Norah falls painfully in love with a handsome, older Ogilvie cousin, who is himself tormented by the decision of whether or not to enlist. No easy solutions are offered although Norah is comforted by an eighty-three-year-old woman who points out that being thirteen doesn't last forever.

The young girl protagonists of Pearson's novels are all shown dealing with problems in their lives—problems of varying degrees of severity —but to call them "problem novels" would misrepresent them: the difficulties and dilemmas the girls encounter are treated as part of the fabric of life, and the world of each novel is larger than the immediate concerns of its protagonist. Although intensely aware of and empathetic with the feelings of her central characters, Pearson is also fair-minded in her portrayal of other people, even such antagonists as Patricia's grandmother and the formidable Mrs. Ogilvie. Not only are such characters given a past history which helps to explain their attitudes, they are also given the capacity to change and to surprise. Mrs. Ogilvie is not just a tyrant who undergoes a necessary change of heart: we come to see that she will always be tyrannical, and that those around her generally accept and even rely on that. Norah learns both to savor the pleasure of surreptitiously laughing at her with the other young cousins and to appreciate her matter-of-fact competence. This generous spirit and humane vision is an important but not altogether common quality in fiction for young adults, and it contributes to the reason that Kit Pearson is one of Canada's leading writers for young people.

—Gwyneth Evans

PECK, Richard (Wayne). American. Born in Decatur, Illinois, 5 April 1934. Educated at University of Exeter, Devon, 1955-56; DePauw University, Greencastle, Indiana, B.A. 1956; Southern Illinois University, Carbondale, M.A. 1959; further graduate study at Washington University, St. Louis, 1960-61. Served in the U.S. Army in Stuttgart, Germany, 1956-58. English instructor, Southern Illinois University, Carbondale, 1958-60; high school English teacher, Glenbrook North High School, Northbrook, Illinois, 1961-63; textbook editor, Scott, Foresman Co., Chicago, 1963-65; instructor in English and education, Hunter College of the City University of New York and Hunter College High School, New York City, 1965-71; writer, since 1971. Assistant director, Council for Basic Education, Washington, D.C., 1969-70; English-Speaking Union fellow, Jesus College, Oxford University, England, 1973; lecturer. Recipient: Child Study Association of America's Children's Book of the Year citations, 1970, for *Sounds and Silences,* 1971, for *Mindscapes,* and 1986, for *Blossom Culp and the Sleep of Death;* Writing award, National Council for the Advancement of Education, 1971; Edgar Allan Poe award runner-up, Mystery Writers of America, 1974, for *Dreamland Lake;* Best Books of the Year citations, American

Library Association (ALA), 1974, for *Representing Super Doll,* 1976, for *Are You in the House Alone?,* and 1977, for *Ghosts I Have Been;* ALA Notable Book citations, 1975, for *The Ghost Belonged to Me,* and 1985, for *Remembering the Good Times;* Friends of American Writers award (older category), 1976, for *The Ghost Belonged to Me;* Edgar Allan Poe award for best juvenile mystery novel, 1977, and Author's award, New Jersey Institute of Technology, 1978, both for *Are You in the House Alone?; School Library Journal*'s Best Books of the Year citations, 1976, for *Are You in the House Alone?,* 1977, for *Ghosts I Have Been,* and 1985, for *Remembering the Good Times; New York Times* Outstanding Book of the Year citation, 1977, for *Ghosts I Have Been;* Illinois Writer of the Year citation, Illinois Association of Teachers of English, 1977; *School Library Journal*'s Best of the Best 1966-1978 citations, for *Dreamland Lake,* and *Father Figure.* New York Public Library Books for the Teen Age citations, 1980, for *Pictures That Storm inside My Head,* 1981, for *Ghosts I Have Been,* and 1982, for *Are You in the House Alone?* and *Close Enough to Touch;* ALA Best Books for Young Adults citations, 1981, for *Close Enough to Touch,* 1985, for *Remembering the Good Times,* and 1987, for *Princess Ashley; School Library Journal*'s Best Books for Young Adults citations, 1981, for *Close Enough to Touch,* 1983, for *This Family of Women,* and 1985, for *Remembering the Good Times;* ALA's Young Adult Services Division's Best of the Best Books 1970-1983 citations, for *Are You in the House Alone?* and *Ghosts I Have Been;* ALA's Margaret Edwards Young Adult Author Achievement award, 1990. Agent: Sheldon Fogelman, 155 East 72nd St., New York, NY 10021.

PUBLICATIONS FOR YOUNG ADULTS

Fiction

Don't Look and It Won't Hurt. New York, Holt, 1972.
Dreamland Lake. New York, Holt, 1973.
Through a Brief Darkness. New York, Viking, 1973; London, Collins, 1976.
Representing Super Doll. New York, Viking, 1974.
The Ghost Belonged to Me. New York, Viking, 1975; London, Collins, 1977.
Are You in the House Alone? New York, Viking, 1976; London, Pan, 1986.
Ghosts I Have Been. New York, Viking, 1977.
Father Figure. New York, Viking, 1978.
Secrets of the Shopping Mall. New York, Delacorte, 1979.
Close Enough to Touch. New York, Delacorte, 1981.
The Dreadful Future of Blossom Culp. New York, Delacorte, 1983.
Remembering the Good Times. New York, Delacorte, 1985.
Blossom Culp and the Sleep of Death. New York, Delacorte, 1986.
Princess Ashley. New York, Delacorte, 1987.
Those Summer Girls I Never Met. New York, Delacorte, 1988.
Unfinished Portrait of Jessica. New York, Delacorte, 1991.
Bel-Air Bambi and the Mall Rats. New York, Delacorte, 1993.

PUBLICATIONS FOR CHILDREN

Fiction

Monster Night at Grandma's House, illustrated by Don Freeman. New York, Viking, 1977.

PUBLICATIONS FOR ADULTS

Novels

Amanda/Miranda. New York, Viking, and London, Gollancz, 1980.
New York Time. New York, Delacorte, and London, Gollancz, 1981.
This Family of Women. New York, Delacorte, and London, Gollancz, 1983.
Voices after Midnight. New York, Delacorte, 1989.

Editor

Edge of Awareness: Twenty-five Contemporary Essays, with Ned E. Hoopes. New York, Dell, 1966.
Sounds and Silences: Poetry for Now. New York, Delacorte, 1970.
Mindscapes: Poems for the Real World. New York, Delacorte, 1971.
Leap into Reality: Essays for Now. New York, Dell, 1973.
Urban Studies: A Research Paper Casebook. New York, Random House, 1973.
Transitions: A Literary Paper Casebook. New York, Random House, 1974.
Pictures That Storm inside My Head. New York, Avon, 1976.

Other

Old Town, A Complete Guide: Strolling, Shopping, Supping, Sipping, with Norman Strasma, 2nd edition. [Chicago], 1965.
A Consumer's Guide to Educational Innovations, with Mortimer Smith and George Weber. Washington, D.C., Council for Basic Education, 1972.
The Creative Word 2, with Stephen N. Judy. New York, Random House, 1974.
Housing and Local Government: A Research Guide for Policymakers and Planners. Massachusetts, Lexington Books, 1975.
Contributor, with Kenneth L. Donelson and Alleen Pace Nilsen, *Literature for Today's Young Adults.* Glenview, Illinois, Scott, Foresman, 1980.
Contributor, *Sixteen: Short Stories by Outstanding Young Adult Writers,* edited by Donald R. Gallo. New York, Delacorte, 1984.
Contributor, *Visions: Nineteen Short Stories by Outstanding Writers for Young Adults,* edited by Donald R. Gallo. New York, Delacorte, 1987.
Write a Tale of Terror. Book Lures, 1987.
Contributor, *Connections: Short Stories by Outstanding Writers for Young Adults, edited by Donald R. Gallo.* New York, Delacorte, 1989.
Anonymously Yours. Morristown, New Jersey, Silver Burdette, 1991.

*

Media Adaptations: *The Ghost Belonged to Me* (audio cassette), Live Oak Media, 1976; *Don't Look and It Won't Hurt* (filmstrip with cassette), New York, Random House; *Remembering the Good Times* (cassette), Listening Library, 1987; *Are You in the House Alone?* (TV movie), CBS, 1977; *Child of Glass* (TV movie based on *The Ghost Belonged to Me*), Walt Disney Productions, 1979; *Father Figure* (TV movie), Time-Life Productions, 1980; *Don't Look and It Won't Hurt* (film rights), Cineville Production Company, 1991.

Biography: Essay in *Something about the Author Autobiography Series,* Volume 2, Detroit, Gale, 1986; essay in *Speaking for Our-*

selves: Autobiographical Sketches by Notable Authors of Books for Young Adults, Volume 1, compiled and edited by Donald R. Gallo, National Council of Teachers of English, 1990.

Critical Study: Entry in *Children's Literature Review,* Volume 15, Detroit, Gale, 1988.

*   *   *

Richard Peck's understanding of young adults and their interests is shown through books whose themes touch young people closely: friendship, loneliness, and relationships with peers and with family. His work shows a concern that young people find a sense of belonging, and that they should not feel alone at times when they must cope with problems that threaten to overwhelm them: the death of a friend or parent, rape, an unwanted pregnancy. At the same time, Peck's protagonists are young adults who are, or come to be, independent of the crowd, who learn to be responsible and to have respect for themselves and others. They "grow," Peck writes in his autobiography, *Anonymously Yours,* "by being backed into corners."

Peck's novels variously incorporating those elements of mystery, melodrama, the supernatural, and humor which have appeal for teenage readers, also extend their horizons by featuring protagonists who venture out on journeys of independence into different locations of time and place. "Characters take trips into wider worlds," he explains in *Anonymously Yours,* in which Peck makes connections between the places and people in his own life with settings and characters in his books.

In these books, adolescents meet a wealth of diverse characters ranging from perceptive and witty elderly people to lovesick teachers. Peck is adept at sketching a character in a few lines. Many of his secondary characters are parents: a father scarred by his Vietnam experience in *Princess Ashley,* an overbearing snobby mother pushing her daughter toward being a "Super Doll" in *Representing Super Doll,* parents who have opted out from the lives of their teenagers, Jessica's father in *Unfinished Portrait of Jessica,* for example, and parents who are often themselves alone, and try singlehandedly to understand and support their teenagers.

Peck writes sensitively about the emotions of boys and their relationships, especially those between father and son. When Jim Atwater's mother commits suicide in *Father Figure,* Jim is left fending off feelings of guilt, and describes his pent-up emotions and subsequent events in a glib tone, as if from a long distance. Left in the care of an elderly, sympathetic, though emotionally distant grandmother, Jim takes responsibility for his younger brother Byron. However, when it is arranged that he and Byron join their father, Jim finds that his buried resentment of his father's leaving the family eight years before causes him to feel anger and jealousy over the bond that grows between Byron and their father.

In *Remembering the Good Times* Buck adjusts to his parents' divorce and makes the decision to live with his father; their easygoing relationship is contrasted by the distant relationship between Trav and his parents. Trav, driven by an inner despair, withdraws from his friends and his parents, and not until it is too late do his friends realize the depth of his withdrawal, and the signals he was giving out to them. Peck offers no solution to the problem of teenage suicide; this he implies concerns everyone. The novel is a story of teenage isolation, a lack of communication, and the loss of roots, but it is also about love and friendship and moving forward with hope.

In *Close Enough to Touch* Matt's father is understanding and supportive when Matt is overwhelmed by grief after the death of his girlfriend Dory. Peck writes sensitively about Matt's emotions and growing love for Margaret, a girl who finally helps Matt free himself from self-pity. In a lighter vein is the plight of sixteen-year-old Drew in *Those Summer Days I Never Met.* It is with dread that Drew looks forward to a Baltic cruise with his sister Steph—a fourteen-year-old "pain"—and their unknown grandmother, when his plans had originally included a driving license and "maybe even girls." However, Drew's growing perceptiveness allows him to gauge the changes in Steph and himself that summer as they grow to love and respect their grandmother and the reason for their grandmother's invitation. Their grandmother, the "sweetheart of Swingtime," who is on the cruise for her last performance, is one of Peck's singular, clear-eyed elderly characters who seems to understand young people intuitively.

Humor and the supernatural are deliciously blended in Peck's four "Blossom Culp" books, whose main setting is Bluff City, USA, during the years 1913-14. The incomparable, spunky Blossom Culp, who carefully distinguishes herself from the popular, beautiful, and wealthy people around her and who goes by rules of her own, is first seen through the eyes of Alexander Armsworth in *The Ghost Belonged to Me.* Together, Blossom and Alexander partake in a myriad of adventures, including a supernatural encounter and a visit to England in *Ghost I Have Been.*

Through displacements of time and place, Peck deftly weaves history in his novels. Young readers are introduced to an Egyptian princess and grave robberies in Ancient Egypt as well as the suffragette movement in Blossom's own time-frame in *Blossom Culp and the Sleep of Death.* An interest in local history sends seventh graders Flip and Brian looking for a roller coaster in an old amusement park in *Dreamland Lake,* where the discovery of a dead tramp leads to a real tragedy; a novel in which perhaps the real mystery is for Brian the different faces of "death" itself. In the suspenseful *Voices After Midnight,* Peck blends elements of history, the supernatural, and romance as Chad and his siblings travel between past and present in their New York rented house and its surroundings and become involved in the romantic lives of the Dunlap family during the 1800s. The rescue of Emily and Tyler Dunlap brings the story full-circle to family roots that prove the Dunlap's are "longlost cousins" of Chad's family. Peck's ghost characters in this title, as in the "Culp" books, are not blurred spectral beings but distinct and memorable characters.

Heidi, Chad's elder sister, deserves "a lot of credit" for the rescue, admits her brother. Like Blossom, Heidi is one of several strong adolescent females in Peck's novels. He portrays intelligent, resourceful girls, who are willing and able to make their own decisions and take on responsibilities for themselves and others. In *Don't Look and It Won't Hurt,* Carol, the dependable middle sister, takes on the responsibility of visiting her sister and persuading her to give her baby up for adoption. Carol, in effect, takes her parents' place in showing love and care to both of her sisters. Similarly, Gail in *Are You in the House Alone?* also has a painful decision to make after she is raped. She is strong enough not to run away from the problem and thinks clearly through her options, realizing her responsibility in protecting others.

Peck also writes of the relationships between mothers and daughters. In *Princess Ashley,* Chelsea distances herself from her mother as much as possible until a tragic event occurs and she learns to value her mother's work as a guidance counselor. It is also a novel about peer pressure and friendship, as Chelsea works out her own values rather than following those of the popular Ashley. Jessica idolizes her absent father in *Unfinished Portrait of Jessica,* and her relationship with her mother is one of criticism and blame. After a vacation with her father in Acapulco, however, she realizes his betrayal and returns to forge a new relationship with her mother whom she now feels she is meeting "for the first time."

Peck writes well and with understanding about the culture, emotions, and relationships of young adults. Using humor, a variety of well-drawn characters, and his knowledge of what young people like to read, Peck creates entertaining books that appeal to both sexes.

—Hilary S. Crew

———

PECK, Robert Newton. American. Born in Vermont, 17 February 1928. Educated at Rollins College, Winter Park, Florida, A.B. 1953; law student, Cornell University, Ithaca, New York. Served in the U.S. Army, Infantry, 1945-47; served with 88th Division in Italy, Germany, and France; received commendation. Married Dorothy Anne Houston in 1958; one son and one daughter. Writer and farmer. Formerly, lumberjack, paper mill worker, hog butcher; advertising executive, New York City. Owner of publishing company, Peck Press; teacher, and speaker at conferences; writer of songs and television commercials and jingles. Recipient: American Library Association best book for young adults citation, Spring Book Festival award older honor, *Book World,* both 1973, *Media & Methods* Maxi award (paperback), 1975, and Colorado Children's Book award, 1977, all for *A Day No Pigs Would Die; New York Times* outstanding book citation, 1973, for *Millie's Boy;* Child Study Association of America children's book of the year citations, 1973, for *Millie's Boy,* 1975, for *Bee Tree and Other Stuff,* 1976, for *Hamilton,* and 1987, for *Soup on Ice;* New York Public Library's books for the teen age citations, 1980 and 1981, for *A Day No Pigs Would Die,* 1980, 1981, and 1982, for *Hang for Treason,* and 1980 and 1982, for *Clunie;* Mark Twain award, Missouri Association of School Librarians, 1981, for *Soup for President;* Notable Children's Trade Book in the Field of Social Studies citations, National Council for Social Studies and the Children's Book Council, 1982, for *Justice Lion,* and 1986, for *Spanish Hoof;* Michigan Young Reader's award, Michigan Council of Teachers, 1984, for *Soup;* Bologna International Children's Book Fair, 1985, for *Spanish Hoof.* Address: 500 Sweetwater Club Circle, Longwood, FL 32779, U.S.A.

<small>Publications for Young Adults</small>

Fiction

A Day No Pigs Would Die. New York, Knopf, 1972; London, Hutchinson, 1973.
Millie's Boy. New York, Knopf, 1973.
Soup, illustrated by Charles Gehm. New York, Knopf, 1974.
Fawn. Boston, Little, Brown, 1975.
Soup and Me, illustrated by Charles Lilly. New York, Knopf, 1975.
Wild Cat, illustrated by Hal Frenck. New York, Holiday House, 1975.
Hamilton, illustrated by Laura Lydecker. Boston, Little, Brown, 1976.
Hang for Treason. New York, Doubleday, 1976.

King of Kazoo, illustrated by William Bryan Park. New York, Knopf, 1976.
Rabbits and Redcoats, illustrated by Laura Lydecker. New York, Walker & Co., 1976.
Last Sunday, illustrated by Ben Stahl. New York, Doubleday, 1977.
Patooie, illustrated by Ted Lewin. New York, Knopf, 1977.
Trig, illustrated by Pamela Johnson. Boston, Little, Brown, 1977.
Eagle Fur. New York, Knopf, 1978.
Soup for President, illustrated by Ted Lewin. New York, Knopf, 1978.
Trig Sees Red, illustrated by Pamela Johnson. Boston, Little, Brown, 1978.
Basket Case. New York, Doubleday, 1979.
Clunie. New York, Knopf, 1979.
Hub, illustrated by Ted Lewin. New York, Knopf, 1979.
Mr. Little, illustrated by Ben Stahl. New York, Doubleday, 1979.
Soup's Drum, illustrated by Charles Robinson. New York, Knopf, 1980.
Trig Goes Ape, illustrated by Pamela Johnson. Boston, Little, Brown, 1980.
Justice Lion. Boston, Little, Brown, 1981.
Kirk's Law. New York, Doubleday, 1981.
Soup on Wheels, illustrated by Charles Robinson. New York, Knopf, 1981.
Banjo, illustrated by Andrew Glass. New York, Knopf, 1982.
Trig or Treat, illustrated by Pamela Johnson. Boston, Little, Brown, 1982.
Soup in the Saddle, illustrated by Charles Robinson. New York, Knopf, 1983.
Dukes. Englewood, Florida, Pineapple Press, 1984.
Soup's Goat, illustrated by Charles Robinson. New York, Knopf, 1984.
Jo Silver. Englewood, Florida, Pineapple Press, 1985.
Soup on Ice, illustrated by Charles Robinson. New York, Knopf, 1985.
Spanish Hoof. New York, Knopf, 1985.
Soup on Fire, illustrated by Charles Robinson. New York, Delacorte, 1987.
Hallapoosa. New York, Walker & Co., 1988.
The Horse Hunters. New York, Random House, 1988.
Soup's Uncle, illustrated by Charles Robinson. New York, Delacorte, 1988.
Arly. New York, Walker & Co., 1989.
Higbee's Halloween. New York, Walker & Co., 1990.
Soup's Hoop, illustrated by Charles Robinson. New York, Delacorte, 1990.
Arly's Run. New York, Walker & Co., 1991.
Little Soup's Birthday. New York, Dell, 1991.
Little Soup's Hayride. New York, Dell, 1991.
FortDog July. New York, Walker & Co., 1992.
Little Soup's Turkey. New York, Dell, 1992.
Soup in Love, illustrated by Charles Robinson. New York, Delacorte, 1992.
Little Soup's Bunny. New York, Dell, forthcoming.
Soup Ahoy. New York, Knopf, forthcoming.
A Part of the Sky. New York, Knopf, forthcoming.

Play

King of Kazoo, music and lyrics by Peck, illustrated by William Bryan Park. New York, Knopf, 1976.

Poetry

Bee Tree and Other Stuff, illustrated by Laura Lydecker. New York, Walker & Co., 1975.

Other

Path of Hunters: Animal Struggle in a Meadow, illustrated by Betty Fraser. New York, Knopf, 1973; London, Macdonald and Jane's, 1974.

PUBLICATIONS FOR ADULTS

Novels

The Happy Sadist. New York, Doubleday, 1962.
The King's Iron. Boston, Little, Brown, 1977.
The Seminole Seed. Englewood, Florida, Pineapple Press, 1983.

Other

Secrets of Successful Fiction. Cincinnati, Writer's Digest Books, 1980.
Fiction Is Folks: How to Create Unforgettable Characters. Cincinnati, Writer's Digest Books, 1983.
My Vermont. Englewood, Florida, Peck Press, 2 vols., 1985, 1988.

*

Media Adaptations: *Soup* (TV), ABC-TV, 1978; *A Day No Pigs Would Die* (cassette), Listening Library; *Soup and Me, Soup for President,* and *Mr. Little,* adapted for television's *Afterschool Specials,* American Broadcasting Companies, Inc. (ABC-TV).

Biography: Entry in *Fifth Book of Junior Authors and Illustrators,* Bronx, New York, H.W. Wilson, 1983; essay in *Something about the Author Autobiography Series,* Volume 1, Detroit, Gale, 1986; essay in *Speaking for Ourselves: Autobiographical Sketches by Notable Authors of Books for Young Adults,* Volume 1, compiled and edited by Donald R. Gallo, National Council of Teachers of English, 1990.

Critical Study: Entry in *Contemporary Literary Criticism,* Volume 17, Detroit, Gale, 1981.

*   *   *

Robert Newton Peck ranks among the more prolific contemporary authors of fiction for children and young adults. His autobiographical and highly successful first novel, *A Day No Pigs Would Die,* has become the critical touchstone for measuring the artistic merit of Peck's fiction. Unfortunately, few novels come close to achieving the warmth and intensity of this classic coming-of-age story. Set in rural Vermont, it is the story of thirteen-year-old Rob Peck whose father makes his meager living slaughtering hogs. The fact that Haven Peck carries the smell of death foreshadows his own dying, which Rob must come to accept. The opening chapter in which Rob helps a neighbor's cow deliver its calf characterizes the realism that is a hallmark of this story. Rob's painful intervention in the birthing leads to his receiving a pig as a reward, and the

pig becomes Rob's pet. Later when the pig proves to be barren, Rob learns that a poor family cannot afford the luxury of feeding a pet when food is scarce, so they must slaughter the pig. In this transition from childhood to the adult world, Rob builds a close, loving relationship with his father which equips him to deal with his father's death with greater maturity and responsibility.

Much of Peck's fiction is rooted in the past. *Eagle Fur, Fawn, Hang for Treason,* and *Rabbits and Redcoats* reach back to Colonial and Revolutionary War times for realistic stories that depict violent events in sometimes graphic detail. Father-son relationships continue to be a familiar Peck theme. In *Eagle Fur,* for instance, the young man, who comes to the new world as an indentured servant, not only develops a quasi father-son relationship with the fur trader to whom he is bound but also falls in love with the Indian women he lives with. While *Eagle Fur* was not initially marketed as a young adult book, it has begun to appear in young adult collections in libraries. *Millie's Boy,* set in Vermont in the late 1890s, is the story of Titmouse Smith's search for his father after someone murders his mother. The close tie between Arly Poole and his father is central to the plot of *Arly,* which is set in rural Florida in 1927.

Peck's penchant for writing adventure stories for younger readers reflects the influence of Twain's *The Adventures of Tom Sawyer* and is particularly evident in his Soup series. Also set in Vermont, these humorous tales trace the adventures of Rob and his pal, Soup (real name Luther Wesley Vinson) in slight and often predictable plots built around childhood escapades. Young readers are drawn to these books, which accounts for the long life of the series and, no doubt, the recent addition of Little Soup stories for beginning readers.

In keeping with his stated goal of writing four books a year, Peck began an adventure series for young female readers featuring Elizabeth Trigman, better known as Trig, but his heroine and her genuine Marvin Purvis Official Junior G-Man Machine Gun retired after her fourth adventure. He has focused on female protagonists in other works of a more serious nature, such as *Clunie,* the story of a retarded girl, and *Spanish Hoof,* which deals with a mother and daughter struggling to manage during the depression without a husband and father. Although these are hardly memorable books, they reflect Peck's efforts to address a range of social issues in his fiction.

Teachers are familiar supporting characters in a number of Peck's novels. Miss Kelly is the boys' favorite teacher in the Soup series, and in *Mr. Little,* Lester Little is the unexpected replacement for Miss Kellogg, the wonderful teacher Finley Streeter and his pal Stanley Dragavich had looked forward to having. Mr. Little weathers the series of pranks Finley and Drag play on him, but in the end his act of heroism ensures their respect and underscores a romantic if not sentimental bent in many books.

In *Arly* and *Arly's Run,* Peck has elevated the role of teacher to a dramatic high in the person of Miss Binnie Hoe, who, ironically, is brought to Jailtown by Miss Liddy Tant, daughter of the man who owns most of Jailtown and who has perpetuated the system that exists there. Miss Hoe offers education as an instrument of freedom to children and youth doomed to slave as farm laborers. Arly's father is in failing health, an added burden for an aging man attempting to meet the weekly rent for their dirt-floor shack and their continuing debt at the local store, which makes all the families on Shack Row virtual prisoners. As Dan Poole grows weaker, field boss Roscos Broda forces Arly and his friend Huff into service, which keeps them from attending Miss Hoe's new school. Miss Hoe realizes that Arly must leave Jailtown if he is to survive, and she and others make arrangements for his secret departure after his father's death. This sets the stage for the story's sequel, *Arly's Run,* in which Arly discovers that other forms of slavery exist beyond Jailtown and that freedom does have its price.

The Arly novels are refreshing in that they show what Peck can do with serious issues of social significance. These books still fall short of the excellence of *A Day No Pigs Would Die,* but Arly is a believable character that young adult readers can admire. Like Arly, readers will be angry that Huff's thirteen-year-old sister elects to go to work in Miss Angel Free's Lucky Leg Social Club rather than work in the fields; that Brother Smith, who longs to be able to read the Bible his wife has left him, would yield to community pressure and stop attending classes with the children, saying "School ain't no place for some old blacky like me." The novels reflect the importance freedom has to an indentured servant or to any humans or animals, as Dodge Yardell notes in *The Horse Hunters* when young Ladd Bodeen urges him to join in capturing the wild stallion his own father had never been able to bring in.

There is no question that Peck is a capable storyteller. However, even *Arly* and *Arly's Run* continue his tendency to capture the folksy language of rural speakers with strained verbs and adjectives that smack of stereotyping. Nevertheless, his work also contains serious fiction that will go beyond mere entertainment and challenge readers to come to grips with the kinds of problems youth face today.

—Hugh Agee

PETERSEN, P(eter) J(ames). American. Born in Santa Rosa, California, 23 October 1941. Educated at Stanford University, California, A.B. 1962; San Francisco State College (now University), California, M.A. 1964; University of New Mexico, Albuquerque, Ph.D. 1972. Married Marian Braun in 1963; two daughters. Writer. English instructor, Shasta College, Redding, California, since 1964. Recipient: National Endowment for the Humanities fellowship, 1976-77; *Would You Settle for Improbable?* and *Nobody Else Can Walk It for You* were named to the American Library Association's list of best books for young adults for 1982 and 1983, respectively. Agent: Ruth Cohen, Inc., P.O. Box 7626, Menlo Park, CA 94025. Address: 1243 Pueblo Court, Redding, CA 96001, U.S.A.

PUBLICATIONS FOR YOUNG ADULTS

Fiction

Would You Settle for Improbable? New York, Delacorte, 1981.
Nobody Else Can Walk It for You. New York, Delacorte, 1982.
The Boll Weevil Express. New York, Delacorte, 1983.
Here's to the Sophomores. New York, Delacorte, 1984.
Corky and the Brothers Cool. New York, Delacorte, 1985.
Going for the Big One. New York, Delacorte, 1986.
The Freshman Detective Blues. New York, Delacorte, 1987.
Good-bye to Good Ol' Charlie. New York, Delacorte, 1987.
How Can You Hijack a Cave? New York. Delacorte, 1988.
The Fireplug Is First Base. New York, Dutton, 1990.
I Hate Camping. New York, Dutton, 1991.

Liars. New York, Simon and Schuster, 1992.
The Sub. New York, Dutton, 1993.
I Want Answers and a Parachute. New York, Simon and Schuster, 1993.

*

Biography: Essay in *Speaking for Ourselves, Too* compiled and edited by Donald R. Gallo, National Council of Teachers of English, 1993.

P.J. Petersen comments:

Because I have tried to avoid repeating myself, my books vary enormously—from adventure novels to comedies to mysteries. The one similar element is in the approach to life taken by my most sympathetic characters: they keep trusting and hoping and caring, even though they're often hurt and disappointed.

*   *   *

P.J. Petersen writes novels with realistic characters, lively dialogue, vivid settings, in a simple briskly paced style easy to read and enjoy, placing him in the top bracket of twentieth century young adult authors.

Going for the Big One is a good example of dealing with problems. Thirteen-year-old Jefferson County Bates, his sister Annie, and his brother Dave have been abandoned by their stepmother who can't handle the job of raising this unwanted family by herself. Their truck-driving father is on the road somewhere in Alaska. After Dave has a run-in with the law for stealing a television, the kids escape to the mountains with camping gear and twenty dollars left by the stepmother, to face an eventful, frightening journey through the High Sierras. When a wounded cocaine dealer takes them hostage, they are faced with even more danger. A Literary Guild selection, this book is filled with excitement, including a fight with a bear, the struggle against starvation, besides facing a coke-crazed drug dealer. The three young people learn that together they can handle almost anything that comes along, even their father's shiftless ways. P.J. Petersen has written a colorfully portrayed, thrill-filled page-turner, filled with sibling love and loyalty.

Good-bye to Good Ol' Charlie is the funny story of a boy trying to be someone other than everyone's pal or a regular "good old boy." He tries on different roles and costumes, acting the parts of Chet the Mysterious, Chad the Poet, Chuck the Cowboy, and Chip the Joe Cool. After he gets in a fight with the town bully, he decides to be just plain Charlie, having learned the world won't stop just because someone doesn't like him, and that his performances are only for somebody else's benefit. Mr. Petersen has written an amusing story of an adolescent coming to grips with reality, filled with humor and affection, frustrations and accomplishments, with the protagonist coming out where he should, just being himself.

The Freshman Detective Blues tells of two friends finding a skeleton weighted down by a boat motor in a lake. Jack is sure the skeleton is that of his father who has been missing for nine years. Jack's friend, Eddie, a freshman in high school, who is falling in love with a seemingly unattainable young beauty in his class, throws himself into trying to solve the mystery of the skeleton. Eddie not only solves the mystery, but solves the problem of being allowed by the parents of his girlfriend to spend time with her. Petersen builds up the suspense, throwing in humor with a little horror, to make a good mystery story with a surprise conclusion.

Liars is also a mystery, taking place in Alder Creek, California. Sam Thompson, whose mother was killed in a car accident a couple of years ago, lives with his forest ranger father in a little town in the mountains. Sam discovers he has the ability to dowse for water and also has the uncanny ability to detect if someone is lying to him. When Uncle Gene's house is burned down by someone searching for the man's map to his gold mine, Sam finds that even his own father is lying to him and things tend to get out of hand. Another exciting story, filled with laughter and family loyalty, this adventure also keeps the reader in suspense until the very end. The setting is memorable, the characters convincing, and the book is another of Petersen's thrillers.

A student teacher brings a juvenile offender into Michael Parker's English class in *Would You Settle for Improbable*. Arnold is not well-received by the class, but when he goes out on a limb to save a classmate from the wrath of the principal because of a prank, the class changes their attitudes. Then when he steals a car and runs away with the class money, another crisis is met and handled. A funny yet touching story with believable characters facing realistic problems, the story is fast-paced, dealing with the challenge of changing destructive behavior patterns, making for thought-provoking but fun reading for young adults.

Here's to the Sophomores is a sequel to *Would You Settle for Improbable* and involves the same characters, telling how they handle being sophomores in high school. The main character, Michael Parker, breaks his leg, gets expelled from school, and lands in a lunchroom brawl. He secretly finds himself in love but still has time for his friend, Warren, who is trying to cope with his parents getting a divorce. Young adults will enjoy reading this book about accepting differences and standing up for convictions.

The Boll Weevil Express is a story of runaways Lars and Doug, two young friends dissatisfied with their lives in general, who decide to run away to San Francisco. Doug's sister insists on going, too, so the three jump a railroad car. Thus ensues an adventure filled with trouble with the law, facing the dangers of San Francisco's Market Street, looking starvation in the eye with no money to buy food, concerning a trio of young people who face hurts and disappointments, trusting and hoping that things will get better, and who learn that life does go on regardless of frustrations and complexities that fill each day.

It is apparent that P.J. Petersen enjoys writing for young adults. He handles difficult ethical problems that young people confront with ease and intelligence. He doesn't preach, but subtly portrays possible solutions to problems encountered by young adults in their ever-changing world. His realistic, exciting stories, filled with emotion, human relationships, the good and evil that fill the world of today, all deal with how young people can and do survive, as they seek and usually find the answers they need.

—Carol Doxey

* * *

PEYTON, K.M. Pseudonym for Kathleen (Wendy) Peyton; also writes as Kathleen Herald. British. Born in Birmingham, England, 2 August 1929. Educated at Wimbledon High School; Kingston School of Art, 1947; Manchester Art School, Art Teacher's Diploma, 1952. Married Michael Peyton in 1950; two daughters. Art teacher,

Northampton High School, England, 1952-56; writer, since 1956. Recipient: Carnegie Medal Commendation from the British Library Association, 1962, for *Windfall*, 1964, for *The Maplin Bird*, 1965, for *The Plan for Birdsmarsh*, 1966, for *Thunder in the Sky*, 1967, for *Flambards*, 1969, for *Flambards in Summer*, and 1977, for *The Team*; *New York Herald Tribune* Spring Book Festival award Honor Book, 1965, for *The Maplin Bird*; Carnegie Medal, 1969, for *The Edge of the Cloud*; *Boston Globe-Horn Book* award Honor Book, 1969, for *Flambards*; *Guardian* award, 1970, for the "Flambards" trilogy; Child Study Association of America's Children's Books of the Year, 1969, for *Fly-by-Night*, 1971, for *Pennington's Last Term*, 1974, for *Pennington's Heir*, and 1976, for *The Team*; American Library Association's Best Books for Young Adults, 1979, for *Prove Yourself a Hero*; *School Library Journal*'s Best Books of Spring, 1979, for *A Midsummer Night's Death*. Seven of Peyton's books have been named American Library Association Notable Books, and six have been named to the *Horn Book* honor list. Address: Rookery Cottage, North Fambridge, Essex CM3 6LP, England.

PUBLICATIONS FOR YOUNG ADULTS

Fiction

North to Adventure. London, Collins, 1958; New York, Platt & Munk, 1965.

Stormcock Meets Trouble. London, Collins, 1961.

The Hard Way Home, illustrated by R. A. Branton. London, Collins, 1962; as *Sing a Song of Ambush,* New York, Platt & Munk, 1964.

Windfall, illustrated by Victor Ambrus. London, Oxford University Press, 1962; as *Sea Fever,* Cleveland, World Publishing, 1963.

Brownsea Silver. London, Collins, 1964.

The Maplin Bird, illustrated by Victor Ambrus. London, Oxford University Press, 1964; Cleveland, World Publishing, 1965.

The Plan for Birdsmarsh, illustrated by Victor Ambrus. London, Oxford University Press, 1965; Cleveland, World Publishing, 1966.

Thunder in the Sky, illustrated by Victor Ambrus. London, Oxford University Press, 1966; Cleveland, World Publishing, 1967.

Flambards. London, Oxford University Press, 1978; as *The Flambards Trilogy,* New York, Puffin Books, 1980.

Flambards, illustrated by Victor Ambrus. London, Oxford University Press, 1967; Cleveland, World Publishing, 1968.

The Edge of the Cloud, illustrated by Victor Ambrus. London, Oxford University Press, 1969; New York, World Publishing, 1969.

Flambards in Summer, illustrated by Victor Ambrus. London, Oxford University Press, 1969; New York, World Publishing, 1970.

Fly-by-Night, illustrated by the author. London, Oxford University Press, 1968; Cleveland, World Publishing, 1969.

Pennington: A Trilogy, Oxford, Oxford University Press, 1984.

Pennington's Seventeenth Summer, illustrated by the author. London, Oxford University Press, 1970; as *Pennington's Last Term,* New York, Crowell, 1971.

The Beethoven Medal, illustrated by the author. London, Oxford University Press, 1971, New York, Crowell, 1972.

Pennington's Heir, illustrated by the author. London, Oxford University Press, 1973; New York, Crowell, 1974.

A Pattern of Roses, illustrated by the author. London, Oxford University Press, 1972; New York, Crowell, 1973.

The Team, illustrated by the author. London, Oxford University Press, 1975; New York, Crowell, 1976.

Prove Yourself a Hero. London, Oxford University Press, 1977; New York, Collins World, 1978.

The Right-Hand Man, illustrated by Victor Ambrus. London, Oxford University Press, 1977; New York, Oxford University Press, 1979.

A Midsummer Night's Death. London, Oxford University Press, 1978; New York, Collins World, 1979.

Marion's Angels, illustrated by Robert Micklewright. London and New York, Oxford University Press, 1979; as *Falling Angel,* London, Methuen, 1983.

Dear Fred. London, Bodley Head, and New York, Philomel Books, 1981.

Flambards Divided. Oxford, Oxford University Press, 1981; New York, Philomel Books, 1982.

Going Home, illustrated by Chris Molan. Oxford, Oxford University Press, and illustrated by Huck Scarry, New York, Philomel Books, 1982.

Free Rein. New York, Philomel Books, 1983; as *The Last Ditch,* Oxford, Oxford University Press, 1984.

Who, Sir? Me, Sir? Oxford and New York, Oxford University Press, 1983.

Frogett's Revenge, illustrated by Leslie Smith. Oxford, Oxford University Press, 1985; illustrated by Maureen Bradley, New York, Puffin Books, 1987.

Downhill All the Way. Oxford, Oxford University Press, 1988.

Darkling. London, Corgi, and New York, Delacorte, 1989.

The Boy Who Wasn't There. New York, Delacorte, 1992.

Fiction as Kathleen Herald

Sabre, the Horse from the Sea, illustrated by Lionel Edwards. London, A. & C. Black, 1948; New York, Macmillan, 1963.

The Mandrake, illustrated by Lionel Edwards. London, A. & C. Black, 1949.

Crab the Roan, illustrated by Peter Biegel. London, A. & C. Black, 1953.

Publications for Children

Fiction

Plain Jack, illustrated by the author. London, Hamish Hamilton, 1988.

Skylark, illustrated by Liz Roberts. Oxford, Oxford University Press, 1989.

Poor Badger. New York, Doubleday, 1990.

Apple Won't Jump, illustrated by the author. London, Hamish Hamilton, 1992.

Publications for Adults

Novels

The Sound of Distant Cheering. London, Bodley Head, 1986.

No Roses Round the Door. London, Methuen, 1990.

*

Media Adaptations: *Flambards* (television series), ITV (Yorkshire, England), 1976; *Going Home* (cassette), G.K. Hall, 1986.

Biography: Entry in *Third Book of Junior Authors,* New York, H.W. Wilson, 1972; essay in *Speaking for Ourselves, Too* compiled and edited by Donald R. Gallo, National Council of Teachers of English, 1993; essay in *Something about the Author Autobiography Series,* Volume 17, Detroit, Gale, 1994.

*   *   *

One of the most enduringly popular of English writers for young adults, K.M. Peyton published her first novel as a schoolgirl, and has continued to grow and develop as a writer for almost half a century since. Her nearly forty novels range in subject matter from historical fiction, to outdoor adventure in sailing and horse racing, to a series about a concert pianist; in tone Peyton's work can range from romance to farce. A gripping storyteller, Peyton transforms her fairly traditional plots by the conviction with which she creates her characters and the situations they find themselves in. Peyton shows an unflagging sympathy for the emotional confusion and needs of adolescence, and a particular empathy with the rebellious young person who does not want to follow the approved path. At the same time, Peyton's work reveals her admiration for those who persevere and show a single-minded commitment to a goal despite the physical, social, and psychological barriers in the way of achieving it. Peyton's adolescent characters come from many different social classes and backgrounds—from the early nineteenth to the late twentieth century—but virtually all of them share qualities of integrity and courage in the pursuit of their various aims which readers continue to find both endearing and inspiring.

After her early work on adventure and horse stories, Peyton explored deeper veins of character and theme through several novels set in her own chosen home ground of the Essex sea coast at different periods in its history. All the young characters—from the Victorian fisherman's son Matt in *Windfall* and housemaid Emily in *The Maplin Bird* to modern-day Paul in *The Plan for Birdsmarsh*—are from working-class families, and the practical need to find employment is an important issue in all of these novels, as indeed it is for most of Peyton's characters in subsequent novels. The value of developing skills and knowledge, as well as the importance of integrity and self-command, is shown through these books largely in terms of the seafaring life: Matt on his fishing smack and Sam, who works on a barge conveying goods across the English Channel during World War I, both do hard and meaningful work which tests them physically and emotionally. In later novels such as *The Right-Hand Man,* about a young coachman in the Regency period; *Dear Fred,* based on the life of the Victorian jockey Fred Archer; and *Darkling,* about a contemporary racing stable, the area of interest is transferred from boats to horses, but Peyton fully persuades us of the discipline and determination needed to master the skill, as well as the thrill of accomplishment.

While Peyton is enough of a realist to write about place in terms of the work that is done there, she is also enough of a romantic to create her most successful trilogy around a beautiful old country house, Flambards, and an orphaned heiress whose choices in marriage affect the fate of the house. The Flambards trilogy (whose epilogue, *Flambards Divided,* was published a decade later) is Peyton's most popular work and was made into a television series. Christina is a strong and determined character, as she needs to be in order to learn to cope with the eccentricities and injustices of

Edwardian life at Flambards; she is eventually obliged to choose between the two cousins who live there, and she is not afraid to marry the lamed and disinherited Will rather than his handsome brother Mark, nor to work to help Will establish himself as a flyer. Will's passion for the flimsy aircraft just being developed is echoed by Christina, Mark, and the gentle groom Dick's passion for horses and hunting. At one point, Dick risks losing his job to help Christina save a horse which Mark had lamed by his reckless riding. After Will and his father die and Mark is presumed dead, Christina turns to Dick to help her restore and manage the Flambards estate, thereby setting herself even more defiantly against the social codes and expectations of her world. Although a romantic heroine, she is also one of Peyton's most successful rebels. Peyton always balances the romantic passions of the landowners with a sense of how the servants may be affected by their demands and with a wry humour and sense of irony.

Peyton writes remarkably well about both young women and young men. Patrick Pennington, the central character in Peyton's second major trilogy, is a moody, rebellious youth from a squalid home. He has a knack for getting into trouble, but he is also a great pianist. He is as convincingly real a contemporary youth as the young people from the historical novels are believably part of their own periods. Penn is the most troubled and the most brilliant of all Peyton's characters, and his escapades, disasters, and triumphs are recounted with breathtaking excitement. While the first, and most humourous, novel of the Pennington series tells the story of Penn's last year at school more or less from his perspective though not in his voice, the second and third novels continue his story from the point of view of Ruth—the girl who falls in love with him, becomes pregnant, and marries him. The events of these later books become more serious as Penn's musical abilities and personal responsibilities increase, and the slapstick escapades of the first novel are replaced by confrontations which have more serious consequences. Penn's resentment of authority, especially that of the police, threatens his career, but the discipline he has gained through his music eventually helps him to control his temper. The various stages of the relationship between Penn and Ruth are vividly depicted, in all their difficulties and moments of joy, and continue as a subplot in the later novel *Marion's Angels*.

An active person of many interests, Peyton excels in writing about people doing things, whether it be playing the piano, flying a small plane, driving a coach, or—most characteristically—sailing a boat or training a horse. The boats of Peyton's early novels give way to horses in the later ones; *Fly-by-Night*, one of the finest books in the traditional English pony story genre, tells how young Ruth in her pre-Pennington days struggles to purchase and train an unbroken pony, and the story is continued with a gradually changing cast of characters through *The Team, Prove Yourself a Hero*, and *Free Rein*. From impecunious but horse-mad Ruth, the series shifts its focus to another Pony Club member, the wealthy Jonathan Meredith who is one of Peyton's few characters to be relatively lazy and uncommitted. His attitude is a response to that of his domineering and ambitious mother and while he is seen first as just one of the members of a riding team, in subsequent novels the story of his struggle for self-assertion takes on many other adventurous dimensions including kidnapping and murder, while horses recede into the background. If one's mother isn't, like Jonathan's, head of the local Pony Club, horses may provide a means to find oneself outside the confines of family life; in *Dear Fred, The Sound of Distant Cheering* (published for adults) and *Darkling*, three very different young women living in the competitive masculine world

of horse racing struggle to maintain their own identities in the face of the conflicting needs of the horses and the men they love. In *Darkling*, a complex tale of love and family hostilities explored in greater depth than is usually found in a horse story, romantic love is not victorious but is rejected in favor of other relationships, quieter but true.

Peyton's main venture outside the realm of realistic fiction, the time-slip fantasy *A Pattern of Roses*, also concerns a young man in conflict with his family, and particularly his domineering mother, over his choice of career. The concern over social injustice which is an undercurrent in many of Peyton's novels is clearly evident in this one. Slipping back into the Edwardian past of the country village to which he has recently moved, Tim learns about the life of young Tom, a farm laborer who shares Tim's artistic gifts but will have no opportunity to develop them because of the rigid traditional class structure. Tim's psychic experience of Tom's early and needless death gives him the courage to stand up to his parents and determine the course of his own life. This fine novel is one of the few which does not focus on some activity like riding, sailing, or flying, nor does it depend for its climax upon a race or competition such as Peyton uses to provide the scene of a final testing or revelation of maturity for many of her characters. Both Tom and Tim are tested, of course, in the decisions which they have to make, and Peyton certainly never implies that winning the race or competition is all important. Paul in *The Plan for Birdsmarsh*, Jonathan in *Free Rein*, and Ruth in *Fly-by-Night* all find that they gain as much or more from losing a competition as they might have done from winning it.

Competition is the central focus in the comic novel *Who, Sir? Me, Sir?*, which like *The Team* shows the emotional maturing of several young people as they prepare to compete together. Very much the underdogs, the four comprehensive-school students of motley backgrounds who find themselves pitted in a tetrathalon against the wealthy and supercilious teams from privileged private schools do rise to the occasion with some hilarious antics and a little cheating on both sides. When more or less the same group of students appears again in *Downhill All the Way* on the ski slopes of France, their misadventures are equally hilarious, although the theme of emotional growth through testing is less convincingly developed than in most of Peyton's novels. The humor emphasized in this pair of novels is a significant element in much of Peyton's fiction, though it is usually subordinated to the more serious themes, and Peyton does seem happier writing from a fundamentally more serious perspective.

That Peyton can write repeatedly about certain characters, such as Jonathan and Ruth, in very different situations and types of novels indicates both the vitality of the characters she has created and her versatility as a novelist. Her style, though it can slip into cliche, is generally clear and serviceable, and she has an excellent ear for colloquial dialogue. Peyton is particularly skillful at writing about action and arousing the reader's interest in various subjects through making her knowledge an intrinsic part of a gripping plot. Her greatest gift as an author for young adults, however, is the empathy with which she creates her characters, whether contemporary or from the past; while she retains a clear-sighted awareness of their limitations, she gives her often moody and difficult young people warm support in their determination to work out their own sense of what really matters in life.

—Gwyneth Evans

PHIPSON, Joan (Margaret). Australian. Born in Warrawee, New South Wales, 16 November 1912. Educated at Frensham School, Mittagong, New South Wales. Married Colin Hardinge Fitzhardinge in 1944; one daughter and one son. Secretary, London, 1935-37; librarian, Frensham School, 1937-39; copywriter, Radio 2-GB, Sydney, 1939-41; telegraphist, Women's Auxiliary Australian Air Force, 1941-44; author of children's books. Recipient: Australian Children's Book award, 1953, for *Good Luck to the Rider;* Australian Children's Book Council Book of the Year award, 1963, for *The Family Conspiracy;* Boys' Clubs of America Junior Book award, 1963, for *The Boundary Riders; New York Herald Tribune* Children's Spring Book Festival award, 1964, for *The Family Conspiracy; Elizabethan* Silver Medal for *Peter and Butch;* Writers award, 1975, for *Helping Horse;* Australian Authors' award, 1975; Honour Book award from International Board on Books for Young People, 1985, for *The Watcher in the Garden.* Agent: A.P. Watt & Son, 20 John St., London WC1N 2DL. Address: Wongalon, Mandurama, NSW 2792, Australia.

PUBLICATIONS FOR YOUNG ADULTS

Fiction

Good Luck to the Rider, illustrated by Margaret Horder. Sydney and London, Angus & Robertson, 1953; New York, Harcourt Brace, 1968.
Six and Silver, illustrated by Margaret Horder. Sydney and London, Angus & Robertson, 1954; New York, Harcourt Brace, 1971.
It Happened One Summer, illustrated by Margaret Horder. Sydney, Angus & Robertson, 1957; New York, Harcourt Brace, 1964.
The Boundary Riders, illustrated by Margaret Horder. Sydney, Angus & Robertson, and London, Constable, 1962; New York, Harcourt Brace, 1963.
The Family Conspiracy, illustrated by Margaret Horder. Sydney, Angus & Robertson, and London, Constable, 1962; New York, Harcourt Brace, 1964.
Threat to the Barkers, illustrated by Margaret Horder. Sydney, Angus & Robertson, and London, Constable, 1963; New York, Harcourt Brace, 1965.
Birkin, illustrated by Margaret Horder. Melbourne, Lothian, and London, Constable, 1965; New York, Harcourt Brace, 1966.
A Lamb in the Family, illustrated by Lynette Hemmant. London, Hamish Hamilton, 1966.
The Crew of the "Merlin," illustrated by Janet Duschesne. Sydney, Angus & Robertson, and London, Constable, 1966; as *Cross Currents,* New York, Harcourt Brace, 1967.
Peter and Butch. Melbourne and London, Longman, and New York, Harcourt Brace, 1969.
The Haunted Night. Melbourne, Macmillan, and New York, Harcourt Brace, 1970.
Bass and Billy Martin, illustrated by Ron Brooks. Melbourne and London, Macmillan, 1972.
The Way Home. London, Macmillan, and New York, Atheneum, 1973.
Polly's Tiger, illustrated by Gavin Rowe. London, Hamish Hamilton, 1973; illustrated by Erik Blegvad, New York, Dutton, 1974.
Helping Horse. London, Macmillan, 1974; as *Horse with Eight Hands,* New York, Atheneum, 1974.
The Cats. London, Macmillan, and New York, Atheneum, 1976.

Hide till Daytime, illustrated by Mary Dinsdale. London, Hamish Hamilton, 1977.
Fly into Danger. New York, Atheneum, 1978; as *The Bird Smugglers,* Sydney, Methuen, 1977; London, Methuen, 1980.
Keep Calm. London, Macmillan, 1978; as *When the City Stopped,* New York, Atheneum, 1978.
No Escape. London, Macmillan, 1979; as *Fly Free,* New York, Atheneum, 1979.
Mr. Pringle and the Prince, illustrated by Michael Charlton. London, Hamish Hamilton, 1979.
A Tide Flowing. Sydney and London, Methuen, and New York, Atheneum, 1981.
The Watcher in the Garden. Sydney, Methuen, and New York, Atheneum, 1982; London, Methuen, 1983.
Beryl the Rainmaker, illustrated by Laszlo Acs. London, Hamish Hamilton, 1984.
The Grannie Season, illustrated by Sally Holmes. London, Hamish Hamilton, 1985.
Dinko. Sydney, Methuen, 1985.
Hit and Run. New York, Atheneum, 1985; London, Methuen, 1986.
Bianca. London, Viking Kestrel, and New York, McElderry, 1988.
The Shadow. Nashville, Tennessee, Nelson, 1989.

Other

Christmas in the Sun, illustrated by Margaret Horder. Sydney and London, Angus & Robertson, 1951.
Bennelong, illustrated by Walter Stackpool. Sydney and London, Collins, 1975.

*

Media Adaptations: *The Boundary Riders, Fly into Danger, A Tide Flowing, Watcher in the Garden, Dinko,* and *Hit and Run* have been recorded on audio cassette. Most of Phipson's books appear in Braille editions, and have been published in foreign editions in seven different languages.

Manuscript Collection: Lu Rees Archives Collection, Canberra College of Advanced Education.

Biography: Essay in *Something about the Author Autobiography Series,* Volume 3, Detroit, Gale, 1987, pp. 205-219.

Critical Study: Entry in *Children's Literature Review,* Volume 5, Detroit, Gale, 1983.

*   *   *

Joan Phipson is not only one of the most prolific Australian writers for young people but one of the most diverse and versatile, and perhaps one of the least appreciated. Her early books were family adventure stories set in the rural Australia of the 1950s and 1960s.

As her own children grew up her characters became older, and Joan Phipson moved gradually, beginning with *The Crew of the "Merlin,"* toward a young adult audience. At the same time she continued to write for young developing readers. The implied readers of her young adult novels are not switched-on, trendy, sophisticated technocrats but thinking, perceptive—albeit imperfect—young people who are aware of their own limitations and shortcomings. They are prepared to learn about themselves and, through their interaction with others, grow in moral stature. But for whatever age group she is writing and whatever her subject—be it the menace of prowling feral cats *(The Cats),* the honors of bird trapping and smuggling *(Fly into Danger* and *Fly Free)* or the city of Sydney crippled by a general strike caused by the threat of building a nuclear reactor *(When the City Stopped)*—this author always tells a wonderfully graphic and suspenseful story.

In *The Haunted Night* four girls spend a night of horror in an old convict-built house, reputed to be haunted. More realistic and chilling is the tension in *Hit and Run* when Roland Fleming, having stolen a car and fearful that he has killed a baby, tries to elude his hunter, Constable Gordon Sutton. The two play a game of physical and psychological cat-and-mouse. Along with *Hit and Run,* inner tension mounts steadily, especially in *The Watcher in the Garden* and *Bianca.* In the former, both the physical landscape and the mind of Catherine, the protagonist, are in a "hushed tension of waiting" as the hoodlum, Terry, bides his time and plans the death of the blind Mr. Lovett who, of all the characters in the book, is in complete harmony with the environment. In *Bianca,* past terrors— her father's death and her mother's instinctual panic—intensify the present horror of a girl suffering from hysterical amnesia.

The power of the mind is a recurring theme in Phipson's writing. Twentieth-century Tom, the protagonist of *Dinko,* can not only see into the future but is a reincarnation of Dinko from Diocletian's time in history. This metaphysical element culminates in Catherine's psychic communication with Terry in *The Watcher in the Garden* and Bianca's refusing to admit her trauma to her conscious mind.

Bianca is at the end of a lengthy line of Phipson characters who have a deep longing for acceptance and a need to be understood. Because of this, they at times follow false gods and have to learn to evaluate what and whom they esteem. Young Charlie in *The Crew of the "Merlin"* unduly and misguidedly admires Jim, an undeserving older youth. The aggressive Butch Watson, who eschews his given name of Peter in *Peter and Butch,* has to learn the hard way that self-satisfaction is not to be gained by associating with the criminal fringe. The basically solid Prue in *The Way Home* is blindly attracted to her urbane but shallow city cousin, Richard. In *No Escape* Wilfred's claustrophobic fears and sensitivity cause him great mental agony. But his less admirable friend, Johnny, a trapper of wild life, when caught in one of his own snares suffers both physically and psychologically. Both boys gain wisdom from a frightening ordeal.

Despite the number of hoodlums, layabouts, robbers, and delinquents among Phipson's characters, they are real, flesh-and-blood people who, although a menace to society, are not beyond redemption. Terry in *The Watcher in the Garden* is, perhaps, the supreme example. She is concerned, too, with social issues—conservation, delinquency, nuclear power, the possibility of another holocaust— but she never succumbs to slick social realism. She indicates that young people can be traumatised by perceived inner inadequacies but also by society and adult imperfection.

At the same time, many of her characters, although dreamers, are self-contained in that they possess rich inner resources, sometimes a metaphysical "gift." The most potent source of this personal strength comes from an affinity with the earth. This power as a life-force to be reckoned with is made explicit in an early historical novel, *Bass and Billy Martin.* In *The Way Home* it is a tangible presence. Peter who is in harmony with the earth and with water (water being another recurring positive image in Phipson's writing) is obviously one of the "elect," as opposed to the sauve, rational

Richard. Water—the ocean—in *A Tide Flowing* obsesses Mark who has been driven, literally, almost to the edge by his mother's suicidal drowning. It is the sea and the redemptive death of his crippled friend, Connie, that bring healing and wholeness to Mark. Bianca, too, in her distress finds lake water "the last, safe, quiet refuge, the first mother." Mr. Lovett's garden is also an image of safety and regeneration. And as Mr. Lovett's life is being threatened by Terry, just beyond the border of the garden the earth slips into a landslide. So the land is not only stronger than people, it protects those who are in harmony with it, punishes those who reject it, but extends forgiveness and reconciliation to those who are open to its essence. A simple country girl, Margaret, in *The Bird Smugglers* and the seemingly slow-witted Willy in *The Cats* are just two of the diverse characters who attest Joan Phipson's passionate belief in the sanctity of the soil, in the firm reliability of the earth, "softened with the comfort of centuries of fallen leaves." *Dinko,* too, is a statement of faith in the perpetuation and renewal of life: an optimism badly needed by today's bewildered and often disillusioned youth.

—Maurice Saxby

———

PIERCE, Meredith Ann. American. Born in Seattle, Washington, 5 July 1958. Educated at University of Florida, B.A. 1978, M.A. 1980. Writer. Teaching assistant, Office of Instructional Resources, 1978, and instructor of creative writing, 1984, Department of English, University of Florida; bookseller, Bookland, 1981, and Waldenbooks, 1981-87, both Gainesville, Florida; since 1987, library assistant, Alachua County (FL) Library District, Gainesville. Recipient: First prize in junior division, *Scholastic*/Hallmark Cards creative writing contest, 1973, for short story "The Snail"; Best Books for Young Adults citation, American Library Association (ALA), Best of the Best Books 1970-1982 citation, ALA, *New York Times* Notable Children's Book citation, and Parents' Choice Award Superbook citation, all 1982, Children's Book Award, International Reading Association, 1983, California Young Reader Medal, 1986, and *Booklist* Best Books of the Decade (1980-89) list, all for *The Darkangel;* Jane Tinkham Broughton Fellow in writing for children, Bread Loaf Writers' Conference, 1984; Best Books for Young Adults semifinalist, ALA, 1985, for *A Gathering of Gargoyles;* Best Books for Young Adults citation, ALA, 1985, Parents' Choice Award for Literature citation, 1985, and New York Public Library Books for the Teen Age exhibit citation, 1986, all for *The Woman Who Loved Reindeer;* Individual Artist Fellowship Special Award for Children's Literature, Florida Department of State, Division of Cultural Affairs, 1987; Best Books for Young Adults citation, 1991, for *The Pearl of the Soul of the World.* Address: 424-H Northeast Sixth St., Gainesville, FL 32601 U.S.A.

PUBLICATIONS FOR YOUNG ADULTS

"Darkangel" trilogy:

The Darkangel. Boston, Little, Brown, 1982; London, Collins, 1983.
A Gathering of Gargoyles. Boston, Little, Brown, 1984.
The Pearl of the Soul of the World. Boston, Little, Brown, 1990.

"Firebringer" series:

Birth of the Firebringer. New York, Four Winds Press, and London, Macmillan, 1985.
The Woman Who Loved Reindeer. Boston, Little, Brown, 1985; London, Hodder and Stoughton, 1987.
Dark Moon. Boston, Little, Brown, 1992.

Other

(Contributor) *Four from the Witch World* (contains novella "Rampion"), edited by Andre Norton. New York, Tor Books, 1989.

PUBLICATIONS FOR CHILDREN

Where the Wild Geese Go (picturebook), illustrated by Jamichael Henterly. New York, Dutton, 1988.

*

Biography: Entry in *Sixth Book of Junior Authors and Illustrators,* New York, H.W. Wilson, 1989.

Critical Study: Entry in *Children's Literature Review,* Volume 20, Detroit, Gale, 1990.

*   *   *

The works of Meredith Pierce reflect the wellspring of myth and magic and religion that have influenced her and have taken new form in her interpretation. The well-read adolescent or adult can revel in both the story that Pierce tells and the search for connections to other stories in the body of fantasy literature.

The Darkangel and *A Gathering of Gargoyles* are the first two books of a trilogy. Ariel, the slave become heroine, had her beginning in a description of a patient's dream in Jung's autobiography. This stimulus-become-story is also influenced by the tales of Beauty and the Beast and Psyche and Eros. The resulting image, however, is Pierce's own. The books are a rich tapestry of love, devotion, faith, and courage; and like a tapestry, the weaving moves slowly but inexorably to its full realization. These are not quick reads for the casual reader, but are books to be savored and pondered. Ariel seeks to avenge her mistress who has been captured by a vampire and in the process first becomes his slave and then his savior. In her need to free Irrylath from his haunted past, Ariel follows a quest to find the missing lons who can become the steeds for Irrylath's brothers in the battle to free the land from the hold of the White Witch and her six vampire sons. The staunch love that Ariel extends to the creatures and beings with whom she comes in contact holds the key to the success of her mission.

The Pearl of the Soul of the World completes the trilogy, and it does so in dramatic fashion as the truth of the origin of Avaric is revealed. The Ancients from Oceanus had created a vibrant world on a lifeless planet, and when they were called back to their world because of a war, a few remained in their cities. Over centuries, entropy threatened the world with collapse into its original state. Ariel comes to Ravenna, the last of the Ancients, and learns that the White Witch is Ravenna's daughter, driven to madness by rage that she is not a true Ancient. There are two entwined plots, one is the doomed love story of Ariel and Irrylath and the other the relentless

path that Ariel must take as she becomes a great sorceress who has the capacity to save her world. Pierce's writing is rich in metaphor, with clever turns of plot that keep the reader racing to the end. For those who have become involved with the characters, though this book completes the trilogy, it is obvious that there is more to come.

When Caribou is thirteen, her sister-in-law foists a bastard child onto her to raise. As the child grows, it is obvious that he is not fully human; indeed he is a trangl who can take both human and stag form. Caribou becomes the woman who loved reindeer in the story by the same name, though she is incapable of feeling human emotion until the end of the book. The elements of sacrifice, love, and devotion take many forms as Caribou becomes a leader and savior of her people as well as a woman who desires one she cannot have. There is a mythic quality to the story that is reminiscent of the tales of the Laplanders, though the setting is a two-mooned world. Pierce has told an adventurous tale, but at times the action seems overwrought.

It is obvious that Pierce is steeped in the mythology of our world, even when she chooses to create new worlds. The main characters in *Birth of the Firebringer* are unicorns who have been driven from their land by vicious wyverns and who inhabit a place that is threatened by deadly gryphons. The unicorns await a savior, the Firebringer, who will lead them back to their promised land. This is a tale of high adventure and of coming-of-age, the first of a proposed trilogy. Though it is a tale of good and evil, Pierce allows the reader to see that both good and evil are dependent on the perception of the viewer. As in life, there are no easy answers.

In *Dark Moon,* the second book of the trilogy, Jan, prince of the unicorns, is fated to be the Firebringer of his people. Separated from his tribe at the annual mating festival, Jan becomes a captive of humans who wish to use him as a sacrifice. Jan's discovery that different species can work together if they listen to each other has implications for the future. His return to the tribe and the birth of his two colts sets the stage for the last book of the trilogy. As with most high fantasy, there are several subplots working within the story, enriching the tale. The problem, in this case, is that the story drags in places and one wishes that it would move at a faster clip. The segment of Jan in captivity is overwritten and arch. That aside, those who have awaited this book will not be disappointed.

Pierce is a compelling storyteller, making use of the classic mythology that resonates with us and placing it within a new context. When she is at her best, the tales are rich and evocative, stirring the reader to question as well as absorb. There are times, however, that her tellings become too intricate, and the reader loses the thread of the tapestry.

—M. Jean Greenlaw

———

PIERCE, Tamora. American. Born in Connellsville, Pennsylvania, 13 December 1954. Educated at University of Pennsylvania, Philadelphia, B.A. 1977. Tax data collector, City of Kingston, New York, 1977-78; Tax clerk, Towns of Hardenburgh and Denning, New York, 1978; social worker and housemother, McAuley Home for Girls, Buhl, Idaho, 1978-79; Associate Editor of *OpenSpace,* 1978-79; assistant to literary agent, 1979-82, Harold Ober Associates, Inc., New York, 1979-82; creative director, ZPPR Productions, Inc. (radio producers), 1982-88; secretary, Chase Investment

Bank, New York, 1985-89; freelance writer, since 1990. Recipient: German Schüler-Express ZDF Preis der Leseratten (fantasy for German translation), 1985, and South Carolina Children's Book award nomination, 1985-86, both for *In the Hand of the Goddess; Lioness Rampant* was a City of Baltimore Enoch Pratt Free Library selection, 1989; Preconference on Genres of the Young Adult Services Division of the ALA Recommended Fantasy Author, 1991, for *Alanna: The First Adventure.* Agent: Claire M. Smith, Harold Ober Associates, Inc. 425 Madison Avenue, New York NY 10017, U.S.A.

PUBLICATIONS FOR YOUNG ADULTS

Novels

Alanna: The First Adventure. New York, Atheneum, 1983.
In the Hand of the Goddess. New York, Atheneum, 1984.
The Woman Who Rides Like A Man. New York, Atheneum, 1986.
Lioness Rampant. New York, Atheneum, 1988.
Wild Magic. New York, Atheneum, 1992.
Wolf-Speaker. New York, Atheneum, 1994.

Other

Contributor, *Digital Deli,* edited by Steve Ditlea. Workman Publishing, 1984.
Contributor, *Planetfall,* edited by Douglas Hill. New York, Oxford University Press, 1985.

*

Biography: Essay in *Speaking for Ourselves, Too* compiled and edited by Donald R. Gallo, National Council of Teachers of English, 1993.

Tamora Pierce comments:

Writing is something which I prefer to keep simple and direct, knowing that whenever I tackle the kind of Byzantine plot which I like to read about, I fall on my rump most painfully. Humor is always integral to my work: I relate best to those who don't take life too seriously. I want characters who are realistic, informal and down-to-earth, a reflection of the people I like and understand. My female and male protagonists try to deal equitably with one another, a reflection of my feeling that life is too hard to reject potential friends and allies on the grounds of sex. Most importantly, I try to work with misfits or outcasts who carve their own unique places in the world. It is my own experience, and in my books it seems to evoke a powerful response from readers.

In my mail I see things that *I* might have said, writing as a teenager to the writers who inspired me. That is a powerful bond, one I try hard to continue to foster. As a high school senior, I once asked a much-adored humanities teacher why she continued to work with high school students rather than college students who would be more committed to learning. She replied, "Because I'm interested in beginnings, not endings." Fifteen years later, I discovered what she meant, and now I do my best to influence beginnings of my own.

*   *   *

Tamora Pierce's fantasy novels capture the attention of the adventurous young adult reader. Her novels include the Song of the Lioness Quartet and her latest book, *Wild Magic,* which includes many of the characters found in her first four books. Pierce creates heroines that break through the sex role barriers in a medieval fantasy kingdom. Heroines of today, both real and fictional—such as women on the battle field, women as religious leaders, and women in roles of authority—are still trying to break through sex role barriers.

Alanna, the main character in the Song of the Lioness Quartet, is certainly not a damsel in distress. *Alanna: the First Adventure* begins with Alanna rebelling against the thought of living in a convent and her brother Thom against the rigorous training necessary to become a knight. Using their wits and Thom's ability to forge their father's signature, Alanna and her brother change identities. Disguising herself as a boy, Alanna begins the lengthy and grueling training toward knighthood. A willingness to stand up for oneself makes the slightly built Alanna/Alan a favorite friend of young Prince Jonathan. Alanna uses the healing power she has tried to hide to save Jonathan from a deadly sickness, one she suspects was magically conjured. While visiting the Bashir desert tribe Alanna and Jonathan ignore the warnings and enter the forbidden Black City and fight the immortals that lure and devour the Bashir young people. Alanna's true identity is exposed to Jonathan during the battle. The immortals taunt Jonathan: "How long do you think she will last?...She is a girl. She is weak." Though the same thoughts "taunted Alanna from within," she destroys her attackers with "a slender thread of violet fire." The first book of the Song of the Lioness Quartet concludes with Jonathan formally asking Alanna to be his squire, proving his acceptance of a female at his side in battle.

In the Hand of the Goddess, the second book, takes Alanna and Jonathan from the castle and into the streets as they become fast friends with George, the King of Thieves. Alanna and her magical sword Lightning battle Duke Roger, Jonathan's uncle, the most powerful sorcerer in the land. The sorcerer dies, but not before a too close swipe of his sword slices through Alanna's chest binding and the entire kingdom discovers her secret.

Having left Jonathan and her other friends behind, Alanna seeks new adventures and the time to accept her identity as a Lady Knight in *The Woman Who Rides Like a Man.* Returning to the desert, she is captured by Bashir tribesmen. Women have their place in this culture, and it certainly isn't upon a horse—thus her name—Woman Who Rides Like a Man. Alanna proves herself to the Bashir and becomes their first female shaman. She devotes her time to teaching magic to apprentices while her thoughts are torn between her love for the two men she has left behind—Prince Jonathan and George, the King of Thieves. She ponders whether love has a place in her life of freedom and adventure.

In *Lioness Rampant* Alanna comes face to face with yet another man after her heart, Liam Ironarm, the Shang Dragon. Alanna is on a quest for the Dominion Jewel, which in the right hands possesses limitless power for good. Thom, Alanna's twin brother and now a sorcerer, brings Duke Roger back from the dead. In the catacombs beneath the castle, Alanna again sends Roger to his death. Fate intervenes to solve her troubles of the heart. Liam, the Shang Dragon, dies in battle and Jonathan falls in love with the princess Thayet. The Song of the Lioness Quartet concludes with Alanna, still the King's champion, agreeing to marry George—on her terms of course.

While Alanna and George live happily at Pirate's Swoop, their seaside castle, Pierce was busy writing *Wild Magic.* The main character, Daine, is a lonely, frightened thirteen-year-old girl. She fears people as well as the power she has over animals before she meets

Onua, a horse-mistress. Onua, sensing Daine's reluctance to share her past, allows the young girl to open up on her own terms. Onua soon learns that Daine has a unique relationship with the animal world. When the stormwings, immortal creatures that feast upon the dead, try to kill a hawk, Daine uses her "wild magic" to protect this hawk as well as to heal the other birds hurt in the fray. The hawk, in true form, is Numair, a mage who teaches Daine to better control her magic. Daine uses her "wild magic" to help save the kingdom. To do so she must let go of the fragile hold she has over the animals. Daine, fearing for their safety, puts a spell on them so they cannot aid the humans. Not until she realizes that they want to help defend their homes does she release them to help in any way they can. Daine, once alone in the world and afraid of her "wild magic," now finds herself surrounded by people and animals who love and accept her.

Adventure and fantasy readers will enjoy Pierce's books. Her characters are strong-willed, be they male or female. Although her main characters are all female, Prince Jonathan, George the King of Thieves, Liam the Shang Dragon, and the devious Duke Roger will attract the male fantasy or adventure reader as well. Pierce creates female heroines that a young adult reader can identify with: from Alanna and her desire to be something society does not find appropriate for a female, to Daine, a medieval animal-rights activist. Each title can be read alone, but for ultimate enjoyment and understanding, the Lioness Quartet should be read before *Wild Magic.*

Tamora Pierce has taken many issues facing adolescents today, especially young women, and addresses them in action packed, thought-provoking adventure fantasy novels.

—Ruth E. Dishnow

PIKE, Christopher (a pseudonym). American. Writer. Worked as a computer programmer. Agent: Joe Rinaldi, St. Martin's Press Publicity Department, 175 Fifth Avenue, New York, NY 10010.

PUBLICATIONS FOR YOUNG ADULTS

Fiction

Slumber Party. New York, Scholastic, 1985.
Chain Letter. New York, Avon, 1986.
Weekend. New York, Scholastic, 1986.
Thrills, Chills, & Nightmares. New York, Scholastic, 1987.
Christopher Pike. New York, Pocket, 1989.

"Final Friends" series:

The Party. New York, Archway, 1989.
The Dance. New York, Archway, 1989.
The Graduation. New York, Archway, 1989.
Gimme A Kiss. New York, Archway, 1989.
Last Act. New York, Archway, 1989.
Remember Me. New York, Archway, 1989.
Scavenger Hunt. New York, Archway, 1989.
Spellbound. New York, Archway, 1989.
Fall Into Darkness. New York, Archway, 1990.

See You Later. New York, Simon & Schuster, 1990.
Witch. New York, Archway, 1990.
Bury Me Deep. New York, Pocket, 1991.
Die Softly. New York, Pocket, 1991.
Whisper of Death. New York, Pocket, 1991.
The Ancient Evil. New York, Pocket, 1992.
Master of Murder. New York, Pocket, 1992.
Monster. New York, Pocket, 1992.
The Season of Passage. New York, Doherty Associates, 1992.
The Eternal Enemy. New York, Pocket, 1993.
The Immortal. New York, Pocket, 1993.
Road to Nowhere. New York, Pocket, 1993.

PUBLICATIONS FOR ADULTS

Fiction

The Tachyon Web. New York, Bantam, 1987.
Sati. New York, St. Martin's, 1990.

* * *

Few authors can lay claim to inventing a genre, but Christopher Pike can. Although there had been mysteries for teens forever, Pike's *Slumber Party* broke the mold and created something new: the teen thriller. Bearing a slight resemblance to mysteries mixed with the horror shocks of movies likes *Friday the 13th,* teen thrillers took over the marketplace in the face of an exhausted romance genre. By 1992 the shelves of book stores and libraries clearly demonstrated the genre was the most popular and Pike its most popular writer, demonstrated by profiles in *Wall Street Journal* and *Entertainment Weekly.*

The reasons for Pike's huge popularity are varied. Like one of his influences, S.E. Hinton, Pike creates a world without adult characters or adult rules of conduct. His novels are filled with teens on their own, making decisions and suffering the consequences. Because of this, his audience is made up of both boys and girls spanning a large age range from high school down to fifth graders. Like another influence, Stephen King, Pike knows how to scare, shock and keep the pages flipping. His books are nothing if not readable; the complicated plot plays out through a series of nail-biting scenes. If his characters are sometimes no more than types, there are different types than stalk other young adult fiction: they aren't all "good kids," they are rarely innocent, some are sexually active, and most of them have a mean streak. And his characters feel intensely: Pike better than most "mainstream" young adult novelists captures the daily drama and roller coaster emotion of his teen characters ping ponging back and forth between emotions and conflicting desires. While he's not writing morality plays, he is writing stories where kids find themselves trapped between intense feelings of love/lust and hate/vengeance. Finally, unlike stupid slasher movies or many teen mysteries, Pike's plots are complex and clever, normally built around righting a past wrong or keeping a secret at all costs.

Slumber Party is textbook Pike: his first young adult novel contains the elements which would make his future work, and those of his many imitators, so successful. Pike takes his characters (six single girls) and puts them in a deserted setting (a snowed-in ski lodge). He lays out unexplained happenings (a snowman that melts), starts making characters disappear (all that's left of one is a ski), and adds a supernatural element (an Ouija board). The climax involves the girls about to be killed, not by some outside force, but by one of their group. It seems the "new girl" of the group, Celeste, is really an old member of the group, Nicole. Nicole, of course, had been wronged by the others in the group. Eight years earlier she had been at another slumber party when a fire broke out which had "killed" Nicole. Now, it is eight years later and she wants revenge. This basic idea: group of kids, deserted setting, unexplained happenings, disappearing characters and supernatural elements would be the guts of *Weekend* and *Spellbound* and remain elements of just about everything else Pike would write.

New ideas were added with *Chain Letter* which lifted its plot from Lois Duncan's *I Know What You Did Last Summer.* Same set-up: a group of kids are out driving when they accidently kill someone. A letter comes telling the group they will be punished and then one by one each group member is terrorized. Yet, hanging from the same plot threads, Pike spins a different kind of tale adding two important elements to his character: the horror of humiliation and the gross out. The services the "caretaker" demands on the teens are not so much to punish them as to embarrass them: a straight A student is to fail a test, another is to "streak" through school, and another is to come to school dressed in a clown suit. When she refuses this humiliation, enter the gross out in the form of a bedroom floor covered with cockroaches. *Chain Letter* is easily one of Pike's best, inspiring a sequel *Chain Letter 2: The Ancient Evil. Last Act* and *The Final Friends* trilogy lost the deserted setting moving the action into the heart of high school life, but the rest of the elements remained. *Final Friends* reflects another of Pike's acknowledged influences, Agatha Christie, as he is working in more of a locked-room mystery than a thriller.

Pike's nastiest book, *Gimme A Kiss,* played heavily off the humiliation/revenge theme with its main character's diary being photocopied and passed around school. It also includes another Pike staple: the faked death. In an audacious act, Pike had a character in *Fall Into Darkness* use *Gimme A Kiss* as inspiration for her revenge plot. Despite this, *Fall Into Darkness* is great Pike and his first work translated to a book-on-tape format. The books concern two teenage girls (Ann and Sharon) who are friends yet intensely jealous of each other and with a shared secret in the past. Ann plots to destroy Sharon by faking her death so that Sharon will be tried for her "murder." Pike intercuts scenes from Sharon's trial with those in the past, building to the usual big, final "all is revealed and now you die" scene.

Remember Me was similar—another dead girl, but this one really is dead and telling the story as a ghost. While Pike often hints at the supernatural, *Remember Me* was the first full-blown "no logical explanation for this" novel. *Scavenger Hunt* followed and although not a really a good book, it is a pivotal one as Pike mixes his old stuff with more pronounced supernatural elements. There's also some heavy religious imagery which would show up in later works like *Witch. See You Later, Die Softly,* and *Bury Me Deep* are reworkings of past themes and even plots twists, plus all are fairly long. *Master of Murder* is a long inside joke: Pike's protagonist Marvin is a best selling author of teen fiction writing under a pen name (that sums up Pike himself) who is in fact a shy guy (Pike once wrote about himself that he was shy in high school). He gets fan letter (ala the chain letter) that says "I know who you are" (this is the plot of Stephen King's 1989 *The Dark Half*).

After getting this autobiographical novel out of his system, Pike switched gears. He had done a ghost story with *Remember Me* and an end of the world tale with *Whisper of Death,* but *Monster* is his first full-blown horror novel and a masterful one. It begins with a

bang: a teen girl enters a party and shotguns away two classmates because they are monsters. The rest of the book is a rave-up: all red eyes and raw meat. It is outstanding horror, and fine young adult fiction. Pike followed with *Road to Nowhere,* a strange tale about good and evil, then *Eternal Enemy,* a *Terminator* style time travel piece. *The Immortal* was another time travel piece, this time back to ancient Greece as Pike continues to work outside of the thriller genre he created almost a decade ago.

In addition to selling a lot of books, Pike's influence has been considerable. Many other authors have imitated him yet none have come close to getting the right mix. Pike is also influencing young would-be teen writers much as he was influenced by S.E. Hinton. Like Hinton, Pike has sold film rights to his books and when those movies are made, his audience might grow even wider. The move to film is natural as Pike's writing is full of bang-bang scenes and characters in conflict. Finally, while known primarily as a thriller writer, Pike's books work with teens not just become of the chills, but also because they are good young adult fiction. While the characters might be broadly drawn, they are still recognizable to his readers. The problems, concerns and fears of his characters are those of his readers. His characters feel deeply and react strongly as they are trying to survive both Pike's mysterious killers and the horror of modern adolescence.

—Patrick Jones

<hr>

PINKWATER, Daniel Manus. Also writes as Manus Pinkwater. American. Born in Memphis, Tennessee, 15 November 1941. Educated at Bard College, Annandale-on-Hudson, New York, B.A. 1964. Married Jill Miriam Schutz in 1969. Art instructor, Children's Aid Society, 1967-69, Lower West Side Visual Arts Center, 1969, and Henry Street Settlement, 1969, all New York, and Bonnie Brae Farm for Boys, Millington, New Jersey, 1969; assistant project director, Inner City Summer Arts Program, Hoboken, New Jersey, 1970. Regular commentator, *All Things Considered,* National Public Radio, 1987—. Exhibitions: various small galleries and university shows. Recipient: New Jersey Institute of Technology award, 1975, for *Fat Elliot and the Gorilla;* American Library Association Notable Book award, 1976, for *Lizard Music;* Junior Literary Guild selection, 1977, for *Fat Men from Space; New York Times* Outstanding Book, 1978, for *The Last Guru;* Children's Choice book award from the International Reading Association and the Children's Book Council, 1981, for *The Wuggie Norple Story;* Parents' Choice award, 1982, for *Roger's Umbrella.* Address: 111 Crum Elbow Rd., Hyde Park, NY 12538, U.S.A.

<small>PUBLICATIONS FOR YOUNG ADULTS</small>

Fiction

Lizard Music, illustrated by the author. New York, Dodd Mead, 1976.
The Last Guru, illustrated by the author. New York, Dodd Mead, 1978.
Alan Mendelsohn: The Boy from Mars. New York, Dutton, 1979.

Yobgorgle: Mystery Monster of Lake Ontario. New York, Clarion, 1979; revised edition, New York, Bantam, 1981.

Java Jack, with Luqman Keele. New York, Crowell, 1980.

The Worms of Kukumlima. New York, Dutton, 1981.

The Snarkout Boys and the Avocado of Death. New York, Lothrop, 1982.

Young Adult Novel. New York, Crowell, 1982.

Young Adults. New York, Tor, 1985.

Borgel. New York, Macmillan, 1990.

Chicago Days, Hoboken Nights. Reading, Massachusetts, Addison-Wesley, 1991.

Spaceburger. New York, Macmillan, 1993.

PUBLICATIONS FOR CHILDREN

Fiction

Wizard Crystal, illustrated by the author. New York, Dodd Mead, 1973.

Magic Camera, illustrated by the author. New York, Dodd Mead, 1974.

The Big Orange Splot, illustrated by the author. New York, Hastings House, 1977.

The Blue Thing, illustrated by the author. Englewood Cliffs, New Jersey, Prentice Hall, 1977.

Fat Men from Space, illustrated by the author. New York, Dodd Mead, 1977.

The Hoboken Chicken Emergency, illustrated by the author. Englewood Cliffs, New Jersey, Prentice Hall, 1977.

Pickle Creature, illustrated by the author. New York, Four Winds Press, 1979.

Return of the Moose, illustrated by the author. New York, Dodd Mead, 1979.

The Magic Moscow, illustrated by the author. New York, Four Winds Press, 1980.

The Wuggie Norple Story, illustrated by Tomie de Paola. New York, Four Winds Press, 1980.

Attila the Pun: A Magic Moscow Book, illustrated by the author. New York, Four Winds Press, 1981.

Tooth-Gnasher Superflash, illustrated by the author. New York, Four Winds Press, 1981.

Roger's Umbrella, illustrated by James Marshall. New York, Dutton, 1982.

Slaves of Spiegel: A Magic Moscow Story. New York, Four Winds Press, 1982.

I Was a Second Grade Werewolf, illustrated by the author. New York, Dutton, 1983.

Devil in the Drain, illustrated by the author. New York, Dutton, 1984.

Ducks!, illustrated by the author. Boston, Little Brown, 1984.

The Snarkout Boys and the Baconburg Horror. New York, Lothrop, 1984.

Jolly Roger, a Dog of Hoboken. New York, Lothrop, 1985.

The Frankenbagel Monster, illustrated by the author. New York, Dutton, 1986.

The Moosepire, illustrated by the author. Boston, Little Brown, 1986.

The Muffin Fiend, illustrated by the author. New York, Lothrop, 1986.

Aunt Lulu, illustrated by the author. New York, Macmillan, 1988.

Guys from Space, illustrated by the author. New York, Macmillan, 1989.

Uncle Melvin, illustrated by the author. New York, Macmillan, 1989.

Doodle Flute, illustrated by the author. New York, Macmillan, 1991.

Wempires. illustrated by the author. New York, Macmillan, 1991.

The Phantom of the Lunch Wagon, illustrated by the author. New York, Macmillan, 1992.

Author's Day, illustrated by the author. New York, Macmillan, 1993.

Fiction as Manus Pinkwater

The Terrible Roar. New York, Knopf, 1970.

Bear's Picture, illustrated by the author. New York, Holt Rinehart, 1972.

Fat Elliot and the Gorilla. New York, Four Winds Press, 1974.

Blue Moose, illustrated by the author. New York, Dodd Mead, 1975; London, Blackie, 1977.

Three Big Hogs. New York, Seabury Press, 1975.

Wingman, illustrated by the author. New York, Dodd Mead, 1975.

Around Fred's Bed, illustrated by Robert Mertens. Englewood Cliffs, New Jersey, Prentice Hall, 1976.

Other

Superpuppy: How to Choose, Raise, and Train the Best Possible Dog for You, with Jill Pinkwater, illustrated by Jill Pinkwater. New York, Seabury Press, 1977.

PUBLICATIONS FOR ADULTS

Fish Whistle: Commentaries, Uncommentaries, and Vulgar Excesses. Reading, Massachusetts, Addison-Wesley, 1989.

*

Media Adaptations: *Wingman* (cassette), Listening Library, 1981; *Blue Moose* (video cassette), Positive Images, 1982; *The Hoboken Chicken Emergency* (television movie), Public Broadcasting System, 1984; *I Was a Second Grade Werewolf* (cassette), Live Oak Media, 1986.

Biography: Essay in *Something about the Author Autobiography Series,* Volume 3, Detroit, Gale, 1987; essay in *Authors and Artists for Young Adults,* Volume 1, Detroit, Gale, 1989.

Critical Study: Marquardt, Dorothy A., and Martha E. Ward, *Authors of Books for Young People,* supplement to the 2nd edition, Scarecrow, 1975; entry in *Children's Literature Review,* Volume 4, Detroit, Gale, 1982; entry in *Contemporary Literary Criticism,* Volume 35, Detroit, Gale, 1985.

Daniel Pinkwater comments:

I have done a great number of interesting and exciting things. Writing is more fun than any of them. If it were not for children's book editors, too many of whom are ignorant, tasteless, officious, and destructive, my life might be perfect, and the gods might be jealous of me. My work is not intended to teach or improve anybody. I think a great deal about how to make Art, but I don't believe it's a suitable topic for polite conversation—because it's apt to spoil the effect. Books purporting to explain how writing is done should be obtainable through the mail, and sent in plain brown wrappers. My books too.

*   *   *

Daniel Pinkwater's books for young adults crackle with antic energy. In a prose style marked by humor and a fondness for puns, he celebrates the eruption of the fantastic into everyday life. Although many of his books can be classified as science fiction or fantasy, his secondary worlds or alternate universes do not quite fit the standard paradigms for those genres because of the irreverent sensibility which informs them. One clue to that sensibility comes from the narrator of *Young Adult Novel,* Charles the Cat, a self-styled Dada artist. He says that the Dadaist expects that things will either go wrong or in an unexpected direction. Pinkwater's characters discover that something has gone wrong with the world or with their own lives, and that the remedy is to strike out in an unexpected direction. No matter how lighthearted, each of Pinkwater's books explores the rewards of being an individual in a society that urges conformity. This is the case even in *The Worms of Kukumlima* and *Yobgorgle: Mystery Monster of Lake Ontario,* books that aim simply at telling a good yarn. In both novels, the young protagonist is in the position of going along for the ride with older, and quite bizarre adults who are pursuing interests that might more accurately be termed "obsessions": in the first book, the search for extraordinarily intelligent, chess-playing earthworms; and the search for a Loch Ness-type beast in the second. Each search involves voyaging to interesting places—Africa or the depths of Lake Ontario—but more importantly, involves the protagonist's exposure to characters with a range of personal eccentricities, most of whom seem to revel in their respective enthusiasms. The reader is left with the impression that passionate interests are what make life worthwhile, so long as the interest does not become an obsession.

The Snarkout Boys and the Avocado of Death and *The Snarkout Boys and the Baconburg Horror* are more typical of Pinkwater's novels in that the young protagonists are themselves full-fledged nonconformists, complete with intense enthusiasms. "Rat" Bently Saunders, a fiercely independent young woman, and Winston Bongo and Walter Galt are movie buffs dedicated to sneaking out of the house in the late evening and making their way to the Snark Theater to see double bill showings of highly unusual foreign and domestic films. The plot of the films feature vampires, intelligent bagels from outer space, and the lives of German composers. Not surprisingly, in each Snarkout adventure the three young people soon find themselves in the middle of their own hybrid science fiction/horror movie/detective story plot. Like most of Pinkwater's fiction, the *Snarkout* books' frenetic energy is fueled by punning allusions and references to other books (some of them Pinkwater titles), to icons of both popular and high culture, and to food. This produces stories in which, for example, James Dean, Beethoven, *The Sorrows of Young Werewolf,* and a giant avocado capable of being modified into a thought-wave producing "Alligatron" all appear within the covers of the same book. The protagonists' madcap adventures serve as necessary antidotes to the boring routine of their days at Genghis Khan High School.

The disruption of boring routine is also the goal of the Wild Dada Ducks, five young men who attend Himmler High School in the short novel, *Young Adult Novel.* Their attempt to recruit a new member to their coterie backfires and they inadvertently create a demagogue who soon rules the high school and uses his power to get back at the Ducks who have disturbed his cherished routines and loner status. The narrator of the book claims that there is no moral to the story because it is a Dada story, but the book seems to have the intent of satirizing the plots and pat resolutions of some young adult "problem" novels. Similarly, *The Last Guru* pokes fun at attempting to solve life's dilemmas through adherence to the doctrines of fake gurus.

As funny as his satires can be, Pinkwater is at his best when his wit is tempered by his compassion for his characters' vulnerabilities. *Lizard Music* and *Alan Mendelsohn, the Boy from Mars* present intelligent and perceptive protagonists whose anxieties are resolved or made less threatening as a result of their fantastic adventures. Leonard Neeble finds friendship in an unexpected direction—from Alan Mendelsohn who claims that he is from Mars. At any rate, both he and Leonard, typical high school nerds, are treated as if they were Martians by the rest of the students and the faculty at the high school which they attend. Alan returns to Mars at the end of the novel, but Leonard returns to his high school better able to cope with its snobberies and ready to make friends with other students similarly written off by the snobs. Victor, of *Lizard Music,* is home alone because his parents have gone on a two-week vacation to try to resolve marital tensions, and Victor's shallow older sister has skipped out on keeping an eye on him. On the cusp of adolescence, Victor is concerned by what he sees as the plastic personalities of most of the people around him. By the end of his adventures with the talking lizards of Invisible Island, he has found friendship and a sense of community with the lizards and their other friends.

Chicago Days/Hoboken Nights, Pinkwater's collection of semi-autobiographical essays first read on public radio, suggests that there are many parallels between his protagonists' adventures and his own life. The parallels and correspondences are rarely one-to-one, however, because the storyteller's art always reshapes the incident from life—even in the autobiographical essays. By turns satiric and serious, Pinkwater's imagination is utopian at heart.

—Janice M. Alberghene

———

PLATH, Sylvia. Also wrote as Victoria Lucas. American. Born in Boston, Massachusetts, 27 October 1932. Educated at Harvard University, Cambridge, Massachusetts, summer, 1954; Smith College, Northampton, Massachusetts, B.A. (summa cum laude) in English 1955; Newnham College, Cambridge (Fulbright Scholar), 1955-57, M.A. 1957. Married Ted Hughes in 1956 (separated, 1962), one daughter and one son. Writer and poet. Worked as a volunteer art teacher at the People's Institute, Northampton, Massachusetts, while in college. Guest Editor, *Mademoiselle* magazine, New York, Summer 1953. Instructor in English, Smith College, 1957-58. Recipient: *Mademoiselle* College Board contest award in fiction, 1953; Irene Glascock Poetry Prize, Mount Holyoke College, South Hadley, Massachusetts, 1955; Bess Hokin Award (*Poetry,* Chicago), 1957; Yaddo Fellowship, 1959; Cheltenham Festival award, 1961; Eugene F. Saxon Fellowship, 1961; Pulitzer Prize in poetry, 1982, for *Collected Poems. Died 11 February 1963.*

PUBLICATIONS FOR ADULTS AND YOUNG ADULTS

Novel

The Bell Jar (as Victoria Lucas). London, Heinemann, 1963; as
    Sylvia Plath, London, Faber, 1966; with drawings, New York,
    Harper, 1971.

Poetry

A Winter Ship (published anonymously). Edinburgh, Tragara Press,
    1960.
The Colossus and Other Poems. London, Heinemann, 1960; New
    York, Knopf, 1962; as *The Colossus,* London, Heinemann, 1967.
Ariel, edited by Ted Hughes and Alwyn Hughes. London, Faber,
    1965; New York, Harper, 1966.
Uncollected Poems (booklet). London, Turret Books, 1965.
Wreath for a Bridal (limited edition). Frensham, Surrey, Sceptre
    Press, 1970.
Crossing the Water, edited by Ted Hughes. London, Faber, 1971; as
    Crossing the Water: Transitional Poems, New York, Harper,
    1971.
Crystal Gazer and Other Poems (limited edition). London, Rain-
    bow Press, 1971.
Fiesta Melons: Poems. Exeter, Devon, Rougemont Press, 1971.
Lyonnesse: Poems (limited edition). London, Rainbow Press, 1971.
Million Dollar Month (limited edition). Frensham, Surrey, Sceptre
    Press, 1971.
Winter Trees, edited by Ted Hughes. London, Faber, 1971; New
    York, Harper, 1972.
Collected Poems, edited by Ted Hughes. New York, Harper, 1981.
The Green Rock. Cambridge, Embers Handpress, 1982.
Stings (drafts). Northampton, Massachusetts, Smith College, 1983.
Sylvia Plath's Selected Poems, edited by Ted Hughes. London, Faber,
    1985.

Plays

Three Women: A Monologue for Three Voices (broadcast, 1962;
    produced New York and London, 1973). London, Turret Books,
    1968.

Radio Play: *Three Women,* 1962 (UK).

Short Stories

Penguin Modern Stories 2, with others. London, Penguin, 1969.

Other

Editor, *American Poetry Now: A Selection of the Best Poems by
    Modern American Writers.* London, Oxford University Press,
    1961.
The Penguin Sylvia Plath. London, Penguin, 1975.
Letters Home: Correspondence, 1950-1963, edited by Aurelia Plath.
    New York, Harper, 1975.
*Johnny Panic and the Bible of Dreams: Short Stories, Prose, and
    Diary Excerpts,* edited by Ted Hughes. New York, Harper, 1979.
The Journals of Sylvia Plath, edited by Frances McCullough and
    Ted Hughes. New York, Ballantine, 1983.

PUBLICATIONS FOR CHILDREN

Poetry

The Bed Book. New York, Harper, 1976.

*

Media Adaptations: *The Bell Jar* (film), Avco-Embassy, 1978; *Letters Home* (play), by Rose Leiman Goldemberg, 1979.

Biography: *Sylvia Plath* by Eileen M. Aird, New York, Harper,
1973, Edinburgh, Oliver and Boyd, 1974; Entry in *Dictionary of
Literary Biography,* Detroit, Gale, Volume 5, 1980, Volume 6, 1980;
Sylvia Plath: A Biography by Linda Wagner-Martin, New York,
Simon & Schuster, 1987; *Bitter Fame: The Undiscovered Life of
Sylvia Plath* by Anne Stevenson, Boston, Massachusetts, Houghton,
1989.

Bibliography: By Mary Kinzie, Daniel Lynn Conrad, and Suzanne
D. Kurman in *The Art of Sylvia Plath: A Symposium* edited by
Charles Newman, Bloomington, Indiana University Press, and London, Faber, 1970; *A Chronological Checklist of the Periodical Publications of Sylvia Plath* by Eric Homberger, Exeter, Devon, University of Exeter American Arts Documentation Centre, 1970.

Critical Study: *The Art of Sylvia: A Symposium* edited by Charles
Newman, Bloomington, Indiana University Press, and London,
Faber, 1970; *A Closer Look at "Ariel": A Memory of Sylvia Plath*
by Nancy Hunter Steiner, New York, Harpers Magazine Press,
1973, London, Faber, 1974; Entry in *Contemporary Literary Criticism,* Detroit, Gale, Volume 1, 1973, Volume 2, 1974, Volume 3,
1975, Volume 5, 1976, Volume 9, 1978, Volume 11, 1979, Volume
14, 1980, Volume 17, 1981, Volume 50, 1988, Volume 51, 1989;
Sylvia Plath: Method and Madness by Edward Butscher, New York,
Seabury Press, 1975; *Sylvia Plath: A Dramatic Portrait* conceived
and adapted from Plath's writing by Barry Kyle, London, Faber,
1976; *A Concordance to The Collected Poems of Sylvia Plath* edited
by Richard M. Matovich, New York, Garland, 1986.

*   *   *

Since her suicide in 1963 at the age of thirty, Sylvia Plath especially has attracted the attention of Women's Studies enthusiasts,
while at the same time she has become recognized as a preeminent
American poet. Often categorized as "confessional," her poems are
primarily inspired by actual events in her life, events that she transforms into probing psychoanalytical studies. For example, "The
Mirror" captures the desperation of a young woman trying unsuccessfully to discern in her own slippery reflection the stable image
of a valued, integrated person.

The mirror imagery that Plath uses so effectively in this poem
pervades her one and only novel, *The Bell Jar,* a work that appeals
to young adults because of its troubled young protagonist, Esther
Greenwood. At a promotional event for *Mademoiselle* magazine,
Esther, unable to smile on cue for the photographer, begins to cry.
Gaining some control of herself, she fumbles in her purse for a gilt
compact "with the side mirror. The face that peered back...seemed
to be peering from the grating of a prison cell after a prolonged
beating. It looked bruised and puffy and all the wrong colors." In
the hospital later, after an unsuccessful suicide attempt, Esther

insists "I want to see a mirror." The nurse reluctantly provides one, and faced with the unfamiliar reflection of her shaved head with the hair sprouting "in bristly chicken feather tufts" and her face with its "supernatural conglomeration of bright colors," Esther smiles.

Like Holden Caulfield in *The Catcher in the Rye,* with whom Esther has been compared, she experiences disillusionment with the compromised adult world, sexual curiosity and resultant guilt, and severe mental depression. Unlike Holden, Esther undergoes electroshock therapy following her suicide attempt.

Esther narrates her story in an eerily detached but precise manner that leads the reader to suspect that all is not well with her even before the undeniable signs of her breakdown (she cannot sleep, read, or write) become evident. In addition to Esther's cold, lucid "voice," there are other signs of her impending collapse. For example, she seems excessively disturbed by the upcoming execution of Julius and Esther Rosenberg, the couple accused and tried as Soviet spies in 1951. *The Bell Jar* opens in June 1953 when, after numerous appeals, the Rosenbergs were finally electrocuted: "It was a queer, sultry summer, the summer they electrocuted the Rosenbergs, and I didn't know what I was doing in New York." This opening reference to a notorious death by electrocution foreshadows numerous passages about death throughout the novel (most significantly Esther's father's death when she was nine) and Esther's own "electrocution" by shock therapy.

Paralleling the death images in the novel are references to difficult births, unwelcome children, and conflicting attitudes about sexual intercourse. All of these concerns might be considered typical for a young woman entering a stage when she might well be asked to choose between marriage and motherhood on one hand or a career on the other. Esther's reactions to these common dilemmas may seem excessive in an age when premarital sex and early sex education have become more the rule than the exception, and when a career does not necessarily preclude marriage and motherhood. However, fear of pregnancy was used as a way of ensuring the virginity of young unmarried women to much greater effect in the 1950s than it is today. Furthermore, in the 1950s, a gifted, intellectual woman like Esther had to make choices that might have contributed to the "splitting" of an already tenuous personality.

Esther is eventually rehabilitated, as Sylvia Plath was for a while, largely through the efforts of a supportive group of women including several friends of her own age, her mother, a literary patron, and her psychiatrist. In a period when teenage suicide rates are increasing, *The Bell Jar* is bound to be a controversial choice for young-adult reading. However, it is an important work by a major American writer, and surely there is as much to be gained from a candid approach to this autobiographical treatment of a young woman's suicide attempt as there is to studying such fictional suicidal antiheroines as Emma Bovary or Anna Karenina.

—Mary Lowe-Evans

———

POTOK, Chaim. American. Born Herman Harold Potok in the Bronx, New York, 17 February 1929. Educated at orthodox Jewish schools; Yeshiva University, New York, 1946-50, B.A. (summa cum laude) in English 1950; Jewish Theological Seminary, New York, 1950-54, M.H.L. and rabbinic ordination 1954; University of Pennsylvania, Philadelphia, 1959-65, Ph.D. in philosophy 1965. Served as a chaplain in the United States Army in Korea, 1955-56: Lieutenant. Married Adena Sara Mosevitsky in 1958; two daughters and one son. National director of Leaders Training Fellowship, Jewish Theological Seminary, 1954-55; director, Camp Ramah, Ojai, California, 1957-59; Instructor, University of Judaism, Los Angeles, 1957-59; scholar-in-residence, Har Zion Temple, Philadelphia, 1959-63; member of the Teachers' Institute faculty, Jewish Theological Seminary, 1964-65; managing editor, *Conservative Judaism,* New York, 1964-65. Associate editor, 1965, editor-in-chief, 1966-74, and since 1974 special projects editor, Jewish Publication Society, Philadelphia. Lived in Israel, 1973-77. Visiting Professor of Philosophy, University of Pennsylvania, 1983, and Bryn Mawr College, Pennsylvania, 1985. Recipient: Edward Lewis Wallant award, 1968, and National Book award nomination, both for *The Chosen;* Athenaeum award for *The Promise.* Address: 20 Berwick Street, Merion, PA 19131, U.S.A.

PUBLICATIONS FOR YOUNG ADULTS

Novels

The Chosen. New York, Simon and Schuster, and London, Heinemann, 1967.
The Promise. New York, Knopf, 1969; London, Heinemann, 1970.
My Name Is Asher Lev. New York, Knopf, and London, Heinemann, 1972.
In the Beginning. New York, Knopf, 1975; London, Heinemann, 1976.
The Book of Lights. New York, Knopf, 1981; London, Heinemann, 1982.
Davita's Harp. New York, Knopf, 1985.
The Gift of Asher Lev. New York, Knopf, and London, Heinemann, 1990.
I Am the Clay. New York, Knopf, 1992.
The Tree of Here, illustrated by Tony Auth. New York, Knopf, 1993.

Uncollected Short Stories

"The Dark Place Inside," in *Dimensions in American Judaism* (New York), Fall 1964.
"The Cats of 37 Alfasi Street," in *American Judaism* (New York), Fall 1966.
"Miracles for a Broken Planet," in *McCall's* (New York), December 1972.
"The Fallen," in *Hadassah* (New York), December 1973.
"Reflections on a Bronx Street," in *May My Words Feed Others,* edited by Chayym Zeldis. Cranbury, New Jersey, A.S. Barnes, 1974.
"A Tale of Two Soldiers," in *Ladies Home Journal* (New York), December 1981.
"The Gifts of Andrea," in *Seventeen* (New York), October 1982.
"Long Distance," in *American Voice* (Louisville, Kentucky), Fall 1986.
"Ghosts," in *Orim* (New Haven, Connecticut), Spring 1987.
"The Seven of the Address," in *Winter's Tales,* edited by Robin Baird Smith. New York, St. Martin's Press, May 1993.

Other

Jewish Ethics (pamphlet series). New York, Leaders Training Fellowship, 14 vols., 1964-69.

The Jew Confronts Himself in American Literature. Hales Corners, Wisconsin, Sacred Heart School of Theology, 1975.

Wanderings: Chaim Potok's History of the Jews. New York, Knopf, and London, Hutchinson, 1978.

Ethical Living for a Modern World. New York, Jewish Theological Seminary of America, 1985.

Contributor, *From the Corners of the Earth,* by Bill Aron. Philadelphia, Pennsylvania, Jewish Publication Society, 1985.

Theo Tobiasse: Artist in Exile. New York, Rizzoli, 1986.

Contributor, *The Jews in America,* edited by David Cohen. San Francisco, Collins Publishers, 1989.

Contributor, *Tales of the Hasidim,* edited by Martin Buber. New York, Pantheon, 1991.

"The Invisible Map of Meaning: A Writer's Confrontations" (essay). *TriQuarterly 84,* Spring/Summer 1992.

Contributor, *Graven Images: Graphic Symbols of the Jewish Grave Stone,* edited by Arnold Schwartzman. New York, Abrams, 1993.

Contributor, *I Never Saw Another Butterfly: Children's Drawings and Poems from Terezin Concentration Camp 1942-1944,* edited by Hana Volavkova. New York, Pantheon, 1993.

*

Media Adaptations: *The Chosen* (film), Landau Productions, distributed by Twentieth Century-Fox, 1981; *The Chosen* (musical, produced New York City, 1987).

Biography: Entry in *Dictionary of Literary Biography* by S. Lilliam Kremer, Volume 28, Detroit, Gale, 1984; entry in *Dictionary of Literary Biography Yearbook: 1984,* Detroit, Gale, 1985; *Chaim Potok* by Edward A. Abramson, Boston, Twayne, 1986.

Critical Study: Entry in *Contemporary Literary Criticism,* Volume 2, Detroit, Gale, 1974; Volume 7, 1977; Volume 14, 1980; Volume 26, 1983; entry in *Studies in American Jewish Literature,* edited by Daniel Walden, State University of New York, 1985.

Chaim Potok comments:

I've been writing about people and events that were of great concern to me as I grew up and began to make my way in this world. My hope has been that if I wrote about those people and events honestly enough, my world would open up and others would be caught up in it. I've been writing about the dreams, thoughts, and passions of individuals confronted by new ways of seeing and explaining the world; how they relate under such difficult and challenging circumstances to parents, friends, teachers, peers, and themselves.

I am deeply gladdened by the fact that young people all over the world read my books. I would like those young people to know James Joyce's response to someone who once asked him why he only wrote about Dublin: "For myself I always write about Dublin, because if I can get to the heart of Dublin I can get to the heart of all the cities of the world. In the particular is contained the universal."

On occasion someone will ask me: Why do you only write about Jews? (No longer quite true since *I Am the Clay.*) I answer that I have used Jews much as Joyce has used Irish, and Ibsen has used Norwegians. People will understand that in time. Many of my young readers understand it already.

Chaim Potok's richly detailed and descriptive novels about young American Jews dealing with the demands of traditional Judaism in a largely Christian and increasingly secular society have had a limited, but very loyal following among young adult readers.

The Chosen and its more ambitious sequel *The Promise* focus on the intellectual, social, and religious conflicts between two groups of religiously observant American Jews: Hasidim who are anti-Zionist (some Hasidim are strongly Zionist) and whose life-style, clothing, and beliefs have changed little from their roots in eighteenth-century Europe; and "modern" Orthodox Jews deeply committed to the state of Israel who strictly observe biblical commandments and rabbinic law but base their beliefs and actions on a rational analysis of biblical text and Talmudic commentary. Metaphor and allegory play a large role in both novels, and the two young protagonists in each reflect the passions of and conflicts between the two groups—as well as the tensions with the larger world around them.

The Chosen begins with a baseball game in which the two protagonists face-off against one another. Reuven Malter, the son of a religiously observant Jewish scholar who argues on the basis of logic and reason rather than unexamined belief, is pitching for his yeshiva team. One of the batters on the opposing team is Danny Saunders, a child-genius son of a Hasidic "rebbe" (rabbi), who has inexplicably chosen to bring his son up in silence—except when study of the Torah or Talmud is concerned. With intensity and seeming purposefulness, Danny hits a line drive at Reuven and almost blinds him. However, as Reuven recovers, the two become close friends and involve themselves in each other's lives. Eventually, with the help of Reuven, Danny is freed from his father's self-imposed vow of silence and is permitted to leave the Hasidic community to become a psychiatrist, while Reuven studies to be a rabbi. The fact that the rigid world of Hasidism is unable to hold a genius like Danny while the more open environment of "modern" orthodox Judaism convinces Reuven to become a rabbi is meant by Potok to be more than a simple statement of irony. Although Potok respects the spiritual intensity of the Hasidim, he is very critical of their communal restrictions on the freedom of individuals within their communities and on the insularity of the communities.

The Promise, like *The Chosen,* begins with an allegory—a carnival where Reuven and a mentally-ill teen friend named Michael are cheated by an unscrupulous Hasid in charge of one of the carnival booths. This sets the stage for the involvement of Reuven—and eventually Danny—in helping Michael confront his illness. A parallel plot deals with Reuven's difficulties with his yeshiva's provincial and mean Talmud teacher, which gives Potok another vehicle for portraying the dichotomy between "enlightened" and "narrow-minded" Orthodox Judaism. The two novels are immersed in the details and the ambience of the study of Jewish texts and the observance of Jewish law. The problem is that the characters are rarely more than effective—and even sometimes dramatic—spokesmen for Potok's view of the Jewish world. Except for the action in the allegorical beginning chapter of the two books, the character changes are described rather than portrayed.

Potok, who grew up in a very strict orthodox Jewish community and was severely criticized by others in his religious community and by family members for the art work he did as a child, also wrote two novels about a fictional Hasidic Jewish artist named Asher Lev (*My Name Is Asher Lev* and *The Gift of Asher Lev*). In traditional Judaism, art has been discouraged because of the biblical injunction against idolatry (worshipping graven images). Feeling compelled and sometimes driven to express himself through his art, Asher has to contend with the deeply ingrained antagonism toward art in the Judaism he practiced and with the hostility within his religious community and even his own family (especially after he paints two pictures dealing with the crucifixion). Twenty years later, he and his family who now live in France return to New York for a funeral of a beloved uncle and once again encounter the harsh criticism that drove him to leave years before.

Potok's novel *In the Beginning* traverses similar territory but in a much broader setting, while *The Book of Lights, Davita's Harp,* and *I Am the Clay* range into different terrain altogether. For example, *Davita's Harp* focuses on a girl whose non-Jewish father and Jewish mother are committed to Communism. When her father is killed in the Spanish Civil War, her mother becomes an Orthodox Jew. Davita enrolls in an all-girls yeshiva and excels in her studies, but she is ultimately frustrated and disillusioned by the gender discrimination she encounters from the religious community. *The Book of Lights* carries his Jewish protagonists to Japan and through the ravages of the Korean War and the memories of Hiroshima. *I Am the Clay* evokes Pearl Buck's *The Good Earth* and concerns Korean peasants trying to act humanely in war's aftermath.

Particularly interesting to teen readers is Potok's only book of nonfiction, *Wanderings: Chaim Potok's History of the Jews.* Like his fiction, this book is highly personalized and richly detailed. Surprisingly, it has perhaps even more appeal to teens than his fiction because history comes alive through Potok's narrative rather than being filtered through one-dimensional fictional characters.

Potok, who is an ordained Conservative Jewish rabbi, writes about what he has experienced in his life—the tensions between the traditional and the modern Jewish religious life; the dichotomy of the letter and spirit of Jewish law; and the mystical and the rational elements within Judaism. His fiction dealing with religious and social issues within a Jewish context touches on issues that most teens grapple with in different contexts, making his novels especially relevant and illuminating for young adult readers.

—Jack Forman

PULLMAN, Philip (N.). British. Born in Norwich, England, 19 October 1946. Educated at Oxford University, England, B.A. 1968. Married Judith Speller in 1970; two sons. Teacher at Ivanhoe, Bishop Kirk, and Marston middle schools, Oxford, England, 1973-86; writer, since 1986. Lecturer at Westminster College, North Hinksey, Oxford. Recipient: Lancashire County Libraries/National and Provincial Children's Book award and a Best Books for Young Adults listing from *School Library Journal,* both 1987, a Children's Book award from the International Reading Association and a Best Books for Young Adults listing from the American Library Association, both 1988, and a Preis der Leseratten from ZDF Television (Germany), for *The Ruby in the Smoke;* Best Books for Young Adults listing from the American Library Association, 1988, and was nominated for an Edgar Allan Poe award by the Mystery Writers of America, Inc., 1989, for *Shadow in the North.* Agent: Ellen Levine, 432 Park Ave. S., Suite 1205, New York, NY 10016. Address: 24 Templar Rd., Oxford OX2 8LT, England.

PUBLICATIONS FOR YOUNG ADULTS

Fiction

The Ruby in the Smoke. London, Oxford University Press, and New York, Knopf, 1985.
The Shadow in the Plate. London, Oxford University Press, 1987; as *The Shadow in the North,* New York, Knopf, 1988.
Spring-Heeled Jack, illustrated by David Mostyn. London, Doubleday, 1989; New York, Knopf, 1991.
The Broken Bridge. London, Macmillan, 1990; New York, Knopf, 1992.
The Tiger in the Well. New York, Knopf, 1990.
The White Mercedes. New York, Knopf, 1993.

Plays

Frankenstein. London, Oxford University Press, 1990.

PUBLICATIONS FOR CHILDREN

Fiction

Ancient Civilizations, illustrated by G. Long. London, Wheaton, 1978.
Count Karlstein. London, Chatto & Windus, 1982; edition with illustrations by Patrice Aggs, London, Doubleday, 1991.
How to Be Cool. New York, Heinemann, 1987.
Penny Dreadful. London, Corgi, 1989.

PUBLICATIONS FOR ADULTS

Novels

Galatea. London, Gollancz, 1978; New York, Dutton, 1979.

Also author of additional plays, including *The Adventure of the Sumatian Devil* and an adaptation of Alexandre Dumas's *The Three Musketeers.*

*

Media Adaptations: *How to Be Cool* (TV), Granada, 1988.

Biography: Essay in *Speaking for Ourselves, Too* compiled and edited by Donald R. Gallo, National Council of Teachers of English, 1993; essay in *Something about the Author Autobiography Series,* Volume 17, Detroit, Gale, 1994.

Critical Study: Entry in *Children's Literature Review,* Volume 20, Detroit, Gale, 1990.

*   *   *

Philip Pullman writes in a variety of genres for a range of children. His greatly readable books for young adults, apart from the flip *How to Stay Cool,* fall into two categories: the historical novel and the realistic novel with a contemporary setting.

His historical books, which comprise a trilogy, are set in the London of the late nineteenth century. This atmosphere has been compared to that of Dickens, although one reviewer has suggested they have more in common with Wilkie Collins, and sometimes they do read like a pastiche of Victorian fiction.

The protagonist in the trilogy is Sally Lockhart. The first book, *The Ruby in the Smoke,* finds sixteen-year-old Sally alone in London. There is a mystery surrounding her father's death on board ship after he has sent Sally an enigmatic message, and she is being pursued by a powerful and ghastly woman, Mrs. Holland. Sally is helped by Frederick Garland, a photographer and detective, his actress sister, an office boy, and a slum child as the plot becomes more complex, involving a ruby which vanished when a maharajah was murdered during the Indian Mutiny. The villain of the piece is the evil Ah Ling, who is supposedly murdered at the end of the book, but whose body is not found.

The second book, *The Shadow in the Plate,* continues the relentless pace. This time the mystery involves the atristocracy, spiritualism, the music hall, high finance, and a conspiracy leading to the production of a Victorian "ultimate weapon": a steam-impelled machine gun to be deployed from railway carriages. Pullman defies all conventions at the end of this book by killing off Frederick, whom Sally has grown to love.

The Tiger in the Well touches on more serious concerns than the previous books. Sally is now a successful business tycoon, as well as an unmarried mother. Her world is thrown awry, however, when Mr. Parrish, a rent collector, claims she is his wife. The real man responsible for trying to destroy her turns out to be Tzaddik, otherwise known as Ah Ling. This book successfully and graphically demonstrates the much greater evil in the London slums where a vicious anti-Semitic campaign is opposed by active socialist groups. Sally's eyes are opened by Goldberg, a middle-aged, tough, and scruffy Jew, and the eccentric Dr. Turner and her compassion for the poor.

Pullman's two contemporary novels are the exciting and punchy *The Broken Bridge* and *The White Mercedes.* The first tells of sixteen-year-old Ginny's search for her true identity. She lives with her father in Wales and is one of only two blacks in her school. She discovers that she has a half brother, and tensions are provoked when he comes to live with them. This novel, named for its mysterious theme concerning a broken bridge, is packed with issues: race, fostering and adoption, sexuality and homosexuality, voodooism. Possibly there is too much going on to be contained in the novel's structure.

The White Mercedes is more assured. Set in Oxford, where Pullman himself lives, it tells of seventeen-year-old Chris, who falls for the mysterious and more experienced Jenny. Her past has been hard, but she has emerged clear-headed and resourceful. This is in contrast to Chris, whose often naive reactions result in his becoming involved with the criminal past of his boss, ultimately leading to tragic consequences. Here, as with *The Shadow on the Plate,* Pullman plays with the rules of fiction as few young-adult writers attempt to do. Even after Jenny's tragic death, Chris remains as naive and innocent as he is at the beginning of the book. He totally misinterprets the situation, and one suspects he will continue to do so for the rest of his life.

Pullman's unpredictability of plot and character coupled with the sheer readability of his novels earn them the right to be widely read.

—Keith Barker

PYLE, Howard. American. Born in Wilmington, Delaware, 5 March 1853. Educated at Friends' School and Clark and Taylor's School, Wilmington; Mr. Van der Weilen's school, Philadelphia, 1868-72; Art Student's League, New York. Married Anne Poole in 1881; seven children. Author, artist, painter, teacher of illustration, and writer of children's stories. Illustrator for *Scribner's Monthly;* freelance illustrator for *St. Nicholas* magazine, *Harper's,* and *Harper's Young People;* taught illustration at Drexel Institute of Arts and Sciences, Philadelphia, 1894-1900, later established his own art school in Wilmington. *Died 9 November 1911.*

PUBLICATIONS FOR YOUNG ADULTS (ILLUSTRATED BY THE AUTHOR)

Fiction

The Merry Adventures of Robin Hood of Great Renown in Nottinghamshire. New York, Scribner, 1883.
Pepper and Salt; or, Seasoning for Young Folk. New York, Harper, 1885.
Otto of the Silver Hand. New York, Scribner, 1888.
The Wonder Clock; or, Four and Twenty Marvellous Tales, Being One for Each Hour of the Day, with verses by sister, Katherine Pyle. New York, Harper, 1888.
The Rose of Paradise. New York, Harper, 1888.
Book of Pirates. New York, Harper, 1891; as *Howard Pyle's Book of Pirates,* edited by Merle Johnson. New York, Harper, 1921.
Men of Iron. New York, Harper, 1892.
A Modern Aladdin; or, The Wonderful Adventures of Oliver Munier. New York, Harper, 1892.
The Garden behind the Moon: A Real Story of the Moon Angel. New York, Scribner, 1895.
The Story of Jack Ballister's Fortunes. Century, 1895.
Twilight Land. New York, Harper, 1895.
The Price of Blood: An Extravaganza of New York Life in 1807. R. G. Badger, 1899.
The Story of King Arthur and His Knights. New York, Scribner, 1903; as *The Book of King Arthur,* Chicago. Children's Press, 1969.
The Story of the Champions of the Round Table. New York, Scribner, 1905.
The Story of Sir Launcelot and His Companions. New York, Scribner, 1907.
Strange Stories of the Revolution, with Winthrop Packard, Molly Elliot Seawell, and others. New York, Harper, 1907.
Adventures of Pirates and Sea-Rovers, with J. H. Upshur, Paul Hull, Reginald Gourlay, and others. New York, Harper, 1908.
The Ruby of Kishmoor. New York, Harper, 1908.
The Story of the Grail and the Passing of Arthur. New York, Scribner, 1910.

Other

Within the Capes. New York, Scribner, 1885.
Editor, *The Buccaneers and Marooners of America,* by Alexandre Olivier Exquemelin. New York, Macmillan, 1891.
School and Playground (stories). New York, D. Lothrop, 1891.
The Divinity of Labor (address). J. Rogers, 1898.
Rejected of Men: A Story of To-day. New York, Harper, 1903.
Contributor, *Shapes that Haunt the Dusk,* edited by Howells. New York, Harper, 1907.

Stolen Treasure (stories). New York, Harper, 1907.

Contributor, *The Book of Laughter,* edited by Katherine N. Birdsall and George Haven Putnam. New York, Putnam, 1911.

King Stork, illustrated by Trina Schart Hyman. Boston, Little, Brown, 1973.

*

Media Adaptations: *Wonder Clock Plays* (play by Sophie L. Goldsmith), Harper, 1925; *Robin Hood Plays Matchmaker* (one act play by Mary T. Pyle), Dramatists Play Service, 1939; *The Apple of Contentment* (one act play by Mary T. Pyle), Dramatists Play Service, 1939; *Three Strangers Come to Sherwood* (one act play by Mary T. Pyle), Dramatists Play Service, 1942; *The Men of Iron* (movie, *The Black Shield of Falworth,* starring Tony Curtis and Janet Leigh), Universal Pictures, 1954. Recording of *Tales of King Arthur and His Knights* (recording, read by Ian Richardson), Caedmon, 1975.

Biography: *Howard Pyle: A Chronicle* by Charles Abbot, Harper, 1923; *Howard Pyle* by Elizabeth Nesbitt, Walek, 1966; *Howard Pyle: Writer, Illustrator, Founder of the Brandywine School* by Henry C. Pitz, Clarkson N. Potter, 1975; entry in *Writers for Children* edited by Jane M. Bingham, Scribner, 1988; entry in *Dictionary of Literary Biography,* Vol. 42, Detroit, Gale, 1985.

Illustrator: *Yankee Doodle: An Old Friend in a New Dress,* 1881; *Lady of Shalott* by Alfred Lord Tennyson, 1881; *Old Times in the Colonies* by Charles Carleton Coffin, 1881; *Phaeton Rogers* by Rossiter Johnson, 1881; *The Chronicle of the Drum* by William Makepeace Thackeray, 1882; *Under Green Apple Boughs* by Helen Campbell, 1882; *Farm Ballads* by Will Carlton, 1882; *Story of Siegfried* by James Baldwin, 1882; *Building the Nation: Events in the History of the United States from the Revolution to the Beginning of the War between the States* by Charles Carleton Coffin, 1883; *A History of the United States of America Preceded by a Narrative of the Discovery and Settlement of North America and of the Events Which Led to the Independence of the Thirteen English Colonies for the Use of Schools and Academies* by Horace E. Scudder, 1884; *Illustrated Poems* by Oliver Wendell Holmes, 1885; *Indian History for Young Folks* by Francis S. Drake, 1885; *A History of New York,* two volumes by Driedrich Knickerbocker (pseudonym of Washington Irving), 1886; *A Larger History of the United States of America* by Thomas Wentworth Higginson, 1886; *City Ballads* by Will Carlton, 1886; *Story of the Golden Age* by James Baldwin, 1887; *The Closing Scene* by Thomas Buchanan Read, 1887; *Storied Holidays: A Cycle of Historic Red-Letter Days* by Elbridge S. Brooks, 1887; *The Star Bearer* by Edmund Clarence Stedman, 1888; *Old Homestead Poems* by Wallace Bruce, 1888; *Youma: The Story of a West Indian Slave* by Lafcadio Hearn, 1890; *In the Valley* by Harold Frederic, 1890; *The Captain's Well* by John Greenleaf Whittier, 1890; *Flute and Violin, and Other Kentucky Tales and Romances* by James Lane Allen, 1891; *One Hoss Shay, with its Companion Poems* by Oliver Wendell Holmes, 1892; *Poetical Works of Oliver Wendell Holmes,* two volumes by Oliver Wendell Holmes, 1892; *Together with A Ballad of the Boston Tea Party and Grandmother's Story of the Bunker Hill Battle* by Dorothy Q. Holmes, 1893; *Autocrat of the Breakfast Table,* two volumes by Oliver Wendell Holmes, 1893; *A Tour around New York* and *My Summer Acre* by John Flavel Mines, 1893; *Abraham Lincoln* by Charles Carleton Coffin,

1893; *Giles Corey* by Mary E. Wilkens, 1893; *In Old New York* by Thomas A. Janvier, 1894; *Stops of Various Quills* by William Dean Howells, 1895; *Great Men's Shoes* by Elbridge S. Brooks, 1895; *The True Story of George Washington* by Elbridge S. Brooks, 1895; *The Parasite: A Story* by Arthur Conan Doyle, 1895; *The Novels and Tales of Robert Louis Stevenson,* three volumes by Robert Louis Stevenson, 1895; *Writings of Harriet Beecher Stowe,* two volumes by Harriet Beecher Stowe, 1896; *Hugh Wynne, Free Quaker* by Silas Weir Mitchell, 1896; *In Ole Virginia* by T.N. Page, 1896; *First Christmas Tree* by Henry Van Dyke, 1897; *George Washington* by Woodrow Wilson, 1897; *Works of Francis Parkman,* three volumes by Francis Parkman, 1897-98; *Odysseus, the Hero of Ithaca* (includes illustrations previously published in *Story of the Golden Age*) by Mary E. Burt, 1898; *Story of the Revolution* by Henry Cabot Lodge, 1898; *The Book of Oceans* by Ernest Ingersoll, 1898; *Silence, and Other Stories* by Mary E. Wilkens, 1898; *Old Chester Tales* by Margaret Deland, 1899; *A Story of the American Revolution,* two volumes by Paul Leicester Ford and Janice Meredith, 1899; *To Have and to Hold* by Mary Johnston, 1900; *The Man with the Hoe, and Other Poems* by Edwin Markham, 1900; *Modern Pen Drawings European and American* (includes illustrations previously published in *The Man with the Hoe*) edited by Charles Holmes, 1901; *Works of John Lothrop Motley* by John Lothrop Motley, 1900; *Complete Writings of Nathaniel Hawthorne* by Nathaniel Hawthorne, 1900; *Sir Christopher: A Romance of a Maryland Manor in 1644* by Maud Wilder Goodwin, 1901; *Captain Renshaw; or, The Maid of Cheapside: A Romance of Elizabethan London* by Robert Neilson, 1901; *A History of American Art* (includes illustrations previously published in *Captain Renshaw*) by Hartman, Sadakichi, 1901; *A History of the American People,* five volumes by Woodrow Wilson, 1902, published with additional illustrations in 1918; *Harper's Encyclopedia of United States History,* ten volumes, 1902; *The Poetical Works of James Russell Lowell,* five volumes by James Russell Lowell, 1904; *A History of the United States* by Wilbur F. Gordy, 1904; *The Island of Enchantment* by Justus Miles Forman, 1905; *The Line of Love* by J.B. Cabell, 1905; *Snow Bound: A Winter Idyl* by John Greenleaf Whittier, 1906; *Gallantry: An Eighteenth Century Dizain* by J.B. Cabell, 1907; *Dulcibel: A Tale of Old Salem* by Henry Peterson, 1907; *Chivalry* by J.B. Cabell, 1909; *Lincoln and the Sleeping Sentinel* by L.E. Chittenden, 1909; *Harper's Book of Little Plays* by Margaret Sutton Briscoe, John Kendrick Bangs, and others, 1910; *The Works of William Makepeace Thackeray* edited by Lady Ritchie, 1910; *On Hazardous Service: Scouts and Spies of the North and South* by William Gilmore Beymer, 1912; *The Buccaneers* by Don Seitz, 1912; *Founders of Our Country* by Fanny E. Coe, 1912; *The Soul of Melicent* by J.B. Cabell, 1913; *Etchings* by W.H.W. Bicknell, 1913; *Around Old Chester* by Margaret Deland, 1915; *Stories of Later American History* by Wilbur F. Gordy, 1915; *Saint Joan Of Arc* by Mark Twain, 1919; *Book of the American Spirit* edited by Francis J. Dowd, 1923; *Robin Hood* by Henry Gilbert, 1964.

*   *   *

Howard Pyle must be considered a giant in American literature for children. An innovative, vastly productive artist-writer-teacher, he was a modest man totally concerned with inspiring good artists and creating good books. But the term giant just might have appealed to him as a description, for his imagination was tuned in to the days of good knights and evil villains, heroes and dragons, magic stools and clever magicians, beautiful maidens and wicked queens, good boys, foolish men, and, surely among them, giants. And of course, King Arthur and Robin Hood.

In his fifty-eight years he accomplished an amazing amount of enduring work. His importance as an artist as well as writer must be mentioned here for several reasons. First, his work spanned a period of vital change in children's books. It began in an era when moralistic stories had themes of illness, suffering, and death, and were usually illustrated by inept saccharine pictures; standards for writing and illustrating were low. It ended with his work, both words and pictures, having produced the highest standards for others to follow. The author-artist Robert Lawson, writing in *Illustrators of Children's Books 1744-1945,* stated, "It is small wonder that the clean-cut, healthy, joyous work of Howard Pyle came to...children...like a fresh breeze flooding a fetid sickroom." Second, his illustration and stories intertwined and enhanced each other, growing equally from his concept of the subject undertaken, even though, to an extent rarely equalled by any other author-artist, each element is strong enough to stand alone. Third, any piece of artwork takes a great deal of time to produce. Thus to research, absorb, recreate, and retell the Robin Hood ballads and the vast lore of King Arthur was a gigantic, time-consuming task. He was a truly prodigious worker.

Although he could easily "see things in image-terms or in the continuity of words," as Henry C. Pitz describes his dual abilities, he was a deliberate craftsman. He actually experimented with various writing styles to achieve the effect of the archaic speech of Robin Hood's days and yet have it understandable to children. Reading it aloud today, now that we are even used to *you* taking the place of *thee-and-thou* in versions of the Bible, it sounds more unreal than ever to hear, "Now will I go too, for fain would I draw a string for the bright eyes of my lass, for so goodly a prize as that," or hear Pauline ask poor little Otto about his mother, "And didst thou never see her?" Such is his thoroughness in setting scene, delineating character, and sweeping all action forward in a dynamic plot—particularly in his own stories such as *Otto of the Silver Hand, Men of Iron* and his pirate tales—that one quickly accepts the language as another rich element of his writing skill.

Although *The Merry Adventures of Robin Hood* (1883) was his first book to be published, *Pepper and Salt* and *The Wonder Clock* contained stories and fables Pyle had written and illustrated for children's magazines. *Twilight Land* was more influenced by Eastern folktales. While at first he borrowed and retold old tales in different guises ("The Salt of Life" is the well-known Catskin motif of universal folklore), so steeped was he in folk and fairy lore that eventually he could turn his own rich imagination out into these forms to perfection, just as Andersen did. *The Garden behind the Moon,* a long allegorical fantasy, is less derivative than his short stories and it contains such strong beautiful prose that it makes him a classic writer of fantasy.

With the grim sad story of medieval revenge, *Otto of the Silver Hand,* and that of fifteenth-century adventure, *Men of Iron,* and in his tales of Robin Hood and King Arthur, Pyle achieved new heights in literature for young people: he gave them an immediate sense of their past, complete with authentic convincing details, replete with drama and pageantry, and taut with adventure.

Elizabeth Nesbitt, commenting on Pyle in *A Critical History of Children's Literature,* mentioned that the era in which Pyle developed his work has been called the Golden Age of children's literature and that "it is difficult to do justice to his contribution to the shining quality of that era. The magnitude and diversity of his work elude definition."

—Lee Kingman

R

RAMPLING, Anne. See RICE, Anne.

RAND, Ayn. American. Born in St. Petersburg, Russia, February 1905; emigrated to the United States in 1926; naturalized, 1931. Educated at the University of Petrograd (now University of Leningrad); graduated with highest honors in history, 1924. Married Charles Francis "Frank" O'Connor in 1929. Worked as tour guide at Peter and Paul Fortress; Cecil B. DeMille Studio, Hollywood, California, movie extra and junior screenwriter, 1926-32, began as filing clerk, became office head in wardrobe department; worked as screenwriter for Universal Pictures, Paramount Pictures, and Metro-Goldwyn-Mayer, 1932-34; worked as free-lance script reader for RKO Pictures, then for Metro-Goldwyn-Mayer, both New York City, 1934-35; worked without pay as a typist for Eli Jacques Kahn, an architect in New York City, doing research work for *The Fountainhead,* 1937; Paramount Pictures, New York City, script reader, 1941-43; Hal Wallis Productions, Hollywood, California, screenwriter (worked under special contract which committed her to work only six months of each year; during the other six months she pursued her own writing), 1944-49; full-time writer and lecturer, 1951-82. Visiting lecturer at Yale University, New Haven, Connecticut, 1960, Princeton University, New Jersey, 1960, Columbia University, New York, 1960 and 1962, University of Wisconsin, 1961, Johns Hopkins University, Baltimore, 1961, Harvard University, Cambridge, 1962, Massachusetts Institute of Technology, Cambridge, 1962. Presenter of annual Ford Hall Forum, Boston, Massachusetts, beginning 1963. Editor, *The Objectivist,* New York, 1962-71, and *The Ayn Rand Letter,* New York, 1971-82. D.H.L.: Lewis and Clark College, Portland, Oregon, 1963. Recipient: Doctor of Humane Letters, Lewis and Clark College, 1963. *Died 6 March 1982.*

PUBLICATIONS

Novels

We the Living. New York, Macmillan, and London, Cassell, 1936.
Anthem. London, Cassell, 1938; revised edition, Los Angeles, Pamphleteers, 1946.
The Fountainhead. Indianapolis, Bobbs Merrill, 1943; London, Cassell, 1947.
Atlas Shrugged. New York, Random House, 1957.

Short Stories

The Early Ayn Rand: A Selection from Her Unpublished Fiction, edited by Leonard Peikoff. New York, New American Library, 1984.

Plays

Night of January 16th (as *Woman on Trial,* produced Hollywood, 1934; New York, 1935; London, 1936; as *Penthouse Legend,* produced New York, 1973). New York, Longman, 1936; revised edition, New York, New American Library, 1987.
The Unconquered, adaptation of her own novel *We the Living* (produced New York, 1940).

Screenplays: *You Came Along,* with Robert Smith, 1945; *Love Letters,* 1945; *The Fountainhead,* 1949.

Other

Textbook of Americanism. New York, Branden Institute, 1946.
Notes on the History of American Free Enterprise. New York, Platen Press, 1959.
Faith and Force: The Destroyers of the Modern World. New York, Branden Institute, 1961.
For the New Intellectual: The Philosophy of Ayn Rand. New York, Random House, 1961.
The Objectivist Ethics. New York, Branden Institute, 1961.
America's Persecuted Minority: Big Business. New York, Branden Institute, 1962.
Conservatism: An Obituary (lecture). New York, Branden Institute, 1962.
The Fascist "New Frontier." New York, Branden Institute, 1963.
The Virtue of Selfishness: A New Concept of Egoism. New York, New American Library, 1964.
Capitalism: The Unknown Ideal, with others. New York, New American Library, 1966.
Introduction to Objectivist Epistemology. New York, Objectivist, 1967; revised edition by Leonard Peikoff and Harry Binswanger, New York, New American Library, 1990.
The Romantic Manifesto: A Philosophy of Literature. Cleveland, World Publishing, 1969.
The New Left: The Anti-Industrial Revolution. New York, New American Library, 1971.
Philosophy: Who Needs It? Indianapolis, Bobbs Merrill, 1982.
The Voice of Reason: Essays in Objectivist Thought. New York, New American Library, 1989.
The Ayn Rand Column: A Collection of Her Weekly Newspaper Articles. Oceanside, California, Second Renaissance Books, 1991.

*

Media Adaptations: *Night of January 16th* (film), Paramount, 1941; *We the Living* (film), Italy, 1942; *We the Living* (a revised and abridged version of the Italian film), United States, 1988.

Biography: Essay in *Authors and Artists for Young Adults,* Volume 10, Detroit, Gale, 1993, pp. 151-62.

Critical Studies: *The Philosophical Thought of Ayn Rand* edited by Douglas J. Den Uyl and Douglas B. Rasmussen, Urbana, University of Illinois Press, 1984; *The Ayn Rand Companion* by Mimi Reisel Gladstein, Westport, Connecticut, Greenwood Press, 1984;

The Passion of Ayn Rand: A Biography by Barbara Branden, New York, Doubleday, 1986, London, W.H. Allen, 1987; *The Ayn Rand Lexicon: Objectivism from A to Z* edited by Harry Binswanger, New York, New American Library, 1986; entry in *Contemporary Literary Criticism,* Detroit, Gale, Volume 3, 1975, Volume 30, 1984, Volume 44, 1987; *Judgment Day; My Years with Ayn Rand* by Nathaniel Branden, New York, Houghton Mifflin, 1989.

*   *   *

Any discussion of the works of Ayn Rand must include a discussion of her philosophy; it is the essence of her work. Rand could not find a philosophy that reflected her beliefs, so she created her own. She called her philosophy "objectivism" because it is based on the premise that reality is an objective absolute; therefore, one's survival depends on one's ability to perceive and understand reality. Since one survives by reason, one's highest value should be one's own ability to reason—one's own mind. To place any concept or consideration above the mind is to act against one's own survival—to choose death instead of life.

Every book Rand wrote is an exploration of the philosophy of objectivism. This does not mean that her novels are dry tomes of academic discourse. The stories are interesting, dramatic, and well-written; and the philosophy is integral to the plot. Her words are not difficult to understand, and her ideas are not difficult to grasp. It simply means that Rand cannot be read casually. The reader must pay attention, because every page is packed with ideas and meanings. Because of this, Rand's novels are not generally considered light reading.

For young adults, the most common introduction to Rand's work is either *Anthem* or *We the Living* because they have young adult protagonists and present a somewhat simplified version of her philosophy. Once exposed to Rand's philosophy, however, many young adults go on to read all her work, hungry for the message at its core: You must value yourself in order to survive.

The novella *Anthem* is Rand's simplest work, and explores objectivism only in terms of the value of the individual's mind. *Anthem* imagines a future society where collectivism has been taken to its extreme. It is a society where singular pronouns—I, me, he, she— are unknown. There is only "the great WE, One, indivisible and forever." Not only is an individual's mind not valued, it is considered a sin to even want to think thoughts that no others think. In fact, it is a sin to want to exist for any reason other than to serve the needs of the great WE.

What young adult whose identity has always been defined as a group—the you're-not-important-you're-just-a-kid group—would not share Equality 7-2521's joy in the discovery of the meaning and the value of the word "I"?

In *We the Living,* objectivism is explored in terms of a young Russian girl, Kira Argounova, entering adulthood just after the Communists came into power. In this, the story reflects Rand's life; she also began her adult life in Russia at the beginning of the Communist regime. Rand says in her forward that, *"We The Living* is as near to an autobiography as I will ever write...the specific events of Kira's life were not mine; her ideas, her convictions, her values were and are."

The title "We the Living" refers to both the character and the author's belief that living means consciously choosing life—by making one's own life one's highest value. When Kira heard the Communists claim that "man must live for the state," she believed that it was monstrous to ask anyone to think so little of his or her own life. Kira's one goal is to escape the monstrosity of communist ideology with the man she loves—to find a place where it is possible to choose life.

It is in *We the Living* that the moral code of objectivism is presented: If one's survival depends on one's own mind, then to claim another's mind is to claim another's life. The only moral course of action is to support one's own life by one's own mind—to live for one's own sake—and to allow others to do the same. Rand makes no distinction between those who seek to claim another's mind, and those who abdicate their own mind. Both are immoral: they act against their own survival; they choose death instead of life.

All young adults who remember the struggle to escape childhood restrictions, and reach the freedom of adulthood—where no one will tell them what to do, what to know, what to think, how to live—can appreciate Kira's struggle to live her own life, and her willingness to accept fully the consequences of fighting against those who would claim her life for their own use.

If these novels strike a responsive cord, the young adult reader will go on to read Rand's more comprehensive explorations of her philosophy, *The Fountainhead* and *Atlas Shrugged.* Both expand the scope of objectivist philosophy and explore the implications of the objectivist moral code in our society. In *The Fountainhead,* the focus is primarily on the objectivist individual's relationship to society; in *Atlas Shrugged,* the focus is on society's relationship to objectivist individuals.

The most striking implication of the objectivist moral code is the role of villains. Villains exist in all of Rand's novels, and their actions affect the protagonists, but they seem strangely irrelevant to the true story. The true story is the conflict between characters who draw different conclusions from the objectivist premise—not good against evil, but good against good-but-different. According to the objectivist moral code, villains are irrelevant. Their existence is granted to them by their victims; they can survive only as long as their victims permit them to survive. This theme is introduced in *The Fountainhead* and explored fully in *Atlas Shrugged.*

By any measure, *Atlas Shrugged* is Rand's masterwork. It superbly integrates a dramatic mystery story with a fully realized philosophy, achieving a scope and maturity of thought only suggested by her earlier works. But all her works deserve the attention of young adults—because growing up is about the quest for individual identity and self-esteem within adult society. Ayn Rand's works represent the epitome of that quest.

—Karen J. Gould

————

RASKIN, Ellen. American. Born in Milwaukee, Wisconsin, 13 March 1928. Educated at University of Wisconsin, Madison, 1945-49. Married Dennis Flanagan in 1960; one daughter by a previous marriage. From 1954 commercial illustrator and designer, New York City: group shows—50 Years of Graphic Arts in America, American Institute of Graphic Arts, 1966; Biennale of Illustrations, Bratislava, Czechoslovakia, 1969; Biennale of Applied Graphic Art, Brno, Czechoslovakia, 1972; author and illustrator of children's books, 1966-1984. Instructor in illustration at Pratt Institute, 1963, Syracuse University, 1976; guest lecturer at University of Berkeley, 1969, 1972, and 1977. Contemporary American Illustrators of

Children's Books, 1974-75. Recipient: Distinctive Merit award, 1958, Silver Medal, 1959, both from Art Directors Clubs; *New York Herald-Tribune* Spring Book Festival award (best picture book), 1966, for *Nothing Ever Happens on My Block; Songs of Innocence* was included in American Institute of Graphic Arts exhibit of 50 best books of the year, 1966; *Spectacles* was named one of the best illustrated children's books by *New York Times Book Review,* 1968; Children's Book Council chose *The Mysterious Disappearance of Leon (I Mean Noel),* 1972, *Who, Said Sue, Said Whoo?,* 1974, and *Figgs & Phantoms,* 1975, for the Children's Book Showcase; *Boston Globe-Horn Book* Honor, 1973, for *Who, Said Sue, Said Whoo?; Figgs & Phantoms* was chosen for the American Institute of Graphic Arts Children's Book Show, 1973-74, and as a Newbery honor book, 1975; Edgar Allan Poe Special award, Mystery Writers of America, 1975, for *The Tattooed Potato and Other Clues; Boston Globe-Horn Book* Best Fiction award, 1978, Newbery Medal, 1979, and American Book award nomination, all for *The Westing Game;* an Ellen Raskin Lecture Symposium has been established in Milwaukee. *Died 8 August 1984.*

PUBLICATIONS FOR YOUNG ADULTS (ILLUSTRATED BY THE AUTHOR)

Fiction

The Mysterious Disappearance of Leon (I Mean Noel). New York, Dutton, 1972.
Figgs & Phantoms. New York, Dutton, 1974.
The Tattooed Potato and Other Clues. New York, Dutton, 1975; London, Macmillan, 1976.
The Westing Game. New York, Dutton, 1978; London, Macmillan, 1979.

Poetry

Silly Songs and Sad. New York, Crowell, 1967.
Who, Said Sue, Said Whoo? New York, Atheneum, 1973.

PUBLICATIONS FOR CHILDREN

Fiction

Nothing Ever Happens on My Block. New York, Atheneum, 1966.
Spectacles. New York, Atheneum, 1968.
And It Rained. New York, Atheneum, 1969.
Ghost in a Four-Room Apartment, illustrated by the author. New York, Atheneum, 1969.
A & THE; or, William T. C. Baumgarten Comes to Town. New York, Atheneum, 1970.
The World's Greatest Freak Show, illustrated by the author. New York, Atheneum, 1971.
Franklin Stein, illustrated by the author. New York, Atheneum, 1972.
Moe Q. McGlutch, He Smokes Too Much, illustrated by the author. New York, Parents Magazine Press, 1973.
Moose, Goose and Little Nobody. New York, Parents Magazine Press, 1974.
Twenty-two, Twenty-three. New York, Atheneum, 1976.

*

Manuscript Collection: Milwaukee Public Library, Wisconsin; Kerlan Collection, University of Minnesota, Minneapolis; Children's Cooperative Book Center, University of Wisconsin, Madison.

Biography: Entry in *Dictionary of Literary Biography,* Volume 52: *American Writers for Children since 1960: Fiction,* Detroit, Gale, 1986, pp. 314-325.

Critical Study: Entry in *Children's Literature Review,* Detroit, Gale, Volume 1, 1976, Volume 12, 1987.

Illustrator: *Happy Christmas: Tales for Boys and Girls* edited by Claire Huchet Bishop, 1956; *A Child's Christmas in Wales* by Dylan Thomas, 1959; *"Mama I Wish I Was Snow, Child" "You'd Be Very Cold"* by Ruth Krauss, 1962; *We Dickensons,* 1965, and *We Alcotts,* 1968, both by Aileen Fisher and Olive Rabe; *Poems of Edgar Allan Poe* edited by Dwight Macdonald, 1965; *The King of Men* by Olivia Coolidge, 1966; *Songs of Innocence* by William Blake, 2 vols., 1966; *The Jewish Sabbath* by Molly Cone, 1966; *The Paths of Poetry: Twenty-five Poets and Their Poems* edited by Louis Untermeyer, 1966; *D.H. Lawrence: Poems Selected for Young People* edited by William Cole, 1967; *Ellen Grae,* 1967, and *Lady Ellen Grae,* 1968, both by Vera Cleaver and Bill Cleaver; *Poems of Robert Herrick* edited by Winfield Townley Scott, 1967; *Probability, The Science of Chance,* 1967, *This Is Four: The Idea of a Number,* 1967, *Symmetry,* 1968, *Three and the Shape of Three,* 1969, *Circles and Curves,* 1969, and *A Question of Accuracy,* 1969, all by Arthur G. Razzell and K.G. Watts; *Books: A Book to Begin On* by Susan Bartlett, 1968; *Inatuk's Friend* by Suzanne Stark Morrow, 1968; *A Paper Zoo: A Collection of Animal Poems by Modern American Poets* by Renée Weiss, 1968; *Piping Down the Valleys Wild: Poetry for the Young of All Ages* edited by Nancy Larrick, 1968; *Come Along!* by Rebecca Caudill, 1969; *Shrieks at Midnight: Macabre Poems, Eerie and Humorous* edited by Sara and John E. Brewton, 1969; *Goblin Market* by Christina Rossetti, 1970; *Elidor* by Alan Garner, 1970.

*   *   *

Ellen Raskin has written that she does not cater to arbitrary reading levels or age groups; instead her books are directed at readers who are curious enough to read slowly and carefully. Her four novels for young adults certainly reflect this philosophy. They tend to break the "rules" of young adult literature by employing literary allusions and puns that many young readers will miss and by using so many characters that one needs a score card to keep track of them. Alice Bach, one of Raskin's closest friends, has admitted that Raskin's work is unconventional and that writing mysteries full of subtle wordplay was a risk. All of Raskin's novels are thematically related, focusing on eccentric outsiders who learn to value their own unique qualities and move beyond the stereotypical roles that society has imposed on them. Generally, Raskin's characters are educated to see the world and themselves in new ways in the course of solving either a series of mysteries or puzzles.

The ability to break out of stereotypes and to look beyond surfaces is very important in Raskin's first novel, *The Mysterious Disappearance of Leon (I Mean Noel).* Its protagonist, Mrs. Carillon, a well-meaning soup heiress, lives her life according to her mistaken notions about her missing husband Noel's interests and preferences in case he reappears. It is not until the end of the novel that she realizes that she has drawn all of the wrong conclusions about her husband and sends her friends and family into shock when she discards the purple-flowered dresses she has worn in Noel's memory. Other characters in the novel are also entrapped by words and names. For example, Noel (Leon) feels that names define the individual, and he changes his twice—once to make himself sound more "genteel" and once to escape his marriage to Mrs. Carillon.

In the course of solving the mystery of Noel's disappearance, the characters learn not to be fooled by either language or appearances. It is Augie Kunkel, misleading other characters into thinking he is stupid because he stutters, who teaches Mrs. Carillon's adopted twins how to try new ways of thinking so they can finally solve the puzzle. It is also Kunkel who shows Mrs. Carillon that there is more to life than her search for Noel.

In many ways *Figgs & Phantoms,* a Newbery Honor book, re-works the ideas in *The Mysterious Disappearance of Leon (I Mean Noel).* The disjunction between surface appearances and reality is presented through Mona Lisa Figg Newton, a younger, more aggressive version of Mrs. Carillon. Like her Uncle Florence, Mona loves cataloging and collecting books. She has difficulty, however, discovering what is inside them. She has even more problems with the outward appearances of the people around her. She frequently projects onto the townspeople her insecurities about her eccentric family. Her family also has its own unusual religion which involves an afterlife in a place called "Capri."

At the end of the novel, however, Mona learns that she has misinterpreted most of the townspeople, whose true natures are revealed during a parade. But before this, Mona must journey to Capri where she realizes that trying to live someone else's dream is destructive. In fact, she gains no joy by finding her Uncle Florence. "Paradise" is not as she has envisioned it, partially because she has nothing to contribute to it. She must first develop her own imaginative faculties, getting beyond the covers of those books Uncle Florence leaves her.

The Tattooed Potato and Other Clues focuses on seventeen-year-old Dickory Dock who takes a job assisting an artist named Garson. In the course of the novel, Dickory and Garson solve a series of mysteries for Chief Quinn. Dickory soon discovers a number of other mysteries, however, which involve the true identities of almost everyone she meets. Through her association with Garson, she learns to observe people more carefully and develop a true artist's vision, one which helps her see the real person hidden behind masks and disguises.

As the case with all of Raskin's books, this novel features ample word play, including humorous names, such as those of a young art student named George Washington and gangsters named Manny Mallomar and Shrimp Marinara, as well as the aliases "Noserag" and "Kod" (Garson and Dock spelled backwards) which the main characters assume while solving mysteries. The novel is also filled with many artistic and literary allusions, including a character named Issac Bickerstaffe and Dickory's alias, "Christina Rossetti."

The Westing Game, which won the Newbery Prize, is Raskin's most well-known novel. Its many characters, representing a variety of ethnic and economic groups, are brought together to discover why paper magnate Sam Westing died. Like Raskin's other works, it also treats the problems of perception. None of the characters in this novel are what they seem. Indeed, part of the task the characters face is to determine who each other is. Mr. Westing, himself, has four different identities, the last of which is the solution to the mystery. Most of the sixteen "heirs" also have at least one "skel-

eton in the closet" (e.g., Angela is a bomber, her father is a bookie, Crowe is Westing's ex-wife, Grace has alcoholic tendencies). Each of the characters also exhibits a number of prejudices. Nevertheless, the game they play is designed to make them look past each other's superficial exteriors. In the end, each character changes and is provided with an appropriate happy ending which is connected to the ways they have changed.

Raskin's four novels have deservedly won a number of awards. In each of these works, the reader is constantly called upon to modify his or her own views of characters and events. Her books invite readers inside, asking them to leave behind their fixed notions about literature in order to experience some of what the novels' characters experience.

—Joel D. Chaston

RAWLINGS, Marjorie Kinnan. American. Born in Washington, D.C., 8 August 1896. Educated at Western High School, Washington, D.C.; University of Wisconsin, Madison, 1914-18, B.A. 1918 (Phi Beta Kappa). Married 1) Charles Rawlings in 1919 (divorced 1933); 2) Norton Sanford Baskin in 1941. Editor, YWCA National Board, New York, 1918-19; assistant service editor, *Home Sector* magazine, 1919; staff member, Louisville *Courier Journal,* Kentucky, and Rochester *Journal,* Rochester, New York, 1920-28; syndicated verse writer ("Songs of a Housewife"), United Features, 1926-28; fulltime writer in Florida from 1928. Recipient: Second place, *McCall's* Child Authorship Contest, 1912, for short story; second place, Scribner Prize Contest, 1931, for novella *Jacob's Ladder;* O. Henry Memorial awards, 1933, for short story "Gal Young Un," and 1946, for short story "Black Secret"; Pulitzer Prize for fiction, 1939, for *The Yearling;* Newbery Medal Honor Book, 1956, for *The Secret River;* Lewis Carroll Shelf award, 1963, for *The Yearling.* LL.D.: Rollins College, Winter Park, Florida, 1939; L.H.D.: University of Florida, Gainesville, 1941; honorary degree, University of Tampa, Florida. *Died 14 December 1953.*

PUBLICATIONS FOR YOUNG ADULTS

Fiction

South Moon Under. New York, Scribner, and London, Faber, 1933.
Golden Apples. New York, Scribner, 1935; London, Heinemann, 1939.
The Yearling, illustrated by Edward Shenton. New York, Scribner, and London, Heinemann, 1938.
Jacob's Ladder. Coral Gables, Florida, University of Miami Press, 1950.
The Sojourner. New York, Scribner, and London, Heinemann, 1953.
The Secret River, illustrated by Leonard Weisgard. New York, Scribner, 1955.

Short Stories

When the Whippoorwill. New York, Scribner, and London, Heinemann, 1940.

Other

Cross Creek. New York, Scribner, and London, Heinemann, 1942.
Cross Creek Cookery. New York, Scribner, 1942; as *The Marjorie Kinnan Rawlings Cookbook,* London, Hammond, 1961.
The Marjorie Kinnan Rawlings Reader, edited by Julia Scribner Bigham. New York, Scribner, 1956.
Selected Letters, edited by Gordon E. Bigelow and Laura V. Monti. Gainesville, University Presses of Florida, 1983.

*

Media Adaptations: *The Yearling* (film), MGM, 1946; *The Sun Comes Up* (film based on several short stories), MGM, 1948; *The Yearling* (musical, by Herbert E. Martin, Lore Noto, and Michael Leonard), 1973; *Gal Young Un* (film), 1980; *Cross Creek* (film), Universal, 1983; *The Yearling* (recording), Caedmon.

Biography: *Marjorie Kinnan Rawlings* by Samuel I. Bellman, New York, Twayne, 1974; entry in *Dictionary of Literary Biography,* Detroit, Gale, Volume 9, 1981; Volume 22, 1983; Volume 102, 1991.

Manuscript Collection: University of Florida Libraries, Gainesville.

Critical Study: *Frontier Eden: The Literary Career of Marjorie Kinnan Rawlings* by Gordon E. Bigelow, Gainesville, University of Florida Press, 1966; Entry in *Twentieth Century Literary Criticism,* Volume 4, Detroit, Gale, 1981; *Marjorie Kinnan Rawlings: Sojourner at Cross Creek* by Elizabeth Silverthorne, New York, Viking, 1988.

*   *   *

Marjorie Kinnan Rawlings is a regional writer. Her work is inhabited by the simple people and natural settings of the Florida backwoods which she adopted as her home. Often paramount in her novels is the struggle against the vicissitudes of an uncertain existence by the poor white—the Florida cracker—commonly epitomized in an archetypical young protagonist with frontier virtues. Her first three major novels and much of her short fiction hold marked appeal for adolescent as well as adult readers.

South Moon Under depicts the difficulties of a hunter scratching out a living as a moonshiner in the Florida scrub country. The novel combines vividly descriptive scenes of rural existence with strong characterizations and an eventful plot. *Golden Apples* recounts the efforts of an orphaned and impoverished brother and sister to survive in late nineteenth-century northern Florida. They "squat" on the estate of an exiled and embittered young Englishman whom they patiently regenerate. The resourceful protagonist is a more convincing figure than the vaguely sketched Englishman in this flawed but dramatically forceful novel. In the novella *Jacob's Ladder* a rootless and destitute young couple encounter adversities in luckless attempts to wrest a living from a bounteous but treacherous environment. The pair's deep mutual reliance and indomitable spirit are a poignant and emotionally powerful testament.

The author's internationally acclaimed novel *The Yearling* represents her finest achievement. The hero is twelve-year-old Jody Baxter, who lives with his parents in the Florida hammock country of the 1870s. As his marginally existing family undergoes severe setbacks, Jody tames a fawn which becomes his forest-roaming companion. When, however, his pet cannot be restrained from eating the precious crops, it must be killed. The anguished boy feels betrayed by his father and severs their close relationship. Eventually they are reconciled. Tragedy has made a man of him. Throughout the story weave such themes as man's need to belong to the land which, in turn, belongs to those who lovingly cultivate it, and the inevitability of unfair and unexpected betrayal by man and nature. Rawlings's compellingly truthful portrait of a boy and his tender relationship is universally appealing. Her striking description of nature's elemental forces and the simple but significant events in the lives of people close to the land enrich an absorbingly ingenuous story. This distinguished novel stands as a classic of adult and children's literature.

Intended primarily for young children is the posthumously published story *The Secret River.* Its heroine is a little girl who on her own helps her empty-handed father by finding in the forest a fish-filled secret river. After sharing her catch with forest animals, she returns home with enough fish to restore her father's modest prosperity which, consequently, restores that of his neighbors. When she looks for the river again it has vanished, since the need for it has gone. Charmingly illustrated, this woodland idyll with simple story and message offers enchantment for the young adult as well as the small child.

Rawlings is a pastoral writer of percipience and power all of whose stories—besides her memorable *The Yearling*—can be enjoyed by young people.

—Christian H. Moe

———

REAVER, Chap. American. Born in Cincinnati, Ohio, 10 June 1935. Educated at Palmer College of Chiropractic, D.C., 1957. Served in the Air Force Reserve. Married Dixie Reece in 1959; two children. Private practice in chiropractic, Cincinnati, Ohio, 1957-80, Marietta, Georgia, since 1980; writer. Part-time writing instructor at Marietta Junior High School, in association with the Marietta Community School Program. Recipient: Delacorte Press Prize for an Outstanding First Young Adult Novel, 1990, and Edgar Allan Poe award for best young adult mystery, Mystery Writers of America, 1991, both for *Mote;* Hugo award nomination for short story, World Science Fiction Society, 1992, for "Feel Good Stuff"; Edgar Allan Poe award for best young adult mystery, 1993, *A Little Bit Dead,* awarded posthumously. *Died 11 January 1993.*

PUBLICATIONS FOR YOUNG ADULTS

Fiction

Mote. New York, Delacorte, 1990.
A Little Bit Dead. New York, Delacorte, 1992.
The Adventures of Jessica Gates. New York, Delacorte, forthcoming.

*   *   *

Chap Reaver's two young adult novels tackle important subjects with a marvelous sense of humor. His adolescent narrators are quick-witted and smart-alecky in their approach to serious situations.

Even though his plots are somewhat contrived, Reaver captures the tone of adolescence with a realistic voice. His humor accompanies a firm sense of right and wrong, and his portrayals depict devoted friendships between adolescent males, as well as strong, though absent, adult male role models.

In Reaver's first young adult novel, *Mote,* sixteen-year-old Chris becomes involved with black detective Stienert when Chris's friend Mote is charged with murder. Through his well-honed sense of a humor, Reaver shows the absurdity of stereotypical beliefs based on black dialect—as when Detective Stienert, talking in a verbless jargon, defends himself by saying, "Doing my part to preserve authentic Negro dialect. Else we all be sounding like Bryant Gumbel."

Reaver also shows the absurdity of racism when Chris attends an "Equal Rights for White Americans" meeting to try to learn who the murderer is. While there, he encounters people who are opposed to any race that is not white, and uses his repartee to make them look like fools.

Chris and his best friend, Billy, are both fatherless and have a close relationship, solidified at Billy's father's funeral. As Chris remembers, "Something happened to us as we watched each other crying across the open grave. Something that joined us in a special friendship." Though close, both boys miss the presence of their fathers, a role that is filled by Mote, a drifting Vietnam veteran who showed up shortly after both boys lost their fathers, and returns for a few weeks each year.

Although Mote is absent in most of the book, Chris and Billy recall conversations in which he has given them guidance and understanding they can't find elsewhere. At one point, Mote tells Chris about his feelings when his parents were divorced, and Chris later reveals how this has helped him: "You don't know this, Mote, but when you talked about the feelings you had when your parents got divorced, well, that helped me too. There were lots of times when you helped me like that." Reaver also uses Mote to speak to teens about growing up and accepting their parents, as when Chris remembers Mote's reflection that "you never really start to grow up until you can look at your parents objectively, see them as they really are."

In his second young adult novel, *A Little Bit Dead,* Reaver again tackles racism with a sharp-witted teen, though this time the setting is 1876. This novel employs some of Reaver's own background, as the main character is named Herbert Reece (but goes by Reece) and chiropractic skills are used to relieve arthritis pain. Like Chris and Billy, Reece and Shanti share a friendship born during a difficult time. Reece rescues Shanti, a Yahi Indian, from torture and hanging by bigoted, greedy men who want directions to the Yahi gold. One of the lynchers, Colby, has only one ear, and Reece shows his sarcastic wit when he first suggests that Colby grow his hair long on one side, then suggests that he do so on both sides: "If you just let one side grow long, people might think you're covering up something. Like maybe you don't have one of your ears or something."

Also like Chris, Reece has an absent father, but one whose memory is strong in Reece's mind, as he recalls much of his father's wisdom. Several times he remembers his father admonishing him to do what is right, and when he can't tell what's right, to trust his feelings. When Reece learns the location of the Yahi gold, he is tempted to take it, but then remembers his father's words and thinks to himself, "Shut up, Dad." His father's memory also serves to point out racism against the Yahi, as when Reece tells them what his father said about equality for everyone: "The white men say these words, but they do not hear them."

After rescuing Shanti, Reece is charged with the murder of one of the lynchers. At the trial, when the judge asks Reece if he'd like to question a witness, Reece can't resist another irreverent comment; instead of asking a question that might help his case, he says, "Do you know what happened to Colby's ear?"

In both of Chap Reaver's young adult novels, the main characters are savvy, witty teens with big hearts who do what is right even though doing so causes them problems. Reaver's humor and insight into adolescence prevent the books from becoming didactic, while conveying strong messages through enjoyable reading.

—Susanne L. Johnston

***

REID BANKS, Lynne. British. Born in London, 31 July 1929. Educated at schools in Canada; Italia Centre Stage School, London, 1946; Royal Academy of Dramatic Art, London, 1947-49. Married Chaim Stephenson in 1965; three sons. Actress in British repertory companies, 1949-54; free-lance journalist, London, England, 1954-55; interviewer, reporter and scriptwriter, Independent Television News, London, 1955-62; English teacher, Kibbutz Yasur School and Na'aman High School, Israel, 1963-71; writer, since 1971. Lecturer, and volunteer teacher of English as foreign language in Tanzania, Zimbabwe, India, Nepal, Navajoland, U.S.A. Recipient: Yorkshire Arts Literary award, 1977, and Best Books for Young Adults award, American Library Association, 1977, both for *Dark Quartet;* West Australian Young Readers' Book award, Library Association of Australia, 1980, for *My Darling Villain;* Outstanding Books of the Year award, *New York Times,* 1981, Young Reader's Choice award, Pacific Northwest Library Association, 1984, California Young Readers Medal, California Reading Association, 1985, Children's Books of the Year award, Child Study Association, 1986, Young Readers of Virginia award, 1988, Arizona Young Readers' award, 1988, and Rebecca Caudill Young Reader's Books award, Illinois Association for Media in Education, 1988, all for *The Indian in the Cupboard;* Parents' Choice award for Literature, Parents' Choice Foundation, 1986, Notable Books award, *New York Times,* 1986, Children's Books of the Year award, 1987, and Indian Paintbrush award, Wyoming Library Association, 1989, all for *The Return of the Indian.* Agent: Sheila Watson, Watson, Little Ltd., 12 Egbert St., London NW1 8LJ, England.

PUBLICATIONS FOR YOUNG ADULTS

Fiction

One More River. London, Vallentine Mitchell, and New York, Simon & Schuster, 1973.
Sarah and After: The Matriarchs. London, Bodley Head, and as *Sarah and After: Five Women Who Founded a Nation,* New York, Doubleday, 1975.
My Darling Villain. London, Bodley Head, and New York, Harper, 1977.

The Writing on the Wall. London, Chatto & Windus, 1981; New York, Harper, 1982.

Melusine: A Mystery. London, Hamish Hamilton, 1988, New York, Harper, 1989.

The Mystery of the Cupboard, illustrated by Tom Newsom. New York, Morrow, 1993.

Nonfiction

Letters to My Israeli Sons: The Story of Jewish Survival. London, W.H. Allen, 1979; New York, Watts, 1980.

PUBLICATIONS FOR CHILDREN

Fiction

The Adventures of King Midas, illustrated by George Him. London, Dent, 1976; illustrated by Joseph A. Smith, New York, Morrow, 1992.

The Farthest-Away Mountain, illustrated by Victor Ambrus. London, Abelard Schuman, 1976; New York, Doubleday, 1977.

I, Houdini: The Autobiography of a Self-Educated Hamster, illustrated by Terry Riley. London, Dent, 1978; New York, Doubleday, 1988.

The Indian in the Cupboard, illustrated by Robin Jacques. London, Dent, 1980; New York, Doubleday, 1981.

Maura's Angel, illustrated by Robin Jacques. London, Dent, 1984.

The Fairy Rebel, illustrated by William Geldart. London, Dent, 1985; New York, Doubleday, 1988.

The Return of the Indian, illustrated by William Geldart. London, Dent, and New York, Doubleday, 1987.

The Secret of the Indian. London, Collins, 1988; New York, Doubleday, 1989.

The Magic Hare, illustrated by Barry Moser. New York, Morrow, 1993.

Plays

It Never Rains (televised 1954; produced Keighley, Yorkshire, 1954). London, Deane, 1954.

Miss Pringle Plays Portia, with Victor Maddern. London, Deane, 1955.

All in a Row. London, Deane, 1956.

The Killer Dies Twice. London, Deane, 1956.

Already It's Tomorrow (televised 1962). London, Samuel French, 1962.

The Unborn (produced London, 1962).

The Gift (produced London, 1965).

The Travels of Yoshi and the Tea Kettle (produced by Polka Children's Theatre, London, 1991); Nelson, 1994.

Radio Plays: *The Stowaway* (produced by BBC, 1967); *Lame Duck* (produced by BBC, 1978); *Purely from Principal* (produced by BBC, 1984; author starred).

Television Plays: *The Wednesday Caller* (produced by BBC, 1963); *The Last Word on Julie* (produced by ATV, 1964); *The Eye of the Beholder* (*She* series, produced by ITV, 1977).

PUBLICATIONS FOR ADULTS

Novels

The L-Shaped Room. London, Chatto & Windus, 1960; New York, Simon & Schuster, 1961.

An End to Running. London, Chatto & Windus, as *House of Hope,* New York, Simon & Schuster, 1962.

Children at the Gate. London, Chatto & Windus, and New York, Simon & Schuster, 1968.

The Backward Shadow. London, Chatto & Windus, and New York, Simon & Schuster, 1970.

Two Is Lonely. London, Chatto & Windus, and New York, Simon & Schuster, 1974.

Dark Quartet: The Story of the Brontës. London, Weidenfeld & Nicholson, 1976; New York, Delacorte, 1977.

Path to the Silent Country: Charlotte Brontë's Years of Fame. London, Weidenfeld & Nicholson, 1977; New York, Delacorte Press, 1978.

Defy the Wilderness. London, Chatto & Windus, 1981.

The Warning Bell. London, Hamish Hamilton, 1984; New York, St. Martin's Press, 1987.

Casualties. London, Hamish Hamilton, 1986; New York, St. Martin's Press, 1987.

Other

The Kibbutz: Some Personal Reflections (address). London, Anglo-Israel Association, 1972.

Torn Country: An Oral History of the Israeli War of Independence. New York, Watts, 1982.

*

Media Adaptations: *The L-Shaped Room* (movie starring Leslie Caron), Davis-Royal Films, 1962; *Indian in the Cupboard,* Imagine, forthcoming.

Biography: Entry in *Sixth Book of Junior Authors,* New York, Wilson, 1989.

Manuscript Collection: Boston University.

Critical Study: Entry in *Contemporary Literary Criticism,* Volume 23, Detroit, Gale, 1983.

*   *   *

Lynne Reid Banks is a versatile writer who casts a wide net, and her novels for young adults are a varied haul strung together with the common thread of history, which she winds and bends through most of her work in a way that reveals its recursive nature and presence in modern life. Whether writing fantasy stories, modern adolescent problem novels, or historical fiction, Banks demonstrates a real understanding of the common questions, struggles and complicated feelings that young adults have and treats these honestly and with humor when appropriate. And while some of her novels are weakened by a heavy authorial presence that doesn't allow characters' actions to establish motives and clunky agendas that aren't believably integrated into plots, Banks's books, on the whole, continue to appeal to young readers because of their diverse and relevant themes and the way they present universal coming-of-age struggles through strong, likeable characters.

In *One More River,*, her first novel for young adults, rewritten in 1992 and made more immediate and approachable than the original 1973 version, Banks presents the classic adolescent themes of rebellion and self-discovery in the context of both political and historical events. Set in 1967, *One More River* is the story of fourteen-year-old Lesley who is forced to leave behind a comfortable and carefree life in Canada when her family emigrates to a kibbutz in Israel because her father believes they have lost touch with their Jewish heritage. The eruption of the Six Day War between the Israelis and Arabs brings the novel to its climax, and Banks personalizes the historic confrontation through a clandestine acquaintance Lesley makes with an Arab boy who lives just across the Jordan River. Lesley's newly developed sense of self is thus tested by "the mysteries of war and peace, friends and enemies, love and hatred," conflicts which remain a part of today's world.

Rebellion and self-discovery themes also mark Banks's other adolescent problem novels. *My Darling Villain* takes a look at class consciousness in British society through the eyes of middle-class Kate, who falls into troubled first love with working-class Mark. *The Writing on the Wall* is about Tracy's rebellion against school and family rules as she takes off on a bicycle trip through Holland with several friends and, with the help of her punked-out boyfriend Kev, becomes involved in more than she can handle. These books follow the same formula: slow exposition of a girl's growing attachment to a boyfriend that her parents find unsuitable brought to an eye-opening climax by a surprising—but not too surprising—disaster, such as a motorbike accident or a brush with the law. Although this self-discovery process is predictable, the characters themselves are not. Banks consistently creates very real young people with unique personalities. She lets her protagonists make their own mistakes and face the consequences, rather than having them learn from friends who get into trouble or parents who step in with the answers. The large social agendas Banks sets out to tackle in the adolescent problem novels—like cultural identity or class prejudice—take a back seat to more immediate and appealing curiosities like falling in love, first sexual encounters, drug and alcohol experimentation, and trying on identities in search of one that fits.

The predictability that characterizes Banks's adolescent problem novels gives way in her fantasy fiction, where she loosens her grip and really lets her stories fly. These are some of her most skillful and engrossing novels, in which she demonstrates an unusual ability for weaving the supernatural into daily life in a way that makes the unbelievable somehow believable. Most of these are geared toward younger readers, and perhaps most notable is the very popular *The Indian in the Cupboard* and its sequels, in which Banks makes real the world of play as miniature plastic historical figures are magically brought to life by a boy in modern-day England. *Melusine*, however, is for young adult readers and is less about magic than it is the mysteries of identities and relationships. Roger, while vacationing in rural France with his family, befriends and becomes fascinated by a chateau owner's elusive daughter Melusine and the secrets—some of them sinister—hidden within the chateau. He happens upon a scene between the girl and her father that indicates sexual abuse and goes on to experience still stranger events which connect Melusine to "a shadowy mythological figure" of the same name who was believed to be a woman by day and a snake by night.

Banks pulls off this fantastic plot by grounding it, first, in the ordinary details of family life, particularly the familiar and often funny banter and spats which are inevitably the result of the forced closeness of a family vacation, and second, in genuine, many-faceted relationships. In this book, Banks overcomes the problems of many of her earlier novels by working out her characters' conflicts through their own mind work and outward actions and not through narrative. She presents the issue of abuse not as her own agenda superimposed onto the lives of her characters but rather as a part of the story's reality. The suspenseful and imaginative use of supernatural elements enhances this reality and makes *Melusine* a compelling place in which to consider the complexities of both healthy and unhealthy relationships.

Historical fiction rounds out the varied body of Banks's work. *Sarah and After* is a sensitive re-creation of the lives of Sarah, Hagar, Rebecca, Leah, Rachel, and Dinah, the Hebrew matriarchs whose stories have always been told in a skimpy and perfunctory manner in most biblical interpretations. *Dark Quartet*, though somewhat scholarly in presentation, brings to life Emily, Charlotte, Anne, and Branwell Brontë, revealing the development of intertwined brilliance in the context of their isolated, harsh upbringing and the creative games of their childhood. *Letters to My Israeli Sons* is a nonfiction historical account of Jewish survival from biblical times up to Israel's war with the Arabs in 1967. Written so that young people, like her own three sons, might understand something of the Jewish nation's historical struggle to maintain cultural and religious identity without a homeland, *Letters to My Israeli Sons* provides insightful background to current, ongoing conflict in the Middle East.

—Tracy J. Sukraw

———

RICE, Anne. Original given name, Howard Allen; name changed c.1947. Also writes as Anne Rampling; A.N. Roquelaure. American. Born in New Orleans, Louisiana, 4 October 1941. Educated Texas Women's University, Denton, Texas, 1959-60; San Francisco State College (now University), California, B.A. 1964, M.A. 1971; graduate study at University of California, Berkeley, 1969-70. Married Stan Rice in 1961; one daughter (deceased), and one son. Writer. Held a variety of jobs, sometimes two at a time, including waitress, cook, theater usherette, and insurance claims examiner. Recipient: Joseph Henry Jackson award honorable mention, 1970. Address: 1239 First St., New Orleans, LA 70130, U.S.A.

Publications

Fiction

The Feast of All Saints. New York, Simon & Schuster, 1980.
Cry to Heaven. New York, Knopf, 1982.
The Mummy: Or Ramses the Damned. New York, Ballantine, 1989.
The Witching Hour. New York, Knopf, 1990.
Lasher. New York, Knopf, 1993.

"Vampire Chronicles" series:

Interview with the Vampire. New York, Knopf, 1976.
The Vampire Lestat. New York, Ballantine, 1985.

The Queen of the Damned. New York, Knopf, 1988.
Vampire Chronicles (contains *Interview with the Vampire, The Vampire Lestat,* and *The Queen of the Damned*). New York, Ballantine, 1989.
The Tale of the Body Thief. New York, Knopf, 1992.

Other

The Claiming of Sleeping Beauty, as A. N. Roquelaure. New York, Dutton, 1983.
Beauty's Punishment, as A.N. Roquelaure. New York, Dutton, 1984.
Beauty's Release, as A.N. Roquelaure. New York, Dutton, 1985.
Exit to Eden, as Anne Rampling. New York, Arbor House, 1985.
Belinda, as Anne Rampling. New York, Arbor House, 1986.
The Sleeping Beauty Novels (contains *The Claiming of Sleeping Beauty, Beauty's Punishment,* and *Beauty's Release*), as A.N. Roquelaure. New York, New American Library/Dutton, 1991.

*

Media Adaptations: Novels that have been recorded onto audio cassette and released by Random House AudioBooks include: *Interview with the Vampire* (read by F. Murray Abraham), 1986, *The Queen of the Damned,* 1988, *The Vampire Lestat* (read by Michael York), 1989, and *The Mummy: Or Ramses the Damned* (read by York), 1990. *The Vampire Lestat* has been adapted into a graphic novel by Faye Perozich, painted by Daerick Gross, New York, Ballantine, 1991. The "Vampire Chronicles" have been optioned for film and stage productions.

Critical Study: Entry in *Contemporary Literary Criticism,* Volume 41, Detroit, Gale, 1987.

*   *   *

Though she writes in a variety of genres, Anne Rice is unmistakably a Southern writer in style and theme. The combined influences of Southern rhetorical syntax and Irish cadence make her language complex and ornate. Like her more traditional colleagues, Rice is also a writer firmly grounded in place—New Orleans' Irish Channel where she grew up and the physically near but spiritually remote Garden District where young Anne O'Brien wandered as an outsider.

The Southerner's interest in place is inextricably linked to a sense of the past; like Southern writers in general, Rice creates a mythic past, in her case based not upon tales of cavalier ancestors but on ancient and oft-repeated stories of ghosts and devils—stories which seem credible in the lush, semi-tropical atmosphere of New Orleans. Thus, like most Southern writers, Rice recreates the mythic past in multi-generational family epics. Clearly Maharet, the red-haired witch twin, speaks for Rice when she says the family is all-important, but Rice's families are matriarchal, differing markedly from conventional patriarchal families.

Though she rejects the limited, negative feminism of Akasha, queen of the damned, Rice considers herself part of the feminist literary tradition, influenced by writers as diverse as Jane Austen and Carson McCullers. She admires Eudora Welty's skill with language and Mary Renault's ability to involve her readers so deeply that they cannot bear for the novel to end. One of the most important influences, though, are the Brontë sisters; Rice's Garden District clearly is the New Orleans equivalent of Emily Brontë's moors.

In an interview transcribed in *Lear's* magazine (W. Kenneth Holditch, "Interview with Anne Rice," *Lear's,* Vol. 2, No.7, October 1989), Rice describes her three voices. As Anne Rice, she writes in the "European-American" tradition, influenced primarily by the Brontës, Charles Dickens, and Leo Tolstoy. Anne Rampling, her "California voice," is influenced by Ernest Hemingway and Raymond Chandler. The A. N. Roquelaure novels, which Rice describes as "the Disneyland of S and M," are the type of pornography she considers legitimate—"literature intended to sexually arouse the reader."

The best known of the Anne Rice novels are the "Vampire Chronicles," begun shortly after her six-year-old daughter died of leukemia and written "out of the deep imagination, with echoes of vegetation gods, blood sacrifice, thousands of images that are more dreamed of than spoken" *(Lear's).* Unlike most vampire tales, which are written from the perspective of the victim, Rice's novels adopt the vampires' point of view. While writing *Interview with the Vampire,* the first of these novels, Rice found herself increasingly identifying with the vampire instead of the interviewer as she had originally intended. In the *Lear's* essay, she explains, "The vampire is a perfect metaphor for people who drain us dry, for our fear of the dead coming back, for the outsider who is in the midst of everything and yet feels monstrous and completely cut off. And I think most people feel that way at heart." Possessing the memory of being human, Rice's vampires enviously compare themselves to humans and often regard immortality as a kind of trap. Their concerns too are human ones: the past, their origin, individual identity and purpose.

Louis de Pointe du Lac, the protagonist of *Interview with the Vampire,* tells a young boy the story of his life in eighteenth-century New Orleans, the encounter with Lestat which resulted in his becoming a vampire, and his subsequent search for human blood. Rice acknowledges the autobiographical elements in the novel: *"Interview* is about grief, guilt, and the search for salvation even though one is, in the eyes of the world and one's own eyes, a total outcast. It's all autobiographical somehow, my story of growing up and losing illusions, losing faith, that sense of a world that has a beginning, a middle, and an end—and a top and bottom" *(Lear's).*

The "Vampire Chronicles" continue with *The Vampire Lestat,* as Lestat awakens from a long sleep to become a popular rock star. His songs and the autobiography he writes as a publicity stunt reveal legends and secrets of the vampires. In fact these constitute a history of vampires from ancient Egypt to modern time. As his popularity increases, the hostility of other vampires also grows, and they converge upon his concert, bent on destroying him.

In *The Queen of the Damned,* various vampire voices continue the story of Lestat's waking Akasha, the mother of all vampires and queen of the damned. As a result of his romance with Akasha, Lestat gains powers beyond those of most vampires and eventually seems prepared for a battle of wills with the Talamasca, who are studying vampires. Meanwhile, he discovers the meaning of his vision of the red-haired twins as Maharet explains the origin of vampires and Mekare fulfills her curse upon Akasha. Rice assures her readers that the "Vampire Chronicles" will continue in *The Tale of the Body Thief,* as Lestat confronts some of the author's moral concerns.

Rice's historical novels deal with social outcasts, many of whom are part of alternative societies. *The Feast of All Saints,* set in the New Orleans of the 1840s, is the story of *gens de couleur libre* (free people of color), especially the coming-of-age of copper-skinned, blue-eyed Marcel Ferronaire and his sister Marie, who appears white. *Cry to Heaven* portrays the life of the Italian *castrati* (male singers castrated before their voices change), as protagonist Tonio Treschi seeks both musical fame and revenge upon the brother who had him castrated and dispossessed.

Rice's continuing interest in the supernatural, especially as associated with ancient Egypt, is evident in *The Mummy: Or Ramses the Damned;* like Akasha, Ramses is a sleeping immortal who is awakened and brought into the modern world.

Rice's own antebellum mansion in New Orleans' Garden District serves as the setting for *The Witching Hour,* another multi-generational family epic. Like Lestat and his fellow vampires, the Mayfair family of witches are the subjects of investigation by the Talamasca. The twelfth of the Mayfair witches, Deidre, has been kept most of her life in a drug-induced catatonic state, attended by female relatives but occasionally accompanied by a mysterious young man who identifies himself as Lasher. Like Amel in *The Queen of the Damned,* Lasher seems to be absolute evil struggling to use Deidre's daughter Rowan to achieve human form. The struggle between Lasher and Rowan continues in the sequel, *Lasher.*

Influenced by Rice's California years, the Anne Rampling novels develop the themes of the conquering power of love and the positive value of sex. Lisa Kelly, the protagonist of *Exit to Eden,* resembles Rice: Lisa too was raised in an Irish-Catholic family but has lost her faith. Virtually obsessed with sadomasochistic fantasies, Lisa establishes the Club, a luxurious Caribbean resort where the guests' fantasies can be fulfilled; however, when she and Elliott fall in love, they decide their ultimate fantasy is to move to New Orleans and establish a conventional romantic relationship.

Belinda, a three-part novel, describes Jeremy Walker, an author and illustrator of children's books, who lives an isolated life in an old house until the teenage runaway Belinda moves in. Jeremy's lost sexuality is evoked by Belinda, a willing participant in his erotic fantasies. Criticized for his drawings of her, as Rice has been criticized for her erotic fiction, Jeremy disregards Belinda's warnings and pries into her past; so she runs away. Following a characteristic Rice pattern, the middle section of the novel relates Belinda's background, and the third part details Jeremy's search for her.

The A. N. Roquelaure novels are frankly erotic, but Rice claims they provide her with the same satisfaction as any of her other books: "setting out to create an illusion, something new, taking the reader someplace he or she has never been and then bringing him or her back" *(Lear's).* In *The Claiming of Sleeping Beauty, Beauty's Punishment,* and *Beauty's Release,* Rice's perspective is again unique, as she uses the traditional fairy tale to make explicit some of the erotic messages psychologists have long insisted are hidden within fairy tales.

Rice insists that there is "a strong moral overview" *(Lear's)* in everything she writes, and the conclusions of her novels reflect her overall optimism. Her protagonists generally have rejected conventional religious and societal values, but a strong sense of personal ethics and the enduring force of love result in lives based upon high principles.

—Charmaine Allmon Mosby

RICHTER, Conrad (Michael). American. Born in Pine Grove, Pennsylvania, 13 October 1890. Educated at the Susquehanna Acad-

emy and Tremont High School, Pennsylvania, graduated 1906. Married Harvena M. Achenbach in 1915; one daughter. Teamster, farm laborer, bank clerk, and journalist, in Pennsylvania, 1906-08; editor, *Weekly Courier,* Patton, Pennsylvania, 1909-10; reporter, Johnstown *Leader,* Pennsylvania, and Pittsburgh *Dispatch,* 1910-11; private secretary in Cleveland, 1911-13; freelance writer in Pennsylvania, 1914-27; settled in New Mexico, 1928. Recipient: National Book award nomination, 1937, for *The Sea of Grass;* Gold Medal for Literature from Society of Libraries of New York University, 1942, for *The Sea of Grass* and *The Trees;* Ohioana Library Medal, 1947; Pulitzer Prize for Fiction, 1951, for *The Town;* National Institute of Arts and Letters grant in literature, 1959; Maggie award, 1959, for *The Lady;* National Book award, 1960, for *The Waters of Kronos;* Litt.D., Susquehanna University, Selinsgrove, Pennsylvania, 1944; University of New Mexico, Albuquerque, 1958; Lafayette College, Easton, Pennsylvania, 1966; LL.D., Temple University, Philadelphia, 1966; L.H.D., Lebanon Valley College, Annville, Pennsylvania, 1966. Member, American Academy. *Died 30 October 1968.*

Publications

Novels

The Sea of Grass. New York, Knopf, and London, Constable, 1937.
The Trees (first book in the "The Awakening Land" trilogy). New York, Knopf, and London, Constable, 1940.
The Fields (second book in "The Awakening Land" trilogy). New York, Knopf, 1946; London, Corgi, 1958.
The Town (third book in "The Awakening Land" trilogy). New York, Knopf, 1950; London, Muller, 1951.
Tacey Cromwell. New York, Knopf, 1942; with *The Free Man,* London, Boardman, 1944.
The Free Man. New York, Knopf, 1943; with *Tacey Cromwell,* London, Boardman, 1944.
Always Young and Fair. New York, Knopf, 1947.
The Light in the Forest. New York, Knopf, 1953; London, Gollancz, 1954.
The Lady. New York, Knopf, and London, Gollancz, 1957.
Dona Ellen. Tübingen, Rauch, 1959.
The Waters of Kronos. New York, Knopf, and London, Gollancz, 1960.
A Simple, Honorable Man. New York, Knopf, and London, Gollancz, 1962.
The Grandfathers. New York, Knopf, 1964.
A Country of Strangers. New York, Knopf, and London, Gollancz, 1966.
The Awakening Land (trilogy). New York, Knopf, 1966.
The Aristocrat. New York, Knopf, 1968.

Short Stories

Brothers of No Kin and Other Stories. New York, Hinds, 1924.
Early Americana and Other Stories. New York, Knopf, 1936.
Smoke over the Prairie and Other Stories. London, Boardman, 1947.
The Rawhide Knot and Other Stories. New York, Knopf, 1978.

Other

Human Vibration: The Mechanics of Life and Mind. Harrisburg, Pennsylvania, Handy Book, 1925.

Principles in Bio-Physics: The Underlying Process Controlling Life Phenomena and Inner Evolution. Harrisburg, Pennsylvania, Good Books, 1927.

The Mountain on the Desert: A Philosophical Journey. New York, Knopf, 1955.

Over the Blue Mountain (for children). New York, Knopf, 1967.

Writing to Survive: The Private Notebooks of Conrad Richter, edited by Harvena Richter. Albuquerque, University of New Mexico Press, 1988.

*

Biography: Entry in *Dictionary of Literary Biography,* Volume 9: *American Novelists, 1910-1945,* Detroit, Gale, 1981.

Critical Studies: *Conrad Richter* by Edwin W. Gaston, Jr., New York, Twayne, 1965; *Conrad Richter* by Robert J. Barnes, Austin, Texas, Steck Vaughn, 1968; *Conrad Richter's Ohio Trilogy: Its Ideas, Themes, and Relationships to Literary Tradition* by Clifford Duane Edwards, Ann Arbor, University of Michigan Press, 1967; *Conrad Richter's America* by Marvin J. LaHood, The Hague, Mouton, 1975; entry in *Contemporary Literary Criticism,* Volume 30, Detroit, Gale, 1984.

*   *   *

Conrad Richter may be best known for his historical Ohio trilogy, *The Trees, The Fields,* and *The Town,* but it is his *Light in the Forest* which has attracted consistent attention in the public schools and has developed an acceptance among adolescent readers and teachers of adolescent literature. Because it is brief, challenging on several different levels of reading appreciation and because it addresses a timeless issue, the novel has continued to appear on many reading lists for adolescents; readers from seventh grade through senior high have enjoyed the story.

The novel has an omniscient author, follows a clear chronology, and provides a circular design. The plot follows the adventures of John Butler, a white boy who is captured and raised by the Delaware Indians and then recaptured by the whites when the boy is fourteen years old. The boy, who assumes the Indian name of True Son, leads an idyllic life with the Indians for ten years until he is forced to return to his natural parents as a result of an Indian treaty. Unable to adjust to his existence in the white world, True Son escapes and returns to the wilderness only to be forced into making a difficult decision that will shape the rest of his life. The Indians wish to use him as a decoy to lure white settlers into an ambush, but he ultimately refuses, leading to his expulsion from the tribe by his Indian father Cuyologa and leaving True Son fatherless and adrift between two worlds.

White men in the novel are not portrayed as the conventional heroes of encounters with Indians. Richter himself at an early age wanted to run away from home and live with the Indians. As an adult studying the lives of Indians, he found numerous accounts of white children who had been captured by Indians but who did not wish to return to their white world. In searching for an answer to why some of these children chose to remain with the Indians, Richter developed the background and the purpose for *Light in the*

Forest. As he said about the novel, "I thought that perhaps if we understood how those First Americans felt toward us even then and toward our white way of life, we might better understand the adverse, if perverted, view of us by some African, European, and Asian peoples today."

The novel offers a valuable perspective on cultural differences. Although set in the American wilderness of the sixteenth century, the emphasis placed upon contrasting ways of life and the manner of thinking and the behaviors exhibited by both cultures dramatizes clearly the dilemma faced by people everywhere. Any individual who automatically accepts his or her culture as superior to others places restrictions on the ability to see good in others. The result is often the inability to see truth clearly and a reliance upon what one wants to believe, regardless of facts, to interpret the world. Through both the white men and the Indians in the story, Richter is able to show the prejudices that lead to misunderstanding and often violence and the effect that can have on young people such as True Son.

True Son loves the freedom of the Indian way of life, primitive as it may be. Richter paints an appealing picture of this life:

> They passed their days in a kind of primitive deliciousness. The past was buried. There was only the present and tomorrow. By day they lived as happy animals. Moonlight nights in the forest they saw what the deer saw. Swimming under water with open eyes, they knew now what the otter knew.

Juxtaposed to this way of life was the view of the white man's life from the Indian perspective and what might lie ahead for True Son if he returned:

> Ahead of him ran the rutted road of the whites. It led, he knew, to where men of their own volition constrained themselves with heavy clothing, like harness, where men chose to be slaves to their own or another's property, and followed empty and desolate lives far from the wild beloved freedom of the Indian.

Deceptive in its brevity, the novel yields both a good adventure and a basis for serious discussion among adolescents. True Son, faced with difficult decisions, shows that he has principles for which he is willing to stand. He also discovers what for him is the "light in the forest"—the age of primitive deliciousness, the spiritual element which links all humans. Adolescent readers continue to respond strongly to True Son's dilemma and teachers, wishing to raise the awareness of their students about the original relationships between whites and Indians during the settling of America, find the book a valuable one.

—Charles R. Duke

————

RICHTER, Hans Peter. German. Born in Cologne, Germany, 28 April 1925. Educated at Universities of Cologne, Bonn, Mainz, and Tuebingen; Technical University Hanover, Dr. rer pol. 1968. Served in the German Army, 1942-45; became lieutenant; wounded in action; received Iron Cross and other decorations. Married Elfriede Feldmann in 1952, (died 1989); four children. Independent social psychologist and writer, since 1954; radio and television broadcaster. Professor of scientific methods and sociology, Darmstadt, Germany, 1973. Recipient: Jugendbuchpreis Sebaldus-Verlag, 1961, for *Damals war es Friedrich;* Cite Internationale des Arts (Paris) stipendiate, 1965-66; Woodward School Book award, 1971, and American Library Association Mildred L. Batchelder award, 1972, Japanese book award, 1981, all for *Friedrich.* Address: 58 Franz-Werfel-Strasse, D-65 Mainz, Germany.

PUBLICATIONS FOR YOUNG ADULTS

Novels

Friedrich, translation by Edite Kroll. New York, Holt, 1970 (originally published as *Damals war es Friedrich,* Sebaldus, 1961).
I Was There, translation by Edite Kroll. New York, Holt, 1972 (originally published as *Wir waren dabei,* Freiburg, Herder, 1962).
The Time of the Young Soldiers. London, Kestrel, 1975 (originally published as *Die Zeit der jungen Soldaten,* Colmar, Alsatia, 1967).

Untranslated Nonfiction

Hoerermeinungsforschung auf einem Dorf. Archiv des Suedwestfunk, 1952.
Hausen vor der Hoehe: Eine Rundfunkuntersuchung. Two volumes, Archiv des Nordwestdeutschen Rundfunks, 1954.
Informationsbriefe fuer Fuehrungskraefte. Industrie-Verlag, 1955.
Geschichte und Quellensammlung zur Geschichte der Hoererforschung im deutschsprachigen Raum. Two volumes, Archiv der Historischen Kommission des deutschen Rundfunks, 1957.
Die Freizeit deines Kindes. Oeffentliches Leben, 1957.
Zwoelf Vorlesungen ueber Marktforschung und Werbung im Aussenhandel. Akademie fuer Welthandel, 1957.
Beitrag zu einer Phaenomenologie der Berufsunfaehigkeit, with Fritz W. Adam. Thieme, 1964.
Editor, *Der jungen Leser wegen.* Schwann, 1965.
Jagd auf Gereon. Styria, 1967.
Einfuehrungen zu Fernsehspielen und Spielfilmen. Archiv des Zweiten Deutschen Fernsehens, 1970.
Mohammed. Balve, Engelbert, 1974.
Saint-Just. Balve, Engelbert, 1975.
Gott—Was ist das? Stuttgart, Thienemanns, 1980.
Gut und boese. Stuttgart, Thienemanns, 1980.
Wissenschaft von der Wissenschaft. Stuttgart, Thienemanns, 1981.

Also author of more than a hundred radio and television scripts and of several book-length publications in journals, including "Einfuehrung in die Philosophie" in *Aufstieg,* 1955, and "Lehrgang der Philosophie," in *Geistesschulung,* 1956.

PUBLICATIONS FOR CHILDREN

Fiction, Translated into English

Uncle and His Merry-Go-Round. Berkeley, California, Bancroft & Co., 1959 (originally published as *Karussell und Luftballon,* Obpacher, 1958).
Hengist the Horse. Berkeley, California, Bancroft & Co., 1960 (originally published as *Das Pferd Max,* Obpacher, 1959).

Untranslated Fiction

Der Heilige Martin. Mainz, Grünewald, 1959.
Nikolaus der Gute (legends about St. Nicholas). Mainz, Grünewald, 1960.
Wie Heinz und Inge sich verlaufen haben. Dessart, 1960.
Hans Kauft ein. Scholz, 1961.
Immer ist etwas los! Bindlach, Loewes, 1961.
Das war eine Reise! Sebaldus, 1962.
Birgitta. Mainz, Grünewald, 1963.
Peter. Mainz, Grünewald, 1963.
Ein Reise um die Erde. Vienna, Ueberreuter, 1963.
Eine wahre Baerengeschichte. Vienna, Ueberreuter, 1964.
Nikolaus. Mainz, Grünewald, 1965.
Ich war kein braves Kind. Colmar, Alsatia, 1967.
Der Hundemord. Colmar, Alsatia, 1968.
Kunibert im Schlafanzug. Balve, Engelbert, 1972.
Katzen haben Vorfahrt. Balve, Engelbert, 1972.
Einschreiben vom Anwalt. Schaffstein, 1974.

Editor, Untranslated Works

Schriftsteller antworten jungen Menschen auf die Frage: Wozu leben wir? Colmar, Alsatia, 1968.
Schriftsteller erzaehlen von ihrer Mutter. Colmar, Alsatia, 1968.
Schriftsteller erzaehlen von der Gewalt. Colmar, Alsatia, 1970.
Harte Jugend. Steyler, 1970.
Schriftsteller erzaehlen aus aller Welt. Balve, Engelbert, 1973.
Schriftsteller erzaehlen von der Gerechtigkeit. Balve, Engelbert, 1977.

*

Biography: Essay in *Something about the Author Autobiography Series,* Volume 11, Detroit, Gale, 1991, pp. 275-287.

Critical Study: Entry in *Children's Literature Review,* Volume 21, Detroit, Gale Research, 1980, pp. 186-190.

*   *   *

Hans Peter Richter's three translated young adult books read better as autobiographical documentaries as opposed to fiction. The trilogy *Friedrich, I Was There,* and *The Time of the Young Soldiers* follows the progression of the narrator through different phases of World War II and Hitler's reign. In each story the unnamed narrator acts as a reporter, describing events in a straightforward and unbiased manner. The stories are first-person confessionals, intense in matter and delivery, conferring an immediate sense of the gravity of the time. The translations are merely satisfactory as they do not detract from the stories.

In *Friedrich,* a young boy describes his early childhood and his family's friendship with a Jewish family, the Schneiders. Friedrich and the narrator are good friends and both families share happy times together before Hitler assumes power. With the rise of Hitler comes the demise of the Schneider family; Frau Schneider is killed, Herr Schneider is sent to a concentration camp and Friedrich dies because none of the German families allow him to enter the air raid shelter during a bombing. Richter explores the effect of the imposed Nazi laws on both families and, without assigning blame, lets the honesty of the narrator and the facts of history speak for themselves. The narrator's ambivalence between being a Nazi or helping the Jews is frightening yet understandable. He feels a rush of excitement when he joins in the trashing of a place that means nothing to him, yet when he returns home and finds the Schneider's apartment destroyed, he feels sick to his stomach. Richter is perhaps most adept at describing what is necessary and allowing only pure unfabricated emotions to pervade. He ends *Friedrich* and *I Was There* by immersing the reader in the history of the novels, with an outline of events running concurrent to the stories.

I Was There continues the story of *Friedrich*'s narrator; Richter, however, shifts the focus from Friedrich, to the narrator and his two friends' initiation into the Hitler Youth. Richter then details the boys' impressions of the movement. The more involved the boys become, the deeper the emotions they feel; from nervousness, excitement, power, and fear to a disenchantment with war and finally, as they arrive at the front, a shattering of all the illusions they held as Nazi Youth. Richter brilliantly escapes melodrama by accurately portraying the characters of the boys. He allows their voices to flourish without superimposing his ideals or messages. Perhaps Richter is so skilled at telling their stories in simple, unadorned language because, as he states in the introduction, "I was there, I was not merely an eyewitness. I believed—and I will never believe again."

In *The Time of the Young Soldiers*, Richter focuses on a seventeen-year-old who volunteers for the army. The chapters are disjointed, each offering a different snapshot or vignette of war experience. The narrator sees his friends killed, his mother's suffering and extreme poverty, and endures the loss of his arm. Instead of portraying a young war hero, Richter realistically describes the intense experiences of a young and ignorant boy who is seemingly oblivious to Hitler's philosophies or the world outside his shell.

In the introduction to *The Time of the Young Soldiers*, Richter states, "When the war broke out, I was fourteen years old; when it ended I was twenty. I was a soldier for three years. I thought the things I saw and the things I did were justified because no one spoke out openly against them." In all three novels, Richter explores why no one spoke out, why people believed in Hitler's policies and what motivated them to act in the ways they did.

In each of the novels, the narrator provides the reader with an honest, unapologetic behind-the-scenes look at what many Germans felt during the Nazi reign. There are no brilliant revelations or completed circles since these are real stories that don't depend on character development or surprise endings. What could be a series of depressing accounts of Nazi Germany are instead gripping and thought-provoking novels. The harsh and sincere tone of the three books will leave lasting impressions on any reader. Richter respects his young adult readers and neither gives in to melodrama or sentimentality; balancing sympathies between characters in each book and he refrains from covering up grim or embarrassing details.

—Kate Lentz

* * *

RINALDI, Ann. American. Born in New York City, 27 August 1934. Educated at a high school in New Brunswick, New Jersey. Married Ronald P. Rinaldi in 1960; two children. Writer; author of column, *Somerset Messenger Gazette,* Somerset, New Jersey, 1969-70; feature writer and author of column, *Trentonian,* Trenton, New Jersey, since 1970. Member of Brigade of the American Revolu-

tion. Recipient: New Jersey Press awards from the New Jersey Press Association, first place, 1978, and several second place awards in subsequent years, all for newspaper columns; Notable Children's Trade Book in the Field of Social Studies by the joint committee of the National Council for Social Studies and the Children's Book Council, 1985, for *But in the Fall I'm Leaving;* one of American Library Association's Best Books for Young Adults, 1986, for *Time Enough for Drums.* Address: 302 Miller Ave., Somerville, NJ 08876, U.S.A.

PUBLICATIONS FOR YOUNG ADULTS

Fiction

Term Paper. New York, Walker & Co., 1980.
Promises Are for Keeping. New York, Walker & Co., 1982.
But in the Fall I'm Leaving. New York, Holiday House, 1985.
Time Enough for Drums. New York, Holiday House, 1986.
The Good Side of My Heart. New York, Holiday House, 1987.
The Last Silk Dress. New York, Holiday House, 1988.
A Ride into Morning: The Story of Tempe Wick. San Diego, Harcourt, 1991.
Wolf by the Ears. New York, Scholastic, 1991.
A Break with Charity: A Story about the Salem Witch Trials. San Diego, Harcourt, 1992.
In My Father's House. New York, Scholastic, 1992.

*

Biography: Essay in *Speaking for Ourselves, Too* compiled and edited by Donald R. Gallo, National Council of Teachers of English, 1993.

* * *

In *Promises Are for Keeping,* Ann Rinaldi's protagonist, Nicki, remarks that Tony, her older brother, "always says I'm observant. He says I should be a writer. I get vibes about people." Rinaldi's readers quickly discover that she, like Nicki, does have good vibes about her characters and is observant of details, especially in her historical fiction. Rinaldi's mother, like Nicki's, died after she was born. For two happy years young Ann lived in the Brooklyn home of an aunt and uncle whose older children—not unlike Nicki's two older brothers—spoiled her, and then her father, a newspaper man, took her to New Jersey to live with her siblings and her new stepmother. While Nicki is more in control of her own future, young Ann's desire to write was subverted as she was steered instead toward secretarial work during and after high school. Her life took a significant turn in 1960; she married Ronald P. Rinaldi, and by 1964 they had a son and a daughter. In 1969 she began her journalism career as a columnist, first for the *Somerset Messenger Gazette* and then the *Trentonian* where she honed her skills and won awards for her writing. During this time she wrote several novels without any success until the publication in 1980 of *Term Paper,* followed by its sequel, *Promises,* in 1982, and *But in the Fall I'm Leaving* in 1985.

In Trenton, which some consider the crossroads of the American Revolution, Rinaldi covered stories of the American bicentennial which, with her son Ron's strong interest in military history, took the family to various Revolutionary War reenactments of encampments and battles. In the process Rinaldi not only learned much history from extensive reading, but she also gained a firsthand feel for lifestyles during these times. When Rinaldi decided to write a historical novel that centered on the War for Independence, her agent said no one would buy it or read it. Nonetheless she proceeded, and the result was *Time Enough for Drums*. Set in Trenton, this is the story of Jemima Emerson, a patriot whose older sister marries a British officer and whose older brother becomes an officer in the Continental army. Jem's parents also support the revolution in their special ways, but her grandfathers have divided loyalties. Jem is torn not only by her concern for her family and the hardships that befall them, but she also is in conflict with John Reid, her handsome Tory tutor who pushes her sternly toward emotional and intellectual maturity. Jem initially is decidedly spoiled and immature, but the realities of war, the death of her father, the support and wise counsel of the family's servant Lucy, and her discovery of Reid's real role in the war bring Jem to maturity and responsibility.

Time Enough for Drums set a new course for Ann Rinaldi, for in historical fiction she had found the vehicle for exploring her interests and developing more fully her talent as a writer. In *Time Enough for Drums* Rinaldi raised the issue of slavery which would figure prominently in several of her later novels. She has said that in the course of her research, Revolutionary War hero Henry "Light-Horse Harry" Lee and father of Robert E. Lee, took her by the hand and led her into the Civil War. From this journey came the novels *The Last Silk Dress* and *In My Father's House*. Set in Richmond during the Civil War, *The Last Silk Dress* traces the coming-of-age of fourteen-year-old Susan Chilmark who gives of her time and energy to support the Confederate cause by tending the wounded and sewing. The title of the book comes from the effort of Susan and her friend Connie to collect silk dresses from women in the city in order to make a balloon to spy on the Yankees who are besieging the city. Susan is burdened by the loss of her father, by the "half-mad" state of her mother who sometimes refers to Susan as a Yankee brat, and by the mysterious circumstances that have alienated her beloved brother Lucien from the family. In the course of the story Susan discovers many family secrets that involve slavery and adultery. She also learns that a devoted Southern woman can fall in love with a Yankee.

In *In My Father's House* Rinaldi builds her story of the Civil War around the fact that the first battle of the war began on property at Manassas owned by Will McLean and his family, and, ironically, ended in his parlor at Appomattox Court House with Lee's surrender to Grant. The narrator, Oscie Mason, begins her story in 1852 when Wilmer McLean begins to court her mother after her father's death. As the oldest child, Oscie is single-minded and resentful of McLean's intrusion. After the marriage McLean brings Miss Buttonworth from the North as the children's tutor. The conflict between Oscie and McLean is one of conflicting visions. Oscie resists change, while McLean is insistent that slavery as an institution cannot survive in the South. "Button," as the children call her, becomes a voice of reason and enlightenment, and even after she returns to the North when the war begins, she corresponds with the children. Oscie matures, accepts change as the war runs its course, and puts aside her infatuation with a dashing Southern officer who is already married in favor of a young man from Appomattox.

Rinaldi's historical research has also resulted in *A Ride into Morning: The Story of Tempe Wick* and *A Break with Charity: A Story about the Salem Witch Trials*. The Tempe Wick story, told by Wick's cousin Mary Cooper, is based on a legend that surrounds a mutiny of Continental troops encamped on the Wick farm. Rinaldi has researched the known facts about the event and has given her own fictional dimensions to the historical details. The dynamics of this story are not as arresting as those of *A Break with Charity*. The Salem Witch Trials are generally known to many literate Americans, yet the details are unfamiliar to most. Her choice of Susanna English as her narrator gives strength to the story, for she is an outsider in the eyes of the village girls who are caught up in playing a deadly game with the lives of innocent people, including Susanna's parents. The struggles within the Salem community make this a compelling story for contemporary American youth.

Wolf by the Ears could be Rinaldi's most creative book while possibly being her most controversial one as well. The title comes from Thomas Jefferson's statement about slavery: "As it is, we have the wolf by the ears, and we can neither hold him, nor safely let him go." The book is the journal of Harriet Hemmings, a Jefferson slave—although she is called a servant—with light skin, red hair, nice clothes, and a good education. Her mother, Sally, is Jefferson's personal servant, and there are rumors that Jefferson may be the father of Harriet and her brothers. The question of parentage continues to be debated among historians. Harriet professes to love the Master and knows that she and her brothers are promised their freedom when they reach twenty-one. She struggles with the notion of freedom, but she begins to consider the alternative of passing as a white woman after the master's son-in-law attempts to rape her. Some readers may raise issues of racism in Harriet's portrayal, in spite of Rinaldi's disclaimer that "I do not know what it felt like to be a slave, to be half black or three-quarters white. But I do know how it feels to be alienated, to wonder about part of one's background, and to be unable to get over the idea that one never quite belongs. These feelings are human, not exclusively belonging to blacks, whites, or anyone else...."

Neither history nor historical fiction can always tell readers exactly what the past holds for the present, but good historical fiction will suggest connections, as *Wolf by the Ears* does in the area of race relations or as *In My Father's House* does, to a lesser degree, about feminist issues. Clearly, Ann Rinaldi has mastered the craft of storytelling, and she has found her niche as a writer of young adult historical fiction. She is an ardent researcher who offers readers background information and lucid explanations about the evolution of her books. Given the richness of American history, there are many stories still waiting for her inquisitive eye.

—Hugh Agee

ROBERTS, Willo Davis. American. Born in Grand Rapids, Michigan, 28 May 1928. Educated at a high school in Pontiac, Michigan, graduated 1946. Married David W. Roberts in 1949; two daughters and two sons. Writer. Worked in hospitals and doctors' offices, 1964-72; co-owner of dairy farm; currently conducts a writers' workshop in Granite Falls, Washington; consultant to executive board of Pacific Northwest Writers' Conference. Founder, Mystery Writers of America Seattle Chapter. Recipient: Named a Notable Children's Trade Book by the National Council for the Social Studies and the Children's Book Council, 1977, for *Don't Hurt Laurie!;* Young Hoosier Book award, Association for Indiana Media Educators, 1980, West Australian Young Readers award, 1981, Georgia Children's Book award, University of Georgia, 1982, all for *Don't Hurt Laurie!;* Mark Twain award, Missouri Library Association and Missouri Association of School Librarians, 1983, and California Young Reader Medal, California Reading Association, 1986, all for *The Girl with the Silver Eyes;* named a West Virginia Children's Book award honor book, 1987, *Eddie and the Fairy Godpuppy;* Pacific Northwest Writers Conference Achievement award, 1986, for body of work; *Baby Sitting Is a Dangerous Job* received the Mark Twain award, the Young Hoosier award, the South Carolina Children's Book award, and the Nevada Young Reader's award; *Sugar Isn't Everything* was named an outstanding science trade book for children by the National Science Teachers Association and the Children's Book Council; Edgar Allan Poe award, 1989, for *Megan's Island;* Governor's award for contribution to the field of children's literature, Washington State, 1990, for body of work. Agent: Curtis Brown, 10 Astor Place, New York, NY 10019. Address: 12020 West Engebretsen Rd., Granite Falls, WA 98252, U.S.A.

PUBLICATIONS FOR YOUNG ADULTS

Fiction

The View from the Cherry Tree. New York, Atheneum, 1975.
Don't Hurt Laurie!, illustrated by Ruth Sanderson. New York, Atheneum, 1977.
The Minden Curse, illustrated by Sherry Streeter. New York, Atheneum, 1978.
The Girl with the Silver Eyes. New York, Atheneum, 1980.
More Minden Curses, illustrated by Sherry Streeter. New York, Atheneum, 1980.
House of Fear. New York, Scholastic, 1983.
No Monsters in the Closet. New York, Atheneum, 1983.
The Pet-Sitting Peril. New York, Atheneum, 1983.
Caroline. New York, Scholastic, 1984.
Eddie and the Fairy Godpuppy, New York, Atheneum, 1984.
Elizabeth. New York, Scholastic, 1984.
Baby Sitting Is a Dangerous Job. New York, Atheneum, 1985.
Victoria. New York, Scholastic, 1985.
The Magic Book. New York, Atheneum, 1986.
Sugar Isn't Everything. New York, Atheneum, 1987.
Megan's Island. New York, Atheneum, 1988.
Nightmare. New York, Atheneum, 1989.
What Could Go Wrong? New York, Atheneum, 1989.
To Grandmother's House We Go. New York, Atheneum, 1990.
Dark Secrets. New York, Fawcett, 1991.
Scared Stiff. New York, Atheneum, 1991.
Jo and the Bandit. New York, Atheneum, 1992.
What Are We Going to Do about David? New York, Atheneum, 1993.

PUBLICATIONS FOR ADULTS

Novels

Murder at Grand Bay. New York, Arcadia House, 1955.
The Girl Who Wasn't There. New York, Arcadia House, 1957.
Murder Is So Easy. Fresno, California, Vega Books, 1961.
The Suspected Four. Fresno, California, Vega Books, 1962.

Nurse Kay's Conquest. New York, Ace Books, 1966.
Once a Nurse. New York, Ace Books, 1966.
Nurse at Mystery Villa. New York, Ace Books, 1967.
Return to Darkness. New York, Lancer Books, 1969.
Devil Boy. New York, New American Library, 1970; London, New English Library, 1971.
The House at Fern Canyon. New York, Lancer Books, 1970.
Invitation to Evil. New York, Lancer Books, 1970.
Shadow of a Past Love. New York, Lancer Books, 1970.
Shroud of Fog. New York, Ace Books, 1970.
The Tarot Spell. New York, Lancer Books, 1970.
The Waiting Darkness. New York, Lancer Books, 1970.
The Gates of Montrain. New York, Lancer Books, 1971.
The Ghosts of Harrel. New York, Lancer Books, 1971.
King's Pawn. New York, Lancer Books, 1971.
The Nurses. London, Pan, 1971; as *The Secret Lives of the Nurses,* New York, Ace Books, 1972.
The Terror Trap. New York, Lancer Books, 1971.
The Watchers. New York, Lancer Books, 1971.
Becca's Child. New York, Lancer Books, 1972.
Dangerous Legacy. New York, Lancer Books, 1972.
The Face of Danger. New York, Lancer Books, 1972.
Inherit the Darkness. New York, Lancer Books, 1972.
The M.D. New York, Lancer Books, 1972.
Nurse in Danger. New York, Ace Books, 1972.
Sing a Dark Song. New York, Lancer Books, 1972.
Sinister Gardens. New York, Lancer Books, 1972.
The Evil Children. New York, Lancer Books, 1973.
The Gods in Green. New York, Lancer Books, 1973.
Nurse Robin. New York, Lennox Hill, 1973.
Didn't Anybody Know My Wife? New York, Putnam, 1974.
Key Witness. New York, Putnam, 1975; London, Hale, 1978.
White Jade. New York, Doubleday, 1975.
Expendable. New York, Doubleday, 1976; London, Hale, 1979.
The Jaubert Ring. New York, Doubleday, 1976.
Act of Fear. New York, Doubleday, 1977; London, Hale, 1978.
Cape of Black Sands. New York, Popular Library, 1977.
The House of Imposters. New York, Popular Library, 1977.

"The Black Pearl" series:

The Dark Dowry. New York, Popular Library, 1978.
The Stuart Strain. New York, Popular Library, 1978.
The Cade Curse. New York, Popular Library, 1978.
The Devil's Double. New York, Popular Library, 1979.
The Radkin Revenge. New York, Popular Library, 1979.
The Hellfire Heritage. New York, Popular Library, 1979.
The Macomber Menace. New York, Popular Library, 1980.
The Gresham Ghost. New York, Popular Library, 1980.
Destiny's Women. New York, Popular Library, 1980.
The Search for Willie. New York, Popular Library, 1980.
The Face at the Window. Toronto, Harlequin, and New York, Raven Press, 1981; London, Hale, 1983.
The Gallant Spirit. New York, Popular Library, 1982.
A Long Time to Hate. New York, Avon, 1982.
Days of Valor. New York, Warner, 1983.
Keating's Landing. New York, Warner, 1984.
The Sniper. New York, Doubleday, 1984.
The Annalise Experiment. New York, Doubleday, 1985.
Different Dream, Different Lands. Toronto, Worldwide, 1985.
My Rebel, My Love. New York, Pocket Books, 1986.

To Share a Dream. Toronto, Worldwide, 1986.
Madawaska. Toronto, Worldwide, 1988.

*

Biography: Essay in *Something about the Author Autobiography Series,* Volume 8, Detroit, Gale, 1989; essay in *Speaking for Ourselves, Too* compiled and edited by Donald R. Gallo, National Council of Teachers of English, 1993.

Manuscript Collections: Bowling Green University, Ohio; (children's books): De Grummond Collection, University of Southern Mississippi, Hattiesburg; Central Missouri State University, Arrensburg.

*   *   *

Willo Davis Roberts possesses the amazing ability to formulate plot after plot and then turn those plots into entertaining mysteries and adventure stories. She is a prolific writer who delivers delightful novels to the youngest of young adults. Besides having a talent for imaginative plots, Roberts also understands young people. She knows what problems young adults have and how they will react to them. Roberts portrays young adults sensitively and with empathy. Her modern realistic novels reflect several serious problems which young adults face. Ideas for her novels come from the young people she visits in schools and from her own children and grandchildren. When she needs some prompting to develop an idea, she does what many writers do to stimulate creativity. Roberts asks herself, "What if?" The answers to that question result in suspenseful plots for her readers and interesting situations for her characters.

Roberts's first novel for young adults, *The View from the Cherry Tree,* was originally written for adults, but her editor saw its potential for a younger audience. In this first mystery, Rob witnesses the murder of a nosy old lady next door. Rob is horrified by the old lady's death and tries to tell someone how she died, but Rob's sister is getting married and everyone is too busy to listen to him. Then someone shoots at Rob, and Rob realizes that the murderer knows he saw something and is trying to kill him.

In her mysteries, Roberts's characters could easily be the kids next door. They are ordinary young adults who find themselves in unusual situations. Her characters must draw on their own resources to be able to solve the mysteries they encounter. In *What Could Go Wrong?* three cousins set out on a flight from Seattle, Washington, to visit their Aunt Molly in San Francisco. It sounds simple enough; their parents will take them to the airport and Aunt Molly will pick them up at their destination. Once the cousins are on board the airplane, however, readers know that Roberts's "what if?" thinking has taken over. After an emergency landing in Portland, a bomb threat, a theft, and a chase through the airport, the cousins solve a mystery and survive their adventure.

Most of Roberts's main characters are eleven or twelve years old, but in *Nightmare* the main character, Nick, is a senior in high school. Nick's adventure begins when a man falls from an overpass just as Nick drives under it. The man's neck breaks when he hits the hood of Nick's old, blue Pinto. Nick consequently has nightmares about the accident. To get away from his policeman stepfather and his thoughts about the tragedy, Nick decides to drive the family motorhome to Texas to see his older brother. Instead of escaping his nightmares at home, Nick is drawn deeper into danger. Someone is

following Nick, and he doesn't know who or why, but he guesses that it has to do with the dead man. Roberts tells a chilling story that keeps young adults reading until the suspenseful ending.

In her modern realistic novels, Roberts is an obvious advocate of young people. *Don't Hurt Laurie!* is the story of a young girl who is being physically abused by her mother. Laurie must get help or she won't survive her mother's anger. *Sugar Isn't Everything* is an informative story about an eleven-year-old girl who discovers that she has diabetes and must learn to adjust her life-style to survive. One of Roberts's most recent realistic novels centers on a theme that can also be found in some of her mysteries and adventure stories. Roberts writes about young adults who suffer because they have been abandoned by their parents. This abandonment may be unintentional, parents are kidnapped or die, but the results are the same. The adolescents feel insecure and unloved. In *What Are We Going to Do about David?* an eleven-year-old boy is sent to live with his grandmother while his mother goes to Hawaii on vacation for a month. David's father is too busy with work to take responsibility for his son. Through his parents' preoccupation with their own problems and concerns David is ignored and feels as if he has been abandoned.

In *Scared Stiff,* Roberts has created a suspenseful mystery about two boys who are abandoned by their parents. Their father leaves after an argument with their mother, then their mother disappears. The last time the boys saw her was when she was talking to some men in a car near a grocery store and they are sure that she has been kidnapped, but it's hard for them to convince anyone else of that. The thoughts and actions of the main characters realistically reflect typical behavior of two boys who are frightened and bewildered by their circumstances.

Although most of Roberts's novels take place in contemporary America, *Jo and the Bandit* is a departure from the contemporary setting. Here is a Western tale set in the late 1860s with plenty of details about daily living to satisfy fans of the Old West. Jo and her little brother Andrew are orphaned and must go out West to live with an uncle they have never met. On their way to Muddy Wells, Texas, their stagecoach is robbed, but Jo is able to draw sketches of some of the men who robbed them. Due to Jo's artistic talent and her bravery, she helps bring the bandits to justice. Roberts again shows her ability to write sympathetically about characters while she lets them meet and survive one heart-stopping challenge after another.

Roberts's knack for imaginative plots combined with her understanding and empathy for young adults result in stories that will entertain readers and leave them with messages of hope.

—Rosemary Chance

————

ROBERTSON, Keith (Carlton). Also writes as Carlton Keith. American. Born in Dows, Iowa, 9 May 1914. Educated at the United States Naval Academy, Annapolis, Maryland, B.S. 1937. Served in the United States Navy: radioman on a battleship, 1930-33; officer, on destroyers, 1941-45; Captain, United States Naval Reserve. Married Elisabeth Hexter in 1946; two daughters, one son. Refrigeration engineer, 1937-41; employee of publishing firm, 1945-47; free-lance writer, 1947-58; Bay Ridge Specialty Co., Inc. (ceramics manufacturer), Trenton, New Jersey, president, 1958-69;

writer, 1969-91. Trustee, Hopewell Museum. Recipient: Spring
Book Festival award, 1956, for *The Pilgrim Goose;* William Allen
White Award, 1961, for *Henry Reed, Inc.;* William Allen White
award, 1969, Pacific Northwest Library Association's "Young
Reader's Choice" award, 1969, and Nene award, 1970, all for *Henry
Reed's Baby-Sitting Service;* New Jersey Institute of Technology
awards, both 1969, for *New Jersey* and *The Money Machine. Died
23 September 1991.*

PUBLICATIONS FOR YOUNG ADULTS

Fiction

Ticktock and Jim, illustrated by Wesley Dennis. Philadelphia, Win-
ston, 1948, as *Watch for a Pony,* London, Heinemann, 1949.
Ticktock and Jim, Deputy Sheriffs, illustrated by Everett Stahl. Phila-
delphia, Winston, 1949.
The Dog Next Door, illustrated by Morgan Dennis. New York,
Viking, 1950.
The Missing Brother, illustrated by Rafaello Busoni. New York,
Viking, 1950; London, Faber, 1952.
The Lonesome Sorrel, illustrated by Taylor Oughton. Philadelphia,
Winston, 1952.
The Mystery of Burnt Hill, illustrated by Busoni. New York, Viking,
1952.
Mascot of the Melroy, illustrated by Jack Weaver. New York, Viking,
1953.
Outlaws of the Sourland, illustrated by Isami Kashiwagi. New York,
Viking, 1953.
Three Stuffed Owls, illustrated by Weaver. New York, Viking, 1954.
Ice to India, illustrated by Weaver. New York, Viking, 1955.
The Phantom Rider, illustrated by Weaver. New York, Viking, 1955.
The Pilgrim Goose, illustrated by Erick Berry. New York, Viking,
1956.
The Pinto Deer, illustrated by Kashiwagi. New York, Viking, 1956.
The Crow and the Castle, illustrated by Robert Grenier. New York,
Viking, 1957.
Henry Reed, Inc., illustrated by Robert McCloskey. New York,
Viking, 1958.
If Wishes Were Horses, illustrated by Paul Kennedy. New York,
Harper, 1958.
Henry Reed's Journey, illustrated by McCloskey. New York, Vi-
king, 1963.
Henry Reed's Baby-Sitting Service, illustrated by McCloskey. New
York, Viking, 1966.
The Year of the Jeep, illustrated by W. T. Mars. New York, Viking,
1968.
The Money Machine, illustrated by George Porter. New York, Vi-
king, 1969.
Henry Reed's Big Show, illustrated by McCloskey. New York, Vi-
king, 1970.
In Search of a Sandhill Crane, illustrated by Richard Cuffari. New
York, Viking, 1973.
Tales of Myrtle the Turtle, illustrated by Peter Parnall. New York,
Viking, 1974.
Henry Reed's Think Tank. New York, Viking Kestrel, 1986.

Other

The Wreck of the Saginaw, illustrated by Jack Weaver. New York,
Viking, 1954.

The Navy: From Civilian to Sailor, illustrated by Charles Geer.
New York, Viking, 1958.
New Jersey. New York, McCann, 1969.

PUBLICATIONS FOR ADULTS

Fiction as Carlton Keith

The Diamond-Studded Typewriter. New York, Macmillan, 1958;
London, Heinemann, 1960; as *A Gem of a Murder,* New York,
Dell, 1959.
Missing, Presumed Dead. New York, Doubleday, 1961.
Rich Uncle. New York, Doubleday, 1963; London, Hale, 1965.
The Hiding Place. New York, Doubleday, 1965; London, Hale,
1966.
The Crayfish Dinner. New York, Doubleday, 1966; as *The Elusive
Epicure,* London, Hale, 1966.
A Taste of Sangria. New York, Doubleday, 1968, as *The Missing
Book-Keeper,* London, Hale, 1969.

*

Biography: Entry in *More Junior Authors,* New York, H.W. Wilson, 1963; essay in *Something about the Author Autobiography
Series,* Volume 15, Detroit, Gale, 1993.

Manuscript Collection: May Massee Collection, Emporia State
University, Kansas.

*   *   *

Keith Robertson's fiction portrays a cozy, 1950s world of small-
town America, where good-natured boys use ingenuity, perseverance, and industry to triumph over external problems. If his books
have a common theme, it's that setting goals and working toward
them with determination and good cheer ensures success.

Animals figure prominently in many of Robertson's early works.
Frequently the protagonist has or wants to acquire a horse or dog,
but must spend considerable time working with it to demonstrate
its worth. Robertson's first book told of Jim Meadows, who trades
a watch for a horse (Ticktock), carefully grooms and trains it, then
launches an all-purpose pony express service. In so doing, he pays
for Ticktock's upkeep and convinces his disapproving father that
Ticktock is a worthwhile investment. Other heroes follow a similar
pattern; their efforts are justified when the animal saves lives, wins
races, or otherwise shows its fine qualities. These books often
emphasize the bond between a pet and its owner, with the animal
languishing when separated from the boy, and the boy anguishing
when he believes his pet may die (one of the only times Robertson's
protagonists experience any deep emotional turmoil). Ironically,
Robertson revamped this plot for a later book, *The Year of the Jeep,*
but with a machine as the object of the boy's devotion. Cloud Selby
works as slavishly and loyally to restore an abandoned jeep as any
of his predecessors do for their pets, and is almost as despondent
when he thinks he may lose it.

Mysteries often provide a plot or subplot with a boy investigating strange happenings. Sometimes this combines with an animal
story, as in *The Phantom Rider,* where Tim Cottrell tries to catch a
mysterious morning rider said to be a ghost from the Revolutionary
War. In others, like the four Carson Street Detective agency books

(*The Mystery of Burnt Hill, The Crow and the Castle, Three Stuffed Owls,* and *The Money Machine*), mysteries form the core of the story. Here, teenaged amateur detectives Neil and Swede take on minor problems—everything from a missing bicycle to photographing a rare chess set—only to discover their cases connect with more serious crimes.

Robertson sets his books in small towns or rural areas. Earlier stories take place in Iowa, later ones in New Jersey, near Princeton, reflecting Robertson's own geographical shift. Nature and wildlife serve as a backdrop, with characters regularly going on hikes or camping out in the woods. The value and beauty of nature appear as a theme as early as *The Pinto Deer,* in which a young boy resolves to capture the title animal to earn money for college, developing a deeper appreciation of wildlife in the process; a similar theme occurs in the more recent *In Search of a Sandhill Crane.* These natural settings also allow the protagonists their own special space, and many have hideouts such as abandoned barns or secluded spots in forests, where they can work or think undisturbed.

Several plot devices and character types recur in the books. One is the value of the printed word or picture. Friendly booksellers or professors with large libraries appear as secondary characters, offering books with useful information (a tactic that also allows Robertson to insert background material). Newspapers and reporters also play a part. In *Ticktock and Jim,* the local paper helps promote Jim and Ticktock's pony express with free advertising; in the sequel, Jim discovers the missing Ticktock through a news photo, and in *The Crow and the Castle* another photo provides a clue about an elusive chess piece.

The protagonists also team up with or receive assistance from unlikely characters. Although it is never explicitly stated, an underlying theme seems to be that good friends can be found in unlikely guises and that kindness reaps rewards. Neil and Swede are one of the few instances of two boys with similar backgrounds working together. Instead, most characters meet an unattractive, unsociable character—such as the irascible, unkempt hermit in *The Missing Brother*—render aid, and thereby form a friendship that benefits both parties. Robertson occasionally varies this by teaming the male protagonist with a strong-minded female—such as the angelic-looking, mischief-creating Wilhelmina (Billy) Atkinson in *The Pinto Deer.* However, this pairing never involves romance; the only objects that claim a Robertson hero's heart are his pet, his car, or his hobbies.

Henry Reed is undoubtedly Robertson's most enduring—and endearing—character, and the five Henry Reed books display most of the above traits. Henry is the quintessential entrepreneur, perpetually embarking on new schemes to test the free enterprise system. His assorted businesses are housed in an unused barn belonging to his mother, and he is aided by the unquenchable Midge Glass, with occasional assistance from his dog Agony. Although many of Robertson's other books incorporate humor, the Henry Reed books are by far the funniest. Poor Henry doesn't try to cause trouble; nonetheless, he has an unerring knack for attracting it, equalled only by his ability to emerge unscathed from the resulting chaos. It is typical of Henry that his stalled tractor (pulling a cart, a bale of hay, a wagon, a bathtub, Midge Glass, and Agony) causes a major traffic jam and delays a dozen distinguished commuters, but also yields favorable publicity and increased business for Henry's new research firm when a local reporter writes about the incident. Although Henry doesn't solve mysteries, he doesn't need to; he fills his days unwittingly creating—and calmly resolving—myriad minor crises.

Robertson's protagonists seem far removed from many of today's more troubled heroes. Well-mannered, respectful, hardworking, and lighthearted—in a word, wholesome—they reflect an earlier time and offer readers a pleasant journey through a lighter, less complicated landscape.

—Deidre Johnson

ROBINSON, Spider. American. Born in New York City, 24 November 1948. Educated at State University of New York, Stony Brook, B.A. 1972; New York State University College, Plattsburgh; Le Moyne College, Memphis, Tennessee. Married Jeanne Rubbicco in 1975; one daughter. Realty editor, *Long Island Commercial Review,* Syosset, New York, 1972-73; science fiction writer, since 1973; Reviewer, *Galaxy,* 1974-77, *Destinies,* 1977-79, and *Analog,* 1978-80. Chairman of the Executive Council, Writers Federation of Nova Scotia, 1981-83. Instructor, Clarion SF Writers Workshop, Michigan State University, 1989. Chairmen of the board of directors, Dance Advance Association. Recipient: John W. Campbell award, 1974, for short story "The Guy with the Eyes"; Hugo award, World Science Fiction Convention, 1977, for best novella, "By Any Other Name," 1978, for best novella, "Stardance," and 1983, for best short story, "Melancholy Elephants"; Skylark award, 1977; Nebula award, Science Fiction Writers of America, 1977, for best novella, "Stardance"; *Locus* (magazine) award, 1976, for best critic, and 1977, for best novella, "Stardance"; E.E. Smith Memorial award, 1977; Pat Terry Memorial award, 1977; Canada Council grant, 1983, and Senior Arts grant, 1984. Agent: Eleanor Wood, Spectrum Literary Agency, 111 Eighth Avenue, Suite 1503, New York, NY 19911, U.S.A. Lives in Vancouver, British Columbia.

PUBLICATIONS

Novels

Telempath. New York, Berkley, 1976; London, Macdonald and Jane's, 1978.
Stardance, with wife, Jeanne Robinson. New York, Dial, and London, Sidgwick & Jackson, 1979.
Mindkiller. New York, Holt, 1982; London, Sphere, 1985.
Night of Power. New York, Baen, 1985.
Callahan's Secret. New York, Ace, 1986.
Callahan and Company (omnibus). West Bloomfield, Michigan, Phantasia Press, 1987.
Time Pressure. New York, Ace, 1987.
Callahan's Lady (Lady Sally's House). New York, Ace, 1989.
Copyright Violation (novella). Eugene, Oregon, Pulphouse, 1990.
Kill the Editor. Pulphouse, 1991.
Starseed (Stardance), with Jeanne Robinson. New York, Ace, 1991.
Lady Slings the Booze. New York, Ace, 1992.
The Callahan Touch. New York, Ace, 1993.

Short Stories

Callahan's Crosstime Saloon. New York, Ace, 1977.
Antinomy. New York, Dell, 1980.

Time Travelers Strictly Cash. New York, Ace, 1981.
Melancholy Elephants. Toronto, Penguin, 1984; New York, Tor, 1985.

Other

Contributor, *Chrysalis 4,* edited by Roy Torgeson. Kensington, 1979.
Contributor, *New Voices 2,* edited by George R.R. Martin. New York, Harcourt, 1979.
Editor, *The Best of All Possible Worlds.* New York, Ace, 1980.

*   *   *

Award-winning science fiction author Spider Robinson prefers crisp humor to lengthy prose to convey his message in his "Callahan's Place" series. Adamantly insisting that the three sequential books are absolutely not a trilogy, Robinson uses his short stories in book form to create a warm and wonderful Place for readers of all ages.

The first book, *Callahan's Crosstime Saloon,* introduces us to the characters who inhabit Callahan's Place, the bar where anything can happen, and usually does. Among the regular denizens of the Place are Jake, the pun-slinging guitar player narrator; Mike, the redheaded Irish barkeep; the Doc, a rotund sawbones who is a master of twisted language; and Fast Eddie, the monkey-faced piano man. During the course of *Callahan's Crosstime Saloon,* these characters interact with a man from outer space, a true time-traveller, two psychics, history's oldest woman, and a swindler, meanwhile saving the world and blowing up the parking lot.

The fictional Callahan's Place is special because only those who need it will find it. Those in pain—emotional, physical, or spiritual—are welcomed, given a drink, and invited to pour out their pain to people who genuinely *care.* The primary theme of these books is love, and Robinson has created a place in which people relate to one another simply as who they are and are accepted absolutely, no matter what their failings or past sins. His humor is alternately broad and sophisticated, with some jokes reserved for technical specialists, and others aimed at ten-year-olds. The characters never stop growing throughout the stories. They constantly change in a mirror of life.

The second Callahan book, *Time Travellers Strictly Cash,* is primarily a collection of Robinson's short stories and essays, including a celebration of the works of Robert A. Heinlein. The three Callahan short stories included in the book are excellent, among them the tale of a true talking dog, and most of the non-Callahan stories bear reading as well.

Callahan's Secret finishes up the plot line loosely begun in *Callahan's Crosstime Saloon.* During the course of the book, Jake falls in love with Callahan's blacksmith daughter, Mary, who eventually marries another man—an alien. Callahan and his family are revealed as not being quite of this world, and the final resolution is as gentle and humorous as the stories that precede it.

Callahan's Lady is for older readers, since the setting is an unusual brothel in Brooklyn. Lady Sally's House is run by Mike Callahan's wife, and their daughter Mary moonlights once in a while as a House "artist" in between blacksmithing and security work. The artists at Lady Sally's are all voluntary employees, well paid and happy with their jobs. When Maureen, a young street prostitute, is stabbed by her pimp, she finds the loving family that she has been searching for in Lady Sally's House. She also finds a husband after rescuing him from the clutches of a Mafia thug.

Like the characters in the Callahan series, the people of *Callahan's Lady* are vividly drawn, sophisticated, and funny. They can, and do, laugh at and with themselves and life, even when life is harsh. At times they lack the depth of characterization of the previous books, but generally the quality of writing in *Callahan's Lady* is high.

Stardance is a very different style, a high-tech science fiction novel. The characters are wooden and lifeless, far different from the vital people of the Callahan's universe. In *Stardance,* a group of performing artists take to space to create a new art form, one that is eventually used to communicate with a new alien life-form. During the course of the story, all of the characters find new goals and new lives, and when the entities from space change them, the stardancers become a new species.

Robinson's award-winning *Telempath* is the story of Isham, a young, black, inner-city assassin who is programmed to kill the man responsible for ending the world as we know it. When he fails to make the kill and then discovers that his father was the man who destroyed society, Isham snaps. Fleeing from his friends and murdering his father, Isham becomes the only human who can communicate with the telepathic "Muskies," gaseous creatures with whom the surviving humans are at war.

Telempath is crisply written, varying in styles and points of view between Isham, his father, friends, and assorted "works of history" to tell the story. Where *Stardance* bogs down in scientific justification, *Telempath* provides just enough to make clear the plot and reasons for action. Both are effective works of science fiction, and both are award winners, but neither has the warm humanity of Callahan's. Robinson's finest and best written works remain the Callahan series, and all ages will enjoy these funny and warm-spirited books.

—Melanie Belviso

———

ROGASKY, Barbara. American. Born in Wilmington, Delaware, 9 April 1933. Educated at University of Delaware, Newark, 1950-54. Held various editorial positions for New York City publishers, including Macmillan Publishing Co., Pyramid Books, and Harcourt Brace Jovanovich, 1955-77; free-lance editorial consultant, editor, and writer, since 1977. Recipient: *Smoke and Ashes: The Story of the Holocaust* was named, in 1988, a notable children's book of the American Library Association, a best nonfiction book for young adults by *Publishers Weekly,* one of the best books of the year by *School Library Journal* and the Young Adult Services Division of the American Library Association, and one of the best books of the year for teenagers by the New York Public Library; it also received the Present Tense/Joel H. Cavior award for children's literature from the American Jewish Committee. Address: Brick Hill Rd., Lyme, NH 03768, U.S.A.

PUBLICATIONS FOR YOUNG ADULTS

Nonfiction

Smoke and Ashes: The Story of the Holocaust. New York, Holiday House, 1988.

Other

Reteller, *Rapunzel.* New York, Holiday House, 1982.
Reteller, *The Water of Life.* New York, Holiday House, 1986.
Compiler, and editor, *Winter Poems,* illustrated by Trina Schart Hyman, New York, Scholastic, 1991.
Photographer, *Light & Shadow,* by Myra Cohn. New York, Holiday House, 1992.

*   *   *

Barbara Rogasky confronts her readers with the brutality of Hitler's war against the Jews in her documentary, *Smoke and Ashes: The Story of the Holocaust.* Accompanied by numerous photographs, Rogasky's text sketches the mistreatment of Jews from the dawn of Christianity to instances of anti-Semitism in the 1980s. However, the bulk of her book deals with the years 1933 to 1950.

Rogasky simplifies her account to the essentials, using short sentences and paragraphs to present her case. She includes many quotations from eyewitnesses to the events that transpired in the countries occupied by Nazi troops and in the camps where they sent their victims.

As she traces Hitler's rise to power, Rogasky explains how Jewish life grew increasingly circumscribed. She poses and answers questions such as why Jews did not flee Nazi-controlled countries. She describes the brutality of life in the ghettos, particularly in Warsaw, and notes the continual escalation of violence and death as German leaders moved toward their development of a "Final Solution" to the Jewish presence in Europe. Rogasky explains how the Jews resisted in overt and covert ways, even in concentration camps. She describes camp life, noting the intense desire to live that enabled at least some Jews to outlast their captors and testify against their brutality. She indicts the governments of other countries, particularly Great Britain and the United States, for failing to intervene to save those in the camps, even after the Nazis' murderous activities became widely known.

Some of the annotated lists, such as brief descriptions of people and governments that helped rescue Jews, or paragraphs noting the fate of Third Reich members judged by the War Crimes Commission, can grow tedious, and without accompanying analysis they may be easy for readers to skip. Yet, lists such as examples of those who fought back against the Nazis cumulate into a picture of resistance that stands without author commentary.

Rogasky acknowledges that her account is not objective. She presents the facts she has accumulated filtered through her underlying assumption that anti-Semitism dominated all governmental and individual decisions during the war. She devotes only four pages of text to other groups killed by the Nazis, including the incurably ill, Gypsies, Polish intellectuals, and Russian prisoners of war. She barely mentions others, such as homosexuals, singled out for persecution. In the introduction she notes that "the war took millions of lives all over the world, not only Jews. Yet this is a story of their destruction, because only they were marked for extinction."

Similarly, Rogasky dismisses other mass exterminations of populations in the recent past as being qualitatively different from the destruction of the Jews. Answering her question "Is the Holocaust Unique?" in the affirmative, Rogasky briefly summarizes such mass killings as the slaughter of the Armenians by the Turks in 1915 and the atrocities of Pol Pot's regime in Cambodia after 1975. Rogasky concludes that such examples do not measure up to the horror perpetrated against the Jews by Nazi Germany because the Holocaust represents the only instance in history when a government and its leaders adopted an avowed policy of murdering an entire group of people solely to exterminate them rather than to achieve some other end. That position might be debatable, particularly in the light of contemporary policies of "ethnic cleansing" aimed at a number of minority groups.

Rogasky's contention that world leaders did not intervene more quickly to save the victims of the Nazis because those victims were Jewish, not Catholic or Protestant, might also be questioned. Government reluctance to interfere in the "internal affairs" of another country seems part of the fabric of twentieth-century history, and the complexity of securing international cooperation on almost any matter has been demonstrated time and again.

Although Rogasky admits her book is not objective, one might still pose the question of its fairness, particularly in light of the fact that it is intended for an audience of young people who may have little knowledge of the topic. For the most part, Rogasky tries to lay out facts to support her contentions. However, in her chapter indicting other governments, she tells readers that presenting the facts is useless. She summarizes the 1943 Bermuda conference as follows: "Several paragraphs could be spent describing the conference. But since from the very beginning the purpose was to lessen some of the public disapproval of both governments, it is wasted space to do so." She says that "much has been left out of this chapter, including the attempts of people in government and elsewhere to change the attitudes and help the dying Jews. But since the result was always the same—little was done—only the most important points and responses seemed necessary to mention."

Astute readers may recognize Rogasky's slant in her presentation, but others may simply absorb her tone of horror and disgrace, experiencing the shock and guilt stemming from the realization that people can be so systematically brutal and disgracefully indifferent.

Rogasky's major achievement lies in the sustained power of her book to indict anti-Semitism in any form. Although the final pages include examples of other recent instances of racism and oppression, she maintains her focus on examples that indicate that suspicion and persecution of Jews has not died. Through her book she tries to recruit a generation of readers to help prevent an escalation of violence that could result in atrocities such as those she graphically documents for them.

—Kathy Piehl

ROQUELAURE, A.N. See **RICE, Anne.**

ROSTKOWSKI, Margaret I. American. Born in Little Rock, Arkansas, 12 January 1945. Educated at Middlebury College, Vermont, B.A. 1967; University of Kansas, Lawrence, M.A.T. 1971. Two sons. Teacher of English, French, and reading at middle schools in Ogden, Utah, 1974-84; teacher of English and writing, since 1984, Ogden High School. Member of Ogden Arts Commission and

Friends of Weber County Library. Recipient: Golden Kite award from the Society of Children's Book Writers, 1986, the Children's Book award from the International Reading Association, 1987, and the Jefferson Cup from the Virginia Library Association, 1987, all for *After the Dancing Days*; the novel was also listed among the Best Books for Young Adults and Notable Children's Books by the American Library Association, 1986. Agent: Ruth Cohen, P.O. Box 7626, Menlo Park, CA 94025. Address: 2830 Marilyn Dr., Ogden, UT 84403, U.S.A.

PUBLICATIONS FOR YOUNG ADULTS

Novels

After the Dancing Days. New York, Harper, 1986.
The Best of Friends. New York, Harper, 1989.
Ghost Women. New York, Harcourt Brace, forthcoming.

*

Biography: Essay in *Speaking for Ourselves, Too* compiled and edited by Donald R. Gallo, National Council of Teachers of English, 1993.

Margaret I. Rostkowski comments:

My books begin with questions, with things I want to explore and learn more about. *After the Dancing Days* began when I wondered what life could be for someone so badly mutilated that people turned away from him in horror. *The Best of Friends* began when my students asked me to write about the period of the Vietnam War, a time they are curious about but find few adults willing to discuss. *Ghost Women* explores the workings of a family, specifically two sisters and their mother, who must learn to shape their love outside the bonds of a traditional family. My next novel explores the effects of illness on a family and on a community.

I enjoy all of writing: the first excitement of falling in love with characters; the thrashing out of the plot; the revision, the hard work of finding the feeling buried beneath the moment.

In trying to write as well and as honestly as I can, I follow a few practices: I don't watch much television; I read, especially writers who work with questions; I listen to and talk to other writers; I explore the land where I live; I walk with my dog almost every day. And always, in my head, I write.

*   *   *

Margaret Rostkowski explores the complexities of emotions engendered by participation in war. Not that she sets her novels in battlefields. Rather she considers the struggles of survivors and the uncertainties of those who might face combat.

After the Dancing Days takes place in 1919, when thirteen-year-old Annie Metcalf waits for her father, Lawrence, to return with some of the wounded veterans he had cared for during the Great War. His decision to work at a medical facility for veterans rather than return to County Hospital in their town near Kansas City puzzles and upsets his wife and other members of the community.

Annie is torn between her desire for life to resume the shape of prewar days, and her growing knowledge that in many ways such an existence can never return. Katherine, Annie's mother, retains an absorption in music that has sustained her through past difficulties.

She opposes Annie's visits to St. John's, where Lawrence works and where Annie's grandfather reads to a blind veteran he had known before the war. At first Annie is frightened and sickened by the condition of the men, particularly Andrew, who had suffered severe burns on his face and hands. Yet, she comes to appreciate the person behind the frightening exterior and helps the embittered Andrew reach out to others.

As the summer progresses, Annie decides that she must risk her mother's anger to do what she believes is right and she directly disobeys her orders to stop her visits to St. John's. Annie also explores the circumstances surrounding the last days of her mother's brother Paul, who had died in France. With Andrew's help, she learns what the official accounts of Paul's death hid. He had died of measles, not of war wounds, a victim of inadequate medical care. Annie's shock on learning that her beloved uncle had not died a heroic death gradually recedes as she acknowledges the truth of Andrew's observation that how men died during the war matters less than the fact that they had to die at all.

Annie's confrontation with her mother over her visits causes Katherine to examine her own attitudes about the war and its victims. By the story's end, Katherine not only invites Andrew to dinner but also agrees to play a concert for the patients at St. John's.

Most townspeople, however, concentrate on forgetting the war, erecting a memorial and putting the past behind them with noble speeches and public pronouncements. When the monument is proposed at the Independence Day celebration, Annie eagerly anticipates seeing her uncle's name chiseled permanently on an appropriate edifice. By the time of its dedication on Armistice Day, she refuses to join her classmates in singing patriotic anthems, in part because the veterans at St. John's are not invited to the ceremony. "The ceremony was for those like my grandmother, those who still believed," Annie concludes.

Although Rostkowski does not minimize the horrible aspects of war, she does not categorize those who participate as villains. Andrew and Paul volunteered to fight, decisions that upset their families. Annie's grandmother makes sense of her son's death by accepting the community's declarations about the nobility of the conflict. Annie realizes that the older woman could not cope with the facts about her son's death and must believe that he died heroically in battle.

Annie's first-person account of her changing view of war and its effects also chronicles an adolescent's growing realization that she must form independent opinions. Although she idolizes her father, Annie confronts him for his attempts to minimize the suffering of the men in order to spare her emotional pain. Yet, Annie too has trouble letting go as Andrew becomes more independent. Her reluctance to allow him to make decisions that will take him away from her parallels her parents' reluctance to have Annie enter adulthood.

From the post-World War I setting of *After the Dancing Days*, Rostkowski shifts to the more recent conflict of the war between the United States and Vietnam in *The Best of Friends*. Dan Ulvang and Will Spencer are about to graduate from high school. Dan's younger sister Sarah has joined the two in a triumvirate of friendship that has lasted for years. However, their relationships undergo a number of changes, some of them precipitated by the escalation of the Vietnam conflict. Sarah's opposition to the war leads her to distribute antiwar materials on the campus of the community college where her father works as a janitor. Mr. Ulvang's devotion to discipline and duty extends to his service as head of the local draft board. Dan, a brilliant student who strives continually to meet his father's standards of perfection, has ignored the war because he is certain to receive a student deferment while he attends college. Will, an indifferent student at best, has allowed Dan to help him through high school and make many decisions for him. Yet, Will refuses to be pushed by Dan into attending college to avoid the military. His enlistment severs the tie between the young men and calls into question his tentative romance with Sarah, whom he had taken to the prom.

What is intriguing about Rostkowski's book is her portrayal of the different decisions young men and women make about their participation in the Vietnam War. Although concern about the political position of the United States is a contributing factor, information about the war is scanty for Will, Dan, and Sarah. Instead, their decisions result from a variety of factors, most of which do not take the Vietnamese into account. Will follows the lead of a classmate and enlists in the army before graduation, as much to prove to Dan he can make his own decisions as to serve his country. Sarah and Dan both react initially to Will's choice in terms of how he had rejected their influences on his life. But Will's action motivates Dan to take a stand against the war and face his father, who sees Will not as a person but as a statistic in filling a monthly draft quota. By turning in his draft card, Dan contemplates a future as uncertain as Will's. At the novel's end, Will and Dan face the consequences of the individual decisions they have made. Rostkowski not only leaves off a happy ending, she refuses to provide a conventional ending at all.

That authorial choice exemplifies one of Rostkowski's themes in her two young-adult novels. For those who stay home during wars and those who participate, the conflict itself shifts the normal course of lives into channels that are not easy to predict or control. Her powerful, thought-provoking books make young adults think about the causes and consequences of war.

—Kathy Piehl

———

RUBINSTEIN, Gillian (Margaret). Australian. Born in Potten End, Hertfordshire, 29 August 1942. Educated at Queen Anne's, Caversham, Berkshire, 1954-60; Lady Margaret Hall, Oxford, 1961-64, B.A. and M.A. (honors) in modern languages; Stockwell College, University of London, postgraduate diploma in education 1973. Married Philip Rubinstein in 1973 (second marriage); one son and two daughters. Research assistant, London School of Economics, 1964-65; administrative officer, Greater London Council, 1965-66; editor, Tom Stacey, publishers, London, 1969-72. Has also worked as a cook, cleaner, script assessor, part-time editor, journalist, and film critic; free-lance writer, since 1986. Recipient: Children's Book Council of Australia honor book, 1987, Australian Children's Literature Peace prize, 1987, Australian National Children's Book award, 1988, and Young Australians Best Book award, 1990, all for *Space Demons;* Australian Council Literature Arts Board fellowship, 1988 and 1989-92; New South Wales Premier's award, 1988, and Children's Book Council of Australia honor book, 1989, both for *Answers to Brut;* Children's Book Council of Australia Book of the Year for Older Readers, 1989, and Adelaide Festival of Arts National Children's Book award, 1990, both for *Beyond the Labyrinth;* Children's Book Council of Australia honor book, 1989, and New South Wales Family Therapy Association Family award for

Children's Books—Highly Recommended, 1989, both for *Melanie and the Night Animal;* Children's Book Council of Australia Shortlist, 1990, for *Skymaze;* Children's Book Council of Australia Honour Book, 1993 and Victorian Premiers award Shortlist, 1993, for *Galax-Arena.* Agent: Caroline Lurie, Australian Literary Management, 2-A Armstrong Street, Middle Park, VIC 3206. Address: 29 Seaview Road, Lynton, SA 5062, Australia.

PUBLICATIONS FOR YOUNG ADULTS

Fiction

Space Demons. Adelaide, Omnibus, 1986; New York, Dial Press, 1988.
Answers to Brut. Adelaide, Omnibus, 1988.
Beyond the Labyrinth. Melbourne, Hyland House, 1988; New York, Orchard Books, 1990.
Melanie and the Night Animal. Adelaide, Omnibus, 1988.
Skymaze. Adelaide, Omnibus, 1989; New York, Orchard Books, 1991.
Flashback: The Amazing Adventures of a Film Horse. Melbourne, Penguin, 1990.
At Ardilla. Adelaide, Omnibus, 1991.
Galax-Arena. Melbourne, Hyland House, 1992.

Other

Editor, *After Dark.* Adelaide, Omnibus, 1988.
Editor, *Before Dawn.* Adelaide, Omnibus, 1988.

PUBLICATIONS FOR CHILDREN

Fiction

Dog in, Cat Out, illustrated by Ann James. New York, Ticknor & Fields, 1993.
Giant's Tooth, illustrated by Craig Smith. New York, Viking, 1993.

* * *

Gillian Rubinstein considers herself a writer for children, yet she is widely read and discussed by young adults and adults. Her status and popularity became instantly established with the publication of her first book, *Space Demons,* which also indicated her interests and concerns. Here, she places a group of children in front of a computer game which turns out to be fiendishly difficult and also fiendish in intent. To play the game fully, the children must be prepared to be physically drawn into it. Their life situations and emotional states influence their game-playing decisions and they must make sophisticated, complex, and moral choices which are eventually refined into "refusing to hate."

Rubinstein came to Australia as an adult from the United Kingdom. She speaks freely of having had an unhappy childhood and having felt totally powerless. These emotions inform and fuel her writing plus her constant interest in the outsider and in the patterns of family scapegoating. Like other writers for young people, Rubinstein is keenly aware of the impact of television, computer, and video games. She actively works towards structuring her books and engaging her readers by using similar strategies: multiple viewpoints, rapid "scene changes," and fast-paced, exciting adventure scenarios.

In *Skymaze,* a sequel to *Space Demons,* the same four children become involved in the hypergame "Skymaze," mysteriously sent to Andrew from Japan. Again a breathtaking, dangerous sequence is played out, and again the children's real life frustrations and anxieties are reflected in how they play and react to the game. Her books are avidly read by young people who admit they are not easily engaged by fiction.

Brenton, the protagonist of *Beyond the Labyrinth,* is an angry, bright, sensitive boy. He is obsessed with a role-playing game where life-determining decisions are made by the roll of a dice. He is also haunted by the threat of nuclear war. His mother is determined to maintain the illusion of a happy family, while his father bullies those around him, often with the help of alcohol and often using Brenton as a scapegoat.

Into their lives come the dark, alien anthropologist Cal and a phantom graffiti artist who daubs variations of the letters "dead end" everywhere. Set against an idyllic seaside landscape, the book questions our attitudes toward the environment, nuclear arms and war, other cultures, and children in the context of a powerful but pared down narrative. At the end of this complex, many faceted, shimmering contemporary tale, the reader is invited to roll the dice and choose alternative endings. Yet a careful reading and the relative placement of the two endings leave little doubt as to the author's view on which ending is the preferred one.

Rubinstein has written for the theatre and also a number of picture books and stories for younger readers. These are generally sunnier, though still devoted to looking at how families function and children see and respond to their world. Several of the stories look with sly humour at pompous power struggles and the human need to claim territory.

At Ardilla is also widely read beyond its implied readership. Rubinstein has frequently commented on the lack of acceptable and safe rite-of-passage activities for young people in western society. She believes this leads to many dangerous risk-taking activities such as experimenting with drugs and reckless driving. "Tense, moody, difficult Jen" is on the cusp of adolescence. Each summer her family moves to their beach house Ardilla, with one other family. This year Jen's father has invited a divorced friend and his children. This invasion is the last straw for Jen whose moodiness and resentment sour the holiday. What Jen is really fighting is change. She does not want to let go of the magic places and emblematic games of childhood. Like Jen's perceptions, the story hovers between a fully realised world of family activities, tensions, conversations, and the fantasy world of Jen's subconscious. After a cathartic near-drowning, Jen is able to "go forward, through the darkness." She is consoled and focused through her commitment to music and the support of her immediate family.

Families in Rubinstein's stories are not always supportive and she has produced a number of tough, unflattering portraits of adults. In *Galax-Arena* the one significant adult character is Hythe. All the images present him as an effective but unfeeling and manipulative animal trainer. Rubinstein is a great animal lover and here she draws possibly unwelcome parallels between methods of capturing, training, and subjugating animals with the way societies in different parts of the world treat children.

The "peb" are children captured after they have been in some way abandoned. Peter, Liane, and Joella are on their way to stay with an aunt because their mother has taken off and their much older father is feckless and erratic. As Joella, the narrator, observes,

"People on journeys are easy to make disappear." Hythe has obviously been on the watch. He drugs them, kidnaps them, and takes them to join the other children at the Galax-Arena. Here the children are isolated and rigorously trained to perform ever more daring acrobatic feats for the invisible Vexa. Those, like Joella, who do not have innate athletic ability or who cannot be cajoled or coerced into becoming single-mindedly competitive are, at worst, disposed of or, at best, placed in a "tank" as playthings for the Vexa.

The children develop an uneasy community and a "patwa" language (there is a glossary) to enable them to communicate.

Galax-Arena is brilliantly imagined and full of tension and menace. The scenes of training and performance are both exhilarating and terrifying, as is the sudden reversal of the plot halfway through. Eventually, the purpose of the Galax-Arena is revealed, and this in turn raises questions about the responsibilities of scientists and the purposes to which science and scarce resources are put.

Joella is an unlikely hero. As Rubinstein has said: "Joella's very ordinariness keeps her whole.... In my books...the boys set the action in motion.... They tend to be less well-adjusted, more vulnerable, more violent.... The girls end up having to put things right again" (*Magpies,* May 1993).

Rubinstein's vision may be bleak, but she shows young people as having the capacity to be compassionate, imaginative, and resourceful. Her tightly plotted narratives move seamlessly from reality to fantasy and, while they incorporate tough issues, they do so in ways that seem to both entertain and empower readers.

—Agnes Nieuwenhuizen

———

RUBY, Lois F. American. Born in San Francisco, California, 11 September 1942. Educated at University of California, Berkeley, B.A. 1964; San Jose State College (now San Jose State University), San Jose, M.A. 1968. Married Thomas Ruby in 1965; three sons. Young adult librarian, Dallas Public Library, Texas, 1965-67; art and music librarian, University of Missouri-Columbia, 1967-68; writer, since 1973. Youth group adviser, since 1976; creative writing instructor, since 1985. Recipient: Best books for young adults citation, American Library Association, 1977, for *Arriving at a Place You've Never Left;* notable children's trade book in the field of social studies citation, National Council for Social Studies and the Children's Book Council, 1982, for *Two Truths in My Pocket;* honorable mention, *Writer's Digest* short story competition, for "Jubilee," 1991. Agent: William Reiss, Paul R. Reynolds, Inc., 71 West 23rd St., New York, NY 10010. Address: 6714 East Tenth St., Wichita, KS 67206, U.S.A.

PUBLICATIONS FOR YOUNG ADULTS

Fiction

Arriving at a Place You've Never Left. New York, Dial, 1977.
What Do You Do in Quicksand? New York, Viking, 1979.
Two Truths in My Pocket (short stories). New York, Viking, 1982.
This Old Man. Boston, Houghton, 1984.
Pig-Out Inn. Boston, Houghton, 1987.
Miriam's Well. New York, Scholastic, 1993.

Skin Deep. New York, Scholastic, forthcoming.
Steal Away, New York, Macmillan, forthcoming.

*

Biography: Essay in *Speaking for Ourselves, Too* compiled and edited by Donald R. Gallo, National Council of Teachers of English, 1993.

*   *   *

Societal conventions do not inhibit Lois Ruby where writing is concerned. Her works deal with taboo subjects including prostitution, teenage pregnancy, child abuse, and interfaith relationships. The pull of modern society on such institutions as marriage and religion is explored from every angle. Ruby's skillful incorporation of these themes into detailed story lines rather than using them to carry a plot and the strength of her characters in confronting these dilemmas head on—sometimes with the help of traditional faith, but often not—results in compelling fiction that is relevant to today's young people.

Ruby's first book, *Arriving at a Place You've Never Left,* is a collection of seven short stories in which the very human characters fail to realize that their problems are universal. "Faces at a Dark Window" is a chillingly accurate portrayal of a mother's nervous breakdown related by her daughter. When a teenager becomes an unwed mother, her boyfriend realizes that he has abandoned not only her but the baby in "Found by a Lost Child." Separation for the sake of finances intervenes in a love affair in "Heads You Go, Tails I Stay." "Justice" and fairness are at issue in the case of an adolescent boy who has killed his abusive father. "Spring" is about a terminally ill teenager coming to terms with his impending death. A boarding school plagued by a rash of thefts is the setting for "Like a Toy on the End of a String." "Arriving at a Place You've Never Left" deals with a Jewish girl whose family escaped the Holocaust only to have to flee a bigoted American town.

Ruby sketches the fine line between normalcy and mental illness in the novel *What Do You Do in Quicksand?* Matt Russell is only seventeen and already a father. Baby Barbara's mother does not want her, and Matt cannot stand the idea of someone else having her, so he accepts his responsibility. Leah McCauley Burke Aaronson, his next-door neighbor and a victim of sexual abuse, takes an instant attraction to Barbara, but things nearly get out of hand as Leah's unstable personality reveals itself. Not a model of perfection himself, Matt grows up in a hurry when necessary and finally leaves with his baby to establish a life for them.

Ruby returns to short fiction with *Two Truths in My Pocket.* Each of the six stories has a Jewish theme. In "Inscriptions on Stone," a boy worries about not becoming a rabbi to follow in his father's footsteps until his sister announces that she will carry on the tradition. A brain-damaged girl gets her wish for religious instruction in "Forgetting Me, Remembering Me." A young Jew falls in love with his English teacher in "Lighter Than Air." "Hasty Vows" deals with a girl's resurgence of faith during the Yom Kippur holiday. "Strangers in the Land of Egypt" is about the relationship of a Jewish couple who are of different races. The "Frail Bridge" of mortality is at issue as a young girl mourns her Bubbie that she never knew as a real person.

Sixteen-year-old Greta Janssen is the common link between two "old men"—one an ancient Chinese patriarch and the other a pimp—in the novel *This Old Man.* Daughter of a prostitute, Greta is living in a group home to escape going to work for the pimp when she meets Wing, a young Chinese-American who is caring for his Chinese-born grandfather. Greta has a love-hate relationship with both old men: the old grandfather resents her because she is not Chinese, and the pimp only sees her as a money-maker. In the end, she realizes that she can stand up to people and choose her own fate.

Dovie Chandler learns that other people's lives can be worse than her own in *Pig-Out Inn.* Dovie feels that her life is rootless because her mother is constantly on the move, but she realizes what real family problems are when a nine-year-old boy is left by his father at the Pig-Out Inn, Dovie's nickname for her mother's truck stop and latest business venture. Tag has been kidnapped from his mother, who has custody of him, and complications follow until a fair visitation schedule is arranged. Dovie's mother gives up the Pig-Out Inn, and the reader finds that a more mature Dovie is ready to face her uncertain future.

Miriam's Well treats both modern legal problems and ancient religious traditions. Seventeen-year-old Miriam Pelham is diagnosed with a treatable bone cancer, but she belongs to a strict religious sect which believes that only faith can cure illness. Her *pro bono* lawyer, Mr. Bergen, is determined to defend her First Amendment rights to refuse treatment. However, his son Adam is falling in love with Miriam and does not want to see her die. Eventually, under duress, Miriam receives some medical treatment (conventional and nonconventional) as well as faith healing. She does recover, but the cause of her remission cannot be determined. Even though "Miriam's well," she and Adam realize that their relationship cannot endure.

While not everyone lives happily ever after in Ruby's books, answers are found that work—at least for the present—and these young adults are able to pick up the pieces and go on with their lives. In Ruby's works, there is no lack of courage on the part of the characters or the writer.

—Sharon Clontz Bernstein

———

RYLANT, Cynthia. American. Born in Hopewell, Virginia, 6 June 1954. Educated at Morris Harvey College (now University of Charleston), West Virginia, 1973-75, B.A. in English 1975; Marshall University, Huntington, West Virginia, 1975-76, M.A. in English 1976; Kent State University, Kent, Ohio, 1980-81, M.L.S. 1982. Has one son. Writer. Part-time English instructor, Marshall University, Huntington, West Virginia, 1979-80; children's librarian, Akron Public Library, Akron, Ohio, 1983; part-time English lecturer, University of Akron, Akron, 1983-84; part-time lecturer, Northeast Ohio Universities College of Medicine, Rootstown, Ohio, since 1991. Recipient: Named a *Booklist* reviewer's choice, 1982, Caldecott Honor Book, American Library Association (ALA) notable book, and Reading Rainbow selection, all 1983, all for *When I Was Young in the Mountains;* American Book award nomination, 1983, and English Speaking Union Book-across-the-Sea Ambassador of Honor award, 1984, both for *When I Was Young in the Mountains;* named an ALA notable book, a *School Library Journal* best book of 1984, a National Council for Social Studies best book, 1984, and a Society of Midland Authors best children's book, 1985, all for *Waiting to Waltz: A Childhood;* named a *New York Times* best illustrated, a *Horn Book* honor book, a Child Study Association of

America's children's book of the year, all 1985, and a Caldecott Honor Book, 1986, all for *The Relatives Came;* named a Child Study Association of America's children's book of the year, 1985, for *A Blue-eyed Daisy;* named a *School Library Journal* best book, 1985, for *Every Living Thing;* named a *Parents' Choice* selection, 1986, and a Newbery Honor Book, 1987, for *A Fine White Dust; Boston Globe/Horn Book* award for nonfiction, 1991, for *Appalachia: The Voices of Sleeping Birds;* Garden State Children's Book award, Children's Services Section of the New Jersey Library Association, 1992, for *Henry and Mudge Get the Cold Shivers; Boston Globe/Horn Book* award, 1992, Newbery medal, 1993, both for *Missing May.*

PUBLICATIONS FOR YOUNG ADULTS

A Blue-eyed Daisy. New York, Bradbury, 1985; as *Some Year for Ellie,* illustrated by Kate Rogers, Viking Kestrel, 1986.
A Fine White Dust. New York, Bradbury, 1986.
A Kindness. New York, Orchard Books, 1989.
A Couple of Kooks: And Other Stories about Love. New York, Orchard Books, 1990.
Missing May. New York, Orchard Books, 1992.

Other

Appalachia: The Voices of Sleeping Birds, illustrated by Barry Moser. New York, Harcourt, 1991.
Best Wishes, photographs by Carlo Ontal. New York, Owen, 1992.
I Had Seen Castles. New York, Harcourt, forthcoming.

Poetry

Waiting to Waltz: A Childhood, illustrated by Stephen Gammell. New York, Bradbury, 1984.
Soda Jerk, illustrated by Peter Catalanotto. New York, Orchard Books, 1990.

Other

But I'll Be Back Again: An Album. New York, Orchard Books, 1989.

PUBLICATIONS FOR CHILDREN

Fiction

When I Was Young in the Mountains, illustrated by Diane Goode. New York, Dutton, 1982.
Miss Maggie, illustrated by Thomas DiGrazia. New York, Dutton. 1983.
This Year's Garden, illustrated by Mary Szilagyi. New York, Bradbury, 1984.
Every Living Thing (stories). New York, Bradbury, 1985.
The Relatives Came, illustrated by Stephen Gammell. New York, Bradbury, 1985.
Night in the Country, illustrated by Mary Szilagyi. New York, Bradbury, 1986.
Birthday Presents, illustrated by Sucie Stevenson. New York, Orchard Books, 1987.

Children of Christmas: Stories for the Season, illustrated by Stephen D. Schindler. New York, Orchard Books, 1987; as *Silver Packages and Other Stories,* London, Orchard Books, 1987.
All I See, illustrated by Peter Catalanotto. New York, Orchard Books, 1988.
Mr. Griggs' Work, illustrated by Julie Downing. New York, Orchard Books, 1989.
An Angel for Solomon Singer, illustrated by Peter Catalanotto. New York, Orchard Books, 1992.
The Everyday Books series: *The Everyday Children, The Everyday Garden, The Everyday House, The Everyday School, The Everyday Town,* illustrated by the author. New York, Bradbury, 5 vols., 1993.

Other (readers)

Henry and Mudge [in Puddle Trouble, in the Green Time, under the Yellow Moon, in the Sparkle Days, and the Forever Sea, Get the Cold Shivers, and the Happy Cat, and the Bedtime Thumps, Take the Big Test, and the Long Weekend, and the Wild Wind, and the Careful Cousin] illustrated by Sucie Stevenson. New York, Bradbury Press, 13 vols., 1987-93; first vol. published London, Gollancz, 1989.

*

Media Adaptations: *When I Was Young in the Mountains* (filmstrip), Random House, 1983; *This Year's Garden* (filmstrip), Random House, 1983; *The Relatives Came* (filmstrip), Random House, 1986. Several of Rylant's books are available on film through American School Publishers.

Biography: Entry in *Sixth Book of Junior Authors,* New York, H.W. Wilson, 1989; essay in *Something about the Author Autobiography Series,* Volume 13, Detroit, Gale, 1991; essay in *Speaking for Ourselves, Too* compiled and edited by Donald R. Gallo, National Council of Teachers of English, 1993; essay in *Authors and Artists for Young Adults,* Volume 10, Detroit, Gale, 1993.

Manuscript Collection: Special Collections, Kent State University, Ohio.

Critical Study: Entry in *Children's Literature Review,* Volume 15, Detroit, Gale, 1988, pp. 167-174.

*   *   *

Reflective, capable teens coping with life in rural or small town settings people the poems, short stories, and novels of Cynthia Rylant. Chip takes care of his single mom in *A Kindness;* Summer overcomes her own grief to encourage her uncle to keep living without his wife in *Missing May;* and the young man behind the fountain in *Soda Jerk* observes a universe of familiar stereotypes even though the drugstore owner thinks, "I've just been making sodas." Some critics question the believability of such perceptive teens, but Rylant respects her protagonists and unveils their individuality and vulnerability in tightly woven plots centering on everyday crises.

Rylant's *A Fine White Dust,* winner of a Newbery Honor Award, is a brave novel dealing with religion, a controversial topic for young-adult books. Peter becomes deeply religious and falls under the spell of the charismatic Preacher Man, who ultimately betrays him, leaving Peter to grapple with the betrayal and disillusionment. As he fingers the fine white dust of a broken ceramic cross he painted in bible school, before he became too cool to attend, he questions his blind faith in God.

It is Rylant's characters that the reader will remember, but she is adept at providing a sense of place within her writings. Small town life in the mountains of Virginia and West Virginia feels slow, almost claustrophobic, yet comfortable, a place the reader recognizes as safe. Summer's Uncle's beat-up house trailer on a hillside with whirligigs in the garden and Maywell's drugstore on Main Street become vivid images in the reader's mind. Rylant has lived in these places and stood elbow to elbow with the local people; she refers to places, characters, and events that turn up in her books in her autobiography, *But I'll Be Back Again: An Album.* Rylant chronicles her own coming of age in the 1960s in *Waiting to Waltz: A Childhood,* a series of autobiographical poems portraying the awkwardness of adolescence as well as the certainty of a young woman who has accomplished a goal. Readers will find themselves matching places from her autobiography and autobiographical poetry to the settings of her stories.

In interviews, Rylant has said she doesn't like neat, happy endings because life is much too complex. In *A Couple of Kooks: And Other Stories about Love,* two teens talk to their unborn baby about the things it should remember once it has been adopted, "And I'd keep you if I could but I truly can't, we don't have money or a place of our own." In another story, a grandfather watching the people and events at his granddaughter's wedding realizes he has missed passion: "I have not yet met anyone for whom I might wear strange hats or sing imbecilic songs or dance the limbo or completely flip-flop religions."

But Rylant's books are hopeful. The characters, although usually odd or different in some way, have humor and compassion. Their futures may not be certain, but they will meet the challenges with the help of the diverse families, friends, and acquaintances that people their tightly knit, rustic communities. In *Missing May,* Cletus, an absolute lunatic according to Summer, uses his collection of unusual photos to distract Uncle Ob from his grief; Chip's wisdom in *A Kindness* helps his mother's situation work out the best it possibly could; and Ernie from *A Couple of Kooks* grows flowers to brighten his days and the lives of the people who visit Stan's hardware store. In her autobiography, Rylant describes the pain of being left with grandparents at the age of four and the restorative power of families and communities: "I lay in my grandparents' bed and cried in agony as everyone stood in the driveway, saying goodbye to my mother as she got in the car.... Luckily, though, in that small white house lived those who could help me heal. I had two uncles and two aunts and two cousins and two grandparents...and they all loved me."

Rylant's books are a celebration of people and places. The picture book format of *Soda Jerk* and *But, I'll Be Back Again* may confuse some young adults, but their sophistication and emotional honesty engage readers of all ages. All of Rylant's stories, including her picture story books marketed for younger readers, create memorable characters and places and provide teens a window on the world. As the soda jerk says, "...and they leave behind / some secret with the jerk. / Tips are okay. / But the secrets are better."

—Hollis Lowery-Moore

S

SACHS, Marilyn (Stickle). American. Born in New York City 18 December 1927. Educated at Hunter College (now of the City University of New York), B.A. 1949; Columbia University, M.S. 1953. Married Morris Sachs in 1947; one daughter, one son. Librarian, Brooklyn Public Library, Brooklyn, New York, 1949-60, and San Francisco Public Library, 1961-67; writer. Recipient: *Veronica Ganz* was named a notable book of 1968 by the American Library Association; *New York Times* outstanding book of the year awards, 1971, for *The Bears' House,* and 1973 *A Pocket Full of Seeds; School Library Journal* best book of the year award, 1971, for *The Bears' House,* and 1973, for *The Truth about Mary Rose;* National Book award finalist, 1972, for *The Bears' House;* Jane Addams Children's Book Honor award, 1974, for *A Pocket Full of Seeds;* Silver Pencil award, Collective Propaganda van het Nederlandse Boek (Netherlands), 1974, for *The Truth about Mary Rose,* and 1977, for *Dorrie's Book;* Austrian Children's Book Prize, 1977, for *The Bears' House;* Garden State Children's Book award, 1978, for *Dorrie's Book; A Summer's Lease* was chosen one of *School Library Journal*'s best books for spring, 1979; *Fleet-Footed Florence* was selected as a children's choice by the International Reading Association, 1982; Association of Jewish Libraries award, 1983, for *Call Me Ruth; The Fat Girl* was chosen one of American Library Association's best books for young adults, 1984; Christopher award, 1986, for *Underdog; Fran Ellen's House* was named a notable book of 1987 by the American Library Association; Bay Area Book Reviewers Association award, 1988, for *Fran Ellen's House;* recognition of merit, George C. Stone Center for Childrens' Books, 1989, for *The Bear's House* and *Fran Ellen's House;* Jane Addams Childrens' Book award, 1990, for *The Big Book for Peace; The Big Book for Peace* was named a notable book for 1991 by the American Library Association. Address: 733 31st Ave., San Francisco, CA 94121. U.S.A.

PUBLICATIONS FOR YOUNG ADULTS

Fiction

A Summer's Lease. New York, Dutton, 1979.
Bus Ride, illustrated by Amy Rowen. New York, Dutton, 1980.
Hello...Wrong Number, illustrated by Pamela Johnson. New York, Dutton, 1981.
Beach Towels, illustrated by Jim Spence. New York, Dutton, 1982.
Fourteen. New York, Dutton, 1983.
The Fat Girl. New York, Dutton, 1984; Oxford, Oxford University Press, 1985.
Thunderbird, illustrated by Jim Spence. New York, Dutton, 1985.
Baby Sister. New York, Dutton, 1986; Oxford, Oxford University Press, 1987.
Almost Fifteen. New York, Dutton, 1987; Oxford, Oxford University Press, 1988.
Fran Ellen's House. New York, Dutton, 1987.
Just Like a Friend. New York, Dutton, 1989.
At the Sound of the Beep. New York, Dutton, 1990.
Circles. New York, Dutton, 1991.
What My Sister Remembered. New York, Dutton, 1992.
Thirteen—Going on Seven. New York, Dutton, 1993.

PUBLICATIONS FOR CHILDREN

Fiction

Amy Moves In, illustrated by Judith Gwyn Brown. New York, Doubleday, 1964.
Laura's Luck, illustrated by Ib Ohlsson. New York, Doubleday, 1965.
Amy and Laura, illustrated by Tracy Sugarman. New York, Doubleday, 1966.
Veronica Ganz, illustrated by Louis Glanzman. New York, Doubleday, 1968; London, Macdonald, 1969.
Peter and Veronica, illustrated by Louis Glanzman. New York, Doubleday, 1969; London, Macdonald, 1970.
Marv, illustrated by Louis Glanzman. New York, Doubleday, 1970.
The Bears' House, illustrated by Louis Glanzman. New York, Doubleday, 1971.
A Pocket Full of Seeds, illustrated by Ben Stahl. New York, Doubleday, 1973; London, Macdonald and Jane's, 1976.
The Truth about Mary Rose, illustrated by Glanzman. New York, Doubleday, and London, Macdonald, 1973.
Dorrie's Book, illustrated by Anne Sachs. New York, Doubleday, 1975; London, Macdonald and Jane's, 1976.
Matt's Mitt, illustrated by Hilary Knight. New York, Doubleday, 1975.
A December Tale. New York, Doubleday, 1976.
A Secret Friend. New York, Doubleday, 1978; London, Corgi, 1988.
Class Pictures. New York, Dutton, 1980.
Fleet-Footed Florence, illustrated by Charles Robinson. New York, Doubleday, 1981.
Call Me Ruth. New York, Doubleday, 1982.
Underdog. New York, Doubleday, 1985; Oxford, Oxford University Press, 1987.

Other

Reading between the Lines (play). New York, Children's Book Council, 1971.
Editor, with Ann Durell, *The Big Book for Peace,* illustrated by Thomas B. Allen. New York, Dutton, 1990.

*

Media Adaptations: *Veronica Ganz* (filmstrip), Insight Media Programs, 1975.

Biography: Entry in *Fourth Book of Junior Authors and Illustrators,* New York, H.W. Wilson, 1978; essay in *Something about the Author Autobiography Series,* Volume 2, Detroit, Gale, 1986; essay in *Speaking for Ourselves: Autobiographical Sketches by Notable Authors of Books for Young Adults,* Volume 1, compiled and edited by Donald R. Gallo, National Council of Teachers of English, 1990.

Manuscript Collection: Kerlan Collection, University of Minnesota.

Critical Study: Entry in *Children's Literature Review,* Volume 2,

Detroit, Gale, 1976; entry in *Contemporary Literary Criticism,* Volume 35, Detroit, Gale, 1985.

Marilyn Sachs comments:

Books have always been a joy and comfort to me. They still are. Whenever the real world becomes too complicated, I can always retreat safely into some other world that books offer. Writing is nearly as great a pleasure as reading. And I feel proud that my books can offer young people another place to go safely.

*   *   *

A writer whose range includes fantasy, realism, history, tragedy, humor, love, and prejudice in a variety of realistic settings and eras, Marilyn Sachs has been one of the most popular writers for young adults for many years. She skillfully delves into the intricacies of family relationships, friendships of young people from entirely different backgrounds, and the horror facing Jewish families under the tyranny of the Nazi regime. She writes about romance, family catastrophes, feelings and fears of young people growing up, death, social issues, and the need for kindness. It is clear that she is sympathetic to losers, because many of her characters are young people that don't "fit in." She depicts them as struggling to find out who they are and where they are going.

Marv is a good example of a young person who doesn't "fit in." He is a dreaming inventor, considered by most of his teachers to be hopelessly stupid and by his older sister to be a failure. He invents worthless objects unrecognizable for what he wants them to be, usually leaving them unfinished, cluttering up the family's backyard. When Marv does invent something useful and cherished by his sister and also by all the little kids in the neighborhood, he wonders why his sister bursts into tears. A story about a dreamer, this is also a story about a sister and brother loving each other in different ways, one showing love and the other not knowing how to receive it.

Being fourteen is tough enough, but having a mother writing books about her life in *Fourteen* makes Rebecca Jamison even more miserable. Sachs has combined humor and mystery in this story of a young girl encountering love for the first time with a boy from a somewhat shady family. This is a delightful story portraying an unusual romance of two young people, similar but different from that of Rebecca's mother when she first met Rebecca's father.

A heartrending story, *A Pocket Full of Seeds* tells of Nicole Nieman living in France during the German occupation of World War II. Being Jewish, Nicole's family is taken away from their home by the Germans while Nicole is in school. When she finds them gone, Nicole wanders around aimlessly but ends up at her school where she decides to stay and wait for the end of the war when she and her family will be reunited. Sachs has written a moving, lifelike story of a young Jewish girl facing the changes of war and the bitter prejudice against the Jews. One can feel the terror and frustration as Nicole loses her family, and the doubt that Nicole will ever be reunited with them again. Sachs has dealt skillfully with the problem of fear that people sometimes have when they are "different" by showing Nicole maturing and becoming capable of facing life alone.

Almost Fifteen portrays Imogen Rogers, a young girl helping to supplement her family's income by babysitting. When she develops a crush on the father of the little boy she babysits for, she can think of nothing else but the young, handsome Adam Derman. Unfortunately, Mr. Derman does not return Imogen's feelings, and

the girl is crestfallen. However, she snaps back to her vivacious self when she finds a new romance at her doctor's office. Sachs has created an amusing yet sometimes affecting story about an adolescent girl who deals with feelings that almost get out of control. As she gets her romantic fantasies and dreams under control, however, she learns to become more responsible and dependable.

Sach's *Dorrie's Book* created an outcry from one mother who picketed her local school protesting the presence of the book. It is a perceptive account cleverly written about a young girl who was always the center of attention in her family because she was an only child but now faces sharing the limelight with a new baby. Dorrie's dialogue and feelings are amusing and not a little pitiable as we tend to sympathize with the young girl who has to deal with not one new sister or brother but screaming triplets.

Another poignant, comical, and thought-provoking book, *Class Pictures* deals with the growing up of two very different best friends. The main character, dark, tall Pat Maddox, sees her friend Lolly Scheiner, in class pictures taken from kindergarten to senior class, changing from fat and very unpopular to a real beauty. Pat begins to feel left out of their friendship as Lolly's popularity increases. Pat turns to a former teacher for consolation and all of a sudden finds herself in love with him, even though he is happily married and a father. Pat and Lolly's friendship becomes strained, but as the two girls mature, each facing problems at home, their friendship revives. Sachs has written sympathetically about a young girl facing the fact that her mother will never grow up, her grandmother whom she has always considered her ally is now happily married and living elsewhere, and her former teacher will always be part of her life, not as a lover, but as a beloved friend.

The recipient of many awards and honors, Marilyn Sachs rates in the top ten percent of young adult writers. A pioneer of contemporary realistic fiction, she deftly introduces appropriate social issues through characters with whom her readers can identify. Her more than thirty books, including those for younger readers, are always enlightening, unpredictable, and entertaining.

—Carol Doxey

SALINGER, J(erome) D(avid). American. Born in New York, New York, 1 January 1919. Educated at McBurney School, New York, 1932-34; Valley Forge Military Academy, Pennsylvania (editor, *Crossed Sabres),* 1934-46; New York University, 1937; Ursinus College, Collegetown, Pennsylvania, 1938; Columbia University, New York, 1939. Married 1) Sylvia Salinger in 1945 (divorced 1947); 2) Claire Douglas in 1955 (divorced 1967), one daughter and one son. Writer. Worked as an entertainer on the Swedish liner *M.S. Kungsholm* in the Caribbean, 1941. Served in the 4th Infantry Division of the United States Army, 1942-45: staff sergeant, received five battle stars. Agent: Dorothy Olding Harold Ober Associates, Inc., 425 Madison Avenue, New York, NY 10017, U.S.A. Lives in Cornish, New Hampshire.

PUBLICATIONS

Novels

The Catcher in the Rye. Boston, Little, Brown, 1951; London, Hamish Hamilton, 1951.

Short Stories

Nine Stories. Boston, Little, Brown, 1953; as *For Esme—With Love and Squalor, and Other Stories,* London, Hamish Hamilton, 1953.
Franny and Zooey. Boston, Little, Brown, 1961; London, Heinemann, 1962.
Raise High the Roof Beam, Carpenters, and Seymour: An Introduction. Boston, Little, Brown, 1963; London, Heinemann, 1963.

*

Media Adaptations: *My Foolish Heart* (film adaptation of "Uncle Wiggily in Connecticut"), 1950.

Biography: Essay in *Authors and Artists for Young Adults,* Volume 2, Detroit, Gale, 1989; entry in *Dictionary of Literary Biography, Volume 2: American Novelists since World War II,* Detroit, Gale, 1978.

Bibliography: *J.D. Salinger: A Thirty Year Bibliography 1938-1968* by Kenneth Starosciak, privately printed, 1971; *J.D. Salinger: An Annotated Bibliography 1938-1981* by Jack R. Sublette, New York, Garland, 1984.

Critical Study: *The Fiction of J.D. Salinger* by Frederick L. Gwynn and Joseph L. Blotner, Pittsburgh, University of Pittsburgh Press, 1958, London, Spearman, 1960; *Salinger: A Critical and Personal Portrait* edited by Henry Anatole Grunwald, New York, Harper, 1962, London, Owen, 1964; *J.D. Salinger and the Critics* edited by William F. Belcher and James W. Lee, Belmont, California, Wadsworth, 1962; *If You Really Want to Know: A Catcher Casebook* edited by Malcolm M. Marsden, Chicago, Scott, Foresman, 1963; *J.D. Salinger* by Warren French, New York, Twayne, 1963, revised edition, 1976, revised edition, as *J.D. Salinger Revisited,* 1988; *Studies in J.D. Salinger* edited by Marvin Laser and Norman Fruman, New York, Odyssey Press, 1963; *J.D. Salinger* by James E. Miller, Jr., Minneapolis, University of Minnesota Press, 1965; *J.D. Salinger: A Critical Essay* by Kenneth Hamilton, Grand Rapids, Michigan, Eerdmans, 1967; entries in *Contemporary Literary Criticism,* Detroit, Gale, Volume 1, 1973; Volume 3, 1975; Volume 8, 1978; Volume 12, 1980; Volume 56, 1989; *Zen in the Art of J.D. Salinger* by Gerald Rosen, Berkeley, California, Creative Arts, 1977; *J.D. Salinger* by James Lundquist, New York, Ungar, 1979; *Salinger's Glass Stories as a Composite Novel* by Eberhard Alsen, Troy, New York, Whitston, 1984; *J.D. Salinger: Modern Critical Views* edited by Harold Bloom, Pennsylvania, Chelsea House, 1987; *In Search of J.D. Salinger* by Ian Hamilton, London, Heinemann, and New York, Random House, 1988.

*   *   *

J.D. Salinger's single most popular work, *The Catcher in the Rye,* has been and probably always will be read by a majority of young adult readers. Part of its appeal lies in the long history of controversy this novel has accrued over its four-decade life. Perhaps, as most teachers know, the best way to ensure adolescents' reading a particular text is to censor or ban it from library access. *Catcher* has been more often removed from bookshelves than any other American young adult novel. Though its censors cite obscene language as the major cause for its removal, it is arguable that the smugly rebellious attitude of its narrator, Holden Caulfield, might be another hidden cause of disfavor. In Holden, Salinger created one of the first characters with whom young adults could identify, and thus influenced the thinking of an entire generation.

Holden's tale spans several days of wanderings in New York City during the late 1940s, after he has been expelled from his fourth private school. Holden views most people as either phonies or victims, whom he must avoid or else he becomes nauseous. Told exclusively from Holden's point of view, this search for authentic human contact and love turns out to be an often hilarious parody of the classical heroic odyssey. The hero separates from a previously intolerable existence, finds in himself new integrity and self-confidence, and returns to his homeland with the quality of leadership.

In the true parodic sense—and at the same time reflecting common adolescent behavior—Salinger arranges for Holden's initiatory wanderings to appear comically haphazard and purposeless most of the time. Holden seems only half conscious that he must find a special someone of substance to bond with in order to fulfill his heroic urge. Like many mythic heroes, Holden's ideal person is a female, making his quest a semi-humorous allegory to unify the masculine and the feminine elements of a complete spiritual entity.

Ultimately, it is his sister Phoebe who epitomizes for Holden the untainted feminine principle within the wasteland of adult hypocrisy, lust, and perversion. Almost pathetically, Holden projects upon Phoebe all that he seeks in others, even though she is only ten years old. At this point the young adult reader senses that Holden is in trouble because he so limits the realization of his ideal. Despite Phoebe's willingness, at novel's end, to accompany Holden on still another separation from intolerable life, he cannot draw her into his unresolved conflict. Young readers are drawn dramatically into an empathetic sharing of a troubled adolescent predicament, involving the withdrawal from family security to forge identity alone.

Again paralleling mythic-quest heroes, Holden seeks counsel from a Merlin-like male figure, Mr. Antolini—his former teacher and family friend—whose status and wisdom qualify him to provide answers to Holden's questions about the world. With a hint of androgynous homosexuality, Mr. Antolini "wakes" Holden by gently caressing his head, in the early morning after the boy spends the night under his protection. Unable to accept this unconventional affection, Holden flees in repulsion, thereby thwarting another rebirth after a descent into the underworld.

In the last chapter, when the young adult reader realizes that Holden has told his story from a West Coast mental institution several months later, he or she can comprehend the full impact of this cautionary tale. In the tradition of other great young adult novels, *Catcher in the Rye* offers its readers vicarious experience and value-clarifying scenarios within troubled lives that echo mythic struggles for identity. In an age of cynicism, the youthful idealist can glean from this novel the message that true heroism means not giving in to frustrations, but continuing to struggle for personal values.

Beyond *Catcher,* Salinger's reputation among young adult readers has been spread by his tales about the Glass family. A mostly northeastern mixture of urban, Catholic-Jewish values and attitudes, this disparate group provides unusual unity of interest and tone for youth. Told in *Nine Stories* (1953), *Franny and Zooey* (1961), and *Raise High the Roof Beam, Carpenter; and, Seymour: An Introduction* (1963), the Glass family portrait includes variable-length individual characterizations of each member. Though few families array the complex makeup of the Glasses', young readers can, once again, find vicarious experience in this imaginative extension of the tradition of the big family.

In the Glass family narratives, Salinger depicts the family members' respective searching for resolution after Seymour's suicide, related in the short story "A Perfect Day for Bananafish" from *Nine Stories*. Because this poetic mystic had mastered Zen and continually taught its truths, the several siblings attempt to grasp and apply his teachings to the smallest details of their own lives. All in all, Salinger's later work seems to balance the dysfunctional family and character of Holden against the spiritually questing Glass family. Arguably, Salinger's shift from hopelessness outside traditional values to a hopefulness and resolution in eastern mysticism mirrors not only a similar shift in his own personality but also a persuasive appeal to young readers to attempt the same. Though sometimes criticized for otherworldly elitism, Salinger's narratives give young adults a perspective for fashioning a spirituality in an age of anti-spiritual consumerism.

Though Salinger's body of work is limited, his books are widely praised for their universal relevance. As one of the first writers to examine and critique the world from the perspective of young characters, he captured the attention of a generation of readers seeking reassurance during the rough transition from childhood to adulthood.

—Ron Evans

SARGENT, Pamela. American. Born in Ithaca, New York, 20 March 1948. Educated at the State University of New York, Binghamton, B.A. in philosophy 1968, M.A. 1970. Model and sales clerk, Monigsbaum's, 1965-66, solderer on assembly line, Endicott Coil Company, 1966, and sales clerk, Towne Distributors, 1966, all Albany, New York; typist in cataloguing department of Harpur College Library, University of New York at Binghamton, 1966-67; office worker and receptionist, Webster Paper Company, Albany, 1969; teaching assistant in philosophy, State University of New York, Binghamton, 1969-71. Managing editor, *Bulletin of the Science Fiction Writers of America,* 1970-73; assistant editor, 1973-75; market report editor, 1973-76; co-editor, *Bullentin of the Science Fiction Writers of America,* 1983-91. Since 1969, writer. Recipient: Nebula award, 1992; Locus award, 1993. Agent: Joseph Elder Agency, 150 West 87th Street, Apartment 6-D, New York, NY 10024. Address: Box 486, Johnson City, New York, NY 13790, U.S.A.

PUBLICATIONS FOR ADULTS AND YOUNG ADULTS

Fiction

Cloned Lives. New York, Fawcett, 1976; London, Fontana, 1981.
Starshadows (short stories). New York, Ace, 1977.
The Sudden Star. New York, Fawcett, 1979; as *The White Death,* London, Fontana, 1980.
The Golden Space. New York, Simon and Schuster, 1982.
The Alien Upstairs. New York, Doubleday, 1983.
Earthseed. New York, Harper, 1983; London, Collins, 1984.
The Mountain Cage, illustrated by Judy King-Rieniets. New Castle, Virginia, Cheap Street, 1983.

The Shore of Women. New York, Crown, 1986; London, Chatto and Windus, 1987.
Venus of Dreams. New York, Bantam, 1986; London, Bantam, 1989.
The Best of Pamela Sargent, edited by Martin H. Greenberg. Chicago, Academy, 1987.
Alien Child. New York, Harper, 1988.
Venus of Shadows. New York, Doubleday, 1988; London, Bantam, 1990.
Ruler of the Sky: A Novel of Genghis Khan. New York, Crown, 1993, London, Chatto and Windus, 1993.

"Earthminds" trilogy:

Watchstar. New York, Pocket Books, 1980.
Eye of the Comet. New York, Harper, 1984.
Homesmind. New York, Harper, 1984.

Other

Editor and contributor, *Women of Wonder: Science Fiction Stories by Women about Women.* New York, Random House, 1975; London, Penguin, 1978.
Editor and contributor, *Bio-Futures: Science Fiction Stories about Biological Metamorphosis.* New York, Random House, 1976.
Editor and contributor, *More Women of Wonder: Science Fiction Novelettes by Women about Women.* New York, Random House, 1976; London, Penguin, 1979.
Editor and contributor, *The New Women of Wonder: Recent Science Fiction Stories by Women about Women.* New York, Random House, 1978.
Editor, with Ian Watson, *Afterlives: Stories about Life after Death.* New York, Random House, 1986.

*

Biography: Entry in *Dictionary of Literary Biography,* Volume 8, Part 2: *Twentieth Century American Science-Fiction Writers,* Detroit, Gale, 1981; essay in *Contemporary Authors Autobiography Series,* Volume 18, Detroit, Gale, 1993; essay in *Speaking for Ourselves, Too* compiled and edited by Donald R. Gallo, National Council of Teachers of English, 1993.

Bibliography: *The Work of Pamela Sargent: An Annotated Bibliography and Guide* by Jeffrey M. Elliot. San Bernardino, California, Borgo Press, 1990.

Manuscript Collection: David Paskow Science Fiction Collection, Temple University, Philadelphia, Pennsylvania.

* * *

Pamela Sargent's work has done much to enhance and advance the role of women in science fiction. As an editor she has compiled three volumes, *Women of Wonder, More Women of Wonder,* and *The New Women of Wonder.* In the introductory essays to these volumes, Sargent addresses the position of women in science fiction. The collections bring together examples of short fiction of the genre by women.

In her own fiction, both for adults and young people, Sargent has created exemplary and exciting female characters who engage her readers. Adult readers find her works like *Venus of Dreams* and *The Shore of Women* to be entertaining and thought provoking. Sargent brings the same strengths to her novels for younger readers. In her introduction to *Women of Wonder* Sargent states: "Science-fiction novels for young adults and children can also offer role models for younger readers. This has happened often enough in the past for boys...There is no reason why this cannot be true for girls as well..."

Sargent's "Earthminds" trilogy begins with *Watchstar.* On a transformed Earth, Daiya belongs to a society of telepaths, but she must undergo her rite of passage to join the mind Net of her village. The ordeal would not be an easy one; there were those who died in their quest and joined the Merged Ones. Daiya's journey takes on an added dimension when a glowing object falls from the sky. Rather than alerting the Village Net, she decides to explore alone. She finds an alien spacecraft and a young man. Reiho, the alien, is without telepathic powers but is connected to Homesmind, a cybernetic intelligence of his world, by an implant. The nature of Daiya's quest changes as she comes to learn more about Reiho, his world, and her own. What she learns makes her unable to rejoin the people of her village, and she accepts Reiho's invitation to visit his comet world. Daiya's powers of mind are lost to her in the comet world. She learns of the beauties and problems of that world, but does not feel at home there and returns to her village. She is rejected by the villagers, even by the young man she loved, for she has changed and become something new. When the comet world tries to connect with the village, there is fear and resentment and the villagers attack the aliens Etey and Reiho. Daiya's mother gives birth to a nontelepathic child, a solitary; but Daiya quickly gives her to Etey to take to the comet world, rather than see her killed. Daiya lives as an outcast of her village, but Homesmind promises to watch over her.

Eye of the Comet continues the saga with Lydee, the solitary sister Daiya rescued from infanticide. Once more Sargent creates a strong female character who must face a test. Lydee journeys to Earth where she was born to be a link between it and the comet world. Lydee is shocked by the primitive life on Earth and finds the ways of Earth's people alien to her. Unlike the action that marked Daiya's quest, Lydee's conflict is more philosophical and psychological. Sargent allows her character to become a sounding board for discussion of questions of death and afterlife, the existence of the soul, and powers of the mind. In *Eye of the Comet* Lydee meets Daiya, Reiho, and other characters from *Watchstar.* Although the cast of characters has grown and the setting is familiar to readers of the first novel, *Eye of the Comet* can stand alone as the story of a girl, searching for identity and love, who is caught in the clash of two cultures.

Homesmind concludes the trilogy and Sargent continues the story of conflict between telepathic earthlings and the comet dwellers whose advanced technology allows them to link minds. Anra, the Earthborn heroine, lacks the gift of telepathy and must use Homesmind technology to enter the Net of her people. Again Sargent explores the philosophical questions raised in the trilogy's previous volumes, as she tells of the conditions of life on Earth and the comet world. Once more, it is a young female character who must deal with portentous events, such as alien invasion and the dissolution of her society.

Sargent explores space colonization in *Earthseed.* A cybernetic spaceship carries genetic material for breeding Earth children through the universe. As the ship nears a habitable planet, the children are readied for the project. Zoheret, with all her adolescent insecurities and fears, must leave the ship and face an ordeal for survival with her peers. A complex examination of the motives for colonization provides part of the novel's conflict, and Sargent again focuses on the developing strengths of a young female character who finds herself in a rite of passage.

Sargent develops some of the same themes in *Alien Child.* Nita believes she is the only human being left on Earth as she lives her life in the Kwalung-Ibarra Institute with her alien guardian Lilpel. Nita's quest for knowledge of her origin leads to her discovery of Sven, a boy raised in the same fashion by Llare, Lilpel's companion. Nita and Sven leave the protection of the Institute to take up a quest to search for other human survivors. In a journey filled with hardship and wonder, they learn they are the only humans left on Earth. Lilpel and Llare are waiting for them at the end of the quest with a visitor from space. Raen is a human, one of those who left Earth in its decaying days, fearful of war, to wander the universe. Those in space have changed and adapted, linking minds telepathically. Nita and Sven are not like them. Yet, Nita and Sven are not alone; there are embryos to revive in the "cold room." Nita and Sven will be their guardians until they can take their places on Earth or with Raen and his people in space.

Sargent's latest anthology explores a new area of interest to young adults. The collection *Afterlives,* which she co-edited with Ian Watson, contains short stories that deal directly with the concept of life after death. These stories, including one of her own "If Ever I Should Leave You," presents a science fiction perspective on this theme. Young adults contemplating afterlife may find this collection to be thought provoking.

While Sargent is best known for her science fiction, she has recently returned to the past in an epic-like novel *Ruler of the Sky.* This biographical novel explores the complex life of Ghengis Khan, the 13th Century warrior. The novel, replete with sex and violence, is told through the women who knew Ghengis Khan—His mother and his wives. This device allows Sargent to do what she does best, create women characters of intelligence and courage who cope with the conditions of their time and place. Sargent's historical fiction may be a departure from her futuristic novels, but her concern about women's roles and issues continues.

Apart from this latest foray into the past, Sargent's stories are filled with science fiction themes of space colonization, telepathy, aliens, and an Earth transformed. She provides the excitement of good storytelling and the intellectual speculations of quality science fiction. Sargent consistently provides strong female characters involved in arduous quest journeys who are the role models she stated girls needed to find. Her work contributes to the demise of the stereotype of women in the world of science fiction.

—Janice Antczak

SAVITZ, Harriet May. American. Born in Newark, New Jersey, 19 May 1933. Educated at Upsala College and Rutgers University. Married Ephraim Savitz; one daughter, one son. Writer. Teacher of writing, Philadelphia Writer's Conference; guest lecturer in English literature, University of Pennsylvania. Holds workshops in novelwriting; helped organize workshop at Philadelphia's Free Library for the Blind to sensitize the media to the needs of the disabled. Recipient: Dorothy Canfield Fisher Memorial Children's Book Award nomination, 1971, for *Fly, Wheels, Fly!; The Lionhearted* was listed in University of Iowa's Books for Young Adults, 1975-76, among the most popular books read by teenagers; Outstanding Author Award, Pennsylvania School Library Association, 1981; received recognition for *Wheelchair Champions,* 1981, from the President's Committee for the Handicapped in celebration of the International Year of Disabled Persons; California Young Reader Medal nomination, high school category, 1983-84, for *Run, Don't Walk.* Agent: Grace Morgan, 45 West 67th Street, Apt. 17A, New York, NY 10023. Address: 412 Park Place Ave., Bradley Beach, NJ 07720, U.S.A.

PUBLICATIONS FOR YOUNG ADULTS

Fiction

The Moon Is Mine (short stories), with Maria Caporale Shecktor, illustrated by Charles Robinson. New York, John Day, 1968.
Peter and Other Stories, with Maria Caporale Shecktor, New York, John Day, 1969.
Fly, Wheels, Fly! New York, John Day, 1970.
On the Move. New York, John Day, 1973.
The Lionhearted. New York, John Day, 1975.
Run, Don't Walk. New York, Watts, 1979.
Wait Until Tomorrow. New York, New American Library, 1981.
If You Can't Be the Sun, Be a Star. New York, New American Library, 1982.
Come Back, Mr. Magic. New York, New American Library, 1983.
Summer's End. New York, New American Library, 1984.
Swimmer. New York, Scholastic Inc., 1986.
The Cats Nobody Wanted. New York, Scholastic Inc., 1989.
The Pail of Nails. with K. Michael Syring, illustrated by Charles Shaw. Nashville, Tennessee, Abingdon, 1989.
The Bullies & Me. New York, Scholastic Inc., 1991.

Nonfiction

Consider—Understanding Disability as a Way of Life. Minneapolis, Minnesota, Sister Kenny Institute, 1975.
Wheelchair Champions: A History of Wheelchair Sports. New York, Crowell, 1978.
The Sweat and the Gold, illustrated by David C. Page. Norristown, Pennsylvania, VEEP, 1984.

*

Media Adaptations: *Run, Don't Walk,* Afterschool Special (television film), American Broadcasting Company.

Biography: Entry in *Fifth Book of Junior Authors and Illustrators,* New York, H.W. Wilson, 1983; essay in *Something about the Author Autobiography Series,* Volume 9, Detroit, Gale, 1990.

Harriet May Savitz comments:

Writing is magic. What other explanation for words that appear without warning, paragraphs that form of their own will, and characters who come to life when yesterday they didn't exist. Only in front of the blank page, do I feel a sense of power. Young people are magic and they possess power. Why would I want to write for anyone else?

*   *   *

Using some factual material, personal experiences, and feelings, Harriet May Savitz writes award-winning books about physically handicapped young people. It is apparent from her writings that she cares deeply about her characters and their disadvantages. She writes to make the public more aware of the disabled, and has published several books, both fiction and nonfiction, based on the lives of handicapped teenagers.

Listed among the most popular books read by teenagers, *The Lionhearted* tells of Rennie who is resigned to spending her life in a wheelchair, but finds friendship with pretty but overweight Bess and handsome, popular Lee. A touching story of a girl coping with being handicapped while finding love, Savitz has written an eye-opening, warm novel for young adults.

Award-winning *Fly, Wheels, Fly!* is a heartwarming story about Jeff Cobb, fourteen years old and confined not only to a wheelchair but to an orphanage where he has been since he was three. It is also the story of Chuck Robbins, athletic senior in high school who crashes through a banister on a stairway and falls, breaking his back, also confined to a wheelchair. Joe Johnson, born black with only three fingers on one deformed hand, dumped at the orphanage where he grew up, is now a recreation therapist in a county home for the handicapped and a coach for a wheelchair team representing the U.S. and headed for the Paralympics. Joe rounds up Jeff and Chuck and enters them in his rehabilitation program, pushing them to become wheelchair athletes, changing their lives. Chuck wins second place in the Paralympics in New York for javelin throwing, and Jeff wins the sixty-yard dash and triumphantly breaks all past wheelchair records. Savitz has written a story of awakening hope, not of two boys expecting to walk again, but to live again. She has also written of love and encouragement, of fighting and winning against staggering odds, of heartache and heartbreak, but of life going on and hope for others confined to wheelchairs.

Wheelchair Champions: A History of Wheelchair Sports depicts paraplegics, amputees, and quadriplegics, all who have been winners in sports, not only of awards and medals, but also of facing life once more in spite of their disabilities. Savitz has recorded the personal frustrations and successes of handicapped athletes, physically disabled men and women who have found sports, especially wheelchair sports, a method of learning to cope with their disadvantages and of relearning skills, establishing themselves as able and useful citizens. She shows that there is little danger involved in wheelchair sports, but that the real danger is the physically handicapped person sitting at home, inactive, not trying to do anything at all, withdrawn and despondent. At the end of the book is a list of names and addresses of organizations where one can write for further information. A very informative book, young adults will learn a great deal about the physically disabled from reading it.

Nineteen-year-old Skip, bitter from losing a leg in a mine explosion in the Vietnam War two years earlier, is the center for the Zippers, a wheelchair basketball team in *On the Move.* Bennie Blue, another Zipper, is a black member of the team, also confined to a wheelchair from being stabbed in the back during high school. Twenty-one-year-old Carrie had polio when she was eight, leaving her crippled for life. She is dependent upon her family and her sister, Sandy, an energetic cheerleader at the local high school. Carrie and Sandy meet the Zippers and their coach, Glen Harris, and Carrie learns from her new friends how to take care of herself, even how to take a bath without the help of others, while Sandy strikes up a loving friendship with Skip. A poignant story filled with love, sharing, struggling, with many disappointments, but a constant determination to move onward, it is about a group of courageous young people who really aren't different from anyone else. They have the same dreams, hopes, and emotions as everyone, and their determination should be an inspiration to all.

Run, Don't Walk portrays a young girl returning to high school in a wheelchair after suffering a paralyzing diving accident. Samantha wants to be left alone, but another student at school, a disabled activist, wants and needs Samantha's help. When a marathon committee rejects her application because of her disability, she turns to him, and a friendship is sparked between them.

It is clear from her writings that Harriet May Savitz knows what she is writing about and has researched her material thoroughly. She portrays her characters realistically and vividly, filling her stories with humor while touching the reader's heart with the frustrations and heartaches of her protagonists, and finally conveying the joyful feelings of their accomplishments.

—Carol Doxey

———

SCOPPETTONE, Sandra. American. Born in Morristown, New Jersey, 1 June 1936. Full-time professional writer. Recipient: Eugene O'Neill award, 1972. Agent: Charlotte Sheedy, 611 Broadway, Suite 428, New York, NY 10012. Address: 131 Prince St., New York, NY 10012, U.S.A.

PUBLICATIONS FOR YOUNG ADULTS

Novels

Trying Hard to Hear You. New York, Harper, 1974.
The Late Great Me. New York, Putnam, 1976.
Some Unknown Person. New York, Putnam, 1977.
Happy Endings Are All Alike. New York, Harper, 1978.
Such Nice People. New York, Putnam, 1980.
Long Time between Kisses. New York, Harper, 1982.
Innocent Bystanders. New York, New American Library, 1983.
Playing Murder. New York, Harper, 1985.

"Lauren Laurano" detective series:

Everything You Have Is Mine. Boston, Little, Brown, 1991.
I'll Be Leaving You Always. Boston, Little, Brown, 1993.
My Sweet Untraceable You. Boston, Little, Brown, 1994.

Plays

Three One-Act Plays (produced at Sheridan Square Playhouse, 1964).
One-Act Play (produced at Sheridan Square Playhouse, 1965).
Two One-Act Plays (produced at Cubiculo Theater, 1968).
Home Again, Home Again Jiggity Jig (produced at Cubiculo Theater, 1969).
Two One-Act Plays (produced at Assembly Theater, 1970).
Something for Kitty Genovese (performed by Valerie Bettis Repertory Company, 1971).
Stuck (produced at Eugene O'Neill Memorial Theater, Waterford, Connecticut, 1972).

Screenplays: *Scarecrow in a Garden of Cucumbers,* Independent, 1972; *The Inspector of Stairs,* Independent (short subject), 1975.

Television Plays: *CBS Playhouse,* 1968; *Where the Heart Is,* 1970; *CBS Playhouse,* 1972; *Love of Life,* 1972; *A Little Bit Like Murder,* ABC Wide World of Entertainment, 1973.

PUBLICATIONS FOR CHILDREN

Fiction

Suzuki Beane. New York, Doubleday, 1961.
Bang Bang You're Dead, with Louise Fitzhugh. New York, Harper, 1968.

*

Biography: Essay in *Speaking for Ourselves: Autobiographical Sketches by Notable Authors of Books for Young Adults,* Volume 1, compiled and edited by Donald R. Gallo, National Council of Teachers of English, 1990.

*   *   *

Sandra Scoppettone's novels for young adults shock. An admitted lesbian and reformed alcoholic, Scoppettone peels the veneer off the lives of middle-class, suburban teenagers to show the emotional conflicts, physical addictions, and potential for violence that lurk near the surface of, and frequently explode into, their seemingly comfortable lives. Dysfunctional "problem" families are her stock in trade. Some may find the subject matter too distasteful to stomach; drunkenness, rape, and homophobia are not pleasant subjects. However, for many young readers she "tells it as it is."

Scoppettone frequently employs a brash but naive female narrator or a point-of-view character who gradually sees her own life or the lives of those she knows implode. In *Trying Hard to Hear You* Camilla Crawford recounts a summer in which a group of Long Island teenagers put on a musical comedy. For much of the novel Camilla recounts the tempestuous tantrums and crushes that occur among the group members. The tone turns serious when the group discovers that two popular males, Jeff Grathwohl and Phil Chrystie, are homosexual lovers. The consequences are tragic as ridicule and ostracism lead Phil to intentionally kill himself in a car accident. In *The Late Great Me* Geri Peters, another Long Island teenager, recounts her junior year in high school when a combination of parental conflicts and an emotional infatuation causes her to start drinking heavily and to be sexually active. Introduced to drinking by an attractive but enigmatic David Townsend, Geri's health deteriorates as she enters the world of drinking bouts and one-night stands. Only gradually through the intervention of a high-school teacher, herself a reforming alcoholic, do Geri and her family begin to mend. In *Happy Endings Are All Alike* Jaret Tyler, still another Long Island teenager, develops a lesbian relationship with Peggy Danziger. Another summer romance novel but with a twist, *Happy Endings* focuses on the deepening relationship between the two girls and the brutal consequences when a male teenager discovers their situation and rapes Jaret. Jaret refuses to be blackmailed and identifies and accuses her assailant. Her family supports her in her plight. In *Long Time between Kisses* Billie James, a teenager living in Greenwich Village and coping with difficult parents, tries to put her life together initially by bizarre behavior and, later, by learning to help others. Finally, in *Playing Murder* Anna Parker, a teenager transplanted from suburban New Jersey to seacoast Maine, finds that the bucolic village where she and her family have moved is the setting for the murder of a young man whose physical attractiveness has overwhelmed her. As she works to identify his killer, she learns secrets about the victim and the community that make her reassess her first impressions.

Chatty is the best way to describe Scoppettone's writing style. Her novels employ the slang and cliches characteristic of young adults. This can become annoying at times as the characters' blithely banter their way through episodes of increasing seriousness. However, Scoppettone's dialogue moves quickly and she does not bog readers down in detailed descriptions and narratives. More mature readers will frequently catch the ironies in the narrators' self-concepts. In some ways the very banality of the language often clearly reflects the shallowness of suburban, middle-class life.

In many ways Scoppettone's young adult novels are melodramas with a liberal, feminist twist. Geri receives considerable advice about the operations and philosophy of Alcoholics Anonymous from a female teacher. Jeff and Phil are dealt with sympathetically while their tormentors are attacked. Jared's rapist is depicted as a mean-spirited, vengeful, irrational boy who stalks his prey. Billie James learns to respect the disabled. Anna Parker comes to appreciate her abandoned, steady boyfriend's concern for her safety even though she no longer wants to date him. For some readers these "politically correct" resolutions may be too pat, although given the controversial nature of much of her material, Scoppettone may have had no alternative than to soften the endings.

Scoppettone's work is often quite violent. Since this violence evolves plausibly from the characters' personalities and circumstances most readers are willing to bear with it. However, for some the violence can become excessive, more like that encountered in Joyce Carol Oates or Stephen King. The most extreme case of this is *Such Nice People,* in which a deranged seventeen-year-old shoots, stabs, and butchers his family and others, and then he is killed. When descriptions of sodomy and masturbation are added, many readers will have had enough.

Scoppettone writes readable novels for young adults in which she bluntly and courageously explores areas of experience that many parents and teachers choose to ignore or deny. At times she deals with the material melodramatically or superficially, but her candor will please readers weary of adult cant. More sophisticated readers will want to explore the problems she deals with most knowledgeably—addiction and sexuality—in works of greater subtlety and complexity. Male readers may find her depictions of heterosexual men troublesome or antagonistic.

—Lawrence B. Fuller

———

SEBESTYEN, Ouida (née Dockery). Has also written as Igen Sebestyen. American. Born in Vernon, Texas, 13 February 1924. Educated at University of Colorado, Boulder. Married Adam Sebestyen in 1960 (divorced, 1966); one son. Writer. Worked previously at a hamburger stand, repairing PT-19s during World War II, cleaning houses, and watching children in her home. Recipient: *New York Times* outstanding book citation, *School Library Journal* best

book citation, and American Library Association (ALA) best book for young adults and notable book citations, all 1979, International Reading Association Children's Book award, 1980, and American Book award, 1982, all for *Words by Heart;* ALA best book for young adults citation, and *School Library Journal* best books of the year citation, both 1980, American Book award nomination, and Child Study Association recommended titles citation, both 1981, William Allen White Master List, 1982-83, and Zilveren Griffel (Silver Pencil) award, 1984, all for *Far from Home;* ALA best book for young adults citation, Library of Congress Children's Books, and National Council of Teachers of English Teacher's Choice-*Parents' Choice* remarkable book citation, all 1982, Child Study Children's Book Committee list, and Texas Institute of Letters Children's Book award, both 1983, and Mark Twain award list nominee, 1985, all for *IOU's; The Girl in the Box* was nominated for the Colorado Blue Spruce Young Adult award. Address: c/o Orchard Books, 95 Madison Ave., New York, NY 10016, U.S.A.

PUBLICATIONS FOR YOUNG ADULTS

Fiction

Words by Heart. Boston, Little, Brown, 1979; London, Hamish Hamilton, 1987.
Far from Home. Boston, Little, Brown, 1980.
IOU's. Boston, Little, Brown, 1982.
On Fire. New York, Atlantic, 1985.
The Girl in the Box. Boston, Little, Brown, 1988; London, Hamish Hamilton, 1989.
Out of Nowhere. New York, Orchard Books, forthcoming.

Also author of short stories under pseudonym Igen Sebestyen. Contributor to anthologies, including *Sixteen,* edited by Donald R. Gallo, Delacorte, 1984.

*

Media Adaptations: *Words by Heart* (television movie), PBS-Wonderworks, 1985.

Biography: Essay in *Something about the Author Autobiography Series,* Volume 10, Detroit, Gale, 1990; essay in *Speaking for Ourselves: Autobiographical Sketches by Notable Authors of Books for Young Adults,* Volume 1, compiled and edited by Donald R. Gallo, National Council of Teachers of English, 1990.

Manuscript Collections: Kerlan Collection, University of Minnesota, Minneapolis; de Grummond Collection, University of Southern Mississippi, Hattiesburg.

Critical Studies: Entry in *Children's Literature Review,* Volume 17, Detroit, Gale, 1989; entry in *Contemporary Literary Criticism,* Volume 30, Detroit, Gale, 1984; *Presenting Ouida Sebestyen,* by Virginia Monseau, Boston, Twayne, forthcoming.

Ouida Sebestyen comments:

I am instinctively, fiercely what is called a homebody. Most of my fiction has been set solidly in a home or a place someone longs to call home. These houses, or temporary rooms, or farms, or little towns where all sorts of people unite as families are rich, complex little worlds to write about while my dog snores and my garden grows. We all deserve to belong, safe within certain spaces, certain hearts, so I like sending out reminders that acceptance is worth fighting for, and something to cherish when we have it.

*   *   *

Ouida Sebestyen's first novel, *Words by Heart,* won numerous awards including the International Reading Association's Children's Book Award given to a promising new writer. Sebestyen was fifty-five at the time, but she had been writing since she was eighteen. She was a new writer only in the sense of being published. The promise is being fulfilled as Sebesteyn has produced five thought-provoking novels.

Sebestyen's novels are about family and love, but there is no easy love in any of her works. She writes of people struggling to understand and accept each other and about families trying to be. *Words by Heart* introduces Lena, a young black girl living in Texas in the early twentieth century. Lena has aspirations to succeed and her father tells her at one point "I want you not to know your place." But it seems that everyone in the community is striving to put the black family in a place of subservience. Papa accepts many slights and Lena struggles with her need for love and acceptance from her father and her anger at his forgiveness of others. The ultimate act of forgiveness comes when Papa saves the life of the boy who mortally wounds him, and asks Lena to forgive him as well. Lena acquiesces, but wonders who will come to fill her Papa's place in her life. The book is rich in detail and both major and minor characters are fully fleshed out. Each is seen with fears and hopes and the actions they use to mask their emotions. Just as one works up a real sense of spite toward a character, Sebestyen reveals an insight that makes the reader reassess. The strength of the book is in the careful rendering of character as well as the poignant story line.

On Fire is the sequel to *Words by Heart,* though it is Sebestyen's fourth novel and her least successful one. Tater Haney is the boy who killed Lena's father and this book picks up the Haney family after they have fled their home in Texas. The book is very disjointed in that it tries to explore the exploitation of mine workers in Colorado, the corruption of the leaders trying to form a union, and the emotions of various Haneys as well as a young woman that Sammy Haney hooks up with. There is little focus to the novel and one never gets emotionally involved as one does with *Words by Heart.*

A shabby boarding house and the emotionally wounded people inhabiting it provides a potent setting for an evocative novel about the tangled web of responsibilities and passions that underlies most human response. Each of the characters is *Far from Home* in the sense that each is lost and trying to make meaning out of a less than perfect life. Sebestyen allows the reader to see the loneliness and near despair of each character, but at the same time the hope that comes when people respond to each other and allow others to touch their lives. There are no easy answers and no happy ending, but the book is filled with the possibilities that hope brings.

None of Sebestyen's families is conventional and *IOU's* family consists of Annie, who is a single parent and determined to live life her way, and her thirteen-year-old son Stowe, who is stoical about their straitened circumstances but laments to himself that everything he wants belongs to someone else or is used. At one point, Annie tells Stowe that they have become pinched from hoarding little bits of money, but most especially from hoarding themselves.

The novel is about enduring and about reaching out and building bridges between those who have lost each other. As in most of her books, Sebestyen's characters are as real as the people you know.

The Girl in the Box is stylistically very different from Sebestyen's earlier works. Told through diary entries and notes, it is written in the voice of a teenage girl who has been kidnapped and thrown in a cellar of some kind by an unknown assailant. There is food and water in the room, but no light. Jackie uses the typewriter and paper that was in her backpack to record her fears and emotions, to question who the assailant might be, to write notes assuring her parents, and to write notes crying for help that she shoves through a crack in the door and that fall on uncaring ground. This is a frightening book in that this is a senseless crime with no motive and an ending that implies Jackie's death. It is at the same time a story of courage and resilience.

Sebestyen's works are provocative and thoughtful. They eschew the typical plot of the young adult novel and probe the inner recesses of human emotion. It took a long time for Sebestyen to find her voice, but it rings clearly. Though she has not written in the past few years, one hopes to see more works by this fine author.

—M. Jean Greenlaw

———

SERRAILLIER, Ian (Lucien). British. Born in London, 24 September 1912. Educated at Brighton College, 1926-30; St. Edmund Hall, Oxford, 1931-35, M.A. 1935. Married Anne Margaret Rogers in 1944; three daughters and one son. Schoolmaster, Wycliffe College, Stonehouse, Gloucestershire, 1936-39, Dudley Grammar School, Worcestershire, 1940-46, and Midhurst Grammar School, Sussex, 1946-61. Since 1950 founder and general editor, with Anne Serraillier, New Windmill series (more than 400 books), Heinemann Educational Books, Oxford. Recipient: *New York Times* Best Illustrated Book citation, 1953, for *Florina and the Wild Bird;* Carnegie Medal commendation, 1956, Spring Book Festival award, 1959, and Boys' Clubs of America Junior Book award, 1960, all for *The Silver Sword.* Address: Singleton, Chichester, Sussex PO18 0HA, England.

PUBLICATIONS FOR YOUNG ADULTS

Fiction

They Raced for Treasure, illustrated by C. Walter Hodges. London, Cape, 1946; abridged edition, as *Treasure Ahead,* London, Heinemann, 1954.

Flight to Adventure, illustrated by C. Walter Hodges. London, Cape, 1947; abridged edition, as *Mountain Rescue,* London, Heinemann, 1955.

Captain Bounsaboard and the Pirates, illustrated by Michael Bartlett and Arline Braybrooke. London, Cape, 1949.

There's No Escape, illustrated by C. Walter Hodges. London, Cape, 1950; New York, Scholastic, 1973.

Making Good, illustrated by Vera Jarman. London, Heinemann, 1955.

The Silver Sword, illustrated by C. Walter Hodges. London, Cape, 1956; New York, Criterion, 1959; as *Escape from Warsaw,* New York, Scholastic, 1963.

The Cave of Death, illustrated by Stuart Tresilian. London, Heinemann, 1965.

Fight for Freedom, illustrated by John S. Goodall. London, Heinemann, 1965.

Plays (in verse)

The Midnight Thief, music by Richard Rodney Bennett, illustrated by Tellosa. London, BBC Publications, 1963.

Ahmet the Woodseller, music by Gordon Crosse, illustrated by John Griffiths. London, BBC Publications, 1965.

The Turtle Drum, music by Malcolm Arnold, illustrated by Charles Pickard. London, BBC Publications, 1967.

A Pride of Lions, music by Phyllis Tate (produced Nottingham, 1970). London, Oxford University Press, 1971.

Poetry

The Weaver Birds, illustrated by the author. London, Macmillan, 1944; New York, Macmillan, 1945.

Thomas and the Sparrow, illustrated by Mark Severin. London, Oxford University Press, 1946.

The Tale of the Monster Horse, illustrated by Mark Severin. London, Oxford University Press, 1950.

The Ballad of Kon-Tiki and Other Verses, illustrated by Mark Severin. London, Oxford University Press, 1952.

Belinda and the Swans, illustrated by Pat Marriott. London, Cape, 1952.

Everest Climbed, illustrated by Leonard Rosoman. London, Oxford University Press, 1955.

Poems and Pictures. London, Heinemann, 1958.

A Puffin Quartet of Poets, with others, edited by Eleanor Graham, illustrated by Diana Bloomfield. London, Penguin, 1958.

The Windmill Book of Ballads, illustrated by Mark Severin and Leonard Rosoman. London, Heinemann, 1962.

Happily Ever After, illustrated by Brian Wildsmith. London, Oxford University Press, 1963.

The Challenge of the Green Knight, illustrated by Victor Ambrus. London, Oxford University Press, 1966; New York, Walck, 1967.

Robin in the Greenwood, illustrated by Victor Ambrus. London, Oxford University Press, 1967; New York, Walck, 1968.

Robin and His Merry Men, illustrated by Victor Ambrus. London, Oxford University Press, 1969; New York, Walck, 1970.

The Ballad of St. Simeon, illustrated by Simon Stern. London, Kaye and Ward, and New York, Watts, 1970.

The Tale of Three Landlubbers, illustrated by Raymond Briggs. London, Hamish Hamilton, 1970; New York, Coward McCann, 1971.

The Bishop and the Devil, illustrated by Simon Stern. London, Kaye and Ward, and New York, Warne, 1971.

Marko's Wedding, illustrated by Victor Ambrus. London, Deutsch, 1972.

Suppose You Met a Witch, illustrated by Ed Emberley. Boston, Little Brown, 1973.

I'll Tell You a Tale: A Collection of Poems and Ballads, illustrated by Charles Keeping and Renate Meyer. London, Longman, 1973; revised edition, London, Kestrel, 1976.

The Robin and the Wren, illustrated by Fritz Wegner. London, Kestrel, 1974.

How Happily She Laughs and Other Poems. London, Longman, 1976.

Other

Translator, with Anne Serraillier, *Florina and the Wild Bird*, by Selina Chönz, illustrated by Alois Carigiet. London, Oxford University Press, 1952.

Jungle Adventure (based on story by R.M. Ballantyne), illustrated by Vera Jarman. London, Heinemann, 1953.

Editor, with Ronald Ridout, *Wide Horizon Reading Scheme*. London, Heinemann, 4 vols., 1953-55.

The Adventures of Dick Varley (based on story by R.M. Ballantyne), illustrated by Vera Jarman. London, Heinemann, 1954.

Translator, *Beowulf the Warrior* (in verse), illustrated by Mark Severin. London, Oxford University Press, 1954; New York, Walck, 1961.

Guns in the Wild (based on story by R.M. Ballantyne), illustrated by Shirley Hughes. London, Heinemann, 1956.

Katy at Home (based on story by Susan Coolidge), illustrated by Shirley Hughes. London, Heinemann, 1957.

Katy at School (based on story by Susan Coolidge), illustrated by Shirley Hughes. London, Heinemann, 1959.

The Ivory Horn: Retold from the Song of Roland, illustrated by William Stobbs. London, Oxford University Press, 1960.

The Gorgon's Head: The Story of Perseus, illustrated by William Stobbs. London, Oxford University Press, 1961; New York, Walck, 1962.

The Way of Danger: The Story of Theseus, illustrated by William Stobbs. London, Oxford University Press, 1962; New York, Walck, 1963.

The Clashing Rocks: The Story of Jason, illustrated by William Stobbs. London, Oxford University Press, 1963; New York, Walck, 1963.

The Enchanted Island: Stories from Shakespeare, illustrated by Peter Farmer. London, Oxford University Press, and New York, Walck, 1964; abridged edition, as *Murder at Dunsinane*, New York, Scholastic, 1967.

A Fall from the Sky: The Story of Daedalus, illustrated by William Stobbs. London, Nelson, and New York, Walck, 1966.

Chaucer and His World. London, Lutterworth Press, 1967; New York, Walck, 1968.

Havelok the Dane, illustrated by Elaine Raphael. New York, Walck, 1967; as *Havelok the Warrior*, London, Hamish Hamilton, 1968.

Heracles the Strong, illustrated by Rocco Negri. New York, Walck, 1970; London, Hamish Hamilton, 1971.

The Franklin's Tale, Retold, illustrated by Philip Gough. London, Kaye and Ward, and New York, Warne, 1972.

Have You Got Your Ticket? (reader), illustrated by Douglas Hall. London, Longman 1972.

Pop Festival (reader), illustrated by Douglas Hall. London, Longman, 1973.

The Sun Goes Free (reader). London, Longman, 1977.

The Road to Canterbury (tales from Chaucer retold), illustrated by John Lawrence. London, Kestrel, 1979.

PUBLICATIONS FOR ADULTS

Poetry

Three New Poets, with Roy McFadden and Alex Comfort. Billericay, Essex, Grey Walls Press, 1942.

Other

All Change at Singleton: For Charlton, Goodwood, East and West Dean (local history). London, Phillimore, 1979.
Goodwood Country in Old Photographs, with Richard Pailthorpe. Gloucester, Sutton, 1987.

*

Media Adaptations: *The Silver Sword* (television series), BBC-TV, 1957 and 1970, and dramatized as *The Play of the Silver Sword* by Stuart Henson, Heinemann Educational Books, 1982, first performed in Oldham, England, 1983.

Biography: Essay in *Something about the Author Autobiography Series,* Volume 3, Detroit, Gale, 1987; entry in *Third Book of Junior Authors,* New York, H.W. Wilson, 1972.

Critical Study: Entry in *Children's Literature Review,* Volume 2, Detroit, Gale, 1976.

*   *   *

Ian Serraillier's love for words is evident. Whether reading his retellings of old ballads and legends, or one of his original works of prose, the text flows with a warmth and rhythm only a poet could impart.

Two of his better works include *Beowulf* and *The Silver Sword.* Both speak of heroes and perhaps this is the reason young adult readers often select these works to read. Infatuated with ballads, Serraillier captures their romance of courage, heroism, and survival in many of his works.

Beowulf is an excellent example of Serraillier's love for the legend and for the heroism it embraces. His success comes in foregoing translation and simply retelling the story in poetry that captures the essence of the original masterpiece. One of the most difficult of the ancient poems to translate, he superbly renders the tale in a style admissible by today's standards. The text rings with the clarity, rhythm, and emotion of the epic.

His introduction and description of Grendel is one example:

Misbegotten son of a foul mother,
Grendel his name, hating the sound of the harp,
The minstrel's song, the bold merriment of men
In whose distorted likeness he was shaped...

The character of Beowulf, with his royal breeding, unwavering composure, and heroic dissolution at the same time relates to ordinary emotions and ideals.

Serraillier also translated and wrote adaptions of many other legends, including tales from Greek mythology, the Bible, Shakespeare, about Robin Hood, and about King Arthur's knights. All attempt to authentically portray scene and the appeal aurally. With a rhythm meant to be spoken aloud, the words roll more easily off the tongue than the eyes can smoothly scan them in silence.

Like his poetry, Serraillier applies the same feeling for rhythm and inspiring word choice in his prose. *The Silver Sword,* written in 1956 and reprinted in 1963 as *Escape from Warsaw,* is undoubtedly his best original work. Because it is fiction based on fact and eyewitness accounts, Serraillier is able to treat it as a modern-day epic.

The Balicki children, separated from their parents, struggle to survive in war-torn Poland. A silver sword, found by a scavenger boy, is the only link they have with their parents and provides hope for the family reuniting in Switzerland.

Allowing both the words and factual circumstances to convey the heroism of the characters in *The Silver Sword* and their determination to survive, a reader has no choice but to reexamine his own personal world views. After all, the book may have fictitious characters but the events actually took place, and Serraillier succeeds in conveying the hope and endurance of both the characters and the Polish people in general. When the Russians begin to drive back the Nazis, the Resistance in Warsaw calls the Poles to arms: "At the same moment thousands of windows in the city were flung open, and a hail of bullets struck the passing Germans. All traffic ceased as the Polish Underground rushed to the attack. Starving people streamed out of the cellars and flung themselves upon the Nazis, with weapons if they had them, with their fists if they had nothing else."

The steadfast strength of the characters, whether modern-day or long-ago legend, offer hope that this endurance and courage lies within us all. We need only allow it to flourish.

—Lisa A. Wroble

———

SERVICE, Pamela. American. Born in Berkeley, California, 8 October 1945. Educated at University of California, Berkeley, B.A. 1967; University of London, M.A. 1969. Married Robert Gifford Service in 1967; one daughter. Publicist for Art Museum, Indiana University, Bloomington, 1970-72; curator, Monroe County Museum, Bloomington, since 1978. Member of Bloomington City Council, since 1979. Recipient: Society of Children's Book Writers Honor Book, 1988, for *The Reluctant God.* Address: 419 North Washington, Bloomington, IN 47408, U.S.A.

PUBLICATIONS FOR YOUNG ADULTS

Fiction

Winter of Magic's Return. New York, Atheneum, 1985.
A Question of Destiny. New York, Atheneum, 1986.
Tomorrow's Magic. New York, Atheneum, 1987.
When the Night Wind Howls. New York, Atheneum, 1987.
The Reluctant God. Athenuem, 1988.
Stinker from Space. New York, Scribner, 1988.
Vision Quest. New York, Atheneum, 1989.
Under Alien Stars. New York, Atheneum, 1990.
Being of Two Minds. New York, Atheneum, 1991.
Weirdos of the Universe, Unite! New York, Atheneum, 1992.
Stinker's Return. New York, Scribner, 1993.
All's Faire. New York, Fawcett, 1993.
Phantom Victory. New York, Scribner, forthcoming.

PUBLICATIONS FOR CHILDREN

Fiction

Wizard of Wind & Rock (picture book), illustrated by Laura Marshall. New York, Atheneum, 1990.

Pamela Service comments:

I write science fiction and fantasy because that is the sort of reading that stretches our minds and imaginations beyond the everyday present world in which we normally live. And it is minds expanded and enriched in this way that are often best equipped to deal inventively and compassionately with that same real world. I write for young people because theirs are the minds most open to the joy and excitement of new ideas and to the wondrous possibilities of this world—or others.

*   *   *

If anyone is a master of genre fiction, it is Pamela F. Service—she writes fantasy, science fiction, and mystery equally well. Many of the fantasy novels deal with ancient civilizations, and her archaeological background is readily apparent.

Winter of Magic's Return is both a retelling of the Arthurian legend and a new twist on the theme of post-nuclear-holocaust civilization. Five hundred years after most of the world has been destroyed, nearsighted Wellington Jones and plain Heather McKenna befriend amnesiac Earl Bedwas. Earl remembers that he is Merlin the magician, who has been spellbound for 2,000 years. The three set out on a quest to find King Arthur; they succeed and go forth to save the world—the age of magic is returning to make up for the lost age of science that ended so tragically. While convoluted explanations are offered as to how magic works, the action is fast-paced and suspenseful.

Tomorrow's Magic takes up two years after *Winter of Magic's Return* left off. The fantasy continues, with King Arthur gradually conquering England. Heather has begrudgingly come to realize that she has magical talent; she also is falling in love with Merlin, who is both respected and shunned for his magic. After Merlin stages a vicarious re-creation of the nuclear disaster that ruined civilization, he and Heather accept both their relationship and their abilities in this new world. Their lives mirror the society as the shortcomings of science are emphasized.

In *A Question of Destiny,* a science fiction work, Don Stratton is just an average fourteen-year-old except that his father is a U.S. senator. When his dad decides to run for president, Dan wants to help with the campaign. He suspects that one of his father's top aides, David Greer, is not what he claims to be. In a dramatic confrontation, Dan discovers that Greer is not a Russian spy but an alien. Greer enlists the help of Dan and Dan's friend Carla Brenner to change the world's fate. Senator Stratton is running on an anti-space exploration platform, believing that problems on earth are more pressing. A top-secret experiment threatens to develop space flight before humans are mature enough to move out into the universe. The three manage to sabotage the research and solve the "question of destiny." The theme of accepting others' differences is treated honestly here: Greer's alienism is truly disconcerting to the humans, yet they manage to overcome their discomfort. And while the earth is saved from itself, the saviors must keep their feat secret, the moral being that the best good deeds should remain anonymous.

A supernatural mystery, *When the Night Wind Howls* portrays Sid, a new member of a local acting troupe whose theater appears to be haunted. Byron Vincenti, a handsome actor, is at the center of the mystery. Along with her friend Joel, Sid investigates. Horror plays a role as they discover a pact Vincenti has made with the Devil in exchange for a successful career. Suspense builds as Joel and Sid concoct a plot to redeem Vincenti's soul. Classic theories of the occult are blended with theatrics to make an enthralling narrative.

With her next novel, Service returns to fantasy. *The Reluctant God* is Ameni, an ancient Egyptian prince. Placed in suspended animation, he is set to guard two urns that are essential to the preservation of Egypt, for their contents represent the eternal afterlife. Four thousand years later, Lorna Padgett, the daughter of an Egyptologist who is following in her father's footsteps, accidentally discovers Ameni's tomb; when one of the urns is then taken from Egypt, Ameni awakens from his long sleep. By hook or by crook, Lorna and Ameni recover the urn, and the gods intervene to let them escape safely. But suddenly Ameni must sacrifice the urn to save Lorna. He does so and is rewarded by the gods, who have decided that life is more precious than objects. Ameni goes forth to live in this modern world, understanding that eternity is found in people. Although the story contains some weaknesses—money and passports present no real problems for the teenagers—the scientific and historical details add to the fantasy's appeal.

Archaeological mysteries are important in the next book too. *Vision Quest* is set in Nevada, where Kate Elliot has just moved. When she encounters a stolen charm stone, sacred to ancient Indian shamans, she realizes she must return it to its rightful place. Wadat and Hizu, two shamans of long ago, relate their tale of suffering: Through misfortune, both their charm stones were lost and not buried properly. Kate then teams up with Jimmy Fong, an amateur archaeologist, to solve the problem. They must find the petroglyphs (rock paintings) that were created by the two shamans. After many misadventures, the stones are properly buried at the petroglyphs, as past and present fuse into one. Again, fantasy is blended with authentic anthropology as Kate and Jimmy fulfill their own "vision quest."

In *Under Alien Stars,* another science fiction work, Earth has become a Tsorian outpost and part of a galactic empire. Aryl is the daughter of Rogav Jy, the Tsorian commander of Earth. Jason Sikes, a young human, resents the invaders and thinks his mother, because she works for Tsorian headquarters, is a collaborator. It turns out, however, that Marilyn Sikes is a part of the organized resistance movement. Her group kidnaps Jy just as the Hykzoi—strange and vicious aliens—arrive. Jason and Aryl manage to rescue their parents from the Hykzoi and rendezvous with the Tsorian forces. The Tsorians defeat the Hykzoi, and Earth is upgraded from military outpost to colony status. In this book, enemies become friends when confronted with worse foes; the message is that technology must incorporate morality. Despite its lack of explanation regarding technical aspects, this is good science fiction.

Service's faculty for writing within multiple genres, coupled with her ability to make good use of her archaeological know-how, offers young adults a fine selection of books that both entertain and inform.

—Sharon Clontz Bernstein

———

SHANGE, Ntozake. American. Born Paulette Williams in Trenton, New Jersey, 18 October 1948; took name Ntozake Shange in 1971. Educated at schools in St. Louis and New Jersey; Barnard College, New York, 1966-70, B.A. (cum laude) in American studies 1970; University of Southern California, Los Angeles, 1971-73, M.A. in American studies 1973. Married David Murray in 1977 (second marriage; divorced); one daughter. Writer and performer.

Faculty member in women's studies, humanities, and Afro-American studies at Sonoma State College, Rohnert Park, California, 1973-75, Mills College, Oakland, California, 1975, and the University of California Extension, 1972-75; artist-in-residence, Equinox Theatre, Houston, from 1981, and New Jersey State Council on the Arts. Creative writing instructor, City College, New York, 1975; currently Associate Professor of drama and creative writing, University of Houston, Texas. Lecturer at Douglass College, New Brunswick, New Jersey, 1978, and other institutions, including Yale University, Howard University, Detroit Institute of Arts, and New York University. Dancer with Third World Collective, Raymond Sawyer's Afro-American Dance Company, Sounds in Motion, West Coast Dance Works, and For Colored Girls Who Have Considered Suicide (her own dance company); has appeared in Broadway and Off-Broadway productions of her own plays, including *For Colored Girls Who Have Considered Suicide/When the Rainbow Is Enuf* and *Where the Mississippi Meets the Amazon.* Director of several productions, including *The Mighty Gents,* produced by the New York Shakespeare Festival's Mobile Theatre, 1979, *A Photograph: A Study in Cruelty,* produced at the Equinox Theatre, Houston, Texas, 1979, and June Jordan's *The Issue* and *The Spirit of Sojourner Truth,* 1979. Has given poetry readings. Recipient: Obie award, Outer Critics Circle award, Audelco award, Mademoiselle award, and Antoinette Perry (Tony), Grammy, and Emmy award nominations, 1977, all for *For Colored Girls Who Have Considered Suicide/When the Rainbow Is Enuf;* Frank Silvera Writers' Workshop award, 1978; *Los Angeles Times* Book Prize for Poetry, 1981, for *Three Pieces;* Guggenheim fellowship, 1981; Medal of Excellence, Columbia University, 1981; Obie award, 1981, for *Mother Courage and Her Children;* Pushcart Prize. Address: Department of Drama, University of Houston-University Park, 4800 Calhoun Rd., Houston, TX 77004, U.S.A.

PUBLICATIONS

Poetry

Melissa and Smith. St. Paul, Bookslinger Editions, 1976.
Natural Disasters and Other Festive Occasions. San Francisco, Heirs, 1977.
Nappy Edges. New York, St. Martin's, 1978; London, Methuen, 1987.
Some Men. Privately printed, 1981.
A Daughter's Geography. New York, St. Martin's, 1983; London, Methuen, 1985.
From Okra to Greens. St. Paul, Coffee House Press, 1984.
Ridin' the Moon in Texas: Word Paintings. New York, St. Martin's, 1987.
The Love Space Demands: A Continuing Saga. New York, St. Martin's, 1991.

Recording: *I Live in Music.* Watershed, 1984.

Plays

For Colored Girls Who Have Considered Suicide/When the Rainbow Is Enuf: A Choreopoem (produced New York, 1975, London, 1980). San Lorenzo, California, Shameless Hussy Press, 1976; revised version, New York, Macmillan, 1977; London, Eyre Methuen, 1978.

A Photograph: Lovers-in-Motion (as *A Photograph: A Still Life with Shadows, A Photograph: A Study of Cruelty* produced New York, 1977; revised version, as *A Photograph: Lovers-in-Motion,* also director: produced Houston, 1979). New York, French, 1981.
Where the Mississippi Meets the Amazon, with Thulani Nkabinda and Jessica Hagedorn (produced New York, 1977).
Black and White Two-Dimensional Planes (produced New York, 1979).
Spell #7: A Geechee Quick Magic Trance Manual (produced New York, 1979; London, 1985). Included in *Three Pieces,* 1981; published separately, London, Methuen, 1985.
Mother Courage and Her Children, adaptation of a play by Bertolt Brecht (produced New York, 1980).
Boogie Woogie Landscapes (produced on tour, 1980). Included in *Three Pieces,* 1981.
From Okra to Greens: A Different Kinda Love Story; A Play with Music & Dance (as *Mouths* produced New York, 1981; as *From Okra to Greens in Three for a Full Moon,* produced Los Angeles, 1982). New York, French, 1983.
Three Pieces: Spell #7, A Photograph: Lovers-in-Motion, Boogie Woogie Landscapes. New York, St. Martin's, 1981.
Educating Rita, adaptation of the play by Willy Russell (produced Atlanta, 1982).
Three for a Full Moon and Bocas (produced Los Angeles, 1982).
Three Views of Mt. Fuji (produced New York, 1987).

Novels

Sassafrass. San Lorenzo, California, Shameless Hussy Press, 1976.
Sassafrass, Cypress & Indigo. New York, St. Martin's, 1982; London, Methuen, 1983.
Betsey Brown. New York, St. Martin's, and London, Methuen, 1985.

Other

See No Evil: Prefaces, Essays, and Accounts, 1976-1983. San Francisco, Momo's Press, 1984.

Author of operetta, *Carrie,* produced 1981.

*

Theatrical Activities:
Director: **Plays**—*The Mighty Gents* by Richard Wesley, New York, 1979; *A Photograph: Lovers-in-Motion,* Houston, 1979.
Actress: **Plays**—The Lady in Orange in *For Colored Girls Who Have Considered Suicide When the Rainbow Is Enuf,* New York, 1976; in *Where the Mississippi Meets the Amazon,* New York, 1977; in *Mouths,* New York, 1981.

Media Adaptations: *Betsey Brown* (musical-operetta), produced Off-Broadway, 1986.

Biography: Entry in *Dictionary of Literary Biography,* Volume 38: *Afro-American Writers after 1955: Dramatists and Prose Writers,* Detroit, Gale, 1985.

Critical Study: Entry in *Contemporary Literary Criticism,* Detroit, Gale, Volume 8, 1978; Volume 25, 1983; Volume 38, 1986.

Ntozake Shange's poems, plays, and stories reveal the unique voice of a strong African-American woman in contemporary society. Her impassioned portrayals of both the joys and the sorrows of women's lives touch on events and emotions, using language that sometimes risks offending traditional western sensibilities. That language, however, is a perfect match for the emotions, and her unconventional spellings and punctuations reflect the sounds of the human voice responding to the full range of lived experiences. There is a musical beat in the language, and even the placement of words on the page often gives the appearance of letters and words dancing to that beat. There is also controlled rage in many of Shange's works, calling attention to the violence, violation, and oppression endured by her characters. This is both a personal and political rage in response to international crises such as apartheid as well as the daily indignities of everyday life. On the other hand, in many of her works there is also the pure, exuberant joy of a young child's playful spirit and her love for her mother.

For Colored Girls Who Have Considered Suicide/When the Rainbow Is Enuf, probably Shange's best known work, is a "choreopoem" in which seven women speak, dance, and sing of the harsh realities of their lives. The beauty of the language of these poems both releases and intensifies the power, the pain, and especially the courage of women coping with the bitter experiences of their lives. The pain in these women's lives was often inflicted by men, and many black men objected to their portrayal in this work. All women, not just women of color, however, recognized themselves in Shange's poems and praised them as a celebration of the oneness of women and the strength they draw from each other.

Betsey Brown is a novel of a young adolescent growing up in St. Louis in the late 1950s during the beginning of school integration and busing. Betsey was reluctant to leave the safety and comfort of her middle-class black community to face the uncertainties and stress of attending an integrated school. In her own home her mother who is "almost white" is more concerned with fashion than with civil rights, but her father begins every day with a black history lesson. Distressed by teachers who devalue her culture and by the fact that she is not welcome in the homes of her white friends, Betsey runs away. She goes to Mrs. Maureen's beauty parlor which she always considered a refuge for black women only to find that it is a brothel where a young woman who had previously cared for the Brown children awaits the birth of her child. Betsey returns home, but before long Jane, her mother, also runs away on her own search for self-discovery. Carrie is brought in to play the role of the "other mother" in caring for the children, but she too is proved unacceptable because she cuts someone and is jailed. Thus, Betsey is repeatedly confronted with challenges to her comfortable life and is forced to rethink her beliefs and her values.

Shange's *Sassafrass, Cypress & Indigo* tells the intergenerational story of three daughters and their mother and explores their individual and very personal points of view. Throughout this novel there is a sense of oral language, of women sharing their lives through music, poetry, dance, and dreams. Mama writes letters which hold her daughters close at the same time that they venture out to explore the choices available to black women in society. Sassafrass is a weaver, a writer, and a dancer who, in her personal vulnerability, cannot extricate herself from an abusive relationship with a man. Cypress, on the other hand, exists in a feminist community and resolves "to have no men." Indigo, the youngest sister, creates large dolls which share her imaginative everyday life. When she reluctantly puts those dolls away, she enters into womanhood, keeping her imagination and her music alive. She also devotes herself to

perhaps the most creative of all female work, that of midwifery. One of the most compelling aspects of this novel is Shange's ability to transform the sometimes mundane work of women such as cooking and weaving into artistic expressions and celebrations of life.

Nappy Edges is a collection of hard-hitting, yet sensitive poems which add to Shange's expressions of the fate of black women in today's world. In "inquiry," we find an encapsulation of her vision of poetry as "whatever runs out / whatever digs my guts / til there's no space in myself." The poem "just as the del vikings stole my heart" exemplifies her ability to write politically devastating poems combined with imaginative visions that both provoke and sustain the reader. Shange is an intellectual as well as emotional poet who uses literary and socio-political references in her poetry. Readers need to bring both knowledge and caring to these poems to fully appreciate the richness within. The first poem in *A Daughter's Geography,* "Mood Indigo," begins and ends with "it hasnt always been this way / ellington was not a street." This, like many of her poems and stories, is taken from her own life experiences of growing up in an affluent black family, but, as always, she calls forth the universal from that which is unique and personal.

Ridin' the Moon in Texas presents a collection of poetry and prose based on the creations of visual artists. Shange writes in response to a selection of paintings, photographs, and artifacts as if she were seeking a verbal dialogue with each work of art. She perceives of the art as metaphor and writes in tandem with a selection of fifteen diverse images. "Who Needs A Heart," her three-part dialogue with Linda Graetz's acrylic painting of the same title, is a poignant and heartrending account of a child and apartheid, letter writing, and in the jubilant segment "Walk, Jump, Fly," a child speaking with her mommy. These word paintings that Shange presents are sometimes harsh and deeply sexual in nature. They scream with pain common to women, but they lift the spirit and provide a validation of women and life through these artistic dialogues.

—Kay E. Vandergrift

SHERBURNE, Zoa (Morin). American. Born in Seattle, Washington, 30 September 1912. Educated at parochial schools in Seattle, Washington. Married Herbert Newton Sherburne in 1935 (deceased); four daughters and four sons. Writer. Teacher of short story writing, Cornish School of Allied Arts, Seattle, Washington, 1957; lecturer on writing. Recipient: Woman of Achievement award, Theta Sigma Phi Matrix, 1950; Woman of the Year, Phi Delta Nu, 1951; Best Book for Young People award, Child Study Association, 1959, for *Jennifer*; Henry Broderick award, 1960; Governor's Writers' Day award, 1967. Agent: Ann Elmo Agency Inc., 52 Vanderbilt Ave., New York, NY 10017. Address: 2401 North East Blakeley, Seattle, WA 98105, U.S.A.

PUBLICATIONS FOR YOUNG ADULTS

Fiction

Almost April. New York, Morrow, 1956.
The High White Wall. New York, Morrow, 1957.
Princess in Denim. New York, Morrow, 1958.

Jennifer. New York, Morrow, 1959.
Evening Star. New York, Morrow, 1960.
Ballerina on Skates. New York, Morrow, 1961.
Girl in the Shadows. New York, Morrow, 1963.
Stranger in the House. New York, Morrow, 1963.
River at Her Feet. New York, Morrow, 1965.
Girl in the Mirror. New York, Morrow, 1966.
Too Bad about the Haines Girl. New York, Morrow, 1967.
The Girl Who Knew Tomorrow. New York, Morrow, 1970.
Leslie. New York, Morrow, 1972.
Why Have the Birds Stopped Singing? New York, Morrow, 1974.

Other

Shadow of a Star. London, Hurst & Blacklett, 1959.
Journey out of Darkness. London, Hurst & Blacklett, 1961.

*

Media Adaptations: *Memories Never Die* (television movie adaptation of *Stranger in the House*), Columbia Broadcast Service, Inc., 1982.

Biography: Essay in *Speaking for Ourselves: Autobiographical Sketches by Notable Authors of Books for Young Adults,* Volume 1, compiled and edited by Donald R. Gallo, National Council of Teachers of English, 1990.

*   *   *

Family life and romance have been strong themes for young adult novels. Louisa May Alcott's *Little Women,* one of the first works written specifically for this age group, described the joys and sorrows of the March sisters. Until the second half of the twentieth century, few books for teenaged readers dealt with life, love, and death as realistically as did Alcott. In 1956, a wife, mother, and writer for *Seventeen Magazine* came onto the literary scene—Zoa Sherburne.

Sherburne's books for young adults span three decades, from the 1950s to the 1970s. When her first books were published, Ike was president, hula hoops were the craze, and the move to suburbia was in full-swing. Elvis had just begun and pink poodle skirts were in fashion as were sock hops. "Ozzie and Harriet" were on television, and it seemed to be a black and white world with very few shades of grey. But for teenagers, the world wasn't quite this simple. While her initial stories portray first kisses and teenage crushes, Sherburne is best known for her contemporary novels which deal with problems real teenagers face in today's society. In a world which does not always have simple problems, her protagonists struggle with family divorce, illness, the death of loved ones, drug usage, being unpopular, and unwanted pregnancy.

Many of Sherburne's novels share the Pacific Northwest as their setting where she was born and raised. It is characteristic of her writing to portray the turbulence of youth in striking scenes of windswept beaches, stormy weather, and majestic snowcapped mountains. Adolescence is a time of considerable growth physically, but also mentally and emotionally. It is a time when young people need to learn to believe in themselves, to be confident, and to make intelligent decisions. Many teens today have never experienced a father and mother's love because of death or divorce. This emptiness can lead to self-doubt, sexual intimacy, alcohol, or drugs.

The mother of eight children, Zoa Sherburne is primarily a realistic writer who shares her observations of contemporary teenagers, not through research, but from experience.

The themes of many of her books are based upon young people's desire for independence. Karen in *Almost April* travels to Oregon after the death of her mother to live with her father and his new wife. Since she has not seen her father for many years, Karen is bitter. But just as love, understanding, and time are healing the wounds, a romance with Nels develops and the division is reopened. Eighteen-year-old Leeann leaves her overcrowded home in *The High White Wall,* to take a summer job as a children's companion for a wealthy family in the exclusive Mountcastle area. She falls in love with Dick, the oldest son of the Kingsley family, and struggles with decisions about her future. Eden, the winner of the local Tulip Princess beauty pageant, learns that the Miss Washington contest is not fun, but a highly competitive and stressful experience. She returns home happy to be a *Princess in Denim.* Fourteen-year-old Nancy, a Native American living in the beautiful San Juan Islands of Puget Sound, also learns that happiness comes from within, in *Evening Star.*

Tragedy and its results upon the lives of all involved are also ingrained within many of Sherburne's plots. *Girl in the Mirror* is the story of a sixteen-year-old who has partially retreated from reality when her widowed father plans to remarry. Ruth Ann is very self-conscious of her problem with obesity. Her father's marriage to a young nurse and the tragic events that follow the honeymoon cause Ruth to re-examine life and to realize that the future holds promise. *Leslie* tells of a teen who has become self-sufficient in many ways as a result of living with her mother who has been embittered by divorce. But a party in which drugs were used is followed by a hit-and-run motor death and Leslie knows that she cannot deal with this problem alone. *Jennifer* is the poignant story of the effect of the death of Jennifer's twin sister upon the Martin family. Her mother's illness with alcoholism affects sixteen-year-old Jennifer who becomes withdrawn and unsocial. Sherburne skillfully considers her audience in this heartwarming story of family grief and adjustment. The characterization is superb, and the depth of the story is blended with humor, dances, conflicting romances, and Jennifer's newfound friend, Patsy. *Stranger in the House* examines the need for love and acceptance—by both youngsters and their parents. After nine years in a hospital where she was treated for mental illness, Kathy's mother returns home. Unfortunately, after such a long absence, she is considered a stranger by members of her own family. Finally, on the night of a party for members of a school play, Kathleen and her mother are able to communicate—and the barrier between them is gradually replaced with understanding and togetherness.

While considering problems that young adults face, Sherburne is also able to share in their fun. Both *Ballerina on Skates* and *River at Her Feet* are light reading and will appeal to young girls. The former tells of seventeen-year-old Karen's escapades as a professional ice-skater. The latter is the story of a teenage crush and its effects upon sixteen-year-old Elizabeth and her family.

Although neither a tragedy nor a comedy, *The Girl Who Knew Tomorrow* blends a little of each in the tale of a fifteen-year-old girl who has been able to see the shadows of events before their occurrence. Angie has ESP. In a conversation with her dying grandmother, Angie is encouraged to use her gift to help others. *Why Have the Birds Stopped Singing?* is a Gothic journey back in time. Sixteen-year-old Katie is epileptic. While on a school tour of Puget Sound, she forgets to take her medicine and falls. Upon awaking, she is in the nineteenth century and is thought to be her own great-great-great-grandmother Kathryn who was also epileptic. It is a historical novel of romance and suspense.

Critics consider *Too Bad about the Haines Girl* to be Sherburne's best work for young adult readers. Westwood High's popular seniors, Lindy and Jeff, are very much in love. Zoa Sherburne has offered a straightforward account which is neither didactic nor conclusive, but instead is an honest discussion of premarital pregnancy and its effect upon many lives. The story ends with Lindy facing the fact that she needs to tell her parents and to receive their support. The final paragraph of the book expresses the change that has taken place in Lindy Haines' life. While listening to the radio, she hears a tune that Jeff and she had called their song. And she reminisces that they had danced to it many times last year, "when they were young."

From boy-next-door type of books for young girls to those dealing with serious problems and concerns that teens experience, Sherburne's work documents the changing scene of American life from the fifties to the seventies. Her characterizations are well written. Confident teenagers are shown as well as those who do not fit into the crowd; family, marriage and divorce, and birth and death are present; and lives in pain from drugs, alcohol, and other choices are vividly depicted. Sometimes her protagonists make mistakes and choices which they regret and sometimes not. There are happy times, sad times, bad times, and fun times. Youth is a time of transition—and Zoa Sherburne has documented the metamorphosis from childhood to adult. Life does not always have a Cinderella ending, but Sherburne's novels show that there is always hope for the future.

—Albert F. Spencer

SINCLAIR, Upton (Beall). Also wrote as Clarke Fitch, Frederick Garrison, and Arthur Stirling. American. Born in Baltimore, Maryland, 20 September 1878. Educated at the City College (now City College of the City University of New York), 1893-97, A.B. 1897; Columbia University, New York, 1897-1901. Married 1) Meta H. Fuller in 1900 (divorced 1913), one son; 2) Mary Craig Kimbrough in 1913 (died 1961); 3) Mary Elizabeth Willis in 1961 (died 1967). Writer from 1893; wrote nearly one hundred pseudonymous "dime novels" while attending graduate school; wrote Clif Faraday stories (as Ensign Clarke Fitch) and Mark Mallory stories (as Lieutenant Frederick Garrison) for various boys' weeklies, 1897-98; founded Intercollegiate Socialist Society (now League for Industrial Democracy), Helicon Home Colony, Englewood, New Jersey, 1906, and EPIC (End Poverty in California) League, 1934; assisted U.S. Government in investigation of Chicago stock yards, 1906; established theater company for performance of socialist plays, 1908. Socialist candidate for Congress, from New Jersey, 1906; settled in Pasadena, California, 1915; Socialist candidate for Congress, 1920, and for the United States Senate, 1922, and for Governor of California, 1926, 1930; moved to Buckeye, Arizona, 1953. Democratic candidate for governor of California, 1934. Occasional lecturer. Recipient: Nobel Prize for literature nomination, 1932; Pulitzer Prize, 1943, for *Dragon's Teeth;* New York Newspaper Guild Page One award, 1962; United Auto Workers Social Justice award, 1962. *Died 25 November 1968.*

PUBLICATIONS

Novels

Springtime and Harvest: A Romance. New York, Sinclair Press, 1901; as *King Midas,* New York and London, Funk, 1901.

The Journal of Arthur Stirling New York, Appleton, and London, Heinemann, 1903.

Prince Hagen: A Phantasy. Boston, Page, and London, Chatto & Windus, 1903.

Manassas: A Novel of the War. New York and London, Macmillan, 1904; as *Theirs Be the Guilt: A Novel of the War between the States,* New York, Twayne, 1959.

A Captain of Industry, Being the Story of a Civilized Man. Girard, Kansas, Appeal to Reason, and London, Heinemann, 1906.

The Jungle. New York, Doubleday, 1906; reprinted, Penguin, 1980; unabridged edition, New York, Doubleday, 1988.

The Metropolis. New York, Moffat, Yard, and London, Laurie, 1908.

The Moneychangers. New York, B.W. Dodge, and London, Long, 1908.

Samuel the Seeker. New York, B.W. Dodge, and London, Long, 1910.

Love's Pilgrimage. New York, M. Kennerley, 1911; London, Heinemann, 1912.

Damaged Goods. Philadelphia, Winston, 1913, and London, Hutchinson, 1913; as *Damaged Goods: A Novel about the Victims of Syphilis,* Girard, Kansas, Haldeman-Julius Publications, 1948.

Sylvia. Philadelphia, Winston, 1913; London, Long, 1914.

Sylvia's Marriage. Philadelphia, Winston, 1914; London, Laurie, 1915.

King Coal. New York, Macmillan, 1917, and London, Laurie, 1917.

Jimmie Higgins. London, Hutchinson, 1918; New York, Boni & Liveright, 1919.

The Spy. London, Laurie, 1919; as *100%: The Story of a Patriot,* privately printed, 1920; excerpt, as *Peter Gudge Becomes a Secret Agent,* Moscow, State Publishing House, 1930.

They Call Me Carpenter: A Tale of the Second Coming. New York, Boni & Liveright, and London, Laurie, 1922.

The Millennium: A Comedy of the Year 2000. Girard, Kansas, Haldeman Julius, 1924; London, Laurie, 1929.

Oil! New York, Boni, and London, Laurie, 1927.

Boston: A Documentary Novel of the Sacco-Vanzetti Case. New York, Boni, 1928; London, Laurie, 1929; abridged edition, as *August 22nd,* New York, Universal, 1965; Bath Chivers, 1971.

Mountain City. New York, Boni, and London, Laurie, 1930.

Roman Holiday. New York, Farrar & Rinehart, and London, Laurie, 1931.

The Wet Parade. New York, Farrar & Rinehart, and London, Laurie, 1931.

Co-op: A Novel of Living Together. New York, Farrar & Rinehart, and London, Laurie, 1936.

The Gnomobile: A Gnice Gnew Gnarrative with Gnonsense, but Gnothing Gnaughty (juvenile). New York, Farrar & Rinehart, and London, Laurie, 1936.

Little Steel. New York, Farrar & Rinehart, and London, Laurie, 1938.

Our Lady. Emmaus, Pennsylvania, Rodale Press, and London, Laurie, 1938.

Marie Antoinette. New York, Vanguard Press, and London, Laurie, 1939; as *Marie and Her Lover,* Girard, Kansas, Haldeman-Julius Publications, 1948.

World's End. New York, Viking, and London, Laurie, 1940.
Between Two Worlds. New York, Viking, and London, Laurie, 1941.
Dragon's Teeth. New York, Viking, and London, Laurie, 1942.
Wide Is the Gate. New York, Viking, and London, Laurie, 1943.
Presidential Agent. New York, Viking, 1944; London, Laurie, 1945.
Dragon Harvest. New York, Viking, and London, Laurie, 1945.
A World to Win, 1940-1942. New York, Viking, 1946; London, Laurie, 1947.
Presidential Mission. New York, Viking, 1947; London, Laurie, 1948.
One Clear Call. New York, Viking, 1948; London, Laurie, 1949.
O Shepherd, Speak. New York, Viking, 1949; London, Laurie, 1950.
Another Pamela; or, Virtue Still Rewarded. New York, Viking, and London, Laurie, 1950.
The Return of Lanny Budd. New York, Viking, and London, Laurie, 1953.
What Didymus Did. London, Wingate, 1954; as *It Happened to Didymus,* New York, Sagamore Press, 1958.
The Cup of Fury. Great Neck, New York, Channel Press, 1956; London, Arco, 1957.
Affectionately Eve. New York, Twayne, 1961.
The Coal War: A Sequel to King Coal, edited by John Graham. Boulder, Colorado Associated University Press, 1976.

Plays

Prince Hagen. adaptation of his own novel (produced San Francisco, 1909). Privately printed, 1909.
Plays of Protest (includes *Prince Hagen, The Naturewoman, The Machine, The Second-story Man*). New York, Kennerley, 1912.
Hell: A Verse Drama and Photo-play. Privately printed, 1923.
The Pot Boiler. Girard, Kansas, Haldeman, Julius, 1924.
Singing Jailbirds: A Drama in Four Acts (produced London, 1930). Privately printed, 1924.
Bill Porter: A Drama of O. Henry in Prison. Privately printed, 1925.
Wally for Queen! The Private Life of Royalty. Privately printed, 1936.
A Giant's Strength. Girard, Kansas, Haldeman-Julius, and London, Laurie, 1948.
The Enemy Had It Too. New York, Viking, 1950.
Three Plays (includes *The Second-Story Man, John D., The Indignant Subscriber*). Moscow, Progress, 1965.

Poetry

Songs of Our Nation (as Frederick Garrison). New York, Marks Music, 1941.

Other

Off for West Point; or, Mark Mallory's Struggle (as Frederick Garrison). New York, Street & Smith, 1903.
On Guard; or, Mark Mallory's Celebration (as Frederick Garrison). New York, Street & Smith, 1903.
The Toy and the Man. Westwood, Massachusetts, Ariel Press, 1904.
Our Bourgeois Literature. Chicago, Kerr, 1905.
Colony Customs. Englewood, New Jersey, Constitution, 1906.
The Helicon Home Colony. Englewood, New Jersey, Constitution, 1906.

A Home Colony: A Prospectus. New York, Jungle, 1906.
What Life Means to Me. Girard, Kansas, Appeal to Reason, 1906.
The Overman. New York, Doubleday, and Boston, Page, 1907.
Good Health and How We Won It, with an Account of the New Hygiene, with Michael Williams. New York, F.A. Stokes, 1909; as *Strength and Health,* 1910; as *The Art of Health,* London, Health and Strength, 1909.
War: A Manifesto Against It. Girard, Kansas, Appeal to Reason, New York, Wilshire, and London, Clarion Press, 1909.
The Fasting Cure. New York, M. Kennerley, and London, Heinemann, 1911.
Four Letters About "Love's Pilgrimage." Privately printed, 1911.
The Sinclair-Astor Letters: Famous Correspondence Between Socialist and Millionaire. Girard, Kansas, Appeal to Reason, 1914.
Editor, *The Cry for Justice: An Anthology of the Literature of Social Protest.* Philadelphia, Winston, 1915.
Upton Sinclair: Biographical and Critical Opinions. Privately printed, 1917.
The Profits of Religion: An Essay in Economic Interpretation. Privately printed, 1918; New York, Vanguard, 1927; London, Laurie, 1936.
The Brass Check: A Study of American Journalism. London, Laurie, 1919; Pasadena, California, privately printed, 1920; excerpt, as *The Associated Press and Labor,* privately printed, 1920.
The High Cost of Living (address). Girard, Kansas, People's Press, 1919.
Russia: A Challenge. Girard, Kansas, Appeal to Reason, 1919.
Press-titution. Girard, Kansas, Appeal to Reason, 1920.
The Crimes of the "Times": A Test of Newspaper Decency. Privately printed, 1921.
The McNeal-Sinclair Debate on Socialism. Girard, Kansas, Haldeman Julius, 1921.
Mind and Body. New York, Macmillan, 1921; revised edition, Girard, Kansas, Halderman-Julius, 4 vols., 1950.
Biographical Letter and Critical Opinions. Privately printed, 1922.
The Book of Life. Pasadena, California, Sinclair Paine, 1922; London, Laurie, 1934.
The Goose-step: A Study of American Education. Privately printed, 1922; revised edition, n.d.; Girard, Kansas, Haldeman-Julius Publications, and London, Laurie, 1923.
Love and Society. Pasadena, California, Sinclair Paine, 1922; revised edition, Girard, Kansas, Haldeman-Julius, 4 vols., n.d.
The Goslings: A Study of the American Schools. Privately printed, 1924; London, Laurie, 1930; excerpt, as *The Schools of Los Angeles,* privately printed, 1924.
Mammonart: An Essay in Economic Interpretation. Privately printed, 1925; London, Laurie, 1934.
Letters to Judd, An American Workingman. Privately printed, 1926; revised edition as *This World of 1949 and What to Do about It: Revised Letters to a Workingman on the Economic and Political Situation,* Girard, Kansas, Haldeman-Julius, 1949.
The Spokesman's Secretary, Being the Letters of Mame to Mom. Privately printed, 1926.
Money Writes! New York, Boni, 1927; London, Laurie, 1931.
The Pulitzer Prize and "Special Pleading." Privately printed, 1929.
Mental Radio. New York, Boni, 1930; as *Mental Radio: Does It Work, and How?,* London, Laurie, 1930, revised edition, Springfield, Illinois, Thomas, 1962.
Socialism and Culture. Girard, Kansas, Haldeman-Julius, 1931.
Upton Sinclair on "Comrade" Kautsky. Moscow, Co-operative Publishing Society of Foreign Workers in the USSR, 1931.

American Outpost: A Book of Reminiscences. New York, Farrar & Rinehart, 1932; as *Candid Reminiscences: My First Thirty Years,* London, Laurie, 1932.

I, Governor of California, and How I Ended Poverty: A True Story of the Future. New York, Farrar & Rinehart, and London, Laurie, 1933.

Upton Sinclair Presents William Fox. Privately printed, 1933.

The Way Out: What Lies Ahead for America. New York, Farrar & Rinehart, and London, Laurie, 1933; revised edition, as *Limbo on the Loose: A Midsummer Night's Dream,* Girard, Kansas, Haldeman-Julius Publications, 1948.

The Book of Love. London, Laurie, 1934.

EPIC Answers: How to End Poverty in California. Los Angeles, End Poverty League, 1934.

The EPIC Plan for California. New York, Farrar & Rinehart, 1934.

The Lie Factory Starts. Los Angeles, End Poverty League, 1934.

An Upton Sinclair Anthology, edited by I.O. Evans. New York, Farrar & Rinehart, and London, Laurie, 1934; revised edition, Culver City, California, Murray & Gee, 1947.

Upton Sinclair's Last Will and Testament. Los Angeles, End Poverty League, 1934.

Depression Island. Pasadena, California, privately printed, and London, Laurie, 1935.

I, Candidate for Governor, and How I Got Licked. New York, Farrar & Rinehart, 1935; as *How I Got Licked and Why,* London, Laurie, 1935.

We, People of America, and How We Ended Poverty: A True Story of the Future. Pasadena, California, National EPIC League, 1935.

What God Means to Me: An Attempt at a Working Religion. New York, Farrar & Rinehart, and London, Laurie, 1936.

The Flivver King: A Story of Ford-America. Girard, Kansas, Haldeman-Julius Publications, 1937; as *The Flivver King: A Novel of Ford-America,* London, Laurie, 1938.

No Pasoran! (They Shall Not Pass): A Story of the Battle of Madrid. New York, Labor Press, and London, Laurie, 1937.

Terror in Russia?: Two Views, with Eugene Lyons. New York, Richard R. Smith, 1938.

Upton Sinclair on the Soviet Union. New York, Weekly Masses, 1938.

Expect No Peace! Girard, Kansas, Haldeman-Julius Publications, 1939.

Telling the World. London, Laurie, 1939.

What Can Be Done about America's Economic Troubles. Girard, Kansas, Haldeman-Julius, 1939.

Your Million Dollars. Privately printed, 1939; as *Letters to a Millionaire,* London, Laurie, 1939.

Is the American Form of Capitalism Essential to the American Form of Democracy? Girard, Kansas, Haldeman-Julius, 1940.

Peace or War in America? Girard, Kansas, Haldeman-Julius, 1940.

Index to the Lanny Budd Story, with others. New York, Viking Press, 1943.

To Solve the German Problem—A Free State? Privately printed, 1943.

A Personal Jesus: Portrait and Interpretation. New York, Evans, 1952; as *The Secret Life of Jesus,* Philadelphia, Mercury Books, 1962.

Radio Liberation Speech to the Peoples of the Soviet Union. New York, American Committee for Liberation from Bolshevism, 1955.

Cicero: A Tragedy of Ancient Rome. Privately printed, 1960.

My Lifetime in Letters. Columbia, University of Missouri Press, 1960.

The Autobiography of Upton Sinclair. New York, Harcourt, 1962; London, Allen & Unwin, 1963.

Upton Sinclair: Four Unpublished Letters. San Francisco, California, Artichoke Press, 1984.

Novels as Clarke Fitch

Courtmartialed. New York, Street & Smith, 1898.

Saved by the Enemy. New York, Street & Smith, 1898.

A Soldier Monk. New York, Street & Smith, 1899.

A Soldier's Pledge. New York, Street & Smith, 1899.

Wolves of the Navy; or, Clif Faraday's Search for a Traitor, New York, Street & Smith, 1899.

Clif, the Naval Cadet; or, Exciting Days at Annapolis. New York, Street & Smith, 1903.

The Cruise of the Training Ship; or, Clif Faraday's Pluck. New York, Street & Smith, 1903.

From Port to Port; or, Clif Faraday in Many Waters. New York, Street & Smith, 1903.

A Strange Cruise; or, Clif Faraday's Yacht Chase. New York, Street & Smith, 1903.

*

Media Adaptations: *The Adventurer* (film), U.S. Amusement Corp., 1917; *The Money Changers* (film), Pathe Exchange, 1920; *Marriage Forbidden* (film), Criterion, 1938; *The Gnome-Mobile* (film), Walt Disney Productions, 1967.

Biography: Entry in *Dictionary of Literary Biography,* Volume 9: *American Novelists, 1910-1945,* Detroit, Gale, 1981.

Bibliography: *Upton Sinclair: An Annotated Checklist* by Ronald Gottesman, Kent, Ohio, Kent State University Press, 1973.

Manuscript Collection: Lilly Library, Indiana University, Bloomington.

Critical Studies: *Upton Sinclair: A Study in Social Protest* by Floyd Dell, New York, Doubleday, 1927; *This Is Upton Sinclair* by James Harte Lambert, Emmaus, Pennsylvania, Rodale Press, 1938; *The Literary Manuscripts of Upton Sinclair* by Ronald Gottesman and Charles L.P. Silet, Columbus, Ohio State University Press, 1972; *Upton Sinclair* by John A. Yoder, New York, Ungar, 1975; *Upton Sinclair, American Rebel* by Leon Harris, New York, Crowell, 1975; *Critics on Upton Sinclair* edited by Abraham Blinderman, Coral Gables, Florida, University of Miami Press, 1975; *Upton Sinclair* by William A. Bloodworth, Boston, Twayne, 1977; entries in *Contemporary Literary Criticism,* Detroit, Gale, Volume 1, 1973; Volume 9, 1979; Volume 15, 1980.

*   *   *

Like a number of other writers, but with more zeal than most, Upton Sinclair dedicated himself to a cause—he once wrote that if his heart were cut in half after his death, the words inscribed there would be "Social Justice." This was his cause, and Sinclair supported it primarily in the form of devotion to the tenets of Socialism. The commitment began early; he joined the Socialist party in

1904. With an astounding production of books, articles, and letters, Sinclair attempted to advance Socialist principles, as he perceived them, all of his long life.

His very accessible fiction, most widely read of his works today, falls generally into two genres: the novel of social protest and the "historical" novel. Fame came early for Sinclair because of one of his social protest novels whose "cause" has largely vanished today but which is still assigned reading in many classrooms because of its realistic portrayal of the life and mistreatment of poor immigrants. His best-known title, *The Jungle* was never a great critical success, yet its fame was deserved: apart from presenting in great detail the grim events in the life of Jurgis Rudkus, a Lithuanian immigrant, and his family, Sinclair painted a naturalistic picture of the Chicago stockyards and the workings of that ghastly place which was so moving that it helped to cause the enactment of the Pure Food and Drug Act of 1906.

The Jungle reveals the strengths that were to mark Sinclair's work for the rest of his career. The ease and fluency with which Sinclair wrote tended to make him occasionally hasty and casual as to literary technique, but this easy-to-read style that lended itself to ready translation—into some forty-five languages in roughly forty countries—broadens Sinclair's appeal to young adults. Another strength of the novel lies in the painstaking research that went into it. Sinclair had an observing eye and strived tirelessly to determine facts; he even worked in a meatpacking plant for a time in order to observe details for himself.

The Jungle was followed by a long series of exposes of various immoral (and occasionally illegal) practices, usually by rich and unscrupulous capitalists. *King Coal* attempted to reveal the mistreatment of miners in Colorado. *Oil!* dealt with the Teapot Dome and other scandals involving the petroleum industry. The novel had considerable journalistic interest for contemporary readers, but it typically closes with a kind of sermon about "the black and cruel demon...an evil Power which roams the earth, crippling the bodies of men and women, and luring the nations to destruction by visions of unearned wealth, and the opportunity to enslave and exploit labor." A number of similar "message" novels followed. The long and comprehensive *Boston* delves into the injustices of the Sacco-Vanzetti case but also presents a sharp outline of Boston society with fine attention to detail. Another such work is Sinclair's vision of the immorality of a society that lives off great amounts of money— *The Metropolis,* in which New York is the central setting and in which, typically, the main character becomes sated with the life of easy wealth and luxury and rejects it.

Possessing a liveliness and spirit that appeals to many readers, Sinclair's historical novels are more pleasurable reading. Lanny Budd is the central character in a series of ten novels in which Sinclair covers leading world events, especially those from 1913 to 1950. Son of a munitions manufacturer and his socialite lady friend, Lanny is raised in Europe, where he begins as politically neutral, later learning to fear and hate the growing immorality which he finds in Nazi Germany. As Lanny grows older, he develops into a deeper and more rounded character, and becomes a secret agent for the president (a career founded on the real-life exploits of Cornelius Vanderbilt, Jr., according to Sinclair). A key aspect of these books, one that was typical of Sinclair himself, is Lanny's power of observation. He seems to overlook almost nothing. While some of Lanny's meetings—with, for example, Joseph Goebbels, Adolf Hitler, Hermann Goering, and Franklin Roosevelt—seem improbable, this series has been highly praised for its accurate reflection of the sometimes calamitous events in the first half of this century. In his

autobiography, Sinclair firmly asserted that no one had ever proved one of his "facts" to be in error.

While the series is strong in historical accuracy, one of the novels also found favor with the literary establishment: *Dragon's Teeth,* which deals with Germany's descent into Naziism during 1930 to 1934, won the Pulitzer Prize for fiction in 1943.

Very probably, Sinclair will be remembered best for *The Jungle;* however, his other works will repay the attention of young adults who desire to learn about social problems and important events in modern history in an easy and readable fashion.

—Fred McEwen

———

SINGER, Marilyn. American. Born in New York City, 3 October 1948. Attended University of Reading, 1967-68; Queens College of the City University of New York, B.A. (cum laude) 1969; New York University, M.A. 1979. Married Steven Aronson in 1971. Editor, Daniel S. Mead Literary Agency, 1967; *Where* (magazine), New York City, assistant editor, 1969; teacher of English and speech, New York City Public High Schools, 1969-74; writer, 1974—. Recipient: Children's Choice Award, International Reading Association, 1977, for *The Dog Who Insisted He Wasn't,* 1979, for *It Can't Hurt Forever,* and 1988, for *Ghost Host;* Maud Hart Lovelace Award, Friends of the Minnesota Valley Regional Library (Mankato), 1983, for *It Can't Hurt Forever;* American Library Association (ALA) best book for young adults citation, 1983, for *The Course of True Love Never Did Run Smooth;* Parents' Choice Award, Parents' Choice Foundation, 1983, for *The Fido Frame-Up;* ALA best book for young adults nomination, 1988, for *Several Kinds of Silence; New York Times* best illustrated children's book citation, *Time* best children's book citation, both 1989, National Council of Teachers of English notable trade book in the language arts, 1990, and Texas Bluebonnet Award nomination, 1992, all for *Turtle in July.* Address: 42 Berkeley Pl., Brooklyn, NY 11217, U.S.A.

PUBLICATIONS FOR YOUNG ADULTS

Fiction

No Applause, Please. New York, Dutton, 1977.
The First Few Friends. New York, Harper, 1981.
The Course of True Love Never Did Run Smooth. New York, Harper, 1983.
Horsemaster. New York, Atheneum, 1985.
Ghost Host. New York, Harper, 1987.
Several Kinds of Silence. New York, Harper, 1988.
Storm Rising. New York, Scholastic, 1989.

PUBLICATIONS FOR CHILDREN

Picture Books

The Dog Who Insisted He Wasn't, illustrated by Kelly Oechsli. New York, Dutton, 1976.

The Pickle Plan, illustrated by Steven Kellogg. New York, Dutton, 1978.

Will You Take Me to Town on Strawberry Day?, illustrated by Trinka Hakes Noble. New York, Harper, 1981.

Archer Armadillo's Secret Room, illustrated by Beth Lee Weiner. New York, Macmillan, 1985.

Minnie's Yom Kippur Birthday, illustrated by Ruth Rosner. New York, Harper, 1989.

Turtle in July, illustrated by Jerry Pinkney. New York, Macmillan, 1989.

Nine O'Clock Lullaby, illustrated by Frane Lessac. New York, HarperCollins, 1991.

The Golden Heart of Winter, illustrated by Robert Rayevsky. New York, Morrow, 1991.

Out-of-Work Dog, illustrated by Cat Bowman Smith. New York, Holt, 1992.

In My Tent, illustrated by Emily Arnold McCully. New York, Macmillan, 1992.

Fiction

It Can't Hurt Forever, illustrated by Leigh Grant. New York, Harper, 1978.

Tarantulas on the Brain, illustrated by Leigh Grant. New York, Harper, 1982.

Lizzie Silver of Sherwood Forest (sequel to *Tarantulas on the Brain*), illustrated by Miriam Nerlove. New York, Harper, 1986.

The Lightey Club, illustrated by Kathryn Brown. New York, Four Winds, 1987.

Mitzi Meyer, Fearless Warrior Queen. New York, Scholastic, 1987.

Charmed. New York, Atheneum, 1990.

Twenty Ways to Lose Your Best Friend, illustrated by Jeffrey Lindberg. New York, Harper, 1990.

California Demon. New York, Hyperion, 1992.

"Sam and Dave" mystery series:

Leroy Is Missing, illustrated by Judy Glasser. New York, Harper, 1984.

The Case of the Sabotaged School Play, illustrated by Judy Glasser. New York, Harper, 1984.

A Clue in Code, illustrated by Judy Glasser. New York,, Harper, 1985.

The Case of the Cackling Car, illustrated by Judy Glasser. New York, Harper, 1985.

The Case of the Fixed Election, illustrated by Richard Williams. New York, Harper, 1989.

The Hoax on You, illustrated by Richard Williams. New York, Harper, 1989.

"Samantha Spayed" mystery series:

The Fido Frame-Up, illustrated by Andrew Glass. New York, Warne, 1983.

A Nose for Trouble, illustrated by Andrew Glass, New York, Holt, 1985.

Where There's a Will, There's a Wag, illustrated by Andrew Glass. New York, Holt, 1986.

Nonfiction

Exotic Birds, illustrated by James Needham. New York, Doubleday, 1990.

PUBLICATIONS FOR ADULTS

Nonfiction

Editor and author of introduction, *A History of Avant-Garde Cinema.* American Federation of Arts, 1976.

Editor and contributor, *New American Filmmakers.* American Federation of Arts, 1976.

The Fanatic's Ecstatic, Aromatic Guide to Onions, Garlic, Shallots and Leeks, illustrated by Marian Perry. New York, Prentice-Hall, 1981.

Also author of several teacher's guides, catalogs, and program notes on films and filmstrips, including Jacob Bronowski's *The Ascent of Man* and David Attenborough's *The Tribal Eye.* Past curator of *SuperFilmShow!,* a series of avant-garde films selected for children. Writer of scripts for the children's television show *The Electric Company.* Contributor of short stories to books, including *Rooms of Our Own,* Holt, 1992.

*   *   *

Winner of numerous awards and honors, Marilyn Singer is a prolific writer of picture books, juvenile books, and young adult novels, which include mysteries and fantasies. Understanding the child in herself, she uses some of her own past experiences in writing for children and young adults because, as she says, she likes to.

Death can be very frightening when one is faced with it, but everyone has to confront it sooner or later. Ellie Simon is terrified that she is going to die in *It Can't Hurt Forever.* She has a patent ductus arteriosus, or heart defect, and must have an operation to repair it. This is a very informative story about Ellie's stay in the hospital, the various tests and diagnoses she has to go through before the operation, and it is also about hospitals and operations in general. Singer writes from experience, having had a similar operation when she was young, and she doesn't want anyone to face the terrifying unknown that she faced as a child. She tells of young people's fears and how ignorance of hospitals and surgery can lead to terror-filled misconceptions of the various medical procedures. Ellie fortunately has parents, doctors, and friends who take the time to tell her generally what she will be going through during her stay in the hospital. Unfortunately, everyone fails to inform her of the pain she must endure when she gets her cardiac catheterization. Her anger and frustration upset everyone, including herself, but she comes through her surgery like a champ, unhappy about the scar that begins in the middle of her chest and ends in the middle of her back, but knowing that she is going to live. Young people will appreciate reading this book, because it is written in a caring, descriptive, factual way, with a little humor woven among the explanations about hospitals and operations. It is simple to understand, and fears will vanish after reading it.

Horsemaster, a fantasy, is an example of Singer's varying genres. Jessica, the main character, is a fourteen-year-old rebellious girl, encouraged in her defiance against her domineering mother by Jessica's friend Jack, also a rebel. When the two young people go for a ride on a "borrowed" motorcycle, they stop at a deserted, ramshackle farmhouse where they find an ancient tapestry hanging on a wall. In the threads of the dusty material is woven the starred head of a horse named Gabdon that mysteriously appears before Jessica and Jack and carries them to another world, far away from Brown Dear, Wisconsin, where they live. In the new world Jessica learns to forgive her father for leaving his family, her mother for the sorrow and bitterness she has caused, and to forgive herself. Jack, too, overcomes his rebellious anger and restlessness, and the two young people realize they must change in order to get along in the real world, learning that there are other important people in their lives. An appropriate story for young adults in this seemingly uncaring contemporary world, readers will gain a new perspective on life after reading it.

Cited best book for young adults, *The Course of True Love Never Did Run Smooth* deals with the difficulties encountered by a gay couple, a rather touchy subject that is gaining more attention every day. Becky plays the part of Helena in the high school play *A Midsummer Night's Dream* and finds she has problems with her feelings toward Blake and her friend Nehemiah. The characters are unique, the dialogue humorously amorous at times, and a controversial topic is handled well, providing an interesting insight into the feelings of a gay couple who are finally admitting their true identities to others.

Ghost Host, another fantasy but more supernatural, portrays a poltergeist named Stryker and a friendly ghost named Millie who enter the lives of star quarterback Bart Hawkins, his girlfriend Lisa, captain of the cheerleading squad, and Arvie, a derisive classmate. An amusing tale, Singer once more has written an appealing story for young adults.

Marilyn Singer's stories include such a variety of genres—mysteries, medical tales, romances, fantasies, as well as picture books for children—one doesn't know what she is going to write next. Every young adult knows, however, that whatever Singer writes for them will be enjoyable, entertaining reading.

—Carol Doxey

SLEATOR, William (Warner III). American. Born in Havre de Grace, Maryland, 13 February 1945. Educated at Harvard University, Cambridge, Massachusetts, 1963-67, B.A. in English 1967; studied musical composition in London, England, 1967-68. Accompanist for ballet classes, Royal Ballet School, London, 1967-68, and Rambert School, London, 1967-68; rehearsal pianist, Boston Ballet Company, Boston, Massachusetts, 1974-83; writer. Recipient: Bread Loaf Writers' Conference fellowship, 1969; Caldecott Medal Honor Book, American Library Association (ALA), and *Boston Globe-Horn Book* award, both 1971, American Book award for Best Paperback Picture Book, 1981, ALA Notable Book citation, and *Horn Book* Honor List citation, all for *The Angry Moon;* Children's Book of the Year award, Child Study Association of America, 1972, and ALA Notable Book citation, both for *Blackbriar;* Best Books for Young Adults citations, ALA, 1974, for *House of Stairs,* 1984, for *Interstellar Pig,* 1985, for *Singularity,* and 1987, for *The Boy Who Reversed Himself;* Best of the Best for Young Adults citation, ALA Notable Book citation, *Horn Book* Honor List citation, and Junior Literary Guild selection, all for *Interstellar*

Pig; Children's Choice award, International Reading Association and Children's Book Council, and Junior Literary Guild selection, both for *Into the Dream;* Best Book of the Year awards, *School Library Journal,* 1981, for *The Green Futures of Tycho,* 1983, for *Fingers,* and 1984, for *Interstellar Pig;* Junior Literary Guild selection, for *Singularity;* Golden Pen award, Spokane Washington Public Library, 1984 and 1985, both for "the author who gives the most reading pleasure." Agent: Sheldon Fogelman, 10 East Fortieth St., New York, NY 10016. Address: 77 Worcester St., Boston, MA 02118, U.S.A.

PUBLICATIONS FOR YOUNG ADULTS

Fiction

Run. New York, Dutton, 1973.
House of Stairs. New York, Dutton, 1974; London, Macdonald, 1988.
Among the Dolls, illustrated by Trina Schart Hyman. New York, Dutton, 1975.
Into the Dream, illustrated by Ruth Sanderson. New York, Dutton, 1979.
The Green Futures of Tycho. New York, Dutton, 1981; London, Macdonald, 1988.
Fingers. New York, Atheneum, 1983.
Interstellar Pig. New York, Dutton, 1984; London, Hodder and Stoughton, 1987.
Singularity. New York, Dutton, 1985; London, Macdonald, 1988.
The Boy Who Reversed Himself. New York, Dutton, 1986; London, Macdonald, 1988.
The Duplicate. New York, Dutton, 1988.
Strange Attractors. New York, Dutton, 1990.
The Spirit House. New York, Dutton, 1991.
Oddballs: Stories. New York, Dutton, 1993.
Others See Us. New York, Dutton, 1993.

PUBLICATIONS FOR CHILDREN

Fiction

Blackbriar, illustrated by Blair Lent. New York, Dutton, 1972.
Once, Said Darlene, illustrated by Steven Kellogg. New York, Dutton, 1979.
That's Silly, illustrated by Lawrence DiFiori. New York, Dutton, 1981.

Other

The Angry Moon (retelling), illustrated by Blair Lent. Boston, Little, Brown, 1970.

Composer of music for film *Why the Sun and Moon Live in the Sky,* 1972.

PUBLICATIONS FOR ADULTS

Other

Take Charge: A Personal Guide to Behavior Modification, with William H. Redd. New York, Random House, 1976.

Media Adaptations: *The Angry Moon* (audiocassette), Read-Along-House; *Interstellar Pig* (audiocassette), Listening Library, 1987.

Biography: Essay in *Speaking for Ourselves: Autobiographical Sketches by Notable Authors of Books for Young Adults,* Volume 1, compiled and edited by Donald R. Gallo, National Council of Teachers of English, 1990; essay in *Authors and Artists for Young Adults,* Volume 5, Detroit, Gale, 1991.

*   *   *

William Sleator's books for young adults present interesting challenges for both the characters in the stories and readers alike. A writer of mysteries initially, Sleator later branched out to create works with science fictional elements—from technology and experimentation gone awry to the capricious machinations of alien beings to supernatural and occult forces. It has become his trademark to place seemingly ordinary young people in extraordinary and often threatening situations involving at least one hidden influence that changes the direction of the outcome. While his novels tend to provide satisfactory endings, with most problems solved and the future of the protagonist somewhat secure, Sleator refuses to leave the reader feeling complacent. There is always the hint that there is more to come, that maybe things aren't quite what they seem, prompting the reader to use his or her own imagination to consider the "what ifs" if the story were to continue.

In *House of Stairs,* six teenagers are placed in an unusual environment, a building full of stairs leading nowhere—or everywhere—with no directions for survival. The teenagers learn to cope by performing strange rituals before a machine that rewards them with food and by forming relationships with others in the group. Although they are not aware of it, the young people are part of a scientific stimulus-response experiment enacted by the government to induce behavior modification. Every reaction, movement, and even bodily function occurs under the watchful eyes of the other young people and hidden observers. When two of the young people refuse to perform the cruelty required to obtain food and are close to starving, the scientists end the experiment. They regard these two as symbols of hope for the survival of the human spirit and its ability to fight against conformity and cruelty.

Other works by Sleator examine the possibility of time travel both into the past and into the future, and the possible futures such travel would bring about. In *The Green Futures of Tycho,* an egglike device dropped—planted—by aliens in prehistoric times is found by eleven-year-old Tycho, who uses it to explore many different futures, each more unpleasant than the last. Time travel also occurs in *Singularity,* in an Illinois field, where time speeds up. Overnight, a twin brother ages one year; he turns seventeen while his twin remains sixteen. Characters in *The Boy Who Reversed Himself* travel in both time and the fourth spatial dimension. In *Strange Attractors,* time travel is made possible by a scientist who inadvertently manages to clone himself and his daughter on one of their trips.

Sibling rivalry is a theme in several of Sleator's books, including *Fingers, Singularity,* and *The Duplicate* in which sixteen-year-old David finds a machine on the beach that can duplicate any living thing. David duplicates himself so that he can spend time with his girlfriend and have fun while his clone goes to school and performs other unpleasant duties. However, the clone duplicates itself, and David has to deal with his two other selves. In this instance, sibling rivalry results in murder.

In *Interstellar Pig,* Barney is quite aware of the beauty and sexuality of the mysterious Zena who lives next door. He is so flattered by her attention that he acquires an acute sunburn to be in her presence. However, since she is really an alien spider-like creature, their relationship progresses no further. Although twins Harry and Barry in *Singularity* are both attracted to Lucy, she chooses Barry as a boyfriend. Jealousy is a major reason why Harry decides to sleep overnight in the time-altering workshop, and when he appears the next day one year older, taller, and more muscular than Barry, Lucy's interest shifts to him. However, the relationship between the brothers proves more important than their competition over Lucy, when they reconcile and return home with their parents at the end, she is left behind.

In *The Duplicate,* David and his clones are all enamored of Angela, one of David's classmates. While David is awkward, hesitant, and inept in his interactions with Angela, his clones are rough and insistent with her, to the point of near rape. Yet Angela realizes that she is not dealing with the real David and helps him destroy the two duplicates. By the end of the novel, she and David have established a good relationship.

Sexuality becomes more overt in some of Sleator's later novels, including *Strange Attractors* in which Max has a definite sexual encounter with Eve's evil clone. While Sleator does not try to shock the reader, as he does not go into detail about Max's experiences. For Max, sexual attraction for a girl who is evil represents one of those strange attractors that makes people do things they might not do otherwise. The reader is left with the hint that even though Max knows better, he will go back into the past to find Eve where he has safely trapped her.

Spirit House marks a change for Sleator in that he creates a female protagonist and uses his fascination with Thailand to supply the unusual twist. The family of fifteen-year-old Julie accepts an exchange student, Bia, from Thailand who turns out to be nothing like his pictures or letters. The Thai spirit house that her little brother builds in the back yard as a gift for Bia turns out to be more than anyone has bargained for. Mysteriously, Julie's health and looks begin to deteriorate until at last she appeases the spirit who inhabits the spirit house. Or does she? In his typical style, Sleator employs a quirky ending that sets the reader up for continuing the story in his or her imagination.

The protagonists in Sleator's fiction are primarily teenage males experiencing difficulties in their relationships with females, siblings, parents and even themselves. The appeal that such characters hold for young readers is that while they are encountering strange and often extraordinary forces and beings, they are also working out their own psychological issues and emerging with a stronger sense of self. Sleator challenges both his characters and his readers, whom he invites to take an active role in the stories by using their own imaginations. Regardless of the scenario, the reader is encouraged to do what Sleator himself does—create a new story.

—Hazel K. Davis

———

SLEPIAN, Jan(ice B.) American. Born in New York City, 2 January 1921. Educated at Brooklyn College, B.A. 1942; University of Washington, M.A. (clinical psychology), 1947; New York University, M.A. (speech pathology), 1964; attended University of California—Berkeley, 1979. Married 1) Urey Krasnopolsky in 1945 (divorced, 1948); 2) David Slepian in 1950, two sons and one daughter. Language therapist, Massachusetts General Hospital, Boston, Massachusetts, 1947-49; private speech therapist, 1952-58; speech therapist, Easter Seal Clinic, Newton, New Jersey, 1953-55; speech therapist, Matheny School for Cerebral Palsy, Far Hills, New Jersey, 1955-57; writer. Recipient: *The Alfred Summer* was named one of the best books of the year by *School Library Journal,* 1980, and was named a notable book by the American Library Association (ALA); American Book Award finalist in children's fiction, and *Boston Globe-Horn Book* Honor for fiction, both 1981, for *The Alfred Summer;* Author's awards, New Jersey Institute of Technology, 1981, for *The Alfred Summer,* and 1983, for *The Night of the Bozos; Lester's Turn* was named one of the best books for children by the *New York Times,* and a notable children's book for older readers by *School Library Journal,* both 1981, a notable children's trade book in social studies by *Social Education,* and one of New York Public Library's books for the teen age, both 1982, and a notable book by the ALA; *The Night of the Bozos* was named one of the best books for young adults by the ALA, one of the children's books of the year by the Child Study Association of America, and one of the books of the year by the Library of Congress, all 1983; *Something beyond Paradise* was named one of the ten great books of the year for teens by *Redbook,* 1987; *The Broccoli Tapes* was named a notable book by the ALA, 1989; *Booklist* Editor's Choice, 1989, for *The Broccoli Tapes,* and 1990, for *Risk n' Roses; Risk n' Roses* was named one of New York Public Library's best books, 1990. Agent: Sheldon Fogelman, 10 East 40th St., New York, NY 10016. Address: 212 Summit Ave., Summit, NJ 07901, U.S.A.

PUBLICATIONS FOR YOUNG ADULTS

Fiction

The Alfred Summer. New York, Macmillan, 1980.
Lester's Turn (sequel to *The Alfred Summer*). New York, Macmillan, 1981.
The Night of the Bozos. New York, Dutton, 1983.
Getting On with It. New York, Four Winds, 1985.
Something beyond Paradise. New York, Philomel, 1987.
The Broccoli Tapes. New York, Philomel, 1989.
Risk n' Roses. New York, Philomel, 1990.
Back to Before. New York, Philomel, 1993.

PUBLICATIONS FOR CHILDREN

"Listen-Hear" picture book series; all with Ann Seidler; all illustrated by Richard E. Martin:

Alphie and the Dream Machine. New York, Follett, 1964.
The Cock Who Couldn't Crow. New York, Follett, 1964.
Lester and the Sea Monster. New York, Follett, 1964.
Magic Arthur and the Giant. New York, Follett, 1964.
Mister Sipple and the Naughty Princess. New York, Follett, 1964.
The Roaring Dragon of Redrose. New York, Follett, 1964.

"Junior Listen-Hear" picture book series; all with Ann Seidler; all illustrated by Richard E. Martin:

Bendemolena. New York, Follett, 1967; as *The Cat Who Wore a Pot on Her Head,* New York, Scholastic, 1981.

Ding-Dong, Bing-Bong. New York, Follett, 1967.
An Ear Is to Hear. New York, Follett, 1967.
The Hungry Thing. New York, Follett, 1967.
The Silly Listening Book. New York, Follett, 1967.

With Ann Seidler

The Best Invention of All, illustrated by Joseph Veno. New York, Crowell-Collier, 1967.
The Hungry Thing Returns, illustrated by Richard E. Martin. New York, Scholastic, 1990.
The Hungry Thing Goes To a Restaurant, illustrated by Elroy Freem. New York, Scholastic, 1992.

Other

Building Foundations for Better Speech and Reading (teachers' training series and cassette tape program; with twelve tapes and discussion guide). Instructional Dynamics Inc., 1974.

*

Biography: Essay in *Something about the Author Autobiography Series,* Volume 8, Detroit, Gale, 1989; essay in *Speaking for Ourselves, Too* compiled and edited by Donald R. Gallo, National Council of Teachers of English, 1993.

Manuscript Collection: Kerlan Collection, University of Minnesota.

Jan Slepian comments:

I never thought of being a writer when I was growing up. The idea never occurred to me. It was on about the same unimaginable level as aiming to be the Pope or a horse. But always, always I was in love with words. I read myself silly, and to this day I get the greatest pleasure from the way words are arranged in a sentence. For me, in writing, the fun is in the way I say a thing.

*   *   *

Jan Slepian began writing picture books because of her work as a speech therapist. Later she wrote books for young adults, two of which were selected by Junior Literary Guild. Many of Slepian's characters are mentally, physically, or socially handicapped, but they learn about themselves and how to cope with their problems and the world around them.

The Alfred Summer, named Boston Globe Horn Book fiction honor book of 1980, portrays four outcasts. Lester has cerebral palsy, Myron is a total klutz, Alfred Burt is retarded, and Claire is a skinny girl with a dream of becoming the world's fastest girl runner. Lester is smart—full of ideas, words and dreams—but can't express himself because of his handicap. Besides, he is attached to his mother by invisible strings and feels he can't get along in life without her. Claire introduces the boys to her Aziff Theory which is to act as if...anything you want, especially as if things don't really bother you when they do, or that you are really happy when you aren't, or that you really have confidence when you don't. Slepian has written a very enlightening story about retardation and cerebral palsy, plus the problems of a boy who is overweight and clumsy, and she has handled all problems with delicacy and light humor, showing that the problems are not as big as they seem when faced with a positive attitude. Although the narrative shifts from the first person to the third unexpectedly, confusing the reader for a moment, the story is moving, the reader can hear and smell Coney Island, and the wit of Lester is hilarious. Slepian has skillfully portrayed four admirable young people dealing with afflictions that cannot be changed, but can be accepted. Young adults will read this book and come away knowing they, too, can face problems using the Aziff Theory with success.

Lester's Turn continues the story of Alfred and Lester. Alfred's mother dies, and Alfred is placed in a hospital. Lester attempts to kidnap Alfred from the institution, but miserably fails. Eventually, Lester is allowed to take Alfred out of the building, but when Alfred becomes ill and dies of a burst appendix, even though Lester is devastated, he realizes he is now more able to face his own problems because of Alfred. Young people can learn that one's problems aren't as great as they seem when compared to those of others.

Death is a difficult subject to write about, but Slepian handles it straight on in *The Broccoli Tapes*. Sara Davidson and her family move to Hawaii for four months while Mr. Davidson teaches a biology class there. Sara records on cassette tapes events that happen in Hawaii for an oral history project for her social studies class back in Boston. Sara and her brother, Sam, find a cat caught in the rocks at the beach and rescue it. They sneak food to it and are amazed to find the animal loves broccoli, thus that is what they name her. They are also amazed when Broccoli has kittens. Sara's grandmother, visiting them for a few weeks, is diagnosed with cancer and dies. The family members deal with her death in different ways, running away from it, holding it inside, or facing it head-on. Then Broccoli also dies and the young people reach their limit. Slepian has written a heartbreaking story of losing a loved person and a pet, but shows that because of love, people can handle loss, knowing that it is better to have loved and lost rather than to have never loved at all. Cleverly written with the unique device of a tape recorder recording happenings and revealing feelings, the book has the added advantage of its setting in beautiful Hawaii.

In *Something Beyond Paradise,* Slepian has written about several people that seem incapable of standing on their own two feet. Franny Simone, sixteen years old, lives with her single mother and somewhat senile grandmother in Hawaii. Franny's best friend, Akiko, joins a cult commune, The House of Regis, run by an overpowering man who seems to mesmerize his followers. Franny decides to leave home and move to New York and join a dance group. This is a disconcerting story, because sixteen seems young for a teenager to be making such an important decision without parental support. Moreover, the girl encourages her nineteen-year-old boyfriend to accompany her to New York, making the situation even more questionable. Although the reader is left not knowing if things are going to work out or not, the story is interesting and shows young people the dangers of becoming involved with cults and the consequences. It certainly gives the reader something to think about.

Getting On With It, a Junior Literary Guild selection, portrays a young girl pushed off on her grandmother for a month while the girl's parents contemplate divorce. Berry Brice is faced with the death of a loved older friend and the lopsided romance of a forty-year-old neighbor woman with a twenty-nine-year-old man, besides the frustration of her parents possibly splitting up. Quite a bit for a thirteen-year-old to manage, but somehow Berry does it, leaving the reader a bit in awe.

Jan Slepian is an intriguing writer, solving a variety of problems dealing with the physically handicapped, death, divorce, and irrational behavior. She writes thought-provoking books, stimulating young adults to think for themselves and to strive to overcome problems that have seemed like mountains until, after Slepian's characters, they seem like mere anthills.

—Carol Doxey

SMITH, Doris Buchanan. American. Born in Washington, D.C., 1 June 1934. Educated at South Georgia College, Douglas. Married 1) R. Caroll Smith in 1954 (divorced 1977), four sons and one daughter; 2) Bill Curtis, c. 1988. Writer since 1971. Recipient: American Library Association Notable Book award and Child Study Association Book of the Year award, both 1973, Georgia Children's Book Author of the Year and Georgia General Author of the Year award, both from Dixie Council of Authors and Journalists, 1974, Georgia Children's Book award, 1975, and Sue Hafner award and Kinderbook award, both 1977, all for *A Taste of Blackberries;* Georgia Children's Book Author of the Year award from Dixie Council of Authors and Journalists and Notable Children's Book award from National Council for Social Studies, both 1975, for *Kelly's Creek;* Breadloaf Writers Conference fellowship, 1975; Georgia Children's Book Author of the Year award from Dixie Council of Authors and Journalists and Best Book of the Year award from *School Library Journal,* both 1982, for *Last Was Lloyd;* Parents' Choice Literature award, 1986, for *Return to Bitter Creek.* Address: P.O. Box 266, Canton, MO 63435, U.S.A.

PUBLICATIONS FOR YOUNG ADULTS

Fiction

A Taste of Blackberries, illustrated by Charles Robinson. New York, Crowell, 1973; London, Heinemann, 1975.
Kick a Stone Home. New York, Crowell, 1974.
Tough Chauncey, illustrated by Michael Eagle. New York, Morrow, 1974.
Kelly's Creek, illustrated by Alan Tiegreen. New York, Crowell, 1975.
Up and Over. New York, Morrow, 1976.
Dreams and Drummers. New York, Crowell, 1978.
Salted Lemons. New York, Four Winds Press, 1980.
Last Was Lloyd. New York, Viking Kestrel, 1981.
Moonshadow of Cherry Mountain. New York, Four Winds Press, 1982.
The First Hard Times. New York, Viking Kestrel, 1983.
Laura Upside-Down. New York, Viking Kestrel, 1984.
Return to Bitter Creek. New York, Viking Kestrel, 1986.
Karate Dancer. New York, Putnam, 1987.
Voyages. New York, Viking Kestrel, 1989.
The Pennywhistle Tree. New York, Putnam, 1991.
Best Girl. New York, Viking Kestrel, 1993.

*

Biography: Essay in *Something about the Author Autobiography Series,* Volume 10, Detroit, Gale.

Critical Study: Entry in *Dictionary of Literary Biography,* Volume 52: *American Writers for Children since 1960: Fiction,* Detroit, Gale, 1986.

*   *   *

Doris Buchanan Smith's fifteen novels, principally for young adult readers, describe teenager's daily lives, feelings, and problems with skill, sensitivity, and honesty. Her books have often broken new ground in realistic treatments of death, divorce, obesity, juvenile delinquency, unwed mothers, dyslexia, sexual drives, foster and stepparents, and child abuse. But they seldom focus on these problems. She begins with a character. Then as she has said, the character has problems because people do in real life. Her books do not force neat solutions. Just as in life some problems cannot be solved but must be adjusted to or lived with.

Certainly Smith's experiences in raising five of her own, and numerous foster children gave insights into the nature of older children and their families. Her first published book, *A Taste of Blackberries* brought critical success and several awards for her sensitivity to the internal life of a child. In dealing directly with the death of a child's playmate, it broke a taboo of twentieth-century American children's fiction. It focuses on the unnamed narrator's feelings of guilt and loss for his best friend Jamie, "a show-off and a clown," who dies from an allergic reaction to a bee sting.

Though her next books *Kick a Stone Home* and *Tough Chauncey* deal with alienation from family and friends, their main characters are very different. The protagonist of *Kick a Stone Home* is Sara Jane Chambers, a fifteen-year-old middle-class Atlanta girl, who has ordinary domestic problems: adjusting to her parents' divorce and moving to a new neighborhood. But Chauncey, a thirteen-year-old poor white, is illiterate, delinquent, belligerent, and disobedient to both parental and school authorities. He is beaten by his religiously fundamentalist grandfather and frequently abandoned by his immature mother, who drifts through life with a low-paying job and a series of rather worthless husbands and lovers. After Jack Levitt, a black boy from another broken home and his "best friend," frames him for the theft of a bike, he seriously injures himself while attempting to hitch a ride on a freight train. He soon realizes that a foster home promises him more of a chance than does his family. It is a powerful story, and well told.

Kelly's Creek deals with the social and educational problems of the dyslexia of nine-year-old Kelly O'Brian. Friendship with a college student who comes to do research in the tidal creek behind their coastal Georgia home helps Kelly to develop confidence and an interest in learning, which leads to success in biology class and a better relationship to his parents and old brother.

This simply written book with sparse yet accurate biological details was followed by *Up and Over,* which seems to crowd in everything remarkable about the 1960s: streaking, student protests, drug addiction, racial tension, teenage marriages or pregnancy, over-rigorous parenting, and mainstreaming of the handicapped. In the much simpler, much less traumatic story of *Dreams and Drummers,* fourteen-year-old Stephanie Stone's only problem is that she fails to agonize over the ordinary teenage woes of studies and dates.

Salted Lemons marked a return to more weighty issues. Set in the Atlanta of 1943 and drawing on details of Smith's youth, the book tells how ten-year-old Darby Bannister finds herself ostracized as a Yankee from Washington, D.C., and as a hick because she can not attend the city school as she lives just inside the county line. The novel focuses on the paradoxes of prejudice, alienation, and friendship, nicely symbolized by the salted lemons that Darby learns to share with Yoko, a Japanese-American girl whose family is subsequently interred in Florida during World War II spy hysteria. Religious extremes are represented by Darby's father's agnosticism; her mother's conventional Methodism; the Fundamentalism of Fancy Potter, a poor white girl and Darby's friend; and the millenarianism of Jeannine, another friend, whose family rents Yoko's empty house. Relating to these people teaches Darby the importance of tolerance.

In *Last Was Lloyd,* twelve-year-old Lloyd Albert, a mother-ridden and overweight sixth grader, is last in everything, especially school sports. As a result he is a bully and a glutton. Lloyd first picks on and then befriends another bright outsider, Ancil Witherspoon. She leads him into changing his behavior and establishing his independence from his over-protective mother.

The First Hard Times takes up where *Last Was Lloyd* left off. Ancil has to adjust to her mother's remarriage to Harvey Hutton and the family's subsequent move to the coastal Georgia town of Hanover. She clings to a futile hope that her real father Alexander will return, though he has been reported missing-in-action for eleven years. Her change from anger and grief to an acceptance of the new marriage is well handled.

Moonshadow of Cherry Mountain, a dog story set in the North Carolina mountains where the author has a simple A frame summer cabin, marked quite a departure in locale and main character. Moonshadow, a Labrador retriever, belongs to Greg, the fifteen-year-old son of school teachers Grant and Peg Riley. Just as the dog has to learn to adjust his territorial boundaries as the mountain lands are developed, so also people must adjust to families with different values who move in. And Greg has to adjust to the Riley's adoption of a daughter, who is allergic to, and frightened of, his beloved dog.

Laura Upside-Down attempts to explore severe religious intolerance and family conflicts. The central character Laura Catherine or "Cat" is happiest seeing the world upside down, hanging from a large tree. The novel deals with her attempts to see religious and family matters right side up. Her own family is agnostic. Her ten-year-old girlfriends Zipporah Greengold and Anna Banner come from an Orthodox Jewish family and a Fundamentalist Christian one. While researching the origins of Halloween, Thanksgiving, Hanukkah, and Christmas in preparation for seasonal parties, they learn tolerance for different views and persons. Unfortunately the messages and didacticism of the novel make for a very talky book, not one of action.

Much simpler and more believable is *Return to Bitter Creek.* Twelve-year-old Lacey Bittner, her mother Ann Campbell Bittner, and David Habib—her mother's lover of three years and a crafts blacksmith—return to the tiny mountain community of Bitter (i.e. Bittner) Creek, North Carolina, where Ann grew up, Lacey was born illegitimately, and from whence Ann fled when Lacey was two. An offer of a job for David at the local craft school brings the trio to Bitter Creek. Though it is another book about cultural, moral, and family differences, these concerns are embodied in the characters, who, major and minor, are strong and convincing. Smith's earlier books have been occasionally faulted for being too episodic or too crowded with peripheral details. This book has a nice unity; the final chapter echoes the opening with its title and action.

Karate Dancer features Smith's kind of paradoxical hero. Fourteen-year-old Troy Matthews, a karate enthusiast and political cartoonist for the local newspaper, is disappointed and resentful that his mother and father are not interested in his growing karate skills. In return he scorns their interests in music and photography. As the story develops, Troy and his family learn to meet each other halfway in their interests, while recognizing their differences. A romantic interest in Liesl Trunzo leads him to become her partner in the ballet *Coppelia.* His conflict with three karate students from a rival studio and his demonstration of karate skills to children with muscular dystrophy at a summer camp help him to redefine masculinity. Smith alludes skillfully to the developing sexuality of Troy and Liesl.

One of the most original current writers of young adult novels, Smith continues to surprise readers by the variety and depth of her books. In *Voyages,* fantasy adventures activate the story of twelve-year-old Janessa Kessel, forced to lie immobile in a hospital bed with a broken arm and back after being kidnapped and thrown from a car. The traumatized Janessa would prefer to isolate herself from parents, her brother and sister, the family dog, her friend Lynn, school, and the world by staying in her safe hospital bed. But when she unfolds a paper origami boat, it suddenly expands into the fabulous skin boat *Skidbladnir* piloted by the god Freyr. Through his help, her spiritual body is taken to the violent world of Norse myth, to such places as Asgard, Valhalla, and the caves of the Elves of Invaldi and to meet Odin, Thor, Loki, Sif, and fabulous animals. Her adventures in this fantasy world give her the courage at last to reject Asgard for Midgard and her life in this world.

The Pennywhistle Tree, a story of ordinary events in Hanover, Georgia, has a profound theme: how to relate to others vastly different in culture, economic class, and background without being either hostile or condescending. In late summer the large, poor white George family moves into a two-storey rental Victorian house on the same block of Carr Street, where Jonathon Douglas, an only child, lives with his atypical upper-middle class family: his mother is a professional restorer of houses; his father stays at home and writes action novels. The invasion of the Georges and their seven children threatens Jonathon's relationship with his closest chums Alex, Benjy, and Craig. Twelve-year-old Sanders George and his six siblings soon take over the Douglas yard and even the large tree where the four boys have played together for years. Sanders makes a pest of himself to get Jonathon's attention in the neighborhood and at school. Jonathon's ambivalent feelings prevent more than half gestures of friendship: giving the illiterate but musically talented Sanders his pennywhistle and some easy readers before the George family suddenly moves away. Only then does he regret the opportunity for friendship that he missed.

Doris Smith's latest book *Best Girl* set in Hanover, Georgia, uses a traumatic event in the author's life—the gutting of her home by an arsonist in 1984—as a catalyst in the life of imaginary heroine Nealy Compton. The author imagines Nealy to have had a secret hiding place beneath the house when it was burned. The story concerns her strained relationships in a modern alienated, divorced family. Docile Nealy is called her mother's "best girl," while she drives her fourteen-year-old sister from the house and later calls the police to arrest her for breaking back in the home. Isolated by her mother's lack of affection, Nealy makes her hiding place under Mrs. Dees's house into a substitute home—keeping books, her drawings, and a butterfly collection there. When it burns, Nealy is forced into forming relationships with others and establishing a sense of community. The sensitive Nealy and her sexually mature sister Noel Anne are believable, but the reader never gets emotionally involved with the other characters or the plot.

Ironically, Mrs. Compton is an official at the local department of human resources, but she cannot deal with the loss of human re-

sources in her life: the death of her mother, two brothers in the Vietnam War, and her divorce. Mrs. Dees, supposedly is a potter, but the story makes little reference to her skills, and Nealy, who has regularly hidden under the house, learns of the existence of her potter's studio only after the fire. A novel about alienation and frozen characters, *Best Girl* leaves readers largely uninvolved.

In all of her varied books, Doris Smith excels best at describing the exterior details and the inner life of all of her protagonists, whether nine or seventeen, male or female. She writes assuredly and honestly about problems and situations that they confront. Awards continue to attest to the high respect of readers and critics of modern young adult novels for her work.

—Hugh T. Keenan

———

SNYDER, Zilpha Keatley. American. Born in Lemoore, California, 11 May 1927. Educated at Whittier College, California, 1944-48, B.A. 1948; University of California, Berkeley, summers 1958-60. Married Larry Allan Snyder in 1950; one daughter, two sons. Writer. Public elementary school teacher, Washington School, Berkeley, California, and in New York, Washington, and Alaska, 1948-62; master teacher and demonstrator for education classes, University of California, Berkeley, 1959-61; lecturer. Recipient: George G. Stone Center for Children's Books award, 1973, Lewis Carroll Shelf award, Spring Book Festival first prize, both 1967, and Newbery honor book, 1968, all for *The Egypt Game;* Christopher Medal, 1971, for *The Changeling;* William Allen White award, Newbery honor book, Christopher Medal, all 1972, and Hans Christian Andersen International honor list of the International Board on Books for Young People, 1974, all for *The Headless Cupid; New York Times* Outstanding Book, 1972, National Book award finalist and Newbery honor book, both 1973, all for *The Witches of Worm; New York Times* Outstanding Book, 1981, for *A Fabulous Creature;* PEN Literary award, 1983, and Parent's Choice award, both for *The Birds of Summer;* Bay Area Book Reviewers award, 1988, William Allen White Master Reading List, 1989-90, and Georgia Children's Book award Master List, 1990-91, all for *And Condors Danced;* New Mexico State award, 1989-90, and on the Notable Trade Books in the Language Arts list of the National Council of Teachers of English, both for *The Changing Maze; Season of Ponies, The Egypt Game, The Headless Cupid, The Witches of Worm,* and *A Fabulous Creature* were all named American Library Association Notable Books; *The Velvet Room* and *The Egypt Game* were named on the *Horn Book* honor list; *The Velvet Room, The Changeling, The Headless Cupid, Below the Root, Until the Celebration,* and *Blair's Nightmare* were all Junior Literary Guild selections; *Blair's Nightmare* was included on state awards master lists in Missouri, Texas, Nebraska, Pacific Northwest, and New Mexico; *Libby on Wednesday* was on the Virginia state award master list. Address: 52 Miller Ave., Mill Valley, CA 94941, U.S.A.

PUBLICATIONS FOR YOUNG ADULTS

Fiction

Eyes in the Fishbowl, illustrated by Alton Raible. New York, Atheneum, 1968.

The Headless Cupid, illustrated by Alton Raible. New York, Atheneum, 1971; Guildford, Surrey, Lutterworth, 1973.

The Witches of Worm, illustrated by Alton Raible. New York, Atheneum, 1972.

Below the Root, illustrated by Alton Raible. New York, Atheneum, 1975.

A Fabulous Creature. New York, Atheneum, 1981.

The Birds of Summer. New York, Atheneum, 1983.

And Condors Danced. New York, Delacorte, 1987; London, Macmillan, 1989.

Libby on Wednesday. New York, Delacorte, 1990.

Song of the Gargoyle. New York, Delacorte, 1991.

Fool's Gold. New York, Delacorte, 1993.

PUBLICATIONS FOR CHILDREN

Fiction

Season of Ponies, illustrated by Alton Raible. New York, Atheneum, 1964.

The Velvet Room, illustrated by Alton Raible. New York, Atheneum, 1965.

Black and Blue Magic, illustrated by Gene Holtan. New York, Atheneum, 1966.

The Egypt Game, illustrated by Alton Raible. New York, Atheneum, 1967.

The Changeling, illustrated by Alton Raible. New York, Atheneum, 1970; Guildford, Surrey, Lutterworth, 1976.

The Princess and the Giants, illustrated by Beatrice Darwin. New York, Atheneum, 1973.

The Truth about Stone Hollow, illustrated by Alton Raible. New York, Atheneum, 1974; as *The Ghosts of Stone Hollow,* Guilford, Lutterworth, 1978.

And All Between, illustrated by Alton Raible. New York, Atheneum, 1976.

Until the Celebration, illustrated by Alton Raible. New York, Atheneum, 1977.

The Famous Stanley Kidnapping Case, illustrated by Alton Raible. New York, Atheneum, 1979.

Come On, Patsy, illustrated by Margot Zemach. New York, Atheneum, 1982.

Blair's Nightmare. New York, Atheneum, 1984.

The Changing Maze, illustrated by Charles Mikolaycak. New York, Macmillan, 1985.

The Three Men. New York, Harper, 1986.

Squeak Saves the Day and Other Tooley Tales, illustrated by Leslie Morrill. New York, Delacorte, 1988.

Janie's Private Eyes. New York, Delacorte, 1989.

Poetry

Today Is Saturday, photographs by John Arms. New York, Atheneum, 1969.

PUBLICATION FOR ADULTS

Novel

Heirs of Darkness. New York, Atheneum, 1978; London, Magnum, 1980.

Media Adaptations: *Black and Blue Magic* (filmstrip with tape), Pied Piper, 1975; *The Egypt Game* (recording and cassette), Miller-Brody, 1975; *The Headless Cupid* (from *Newbery Award Cassette* stories; recording and cassette), Miller-Brody, 1976, also (filmstrip with tape) Pied Piper, 1980; *The Witches of Worm* (recording), Miller-Brody, 1978; *Below the Root* (computer game), Spinnaker Software's Windham Classics, 1985; *The Egypt Game* (filmstrip and tape), Piped Piper.

Biography: Essay in *Something about the Author Autobiography Series,* Volume 2, Detroit, Gale, 1986; essay in *Speaking for Ourselves: Autobiographical Sketches by Notable Authors of Books for Young Adults,* Volume 1, compiled and edited by Donald R. Gallo, National Council of Teachers of English, 1990.

Manuscript Collection: Kerlan Collection, University of Minnesota, Minneapolis.

Critical Study: Entry in *Contemporary Literary Criticism,* Volume 17, Detroit, Gale, 1981.

*   *   *

Zilpha Keatley Snyder decided to become a writer at age eight when she discovered that books were written by real people. Snyder's books appeal to a wide range of readers from upper elementary to high school. Her topics are just as diverse covering magic, ghosts, mystery, murder, integration, witchcraft, drugs, dysfunctional families, and environmental awareness. For inspiration Snyder draws on memories of her own childhood and the stories told to her then, her students, and from some mysterious source outside herself.

Most of Snyder's books have a young girl as the main character, but she did change that format with her first book for young adults, *A Fabulous Creature,* about fifteen-year-old James Fielding, a professor's son on vacation in the Sierra Nevada mountains. Lonely and bored, James discovers a magnificent stag in a hidden canyon whom he begins to visit and ply regularly with apples. Then, in his adolescent need to impress the daughter of a rich game hunter, he inadvertently betrays the deer and must confront the consequences.

Snyder's second and best-known young adult novel, *Birds of Summer,* is just as timely today as it was in 1983. Fifteen-year-old Summer must deal with her emerging sexuality; the irresponsibility of her mother, Oriole, who leaves the rearing of seven-year-old Sparrow to Summer; loneliness; drugs; and friendship. Summer handles these problems with understanding and sophistication. Set in California in the 1980s, Summer's family lives in a trailer on property owned by the Fishers who have a son, Nicky, the same age as Summer. Oriole and the Fishers once lived in the same commune. Oriole tries to live as she did in those carefree days of the 70s, but now must depend on government welfare to do so. She has had many men in her life, but none ever stays long, including the fathers of her two daughters. Summer is especially bothered by the fact that she does not know her father who left before he knew Oriole was pregnant.

The only stable adults in her life are Mr. Pardell, her English teacher, and the Olivers, a rich family who hire Summer to clean house for them. Each of them knows the problems Summer faces, but the solution offered by the Olivers is for Summer to come live with them, which she agrees to do if they will also take Sparrow. They agree since they want Summer to work for them and they too have come to love Sparrow. In the end Summer sends Sparrow to the Olivers, and she stays with her mother.

Snyder deals with Summer's emerging sexuality with sensitivity. Summer and a girlfriend discuss sex, but it is of minor importance to Summer who must deal with the problems Oriole has managed to get the family into with her drug-raising boyfriend. Nicky had always been her best friend, but now, he, too, has discovered sex. She and Nicky realize that they are not ready for intimacy yet and join together in trying to extricate their parents from the difficulties they are in with the drug gang.

Snyder's "Green-sky" trilogy takes on the issues of violence as part of human nature, free access to knowledge, and the moral issues of governmental actions. Green-sky is a fantasy world of people living high above the forest floor in trees. The forest floor, a place of mystery and fear, is covered by impenetrable roots and below them are monsters trapped from entering the world of Green-sky. The falsification of history and governmental secrecy are a major motif as Raamo and Genaa, both thirteen, begin to find out the truth about the Pash-shan, the monsters who are below the roots.

Snyder is able to draw her readers into the worlds she creates, whether that is the fantasy world of Green-sky, or the real world of California or Nevada today. A versatile writer, Snyder has also written numerous books for younger children and one novel for adults.

—Hazel K. Davis

———

SOTO, Gary. American. Born in Fresno, California, 12 April 1952. Educated at California State University, Fresno, B.A. (magna cum laude) 1974; University of California, Irvine, M.F.A. 1976. Married Carolyn Oda in 1975; one daughter. Senior Lecturer in English, University of California, Berkeley. Recipient: Academy of American Poets Prize, 1975; award from *Nation,* 1975, for "The Discovery"; United States award from International Poetry Forum, 1976, for *The Elements of San Joaquín;* Bess Hokin Prize from *Poetry,* 1978; Guggenheim fellowship, 1980; creative writing fellowship from Endowment for the Arts, 1982 and 1991; Levinson award from *Poetry,* Chicago, 1984; American Book award from Before Columbus Foundation, 1985, for *Living up the Street;* California Arts Council fellowship, 1989; Andrew Carnegie Medal for video, 1993, with John Kelly, for *The Pool Party.* Address: 43 The Crescent, Berkeley, CA 94708-1701, U.S.A.

PUBLICATIONS FOR YOUNG ADULTS

Poetry

Editor and contributor, *Entrance: Four Chicano Poets,* with others. Greenfield Center, New York, Greenfield Review Press, 1976.
The Elements of San Joaquín. Pittsburgh, University of Pittsburgh Press, 1977.
The Tale of Sunlight. Pittsburgh, University of Pittsburgh Press, 1978.
Father Is a Pillow Tied to a Broom. Pittsburgh, Slow Loris Press, 1980.

Where Sparrows Work Hard. Pittsburgh, University of Pittsburgh Press, 1981.
Black Hair. Pittsburgh, University of Pittsburgh Press, 1985.
A Fire in My Hands. New York, Scholastic, 1990.
Who Will Know Us? San Francisco, Chronicle, 1990.
Home Course in Religion. San Francisco, Chronicle, 1991.
Neighborhood Odes, illustrated by David Diaz. San Diego, Harcourt, 1992.
Contributor, *I Thought I'd Take My Rat to School: Poems for September to June,* by Russell Hoban. Boston, Little, Brown, 1993.

Fiction

Small Faces. Houston, Texas, Arte Publico, 1986.
Taking Sides. San Diego, Harcourt, 1991.
Pacific Crossing. San Diego, Harcourt, 1992.
The Pool Party, illustrated by Robert Casilla. New York, Delacorte, 1993.
Crazy Weekend. New York, Scholastic, 1994.
Jesse. San Diego, Harcourt, 1994.

Short Stories

Baseball in April and Other Stories. San Diego, Harcourt, 1990.
Local News. San Diego, Harcourt, 1993.

Other

Living up the Street: Narrative Recollections. San Francisco, Strawberry Hill Press, 1985.
The Sadness of Days, edited by Luis O. Salinas. Houston, Texas, Arte Publico, 1987.
Editor, *California Childhood: Recollections and Stories of the Golden State.* Berkeley, California, Creative Arts, 1988.
Lesser Evils: Ten Quartets (essays). Houston, Texas, Arte Publico, 1988.
A Summer Life (essays). Hanover, New Hampshire, University Press of New England, 1990.
Editor, *Pieces of the Heart: New Chicano Fiction.* San Francisco, Chronicle Books, 1993.

PUBLICATIONS FOR CHILDREN

Fiction

The Cat's Meow. San Francisco, Strawberry Hill Press, 1987.
Too Many Tamales, illustrated by Ed Martinez. New York, Putnam, 1993.
The Skirt, illustrated by Eric Velasquez. New York, Delacorte, 1992.

*

Biography: Entry in *Dictionary of Literary Biography,* Volume 82: *Chicano Writers, First Series,* Detroit, Gale, 1989; essay in *Speaking for Ourselves, Too* compiled and edited by Donald R. Gallo, National Council of Teachers of English, 1993.

Critical Study: Entry in *Contemporary Literary Criticism,* Volume 32, Detroit, Gale, 1985.

Gary Soto comments:

For me, streets have always mattered. When I'm ready to write, ready to sit down, usually at our kitchen table, I conjure up inside my head an image of our old street in south Fresno, one that was torn down in the name of urban renewal at the beginning of the 1960s. It was, as one might imagine, a blighted area: a junk yard to the left of our house, Coleman Pickle across the street, a broom factory with its nightly *whack-whack* of straw taking shape and warehouses humming with machinery down the alley, and the almighty Sun-Maid Raisin factory in the distance. There were also weed-choked vacant lots where orange-colored cats wandered cautiously and gophers burrowed holes large enough to push a child's first through. I did this a number of times and usually just came up with a fist of loose dirt and feathery seed.

These are pictures that I take into my work, both in poetry and prose, pictures that stir the past, which I constantly haunt with an inventory list. They muster up a power inside me, a delicious feeling of memory, imagination, and the willingness to care for the smallest of objects—shards of glass, taps on my shoes, a chicken claw that I worked like a lever, a bicycle part, and an inner tube I rolled from one end of the yard to the other. In short, all the raw and discarded elements of the world.

*   *   *

Gary Soto has been called "one of the finest natural talents to emerge" from among today's Chicano writers by Alan Cheuse in the *New York Times Book Review.* An award-winning author best known for his poetry, short stories, and novels for young adults, Soto brings the sights and sounds of the barrio, the urban Spanish-speaking neighborhood where he was raised, vividly to life within the pages of his books. The shrill whistle of a nearby factory piercing the gleeful screams of playing children, the coarse oaths of playground brawls, picking grapes in the fields beneath a harsh sun that turns the air to dust—the reader experiences an abundance of small details characteristic of growing up in a Mexican American tradition. Soto recreates telling, intimate vignettes from his own childhood and adolescence: He allows us to stand beside him in his mother's kitchen amid the aroma of warm butter and tortillas browning in a black, cast-iron pan and shares with us the strong sense of love and loyalty characteristic of his working-class Hispanic heritage.

Although his parents were both American-born, their Mexican heritage figured strongly in his upbringing. Like many Mexican Americans, both Soto's parents and his grandparents labored in the fields picking grapes, oranges, and cotton, worked in the packing houses of the Sun Maid Raisin Company, or found jobs as factory or warehouse workers; their lives were typical of the Mexican American employed in the areas around Fresno, the industrial center of the agriculture-based San Joaquin Valley.

Memories of a childhood spent in the barrio, including recollections of growing up in impoverished surroundings as his mother, step-father, and grandparents struggled to provide the children with a secure home, of neighbors and friends, and of the ethnic cultural traditions he experienced throughout his youth, serve as a basis for Soto's writing. In *Living up the Street,* a collection of narratives first published in 1985, he vividly recreates incidents of his youth.

Soto was greatly influenced by what he calls "very rambunctious, lively, irreverent writers" such as Gregory Corso, Edward Field, Kenneth Koch, and, later, Weldon Kees, Theodore Roethke, Gabriel Garcia Marquez, and W. S. Merwin, writers whom Soto considers more sophisticated. Another major influence on Soto was the noted poet Philip Levine, his instructor in creative writing from 1972 to 1973.

Living up the Street was followed by *Small Faces,* a selection of prose memoirs published in 1986, and *Lesser Evils: Ten Quartets,* a collection of autobiographical essays about growing up near Fresno, California, that Soto published in 1988. In each of these works, the element of youthful fantasy figures largely, and vivid details and Soto's obvious fondness for people and places from his youth effectively recreate his own childhood for the reader. As a *Publishers Weekly* reviewer noted, Soto has an ability to make "the personal universal, and readers will feel privileged to share the vision of this man who finds life perplexing but a joy." His work may be imbued with his personal optimism and a sometimes poignant nostalgia, but it is poverty that serves as the thread binding the author, his friends, and his family together within Soto's narratives.

Soto has gone on to write several collections of short stories and novels specifically geared for youth. *Baseball in April, and Other Stories,* published in 1990, received both the American Library Association's "Best Book for Young Adults" designation and the Beatty Award. A collection of eleven short stories about everyday events in a modern-day Mexican American neighborhood, *Baseball in April* is praised by a *Horn Book* reviewer as "an acute [observation] of the desires, fears, and foibles of children and teenagers going about the business of daily living." The ethnic flavor of the barrio setting is intensified by the Spanish vocabulary that Soto scatters throughout the text—many of his books contain a glossary of Spanish terms at the back to aid non-Spanish speaking readers. Soto focuses on a different young person as the subject of each of his stories. Alfonso wants to transform himself from an awkward young man to an Aztec warrior in "Broken Chain": "Last week he did fifty sit-ups a day, thinking that he would burn those already apparent ripples on his stomach to even deeper ripples, dark ones, so when he went swimming at the canal next summer, girls in cutoffs would notice. And the guys would think he was tough, someone who could take a punch and give it back." But Alfonso finds that the girl he likes accepts him just the way he is. In "Mother and Daughter," Yollie is looking forward to the eighth-grade dance, but has no dress to wear. Her mother dyes Yollie's white summer dress black, but the night of the school dance turns into a disaster when Yollie gets caught in a cloudburst and the rain causes the black dye to run.

Soto's depiction of the Americanization of a generation of Latino teenagers is one of the themes unifying his writing for young adults. Media pressures figure strongly in the lives of his characters: Alfonso wants his hair to look like that of the rock singer, Prince. Young Veronica covets a Barbie doll after watching numerous Barbie commercials, and a pretend one won't do. Fausto covets a guitar so that he can accomplish his mission in life: "to play guitar in his own band; to sweat out his songs and prance around the stage; to make money and dress weird." Unconscious of the threat of poverty weighing upon the shoulders of their parents—hard-working men and women trying to support their families as night watchmen, warehousemen, auto mechanics, and teacher's aides—the young people in Soto's stories are caught up in the commercialism aimed at a more affluent, primarily white culture.

While Soto's writing takes place in the ethnic neighborhoods that are familiar to him, the conflicts faced by his young protagonists are universal. One example is Soto's 1991 novel, *Taking Sides,* about an eighth-grade Mexican American boy named Lincoln

Mendoza. One of the best basketball players on his school team, Lincoln's loyalties become divided after he and his mother move from the Mission District barrio in San Francisco, where he grew up, to the wealthier white suburb of Sycamore, California. Although he has problems fitting in at his new school, Lincoln joins the basketball team in his new junior high school. As a crucial basketball game between his old team and his new team approaches, Lincoln finds himself involved in confrontations with his coach and teammates, as well as with himself, as he wrestles with the fear that he is somehow a traitor to his old neighborhood. Soto's study of sportsmanship and loyalty ends on a positive note as the young man adapts to his circumstances in a mature way, makes peace with both his old and new friends, and learns a valuable lesson about maintaining his individuality and trusting in himself.

While much of his inspiration comes from the events of his Mexican American upbringing, Soto has expressed concern that limitations might be placed upon him because of his ethnic background. Rather than remain in a separate category and be judged solely against other Chicano writers, Soto wants his work to be considered on its own merits: "One of the things I would like to do is make that leap from being a Chicano writer to being simply a writer," he told Jean W. Ross in an interview for *Contemporary Authors.*

Soto's ability to tell a story, to recreate moments of his own past in a manner that transcends the boundaries of race or age, to transport his reader to the world of his own childhood is felt within each of his written works. "Soto's remembrances are as sharply defined and appealing as bright new coins," writes Alicia Fields in the *Bloomsbury Review.* "His language is spare and simple yet vivid." But it is his joyful outlook, strong enough to transcend the poverty of the barrio, that makes his work so popular. The optimism with which he views his own life radiates from each of his young characters—Soto views life as a gift and his talent for expression is his gift to his readers.

—Pamela L. Shelton

———

SOUTHALL, Ivan (Francis). Australian. Born in Canterbury, Victoria, 8 June 1921. Educated at Chatham State School; Mont Albert Central School; Box Hill Grammar School; Melbourne Technical College, 1937-41. Served in the Australian Army, 1941, the Royal Australian Air Force, 1942-46, pilot, 1942-44, and war historian, 1945-46; became flight lieutenant; received Distinguished Flying Cross. Married 1) Joyce Blackburn in 1945 (divorced), one son and three daughters; 2) Susan Stanton in 1976. Engraver, Melbourne *Herald and Weekly Times,*, 1936-41, 1947; free-lance writer, since 1948. Whittall Lecturer, Library of Congress, Washington, D.C., 1973; May Hill Arbuthnot Honor Lecturer, University of Washington, Seattle, 1974; writer-in-residence, MacQuarie University, Sydney, 1978. Past president, Community Youth Organization, Victoria; foundation president, Knoxbrooke Training Centre for the Intellectually Handicapped, Victoria. Recipient: Australian Children's Council Book of the Year award, 1966, for *Ash Road,* 1968, for *To the Wild Sky,* 1971, for *Bread and Honey,* and 1976, for *Fly West;* Australian picture book of the year award, 1969, for *Sly Old Wardrobe;* Japanese Government's Children's Welfare and Culture Encouragement award, 1969, for *Ash Road;* Carnegie Medal, British Library Association, 1971, for *Josh;* Zilver

Griffel (Netherlands), 1972, for *To the Wild Sky;* Australian Writers award, 1974, for *Matt and Jo;* member, Order of Australia, 1981; National Children's Book award (Australia), 1986, for *The Long Night Watch.* Address: P.O. Box 25, Healesville, VIC 3777, Australia.

PUBLICATIONS FOR YOUNG ADULTS

Fiction

Finn's Folly. Sydney and London, Angus & Robertson, and New York, St. Martin's, 1969.
Bread and Honey. Sydney and London, Angus & Robertson, 1970; as *Walk a Mile and Get Nowhere,* Englewood Cliffs, New Jersey, Bradbury, 1970.
Josh. Sydney and London, Angus & Robertson, 1971; New York, Macmillan, 1972.
Matt and Jo. Sydney, Angus & Robertson, and New York, Macmillan, 1973; London, Angus & Robertson, 1974.
Fly West. London, Angus & Robertson, 1974; New York, Macmillan, 1975.
What about Tomorrow? Sydney and London, Angus & Robertson, and New York, Macmillan, 1977.
King of the Sticks. Sydney, Collins, London, Methuen, and New York, Greenwillow, 1979.
The Golden Goose. London, Methuen, and New York, Greenwillow, 1981.
The Long Night Watch. London, Methuen, 1983; New York, Farrar, Straus, 1984.
A City out of Sight. Sydney, Angus & Robertson, 1984; London, Angus & Robertson, 1985.
Rachel. Sydney and London, Angus & Robertson, and New York, Farrar, Straus, 1986.
Blackbird. New York, Farrar, Straus, 1988; Melbourne, Heinemann, 1992.
The Mysterious World of Marcus Leadbeater. New York, Farrar, Straus, 1990; Melbourne, Heinemann, 1991.

Other

Seventeen Seconds. Sydney, Hodder & Stoughton, 1973; Leicester, Brockhampton, and New York, Macmillan, 1973.
Let the Balloon Go (screenplay), with others, 1976.

PUBLICATIONS FOR CHILDREN

Fiction

Meet Simon Black, illustrated by Frank Norton. Sydney and London, Angus & Robertson, 1950.
Simon Black in Peril [in Space, in Coastal Command, in China, and the Spaceman, in the Antarctic, Takes Over, at Sea], illustrated by I. Maher and Wal Stackpool. Sydney and London, Angus & Robertson, 1951-62.
Hills End, illustrated by Jim Phillips. Sydney and London, Angus & Robertson, 1962; New York, St. Martin's, 1963.
Ash Road, illustrated by Clem Seale. Sydney and London, Angus & Robertson, 1965, New York, St. Martin's, 1966.
The Fox Hole, illustrated by Ian Ribbons. Sydney, Hicks Smith, London, Methuen, and New York, St. Martin's, 1967.

To the Wild Sky, illustrated by Jennifer Tuckwell. Sydney and London, Angus & Robertson, and New York, St. Martin's 1967.

Let the Balloon Go, illustrated by Ian Ribbons. Sydney, Hicks Smith, London, Methuen, and New York, St. Martin's, 1968.

Sly Old Wardrobe, illustrated by Ted Greenwood. Melbourne, Cheshire, and London, Angus & Robertson, 1968; New York, St. Martin's, 1969.

Chinaman's Reef Is Ours. Sydney and London, Angus & Robertson, and New York, St. Martin's 1970.

Head in the Clouds, illustrated by Richard Kennedy. Sydney and London, Angus & Robertson, 1972; New York, Macmillan, 1973.

Over the Top, illustrated by Ian Ribbons. Sydney, Hicks Smith, and London, Methuen, 1972; as *Benson Boy,* illustrated by Ingrid Fetz, New York, Macmillan, 1972.

Three Novels (contains *The Fox Hole, Let the Balloon Go,* and *Over the Top*). London, Methuen, 1975.

Christmas in the Tree. Sydney, Hodder & Stoughton, 1985.

Other

Journey into Mystery: A Story of the Explorers Burke and Willis, illustrated by Robin Goodall. Melbourne, Lansdowne, 1961.

Lawrence Hargrave. Melbourne, Oxford University Press, 1964.

Rockets in the Desert: The Story of Woomera. Sydney, Angus & Robertson, 1964; London, Angus & Robertson, 1965.

Indonesian Journey. Melbourne, Lansdowne, 1965; London, Newnes, and Boston, Ginn, 1966.

The Sword of Esau: Bible Stories Retold, illustrated by Joan Kiddell-Monroe. Sydney, Angus and Robertson, 1967; New York, St. Martin's, 1968.

Bushfire!, illustrated by Julie Mattox. Sydney, Angus & Robertson, 1968.

The Curse of Cain: Bible Stories Retold, illustrated by Joan Kiddell-Monroe. Sydney, Angus & Robertson, and New York, St. Martin's, 1968.

PUBLICATIONS FOR ADULTS

Novels

Flight to Gibraltar. Sydney, Horwitz, 1958; as *Terror Flight,* 1962.

Third Pilot. Sydney, Horwitz, 1958.

Mediterranean Black. Sydney, Horwitz, 1959.

Mission to Greece. Sydney, Horwitz, 1959.

Sortie in Cyrenaica. Sydney, Horwitz, 1959

Atlantic Pursuit. Sydney, Horwitz, 1960.

Short Stories

Out of the Dawn: Three Short Stories. Privately printed, 1942.

Other

The Weaver from Meltham (biography of Godfrey Hirst), illustrated by George Colville. Melbourne, Whitcombe & Tombs, 1950.

The Story of the Hermitage: The First Fifty Years of the Geelong Church of England Girls' Grammar School. Melbourne, Cheshire, 1956.

They Shall Not Pass Unseen. Sydney, Angus & Robertson, 1956.

A Tale of Box Hill: Day of the Forest. Box Hill, Victoria, Box Hill City Council, 1957.

Bluey Truscott: Squadron Leader Keith William Truscott, R.A.A.F., D.F.C. and Bar. Sydney, Angus & Robertson, 1958.

Softly Tread the Brave: A Triumph over Terror, Devilry, and Death by Mine Disposal Officers John Stuart Mould and Hugh Randall Syme. Sydney, Angus & Robertson, 1960.

Parson on the Track: Bush Brothers in the Australian Outback. Melbourne, Lansdowne, 1962.

Woomera. Sydney, Angus & Robertson, 1962.

Indonesia Face to Face. Melbourne, Lansdowne, 1964; London, Angus & Robertson, 1965.

Editor, *The Challenge—Is the Church Obsolete? An Australian Response to the Challenge of Modern Society* (essays). Melbourne, Lansdowne, 1966.

A Journey of Discovery: On Writing for Children. London, Kestrel, 1975; New York, Macmillan, 1976.

*

Biography: Essay in *Something about the Author Autobiography Series,* Volume 3, Detroit, Gale, 1987; essay in *Speaking for Ourselves, Too* compiled and edited by Donald R. Gallo, National Council of Teachers of English, 1993.

Critical Study: Entry in *Children's Literature Review,* Volume 2, Detroit, Gale, 1976.

Ivan Southall comments:

I wrote my first book for young people before the outbreak of the Second World War. It was published in 1950. Since then the world has changed. So have I. I played a part in the change that came upon the books that young people read, but few people of mature years can fail to observe that books and the world have gone on changing. I have become less and less concerned with the external adventure that once challenged me on paper and in life; more and more I'm concerned with the remarkable world that we inhabit internally.

*   *   *

In forty years as a novelist Ivan Southall has lived through great changes in Australian children's literature. His range is dazzling—from entertainment to profound philosophical enquiry—and yet in another sense he has spent the whole of his writing life in an attempt to make sense of a single theme, which he describes as "the thrust for personal survival, whilst struggling with duty, discipline and the expectation of others."

Southall began his career as a writer of children's fiction with the "Simon Black" series about a Royal Australian Air Force pilot who "possessed an incredible measure of virtue, honour, righteous anger, courage and inventiveness." In 1962 readers were startled and impressed by his new novel, *Hills End,* the story of a group of children who have to cope on their own when their town is cut off by floods, a book very different from Simon Black's formulaic adventures and from the holiday adventures of writers like Arthur Ransome, where middle-class children escape from parental restraints to go boating or camping without ever running into any real danger.

Indeed, Southall's next series of novels might better be described as survival stories than as adventure stories. In successive books during the next eight years, groups of children faced a bushfire in *Ash Road,* a fall into a mine shaft in *The Fox Hole,* being marooned on a deserted island in *To the Wild Sky,* a multiple-car crash in *Finn's Folly,* and a takeover of their town by a mining company in *Chinaman's Reef Is Ours.* In each book one of the boy characters faces a struggle with courage at a significant point in the novel, although this struggle never provides the central narrative impetus. The group itself, greater than the sum of its parts, is the true hero of the survival stories, and Southall's special achievement is the way he charts the fluctuations of the group mood.

During the 1970s, along with the majority of Australian children's writers, Southall began to pay more attention to notions of masculinity and femininity. However, where most writers concentrated on stretching the limits for their female characters, Southall zeroed in on the boys in his survival stories to construct a searching analysis of masculinity. This shift of focus, prefigured in *Let the Balloon Go,* becomes fully apparent in *Bread and Honey,* set around Australia's most masculine institution, Anzac Day, a commemoration of the Australian force's heroic stand at Gallipoli in World War I. Torn between the opposing philosophies of his scientist father and his story-telling grandmother, Michael Cameron is gradually forced to take his own semi-heroic stand against Bully Boy MacBaren in a novel where every word counts and every action raises simultaneous questions about the scientific and romantic perspectives of war, about civilization and violence.

By contrast, *Josh* is a more leisurely and expansive novel, giving full play to the characteristic Southall interior monologue with its carefully crafted rhythms that are sometimes biblical, sometimes Shakespearean, and always Australian. Josh Plowman goes to Ryan's Creek expecting to take a thoughtful look at his family history but instead finds himself staggering through a series of Chaplinesque accidents, mocked by the local children and lectured by his formidable Aunt Clara. However, the intensely normative pressures on Josh in fact make him more aware of his own choices, and while he looks back without anger at Ryan's Creek, he heads forward into a different kind of future: "Go away, crows. Find yourself a body that's had its day. I'm walking mine back to Melbourne town and living every mile."

After these substantial achievements came an interlude of playfulness with the mellow comedy of *Over the Top* and the romantic mood of *Matt and Jo.* Following two books based on his wartime experiences, there came a period described in the cover notes to *What about Tomorrow* as three years of personal anguish, during which Southall believed "his sun had set." An intriguing mixture of folklore patterns with an uncharacteristic abundance of realistic detail about the Depression, *What about Tomorrow* led directly into Southall's most purely celebratory novel, *King of the Sticks,* where the gold rush setting suitably distances a tale of forests and bandits and younger sons who start as simpletons but turn out to possess a special intuition. Its sequel, *The Golden Goose,* however, was completely overwhelmed by the riot of language, and Southall never finished the planned trilogy.

Instead he turned back to some of his earlier narrative modes. *The Long Night Watch* recalls the documentary fiction of his wartime books; *A City out of Sight,* the sequel to *To the Wild Sky,* is disturbingly similar in style to its predecessor, written seventeen years earlier; *Rachel,* Southall's only novel about a young woman, is basically another survival story, and interestingly, his girl character faces the same rites of passage as the boys.

But Southall is an expert at stepping back in order to leap forward. In *Blackbird,* set during World War II, he confronts Will

Houghton with a classic choice between heroism and self-preservation, expanding on these choices in an inspired and surreal dialogue between Will and a vengeful blackbird whose fledgling has been killed by flying against the Houghtons' window. As Will explains consequences and responsibility to the bird, he begins to understand them for himself, turning from his war games to start clearing away the dangerous debris around his house. Will's decision carries the questioning of *Bread and Honey* and *Josh* to an authoritative conclusion—until Southall throws all the questions open again in his next novel.

The Mysterious World of Marcus Leadbeater is a wild book where dreams and metaphors have the validity of facts, and facts themselves are not to be relied on. Gramps, a charismatic wit and womanizer, impresses Marcus far more than does his steady and reliable father, but Marcus's identification with his grandfather's life carries over to an identification with his grandfather's death, and the powerful but enigmatic ending represents Southall's most strenuous testing of concepts of masculinity to date.

—Jenny Pausacker

SPARK, Muriel (Sarah). British. Born in Edinburgh, Scotland, 1 February 1918. Educated at James Gillespie's School for Girls and Heriot Watt College, both Edinburgh. Married S.O. Spark in 1937 (divorced); one son. Writer. Employed in the Political Intelligence Department of the British government's Foreign Office, 1944-45; affiliated with *Argentor* (jewelry trade magazine); general secretary, Poetry Society, 1947-49; founder, *Forum* (literary magazine), and editor of *Poetry Review,* London, 1949; part-time editor, Peter Owen Ltd. (publishing company); writer. Recipient: *Observer* short story prize, 1951, for "The Seraph and the Zambesi"; Prix Italia, 1962, for radio play adaptation of *The Ballad of Peckham Rye;* Yorkshire Post Book of the Year award, 1965, and James Tait Black Memorial Prize, 1966, both for *The Mandelbaum Gate;* Order of the British Empire, 1967; Booker McConnell Prize nomination, 1981, for *Loitering with Intent;* First Prize, F.N.A.C. La Meilleur Recueil des Nouvelles Etrangeres, 1987, for the Editions Fayard translation of *The Stories of Muriel Spark;* Officier de l'Ordre des Arts et des Lettres, France, 1988; Bram Stoker award, 1988; Royal Bank of Scotland—Saltire Society award, 1988. D.Litt., University of Strathclyde, Glasgow, 1971; University of Edinburgh, 1989. Fellow, Royal Society of Literature, 1963; Honorary Member, American Academy, 1978. O.B.E. (Officer, Order of the British Empire), 1967; Officer, Order of Arts and Letters (France), 1988. Agent: Georges Borchardt, Inc., 136 E. 57th St., New York, NY 10022.

PUBLICATIONS

Novels

The Comforters. London, Macmillan, and Philadelphia, Lippincott, 1957.
Robinson. London, Macmillan, and Philadelphia, Lippincott, 1958.
Memento Mori. London, Macmillan, and Philadelphia, Lippincott, 1959.

The Bachelors. London, Macmillan, 1960; Philadelphia, Lippincott, 1961.

The Ballad of Peckham Rye. London, Macmillan, and Philadelphia, Lippincott, 1960.

The Prime of Miss Jean Brodie. London, Macmillan, 1961; Philadelphia, Lippincott, 1962.

The Girls of Slender Means. London, Macmillan, and New York, Knopf, 1963.

The Mandelbaum Gate. London, Macmillan, and New York, Knopf, 1965.

The Public Image. London, Macmillan, and New York, Knopf, 1968.

The Driver's Seat. London, Macmillan, and New York, Knopf, 1970.

Not to Disturb. London, Macmillan, 1971; Viking, 1972.

The Abbess of Crewe. London, Macmillan, and New York, Viking, 1973.

The Hothouse by the East River. London, Macmillan, and New York, Viking, 1973.

The Takeover. London, Macmillan, and New York, Viking, 1976.

Territorial Rights. London, Macmillan, and New York, Coward, 1979.

Loitering with Intent. London, Bodley Head, and New York, Coward, 1981.

The Only Problem. London, Bodley Head, and New York, Coward, 1984.

A Far Cry from Kensington. London, Constable, and Boston, Houghton, 1988.

Symposium. London, Constable, and Boston, Houghton, 1990.

Short Stories

The Go-Away Bird and Other Stories. London, Macmillan, 1958; Philadelphia, Lippincott, 1960.

Voices at Play (includes the radio plays *The Party through the Wall, The Interview, The Dry River Bed, The Danger Zone*). London, Macmillan, 1961; Philadelphia, Lippincott, 1962.

Collected Stories I. London, Macmillan, 1967; New York, Knopf, 1968.

Bang-Bang You're Dead and Other Stories. London, Granada, 1982.

The Stories of Muriel Spark. New York, Dutton, 1985; London, Bodley Head, 1987.

Poetry

Out of a Book (as Muriel Camberg). Leith, Midlothian, Millar & Burden, 1933.

The Fanfarlo and Other Verse. Aldington, Kent, Hand and Flower Press, 1952.

Collected Poems I. London, Macmillan, 1967; New York, Knopf, 1968.

Going Up to Sotheby's and Other Poems. London, Granada, 1982.

Plays

Doctors of Philosophy (produced London, 1962). London, Macmillan, 1963; New York, Knopf, 1966.

Radio Plays: *The Party through the Wall,* 1957; *The Interview,* 1958; *The Dry River Bed,* 1959; *The Ballad of Peckham Rye,* 1960; *The Danger Zone,* 1961.

Other

Editor, with Derek Stanford, *Tribute to Wordsworth.* London, Wingate, 1950.

Child of Light: A Reassessment of Mary Wollstonecraft Shelley. London, Tower Bridge Publications, 1951; revised edition, as *Mary Shelley: A Biography,* New York, Dutton, 1987; London, Constable, 1988.

Editor, *A Selection of Poems,* by Emily Brontë. London, Grey Walls Press, 1952.

Emily Brontë: Her Life and Work, with Derek Stanford. London, Owen, 1953; New York, British Book Centre, 1960.

John Masefield. London, Nevill, 1953.

Editor, with Derek Stanford, *My Best Mary: The Letters of Mary Shelley.* London, Wingate, 1953.

Editor, *The Brontë Letters.* London, Nevill, 1954; as *The Letters of the Brontës: A Selection,* Norman, University of Oklahoma Press, 1954.

Editor, with Derek Stanford, *Letters of John Henry Newman.* London, Owen, 1957.

The Very Fine Clock (for children). New York, Knopf, 1968; London, Macmillan, 1969.

Curriculum Vitae: Autobiography. Boston, Houghton, 1993.

*

Media Adaptations: Several of Muriel Spark's novels have been adapted for the stage, film, and television. *Memento Mori* (dramatization on stage), in 1964; *The Prime of Miss Jean Brodie* (Jay Presson Allen's dramatization, published by Samuel French, 1969, in Torquay, England, at the Princess Theatre beginning April 5, 1966, then in Boston at the Colonial Theatre from December 26, 1967, to January 6, 1968, and finally on Broadway at the Helen Hayes Theatre beginning January 9, 1968); Allen also wrote the screenplay for the 1969 film version of the same novel, a Twentieth Century-Fox production starring Maggie Smith; John Wood's dramatization of *The Prime of Miss Jean Brodie* was produced in London at Wyndham's Theatre in 1967, and on Broadway in 1968; a six-part adaptation of the novel appeared on public television in England in 1978 and in the United States in 1979; *The Driver's Seat* (film), 1972; *The Girls of Slender Means* (T.V.), 1974; *Nasty Habits* (film), 1976.

Biography: Entry in *Dictionary of Literary Biography,* Volume 15: *British Novelists, 1930-1959,* Detroit, Gale, 1983.

Bibliography: *Iris Murdoch and Muriel Spark: A Bibliography* by Thomas A. Tominaga, and Wilma Schneidermeyer, Metuchen, New Jersey, Scarecrow Press, 1976.

Critical Studies: *Muriel Spark: A Biographical and Critical Study* by Derek Stanford, Fontwell, Sussex, Centaur Press, 1963; *Muriel Spark* by Karl Malkoff, New York, Columbia University Press, 1968; *Muriel Spark* by Patricia Stubbs, London, Longman, 1973; entry in *Contemporary Literary Criticism,* Detroit, Gale, Volume 2, 1974; Volume 3, 1975; Volume 5, 1976; Volume 8, 1978; Volume 13, 1980; Volume 18, 1981; Volume 40, 1987; *Muriel Spark* by Peter Kemp, London, Elek, 1974, New York, Barnes & Noble, 1975; *Muriel Spark* by Allan Massie, Edinburgh, Ramsey Head Press, 1979; *The Faith and Fiction of Muriel Spark* by Ruth Whittaker, London, Macmillan, 1982, New York, St. Martin's Press, 1983;

Comedy and the Woman Writer: Woolf, Spark, and Feminism by Judy Little, Lincoln, University of Nebraska Press, 1983; *Muriel Spark: An Odd Capacity for Vision* edited by Alan Bold, London, Vision Press, and New York, Barnes and Noble, 1984, and *Muriel Spark* by Bold, London, Methuen, 1986; *Muriel Spark* by Belma Bourgeois Richmond, New York, Ungar, 1984; *The Art of the Real: Muriel Spark's Novels* by Joseph Hynes, Rutherford, New Jersey, Fairleigh Dickinson University Press, 1988; *Muriel Spark* by Norman Page, London, Macmillan, 1990; *Vocation and Identity in the Fiction of Muriel Spark* by Rodney Stenning Edgecombe, Columbia, University of Missouri Press, 1990.

*   *   *

The Prime of Miss Jean Brodie, like all of Muriel Spark's books, is not a young adult novel in the sense that it was not written particularly for young adults. But because it is the story of six girls who come of age under the influence of an eccentric woman in the extremes of her prime, the book has "infiltrated" (a suitable word for a book written by someone as sly as Spark) the young adult shelves, and is therefore the Spark novel one is most likely to discover while in the young adult reading years. It's one of those little books that is not as little it as seems; the largeness of the matters at its heart—some of them rather dark—and the liberties taken with its form are disguised by wit, charm, and faultless craftsmanship. In that way, it's a deceptive kind of book, just as Muriel Spark is a deceptive kind of writer.

In many ways, she is a traditional novelist, as she goes about creating intellectual narratives with more or less complex plot schemes and patterns of events about people and their thoughts, feelings, and actions. At the same time, however, she takes the traditional conventions of the novel—things like point of view, climax, chronological progression—and does surprising, crafty things with them. The mysteries of religion and human behavior are at the core of all her work, and she very often makes use of bizarre, supernatural events that raise more questions than they answer. One gets the feeling that Spark would be a formidable chess opponent with her ability to see into space and then somehow create a pattern of calculated moves that bring her work to its desired conclusion. For Spark, creating forms seems to be just as important as creating fictions.

Miss Jean Brodie is a teacher in an Edinburgh school for girls who decides to devote her prime years to six chosen students whom she believes, under her tutelage, will become "the creme de la creme." An authoritarian who bucks authority, Miss Brodie follows her own progressive principles of education, schooling her girls in her favorite subjects—romance, art, and Italian politics—all the while keeping a sample math problem on the blackboard or instructing the girls to keep their history books in front of them in case her nemesis, the headmistress, should appear. The six soon become like "a body with Miss Brodie for the head." (The story is set in the 1930s, and the rise of fascism in Italy, where Miss Brodie spends her holidays, provides an obvious and interesting parallel to her methods.) However, beneath the surface along which the story does its amusing hops, skips, and jumps, larger motivational concerns are at the boil and begin to bubble up into the story. As the girls grow older, it becomes clear that Miss Brodie's intentions are not selfless ones. She has been grooming her girls so that she might vicariously experience through them the life and love that has been otherwise unattainable to her. She goes too far and one of the girls betrays her.

Spark tells us up front this is going to happen. She even tells us who will do it. These details come in unexpected bits and pieces as she moves back and forth in time in order to reveal what the Brodie girls will become later in life and what they will think about events that have yet to unfold. She doesn't bother much with the things her characters do so much as why they do them and what effects such motives have. This is characteristic of all Spark's fiction. She routinely gives away her endings, "spoils" what might have been climactic surprises, and moves back and forth with ease between past, present, and future. By doing this, she dispenses with the questions readers traditionally ask of plots (What will happen next? Who is responsible? When will we find out?) so that we might begin to ask deeper ones: Is Miss Brodie really leading out what is already in her students's souls, as she claims, or is she really thrusting in her own ideas, a method for which she criticizes traditional educators? At what point does nonconformity become conformity? Does one of Miss Brodie's girls betray her merely to stop her or is the motivation something deeper, something as much spiritual as it is personal? To what extent is loyalty a part of the betrayal? What is the truth of this novel? How, by thwarting, manipulating, and repatterning readers's expectations does the author make her fiction like life?

If Spark's fiction is sometimes steely and surgical and always lacking in the lifelike clutter of emotional response, it is because she seems to be dealing in carefully patterned parables; her fiction presents real life only to the extent that deeper truths about human nature, its good and its evil, can emerge. She leaves her readers in a Miss Brodie-like position to experience these truths vicariously through her fiction. Spark does this with the same instinct, insight, and economy of method that her characters admire and congratulate each other for. *The Prime of Miss Jean Brodie,* as it provides readers with a new way to experience and consider the novel, is a good introduction to Spark's other work as well as to further exploration of modern fiction.

—Tracy J. Sukraw

———

SPEARE, Elizabeth George. American. Born in Melrose, Massachusetts, 21 November 1908. Educated at Smith College, Northampton, Massachusetts, 1926-27; Boston University, Massachusetts, A.B. 1930, M.A. 1932. Married Alden Speare, 26 September 1936; one daughter and one son. English teacher, Rockland High School, Rockland, Massachusetts, 1932-35, and Auburn High School, Auburn, Massachusetts, 1935-36. Since 1955, writer. Recipient: Society of Colonial Wars Award from the State of New York, and Newbery Medal from the American Library Association, both 1959, International Board on Books for Young People (IBBY) Honor List, and selected one of American Institute of Graphic Arts Children's Books, both 1960, and New England Round Table Children's Librarians Award, 1976, all for *The Witch of Blackbird Pond;* Newbery Medal, 1962, and IBBY Honor List, 1964, both for *The Bronze Bow;* one of American Library Association's Best Young Adult Books, Teachers' Choice from the National Council of Teachers of English, one of Child Study Association of America's Children's Book of the Year, one of *School Library Journal*'s Best Books of the Year, a *Booklist* Children's Reviewers Choice, and one of *New York Times* Outstanding Books, all 1983, and Newbery Medal Honor Book, Scott O'Dell Award for Historical Fiction, and Christopher Award, all 1984, all for *The Sign of the Beaver;* Laura Ingalls Wilder Award, 1989, for a distinguished and enduring contribution to children's literature. Address: 7500 Calla Sin Envidia, Tucson, AZ, 85718, U.S.A.

PUBLICATIONS FOR YOUNG ADULTS

Novels

Calico Captive, illustrated by W.T. Mars. Boston, Houghton Mifflin, 1957; London, Gollancz, 1963.
The Witch of Blackbird Pond, illustrated by Nicholas Angelo. Boston, Houghton Mifflin, 1958; London, Gollancz, 1960.
The Bronze Bow. Boston, Houghton Mifflin, 1961; London, Gollancz, 1962.
The Sign of the Beaver, illustrated by Robert Andrew Parker. Boston, Houghton Mifflin, 1983; London, Gollancz, 1984.

Other

Child Life in New England, 1790-1840. Sturbridge, Massachusetts, Old Sturbridge Village, 1961.
Life in Colonial America. New York, Random House, 1963.

PUBLICATIONS FOR ADULTS

Novel

The Prospering. Boston, Houghton Mifflin, and London, Gollancz, 1967.

*

Media Adaptations: *Abby, Julia and the Cows* (television play; based on an article for *American Heritage),* Southern New England Telephone Company, 1958; *The Bronze Bow* (record, cassette, filmstrip with cassette), Random House; *The Witch of Blackbird Pond* (cassette), Random House; *The Sign of the Beaver* (cassette, filmstrip with cassette), Random House.

Manuscript Collection: Mugar Memorial Library, Boston University, Massachusetts.

Biography: *More Junior Authors,* New York, H.W. Wilson, 1963; *Elizabeth George Speare* by Marilyn Fain Apseloff, New York, Twayne, 1991; essay in *Speaking for Ourselves, Too* compiled and edited by Donald R. Gallo, National Council of Teachers of English, 1993.

Critical Study: Entry in *Children's Literature Review,* Volume 8, Detroit, Gale.

*   *   *

Elizabeth George Speare's stories illuminate history through her well-defined characters and fascinating plots. Four out of five of her novels display a particular interest in North American life in the late seventeenth and early eighteenth centuries. Two are based on

the lives of historically documented personages, while in the other two, the main characters are believable composites; all provide unique vision into their specific historical periods as well as underlining the universality of the themes presented. A fifth historical novel is set in Palestine at the time of Christ and is also linked to the others by common themes which transcend issues of race and culture.

The protagonists in Speare's work—two young men and three young women—range in age from thirteen to nineteen, and all struggle with issues of maturity and self-determination. Confronted with rigid legalism, bigotry, and injustice, these characters often find themselves acting outside of society's prescribed roles in order to follow their developing convictions. Although a strong moral tone pervades Speare's work, the vitality and ever present humanity of her characters excludes didacticism.

In her first novel, *Calico Captive,* (1957) Speare spins a fast-moving tale, based on the real experience of Susanna Johnson, captured from her New England home in an Indian raid, forced to march north where she is caught up in the French and Indian War, and finally sold as a servant to a rich family in Montreal. The detailed descriptions and active use of dialogue create a compelling picture of both the geographical terrain and the colonial conflicts of the time; however Speare's depiction of the Abenaki Indian captors is stereotypical at best, and even her principal characters appear somewhat predictable and idealized.

This is not the case in her next work, *The Witch of Blackbird Pond* (1961), however, in which the sixteen-year-old Kit presents a strong and well-defined female protagonist. Kit arrives on a ship from Barbados to stay with her uncle's family at the colony of Wethersfield, Connecticut. With her "foreign" ways and boyish assertiveness, Kit is regarded suspiciously by the puritan community as she struggles to reconcile her own spontaneity with the rigid constrictions of that society. Defying convention, she befriends an isolated old woman and teaches a young girl to read, but in doing so brings upon herself hysterical accusations of witchcraft which eventually lead to a trial. In this captivating story, well worthy of its Newbery Medal, the adversity Kit faces, serves to mature the strength and exuberance of her character as she works through disillusionment and alienation to understanding and compassion.

Speare introduces a male protagonist in her second Newbery Medal winner, *The Bronze Bow* (1961), Daniel, the nineteen-year-old Galilean patriot, is bent on revenging the brutal death of his parents and driving the occupying Romans out of Palestine. The relationships Daniel develops, like those of Kit, lead him into danger, growth, and the chance to resolve his bitterness. Carefully sketched characters such as a fellow Galilean, Joel, a group of outlaws and a black slave, Daniel's own mentally ill sister, a roman guard, and finally Jesus himself, provide the story with a rich interweaving of personalities and motivations. Although the novel could be criticized for imposing a western bias on a middle eastern setting, as well as for its unabashed presentation of this early period in the Christian religion, its predominant themes of hatred and forgiveness, coming of age, and war and peace are universal ones with relevance to any society and culture.

In contrast, *The Prospering* (1967) is less accessible to young adults because of its deep emphasis on religious division and fanaticism. The novel is based on the true story of the Williams family who left Boston in 1737 to take part in a social and religious experiment. This involved the establishment of the integrated community of Stockbridge in which Indians were to be taught the beliefs, the manners, and the livelihood compatible to the English way of life.

The story is narrated in the first person by Elizabeth, another strong female protagonist whose inner depth and development is offset by her lack of outward beauty. Her story conveys a rich awareness of place as it details the growth of the small mission settlement through conflicts with the Indians, wars and revolution, to establishment as a town. However, its lengthy treatment of Elizabeth's both religious and romantic fantasies detract from her genuine struggles to find a place of her own in the adult world.

The Sign of the Beaver (1988) has a younger protagonist who introduces themes of survival and interracial understanding. Thirteen-year-old Matt comes of age in the wilderness of eighteenth-century Maine. Left alone for several months to guard the family homestead, Matt learns to survive physically as well as discovering new strengths and resources in his inner person. Through an unexpected friendship with Attean, a Penobscot Indian, Matt becomes familiar with the woodland culture of this endangered race and develops a deep appreciation for their way of life. Speare's factual depiction of the Indians, so different from *Calico Captive,* shows both respect and sensitivity, and renders the book particularly relevant today.

Elizabeth George Speare's body of fictional work spans just five novels written over the course of thirty-one years. Her careful research, vivacious plots, and convincing characterization make it a selection of fine historical literary works which will continue to enlighten and encourage readers.

—Patricia Hill

* * *

SPENCE, Eleanor (Rachel). Australian. Born in Sydney, New South Wales, Australia, 21 October 1928. Educated at Erina Primary School, 1935-40; Gosford High School, 1941-45; University of Sydney, 1946-48, B.A. 1949. Married John A. Spence in 1952; two sons and one daughter. Author of children's books. Teacher, Methodist Ladies' College, Burwood, New South Wales, 1949; librarian, Commonwealth Public Service Board, Canberra, Australia, 1950-52; children's librarian, Coventry City Libraries, Coventry, England, 1952-54; teaching assistant, 1974-75, and since 1976 teacher, Autistic Children's Association of New South Wales, Sydney, Australia. Recipient: Australian Children's Book of the Year award, 1964, for *The Green Laurel,* and 1977, for *The October Child;* Facilities for Autistic Handicapped Winston Churchill fellow, 1978; Australian Literature Board writer's fellowship, 1980; Australian Children's Book Honor award, 1991, for *The Family Book of Mary Claire.* Address: 11 Handley Ave., Turramurra, NSW 2074, Australia.

PUBLICATIONS FOR YOUNG ADULTS

Fiction

Patterson's Track, illustrated by Alison Forbes. Melbourne, Oxford University Press, 1958; London, Angus & Robertson, 1959.
The Summer in Between, illustrated by Marcia Lane Foster. London, Oxford University Press, 1959.
Lillipilly Hill, illustrated by Susan Einzig. London, Oxford University Press, 1960; New York, Roy, 1963.

The Green Laurel, illustrated by Geraldine Spence. London, Oxford University Press, 1963; New York, Roy, 1965.
The Year of the Currawong, illustrated by Gareth Floyd. London, Oxford University Press, and New York, Roy, 1965.
The Switherby Pilgrims, illustrated by Corinna Gray. London, Oxford University Press, and New York, Roy, 1967.
Jamberoo Road, illustrated by Doreen Roberts. London, Oxford University Press, and New York, Roy, 1969.
The Nothing Place, illustrated by Geraldine Spence. London, Oxford University Press, 1972; New York, Harper, 1973.
Time to Go Home, illustrated by Fermin Rocker. London, Oxford University Press, 1973.
The Travels of Hermann, illustrated by Noela Young. Sydney, Collins, 1973.
The October Child, illustrated by Malcolm Green. London, Oxford University Press, 1976; as *The Devil Hole,* New York, Lothrop, 1977.
A Candle for St. Anthony. London, Oxford University Press, 1977; New York, Oxford University Press, 1979.
The Seventh Pebble, illustrated by Sisca Verwoert. Melbourne and London, Oxford University Press, 1980.
The Left Overs. Sydney, Methuen, 1982; London, Methuen, 1983.
Me and Jeshua. Melbourne, Dove, 1984.
Miranda Going Home. Melbourne, Dove, 1985.
Mary and Frances. Melbourne, Dove, 1986.
Deezle Boy. Melbourne, Dove, 1987.
Another Sparrow Singing. Melbourne, Dove, 1991; London, Oxford University Press, 1992.
The Family Book of Claire. Melbourne, Dove, 1991.

Other

A Schoolmaster, illustrated by Jane Walker. Melbourne, Oxford University Press, 1969.
A Cedar-Cutter, illustrated by Barbara Taylor. Melbourne, Oxford University Press, 1971.

PUBLICATIONS FOR ADULTS

Other

Another October Child: Recollections of Eleanor Spence. Melbourne, Dove, 1988.

* * *

Eleanor Spence has been publishing books for young people since 1958, and her novels chart the changes that have occurred in Australian children's fiction since that time. Spence began by writing simple, outdoor family stories based on her own recollections of a happy childhood. The families in her early books were largely conventional two-parent ones, where children followed the patterns of behaviour set down by their elders. As the years went on Spence recognised the changes in society and the family, and in the late 1960s began weaving these threads into such novels as *The Nothing Place* (1972) and *Time to Go Home* (1973), where she takes special interest in characters who are disadvantaged in some way. This process reached its peak with *The October Child* (1976), a book largely written from her experience working with autistic children. This interest in characters who are disadvantaged physically or socially remains the focus of her work. Spence's two religious novels, centring upon the life of Jesus, are sometimes seen as aberrations, but they deal directly with characters who are different, displaced, or oppressed, and her interest in historical settings and the nature of families is also apparent.

Spence's first novel, *Patterson's Track* (1958), is written within the established tradition of its time. With their parents conveniently out of the way, the children undertake a series of adventures, and though danger is present, the outcome of their exploits is never in any serious doubt. Karen Winter, the heroine—self-conscious, untidy, poor at school work and sport—finds self-worth and self-discovery at the end. Leadership qualities and the operation of group dynamics play an important part in the workings of the story. The impetus for the book is local history, as Karen decides to find out the truth about an incident that happened in 1820, when she believed a convict was treated unjustly.

An interest in history is an important feature of Spence's work. *Lillipilly Hill* (1963) concentrates on developing relationships among young people, but it is also a fine historical novel. Its heroine, Harriet Wilmot, tries to convince her family to remain in the Australia of the 1800s rather than return to a more comfortable life in England. *Lillipilly Hill* is an absorbing book which is carefully researched and crafted and expresses the need to belong and to put roots down in permanent surroundings. *The Green Laurel* (1963), for which Spence won her first Book of the Year Award, expresses this idea too, as itinerant children long for stability, though the book has a contemporary setting.

Spence wrote two novels of straight historical fiction in the sixties, *The Switherby Pilgrims* (1967) and *Jamberoo Road* (1969). The first begins the story of Arabella Braithwaite, who brings a group of ten orphans to Australia to give them a better chance in life, and its sequel continues her efforts to find careers for them. The background of these stories is again well researched, and the wealth of characters in each draws the reader into a rich family saga. In the 1980s Spence published two more historical novels, *Me and Jeshua* (1984) and *Miranda Going Home* (1985), which tell of the extended family of Jeshua, whom readers come to realise is the young Jesus when his family returned from Egypt and settled in Nazareth. In the first story the events are seen through the eyes of Jeshua's cousin Jude, who is a protector of Jeshua as he comes to learn about his growing divinity. The second story stands in its own right, as Miranda, living in Palestine at the time of the Roman occupation, finds herself in a world of upheaval, racism, and the aftermath of war. Nevertheless, its setting and the presence of Jeshua and his family link it strongly to *Me and Jeshua*.

Spence's novel *The Family Book of Mary-Claire* (1991) is a triumph of historical writing. It presents the history of one family in New South Wales and reflects the changing society over time. The story is told in three parts with a short epilogue and is built around four young characters, each representing a generation. When each character tells his or her own story, that character is aged between ten and thirteen years. Each child makes an entry in the family Bible and is curious about the lives of earlier family members. The family provides a structure in time and is at the heart of the novel. Through the generations the reader is able to see inherited traits and talents being passed on. The documenting of nearly 100 years of history in 300 large-print pages is masterly, as each child character attempts to pass on the truth of the past that has created them. In addition, the book records much social history.

In the 1970s Spence's focus began to shift from the happy family to more specific and social problems centred within the family.

In *The Nothing Place,* Glen Calder is deaf and lacks the support of his family. In *Time to Go Home,* Rowan Price comes from a one-parent family and has to learn some difficult lessons through hard experience. Rowan is irritable, deceitful, swears, and steals, though he has another side which gains the reader's sympathy. Feeling he is useless at everything but football, Rowan hopes to achieve there but loses his chance to play when he is beaten up by his pot-smoking rival. Plots in Spence's later books, when summarised, often appear sensational, but Spence is keenly aware of what young people do and never sensationalises the issues.

Spence won her second Book of the Year Award for *The October Child,* which explores the effect an autistic child has on a family. Most of the responsibility for the autistic Carl falls on his ten-year-old brother Douglas, who survives through his music and the help of friends. There is a powerful scene at the end of the book when Carl goes berserk and turns on Douglas, biting his arm and publicly humiliating him. The frenzy drives Douglas to disown the child, but he comes to terms with the situation at the end.

A Candle for St. Anthony (1977), one of Spence's most sensitively written novels, presents a situation new to Australian children's literature at the time. It deals with the adolescent friendship of Justin and Rudi, two boys from different backgrounds and cultures. Justin is Australian, affluent, middle-class, handsome, and macho, while Rudi is European, poor, industrious, sensitive, and pretty. Justin immediately dislikes Rudi for reasons he cannot understand, but later the boys become firm friends. Eventually a mutual friend makes their friendship appear a homosexual one when he hears Rudi tell Justin he loves him, and the embarrassment this causes ends the friendship. But the novel is not about covert homosexuality. It is a compelling and involving book with haunting overtones at different levels. It is about the strong friendship of adolescence and the importance of finding someone who completely understands you. It is also about opposing lifestyles and the meeting of two cultures, and Spence implies that a combination of elements from both cultures would be a good thing.

The Seventh Pebble (1980) presents an authentic picture of religious and social prejudice in a small Australian town before World War II. Rachel Blackwood, the daughter of the highly respected town doctor, befriends Bridget Connell, a member of a large Irish Catholic family who are poor, and discovers for herself what it means to be different. *The Left Overs* (1982) is about four foster children whose home is being demolished to make way for a freeway and their attempt to find a home where they can still be together. Despite the seriousness of their themes, the books have many lighthearted moments.

As Spence's work progresses she moves from stories for the younger child to stories for the young adult; this probably goes hand in hand with the growth of her own three boys. But two later novels are again directed at a younger child, perhaps because Spence reached the grandmother stage. The hero of *Deezle Boy* (1987) has low self-esteem and is slow at working things out. He is adopted but then is kidnapped by his birth mother. Spence uses the situation to analyse parental custody, illiteracy, unemployment, and social change within the family. How family matters were handled in the past, the arrival of children out of wedlock, and the question of the elderly remaining part of the family are placed before the reader in a non-didactic, compassionate way, so once again readers are able to draw their own conclusions about issues. *Another Sparrow Singing* (1991) is a gentle and sympathetic book about children living in a caravan park after their father has deserted them. This novel brings together many of Spence's beliefs in the value of the human spirit, the need to belong, and the need for a peaceful place to resolve life's difficulties. Throughout her work readers are asked to avoid the insularity of life and become involved in useful and creative work.

Eleanor Spence's novels reflect the concerns of a complex Australian society over time. She has kept abreast of the times through observing the changing dress, habits, and language of young people. Although family structures may change, family relationships, peer group pressures, and school difficulties remain much the same. Though her work is often low-key, the more one comes to examine her novels, the more one comes to highly regard them. Their craftsmanship and literary worth is of a high order, and close rereading will often reveal new aspects and insights.

—Michael Stone

SPIEGELMAN, Art. American. Born in Stockholm, Sweden, 15 February 1948; immigrated to United States. Educated Harpur College (now State University of New York at Binghamton), 1965-68. Married Francoise Mouly in 1977; two children. Attended Harpur College (now State University of New York at Binghamton), 1965-68. Free-lance artist and writer, since 1965; creative consultant, artist, designer, editor, and writer for novelty packaging and bubble-gum cards and stickers, Topps Chewing Gum, Inc., Brooklyn, New York, since 1966. Instructor in studio class on comics at San Francisco Academy of Art, 1974-75, and in history and aesthetics of comics at New York School of Visual Arts, since 1979. On advisory board of Swann Foundation. Art work featured in numerous exhibitions at galleries and museums in the United States and abroad, including the New York Cultural Center, the Institute of Contemporary Art in London, and the Seibu Gallery in Tokyo. Editor, *Douglas Comix,* 1972; contributing editor with Bill Griffith, *Arcade, the Comics Revue,* 1975-76; founding editor with Francoise Mouly, *Raw,* since 1980; contributing artist and editor, *New Yorker,* since 1992. Recipient: Annual *Playboy* Editorial award for best comic strip and Yellow Kid award (Italy) for best comic strip author, both 1982; Regional Design award from *Print* magazine, 1983, 1984, and 1985; Joel M. Cavior award for Jewish Writing, and National Book Critics Circle nomination, both 1986, both for *Maus;* Inkpot award from San Diego Comics Convention and Stripschappenning award (Netherlands) for best foreign comics album, both 1987; Guggenheim fellowship, 1990; Pulitzer prize special award, 1992; *Los Angeles Times* book prize for fiction, 1992. Agent: Wylie, Aitken & Stone, 250 West 57th St., Suite 2106, New York, NY 10107. Lives in New York City.

PUBLICATIONS

Comics

The Complete Mr. Infinity. New York, S.F. Book Co., 1970.
The Viper Vicar of Vice, Villainy, and Vickedness. Privately printed by Spiegelman, 1972.
Zip-a-Tune and More Melodies. New York, S.F. Book Co., 1972.
Ace Hole, Midge Detective. New York, Apex Novelties, 1974.

Contributor, *The Apex Treasury of Underground Comics,* edited by Don Donahue and Susan Goodrich. New York, D. Links, 1974.
Language of Comics. State University of New York at Binghamton, 1974.
Breakdowns; From Maus to Now: An Anthology of Strips. New York, Belier Press, 1977.
Every Day Has Its Dog. New York, Raw Books, 1979.
Work and Turn. New York, Raw Books, 1979.
Two-Fisted Painters Action Adventure. New York, Raw Books, 1980.
Maus: A Survivor's Tale. New York, Pantheon, 1986.
Read Yourself Raw: Comix Anthology for Damned Intellectuals. with wife, Francoise Mouly. New York, Pantheon, 1987.
Jimbo: Adventures in Paradise, with Francoise Mouly. New York, Pantheon, 1988.
Raw. New York, Penguin, 1990.
Maus II: A Survivor's Tale; and Here My Troubles Began. New York, Pantheon, 1991.
Raw—Number Three: High Culture for Low Brows. New York, Viking, 1991.

Other

Compiling editor with Bob Schneider, *Whole Grains: A Book of Quotations.* New York, D. Links, 1972.
Contributor, *Drawn Together: Relationships Lampooned, Harpooned, and Cartooned,* edited by Nicole Hollander, Skip Morrow, and Ron Wolin. New York, Crown, 1983.
Contributor, *The Complete Color Polly & Her Pals, Vol. 1: The Surrealist Period, 1926-1927.* New York, Remco Worldservice Books, 1990.
Editor, with R. Sikoryak and Francoise Mouly, *Warts and All/Drew Friedman and Josh Alan Friedman.* New York, Penguin, 1990.

*

Illustrator: *Argonaut: Rediscovering American Resources* by Warren Hinckle, 1992.

* * *

A father who is difficult to get along with, a mother who commits suicide, an only brother who is thought of as a perfect child, impossible to compete with because he is dead, are all issues for Art Spiegelman in his life and in his art. The Holocaust looms over all. Survivors of the Holocaust, Spiegelman's parents eventually relocated in the United States. Before his birth, his brother and most of Art Spiegelman's relatives had all been murdered as a result of the Holocaust.

Spiegelman created in comic-book form *Maus: A Survivor's Tale (Maus I)* and *Maus II: A Survivor's Tale II; and Here My Troubles Began, (Maus II)* to tell his father's story, his own story, and a universal story of the Holocaust. The action takes place on multiple levels, sometimes in the past and at other times in the present. The narration alternates between father, Vladek, and son, Artie.

Creator, artist, writer, and one of the two narrators of *Maus I* and *Maus II,* Spiegelman assumes the identity of the autobiographical character, Artie. Struggling to understand not only his father's past but the man his father has become, Spiegelman portrays the duality he sees in his father: the incredibly resistant and resourceful survivor of the Holocaust and the present-day cantankerous, stingy, fearful man. In coping with his own life, Art Spiegelman, the author and the character, is clearly a survivor as well.

Maus I and *Maus II* differ on many levels from what is most commonly thought of as traditional comics. Not flimsy in format or narration, nor frivolous in nature, *Maus I* and *Maus II* are substantial graphic novels, available as trade paperbacks. With a strong narrative voice, and a unique blend of words and illustrations, the overall effect of reading these books is similar to watching a riveting movie.

"The Jews are undoubtedly a race but they are not human." With this quote of Adolph Hitler, Art Spiegelman begins *Maus I.* The novel jumps in time and setting from pre-World War II Poland, near the border with Germany, to the trenches on the battlefields of the war, to prisoner of war camps, to a Jewish ghetto, and to the concentration camp Auschwitz. Not following strict chronological order, Spiegelman occasionally cuts away from his father's recollections of the past and moves to present-day events.

Just as Vladek recalls incidents of his past, Artie too has his memories. At ten years of age, Vladek tells Artie how to distinguish real friends. In his own particular manner of speaking English, Vladek says: "If you lock them together in a room with no food for a week, then you could see what it is friends." Vladek recalls how people act toward one another in situations far worse than in a locked room. Readers see both the heroic and the horrible.

Maus II continues the narrative begun in *Maus I.* Vladek remembers Auschwitz and Birkenau, the workshops, crematoriums with underground gas chambers, incineration rooms, ovens, and mass graves. He tells of forced marches, confinement on boxcars, and recounts the continued suffering after the official ending of the war. As in *Maus I,* interspersed with Vladek's narrative of the past is Artie's story of his father's difficult personality in the present. Spiegelman does not romanticize either story.

In *Maus II,* Artie reveals to his "shrink" the ambiguity he feels toward his father, and even readers who have lived without personal experience of the Holocaust may identify with this ambiguity. Artie discloses his mixed feelings about writing the *Maus* books. He says: "Some part of me doesn't want to draw or think about Auschwitz."

In both *Maus* books, Spiegelman uses animals to represent people. Jews are depicted as mice, Germans as cats, Poles as pigs, the British as fish, the French as frogs, Americans as dogs, the Swedes as reindeer, and gypsies as moths. Often not much beyond clothing differentiates characters.

The only scene in either book that depicts individuals as real people instead of animals is the self-contained comic strip, entitled "Prisoner on the Hell Planet." Located within *Maus I,* it tells of Artie's strong personal reaction to his mother's suicide. Drawn in an exaggerated, surrealistic manner, the change in the artistic style and character representation helps create a mood of heightened emotionalism. In contrast, the drawings that make up the rest of the books emphasize the factual, nonfictional aspects of the story.

Spiegelman worked hard to attain accuracy in recording even small details. He not only taped his father's recollections but traveled to his parents' house in Sosnowiec, to the concentration camps of Auschwitz and Birkenau, studied old family and archival photographs, read the accounts of other survivors, and looked at documentary film footage, drawings and paintings made by camp inmates.

Spiegelman uses only black-and-white drawings throughout *Maus I* and *Maus II.* Often the illustrations supply information not expressed in the narrative. Different sizes of cartoon frames co-exist on a single page, some traditionally rectangular or square, others round, and some without borders. Each frame fluidly moves the reader ahead in the narrative. Both *Maus* books contain some maps, charts, and diagrams to enhance visualization of places and events.

Maus I and *Maus II* have received wide critical acclaim. *Maus I* was nominated for the 1987 National Book Critics Circle Award and *Maus II* won a Pulitzer Prize. The animal metaphor, distilled language, and deliberately simple drawings create a powerful and moving story, accessible on many levels. Spiegelman's use of flashbacks and fast-forwards in both *Maus* books enhances multiple interpretations.

By dealing with the most serious of history in *Maus I* and *Maus II* and by telling his story eloquently, Art Spiegelman has done much to redefine the comic book. In so doing, he has shown that his chosen format need not be stereotyped as frivolous or trivial. Instead he has shown that graphic novels and comics can be multidimensional literature, capable of irony, emotional depth, and sophistication.

—Karen Ferris Morgan

————

SPINELLI, Jerry. American. Born in Norristown, Pennsylvania, 1 February 1941. Educated at Gettysburg College, Pennsylvania, A.B. 1963; Johns Hopkins University, Baltimore, Maryland, M.A. 1964; Temple University, Philadelphia, Pennsylvania, 1964. Served in the U.S. Naval Air Reserve, 1966-72. Married Eileen Mesi in 1977; four sons and two daughters. Editor, Chilton Company (magazine publishers), Radnor, Pennsylvania, 1966-89; writer. Recipient: *Boston Globe/Horn Book* award, 1990, and Newbery Medal, American Library Association, 1991, both for *Maniac Magee;* Carolyn Field award, 1991; Dorothy Canfield Fisher award, 1992; Indian Paintbrush award, Rhode Island Children's Book award, Flicker Tale award, Charlotte award, Mark Twain award, Nevada Young Readers' award, all 1992, William Allen White award, Pacific Northwest award, Massachusetts Children's Book award, Rebecca Caudill award, West Virginia Children's Book award, Buckeye Children's Book award, Land of Enchantment award, all 1993, all for *Maniac Magee.* Agent: Ms. Ray Lincoln, Ray Lincoln Literary Agency, 7900 Old York Rd., Apt. 107-B, Elkins Park, PA 19117. Address: 331 Melvin Rd., Phoenixville, PA 19460, U.S.A.

PUBLICATIONS FOR YOUNG ADULTS

Fiction

Space Station Seventh Grade. Boston, Little, Brown, 1982.
Who Put That Hair in My Toothbrush? Boston, Little, Brown, 1984.
Night of the Whale. Boston, Little, Brown, 1985.
Jason and Marceline. Boston, Little, Brown, 1986.
Dump Days. Boston, Little, Brown, 1988.
The Bathwater Gang, illustrated by Meredith Johnson. Boston, Little, Brown, 1990.
Maniac Magee. Boston, Little, Brown, 1990.
Fourth Grade Rats. New York, Scholastic, 1991.

Report to the Principal's Office. New York, Scholastic 1991.

There's a Girl in My Hammerlock. New York, Simon & Schuster, 1991.

The Bathwater Gang Gets down to Business, illustrated by Meredith Johnson. Boston, Little, Brown, 1992.

Do the Funky Pickle. New York, Scholastic, 1992.

Who Ran My Underwear up the Flagpole? New York, Scholastic, 1992.

Picklemania. New York, Scholastic, 1993.

Contributor to books, including *Our Roots Grow Deeper Than We Know: Pennsylvania Writers—Pennsylvania Life,* edited by Lee Gutkind, University of Pittsburgh Press, 1985, and *Noble Pursuits,* edited by Virginia A. Arnold and Carl B. Smith, Macmillan, 1988. Work represented in anthologies, including *Best Sports Stories of 1982,* Dutton, and *Connections: Short Stories by Outstanding Writers for Young Adults,* edited by Donald R. Gallo, Delacorte, 1989.

*

Biography: Essay in *Speaking for Ourselves: Autobiographical Sketches by Notable Authors of Books for Young Adults,* Volume 1, compiled and edited by Donald R. Gallo, National Council of Teachers of English, 1990.

Jerry Spinelli comments:

Don't tell my English teachers, but not much planning goes into my novels. Oh, plenty of experience and imagination and hard work and such go into them, and I do jot down lots of notes, and I do have some idea where to start a story and maybe where to end it. But there's no outline telling me how to get from here to there, because I have found that there is no way to know what is inside the story until I am in there myself. In other words, for me, the product and the process are pretty much the same thing.

* * *

Jerry Spinelli creates realistic fiction with humorous dialog and situations, but his stories go beyond humor; Spinelli's characters stumble and blunder through their lives until they emerge from the fog of adolescence guided by an optimistic light that readies them for their next challenge. While entertaining readers, Spinelli's protagonists face today's social issues, such as racism and sex stereotyping.

In his first book for young adults Spinelli introduces Jason Herkimer, a seventh grader entering junior high school. *Space Station Seventh Grade* chronicles the dilemmas and struggles through puberty that Jason and other young teens face. When Jason is suspended from school, Jason's mother is upset but Ham, Jason's stepfather, explains that the boy sprawled on the recliner is not the Jason they used to know. That Jason disappeared when Jason turned thirteen. Ham tells Jason's mother, "The thirteen-year-old does not change from a worm to a butterfly, you know. It changes from a butterfly to a worm." Jason's humanism, as he suffers through his first pimple and his first crush, allows readers to identify personally with him. The slang words related to sexual activity used in the text may offend some readers, but, Spinelli does not mince words when relating how teens act and speak. The book will be funny for adults who remember their own adolescence, while teens relate the story to their own strange feelings and alien urges.

Jason first discovers romance in *Space Station Seventh Grade,* in the guise of the beautiful cheerleader, Debbie. But he realizes that she is interested in other boys, and not him. At the end of the book, Jason falls in love with Marceline McAllister, which is elaborated on in *Jason and Marceline.* In this novel, Jason has more to learn about girls and relationships. According to his friends, the main reason to have a steady girlfriend is to make out. Marceline sets Jason straight right away. She refuses to let him give her hickeys as proof of his affection. Jason asks himself, "Who ever heard of a girl like this?" Through the ups and downs of their relationship, Spinelli treats readers to his sense of humor as Jason tries to drive down a romantic road filled with emotional potholes. Spinelli exaggerates conversations and situations enough to be witty without getting too far from reality. Young adults will sympathize with Jason and laugh when Marceline tells Jason at the end of the novel, "There's one thing that hasn't changed, and isn't going to change. I hate to tell you. No hickeys!"

Spinelli claims that his ideas for his characters and plots come from the children in his house. The situations and people in *Who Put That Hair in My Toothbrush?* make this statement believable. Greg and Megin take turns narrating their individual lives over a background of sibling rivalry. Their hostilities toward each other lean toward slapstick humor as they jostle and grate against one another but, despite the insults and humor, Spinelli does provide readers with some sensitive moments: Greg's devotion to beautiful Jennifer Wade; Megin's grief over her friend Emily's death.

With *There's a Girl in My Hammerlock,* Spinelli shows readers his wittiest dialog, his most focused social issue, and his uncanny ability to write from a girl's viewpoint. Maisie tries out for the wrestling team when she learns that the boy she's interested in, Eric Delong, is on the team. When she makes the team an uproar follows. The coach, the boys on the team, the kids at school, her best friend, her brother, Eric's girlfriend, and the townspeople all try to dissuade her from wrestling. But Maisie endures ridicule and forfeits. At last she has Eric's attention, but his ungentlemanly advances are not her idea of romance. Maisie's independence and self-sufficiency serves as an inspiration to girls who have unconventional talents and want to develop them.

In 1991 Spinelli was awarded the Newbery Medal for *Maniac Magee.* This novel is a departure from Spinelli's other writing in the respect that it was written for younger readers and lacks his irreverent style of writing. Jeffrey Lionel Magee is not a mixed-up teenager. Instead, he represents the best in each of us: he's generous, sensitive, and lacks any inclinations for prejudice. At first, *Maniac Magee* appears to be another realistic novel. Maniac is a homeless, orphaned boy who changes the lives of many residents of Twin Mills. Then readers learn about the legends. Maniac can run faster, jump higher, and untie knots quicker than anyone the kids of Twin Mills have ever seen. Maniac functions as a Johnny Appleseed or a Paul Bunyon, a folk hero for modern times.

Spinelli's specialty is his humorous view of adolescence. His readers know that he's laughing with them at the absurdities of growing up. It takes special talent to combine humor with sensitivity, but Spinelli manages this challenging combination well.

—Rosemary Chance

———

STAPLES, Suzanne Fisher. American. Born in Philadelphia, Pennsylvania, 27 August 1945. Educated at Cedar Crest College, Allentown, Pennsylvania, B.A. 1967. Married 1) Nicholas Green in 1967 (divorced, 1976); 2) Eugene Staples in 1980. Asian marketing director, Business International Corp., 1974-76; news editor and correspondent in New York, Washington, D.C., Hong Kong, and India, United Press International, Washington, D.C., 1975-83; part-time editor for foreign desk, *Washington Post,* 1983-85; consultant, U.S. Agency for International Development, 1986-87; fiction writer, since 1988. Lecturer on the status of women in the Islamic Republic of Pakistan. Citizens for a Better Eastern Shore, board member. Recipient: Newbery Honor, American Library Association, 1990, and Ibby Honor List, 1992, both for *Shabanu: Daughter of the Wind.* Agent: Jeanne Drewsen, 250 Mercer, New York, NY 10012. Lives in New York City.

PUBLICATIONS FOR YOUNG ADULTS

Fiction

Shabanu: Daughter of the Wind. New York, Knopf, 1989.
Haveli. New York, Knopf, 1993.

*   *   *

Shabanu: Daughter of the Wind is a Newbery Honor book and a first offering by Suzanne Fisher Staples. It is the story of a spirited eleven-year-old girl, who lives with her nomad family in the Cholistan Desert of present-day Pakistan. Staples brings to us the experiences of a girl whose playfulness is not unlike an American girl her age. However, the carefree youth of a Pakistani girl is fleeting, for Muslim tradition in their country dictates that she marry young.

Phulan, her thirteen-year-old sister, is betrothed to Hamir. Their arranged marriage is planned for the summer monsoon rains. Shabanu (Shah-*bah*-noo) contentedly plays with her camel, Guluband, and plans to go to the great annual fair at Sibi with her father. However, as her family prepares for her sister's upcoming wedding, Shabanu realizes her own freedom will soon end, as it has been arranged that she will wed Murad, Hamir's brother.

Shabanu loves the camels and helps care for them. One day while tending to the herd, she sees the circling of vultures overhead. She runs to the side of a camel, who while giving birth has been bitten by a poisonous snake. Shabanu struggles to birth the young camel herself before its mother dies. She saves the baby and names him Mithoo, a name that means "sweet."

Leaving Mithoo behind with her sister and mother, Shabanu and her father begin the journey to Sibi where they hope to sell some of their camels, with the exception, she hopes, of Guluband. The money they make will be used for Phulan's wedding and dowry. On the way, they meet a band of men who are looking for one of their daughters. The young girl had eloped with a Marri tribesman. After they have left, Shabanu's father tells her that they will kill the young woman when they find her: a reminder that she must always do as she is told.

Shabanu loves the fair and when they arrive, they hurriedly set up camp so they can go to the carnival. Her father takes her on the rides. Little does she realize that it will be the last time she can be young and free.

They receive several offers for their fine camels. But Shabanu's greatest fear is realized when her father's outrageous asking price for the entire herd is met. They will now have enough for not only Phulan's wedding, but Shabanu's wedding as well. Her parents will no longer have to struggle, they are now wealthy. Shabanu is numb, her beloved Guluband is gone. Her father has given her a puppy to replace her sorrow. But it doesn't help, for her childhood is now behind her. She must learn to sacrifice for the benefit of her family. This is only the beginning of her ascent into adulthood.

One day, Shabanu and her sister narrowly escape rape attempted by the hated landlord of Hamir's family property. In retaliation, the despised landowner takes the life of Hamir. To resolve the fury, the landowner has agreed to leave the families alone on one condition: Shabanu agrees to marry his wealthy brother, Rahim-*sahib.* The plans for the marriages are rearranged: Phulan will now marry Murad, Shabanu's intended; and Shabanu will wed Rahim-*sahib.* Her parents are very pleased as Shabanu's marriage will bring prestige to their family. However, Shabanu is not happy to wed an older man with three wives. She wonders whether these women will make her a slave. How will she survive?

"It isn't a matter of what she wants!" says her father.

"She is intelligent and..." her mother hopes to explain.

"She'll find out where her intelligence will get her." Shabanu hasn't a choice according to her father.

Shabanu calls upon the wise words of a respected elder: "No matter what happens—you have *you."*

The story of *Shabanu* offers so much more than the tale of a young girl coming-of-age. From the colorful *chadr* draped over the head and shoulders of every woman in public view, to the making of *chapati,* a pan bread made of wheat flour and water, Staples takes you to another culture, teaches you another language, and makes you feel the pain and torment of a spirit struggling to survive when the rules of tradition seem destined to destroy it. It is a lesson for all who are determined to soar above that which seeks to keep them down.

This is a wonderful beginning for Suzanne Fisher Staples. In addition to being a Newbery Honor book, *Shabanu* was named an ALA Best Book for Young Adults, an ALA Notable Children's Book, and a New York Times Notable Book of the Year. For those who want to read more of the life of Shabanu, see Staples's new sequel, published in 1993, called *Haveli.*

—Suzanne M. Valentic

———

STEINBECK, John (Ernst). Born in Salinas, California, 27 February 1902. Educated at Stanford University, special student, 1919-25. Married 1) Carol Henning in 1930 (divorced 1943); 2) Gwyn Conger in 1943 (divorced 1948), two sons; 3) Elaine Scott in 1950. Variously employed as hod-carrier, fruit-picker, apprentice painter, laboratory assistant, caretaker, surveyor, and reporter; writer. Foreign correspondent in North Africa and Italy for *New York Herald Tribune,* 1943; correspondent in Vietnam for *Newsday,* 1966-67. Special writer for U.S. Army Air Forces, during World War II. Recipient: General Literature Gold Medal, Commonwealth Club of California, 1936, for *Tortilla Flat,* 1937, for *Of Mice and Men,* and 1940, for *The Grapes of Wrath;* New York Drama Critics Circle award, 1938, for play, "Of Mice and Men"; Pulitzer Prize, 1940, for *The Grapes of Wrath;* Academy award nomination for best original story, Academy of Motion Picture Arts and Sciences, 1944, for "Lifeboat," and 1945, for "A Medal for Benny"; Nobel Prize for literature, 1962; Paperback of the Year award, Best Sellers, 1964, for *Travels with Charley: In Search of America. Died 20 December 1968.*

PUBLICATIONS

Novels

Cup of Gold: A Life of Henry Morgan, Buccaneer. New York, Robert McBride, 1929.
The Pastures of Heaven. New York, Viking, 1932.
To a God Unknown. New York, Viking, 1933.
Tortilla Flat. New York, Viking, 1935.
In Dubious Battle. New York, Viking, 1936.
Of Mice and Men. New York, Viking, 1937.
The Red Pony. Covici, Friede, 1937.
The Grapes of Wrath. New York, Viking, 1939; revised edition, edited by Peter Lisca, New York, Viking, 1972.
The Forgotten Village. New York, Viking, 1941.
The Moon Is Down. New York, Viking, 1942.
Cannery Row. New York, Viking, 1945; new edition (includes manuscript, corrected typescript, corrected galleys, and first edition), Stanford Publications Service, 1975.
The Wayward Bus. New York, Viking, 1947.
The Pearl. New York, Viking, 1947.
Burning Bright: A Play in Story Form. New York, Viking, 1950.
East of Eden. New York, Viking, 1952.
Sweet Thursday. New York, Viking, 1954.
The Short Reign of Pippin IV: A Fabrication. New York, Viking, 1957.
The Winter of Our Discontent. New York, Viking, 1961.

Short Stories

Saint Katy the Virgin. Covici, Friede, 1936.
Nothing So Monstrous. Pynson Printers, 1936.
The Long Valley. New York, Viking, 1938; as *Thirteen Great Short Stories from the Long Valley,* New York, Avon, 1943; as *Fourteen Great Short Stories from the Long Valley,* New York, Avon, 1947.
How Edith McGillicuddy Met R.L.S. Cleveland, Ohio, Rowfant Club, 1943.
The Crapshooter. New York, Mercury Publications, 1957.

Plays

Of Mice and Men: A Play in Three Acts (produced Broadway, 1937), with George S. Kaufman. New York, Viking, 1937.
The Moon Is Down: Play in Two Parts (produced Broadway, 1942). New York, Dramatist's Play Service, 1942.
Burning Bright: Play in Three Acts (produced Broadway, 1950). New York, Dramatist's Play Service, 1951.

Screenplays: *Forgotten Village,* independently produced, 1939; *Lifeboat,* Twentieth Century-Fox, 1944; *A Medal for Benny,* Paramount, 1945, in *Best Film Plays—1945,* edited by John Gassner and Dudley Nichols, New York, Crown, 1946; *The Pearl,* RKO, 1948; *The Red Pony,* Republic, 1949; *Viva Zapata!,* Twentieth Century-Fox, 1952, edited by Robert E. Morsberger, New York, Viking, 1975.

Other

Their Blood Is Strong. Simon J. Lubin Society of California, 1938.

A Letter to the Friends of Democracy. Mountain Brook, Alabama, Overbrook Press, 1940.
Sea of Cortez, with Edward F. Ricketts. New York, Viking, 1941; as *Sea of Cortez: A Leisurely Journal of Travel,* Mount Vernon, New York, Appel, 1971; revised edition, as *The Log from the "Sea of Cortez": The Narrative Portion of the Book, "Sea of Cortez,"* New York, Viking, 1951.
Bombs Away: The Story of a Bomber Team. New York, Viking, 1942.
Steinbeck, edited by Pascal Covici. New York, Viking, 1943; expanded edition, as *The Portable Steinbeck,* 1946; as *Steinbeck Omnibus,* Australia, Oxford University Press, 1946; revised edition, New York, Viking, 1971.
A Russian Journal, photographs by Robert Capa. New York, Viking, 1948.
Short Novels: Tortilla Flat, The Red Pony, Of Mice and Men, The Moon Is Down, Cannery Row, The Pearl. New York, Viking, 1953; new edition, New York, Viking, 1963.
Once There Was a War. New York, Viking, 1958.
East of Eden and *The Wayward Bus.* New York, Viking, 1962.
Travels with Charley: In Search of America. New York, Viking, 1962.
The Red Pony, Part I: The Gift and *The Pearl.* Toronto, Macmillan, 1963.
Letters to Alicia (collection of newspaper columns written as a correspondent in Vietnam). Garden City, New Jersey, 1965.
The Pearl and *The Red Pony.* New York, Viking, 1967.
America and Americans. New York, Viking, 1969.
Cannery Row and *Sweet Thursday.* San Francisco, California, Heron Books, 1971.
To a God Unknown and *The Pearl.* San Francisco, California, Heron Books, 1971.
Of Mice and Men and *Cannery Row.* Harmondsworth, England, Penguin, 1973; New York, Penguin, 1978.
Steinbeck: A Life in Letters, edited by Elaine Steinbeck and Robert Wallsten. New York, Viking, 1975.
The Acts of King Arthur and His Noble Knights: From the Winchester Manuscripts of Thomas Malory and Other Sources, edited by Chase Horton. New York, Farrar, Straus, 1976.
The Collected Poems of Amnesia Glasscock (as Amnesia Glasscock) San Francisco, California, Manroot Books, 1976.
The Grapes of Wrath, The Moon Is Down, Cannery Row, East of Eden, and *Of Mice and Men.* North Pomfret, Vermont, Heinemann, 1976.
John Steinbeck, 1902-1968 (includes *Tortilla Flat, Of Mice and Men,* and *Cannery Row*). Franklin Center, Pennsylvania, Franklin Library, 1977.
Letters to Elizabeth: A Selection of Letters from John Steinbeck to Elizabeth Otis, edited by Florian J. Shasky and Susan F. Kiggs. San Francisco, California, Book Club of California, 1978.
Contributor, *Famous American Plays of the Nineteen Thirties,* edited by Harold Clurman. New York, Dell, 1980.
The Short Novels of John Steinbeck (includes *Tortilla Flat, The Red Pony, Of Mice and Men, The Moon Is Down, Cannery Row, and The Pearl*). New York, Viking, 1981.
The Harvest Gypsies: On the Road to the Grapes of Wrath. Berkeley, California, Heyday, 1988.
Working Days: The Journals of the Grapes of Wrath, edited by Robert DeMott. New York, Penguin, 1989.

*

Media Adaptations: *Of Mice and Men* (film), United Artists, 1939; (opera adapted by Carlisle Floyd), 1970; (teleplay by E. Nick Alexander); (film, starring Sherilyn Fenn), 1992; *The Grapes of Wrath* (film), Twentieth Century-Fox, 1940; *Tortilla Flat* (film), MGM, 1942; *The Moon Is Down* (film), Twentieth Century-Fox, in 1943; *The Red Pony* (film), Republic, 1949; *East of Eden* (film), Warner Bros., 1954; (musical, *Here's Where I Belong*), 1968; (television mini-series); *Pipe Dream* (musical, adapted by Oscar Hammerstein II, with music by Richard Rogers, based on *Sweet Thursday*), 1955; *The Wyaward Bus* (film), Twentieth Century-Fox, 1957; *America and Americans* (television movie), NBC-TV, 1967; *Travels with Charley* (television movie), NBC-TV, 1968; *The Harness* (television movie), 1971; *The Red Pony* (television movie), 1973; *Cannery Row* (film), MGM, 1982.

Biography: Entry in *Concise Dictionary of American Literary Biography: The Age of Maturity, 1929-1941*, Detroit, Gale, 1989; entry in *Dictionary of Literary Biography*, Detroit, Gale, Volume 7, 1981; Volume 9, 1981; entry in *Dictionary of Literary Biography Documentary Series*, Volume 2, Detroit, Gale, 1982; *John Steinbeck* by Warren French, Boston, Twayne, 1961.

Critical Studies: Entry in *Contemporary Literary Criticism*, Volume 1, Detroit, Gale, 1973; Volume 5, 1976; Volume 9, 1978; Volume 13, 1980; Volume 21, 1982; Volume 34, 1985; Volume 45, 1987; *Steinbeck: A Collection of Critical Essays* edited by Robert Murray Davis, Englewood Cliffs, New Jersey, Prentice-Hall, 1972; *John Steinbeck: An Introduction and Interpretation* by Joseph Fontenrose, New York, Barnes and Noble, 1963; *John Steinbeck: A Dictionary of His Fictional Characters* edited Tetsumaro Hayashi, Metuchen, New York, Scarecrow, 1976; *The Novels of John Steinbeck: A Critical Study* by Howard Levant, Columbia, University of Missouri Press, 1974; *The Wide World of John Steinbeck* by Peter Lisca, New Brunswick, New Jersey, Rutgers University Press, 1958; *Steinbeck: The Man and His Work* by Peter Lisca, Corvallis, Oregon State University Press, 1971; *John Steinbeck* by Paul McCarthy, Ungar, 1980; *The Novels of John Steinbeck: A First Critical Study* by Harry Thornton Moore, New York, Normandie House, 1939; *Steinbeck and His Critics: A Record of Twenty-Five Years* edited by E.W. Tedlock, Jr., and C.V. Wicker, Albuquerque, University of New Mexico Press, 1957; *John Steinbeck's Fiction: The Aesthetics of the Road Taken* by John H. Timmerman, Norman, University of Oklahoma Press, 1986; *John Steinbeck* by F.W. Watt, New York, Grove, 1962.

*   *   *

Justly renowned as one of America's classic modern writers, John Steinbeck is not an author for young adults in terms of his own intentions. He intended his fiction for a general audience, and, though he welcomed younger readers (as well as the use of his books in the schools), he wrote no important works specifically for young adults. However, his volumes of both fiction and nonfiction remain so readable and accessible for any audience that they have become favorites of both young adults and their teachers. Most of his novels would interest advanced readers at the secondary level, but his best stories for young adults are those which grow from his own childhood, adolescence, and young manhood.

The Depression had elicited a reevaluation of American culture, a reassessment of the American dream; a harsh realism of observation was balanced by a warm emphasis on human dignity. A writer of great talent, sensitivity, and imagination, John Steinbeck entered in the mood of the country in the late 1930s with an extraordinary responsiveness. Literature and the other arts joined social, economic, and political thought in contrasting traditional American ideals with the bleak reality of breadlines and shantytowns. Perhaps the major symbol of dislocation was the Dust Bowl, depicted in Steinbeck's classic *The Grapes of Wrath* (1939). The arts in the 1930s focused on these harsh images and tried to find in them the human dimensions which promised a new beginning.

The best of Steinbeck's works strikes this very balance. Although its attitude toward Hispanic Americans seems dated, Steinbeck's first successful novel, *Tortilla Flat* (1935), provides entertaining reading as do its sequels, *Cannery Row* (1945) and *Sweet Thursday* (1954). Several stories in *The Long Valley* are often collected in high school anthologies, most notably "Flight," (1938) a harsh story of a young Chicano boy's initiation into manhood. *Of Mice and Men* (1939) is also harsh and realistic, but its beautiful evocation of friendships and dreams makes it a timeless American classic. Another classic is Steinbeck's symbolic tale of a Mexican fisherman, *The Pearl* (1947). Although Steinbeck's epic *The Grapes of Wrath* is somewhat long and complex, the mature young person will enjoy and profit from reading it. Steinbeck also wrote some fine works of nonfiction, such as *Log from the "Sea of Cortez"* (1941) and *Travels with Charley: In Search of America* (1962).

Steinbeck also has fared better at the hands of Hollywood than have most classic American writers. *Of Mice and Men* has received three fine film treatments (1939, 1973, 1993). Director John Ford's film version of *The Grapes of Wrath* (1940) remains as important a part of Americana as the novel. The Mexican film version of *The Pearl* (1947) is more than adequate. Steinbeck wrote the screenplay for the successful 1949 film treatment of *The Red Pony*, and Lewis Milestone produced and directed the film which starred Robert Mitchum and Peter Miles. A 1973 production of *The Red Pony*, directed by Robert Totten and starring Henry Fonda and Maureen O'Hara, received more favorable reviews. One of Steinbeck's best works of the postwar period was the script for the powerful film *Viva Zapata!* (1952), which was directed by Elia Kazan and starred Marlon Brando. Many of the films based on Steinbeck's work continue to appear on television, including the two versions of *East of Eden* (1955, 1981) and the 1982 adaptation of *Cannery Row*.

Perhaps Steinbeck's finest work for young adults is *The Red Pony*. The writer began *The Red Pony* fairly early in his career; his letters indicate he was working on a pony story in 1933, and the first two sections of the story sequence, "The Gift" and "The Great Mountains," were published in the *North American Review* in November and December of that year. The third section, "The Promise," did not appear in *Harpers* until 1937, and these three parts were published in a slim volume in 1937. "The Leader of the People," the final section, was not added until the publication of the fiction story collection *The Long Valley* in 1938. However, manuscript and textual evidence suggests that the later sections were written some time before their publication, not very long after the first two stories. The four sections are connected by common characters, settings, and themes, forming a clearly unified story sequence which was published separately as *The Red Pony* in 1945. A modestly successful movie version, for which Steinbeck wrote the screenplay, followed in 1949, and a television movie was even better received in 1973.

The Red Pony is among Steinbeck's finest works. This story sequence traces a young boy's initiation into adult life with both realism and sensitivity, a balance that Steinbeck did not always achieve. The vision of characters caught up in the harsh world of nature is balanced by their deep human concerns and commitments. The story takes place on the Tiflin ranch in the Salinas Valley, California. Steinbeck's evocation of the vital beauty of the ranch matches his fine work in *Of Mice and Men,* and his symbols grow naturally out of this setting. The setting stresses the end of the frontier and of the American dream; so in a sense Jody's maturation matches that of modern America. In its depiction of an American variation of a universal experience, *The Red Pony* deserves comparison with the finest of modern American fiction, especially initiation tales such as Williams Faulkner's *The Bear* (1942) or Ernest Hemingway's "Nick Adams" stories.

The literary qualities in *The Red Pony* typify the style that won Steinbeck immense popularity. Rising to prominence at the height of the Depression, Steinbeck seemed to reflect the mood of the era with his strong lines of simple prose. Yet Steinbeck derives his literary power from his use of symbolism for ironic effect. The symbolic images in the plot allow the reader to perceive the significance of an event on a much deeper level than do the characters. The pony in *The Red Pony,* for example, functions as a symbol of Jody's boyhood and innocence as well as a symbol of his maturation. When the pony dies, the reader experiences a sense of loss, because the pony's death represents Jody's loss of innocence. But while the reader understands that Jody's life has been dramatically altered by the death of the pony, Jody, ironically, grieves for his pony without the ability to fully see the death in a larger context.

During World War II, Steinbeck's development as a novelist faltered, and he never recovered his artistic momentum. Even *East of Eden,* the work he thought his masterpiece, proved a critical failure although it was a popular success. Since his death, Steinbeck's books have remained widely read, both in America and abroad. His critical reputation has enjoyed a modest revival, and will most likely continue to develop, for few writers have better celebrated the American dream or traced the dark shape of the American nightmare.

Although Steinbeck appeals to readers of all ages, much of his work is excellent fare for young adult readers. At least a dozen of his titles, along with the film versions made from them, prove excellent classroom reading. Perhaps the most accessible and readable of these are the narratives based on his own younger life. In particular *The Red Pony* remains a classic of young adult fiction, a sensitive yet realistic story of both personal and cultural maturation which becomes universal in its insights. For fiction like this, John Steinbeck will continue to be regarded as an important young adult author, despite the fact that he did not intend this aspect of his literary reputation.

—Joseph R. Millichap

* * *

STEVENSON, Robert Louis (Balfour). Also wrote as Captain George North. British. Born in Edinburgh, 13 November 1850. Educated at Edinburgh Academy; Edinburgh University, 1867-72; studied law in the office of Skene Edwards and Gordon, Edinburgh; called to the Scottish bar, 1875. Married Fanny Van de Grift Osbourne in 1880; two stepsons, including Lloyd Osbourne. Con-

tributor, *Cornhill Magazine,* London, 1876-82. Novelist, poet, essayist, and writer of travel books. Called to the Scottish bar, 1875, but never practiced. Traveled widely in Europe, America, and the South Sea Islands, finally settling in Samoa in 1899. Recipient: Silver medal, Royal Scottish Society of Arts, 1871, for a scientific essay on lighthouses. *Died 3 December 1894.*

PUBLICATIONS

Novels

Treasure Island (first published serially under the pseudonym Captain George North in *Young Folks,* 1881-82). London, Cassell, 1883.
Prince Otto: A Romance. London, Chatto & Windus, 1885; Boston, Roberts Brothers, 1886.
Kidnapped. New York, Scribner, 1886.
The Strange Case of Dr. Jekyll and Mr. Hyde. New York, Scribner, 1886.
The Black Arrow: A Tale of the Two Roses. New York, Scribner, 1888.
The Master of Ballantrae: A Winter's Tale. New York, Scribner, 1889.
The Wrong Box, with Lloyd Osbourne. New York, Scribner, 1889.
The Wrecker, with Lloyd Osbourne, illustrated by William Hole and W.L. Metcalf. New York, Scribner, 1892.
David Balfour. New York, Scribner, 1893; as *Catriona: A Sequel to Kidnapped,* London, Cassell, 1893.
The Ebb-Tide: A Trio and a Quartette, with Lloyd Osbourne. Chicago, and Cambridge, Stone & Kimball, 1894.
Weir of Hermiston: An Unfinished Romance. New York, Scribner, 1896.
St. Ives; Being the Adventures of a French Prisoner in England (completed by Arthur T. Quiller-Couch). New York, Scribner, 1897.

Short Stories

New Arabian Nights. New York, Holt, 1882.
The Story of a Lie. Hayley & Jackson, 1882; as *The Story of a Lie and Other Tales,* Boston, Turner, 1904.
More New Arabian Nights: The Dynamiter, with Fanny Stevenson. New York, Holt, 1885.
The Merry Men and Other Tales and Fables. New York, Scribner, 1887.
The Misadventures of John Nicholson: A Christmas Story. New York, Lovell, 1887.
Island Nights' Entertainments: Consisting of The Beach of Falesa, The Bottle Imp, The Isle of Voices, illustrated by Gordon Browne. New York, Scribner, 1893.
The Body-Snatcher. Springfield, Merriam, 1895.
Fables. New York, Scribner, 1896.
Tales and Fantasies. London, Chatto & Windus, 1905.
The Waif Woman. London, Chatto & Windus, 1916.
When the Devil Well, edited by W.P. Trent. Boston, Bibliophile Society, 1921.
Two Mediaeval Tales, illustrated by C.B. Falls. New York, Limited Editions Club, 1929.
Tales and Essays, edited by G.B. Stern. Falcon, 1950.

The Complete Short Stories of Robert Louis Stevenson, edited by Charles Neider. New York, Doubleday, 1969.

Poetry

Not I, and Other Poems, illustrated by the author. Davos, S.L. Osbourne, 1881.
Moral Emblems, illustrated by the author. Davos, S.L. Osbourne, 1882.
A Child's Garden of Verses. New York, Scribner, 1885.
Underwoods. New York, Scribner, 1887.
Ballads. New York, Scribner, 1890.
The Poems and Ballads of Robert Louis Stevenson. New York, Scribner, 1896.
Songs of Travel and Other Verses, edited by Sidney Colvin. London, Chatto & Windus, 1896.
R. L. S. Teuila (fugitive lines and verses). Privately printed, 1899.
Poetical Fragments. Privately printed, 1915.
An Ode of Horace. Privately printed, 1916.
Poems Hitherto Unpublished, edited by G.S. Hellman. Two volumes, Boston, Bibliophile Society, 1916.
New Poems and Variant Readings. London, Chatto & Windus, 1918.
The Poems of Robert Louis Stevenson (the complete poems). New York, Gordon Press, 1974.

Plays

Deacon Brodie; or, The Double Life, with William E. Henley. Privately printed, 1880.
Admiral Guinea, with William E. Henley. Privately printed, 1884.
Beau Austin, with William E. Henley. Privately printed, 1884.
Macaire, with William E. Henley. Privately printed, 1885.
Three Plays: Deacon Brodie, Beau Austin, Admiral Guinea, with William E. Henley. New York, Scribner, 1892.
The Hanging Judge, with Fanny Stevenson, edited by Edmund Gosse. Privately printed, 1914.
Monmouth: A Tragedy, edited by C. Vale. New York, Rudge, 1928.

Travel Books

An Inland Voyage. Carmel, California, Kegan Paul, 1878; Boston, Roberts Brothers, 1883.
Edinburgh: Picturesque Notes, with Etchings. London, Seeley, Jackson & Halliday, 1879; London, Macmillan, 1889.
Travels with a Donkey in the Cevennes. Boston, Roberts Brothers, 1879.
The Silverado Squatters. London, Chatto & Windus, 1883; New York, Munro, 1884.
Across the Plains, with Other Memories and Essays. New York, Scribner, 1892.
The Amateur Emigrant from the Clyde to Sandy Hook. Chicago, Stone & Kimball, 1895.
In the South Seas. New York, Scribner, 1896.
A Mountain Town in France: A Fragment, illustrated by the author. New York, and London, J. Lane, 1896.
Essays of Travel. London, Chatto & Windus, 1905.
Silverado Journal, edited by John E. Jordan. San Francisco, Book Club of California, 1954.
From Scotland to Silverado, edited by James D. Hart. Cambridge, Massachussetts, Harvard University Press, 1966.

The Amateur Emigrant with Some First Impressions of America, edited by Roger G. Swearingen. Two volumes, Osborne, 1976-77.

Essays

The Pentland Rising. Privately printed, 1866.
An Appeal to the Clergy. Blackwood, 1875.
Virginibus Puerisque and Other Papers. New York, Collier, 1881.
Familiar Studies of Men and Books. London, Chatto & Windus, 1882; New York, Dodd, Mead, 1887.
Some College Memories. Edinburgh, University Union Committee, 1886; New York, Mansfield & Wessels, 1899.
Memoir of Fleeming Jenkin. New York, Longmans, Green, 1887.
Memories and Portraits. New York, Scribner, 1887.
Father Damien: An Open Letter to the Reverend Dr. Hyde of Honolulu. London, Chatto & Windus, 1890; Portland, Maine, Mosher, 1897.
A Footnote to History: Eight Years of Trouble in Samoa. New York, Scribner, 1892.
War in Samoa. Privately printed, 1893.
Essays and Criticisms. Boston, Turner, 1903.
Prayers Written at Vailima, with an Introduction by Mrs. Stevenson. New York, Scribner, 1904.
Essays in the Art of Writing. London, Chatto & Windus, 1905.
Essays, edited by W.L. Phelps. New York, Scribner, 1906.
Lay Morals and Other Papers. New York, Scribner, 1911.
Memoirs of Himself. Privately printed, 1912.
Records of a Family of Engineers. London, Chatto & Windus, 1912.
On the Choice of a Profession. London, Chatto & Windus, 1916.
Confessions of a Unionist: An Unpublished Talk on Things Current, Written in 1888, edited by F.V. Livingstone. Privately printed, 1921.
The Best Thing in Edinburgh: An Address to the Speculative Society of Edinburgh in March 1873, edited by K.D. Osbourne. New York, Howell, 1923.
Selected Essays, edited by H.G. Rawlinson. London, Oxford University Press, 1923.
The Manuscripts of Robert Louis Stevenson's "Records of a Family of Engineers": The Unfinished Chapters, edited by J. Christian Bay. Chicago, Hill, 1929.
The Essays of Robert Louis Stevenson, edited by M. Elwin. London, Macdonald, 1950.

Letters and Diaries

Vailima Letters: Robert Louis Stevenson to Sidney Colvin, 1890-1894. Chicago, Stone & Kimball, 1895.
The Letters of Robert Louis Stevenson to His Family and Friends, edited by S. Colvin. New York, Scribner, 1899.
Autograph Letters, Original Mss., Books, Portraits and Curios from the Library of the Late R.L. Stevenson (catalog of the Anderson Galleries sale of Stevenson's literary property). Three volumes, London, Brown, 1914-16.
Our Samoan Adventure, with Fanny Stevenson, edited by Charles Neider. New York, Harper, 1955.
R.L.S.: Stevenson's Letters to Charles Baxter, edited by De Lancey Ferguson and Marshall Waingrow. New Haven, Connecticut, Yale University Press, 1956.

Collections

The Works of R.L. Stevenson. Edinburgh edition, eighteen volumes, edited by S. Colvin. London, Chatto & Windus, 1894-98; Thistle edition, twenty-six volumes, New York, Scribner, 1902; Biographical edition, thirty-one volumes, New York, Scribner, 1905-39; Pentland edition, twenty volumes, edited by Edmund Gosse, London, Cassell, 1906-07; Swanston edition, twenty-five volumes, London, Chatto & Windus, 1911-12; Tusitala edition, thirty-five volumes, London, Heinemann, 1923-24; South Seas edition, thirty-two volumes, New York, Scribner, 1925.

Other

A Stevenson Medley, edited by S. Colvin. London, Chatto & Windus 1899.

Robert Louis Stevenson: Hitherto Unpublished Prose Writings, edited by H.H. Harper. Boston, Bibliophile Society, 1921.

Castaways of Soledad: A Manuscript by Stevenson Hitherto Unpublished, edited by G.S. Hellman. Privately printed, 1928.

The Charity Bazaar: An Allegorical Dialogue. Portland, Oregon, Georgian Press, 1929.

Salute to RLS, edited by F. Holland. Cousland, 1950.

A Newly Discovered Long Story "An Old Song" and a Previously Unpublished Short Story "Edifying Letters of the Rutherford Family," edited by Roger G. Swearingen. Hamden, Connecticut, Archon, 1982.

Robert Louis Stevenson and "The Beach of Falesá": A Study in Victorian Publishing with the Original Text, edited by Barry Menikoff. Palos Verdes Estates, California, Stanford University Press, 1984.

*

Manuscript Collection: Beinecke Rare Book and Manuscript Library, Yale University; the Pierpont Morgan Library, New York City; the Henry E. Huntington Library, San Marino, California; the Widener Library, Harvard University; the Edinburgh Public Library; the Silverado Museum, Saint Helena, California; and the Monterey State Historical Monument Stevenson House, Monterey, California.

Media Adaptations: *Robert Louis Stevenson's "Markheim"* (one-act play), Eldridge Publishing, 1963; *Robert Louis Stevenson's "The Suicide Club"* (one-act play), Eldridge Publishing, 1964; *The Bottle Imp* (film, starring Sessue Hayakawa), Jesse L. Lasky Feature Play Co., 1917; *Kidnapped* (film), Thomas A. Edison, Inc., 1917, Twentieth Century-Fox, starring Freddie Bartholomew and Warner Baxter, 1938, Teaching Film Custodians, 1947, Monogram Pictures, starring Roddy McDowall and Dan O'Herlihy, 1948, and Walt Disney, starring James MacArthur and Peter Finch, 1950; *Treasure Island* (film), Fox Film Corp., 1917, Famous Players-Lasky Corp., starring Lon Chaney, 1920, Metro-Goldwyn-Mayer, starring Jackie Cooper, Wallace Beery, and Lionel Barrymore, 1934, Teaching Film Custodians, 1945, Walt Disney Productions, starring Bobby Driscoll and Robert Newton, 1950, and Turner Network Television and Agamemnon Films, starring Charlton Heston, Christian Bale, and Oliver Reed, 1990; *Dr. Jekyll and Mr. Hyde* (film), Pioneer Film Corp., 1920, Famous Players-Lasky Corp., starring John Barrymore and Nita Naldi, 1920, Paramount Publix Corp., starring Fredric March and Miriam Hopkins, 1932, Metro-Goldwyn-Mayer, star-

ring Spencer Tracy and Ingrid Bergman, 1941, and Sterling Educational Films, 1959; *The White Circle* (film adaptation of "The Pavilion on the Links," starring John Gilbert), Famous Players-Lasky Corp., 1920; *Ebb Tide* (film), Famous Players-Lasky Corp., starring Milton Sills, 1922, and Paramount Pictures, starring Ray Milland and Barry Fitzgerald, 1937; *Trouble for Two* (film adaptation of *The Suicide Club,* starring Robert Montgomery and Rosalind Russell), Metro-Goldwyn-Mayer, 1936; *The Body Snatcher* (film, starring Boris Karloff and Bela Lugosi), RKO Radio Pictures, 1945; *Adventure Island* (film adaptation of *Ebb Tide,* starring Rory Calhoun and Rhonda Fleming), Paramount Pictures, 1947; *Adventures in Silverado* (film adaptation of *The Silverado Squatters,* starring William Bishop and Forrest Tucker), Columbia Pictures, 1948; *The Black Arrow* (film, starring Louis Hayward and Janet Blair), Columbia Pictures, 1948, and Walt Disney, starring Oliver Reed and Stephan Chase; *Lodging for the Night* (film), Realm Television Productions, 1949; *Lord Maletroit's Door* (film), Realm Television Productions, 1949; *The Secret of St. Ives* (film, starring Richard Ney and Vanessa Brown), Columbia Pictures, 1949; *The Treasure of Franchard* (film), Realm Television Productions, 1949; *The Imp in the Bottle* (film), General Television Enterprises, 1950; *The Strange Door* (film adaptation of "The Sire de Maletroit's Door," starring Charles Laughton and Boris Karloff), Universal International Pictures, 1951; *The Treasure of Lost Cannon* (film adaptation of "The Treasure of Franchard"), Universal International Pictures, starring William Powell, 1951; *The Master of Ballantrae* (film, starring Errol Flynn), Warner Brothers, 1953, and six half-hour episodes by Time Life Television and BBC Enterprises, starring Julian Glover and Brian Cox; *Long John Silver* (film based on characters from *Treasure Island,* starring Robert Newton), Distributors Corp. of America, 1955; *The Wrong Box* (film, starring John Mills, Peter Sellers, Ralph Richardson, and Michael Caine), Columbia Pictures, 1966; *A Child's Garden of Verses* (film), Sterling Educational Films, 1967; McGraw-Hill, 1968, and University of California Extension Media Center, 1974; *Treasure Island* (adapted to films *Treasure Island Revisited* and *Treasure Island with Mr. Magoo*), both by Macmillan Films; *Treasure Island with Mr. Magoo* (thirty minute television series with Robert Newton); *Kidnapped* (filmstrip), Eye Gate House, 1958, Encyclopaedia Britannica Films, 1961, and Carman Educational Associates, 1966; *Treasure Island* (filmstrip), Encyclopaedia Britannica Films, 1960, Carman Educational Associates, 1966, Jam Handy School Service, 1968, Dufour Editions, 1969, Walt Disney Educational Materials, 1970, Universal Education and Visual Arts, 1971, Educational Record Sales, 1971, McGraw-Hill, 1972, and Teaching Resources Films, 1974; *The Owl and the Pussy-Cat [and] My Shadow* (filmstrips of the first poem by Edward Lear, the second by Stevenson), Cooper Films and Records, 1969; *Garden of Verses* (transparencies), Creative Visuals, 1970; *Highlights from Treasure Island* (filmstrips), Encyclopaedia Britannica Educational Corp., 1973; *Treasure Island* (record or cassette), read by Ian Richardson, Caedmon, Spoken Arts, 1971; *Treasury of Great Educational Records* (includes *Treasure Island;* twelve records), Miller-Brody Productions, also with *Robin Hood,* Columbia Special Products, 1977; *Adventure Library* (includes *Kidnapped* and *Treasure Island;* ten records or sixteen cassettes), Miller-Brody Productions; *Adventure Poets* (five cassettes), United Learning; *A Child's Garden of Verses* (two records), read by Nancy Wickwire and Basil Langton, Miller-Brody Productions, also read by Dame Judith Anderson, Caedmon; *Dr. Jekyll and Mr. Hyde* (three records or cassettes), read by Patrick Horgan, Miller-Brody Productions; *Kidnapped* (parts 1 and 2, cassettes only), read by John Franklyn, Alan MacDonald, Pamela Mant, David Thorndike, and Derek Young, Spoken Arts; *Markheim by Robert Louis Stevenson,* CMS Records; *Poetry in Song,* Crofut Productions; *The Strange Case of Dr. Jekyll and Mr. Hyde,* Caedmon, (parts 1 & 2, cassettes only), Spoken Arts.

Critical Studies: Entry in *Dictionary of Literary Biography,* Detroit, Gale, Volume 18: *Victorian Novelists after 1885,* 1983, Volume 57: *Victorian Prose Writers after 1867,* 1987.

*   *   *

Nearly all Robert Louis Stevenson's mature fiction, with the exception of *Dr. Jekyll,* takes the form of the historical romance. *Treasure Island, Kidnapped, Catriona, The Master of Ballantrae, St. Ives,* and *Weir of Hermiston* all fall into this category, with the action mainly taking place in eighteenth-century Scotland. The two exceptions are *The Black Arrow,* which is set in the Middle Ages, and *Treasure Island,* which has an English and exotic background.

The plots are nearly always concerned with long journeys, the search for treasure, or flight from capture, and they are usually fraught with great hazards—piracy, murder, intrigue—against which the hero, normally a young person of some resourcefulness, struggles to survive. But Stevenson does not merely use the ingredients of the historical romance for dramatic effects; he also tries to integrate them into a design by which they throw light on various aspects of the human situation as he saw it.

Many of the stories have not a single hero at the centre, but a pair. David and Alan in *Kidnapped,* Jim and Long John in *Treasure Island,* Dr. Jekyll and Mr. Hyde are the best known examples, and they seem to achieve a kind of complementarity as if each partner compensates for the defects of the other. Many of the books also deal with conflicts between clearly defined sides, such as pirates versus honest sailors, English versus Scots, or York versus Lancaster. But there is usually a good deal of changing sides between these antagonists. Long John Silver, for example, begins as an apparently honest sea cook, reveals himself as leader of the mutiny, then deserts the pirates, and finishes up by jumping Captain Smollett's ship. Dick Shelton in *The Black Arrow* switches his allegiance from Lancaster to York, while Alan Breck actually deserts King George at the Battle of Prestonpans. James in *The Master of Ballantrae* seems to have the best of both worlds, fighting for Bonnie Prince Charlie but spying for the other side. Finally, there is a good deal of intrigue and duplicity in the way Stevenson's characters behave, and physical disguises are frequently adopted. In *Catrion* the heroine pretends to be David's sister; in *The Black Arrow* Joanna passes herself off as a boy; and Dr. Jekyll's disguise is even more fundamental.

Stevenson's use of the dual hero, the changing of sides, and the adoption of disguises is not only appropriate to the kinds of stories he wrote, and adds to their dramatic effectiveness, but reveals his passionate concern with the problems of identity and morality. From Stevenson's biographers we know of the ambiguities of his own life, his troubled relations with his parents, whom he adored, and with Scotland, which he worshipped from afar. It may be that his literary interests developed there, but, from the evidence of the fiction, it is clear that Stevenson saw man's nature as constantly shifting, and therefore all the more difficult to define and come to terms with. Dr. Jekyll, who can transform himself physically into a murderous villain, and Deacon Brodie, the clergyman who becomes a robber by night, are simply extreme examples of such shifts. Long

John Silver and Alan Breck are much more equivocal as their personalities and virtues fluctuate.

Long John, for example, is a pirate, thief, and murderer, and, as such, quite ruthless in pursuit of gold. But he is also cheerful, brave, witty, and above all kind to Jim, who has no father. In this way Stevenson is constantly challenging our responses. Who is good or bad? he seems to be saying. In your final judgment, do you find Long John sympathetic or not? Are these sorts of questions even relevant? David Balfour operates as a kind of moral censor of Alan Breck's behaviour in *Kidnapped,* but in the end, though he may be "right" in his quarrel with Alan in "The Flight in the Heather," he comes to see that their love complicates the whole matter of knowing who is right or wrong.

Stevenson's influence on later writers is less specific, more pervasive. The historical romance, first established by Scott at the beginning of the nineteenth century, and then adapted for children by such authors as Marryat and Henty, went from strength to strength, until it reached its Victorian peak with Stevenson himself. Though the quality of many early twentieth-century historical novels deteriorated, honourable exceptions can be found in the work of John Masefield and Geoffrey Trease, and since the 1950s the emergence of such writers as Leon Garfield, Cynthia Harnett, and Rosemary Sutcliff has sparked a renaissance of the form.

Though the influence of Stevenson on the specific narrative techniques of the adventure story is doubtful, the influence of his moral values issuing into literary attitudes is everywhere absolutely pervasive, even among those authors who would say they had never read him, and this for two reasons. First, he showed how it was possible to write books for young people that were both thrilling in the most fundamental sense, and yet at the same time deeply serious. The loss of innocence—for example, by Jim Hawkins—is as prevalent in Stevenson's work as in that of Henry James, and the friendship of the two writers was, of course, very significant. And second, in his treatment of the complexities of human behaviour, in his refusal to compartmentalise characters as either "good" or "bad," his writing revealed a maturity which the best children's writers of today can only hope to emulate but not excel. It is significant that a novelist like Leon Garfield, whose stories of the eighteenth century differ so much from Stevenson's, should return time and again to the equivocal nature of human relationships, and the difficulties of distinguishing appearance from reality in exciting books such as *Smith* and *Jack Holborn.* Without the achievement of Stevenson so much of today's best writing would never have appeared.

—Dennis Butts

————

STEWART, Mary (Florence Elinor). British. Born in Sunderland, County Durham, 17 September 1916. Educated at Eden Hall, Penrith, Cumberland; Skellfield School, Ripon, Yorkshire; St. Hild's College, University of Durham, B.A. (honors) 1938, M.A. 1941. Served in the Royal Observer Corps during World War II. Married Sir Frederick Henry Stewart in 1945. Lecturer in English, Durham University, 1941-45; Part-time Lecturer in English, St. Hild's Training College, Durham, and Durham University, 1948-56; writer, since 1954. Recipient: Crime Writers Association Silver Dagger award, 1960, for *My Brother Michael;* Mystery Writers of America award, 1964, for *This Rough Magic;* Frederick Niven award, 1971, for *The*

Crystal Cave; Scottish Arts Council award, 1974, for *Ludo and the Star Horse.* Fellow, Royal Society of Arts, 1968; Fellow, Newnham College, Cambridge, 1986. Agent: c/o Hodder & Stoughton Ltd., Mill Road, Dunton Green, Sevenoaks, Kent TN13 2YA, England.

PUBLICATIONS FOR ADULTS AND YOUNG ADULTS

Novels

Madam, Will You Talk? London, Hodder & Stoughton, 1955; New York, Mill, 1956.
Wildfire at Midnight. London, Hodder & Stoughton, and New York, Appleton Century Crofts, 1956.
Thunder on the Right. London, Hodder & Stoughton, 1957; New York, Mill, 1958.
Nine Coaches Waiting. London, Hodder & Stoughton, 1958; New York, Mill, 1959.
My Brother Michael. London, Hodder & Stoughton, and New York, Mill, 1960.
The Ivy Tree. London, Hodder & Stoughton, and New York, Mill, 1961.
The Moon-Spinners. London, Hodder & Stoughton, 1962; New York, Mill, 1963.
This Rough Magic. London, Hodder & Stoughton, and New York, Mill, 1964.
Airs above the Ground. London, Hodder & Stoughton, and New York, Mill, 1965.
The Gabriel Hounds. London, Hodder & Stoughton, and New York, Mill, 1967.
The Wind off the Small Isles. London, Hodder & Stoughton, 1968.
The Crystal Cave (first book in the "Merlin Trilogy"). London, Hodder & Stoughton, and New York, Morrow, 1970.
The Hollow Hills (second book in the "Merlin Trilogy"). London, Hodder & Stoughton, and New York, Morrow, 1973.
Touch Not the Cat. London, Hodder & Stoughton, and New York, Morrow, 1976.
The Last Enchantment (third book in the "Merlin Trilogy"). London, Hodder & Stoughton, and New York, Morrow, 1979.
Merlin Trilogy. New York, Morrow, 1980.
The Wicked Day. London, Hodder & Stoughton, and New York, Morrow, 1983.
Thornyhold. London, Hodder & Stoughton, and New York, Morrow, 1988.
The Stormy Petrel. London, Hoddard & Stoughton, and New York, Morrow, 1991.

Other

Frost on the Window (poetry). New York, Morrow, 1990.
Contributor, *Three Women Alone in the Woods.* West Liberty, Kentucky, Trillium, 1992.

Radio Plays: *Lift from a Stranger, Call Me at Ten-Thirty, The Crime of Mr. Merry,* and *The Lord of Langdale,* 1957-58.

PUBLICATIONS FOR CHILDREN

Fiction

The Little Broomstick. Leicester, Brockhampton Press, 1971; New York, Morrow, 1972.

Ludo and the Star Horse. Leicester, Brockhampton Press, 1974; New York, Morrow, 1975.
A Walk in Wolf Wood. London, Hodder & Stoughton, and New York, Morrow, 1980.
Yoga for Children. New York, Simon & Schuster, 1993.

*

Manuscript Collection: National Library of Scotland, Edinburgh.

Critical Study: Entry in *Contemporary Literary Criticism,* Volume VII, Detroit, Gale, 1977.

*   *   *

Mary Stewart's novels fall into two distinct categories. Her early books were all romantic thrillers, in which the spirited heroines invariably arrived at happy marriages after preparatory ordeals of involvement with violent crime, perplexing mystery, and serious personal danger. In the last few years she has added some gentler novels to her list—*Thornyhold* and *Stormy Petrel*—which are simple romances, still containing elements of mystery and wrongdoing but without the strong plotting and excitements of the early romantic adventures. Since settings are always important in Stewart's work, one can see the difference between her early and more recent romances by comparing *Stormy Petrel* with *Wildfire at Midnight,* both of which are set in the Scottish islands. *Stormy Petrel* is a pleasant low-key story, but it has nothing to compare with the psychotic menace which threatens the heroine of the earlier book.

In contrast to these romantic stories of the present day are Stewart's reworkings of the Arthurian legend. These are romances of an altogether different kind. Based on careful research into medieval sources, from the imaginative historian Geoffrey of Monmouth to Malory's *Morte d'Arthur,* these books transcribe the Matter of Britain into a modern idiom - not with the modernist ironic distance of T.H. White's *The Once and Future King* but with an eye to the realistic explanations and psychological plausibilities that might have underlain the more spectacular magic of the legend. These books offer to older readers the sensitive re-enactment of Arthurian romance in modern terms that Rosemary Sutcliff achieved for a younger audience in *The Lantern-Bearers.* Retaining the magic of the original tellings and respecting the essentials of the legend, Stewart's books nevertheless open up the psychology of romance and successfully reactivate the Arthurian story for a contemporary readership.

All Stewart's books were originally published for adults, but both categories of her work are popular with and have much to offer to an young adult audience. The romances, whether thrillers or not, will appeal predominantly to girls, because they have female protagonists, are written almost exclusively from a woman's viewpoint, and usually (the brilliant *Thunder on the Right* is an exception) are narrated in the first person. Male teenage readers free of prejudice against female narrators will find a great deal in these to enjoy. The Arthurian stories appeal equally to readers of both sexes, especially those who have previously enjoyed Arthurian retellings aimed at younger children.

For young adults the attraction of Stewart's romantic thrillers lies particularly in their use of a conventional romance framework to present a succession of intelligent and resourceful women who are fully equal to their male coadventurers in virtually every quality except brute muscular strength. Book after book ends with some impressive male chivalry, but one is often aware of a tongue-in-cheek quality in Stewart's depiction of these sexual partnerships, and when the story ends, as it invariably does, in the female protagonist's delighted surrender to protective marital union, the motive is clearly shown to be instinctive natural pleasure, not weakness or social necessity. The point is underlined by those stories—*The Gabriel Hounds* and *Touch Not the Cat*—in which the lovers are also cousins, equalised in status by family relationships. As if to underscore the point still further, the lovers in *The Gabriel Hounds* have fathers who are identical twins, and those in *Touch Not the Cat* are linked by shared telepathic powers. Stewart is interested in isolated and hence self-reliant, independent heroines but also in closer than usual family bonding, and through permutations on these two extremes she subverts the cliches of dominant male and submissive female, presenting some formidable protagonists. They need to be formidable, too, because they inhabit excitingly treacherous worlds where appearances can never be trusted.

Although small period details have dated in some of the books, their tone is remarkably modern and up-to-date. The exotic but accessible settings (Crete in *The Moon-Spinners,* Austria in *Airs above the Ground,* southern France in *Madam, Will You Talk?*) are vividly realised in authentic local detail and are Stewart's particular strength.

The Arthurian stories are likewise marked by their precise geographical locale and vivid sense of place and atmosphere. Above all, however, the power of the Arthurian stories lies in the humanising of a legend. The books comprise a trilogy (*Merlin of the Crystal Cave,* originally published as *The Crystal Cave, The Hollow Hills,* and *The Last Enchantment*) which forms the first-person story of the life of Merlin, the magician and seer who was King Arthur's guardian and teacher. *The Wicked Day* is a kind of coda to the trilogy, which is the third-person story of Arthur's bastard son Mordred. This last book is in many ways the most interesting and original of all. In the traditional legend Mordred is an evil figure, finally the cause of Arthur's ruin. He destroys Arthur in Stewart's story also, but against his will, and only as tragic proof that determined historical process is too powerful to be frustrated by the individual human will.

The Wicked Day has much to offer young adult readers and deserves to be widely known, but inevitably it is overshadowed by the Merlin trilogy. This is a fine piece of storytelling—immensely readable, full of action, incident, and suspense. It is extremely skilful in combining believable character, motive, and the actions of men in a stylised but intricate political world with the overarching sense of destiny and fatefulness which is true to the legend in all its classic forms. *The Last Enchantment,* which tells the story of Arthur's adult life at a time when the narrator Merlin was somewhat removed from it, is perhaps the least successful of the three, but the stories of Merlin's boyhood, in *Merlin of the Crystal Cave,* and of Arthur's, in *The Hollow Hills,* are triumphant narratives which take an honourable place in the literary history of Arthurian legend.

Mary Stewart's work represents popular romantic storytelling at its best, and both categories of her work deserve a large young adult readership.

—Peter Hollindale

———

STINE, R(obert) L(awrence). Also writes as Eric Affabee; Zachary Blue; Jovial Bob Stine. American. Born in Columbus, Ohio, 8 October 1943. Educated at Ohio State University, B.A. 1965; New York University, 1966-67. Married Jane Waldhorn in 1969; one son. Social Studies teacher at junior high schools in Columbus, Ohio, 1967-68; associate editor, *Junior Scholastic* (magazine), New York City, 1969-71; editor, *Search* (magazine), New York City, 1972-75; editor, *Bananas* (magazine), New York City, 1972-83; editor, *Maniac* (magazine), New York City, 1984-85.

PUBLICATIONS FOR YOUNG ADULTS

Fiction

The Time Raider, illustrated by David Febland. New York, Scholastic, 1982.
The Golden Sword of Dragonwalk, illustrated by David Febland. New York, Scholastic, 1983.
Horrors of the Haunted Museum. New York, Scholastic, 1984.
Indiana Jones and the Curse of Horror Island. New York, Ballantine, 1984.
Indiana Jones and the Giants of the Silver Tower. New York, Ballantine, 1984.
Instant Millionaire, illustrated by Jowill Woodman. New York, Scholastic, 1984.
Through the Forest of Twisted Dreams. New York, Avon, 1984.
The Badlands of Hark, illustrated by Bob Roper. New York, Scholastic, 1985.
Challenge of the Wolf Knight. New York, Avon, 1985.
Conquest of the Time Master. New York, Avon, 1985.
Demons of the Deep, illustrated by Fred Carrillo. New York, Golden Books, 1985.
Indiana Jones and the Cult of the Mummy's Crypt. New York, Ballantine, 1985.
The Invaders of Hark. New York, Scholastic, 1985.
Blind Date. New York, Scholastic, 1986.
Cavern of the Phantoms. New York, Avon, 1986.
Mystery of the Imposter. New York, Avon, 1986.
Operation: Deadly Decoy. New York, Ballantine, 1986.
Twisted. New York, Scholastic, 1986.
Jungle Raid. New York, Ballantine, 1988.
The Baby-Sitter. New York, Scholastic, 1989.
Beach Party. New York, Scholastic, 1990.
The Boyfriend. New York, Scholastic, 1990.
Curtains. New York, Pocket, 1990.
Fear Street: The Wrong Number. New York, Pocket, 1990.
Halloween Party. New York, Pocket, 1990.
How I Broke up with Ernie. New York, Pocket, 1990.
Missing. New York, Pocket, 1990.
Phone Calls. New York, Pocket, 1990.
The Stepsister. New York, Pocket, 1990.
The Surprise Party. New York, Pocket, 1990.
Baby-Sitter II. New York, Scholastic, 1991.
Broken Date. New York, Pocket, 1991.
Fear Street: Fire Game. New York, Pocket, 1991.
The Girlfriend. New York, Scholastic, 1991.
Haunted. New York, Pocket, 1991.
Jerks-In-Training. New York, Scholastic, 1991.
Lights Out. New York, Pocket, 1991.
Losers in Space. New York, Scholastic, 1991.

The New Girl. New York, Pocket, 1991.
The Overnight. New York, Pocket, 1991.
Party Summer. New York, Pocket, 1991.
The Secret Bedroom. New York, Pocket, 1991.
Silent Night. New York, Pocket, 1991.
Ski Weekend. New York, Pocket, 1991.
The Sleepwalker. New York, Pocket, 1991.
Snowman. New York, Scholastic, 1991.
Beach House. New York, Scholastic, 1992.
The Best Friend. New York, Pocket, 1992.
Bozos on Patrol. New York, Scholastic, 1992.
First Date. New York, Pocket, 1992.
The First Evil. New York, Pocket, 1992.
Goodnight Kiss. New York, Pocket, 1992.
Goosebumps: Monster Blood. New York, Scholastic, 1992.
Goosebumps: Say Cheese & Die! New York, Scholastic, 1992.
Goosebumps: Welcome to the Deadhouse. New York, Scholastic, 1992.
The Knife. New York, Pocket, 1992.
Prom Queen. New York, Pocket, 1992.
The Second Evil. New York, Pocket, 1992.
Stay out of the Basement. New York, Scholastic, 1992.
The Third Evil: Fear Street. New York, Pocket, 1992.
Broken Hearts. New York, Pocket, 1993.
The Cheater. New York, Pocket, 1993.
Goosebumps: The Curse of the Mummy's Tomb. New York, Scholastic, 1993.
Hitchhiker. New York, Scholastic, 1993.
Sunburn. New York, Pocket, 1993.
Hit and Run, forthcoming.

As Jovial Bob Stine

The Absurdly Silly Encyclopedia and Flyswatter, illustrated by Bob Taylor. New York, Scholastic, 1978.
How to Be Funny: An Extremely Silly Guidebook, illustrated by Carol Nicklaus. New York, Dutton, 1978.
The Complete Book of Nerds, illustrated by Sam Viviano. New York, Scholastic, 1979.
The Dynamite Do-It-Yourself Pen Pal Kit, illustrated by Jared Lee. New York, Scholastic, 1980.
Dynamite's Funny Book of the Sad Facts of Life, illustrated by Jared Lee. New York, Scholastic, 1980.
Going Out! Going Steady! Going Bananas!, photographs by Dan Nelken. New York, Scholastic, 1980.
The Pigs' Book of World Records, illustrated by Peter Lippman. New York, Random House, 1980.
The Sick of Being Sick Book, with wife, Jane Stine, edited by Ann Durrell, illustrated by Carol Nicklaus. New York, Dutton, 1980.
Bananas Looks at TV. New York, Scholastic, 1981.
The Beast Handbook, illustrated by Bob Taylor. New York, Scholastic, 1981.
The Cool Kids' Guide to Summer Camp, with Jane Stine, illustrated by Jerry Zimmerman. New York, Scholastic, 1981.
Gnasty Gnomes, illustrated by Peter Lippman. New York, Random House, 1981.
Don't Stand in the Soup, illustrated by Carol Nicklaus. New York, Bantam, 1982.
Bored with Being Bored!: How to Beat the Boredom Blahs, with Jane Stine, illustrated by Jerry Zimmerman. New York, Four Winds, 1982.

Blips!: The First Book of Video Game Funnies, illustrated by Bryan Hendrix. New York, Scholastic, 1983.
Everything You Need to Survive: Brothers and Sisters, with Jane Stine. New York, Random House, 1983.
Everything You Need to Survive: First Dates, with Jane Stine. New York, Random House, 1983.
Everything You Need to Survive: Homework, with Jane Stine. New York, Random House, 1983.
Everything You Need to Survive: Money Problems, with Jane Stine. New York, Random House, 1983.
Jovial Bob's Computer Joke Book. New York, Scholastic, 1985.
The Doggone Dog Joke Book. Dayton, Parachute Press, 1986.
Miami Mice, illustrated by Eric Gurney. New York, Scholastic, 1986.
One Hundred and One Silly Monster Jokes. New York, Scholastic, 1986.

As Eric Affabee

Attack on the King. New York, Avon, 1986.
G.I. Joe and the Everglades Swamp Terror. New York, Ballantine, 1986.

As Zachary Blue

The Jet Fighter Trap. New York, Scholastic, 1987.
The Petrova Twist. New York, Scholastic, 1987.

*

Biography: Essay in *Speaking for Ourselves, Too* compiled and edited by Donald R. Gallo, National Council of Teachers of English, 1993.

*   *   *

Robert L. Stine is a publisher's dream: a prolific writer who turns out compact, marketable best sellers almost monthly. Between 1988 and 1993, Stine had over fifty books published under his name, most of them in the teen thriller genre. His thriller series, *Fear Street,* is among the most popular series in all YA fiction, spinning off series like *The Cheerleaders, Fear Street Saga, Fear Street Super Chillers* and *Goosebumps.* Each one is unquestionably Stine: a collection of cliffhanging scenes creating a "safe scare."

Stine's background is writing for humor magazines and jokebooks which shows in his thrillers. Unlike other writers in the genre, Stine's books have a comic edge to them and are filled with characters playing practical jokes which more than often backfire or have unexpected tragic results. If writing jokes is about setting up the joke then providing the punchline, Stine operates the same way in a thriller as he sets up the situation then adds the punchline in the form of a cliffhanger scene. In addition to humor, Stine also wrote books in the *Find Your Fate, Wizards, Warriors & You* and *Twist-A-Plot* series. The seeds of Stine's thriller are also here in the multiple-ending adventure series titles as he builds the action, gets to a cliffhanging sequences, then builds the action again. Characters are secondary to the twisting "you'll never guess what happens next" plots.

Blind Date and *Twisted* were Stine's first two novels and along with Christopher Pike's books, represented the beginning of the teen thriller. *Blind Date* is an almost perfect thriller containing all the elements of the mix: a teenage boy with a secret in his past, some mysterious phone calls, lots of scenes set in school filled with realistic teen dialogue and concerns, and a scene where Kerry shows up for his date only to have the girl's mother tell him "she's dead." The book then kicks along briskly as Kerry gets into more trouble, there are more cliffhangers and red herrings, and finally the big "saved just in the nick of time" finish where the killer's identity is revealed. *Twisted* is more of the same including the switched identity ending, but this time the setting is in a sorority rather than a high school. *Broken Date* originally came out in the *Crosswinds* romance series and is to form: the book begins with blood (from a paper cut) and ends with a struggle involving a knife.

Then, Stine came upon *Fear Street*. Set in the town of Shadyside, the *Fear Street* series is held together only by a common location and all too familiar plots. Violence hangs in the air: almost every book features the words "murder" or "kill" on the front cover blurb, several covers feature knives, and every cover shows a young woman or women in danger. Some, of course, are better than others, but considering they are chucked out almost once a month, the actual quality of them is quite surprisingly good. Rarely does Stine fail to entertain and/or frighten. From the early creepiness of *The Surprise Party* or *Missing* (a truly scary book), to the more bared down stalking of *The Knife* or *The Cheater,* Stine loads every book with false endings, "it was only a paper maché severed hand" gross outs, and "so it was you!" endings, thus supplying his audience, somewhat younger than that of Christopher Pike's crowd, with their daily minimum requirement of chills. And while the plots are fantastic, the characters are very real high school age kids. They worry a lot about grades, friends, dating, being popular and the like. That realistic backdrop of anxiety sets up wonderfully for high anxiety as Stine turns every day worries into outlandish thrillers. If being a teenager is about fitting in, then Stine writes books about where "fitting in" is translated into being "singled out" for terror.

In addition to the *Fear Street* series, Stine also writes *Fear Street Super Chillers* which are the same idea, just expanded by about fifty pages. His *Cheerleaders* series is also spun off from *Fear Street.* Choosing cheerleaders to be the victims *and* the villains shows Stine knows his audience, plus he adds even more supernatural mumbo jumbo than usual. There's also his *Baby Sitter* trilogy which started with *The Baby Sitter,* followed by *Baby Sitter II,* and finally *Baby Sitter III.* These feature the recurrent character of Jenny, the stalked baby sitter, and read like movie ties to as yet unmade slasher films. Finally, *Goosebumps* contains many of the same tricks but rarely any real violence or body counts since they are aimed at younger readers. *Stay out of the Basement* is another reworking of an old horror staple—the mad scientist. The Stine angle is simple: what if that mad scientist was your father? Margaret and Casey's father is conducting experiments in the basement that get out of hand. Stine's style in *Goosebumps* is the same, yet even more compact: chapters are less than five pages and almost everyone has a cliffhanger. The scares are more cartoonish and the humor is also more evident.

Stine's non-*Fear Street* novels are both scarier yet less violent. This toning down might have something to do with the publisher, Scholastic, who market their YA novels through schools and therefore avoid controversial/violent novels. Unlike the "girls in trouble" covers of the *Fear Street,* Stine's Scholastic novels feature no such imagery, nor do the books as a rule rely as heavily on mayhem. In *The Boyfriend* Stine presents an evil character, Joanna, as the protagonist. Joanna feels no regret after causing the death of her boyfriend Dexter, only to feel fear when Dexter returns from the grave.

Of course, he never really died and it was all part of a plan, but that is beside the point. In *The Girlfriend,* Stine works off a *Fatal Attraction* riff of the obsessed scorned woman, where in *Beach Party* and *Beach House,* he's taken the thriller formula of a deserted exotic location, kids in trouble and a stalking killer and applied it to great success. *Hit and Run* covers the same "they hit someone with a car now they have to pay" ground as Pike's *Slumber Party* and Lois Duncan's *I Know What You Did Last Summer,* yet is still enjoyable as Stine applies his bag-of-tricks to the formula. Even a book like *Hitchhiker* is not terribly original with a stock premise (two girls pick up a mysterious hitchhiker) and writing that is not that special, Stine still manages to tell a good tale by pacing the novel so that chills happen at a regular interval and like those readers of his *Twist-A-Plot* books, readers are kept guessing how it will all turn out.

Stine has broken from the thriller genre for the YA audience with *Phone Calls* and *How I Broke up with Ernie.* Both rely on situations similar to thrillers, *Phone Calls* even includes a revenge plot, albeit wacky. *Phone Calls* fails because of the all dialogue gimmick, but *Ernie* works like a funny flipside to *The Girlfriend* about a person who just won't go away after a break-up. As always the story begins with a bang, with "I've decided to break up with Ernie," and ends with one; rather than getting a knife thrown at him Ernie gets a cake shoved in his face. But it is all done with enough character development to make the reader care about the fate of Ernie and the other characters.

That ability is what keeps Stine's audience waiting for his next book. While his characters are normally faceless suburban kids, they are so real to readers that when Stine puts them in jeopardy, over and over and over again, the readers care enough to read on. The plots are simpler than those in Pike's novels and the violence is more imagined than actual, thus keeping Stine popular with younger readers. Reading Stine is a lot like a roller coaster ride: the trip is quite short (most of his books are under 175 pages), the thrills plenty and smartly spaced, and after a while the fear is gone (because the experience ends) but the thrills are not.

—Patrick Jones

———

STIRLING, Arthur. See **SINCLAIR, Upton (Beall).**

———

STOLZ, Mary (née Slattery). American. Born in Boston, Massachusetts, 24 March 1920. Educated at Birch Wathen School, New York; Columbia University Teacher's College, New York, 1936-38; Katharine Gibbs School, New York, 1938-39. Married 1) Stanley Burr Stolz in 1940 (divorced 1956), one son; 2) Thomas C. Jaleski in 1965. Writer of books for children and young adults. Worked at R.H. Macy's, New York, and as secretary at Columbia University Teachers College. Recipient: Notable Book citation, American Library Association (ALA), 1951, for *The Sea Gulls Woke Me;* Children's Book award, Child Study Children's Book Committee at Bank Street College, 1953, for *In a Mirror;* Spring Book Festival Older Honor award, *New York Herald Tribune,* 1953, for *Ready or Not,* 1956, for *The Day and the Way We Met,* and 1957, for *Because of Madeline;* ALA Notable Book citation, 1961, for *Belling the Tiger;* Newbery award Honor Book designation, 1962, for *Belling the Tiger,* and 1966, for *The Noonday Friends;* Junior Book award, Boys' Club of America, 1964, for *The Bully of Barkham Street;* Honor List citation, *Boston Globe/Horn Book* and National Book award finalist, Association of American Publishers, both 1975, for *The Edge of Next Year;* Recognition of Merit award, George G. Stone Center for Children's Books, 1982, for entire body of work; ALA Notable Book citation, 1985, for *Quentin Corn;* Children's Science Book Younger Honor award, New York Academy of Sciences, 1986, for *Night of Ghosts and Hermits: Nocturnal Life on the Seashore;* German Youth Festival award; ALA Notable Book citation, Notable Children's Trade Books in Social Studies, Children's Book Council, both 1988, and Teacher's Choice citation, International Reading Association, 1989, all for *Storm in the Night;* numerous other ALA Notable Book citations; Kerlan award, 1993. Agent: Roslyn Targ Literary Agency, 105 West 13th St., Suite 15E, New York, NY 10011. Address: P.O. Box 82, Longboat Key, FL 34228, U.S.A.

PUBLICATIONS FOR YOUNG ADULTS

Fiction

To Tell Your Love. New York, Harper, 1950.
The Organdy Cupcakes. New York, Harper, 1951.
The Sea Gulls Woke Me. New York, Harper, 1951.
In a Mirror. New York, Harper, 1953.
Ready or Not. New York, Harper, 1953; London, Heinemann, 1966.
Pray Love, Remember. New York, Harper, 1954.
Two by Two. Boston, Houghton, 1954; London, Hodder & Stoughton, 1955; revised version, as *A Love, or a Season,* New York, Harper, 1964.
Rosemary. New York, Harper, 1955.
The Day and the Way We Met. New York, Harper, 1956.
Hospital Zone. New York, Harper, 1956.
Because of Madeline. New York, Harper, 1957.
Good-by My Shadow. New York, Harper, 1957; London, Penguin, 1964.
And Love Replied. New York, Harper, 1958.
Second Nature. New York, Harper, 1958.
Some Merry-Go-Round Music. New York, Harper, 1959.
The Beautiful Friend and Other Stories. New York, Harper, 1960.
Wait for Me, Michael. New York, Harper, 1961.
Who Wants Music on Monday? New York, Harper, 1963.
By the Highway Home. New York, Harper, 1971.
Leap before You Look. New York, Harper, 1972.
The Edge of Next Year. New York, Harper, 1974.
Cat in the Mirror. New York, Harper, 1975.
Ferris Wheel. New York, Harper, 1977.
Cider Days. New York, Harper, 1978.
Go and Catch a Flying Fish. New York, Harper, 1979.
What Time of Night Is It? New York, Harper, 1981.
Ivy Larkin: A Novel. San Diego, Harcourt, 1986.

PUBLICATIONS FOR CHILDREN

Fiction

The Leftover Elf, illustrated by Peggy Bacon. New York, Harper, 1952.
Emmett's Pig, illustrated by Garth Williams. New York, Harper, 1959; Kingswood, Surrey, World's Work, 1963.
A Dog on Barkham Street, illustrated by Leonard Shortall. New York, Harper, 1960.
Belling the Tiger, illustrated by Beni Montresor. New York, Harper, 1961.
The Great Rebellion, illustrated by Beni Montresor. New York, Harper, 1961.
Fredou, illustrated by Tomi Ungerer. New York, Harper, 1962.
Pigeon Flight, illustrated by Murray Tinkelman. New York, Harper, 1962.
The Bully of Barkham Street, illustrated by Leonard Shortall. New York, Harper, 1963.
Siri, the Conquistador, illustrated by Beni Montresor. New York, Harper, 1963.
The Mystery of the Woods, illustrated by Uri Shulevitz. New York, Harper, 1964.
The Noonday Friends, illustrated by Louis S. Glanzman. New York, Harper, 1965.
Maximilian's World, illustrated by Uri Shulevitz. New York, Harper, 1966.
A Wonderful, Terrible Time, illustrated by Louis S. Glanzman. New York, Harper, 1967.
Say Something, illustrated by Edward Frascino. New York, Harper, 1968; revised edition illustrated by Alexander Koshkin, 1993.
The Dragons of the Queen, illustrated by Edward Frascino. New York, Harper, 1969.
The Story of a Singular Hen and Her Peculiar Children, illustrated by Edward Frascino. New York, Harper, 1969.
Juan, illustrated by Louis Glanzman. New York, Harper, 1970.
Land's End, illustrated by Dennis Hermanson. New York, Harper, 1973.
Cat Walk, illustrated by Erik Blegvad. New York, Harper, 1983; London, Armada, 1985.
The Explorer of Barkham Street, illustrated by Emily Arnold McCully. New York, Harper, 1985.
Quentin Corn, illustrated by Pamela Johnson. Boston, David Godine, 1985.
The Cuckoo Clock, illustrated by Pamela Johnson. Boston, David Godine, 1986.
The Scarecrows and Their Child, illustrated by Amy Schwartz. New York, Harper, 1987.
Pangur Ban, illustrated by Pamela Johnson. New York, Harper, 1988.
Storm in the Night, illustrated by Pat Cummings. New York, Harper, 1988.
Zekmet, the Stone Carver: A Tale of Ancient Egypt, illustrated by Deborah Nourse Lattimore. San Diego, Harcourt, 1988.
Barkham Street Trilogy (contains *A Dog on Barkham Street, The Bully of Barkham Street,* and *The Explorer of Barkham Street*). New York, Harper, 1989.
Bartholomew Fair. New York, Greenwillow, 1990.
Tales at the Mousehole (contains revised versions of *The Great Rebellion, Maximilian's World,* and *Siri, the Conquistador*), illustrated by Pamela Johnson. Boston, David Godine, 1990.

Deputy Shep, illustrated by Pamela Johnson. New York, HarperCollins, 1991.

Go Fish, illustrated by Pat Cummings. New York, HarperCollins, 1991.

King Emmett the Second, illustrated by Garth Williams. New York, Greenwillow, 1991.

Stealing Home. New York, HarperCollins, 1992.

Say Something, illustrated by Alexander Koshkin. New York, HarperCollins, 1993.

Cezanne Pinto: A Memoir. New York, Knopf, 1994.

Coco Grimes. New York, HarperCollins, 1994.

The Weeds and the Weather. New York, Greenwillow, 1994.

Other

Night of Ghosts and Hermits: Nocturnal Life on the Seashore, illustrated by Susan Gallagher. San Diego, Harcourt, 1985.

PUBLICATIONS FOR ADULTS

Novel

Truth and Consequence. New York, Harper, 1953.

*

Media Adaptations: "Baby Blue Expression" (short story; first published in *McCall's*) adapted for television by Alfred Hitchcock. *The Noonday Friends* (recording), Miller-Brody, 1976.

Biography: Entry in *More Junior Authors,* New York, H.W. Wilson, 1963; essay in *Something about the Author Autobiography Series,* Volume 3, Detroit, Gale, 1986; essay in *Speaking for Ourselves: Autobiographical Sketches by Notable Authors of Books for Young Adults,* Volume 1, compiled and edited by Donald R. Gallo, National Council of Teachers of English, 1990.

Manuscript Collection: Kerlan Collection, University of Minnesota, Minneapolis.

Critical Studies: Entry in *Contemporary Literary Criticism,* Volume 12, Detroit, Gale, 1980.

*   *   *

Mary Stolz is a prolific writer who perceptively addresses the feelings and concerns of children and young adults. The themes of her early young adult works include coming of age and dealing with love. Her later books focus upon the interactions of family members who are coping with the stresses of modern life.

Stolz's work is particularly noteworthy for her strong characterization. Her characters are well-rounded and introspective. They observe and analyze their own behavior and feelings as well as the actions and emotions of family and friends.

One of Stolz's early works, *Because of Madeline,* is set in a posh private school. The main character is disdainful of her snobbish classmates and considerate of the scholarship students until Madeline arrives. Madeline, one of the girls accepted on scholarship, challenges the main character's egalitarian attitudes by her refusal to conform in any way to what others expect of her.

Madeline's intellectual brilliance makes her schoolmates feel inferior and her nonchalance about her singing ability aggravates them. After reflecting about her relationship with Madeline, the protagonist recognizes and regrets her own hypocrisy. Despite the message about accepting others on their own merits without regard to appearances, this book's descriptions of prep schools and coming out parties has the haughty tone of a wealthy egocentric. For example, the main character considers herself thoughtful for not inviting her friend on a shopping trip to Bonwit's since, after all, she couldn't really afford to shop there.

The main characters in Stolz's recent books do not come from such privileged homes. Their conflicts do not center on acceptance of others but on the interactions of family members as they struggle to cope with some of the senseless suffering many people face.

By the Highway Home is the story of a family reeling from the tragic loss of a son in Vietnam. This loss is compounded by financial difficulties arising from the father's unemployment. Catty's outburst, descrying her family's unrelenting sadness and despair helps to break the hold of grief upon their lives. As they begin their lives in a new home they learn to feel joy with each other and with the memory of their dead child. The author's description of the effect that cold, empty silence can have on a child is reminiscent of *The Noonday Friends.*

The Edge of Next Year also addresses the difficulty of coping with death. In this story, Orin is given the responsibility of keeping house and caring for his younger brother after his mother is killed in an automobile accident. As Orin attempts to cope with his own sense of loss he is baffled by his brother's lack of grief and embittered by his father's gradual decline into alcoholism. Interestingly, Orin seems more troubled by his crushing domestic responsibilities than by the loss of his mother. Her importance, it would seem, was as a care-giver although Orin's recollections of his mother are riddled with conflict. He recalls her drinking and feels disdain; he remembers his inability to share her interest in ornithology; and he feels a mixture of frustration and admiration for the way she refused to adhere to conventional behavior.

The loss of a mother is anticipated throughout the book *Go and Catch a Flying Fish.* The mother in this story is also a nonconformist and her children seem rather troubled by her lack of interest in housekeeping. As the tensions between their parents rise, the children assume protective stances, attempting to defuse conflict between their parents. When their mother leaves they are hurt but display an understanding surprising for their years. The eldest child who collects fish for an aquarium uses the metaphor of a flying fish for his mother—if captured and contained, it would not be beautiful and may even die. *What Time of Night Is It?* continues the story as the family adjusts to life without a mother.

The plots of these stories are simple and revolve around the daily life of a family; eating, sleeping, and reacting to each other but remaining largely uninvolved with the outside world.

The setting of each story is fully described and becomes a backdrop for Stolz's love of nature. Each of her characters has a fascination for a type of animal. Catty, in *By the Highway Home,* loved wildlife and longed for a cat but her older brother was allergic to them. After the family accepts his death, Catty is given permission to have a cat. Orin's little brother, in *The Edge of Next Year,* is a budding herpetologist and convinces Orin to turn their attic into a life-scale vivarium. Taylor, in *Go and Catch a Flying Fish,* loves the birds of Florida and compiles an impressive lifetime list as her brother Jim collects fish for his aquarium. These interests provide another dimension for Stolz's characters who often seem too mature for their age. These children spend much of their time thinking about their parents' actions and emotions. They show striking perceptiveness about adult behavior, perhaps more than can be expected of adolescents.

Interaction between siblings is remarkably high and typifies the adolescent's tendency to settle differences in the face of stress. The closeness of the protagonists and their younger siblings is noteworthy and admirable if not entirely realistic.

In recent years, Stolz has discontinued writing for young adults because she does not wish to write about children involved with the drug scene. This is a pity because her books which deal with family stress are invaluable. These are not books for those seeking fast-paced adventure. They are, instead, for the reader who wants a reflective look at difficulties within the home and models for coping with them.

—Anne Drolett Creany

* * *

SUTCLIFF, Rosemary. British. Born in West Clanden, Surrey, 14 December 1920. Educated privately and at Bideford School of Art, 1935-39. Writer, 1945—. Recipient: Carnegie Medal commendation, 1955, and American Library Association (ALA) Notable Book, both for *The Eagle of the Ninth;* Carnegie Medal commendation and *New York Herald Tribune*'s Children's Spring Book Festival honor book, both 1957, and ALA Notable Book, all for *The Shield Ring;* Carnegie Medal commendation and *New York Herald Tribune*'s Children's Spring Book Festival honor book, both 1958, both for *The Silver Branch;* Carnegie Medal commendation and Hans Christian Andersen Award honor book, both 1959, International Board on Books for Young People honor list, 1960, Highly Commended Author, 1974, and ALA Notable Book, all for *Warrior Scarlet;* Carnegie Medal, 1960, and ALA Notable Book, both for *The Lantern Bearers;* ALA Notable Book, 1960, for *Knight's Fee; New York Herald Tribune*'s Children's Spring Book Festival Award, 1962, ALA Notable Book, and *Horn Book* honor list, all for *Dawn Wind;* ALA Notable Book and *Horn Book* honor list, both 1962, both for *Beowulf;* ALA Notable Book and *Horn Book* honor list, both 1963, both for *Hound of Ulster;* ALA Notable Book and *Horn Book* honor list, both 1965, and Children's Literature Association Phoenix Award, 1985, all for *The Mark of the Horse Lord; Horn Book* honor list, 1967, for *The High Deeds of Finn MacCool;* Lewis Carroll Shelf Award, 1971, ALA Notable Book, and *Horn Book* honor list, all for *The Witch's Brat; Boston Globe-Horn Book* Award for outstanding text and Carnegie Medal runner-up, both 1972, ALA Notable Book, and *Horn Book* honor list, all for *Tristan and Iseult; Heather, Oak, and Olive: Three Stories* was selected one of Child Study Association's "Children's Books of the Year," 1972, and *The Capricorn Bracelet* was selected, 1973; Officer, Order of the British Empire, 1975; *Boston Globe-Horn Book* honor book for fiction, 1977, and *Horn Book* honor list, both for *Blood Feud; Children's Book Bulletin* Other Award, 1978, for *Song for a Dark Queen; Horn Book* honor list, 1978, for *Sun Horse, Moon Horse;* Children's Rights Workshop Award, 1978; ALA Notable Book, 1982, for *The Road to Camlann: The Death of King Arthur;* Royal Society of Literature fellow, 1982; Commander, Order of the British Empire, 1992. *Died 23 July 1992.*

PUBLICATIONS FOR YOUNG ADULTS

Fiction

The Armourer's House, illustrated by C. Walter Hodges. London and New York, Oxford University Press, 1951.

Brother Dusty-Feet, illustrated by Hodges. London, Oxford University Press, 1952.

Simon, illustrated by Richard Kennedy. London, Oxford University Press, 1953.

The Eagle of the Ninth, illustrated by Hodges. London, Oxford University Press, 1954; New York, Walck, 1961.

Outcast, illustrated by Kennedy. London, Oxford University Press; New York, Walck, 1955.

The Shield Ring, illustrated by Hodges. London, Oxford University Press; New York, Walck, 1956.

The Silver Branch, illustrated by Charles Keeping. London, Oxford University Press, 1957; New York, Walck, 1959.

Warrior Scarlet, illustrated by Charles Keeping. London, Oxford University Press; New York, Walck, 1958.

The Bridge-Builders. Oxford, Blackwell, 1959.

The Lantern Bearers, illustrated by Charles Keeping. London, Oxford University Press and New York, Walck, 1959.

Knight's Fee, illustrated by Charles Keeping. London, Oxford University Press and New York, Walck, 1960.

Dawn Wind, illustrated by Charles Keeping. London, Oxford University Press, 1961; New York, Walck, 1962.

The Mark of the Horse Lord, illustrated by Charles Keeping. London, Oxford University Press and New York, Walck, 1965.

The Chief's Daughter, illustrated by Ambrus. London, Hamish Hamilton, 1967.

A Circlet of Oak Leaves, illustrated by Ambrus. London, Hamish Hamilton, 1968.

The Witch's Brat, illustrated by Robert Micklewright, London, Oxford University Press, 1970; illustrated by Richard Lebenson, New York, Walck, 1970.

The Truce of the Games, illustrated by Ambrus. London, Hamish Hamilton, 1971.

Heather, Oak, and Olive: Three Stories (contains *The Chief's Daughter, A Circlet of Oak Leaves,* and *A Crown of Wild Olive*), illustrated by Ambrus, New York, Dutton, 1972.

The Capricorn Bracelet, illustrated by Charles Keeping, London, Oxford University Press, and New York, Walck, 1973.

The Changeling, illustrated by Ambrus. London, Hamish Hamilton, 1974.

We Lived in Drumfyvie, with Margaret Lyford-Pike. London, Blackie, 1975.

Blood Feud, illustrated by Charles Keeping. London, Oxford University Press, 1976, New York, Dutton, 1977.

Shifting Sands, illustrated by Laszlo Acs. London, Hamish Hamilton, 1977.

Sun Horse, Moon Horse, illustrated by Shirley Felts. London, Bodley Head, 1977; New York, Dutton, 1978.

Song for a Dark Queen. London, Pelham Books, 1978; Crowell, 1979.

Frontier Wolf. London, Oxford University Press, 1980; New York, Dutton, 1981.

Three Legions: A Trilogy (contains *The Eagle of the Ninth, The Silver Branch,* and *The Lantern Bearers*), London, Oxford University Press, 1980.

Eagle's Egg, illustrated by Ambrus. London, Hamish Hamilton, 1981.

Bonnie Dundee. London, Bodley Head, 1983; New York, Dutton, 1984.

Flame-Coloured Taffeta. London, Oxford University Press, 1985; New York, Farrar, Straus, 1986.

The Shining Company. New York, Farrar, Straus, 1990.

The Minstrel and the Dragon Pup, illustrated by Emma Chichester Clark. Boston, Candlewick, 1993.

Nonfiction

The Chronicles of Robin Hood, illustrated by C. Walter Hodges, London, Oxford University Press, 1950; New York, Walck, 1950.

The Queen Elizabeth Story, illustrated by Hodges. London, Oxford University Press, 1950; New York, Walck, 1950.

Houses and History, illustrated by William Stobbs. London, Batsford, 1960; New York, Putnam, 1965.

Beowulf, illustrated by Charles Keeping. London, Bodley Head, 1961; New York, Dutton, 1962; as *Dragon Slayer: The Story of Beowulf.* London, Penguin, 1966.

Hound of Ulster (Cuchulain Saga), illustrated by Victor Ambrus. London, Bodley Head, and New York, Dutton, 1963.

Heroes and History, illustrated by Charles Keeping. New York, Putnam, 1965.

A Saxon Settler, illustrated by John Lawrence. London, Oxford University Press, 1965.

The High Deeds of Finn MacCool, illustrated by Michael Charlton. New York, Dutton, 1967.

Tristan and Iseult, illustrated by Victor Ambrus. New York, Dutton, 1971.

Editor, *Is Anyone There?,* with Monica Dickens. New York, Penguin, 1978.

The Light beyond the Forest: The Quest for the Holy Grail, illustrated by Shirley Felts. London, Bodley Head, 1979; New York, Dutton, 1980.

The Sword and the Circle: King Arthur and the Knights of the Round Table, illustrated by Felts. New York, Dutton, 1981.

The Road to Camlann: The Death of King Arthur, illustrated by Felts. London, Bodley Head, 1981; New York, Dutton Children's Books, 1982.

Black Ships before Troy, illustrated by Alan Lee. New York, Delacorte, 1993.

PUBLICATIONS FOR CHILDREN

Fiction

The Roundabout Horse, illustrated by Alan Marks. London, Hamilton Children's, 1986.

A Little Dog Like You, illustrated by Jane Johnson. London, Orchard, 1987; New York, Simon and Schuster, 1990.

Little Hound Found, illustrated by Jo Davies. London, Hamish Hamilton, 1989.

PUBLICATIONS FOR ADULTS

Fiction

Lady in Waiting. London, Hodder and Stoughton, 1956; New York, Coward, 1957.

The Rider of the White Horse. London, Hodder and Stoughton, 1959, as *Rider on a White Horse.* New York, Coward, 1960.

Sword at Sunset, illustrated by John Vernon Lord. London, Hodder and Stoughton, 1963; New York, Coward, 1964.

The Flowers of Adonis. London, Hodder and Stoughton, 1969; New York, Coward, 1970.

Blood and Sand. London, Hodder and Stoughton, 1987.

Nonfiction

Rudyard Kipling. London, Bodley Head, 1960; New York, Walck, 1961, bound with *Arthur Ransome,* by Hugh Shelley, and *Walter de la Mare,* by Leonard Clark, Bodley Head, 1968.

Blue Remembered Hills: A Recollection (autobiography). London, Bodley Head, 1983; New York, Morrow, 1984.

Plays

Mary Bedell (produced Chichester, England, 1986).

Screenplay: *Ghost Story,* with Stephen Weeks). 1975.

*

Media Adaptations: *Song for a Dark Queen* was adapted for stage by Nigel Bryant, Heinemann, 1984; *Dragon Slayer: The Story of Beowulf* has been recorded onto audio cassette (read by Sean Barrett), G.K. Hall Audio, 1986.

Biography: Entry in *More Junior Authors,* New York, H.W. Wilson, 1963; essay in *Speaking for Ourselves: Autobiographical Sketches by Notable Authors of Books for Young Adults,* Volume 1, compiled and edited by Donald R. Gallo, National Council of Teachers of English, 1990.

Critical Study: *Rosemary Sutcliff* by Margaret Meek, London, Bodley Head, and New York, Walck, 1962; entry in *Children's Literature Review,* Volume 1, Detroit, Gale, 1983; entry in *Contemporary Literary Criticism,* Volume 26, Detroit, Gale, 1983.

*   *   *

Rosemary Sutcliff had suffered from a chronic arthritic condition since childhood which, after numerous painful operations, left her, at forty, with a crippled body (many of her characters have physical disabilities of one kind or another), no movement in her legs, and hands whose work (including writing and painting) was done with a forefinger and a tiny, rudimentary thumb. This may partially explain why someone who was prevented from having any concerted education (what she had was provided by her mother) would re-create complete worlds from the past, and in doing so confound military historians with her understanding of the art of battle in any situation she cared to devise.

Sutcliff's particular sense of detail pervades all her writing: it might be the glint of an earring or the appearance, in a swathe of grass laid down as bedding, of "the withered head of a moon daisy," which becomes the talisman of the war-host of Artos the Bear. And then there are the colours: not just the copper and scarlet of the Golden People in stark contrast to the muted, mysterious aspects of the dark races of Britain, or the gold of the Roman eagle standard at the head of "a shining serpent of men," but also the greens and browns of the forests and the land, the grey and tawny marshes, blue sails, bronze accoutrements, intricate jewelry, embroidered wall-coverings, striped blankets, and, always, the precise shades of people's hair, eyes, and complexions—even the particular colours of their horses.

Sutcliff's *Blue Remembered Hills: A Recollection* is an autobiographical study of her youth and young adulthood which, as is often the way with such recollections, offers little insight into the source of her particular creative inspiration. The severely restricted and painful nature of her existence was such that her romantic fantasies lacked the naturalism with which she imbued her reconstructions of civilisations, cultures, and historical issues. Yet it was a writer of romances that Sutcliff always aspired to be, and it was with two romantic period dramas, *Lady in Waiting* and *The Rider of the White Horse,* that she was first published as an adult novelist. She had already, slowly and with an assurance first demonstrated in *The Eagle of the Ninth,* established a literary style, and achieved a balance of passion, insight, and depth. Sutcliff further refined these qualities when she wrote *The Silver Branch* and *The Lantern Bearers,* the two succeeding books in her Roman Britain sequence, and the other children's novels of this period in her writing career: *Warrior Scarlet, Knight's Fee, Dawn Wind,* and *The Mark of the Horse Lord.*

The Mark of the Horse Lord follows the fortunes of a freed gladiator pressed into impersonating the Lord of the Horse People (the Dalriada of Scottish history). From its tremendous opening sequence in the gladiatorial ring, it continually progresses to a totally unexpected ending, and treats with mature understanding the gladiator's strange relationship with his ritual wife. Though published for children, it has more than any of her books satisfied young adult readers, and is arguably her finest novel.

Much longer, but still eminently accessible to young adults is *Sword at Sunset.* This is the best of the several modern novels in which the King Arthur of legend is given historical substance as Artos the Bear, who after the exodus of the Romans from Britain established his own band of cavalry to defend the land against the Saxon incomers.

Between 1965 and 1977 Sutcliff published no major works specifically for young people, and for adults just *The Flowers of Adonis,* a novel of ancient Greece in which she was able to demonstrate her knowledge of naval as well as military tactics. When she resumed writing young adult literature, with *Blood Feud,* whose background is the Viking excursions to the Black Sea during the Byzantine regime, something of the old mystique had, for some reason, faded, though her talents remained for creating rich scenes and violent action, and for the convincing representation of historical dialogue. Sutcliff was never at her most assured when called upon to embroider historical facts or events whose detail has survived, or when imbuing actual characters with motivation, such as she does in *Song for a Dark Oueen.* Her forte was to invest with flesh and blood the merest slivers of bone that have come down through the ages, often as mere legend, and to create her own characters to illuminate the conflicts of the times. She managed to do this again in *Frontier Wolf,* an extension of her Romano-British sequence, and in *The Shining Company,* inspired by the Welsh bard Aneirin's elegy on the band of knights organised and trained by the King of the British kingdom of Gododdin.

When she started the research for *The Shining Company* in 1983 she envisaged it as an adult novel along the lines of *Sword at Sunset,* with, as "hero," any character who emerged as a leader of the expedition. A subsequent letter she wrote at the time further illustrates

her researching method: "The '300' who got themselves mopped up at Catterick seem to have been (in spite of the name of [the poem] 'The Gododdin') actually drawn from lots of different little kingdoms. I found mention of only one of them, Garfyl or the like, who actually came from Gwynedd with a following. I don't think there's going to be, anywhere, an actual person with an actual story; I think it's going to be more of a matter of getting as much background as possible, and then simply picking someone out of the general mix-max of people mentioned, who has a memorable name, and an interesting attribute and perhaps just a scrap of personal history behind him, such as that he came from such and such a place and was so and so's nephew, and weaving a story round him. You see what I'm getting at?"

In the end she found no participant around whom she could weave her story, which she eventually wrote as a children's book. It is a *Bildungsroman* of the second son of a minor chief in Gwynedd, who accompanies the Prince of Gwynedd on the exploit, as his shieldbearer. For it she created, out of the sparsest of clues, a complete Dark Age society, including its beliefs, rules, customs, and taboos.

Latterly, the romantic strain within her resurfaced. So much is known, however, about John Graham of Claverhouse, the eponymous hero of *Bonnie Dundee,* that the introduction of secondary characters through whom his exploits are seen in the novel detracts from rather than embellishes the facts. *Flame-Coloured Taffeta,* on the other hand, an eighteenth-century tale of smugglers on the Sussex coast, is an almost entirely fictional adventure. With *Blood and Sand,* her last adult novel, the circle was complete: the facts about the extraordinary events in the life of Thomas Keith, who fought as a private in the 78th Highlanders against the Turks in 1807 and became Emir of the Islamic city of Medina, are attested, but they are elaborated enough to make an adolescent action story which is recognisable as Sutcliffian only if one recalls her innate aspirations.

—Antony Kamm

———

SWARTHOUT, Glendon (Fred). American. Born in Pinckney, Michigan, 8 April 1918. Educated at the University of Michigan, Ann Arbor, 1935-39, A.B. 1939, A.M. 1946; Michigan State University, East Lansing, 1952-55, Ph.D. 1955. Served in the United States Army Infantry, 1943-45: Sergeant; awarded two battle stars. Married Kathryn Blair Vaughn in 1940; one son. Teaching fellow, University of Michigan, 1946-48; Instructor, University of Maryland, College Park, 1948-51; Associate Professor of English, Michigan State University, 1951-59; lecturer in English, Arizona State University, Tempe, 1959-62. Writer. Recipient: Theatre Guild Playwriting award, 1947; Hopwood award in Fiction, 1948; O. Henry Prize Short Story, 1960; gold medal, National Society of Arts and Letters, 1972; Western Writers of America Spur award, 1975, 1988; Wrangler award, 1988; Owen Wister Lifetime Achievement award, Western Writers of America, 1991. *Died 23 September 1992.*

PUBLICATIONS FOR YOUNG ADULTS

Fiction

Where the Boys Are. New York, Random House, and London, Heinemann, 1960.

Loveland. New York, Doubleday, 1968.

Bless the Beasts and Children. New York, Doubleday, and London, Secker & Warburg, 1970.

TV Thompson, with Kathryn Swarthout, illustrated by Barbara Ninde Byfield. New York, Doubleday, 1972.

Luck and Pluck. New York, Doubleday, and London, Secker & Warburg; 1973.

Whales to See The, with Kathryn Swarthout, illustrated by Paul Bacon. New York, Doubleday, 1975.

The Melodeon (autobiographical), illustrated by Richard Cuffari. New York, Doubleday, and London, Secker & Warburg, 1977; as *A Christmas Gift,* New York, St. Martin's, 1992.

Cadbury's Coffin. New York, Doubleday, 1982.

PUBLICATIONS FOR ADULTS

Fiction

Willow Run. New York, Crowell, 1943.

They Came to Cordura. New York, Random House, and London, Heinemann, 1958.

Welcome to Thebes. New York, Random House, 1962; London, Heinemann, 1963.

The Cadillac Cowboys. New York, Random House, 1964.

The Eagle and the Iron Cross. New York, New American Library, 1966; London, Heinemann, 1967.

The Tin Lizzie Troop. New York, Doubleday, and London, Secker & Warburg, 1972.

The Shootist. New York, Doubleday, and London, Secker & Warburg, 1975.

Skeletons. New York, Doubleday, and London, Secker & Warburg, 1979.

The Old Colts. New York, Fine, and London, Secker & Warburg, 1985.

The Homesman. New York, Weidenfeld and Nicolson, and London, Deutsch, 1988.

PUBLICATIONS FOR CHILDREN

Fiction

The Ghost and the Magic Saber, with wife, Kathryn Swarthout. New York, Random House, 1963.

Whichaway, with Kathryn Swarthout, drawings by Richard M. Powers. New York, Random House, 1966; London, Heinemann, 1967.

The Button Boat, with Kathryn Swarthout. New York, Doubleday, 1969; London, Heinemann, 1971.

*

Manuscript Collection: Hayden Memorial Library, Arizona State University, Tempe.

Media Adaptations: "Where the Boys Are," starring George Hamilton and Delores Hart, Metro-Goldwyn-Mayer, 1961.

*   *   *

Novelist, short story writer, and dramatist, Glendon Swarthout is a master storyteller who sets many of his novels in Michigan, where he was born and raised, or the Western part of the United States, where he lived during the latter part of his life. His most acclaimed and enduring work is unquestionably *Bless the Beasts and Children* (1970) which focuses on a collection of misfit adolescents sent to Box Canyon Camp in Arizona.

The camp, which boasts the motto: "Send us a boy. We'll send you a cowboy!" focuses on competition among the cabins in sports and crafts which in turn decides one's position in the camp. The group with the least points becomes known officially around the camp as the "Bedwetters." Formed by a process of elimination, they are composed of individuals driven out of other cabins into that of John Cotton, who establishes himself as their leader by accepting such immature behavior as thumb sucking, bedwetting, and teeth grinding. The camp director assures the campers that if a cabin really wants to be the top group in the camp but fails in the competition system (success in riflery, swimming, etc.), they could steal their way to the summit by raiding the leaders' cabins and making off with their trophy of an animal head. To avenge previous humiliation at the hands of the other campers, the misfits release the camp's horses and, as the entire camp rounds them up again, they successfully steal the trophies of every cabin.

Following the above success, the boys next persuade their counselor to allow them to visit a government holding area for buffalo. To their horror, they discover that the bison are being slaughtered by "hunters" who shoot rifles inaccurately from behind the safety of a fence. The display of unskilled brutality binds them together and delivers their only chance at making the summer meaningful: save the bison. The night escape from the camp to free the beasts is supremely suspenseful and tautly written, with the tension enhanced by prior incidents which elaborate and underscore lives full of unkept promises and self-doubt. Swarthout successfully cultivates the feeling of anxiety and excitement the boys feel as they break free of the camp.

In a novel with such simple characterization and plot, one might expect their mission to be accomplished with some effort and then conclude with a heroes' return to the camp to be welcomed and accepted by those who had once scorned them. This is not the case. On the contrary, once the boys get to the holding pens they realize they must overcome their own fears of the massive animals before they can act. Freeing the bison proves to be an undertaking which requires the ultimate sacrifice. The suspense finally breaks with the death of John Cotton when he goes over a rim in the "Judas truck" which has led the buffalo herd to freedom.

Although contemporary readers may find the references to films, music, and transistor radios to be somewhat dated, the urgent need these young men exhibit for acceptance and brotherhood holds a timeless appeal for young adults. The alienation of these losers from their parents, peers, and counselors is so great that comparisons to the more complex and subtle *Lord of the Flies* arise easily. Unlike Golding's characters, however, these boys band strongly together as nonhunters, preserving and supporting not only themselves but the mighty bison as well. Swarthout's description of the slaughter is horribly graphic and authentic, but anything less would leave the reader unsympathetic to the boys.

Swarthout's novels *The Shootist* and *The Homesman* are set in the "old West" and may be helpful to the young adult reader in challenging myths about life on the American frontier. *The Shootist* deals with the last days of a renowned gunfighter dying of cancer alone in a boarding house in El Paso. The year 1901 sees the passing of Queen Victoria and the era of the gunfighter. He discovers that somewhere between those who admire his skill with a gun and ability to survive and those who view him as a ruthless assassin, he is friendless. Those who come to visit him seek only to cash in on his former glory. The final scene in *The Shootist,* like the slaughter of the buffalo in *Bless the Beasts and Children,* is described in visceral detail, unlike a "clean" Hollywood death, slowing down the instantaneous destruction wrought by a gun.

The Homesman details the journey of a strong pioneer woman and a man of dubious character leading three women who have lost their minds as a result of the wrenching hardships of life on the American frontier. Unable to be cared for on the plains, these women are being shipped back east. As in Swarthout's other novels, the specifics of their ordeals are gruesome, but as they head east, the women seem to improve, and the real challenge emerges for the duo who lead them, avoiding eager pilgrims heading west who are fearful their own women will see what hardships may possibly lie ahead.

A number of Swarthout's books have been adapted for the screen. Among them are *Bless the Beasts and Children, The Shootist,* and *Where the Boys Are,* a story set in Ft. Lauderdale, Florida, during spring break. Swarthout has also collaborated with his wife, Kathryn Vaughn Swarthout, on books for children as well as young adults.

—Parish Lentz

———

SWINDELLS, Robert (Edward). British. Born in Bradford, Yorkshire, 20 March 1939. Educated at Huddersfield Polytechnic, Yorkshire, 1969-72, teaching certificate, 1972; Bradford University, Yorkshire, 1986-87, M.A. in peace studies 1987. Served in the Royal Air Force, 1957-60. Married Brenda Marriott in 1982 (second marriage); two daughters (from first marriage). Copyholder, 1954-57, advertising clerk, 1960-67, *Telegraph and Argus,* Bradford; engineer, Hepworth & Grandage (turbine manufacturer), Bradford, 1967-69; elementary school teacher, Undercliffe First, Bradford, 1972-77; part-time teacher, Southmere First, Bradford, 1977-80; full-time writer, since 1980. Recipient: Child Study Association of America's Children's Books of the Year, 1975, for *When Darkness Comes;* National Book award nomination, children's category, Arts Council of Great Britain, 1980, for *The Moonpath and Other Stories;* Other award, 1984, Children's Book award, Federation of Children's Book Groups, and Carnegie Medal runner-up, British Library Association, both 1985, all for *Brother in the Land;* Children's Book award, 1990, for *Room 13.* Agent: Jennifer Luithlen, "The Rowans," 88 Holmfield Rd., Leicester LE2 1SB. Address: 3 Upwood Park, Black Moor Rd., Oxenhope, Keighley, West Yorkshire BD22 9SS, England.

PUBLICATIONS FOR YOUNG ADULTS

Fiction

When Darkness Comes, illustrated by Charles Keeping. Leicester, Brockhampton Press, 1973; New York, Morrow, 1975.
A Candle in the Night. Newton Abbot, Devon, David & Charles, 1974; as *A Candle in the Dark,* Sevenoaks, Kent, Knight, 1983.

Voyage to Valhalla, illustrated by Victor Ambrus. London, Hodder & Stoughton, 1976; Portsmouth, New Hampshire, Heinemann Educational, 1977.
The Ice-Palace, illustrated by June Jackson. London, Hamish Hamilton, 1977.
The Very Special Baby, illustrated by Victor Ambrus. London, Hodder & Stoughton, 1977; Englewood Cliffs, New Jersey, Prentice-Hall, 1978.
Dragons Live Forever, illustrated by Petula Stone. London, Hodder & Stoughton, and Englewood Cliffs, New Jersey, Prentice-Hall, 1978.
The Moonpath and Other Stories. Exeter, Wheaton, 1979; as *The Moonpath and Other Tales of the Bizarre,* illustrated by Reg Sandland, Minneapolis, Carolrhoda Books, 1983.
Norah's Ark, illustrated by Avril Haynes. Exeter, Wheaton, 1979.
Norah's Shark, illustrated by Avril Haynes. Exeter, Wheaton, 1979.
The Weather-Clerk, illustrated by Petula Stone. London, Hodder & Stoughton, 1979.
Ghost Ship to Ganymede, illustrated by Jeff Burns. Exeter, Wheaton, 1980.
Norah and the Whale, illustrated by Avril Haynes. Exeter, Wheaton, 1981.
Norah to the Rescue, illustrated by Avril Haynes. Exeter, Wheaton, 1981.
World Eater. London, Hodder & Stoughton, 1981.
The Wheaton Book of Science Fiction Stories, illustrated by Gary Long. Exeter, Wheaton, 1982.
Brother in the Land. Oxford, Oxford University Press, 1984; New York, Holiday House, 1985.
The Thousand Eyes of Night. London, Hodder & Stoughton, 1985.
The Ghost Messengers. London, Hodder & Stoughton, 1986.
Staying Up. Oxford, Oxford University Press, 1986.
Mavis Davis. Oxford, Oxford University Press, 1988.
The Postbox Mystery, illustrated by Kate Rogers. London, Hodder & Stoughton, 1988.
A Serpent's Tooth. London, Hamish Hamilton, 1988; New York, Holiday House, 1989.
Follow a Shadow. London, Hamish Hamilton, 1989, New York, Holiday House, 1990.
Night School. Paperbird, 1989.
Room 13. New York, Doubleday, 1989.
Daz 4 Zoe. London, Hamish Hamilton, 1990.
Tim Kipper. London, Macmillan, 1990.
Dracula's Castle. New York, Doubleday, 1991.
Fallout. New York, Morrow, 1992.
Rolf and Rosie. Ann Arbor, Michigan, Andersen Press, 1992.
You Can't Say I'm Crazy. London, Hamish Hamilton, 1992.
When Darkness Comes. London, Hodder & Stoughton, in press.

Other

Translator, *Alfie* series (*Alfie and His Secret Friend; Who'll Save Alfie Atkins?; Alfie and the Monster; You're a Sly One, Alfie Atkins!*), by Gunilla Bergström. Exeter, Wheaton, 4 vols., 1979.
Contributor, *The Methuen Book of Strange Tales,* edited by Jean Russell, London, Methuen, 1980.

*

Biography: Essay in *Something about the Author Autobiography Series,* Volume 14, Detroit, Gale, 1992.

Robert Swindells lives in Yorkshire, England. His novels are usually set near the city of Bradford. However, in no sense can he be regarded purely as a regional novelist: the area and its people are what he knows best, but his narratives roam freely between past, present, and future, and his concerns are urgent and universal.

His stories exhibit sheer narrative energy to a high degree: common assent among readers is that few writers' pages are more compulsively turned over. Through an acute historical sense, profound understanding and unease about today's social conditions, and logical projection of them into convincing and disturbing dystopias, Swindells uses narrative to dramatise human failings and young adult possibility highly effectively.

Two among his earlier novels may serve to demonstrate important facets of his achievement. In *A Candle in the Night* (1974: later entitled *A Candle in the Dark),* we are in the Yorkshire coalfield at the time of Victorian child labour. Orphan Jimmy Booth is taken out of the workhouse to be a collier's apprentice. The apprentices are brutalised: the story chronicles a struggle between cruel ignorance and a possibility of better things. *World Eater* (1981) is an engaging science-fiction fantasy with a north-country background of pigeon racing: Orville loves his pigeons and is the only person to realize the errant planet threatening the entire solar system is a gigantic egg.

Swindells's best known novel, *Brother in the Land,* appeared in 1984. Few post-nuclear holocaust novels are as grim and uncompromising. Swindells himself wrote of other such novels: "...all shared a major flaw: they presented a picture of postcatastrophe which young readers might find attractive..." His novel, he says, shows "...no hope." Total desolation and a savage view of human nature in extremity present a Hobbesian future. In Danny and Kim, the young adult central characters, are vestiges of optimism: hope, the tenor of the narrative suggests, born to die. Swindells looks fearlessly at the overwhelming nature of his subject: a deserved award-winner, the novel has had great effect in schools and must rank at the top of its particular sub-genre.

Staying Up (1986) centres on Brian and Debbie. This severely contemporary novel revolves around the fictional town of Barfax and its third division football team whose fortunes mirror those of its people. Brian lives on a run-down estate: Debbie's parents aspire. Both are in a state of struggle, of finding out as the relationship develops—Brian between escape from his background and the attractions of "The Ointment" (a football hooligan gang), booze, and drugs, Debbie between Brian and her parents' restrictive views. All choices involve loss: the breakup of social and economic values in Barfax is typified by a serial killer—Debbie is nearly his last victim.

A Serpent's Tooth (1988) involves the supernatural. Lucy's parents—activist mother, careerist father—move to Yorkshire. Lucy is a pawn in their mutual animosities. The nearby Pitfield is to be used for nuclear dumping: Lucy's mother forms a noisy protest group (which becomes a women's camp similar to Greenham Common). But Lucy sees a strange, recurring vision—two shadowy figures wheeling a handcart. From the old recluse Alice Hazelborne she finds she has second sight. The Pitfield was a mass burial ground in the Black Death. The novel moves to a gripping climax, acutely observant about contemporary values.

In *Follow a Shadow* (1989) the themes of choice and loyalty in *Staying Up* and the supernatural as an image of continuity as in *A Serpent's Tooth* are combined. Tim South—small, unprepossessing, talented but dreamy—is torn between the gang values of the Barracloghs and Janis Lee and the stability offered by Dilys, his girlfriend. The discovery of a sketch dated 1835 of a face like his, strange experiences of seeming taken out of place and time, conversation with his grandmother about family traditions, and a school trip to Howarth, home of the Brontes, convince him he is directly descended from Branwell Bronte. The contemporary narrative is handled surely: a shrewdly interspersed element involves nineteenth-century pastiche—Branwell's own diary chronicling his disastrous visit to London in 1835: opium, drink, failure to enter the Royal Academy, and a brief affair with a barmaid. Tim is not only descended from Branwell, he is a present-day version. In a brilliantly realised climax, the ghost of Branwell Bronte rescues Tim and the Barracloghs from death from exposure on the moors. Tim makes resolutions about himself—starting with the confession of stealing from his grandmother's savings for the gang.

A Serpent's Tooth and *Follow a Shadow,* though pessimistic about much in modern life, have optimistic outcomes. *Daz 4 Zoe* (1990), like *Brother in the Land,* offers little hope except through its young main characters. Here is a different, no less frightening future: by extending present trends logically, Swindells depicts a society where the haves and have-nots—the "Subbies" and the "Chippies"—are institutionally separated. Zoe lives in a wealthy, protected suburb, Daz in an inner-city wasteland. Force and propaganda maintain this status-quo. Daz, till he meets Zoe and their irresistible Romeo and Juliet love begins, wants to join Dred, the Chippy terrorist gang.

The novel is formally and stylistically advanced. Two first-person narratives are intertwined, that by Daz is eloquently illiterate. The power of this dystopia comes from its awful lausibility: Swindells is making a devastating critique of contemporary Western society. This novel is as much a warning for a new generation as *Brother in the Land.* With deepest irony, Swindells suggests that in the two centuries which separate *A Candle in the Night* and *Daz 4 Zoe* society will merely come back full circle to its old iniquitous barbarities. This pessimistic but consistent view has generated many fine novels.

—Dennis Hamley

T

TAN, Amy. American. Born in Oakland, California, 19 February 1952. Educated at San Jose State, California, B.A. 1973, M.A. 1974; postgraduate study at University of California, Berkeley, 1974-76. Married Lou DeMattei in 1974. Writer. Worked as language consultant to programs for disabled children, 1976-81, and as reporter, managing editor, and associate publisher for *Emergency Room Reports* (now *Emergency Medicine Reports*), 1981-83; freelance technical writer, 1983-87. Recipient: Commonwealth Club gold award for fiction, Bay Area Book Reviewers award for best fiction, American Library Association's best book for young adults citation, nomination for National Book Critics Circle award for best novel, and nomination for *Los Angeles Times* book award, all 1989, all for *The Joy Luck Club*; *The Kitchen God's Wife* was a 1991 *Booklist* editor's choice and was nominated for Bay Area Book Reviewers award. Lives in San Francisco, California.

PUBLICATIONS FOR ADULTS AND YOUNG ADULTS

Novels

The Joy Luck Club. New York, Putnam, 1989.
The Kitchen God's Wife. New York, Putnam, 1991.

PUBLICATIONS FOR CHILDREN

Fiction

The Moon Lady. New York, Macmillan, 1992.

*

Media Adaptations: *The Joy Luck Club* (audiocassette); *The Kitchen God's Wife* (audiocassette), Dove, 1991.

Critical Study: Entry in *Contemporary Literary Criticism*, Volume 59, Detroit, Gale, 1990, pp. 89-99.

* * *

Amy Tan would probably identify herself as a successful adult writer who also happens to enjoy a large young adult audience. Nevertheless, when the American Library Association added to the many awards already received by *The Joy Luck Club* by naming it a Best Book for Young Adults in 1990, Tan's reputation as a young adult writer was cemented. *The Kitchen God's Wife*, Tan's second novel, has only intensified her appeal to adolescent readers.

Because Tan is a relatively new writer, one who has published only two novels to date, it would seem ludicrous to generalize about such things as her "development" as a novelist or her "style." Both critically acclaimed, *The Joy Luck Club* and *The Kitchen God's Wife* tell different stories through markedly divergent structures. Still, the two novels share thematic concerns suggestive of reasons for Tan's popularity among young adults. Both are built around generational conflicts (specifically, the points of tension between mothers and their daughters) and the challenge of establishing personal identity. While such conflicts and challenges are circumscribed by a specific ethnic culture—the Chinese-American culture of northern California—they are universal in nature and significance. That the mothers in Tan's fiction are foreign-born Americans with American-born daughters is rarely off-putting to young readers outside the Chinese-American culture. Instead, Tan's novels stimulate ethnic appreciation while allowing readers to objectify their own situations, making connections between their own lives and the geographically/culturally distant lives of Tan's characters.

A reader's gender often determines the significance he or she assigns to Tan's work. While Tan's characters are often much older than themselves, young adult females find Tan to be a trustworthy guide to the challenges of adolescent identity crisis and familial conflicts, especially mother-daughter conflicts. Perhaps more than anything else, a young woman is moved by Tan's portrayals of a daughter's opposing desires concerning her mother: on one hand, the daughter wants to be like her mother, to be bound to her; on the other, she feels the unassailable need to separate herself from her mother, to establish a unique identity. The young adult male who is sufficiently mature and self-assured to read what are often perceived as "women's novels" will learn much about his own behavior towards women—and reasons for possibly changing his behavior. Few young men who read Tan's novels feel threatened by her. Instead, they are delighted by her humor and her life-affirming stance; they grow to respect her objectivity and fairness.

The Joy Luck Club is, in its most rudimentary form, a collection of related short stories told by four Chinese-American mothers and their four American-born daughters. (In actuality, one of the daughters is a voice for herself as well as her recently-deceased mother; she becomes a kind of "generational bridge" and the thematic focus of the novel.) While the novel is rather loosely plotted, its themes are wonderfully controlled: they are introduced, modified, and reprised with technical and aesthetic brilliance. The novel suggests that a woman's identity must be measured against her ethnic and cultural roots and that her mother is the most immediate embodiment of such roots. Accordingly, a central theme of the novel is that connections between daughters and their mothers are tenuous but priceless, the very key to selfhood.

The Kitchen God's Wife echoes the mother/daughter themes of *The Joy Luck Club* while also implying that male-centered social traditions subvert a woman's self-awareness and her relationships with other women. It also suggests that withholding one's "stories" (one's past experiences) from those one cares about is a kind of deception, a failure of trust which undermines mature and enduring relationships. The novel begins as the narrative of the American-born daughter of a Chinese-American mother; before the novel has progressed very far, however, the mother has wrested the narrator's responsibilities away from her daughter, recounting her own experiences to reveal her daughter's identity and potential. In the end, *The Kitchen God's Wife* is a profoundly moving, profoundly optimistic story of endurance, reconciliation, and love.

The Moon Lady is a picture book adaptation of a chapter by the same title in *The Joy Luck Club*. While *The Moon Lady* appeals to few teenage readers, and while it seems designed to be read aloud to young children, preteens nevertheless find it an accessible introduction to the style and themes of Tan's novels.

—Keith Lawrence

TATE, Eleanora E(laine). American. Born in Canton, Montana, 16 April 1948. Educated at Drake University, Des Moines, Iowa, B.A. 1973. Married Zack E. Hamlett III in 1972; one daughter. News editor, *Iowa Bystander,* West Des Moines, 1966-68; staff writer, *Des Moines Register,* and *Des Moines Tribune,* Des Moines, Iowa, 1968-76; staff writer, *Jackson Sun,* Jackson, Tennessee, 1976-77; writer and researcher, Kreative Koncepts, Inc., Myrtle Beach, South Carolina, 1979-81; president and co-owner (with husband Zack E. Hamlett III), Positive Images, Inc., Myrtle Beach, since 1983. Writer-in-residence, Elgin, South Carolina, Chester, South Carolina, and the Amana colonies, Middle, Iowa, all 1986. Free-lance writer for *Memphis Tri-State Defender,* 1977. Contributor to black history and culture workshops in Des Moines, 1968-76; giver of poetry presentations, including Iowa Arts Council Writers in the Schools program, 1969-76, Rust College, 1973, and Grinnell College, 1975. Guest author of South Carolina School Librarians Association Conference, 1981 and 1982. Member, Iowa Arts Council's Writers in the Schools/Community, since 1986; member, South Carolina Arts Commission, Artist in Education; member of Board of Governors, South Carolina Academy of Authors. Recipient: Fifth Annual Third World Writing Contest finalist, 1973; Unity award from Lincoln University, 1974, for educational reporting; Community Lifestyles award from Tennessee Press Association, 1977; fellowship in children's fiction for Bread Loaf Writer's Conference, 1981; "Just an Overnight Guest" (film adaptation of her juvenile novel of the same name) was named to the "Selected Films for Young Adults 1985: list by the Young Adult Committee of the American Library Association. Agent: Charlotte Sheedy, Charlotte Sheedy Literary Agency, 145 West 86th Street, New York, NY 10024, U.S.A.

PUBLICATIONS FOR YOUNG ADULTS

Fiction

Just an Overnight Guest. New York, Dial, 1980.
The Secret of Gumbo Grove. New York, F. Watts, 1987.
Thank You, Dr. Martin Luther King, Jr! New York, F. Watts, 1990.
Front Porch Stories at the One-room School, illustrated by Eric Velasquez. New York, Bantam, 1992.
Retold African Myths, illustrated by Don Tate. Des Moines, Perfection Learning Corporation, 1992.

Other

Contributor, *Children of Longing,* edited by Rosa Guy. New York, Bantam, 1970.
Contributor, *Broadside Annual 1972.* Detroit, Broadside Press, 1972.
Contributor, *Impossible?* Boston, Houghton, 1972.
Contributor, *Communications.* Lexington, Massachusetts, Heath, 1973.
Contributor, *Off-Beat.* New York, Macmillan, 1974.
Editor, and contributor, *Eclipsed,* with husband Zack E. Hamlett, III. Privately printed, 1975.
Contributor, *Sprays of Rubies.* Ragnarok, 1975.
Editor, and contributor, *Wanjiru: A Collection of Blackwomanworth.* Privately printed, 1976.
Contributor, *Valhalla Four.* Ragnarok, 1977.

Media Adaptations: *Just an Overnight Guest* (film, starring Fran Robinson, Tiffany Hill, Rosalind Cash, and Richard Roundtree), Phoenix/B.F.A. Films & Videos, 1983.

*   *   *

Eleanora Tate focuses on black families, yet this black writer's themes have universal appeal. Through her characters, she inspires young adults to have a strong sense of self as they accept their lives and their past. Her books challenge them to be compassionate, to explore their heritage, to satisfy their intellectual curiosity, and to pass on stories to others.

Just an Overnight Guest portrays a middle-class Missouri family suddenly confronted by change. Margie Carson, nine, enjoys a comfortable life with her parents and older sister until a four-year-old social misfit, Ethel Hardisen, intrudes as an unwelcome "overnight guest" dropped off by her mother but then never picked up. Margie, who hates this ill-mannered half-white, half-black, "trashy little kid" explains, "Some folks said she was half white and other folks said she was half Black. To me she was all bad." Margie hates this bed-wetter who shares her bed; moreover, Margie's mother does not punish Ethel's destructive, disruptive misbehavior. Margie also bitterly resents Ethel's calling *her* mother "Momma" and *her* father "Daddy." But the worst shock is learning that Ethel is blood kin (her uncle's child) and will be living with them for a long time. Margie's father gently consoles the heartbroken Margie, explaining that life is not fair, but "some things won't change. People have to change." The *New York Times Book Review* praises Tate's sensitive presentation of this adolescent's initiation into life's moral ambiguities. The novel's award-winning film version has reached large audiences on Nickelodeon cable television and the Public Broadcasting System's *Wonderworks* series.

The Secret of Gumbo Grove depicts a close-knit South Carolina family. Raisin Stackhouse, age eleven, is discouraged when her history teacher says local blacks never did anything worth mentioning, but Raisin desperately wants more black heroes like Harriet Tubman and Sojourner Truth. "I liked heroes. And I liked to feel good about what people did back in the old days, because it helped me go ahead and feel good about now." Consequently, she accepts the challenge of Miss Effie Pfluggins, the black community's respected elder, to restore an abandoned black church cemetery, and she discovers Gumbo Grove's "secret": the city's founder, assumed to be white, lies buried in the black cemetery. His story and equally fascinating tales of other black ancestors enable Raisin and her friends to take pride in their heritage. Honored as the first recipient of a community service award, Raisin proudly accepts it, feeling good that she at last knows her community's history. By appreciating the past, the adolescents can understand the present. Tate researched local history of the black community in Myrtle Beach, South Carolina; she also helped to rally people to renovate a run-down black church cemetery, having been moved by voices from those neglected headstones. Inspired by factual events, this novel reflects her strong conviction that involving youth in history connects them to their roots and instills pride in who they are.

In *Thank You, Dr. Martin Luther King, Jr.!* (a sequel to *The Secret of Gumbo Grove*), Mary Elouise Avery, nine, laments her dark skin and dreads hearing her white teacher and classmates discuss black history with negative, stereotyped images of slavery. The teacher uses books, filmstrips, and movies that make her ashamed, showing "dead Black people hanging from tree limbs, or German shepherd dogs biting on them" or "starving Africans...

with flies crawling on their faces, white crud around their mouths, and big bellies. Nasty!" These frightening images from the past and present make Mary Elouise wonder if these people somehow deserved their fate; furthermore, they confuse her because she does not understand why blacks have been exploited and abused. Her low self-esteem receives another blow when her mother mocks the child's dark skin. However, when a visiting black storyteller encourages Mary Elouise to take pride in her African ancestors and gives her a book about African history, she changes from an insecure child, embarrassed to be black, to a confident narrator of the black history play. As Mary Elouise thanks Dr. King and other African American heroes, she realizes she can be anything she wants to be.

Front Porch Stories at the One-Room School, a companion piece to *Just an Overnight Guest,* celebrates storytelling's rich traditions of entertaining and transmitting the past. Three years after Ethel Hardisen intruded into her home, Margie Carson has not quite fully accepted her abandoned cousin: she teases Ethel unmercifully and still resents her father's affection toward his niece. One boring, hot summer night on the front porch steps of the abandoned one-room Douglass School, they hear Mr. Carson's stories about meeting Eleanor Roosevelt, surviving a dangerous flood, and attending the all-black, one-room school. Other tales are scary, such as the mysterious bright light hovering over Grandpa's couch the night after his funeral or the huge shadow that terrified Aunt Daisy. Then it is the girls' turn. After Margie recounts the true story about an eight-foot-four-inch giant woman, born in 1872 and lived in a town nearby, she hears Ethel's poignant story about a little girl abandoned by her mother. When Margie empathizes with Ethel's devastating parental neglect—being abandoned by her mother and never being claimed by her father—she finally can accept her cousin's place in the family.

Tate's characters are learning to be strong young adults, confident of where they came from and who they are. Her universal themes of human compassion, historical awareness, and family unity relate to readers no matter what race or culture. Indeed, Tate offers rewarding learning experiences to all young adults in our multicultural society.

—Laura M. Zaidman

———

TAYLOR, Mildred D. American. Born in Jackson, Mississippi, 13 September 1943. Educated at University of Toledo, B.Ed. 1965; University of Colorado, M.A. 1969. Married Errol Zea-Daly in 1972 (divorced 1975). Writer. English and history teacher with the Peace Corps, Tuba City, Arizona, 1965, and Yirgalem, Ethiopia, 1965-67, recruiter, 1967-68, instructor in Maine, 1968; study skills coordinator, University of Colorado, 1969-71; proofreader and editor in Los Angeles, California, 1971-73. Recipient: First prize (African-American category), Council on Interracial Books for Children, 1973, outstanding book of the year citation, *New York Times,* 1975, and Jane Addams Honor citation, 1976, all for *Song of the Trees;* notable book citation, American Library Association, 1976, National Book Award (finalist), honor book citation, *Boston Globe-Horn Book,* Jane Addams Honor citation, and Newbery Medal, all 1977, and Buxtehuder Bulle Award, 1985, all for *Roll of Thunder, Hear My Cry;* outstanding book of the year citation, *New York*

Times, 1981, Jane Addams Honor citation, 1982, American Book Award nomination, 1982, and Coretta Scott King Award, 1982, all for *Let the Circle be Unbroken;* Coretta Scott King Award, and fiction award, *Boston Globe-Horn Book,* both 1988, both for *The Friendship;* notable book citation, *New York Times,* 1987, and Christopher Award, 1988, both for *The Gold Cadillac;* Coretta Scott King Award, 1990, for *The Road to Memphis.*

PUBLICATIONS FOR YOUNG ADULTS

Fiction

Roll of Thunder, Hear My Cry. New York, Dial, 1976; London, Gollancz, 1977.
Let the Circle Be Unbroken. New York, Dial, 1981; London, Gollancz, 1982.
The Friendship, illustrated by Max Ginsburg. New York, Dial, 1987; London, Gollancz, 1989.
The Road to Memphis. New York, Dial, 1990.

PUBLICATIONS FOR CHILDREN

Fiction

Song of the Trees, illustrated by Jerry Pinkney. New York, Dial, 1975.
The Gold Cadillac, illustrated by Michael Hays. New York, Dial, 1987.
Mississippi Bridge. New York, Dial, 1990.

*

Media Adaptations: *Roll of Thunder, Hear My Cry* was recorded by Newbery Awards Records, 1978, and adapted as a three-part television miniseries of the same title, American Broadcasting Companies, Inc. (ABC-TV), 1978.

Biography: Entry in *Fifth Book of Junior Authors and Illustrators,* New York, H.W. Wilson, 1983; entry in *Dictionary of Literary Biography: American Writers for Children since 1960: Fiction,* Volume 52, Detroit, Gale, 1986; essay in *Something about the Author Autobiography Series,* Volume 5, Detroit, Gale, 1988; essay in *Authors and Artists for Young Adults,* Volume 10, Detroit, Gale, 1993.

Critical Study: *Contemporary Literary Criticism,* Volume 21, Detroit, Gale, 1982; *Children's Literature Review,* Volume 9, Detroit, Gale, 1985.

*   *   *

Upon examining the works of Mildred D. Taylor, one cannot fail to be inspired by her unusually cohesive and consistent approach to historical writing for young people. For each of her works to date Taylor has chosen an autobiographical base upon which to create stories of amazing power and spiritual ethos. Black experience of the 1930s through 1950 provides the framework for the stories. Taylor has selected various episodes both from her personal experience and from the stories related to her by her father, a powerful role model throughout her life.

The stories offer a moving and honest perspective on the perils and the joys of black family life, primarily in Mississippi. The strength of the black family as a unit is emphasized as is the successful potential for confronting and dealing with adversity, when one has spiritual and family resources upon which to call. Taylor's works would be welcome at any point in time, but particularly so during a period when the problems and/or dissolution of minority family life are stressed in the media. Taylor's writing communicates a natural and fluid style. The storylines are clear-cut, easy to follow but never simplistic. The reader is always left to muse and indeed wonder at human action, inaction, and the far-reaching effects these factors may have upon the lives of others.

The Logan family, consisting of David, Mary, Caroline ("Big Ma"), and the children—Stacey, Cassie, Christopher-John, and Little Man—are first introduced in *Song of the Trees,* a short novel. The basic story, told from Cassie's perspective, involves the threat to land owned by the Logan family posed by an unscrupulous white neighbor who wishes to exploit their property by cutting down and selling the trees. The land, passed down from David Logan's father, is symbolic of the fortitude and strength of the family. The conflict is a spiritual as well as physical one. The image of the trees and the land are dominant and almost mystical, almost placing the work within the category of a romance. Even before Cassie, the major protagonist, sights the men illegally marking the trees to be cut, she notes that the "song of the trees" (the sound made by the wind blowing through the branches), has stopped and senses that something is amiss. It is the return of Mr. Logan from his railroad job in Louisiana that halts the progress of the evil plan. Damage has been done, but total desecration has been avoided. The family has been shaken but strengthened through the experience.

Cassie Logan also figures prominently in *Roll of Thunder, Hear My Cry, Let the Circle Be Unbroken, The Friendship, The Road to Memphis,* and *Mississippi Bridge.* She is portrayed as a young woman whose feisty spirit becomes fully developed during the course of the works; an innocent with a far-seeing vision, questioning what others of her time fear to question. Knowingly and unknowingly, she risks both the futility and the danger of confrontation. Cassie is often shocked by what she learns, but in the true Logan tradition refuses to let her spirit be dominated or crushed.

Roll of Thunder, Hear My Cry traces the incidents in the lives of the Logan family over the period of about a year. The family continues its struggle to maintain balance and dignity in the face of Southern racism. Educational inequities are laid bare, and the terrifying visits of the night riders, who descend upon defenseless blacks, become a reality. The prosecution of the misguided teenager T.J. for a crime perpetrated by whites also shakes the family, but serves to bind them to each other even more tightly.

Let the Circle Be Unbroken is the powerful sequel in which Cassie continues the story of her family and its attempts to cope with the inequities of Southern justice. A foreshadowing of civil rights initiatives is seen in the actions of Mrs. Lee Annie who at the age of sixty-five decides she is going to register to vote, a dangerous aspiration in the Mississippi of the 1930s.

The Gold Cadillac departs from the lives of the Logan family and introduces a new family and a new era—1950. Lois is the narrator of this story about a family of four who encounter the realities of racism when they travel from Ohio to Mississippi to visit relatives in a new gold cadillac. Again, the protagonist begins as an innocent who must adjust to the injustices of contemporary society, but who does so with the support of a loving family.

In *The Friendship,* Taylor returns to the lives of the Logan family. This story focuses on the events of one day in the life of the Logan children who witness an incident in the local country store. Mr. Tom Bee, a neighbor who has appeared earlier in *Let the Circle Be Unbroken,* confronts John Wallace, owner of the store, in a test of wills. Tom Bee insists upon calling John Wallace by his first name, an "offense" not tolerated by white society of the 1930s. Bee is shot by Wallace for this "infraction," but in a scene filled with pathos and courage, he crawls away from the store still refusing to acquiesce to the store owner's demands. This is a drama within drama; an incident involving Little Man in which he is insulted and threatened by Wallace's sons foreshadows the viciousness of the scene which follows. The reader is shown that the honesty of childhood and old age are treated with callous indifference by those who are steeped in racist philosophy. Yet the reader triumphs in the pride of both characters and (despite battles lost on the surface) in their continued strength.

While Taylor's two most recent books *The Road to Memphis* and *Mississippi Bridge* continue the narrative of the Logan family and its associates, they add a new dimension to the author's work. The two books act as a duo; each appears designed to complement the other and makes a statement regarding all that has taken place before. Set in 1941, the riveting narrative of *The Road to Memphis* chronicles events surrounding a violent incident involving a young black man. Moe, a friend to the Logan family, is goaded by the evil taunts and actions of a group of young white men. He responds by hitting three of them with a crowbar, an incident which causes him to have to flee the town, aided by Cassie, Stacey, and a friend, Clarence. Taylor creates a spellbinding plot as the young people make their way through danger-filled Mississippi towards Memphis where Moe will be able to catch a train bound for Chicago—north and freedom. The desolation of black life here is shown as arguably more intense than in Taylor's other work, as incident upon incident serves to underscore the total disenfranchisement of the black populace in the 1940s.

Mississippi Bridge, while set years earlier, acts as biblical commentary upon the actions not only of those in *The Road to Memphis* but actually, the actions of those in all other books which precede it. Told from the point of view of ten-year-old Jeremy Simms, the story involves the tragedy of a bus which goes over the side of a bridge in heavy fog, drowning all the passengers in the swirling waters below. All of the dead are white passengers—since blacks had been ordered off of the bus before it left town on its journey, in order to make space for white passengers. Ironically, it is a young black man, named Josias, previously ordered off of that very bus, who selflessly dives into the water in a fruitless attempt to save white lives. Taylor's irony seems less a contrivance of fate than a startling portrayal of Old Testament justice, enacting an event designed to exact payment for all of the injustices experienced in past stories, and in the past, collectively. Josias' desire to save human beings who represent the very race which constantly seeks his humiliation makes *Mississippi Bridge* at once a study in deific payment for wrongs and human kindness.

A poetic vision, the art of the storyteller, and the ability to recreate the past in a thoroughly convincing manner distinguish Mildred Taylor's work. She has provided us with important vignettes from an unforgettable era, which stand as classics in the genre of American historical fiction for young people.

—Karen Patricia Smith

TAYLOR, Theodore. Also writes as T.T. Lang. American. Born in Statesville, North Carolina, 23 June 1921. Educated at Cradock High School, Virginia, 1934-1939; Fork Union Military Academy, Virginia, 1939-40; studied with American Theatre Wing, 1947-48. Served in U.S. Merchant Marine, 1942-44; U.S. Naval Reserve, active duty, 1944-46, 1950-55; became lieutenant. Married Gweneth Goodwin in 1946 (divorced 1977), children: (first marriage) two sons and one daughter; married Flora Gray Schoenleber in 1981. Cub reporter, *Portsmouth Star,* Portsmouth, Virginia, 1934-39, sports editor, 1941-42; copyboy, *Washington Daily News,* Washington, DC; sports writer, National Broadcasting Co. Radio, New York City, 1942; sports editor, *Sunset News,* Bluefield, West Virginia, 1946-47; assistant director of public relations, New York University, New York City, 1947-48; director of public relations, YMCA schools and colleges, New York City, 1948-50; reporter, *Orlando Sentinel Star,* Orlando, Florida, 1949-50; publicist, Paramount Pictures, Hollywood, California, 1955-56; story editor, writer and associate producer, Perlberg-Seaton Productions, Hollywood, 1956-61; associate producer and free-lance press agent for Hollywood studios, 1961-68. Producer and director of documentary films. Recipient: Commonwealth Club of California Silver Medal, 1969; Jane Addams Children's Book Award from Women's International League for Peace and Freedom (returned, 1975); Lewis Carroll Shelf Award, Southern California Council on Literature for Children and Young People Notable Book Award, Woodward Park School Annual Book Award, California Literature Medal Award, and Best Book Award from University of California, Irvine, all 1970, all for *The Cay; Battle in the Arctic Seas* was selected one of *New York Times* Outstanding Books of the Year, 1976; Spur Award for Best Western for Young People, Western Writers of America, and Commonwealth Club of California Silver Medal for the best juvenile book by a California author, both 1977, both for *A Shepherd Watches, a Shepherd Sings;* Southern California Council on Literature for Children and Young People Award, 1977, for distinguished contribution to the field of children's literature and body of work; George G. Stone Center for Children's Books Recognition of Merit Award, 1980, for body of work; Young Reader Medal from the California Reading Association, 1984, for *The Trouble with Tuck;* Jefferson Cup Honor Book, Virginia Library Association, 1987, for *Walking Up a Rainbow: Being the True Version of the Long and Hazardous Journey of Susan D. Carlisle, Mrs. Myrtle Dessery, Drover Bert Pettit, and Cowboy Clay Carmer and Others*; American Library Association Best Young Adult Book Award, 1989; Young Reader Medal Award, California Reading Association, 1992; 1993 Utah Young Adult Book Award, *Sniper;* American Library Association Best Young Adult Book Award, *The Weirdo.* Edgar Allan Poe Award, 1993, Mystery Writers of America, *The Weirdo.* Agent: Gloria Loomis, Watkins Loomis Agency, Inc., 150 East 35th St., Suite 530, New York, NY 10016. Address: 1856 Catalina St., Laguna Beach, CA 92651, U.S.A.

<small>PUBLICATIONS FOR YOUNG ADULTS</small>

Fiction

The Cay. New York, Doubleday, 1969; London, Bodley Head, 1970.
The Children's War. New York, Doubleday, 1971.
The Maldonado Miracle. New York, Doubleday, 1973.
Teetoncey, illustrated by Richard Cuffari. New York, Doubleday, 1974.

Teetoncey and Ben O'Neal, illustrated by R. Cuffari. New York, Doubleday, 1975.
The Odyssey of Ben O'Neal, illustrated by R. Cuffari. New York, Doubleday, 1977.
The Trouble with Tuck. New York, Doubleday, 1981.
Sweet Friday Island. New York, Scholastic Inc., 1984.
Walking Up a Rainbow: Being the True Version of the Long and Hazardous Journey of Susan D. Carlisle, Mrs. Myrtle Dessery, Drover Bert Pettit, and Cowboy Clay Carmer and Others. New York, Delacorte, 1986.
The Hostage, illustrated by Thomas McKeveny. New York, Delacorte, 1987.
Sniper. New York, Harcourt, 1989.
Tuck Triumphant. New York, Doubleday, 1991.
The Weirdo. New York, Harcourt, 1992.
Timothy of the Cay. New York, Harcourt, 1993.

Nonfiction

People Who Make Movies. New York, Doubleday, 1967.
Air Raid—Pearl Harbor! The Story of December 7, 1941, illustrated by W. T. Mars. New York, Crowell, 1971.
Rebellion Town: Williamsburg, 1776, illustrated by R. Cuffari. New York, Crowell, 1973.
Battle in the Arctic Seas: The Story of Convoy PQ 17, illustrated by Robert Andrew Parker. New York, Crowell, 1976.
A Shepherd Watches, a Shepherd Sings, with Louis Irigaray. New York, Doubleday, 1977.
The Battle off Midway Island, illustrated by Andrew Glass. New York, Avon, 1981.
H.M.S. Hood vs. Bismarck: The Battleship Battle, illustrated by A. Glass. New York, Avon, 1982.
Battle in the English Channel, illustrated by A. Glass. New York, Avon, 1983.
Rocket Island. New York, Avon, 1985.

Television Plays: *Sunshine, the Whale.* 1974; *Threepersons,* 1962.

<small>PUBLICATIONS FOR ADULTS</small>

Fiction

The Body Trade. New York, Fawcett, 1968.
The Stalker. New York, D. I. Fine, 1987.
Monocolo. New York, D. I. Fine, 1989.
To Kill the Leopard, New York, Harcourt Brace, 1993.

Nonfiction

The Magnificent Mitscher (biography), foreword by Arthur W. Radford. New York, Norton, 1954.
Fire on the Beaches. New York, Norton, 1958.
Special Unit Senator: The Investigation of the Assassination of Senator Robert F. Kennedy, with Robert A. Houghton. New York, Random House, 1970.
The Amazing World of Kreskin. New York, Random House, 1973.
Jule: The Story of Composer Jule Styne. New York, Random House, 1979.
The Cats of Shambala, with Tippi Hedren. New York, Simon & Schuster, 1985; London, Century Hutchinson, 1986.

Screenplays: *Night without End,* 1959; *Showdown,* Universal, 1973; *Diplomatic Immunity,* 1989; *The Hold-Up;* and seventeen documentaries.

Television Plays: *Tom Threepersons* (adult mystery), TV Mystery Theatre, 1964, and *The Girl Who Whistled the River Kwai,* 1980.

*

Media Adaptations: *The Cay* was adapted as a movie by NBC-TV, 1974, and as a filmstrip by Pied Piper Productions, 1975. *The Trouble with Tuck* was adapted as a filmstrip by Pied Piper Productions, 1986.

Biography: Entry in *Authors of Books for Young People,* supplement to the 2nd edition, edited by Dorothy A. Marquardt and Martha E. Ward, Scarecrow, 1979; essay in *Something about the Author Autobiography Series,* Volume 4, Gale, 1987; essay in *Authors and Artists for Young Adults,* Volume 2, Gale, 1989; essay in *Speaking for Ourselves, Too* compiled and edited by Donald R. Gallo, National Council of Teachers of English, 1993.

Manuscript Collection: Kerlan Collection, University of Minnesota.

Critical Study: Bagnall, Norma, "Theodore Taylor: His Models of Self-reliance," *Language Arts,* January, 1980, pp. 86-91.

*   *   *

Although Theodore Taylor's young adult novels touch current concerns of our society, they also include life-and-death adventures in which young people struggle to make decisions and/or solve mysteries that would challenge mature adults.

In these novels for young adults, *The Hostage, The Weirdo,* and *Sniper,* the theme of wildlife preservation is the background for tales of adventure and suspense. There's also a bit of romance. Each book portrays young characters risking their lives for a specific environmental issue. Also, the teenagers summon up previously unrecognized initiative and strength as they face up to their parents and other adults who sometimes seem insensitive to the issues involved.

In *The Hostage,* fourteen-year-old Jamie Tidd and his father capture a large killer whale for a marine park being established in California. The developers of the park offer $100,000 for the whale. This money would be a windfall which would permit Jamie's family to leave the isolated fishing camp in British Columbia and enjoy such benefits of town life as better schooling for their son. Jamie's mother dreams of taking a trip to Hawaii.

However, Angie, a girlfriend home for the summer, along with the television crew that comes to film the whale and other active environmentalists work to convince Jamie and his parents that to confine this large whale to an exhibit for humans would be cruel.

Interspersed with information about the Orca whale and the Tidd's conflict with environmentalists are such exciting episodes as the one in which Jamie saves Angie from drowning as she takes it upon herself to release the whale from the cove where it is held captive.

In *The Weirdo,* seventeen-year-old Chip Clewt, disfigured in a fiery airplane accident ten years ago and hiding from civilization in Powhatan Swamp in North Carolina, meets sixteen-year-old native Samantha (called "Sam") and an older graduate student from the state university who is doing research on the bear population of the swamp. The student (Tom) works with Chip and Sam to track bears and mark them for a project to help the government decide whether or not to allow bear hunting on the designated Natural Wildlife Refuge. Some hunters, feeling threatened, turn guns on the young people in their determination to win back their bear hunting privileges. Tom disappears. Chip and Samantha attempt to prove their belief that Tom has met with foul play from poachers.

Human relationships are important here as well as the action and the unusual setting. Chip comes to face up to the fact that physical scars need not cause him to continue to hide from people. Sam is torn between her feelings for Chip and her loyalty to her father who is a hunter.

Taylor is at his best in building suspense and creating action. As for the setting, Chip describes the swamp environment and the animals and birds who live there in short essays throughout the book. Although the essays tend to slow the action, they help you understand Chip and see the swamp through the eyes of someone who loves the area. Teenagers will want to finish this book once they start to read it.

A third novel for young adults, *Sniper,* provides even more suspense in the adventures of a youth, facing danger toward himself and the animals of a private zoological preserve. Ben Jepson ends up in charge of his family's Los Coyotes Preserve in Orange County, California. It's an area with compounds for lions, tigers, and other animals along with Ben's home and trailors for animal handlers.

Ben's parents are on assignment for a National Geographic piece about poaching and cannot be reached by telephone when someone attacks the animals and the boy at night with a gun equipped with a telescopic night vision lens. Alfredo, the man whom Ben's parents left in charge of the preserve during their absence, has met with a serious automobile accident. This leaves Ben, who's just turning fifteen, to make life and death decisions to protect the captive animals and the preserve itself. He does have the help of a resident veterinarian from Africa who is studying for the California veterinary exams and two Spanish-speaking handlers, Luis Vargas who also speaks English and Rafael Soto. Ben's girlfriend is his reliable confidant. This novel is so filled with suspense, action, and mystery that it seems like a good candidate for a screenplay, a type of writing with which Taylor has had much experience.

Over his long writing career, Mr. Taylor has also written historical fiction and nonfiction. *Walking up a Rainbow,* set on the American frontier in 1851 and 1852, is a young adult story of a fourteen-year-old orphan Susan and her guardian who attempt to drive sheep—which Susan has inherited—over the plains and deserts toward California. The first and third sections of the book are told by Susan and the middle section by her handsome cowboy Clay Carmer. The book has humor, characters who are lively, and an interesting historical setting.

Taylor's best known novel for children, *The Cay,* is a survival tale about the boy Phillip who finds himself on a life raft in the Caribbean with only Timothy—an old West Indian man who is black—as a companion. Phillip is blinded as a result of the injuries to him in a torpedo attack on the freighter which was taking Phillip and his mother from a 1942 war zone to the United States.

In the biographical sketch about Taylor in *Something about the Author* (Gale, 1986), Taylor says that he doesn't have a very good imagination. He writes from life experience. He lives in California which is the setting for *Sniper.* He has lived and worked around ocean ports and served in the Merchant Marines and the U.S. Navy. He grew up in North Carolina not far from the swampland in *The Weirdo.* He may use familiar locations for his settings, but his novels prove that he really does have a vivid imagination.

—Virginia L. Gleason

TCHUDI, Stephen N. Also writes as Stephen Judy; Stephen N. Judy. American. Born in Waterbury, Connecticut, 31 January 1942. Educated at Hamilton College, Clinton, New York, B.A. 1963; Northwestern University, Evanston, Illinois, M.A. 1964, Ph.D. 1967. Married Susan Jane Schmidt in 1979; three sons and one daughter. Assistant professor of English and education, Northwestern University, Evanston, Illinois, 1967-69; assistant professor, 1969-71, associate professor, 1971-76, professor of English, since 1976, director of the Center for Literacy and Learning, since 1987, Michigan State University, East Lansing, MI. Visiting professor, University of British Columbia, 1975, Northeastern University, 1981, 1983, University of Sydney, 1986; editor of *English Journal,* 1973-80. Recipient: Eight awards from the Educational Press Association for excellence in educational journalism, for *English Journal;* Charles Carpenter Fries award from the Michigan Council of Teachers of English, 1978, for distinguished service to the profession of English teaching; *The Burg-O-Rama Man* was chosen as a Notable Children's Trade Book in the Field of Social Studies by the National Council for Social Studies and the Children's Book Council, 1985; *Soda Poppery* was selected one of Child Study Association of America's Children's Books of the Year, 1987. Address: 2011 Pawnee Trail, Okemos, MI 48864. U.S.A.

PUBLICATIONS FOR YOUNG ADULTS

Fiction

The Burg-O-Rama Man. New York, Delacorte, 1984.
The Green Machine and the Frog Crusade. New York, Delacorte, 1987.

Nonfiction

Gifts of Writing Creative Projects with Words and Art (as Stephen Judy), with wife, Susan J. Judy. New York, Scribner, 1980.
Putting on a Play: A Guide to Writing and Producing Neighborhood Drama (as Stephen Judy), with wife, Susan J. Judy. New York, Scribner, 1982.
The Young Writer's Handbook: A Practical Guide for the Beginner Who Is Serious about Writing, with Susan J. Tchudi. New York, Scribner, 1984.
Soda Poppery: The History of Soft Drinks in America. New York, Scribner, 1986.
The Young Learner's Handbook: A Guide to Solving Problems, Mastering Skills, Thinking Creatively. New York, Scribner, 1987.
Lock and Key: The Secret of Locking Things Up, In, and Out. New York, Scribner, 1993.

PUBLICATIONS FOR ADULTS

NONFICTION

Teaching Writing in the Content Areas: Elementary School, with Susan J. Tchudi. Washington, D.C., National Education Association, 1983.
Teaching Writing in the Content Areas: Middle School/Junior High, with Margie C. Huerta. Washington, D.C., National Education Association, 1983.
Teaching Writing in the Content Areas: Senior High School, with Joanne Yates. Washington, D.C., National Education Association Professional Library, 1983.
Probing the Unknown: From Myth to Science. New York, Scribner, 1990.
The English-Language Arts Handbook: Classroom Strategies for Teachers, with Susan J. Tchudi. Portsmouth, New Hampshire, 1991.
Planning and Assessing the Curriculum in English Language Arts. Alexandria, Virginia, Association for Supervision and Curriculum Development, 1991.

Other

Editor, *Language, Schooling, and Society.* Portsmouth, New Hampshire, Boynton Cook, 1985.
Editor, *English Teachers at Work: Ideas and Strategies from Five Countries.* Portsmouth, New Hampshire, Boynton Cook, 1986.

Nonfiction as Stephen N. Judy

The Creative Word, with others. 6 vols., New York, Random House, 1973-74.
Explorations in the Teaching of Secondary English: A Source Book for Experimental Teaching. Palos Verdes, California, Dodd, 1974.
Writing in Reality, with James Edwin Miller. New York, Harper, 1978.
The English Teacher's Handbook: Ideas and Resources for Teaching English, with Susan J. Judy. Englewood Cliffs, New Jersey, Winthrop Publishers, 1979.
Editor, *Teaching English: Reflections on the State of the Art.* Rochelle Park, New Jersey, Hayden Book, 1979.
The ABCs of Literacy: A Guide for Parents and Educators. Oxford University Press, New York, 1980.
An Introduction to the Teaching of Writing, with Susan J. Judy. New York, Wiley, 1981.
Editor, *Publishing in English Education.* Portsmouth, New Hampshire, Boynton Cook, 1982.

*   *   *

For many teenagers, in fact as well as fiction, the high-school years constitute a wasteland journey. Excessive self-absorption, concern with trivia, uncaring adults, and a fragmented instructional curriculum stultify rather than stimulate the life of the young on their way to adulthood. Stephen Tchudi, obviously not unaware of that bleak scenario, undercuts it by creating characters who have brains, convictions, commitment, and courage as they confront issues that deal with the ecology of the body and the environment.

Karen Wexler in *The Burg-O-Rama Man* is editor of the school newspaper. She is gifted with a keen eye for the praiseworthy and the tawdry. And when a national fast food chain selects Crawford City High School as its source for a new series of TV commercials, that critical faculty gets plenty of exercise. She watches as the silver-tongued company rep, the Burg-O-Rama man, easily gains the enthusiastic cooperation of all, through the allure of fame and money; as the camera man invades the school, and students turn into junk food hucksters; as the school's most respected and principled educator turns out to be merely another opportunist when, for a hefty fee, he accepts a starring role in one of the commercials. When the Burg-O-Rama man finally selects Karen as the star for his last commercial, she refuses and thereby establishes the author's thematic intent.

There's plenty of stuff here for hard-hitting confrontations. But Tchudi tries hard for balance; perhaps too hard. Junk food may be bad for the body, but it's popular and it tastes good. Commercial exploitation of an educational institution may be questionable, but the money is much needed and can be put to good use. Sports fanatics may be bad for the game, but stars still emerge and feel good about their heroics. In that kind of context, Karen's lone act of ethical nonconformity signifies too little.

In *The Green Machine and the Frog Crusade,* Tchudi is less timid. Again the issue focuses on commercial versus personal values. Here the hero is sixteen-year-old David Morgan who becomes an environmental crusade leader when plans for a shopping mall threaten to turn his favorite swampland, with its unique wildlife, into concrete. The courage of his convictions impels him to oppose his father, city hall, and most of the town's leading citizens. With the help of a gadfly lawyer, his best friend, and his impetuous sister who rounds up half the school as coactivists, David is able to achieve a temporary victory. Yes, commercial interests predictably have the last word, but David's commitment has at least inspired the respect of his family, his town, his cute new girlfriend, as well as the reader. The last touch is too sentimental as David and girlfriend Sharon say good-bye to the doomed swamp: "I won't forget you. I'll never forget you." But the author has at least explored and pursued the main issue here in considerable depth.

However, Stephen Tchudi's most important contribution to literature for the young adult may rest not so much in his two novels, but in his nonfiction books that try to inspire the student's quest for knowledge and self-development. *Soda Poppery* not only traces the fascinating history of soft drinks in America but also educates the student through interesting side excursions in history, science, economics, and marketing. Deftly integrated ideas for experiments or further research appeal especially to the scientifically curious. Relevant stories, myths, and legends keep the tone light and the content consistently highly informative. And for readers eager to become do-it-yourselfers, the last section in the book offers them all the instructions they need.

The Young Writer's Handbook, a book cowritten by Susan Tchudi, is intended for the young writer but would serve well writers of any age who are still young in craft but have dreams of becoming accomplished. The title is unfortunate, with its connotations of rhetorical rules and grammar exercises. This book has none of that. Ironically, however, it accomplishes the aim of the typical handbook—the development of a better writer—far more effectively. It does so through an engaging, personal voice that motivates, advises, illustrates, guides, and inspires with a wide range of creative ideas for writing. As such, this book constitutes an ideal individualized program in writing instruction. But it needs updating; written at the dawn of the classroom computer age, the book still assumes the pen-and-paper writer.

The Young Learner's Handbook is less narrowly focused. It aims to reach and stimulate the young questing minds that are curious about much and perhaps in need of some method and guidance in their pursuits. The author introduces questing as a process, then goes on to discuss the art of questioning, the importance of data gathering, and the various information sources such as print, media, people, and places. An excellent guide to library literacy serves as an invaluable aid to the research-minded. Among the most important chapters are the last two in which young questers are challenged to apply and share what they learn through such activities as science fair projects, contests, exhibits, and videos. Again, a real strength of this handbook is the plethora of imaginative suggestions that are sure to incite the interest of readers. And now ComputerQuest sections are included as well for the computerphile.

Stephen Tchudi's pervasive aim in both his fiction and nonfiction is clearly to educate the middle and high-school age student. He does so in a personable voice that respects the student's intelligence and capacity for mature action. His fiction, so far, suffers at times from too heavy a theme or message orientation. The young reader would be served better by a spicier writing style that exudes more of the liveliness and excitement the author tries to engender in his audience. But it is refreshing to have a writer who can write entertainingly and offer a substantive learning experience.

—Henry J. Baron

THIELE, Colin (Milton). Australian. Born in Eudunda, South Australia, 16 November 1920. Educated at Adelaide Teachers College, South Australia, 1937-38; University of Adelaide, B.A. 1941, Dip.Ed. 1947, Dip.T. Served in the Royal Australian Air Force, 1942-45. Married Rhonda Gill in 1945; two daughters. Teacher, Port Lincoln High School, South Australia, 1946-55, and Brighton High School, 1956; Lecturer, 1957-62, Senior Lecturer in English, 1962-63, Vice Principal, 1964, and Principal, 1965-72, Wattle Park Teachers College, Adelaide; Director, Murray Park College of Advanced Education, 1973; Principal, Wattle Park Teachers Centre, 1973-81. Formerly national book reviewer, Australian Broadcasting Commission; Commonwealth Literary Fund Lecturer in Australian Literature. Member, 1964-68, and since 1969 fellow, Australian College of Education; since 1967 council member, and president, 1987-89, Australian Society of Authors. Recipient: W.J. Miles Memorial prize, for poetry, 1944; Commonwealth Jubilee prize, for radio play, 1951; Fulbright scholarship, 1959; Grace Leven prize, for poetry, 1961; Commonwealth Literary Fund fellowship, 1967; Children's Literature prize (Austria), 1979, 1986; Australian Children's Book Council Book of the Year award, 1982; Silver Pencil award (Netherlands), 1986. Companion, Order of Australia, 1977. Address: 24 Woodhouse Crescent, Wattle Park, SA 5066, Australia.

PUBLICATIONS FOR YOUNG ADULTS

Fiction

The Sun on the Stubble. Adelaide, Rigby, 1961; London, White Lion, 1974.
Storm Boy, illustrated by John Baily. Adelaide, Rigby, 1963; London, Angus & Robertson, 1964; Chicago, Rand McNally, 1966.

February Dragon. Adelaide, Rigby, 1965; London, Angus & Robertson, 1966; New York, Harper, 1976.

The Rim of the Morning: Six Stories. Adelaide, Rigby, 1966; as *Storm Boy and Other Stories,* 1986.

Blue Fin, illustrated by Roger Haldane. Adelaide, Rigby, 1969; New York, Harper, 1974; London, Collins, 1976.

Yellow-Jacket Jock, illustrated by Clifton Pugh. Melbourne, Cheshire, 1969.

Flash Flood, illustrated by Jean Elder. Adelaide, Rigby, 1970.

The Fire in the Stone. Adelaide, Rigby, 1973; New York, Harper, 1974; London, Penguin, 1981.

Albatross Two. Adelaide, Rigby, 1974; London, Collins, 1975; as *Fight against Albatross Two,* New York, Harper, 1976.

Magpie Island, illustrated by Roger Haldane. Adelaide, Rigby, 1974; London, Collins, 1975.

Uncle Gustav's Ghosts. Adelaide, Rigby, 1974.

The Hammerhead Light. Adelaide, Rigby, 1976; New York, Harper, 1977.

The Shadow on the Hills. Adelaide, Rigby, 1977; New York, Harper, 1978.

Chadwick's Chimney, illustrated by Robert Ingpen. Sydney, Methuen, 1979; London, Methuen, 1980.

River Murray Mary, illustrated by Robert Ingpen. Adelaide, Rigby, 1979.

The Best of Colin Thiele. Adelaide, Rigby, 1980.

The Valley Between. Adelaide, Rigby, 1981.

Patch Comes Home. Melbourne, Rigby, 1982.

The Undercover Secret. Adelaide, Rigby, 1982.

Pitch the Pony. Melbourne, Rigby, 1984.

Potch Goes down the Drain. Melbourne, Rigby, 1984.

Coorong Captive. Melbourne, Rigby, 1985.

Seashores and Shadows. Glebe, New South Wales, McVitty, 1985; as *Shadow Shark,* New York, Harper, 1988; as *Sharks in the Shadows,* London, Dent, 1988.

Skipton's Landing; and River Murray Mary, illustrated by Robert Ingpen. Adelaide, Rigby, 1986.

Shatterbelt. Glebe, New South Wales, McVitty, 1987.

Jodie's Journey. Glebe, New South Wales, McVitty, 1988.

Klontarf. Melbourne, Rigby, 1988.

Stories Short and Tall. Melbourne, Rigby, 1988.

Aftershock, forthcoming.

Other

The State of Our State. Adelaide, Rigby, 1952.

Editor, *Looking at Poetry.* London, Longman, 1960.

Editor, with Greg Branson, *One-Act Plays for Secondary Schools.* Adelaide, Rigby, 3 vols., 1962-64; revised edition, as *Setting the Stage* and *The Living Stage,* 2 vols., 1969-70.

Editor, with Greg Branson, *Beginners, Please.* Adelaide, Rigby, 1964.

Editor, with Greg Branson, *Plays for Young Players.* Adelaide, Rigby, 1970.

PUBLICATIONS FOR CHILDREN

Fiction

Mrs. Munch and Puffing Billy, illustrated by Nyorie Bungey. Adelaide, Rigby, 1967.

Flip-Flop and the Tiger Snake, illustrated by Jean Elder. Adelaide, Rigby, 1970.

The Skunks, illustrated by Mary Milton. Adelaide, Rigby, 1977.

Ballander Boy, photographs by David Simpson. Adelaide, Rigby, 1979.

Tanya and Trixie, photographs by David Simpson. Adelaide, Rigby, 1980.

Little Tom Little, photographs by David Simpson. Adelaide, Rigby, 1981.

Pinquo, illustrated by Mary Milton. Melbourne, Rigby, 1983.

Farmer Schulz's Ducks. Glebe, New South Wales, McVitty, 1986; New York, Harper, 1988.

Rotten Egg Paterson to the Rescue, illustrated by Karen Ritz. New York, Harper, 1991.

Poetry

Gloop the Gloomy Bunyip, illustrated by John Baily. Brisbane, Jacaranda Press, 1962; revised version, in *Gloop the Bunyip,* 1970.

Gloop the Bunyip, illustrated by Helen Sallis. Adelaide, Rigby, 1970.

Songs for My Thongs, illustrated by Sandy Burrows. Adelaide, Rigby, 1982.

PUBLICATIONS FOR ADULTS

Novels

Labourers in the Vineyard. Adelaide, Rigby, and London, Hale, 1970.

The Seed's Inheritance. Adelaide, Lutheran Publishing, 1986.

Plays

Burke and Wills (broadcast 1949). Included in *Selected Verse (1940-1970),* 1970.

Radio Plays: *Burke and Wills,* 1949; *Edge of Ice,* 1951; *The Shark Fishers,* 1953; *Edward John Eyre,* 1962.

Poetry

Progress to Denial. Adelaide, Jindyworobak, 1945.

Splinters and Shards. Adelaide, Jindyworobak, 1945.

The Golden Lightning. Adelaide, Jindyworobak, 1951.

Man in a Landscape. Adelaide, Rigby, 1960.

In Charcoal and Cont. Adelaide, Rigby, 1966.

Selected Verse (1940-1970). Adelaide, Rigby, 1970.

Other

Editor, *Jindyworobak Anthology.* Adelaide, Jindyworobak, 1953.

Editor, with Ian Mudie, *Australian Poets Speak.* Adelaide, Rigby, 1961.

Editor, *Favourite Australian Stories.* Adelaide, Rigby, 1963.

Editor, *Handbook to Favourite Australian Stories.* Adelaide, Rigby, 1964.

Barossa Valley Sketchbook. Adelaide, Rigby, 1968.

Heysen of Hahndorf (biography). Adelaide, Rigby, 1968; revised edition, 1974.

Coorong, photographs by Mike McKelvey. Adelaide, Rigby, and London, Hale, 1972.

Range without Man: The North Flinders, photographs by Mike McKelvey. Adelaide, Rigby, 1974.

Grains of Mustard Seed (on state education). Adelaide, South Australia Education Department, 1975.

The Little Desert, photographs by Jocelyn Burt. Adelaide, Rigby, 1975.

The Bight. Adelaide, Rigby, 1976.

Heysen's Early Hahndorf. Adelaide, Rigby, 1976.

Lincoln's Place. Adelaide, Rigby, 1978.

Maneater Man: The Story of Alf Dean, The World's Greatest Shark Hunter. Adelaide, Rigby, 1979.

The Adelaide Story. Nambour, Peacock, 1982.

Writing for Children: A Personal View (lecture). Dromkeen, Victoria, Oldmeadow, 1983.

Coorong. Adelaide, Wakefield Press, 1986.

Something to Crow About. N.p., Commonwealth, 1986.

South Australia Revisited. Adelaide, Rigby, 1986.

A Welcome to Water. Adelaide, Wakefield Press, 1986.

Ranger's Territory: The Story of Frank Woerle. Sydney, Angus & Robertson, 1987.

*

Media Adaptations: *Storm Boy* (feature film), screenplay by Sonia Borg, South Australian Film Corporation, 1976; *Blue Fin* (feature film), South Australian Film Corporation, 1978; *The Fire in the Stone* (television film), screenplay by Graeme Koestveld, South Australian Film Corporation, 1983; *Danny's Egg* (television film), Channel Nine (Sydney), 1987; *The Water Trolley* (television film, adapted from the short story by the same name in *The Rim of the Morning),* Channel Nine, (Sydney), 1989.

Critical Study: Entry in *Contemporary Literary Criticism,* Volume 17, Detroit, Gale, 1981.

*   *   *

Colin Thiele is one of Australia's most admired writers, best known for the classic tale *Storm Boy* and another story of the sea, *Blue Fin.* Although very much a regional writer representing aspects of his home state South Australia in almost all his books, numerous translations point to his considerable international appeal. Many of his books such as *February Dragon, Chadwick's Chimney, Albatross Two, Coorong Captive,* and *Seashores and Shadows* feature breathtaking adventures but also reflect a love of, and concern for, the natural world. Adventure and slapstick humour are undoubtedly part of his appeal to readers the world over, but the special strength of Thiele's writing is its strong emotional core that recognises the joy and tragedy of ordinary lives. Thiele has written in Walter McVitty's *Authors and Illustrators of Australian Children's Books,* "...My observation that the world and the people in it could be happy and sad, cruel and kindly, stupid and wise, all at the same time, and my belief that our daily experiences often educated us more profoundly than formal lessons...all these and more were part of the general background which I carried forward into my writing."

Two major settings for his novels are the countryside—particularly the Barossa Valley, a general farming and wine making area

settled by German immigrants north of Adelaide where Thiele was born and spent his youth—and the sea, based especially on his experiences as a teacher in the Eyre Peninsula region of South Australia. One of the "Barossa" novels, *The Valley Between* was Australian Book of the Year for 1982, the top award after earlier works achieved numerous commended listings. This is the fourth book set in the German community of a fictional town Gonunda. All the incidents involve a thirteen-year-old boy, Benno, who attracts trouble like sheep attract flies. The dramatic focus is on an ongoing feud between Jack Ryan, an easy going Irish farmer, and malicious Adolf Heinz who displays the worst characteristics of the dour Germans. The first in the series is *The Sun on the Stubble,* a humourous tale of an adolescent boy, Bruno Gunther, growing up in the Barossa Valley in the 1920s, and the pain he feels at leaving the farm when it is time to go to Adelaide to school. *The Sun on the Stubble* was initially published for a general readership with Thiele dedicating the book "To the boys who were boys with me." Indeed the Barossa novels are still read with equal enjoyment by adults and children, not least of all the hilarious *Uncle Gustav's Ghosts,* where the hapless Uncle Gustav is plagued with "Unseen Presences." The tin-kettling episode, a noisy and drunken ceremony that welcomes newlyweds to their new home, is one of the funniest in Australian literature.

There are boyish high jinks too in *The Shadow on the Hills* recounting the life of Bodo Schneider from birth to leaving school at Gonunda. Prominent is the special relationship between Bodo and old Ebenezer Blitz, a hermit who preaches from the hills each day accompanied by his dog Elijah. But as the sombre title suggests there are darker things. Ebenezer has supposedly been driven to madness by storekeeper Moses Mibus, whose greedy ways also bring financial ruin to Bodo's parents and other farmers. Eventually Moses is caught due to Bodo's testimony, but telling the truth brings unhappy consequences for Bodo and many changes, not least being the end of his childhood. But in Thiele's writing, change, however painful, brings hope of new beginnings. The title lines of the short story collection, *The Rim of the Morning,* reflects this conviction, "The Boy and the Man went up the hill of the world together. But the Man grew old and stayed behind to rest. Then the Boy went on until he reached the rim of the morning, and there, in magic and pain and wonder, he looked out alone...." Bodo too is "a dark figure silhouetted on the rim of the world" and as unhappy Bruno of *The Sun on the Stubble* is being driven away to school, "The car topped the rise and seemed to pause before moving down the other side." Similarly change, and a special relationship between young and old is the subject of the emotional story *The Hammerhead Light.*

Thiele's *Storm Boy,* first published as a short story in *The Rim of the Morning,* is a moving portrayal of a boy's transition from childhood to adulthood. Storm Boy and his father Hide-Away Tom live in a hut in the seashore wilderness known as the Coorong in South Australia. Their only friend is another solitary man, the Aboriginal Fingerbone Bill. Storm Boy loves his life by the sea and revels in its changing phases. One day he finds three orphaned pelicans and raises them. Mr. Percival is his special friend until the bird is cruelly killed by shooters, and the special happiness of Storm Boy's solitary life is altered forever. This story has been particularly popular since the 1976 film version. Also made into successful films are *Blue Fin* and *The Fire in the Stone,* both featuring boys with unsatisfactory fathers. Snook, in *Blue Fin,* proves himself a hero after a series of adventures, but for Ernie Ryan in *The Fire in the Stone* life on the opal fields is harsh and eventually tragic.

Most of Thiele's books feature boys, but more recent novels have major girl characters. Emma in *Emma Keppler,* the fifth Barossa novel, decides to stand up for herself at a time when woman were meant to "hold their tongues." She is a clever girl and her teacher wants her to go to high school, but her father thinks this is a joke. Like *Storm Boy, River Murray Mary* is an illustrated book that has much appeal for adolescents although the format might suggest a younger readership. These are delightful stories about the life of a resourceful young girl, Mary, whose father has a small farm on the banks of the Murray River. Two recent adventures also featuring resourceful heroines, *Jodie's Journey* and *Shatterbelt,* are set in the Adelaide Hills and are about real disasters in that part of Australia, bushfire and earthquakes. Jodie is a happy twelve-year-old girl but life changes dramatically for her when she is diagnosed as arthritic. This novel gives details of her treatment and also tells of a dramatic incident when Jodie and her horse are almost killed in the 1983 Ash Wednesday fires. In *Shatterbelt* Tracy starts to have dreams that forewarn her of disasters. Nobody believes her so she has to save the people of the Adelaide Hills from a mine collapse single-handedly. This is an exciting story that ends with many questions left unanswered. Was it sabotage that collapses the mine or an earthquake? Will Tracy continue to have special powers or was it just this one event? A sequel, *Aftershock* answers some of the questions.

—Kerry White

THOMAS, Joyce Carol. American. Born in Ponca City, Oklahoma, 25 May 1938. Educated at San Francisco City College, California, 1957-58, and University of San Francisco, 1957-58; College of San Mateo, A.A. 1964; San Jose State College (now University), B.A. 1966; Stanford University, M.A. 1967. Married 1) Gettis L. Withers, 31 May 1959 (divorced, 1968); 2) Roy T. Thomas, Jr., 7 September 1968 (divorced, 1979); one daughter and three sons. Telephone operator, San Francisco, California, 1957-58; teacher of French and Spanish, Ravenwood School District, East Palo Alto, California, 1968-70; assistant professor of black studies, San Jose State College (now University), California, 1969-72; teacher of drama and English, Contra Costa College, San Pablo, California, 1973-75; professor of English, 1975-77, St. Mary's College, Moranga, California; reading program director, San Jose State University, San Jose, 1979-82, and professor of English, 1982-83; visiting associate professor of English at Purdue University, spring 1983; member of Berkeley Civic Arts Commission. Since 1982, full-time writer; since 1989, professor of English, University of Tennessee. Recipient: Danforth Graduate Fellow, University of California at Berkeley, 1973-75; Stanford University scholar, 1979-80, and Djerassi Fellow, 1982 and 1983; *New York Times* outstanding book of the year citation, American Library Association (ALA) best book citation, and Before Columbus American Book Award, Before Columbus Foundation (Berkeley, California), all 1982, and the American Book Award for children's fiction (National Book Award), Association of American Publishers, 1983, all for *Marked by Fire;* Coretta Scott King Award, ALA, 1984, for *Bright Shadow;* named Outstanding Woman of the Twentieth Century, Sigma Gamma Rho, 1986. Agent: Mitch Douglas, International Creative Management, 40 West 57th St., New York, NY 10019, U.S.A.

PUBLICATIONS FOR YOUNG ADULTS

Novels

Marked by Fire. New York, Avon, 1982.
Bright Shadow (sequel to *Marked by Fire*). New York, Avon, 1983.
Water Girl. New York, Avon, 1986.
The Golden Pasture. New York, Scholastic, 1986.
Journey. New York, Scholastic, 1988.
When the Nightingale Sings. New York, HarperCollins, 1992.

Poetry

Bittersweet. San Jose, Firesign Press, 1973.
Crystal Breezes. San Jose, Firesign Press, 1974.
Blessing. Berkeley, Jocato Press, 1975.
Black Child, illustrated by Tom Feelings. Zamani Productions, 1981.
Inside the Rainbow. Zikawana Press, 1982.
Brown Honey in Broomwheat Tea, illustrated by Floyd Cooper. New York, HarperCollins, 1993.

Plays

And producer, *A Song in the Sky* (two-act; produced San Francisco, 1976).
Look! What a Wonder! (two-act; produced Berkeley, 1976).
And producer, *Magnolia* (two-act; produced San Francisco, 1977).
And producer, *Ambrosia* (two-act; produced San Francisco, 1978).
Gospel Roots (two-act; produced Carson, California, 1981).
I Have Heard of a Land (produced Oklahoma City, Oklahoma, 1989).
When the Nightingale Sings (produced Knoxville, Tennessee, 1991).

Other

Editor, *A Gathering of Flowers: Stories about Being Young in America.* New York, HarperCollins, 1990.

*

Biography: *Dictionary of Literary Biography,* Volume 33: *Afro-American Fiction Writers after 1955,* Detroit, Gale, 1984; essay in *Speaking for Ourselves: Autobiographical Sketches by Notable Authors of Books for Young Adults,* Volume 1, compiled and edited by Donald R. Gallo, National Council of Teachers of English, 1990.

Critical Studies: Entries in *Children's Literature Review,* Volume 19, Detroit, Gale, 1990; *Contemporary Literary Criticism,* Volume 35, Detroit, Gale, 1985.

*   *   *

Joyce Carol Thomas knows stories; she heard them from her mother, her aunts, and from the women of Ponca City, Oklahoma, where she lived until she was ten. She knows stories from the African American culture and from her own imagination. She has listened and recorded. Her novels are infused with the rich folklore of her people. She has written since she was a young girl, starting with poetry and eventually plays.

In 1982 Thomas wrote her first novel, and it won the American Book Award. *Marked by Fire* begins in 1951 with Patience Jackson working in the cotton fields of Oklahoma where she gives birth to Abyssinia. The child is marked by fire and water: the water for birthing and baptism and the fire which causes an ember to burst from a blaze and places a mark on her cheek. The child has many gifts: a keen and curious mind, the gift of singing, and the ability to tell stories, to love and care for others, and to solve problems. Abyssinia becomes an important member of her community. But life is not easy, and though a myriad of events scar Abyssinia emotionally, she learns how to heal.

Thomas's book *Journey* is a horror story in which Meggie Alexander discovers a horrible series of crimes and their perpetrator. This intriguing story begins when Meggie is a baby giggling in her crib while watching a tarantula above her head. As a result, she begins a kind of kinship with spiders, a unique relationship that works well for her when her life is later in danger.

A "Cinderella" story, *When the Nightingale Sings,* is about Marigold who was found in a swamp and raised to do all of the work by a woman named Ruby and her twin daughters. Marigold has the gift of song, but she doesn't believe in her talent until she is discovered while attending the Great Gospel Convention.

Thomas's use of the language is exquisite; this craftsmanship provides words that are of music, voice, and song. Her characters are often musical, and the church—the gospel music, rhythm, movement, and harmony—provides not only a backdrop, but a language that expresses the spirit of the community. Proverbs, folk wisdom, scripture, and prophecy are liberally scattered among the voices of the characters.

In *Bright Shadow,* the sequel to *Marked by Fire,* Abyssinia is going to college and has fallen in love with Carl Lee Jefferson. Her father is not happy to see his daughter's love interest, and he discourages the relationship. In this story as in *Marked by Fire,* there is tragedy, brutality, and pain, but Abyssinia is once again able to see beauty, hope, and courage. The title suggests numerous symbols and images: the dark and light of human experience, the difficulty of knowing and seeing clearly, and, specifically, "Bright Shadow" is used to describe Carl Lee's mother, a Cherokee Indian, who spent her life in the woods and the shadows watching over her child from a distance. In *The Golden Pasture,* Thomas goes back to when Carl Lee was thirteen and spent most of his summers with his grandfather. He finds a beautiful horse and through the challenge of breaking him in, establishes a new relationship with his father.

California is the common setting for *Water Girl* and *Journey* although these two novels are quite different. *Water Girl* is a story of quest and self-discovery for Amber Wetbrook who is seeking to understand her place in a society that has allowed inhumanity such as the slave trade. Not only does the setting matter, but the physical elements also impact the fate of Thomas's characters. These elements shape and define events and sometimes destiny. Wind, rain, fire, hurricane, or tornado have the power to direct and change lives and sometimes they provide Thomas with metaphors for human emotions, behaviors, and experiences. The swamp, the fields, hills, flowers, heat and cold, insects, rocks, quicksand, grasses, all have color, texture, life and they frame the days of the characters.

Thomas has also edited *A Gathering of Flowers* which features eleven stories representing different cultures in America. Her contribution is "Young Reverend Zelma Lee Moses," a short story about a gospel preacher and singer in a rural Oklahoma church. It pulsates with rhythm and energy, and the reader can almost feel the electricity and the swaying energy as Zelma attempts to fly.

Some of her characters reach for impossible notes and make them happen. Others reach for something else: a flight of the soul, a finding of the spirit, a knowing and understanding. They don't have money or the opportunity to go on a quest, so they look within. Their invisible flight is inside the human heart and soul wherein they reach incredible heights.

—Caroline S. McKinney

———

TOLKIEN, J(ohn) R(onald) R(euel). British. Born in Bloemfontein, Orange Free State, South Africa, 3 January 1892; came to England, 1895. Educated at King Edward's VI's School, Birmingham, 1900-02, 1903-11; St. Philip's School, Birmingham, 1902-03; Exeter College, Oxford (open classical exhibitioner; Skeat prize, 1914), 1911-15, B.A. (honours), 1915, M.A. 1919. Served in the Lancashire Fusiliers, 1915-18: Lieutenant. Married Edith Mary Bratt in 1916 (died 1971); three sons and one daughter. Writer. Free-lance tutor, 1919. Assistant, Oxford English Dictionary, 1919-20; Reader in English, 1920-23, and Professor of the English Language, 1924-25, University of Leeds, Yorkshire; at Oxford University: Rawlinson and Bosworth Professor of Anglo-Saxon, 1925-45; Fellow, Pembroke College, 1926-45; Leverhulme Research Fellow, 1934-36; Merton Professor of English Language and Literature, 1945-59; Honorary Fellow, Exeter College, 1963; Emeritus Fellow, Merton College; Honorary resident fellow of Merton College, 1972-73. Sir Israel Gollancz Memorial Lecturer, British Academy, 1936; Andrew Lang Lecturer, University of St. Andrews, Fife, 1939; W.P. Ker Lecturer, University of Glasgow, 1953; O'Donnell Lecturer, Oxford University, 1955. Artist: individual show: Ashmolean Museum, Oxford, 1977. Recipient: *New York Herald Tribune* Children's Spring Book Festival award, 1938, for *The Hobbit*; International Fantasy award, 1957, for *The Lord of the Rings*; Royal Society of Literature Benson Medal, 1966; Foreign Book prize (France), 1973; World Science Fiction Convention Gandalf award, 1974; Hugo award, 1978; *Locus* award for best fantasy novel, 1978, for *The Silmarillion*. D.Litt.: University College, Dublin, 1954; University of Nottingham, 1970; Oxford University, 1972; Dr. en Phil et Lettres: Liège, 1954; honorary degree: University of Edinburgh, 1973. Fellow, Royal Society of Literature, 1957. C.B.E. (Commander, Order of the British Empire), 1972. *Died 2 September 1973.*

PUBLICATIONS FOR ADULTS AND YOUNG ADULTS

Novels

The Hobbit; or, There and Back Again, illustrated by the author. London, Allen and Unwin, 1937; Boston, Houghton Mifflin, 1938; revised edition, 1951; revised edition, 1966; *The Annotated Hobbit,* edited by Douglas A. Anderson, London, Unwin Hyman, and Boston, Houghton Mifflin, 1989.
The Silmarillion, edited by Christopher Tolkien. London, Allen and Unwin, and Boston, Houghton Mifflin, 1977.

"The Lord of the Rings" trilogy:

The Fellowship of the Ring. London, Allen and Unwin, and Boston, Houghton Mifflin, 1954; revised edition, Allen and Unwin, 1966; Houghton Mifflin, 1967.

The Two Towers. London, Allen and Unwin, 1954; Boston, Houghton Mifflin, 1955; revised edition, Allen and Unwin, 1966; Houghton Mifflin, 1967.

The Return of the King. London, Allen and Unwin, 1955; Boston, Houghton Mifflin, 1956; revised edition, Allen and Unwin, 1966; Houghton Mifflin, 1967.

Short Stories

Unfinished Tales of Númenór and Middle-Earth, edited by Christopher Tolkien. London, Allen and Unwin, and Boston, Houghton Mifflin, 1980.

Plays

The Homecoming of Beorhtnoth Beorhthelm's Son (broadcast, 1954). Included in *The Tolkien Reader,* 1966; in *Tree and Leaf, Smith of Wootton Major, The Homecoming of Beorhtnoth Beorhthelm's Son,* 1975.

Radio Play: *The Homecoming of Beorhtnoth Beorhthelm's Son,* 1954.

Poetry

Songs for the Philologists, with others. Privately printed, 1936.

The Road Goes Ever On: A Song Cycle, music by Donald Swann. Boston, Houghton Mifflin, 1967; London, Allen and Unwin, 1968; revised edition, Houghton Mifflin, 1978.

Poems and Stories. London, Allen and Unwin, 1980.

Other

A Middle English Vocabulary. Oxford, Clarendon Press, and New York, Oxford University Press, 1922.

Beowulf: The Monsters and the Critics. London, Oxford University Press, 1937.

Chaucer as a Philologist. London, Oxford University Press, 1943.

Tree and Leaf (includes short story "Leaf by Niggle" and essay "On Fairy-Stories"). London, Allen and Unwin, 1964; Boston, Houghton and Mifflin, 1965; revised edition, London, Unwin Hyman, 1975.

The Tolkien Reader. New York, Ballantine, 1966.

Smith of Wootton Major and Farmer Giles of Ham. New York, Ballantine, 1969.

Farmer Giles of Ham, The Adventures of Tom Bombadil. London, Allen and Unwin, 1975.

Tree and Leaf, Smith of Wootton Major, The Homecoming of Beorhtnoth Beorhthelm's Son. London, Allen and Unwin, 1975.

Pictures by J.R.R. Tolkien. London, Allen and Unwin, and Boston, Houghton Mifflin, 1979.

The Letters of J.R.R. Tolkien, edited by Humphrey Carpenter. London, Allen and Unwin, and Boston, Houghton Mifflin, 1981.

Finn and Hengest: The Fragment and the Episode, edited by Alan Bliss. London, Allen and Unwin, 1982; Boston, Houghton Mifflin, 1983.

The Monsters and the Critics and Other Essays, edited by Christopher Tolkien. London, Allen and Unwin, 1983; Boston, Houghton Mifflin, 1984.

The Book of Lost Tales 1-2. London, Allen & Unwin, 2 vols., 1983-84; Boston, Houghton Mifflin, 2 vols., 1984.

The Lays of Beleriand. London, Allen and Unwin, and Boston, Houghton Mifflin, 1985.

The Shaping of Middle-Earth: The Quenta, the Ambarkanta, and the Annals. London, Allen and Unwin, and Boston, Houghton Mifflin, 1986.

The Lost Road and Other Writings: Language and Legend before The Lord of the Rings. London, Unwin Hyman, and Boston, Houghton Mifflin, 1987.

The Return of the Shadow: The History of The Lord of the Rings, Part 1. London, Unwin Hyman, 1988; Boston, Houghton Mifflin, 1989.

The Treason of Isengard: The History of The Lord of the Rings, Part 2. Boston, Houghton Mifflin, 1989.

The War of the Ring: The History of The Lord of the Rings, Part 3. Boston, Houghton Mifflin, 1990.

Sauron Defeated: The History of The Lord of the Rings, Part 4. Boston, Houghton Mifflin, 1992.

Editor, with C.L. Wiseman, *A Spring Harvest,* by Geoffrey Bache Smith. Erskine Macdonald, 1918.

Editor, with Eric V. Gordon, *Sir Gawain and the Green Knight.* Oxford, Clarendon Press, and New York, Oxford University Press, 1925; revised by Norman Davis, 1967.

Editor, *Ancrene Wisse: The English Text of the Ancrene Riwle.* London, Oxford University Press, 1962; New York, Oxford University Press, 1963.

Translator, *Sir Gawain and the Green Knight, Pearl, and Sir Orfeo,* edited by Christopher Tolkien. London, Allen and Unwin, and Boston, Houghton Mifflin, 1975.

Translator, *The Old English Exodus,* edited by Joan Turville-Petre. Oxford, Clarendon Press, 1981.

Contributor, *Oxford Poetry, 1915,* edited by G.D.H. Cole and T.W. Earp. B.H. Blackwell, 1915.

Contributor, *A Northern Venture: Verses by Members of the Leeds University English School Association.* Swan Press, 1923.

Contributor, *Realities: An Anthology of Verse,* edited by G.S. Tancred. Gay and Hancock, 1927.

Author of foreword, *A New Glossary of the Dialect of the Huddersfield District,* edited by Walter E. Haigh. London, Oxford University Press, 1928.

Contributor, *Report on the Excavation of the Prehistoric, Roman, and Post-Roman Sites in Lydney Park.* Gloucestershire, Reports of the Research Committee of the Society of Antiquaries of London, Oxford University Press, 1932.

Author of preface, *Beowulf and the Finnesburg Fragment: A Translation into Modern English Prose,* by John R. Clark Hall, edited by C.L. Wrenn. London, Allen and Unwin, 1940.

Contributor, *Essays Presented to Charles Williams.* London, Oxford University Press, 1947.

Author of preface, *The Ancrene Riwle,* translated by M. Salu. Burns and Oates, 1955.

Contributor, *Angles and Britons: O'Donnell Lectures.* University of Wales Press, 1963.

Contributor, *Winter's Tales for Children: 1,* edited by Caroline Hillier. New York, St. Martin's, 1965.

Contributor, *The Image of Man in C.S. Lewis,* by William Luther White. Nashville, Tennessee, Abingdon Press, 1969.

Contributor, *The Hamish Hamilton Book of Dragons,* by Roger Lancelyn Green. Hamish Hamilton, 1970.

Contributor, *A Tolkien Compass,* edited by Jared Lobdell. Chicago, Open Court, 1975.

Contributor, *J.R.R. Tolkien: Scholar and Storyteller,* by Mary Salu and Robert T. Farrell. Ithaca, New York, Cornell University Press, 1979.

PUBLICATIONS FOR CHILDREN

Fiction

Farmer Giles of Ham, illustrated by Pauline Baynes. London, Allen and Unwin, 1949; Boston, Houghton Mifflin, 1950.
Smith of Wootton Major, illustrated by Pauline Baynes. London, Allen & Unwin, and Boston, Houghton Mifflin, 1967.
The Father Christmas Letters, edited by Baillie Tolkien, illustrated by the author. London, Allen and Unwin, and Boston, Houghton Mifflin, 1976.
Mr. Bliss, illustrated by the author. London, Allen and Unwin, 1982; Boston, Houghton Mifflin, 1983.
Oliphaunt, illustrated by Hank Hinton. Chicago, Contemporary Books, 1989.

Poetry

The Adventures of Tom Bombadil and Other Verses from the Red Book, illustrated by Pauline Baynes. London, Allen and Unwin, 1962; Boston, Houghton Mifflin, 1963.
Bilbo's Last Song, illustrated by Pauline Baynes. London, Allen and Unwin, and Boston, Houghton Mifflin, 1974.

Contributor of translations to *The Jerusalem Bible,* New York, Doubleday, 1966. Contributor to *The Year's Work in English Studies,* 1924 and 1925, *Transactions of the Philological Society,* 1934, *English Studies,* 1947, *Studia Neophilologica,* 1948, and *Essais de philologie moderne,* 1951.

*

Media Adaptations: *The Filmbook of J.R.R. Tolien's The Lord of the Rings,* Toronto, Methuen, 1978; Recordings of J.R.R. Tolkien reading from his own works, including "Poems and Songs of Middle-Earth," "The Hobbit and The Fellowship of the Ring," and "The Lord of the Rings," have all been released by New York, Caedmon; Christopher Tolkien reads "The Silmarillion: Of Beren and Luthien," also for Caedmon; Tolkien's illustrations from *Pictures by J.R.R. Tolkien* have been published in various editions of his books and have appeared on calendars, posters, and postcards; Rankin-Bass animated a version of *The Hobbit* for television, which aired in 1977; Ralph Bakshi directed a theater film based on *The Fellowship of the Ring* and bits and pieces of *The Two Towers,* which was released as *The Lord of the Rings* in 1978; A Bunraku-style puppet version of *The Hobbit* was produced in Los Angeles in 1984 by Theatre Sans Fil of Montreal.

Biography: *J.R.R. Tolkien* by Catherine Stimpson, New York, Columbia University Press, 1969; *J.R.R. Tolkien: A Biography* (includes bibliography) by Humphrey Carpenter, London, Allen and Unwin, and Boston, Houghton Mifflin, 1977; entry in *Dictionary of Literary Biography* by Augustus Kolich, Detroit, Gale, Volume 15, 1983.

Bibliography: *Tolkien Criticism: An Annotated Checklist* by Richard C. West, Kent, Ohio, Kent State University Press, 1970; revised edition, 1981.

Manuscript Collections: Marquette University, Milwaukee; Various of Tolkien's letters are in the collections of the BBC Written Archives, the Bodleian Library of Oxford University, the Oxford University Press and its Dictionary Department, the Humanities Research Center of the University of Texas at Austin, and the Marion E. Wade Collection of Wheaton College, Wheaton, Illinois.

Critical Studies: *Tolkien and the Critics* edited by Neil D. Harvey and Rose A. Zimbardo, Notre Dame, Indiana, University of Notre Dame Press, 1968; *The Tolkien Relation: A Personal Inquiry* by William B. Ready, Washington D.C., Regnery, 1968; *A Look behind The Lord of the Rings* by Lin Carter, Boston, Houghton Mifflin, 1969; *Good New from Tolkien's Middle-Earth: Two Essays on the Applicability of The Lord of the Rings* by Gracia F. Ellwood, Grand Rapids, Michigan, Eerdmans, 1970; *A Guide to Middle-Earth* by Robert Foster, Mirage Press, 1971, revised edition, *The Complete Guide to Middle-Earth,* New York, Del Rey, 1981; *Master of Middle-Earth: The Fiction of J.R.R. Tolkien* by Paul Kocher, Boston, Houghton Mifflin, 1972, London, Thames and Hudson, 1973; entries in *Contemporary Literary Criticism,* Detroit, Gale, Volume 1, 1973; Volume 2, 1974; Volume 3, 1975; Volume 8, 1978; Volume 12, 1980; Volume 38, 1986; *Lord of the Elves and Eldils: Fantasy and Philosophy in C.S. Lewis and J.R.R. Tolkien* by Richard L. Purtill, Grand Rapids, Michigan, Zondervan, 1974; *Myth, Allegory and Gospel: An Interpretation; J.R.R. Tolkien, C.S. Lewis, G.K. Chesterton, Charles Williams* by Edmund Fuller and others, Minneapolis Minnesota, Bethany Fellowship, 1974; *Tolkien's World,* London, Thames and Hudson, and Boston, Houghton Mifflin, 1974, and *Tolkien and the Silmarils,* Thames and Hudson, 1981, both by Randel Helms; *The Tolkien Companion* by J.E.A. Tyler, New York, St. Martin's Press, 1976; *The Mythology of Middle-Earth* by Ruth S. Noel, London, Thames and Hudson, and Boston, Houghton Mifflin, 1977; *The Complete Guide to Middle-Earth* by Robert Foster, London, Allen and Unwin, and New York, Ballantine, 1978; *A Hobbit's Journal* by Michael Green, Philadelphia, Running Press, 1979; *Tolkien's Art: A Mythology for England* by Jane C. Nitzche, London, Macmillan, 1979; *A Tolkien Bestiary* by David Day, New York, Ballantine, 1979; *The Languages of Tolkien's Middle-Earth* by Ruth S. Noel, Boston, Houghton Mifflin, 1980; *The Atlas of Middle-Earth* by Karen Wynn Fonstad, Boston, Houghton Mifflin, 1981; *Journeys of Frodo: An Atlas of J.R.R. Tolkien's The Lord of the Rings* by Barbara Strachey, New York, Ballantine, 1981; *Tolkien Criticism: An Annotated Checklist* compiled by Richard C. West, Kent, Ohio, Kent State University Press, 1970, revised edition, 1981; *Tolkien: New Critical Perspectives* edited by Neil D. Isaacs and Rose A. Zimbardo, Lexington, University Press of Kentucky, 1981; *The Road to Middle-Earth* by T.A. Shippey, London, Allen and Unwin, 1982, Boston, Houghton Mifflin, 1983; *J.R.R. Tolkien: This Far Land* edited by Robert Giddings, London, Vision, 1983; *The Song of Middle-Earth: J.R.R. Tolkien's Themes, Symbols, and Myths* by David Harvey, London, Allen and Unwin, 1985; *J.R.R. Tolkien: Six Decades of Criticism* by Judith A. Johnson, Westport, Connecticut, Greenwood Press, 1986; *The Magical World of the Inklings: J.R.R. Tolkien, C.S. Lewis, Charles Williams, Owen Barfield* by Gareth Knight, Shaftesbury, Element, 1990; *A Tolkien Thesaurus* by Richard E. Blackwelder, New York, Garland, 1990.

*   *   *

The Lord of the Rings has become one of the key books which teachers and librarians recommend to young adults to lead them towards adult literature; but it was not always so. The making of the book was a series of accidents, and, once published, young people insisted on reading it despite the hostility of literary critics and some educationalists, and the sheer difficulty of obtaining all three instalments in the right order.

Professor J.R.R. Tolkien made up the story of *The Hobbit* for his children, without intending to publish it. While Tolkien was advising the publishers Allen and Unwin on a translation of the Old English poem *Beowulf,* an editor read *The Hobbit* in manuscript and recommended it for publication. Tolkien had not even written the final chapters! After *The Hobbit* was successfully published in 1937, Stanley Unwin, Tolkien's publisher, asked him for a sequel. After beginning a supposed companion piece for children, Tolkien's creativity led him on an unexpected journey.

Ever since he left his newly-wed wife to fight in World War I, Tolkien had been developing a mythology based on a series of invented languages, into which he had poured his feelings about religion, love, and war. This saga, later to be called *The Silmarillion,* told of the creation of the world of Middle-Earth, and how God's purpose was continually thwarted by Melkor, the Spirit of Evil, once one of His greatest angels or Valar, and how God still brought Good out of Evil. In this world, purporting to be ours at its earliest stage, Elves were created first, then Men, Dwarves, and Ents, while Melkor distorted creation to make Orcs, Trolls, and other creatures like Dragons and Balrogs. Elves and Men made war on Melkor, now named Morgoth, for the three magical Silmarils which he had stolen, and at the end of the First Age, with the aid of the Valar, Morgoth was permanently imprisoned. Morgoth's chief lieutenant, Sauron, remained on Middle-Earth to cause further trouble, especially the drowning of Numenor, the island given by the Valar as a reward to those Men who fought against Morgoth.

In composing *The Hobbit,* Tolkien drew on this mythology, setting the story in the same Secondary World of Middle-Earth in a later era; thus, as he developed the sequel, he began to make connections with *The Silmarillion.* He had already said that Bilbo's sword was made in Gondolin (an Elven city at war with Morgoth); now he discovered that Bilbo's magic ring had been made by Sauron; it was the Ruling Ring which governed all the others; and Sauron was also the Necromancer, the sorcerer whom Gandalf had defeated in *The Hobbit.*

Over twelve years *The Lord of the Rings* developed into a massive typescript, not the children's book his publishers had requested, and initially they rejected it, for Tolkien wanted *The Silmarillion* published as well. Several years later, owing to the enthusiasm of Stanley Unwin's son Rayner, Unwin and Tolkien reconsidered, and over 1954-55 *The Lord of the Rings* was published in three installments, with the cliff-hanger at the end of Volume Two causing tremendous frustration to many devoted readers.

Many critics, however, were hostile because the book did not fit current fashions of adult fiction: it was not a realistic contemporary novel, and in the words of Edmund Wilson, "It is essentially a children's book—a children's book which has somehow got out of hand." Such misunderstandings were anticipated by the three authors commissioned to write the jacket "blurb," who concentrated on genre and comparable authors: Malory, Ariosto, science fiction, "an heroic romance." As we now know, Tolkien re-awakened an appetite for fantasy literature among readers and inadvertently founded the genre of "adult fantasy." Since publication, those critics who enjoy Tolkien have striven to establish criteria by which Tolkien and other fantasists should be judged.

Among them was Elizabeth Cook, who wrote: "The inherent greatness of myth and fairy tale is a poetic greatness. Childhood reading of symbolic and fantastic tales contributes something irreplaceable to any later experience of literature...The whole world of epic, romance, and allegory is open to a reader who has always taken fantasy for granted, and the way into it may be hard for one who never heard fairy tales as a child." *(The Ordinary and the Fabulous,* Cambridge University Press, 1969, 1976).

Tolkien's reception in the USA was more whole-hearted. Independently of Tolkien, a popular style of heroic fantasy had developed, entitled "Sword-and-sorcery," usually written by science-fiction authors as recreation from stories of space-ships and aliens. Barbarians, sorcerers, seductive princesses, and treasure hoards were common features of yarns set amid a mix of fantasy cultures and periods, from Viking saga to the Arabian Nights. So, although Tolkien saw himself in a literary tradition running from the Volsung Saga and Celtic legend through Rider Haggard, William Morris, Dunsany, and Eddison, there was another "pulp" tradition from legend, Haggard, Dunsany, E.R. Burroughs, Cabell, H.E. Howard's Conan the Barbarian, Fritz Leiber and L. Sprague de Camp. Typical of this American style is an anti-heroic, tongue-in-cheek attitude to great deeds which invites the reader to bridge the gulf between "real life" and fantasy: Tolkien does employ this anachronistic approach in *The Hobbit,* in the person of Bilbo and in the authorial comments, but in *The Lord of the Rings* this self-consciousness disappears, replaced by a pervading down-to-earth quality in the four hobbits' response to the heroic world, to accustom readers to heroic attitudes and archaic language, without inviting ridicule.

After hardback publication of *The Lord of the Rings,* American SF fans put the word out that Tolkien was an essential read. Paperback reprints of the Conan stories popularised sword-and-sorcery in SF bookshops, and the market was prepared for paperback Tolkien, but there were more obstacles in the way. Tolkien disliked paperback editions and wanted to revise the text. In 1965 Ace Books forced his hand by publishing a legal but unauthorised paperback, with cover illustrations and blurb to appeal to fans of SF and fantasy, and *The Lord of the Rings* became a best-seller twice over: selling well in the Ace edition, and then as a controversial book when the story of the author's disapproval broke, and an authorised, revised edition came out months later. At last young people could afford to buy Tolkien for themselves: in England a one-volume paperback appeared in 1968.

Since then youngsters have continued to fall in love with the Middle-Earth sagas, overwhelmed by the suspense, joy, beauty, and poignancy of this unique reading experience. In fairness, Tolkien's work should be judged by the conventions of its genre, not by criteria devised for contemporary fiction. I will now propose reasons for asserting its literary value and attempt to counter some anti-Tolkien views.

First, the book's readability throughout its epic length helps novice readers to progress, giving them confidence and a sense of achievement so that they may tackle other long works. A series of cliff-hangers and surprise confrontations maintain the suspense, the whole epic being intricately patterned so that characters separate and reunite, and all tends towards the climaxes of Volume three, when the reader is thrilled by first, the arrival of the Riders of Rohan to relieve the Siege of Gondor, then Eowyn's challenge to the Lord of the Nazgul and his death, which fulfils the prophecy that "no man" would slay him, and finally Aragorn's arrival in the fleet of corsairs' ships.

Then the book is written by a master of language, ranging from plain English through archaisms to poetic prose in such scenes as Gandalf's defiance of the Lord of the Nazgul, and Aragorn's healing of Eowyn. Tolkien's use of epic diction has earned him much criticism: he responded that high deeds in a heroic setting needed that "ancient style," and he revelled in "the wealth of English which leaves us a choice of styles." Tom Shippey points out that Tolkien's success with millions of ordinary readers proved the critics wrong, and that Tolkien did the best he could to bring the heroic world close to the modern reader through the eyes of the hobbits.

In recalling features of myth and legend, *The Lord of the Rings* inspires its readers to search the past: Norse and Welsh legend, and Old English poetry. Teachers might encourage this, and also recommend fantasy authors who owe Tolkien a debt: he created the appetite for fantasy by which they have profited: published for children are C.S. Lewis, Alan Garner, Susan Cooper, Lloyd Alexander, and Ursula Le Guin; for adults and young adults, Jane Yolen, Robin McKinley, David Eddings, Terry Pratchett, and Stephen Donaldson.

Tolkien has been criticised for flat characterisation: but in genre literature the reader must identify with the main character (or his partner, e.g. Dr. Watson), who must be an ordinary individual facing extraordinary pressures. Tolkien's main characters are drawn to three patterns: they have individual qualities; archetypal qualities; and they represent their species. All the main characters are well differentiated: the five hobbits, of course, and also the four heroes, Aragorn, Boromir, Eomer, and Faramir. Gimli and Legolas represent their races, and in the experiences of Gimli Tolkien includes a plea for racial tolerance. Wherever the Company goes, Gimli meets hostility because he is a Dwarf, but the Company stands by him and he wins the esteem of Elves and Men.

Tolkien's view of Evil has also been criticised. However, it is appropriate for supernatural genres to depict creatures of ultimate evil, like aliens and monsters, whereas fictions set in the real world cannot do this. So we need fantasy to experience the extremes of Good and Evil, testing real life against the fantasy. Sauron, in his desire to conquer and control the world, is not very different from a real-world dictator: it is his methods which count. Don't real-life soldiers deport and even massacre civilians? Consider the Nazi Holocaust of the Jews, taking place at the time when Tolkien wrote *The Lord of the Rings.* Issues in the real world may date: Shakespeare's play *Richard III* is a timeless portrait of a tyrant, but the real Richard III was probably not guilty of all the murders he commits or orders in the play.

Tolkien's orcs are not of course intended to stand for Germans or any other nation of the "real world"; they represent the worst aspect of humankind when engaged in indiscriminate violence. Tolkien does not show his orcs at their worst, in rape and massacre, and there is nothing observed or reported of the orcs which has not happened in our world. The human-like characters who choose evil, however—Denethor, Saruman, Wormtongue, and Gollum—are tempted, fall, and are given chances to repent. Moreover, throughout the epic Gollum's life is frequently spared: part of the essential patterning of the plot in order for Gollum to reach the Crack of Doom and save Frodo from the Ring.

Tolkien urges his readers to choose Good over Evil; but as a Roman Catholic believing the doctrine of original sin, he feared for the world's future. He was particularly concerned about ultimate war, which he predicted before the atom bomb was dropped on Hiroshima: "Shall there be two cities of Minas Morgul, grinning at each other across a dead land filled with rottenness?" In his hatred of industrial pollution and his portrayal of the Ents, he was also

ahead of his time. Meanwhile the contemporary novel of personal relationships may ignore wider issues which Tolkien pondered throughout his life.

Of Tolkien's works, the YA library should have *The Hobbit, The Lord of the Rings* and *The Silmarillion,* and also *Unfinished Tales*— more material from *The Silmarillion* and an adult love story, "Aldarion and Erendis." Tolkien's son Christopher has edited Tolkien's early versions of *The Silmarillion* and *The Lord of the Rings:* under the overall title *The History of Middle-Earth* the series has reached ten volumes; the YA library could acquire these in paperback if there is demand, and also Tolkien's *Letters* and the *Biography.* Tolkien's work is not only enjoyable, but also relevant to contemporary life: we should recommend it to young people and rejoice when they become enthusiastic for tales of Middle-Earth.

—Jessica Yates

TOWNSEND, John Rowe. British. Born in Leeds, England, 10 May 1922. Educated at Leeds Grammar School, 1933-40; Emmanuel College, Cambridge, B.A. 1949, M.A. 1954. Served in the Royal Air Force, 1942-46: Flight Sergeant. Married Vera Lancaster in 1948 (died 1973); two daughters and one son. Journalist, *Yorkshire Post,* Leeds, 1946, and *Evening Standard,* London, 1949; sub-editor, 1949-54, and art editor, 1954-55, Manchester *Guardian,* and editor of *Guardian Weekly,* 1955-69; part-time children's books editor, *Guardian,* Manchester and London, 1968-79, columnist, 1968-81; writer and lecturer, since 1969. Adjunct professor, Simmons College Center for the Study of Children's Literature, Boston, 1978-86; faculty member since 1987, member of adjunct board since 1990, Children's Literature New England; chairman of children's writers and illustrators group, British Society of Authors, 1977-78, 1990-91, member of management committee, 1982-85. Member of Harvard International Seminar, 1956. Visiting lecturer, University of Pennsylvania, Philadelphia, 1965, and University of Washington, Seattle, 1969, 1971; May Hill Arbuthnot Honor Lecturer, Atlanta, 1971; Anne Carroll Moore Lecturer, New York Public Library, 1971; Whittall Lecturer, Library of Congress, Washington, D.C., 1976. Recipient: Carnegie Medal honors list, 1963, for *Hell's Edge;* Carnegie Medal honors list, 1969, Silver Pen award from English Centre of International PEN, 1970, *Boston Globe-Horn Book* award, and 1971, Edgar Allan Poe award from Mystery Writers of America, all for *The Intruder;* Christopher award, 1982, for *The Islanders; Trouble in the Jungle, Good-bye to the Jungle, Pirate's Island, The Intruder, The Summer People, Noah's Castle,* and *Good-night, Prof, Dear* appeared on the American Library Association notable books list; *Trouble in the Jungle, The Intruder, The Islanders,* and *A Sense of Story* appeared on the *Horn Book* Honor List. Address: 72 Water Lane, Histon, Cambridge CB4 4LR, England.

PUBLICATIONS FOR YOUNG ADULTS

Fiction

Hell's Edge. London, Hutchinson, 1963; New York, Lothrop, 1969.
The Hallersage Sound. London, Hutchinson, 1966.
The Intruder, illustrated by Graham Humphreys. London, Oxford University Press, 1969, illustrated by Joseph A. Phelan, Philadelphia, Lippincott, 1970.

Good-night, Prof, Love, illustrated by Peter Farmer. London, Oxford University Press, 1970; as *Good-night, Prof, Dear,* Philadelphia, Lippincott, 1971; as *The Runaways,* edited by David Fickling, London, Oxford University Press, 1979.

The Summer People, illustrated by Robert Micklewright. London, Oxford University Press, and Philadelphia, Lippincott, 1972.

Forest of the Night, illustrated by Peter Farmer. London, Oxford University Press, 1974; illustrated by Beverly Brodsky McDermott, Philadelphia, Lippincott, 1975.

Noah's Castle. London, Oxford University Press, 1975; Philadelphia, Lippincott, 1976.

The Xanadu Manuscript, illustrated by Paul Ritchie. London, Oxford University Press, 1977; as *The Visitors,* Philadelphia, Lippincott, 1977.

King Creature, Come. Oxford, Oxford University Press, 1980; as *The Creatures,* New York, Lippincott, 1980.

The Islanders. Oxford, Oxford University Press, and New York, Lippincott, 1981.

A Foreign Affair. London, Kestrel Books, 1982; as *Kate and the Revolution,* New York, Lippincott, 1982.

Cloudy-bright. London, Viking Kestrel, and New York, Lippincott, 1984.

Downstream. New York, Lippincott, 1987; London, Walker, 1988.

The Golden Journey. London, Viking Kestrel, 1989; as *The Fortunate Isles,* New York, Lippincott, 1989.

The Invaders. Oxford, Oxford University Press, 1992.

PUBLICATIONS FOR CHILDREN

Fiction

Gumble's Yard, illustrated by Dick Hart. London, Hutchinson, 1961; as *Trouble in the Jungle,* illustrated by W. T. Mars, Philadelphia, Lippincott, 1969.

Pirate's Island, illustrated by Douglas Hall. London, Oxford University Press, and Philadelphia, Lippincott, 1968.

Widdershins Crescent. London, Hutchinson, 1965; as *Good-bye to the Jungle,* Philadelphia, Lippincott, 1967; as *Good-bye to Grumble's Yard,* London, Penguin, 1981.

Top of the World, illustrated by Nikki Jones. London, Oxford University Press, 1976; pictures by John Wallner, Philadelphia, Lippincott, 1977.

Dan Alone. London, Kestrel, and New York, Lippincott, 1983.

Tom Tiddler's Ground, illustrated by Mark Peppé. London, Viking Kestrel, 1985; New York, Lippincott, 1986; as *The Hidden Treasure,* New York, Scholastic, Inc., 1988.

The Persuading Stick. London, Viking Kestrel, and New York, Lothrop, 1986.

Rob's Place. London, Viking Kestrel, 1987; New York, Lothrop, 1988.

Nonfiction

Written for Children: An Outline of English Children's Literature. London, J. Garnet Miller, 1965; New York, Lothrop, 1967; revised edition, London, Kestrel, 1974; Philadelphia, Lippincott, 1975; revised edition, Kestrel, and New York, Harper, 1983; revised edition, London, Penguin, 1987; Harper, 1988; 5th edition, London, Bodley Head, 1990; New York, HarperCollins, 1992.

PUBLICATIONS FOR ADULTS

Nonfiction

Editor, *Modern Poetry: A Selection for Young People.* London, Oxford University Press, 1971, with photographs by Barbara Pfeffer, Philadelphia, Lippincott, 1974.

A Sense of Story: Essays on Contemporary Writers for Children. London, Longman, and Philadelphia, Lippincott, 1971; revised edition, as *A Sounding of Storytellers: New and Revised Essays on Contemporary Writers for Children,* London, Kestrel, and New York, Lippincott, 1979.

Editor, *Twenty-five Years of British Children's Books.* London, National Book League, 1977.

Contributor, Virginia Haviland, editor, *The Openhearted Audience: Ten Authors Talk about Writing for Children.* Washington, D.C., Library of Congress, 1980.

Cranford Revisted, illustrated by Jane Langton. Cambridge, England, Green Bay Publications, 1989.

*

Media Adaptations: *Gumble's Yard* (television); *The Intruder* (ITV television series), 1972; *Noah's Castle* (ITV television series), 1980.

Biography: Essay in *Something about the Author Autobiography Series,* Volume 2, Detroit, Gale, 1986; essay in *Speaking for Ourselves: Autobiographical Sketches by Notable Authors of Books for Young Adults,* Volume 1, compiled and edited by Donald R. Gallo, National Council of Teachers of English, 1990.

Manuscript Collections: Kerlan Collection, University of Minnesota, Minneapolis; International Youth Library, Munich.

Critical Study: Entry in *Children's Literature Review,* Volume 2, Detroit, Gale, 1976.

*   *   *

John Rowe Townsend—historian, critic, and author—is probably best known for his realistic portrayal of adolescents attempting to traverse the chasm which separates the child from the adult. Best known as a British realist, Townsend has directed his talents in a number of different directions: writing fantasies, pseudo-historical novels, science fiction, and a novel of teenage angst which gives dimensions to the internal quest for maturity (*Forest of the Night,* 1974). The result has been books of mixed quality, but the author remains true to his audience.

In his early works, *Trouble in the Jungle* (as *Gumble's Yard,* 1961), *Hell's Edge* (1963), *Good-bye to the Jungle* (as *Widdershins Crescent,* 1965), *The Hallersage Sound* (1966), and *Pirate's Island* (1968), Townsend frequently presents very young protagonists in bleak surroundings, allowing them to survive and even thrive without the help of, and often in spite of, the grown-ups in their lives. In the first of the "Jungle" books, Kevin (thirteen) and Sandra (twelve) are orphans being cared for by an alcoholic uncle; the two children must grow up before their time as they try to manage the family finances and protect their cousins Harold and Jean. While the surroundings are bleak and the situation nearly hopeless, Kevin, the narrator, manages to remain cheerful and hopeful.

What becomes clear as the reader examines Townsend's early work is that while he creates believable characters and setting, his plots often contain elements of the fantastic. The idea that Kevin and Sandra might be able to care for their cousins for a few days is believable, but when they find stolen diamonds and help stop an escaped convict, the story moves into the realm of fantasy. Most surprising, however, is the note of hope on which the novel ends. The return of Uncle Walter in the first book leaves the young protagonists with a sense of contentment—their lives are not great, but at least they are back to normal. In the second book, Kevin, now fifteen, loses his own scholarship but takes pride in seeing young Harold receive honors, both in school and in the neighborhood.

In his later books, Townsend becomes less concerned about the teenager who is buffeted about by the winds of the adult world and focuses on the internal angst—particularly the tension caused by love and sexual experience—of his young protagonists. In *The Intruder* (1969), Townsend gives concrete form to the natural anxieties teenagers face in developing their own identities. Rather than wrestle with the abstract concept of identity, Townsend creates Arnold Haithwaite who is confronted by an evil man who claims that he is Arnold Haithwaite. The young boy must then discover who he is and ascertain his place in his world.

Several of Townsend's books struggle with the problems of love, many of them focusing on the trepidations brought on through early sexual encounters. *Good-night, Prof, Dear* (as *Good-night, Prof, Love* 1970) is a realistic novel in which a shy young Graham Hollis falls in love with a woman slightly older in age but years older in experience. The love affair is doomed almost from the start, but his sexual initiation is successful and his broken heart is soothed by the recognition that in her own way Lynn has loved him.

Downstream (1967) presents a darker version of young love and initiation. Alan Dollis also falls in love, and in lust, with an older woman, his tutor. Alan's own misdirected sexual energy and his discovery of his father's unfaithfulness add grim dimensions to the problems faced by young people as they are introduced to the adult world.

Perhaps the most haunting of Townsend's books on teenage initiation is his very difficult *Forest of the Night* (1974). It is unbelievable that this abstract journey through a symbolic sexual awakening can be intended for Townsend's usual young adult audience. The book is compelling as well as frightening. It must be sensed and becomes more difficult to put into perspective because of the structure which lies almost outside the scope of the analytical mind. The boy must, as all boys, face his monster or remain a child; in this book, the author invites others to share the experience, to become a guide or to be guided on the journey.

Another kind of tension the maturing teenager must face is the tension inherent in forming his or her own value system, especially if those values prove to be different than those of their parents. It is this belief that children can develop values which surpass their parent's which gives Townsend's works their spark of hope. In *Noah's Castle* (1975), Barry Mortimer must choose between his father's concern for the family's welfare and Barry's own desire to help his community. While Barry's father is not condemned by the author for hoarding food while others starve, his behavior is explained as a type of insanity, and it is Barry and other young people of England who offer the country hope in its darkest hour.

Townsend examines teenage problems and successes in many forms and genres. *The Summer People* (1972) is a realistic novel which examines a thwarted love over a period of twenty years. *The Visitors* (*The Xanadu Manuscript* 1977), on the other hand, is a time travel fantasy which scrutinizes the same issue. *The Creatures* (*King Creature, Come* 1980) is a science fiction story of young people changing their society, and *Kate and the Revolution* is nearly a satire on modern wars and intrigue, where change, though initiated by the young, is nearly meaningless.

Throughout his work Townsend emphasizes both the resilience of the young, and their ability to overcome the problems and the obstacles which block the path to maturity. Although he is a realist, it is hope not despair which crowds most of the pages of his novels. Generally, he acknowledges the pain, the fear, and the heartbreak of growing up, but he tells his audience that they can survive and that in surviving, they will gain hope for themselves and for the whole world.

—Judith Gero John

TOWNSEND, Sue. British. Born in Leicester, Leicestershire, 2 April 1946. Educated at an English secondary school. Worked in various capacities, including garage attendant, hot dog saleswoman, dress shop worker, factory worker, and trained community worker; full-time writer, since 1982. Recipient: Thames Television Bursary, 1979, for *Womberang.* Agent: Giles Gordon, 43 Doughty Street, London WC1N 2LF, England. Lives in Leicester, Leicestershire.

PUBLICATIONS FOR YOUNG ADULTS

Fiction

The Secret Diary of Adrian Mole, Aged 13 3/4. London, Methuen, 1982.
The Growing Pains of Adrian Mole. London, Methuen, 1984.
Rebuilding Coventry: A Tale of Two Cities. London, Methuen, 1988.
Mr. Bevan's Dream. North Pomfret, Vermont, Trafalgar Square, 1990.
True Confessions of Adrian Albert Mole, with Margaret Hilda Roberts. London, Teen, 1991.

Plays

Womberang (produced Leicester, England, 1979).
Groping for Words (produced London, 1983).
Bazaar and Rummage, Groping for Words [and] Womberang (play collection). London, Methuen, 1984.
The Great Celestial Cow (produced Leicester, 1984).
The Secret Diary of Adrian Mole, Aged 13 3/4 (produced Leicester, 1984), with songs by Ken Howard and Alan Blaikley. London, Methuen, 1985.
Ear, Nose and Throat (produced Cambridge, England, 1989).
Ten Tiny Fingers, Nine Tiny Toes. London, Heinemann, 1991.

Television Play: *Bazaar and Rummage,* British Broadcasting Corporation, 1983.

Radio Play: *Secret Diary of A. Mole,* British Broadcasting Corporation Radio 4, 1982.

*

Media Adaptations: *Secret Diary of A. Mole* (television series) Thames TV, first broadcast 1986.

Although she has been a fairly prolific stage and television dramatist and has written other novels, Sue Townsend's reputation and popularity have been founded on her creation of a spotty, self-absorbed and pretentious schoolboy called Adrian Mole. Mole's "growing pains," his rather halting progress through post-pubertal anxiety and secondary education, form the subject of his "secret diary," a document as rich in comic banality and inadvertent self-disclosure as its prototype, George and Weedon Grossmith's *Diary of a Nobody* (1892). Adrian's problems and preoccupations are the universal problems and preoccupations of moderately intelligent adolescent males. He is worried about his disfiguring acne, the unpredictable and uncontrollable behaviour of his sexual organs, the social embarrassments he is forced to suffer at his parents' hands, about whether or not he will pass his exams, and whether the beautiful Pandora (who sits next to him in geography) will ever return his love. He writes poems, reads voraciously and indiscriminately (at one point sprinting through *War and Peace* in the space of twenty-four hours), regards himself as politically radical, and adores the Royal Family. Beneath all of the teenage confusions and affectations, however, Adrian emerges as a genuinely sympathetic figure. His messily unsystematic reading, for example, suggests a real inquisitiveness which his school appears almost purposely designed to frustrate, and he becomes, albeit reluctantly, devoted to the cantankerous octogenarian Bert Baxter, whose care he is assigned in a community aid project.

The Mole books succeed partly because they credibly portray a character who is at the same time a target for comic irony and an object of affection. But Adrian is also very much the product of his time and place, and the books evoke, in sharply circumstantial detail, the England of the 1980s, a nation itself beset by "growing pains" as the conservative social and economic policies of Margaret Thatcher's successive governments take an increasing hold on people's lives. Adrian's father, for example, loses his job early on and remains unemployed apart from a brief stint as a Canal Bank Renovation Supervisor overseeing a reluctant group of similarly unemployed (and unemployable) school-leavers. The state education system is tottering towards terminal collapse: the school that Adrian attends is staffed by a succession of transient incompetents and presided over by an unstable autocrat who has a portrait of Mrs. Thatcher hanging in his office. Political opposition seems confined to the ineffectual gestures of Pandora's vaguely leftist parents and to the anachronistic Labour fundamentalism of Bert Baxter. Most of the diary's inhabitants, indeed, seem happy enough to be distracted from their immediate troubles by stirring displays of national grandeur like royal weddings ("We truly lead the world when it comes to pageantry!" notes Adrian approvingly) or the Falklands War ("Grandma has got a funny look in her eyes. My mother says it is called jingoism..."). Barry Kent, the school bully, proudly wears a Union Jack tee shirt while his family (his father is another of the book's many unemployed males) has to furnish his home with pickings from the local garbage-tip.

The confusions which beset Adrian as he gropes his way towards adulthood are, thus, not solely the result of patchy knowledge and immature judgment; rather, they reflect broader confusions within the society of which he is a part. He can be, simultaneously, buoyantly patriotic and dimly aware of a deepening social malaise; sometimes, he confesses, he thinks of Mrs Thatcher as a "nice kind sort of woman" but the next day discovers that "she frightens me rigid." During the Falklands campaign he enthusiastically plots troop movements on a map, but he disgustedly throws the map away after seeing the official memorial service on television.

This account has perhaps made Adrian's fictional journals sound rather sombre. They are not, but their comic success is nevertheless based firmly on the sometimes satirical and always precise observation of an exactly defined social situation. Townsend is extremely adept at extracting humour from the specific detail of lower middle-class daily living in a Midlands town. Adrian's mother, for example, belatedly discovers feminism through reading Germaine Greer, but Adrian's hasty glance at *The Female Eunuch* results only in his first wet dream. Having been introduced at school to notions of dietary correctness, Adrian is despatched to do the family shopping and proudly returns laden with a huge assortment of lentils, brown rice, and other nutritious comestibles, only to have his mother complain that he has forgotten the frozen black forest gateaux.

The first two Adrian Mole books, then, owe their deserved popularity to a shrewd combination of comic action with informed social observation. Some of Townsend's more recent work has suggested the difficulty of sustaining such a combination. The third Mole book (*True Confessions*) takes Adrian fully into adulthood but makes him over as a grotesque eccentric whose earlier curiosity has become undiluted pretension and whose kindliness has been largely replaced by egotism. Conversely, *Rebuilding Coventry,* a lightly feminized pilgrim's progress through the "two nations" of Margaret Thatcher's England, is too angry to be able to realize more than intermittently its comic purpose. Therefore, it seems, probable that Townsend's durability as a writer will rest on her invention of the younger Adrian, a figure who manages to be representative both of his age-group and of English society at a particular moment in its evolution.

—Robert Dingley

TREASE, (Robert) Geoffrey. British. Born in Nottingham, 11 August 1909. Educated at Nottingham High School, 1920-28; Queen's College, Oxford (scholar), 1928-29. Served in the British Army, 1942-46; infantry and educational corps, England and India. Married Marian Haselden Granger Boyer in 1933 (died 1989); one daughter. Journalist and social worker, London, 1929-32; teacher, Clacton-on-Sea, Essex, 1932-33; full-time writer, since 1933. Lecturer on children's literature; Chairman, Children's Writers Group, 1962-63. Chairman, 1972-73, and since 1974 member of the Council, Society of Authors. Fellow, Royal Society of Literature, 1979. Recipient: Welwyn Festival award (England), 1938, for *After the Tempest* (play); *New York Herald Tribune* Spring Book Festival award for Nonfiction, 1966, for *This Is Your Century.* Agent: Murray Pollinger, 222 Old Brompton Road, London SW5 0BZ. Address: 1 Yomede Park, Newbridge Rd., Bath, Avon BA1 3LS, England.

PUBLICATIONS FOR YOUNG ADULTS

Fiction

Bows against the Barons, illustrated by Michael Boland. London, Lawrence, and New York, International Publishers, 1934; revised edition, Leicester, Brockhampton Press, 1986; revised edition, illustrated by C. Walter Hodges, New York, Meredith Press, 1966.

Comrades for the Charter, illustrated by Michael Boland. London, Lawrence & Wishart, 1934; revised edition illustrated by Douglas Phillips, Leicester, Brockhampton Press, 1972.

The Call to Arms. London, Lawrence, and New York, International Publishers, 1935.

Missing from Home, illustrated by Scott. London, Lawrence & Wishart, 1936.

Red Comet, illustrated by Fred Ellis. Moscow, Co-operative Publishing Society of Foreign Workers, 1936; as *Red Comet: A Tale of Travel in the U.S.S.R.,* London, Lawrence & Wishart, 1937.

The Christmas Holiday Mystery, illustrated by Alfred Sindall. London, A. & C. Black, 1937; as *The Lakeland Mystery,* 1942.

Mystery on the Moors, illustrated by Alfred Sindall. London, A. & C. Black, 1937.

Detectives of the Dales, illustrated by A.C.H. Gorham. London, A. & C. Black, 1938.

In the Land of the Mogul: A Story of the East India Company's First Venture in India, illustrated by J.C.B. Knight. Oxford, Basil Blackwell, 1938.

North Sea Spy. London, Fore, 1939.

Cue for Treason, illustrated by Beatrice Goldsmith. Oxford, Basil Blackwell, 1940; illustrated by L.F. Grant, New York, Vanguard Press, 1941.

Running Deer, illustrated by W. Lindsay Cable. London, Harrap, 1941; as *The Running of the Deer,* illustrated by Maureen Bradley, London, Hamish Hamilton, 1982.

The Grey Adventurer, illustrated by Beatrice Goldsmith. Oxford, Basil Blackwell, 1942.

Black Night, Red Morning, illustrated by Donia Nachsen. Oxford, Basil Blackwell, 1944.

Army without Banners. London, Fore, 1945.

Trumpets in the West, illustrated by Alan Blyth. Oxford, Basil Blackwell, 1947; illustrated by Joe Krush, New York, Harcourt, 1947.

The Hills of Varna, illustrated by Treyer Evans. London, Macmillan, 1948; as *Shadow of the Hawk,* illustrated by Joe Krush, New York, Harcourt, 1949.

Silver Guard, illustrated by Alan Blyth. Oxford, Basil Blackwell, 1948.

The Mystery of Moorside Farm, illustrated by Alan Blyth. Oxford, Basil Blackwell, 1949.

No Boats on Bannermere, illustrated by Richard Kennedy. London, Heinemann, 1949; New York, Norton, 1965.

The Secret Fiord, illustrated by H.M. Brock. London, Macmillan, 1949; illustrated by Joe Krush, New York, Harcourt, 1950.

Under Black Banner, illustrated by Richard Kennedy. London, Heinemann, 1950.

The Barons' Hostage: A Story of Simon de Montfort, illustrated by Alan Jessett. London, Phoenix House, 1952; revised edition, Leicester, Brockhampton Press, 1973; Nashville, Thomas Nelson, 1975.

Black Banner Players, illustrated by Richard Kennedy. London, Heinemann, 1952.

The Crown of Violet, illustrated by C. Walter Hodges. London, Macmillan, 1952; as *Web of Traitors: An Adventure Story of Ancient Athens,* New York, Vanguard Press, 1952.

The New House at Hardale. London, Lutterworth, 1953.

The Silken Secret, illustrated by Alan Jessett. Oxford, Basil Blackwell, 1953; New York, Vanguard Press, 1954.

Black Banner Abroad. London, Heinemann, 1954; New York, Warne, 1955.

The Fair Flower of Danger. Oxford, Basil Blackwell, 1955.

Editor, *Six of the Best: Stories.* Oxford, Basil Blackwell, 1955.

The Gates of Bannerdale. London, Heinemann, 1956; New York, Warne, 1957.

Word to Caesar, illustrated by Geoffrey Whittam. London, Macmillan, 1956; as *Message to Hadrian,* New York, Vanguard Press, 1956.

Mist over Athelney, illustrated by R.S. Sherriffs and J.L. Stockle. London, Macmillan, 1958; as *Escape to King Alfred,* New York, Vanguard Press, 1958,

The Maythorn Story, illustrated by Robert Hodgson. London, Heinemann, 1960.

Thunder of Valmy, illustrated by John S. Goodall. London, Macmillan, 1960; as *Victory at Valmy,* New York, Vanguard Press, 1961.

Change at Maythorn, illustrated by Robert Hodgson. London, Heinemann, 1962.

Follow My Black Plume, illustrated by Brian Wildsmith. New York, Vanguard Press, 1963.

A Thousand for Sicily, illustrated by Brian Wildsmith. London, Macmillan, and New York, Vanguard Press, 1964.

Bent Is the Bow, illustrated by Charles Keeping. London, Thomas Nelson, 1965; New York, Nelson, 1967.

The Dutch Are Coming, illustrated by Lynette Hemmant. London, Hamish Hamilton, 1965.

The Red Towers of Granada, illustrated by Charles Keeping. London, Macmillan, 1966; New York, Vanguard Press, 1967.

The White Nights of St. Petersburg, illustrated by William Stobbs. London, Macmillan, and New York, Vanguard Press, 1967.

The Runaway Serf, illustrated by Mary Russon. London, Hamish Hamilton, 1968.

A Masque for the Queen, illustrated by Krystyna Turska. London, Hamish Hamilton, 1970.

Horsemen on the Hills. London, Macmillan, 1971.

A Ship to Rome, illustrated by Leslie Atkinson. London, Heinemann, 1972.

Popinjay Stairs: A Historical Adventure about Samuel Pepys. London, Macmillan, 1973; New York, Vanguard Press, 1982; as *The Popinjay Mystery,* London, Pan Macmillan, 1993.

A Voice in the Night, illustrated by Sara Silcock. London, Heinemann, 1973.

The Chocolate Boy, illustrated by David Walker. London, Heinemann, 1975.

The Iron Tsar. London, Macmillan, 1975.

The Seas of Morning, illustrated by David Smee. London, Penguin, 1976.

The Spy Catchers, illustrated by Geoffrey Bargery. London, Hamish Hamilton, 1976.

Violet for Bonaparte. London, Macmillan, 1976.

When the Drums Beat, illustrated by Janet Marsh. London, Heinemann, 1976; augmented edition, as *When the Drums Beat and Other Stories,* London, Pan Books, 1979.

The Claws of the Eagle, illustrated by Ionicus. London, Heinemann, 1977.

The Field of the Forty Footsteps. London, Macmillan, 1977.

Mandeville. London, Macmillan, 1980.

A Wood by Moonlight, and Other Stories. London, Chatto & Windus, 1981.

Saraband for Shadows. London, Macmillan, 1982.

The Cormorant Venture. London, Macmillan, 1984.

Tomorrow Is a Stranger. London, Heinemann, 1987.

The Arpino Assignment, illustrated by Paul Leith. London, Walker Books, 1988.

A Flight of Angels, illustrated by Eric Stemp. London, Macmillan, 1988; Minneapolis, Minnesota, Lerner Publications, 1989.

Hidden Treasure, illustrated by Chris Molan. London, Hamish Hamilton, 1989; New York, Lodestar, 1989.

Calabrian Quest. London, Walker Books, 1990.

Shadow under the Sea. London, Walker Books, 1990.

Aunt Augusta's Elephant, illustrated by Jean Foster. London, Macmillan, 1991.

Song for a Tattered Flag, London, Walker Books, 1992.

Fire on the Wind, London, Macmillan, 1993.

Bring out the Banners, London, Walker Book, 1994.

No Horn at Midnight, London, Macmillan, forthcoming.

Plays

The Dragon Who Was Different, and Other Plays (includes *The Mighty Mandarin, Fairyland Limited, The New Bird*). London, Muller, 1938.

The Shadow of Spain, and Other Plays (includes *The Unquiet Cloister* and *Letters of Gold*). Oxford, Basil Blackwell, 1953.

Radio Play: *Popinjay Stairs,* from his own story, 1973.

Other

Fortune, My Foe: The Story of Sir Walter Raleigh, illustrated by Norman Meredith. London, Methuen, 1949; as *Sir Walter Raleigh, Captain and Adventurer,* New York, Vanguard Press, 1950.

The Young Traveller in India and Pakistan [England and Wales, Greece]. London, Phoenix House, 3 vols., 1949-56; New York, Dutton, 3 vols., 1953-56.

Enjoying Books. London, Phoenix House, 1951; revised edition, 1963.

Translator, *Companions of Fortune.* by René Guillot, illustrated by Pierre Collot. London, Oxford University Press, 1952.

The Seven Queens of England. London, Heinemann, and New York, Vanguard Press, 1953; revised version, Heinemann, 1968.

Translator, *The King's Corsair,* by René Guillot, illustrated by Pierre Rousseau. London, Oxford University Press, 1954.

Seven Kings of England, illustrated by Leslie Atkinson. London, Heinemann, and New York, Vanguard Press, 1955.

Edward Elgar: Maker of Music. London, Macmillan, 1959.

Wolfgang Mozart, The Young Composer. London, Macmillan, 1961; New York, St. Martin's, 1962.

The Young Writer: A Practical Handbook, illustrated by Carl Hollander. London, Thomas Nelson, 1961.

Seven Stages. London, Heinemann, 1964; New York, Vanguard Press, 1965.

This Is Your Century. London, Heinemann, and New York, Harcourt, 1965.

Seven Sovereign Queens. London, Heinemann, 1968; New York, Vanguard Press, 1968.

Byron: A Poet Dangerous to Know. London, Macmillan, and New York, Holt, 1969.

Days to Remember: A Garland of Historic Anniversaries, illustrated by Joanna Troughton. London, Heinemann, 1973.

D.H. Lawrence: The Phoenix and the Flame. London, Macmillan, 1973; as *The Phoenix and the Flame: D.H. Lawrence, A Biography,* New York, Viking, 1973.

Britain Yesterday, illustrated by Robert Hodgson. Oxford, Basil Blackwell, 1975.

Timechanges: The Evolution of Everyday Life. London, Kingfisher Books, 1985; New York, Watts, 1986.

Living through History: The Edwardian Era. London, Batsford, 1986.

Hidden Treasure, illustrated by Chris Molan. London, Hamish Hamilton, and New York, Lodestar, 1989.

PUBLICATIONS FOR ADULTS

Novels

Such Divinity. London, Chapman & Hall, 1939.

Only Natural. London, Chapman & Hall, 1940.

Snared Nightingale. London, Macmillan, 1957; New York, Vanguard Press, 1958.

So Wild the Heart. London, Macmillan, and New York, Vanguard Press, 1959.

Short Stories

The Unsleeping Sword. London, Lawrence, 1934.

Plays

After the Tempest (produced Welwyn, Hertfordshire, 1938; London, 1939). Published in *Best One-Act Plays of 1938,* edited by J.W. Marriott, London, Harrap, 1939; published separately, Boston, Baker, n.d.

Colony. (produced London, 1939).

Time out of Mind (televised, 1956; produced London, 1967).

Radio Plays: *Mr. Engels of Manchester Change,* 1947; *Henry Irving,* 1947; *Lady Anne,* 1949; *The Real Mr. Ryecroft,* 1949; *Elgar of England,* 1957.

Television Plays: *Time out of Mind,* 1956; *Into Thin Air,* 1973.

Poetry

The Supreme Prize and Other Poems. London, Stockwell, 1926.

Nonfiction

Walking in England. Wisbech, Cambridge, Fenland, 1935.

Clem Voroshilov: The Red Marshal. London, Pilot Press, 1940.

Tales out of School: A Survey of Children's Fiction. London, Heinemann, 1949; revised edition, 1964.

The Italian Story: From the Earliest Times to 1946. London, Macmillan, 1963; *The Italian Story: From the Etruscans to Modern Times,* New York, Vanguard Press, 1963.

The Grand Tour. London, Heinemann, and New York, Holt, 1967.

Editor, *Matthew Todd's Journal: A Gentleman's Gentleman in Europe, 1814-1820.* London, Heinemann, 1968.

Nottingham: A Biography. London, Macmillan, 1970.

The Condottieri: Soldiers of Fortune. London, Thames & Hudson, 1970; New York, Holt, 1971.

A Whiff of Burnt Boats: An Early Autobiography. London, Macmillan, and New York, St. Martin's, 1971.

Samuel Pepys and His World. London, Thames & Hudson, and New York, Putnam, 1972.
Laughter at the Door: A Continued Autobiography. London, Macmillan, and New York, St. Martin's, 1974.
London: A Concise History. London, Thames & Hudson, and New York, Scribner, 1975.
Portrait of a Cavalier: William Cavendish, First Duke of Newcastle. London, Macmillan, and New York, Taplinger, 1979.

*

Media Adaptations: *Popinjay Stairs* (radio play), BBC, 1973; *Cue for Treason* (adapted for the stage by David Craig), produced by Toronto Young People's Theatre, Canada, 1986; *The Red Towers of Grenada* dramatized in a TV biographical film on Trease's life and work, London, Channel 4, 1992.

Biography: Essay in *Something about the Author Autobiography Series,* Volume 6, Detroit, Gale, 1988, pp. 237-256.

Manuscript Collections: Nottingham Central Library; Kerlan Collection, University of Minnesota, Minneapolis; University of Nottingham Library.

Critical Study: *Geoffrey Trease* by Margaret Meek, London, Bodley Head, 1960; New York, Walck, 1964.

Geoffrey Trease comments:
I have always disliked age-group classifications, though I can see why overworked adults demand them for timesaving reassurance. I despise the arrogant generalizations implied in "catering" for this group or that. Now, well into my eighties, with over a hundred books behind me, I do as I have always done—I write about what interests *me* and hope it will find enough readers to keep my publishers happy. My work has appeared in twenty languages. How could I cater to the young Estonian or Brazilian, the Icelander or the Japanese? As for age-groups, the reader I am proudest to have roused to enthusiasm was the great historian G.M. Trevelyan, who, when old and going blind, told me what pleasure he had found in my adventure stories. Though I sometimes write shorter books with child characters, I am happiest with what I call my "junior novels," in which adult life is seen through the eyes of adolescents or the slightly older. Writing fiction remains my absolute lifeline. There are still so many themes and so many backgrounds, crying out for treatment—and on the whole, so much more freedom of expression than in the strait-laced 1930s when I began. (Only the creeping censorship of political correctness worries me.) Though still loyal to my old favourite periods, such as Pepys's London, I have been specially drawn, in recent novels, to the dramas of my own century, from the women's struggle for the vote to post-Communist Russia and the Bucharest rising of 1989.

*   *   *

The excellence of modern English historical fiction for young people is in no small part due to the pioneering efforts and achievement of Geoffrey Trease. When his first novels were published in the early 1930s, realistic fiction for children in general, and historical fiction in particular, had few notable practitioners. The historical novels available for children tended to romanticize upper-class life, to ignore the poor, and to glorify warfare and picturesque,

aristocratic lost causes. Trease was to change all this by writing historical fiction from the perspective of middle- or working-class children and from a position of support for liberal or radical and democratic movements in history. Although as a youth Trease won a scholarship to Oxford to study the classics, he left the university after one year, and his future studies in history were self-directed. Intensely aware of the social and economic distress throughout Britain as the Depression deepened, he first went to work with slum children in the east end of London, and then while employed as a teacher and journalist, he became a pacifist and adherent of the idealistic left-wing movement that flourished in Britain in the 1930s. Working with children, he was struck by the realization, as he noted in his later *Tales out of School,* that "children's books were not reflecting the changed values of the age." Trease set about to remedy the situation with a novel about the age of Robin Hood, *Bows against the Barons,* whose very title reflects Trease's lifelong sympathy with the ordinary man and the underdog against the wealthy and powerful.

Partly inspired by the Soviet children's book *Moscow Has a Plan,* Trease's first novel presented Robin Hood as the people's hero, and had a fairly heavy political message which was toned down in a later edition. As well as its stirring presentation of the struggle of right against privileged wrong, *Bows against the Barons* revealed Trease's gift for telling an exciting story whose well-crafted incidents grip the reader's attention throughout the tale. As a child he had loved to read the adventure stories of writers like Henty and Ballantyne, and he proved able in his own writing to combine the dash of the adventure story with a serious view of the significance of historical events. While at this time even an innovative and relatively successful children's author received little recognition or pecuniary reward, Trease continued to write and steadily gained command over his craft. Showing the relevance of history to the concerns of our own day has always been his aim although he admitted that *Comrades for the Charter,* his second novel, savoured more of the 1930s socialists than the 1830s Chartists who were its subject. Trease did, however, rapidly increase his own grasp of historical detail to add depth to his vision of the significance of historical movements, and learned to adapt contemporary speech patterns to characters in different historical settings.

The young characters of Trease's novels are almost always involved in important political events of their era as well as some aspect of its cultural and intellectual life. In one of the earliest and most popular of Trease's novels, *Cue for Treason,* two young people manage to foil a plot against the life of Queen Elizabeth I and to join Shakespeare's company and act in his plays. Apart from this exciting action, however, the novel is notable for its pairing of the fourteen-year-old narrator, Peter, with a spirited and resourceful heroine, Kit. Unlike the passive girls who had played largely decorative roles in most previous historical fiction which was aimed at young male readers, Kit is an active and interesting character who takes her fate into her own hands, runs away from a forced engagement disguised as a boy, and in that disguise has the opportunity to perform some of Shakespeare's great female roles. Trease was to retain through many of his novels this device of a paired hero and heroine who are fully equal as they travel and have adventures together. Sometimes they arrive at a mature appreciation of each other which is romantic but never cloying or sentimental and does not require the girl to give up the independence and self-assertion she has demonstrated throughout their adventures. Trease has received too little credit for his creation of these lively and strong-minded girls; while their disguises and successes may sometimes seem implausible in the historical context, they were a refreshing innovation to the genre and created at a time when the roles of young female characters were sadly limited.

While many of Trease's early novels were concerned with young people caught up in major events of English history (such as the Civil War, the Monmouth rebellion, and King Alfred's resistance against Danish invaders), later novels went further afield to deal with the Garibaldi uprising, the Russian Revolution, and the early years of the French Revolution. Yet others depict English characters travelling to far-off places, the link with the familiar being provided for his English readers by the age and English perspective of the central character. In *The Hills of Varna* a young English student of the early sixteenth century is sent by Erasmus to search in Italy and Dalmatia for a lost manuscript of a Greek play. Through all the ensuing dramatic adventures, Trease manages to evoke a real sense of the intellectual excitement of the rediscovery of Greek learning in the Renaissance, excitement shared not only by Alan and his fellow students but also by Angela, the clever and intrepid Italian girl who joins Alan in fulfilling the quest. Trease often gives a sense of historical development and perspective by linking elements from one novel to another: the manuscript sought by Alan and Angela reappears in *The Crown of Violet* as it is actually being written and then performed in the Theatre of Dionysus in fifth-century Athens. Athenian Alexis and Corinna, like many of Trease's paired young characters, are fascinated by the theatre, and Alexis writes the prizewinning comedy as well as engages in exciting maneuvers to foil a band of traitors who seek to undermine Athenian democracy.

Interestingly, when *The Crown of Violet* appeared in the U.S. at the height of the McCarthy era, it was given the title *Web of Traitors* and presented by its publishers as a kind of anticommunist allegory, with Alexis compared to an F.B.I. agent—a curious fate for an author of Trease's left-wing sympathies. Those sympathies were never rigidly doctrinaire, however; while writing from the Roundhead or Cromwellian point of view in his early Civil War novel *Silver Guard* and in the later *The Field of the Forty Footsteps,* he shows the harsh consequences resulting from the imposition of Puritan rule under Cromwell. But although he is willing and able to show two sides of a question and to grant that good people may be found on both sides, Trease always takes a stand on issues and directs his readers' support to defend popular and/or individual rights against assault by the privileged and powerful. Necessity, often rooted in social injustice, usually sends his young characters out on the road to adventure: farmer's son Peter in *Cue for Treason* has to leave home because he is in trouble for protesting against the enclosure of common land, sailor Denzil in *Popinjay Stairs* is penniless because the Navy can not afford to employ sailors through the winter, and Robin in *The Red Towers of Granada* is driven away from his home village because he is suspected of having leprosy; he is befriended by another medieval outcast, a Jew. Despite their breathtaking plots and the encounters with famous historical figures, Trease's historical novels are realistic in conveying a sense of the economic pressures and physical discomforts experienced by the characters, and Trease's conclusions rarely promise a simple solution to the problems—whether personal or political.

While he is best known for his historical fiction, Trease has written a number of novels about modern young people as well. The novels of the Bannermere sequence, set in the English Lake District, depict the gradual maturing of a group of adolescent friends of both sexes; they rely less on dramatic events than do the historical novels and were both innovative and successful in depicting the school and home lives of ordinary young people at a time when the exclusive world of the boarding school stories dominated the field. The Maythorn novels and other more recent books also explore settings and characters from contemporary working-class life. Trease has also written a number of nonfiction books for young people, mostly on subjects from English history but including well-regarded biographies of the writers Byron and D.H. Lawrence, both of whom had a connection with his own family home of Nottingham. In the first volume of his autobiography, *A Whiff of Burnt Boats,* Trease remarks that he is much more interested in older children than younger ones, and rather than encouraging them to cling to the magical world of childhood "my impulse was to beckon them on and shout: 'There is a wider view from the next bend.'" In well over half a century of writing for young people, Trease has beckoned his readers around many bends in the river of human experience, and widened the view for all of them.

—Gwyneth Evans

TREECE, Henry. British. Born in Wednesbury, Staffordshire, 22 December 1911. Educated at Wednesbury High School for Boys; Birmingham University, B.A. 1933, Dip. Ed. 1934; University of Santander, diploma, 1933. Served in the Royal Air Force, Bomber Command, 1941-46; served as intelligence officer; Flight Lieutenant. Married Mary Woodman in 1939; two sons and one daughter. Teacher, Leicestershire Home Office School, Shustoke, 1933-34; English master, The College, Cleobury Mortimer, Shropshire, 1934-35, and Tynemouth School for Boys, Northumberland, 1935-38; English master, 1938-41, and senior English master, 1946-59, Barton on Humber Grammar School, Lincolnshire; full-time writer, 1959-66. Made numerous appearances on British radio and television, 1948-66; lectured in the United States, 1950-51. Recipient: Art Council Play Prize, 1955; Carnegie Medal nomination, 1967, for *The Dream-Time. Died 10 June 1966.*

PUBLICATIONS FOR YOUNG ADULTS

Fiction

Desperate Journey, illustrated by Richard Kennedy. London, Faber, 1954.
The Eagles Have Flown, illustrated by Christine Price. London, Lane, and New York, Criterion, 1954.
Legions of the Eagle, illustrated by Christine Price. London, Lane, and New York, Criterion, 1954.
Ask for King Billy, illustrated by Richard Kennedy. London, Faber, 1955.
Hounds of the King, illustrated by Christine Price. London, Lane, and New York, Criterion, 1955.
Viking's Dawn, illustrated by Christine Price. London, Lane, 1955; New York, Criterion, 1956.
The Golden Strangers. London, Lane, 1956; New York, Random House, 1957; as *The Invaders,* New York, Avon, 1960.
The Great Captains. London, Lane, and New York, Random House, 1956.

Hunter Hunted, illustrated by Richard Kennedy. London, Faber, 1957.

Men of the Hills, illustrated by Christine Price. London, Lane, 1957; New York, Criterion, 1958.

The Road to Miklagard, illustrated by Christine Price. London, Lane, and New York, Criterion, 1957.

The Children's Crusade, illustrated by Christine Price. London, Bodley Head, 1958; as *Perilous Pilgrimage,* New York, Criterion, 1959.

Don't Expect Any Mercy! London, Faber, 1958.

Red Queen, White Queen. London, Bodley Head, and New York, Random House, 1958; as *The Pagan Queen,* New York, Avon, 1959.

The Return of Robinson Crusoe, illustrated by Will Nickless. London, Hulton Press, 1958; as *The Further Adventures of Robinson Crusoe,* New York, Criterion, 1958.

The Bombard, illustrated by Christine Price. London, Bodley Head, 1959; as *Ride to Danger.* New York, Criterion, 1959.

Wickham and the Armada, illustrated by Hookway Cowles. London, Hulton Press, 1959.

Red Settlement. London, Bodley Head, 1960.

Viking's Sunset, illustrated by Christine Price. London, Bodley Head, 1960; New York, Criterion, 1961.

The Golden One, illustrated by William Stobbs. London, Bodley Head, 1961; New York, Criterion, 1962.

The Jet Beads, illustrated by W.A. Sillince. Leicester, Brockhampton Press, 1961.

Man with a Sword, illustrated by W. Stobbs. London, Bodley Head, 1962; New York, Pantheon, 1964.

War Dog, illustrated by Roger Payne. Leicester, Brockhampton Press, 1962; New York, Criterion, 1963.

Horned Helmet, illustrated by Charles Keeping. Leicester, Brockhampton Press, and New York, Criterion, 1963.

The Last of the Vikings, illustrated by Charles Keeping. Leicester, Brockhampton Press, 1964; as *The Last Viking,* New York, New York, Pantheon, 1966.

Killer in Dark Glasses. London, Faber, 1965.

Splintered Sword, illustrated by Charles Keeping. Leicester, Brockhampton Press, 1965; New York, Duell, 1966.

Bang, You're Dead! London, Faber, 1966.

The Bronze Sword, illustrated by Mary Russon. London, Hamish Hamilton, 1966; augmented edition as *The Centurian,* New York, Meredith Press, 1967.

The Dream-Time, illustrated by Charles Keeping. Leicester, Brockhampton Press, 1967; New York, Meredith Press, 1968.

The Queen's Brooch. London, Hamish Hamilton, 1966; New York, Putnam, 1967.

Swords from the North, illustrated by Charles Keeping. London, Faber, and New York, Pantheon, 1967.

Vinland the Good, illustrated by William Stobbs. London, Bodley Head, 1967; as *Westward to Vinland,* New York, Phillips, 1967.

The Windswept City, illustrated by Faith Jacques. London, Hamish Hamilton, 1967; New York, Meredith Press, 1968.

The Invaders: Three Stories, illustrated by Charles Keeping. Leicester, Brockhampton Press, and New York, Crowell, 1972.

Plays

Hounds of the King, with Two Radio Plays. (includes *Harold Godwinson* and *William, Duke of Normandy*), illustrated by Stuart Tresilian. London, Longman, 1965.

Radio Plays: *Harold Godwinson,* 1954; William, *Duke of Normandy,* 1954.

Other

Castles and Kings, illustrated by C. Walter Hodges. London, Batsford, 1959; New York, Criterion, 1960.

The True Book about Castles, illustrated by G.H. Channing. London, Muller, 1960.

Fighting Men: How Men Have Fought through the Ages, with Ewart Oakeshott. Leicester, Brockhampton Press, 1963; New York, Putnam, 1965.

Know about the Crusades. London, Blackie, 1963; as *About the Crusades,* Chester Springs, Pennsylvania, Dufour, 1966.

The Burning of Njal (saga retold), illustrated by Bernard Blatch. London, Bodley Head, and New York, Criterion, 1964.

PUBLICATIONS FOR ADULTS

Novels

The Dark Island. London, Gollancz, and New York, Random House, 1952; as *The Savage Warriors,* New York, Avon, 1959.

The Rebels. London, Gollancz, 1953.

The Master of Badger's Hall. New York, Random House, 1959; as *A Fighting Man,* London, Bodley Head, 1960.

Jason. London, Bodley Head, and New York, Random House, 1961.

The Amber Princess. New York, Random House, 1962; as *Electra,* London, Bodley Head, 1963.

Oedipus. London, Bodley Head, 1964; as *The Eagle King,* New York, Random House, 1965.

The Green Man. London, Bodley Head, and New York, Putnam, 1966.

Short Stories

I Cannot Go Hunting Tomorrow. London, Grey Walls Press, 1946.

Plays

Carnival King (produced Nottingham, 1954). London, Faber, 1955.
Footsteps in the Sea (produced Nottingham, 1955).

Poetry

38 Poems. London, Fortune Press, 1940.

Towards a Personal Armageddon. Prairie City, Illinois, Press of James A. Decker, 1941.

Invitation and Warning. London, Faber, 1942.

The Black Seasons. London, Faber, 1945.

Collected Poems. New York, Knopf, 1946.

The Haunted Garden. London, Faber, 1947.

The Exiles. London, Faber, 1952.

The Magic Wood, paintings by Barry Moser. New York, HarperCollins, 1992.

Other

Editor, with J.F. Hendry, *The New Apocalypse.* London, Fortune Press, 1939.

Editor, with J.F. Hendry, *The White Horseman: Prose and Verse of the New Apocalypse.* London, Routledge, 1941.

Editor, with Stefan Schimanski, *Transformation.* London, Gollancz, 1943.

Editor, with Stefan Schimanski, *Wartime Harvest.* London, Bale and Staples, 1943.

Editor, with John Pudney, *Air Force Poetry.* London, Lane, 1944.

Editor, *Herbert Read: An Introduction.* London, Faber, 1944; Port Washington, New York, Kennikat Press, 1969.

Editor, with Stefan Schimanski. *A Map of Hearts: A Collection of Short Stories.* London, Drummond, 1944.

Editor, with Stefan Schimanski, *Transformation 2-4.* London, Drummond, 3 vols., 1944-47.

Editor, with J.F. Hendry, *The Crown and the Sickle: An Anthology.* London, King and Staples, 1945.

How I See Apocalypse. London, Drummond, 1946.

Editor, with Stefan Schimanski, *Leaves in the Storm: A Book of Diaries.* London, Drummond, 1947.

Editor, *Selected Poems,* by Algernon Charles Swinburne. London, Grey Walls Press, 1948.

Dylan Thomas: "Dog among the Fairies." London, Drummond, 1949; New York, de Graff, 1954; revised edition, London, Benn, and New York, de Graff, 1956.

Editor, with Stefan Schimanski, *New Romantic Anthology.* London, Grey Walls Press, 1949.

The Crusades. London, Bodley Head, and New York, Random House, 1962.

*

Biography: Entry in *More Junior Authors,* edited by Muriel Fuller, New York, Wilson, 1963, pp. 209-11.

Critical Study: Entry in *Children's Literature Review,* Volume 2, Detroit, Gale, 1976.

*   *   *

Henry Treece was a Romantic poet in the 1930s and 1940s who, with the Scottish poet J. F. Hendry, founded the literary movement the "New Apocalypse": "In my definition, the writer who senses the chaos, the turbulence, the laughter and the tears, the order and the peace of the world in its entirety, is an Apocalyptic writer. His utterance will be prophetic, for he is observing things which less sensitive men have not yet come to notice..." Treece's last collection of verse appeared in 1952, when he also published his first novel. Between then and his death from heart trouble fourteen years later, Treece wrote, among other prose works, nine historical novels for adults and more than twenty for children, in which he played out his poetic philosophy in prose. History, mythology, and, most often, the rationalisation of historical legend were the means through which Treece expounded his universal messages of loyalty, toleration, reconciliation, redemption, and self-realisation, choosing as his settings times of upheaval and change, which he termed "cross-roads of history."

From Treece's experience as a teacher (his full-time profession until afflicted with ill health in 1959), as well as from his poetic instinct came his penchant for experimenting with form and language, and also for treating the same theme from different angles and at different levels of understanding and reading interest. His works are thus quite suitable for young adults even though Treece was not consciously writing to fulfil the criteria of this genre.

Considered from this perspective, the novels which Treece set in northern Europe follow a meaningful pattern when placed in order of historical time. *Men of the Hills* has as its counterpart *The Golden Strangers,* in which the dark Celtic race of Britain, the Barley Folk, confront the blond invaders from the continent, the Beaker Folk. Treece returned to this thematic territory with visionary insight in the allegorical *The Dream-Time,* the last book he wrote—he packed up the manuscript for posting to his publisher a few hours before he died. The conflict between Roman tradition and Celtic passion described in *Legions of the Eagle* is elaborated upon in *The Dark Island.* The revolt of Boudicca against Roman domination motivates the plots of *The Bronze Sword (The Centurian), The Queen's Brooch,* and *Red Queen, White Queen,* in the latter of which there is a full-scale study of this legendary leader of the Iceni. The literary forerunner of these is a short story, "I Cannot Go Hunting Tomorrow" (reprinted in *The Invaders: Three Stories),* which postulates that in the light of the mutual incomprehension of values that divides Roman and Celt, a unified Britain can only be developed from within. Consequently *The Eagles Have Flown* and *The Great Captains* present versions of the King Arthur story, in historical terms.

Treece abhorred violence but respected the skill and courage of the fighter. His fascination with the Vikings was evident in many books, beginning with *Viking's Dawn,* which, with *The Road to Miklagard* and *Viking's Sunset,* became an adventure trilogy spanning not only the Viking world but ranging also from Kiev in the west to Vinland in the east, in which a youth grows to manhood. Treece expanded his chronological framework with *Hounds of the King,* which ends with the death of Harold II (Godwinson) at Hastings, but whose earlier climax centres on Harold's victory at Stamfordbridge over Harald Hardrada, the Norwegian king. Hardrada was a folk hero after Treece's heart and recurs as the father figure and early mentor of Hereward (the Wake), whose opposition to and final reconciliation with William (the Conqueror) Treece brilliantly sketches in *Man with a Sword.* Hardrada also has two books to himself: *Swords from the North* covers his life and exploits; *The Last of the Vikings* is a deceptively simple hero tale which concentrates on Hardrada's young adulthood, for which Treece supplies him with a mentor of his own, the mysterious Arsleif Summerbird, a character so fully rounded and sympathetic that he almost steals the show.

All these novels have adult protagonists or feature young adults growing to maturity. Treece's six modern thrillers, *Desperate Journey, Ask for King Billy, Hunter Hunted, Don't Expect Any Mercy!, Killer in Dark Glasses,* and *Bang, You're Dead,* also have adult heroes, whom he sets in improbable situations, from which they escape, or otherwise emerge, with justice or honour prevailing. A similar bent and attitude to danger and skulduggery are discernible in *Red Settlement,* a story of the earliest colonial days in Pennsylvania. It was the only historical novel which Treece wrote consciously for the young adult market; while it is not a particularly distinguished piece of work, it has an ending which is, in Treece's terms, eminently "Apocalyptic."

—Antony Kamm

TRUMBO, Dalton. Also wrote as Sam Jackson; Robert Rich. American. Born in Montrose, Colorado, 9 December 1905. University of Colorado, 1924-25, Southern Branch, University of California (now University of California, Los Angeles), 1926, and University of Southern California, Los Angeles, 1928-30. Served in the United States Army Air Forces as War correspondent, 1945. Married Cleo Beth Fincher in 1939; two daughters and one son. Screenwriter and novelist. Car washer; section hand; worked for nine years as a bread-wrapper and later as an estimator ont he night shift for Divis Perfection bakery, Los Angeles, California; reader at Warner Brothers. Served as national chairman of Writers for Roosevelt, 1944. Recipient: National Book award, 1939, for *Johnny Got His Gun;* Academy award, 1957, for "The Brave One"; Teachers Union of New York annual award, 1960; Writers Guild Laurel award for achievement in screenwriting, 1970; Cannes Film Festival Special Jury Grand Prize, International Critics Prize, Interfilm Jury World Council of Churches Prize, Atlanta Film Festival Golden Dove Peace Prize, and Golden Phoenix for Best of Festival, all 1971, and Belgrade Film Festival Audience and Director's award and Japanese International Festival of the Arts Grand Prize, both 1972, all for "Johnny Got His Gun. *Died 10 September 1976.*

PUBLICATIONS

Novels

Eclipse. London, L. Dickson & Thompson, 1935.
Washington Jitters. New York, Knopf, 1936.
Johnny Got His Gun. Philadelphia, Lippincott, 1939.
The Remarkable Andrew. Philadelphia, Lippincott, 1941.
Night of the Aurochs, edited by Robert Kirsch. New York, Viking, 1979.

Plays

The Biggest Thief in Town (produced New York, 1949). New York, Dramatists Play Service, 1949.

Screenplays: *Jealousy,* 1934; *The Story of Isadore Bernstein,* 1936; *Love Begins at Twenty,* with Tom Reed, 1936; *Road Gang,* 1936; collaborator, *Devil's Playground,* 1937; *A Man to Remember* (based on Katharine Haviland-Taylor's short story *Failure,* 1938; *Fugitives for a Night,* 1938; *Sorority House,* 1939; *Career,* 1939; *Five Came Back,* with Nathanael West and Jerry Cady, 1939; *The Flying Irishman,* with Ernest Pagano, 1939; *Heaven with a Barbed Wire Fence,* 1939; *Half a Sinner,* 1940; *We Who Are Young,* 1940; *Kitty Foyle* (adaptation of the book by Christopher Morley), 1940; *A Bill of Divorcement,* 1940; *Curtain Call,* 1940; *The Remarkable Andrew,* 1942; *Tender Comrade,* 1943; *A Man Named Joe,* 1943; *Thirty Seconds Over Tokyo,* 1944; *Our Vines Have Tender Grapes* (adaptation of the book by George Victor Martin), 1945; *The Brave One,* as Robert Rich, King Brothers Production, 1957; *Exodus* (adaptation of the book by Leon Uris), 1960; *Spartacus* (based on the novel by Howard Fast), 1960; *The Last Sunset* (based on *Sundown at Crazy Horse* by Howard Rigsby), 1961; *Lonely Are the Brave* (based on *The Brave Cowboy* by Edward Abbey), 1962; *The Sandpiper,* 1965; *Hawaii* (adaptation of the book by James A. Michener, 1966; *The Fixer* (adaptation of the book by Bernard Malamud), 1968; *The Horsemen,* 1971; (and director) *Johnny Got His Gun,*

1971; *Papillon,* with Lorenzo Semple, Jr., 1973; *Executive Action* (based on a story by Donald Freed and Mark Lane), 1973.

Other

Harry Bridges (pamphlet). League of American Writers, 1941.
Additional Dialogue: Letters of Dalton Trumbo, 1942-1962, edited by Helen Manfull. New York, M. Evans, 1970.
The Time of the Toad: A Study of the Inquisition in American and Two Related Pamphlets (includes *The Time of the Toad, The Devil in the Book,* and *Honor Bright and All that Jazz*) New York, Harper, 1972.

*

Media Adaptations: *Washington Jitters* was dramatized by John Boruft and Walter Hart and produced at the Guild Theatre, New York, City, May 2, 1938. The films *The Kid from Kokomo,* Warner Brothers, 1939, *The Lone Wolf Strike,* Columbia, 1940, *Accent on Love,* Twentieth Century-Fox, 1941, and *You Belong to Me,* Columbia, 1941, refilmed as *Emergency Wedding,* Columbia, 1950, were based on Trumbo's stories. A novelization by Randall M. White of *A Man Named Joe* was published as *A Guy Named Joe,* Grossett, 1944. *The Biggest Thief in Town* was adapted for television and shown on the British Broadcasting Corp., 1957.

Critical Study: Entry in *Contemporary Literary Criticism,* Volume 19, Detroit, Gale, 1981.

*   *   *

World War I killed more than people, it killed an age of innocence. When the fighting began, singing mothers and wives who expected to see their men home by Christmas sent young men away with fanfare to the battlefields of the "war to end all wars." That Christmas did not come until four years later, and many of the men never returned. Armed primarily with a sense of national pride, the desire to serve God and country, and an archaic albeit glorious notion of war, the young soldiers were faced with a brutal reality. Modern war with its machine guns, chemicals, grenades, and mines ravaged the European countryside and the armies along with it. Not until Vietnam would the United States experience such trauma again.

In fact, the worst of the trauma was never revealed. This is the story Dalton Trumbo tells in his sole completed novel, *Johnny Got His Gun.* His compelling yet chilling account, though published in 1939, still wrenches the soul of the reader. Trumbo, best known for his screenplays and political activities, relates in his novel the story of Joe Bonham, a young veteran who was wounded during the war. Bonham was not simply wounded, however, he was marred beyond recognition as a human being. His face was completely disfigured and all four of his limbs were lost. He was, in essence, a stump. His mental functions, however, were completely intact—and trapped inside a body that allowed him no expression. The story is told completely from Bonham's perspective, thus the reader becomes engaged in the character's struggle to figure out what has happened to him, create order in a new universe of which he is the only inhabitant, and establish contact with the outside world.

Part of Trumbo's success with *Johnny Got His Gun* was his use of cinematic techniques to keep his audience involved. Most of the novel takes place in Joe Bonham's head, but Trumbo kept the reader engaged in the stream of consciousness flow through the extensive use of flashbacks and even, on one occasion, a montage. The sensual detail of Bonham's flashbacks is exquisite. Often the character remembers the sights, sounds, smells, and tastes of his childhood. Trumbo describes these memories with such clarity and finesse that the reader lives these scenes along with the character. Not only are these flashbacks individually well-crafted, each of them is essential to the progression of the plot. Each flashback reveals new bits of information about Joe's present condition and together, they provide fascinating suggestions about how the human mind uses memory.

Although the book is a cogent and passionate argument for pacificism, it retains a vital significance even in times of peace. Because of Bonham's severe injuries, one of the central issues with which he must grapple is what gives life meaning? What makes one human? Clearly, Bonham is still human and keeps the reader engaged as such. Yet he is one over whom debate would rage on the outside world. Is his life worth continuing? To what lengths should society go to sustain him?

Trumbo also invites an examination of society in this book. Interestingly, Bonham becomes more of a problem to society once he regains access to it. When he was non-responsive, the outside world could more or less ignore him. Once he could make his wishes known, however, they knew he still was an alert and aware human being. The thought of that—the obligations that implied—were beyond society's ability to handle. He held an unkind mirror to society. The people within the system wanted to appear magnanimous as is evidenced by their bestowing Bonham with medals and offering him such extensive care for the rest of his life. But once Bonham could make his desires known, the system was revealed to be cruel, callous, and self-serving.

Perhaps this reflective aspect of the book is its most significant contribution to young adults. The pacifist argument is certainly an important one—war is not a glorious undertaking and should not be portrayed as such. Yet war is not always at issue. The more constant issue within society is the meaning and value of life. Teaching young people to ponder these issues and form conscious convictions about them is, perhaps, the more urgent matter at hand. Trumbo provides a vehicle through which both sets of issues can be addressed.

—Linda Ross

——————

TUNIS, John R(oberts). American. Born in Boston, Massachusetts, 7 December 1889. Educated at Harvard University, Cambridge, Massachusetts, A.B. 1911; Boston University Law School, 1916. Served in the United States Army in France during World War I: Lieutenant. Married Lucy Rogers in 1918. Sportswriter, New York *Evening Post*, 1925-32, and Universal Service, New York, 1932-35; tennis commentator, NBC, New York, 1934-42. Regular contributor to *Harper's, Atlantic Monthly, Saturday Evening Post,* and other periodicals; sports columnist, the *New Yorker.* Recipient: Spring Book Festival award, *New York Herald Tribune,* 1938, for *The Iron Duke,* 1940, for *The Kid from Tomkinsville,* 1948, for *Highpockets,* and 1949, for *Son of the Valley;* Child Study Children's Book award, 1943, for *Keystone Kids;* Junior Book award, Boys' Clubs of America, 1949, for *Highpockets. Died 4 February 1975.*

PUBLICATIONS FOR YOUNG ADULTS

Fiction

Iron Duke, illustrated by Johan Bull. New York, Harcourt Brace, 1938.
The Duke Decides, illustrated by James MacDonald. New York, Harcourt Brace, 1939.
Champion's Choice, illustrated by Jay Hyde Barnum. New York, Harcourt Brace, 1940.
The Kid from Tomkinsville, illustrated by Jay Hyde Barnum. New York, Harcourt Brace, 1940.
World Series, illustrated by Jay Hyde Barnum. New York, Harcourt Brace, 1941.
All-American, illustrated by Hans Walleen. New York, Harcourt Brace, 1942.
Keystone Kids. New York, Harcourt Brace, 1943.
Rookie of the Year. New York, Harcourt Brace, 1944.
Yea! Wildcats! New York, Harcourt Brace, 1944.
A City for Lincoln. New York, Harcourt Brace, 1945.
The Kid Comes Back. New York, Morrow, 1946.
Highpockets. New York, Morrow, 1948.
Son of the Valley. New York, Morrow, 1949.
Young Razzle. New York, Morrow, 1949.
The Other Side of the Fence. New York, Morrow, 1953.
Go, Team, Go! New York, Morrow, 1954.
Buddy and the Old Pro, illustrated by Jay Hyde Barnum. New York, Morrow, 1955.
Schoolboy Johnson. New York, Morrow, 1958.
Silence over Dunkerque. New York, Morrow, 1962.
His Enemy, His Friend. New York, Morrow, 1967.
Grand National. New York, Morrow, 1973.

Other

$port$, Heroics, and Hysterics. New York, Day, 1928.
Was College Worth While? New York, Harcourt Brace, 1936.
Choosing a College. New York, Harcourt Brace, 1940.
Sport for the Fun of It. New York, A.S. Barnes, 1940; revised edition, 1950.
Democracy and Sport. New York, A.S. Barnes, 1941.
This Writing Game: Selections from Twenty Years of Free-Lancing. New York, A.S. Barnes, 1941.
Million-Miler: The Story of an Air Pilot. New York, Messner, 1942.
Lawn Games. New York, A.S. Barnes, 1943.
The American Way of Sport. New York, Duell, 1958.

PUBLICATIONS FOR ADULTS

Novel

American Girl. New York, Brewer and Warren, 1930.

Other

A Measure of Independence (autobiography). New York, Atheneum, 1964.

*

Media Adaptations: *American Girl* (as film called *Hard, Fast and Beautiful*), RKO.

Manuscript Collection: Mugar Memorial Library, Boston University.

* * *

John R. Tunis was from early youth fascinated with sports. He competed in high school; at Harvard he was active in tennis and long-distance track. Following service in France during World War I, he wrote sports articles for the New York *Evening Post* and at the same time announced major sporting events. He wrote literally thousands of articles on sports and education, about which he felt keenly.

Most of his books for children are about college athletics or professional sports. He covers equally well baseball, basketball, football, and tennis. *All-American* was deemed by the New York *Herald Tribune* as the best story offered to boys in 1942. *Keystone Kids* was chosen by the Child Study Association as the most challenging book of 1943 for young people. Tunis's plots are fast moving, as are professional games; his dialogue is clipped and colorful, as are radio and TV sportscasts. The drama of challenge and skill set against competition and effort is the basis of the books. In addition the books promulgate the ideal American sports values of fair play and of consideration for individuals and for teams. Tunis's concern with sportsmanship as well as sports is evident in his focus on respect for others. Long before it was well understood, Tunis discussed racial and religious discrimination in sports. *All-American* focuses on a well-to-do boy who comes to an economically mixed high school and makes the football team. How this boy learns to admire his fellow players and how he is able to help with the special problems of one black player are realistically and forcefully presented. Also clearly shown are the difficulties of teamwork, of caring and looking out for one's fellow player. Among Tunis's other first-rate sports stories are: *Champion's Choice, The Kid from Tomkinsville, World Series, Rookie of the Year, Young Razzle*, and *Go, Team, Go!*

In addition to his stories of American sports, Tunis also wrote stories of politics—of American democracy (*A City for Lincoln*) and of world war (*Silence over Dunkerque* and *His Enemy, His Friend*). These works are more didactic, less exciting, and less suspenseful than the sports stories. They express, though, Tunis's deep concern for human beings and their interrelatedness.

—Mary Lystad

———

TWAIN, Mark. Pseudonym for Samuel Langhorne Clemens. American. Born in Florida, Missouri, 30 November 1835; moved to Hannibal, Missouri, 1839. Married Olivia Langdon in 1870 (died 1904); one son and three daughters. Printer's apprentice and typesetter for Hannibal newspapers, 1847-50; helped brother with Hannibal *Journal*, 1850-52; typesetter and printer in St. Louis, New York, Philadelphia, for Keokuk *Saturday Post*, Iowa, 1853-56,

and in Cincinnati, 1857; apprentice river pilot, on the Mississippi, 1857-58; licensed as pilot, 1859-60; went to Nevada as secretary to his brother, then on the staff of the Governor, and also worked as goldminer, 1861; staff member, Virginia City *Territorial Enterprise,* Nevada, 1862-64 (first used pseudonym Mark Twain, 1863); reporter, San Francisco *Morning Call,* 1864; correspondent, Sacramento *Union,* 1866, and San Francisco *Alta California,* 1866-69: visited Sandwich (i.e., Hawaiian) Islands, 1866, and France, Italy, and Palestine, 1867; lecturer from 1867; editor, *Express,* Buffalo, New York, 1869-71; moved to Hartford, Connecticut and became associated with Charles L. Webster Publishing Company, 1884; invested in unsuccessful Paige typesetter and went bankrupt, 1894 (last debts paid, 1898); lived mainly in Europe, 1896-1900, New York, 1900-07, and Redding, Connecticut, 1907-10. M.A.: Yale University, New Haven, Connecticut, 1888; Litt.D.: Yale University, 1901; Oxford University, 1907; LL.D.: University of Missouri, Columbia, 1902. Member, American Academy, 1904. *Died 21 April 1910.*

PUBLICATIONS

Novels

The Gilded Age: A Tale of Today, with Charles Dudley Warner, illustrated by Augustus Hoppin and others. Hartford, Connecticut, American Publishing, 1873; London, Routledge, 1874; Twain's portion published separately as *The Adventures of Colonel Sellers,* edited by Charles Nelder, New York, Doubleday, 1965.

The Adventures of Tom Sawyer, illustrated by True Williams. Hartford, Connecticut, American Publishing, and London, Chatto & Windus, 1876.

The Prince and the Pauper. London, Chatto & Windus, 1881; Boston, Osgood, 1882.

The Adventures of Huckleberry Finn, Tom Sawyer's Comrade, illustrated by Edward Windsor Kemble. London, Chatto & Windus, 1884; New York, Webster, 1885.

A Connecticut Yankee in King Arthur's Court, illustrated by Dan Beard. New York, Webster, 1889; as *A Yankee at the Court of King Arthur,* London, Chatto & Windus, 1889.

The American Claimant, adapted from the play by Twain and William Dean Howells. New York, Webster, and London, Chatto & Windus, 1892.

Tom Sawyer Abroad, by Huck Finn, illustrated by Dan Beard. New York, Webster, and London, Chatto & Windus, 1894.

Pudd'nhead Wilson: A Tale. London, Chatto & Windus, 1894; expanded as *The Tragedy of Pudd'nhead Wilson, and the Comedy of Those Extraordinary Twins,* Hartford, Connecticut, American Publishing, 1894.

Personal Recollections of Joan of Arc (under pseudonym Sieur Louis de Conte), illustrated by E. V. Du Mond, New York, Harper, and London, Chatto & Windus, 1896.

Extract from Captain Stormfield's Visit to Heaven. New York and London, Harper, 1909.

The Mysterious Stranger: A Romance, illustrated by N. C. Wyeth, edited by Albert Bigelow Paine and Frederick A. Duneka. New York and London, Harper, 1916; expanded as *The Mysterious Stranger and Other Stories,* New York and London, Harper, 1922.

Simon Wheeler: Detective (unfinished novel), edited by Franklin R. Rogers. New York, New York Public Library, 1963.

Short Stories

The Celebrated Jumping Frog of Calaveras County, and Other Sketches, edited by John Paul. New York, Webb, and London, Routledge, 1867.
Screamers: A Gathering of Scraps of Humour, Delicious Bits, and Short Stories. London, Hotten, 1871.
Eye Openers: Good Things, Immensely Funny Sayings, and Stories. London, Hotten, c. 1871.
A Curious Dream, and Other Sketches. London, Routledge, 1872.
Mark Twain's Sketches, illustrated by R. T. Sperry. New York, American News, 1874.
Mark Twain's Sketches: New and Old. Hartford, Connecticut, American Publishing, 1876.
Merry Tales. New York, Webster, 1892.
The 1,000,000 Pound Bank-Note, and Other New Stories. New York, Webster, 1893.
Tom Sawyer, Detective, as Told by Huck Finn, and Other Stories. London, Chatto & Windus, 1896.
The Man that Corrupted Hadleyburg, and Other Stories and Essays. New York and London, Harper, 1900; revised edition, London, Chatto & Windus, 1900.
A Double Barrelled Detective Story, illustrated by Lucius Hitchcock. New York and London, Harper, 1902.
A Dog's Tale, illustrated by W. T. Smedley. New York, Harper, 1904.
Extracts from Adam's Diary illustrated by F. Strothmann. New York and London, Harper, 1904.
Eve's Diary Translated from the Original Ms, illustrated by Lester Ralph. New York and London, Harper, 1906.
The $30,000 Bequest, and Other Stories. New York and London, Harper, 1906.
A Horse's Tale, illustrated by Lucius Hitchcock. New York and London, Harper, 1907.
The Curious Republic of Gondour, and Other Whimsical Sketches. New York, Boni & Liveright, 1919.
Sketches of the Sixties, with Bret Harte. San Francisco, Howell, 1926.
Short Stories of Mark Twain. New York, Funk & Wagnall, 1967.
Early Tales and Sketches, Volume 1: *1851-1864,* edited by Edgar M. Branch and Robert H. Hirst. Berkeley, University of California Press, 1979.

Plays

Colonel Sellers (five-act, produced New York, 1874).
Ah Sin, with Bret Harte (produced Washington, DC, 1877).

Travel Books

The Innocents Abroad; or, The New Pilgrims' Progress, illustrated by True Williams. Hartford, Connecticut, American Publishing, 1869; as Volume 1: *Innocents Abroad,* London, Hotten, 1870, Volume 2: *The New Pilgrims' Progress,* London, Hotten, 1870.
The Innocents at Home. London, Routledge, 1872.
Roughing It. London, Routledge, 1872; revised edition (includes *The Innocents at Home*), Hartford, Connecticut, American Publishing, 1872.
An Idle Excursion. Toronto, Rose-Belford, 1878; revised as *Punch, Brothers, Punch!, and Other Sketches,* New York, Slote, Woodman, 1878.

A Tramp Abroad, illustrated by Twain and others. Hartford, Connecticut, American Publishing, 1880.
Following the Equator: A Journey around the World. Hartford, Connecticut, American Publishing, 1897; as *More Tramps Abroad,* London, Chatto & Windus, 1897.
Europe and Elsewhere, edited by Albert Bigelow Paine. New York, Harper, 1923.
Traveling with the Innocents Abroad: Mark Twain's Original Reports from Europe and the Holy Land, edited by Daniel Morley McKelthan. Norman, University of Oklahoma Press, 1958.

Essays

How to Tell a Story, and Other Essays. New York, Harper, 1897.
English as She Is Taught. Mutual Book Co., 1900.
King Leopold's Soliloquy: A Defense of His Congo Rule. P. R. Warren, 1905.
Editorial Wild Oats. New York, Harper, 1905.
My Debut as a Literary Person, with Other Essays and Stories. Hartford, Connecticut, American Publishing, 1906.
What Is Man? (originally published anonymously). New York, De Vinne Press, 1906; revised as *What Is Man?, and Other Essays,* New York and London, Harper, 1917.
Christian Science, with Notes Containing Corrections to Date. New York and London, Harper, 1907.
Is Shakespeare Dead? New York and London, Harper, 1909.
In Defense of Harriet Shelley, and Other Essays. New York, Harper, 1918.
Concerning the Jews. New York, Harper, 1934.

Autobiographical Works

Old Times on the Mississippi. Toronto, Belford, 1876; reprinted as *The Mississippi Pilot,* London, Ward, Lock & Tyler, 1877; revised as *Life on the Mississippi,* Boston, Osgood, and London, Chatto and Windus, 1883.
Mark Twain's Autobiography (two volumes), edited by Albert Bigelow Paine. New York and London, Harper, 1924; edited as one volume by Charles Neider, New York, Harper, 1959.

Collected Journalism

Letters from the Sandwich Islands Written for the Sacramento Union, edited by G. Ezra Dane. San Francisco, Grabhorn, 1937.
The Washoe Giant in San Francisco, edited by Franklin Walker. San Francisco, Fields, 1938.
Mark Twain's Letters in the Muscatine Journal, edited by Edgar M. Branch. Mark Twain Association of America, 1942.
Mark Twain of the Enterprise: Newspaper Articles and Other Documents, 1862-1864, edited by Henry Nash Smith. Berkeley, University of California Press, 1957.
Contributions to the Galaxy, 1868-1871, edited by Bruce R. McElderry. Jr. Scholars' Facsimiles and Reprints, 1961.
Mark Twain's San Francisco, edited by Bernard Taper. New York, McGraw, 1963.
Clemens of the "Call": Mark Twain in San Francisco, edited by Edgar M. Branch. Berkeley, University of California Press, 1969.

Other

Mark Twain's (Burlesque) Autobiography and First Romance. New York, Sheldon, and London, Hotten, 1871.

Practical Jokes with Artemus Ward, with others. London, Hotten, 1872.

A True Story [and] *The Recent Carnival of Crime.* Boston, Osgood, 1877.

"1601"; or, Conversation as It Was by the Social Fireside in the Time of the Tudors. Published in Cleveland, 1880.

The Stolen White Elephant, Etc. Boston, Osgood, 1882; as *The Stolen White Elephant,* London, Chatto & Windus, 1882.

Editor, with William Dean Howells and others, *Mark Twain's Library of Humor,* illustrated by E.W. Kemble. New York, Webster, 1888.

Mark Twain's Speeches, edited by F.A. Nast. New York and London, Harper, 1910.

Mark Twain's Speeches (two volumes), edited by Albert Bigelow Paine. New York and London, Harper, 1924.

The Adventures of Thomas Jefferson Snodgrass (under pseudonym Thomas Jefferson Snodgrass), edited by Charles Honce. Chicago, Pascal Covici, 1928.

Mark Twain's Notebook, edited by Albert Bigelow Paine. New York and London, Harper, 1935.

Mark Twain's Travels with Mr. Brown, edited by Franklin Walker and G. Ezra Dane. New York, Knopf, 1940.

Mark Twain's First Story. Prairie Press, 1952.

Life as I Find It, edited by Charles Nelder. Hanover House, 1961.

Mark Twain's "Mysterious Stranger" Manuscripts, edited by William G. Gibson. Berkeley, University of California Press, 1969.

Mark Twain's Notebooks and Journals. Berkeley, University of California Press, Volume 1: *1855-1873,* edited by Frederick Anderson, Michael B. Frank, and Kenneth M. Sanderson, 1975, Volume 2: *1877-1883,* edited by Anderson, Lin Salamo, and Bernard L. Stein, Volume 3: *1883-1891,* edited by Robert Pack Browning, Frank, and Salamo, 1979.

*

Media Adaptations: *The Adventures of Huckleberry Finn* was adapted as a motion picture titled *Huckleberry Finn,* in 1931 by Paramount, in 1939 by Metro-Goldwyn-Mayer (MGM), and in 1974 by United Artists, and as a motion picture of the same title in 1960 by MGM; *The Adventures of Tom Sawyer* was adapted as *Tom Sawyer* in 1930 by Paramount, and as a motion picture of the same title in 1938 by Selznick International and in 1973 by United Artists; *The Adventures of Tom Sawyer* was adapted as the film *Tom Sawyer, Detective,* Paramount, 1939; *A Connecticut Yankee in King Arthur's Court* was adapted as the film *A Connecticut Yankee* in 1931 by Twentieth Century-Fox, and as *A Connecticut Yankee in King Arthur's Court* in 1949 by Paramount; *The Prince and the Pauper* was adapted as motion pictures of the same title in 1937 by Warner Brothers, and in 1969 by Childhood Productions; *The Prince and the Pauper* was adapted as a film titled *Crossed Swords* in 1978 by Warner Brothers; *A Double Barrelled Detective Story* was adapted as a film of the same title in 1965 by Saloon Productions; *The Celebrated Jumping Frog of Calaveras County, and Other Sketches* was adapted as a film titled *Best Man Wins* in 1948 by Columbia. Among the many stagings of Twain's works are *Tom Sawyer* and *Huckleberry Finn;* some of Twain's writings have also been adapted as radio plays; *Huckleberry Finn* has also been staged as a musical. Twain's own life inspired *The Adventures of Mark Twain,* filmed by Warner Brothers in 1944, and such stage productions as *Mark Twain Tonight!*

Biography: *Mark Twain: A Biography; the Personal and Literary Life of Samuel Langhorne Clemens* (four volumes) by Albert Bigelow Paine, Harper, 1912; *A Lifetime with Mark Twain* by Mary Lawton, Harcourt, 1925, reprinted, Haskell House, 1972; *Mark Twain: A Portrait* by Edgar Lee Masters, Scribner's, 1938; *Sam Clemens of Hannibal* by Dixon Wecter, Houghton, 1952; *Mark Twain Himself* by Milton Meltzer, Crowell, 1960; *Mr. Clemens and Mr. Twain* by Justin Kaplan, Simon & Schuster, 1966; *Mark Twain* by Charles Neider, Horizon, 1967; entries in *Dictionary of Literary Biography,* Gale, Volume 11: *American Humorists, 1800-1950,* 1982, pp. 526-55, Volume 12: *American Realists and Naturalists,* 1982, pp. 71-94, Volume 23: *American Newspaper Journalists, 1873-1900,* 1983, pp. 31-46, Volume 64: *American Literary Critics and Scholars, 1850-1880,* 1988, pp. 34-47, Volume 74: *American Short-Story Writers before 1880,* 1988, pp. 54-83.

Critical Study: *The Innocent Eye: Childhood in Mark Twain's Fiction* by Albert E. Stone, Yale University Press, 1961; *Mark Twain: A Collection of Critical Essays* edited by Henry Nash Smith, Prentice-Hall, 1963; *Plots and Characters in the Works of Mark Twain* (two volumes) by Robert L. Gale, Shoe String, 1973; *The Art of Mark Twain* by William H. Gibson, Oxford University Press, 1976; entries in *Twentieth-Century Literary Criticism,* Gale, Volume 6, 1982; Volume 12, 1984; *Mark Twain* by Robert Keith Miller, Ungar, 1983; essay by Michael Patrick Hearn in *Writers for Children,* edited by Jane Bingham, Scribner's, 1988.

*   *   *

Ernest Hemingway wrote, in *Green Hills of Africa,* "All modern American literature comes from one book by Mark Twain called *Huckleberry Finn*...it's the best book we've had. All American writing comes from that. There was nothing before. There has been nothing as good since."

As criticism, Hemingway's statement is admittedly overstated. Samuel Clemens, or Mark Twain, has always been an enigma for critics, many of whom have had great difficulty in analyzing his works, and others in psychoanalyzing him. Hemingway, however, was not speaking as a critic, but rather as a reader, as a devotee, as a writer who recognized his debt to one who came before him. In that role he is an apt and accurate spokesman for all of us who rejoice in listening to the voice of Mark Twain. Just as Lincoln remains the folk symbol of the American spirit, for many Twain remains the folk symbol of the American writer.

It is significant that Hemingway specifically referred to *The Adventures of Huckleberry Finn,* for it is in that work, along with *The Adventures of Tom Sawyer* and *Life on the Mississippi,* that Twain's narrative genius is self-evident. Today *Tom Sawyer* is usually categorized as a book for children, while *Huck Finn* is considered adult fiction. Nevertheless, in any discussion of Twain's influence on American authors of books for young people, both must be considered.

Oddly enough, when Twain wrote *Tom Sawyer* he did not have a young audience in mind. It wasn't until his friend William Dean Howells suggested that it was a story most appropriate for children that Twain "cleaned up" the manuscript and added a preface in which he said: "Although my book is intended mainly for the entertainment of boys and girls, I hope it will not be shunned by men and women on that account, for part of my plan has been to try to pleasantly remind adults of what they once were themselves, and of how they felt and thought and talked, and what queer enterprises they sometimes engaged in." That he did not consciously write it for children is perhaps the book's strongest attribute, though occasionally Twain as narrator speaks directly to the adult readers he originally had in mind. This is overwhelmingly outweighed by the absence of any condescension or moralizing. In fact at the time of its publication (1876) it came under attack as a children's book. The *New York Times* book review concluded: "In the books to be placed into children's hands for purposes of recreation, we have a preference for those of a milder type than *Tom Sawyer*."

Tom Sawyer is much more than a grown man's reminiscences about the idyllic joys and pains of childhood. Twain stands high on the list of eminent writers like Stevenson, Dickens, and Saroyan who successfully depicted how young people "felt and thought and talked." Though they did not write specifically for children, they demonstrated for those who would how necessary it is to retain the heart of a child if your work is to have the ring of truth. Twain above all else sets out to entertain. One should not overlook the word "Adventures" in the titles of his "boy" books. He takes the blood and thunder stuff of the old-fashioned dime novels and the serial boy romances and makes it literature.

In *Huck Finn,* intended as a sequel to *Tom Sawyer,* Twain gets into the skin of Huck and tells the story through him, and by so doing he happens upon the narrative mode that is explicitly suited for his special talents. Huck, who could not possibly *write* a story, *tells* us the story. And that is how Twain himself would have it; as he says in his *Autobiography:* "With the pen in one's hand, narrative is a difficult art; narrative should flow as flows the brook down through the hills and leafy woodlands." This also was one of the reasons for Hemingway's acclaim, for he too, like many storytellers, was at heart a raconteur and a minstrel rather than a scribbler.

But there was even a more important reason. Hemingway recognized the straightforward honesty in *Huck Finn.* Twain possessed, as H.L. Mencken put it, "a truly amazing instinct for the truth." Today many writers of books for children and young adults have turned to first-person narrative, with only a meager few of them handling it successfully. They would do well to look closely at *Huckleberry Finn,* for there they will find Mark Twain's greatest legacy to them—his integrity. He doesn't use the first-person point of view as a literary device for simulating a peer relationship with young readers; but rather he turns over the complete narrative to Huck, allowing him to tell the story as only he can do it. Huck's understated and innocent "telling" is the primary reason that this story of a boy's adventure is, at the same time, a devastating denunciation of the society in which the tale takes place.

A final word of caution. Too often *Huck Finn* appears on children's reading book lists as a companion piece to *Tom Sawyer,* when in fact it is a work best suited for a more mature audience. Indeed, anyone who recommends *The Adventures of Huckleberry Finn* to a young reader must first consider whether that reader is capable or not of handling the intricacies of its ironic thrust.

—James E. Higgins

TYLER, Anne. American. Born in Minneapolis, Minnesota, 25 October 1941. Educated at Duke University, Durham, North Carolina, 1958-61, B.A. 1961; Columbia University, New York, 1961-62. Married Taghi Modarressi in 1963; two daughters. Writer. Rus-

sian bibliographer, Duke University Library, 1962-63; assistant to the librarian, McGill University Law Library, Montreal, 1964-65. Recipient: *Mademoiselle* award for writing, 1966; award for Literature, American Academy and Institute of Arts and Letters, 1977; National Book Critics Circle fiction award nomination, 1980, Janet Heidinger Kafka prize, 1981, and American Book award nomination in paperback fiction, 1982, all for *Morgan's Passing;* National Book Critics Circle fiction award nomination, 1982, and American Book award nomination in fiction, P.E.N./Faulkner award for fiction, and Pulitzer Prize nomination for fiction, all 1983, all for *Dinner at the Homesick Restaurant;* National Book Critics Circle fiction award and Pulitzer Prize nomination for fiction, both 1985, both for *The Accidental Tourist;* Pulitzer Prize, 1989, *Breathing Lessons.* Agent: Russell & Volkening, 50 West 29th St., New York, NY 10001. Address: 222 Tunbridge Rd., Baltimore, MD 21212, U.S.A.

PUBLICATIONS

Novels

If Morning Ever Comes. New York, Knopf, 1964; London, Chatto & Windus, 1965.
The Tin Can Tree. New York, Knopf, 1965; London, Macmillan, 1966.
A Slipping-Down Life. New York, Knopf, 1970; London, Severn House, 1983.
The Clock Winder. New York, Knopf, 1972; London, Chatto & Windus, 1973.
Celestial Navigation. New York, Knopf, 1974; London, Chatto & Windus, 1975.
Searching for Caleb. New York, Knopf, and London, Chatto & Windus, 1976.
Earthly Possessions. New York, Knopf, and London, Chatto & Windus, 1977.
Morgan's Passing. New York, Knopf, and London, Chatto & Windus, 1980.
Dinner at the Homesick Restaurant. New York, Knopf, and London, Chatto & Windus, 1982.
The Accidental Tourist. New York, Knopf, and London, Chatto & Windus, 1985.
Breathing Lessons. New York, Knopf, 1988; London, Chatto & Windus, 1989.
Saint Maybe. New York, Knopf, and London, Chatto & Windus, 1991.
Tumble Tower, pictures by Mitra Modarressi. New York, Orchard, 1993.

Other

Editor, with Shannon Ravenel, *The Best American Short Stories 1983.* Boston, Houghton, 1983; as *The Year's Best American Short Stories,* London, Severn House, 1984.
Anne Tyler: Three Complete Novels. New York, Wings Books, 1991.

*

Media Adaptation: *The Accidental Tourist* (film), Warner Brothers, 1988.

Biography: Entry in *Dictionary of Literary Biography,* Volume 6; *Dictionary of Literary Biography, Yearbook: 1982,* Detroit, Gale, 1983.

Critical Study: Entry in *Contemporary Literary Criticism,* Detroit, Gale, Volume 7, 1977, Volume 11, 1979, Volume 18, 1981, Volume 28, 1984, Volume 44, 1987; *Art and the Accidental in Anne Tyler* by Joseph C. Voelker, Jackson, University Press of Mississippi, 1989; *The Temporal Horizon: A Study of the Theme of Time in Anne Tyler's Major Novels* by Karin Linton, Uppsala, Sweden, Studia Anglistica, 1989; *The Fiction of Anne Tyler* edited by C. Ralph Stephens, Jackson, University Press of Mississippi, 1990; *Understanding Anne Tyler* by Alice Hall Petry, Columbia, University of South Carolina Press, 1990.

* * *

Perhaps more forcefully than any other writer of her generation, Anne Tyler portrays disintegration of the traditional family structure and the resulting effect on the individual.

In her first novel, *If Morning Ever Comes,* Tyler shows the emptiness behind the facade of a conventional family: for several years Ben Joe Hawkes has known that his father has lived alternately with wife and mistress, dying at the mistress' home because, ironically, on the night of his death he forgot which was his current residence. Ben Joe also learns that his grandmother, actually in love with another man, married his grandfather as a matter of expediency. As with many of Tyler's protagonists, Ben Joe is lost until jolted out of his routine by a more forceful individual who demands commitment. Ben Joe resists any definite commitment regarding his possessions, his place of residence, or his relationship with his girlfriend until his ex-girlfriend demonstrates her love by her willingness to abandon the man she is supposed to marry.

Births and deaths upset the balance in several Tyler families. The Bedloes, another quasi-traditional, middle-class family in *Saint Maybe,* reluctantly adjust when thirty-year-old Danny marries opportunistic Lucy, a divorcee with two children. The supposedly premature birth of their child begins a chain of events which culminates in the deaths, probable suicides, of both Danny and Lucy, and radically changes the life of Ian, Danny's seventeen-year-old brother. Ian cannot forgive himself for his role in their deaths until years later when he marries Rita, originally hired to reorganize the house after his mother's death, who not only changes his life but shows him that change is a vital part of life.

The senseless murder of their son highlights the differences between Sarah and Macon Leary and leads to their separation in *The Accidental Tourist.* Macon, who writes travel guides for people like himself whose business forces them to travel but who hate to leave familiar surroundings, is lost and helpless until Muriel Pritchett not only trains his dog but shows him that accepting the unfamiliar makes him feel more alive.

There are few genuinely happy families in Tyler's novels. Pamela Emerson in *The Clock Winder* says the neighbors thought her family

was happy, but she knew she had never really devoted her life to her seven children. Her husband dead and her children scattered, Pamela is alone until a new handyman appears and the family begins to draw together.

The most dysfunctional of Tyler's families is the Tulls in *Dinner at the Homesick Restaurant.* Having married to avoid the incompleteness of being alone, Pearl Cody Tull has three children when her husband leaves the family. Each child sees different facets of Pearl's personality: Cody remembers her as violently abusive, Ezra as nurturing, and Jenny as suspicious and accusative. Pearl's last request—that her entire family gather for dinner after her funeral—brings her husband and their children together at the Homesick Restaurant. Unlike previous attempts, this family meal concludes with everyone still together, suggesting that family bonds not only are inescapable but also can be healing.

Tyler vividly draws her characters, both major and minor. Morgan Gower, her most bizarre character, collects identities in the same way he collects hats and changes both with the same ease, posing as a glassblower, a tugboat captain, a lobster fisherman, a politician, a Mohawk Indian high-rise worker, and the only undefeated jockey in the history of Pimlico. Answering the appeal for a doctor to deliver the Meredith's baby, he becomes so involved with Emily and Leon that he assumes Leon's identity and eventually even his name. Other eccentrics include Morgan's sister Brindle, who marries her "one true love" only to feel the marriage threatened by her own high school photograph; Serena in *Breathing Lessons,* who attempts to reenact her wedding at her husband's funeral; and the Peck family in *Searching for Caleb,* especially the "genius," Duncan, who makes his own fertilizer by processing the household's organic garbage in a blender.

Most of Tyler's elderly characters possess a dignity which makes their memory lapses and erratic behavior seem endearing. *Breathing Lessons'* Daniel Otis is a stubborn and exasperating old man, but he manipulates the reader just as he manipulates his nephew and the Morans. Tyler also treats with sympathetic humor her emotionally disturbed characters, such as Dorrie Moran, who carries a department store suitbox filled with marshmallows wherever she goes, and Junie Moran, who can leave home only when she is disguised as someone else.

While there is much unhappiness in Tyler's works, her tone is essentially optimistic. Many of her characters achieve almost Joycean epiphanies and, at the very least, a kind of peaceful acceptance. Young-adult readers struggling with family problems may be able to relate to these characters and find, as Maggie found in *Breathing Lessons,* that life, like her husband's perpetual game of solitaire, is a series of narrowing options which one can only play with as much skill and judgment as possible.

—Charmaine Allmon Mosby

U-V

URE, Jean. Also writes as Ann Colin; Jean Gregory; Sarah McCulloch. British. Born in Surrey, England, 1 January 1943. Educated at Croyden High School, Surrey, 1954-60; Webber-Douglas Academy of Dramatic Art, London, 1966-68. Married Leonard Gregory in 1967. Educated at Webber-Douglas Academy of Dramatic Art, 1965-67. Writer. Worked variously as a waitress, cook, washer-up, nursing assistant, newspaper seller, shop assistant, theatre usherette, temporary shorthand-typist, translator, secretary with NATO and UNESCO, and television production assistant. Since 1968, full-time writer. Recipient: American Library Association best book for young adult citation, 1983, for *See You Thursday*. Agent: Maggie Noach, 21 Redan St., London W14 0AB. Address: 88 Southbridge Rd., Croydon, Surrey CR0 1AF, England.

PUBLICATIONS FOR YOUNG ADULTS

Novels

See You Thursday. London, Kestrel, 1981; New York, Delacorte, 1983.
A Proper Little Nooryeff. London, Bodley Head, 1982; as *What If They Saw Me Now?*, New York, Delacorte, 1982.
If It Weren't for Sebastian. London, Bodley Head, 1982; New York, Delacorte, 1985.
You Win Some, You Lose Some. London, Bodley Head, and New York, Delacorte, 1984.
After Thursday. London, Kestrel, and New York, Delacorte, 1985.
The Other Side of the Fence. London, Bodley Head, 1986; New York, Delacorte, 1988.
Trouble with Vanessa. London, Corgi, 1988.
One Green Leaf. London, Bodley Head, 1987; New York, Delacorte, 1989.
There's Always Danny. London, Corgi, 1988.
Say Goodbye, London, Corgi, 1989.
Tomorrow Is Also a Day. London, Methuen, 1989.
Plague 99. London, Methuen, 1990; New York, Harcourt, 1991.
Play Nimrod for Him. London, Bodley Head, 1990.
Dreaming of Larry. New York, Doubleday, 1991.

PUBLICATIONS FOR CHILDREN

Fiction

Ballet Dance for Two. New York, Watts, 1960; as *Dance for Two*, illustrated by Richard Kennedy, London, Harrap, 1960.
Hi There, Supermouse!, illustrated by Martin White. London, Hutchinson, 1983; as *Supermouse*, illustrated by Ellen Eagle, New York, Morrow, 1984.
You Two, illustrated by Ellen Eagle. New York, Morrow, 1984; as *The You-Two*, illustrated by Martin White, London, Hutchinson, 1984.
Megastar. London, Blackie, 1985.
Nicola Mimosa, illustrated by Martin White. London, Hutchinson, 1985; as *The Most Important Thing*, illustrated by Ellen Eagle, New York, Morrow, 1986.

A Bottled Cherry Angel. London, Hutchinson, 1986.
Brenda the Bold, illustrated by Glenys Ambrus. London, Heinemann, 1986.
Swings and Roundabouts. London, Blackie, 1986.
The Fright, illustrated by Beverley Lees. London, Orchard, 1987.
Tea-Leaf on the Roof, illustrated by Val Sassoon. London, Blackie, 1987.
War with Old Mouldy!, illustrated by Alice Englander. London, Methuen, 1987.
Who's Talking?, illustrated by Beverley Lees. London, Orchard, 1987.
Frankie's Dad. London, Hutchinson, 1988.
Loud Mouth, illustrated by Lynne Willey. London, Orchard, 1988.
A Muddy Kind of Magic, illustrated by Michael Lewis. London, Blackie, 1988.
Soppy Birthday, illustrated by Michael Lewis. London, Orchard, 1988.
Two Men in a Boat, illustrated by Michael Lewis. London, Blackie, 1988.
King of Spuds. London, Orchard, 1989.
Who's for the Zoo? London, Orchard, 1989.
Cool Simon. London, Orchard, 1990.
Jo in the Middle. London, Hutchinson, 1990.
The Wizard in the Woods. New York, Walker, 1990.
Fat Lollipop. London, Hutchinson, 1991.
William in Love. London, Blackie, 1991.
Wizard in Wonderland. New York, Walker, 1991.

PUBLICATIONS FOR ADULTS

Novels

The Other Theatre. London, Corgi, 1966.
The Test of Love. London, Corgi, 1968.
Had We But World Enough and Time. London, Corgi, 1972.
If You Speak Love, London, Corgi, 1972.
The Farther off from England. London, Corgi, 1973.
Daybreak. London, Corgi, 1974.
All Thy Love. London, Corgi, 1975.
Marriage of True Minds. London, Corgi, 1975.
Hear No Evil. London, Corgi, 1976.
No Precious Time. London, Corgi, 1976.
All in a Summer Season. London, Corgi, 1977.
Dress Rehearsal. London, Corgi, 1977.
Early Stages. London, Corgi, 1977.
Bid Time Return, London, Corgi, 1978.
Curtain Fall, London, Corgi, 1978.
A Girl Like That, London, Corgi, 1979.
Masquerade, London, Corgi, 1979.
A Different Class of Doctor, as Ann Colin. London, Corgi, 1980.
Doctor Jamie, as Ann Colin. London, Corgi, 1980.
Love beyond Telling, as Jean Gregory. London, Corgi, 1986.

Novels as Sarah McCulloch

Not Quite a Lady. London, Corgi, 1980; New York, Fawcett, 1981.

A Lady for Ludovic. London, Corgi, 1981.
A Most Insistent Lady. London, Corgi, 1981.
Merely a Gentleman. London, Corgi, 1982.
A Perfect Gentleman. London, Corgi, 1982.

Other

Translator, *City of a Thousand Drums,* by Henri Vernes. London, Corgi, 1966.
Translator, *The Dinosaur Hunters,* by Henri Vernes. London, Corgi, 1966.
Translator, *The Yellow Shadow,* by Henri Vernes. London, Corgi, 1966.
Translator, *Cold Spell,* by Jean Bruce. London, Corgi, 1967.
Translator, *Top Secret,* by Jean Bruce. London, Corgi, 1967.
Translator, *Treasure of the Golcondas,* by Henri Vernes. London, Corgi, 1967.
Translator, *The White Gorilla,* by Henri Vernes. London, Corgi, 1967.
Translator, *Operation Parrot,* by Henri Vernes. London, Corgi, 1968.
Translator, *Strip Tease,* by Jean Bruce. London, Corgi, 1968.
Translator, *The Snare,* by Noel Calef. London, Souvenir Press, 1969.
Translator, *March Battalion,* by Sven Hassel. London, Corgi, 1970.
Translator, *Assignment Gestapo,* by Sven Hassel. London, Corgi, 1971.
Translator, *Hitler's Plot to Kill the Big Three,* by László Havas. London, Corgi, 1971.
Translator, *SS General,* by Sven Hassel. London, Corgi, 1972.
Translator, *Reign of Hell,* by Sven Hassel. London, Corgi, 1973.

*

Biography: Essay in *Something about the Author Autobiography Series,* Volume 14, Detroit, Gale, 1992.

*   *   *

Jean Ure is a prolific author with whom children can progress from first readers to challenging young adult novels.

Increasingly, her teenage books have tackled serious themes, but even the lightest novels have convincing backgrounds. Two books which bring together teenagers from differing social settings are *A Proper Little Nooryeff,* published in the United States as *What If They Saw Me Now?,* dealing with the embarrassment of a boy pushed into taking part in a ballet, and *The Other Side of the Fence,* in which Richard rows with his affluent parents and teams up with Bonny, a streetwise, amoral, and chronic liar; each gains strength from the unlikely pairing.

Another early novel, *See You Thursday,* followed by *After Thursday* and *Tomorrow Is Also a Day,* rises above the usual boy-meets-girl story because of its subtle delineation of character. Marianne, initially a self-doubting sixteen-year old, befriends blind musician Abe, eight years her senior. The relationship—deepening into love—falters when Abe's musical career prospers, Marianne matures, and each wonders whether the other is being stifled. The trilogy involves the reader completely with its likeable, realistically fallible main characters.

Animal rights have always featured in Ure's novels, even when not a central issue. The subject takes centre stage in a trilogy begin-

ning with *If It Weren't for Sebastian* and continuing eleven years later with *Always Sebastian* and *Seven for a Secret.* In the first novel, Maggie learns through Sebastian of the cruelties inflicted on animals in farms and laboratories. His disturbed, obsessive fear of violence has led to criticism of the novel for suggesting that only someone mentally unstable could be so sensitive; the possibility is left open, however, that Sebastian is perfectly sane, while the rest of the world is at fault.

In *Always Sebastian,* Ure moves on a generation, shifting the focus to Maggie's daughter, Martha, who hands out leaflets in the high street and argues with her science teacher about dissection. Sebastian, now Maggie's lover, is an animal rights activist; the dubious morality of using violence to make a point is questioned when a bomb is planted in a shopping centre. Unlike many current novels which have characters mouthing token protests about animal rights as if the issue is merely the trendiest bandwagon to be seen riding on, Ure treats the topic seriously, confronting her characters with realistic grey areas. Here, the younger daughter Sophie is a purist to the extent of being maddening to live with, and even tolerant Maggie experiences "compassion fatigue."

Career choices are often of crucial importance to Ure's characters, who frequently come to a decision after spurning the values of their parents, schools, peers, and the government. *A Place to Scream* shows a future Thatcher-like England sharply divided into haves and have-nots under a repressive, materialistic government with beggars on the streets and where old people are regarded as useless burdens. Gillian, sick of the undemanding job she is thought lucky to have, is tempted to escape abroad with Rick, an intelligent dropout who shares her humane values. The plan is abandoned when Gillian's ailing Grandfather needs her, and she finds fulfillment in nursing the elderly, even though it's a low-paid, squalid job. The serious theme is mediated by lightness of tone, although the warning note is unmistakable: Is this the sort of future we are heading for?

Plague 99 combines a survival story with a topical environmental theme. An accident with germ-warfare research releases a deadly plague virus; three teenagers, Fran, Harriet, and Shahid, join forces in an attempt to survive. The government and the passivity of citizens are blamed; Shahid comments: "We all thought it would be the Bomb or the ozone layer. We forgot all the nasty little bacterial messes they were cooking up behind their closed doors."

Although grim, *Plague 99* ends with a suggestion that Fran and Shahid will escape to Cornwall. The story is continued in *Come Lucky April.* Set a hundred years later, it brings together two societies with contradictory values. The main characters are descendants of those in *Plague 99;* April is living in Croydon in a society dominated by women, while Daniel comes from an isolated patriarchal community in Cornwall, and is shocked to discover that the Croydon group controls male aggression by castrating men. The balance between the need for harmony and communal safety on the one hand and individual freedom on the other is illustrated by April's choice: to go with Daniel to the male-dominated Cornwall society or stay with the eunuch, David, who has the courage to challenge the status quo.

Listing Ure's themes might suggest that her books are uniformly earnest, yet her lightness of touch makes this far from the case. *One Green Leaf,* about a teenager dying of cancer, could in other hands have been mawkish or morbid. Ure avoids this by giving the narrative to Robyn, whose friend Abbey is the victim's girlfriend. This enables Robyn to observe the effect of David's illness on both himself and Abbey, who has to put up with his frequent unkind-ness. Robyn's narrative gives humour to the story, and a skillfully-controlled ending shows the friends remembering David in a positive way after his death.

Some of Ure's strengths are also her weaknesses. Her crisp, easily-readable style lacks variety; conversations in a futuristic community of survivors are indistinguishable from exchanges in form room or ballet class. Ure admits that there is little sense of place in her writing, and certainly she does not achieve the easy, evocative scene-setting of, say, K. M. Peyton or Katherine Paterson. On the other hand, her novels are always expertly-paced, fast-moving without being rushed, and there is no doubt that she knows her readership. Ure has never produced the sort of book which librarians and award panels adore but which stay on the shelves unread. She writes that one of her aims is "to make people think: to make them examine their motives and question their assumptions," and she unfailingly goes for topical and relevant issues on which to challenge her readers. The successful blend of provocation and entertainment ensures her continuing popularity.

—Linda Newbery

VINGE, Joan (Carol) D(ennison). American. Educated at San Diego State University, California, B.A. in anthropology 1971. Married 1) Vernor Vinge, in 1972 (divorced 1979); 2) James R. Frenkel in 1980. Salvage archaeologist, San Diego County, 1971; writer since 1974. Recipient: Hugo award for best novelette from World Science Fiction Convention, 1978, for "Eyes of Amber," and for best science fiction novel, 1981, for *The Snow Queen; Locus* award, 1981; North Dakota Children's Choice (older) award, 1984, for *Return of the Jedi: The Storybook.* Agent: Merrilee Heifetz, Writers House Inc., 21 West 26th Street, New York, NY 10010, U.S.A.

PUBLICATIONS FOR ADULTS AND YOUNG ADULTS

Novels

The Outcasts of Heaven Belt. New York, New American Library, 1978; London, Futura, 1981.
The Snow Queen. New York, Dial Press, and London, Sidgwick & Jackson, 1980.
Psion. New York, Delacorte Press, 1982; London, Futura, 1983.
World's End. New York, Bluejay, 1984; London, Futura, 1985.
Ladyhawke (novelization of screenplay). New York, New American Library, 1985; London, Piccolo, 1985.
Mad Max: Beyond the Thunderdome. New York, Warner, and London, W.H. Allen, 1985.
Return to Oz. New York, Ballantine, and London, Purnell, 1985.
Santa Claus. New York, Berkley, and London, Sphere, 1985.
Catspaw. New York, Warner, 1988; as *Cat's Paw,* London, Gollancz, 1989.
Willow (novelization of screenplay). New York, Random House, 1988.
Heaven Chronicles (includes "Legacy" and *The Outcasts of Heaven Belt*). New York, Warner, 1991.
The Summer Queen. New York, Warner, 1991.
Refuge. New York, Warner, 1993.

Short Stories

Fireship. New York, Dell, 1978; as *Fireship, and Mother and Child,* London, Sidgwick & Jackson, 1981.
Eyes of Amber and Other Stories. New York, New American Library, 1979; London, Futura, 1981.
Phoenix in the Ashes. New York, Bluejay, 1985; London, Futura, 1986.

PUBLICATIONS FOR CHILDREN

Fiction

Return of the Jedi Storybook (novelization of screenplay). New York, Random House, and London, Futura, 1983.
Tarzan, King of Apes. New York, Random House, 1983.
The Dune Storybook (novelization of screenplay). New York, Putnam, 1984; London, Sphere, 1984.
The "Santa Claus—The Movie" Storybook. New York, Grosset & Dunlap, 1985.

*

Biography: Essay in *Speaking for Ourselves, Too* compiled and edited by Donald R. Gallo, National Council of Teachers of English, 1993.

Manuscript Collection: Elizabeth Charter Science Fiction Collection, San Diego University.

Critical Study: *Suzy Charnas, Joan Vinge, and Octavia Butler* by Richard Law, with others, San Bernardino, California, Borgo Press, 1986.

*   *   *

This quote from *The Snow Queen* is the essence of Joan D. Vinge's work: "There is more to me, more to the universe, than I suspected. Room for all the dreams I ever had, and all the nightmares...Anything becomes possible after you find the courage to admit that nothing is certain...Life used to look like cut crystal to me—sharp and clear and perfect. But now those clean hard edges break up the light into rainbows, and everything gets soft and hazy." There are no simple characters in her work, no simple truths, and no simple answers—the conflict is not between good and evil, but between different facets of human nature; winning is sometimes indistinguishable from losing, success can sometimes feel like failure, and one person's dream is often someone else's nightmare.

While the societies Vinge creates for her stories are richly textured, they are primarily a device for exploring human nature. By taking humanity out of our own cultural context, Vinge can focus more clearly on universal human interactions—power, greed, honor, duty, love, justice—and on the human nature that is a part of those interactions.

Vinge's works are not specifically targeted to young adults. However, the "Snow Queen" series and the "Psion" novels have young adult protagonists, and deal with issues of interest to young adult readers.

The Snow Queen is a story of power—the validity of gaining it, keeping it, using it—and a story of the permutations of right and wrong. Its setting is Tiamat, a world where power ritually changes hands every 150 years. Arienrhod, the Snow Queen, is at the end of her rule, and "the Change" requires her death. She has one last scheme to carry out—a plan to save her world, not her life. But she does despicable things in pursuit of this worthy goal—is she right or wrong? Moon, Arienrhod's unknowing young pawn, is honorable and innocent, but her actions cause pain and suffering—is she right or wrong? Vinge's answer is that they are both only human, with flaws and virtues which are ultimately the source of both their successes and their failures. All of the characters are quite sure they know what is right—and all of their certainties are turned upside down and inside out before the story ends.

World's End, the second book in the "Snow Queen" series, is only tangentially related to the events in *The Snow Queen;* it follows B.Z. Gundhalinu as he leaves Tiamat, and tries to fit his new worldview into the rigid structure of his old world. What he learns, however, plays a significant role in the final book of the series, the story of Moon's reign as Summer Queen.

In *The Summer Queen,* Vinge explores the interplay of the facets of human nature. All of her characters' flaws and virtues are heaped together like a precarious pile of pickup sticks, making unpredictable connections and supporting each other in unanticipated ways.

Psion focuses on the inner life of its protagonist, the half-human psion Cat, and his responses to the shifting circumstances of his life. Alone on the streets of Oldcity, Cat is a teenage pickpocket, prostitute, panhandler—whatever it takes to stay alive. His life disgusts him, and the price he must pay to keep it disgusts him. All of that changes when he's arrested, then released to participate in a psionic research project. For the first time in his memory, he's safe, well-fed, and cared about. But he soon learns that every kind of life has a price, and this life's price is to use the psionic ability he has suppressed to help the authorities he hates.

Catspaw takes the character Cat into the high-stakes world of the hereditary Combines—corporations so powerful that one member's flaws and virtues can affect the entire Interplanetary Human Federation. Cat is hired to use his psionic power to protect a woman of those Combines from enemies he doesn't know and whose power he can't even comprehend.

Vinge has also written a number of novellas and short stories published in magazines and anthologies. Some of these have been collected in *Phoenix in the Ashes, Fireship,* and the recently republished *Heaven Chronicles.* The brevity of the short story and novella formats require some simplification of detail, but her short-form work is no less thought-provoking than her novels are; the focus is still on the permutations of human nature within the society she creates.

To read Vinge is to have one's assumptions challenged; to see that faults can sometimes cause success, and virtues can sometimes cause failure; to understand that right and wrong do not exist in a vacuum. But life is not clear-cut, and blind assumptions should be challenged. Like B.Z. Gundhalinu, the young adult reader may discover through Vinge's works that, indeed, "There is more to me, more to the universe, than I suspected."

—Karen J. Gould

VINING, Elizabeth Gray. Also writes as Elizabeth Janet Gray. American. Born in Philadelphia, Pennsylvania, 6 October 1902. Educated at Bryn Mawr College, A.B. 1923; Drexel Institute School of Library Science (now Drexel University), B.S. 1926. Married Morgan Gray Vining in 1929 (died 1933). Tutor to Crown Prince Akihito of Japan, 1946-50; vice-president of board of trustees and vice-chairman of board of directors, Bryn Mawr College, 1952-71; American Friends Service Committee staff member. Writer. Recipient: American Women's Eminent Achievement Award; named Distinguished Daughter of Pennsylvania; Third Order of the Sacred Crown, Japan; Newbery Medal, 1943, for *Adam of the Road; Herald Tribune* Spring Festival Award, 1945, for *Sandy;* Constance Lindsay Skinner Award, Women's National Book Association, 1954; *Philadelphia Athenaeum* Literary Award, 1964, for *Take Heed of Loving Me,* and special award, 1980, for *Being Seventy.* Litt.D., Drexel Institute of Technology (now Drexel University), 1951, Tufts College (now Tufts University), 1952, Douglas College, 1953, Women's Medical College, 1953, Lafayette College, 1956, and University of North Carolina at Greensboro, 1968; L.H.D., Russell Sage College, 1952, Haverford College, 1958, Western College for Women (now Western College), 1959, Cedar Crest College, 1959, Moravian College, 1961, Wilmington College, 1962, and International Christian University, 1966; D.Ed., Rhode Island College of Education (now Rhode Island College), 1956.

PUBLICATIONS FOR YOUNG ADULTS AS ELIZABETH JANET GRAY

Fiction

Meredith's Ann, illustrated by G.B. Cutts. New York, Doubleday, 1927.

Tangle Garden, illustrated by G.B. Cutts. New York, Doubleday, 1928.

Tilly-Tod, illustrated by Mary Hamilton Frye. New York, Doubleday, 1929.

Meggy MacIntosh, illustrated by Marguerite de Angeli. New York, Doubleday, 1930.

Jane Hope. New York, Viking, 1933; London, Dickson, 1935.

Beppy Marlowe of Charles Town, illustrated by Loren Barton. New York, Viking, 1936.

The Fair Adventure, illustrated by Alice K. Reischer. New York, Viking, 1940.

Adam of the Road, illustrated by Robert Lawson. New York, Viking, 1942; London, A. and C. Black, 1943.

Sandy. New York, Viking, 1945.

The Cheerful Heart, illustrated by Kazue Mizumura. New York, Viking, 1959; London, Macmillan, 1961.

I Will Adventure, illustrated by Corydon Bell. New York, Viking, 1962.

The Taken Girl (as Elizabeth Gray Vining). New York, Viking, 1972.

Other

Young Walter Scott. Viking, 1935; London, Nelson, 1937.

Penn, illustrated by George Whitney. New York, Viking, 1938.

Mr. Whittier (as Elizabeth Gray Vining). New York, Viking, 1974.

PUBLICATIONS FOR ADULTS

Fiction

The Virginia Exiles. Philadelphia, Lippincott, 1955.
Take Heed of Loving Me. Philadelphia, Lippincott, 1963.
I, Roberta. Philadelphia, Lippincott, 1967.

Other

The Contributions of the Quakers (as Elizabeth Janet Gray). Philadelphia, F. A. Davis, 1939.
Windows for the Crown Prince (autobiography). Philadelphia, Lippincott, 1952.
The World in Tune. Wallingford, Pennsylvania, Pendle Hill, 1952.
Friend of Life: The Biography of Rufus M. Jones. Philadelphia, Lippincott, 1958.
Return to Japan. Philadelphia, Lippincott, 1960.
Flora: A Biography. Philadelphia, Lippincott, 1966; as *Flora MacDonald: Her Life in the Highlands and America,* London, Bles, 1967.
William Penn, Mystic. Wallingford, Pennsylvania, Pendle Hill, 1969.
Quiet Pilgrimage (autobiography). Philadelphia, Lippincott, 1970.
The May Massee Collection: Creative Publishing for Children, with Annis Duff. Emporia, Kansas, William Allen White Library, 1972.
Being Seventy: The Measure of a Year. New York, Viking, 1978.
John Woolman, Quaker Saint. Philadelphia, Wider Quaker Fellowship, 1981.
A Quest There Is. Wallingford, Pennsylvania, Pendle Hill, 1982.

Editor as Elizabeth Janet Gray

Anthology with Comments. Wallingford, Pennsylvania, Pendle Hill, 1942.

*

Biography: Entry in *The Junior Book of Authors,* New York, H.W. Wilson, 1951.

Manuscript Collection: Quaker Collection, Haverford College Library, Pennsylvania.

*   *   *

Elizabeth Gray Vining will well be remembered for her historical novels and biographies for young people as well as the autobiographical account of her four years in Japan as tutor to the crown prince. Her books reflect her talents as a storyteller and careful historian, but also her belief in the worth and dignity of the individual, real or fictional.

Vining's storytelling skill lies in her ability to recreate a period in history and give it life and color through imagery and carefully chosen details. Although her attention to authenticity in her historical portrayal is evident, it is subordinated to the story she is telling, and her research is painlessly assimilated into the story. Vining uses a variety of narrative techniques to move her story along, but it is through the eyes and ears of her invariably delightful characters that the reader sees and hears the story unfold. Even her minor characters are thoughtfully and humanly portrayed, and the reader can readily identify with them.

Vining's best-known work, *Adam of the Road,* winner of the 1943 John Newbery Award, is a vivid recreation of the people and places of thirteenth-century England as seen through the eyes of a young boy. Historically accurate, medieval England comes to life with a diverse assortment of characters and settings. A series of incidents with relatively mild conflicts and few surprises for the reader comprises the story, but the book is ultimately satisfying because of the reader's immersion in time and place. All five senses are evoked in Vining's vivid descriptions, but most memorably in the sounds of minstrel songs and stories that are interwoven throughout the novel. It is through Adam's consciousness that the reader views this era of English history with the freshness and excitement with which a young person views life.

I Will Adventure is similar in setting and plot. Andrew, on the way to London, meets a traveling company of players which includes William Shakespeare. The reader encounters the noisy richness of Elizabethan England with inside glimpses of the theater through Andrew's consciousness.

Meggy MacIntosh, a historical romance, is based on the true accounts of Flora MacDonald and the Scottish immigrants who settled in North Carolina before the revolution. Meggy is an unspoiled, lovable heroine, and the book paints a vivid picture of the settlers.

The Taken Girl, set in the period before the Civil War, presents a picture of Quaker abolitionists in Philadelphia. Vining once more reflects her depth of knowledge and her compassionate understanding for the period and is especially effective in her portrayal of the poet Whittier. The story is quietly told except for a dramatic climax in the burning of the abolitionist hall.

Written for adults but accessible to mature teens, *Take Heed of Loving Me,* is based on the life of the English poet John Donne. Vining has again carefully researched her historical background and atmosphere in this very human, warmly felt story, but presents a debatable interpretation of Donne's poetry.

Vining's biographies for young adults include *Young Walter Scott, Penn,* and *Mr. Whittier.* The first is written with grace and understanding but in too romantic a vein to be good history. *Penn,* on the other hand, is most readable and authentic. William Penn comes alive as brilliant statesman, resolute defender of religious liberty, and uncompromising member of the Society of Friends (Quakers). *Mr. Whittier* is a quiet account of the abolitionist Quaker poet focusing on his involvement in political issues and the social ills of the nineteenth century. Vining reveals her deep attachment to literature as well in this portrait of a shy, sensitive, but determined man.

Perhaps Vining's most famous work is the adult *Windows for the Crown Prince,* an account of her four years as a tutor for Prince Akihito in Japan following World War II. Her story is simply and directly told with color and feeling for the cultural beauty of Japan and accurately depicts a people recovering from the devastation of war.

Always readable, Vining is the consummate storyteller despite a lack of exciting climaxes. Indeed, her books are worth returning to for the beauty of her language, especially her use of imagery.

—Mattie J. Mosley

———

VOIGT, Cynthia. American. Born in Boston, Massachusetts, 25 February 1942. Educated at Smith College, Northampton, Massachusetts, B.A. 1963; graduate study at St. Michael's College (now College of Santa Fe), New Mexico. Married Walter Voigt in 1974 (second marriage); one daughter and one son. Secretary, J. Walter Thompson Advertising Agency, New York City, 1964; high school English teacher, Glen Burnie, Maryland, 1965-67; English teacher, 1968-69, department chair, 1971-79, and since 1981 part-time teacher and department chair, Key School, Annapolis, Maryland; author of books for young readers, since 1981. Recipient: Notable Children's Trade Book in the Field of Social Studies, National Council for Social Studies/Children's Book Council, *New York Times* Outstanding Books citation, and American Book award nomination, all 1981, all for *Homecoming;* American Library Association (ALA) Best Young Adult Books citation, 1982, for *Tell Me If the Lovers Are Losers,* and 1983, for *A Solitary Blue;* Newbery Medal, ALA, and *Boston Globe-Horn Book* Honor Book citation, both 1983, and ALA Notable Book citation, all for *Dicey's Song;* Parents' Choice award, 1983, Newbery Honor Book, and *Boston Globe-Horn Book* Honor Book citation, both 1984, all for *A Solitary Blue;* Edgar Allan Poe award for best juvenile mystery, Mystery Writers of America, 1984, for *The Callender Papers;* Child Study Association of America's Children's Books of the Year citation, 1987, for *Come a Stranger;* Silver Pencil award (Holland), 1988, and Deutscher Jugend Literatur Preis (Germany), 1989, both for *The Runner;* California Young Readers' Medal, 1990, for *Izzy, Willy-Nilly.* Address: c/o Atheneum, 866 Third Ave., New York, NY 10022, U.S.A.

PUBLICATIONS FOR YOUNG ADULTS

Fiction

Homecoming. New York, Atheneum, 1981; London, Collins, 1983.
Dicey's Song. New York, Atheneum, 1982; London, Collins, 1984.
Tell Me If the Lovers Are Losers. New York, Atheneum, 1982.
The Callender Papers. New York, Atheneum, 1983.
A Solitary Blue. New York, Atheneum, 1983; London, Collins, 1985.
Building Blocks. New York, Atheneum, 1984; London, Fontana, 1988.
Jackaroo. New York, Atheneum, 1985; London, Collins, 1988.
The Runner. New York, Atheneum, 1985; London, Collins, 1986.
Come a Stranger. New York, Atheneum, 1986; London, Collins, 1987.
Izzy, Willy-Nilly. New York, Atheneum, 1986; London, Collins, 1987.
Stories about Rosie, illustrated by Dennis Kendrick. New York, Atheneum, 1986.
Sons from Afar. New York, Atheneum, 1987; London, Collins, 1988.
Tree by Leaf. New York, Atheneum, 1988; London, Collins, 1989.
Seventeen against the Dealer. New York, Atheneum, 1989.
On Fortune's Wheel. New York, Atheneum, 1990.
Tillerman Saga. New York, Fawcett, 1990.
Glass Mountain (for adults). New York, Harcourt, 1991.
The Vandemark Mummy. New York, Atheneum, 1991.
David and Jonathan. New York, Scholastic, 1992.
Orfe. New York, Atheneum, 1992.

Other

Editor, with David Bergman, *Shore Writers' Sampler II.* Easton, Maryland, Friendly Harbor Press, 1988.

*

Media Adaptations: *Dicey's Song* (filmstrip-cassette set), Guidance Associates, 1986.

Biography: Essay in *Speaking for Ourselves: Autobiographical Sketches by Notable Authors of Books for Young Adults,* Volume 1, compiled and edited by Donald R. Gallo, National Council of Teachers of English, 1990.

Critical Studies: Entry in *Contemporary Literary Criticism,* Volume 30, Detroit, Gale, 1984; entry in *Children's Literature Review,* Volume 13, Detroit, Gale, 1987.

*   *   *

Cynthia Voigt depicts adolescents with dignity and compassion in her impressive novels; her characters generally possess a streak of independence or self-reliance enabling them to succeed in tangible endeavors and in creating bonds of friendship and family ties despite serious hardships, such as the loss of one or both parents. The tragedy of dysfunctional families is usually overturned and triumphantly replaced by loving relationships in the earlier novels, but less often in the later ones. Voigt's characters, frequently outsiders initially, are fleshed out until they seem to breathe and ultimately belong in their settings. As a result, Voigt has won several literary prizes—a Newbery Medal for *Dicey's Song,* a Newbery Honor Award for *A Solitary Blue,* an Edgar Award for *The Callender Papers,* and the 1989 ALAN Award for her outstanding contribution to the young adult field.

Except for *Stories about Rosie,* an illustrated book for younger readers about a pet dog, and *Glass Mountain,* an adult novel, Voigt writes for young adults in genres that vary from fantasy (*Building Blocks*), to mystery (*The Callender Papers* and *The Vandemark Mummy*), to realism set in the past (*Jackaroo, On Fortune's Wheel,* and *Tree by Leaf*), to Voigt's forte, realistic contemporary (*Tell Me If the Lovers Are Losers, Izzy, Willy-Nilly, Orfe, David and Jonathan,* and the seven novels comprising the Tillerman family "saga"). The four Tillerman children of the second generation—Dicey, James, Maybeth, and Sammy—travel to Maryland from Connecticut in *Homecoming* and are adopted by their grandmother in *Dicey's Song.* James and Sammy search for their father in *Sons from Afar;* the children's uncle "Bullet" stars in *The Runner;* and friends of Dicey, Jeff Greene, and Mina Smiths become protagonists in *A Solitary Blue* and *Come a Stranger,* respectively. The final book of the saga, *Seventeen against the Dealer,* depicts the children as older teens and focuses on Dicey who attempts to realize her lifelong dream of becoming a boat builder.

Heroes and heroines, about equal in number, vary in age from six-year-old Sammy Tillerman to the college-age young women of *Tell Me If the Lovers Are Losers.* Voigt adeptly depicts blacks as well as whites; in *The Runner* she addresses the situation of the racially troubled 1960s without mincing words, focusing in part on the prejudicial attitude of a white boy against a black teammate. Advancing a step further in *Come a Stranger* with protagonist Mina Smiths, a black girl rejected from a dance camp by an all-white group whom she has tried to emulate and from whom she expected friendship, Voigt deftly and sensitively depicts Mina's awakening to the reality of racial prejudice.

When Voigt plots her novels around other contemporary dilemmas, usually familial ones, she evokes sympathy for the characters who may have lost parents or who may feel forced to separate from their families because of intolerable home situations. The younger

Tillermans, for example, when deserted by their mother in a parking lot, initiate an odyssey that leads them to their "crazy" grandmother, Gram. That the group becomes a warm, loving family who grow individually by reaching out or communicating with others, even with those who do not reciprocate, is a measure of the journey's success in spite of its inauspicious origin.

The characters, although distinct individuals, possess many similar traits. Those who suffer from separation anxiety created by a missing or too reticent parent such as Professor Greene (*A Solitary Blue*), Mr. Thiel (*The Callender Papers*), or Mrs. Hall (*The Vandemark Mummy*), rely upon a surrogate. Dicey and then Gram provide for the younger Tillerman children; Patrice offers Bullet Tillerman work, food, and advice in *The Runner;* Brother Thomas, a close family friend, on occasion provides the affection that Jeff Greene lacks in *A Solitary Blue;* Aunt Constance cares for the "orphaned" Jean Wainwright in *The Callender Papers;* and news journalist O'Meara substitutes for Phineas Hall's absent mother in *The Vandemark Mummy.*

Voigt oversees the maturation of her youthful characters as they accept responsibility and plan future goals in the face of unsettling, often severe, obstacles, partially through her belief in the work ethic. Most learn self-reliance by assisting with family chores and by holding part-time jobs, such as working in a grocery, delivering papers, selling crabs, and baby-sitting. The children capitalize upon their own unique abilities whether they are a gift for music, a talent for academics or for organization, a deep spirituality, or an ability at sports. Maybeth Tillerman, though "slow" in school, excels in music. James, her brother, is the family's academic achiever. Jean Wainwright, although only twelve years old, sorts, organizes, and classifies the documents of the Callender family. Clothilde in *Tree by Leaf* relies on her strong religious faith; she believes that the voice she hears is God's, and she makes four requests of him. Although three are granted, they are not as she had imagined they would be. Other characters excel at sports, such as Bullet Tillerman at running or Hildegarde Koenig in *Tell Me If the Lovers Are Losers,* who so capably organizes and teaches a college freshman volleyball team about unity that they beat every opponent, even the seniors. The characters' participation in a variety of jobs and sports suggests that every child can find one he or she will enjoy and in pursuing it will become more well-rounded, less an outsider.

Voigt sets many novels in Crisfield, Maryland, just inland from Chesapeake Bay, where boating and crabbing provide sport, food, entertainment, and occasionally employment. Later novels, such as *The Vandemark Mummy* and *Tree by Leaf,* are set in Maine; the principal setting of *David and Jonathan* is Cape Cod. In all three settings a love of nature and the seashore appears side by side with a concern for protecting the environment. Even in a fantasy like *Building Blocks,* set primarily in Pennsylvania in 1939, pollution of the Ohio River prevents children from swimming. Brann Connell, a child in 1974 who travels backward in time and befriends his own father-to-be, Kevin Connell, is surprised to learn that pollution was a problem in the 1930s as well as the 1970s.

A thread of women's liberation or independence unites all of the novels, regardless of their time period. Two, although set in medieval times, depict their heroines in modern gender roles: *Jackaroo,* in which Gwyn is a type of precursor to Robin Hood but one who realizes that she must abide by society's rules, and *On Fortune's Wheel,* in which Birle embarks on a dangerous journey reneging on her rash commitment to marry and is at one point a slave, but ultimately becomes an independent landowner. The novels with more modern settings feature characters such as fearless Jean Wain-

wright, who solves the intriguing, exciting mystery in *The Callender Papers;* Althea Hall, who cleverly solves the mystery of the mummy's disappearance in the less exciting, but still provoking *Vandemark Mummy;* and high school sophomore Izzy who, with a leg amputated after an automobile accident caused by a drunk senior, subsequently learns independence and the meaning of true friendship in *Izzy, Willy-Nilly,* a book important for all high school students to read.

The theme of friendship appears in many guises: racist Bullet Tillerman learns to accept that his mentor is part black in *The Runner,* Burl dons the mark of Jackaroo to protect his friend Gwyn, and Birle risks her life to save her friend's in *On Fortune's Wheel.* But perhaps the most extensive treatment of the theme of friendship occurs in Voigt's most sophisticated novel to date, *David and Jonathan,* when Henry Marr and his longtime Jewish friend, Jonathan Nafishe, try to adjust to David, a Holocaust survivor, who comes to live with his relatives, the Nafishes, and causes problems not only for Henry and Jonathan, but also for the entire Nafishe family. Set in both 1967 and some fifteen years earlier, *David and Jonathan,* explores themes of war, death, suicide, survival, and religion in addition to friendship.

Although Voigt adopts an appropriate vocabulary and style for the imaginary medieval kingdom in *Jackaroo* and *On Fortune's Wheel,* and accurately treats the settings (*The Callender Papers* in 1894, *Tree by Leaf* during World War I, and *Building Blocks* in 1939), her greatest strength lies in characterizing contemporary high school and college students and in depicting situations such as desertion and poverty which plague the modern family. Her characters learn middle-class values and other lessons without overt didacticism. For example, when one character tutors another in writing about a classic, the character and the reader derive a lesson and hopefully a greater appreciation for literature.

Voigt often uses her knowledge of myth and legend, the classics, and the Bible to enhance her stories' plots or characters' names; for example, *Homecoming* features an odyssey of the Tillerman children; Bucephalus, the horse of Clothilde's father in *Tree by Leaf,* was named after Alexander the Great's horse; *David and Jonathan* depicts characters with Biblical names, including one who frequently refers to Biblical parables or creates his own; and *Orfe* retells the Orpheus and Eurydice myth with a reversal of the main characters' roles. Without knowledge of this myth, however, readers may be less satisfied with this book which focuses on Orfe, a singer and songwriter who tries without success to rescue her boyfriend, Yuri, from drug addiction.

A skilled craftsman, Voigt excels in creating characters who resonate in the reader's mind, particularly those in the Tillerman series; readers recognize with approbation the narrative links and repetitions of scenes, which aid in uniting the saga. For example, a scene in which Jeff Greene plays his guitar for Dicey is told from Dicey's point of view in *Dicey's Song,* but from Jeff's point of view in *A Solitary Blue.* The recognition of previously known characters and the déjà vu effect heighten the realism. Voigt's understanding of narrative techniques, power to create memorable characters, admirable but not goody-goody knowledge of the problems of youth, and desire to teach by transporting readers into the characters' inner lives usually result in reversing unpromising, perhaps even tragic, situations into positive, optimistic ones. Her novels make excellent reading.

—Sylvia Patterson Iskander

VONNEGUT, Kurt, Jr. American. Born in Indianapolis, Indiana, 11 November 1922. Educated at Cornell University, Ithaca, New York, 1940-42; Carnegie Institute, Pittsburgh, 1943; University of Chicago, 1945-47. Served in the United States Army Infantry, 1942-45; Purple Heart. Married 1) Jane Marie Cox in 1945 (divorced 1979), one son and two daughters; 2) Jill Krementz in 1979, one daughter. Police reporter, Chicago City News Bureau, 1946; worked in public relations for the General Electric Company, Schenectady, New York, 1947-50. Since 1950, freelance writer. Since 1965, teacher, Hopefield School, Sandwich, Massachusetts. Visiting Lecturer, Writers Workshop, University of Iowa, Iowa City, 1965-67, and Harvard University, Cambridge, Massachusetts, 1970-71; Visiting Professor, City University of New York, 1973-74. Actor in several films, including *Between Time and Timbuktu*, 1972, *Back to School*, Orion, 1986, *Storytellers: PEN Celebration*, 1987, and *That Day in November*, 1988. Speaker, National Coalition against Censorship briefing for the Attorney General's Commission on Pornography hearing, 1986. One-man exhibition of drawings, 1980. Recipient: Guggenheim Fellowship, 1967; American Academy grant, 1970; *Slaughterhouse Five* was selected one of American Library Association's Best Books for Young Adults, 1975, and *Jailbird*, 1979; *Jailbird* was selected one of New York Public Library's Books for the Teen Age, 1980, and *Slaughterhouse Five*, 1980, 1981, and 1982; Literary Lion from the New York Public Library, 1981; Eugene V. Debs award from the Eugene V. Debs Foundation, 1981, for public service; Freedom to Read award from Playboy Enterprises and the Friends of the Chicago Public Library, 1982, for his support against the suppression of books and his work to preserve First Amendment rights; Emmy award for Outstanding Children's Program from the National Academy of Television Arts and Sciences, 1985, for *Displaced Person*. M.A.: University of Chicago, 1971; Litt. D.: Hobart and William Smith Colleges, Geneva, New York, 1974. Agent: Donald C. Farber, 99 Park Avenue, New York, NY 10016, U.S.A. Lives in New York City.

PUBLICATIONS

Novels

Player Piano. New York, Scribner, 1952; London, Macmillan, 1953; as *Utopia 14*, New York, Bantam, 1954.
The Sirens of Titan. New York, Dell, 1959; London, Gollancz, 1962.
Mother Night. New York, Fawcett, 1962; London, Cape, 1968.
Cat's Cradle. New York, Holt Rinehart, and London, Gollancz, 1963.
God Bless You, Mr. Rosewater; or, Pearls before Swine. New York, Holt Rinehart, and London, Cape, 1965.
Slaughterhouse Five; or, The Children's Crusade: A Duty-Dance with Death, by Kurt Vonnegut, Jr., a Fourth-Generation German-American Now Living in Easy Circumstances on Cape Cod (and Smoking Too Much) Who, as an American Infantry Scout Hors de Combat, as a Prisoner of War, Witnessed the Fire-Bombing of Dresden, Germany, the Florence of the Elbe, a Long Time Ago, and Survived to Tell the Tale: This Is a Novel Somewhat in the Telegraphic Schizophrenic Manner of Tales of the Planet Tralfamadore, Where the Flying Saucers Come From. New York, Delacorte Press, 1969; London, Cape, 1970.
Breakfast of Champions; or, Goodbye Blue Monday. New York, Delacorte Press, and London, Cape, 1973.

Slapstick; or, Lonesome No More! New York, Delacorte Press, and London, Cape, 1976.
Jailbird. New York, Delacorte Press, and London, Cape, 1979.
Deadeye Dick. New York, Delacorte Press, 1982; London, Cape, 1983.
Galápagos: A Novel. New York, Delacorte Press, and London, Cape, 1985.
Bluebeard. New York, Delacorte Press, 1987; London, Cape, 1988.
Hocus Pocus; or, What's the Hurry, Son? New York, Putnam, and London, Cape, 1990.
The Lie, edited by Vaughn McBride. Woodstock, Illinois, Dramatic Publishing Company, 1992.

Short Stories

Canary in a Cathouse. New York, Fawcett, 1961.
Welcome to the Monkey House: A Collection of Short Works. New York, Delacorte Press, 1968; London, Cape, 1969.
Who Am I This Time? For Romeos and Juliets, illustrated by Michael McCurdy. Minneapolis, Minnesota, Redpath Press, 1987.

Plays

Happy Birthday, Wanda June (as *Penelope*, produced Cape Cod, Massachusetts, 1960; revised version, as *Happy Birthday, Wanda June*, produced New York, 1970; London, 1977). New York, Delacorte Press, 1970; London, Cape, 1973.
The Very First Christmas Morning, in *Better Homes and Gardens* (Des Moines, Iowa), December 1962.
Between Time and Timbuktu; or, Prometheus-5: A Space Fantasy (televised, 1972; produced New York, 1976). New York, Delacorte Press, 1972; London, Panther, 1975.
Fortitude, in *Wampeters, Foma, and Granfalloons*, 1974.
Timesteps (produced Edinburgh, 1979).
God Bless You, Mr. Rosewater, adaptation of his own novel (produced New York, 1979).

Television Plays: "Auf Wiedersehen," with Valentine Davies, 1958; *Between Time and Timbuktu*, 1972.

Other

Wampeters, Foma, and Granfalloons: Opinions. New York, Delacorte Press, 1974; London, Cape, 1975.
Sun, Moon, Star (for young adults), with Ivan Chermayeff. New York, Harper, and London, Hutchinson, 1980.
Palm Sunday: An Autobiographical Collage. New York, Delacorte Press, and London, Cape, 1981.
Contributor, *Bob and Ray: A Retrospective, June 15-July 10, 1982*. Museum of Broadcasting, 1982.
Contributor, *Discrimination, Affirmative Action, and Equal Opportunity: An Economic and Social Perspective*, edited by W.E. Block and M.A. Walker. Vancouver, Canada, Fraser Institute, 1982.
Nothing Is Lost Save Honor: Two Essays. Jackson, Mississippi, Noveau Press, 1984.
Conversations with Kurt Vonnegut (interview), edited by William Rodney Allen. Jackson, University of Mississippi Press, 1988.
Fates Worse Than Death: An Autobiographical Collage of the 1980's. Nottingham, Spokesman, 1980(?); New York, Putnam, 1991.

*

Media Adaptations: *Happy Birthday, Wanda June* (film), Red Lion, 1971; *Slaughterhouse Five* (film), Universal, 1972; *Who Am I This Time?* (film), Rubicon Films, 1982; *Slapstick of Another Kind* (film based on *Slapstick),* Paul-Serendipity, 1984; *Displaced Person* (film), Hemisphere, 1985; *Slaughterhouse Five* (cassette), Listening for Pleasure, 1985; *Jailbird* (cassette), Warner Audio Publishers, 1985; *Breakfast of Champions* (cassette), Caedmon; *Cat's Cradle* (cassette), Books on Tape, (abridged cassette), Caedmon; *Galapagos* (cassette), Simon and Schuster; *Slapstick* (cassette), Books on Tape; *The Sirens of Titan* (cassette), Books on Tape; *Welcome to the Monkey House* (cassette), Books on Tape; *Vonnegut Soundbook* (recording), Caedmon; *Kurt Vonnegut, Jr. Reads Slaughterhouse Five* (cassette), Caedmon.

Biography: Entry in *Dictionary of Literary Biography,* Detroit, Gale, Volume 2, 1978; Volume 8, 1981; *Kurt Vonnegut, Jr.* by Stanley Schatt, Boston, Twayne, 1976; entry in *Dictionary of Literary Biography Yearbook 1980,* Detroit, Gale, 1981; entry in *Dictionary of Literary Biography Documentary Series,* Detroit, Gale, Volume 3, 1983.

Bibliography: *Kurt Vonnegut, Jr.: A Descriptive Bibliography and Annotated Secondary Checklist* Asa B. Pieratt, Jr., and Jerome Klinkowitz, Hamden, Connecticut, Shoe String Press, 1974; *Kurt Vonnegut: A Comprehensive Bibliography* by Asa B. Pieratt, Jr., Julie Huffman-Klinkowitz, and Jerome Klinkowitz, Hamden, Connecticut, Archon, 1987.

Critical Studies: *Kurt Vonnegut, Jr.: A Checklist* by Betty Lenhardt Hudgens, Detroit, Gale, 1972; *Kurt Vonnegut, Jr.* by Peter J. Reed, New York, Warner, 1972; *Kurt Vonnegut: Fantasist of Fire and Ice* by David H. Goldsmith, Bowling Green, Ohio, Popular Press, 1972; *The Vonnegut Statement* edited by Jerome Klinkowitz and John Somer, New York, Delacorte Press, 1973, London, Panther, 1975, *Vonnegut in America: An Introduction to the Life and Work of Kurt Vonnegut* edited by Jerome Klinkowitz and Donald L. Lawler, New York, Delacorte Press, 1977, and *Kurt Vonnegut* by Jerome Klinkowitz, London, Methuen, 1982; entry in *Contemporary Literary Criticism,* Detroit, Gale, Volume 1, 1973; Volume 2, 1974; Volume 3, 1975; Volume 4, 1975; Volume 5, 1976; Volume 8, 1978; Volume 12, 1980; Volume 22, 1982; Volume 40, 1986; *Vonnegut's Major Works* by Thomas R. Holland, Lincoln, Nebraska, Cliff's Notes, 1973; *Something to Believe In: Is Kurt Vonnegut Exorcist of Jesus Christ Superstar?* by Robert Short, New York, Harper, 1976; *Kurt Vonnegut* by James Lundquist, New York, Ungar, 1977; *Kurt Vonnegut: The Gospel from Outer Space* by Clark Mayo, San Bernardino, California, Borgo Press, 1977; *Vonnegut: A Preface to His Novels* by Richard Giannone, Port Washington, New York, Kennikat Press, 1977; *Vonnegut Talks!* edited by Michael Chernuchin, Pylon, 1977; *Vonnegut's Duty-Dance with Death: Theme and Structure in Slaughterhouse-Five* by Monica Loeb, Umeå Studies in the Humanities, 1979; *Happy Birthday, Kurt Vonnegut: A Festschrift for Kurt Vonnegut on His Sixtieth Birthday* edited by Jill Krementz, New York, Delacorte Press, 1982.

*   *   *

Although Kurt Vonnegut, Jr., has not written any novels specifically for young adults, his works are broadly popular among students from late middle school through college. Certainly a part of this appeal derives from his clear, readable prose telling an interesting, though often puzzling story. Vonnegut informs young readers about the complexity of attitudes in modern life and delights them with a flippancy of tone which teenagers admire as a way of communicating early sophistication.

Many of Vonnegut's novels are tied together by recurring characters and settings such as the fumbling, failed science-fiction writer, Kilgore Trout, and the cerebral planet Tralfamadore. This continuity captures the fancy of young readers brought up on either print serials like Nancy Drew and the Hardy Boys or cartoons and television series. A comfortable Vonnegut "family" of literary style thus invites young readers back to familiar ground, even though the stories may be bizarre satires.

Vonnegut's novels span the years 1952 to 1990, a forty-year career beginning with *Player Piano* and recently culminating with *Hocus Pocus.* At first, he was labeled a "science-fiction" writer because of the futuristic settings and imaginative detailing of such early works as *Player Piano, Sirens of Titan,* and *Mother Night.* In the first of these, Paul Proteus, a brilliant, young executive with the megacorporate power industry of the future USA, is stifled by the utopian perfection imposed by "the company." He longs for the nostalgia of the old days, found in the player piano in a bar across the river in Homestead, where the workers live. To realize his longing, he becomes involved with the "Ghost Shirt," society's revolution, in which he gains independent integrity though losing the struggle.

Like Proteus's mythic crossing of the water and descent into Homestead, Malachi Constant, hero of *Sirens of Titan,* descends into the caves of Mercury and passes a series of trials on Mars. He then returns heroically with the boon of being a messiah of the new Church of God the Utterly Indifferent, only to be scapegoated for its failure. Vonnegut's adapting of the mythic initiation theme bridges old and new narrative styles for young readers, again creating a more accessible route for reading.

In perhaps the best of his early novels for young adults, *Slaughterhouse Five,* subtitled *The Children's Crusade,* Vonnegut combines many of his narrative experiments. Child-like Billy Pilgrim narrates the entire tale of a young draftee's horrible experiences during World War II, his return to settled life with a family, his involuntary transportation to and secret life on Tralfamadore, and his assassination by a former antagonist in the German prison camp in Dresden. But this narration does not follow any linear, chronological plan. "Unstuck in time," because of his all-knowing Tralfamadorian perspective, Billy's mind, along with the narrative, jump about between 1945 and 1968 with the disjointed abandon common to adolescent perspectives. In such juxtapositions of consciousness, the reader, together with Billy, knows all along about his death, the birth of his son on Tralfamadore by blue-movie queen Montana Wildhack, the firebombing of Dresden, the accidental death of his wife rushing to him after a foreknown plane crash, and the destruction of the universe by a Tralfamadorian accident. Although the book may be challenging at first, young readers find, after reading and discussing it, a dungeon-and-dragon-like confidence—awareness of all the variables and outcomes in Billy's life which brings to the forefront their powers of informed imagination.

The difficulty in understanding Vonnegut's works is offset by his direct simplicity of prose. Like the Tralfamadorian model of the novel, one may clearly read "each clump of symbols" all at once without there being any initial relationship among them, save that in retrospect one can see how the moment is structured in the whole image of life. Not unlike the notions of modern physics, this view offers a fascinating cross-disciplinary link between speculative science and literature.

By tracing symbolic links, the young reader can easily associate Billy with Christian in Bunyan's *Pilgrim's Progress* and find an updated initiation quest for moral vision and behavior. The modern version speaks as persuasively to its readers about finding the virtuous life as does its seventeenth-century counterpart, but in allegory more allusive and fitting our times. Bunyan's Mr. Wiseman and the lions are replaced by Vonnegut's Howard Campbell and a brutal humanity instrumental in the firebombing of Dresden. Ultimately, the quest for Christian love parallels Billy's quest for "common, human decency."

In all, Vonnegut's novels engage the young-adult reader who is seeking some transition between the accepting, unifying views of youth and the cynical, compartmentalizing frustration of the adult world. Bright readers will always be drawn to this writer because his work anticipates the future while speaking clearly to us in the present.

—Ron Evans

W

WALDEN, Amelia Elizabeth. American. Born in New York. Educated at Danbury State Teachers College (now Western Connecticut State College), Danbury, diploma (summa cum laude) 1928; Columbia University, New York, B.S. 1934; American Academy of Dramatic Arts, New York, certificate. Married John William Harmon in 1946 (died 1950). Teacher of English, speech, and drama, Benjamin Franklin School, Norwalk, Connecticut, 1935-45; novelist, since 1946. Playwright, producer, and director of several community theatre groups in Connecticut. Address: 89 North Compo Rd., Westport, CT 06880, U.S.A.

PUBLICATIONS FOR YOUNG ADULTS

Novels

Gateway. New York, Morrow, 1946.
Waverly. New York, Morrow, 1947.
Skymountain. New York, Morrow, 1948.
Sunnycove. New York, Morrow, 1948.
A Girl Called Hank. New York, Morrow, 1951.
Marsha on Stage. New York, Morrow, 1952.
Victory for Jill. New York, Morrow, 1953.
All My Love. New York, Morrow, 1954.
Daystar. Philadelphia, Westminster, 1955.
Three Loves Has Sandy. New York, McGraw, 1955.
I Found My Love. Philadelphia, Westminster, 1956.
My Sister Mike. New York, McGraw, 1956.
Palomino Girl. Philadelphia, Westminster, 1957.
Today Is Mine. Philadelphia, Westminster, 1958.
Queen of the Courts. Philadelphia, Westminster, 1959.
A Boy to Remember. Philadelphia, Westminster, 1960.
Where Is My Heart? Philadelphia, Westminster, 1960.
Shadow on Devil's Peak. Philadelphia, Westminster, 1961.
When Love Speaks. New York, McGraw, 1961.
How Bright the Dawn. Philadelphia, Westminster, 1962.
So Near the Heart. New York, McGraw, 1962.
My Dreams Ride High. Philadelphia, Westminster, 1963.
My World's the Stage. New York, McGraw, 1964.
To Catch a Spy. Philadelphia, Westminster, 1964.
Race the Wild Wind. Philadelphia, Westminster, 1965.
The Spy on Danger Island. Philadelphia, Westminster, 1965.
In Search of Ophelia. New York, McGraw, 1966.
The Spy with Five Faces. Philadelphia, Westminster, 1966.
A Name for Himself. Philadelphia, Lippincott, 1967.
A Spy Called Michel-E. Philadelphia, Westminster, 1967.
The Spy Who Talked Too Much. Philadelphia, Westminster, 1968.
Walk in a Tall Shadow. Philadelphia, Lippincott, 1968.
The Case of the Diamond Eye. Philadelphia, Westminster, 1969.
Same Scene, Different Place. Philadelphia, Lippincott, 1969.
A Spycase Built for Two. Philadelphia, Westminster, 1969.
Basketball Girl of the Year. New York, McGraw, 1970.
What Happened to Candy Carmichael? Philadelphia, Westminster, 1970.
Stay to Win. Philadelphia, Lippincott, 1971.
Valerie Valentine Is Missing. Philadelphia, Westminster, 1971.
Play Ball, McGill! Philadelphia, Westminster, 1972.

Where Was Everyone When Sabrina Screamed? Philadelphia, Westminster, 1973.
Go, Phillips, Go! Philadelphia, Westminster, 1974.
Heartbreak Tennis. Philadelphia, Westminster, 1977.

PUBLICATIONS FOR ADULTS

Novels

The Bradford Story. New York, Appleton, 1956.
Flight into Morning. New York, Appleton, 1957.
Escape on Skis. Philadelphia, Westminster, 1975.

*

Amelia Elizabeth Walden comments:

In the summer of 1945, I made one of the most momentous decisions of my life. I chose to give up the emotional, intellectual, and financial security of the teaching profession and cast my net into the unknown world outside the classroom. I was at that time writing short stories, which were returned from publishers as fast as I sent them out. Someone in the field told me I was writing in the wrong form and that I should try a novel.

The idea was challenging, and when a plot formed itself almost unbidden in my mind, the thought of writing for and about young people in a new and different way impelled me to start my first book. That Christmas Eve, I received a letter from William Morrow's new editor of young peoples' books saying they liked and would publish *Gateway.* I never deviated from my original idea of writing for young readers in an adult style, using an adult vocabulary.

I never had an agent and sold my forty-seven books by going personally into the top offices of the five publishers with whom I dealt. At that time, women were not thought to have the talent, strength, and staying power of men. I have been told that the curator of manuscripts at the university which will receive my collections made inquiries of my publishers and was told by all of them, "She's the best business person in the field."

*   *   *

If the success of any writer depends upon the number of times his or her books are taken out of the library to be read, Amelia Elizabeth Walden considers herself successful. She has written many books for young people, her first book, *Gateway,* being published in 1946. She considers herself to be the first to have written a genuine "young adult" novel, writing novels in the young adult language about young adult problems and interests.

One good example of Walden's young adult novels is *My Dreams Ride High,* portraying eighteen-year-old Jay Wyndham Gilbert, daughter of the boss of Wyndham Engineering Company, a factory producing marine pumps and government projects (some secret). Jay prefers calculus to cooking and hates femininity, until she meets and falls in love with Shane Rogers, sent by the Navy to Wyndham Engineering to help develop a secret turbocraft. An exciting story about the perils of skin diving, sabotage, and a romance between two people of conflicting personalities, Walden has written a book that young adults will not put down until the end.

Walden's many novels of suspense and international intrigue include *To Catch a Spy* which features Sally Templeton, a young lady in her early twenties, who helps solve the mystery of an airplane crash in the Nigerian jungle, falls in love with one of two brothers raised by the infamous head of a spy ring, and keeps the reader guessing until the case is solved.

Walden has written many novels for young adults dealing with sports. *Race the Wild Wind* is about Marty Conover, senior in high school, who is following in the footsteps of famous ski champion, winner of Olympic medals, beautiful older sister Glory Conover. Marty struggles to be herself while fighting the nightmare from the past of her only brother being killed on a ski slope while saving Marty's life. Marty flirts with danger on the ski slopes, plays the clown to gain the attention of others, stuffs herself with food for consolation, adding a weight problem to her frustrations. Then she meets Garth Falkner, not at all her idea of Prince Charming, but a young man who helps her realize how she must change. Walden's keen knowledge of skiing and also of young people's feelings come through.

To Pat Palmer, tomboy and captain of Greenport's girl basketball team in *Basketball Girl of the Year,* life is mainly a rectangle with a hardwood floor, a ceiling overhead, with two backboards with metal hoops attached. Basketball is her life, until she meets Chris Landry who shows her there is more to life than winning the coveted Basketball Girl of the Year award. Because Pat learns to put her team first instead of herself, she loses the award but wins the Girl Athlete for All Seasons instead, and she wins it because she learns to grow up with the help of Chris Landry and a coach who teach her to open her eyes and see more around her than just her own little world.

Softball is the theme of *Play Ball, McGill!,* about Ginger McGill, a feisty senior in high school, who has hot-rods, especially her souped-up Studebaker, and Snake Anderson, new handsome boy on the block, all on her mind. Ginger is the best pitcher in her school, but she comes by it naturally, having two older brothers in the pros. When she hits a bad streak of luck playing ball, she turns to Snake and cars for consolation. Snake not only helps Ginger, he also helps her brother, Karl, when he too has a bad streak of luck at baseball and at love. Walden has written another knowledgeable book about sports, including auto racing and the building of cars themselves.

Amelia Elizabeth Walden writes vividly about the emotional upheavals and confusion that fill young adult lives because she has never forgotten her own adolescence. Her novels appeal not only to sports-minded young people, but to a larger teenage audience because she portrays situations that have appeal for her readers: romance, espionage, mysteries, and most of all, feelings. Her books are well-plotted with vivid backgrounds, whether on ski slopes, basketball courts, or in the ghetto. She is also known for her Shakespeare Festival books.

—Carol Doxey

WALKER, Alice (Malsenior). American. Born in Eatonton, Georgia, 9 February 1944. Educated at Spelman College, Atlanta, 1961-

63; Sarah Lawrence College, Bronxville, New York, 1963-65; B.A. 1965. Married Melvyn Rosenman Leventhal in 1967 (divorced 1976); one daughter. Writer. Co-founder and publisher, Wild Trees Press, Navarro, California, 1984-88. Voter registration worker, Georgia; Head Start program worker, Mississippi, and with New York City Department of Welfare, mid-1960s. Writer-in-residence and teacher of black studies at Jackson State College, 1968-69, and Tougaloo College, 1970-71, both Mississippi; lecturer in literature, Wellesley College, Massachusetts, 1972-73, and University of Massachusetts, Boston, 1972-73; Associate Professor of English, Yale University, New Haven, Connecticut, after 1977. Distinguished Writer in Afro-American studies department, University of California, Berkeley, spring 1982; Fannie Hurst Professor of Literature, Brandeis University, Waltham, Massachusetts, fall 1982. Lecturer and reader of own poetry at universities and conferences. Member of board of trustees of Sarah Lawrence College. Consultant on black history to Friends of the Children of Mississippi, 1967. Recipient: Bread Loaf Writer's Conference scholarship, 1966; first prize, *American Scholar* essay contest, 1967; Merrill writing fellowship, 1967; MacDowell Colony fellowship, 1967, 1977-78; National Endowment for the Arts grant, 1969, 1977; Radcliffe Institute fellowship, 1971-73; Ph.D., Russell Sage College, 1972; National Book award nomination, 1973, for *Revolutionary Petunias and Other Poems;* Lillian Smith award, for poetry, Southern Regional Council, 1973, for *Revolutionary Petunias;* Richard and Hinda Rosenthal Foundation award, American Academy and Institute of Arts and Letters, 1974, for *In Love and Trouble;* Guggenheim award, 1977-78; National Book Critics Circle award nomination, 1982, Pulitzer Prize, 1983, and American Book award, 1983, all for *The Color Purple;* D.H.L., University of Massachusetts, 1983; O. Henry Award, 1986, for "Kindred Spirits;" Ph.D.: Russell Sage College, Troy, New York, 1972; D.H.L.: University of Massachusetts, Amherst, 1983. Agent: Wild Trees Press, P.O. Box 378, Navarro, CA 95463. Lives in San Francisco, California.

PUBLICATIONS

Novels

The Third Life of Grange Copeland. New York, Harcourt, 1970; London, Women's Press, 1985.
Meridian. New York, Harcourt, and London, Deutsch, 1976.
The Color Purple. New York, Harcourt, 1982.
The Temple of My Familiar. San Diego, Harcourt, and London, Women's Press, 1989.
Possessing the Secret of Joy. New York, Harcourt, 1992.

Poetry

Once. New York, Harcourt, 1968; London, Women's Press, 1986.
Five Poems. Detroit, Broadside Press, 1972.
Revolutionary Petunias and Other Poems. New York, Harcourt, 1973; London, Women's Press, 1988.
Goodnight, Willie Lee, I'll See You in the Morning. New York, Dial, 1979; London, Women's Press, 1987.
Horses Make a Landscape Look More Beautiful. New York, Harcourt, 1984; London, Women's Press, 1985.
Her Blue Body Everything We Know: Earthling Poems 1965-1990. San Diego, Harcourt, 1991.

Short Stories

In Love and Trouble: Stories of Black Women. New York, Harcourt, 1973; London, Women's Press, 1984.
You Can't Keep a Good Woman Down. New York, Harcourt, 1981; London, Women's Press, 1982.

Other

Langston Hughes: American Poet (children's biography). New York, Crowell, 1974.
Editor, *I Love Myself When I'm Laughing...and Then Again When I Am Looking Mean and Impressive: A Zora Neale Hurston Reader.* Old Westbury, New York, Feminist Press, 1979.
In Search of Our Mothers' Gardens: Womanist Prose. New York, Harcourt, 1983; London, Women's Press, 1984.
Living by the Word: Selected Writings, 1973-1987. San Diego, Harcourt, and London, Women's Press, 1988.
To Hell with Dying (for children), illustrated by Catherine Deeter. San Diego, Harcourt, and London, Hodder & Stoughton, 1988.
Finding the Green Stone, paintings by Catherine Deeter. San Diego, Harcourt, 1991.

*

Media Adaptations: *The Color Purple* (feature film directed by Steven Spielberg), Warner Brothers, 1985.

Biography: Entry in *Dictionary of Literary Biography,* Detroit, Gale, Volume 6: *American Novelists since World War II, 2nd series,* 1980, Volume 33: *Afro-American Fiction Writers after 1955,* 1984.

Critical Study: Entry in *Contemporary Literary Criticism,* Detroit, Gale, Volume 5, 1976, Volume 6, 1976, Volume 9, 1978, Volume 19, 1981, Volume 27, 1984, Volume 46, 1988.

*   *   *

Alice Walker is a novelist, short story writer, essayist, poet, and author of children's books. Of particular interest to young adults are her novels: powerful, strident stories principally set in America's rural and poor South. But Walker cannot be labeled as a southern writer, a black writer, a feminist writer. Her works speak of universal struggles for dignity and meaning and connectedness in life. She does view the African American woman as a symbol of hope for humanity, and stresses the importance of bonds between women in combatting racism and sexism, inequalities of any kind. Her prose is lyrical, and her skill at portraying grace and goodness in the lives of ordinary people is remarkable.

Walker's first novel, *The Third Life of Grange Copeland,* introduces themes she will use again and again, such as the domination of powerless women by also powerless men. This work details the life of three generations of a black sharecropping family during the years between the depression and the beginning of the civil rights movement. The terrible effects of poverty and racism on the lives of the Copelands, resulting in suicide of a wife in the first generation, murder of a wife in the second generation, and murder of a son to provide freedom for the son's daughter in the third generation, are told with intensity and with clarity. Walker's message is that family members must not ignore family functioning and commu-

nity relationships; if they do, they lose the major basis for understanding themselves.

Meridian, Walker's second novel, is a powerful story of black strength and perseverance. Also set in the rural South, it focuses on the civil rights movement. Meridian is a southerner who goes north to college and then returns to the South, committing her life to aiding southern blacks in gaining political and social equality. She joins a black militant group but is forced to leave when she refuses to agree to violence. Meridian continues her activist work, mostly alone, and becomes a legendary figure throughout the South. In order to align herself, though, with the larger social problems of blacks, she divests herself of immediate family relationships—her parents and her child. This rupture in family in the end allows Meridian to define herself. At the end of the novel, Meridian's self-identity is a collective identity, and Meridian becomes a model for others to take up the civil rights cause.

The Color Purple is Walker's most highly acclaimed book. It won both the Pulitzer Prize and the American Book Award for fiction, and became a well received movie. The novel describes thirty years in the life of Celie, a poor southern black who is subjected to physical and emotional abuse by her stepfather and her husband. The story begins when Celie is fourteen years old. She has been repeatedly raped by her stepfather, and the children she bore him were sold. She is then placed in a loveless marriage by her stepfather, with a widower who beats and ridicules her. The book is in the form of letters describing her ordeals to God and to her sister Nettie, who escapes a similar life by becoming a missionary in Africa. Celie finally finds comfort and love in her husband's mistress, Shug Avery, a flamboyant blues singer who treats her with dignity, provides her with love, and helps her leave her marriage. In the end Celie is reunited with her children and with Nettie. This is a rare and beautiful book, filled with characters who live and breathe. Its descriptions of adolescence as well as adulthood are moving, painful, and unforgettable.

The Temple of My Familiar continues Walker's fascination with African history in more detail. It attempts to record five hundred thousand years of human history, using multiple settings and narrative voices, shifting rapidly between past and present. It moves from the Americas, Europe, and Africa to nameless primal worlds. At center stage is Miss Lissie, an African goddess who has been incarnated hundreds of times—usually as a woman, sometimes as a man, once as a lion. Lissie enables Walker to go back in time to beginnings of (wo)man. This book, a mixture of fantasy and revisionary history, is more difficult to read and less eloquent than *The Color Purple.*

Alice Walker is a passionate writer. Her portrayals of young, poor, southern, black women are unsurpassed. These women may be uneducated and unappreciated, they may be abused, but they survive and they affirm themselves. All young people need to read *The Color Purple.* They will see in it their own doubts and fears, and they will see in it strength and staying power.

—Mary Lystad

WALTER, Mildred Pitts. American. Born in Sweetville, Louisiana, 9 September 1922. Educated at Southern University, Louisiana, B.A. 1944; University of California, Los Angeles; California

State College, 1950-52; University of Southern California, Los Angeles; Antioch College, Yellow Springs, Ohio, M.Ed. 1977. Married Earl Lloyd Walter in 1947 (died 1965); two sons. Shipwright helper in Vancouver, Washington, 1943-44; salesperson, City Dye Works, Los Angeles, California, 1944-48; personnel clerk, 1949-52, elementary schoolteacher, 1952-70, Los Angeles Public Schools; educational consultant and lecturer on cultural diversity for educational institutions, 1971-73. Civil rights activist for Congress of Racial Equality (CORE), during 1950s and 1960s. Northeast Women's Center, Denver, Colorado, cofounder and administrator, 1982-86. Delegate to Second World Black and African Festival of the Arts and Culture, Lagos, Nigeria, 1977. Recipient: Runner-up for Irma Simonton Black award, 1981, for *Ty's One-Man Band; Parents' Choice* awards, 1984, for *Because We Are,* and 1985, for *Brother to the Wind;* Coretta Scott King awards from Social Responsibility Round Table of American Library Association, honorable mention, 1984, for *Because We Are,* honorable mention, 1986, for *Trouble's Child,* winner 1987, for *Justin and the Best Biscuits in the World,* for *Mississippi Challenge,* Honor award 1993. Address: c/o Bradbury Press, 866 Third Avenue, New York, NY 10022, U.S.A.

PUBLICATIONS FOR YOUNG ADULTS

Fiction

Lillie of Watts: A Birthday Discovery, illustrated by Leonora E. Prince. Los Angeles, Ward Ritchie Press, 1969.
Lillie of Watts Takes a Giant Step, illustrated by Bonnie Helene Johnson. New York, Doubleday, 1971.
The Girl on the Outside. New York, Lothrop, 1982.
Because We Are. New York, Lothrop, 1983.
Trouble's Child. New York, Lothrop, 1985.
Mariah Loves Rock. New York, Bradbury Press, 1988.

Nonfiction

Mississippi Challenge. New York, Bradbury Press, 1992.

PUBLICATIONS FOR CHILDREN

Fiction

Ty's One-Man Band, illustrated by Margot Tomes. New York, Four Winds Press, 1980.
My Mama Needs Me, illustrated by Pat Cummings. New York, Lothrop, 1983.
Brother to the Wind, illustrated by Diane and Leo Dillon. New York, Lothrop, 1985.
Justin and the Best Biscuits in the World, illustrated by Catherine Stock. New York, Lothrop, 1986.
Have a Happy..., illustrated by Carole Byard. New York, Lothrop, 1989.
Mariah Keeps Cool, illustrated by Pat Cummings. New York, Bradbury, 1990.
Two and Too Much, illustrated by Pat Cummings. New York, Bradbury, 1990.

*   *   *

In Mildred Pitts Walter's books for adolescents and young adults, metamorphosis is a predominant theme. When Martha of *Trouble's Child* realizes at the novel's end that "she was on the threshold of searching, learning, knowing, of stretching her mind," her thoughts represent not only the growing recognition of her own identity but the transformations that occur in all of Walter's black characters. Walter writes with power, determination, and truth about how young black people achieve self-awareness in diverse social environments in the United States. She focuses on the cultural defamation of black Americans and their struggle to face the realities of their racial heritage and become fully integrated human beings. While Walter writes about black Americans, her books transcend that particular experience to speak movingly about the connectedness of people despite differences in color, race, or creed.

In *Lillie of Watts,* eleven-year-old Lillie must find meaning in a world where racial differences parallel social and economic privileges. Advertisements bombard Lillie with the message that to be white means to be valued by society while to be black means to be overlooked. Over the course of the story, Lillie learns that "people are more important than cats, sweaters, and cars." Her mother's unconditional love helps Lillie appreciate and understand that pride and a sense of self cannot be measured in material goods but by how an individual conducts his or her life.

The setting for *Trouble's Child,* a young adult novel that was named a Coretta Scott King Honor Book, is the lush Louisiana bayou community of Blue Isle. In this coming-of-age story, Martha, who dreams of finishing her high-school education, tries to free herself from the binding ties of her small, isolated community and its expectation that she marry and follow in her grandmother's footsteps by becoming a midwife. Martha achieves her aspirations when she finds the courage to stand by her choices despite community disapproval. Rich in detail and written in the soft cadences of Louisiana speech, the book strongly but tenderly portrays a universal adolescent experience.

The Girl on the Outside is a fictional re-creation of the integration of Central High School in Little Rock, Arkansas, in 1957. Resonating with honesty and integrity, the novel focuses on the experiences of two students: Sophie, a white girl who is caught in a web of unconscious racism, and Eva, a black girl who volunteers to be bused to the new school. *The Girl on the Outside* takes a powerful and poignant look at the problems, fears, and prejudices that must be faced during the process of accepting integration.

Themes of racial pride and adolescent maturation also occur in *Because We Are,* a recipient of the Coretta Scott King Award. A misunderstanding between Emma Walsh, a black honor student, and one of her teachers at a predominantly white high school results in her transfer to an all-black high school. In dealing with the discrimination against her, the African proverb "Because we are, I am" resonates for Emma, who discovers strength in her community's collective racial heritage.

Mississippi Challenge, Walter's only nonfiction book to date and a Coretta Scott King Honor Book, documents the struggles of blacks in Mississippi from the pre-Civil War era through the organization of the Mississippi Freedom Democratic Party (MFDP) in the 1960s, and its role in changing the course of Mississippi history. Using a reportorial style and aimed at a junior-high audience, the book moves from recounting some of the dire injustices committed against blacks during this time to detailing the civil rights work of both the MFDP and the Student Nonviolent Coordinating Committee (SNCC). Courage, choice, and change-themes that are so integral to Walter's fiction—are also the cornerstones of this probing examination of a dark period in American history.

Integration of a different kind occurs in *Mariah Loves Rock,* in which eleven-year-old Mariah must confront her feelings about her father's daughter from his first marriage coming to live with them. As she anticipates Denise's arrival, Mariah's concern that she will lose her father's affections to this new family member fosters jealousy and resentment. In the novel's sequel, *Mariah Keeps Cool,* Mariah moves from viewing Denise as a rival to accepting her as a sister. With keen insight into the psyche of the family unit, Walter realistically and warmly chronicles Mariah's transformation.

Walter's imbues her work with feeling and conviction of purpose. Thematically complex yet stylistically accessible, her writing addresses issues of race relations, family life, and adolescent maturation. It also celebrates change—at times frightening, exhilarating, comforting, and perplexing—as an essential and liberating force in coming to terms with oneself and society. Wellsprings of hope, Walter's books embrace life even as they acknowledge the sometimes seemingly insurmountable difficulties of living.

—Carolyn Shute

* * *

WANGERIN, Walter, Jr. American. Born in Portland, Oregon, 13 February 1944. Educated at Concordia Senior College (now Concordia Theological Seminary), Fort Wayne, Indiana, B.A. 1966; Miami University, Oxford, Ohio, M.A. 1968; Christ Seminary, Seminex, M.Div. 1976. Married Ruthanne Bohlmann in 1968; two sons and two daughters. Full-time writer. Worked at a variety of jobs, including migrant peapicker, lifeguard, and ghetto youth worker; producer, announcer, KFUO-Radiocomments, St. Louis, Montana, 1969-70; instructor in English literature, University of Evansville, Evansville, Indiana, 1970-74; ordained Lutheran minister, 1976; assistant pastor, Lutheran Church of Our Redeemer, Evansville, beginning 1974; assistant pastor, beginning 1974, senior pastor, 1977-85, Grace Lutheran Church, Evansville; Jockum Professor in English and Theology, Valparaiso University, Valparaiso, Indiana, beginning 1991. Recipient: Best Children's Book of the Year, *School Library Journal* and *New York Times,* both 1978; National Religious Book award (children/youth category), 1980, American Book award for paperback science fiction, 1981, and American Library Association Notable Book citation, all for *The Book of the Dun Cow;* Best Book of 1983, School Library Journal, for *Thistle;* Best Fiction, Association of Logos Bookstores, 1986, for *The Book of Sorrows.* Lives in Evansville, Indiana.

PUBLICATIONS FOR ADULTS AND YOUNG ADULTS

Fiction

The Book of the Dun Cow. New York, Harper, 1978.
The Book of Sorrows. New York, Harper, 1985.
The Orphean Passages: The Drama of Faith. New York, Harper, 1986.

Other

Ragman and Other Cries of Faith. New York, Harper, 1984.

Miz Lil and the Chronicles of Grace. New York, Harper, 1988.
The Manger Is Empty. New York, Harper, 1989.

Poetry

A Miniature Cathedral and Other Poems. New York, Harper, 1986.

Other

As for Me and My House: Crafting Your Marriage to Last. Nelson, 1987.
Mourning into Dancing. Grand Rapids, Michigan, Zondervan, 1992.
Reliving the Passion: Meditations on the Suffering, Death, and Resurrection of Jesus as Recorded in Mark. Grand Rapids, Michigan, Zondervan, 1992.

PUBLICATIONS FOR CHILDREN

Fiction

The Glory Story. Concordia, 1974.
God, I've Gotta Talk to You. Concordia, 1974.
A Penny Is Everything, with A. Jennings. Concordia, 1974.
The Baby God Promised. Concordia, 1976.
The Bible for Children. Rand McNally, 1981.
O Happy Day! Concordia, 1981.
My First Bible Book about Jesus, illustrated by Jim Cummins. Rand McNally, 1983.
Thistle, illustrated by Marcia Sewall. New York, Harper, 1983.
Potter, Come Fly to the First of the Earth, illustrated by Daniel San Souci. Cook, 1985.
In the Beginning There Was No Sky. Nelson, 1986.
The Bible for Children. Macmillan, 1987.
Elisabeth and the Water Troll. New York, Harper, 1991.
Branta and the Golden Stone, illustrated by Deborah Healey. New York, Simon & Schuster, 1993.

* * *

Walter Wangerin, Jr., is a master storyteller who is at his best in books in which he resurrects the fable and fairy tale, those age-old grandparents of storytelling forms, and fills them with rich, multilevel stories that are unique for their modern resonance and elusive use of symbols and religious parallels. Fables and fairy tales have always been a means of delivering stories to people of all ages, and Wangerin's are no exception. His first novel, *The Book of the Dun Cow,* and his more recent picture book, *Elisabeth and the Water-Troll,* deal with timeless themes—good versus evil, the nature of appearances and reality—and fall somewhere in between his books written specifically for children and his poetry, plays, and other adult books. *Elisabeth and the Water-Troll,* with folksy illustrations by Deborah Healy that incorporate the story's elements of wonder and adventure, is a "Beauty and the Beast" sort of fairy tale which, through its beautifully implied lessons of trust, loss, love, and inner beauty, invites older readers to enjoy it alongside children. *The Book of the Dun Cow* even more decidedly defies age appropriate categorization. Young readers and listeners are drawn to it for its lively and sometimes humorous animal characterization, lyrical language, and dramatic conflict that does not spare gruesome details. Full appreciation of these books, however, requires a more mature grasp of symbol and allusion and an ability to deal with questions for which there are no ultimate answers.

The Book of the Dun Cow is a beast fable, a story form that isolates, characterizes, and interprets human behavior by giving its unchanging aspects familiar animal forms—the industrious ant, the crafty fox, the prideful rooster. Other modern novels of appeal to young adults make powerful use of the form; George Orwell's *Animal Farm* and Richard Adams's *Watership Down* are examples. These give our virtues and vices names and faces and create a microcosm which helps us interpret the larger world. But what distinguishes *The Book of the Dun Cow* is that Wangerin works within the fable, demonstrating a working knowledge of medieval literature and a poetic facility with language that makes his tales sound old and familiar, stories that might have once been told aloud or sung, stories you would crowd up against others to hear. Additionally, in *The Book of the Dun Cow*, Wangerin goes beyond recreating the microcosmic barnyard or rabbit warren. His attempt is to take readers back to a time "when the animals could both speak and understand speech," "the earth was still fixed in the absolute center of the universe...And the sun still traveled around the moored earth, so that days and nights belonged to the earth and to the creatures thereon, not to a ball of silent fire." The barnyard of his story is just one barnyard of many operating as one part of an infinitely larger scheme. Thus, he ambitiously creates an entire cosmology of the universe and the good and evil within it.

In *The Book of the Dun Cow*, the rooster Chauncticleer, a cocky, often cranky fellow, rules his roost and the land beyond with few cares beyond marking each part of the day with his crowing and trying to sleep, strut, and sun himself without too many interruptions from the egg-sucking Ebenezer Rat, the tattletale John Wesley Weasel or the mournful boot-nosed dog Mundo Cani, who arrives out of nowhere and stays. But unbeknownst to Chauncticleer and the other animals, evil embodied in a monstrous, putrescent snake called Wyrm is imprisoned within the earth and they are its keepers. When Wyrm's minion Cockatrice—an unnaturally born snake-like rooster—gets a foothold in a neighboring land and the death and destruction he brings to it begin to spread like a choking odor, Chauncticleer and his fellow creatures must wage war. Their efforts seem doomed from the start. For what is a ragtag band of God's creatures—representing good in all its meekness—against the insidious powers of evil? The animals admirably defeat an army of basilisks and Chauncticleer goes on to kill Cockatrice, but these make a weak victory won at the cost of too many animal lives and Chauncticleer's own faith, which is lost with the realization that "it is entirely possible to win against the enemy, it is possible even to kill the enemy, and still to be defeated by the battle." Wyrm is subdued for an indefinite time when Mundo Cani sacrifices himself for the others by throwing himself into the serpent's eye, armed with the horn of the mysterious Dun Cow.

The war in *The Book of the Dun Cow* is a Vietnam-like experience—how many battles make the war?—and is just one of the modern infusions Wangerin gives to his fable. What also lends to the modern resonance of Wangerin's work, and what makes it truly original, is his ability to deliver a tale about morality that contains no moralisms. The book is full of obvious biblical parallels: Chauncticleer, for instance, is Job-like as he rails at God over the loss of his children, Moses-like as he doubts his abilities to be the chosen leader, and Noah-like as he calls all creatures together against impending doom. But he never really becomes any of those characters, just as the dog Mundo Cani is Christ-like but is clearly not

Christ. Readers are left to make what they will of Wangerin's changeable allusions and symbols, as well as his endings, which bring unsettling events to a conclusion but leave things far from settled.

—Tracy J. Sukraw

WARTSKI, Maureen (Ann) Crane. Also writes as M.A. Crane. American. Born in Ashiya, Japan, 25 January 1940: naturalized U.S. citizen, 1962. Educated at University of Redlands, 1958-59; Sophia University, B.A. 1962. Married Maximilian Wartski in 1962; two sons. Free-lance writer. *English Mainichi*, Kobe, Japan, reporter, 1957-58; teacher at public schools in Sharon, Massachusetts, 1968-69; high school history teacher in Sharon, 1978-79. Has also taught creative writing, conducted workshops and lectured on writing. Recipient: annual book award of the Child Study Committee at Bank Street College of Education, for *A Boat to Nowhere,* and honor book, for *A Long Way from Home,* both 1980; Magazine Merit award, Society of Children's Book Writers, 1990, for "A Watcher in the Shadows," *Boys' Life.* Agent: Howard Morhaim Literary Agency, 175 5th Ave., Suite 709, New York, NY 10010. Address: 15 Francis Rd., Sharon, MA 02067, U.S.A.

PUBLICATIONS FOR YOUNG ADULTS

Fiction

My Brother Is Special. Philadelphia, Westminster, 1979.
A Boat to Nowhere, illustrated by Dick Teicher. Philadelphia, Westminster, 1980.
A Long Way from Home. Philadelphia, Westminster, 1980.
The Lake Is on Fire. Philadelphia, Westminster, 1981.
My Name is Nobody. New York, Walker, 1988.
Belonging. New York, Fawcett, 1993.
Dark Silence. New York, Fawcett, forthcoming.

*

Maureen Crane Wartski comments:

Writing for me is reflective communication. It means seizing the heartbeat of the moment and burnishing it with thought and experience. We all were young once, and we all experienced the exhilarating, sometimes painful, often wonderful world of the young. In my writing for young adults I try to renew these moments.

Writing also means responsibility. When I was younger, the book that most held my attention was one that took me into myself and beyond myself. Now I try to present readers with their world, the problems of their world, and the choices they themselves have as they interact with this world.

*   *   *

Maureen Crane Wartski, who has a knack for telling realistic stories, writes equally well about both children of other countries and American teenagers. Courage is the common theme of her fiction, in which believable characters must contend with difficult situations.

A Boat to Nowhere relates the adventures of Mai, an adolescent Vietnamese girl; her little brother Loc; and their grandfather Van Chi. The time is shortly after the Communist takeover of Vietnam;

the setting, a remote Vietnamese fishing village. Mai, Loc, and their grandfather are forced to flee their homeland with Kien, a fourteen-year-old orphan who has come to live in their village. Wartski portrays their experiences through the eyes of children who do not understand why the world is so cruel and provides a bittersweet ending. Yet the ending is just a pause in the lives of the characters, for it is obvious there will be a sequel relating their new lives.

The sequel, *A Long Way from Home,* begins in a Hong Kong refugee camp, where the three children are awaiting word from Steve Olson, their American sponsor. Soon they are living in California. Kien, however, has trouble adjusting—he runs away to a fishing village where many Vietnamese refugees have settled, and finds himself mediating a dispute between the new arrivals and the American fishermen of the town. Even though he is a hero, he realizes that home is with the Olsons, and the book ends with his return to their house to take up the task of finding a place in American life. Wartski deals with prejudice directly in this story, making it clear that there are no easy answers.

Wartski's next two books deal with children who are physically rather than culturally different. In *My Brother Is Special,* Noni (Nora) Harlow is in the eighth grade, and her brother Kip is eight years old and mentally retarded; they have moved from California to Massachusetts, where the whole family is experiencing problems. Then Noni goes out for the track team and finds out about the Special Olympics, in which Kip eventually participates. Though Kip does not win the race, Noni learns that winning and popularity are not everything. Despite a few inconsistencies, such as Kip not being enrolled in school as legally required, the book treats the subject of families with handicapped children thoughtfully.

In *The Lake Is on Fire,* Ricky Talese, after being blinded in a freak accident, can only feel sorry for himself. When Ricky tries to commit suicide, some family friends take him to their mountain cabin. Though he used to love the cabin, nothing is the same since the accident that blinded him and killed his best friend. Moreover, Ricky now has to deal with King, a German shepherd, who dislikes people because a former owner mistreated him. Inadvertently, Ricky ends up alone in the cabin in the midst of a forest fire, with only King for company. He and the dog manage to survive by learning to trust each other, as Ricky risks his own life in order to rescue King and, through that action, regains his sense of competency. The depression often associated with sudden blindness is described very well here.

Holland, who has been abused by his alcoholic father, is the subject of *My Name Is Nobody,* in which the youth's severe emotional problems are profiled from his confused viewpoint. Abandoned by his father, Rob is taken in by Kurt Doyle, a retired policeman, after trying to kill himself. Under Kurt's tutelage, Rob learns how to sail a boat, and gradually develops some self-esteem. But he is continually beset by new problems, and once again suicide seems like the answer. Only when Kurt risks his own life intervening does Rob change his mind and, in a dramatic, save both of them. Again, the social commentary is gentle here, as Wartski shows societal institutions to be susceptible to human error.

Whether depicting youths confronting cultural, physical, or psychological problems, Wartski's young adult novels consistently evince both sensitivity and authenticity, and hold considerable appeal for contemporary adolescents struggling with issues of courage.

—Sharon Clontz Bernstein

WATSON, Sally (Lou). American. Born in Seattle, Washington, 28 January 1924. Educated at Reed College, B.A. 1950. Served in the United States Navy, 1944-46. Area representative, Great Books Foundation, Los Angeles, California, 1953-56; executive secretary, writer, and artist, Listen and Learn With Phonics (basic reading instruction), Oakland, California, 1957-63. Member of juvenile panel, Pacific Northwest Writers Conference, Seattle, Washington, 1962. Judo instructor, referee, and examiner, 1969-80. Copper enamelist, since 1976. Recipient: Brooklyn Community Woodward School's annual book award, 1959, for *To Build a Land;* named to *Hornbook* honor list, 1963, for *Witch of the Glens.* Agent: McIntosh and Otis, Inc., 475 Fifth Ave., New York, NY 10017. Address: "Sutemi," Fairview Rd., Headley Down, Bordon, Hampshire, England.

PUBLICATIONS FOR YOUNG ADULTS

Fiction

Highland Rebel. New York, Holt, 1954.
Mistress Malapert. New York, Holt, 1955.
To Build a Land. New York, Holt, 1957.
Poor Felicity. New York, Doubleday, 1961.
Witch of the Glens. New York, Viking, 1962.
Lark. New York, Holt, 1964.
Other Sandals. New York, Holt, 1966.
Hornet's Nest. New York, Holt, 1967.
The Mukhtar's Children. New York, Holt, 1968.
Jade. New York, Holt, 1969.
Magic at Wychwood. New York, Knopf, 1970.
Linnet. New York, Dutton, 1971.

*   *   *

The central theme of Sally Watson's fiction, from her historical novels to her stories about emergent Israel, is the difficulty that adolescents experience in adjusting to adult society, their peers, and even themselves. Her heroines and heroes struggle against political upheaval, exile from their homes, and cultural codes too rigid to contain them comfortably. But despite the daunting problems facing Watson's beleaguered teenagers, her novels not only trace the protagonists' attainment of the blend of wisdom, courage, and flexibility that will prepare them for happiness in the adult world, but suggest that these qualities also help young adults to change adult society to suit themselves. It is this respect for the good sense, emotional strength, and capability of her main characters (and, by implication, the reader who identifies with them), as much as the wit of the dialogue or the suspense of the plots, that makes Watson's works so engaging.

A major source of conflict in these novels is the practice of stereotyping. In the Middle Eastern fictions—*To Build a Land, Other Sandals,* and *The Mukhtar's Children*—the problems that stem from judging people in terms of their membership in a group instead of individually are most obvious in a religious context. The young refugees of *To Build a Land,* for instance, are survivors of Hitler's Europe whose attempts to turn the Israel of 1947 into a home are complicated by the violent resentments of some of their Arab neighbors. The narrative makes clear, however, that neither side can afford to condemn the other *en masse,* and that seeing an opponent's viewpoint is essential to national concord and even to inner peace. Similarly, *Other Sandals* (set in the mid-1960s) traces the parallel development of a city boy, Eytan, and a kibbutz girl, Devra, when they trade places for a summer: Eytan abandons his fear-based prejudice against belonging to a community, while Devra overcomes her hatred of Arabs. Meanwhile, *The Mukhtar's Children* provides a sympathetic look at a family on the other side of the Arab-Israeli conflict.

If xenophobia (ranging from Devra's pathological dislike of the culturally alien to Eytan's bitterness against anyone other than himself) is the major issue in Watson's Middle East novels, her historical works often focus on the frustrations felt by girls confronting the rigid rules that surround gender, class, or race. As the eponymous heroine of *Jade* puts it, few relish "being marked down as a sort of second-rate human just because of the body [they] happened to get born into." For many of Watson's heroines, the solution is to take on, at least temporarily, the attributes of another "body." Thus Valerie Leigh of *Mistress Malapert* and Lauren Cameron of *Highland Rebel* disguise themselves as boys, the one to go on the Elizabethan stage, the other to fight for Bonnie Prince Charlie. Lauchlin MacLeod trades her Scottish heritage for American citizenship in *The Hornet's Nest,* simultaneously learning to combine young ladyhood with revolutionary fervor; similarly, pioneer Felicity Dare moves from Virginia to Seattle and from invalid to capable tomboy in *Poor Felicity*. Kelpie in *Witch of the Glens* and Lark Lennox in *Lark* alternately adopt and shed Roundhead garb in their efforts to defeat the narrow-minded cruelty Puritanism represents in these novels. Finally, Jade Lennox, perhaps the most outspokenly rebellious of Watson's many feisty heroines, cuts her hair and puts on velvet breeches to sail with the cross-dressing pirates Anne Bonney and Mary Read, mounting her own crusade against hypocrisy, slavery, and boredom.

Each of these novels suggests that adolescence, and ultimately adulthood, is the state of becoming a new person. But if growing up holds out on the promise of sexual maturity (each heroine meets a male counterpart who appreciates her intelligence and spirit), it also threatens to enforce conformity and shatter idealism. The challenge for Watson's protagonists is to retain the virtues of childhood—resilience, honesty, impatience with convention—while developing the empathy and self-knowledge essential to wisdom. Her focus on the unjust social practices that disturb her central characters, such as slavery in Virginia or the Act of Proscription in Scotland, emphasizes that those in power all too often fail the moral tests that age imposes.

If these novels identify rigidity and lack of fellow feeling as the root of most evil, the solution to these flaws is implied in the structure of Watson's oeuvre. The Israeli tales trace the experiences of the "family" of Gan Shalom over two generations; the historical novels sketch a ten-generation pedigree within which each heroine is ultimately tied to the heroines of the other novels in the sequence, whether by birth or by marriage. (For instance, Valerie of *Mistress Malapert* is the ancestress of every protagonist save Kelpie, who eventually joins the bloodline when her grandson marries Valerie's great-great-great-granddaughter Jade.) This narrative strategy not only rewards the assiduous reader with glimpses at the later lives of favorite characters and makes plausible the strong likeness among all these young people, but suggests a sense of kinship as a remedy for the bigotry and lack of sympathy that darkens the historical picture the novels describe.

Watson's works clearly continue a tradition of American historical novels dealing with the maturation of a hoyden into a woman of character and competence (Carol Ryrie Brink's *Caddie Woodlawn*

and Caroline Dale Snedeker's *Downright Dencey* are earlier examples). Equally clear in their emphasis on youthful idealism, freedom, and the rights of the oppressed, they reflect the concerns of the 1960s, the decade in which most of Watson's fiction was published. But because of the skill with which she mixes moralism with humor, adventure, and lively characterization in her most successful works—*Jade, The Hornet's Nest,* and *Witch of the Glens*—they are by no means dated. Although in the absence of reissues Watson's novels are increasingly difficult to find, they retain their appeal for young readers seeking strong heroines and vividly drawn settings.

—Claudia Nelson

WELLS, H(erbert) G(eorge). British. Born in Bromley, Kent, 21 September 1866. Educated at Mr. Morley's Bromley Academy until age 13; certificate in book-keeping; apprentice draper, Rodgers and Denyer, Windsor, 1880; pupil-teacher at a school in Wookey, Somerset, 1880; apprentice chemist in Midhurst, Sussex, 1880-81; apprentice draper, Hyde's Southsea Drapery Emporium, Hampshire, 1881-83; student/assistant, Midhurst Grammar School, 1883-84; studied at Normal School (now Imperial College) of Science, London (editor, *Science School Journal*) 1884-87; teacher, Holt Academy, Wrexham, Wales, 1887-88, and at Henley House School, Kilburn, London, 1889; B.Sc. (honours) in zoology 1890, and D.Sc. 1943, University of London. Married 1) his cousin Isabel Mary Wells in 1891 (separated 1894; divorced 1895); 2) Amy Catherine Robbins in 1895 (died 1927), two sons; had one daughter by Amber Reeves, and one son by Rebecca West, the writer Anthony West. Rodgers and Denyer, Windsor, England, apprentice draper, 1880; pupil-teacher at school in Wookey, England, 1880; apprentice pharmacist in Midhurst, England, 1880-81; Hyde's Southsea Drapery Emporium, Hampshire, England, apprentice draper, 1881-83; student-assistant at grammar school in Midhurst, 1883-84; teacher at schools in Wrexham, Wales, 1887-88, and London, 1889; Tutor, University Tutorial College, London, 1890-93; full-time writer from 1893; theatre critic, *Pall Mall Gazette,* London, 1895; member of the Fabian Society, 1903-1908; Member of Research Committee for the League of Nations, 1917; affiliated with British Ministry of Information, 1918; director of Policy Committee for Propaganda in Enemy Countries, 1918; Labour candidate for Parliament, for the University of London, 1922, 1923; lived mainly in France, 1924-33. International president, PEN, 1934-46. Recipient: D.Litt: Universtity of London, 1936. Honorary fellow, Imperial College of Science and Technology, London. *Died 13 August 1946.*

PUBLICATIONS

Novels

The Time Machine: An Invention. London, Heinemann, and New York, Holt, 1895; as *The Definitive Time Machine: A Critical Edition,* edited by Harry M. Geduld, Bloomington, Indiana University Press, 1987.
The Wonderful Visit. London, Dent, and New York, Macmillan, 1895.

The Island of Doctor Moreau: A Possibility. London, Heinemann, and New York, Stone and Kimball, 1896.

The Wheels of Chance: A Holiday Adventure, illustrated by J. Ayton Symington. London, Dent, 1896; as *The Wheels of Chance: A Bicycling Idyll,* New York, Macmillan, 1896.

The Invisible Man: A Grotesque Romance. London, Pearson, and New York, Arnold, 1897; as *The Invisible Man: A Fantastic Sensation,* Cambridge, Massachusetts, Bentley, 1981.

The War of the Worlds. London, Heinemann, and New York, Harper, 1898.

When the Sleeper Wakes. London and New York, Harper, 1899; revised edition, as *The Sleeper Awakes,* London, Nelson, 1910.

Love and Mr. Lewisham: The Story of a Very Young Couple. London, Harper, and New York, Stokes, 1900.

The First Men in the Moon. London, Newnes, and Indianapolis, Bowen Merrill, 1901.

The Sea Lady: A Tissue of Moonshine. London, Methuen, 1902; as *The Sea Lady,* New York, Appleton, 1902.

The Food of the Gods, and How It Came to Earth. London, Macmillan, and New York, Scribner, 1904.

Kipps: A Monograph. London, Macmillan, and New York, Scribner, 1905; as *Kipps: The Story of a Simple Soul.* 1905.

A Modern Utopia, illustrated by E.J. Sullivan. London, Chapman and Hall, and New York, Scribner, 1905.

In the Days of the Comet. London, Macmillan, and New York, Century, 1906.

Tono-Bungay. New York, Duffield, 1908; London, Macmillan, 1909.

The War in the Air, and Particularly How Mr. Bert Smallways Fared While It Lasted. London, Bell, and New York, Macmillan, 1908.

Ann Veronica: A Modern Love Story. London, Unwin, and New York, Harper, 1909.

The History of Mr. Polly. London, Nelson, and New York, Duffield, 1910.

The New Machiavelli. London, Lane, and New York, Duffield, 1911.

Marriage. London, Macmillan, and New York, Duffield, 1912.

The Passionate Friends: A Novel. London, Macmillan, and New York, Harper, 1913.

The Wife of Sir Isaac Harman. London and New York, Macmillan, 1914.

The World Set Free: A Story of Mankind. London, Macmillan, and New York, Dutton, 1914.

Bealby: A Holiday. London, Methuen, and New York, Macmillan, 1915.

Boon, The Mind of the Race, The Wild Asses of the Devil, and The Last Trump: Being a First Selection From the Literary Remains of George Boon, Appropriate to the Times, Prepared for Publication by Reginald Bliss With an Ambiguous Introduction by H.G. Wells (as Reginald Bliss). London, Unwin, and New York, Doran, 1915; under name H.G. Wells, London, Unwin, 1920.

The Research Magnificent. London and New York, Macmillan, 1915.

Mr. Britling Sees It Through. London, Cassell, and New York, Macmillan, 1916.

The Soul of a Bishop: A Novel—With Just a Little Love in It—About Conscience and Religion and the Real Troubles of Life. London, Cassell, 1917; as *The Soul of a Bishop,* New York, Macmillan, 1917.

Joan and Peter: The Story of an Education. London, Cassell, and New York, Macmillan, 1918.

The Undying Fire: A Contemporary Novel. London, Cassell, and New York, Macmillan, 1919.

The Secret Places of the Heart. London, Cassell, and New York, Macmillan, 1922.

Men Like Gods: A Novel. London, Cassell, and New York, Macmillan, 1923.

The Dream: A Novel. London, Cape, and New York, Macmillan, 1924.

Christina Alberta's Father. London, Cape, and New York, Macmillan, 1925.

The World of William Clissold: A Novel at a New Angle. London, Benn, 3 vols., and New York, Doran, 2 vols., 1926.

Meanwhile: The Picture of a Lady. London, Benn, and New York, Doran, 1927.

Mr. Blettsworthy on Rampole Island. London, Benn, and New York, Doubleday, 1928.

The King Who Was a King: The Book of a Film. London, Benn, 1929; as *The King Who Was a King: An Unconventional Novel,* New York, Doubleday, 1929.

The Autocracy of Mr. Parham: His Remarkable Adventures in This Changing World. London, Heinemann, and New York, Doubleday, 1930.

The Bulpington of Blup: Adventures, Poses, Stresses, Conflicts, and Disaster in a Contemporary Brain. London, Hutchinson, 1932; New York, Macmillan, 1933.

The Shape of Things to Come: The Ultimate Revolution. London, Hutchinson, and New York, Macmillan, 1933; revised edition, as *Things to Come* (film story), London, Cresset Press, and New York, Macmillan, 1935.

The Croquet Player. London, Chatto and Windus, 1936; New York, Viking Press, 1937.

Brynhild. London, Methuen, 1937; as *Brynhild; or, The Show of Things,* New York, Scribner, 1937.

The Camford Visitation. London, Methuen, 1937.

Star Begotten: A Biological Fantasia. London, Chatto and Windus, and New York, Viking Press, 1937.

Apropos of Dolores. London, Cape, and New York, Scribner, 1938.

The Brothers: A Story. London, Chatto and Windus, and New York, Viking Press, 1938.

The Holy Terror. London, Joseph, and New York, Simon and Schuster, 1939.

All Aboard for Ararat. London, Secker and Warburg, 1940; New York, Alliance, 1941.

Babes in the Darkling Wood. London, Secker and Warburg, and New York, Alliance, 1940.

You Can't Be Too Careful: A Sample of Life, 1901-1951. London, Secker and Warburg, 1941; New York, Putnam, 1942.

The Wealth of Mr. Waddy: A Novel, edited with an introduction by Harris Wilson, preface by Harry T. Moore. Carbondale, Southern Illinois University Press, 1969.

A Story of the Days to Come. Corgi, 1976.

Short Stories

Select Conversations With an Uncle (Now Extinct) and Two Other Reminiscences. London, Lane, and New York, Merriam, 1895.

The Stolen Bacillus and Other Incidents. London, Methuen, 1895.

The Red Room. New York, Stone and Kimball, 1896.

The Plattner Story, and Others. London, Methuen, 1897.

Thirty Strange Stories. New York, Arnold, 1897.

A Cure for Love. New York, Scott, 1899.

Tales of Space and Time. London, Harper, and New York, Doubleday, 1899.

The Vacant Country. New York, Kent, 1899.

Twelve Stories and a Dream. London, Macmillan, 1903; New York, Scribner, 1905.

The Country of the Blind, and Other Stories. London, Nelson, 1911; revised edition of *The Country of the Blind,* London, Golden Cockerel Press, 1939.

The Door in the Wall, and Other Stories. New York, Kennerley, 1911; London, Richards, 1915.

The Star. Pitman, 1913.

Tales of the Unexpected [of Life and Adventure, of Wonder], edited by J.D. Beresford, introduction by Frank Wells. London, Collins, 3 vols., 1922-23.

The Short Stories of H.G. Wells. London, Benn, 1927; New York, Doubleday, 1929; as *The Complete Short Stories of H.G. Wells,* London, Benn, 1966, and New York, St. Martin's, 1970.

The Adventures of Tommy (for children), illustrated by the author. London, Harrap, and New York, Stokes, 1929.

The Stolen Body, and Other Tales of the Unexpected. London Book, 1931.

The Favorite Short Stories of H.G. Wells. New York, Doubleday, 1937; as *The Famous Short Stories of H.G. Wells,* Garden City Publishing, 1938.

Short Stories by H.G. Wells. London, Nelson, 1940.

The Empire of the Ants. Todd, 1943.

The Inexperienced Ghost. Todd, 1943.

The Land Ironclads. Todd, 1943.

The New Accelerator. Todd, 1943.

The Truth About Pyecraft, and Other Short Stories. Todd, 1943.

The Inexperienced Ghost and The New Accelerator. Vallancey Press, 1944.

Twenty-eight Science Fiction Stories. New York, Dover, 1952.

Seven Stories. New York, Oxford University Press, 1953.

The Desert Daisy (for children), introduction by Gordon N. Ray. Pittsburg, Pennsylvania, Beta Phi Mu, 1957.

Selected Short Stories. London, Penguin, 1958.

The Valley of Spiders. London, Collins, 1964.

The Cone. London, Collins, 1965.

The Inexperienced Ghost, and Nine Other Stories. New York, Bantam, 1965.

Best Science Fiction Stories of H.G. Wells. New York, Dover, 1966.

The Man With a Nose: And the Other Uncollected Short Stories of H.G. Wells, edited with an introduction by J.R. Hammond. London, Athlone Press, 1984.

The Complete Short Stories of H.G. Wells. London, Black, and New York, St. Martin's Press, 1987.

Plays

Kipps, with Rudolf Besier, adaptation of the novel by Wells (produced London, 1912).

The Wonderful Visit, with St. John Ervine, adaptation of the novel by Wells (produced London, 1921).

Things to Come: A Film Story Based on the Material Contained in His History of the Future "The Shape of Things to Come". New York, Macmillan, 1935.

The Man Who Could Work Miracles: A Film Story Based on the Material Contained in His Short Story "Man Who Could Work Miracles." London, Cresset Press, 1936; as *The Man Who Could Work Miracles: A Film by H.G. Wells, Based on the Short Story Entitled "The Man Who Could Work Miracles,"* New York, Macmillan, 1936.

Hoopdriver's Holiday, adaptation of his novel *The Wheels of Chance,* edited by Michael Timko. Lafayette, Indiana, Purdue University English Department, 1964.

Also author of *H.G. Wells Comedies (Bluebottle, The Tonic, Daydreams),* with Frank Wells, 1928.

Nonfiction

Text-Book of Biology, introduction by G.B. Howes. London, Clive, Volume 1, 1892; Volume 2, 1893; revised edition, as *Text-Book of Zoology* by A.M. Davies, 1898; revised edition, by J.T. Cunningham and W.H. Leigh-Sharpe, 1929.

Honours Physiography, with R.A. Gregory. London, Hughes, 1893.

Certain Personal Matters: A Collection of Material, Mainly Autobiographical. London, Lawrence and Bullen, 1897.

Anticipations of the Reaction of Mechanical and Scientific Progress Upon Human Life and Thought. London, Champman and Hall, 1901; New York, Harper, 1902.

The Discovery of the Future (lecture). London, Unwin, 1902; New York, Huebsch, 1913; revised edition, London, Cape, 1925.

Mankind in the Making. London, Chapman and Hall, 1903; New York, Scribner, 1904.

Faults of the Fabian (lecture). Privately printed, 1906.

The Future in America: A Search After Realities. London, Chapman and Hall, and New York, Harper, 1906.

Reconstruction of the Fabian Society. Privately printed, 1906.

Will Socialism Destroy the Home? London, Independent Labour Party, 1907.

First and Last Things: A Confession of Faith and a Rule of Life. London, Constable, and New York, Putnam, 1908; revised edition, London, Cassell, 1917; London, Watts, 1929.

New Worlds for Old. London, Constable, and New York, Macmillan, 1908; revised edition, London, Constable, 1914.

Floor Games (for children), illustrated by the author. London, Palmer, 1911; Boston, Small Maynard, 1912.

Editor with G.R.S. Taylor and Frances Evelyn Warwick, *The Great State: Essays in Construction.* London, Harper, 1912; as *Socialism and the Great State: Essays in Construction,* New York, Harper, 1914.

The Labour Unrest. London, Associated Newspapers, 1912.

Liberalism and Its Party. London, Good, 1913.

Little Wars: A Game for Boys From Twelve Years of Age to One Hundred and Fifty and for That More Intelligent Sort of Girls Who Like Boys' Games and Books With an Appendix on Kriegspiel (children's games). London, Palmer, and Boston, Small Maynard, 1913.

War and Common Sense. London, Associated Newspapers, 1913.

An Englishman Looks at the World: Being a Series of Unrestrained Remarks Upon Contemporary Matters. London, Cassell, 1914; as *Social Forces in England and America,* New York, Harper, 1914.

The War That Will End War. London, Palmer, and New York, Duffield, 1914; repirnted in part as *The War and Socialism,* London, Clarion Press, 1915.

The Peace of the World. London, Daily Chronicle, 1915.

The Elements of Reconstruction. London, Nisbet, 1916.

What Is Coming? A Forecast of Things After the War. London, Cassell, 1916; as *What Is Coming? A European Forecast,* New York, Macmillan, 1916.

God the Invisible King. London, Cassell, and New York, Macmillan, 1917.

Introduction to Nocturne. New York, Doran, 1917.

A Reasonable Man's Peace. London, Daily News, 1917.

War and the Future: Italy, France, and Britain at War. London, Cassell, 1917; as *Italy, France, and Britain at War,* New York, Macmillan, 1917.

British Nationalism and the League of Nations. London, League of Nations Union, 1918.

In the Fourth Year: Anticipations of a World Peace. London, Chatto and Windus, and New York, Macmillan, 1918; abridged edition, as *Anticipations of a World Peace,* London, Chatto and Windus, 1918.

History Is One. Boston, Ginn, 1919.

The Idea of a League of Nations: Prolegomena to the Study of World-Organisation, with Viscount Grey, Lionel Curtis, William Archer, H. Wickham Steed, A.E. Zimmern, J.A. Spender, Viscount Bryce, and Gilbert Murray. New York, Atlantic Monthly Press, 1919.

The Way to the League of Nations: A Brief Sketch of the Practical Steps Needed for the Formation of a League, with Viscount Grey, Gilbert Murray, J.A. Spender, A.E. Zimmern, H. Wickham Steed, Lionel Curtis, William Archer, Ernest Barker, G. Lowes Dickinson, John Hilton, and L.S. Woolf. New York, Oxford University Press, 1919.

Frank Swinnerton: Personal Sketches; Together With Notes and Comments on the Novels of Frank Swinnerton, with Arnold Bennett and Grant Overton. New York, Doran, 1920.

The Outline of History, Being a Plain History of Life and Mankind, with advice and editorial help of Ernest Barker, H.H. Johnston, E. Ray Lankester, and Gilbert Murray, illustrated by J.F. Horrabin. London, Newnes, 2 vols., and New York, Macmillan, 2 vols., 1920; as *The New and Revised Outline of History: Being a Plain History of Life and Mankind,* Garden City Publishing, 1931; as *The Enlarged and Revised Outline of History: Being a Plain History of Life and Mankind,* Kemp, Texas, Triangle Books, 1940; under original title revised and brought up to the end of World War II by Raymond Postgate, Garden City Publishing, 1949; as *The Outline of History: Being a Plain History of Life and Mankind From Primordial Life to Nineteen-sixty,* London, Cassell, 1961; under original title revised and brought up to date by Postgate and G.P. Wells, New York, Doubleday, 1971.

Russia in the Shadows. London, Hodder and Stoughton, 1920; New York, Doran, 1921.

The New Teaching of History, with a Reply to Some Recent Criticisms of "The Outline of History." London, Cassell, 1921.

The Salvaging of Civilization: The Probable Future of Mankind. London, Cassell, and New York, Macmillan, 1921.

A Short History of the World. London, Cassell, and New York, Macmillan, 1922; revised edition, London, Penguin, 1946.

Washington and the Hope of Peace. London, Collins, 1922; as *Washington and the Riddle of Peace,* New York, Macmillan, 1922.

The World, Its Debts, and the Rich Men. London, Finer, 1922.

Socialism and the Scientific Motive (lecture). Privately printed, 1923.

Contributor, *Thirty-one Stories by Thirty and One Authors,* edited by Ernest Rhys and C.A. Dawson Scott. Butterworth, 1923.

The P.R. Parliament. London, Proportional Representation Society, 1924.

The Story of a Great Schoolmaster: Being a Plain Account of the Life and Ideas of Sanderson of Oundle. London, Chatto and Windus, and New York, Macmillan, 1924.

Works (Atlantic edition). London, Unwin, and New York, Scribner, 28 vols., 1924.

A Year of Prophesying. London, Unwin, 1924; New York, Macmillan, 1925.

A Forecast of the World's Affairs. New York, Encyclopaedia Britannica, 1925.

A Short History of Mankind (adapted from *A Short History of the World* by E.H. Carter). New York, Macmillan, 1925.

Mr. Belloc Objects to "The Outline of History." London, Watts, 1926.

Works (Essex edition). London, Benn, 24 vols., 1926-27.

In Memory of Amy Catherine Wells. Privately printed, 1927.

Wells' Social Anticipations, edited by Harry W. Laidler. New York, Vanguard Press, 1927.

Editor and author of introduction, *The Book of Catherine Wells.* London, Chatto and Windus, 1928.

The Open Conspiracy: Blue Prints for a World Revolution. London, Gollancz, and New York, Doubleday, 1928; revised edition, as *The Open Conspiracy: Blue Prints for a World Revolution; a Second Version of This Faith of a Modern Man Made More Explicit and Plain,* London, Hogarth Press, 1930; revised edition, as *What Are We to Do With Our Lives?,* London, Heinemann, and New York, Doran, 1931; as *The Open Conspiracy,* New York, Gordon Press, 1979.

The Way the World Is Going: Guesses and Forecasts of the Years Ahead; Twenty-six Articles and a Lecture. London, Benn, 1928; New York, Doubleday, 1929.

The Common Sense of World Peace (lecture). London, Hogarth Press, 1929.

Imperialism and the Open Conspiracy. London, Faber, 1929.

Divorce as I See It, with Bertrand Russell, Fannie Hurst, Theodore Dreiser, Warwick Deeping, Rebecca West, Andre Maurois, and Lionel Feuchtwanger. Douglas, 1930.

Points of View: A Series of Broadcast Addresses, with G. Lowes Dickinson, Dean Inge, J.B.S. Haldane, Sir Oliver Lodge, and Sir Walford Davis. London, Unwin, 1930.

The Problem of the Troublesome Collaborator. Privately printed, 1930.

The Science of Life: A Summary of Contemporary Knowledge about Life and Its Possibilities, with Julian S. Huxley and G.P. Wells. London, Amalgamated Press, 3 vols., 1930; New York, Doubleday, 4 vols., 1931; revised edition, as "The Science of Life" series, New York, Doubleday, 1932; revised editon, as *Science of Life Series,* London, Cassell, 9 vols., 1934-37.

Settlement of the Trouble Between Mr. Thring and Mr. Wells: A Footnote to the Problem of the Troublesome Collaborator. Privately printed, 1930.

The Way to World Peace. London, Benn, 1930.

The New Russia: Eight Talks Broadcast, with H.R. Knickerbocker, Sir John Russell, Sir Bernard Pares, Margaret S. Miller, B. Mouat-Jones, Stafford Talbot, and Frank Owen. London, Faber, 1931.

Selections From the Early Prose Works of H.G. Wells. University of London Press, 1931.

The Work, Wealth, and Happiness of Mankind. New York, Doubleday, 2 vols., 1931; London, Heinemann, 1 vol., 1932; revised edition, Heinemann, 1934; as *The Outline of Man's Work and Wealth,* New York, Doubleday, 1936.

After Democracy: Addresses and Papers on the Present World Situation. London, Watts, 1932.

What Should Be Done—Now. New York, Day, 1932.

Experiment in Autobiography: Discoveries and Conclusions of a Very Ordinary Brain (since 1866), illustrated by the author. London, Gollancz-Cresset Press, 2 vols., and New York, Macmillan, 1 vol., 1934.

Stalin-Wells Talk: The Verbatim Record, and A Discussion, with others. London, New Statesman and Nation, 1934.

The New America: The New World. London, Cresset Press, and New York, Macmillan, 1935.

The Anatomy of Frustration: A Modern Synthesis. London, Cresset Press, and New York, Macmillan, 1936.

The Idea of a World Encyclopaedia. London, Hogarth Press, 1936.

World Brain. London, Methuen, and New York, Doubleday, 1938.

The Fate of Homo Sapiens: An Unemotional Statement of the Things That Are Happening to Him Now and of the Immediate Possibilities Confronting Him. London, Secker and Warburg, 1939; as *The Fate of Man: An Unemotional Statement of the Things That Are Happening to Him Now and of the Immediate Possibilities Confronting Him,* New York, Alliance, 1939.

Travels of a Republican Radical in Search of Hot Water. London, Penguin, 1939.

The Common Sense of War and Peace: World Revolution or War Unending? London, Penguin, 1940.

H.G. Wells, S. de Madariaga, J. Middleton Murry, C.E.M. Joad on the New World Order. National Peace Council, 1940.

The New World Order, Whether It Is Attainable, How It Can Be Attained, and What Sort of World a World at Peace Will Have to Be. London, Secker and Warburg, and New York, Knopf, 1940.

The Rights of Man; or, What Are We Fighting For? London, Penguin, 1940.

Guide to the New World: A Handbook of Constructive World Revolution. London, Gollancz, 1941.

The Pocket History of the World. New York, Pocket Books, 1941.

The Conquest of Time. London, Watts, 1942.

Modern Russian and English Revolutionaries: A Frank Exchange of Ideas Between Commander Lev Uspensky, Soviet Writer, and H.G. Wells. Privately printed, 1942.

The New Rights of Man. Girard, Kansas, Haldeman Julius, 1942.

The Outlook for Homo Sapiens: An Unemotional Statement of the Things That Are Happening to Him Now, and of the Immediate Possibilities Confronting Him (revised versions of *The Fate of Homo Sapiens* and *The New World Order*). London, Secker and Warburg, 1942.

Phoenix: A Summary of the Inescapable Conditions of World Reorganisation. London, Secker and Warburg, 1942; Girard, Kansas, Haldeman Julius, n.d.

Science and the World-Mind. London, New Europe, 1942.

A Thesis on the Quality of Illusion in the Continuity of Individual Life of the Higher Metazoa, with Particular Reference to the Species Homo Sapiens. Privately printed, 1942.

Crux Ansata: An Indictment of the Roman Catholic Church. London, Penguin, 1943; New York, Agora, 1944.

The Mosley Outrage. London, Daily Worker, 1943.

'42 to '44: A Contemporary Memoir Upon Human Behaviour During the Crisis of the World Revolution. London, Secker and Warburg, 1944.

Reshaping Man's Heritage: Biology in the Service of Man, with J.S. Huxley and J.B.S. Haldane. London, Unwin, 1944.

The Happy Turning: A Dream of Life. London, Heinemann, 1945.

Marxism vs. Liberalism: An Interview (interview with Joseph Stalin). New York, Century, 1945; as *H.G. Wells' Interview With J.V. Stalin (Marxism v. Liberalism),* Sydney, Australia, Current Book Distributors, 1950.

Mind at the End of Its Tether. London, Heinemann, 1945.

Mind at the End of Its Tether, and The Happy Turning. New York, Didier, 1945.

The Desert Daisy (for children), edited by Gordon N. Ray. Urbana, University of Illinois Press, 1957.

Henry James and H.G. Wells: A Record of Their Friendship, Their Debate on the Art of Fiction, and Their Quarrel, edited by Leon Edel and Gordon N. Ray. Urbana, University of Illinois Press, and London, Hart Davis, 1958.

Arnold Bennett and H.G. Wells: A Record of a Personal and a Literary Friendship, edited by Harris Wilson. London, Hart Davis, 1960.

George Gissing and H.G. Wells: Their Friendship and Correspondence, edited by Royal A. Gettmann. London, Hart Davis, 1961.

Journalism and Prophecy, 1893-1946: An Anthology, edited by W. Warren Wagar. Boston, Houghton Mifflin, 1964; revised edition, London, Bodley Head, 1965.

Contributor, *Masterpieces of Science Fiction,* edited by Sam Moskowitz. World Publishing, 1967.

H.G. Wells's Literary Criticism, edited by Patrick Parrinder and Robert M. Philmus. Brighton, Harvester Press, 1980.

H.G. Wells in Love: Postscript to an Experiment in Autobiography, edited by G.P. Wells. London, Faber, 1984.

Treasury of H.G. Wells. New York, Octopus Books, 1985.

Other

Socialism and the Family (pamphlet; contains "Socialism and the Middle Classes" and "Modern Socialism and the Family"). London, Fifield, 1906; Boston, Ball, 1908.

This Misery of Boots (pamphlet). London, Fabian Society, 1907; Boston, Ball, 1908.

The H.G. Wells Calendar: A Quotation From the Works of H.G. Wells for Every Day in the Year, selected by Rosamund Marriott Watson. London, Palmer, 1911.

Great Thoughts From H.G. Wells, selected by Rosamund Marriott Watson. Dodge, 1912.

Thoughts From H.G. Wells, selected by Elsie E. Morton. London, Harrap, 1913.

Democracy Under Revision: A Lecture Delivered at the Sorbonne, March 15th, 1927 (pamphlet). London, Hogarth Press, and New York, Doran, 1927.

The H.G. Wells Papers at the University of Illinois, edited by Gordon N. Ray. Urbana, University of Illinois Press, 1958.

H.G. Wells: Early Writings in Science and Science Fiction, edited by Robert M. Philmus and David Y. Hughes. Berkeley, University of California Press, 1975.

H.G. Wells Science Fiction Treasury. New York, Crown, 1987.

The Discovery of the Future, with The Common-Sense of World Peace and The Human Adventure, edited by Patrick Parrinder. London, PNL, 1989.

Also author of *Two Hemispheres or One World?,* 1940.

*

Media Adaptations: Numerous works by Wells have been adapted as comic books, films, plays, sound recordings, and radio and television productions, including *The Shape of Things to Come* (film), 1936; *The War of the Worlds* (radio broadcast), Columbia Broadcasting System, 1938.

Biography: *H.G. Wells: A Sketch for a Portrait* by Geoffrey H. West, Howe, 1930; *H.G. Wells: A Biography,* London, Longman, 1951; *H.G. Wells and His Family, As I Have Known Them* by Mathilde Marie Meyer, Chicago, Illinois, International Publishing, 1956; *The Life and Thought of H.G. Wells* by Julius Kagarlitsky (translated by Moura Budberg), London, Sidgwick and Jackson, 1966; *H.G. Wells* by Richard Hauer Costa, New York, Twayne, 1967, revised edition, 1985; *H.G. Wells: His Turbulent Life and Times* by Lovat Dickson, London, Macmillan, 1969; *I Told You So! A Life of H.G. Wells* by James Playsted Wood, New York, Pantheon, 1969; *Bertie: The Life After Death of H.G. Wells* by Elizabeth Hawley and Columbia Rossi, London, New English Library, 1973; Entry in *Dictionary of Literary Biography,* Volume 34, Detroit, Gale, 1985; Volume 70, 1988; *The Time Traveller: The Life of H.G. Wells* by Norman and Jeanne Mackenzie, London, Weidenfeld and Nicolson, 1973, as *H.G. Wells: A Biography,* New York, Simon and Schuster, 1973; *H.G. Wells: A Pictorial Biography* by Frank Wells, London, Jupiter, 1977; *H.G. Wells: Aspects of a Life* by Anthony West, London, Hutchinson, and New York, Random House, 1984; *H.G. Wells: Desperately Mortal: A Biography* by David C. Smith, New Haven, Connecticut, Yale University Press, 1986.

Bibliography: *The Works of H.G. Wells, 1887-1925: A Bibliography, Dictionary, and Subject-Index* by Geoffrey H. Wells, London, Routledge, 1926; *H.G. Wells: A Comprehensive Bibliography,* London, H.G. Wells Society, 1966, revised editions, 1968, 1972, 1986; *Herbert George Wells: An Annotated Bibliography of His Works* by J.R. Hammond, New York, Garland, 1977; *An H.G. Wells Companion: A Guide to the Novels, Romances, and Short Stories* by J.R. Hammond, New York, Macmillan, 1979.

Manuscript Collection: University of Illinois, Urbana.

Critical Studies (selection): *H.G. Wells* by John Davys Beresford, London, Nisbet, 1915, reprinted, Brooklyn, New York, Haskell House, 1972; *The World of H.G. Wells* by Van Wyck Brooks, New York, Mitchell Kennerley, and London, T. Fisher Unwin, 1915; *A Companion to Mr. Wells's "Outline of History,"* by Hilaire Belloc, Kansas City, Missouri, Sheed and Ward, 1926; *Mr. Belloc Still Objects* by Hilaire Belloc, Kansas City, Missouri, Sheed and Ward, 1926; *The Early H.G. Wells: A Study of the Scientific Romances* by Bernard Bergonzi, Manchester, Manchester University Press, 1961, and *H.G. Wells: A Collection of Critical Essays* edited by Bernard Bergonzi, Englewood Cliffs, New Jersey, Prentice Hall, 1976; *H.G. Wells: An Outline* by F.K. Chaplin, London, P.R. Macmillan, 1961; *H.G. Wells and the World State* by W. Warren Wagar, New Haven, Connecticut, Yale University Press, 1961; *H.G. Wells and His Critics* by Ingvald Raknem, London, Unwin, 1962; essay in *A Soviet Heretic* by Yevgeny Zamyatin (translated by Mirra Ginsburg), Chicago, University of Chicago Press, 1970; *H.G. Wells* by Patrick Parrinder, Edinburgh, Oliver and Boyd, 1970, New York, Capricorn, 1977, and *H.G. Wells: The Critical Heritage* edited by Patrick Parrinder, London, Routledge, 1972; *H.G. Wells: Critic of Progress* by Jack Williamson, Baltimore, Mirage Press, 1973; *H.G. Wells and Rebecca West* by Gordon N. Ray, New Haven, Connecticut, Yale University Press, and London, Macmillan, 1974; *The Scientific Romances of H.G. Wells* by Stephen Gill, Cornwall, Ontario, Vesta, 1975; *Anatomies of Egotism: A Reading of the Last Novels of H.G. Wells* by Robert Bloom, Lincoln, University of Nebraska Press, 1977; *H.G. Wells in the Cinema* by Alan Wykes, London, Jupiter, 1977; *H.G. Wells and Modern Science Fiction* edited by Darko Suvin and Robert M. Philmus, Lewisburg, Pennsylvania, Bucknell University Press, 1977; *The H.G. Wells Scrapbook* edited by Peter Haining, London, New English Library, 1978; *Who's Who in H.G. Wells* by Brian Ash, London, Elm Tree, 1979; *H.G. Wells, Discoverer of the Future: The Influence of Science on His Thought* by Roslynn D. Haynes, New York, New York University Press, and London, Macmillan, 1980; *H.G. Wells: Interviews and Recollections* edited by J.R. Hammond, London, Macmillan, 1980; *The Science Fiction of H.G. Wells: A Concise Guide* by P.H. Niles, Clifton Perk, New York, Auriga, 1980; *The Science Fiction of H.G. Wells* by Frank McConnell, New York, Oxford University Press, 1981; *H.G. Wells and the Culminating Ape: Biological Themes and Imaginative Obsessions* by Peter Kemp, London, Macmillan, and New York, St. Martin's Press, 1982; *The Logic of Fantasy: H.G. Wells and Science Fiction* by John Huntington, New York, Columbia University Press, 1982; *H.G. Wells* by Robert Crossley, Mercer Island, Washington, Starmont House, 1984; *H.G. Wells* by John Batchelor, London, Cambridge University Press, 1985; *H.G. Wells: Reality and Beyond* edited by Michael Mullin, Champaign, Illinois, Public Library, 1986; *The Prophetic Soul: A Reading of Things to Come* by Leon Stover, Jefferson, North Carolina, and London, McFarland, 1987; *H.G. Wells* by Michael Draper, London, Macmillan, and New York, St. Martin's Press, 1987; *Bennett, Wells, and Conrad: Narrative in Transition* by Linda R. Anderson, London, Macmillan, and New York, St. Martin's Press, 1988; *H.G. Wells* by Christopher Martin, Howe, Wayland, 1988; *H.G. Wells under Revision* edited by Patrick Parrinder and Christopher Rolfe, Selinsgrove, Pennsylvania, and London, Susquehanna University Presses, 1990; *H.G. Wells* by Brian Murray, New York, Continuum, 1990.

*   *   *

H.G. Wells, often considered the father of modern science fiction, helped popularize this genre and gave it a more solid foundation in science than it had ever enjoyed before. Wells was influenced by earlier writers—from Jonathan Swift to Jules Verne—but the prolific English author was better educated in science than any of them, and he developed a writing style that surpasses those of all but a few writers of science fiction.

Wells wrote over a hundred books, about fifty of them novels. His principal interest was the improvement of society—largely through the sensible application of scientific principles. While his nonfiction volumes contain some quite respectable titles, such as his *Outline of History* and *A Modern Utopia,* it is through his fiction that Wells became famous and is now still remembered and read. His novels generally fall into three categories—scientific romances, novels of personality and character, and novels of ideas—and Wells's reputation rests mainly upon the works of his early, "scientific" period: *The Time Machine, The Invisible Man,* and *The War of the Worlds.*

When *The Time Machine* was published, in 1895, it established Wells as a popular and influential writer. Some readers believe *The Time Machine* to be Wells's finest work, and several experts claim for it the distinction of being the best science fiction book ever written. Perhaps the most compelling feature of this novel is its realism, much of which is achieved by specific details and scientifically persuasive explanations that, if they do not supply absolute authenticity, do provide plausibility. When the Time Traveller (who is not named in the text) is explaining how his machine works, the details of his monologue contain materials regarding time as the fourth dimension that predate Einstein's theory by some years.

Wells's scientific novels gain much of their credibility from the fact that once the premise (as in this case, time travel) is accepted by the reader, the rest of the action seems quite believable. So, when the Time Traveller lands in the year 802701 and finds the Eloi (the weak little people who live above ground) and the Morlocks (the large, carnivorous creatures that live below ground), the situation may seem extreme, but not impossible, given the enormous amount of time that has passed. The book ends in a typically Wellsian fashion, with the Traveller lost somewhere in time.

One of Wells's most popular novels is *The Invisible Man,* which has been adapted for film, like several other of his books. The premise of invisibility is based on a known physical phenomenon: the refraction of light. The principal character, Griffin, is a scientist (as are many of Wells's protagonists) who has discovered this secret and has made himself invisible to all. The story is grim, owing something to the tradition of the Gothic novel, but it is replete with adventure as Griffin turns against everyone and finally meets his destruction by being beaten to death with shovels in the hands of irate citizens. The detailed and vivid style of Wells's writing in this novel is particularly effective, as when Griffin's dead body returns to visibility at the end: "his crushed chest...the dim outline of his drawn and battered features...there lay, naked and pitiful on the ground, the bruised and broken body of a young man about thirty."

Several critics have noted that Wells displayed, perhaps for the first time in English literature, a truly global view of the earth in *War of the Worlds.* This story of Martian invaders came at a time when readers were more interested in science than ever before and when there had been discovered on Mars indentations that resembled canals and thus which intensified speculation that there could be life on the Red Planet. The novel is a triumph of detail, even to the logical "fact" that the Martians have trouble moving about, since their planet, smaller than Earth, has less gravitational pull and therefore they feel much heavier here. Once more, the style is both realistic and expressive, as when one of the Martians is first seen leaving the spaceship: "A big greyish rounded bulk, the size, perhaps, of a bear, was rising slowly and painfully out of the cylinder. As it bulged up and caught the light, it glistened like wet leather." One of the most clever passages—a truly brilliant combination of a vivid imagination coupled with a sound knowledge of science—is the climax, where the Martians start to die off because they have no immunity to the bacteria of Earth. While the death rays they have used (not unlike the laser beams known today) and the poisonous gas (in a novel published well before the first such use, in World War I) employed are striking, the unexpected but quite believable ending is eminently satisfactory.

In this novel, Wells tried to do what he attempted in most of what he wrote: to help mankind attain a wiser, more informed attitude about the future of the human race. He wrote to a friend that perhaps such a catastrophe as a Martian invasion could bring the world's people to their senses and improve the state of society. Plenty of disasters have struck (many of them foretold by the insightful Englishman), and yet the problems remain. One can, though, give credit to H.G. Wells for a noble attempt to improve the future—his efforts in the scientific fiction novel remain among the most sensible and readable to be found anywhere.

—Fred McEwen

———

WELLS, Rosemary. American. Born in New York City, 29 January 1943. Educated at Red Bank High School, New Jersey; Museum School, Boston. Married Thomas Moore Wells in 1963; two daughters. Art editor, Allyn and Bacon, Inc., Boston, Massachusetts; art designer, Macmillan Publishing Co., Inc., New York City; free-lance author and illustrator, since 1968. Recipient: Children's Book Showcase award, Children's Book Council, 1974, for *Noisy Nora;* Art Book for Children citation, Brooklyn Museum and Brooklyn Public Library, 1975, 1976, 1977, for *Benjamin and Tulip;* Irma Simonton Black award, for *Benjamin and Tulip,* and 1975, for *Morris's Disappearing Bag: A Christmas Story;* runner-up for Edgar Allan Poe award, Mystery Writers of America, for *Through the Hidden Door,* and 1981, for *When No One Was Looking; Hazel's Amazing Mother* was named one of the *New York Times* Best Illustrated Books, 1985; Washington Irving Children's Book Choice award, Westchester Library Association, 1986, for *Peabody,* and 1988, for *Max's Christmas; Boston Globe-Horn Book* award, 1989, for *Shy Charles. Noisy Nora, Morris's Disappearing Bag, Leave Well Enough Alone, Stanley and Rhoda, Max's Toys, Max's Breakfast, Max's Bedtime, Max's Bath, When No One Was Looking, Max's Christmas, Shy Charles,* and *Max's Chocolate Chicken* were named among the best books of the year by *School Library Journal;* American Library Association (ALA) Notable Book citations for *Noisy Nora, Benjamin and Tulip, Morris's Disappearing Bag, Max's Breakfast, Max's Christmas, Max's Chocolate Chicken,* and *Max's Dragon Shirt;* ALA Best Books for Young Adults citation for *Through the Hidden Door;* Bulletin of the Center for Children's Books Blue Ribbon for *The Little Lame Prince; American Bookseller* Pick of the Lists citations for *Abdul, Stanley and Rhoda, Goodnight Fred, Timothy Goes to School, A Lion for Lewis, Forest of Dreams,* and *Max's Chocolate Chicken; Booklist* Children's Editor's Choice citations for *Max's Toys, Timothy Goes to School,* and *Through the Hidden Door;* Child Study Association Children's Books of the Year citations for *Morris's Disappearing Bag* and *Don't Spill It Again, James; Horn Book* Fanfare citation and West Australian Young Readers' Book award, both for *When No One Was Looking;* Virginia Young Readers award and New York Public Library Books for Teenagers citation, both for *The Man in the Woods;* Parents' Choice award, Parents' Choice Foundation, for *Shy Charles;* Golden Kite award, Society of Children's Book Writers, and International Reading Association Teacher's Choices List, both for *Forest of Dreams;* International Reading Association Children's Choices citation for *Max's Chocolate Chicken;* International Reading Association/Children's Book Council Children's Choice citations for *Timothy Goes to School, A Lion for Lewis,* and *Peabody;* Cooperative Children's Book Center citation for *Max's Bedtime.* Address: 732 Sleepy Hollow Rd., Briarcliff Manor, NY 10510, U.S.A.

PUBLICATIONS FOR YOUNG ADULTS

Fiction (illustrated by the author)

The Fog Comes on Little Pig Feet. New York, Dial, 1972.
None of the Above. New York, Dial, 1974.
Leave Well Enough Alone. New York, Dial, 1977.
When No One Was Looking. New York, Dial, 1980; London, Deutsch, 1984.
The Man in the Woods. New York, Dial, 1984; London, Deutsch, 1985.

Waiting for the Evening Star, paintings by Susan Jeffers. New York, Dial, 1993.

PUBLICATIONS FOR CHILDREN

Fiction (illustrated by the author)

John and the Rarey. New York, Funk & Wagnalls, 1969.
Michael and the Mitten Test. Englewood Cliffs, New Jersey, Bradbury, 1969.
The First Child. New York, Hawthorn, 1970.
Martha's Birthday. Englewood Cliffs, New Jersey, Bradbury, 1970.
Miranda's Pilgrims. Englewood Cliffs, New Jersey, Bradbury, 1970.
Unfortunately Harriet. New York, Dial, 1972.
Benjamin and Tulip. New York, Dial, 1973; London, Kestrel, 1977.
Abdul. New York, Dial, 1975.
Morris's Disappearing Bag: A Christmas Story. New York, Dial, 1975; London, Kestrel, 1977.
Stanley and Rhoda. New York, Dial, 1978; London, Kestrel, 1980.
Max's First Word [*New Suit, Ride, Toys, Bath, Bedtime, Breakfast, Birthday, Hooray for, Christmas, Chocolate Chicken, Dragon Shirt*]. New York, Dial, 12 vols., 1979-1991; London, Benn, 4 vols., 1980; London, Collins, 5 vols., 1985-86.
Good Night, Fred. New York, Dial, 1981; London, Macmillan, 1982.
Timothy Goes to School. New York, Dial, and London, Kestrel, 1981.
A Lion for Lewis. New York, Dial, and London, Macmillan, 1982.
Peabody. New York, Dial, 1983; London, Macmillan, 1984.
Hazel's Amazing Mother. New York, Dial, 1985; London, Collins, 1986.
Through the Hidden Door. New York, Dial, 1987.
Forest of Dreams, illustrated by Susan Jeffers. New York, Dial, and London, Collins, 1988.
Shy Charles. New York, Dial, and London, Collins, 1988.
The Little Lame Prince. New York, Dial, 1990.
Fritz and the Mess Fairy. New York, Dial, 1991.
First Tomato. New York, Dial, 1992.
The Island Light. New York, Dial, 1992.
Lucy's Come to Stay, pictures by Patricia Cullen-Clark. New York, Dial, 1992.
Moss Pillows. New York, Dial, 1992.
Max and Ruby's First Greek Myth: Pandora's Box. New York, Dial, 1993.

Poetry

Noisy Nora. New York, Dial, 1973; London, Collins, 1976.
Don't Spill It Again, James. New York, Dial, 1977.

Other

Contributor, *So I Shall Tell You a Story: The Magic World of Beatrix Potter.* New York, Warne, 1993.

PUBLICATIONS FOR ADULTS

Other

Cooking for Nitwits, with Joanna Hurley. New York, Dutton, 1989.

Media Adaptations: *Max's Christmas* and *Morris's Disappearing Bag* have been adapted as short films by Weston Woods.

Biography: Essay in *Something about the Author Autobiography Series,* Volume 1, Detroit, Gale, 1986.

Critical Studies: Entry in *Children's Literature Review,* Volume 16, Detroit, Gale, 1989; entry in *Contemporary Literary Criticism,* Volume 12, Detroit, Gale, 1980.

Illustrator: *A Song to Sing, O!* (from *Yeoman of the Guard*), 1968, and *The Duke of Plaza Toro* (from *The Gondoliers*), 1969, both by Williams Schwenck Gilbert and Arthur Sullivan; *Hungry Fred* by Paula Fox, 1969; *Why You Look Like You Whereas I Tend to Look Like Me* by Charlotte Pomerantz, 1969; *The Shooting of Dan McGrew and The Cremation of Sam McGee* by Robert Service, 1969; *The Cat That Walked by Himself* by Rudyard Kipling, 1970; *Marvin's Manhole* by Winifred Rosen, 1970; *Impossible, Possum* by Ellen Conford, 1971; *A Hot Thirsty Day* by Marjorie Weinman Sharmat, 1971; *Two Sisters and Some Hornets* by Beryl Epstein and Dorrit Davis, 1972; *With a Deep-Sea Smile* edited by Virginia A. Tashjian, 1974; *Tell Me a Trudy* by Lore Segal, 1977.

*   *   *

Although Rosemary Wells is more famous for her picture books, like *Noisy Nora* and *Stanley and Rhoda* in which anthropomorphic animals explore typical family problems, she has also developed another area of creativity: thrillers written for a teenage audience. In *When No One Was Looking* Kathy is a tennis champion with a determination to win and a fierce temper. However, when one of her opponents is murdered, Kathy has to discover who has drowned the girl. This is a book which is intriguing in its detection and also shows insights into teenage friendships. More intricately plotted and suitably tense is *The Man in the Woods,* in which Helen discovers a mysterious man in the woods who is supposed to be throwing rocks at car windscreens, a discovery that leads Helen and her friend Pinky into a deeper mystery involving drug trafficking.

These thrillers help to demonstrate Wells's versatility. Whichever direction her talent leads her in future years, thousands of children will be grateful to her for her creations of Nora, Morris, and all those other characters with sibling problems.

—Keith Barker

WERSBA, Barbara. American. Born in Chicago, Illinois, 19 August 1932. Educated at Bard College, B.A. 1954; studied acting at Neighborhood Playhouse and at the Paul Mann Actors Workshop; studied dance with Martha Graham. Actress in radio and television, summer stock, Off-Broadway, and touring companies, 1944-59; full-time writer, 1960—. Summer lecturer at New York University; writing instructor at Rockland Center for the Arts. Recipient: Deutscher Jugend Buchpreis, 1973, for *Run Softly, Go Fast;* American Library Association (ALA) Best Book for Young Adults and Notable Children's Book lists, both 1976, and National Book Award nomination, 1977, all for *Tunes for a Small Harmonica;* ALA Best Book for Young Adults, 1982, for *The Carnival in My Mind;* D.H.L.

from Bard College, 1977. Agent: McIntosh and Otis, Inc., 310 Madison Ave., New York, NY 10017. Address: Box 1892, Sag Harbor, NY 11963, U.S.A.

PUBLICATIONS FOR YOUNG ADULTS

Fiction

The Dream Watcher also see below. New York, Atheneum, 1968; London, Bodley Head, 1988.
Run Softly, Go Fast. New York, Atheneum, 1970.
The Country of the Heart. New York, Atheneum, 1975.
Tunes for a Small Harmonica. New York, Harper, 1976; London, Bodley Head, 1979.
The Carnival in My Mind. New York, Harper, 1982.
Crazy Vanilla. New York, Harper, 1986; London, Bodley Head, 1987.
Fat: A Love Story. New York, Harper, and London, Bodley Head, 1987.
Love Is the Crooked Thing. New York, Harper, and London, 1987.
Beautiful Losers. New York, Harper, and London, Bodley Head, 1988.
Just Be Gorgeous. New York, Harper, 1988; London, Bodley Head, 1989.
Wonderful Me. New York, Harper, 1989.
The Farewell Kid. New York, Harper, 1990.
The Best Place to Live Is the Ceiling. New York, Harper, 1990.
You'll Never Guess the End. New York, Harper, 1992.

Play

The Dream Watcher (adaptation of her novel of the same title), first produced in Westport, Connecticut, 1975; Seattle Repertory Theater, 1977.

PUBLICATIONS FOR CHILDREN

Fiction

The Boy Who Loved the Sea, illustrated by Margot Tomes. New York, Coward, 1961.
The Brave Balloon of Benjamin Buckley, illustrated by Tomes, New York, Atheneum, 1963.
The Land of Forgotten Beasts, illustrated by Tomes. New York, Atheneum, 1964; London, Gollancz, 1965.
A Song for Clowns, illustrated by Mario Rivoli. New York, Atheneum, 1965; London, Gollancz, 1966.
Let Me Fall before I Fly. New York, Atheneum, 1971.
Amanda, Dreaming, illustrated by Mercer Mayer. New York, Atheneum, 1973.
The Crystal Child, illustrated by Donna Diamond. New York, Harper, 1982.

Poetry

Do Tigers Ever Bite Kings?, illustrated by Rivoli. New York, Atheneum, 1966.
Twenty-six Starlings Will Fly through Your Mind, illustrated by David Palladini. New York, Harper, 1980.

Biography: Entry in Martha E. Ward and Dorothy A. Marquardt's *Authors of Books for Young People,* 2nd edition, New York, Scarecrow Press, 1971; essay in *Something about the Author Autobiography Series,* Volume 2, Detroit, Gale, 1986.

Critical Study: *Children's Literature Review,* Volume 3, Detroit, Gale, 1977. *Contemporary Literary Criticism,* Volume 30, Detroit, Gale, 1984; Kay E. Vandergrift, "Barbara Wersba," *Dictionary of Literary Biography,* Volume 52, Detroit, Gale, 1986, pp. 374-380.

*   *   *

Barbara Wersba began writing for children and young adults only after a fifteen-year career as a professional actress. As she recuperated from hepatitis in a friend's house on Martha's Vineyard, she began to realize that her acting career was over. When the friend said to her, "Barbara, why don't you write something?" she decided to do just that, and a few weeks later had completed a children's fantasy called *The Boy Who Loved the Sea.* The book was accepted for publication, and a new career had begun for her. Over the next five years, she wrote three more well-received children's fantasies and a volume of children's poetry, but it was her first novel for young adults, *The Dream Watcher,* that launched her on the most successful area of her career.

The Dream Watcher is the story of Albert Scully, a teenager who just doesn't fit into the society in which he must live; he does not want to go to college, get a job, or be a success. Then he meets Mrs. Orpha Woodfin, an aged grande dame and former actress, and they become friends. Before Orpha dies, she has helped Albert to come to terms with his "differentness" and to be proud of it. The book so impressed actress Eva LeGallienne that she asked Wersba to turn it into a play in which LeGallienne would act the role of Orpha Woodfin. *The Dream Watcher* was followed by *Run Softly, Go Fast,* a conflict-of-generation story of life in the 1960s also featuring a young misfit, who survives that era's drug scene and comes to terms with both himself and his alienated father.

In *The Country of the Heart,* Wersba again presents a story of an alienated young person, who finds himself as an artist and as a man through his relationship with an older woman. Steven's brief love affair with Hadley Norman is told in the form of a memoir after Hadley's death from cancer; as Steven remembers, he realizes that Hadley has given him much more than love, and he is a far better person for it. *Country* was followed by one of Wersba's best novels, *Tunes for a Small Harmonica. Tunes* is the story of J. F. McAllister, a brash young New York woman who falls in love with her rather dim and pale poetry teacher, Harold Murth. Believing him to be too poor to return to Cambridge and finish his thesis, McAllister learns to play the harmonica so that she can earn enough money as a street performer to send him to England. As it turns out, however, Harold is neither poor nor single, and he has completed his thesis; devastated, McAllister decides on suicide but is saved only when her best friend gives her a brand-new Hohner Chromatic harmonica in the key of C. McAllister is a spunky character with a wonderful sense of humor who is at the same time, like so many of Wersba's other characters, vulnerable; the reader admires her pluck and determination and rejoices when she resolves her problems.

Wersba's next book, *The Carnival in My Mind,* is another story of a New York loner, Harvey Beaumont. Fourteen years old and only five feet tall, he is struggling to get along until he meets aspiring young actress Chandler Brown. While not as strong as *Tunes,* this is a charming, tender, and sad love story.

Wersba's next novel, *Crazy Vanilla,* is a book which does reach the level of *Tunes for a Small Harmonica.* A son of privilege, Tyler Woodruff is still not a happy young man, feeling stifled by the demands of his socialite parents and his ambivalent relationship with his older brother Cameron, who has been banished from the family because he is gay. Tyler's only salvation is in photography; this coupled with his interest in wildlife leads him to use his camera in shooting the fauna of Long Island, but it also leads him to further isolation. Then he meets Mitzi, an impoverished young waitress whose life with her unstable mother is as bleak as Tyler's. Miraculously, however, Mitzi is also a fine amateur wildlife photographer, and from this shared interest, a warm and loving bond is created which leads both Tyler and Mitzi to grow and mature in the face of very real obstacles in their lives.

Three of Wersba's more recent books were something of a departure for her. *Fat: A Love Story, Love Is the Crooked Thing,* and *Beautiful Losers* all tell the tale of Rita Formica, a fat, five-foot-three extrovert who is a compulsive eater. In *Fat,* Rita, who works in a cheesecake bakery run by an older man called Arnold Bromberg, meets the love of her life, gorgeous athlete Robert Swann. She resolves to become thin and svelte, as well as tone down her personality. However, Robert is interested only in Rita's friend Nicole, so despite Rita's best attempts Robert remains aloof. A series of very funny misadventures leads brokenhearted Rita into the arms of—of all people—Arnold Blomberg, and the two sequels chart the ups and downs of their very unconventional romance. Along the way, Rita goes from child to woman and from everybody's clown to a self-sufficient adult at peace with herself.

Another popular character in three of Wersba's books is Heidi Rosenbloom, a sixteen-year-old resident of Manhattan who feels unattractive, untalented, and misunderstood by her parents. In *Just Be Gorgeous* she meets a homeless street performer, Jeffrey, and falls in love. He is gay, and Heidi finally accepts this but not before Jeffrey has given Heidi some appreciation of her worth as a human being. In *Wonderful Me* we meet Heidi again, still a little weird and still not totally convinced that she is at all attractive. She has informed her parents that she is not going to college but is going to be a professional dog walker, when suddenly she begins to receive sensitive and passionate love letters from a secret admirer—who turns out to be her English teacher, Mr. Moss. In *The Farewell Kid,* Heidi is eighteen and emancipated from parents, college, and men (at least in her own mind). Her passion for dogs (canine ones) leads her to start a business (Dog Rescue, Inc.) to help the strays she finds in the city's streets, but she soon realizes that she needs a partner to handle the business end while she handles the dogs. She finds a partner—and not only a business partner—in Harvey, in a funny and tender love story.

All of Wersba's novels have as their protagonists young men or women who refuse to shape themselves to society's mold. They are often alienated from their families and loners among their peers; they face their problems alone until someone equally unconventional enters the picture, and together they learn to accept themselves and a world that will always have sharp corners. Critics have sometimes faulted her books for these "unrealistic" characters and situations, but Wersba's sensitivity and honesty in dealing with her characters have made her a favorite with a whole generation of young readers.

—Audrey Eaglen

WEST, (Mary) Jessamyn. American. Born in Jennings County, Indiana, 18 July 1902. Educated at Union High School, Fullerton, California, graduated 1919; Whittier College, California, 1919, 1921-23; A.B. in English 1923; Fullerton Junior College, 1920-21; University of California, Berkeley, 1929-31; Oxford University, 1929. Married Harry Maxwell McPherson in 1923; one adopted daughter. Writer, 1935-84. Teacher and secretary, Hemet, California, 1924-29; taught at Bread Loaf Writers Conference, Vermont, Indiana University, Bloomington, University of Notre Dame, Indiana, University of Colorado, Squaw Valley University of Utah, Salt Lake City, University of Washington, Seattle, Stanford University, California, University of Montana, Portland University, University of Kentucky, and Loyola Marymount University. Visiting professor at Wellesley College, Massachusetts, University of California at Irvine, Mills College, and Whittier College. Visiting lecturer at numerous colleges. Recipient: Indiana Authors' Day award, 1956, for *Love, Death, and the Ladies' Drill Team;* Thermod Monsen award, 1958, for *To See the Dream;* California Commonwealth Club award, 1970, and California Literature Medal, 1971, both for *Crimson Ramblers of the World, Farewell;* Janet Kafke prize for fiction, 1976; Indiana Arts Commission award for Literature, 1977, for body of work. Honorary doctorates from Whittier College; Mills College, Oakland, California; Swarthmore College, Pennsylvania; Indiana University; University of Indiana—Terre Haute, Western College for Women, Oxford, Ohio; Wheaton College, Juniata College, and Wilmington College. *Died 23 February 1984.*

PUBLICATIONS

Novels

The Witch Diggers. New York, Harcourt, 1951; London, Heinemann, 1952.

Little Men, in *Star Short Novels,* edited by Frederik Pohl. New York, Ballantine, 1954; published separately, as *The Chile Kings,* 1967.

South of the Angels. New York, Harcourt, 1960; London, Hodder & Stoughton, 1961.

A Matter of Time. New York, Harcourt, 1966; London, Macmillan, 1967.

Leafy Rivers. New York, Harcourt, 1967; London, Macmillan, 1968.

The Massacre at Fall Creek. New York, Harcourt, and London, Macmillan, 1975.

The Life I Really Lived. New York, Harcourt, 1979.

The State of Stony Lonesome. New York, Harcourt, 1984.

Short Stories

The Friendly Persuasion. New York, Harcourt, 1945, reprinted, Buccaneer Books, 1982.

Cress Delahanty. New York, Harcourt, 1953; London, Hodder & Stoughton, 1954.

Love, Death, and the Ladies' Drill Team. New York, Harcourt, 1955; as *Learn To Say Goodbye,* London, Hodder & Stoughton, 1956.

Except for Me and Thee: A Companion to The Friendly Persuasion. New York, Harcourt, and London, Macmillan, 1969.

Crimson Ramblers of the World, Farewell. New York, Harcourt, 1970; London, Macmillan, 1971.

The Story of a Story and Three Stories. Berkeley, University of
California, 1982.
The Collected Stories of Jessamyn West. San Diego, Harcourt, 1986.

Plays

A Mirror for the Sky, music by Gail Kubik (produced Eugene,
Oregon, 1958). New York, Harcourt, 1948.

Screenplays: *Friendly Persuasion* (uncredited), with Michael Wilson, 1956; *The Big Country,* with others, 1958; *The Stolen Hours,*
1963.

Poetry

The Secret Look. New York, Harcourt, 1974.

Other

Contributor, *Cross Section 1948: A Collection of New American
Writing.* New York, Simon & Schuster, 1948.
The Reading Public (address). New York, Harcourt Brace, 1952.
Friends and Violence. Philadelphia, Friends General Conference,
n.d.
To See the Dream. New York, Harcourt, 1957; London, Hodder &
Stoughton, 1958.
Love Is Not What You Think. New York, Harcourt, 1959; as *A
Woman's Love,* London, Hodder & Stoughton, 1960.
Editor, *A Quaker Reader.* New York, Viking, 1962.
Hide and Seek: A Continuing Journey. New York, Harcourt, and
London, Macmillan, 1973.
The Woman Said Yes: Encounters with Life and Death: Memoirs.
New York, Harcourt, 1976; as *Encounters with Death and Life,*
London, Gollancz, 1977.
Double Discovery: A Journey. New York, Harcourt, 1980.

*

Biography: Entry in *Dictionary of Literary Biography,* Volume 6:
American Novelists since World War II Second Series, Detroit,
Gale, 1980; entry in *Dictionary of Literary Biography Yearbook
1984,* Detroit, Gale, 1985.

Critical Studies: *Jessamyn West* by Alfred S. Shivers, New York,
Twayne, 1972; entry in *Contemporary Literary Criticism,* Detroit,
Gale, Volume 7, 1977, Volume 17, 1981; *Jessamyn West* by Ann
Dahlstrom Farmer, Boise, Idaho, Boise State University, 1982.

Manuscript Collection: Whittier College, California.

*   *   *

During a writing career spanning more than forty years, Mary
Jessamyn West wrote seventeen books, numerous short stories,
several screenplays, an operetta (*A Mirror for the Sky*), and a collection of poetry (*The Secret Look*)—none of which, technically, is
categorized as young adult literature. But for many years, certain of
the "Cress Delahanty" stories were a staple of middle and junior
high school literature anthologies. Motion picture versions of West's
novels were popular among young audiences of the 1950s and 1960s.

And with all her books, a large percentage of her readership has
been comprised of young adult women (and some young adult men)
who are attracted by her unadorned but powerful style and her
knowing, memorable portraits of adolescent experience.

That West is often remembered as a warm, humanistic, and morally grounded Quaker writer (a perception which she is said to have
struggled against as long as she lived) is the consequence of the
immense popularity of her first book. Often referred to as a novel,
The Friendly Persuasion is more accurately described as a collection of short stories about the Birdwells, a Quaker family in rural
Indiana during the late 1800s. The mixture of humorous, serious,
and nostalgic narratives follows a loose chronological structure;
half the stories are about Jess Birdwell, while the other half tell
about Jess's wife Eliza (a beautiful Quaker minister), two of their
children, and one grandchild. The collection has no one emphatic
recurring theme but is an implicit restatement of a guiding maxim
about American transcendentalism: "The unexamined life is not
worth living." A secondary theme is that religious morality, while
vital to the continuance of society as we know it, must be tempered
by humanity and common sense if it is to be an entirely positive
force. *Except for Me and Thee,* another collection of short stories
which constitutes a kind of prequel to *The Friendly Persuasion,*
was published nearly twenty-five years after the first work; among
other things, it recounts Jess's late adolescence, his and Eliza's
courtship, and their early years of marriage. For the most part, it
shares the tone and themes of the earlier collection.

West's first novel was *The Witch Diggers,* the tragicomic history
of Cate Conboy, a highly individualistic but misguided eighteen-
year-old who turns her back on the one fulfilling relationship of her
life because she denies her sexual self. Set in the nondescript environs of a poor county farm, the novel relies upon a variety of
unusual if not altogether bizarre secondary characters to underscore
its themes of confusion, alienation, sexual repression, and futility.
Critically acclaimed at its initial appearance, *The Witch Diggers*
remains a tightly structured and highly readable work.

Among baby boomers, perhaps West's best-known work is her
second collection of short stories, *Cress Delahanty,* whose title
character seems based—at least in part—on West herself. In language that is often poetic but rarely sentimental or melodramatic,
West shows carefully chosen moments in the gradual transformation of twelve-year-old awkwardness, promise, and wonder into
the self-confident and newly-born womanhood of a sixteen-year-
old. Many of the details of the stories are dated, as are certain of its
cultural norms and social conflicts. Still, *Cress Delahanty* speaks to
young readers who look past its surface to what it finally says
about the responsibilities, challenges, and joys of being young.

Other works of fiction by West include *Love, Death, and the
Ladies' Drill Team,* whose stories are now available in the *Collected Stories of Jessamyn West; South of the Angels,* an involved
novel recounting the romantic and social history of the inhabitants
of a small agricultural tract near Los Angeles in the early 1900s;
Leafy Rivers, whose "formula plot" of adultery, guilt, and redemption has provoked more critical disfavor than any other West novel;
The Massacre at Fall Creek, West's best-selling fictionalization of
the 1824 execution of three Indiana whites for the brutal massacre
of the women and children of a Seneca Indian encampment; and *The
State of Stony Lonesome,* West's last novel (which was published
posthumously), an intriguing but finally disturbing and dissatisfy-
ing account of a young woman's apparently innocent love for an
uncle that the reader perceives as calculating, sexually aggressive,
and at least potentially abusive.

For contemporary young readers, none of West's fiction can match the appeal of her autobiographical works, especially *Hide and Seek* and *The Woman Said Yes*. Sometimes compared to Thoreau's *Walden, Hide and Seek* is a highly introspective record of West's experiences with nature and with human "neighbors" during a period of encampment on the banks of the Colorado River. Included in her musings are memories of her childhood and her mother's hesitancy to discuss sex, muted observations on the significance of life and the worth of other people, and overt references to Thoreau and his philosophy. *The Woman Said Yes,* perhaps the most controversial of all West's books, is a somewhat discursive but emotionally gripping history of West's family, focusing on her mother and on West's sister, Carmen, who committed suicide five days before Halloween in 1963. In these two works, West's voice is immediate, insistent, real; young readers seem to find in them a haunting timelessness that often eluded her short stories and novels.

—Keith Lawrence

———

WEST, Owen. See **KOONTZ, Dean R.**

———

WESTALL, Robert (Atkinson). British. Born in Tynemouth, Northumberland, England, 7 October 1929. Educated at Durham University, B.A. 1953; University of London, D.F.A. 1957. Served in British Army, Royal Signals, 1953-55. Married Jean Underhill in 1958 (divorced 1990), one son (deceased). Art master, Erdington Hall Secondary Modern School, Birmingham, 1957-58, and Keighley Boys' Grammar School, Yorkshire, 1958-60; Head of Art, 1960-85, and Head of Careers, 1970-85, Sir John Deane's College, Northwich, Cheshire; antiques dealer, 1985-86. Writer, Whitehorn Press, Manchester, 1968-71; Northern art critic, *Guardian,* London, 1970, 1980; art critic, Chester *Chronicle,* 1962-1973. Director of Telephone Samaritans of Mid-Cheshire, 1965-75. Recipient: Carnegie Medal from Library Association of Great Britain, 1976, for *The Machine-Gunners,* and 1982, for *The Scarecrows;* Boston *Globe/Horn Book* Honor Books citations, 1978, for *The Machine-Gunners,* 1982, for *The Scarecrows,* and 1983, for *Break of Dark; The Devil on the Road* was selected by the American Library Association as a best book for young adults, 1979; Carnegie Medal nomination, 1979, for *The Devil on the Road;* Leseratten Prize (Germany), 1988, for *The Machine-Gunners,* 1990, for *Futuretrack Five,* and 1991, for *The Promise;* Children's Book prize nomination, 1988, for *Urn Burial;* Senior Smarties Prize, 1989, and Children's Book Award commendation, both for *Blitzcat;* Carnegie Award commendation, and Sheffield Children's Book Prize, both 1991, both for *The Promise; Guardian* Award and Carnegie Award runner-up, both 1991, both for *The Kingdom by the Sea. Died 22 April 1993.*

PUBLICATIONS FOR YOUNG ADULTS

Fiction

The Machine-Gunners. London, Macmillan, 1975; New York, Greenwillow, 1976.

The Wind Eye. London, Macmillan, 1976; New York, Greenwillow, 1977.

The Watch House. London, Macmillan, 1977; New York, Greenwillow, 1978.

The Devil on the Road. London, Macmillan, 1978; New York, Greenwillow, 1979.

Fathom Five. London, Macmillan, 1979; New York, Greenwillow, 1980.

The Scarecrows. London, Chatto & Windus, and New York, Greenwillow, 1981.

Break of Dark. London, Chatto & Windus, and New York, Greenwillow, 1982.

The Haunting of Chas McGill and Other Stories. London, Macmillan, and New York, Greenwillow, 1983.

Futuretrack Five. London, Kestrel, 1983; New York, Greenwillow, 1984.

The Cats of Seroster. London, Macmillan, and New York, Greenwillow, 1984.

The Other: A Christmas Story. London, Macmillan, 1985.

The Witness. London, Macmillan, 1985.

Rachel and the Angel and Other Stories. London, Macmillan, 1986; New York, Greenwillow, 1987.

Rosalie. London, Macmillan, 1987.

Urn Burial. London, Viking Kestral, 1987; New York, Greenwillow, 1988.

The Creature in the Dark, illustrated by Liz Roberts. London, Blackie, 1988.

Ghosts and Journeys. London, Macmillan, 1988.

Ghost Abbey. London, Macmillan, 1988; New York, Scholastic, 1989.

Antique Dust: Ghost Stories. London, Viking Kestral, and New York, Viking, 1989.

Blitzcat. London, Macmillan, 1989; New York, Scholastic, 1990.

Old Man on a Horse. London, Blackie, 1989.

A Walk on the Wild Side. London, Methuen, 1989.

The Call, London, Viking Kestral, 1989.

Echoes of War. London, Viking Kestral, 1989.

Cat! London, Methuen, 1989.

The Kingdom by the Sea. London, Methuen, 1990; New York, Farrar, Straus, 1991.

Stormsearch. London, Blackie, 1990.

If Cats Could Fly...? London, Methuen, 1990.

The Promise. New York, Scholastic, 1991.

The Christmas Cat. London, Methuen, 1991.

The Stones of Muncaster Cathedral. London, Kestral, 1991.

Yaxley's Cat. London, Macmillan, 1991; New York, Scholastic, 1992.

The Fearful Lovers. London, Macmillan, 1992.

Size Twelve. London, Heinemann, 1992.

The Ghost in the Tower. London, Methuen, 1992.

A Place for Me. London, Macmillan, 1993.

In Camera and Other Stories. New York. Scholastic, 1993.

Plays

The Machine-Gunners (adapted from his own story). London, Macmillan, 1986.

PUBLICATIONS FOR ADULTS

Other

Editor, *Children of the Blitz: Memories of Wartime Childhood.* London, Viking, 1985.

Biography: Entry in *Fifth Book of Junior Authors and Illustrators,* New York, H.W. Wilson, 1983; essay in *Something about the Author Autobiography Series,* Volume 2, Detroit, Gale, 1986; essay in *Speaking for Ourselves, Too* compiled and edited by Donald R. Gallo, National Council of Teachers of English, 1993.

Critical Study: *Children's Literature Review,* Volume 13, Detroit, Gale, 1987; *Contemporary Literary Criticism,* Volume 17, Detroit, Gale, 1981.

*   *   *

Robert Westall's first book, *The Machine Gunners* (winner of the Carnegie Medal), has been one of those rare novels that has proven equally popular with English teachers, seeking contemporary fiction for school use, and with young adult readers who have responded to this view of growing up during World War II. Twenty years later, it remains widely read as a vivid and authentic re-creation of that experience, and in *Fathom Five* Westall explored what might later have happened to some of the characters from the original novel. Westall has occasionally returned to the wartime setting. In *The Kingdom by the Sea,* for example, he describes how Harry's home and family are destroyed by bombs, and how the boy sets out on a series of adventures in wartime Northumbria. A similar theme is more light-heartedly handled in *Blitzcat,* the story of a lost cat, Lord Gort, seeking his owners (an RAF pilot and his wife) through the chaos of bombed and rationed Britain, which entertainingly juxtaposes the cat's views of adults with theirs of him. Perhaps the best of the five stories in *Break of Dark* is "Blackham's Wimpie," about the experiences of a Wellington bomber crew, told in the characteristic tones of their wireless radio operator. However, it would be a mistake to read these works simply as documentaries the past. *The Machine Gunners* is also an analysis of dual roles, relationships, moral issues, and choices, that remains relevant in the present.

Westall's later work generally consisted of tough stories, set firmly in contemporary times, where conventional patterns of marriage and family life are breaking up and where new fears and threats have replaced the wartime bombs, or in an even more chilling future. The young characters of the books are repeatedly faced by twin sets of problems: moral dilemmas springing from family tensions and pressures from usually evil or malevolent supernatural forces. What might seem a conventional theme, a family's boating holiday, is given a very different treatment in *The Wind Eye.* The recently married scientist and his wife quarrel endlessly and their children from previous marriages are caught up in a complex emotional web. These tensions are counterpointed with the forces unleashed when one of the characters deliberately challenges superstition by stepping on the tomb of St Cuthbert in Durham Cathedral. In *The Watch House,* Anne spends the summer at Garmouth because she has been deserted by her father and is unwanted by her mother. She becomes conscious of manifestations from the old Watch House with its relics of an ancient shipwreck, and her immediate anxieties are intercut with her growing understanding of the past.

Several of Westall's novels raise social issues in an accessible, if sometimes over-simplified, form. *Futuretrack 5* explores the nature of a future hierarchical society in an England run by a giant computer, where new state examinations are used to determine the future lives of the inhabitants. The most successful ("Ests") have a privileged life of sex and leisure; the less able are sent to the cities to fight and survive as best they can. Real power is in the hands of the "Techs," who programme the computer and are plotting to repopulate the country with artificially bred and conditioned citizens. *Urn Burial* also tackles major problems of goodness and human destructiveness, but the two sides of the book are awkwardly integrated. The Cumbrian setting is lively and convincing, with Ralph the young shepherd, his fearsome mother, his girlfriend Ruby working in the supermarket check-out, and country scenes like the sheep-dipping festival. Investigating a hill-top cairn, Ralph discovers a glass coffin wherein space warriors had buried two of their leaders, and so he unintentionally unleashes intergalactic forces. The ensuing "star wars" plot is rather predictable, with a last minute victory of good over evil and a heavily moralising view of Ralph as the "good shepherd," an embodiment of simple wisdom.

The central critical debate over Westall's novels has concerned his treatment of violence and destructive emotions, which has seemed over-intense or even disturbed to some readers. Westall has made clear the influence of his son's death on a motorbike at the age of eighteen on emotionally powerful books like *The Devil on the Road,* in which John Webster narrates the strange biking experiences that lead him back into a world of witchcraft and the Civil War. Some reviewers were unhappy about what they saw as the obsessional feelings vividly realised in *The Scarecrows.* Simon still worships his father who was killed in Aden and bitterly resents his new stepfather. He eavesdrops on his mother making love with her new husband, and is filled with such ferocious anger that he awakens the spirits of three murderers, so that they will return from haunting the old mill in the form of threatening scarecrows and execute vengeance. What is at issue, here and elsewhere, is the extent to which the reader is encouraged to identify with emotions or to be detached and judge them.

Westall's sudden death meant the loss of a versatile and skilful writer who had drawn on his many years of teaching experience for books that might provide what he called "the survival equipment" needed by adolescents. He was strikingly successful in reaching reluctant male readers. Collections like *The Call* or *Fearful Lovers* demonstrate a range of short story skills: the use of different narrative voices, a physical sense of objects and surroundings, a lively sense of humour, and an ability to suggest strangeness by simple means. The novels have enormous narrative drive, impelling the reader to discover what happens next. There is little description or discussion to hold up the action, although there is always a strong sense of atmosphere. Westall was always a skilful and uncompromising storyteller, and his books thoroughly deserve the popularity they have achieved.

—Robert Protherough

————————

WHITE, Ellen E(merson). Also writes as Zack Emerson. American.

PUBLICATIONS FOR YOUNG ADULTS

Fiction

Romance Is a Wonderful Thing. New York, Avon, 1983.
Friends for Life. New York, Avon, 1983.

The President's Daughter. New York, Avon, 1984.
White House Autumn. New York, Avon, 1985.
Life without Friends. New York, Scholastic, 1987.
Long Live the Queen. New York, Scholastic, 1989.
Jennifer Capriati. New York, Scholastic, 1991.

"Echo Company" series, as Zack Emerson

Welcome to Vietnam. New York, Scholastic, 1991.
Hill 568. New York, Scholastic, 1991.
'Tis the Season. New York, Scholastic, 1991.
Stand Down. Scholastic, New York, 1992.
Grateful Nation. New York, Scholastic, forthcoming.

Nonfiction

Bo Jackson: Playing the Game. New York, Scholastic, 1990.
Jim Abbott against All Odds. New York, Scholastic, 1990.

*

Biography: Essay in *Speaking for Ourselves, Too* compiled and edited by Donald R. Gallo, National Council of Teachers of English, 1993.

*   *   *

Ellen Emerson White was in college when she published her first novel, and she has been consistently putting out books ever since: seven young adult titles, three nonfiction books for younger readers and four Vietnam novels for young adults under the name Zack Emerson. She is a versatile writer who enjoys researching her books thoroughly (for example, she likes to make each character a Red Sox fan so that she can attend the games!) She brings to her writing a kind of toughness and realism that young readers appreciate.

Her characters speak honestly with a sophisticated humor and sometimes a savvy cynicism. They are tough, but vulnerable, and often become victims of circumstances over which they have little control. They frequently find themselves becoming heroic and exhibiting an unexpected courage. Sometimes they have to assume leadership or demonstrate maturity when they feel unprepared. Emerson's characters often exist in an unkind world where friendship, loyalty, support, encouragement, and trust are sought and found after considerable efforts. They must be problem solvers, and they are forced to be independent.

Friends for Life, published in 1983, tells the story of Susan McAllister who moves back to her childhood community and hopes to enjoy her senior year with her best friend. However, she becomes involved in a very dangerous mystery when her friend Colleen is found dead of a drug overdose. Only Susan believes that her friend was murdered, and in this page-turning suspense novel, she proves to be correct, but almost loses her own life in the process.

Emerson's first novel was quickly followed by *Romance Is a Wonderful Thing* which describes the relationship between Colin McNamara and Trish Masters. Trish is an honors student and Colin is a silly, fun-loving character who needs to grow up and find confidence in himself.

The next year the first of a very popular series, *The President's Daughter,* was published. The President is a woman, and her daughter, Meg, is completely unprepared for the tremendous changes in her life as her mother assumes the office. The sequel, *White House Autumn,* continues the story of Meg as she adjusts to the fish bowl life of the White House. Her mother survives an assassination attempt, and the family learns how to pull together and support each other through the extraordinary circumstances in which they find themselves.

The last of the series, *Long Live the Queen,* begins six months after the attempt on the President's life. Meg has managed to construct a social life of friends and activities in spite of the constant surveillance of the Secret Service. However, Meg is kidnapped by terrorists and undergoes a horrifying experience at the hands of her captors until she is able to free herself. Left with severe injuries, she strives to cope with coming to terms with the uncertainty about her future, her relationship with her family, and her anger about what happened to her. Chosen as an ALA Best Book for Young Adults, this story doesn't spare any words. Meg's experience is not glamorized or romanticized, and the violence of her kidnapping is told in vivid detail.

In *Life without Friends,* Emerson picks up part of the story from *Friends for Life* with Beverly, who had known about the murders and the person who had committed them but was unable to muster up the courage to tell. As a result, everyone judges her, believing that she failed to speak up and prevent the tragedies. Feeling the ostracism, Beverly pulls more and more into an isolated and lonely existence until she finally learns that there are some people she can trust to forgive her. This is a painful story depicting the enormous difficulty some young people have in communicating with both adults and peer groups.

The "Echo Company" series was written under the name Zach Emerson. This highly regarded series about Vietnam is brutal, violent, and realistic in its portrayal of war. Eighteen-year-old Michael Jennings is totally unprepared for the horrors of war, and the first novel, *Welcome to Vietnam,* describes in graphic detail Michael's experiences there. He is forced to grow up and gain confidence quickly as he lives through unmitigated misery. The second book, *Hill 568,* continues Michael's story and takes him into a leadership position. With somewhat less action than in the first book, *Hill 568* provides the reader with another side of the war experience; boredom. Sometimes the days are all exactly the same, and there is too much time to think, contemplate and despair. However, when they battle for the hill, the description is so intense that it becomes excruciating.

The third book in the series, *'Tis the Season,* introduces a new character—Rebecca, an army nurse. She is seriously injured in a helicopter crash in the jungle. The story describes her terror and physical pain in raw detail and ends with her rescue. However, the reader is left not knowing the extent of her injuries or what happens next. A smart, tough, and courageous heroine, the reader is eager to move into the fourth book to find out if she lives.

Stand Down brings Rebecca and Michael together. Anxious to know how she survived after he found her in the jungle, he locates her still working as a nurse, even though she is recovering from serious injuries. He convinces her to spend an evening together, and they strike up a kind of instant romance, enjoying a brief respite from the realities of the war. Included in each book is a map and a glossary of terms providing definitions for the slang used by the military personnel. Many of these terms are medical, and the listing seems to highlight the grim and horrifying effects of war. *The Grateful Nation,* due to be published in fall of 1993, continues the Vietnam story.

Emerson's talent for creating interesting characters and spellbinding plots has earned her the status of an important writer for and about young adults. Her readers can count on her to find the words to describe feelings and experiences that are often so difficult to explain. Although her characters find themselves in extreme situations, they are always survivors, though not without great effort and cost.

—Caroline S. McKinney

———

WHITE, Robb. Born in Baguio, Luzon, the Philippines, 20 June 1909. Educated at U.S. Naval Academy, Annapolis, Maryland, B.S. 1931. Married 1) Rosalie Mason in 1937 (divorced 1964), one son, two daughters; 2) Ann C. Saunders in 1985. Captain, U.S. Navy. Recipient: Commonwealth Club medal for best juvenile book, for *No Man's Land.*

PUBLICATIONS FOR YOUNG ADULTS

Fiction

The Nub, illustrated by Andrew Wyeth. Boston, Little, Brown, 1935.
Smuggler's Sloop, illustrated by Andrew Wyeth. Boston, Little, Brown, 1937.
Midshipman Lee, illustrated by Anton Otto Fischer). Boston, Little, Brown, 1938.
Run Masked. New York, Knopf, 1938; as *Jungle Fury,* New York, Berkley Publishing, 1956.
In Privateer's Bay. New York, Harper, 1939.
Three against the Sea, illustrated by Aldren A. Watson. New York, Harper, 1940.
Sailor in the Sun, illustrated by Edward Shenton. New York, Harper, 1941.
The Lion's Paw, illustrated by Ralph Ray. Garden City, New York, Doubleday, 1946.
Secret Sea, illustrated by Jay Hyde Barnum. Garden City, New York, Doubleday, 1947.
Sail Away, illustrated by Dorothy Bayley Morse. Garden City, New York, Doubleday, 1948.
Candy, illustrated by Gertrude Howe. Garden City, New York, Doubleday, 1949.
The Haunted Hound, illustrated by Louis Glanzman. Garden City, New York, Doubleday, 1950.
Deep Danger. Garden City, New York, Doubleday, 1952.
Our Virgin Island. Garden City, New York, Doubleday, 1953.
Midshipman Lee of the Naval Academy. New York, Random House, 1954.
Up Periscope. Garden City, New York, Doubleday, 1956.
Flight Deck. Garden City, New York, Doubleday, 1961.
Torpedo Run. Garden City, New York, Doubleday, 1962.
The Survivor. Garden City, New York, Doubleday, 1964.
Surrender. Garden City, New York, Doubleday, 1966.
Silent Ship, Silent Sea. Garden City, New York, Doubleday, 1967.
No Man's Land. Garden City, New York, Doubleday, 1969.
Deathwatch. Garden City, New York, Doubleday, 1972.
The Frogmen. Garden City, New York, Doubleday, 1973.
The Long Way Down. Garden City, New York, Doubleday, 1977.

Fire Storm. Garden City, New York, Doubleday, 1979.
Two on the Isle: A Memory of Marina Cay. New York, W.W. Norton, 1985.

Screenplays: *House on Haunted Hill,* Allied Artists Pictures Corporation, 1958; *Macabre,* Allied Artists Pictures Corporation, 1958; *The Tingler,* Columbia Pictures Corporation, 1959; *Up Periscope,* Warner Brothers Pictures, 1959; *13 Ghosts,* William Castle Productions, 1960; *Homicidal,* William Castle Productions, 1961.

*

Biography: Essay in *Something about the Author Autobiography Series,* Volume 1, Detroit, Gale, 1986.

*   *   *

One of the most prolific young adult authors of our century, Robb White has written more than two dozen novels, a half dozen screenplays, and three war/travel memoirs. Although most of these are not now in print, the well-worn (and still circulating) editions of White's works held by school and public libraries are testament to his appeal, to his capacity for spinning a good yarn.

More than half of White's novels are set wholly or in part in the islands and waterways of the Pacific Ocean during World War II. The majority of these novels, while dated, retain their ability to engage readers who possess enough historical interest in the Second World War to be willing to overlook recurrent similarities in characterization, plot, and viewpoint—and, unfortunately, to ignore the unedited and all-too-accurate portrayal of omnipresent American racism towards Japanese during the war. Though there are important exceptions, White's novels stress two important themes. The first, central to such novels as *Up Periscope, Flight Deck, Silent Ship, Silent Sea,* and *Deathwatch,* is the capacity of the underdog—through ingenuity and effort—to triumph over incredible odds; the second, best exemplified by *Torpedo Run, The Survivor,* and *The Frogmen,* is the all-too-human tendency to misjudge and alienate others. Several White novels explore both themes simultaneously.

The novels written during the first decade or so of White's career are stylistically uneven, beginning with *Run Masked* (ostensibly written as an "adult novel") and *Midshipman Lee,* and continuing through *The Haunted Hound,* a second-rate boy/dog story. While the early novels include passages of taut prose and absolutely convincing dialogue, there are also glaring instances of overwriting, of obvious cleverness, of melodrama. This is especially true of such novels as *The Lion's Paw* and *Secret Sea,* where primary characters are young adolescents. *The Lion's Paw,* the story of a fifteen-year-old boy who escapes from his uncle on a small boat, accompanied by two orphans who join in his search for a rare seashell (which becomes a metaphorical search for the boy's father, for parents and home), has been in print longer than any other White novel. The characters themselves are rather well drawn; their search for love and security, while superficial, is nevertheless believable to preteens. But their dialogue repeatedly rings false to older readers: sometimes it is too childish, sometimes too wise, too "adult." Such readers will also find that emotional scenes involving the children quickly degenerate into melodrama. There are similar problems in *The Haunted Hound* as well as *Secret Sea,* the story of a former Navy commander who hires a fifteen-year-old renegade orphan to help him search for sunken treasure.

What might be called White's "middle period" stretches from the early 1950s to 1970. White wrote less quickly during this period than he had during the early years of his career, and the writing is much more careful, more mature. The World War II novels of this period are markedly influenced by White's increasingly objective and analytical view of the war: the plots are leaner; the characters more deftly drawn; the dialogue a sharper, wittier rendering of the serious exchanges and bantering of adult males. White's most famous war novels come from this period. They include *Up Periscope* (the screenplay of the popular movie was also written by White), whose protagonist is sent on a secret mission to locate a Japanese radar base and copy its codes; *Flight Deck,* the adventures of a Navy pilot who, after being grounded because of injuries, takes upon himself a covert reconnaissance operation on a small uninhabited island; *Torpedo Run,* where plot is encapsulated in the subtitle; and *Silent Ship, Silent Sea,* which tells how a boot-camp graduate and his Navy captain, the sole survivors of an air attack on their destroyer, attempt to torpedo the Japanese ship that has their damaged destroyer in tow. A somewhat unusual novel of this period is *The Survivor,* whose protagonist, a naval aviator assigned to a unit of Marines sent to explore a Japanese-inhabited island, dies after rescuing the companions that have never truly accepted him.

White's later period extends from 1971 to the mid-1980s. Works from this period include *Deathwatch,* White's best-selling novel pitting man against man in a struggle for survival; *The Frogmen,* the account of a World War II underwater demolition team commanded by a Japanese-American (White's largely unsuccessful effort, due to plotting difficulties and blurred characterizations, to redress the racism of his earlier World War II fiction); *The Long Way Down,* the story of a young woman who wants to become a trapeze artist and who falls in love with her trainer (one of only a few White novels with a female protagonist and perhaps the only one directed to a feminine audience); *Fire Storm,* a very short novel about two brothers caught in a forest fire; and *Memory of Marina Cay,* the best of White's war/travel memoirs, this with a Virgin Islands setting.

One novel from this later group merits additional comment, not simply because of its immense popularity but because of its aesthetic achievement. *Deathwatch,* the most unified and carefully plotted of all White's novels—never out of print since its initial publication—is set in California's Mojave Desert, pitting a young loner against the wealthy and determined businessman/hunter who has hired him to track bighorn sheep. When the hunter mistakenly kills a grizzled desert prospector, the young man insists they take the body to the authorities. Angered, knowing that he cannot trust his guide not to turn him in, the hunter resolves to let the younger man die in the desert. The resulting conflict is an intensely gripping drama; it is also the stuff of myth, where spirited, ingenious and uncorrupted youth holds its own and eventually triumphs over the selfish, worldly-wise, and privileged ruthlessness of age. In cementing White's reputation as an intelligent writer with an exciting and significant story to tell, *Deathwatch* has attracted young readers to library holdings of other White fiction, fiction that remains an engrossing portrait of its era.

—Keith Lawrence

———

WHITE, T(erence) H(anbury). Also wrote as James Aston. British. Born in Bombay, India, 29 May 1906; brought to England,

1911. Educated at Cheltenham College, 1920-24; Queens' College, Cambridge (exhibitioner), 1925-27, 1928-29, B.A. 1929. Taught at a preparatory school, 1930-32; head of the English department, Stowe School, Buckinghamshire, 1932-36. *Died 17 January 1964.*

PUBLICATIONS FOR YOUNG ADULTS

Fiction

The Sword in the Stone, illustrated by the author. London, Collins, 1938; New York, Putnam, 1939; revised edition, in *The Once and Future King,* 1958.

The Witch in the Wood, illustrated by the author. New York, Putnam, 1939; London, Collins, 1940; revised edition, as *The Queen of Air and Darkness,* in *The Once and Future King,* 1958.

The Ill-Made Knight, illustrated by the author. New York, Putnam, 1940; London, Collins, 1941; revised edition, in *The Once and Future King,* 1958.

Mistress Masham's Repose, illustrated by Fritz Eichenberg. New York, Putnam, 1946; London, Cape, 1947.

The Master: An Adventure Story. London, Cape, and New York, Putnam, 1957.

The Once and Future King. London, Collins, and New York, Putnam, 1958.

The Book of Merlyn: The Unpublished Conclusion to The Once and Future King, illustrated by Trevor Stubley. Austin, University of Texas Press, 1977; London, Collins, 1978.

PUBLICATIONS FOR ADULTS

Novels

Dead Mr. Nixon, with R. McNair Scott. London, Cassell, 1931.

Darkness at Pemberley. London, Gollancz, 1932; New York, Century, 1933.

First Lesson (as James Aston). London, Chatto and Windus, 1932; New York, Knopf, 1933.

They Winter Abroad (as James Aston). London, Chatto and Windus, and New York, Viking Press, 1932.

Farewell Victoria. London, Collins, 1933; New York, Smith and Haas, 1934.

Earth Stopped; or, Mr. Marx's Sporting Tour. London, Collins, 1934; New York, Putnam, 1935.

Gone to Ground. London, Collins, and New York, Putnam, 1935.

The Elephant and the Kangaroo. New York, Putnam, 1947; London, Cape, 1948.

Short Stories

The Maharajah and Other Stories, edited by Kurth Sprague. London, Macdonald, and New York, Putnam, 1981.

Poetry

The Green Bay Tree; or, The Wicked Man Touches Wood. Cambridge, Heffer, 1929.

Loved Helen and Other Poems. London, Chatto and Windus, and New York, Viking Press, 1929.

Verses. Privately printed, 1962.

A Joy Proposed. London, Rota, 1980; Athens, University of Georgia Press, 1983.

Other

England Have My Bones. London, Collins, and New York, Macmillan, 1936.

Burke's Steerage; or, The Amateur Gentleman's Introduction to Noble Sports and Pastimes. London, Collins, 1938; New York, Putnam, 1939.

The Age of Scandal: An Excursion Through a Minor Period. London, Cape, and New York, Putnam, 1950.

The Goshawk (on falconry). London, Cape, 1951; New York, Putnam, 1952.

The Scandalmonger (on English scandals). London, Cape, and New York, Putnam, 1952.

Editor and Translator, *The Book of Beasts, Being a Translation from a Latin Bestiary of the Twelfth Century.* London, Cape, 1954; New York, Putnam, 1955.

The Godstone and the Blackymor (on Ireland). London, Cape, and New York, Putnam, 1959.

America at Last: The American Journal of T.H. White. New York, Putnam, 1965.

The White/Garnett Letters, edited by David Garnett. London, Cape, and New York, Viking Press, 1968.

Letters to a Friend: The Correspondence Between T.H. White and L.J. Potts, edited by Franois Gallix. New York, Putnam, 1982; Gloucester, Sutton, 1984.

*

Bibliography: *T.H. White: An Annotated Bibliography* by Franois Gallix, New York, Garland, 1986.

Critical Studies: *T.H. White: A Biography* by Sylvia Townsend Warner, London, Cape-Chatto and Windus, 1967, New York, Viking Press, 1968; *T.H. White* by John K. Crane, New York, Twayne, 1974.

*   *   *

"T.H. White, 1906-1964, author who from a troubled heart delighted others, loving and praising this life" reads the inscription on his grave marker in Athens, Greece. It sums up well his life and work. Troubled by an abusive childhood and adolescence, a love-hate relationship with his mother, and the constant necessity of writing to support himself, he also had a passion for life, and a love of all sorts of animals—especially red setters—new experiences and skills, and voracious reading. His life and works are a series of paradoxes. While he loved to play various roles, he took equal delight in satirizing role-playing. His young adult books are both highly original and pastiches of the works of others.

His young adult books, a minor portion of his twenty-three books, are a major portion of his most memorable works. General readers best remember *The Once and Future King,* the book for the popular romantic 1960s musical *Camelot* and the subsequent film. *The Sword in the Stone* was the first book, and the most successful part, of that tetralogy. While it delighted children, its very learned and sophisticated content challenges and appeals to young adults.

Exceedingly popular, *The Sword in the Stone* probably remains his best known story.

In a letter to L.J. Potts, his former Cambridge tutor, White describes *The Sword in the Stone* as a "warm-hearted" story "mainly about bird and beasts" and observes that it "seems impossible to determine whether it is for grown-ups or children."

The Sword in the Stone begins with a famous parody of medieval education reduced to a public school week schedule: "On Mondays, Wednesdays and Fridays it was Court Hand and Summulae Logicales, while the rest of the week it was the Organon, Repetition and Astrology." Because Merlyn lives backwards, from the twentieth century to the fifteenth, White gets to satirize both contemporary and medieval culture. The book has several themes. The first is Sir Ector's search for a proper tutor for Arthur, called Wart. Another is Wart's discovery of his identity and fate. A general theme throughout the book is the pleasures of country life as expressed through accurate details of medieval farming, haymaking, and hunting.

When Wart finds Merlyn, his education begins. Following Rousseau's model for a teacher, a familiar pattern for many children's books, Merlyn waits for Wart to ask questions. Proclaiming that "Education is experience," he transforms him into various animals for his learning. Wart learns about war, peace, and wisdom by becoming a fish, a hawk, a grass snake, an owl, and a badger. In the revised 1958 version, he also becomes an ant and a goose. The novel is full of autobiographical details: Merlyn's study, like White's, is messily full of books, animals, and insects; an owl Archimedes sits on Merlyn's head just as it did on White's. From his experience in the human world, Wart learns responsibility, courage, and the need for rules, humility, and honesty.

The novel gives explicit details about medieval life and compares it to contemporary country life; it also parodies medieval themes and situations such as the interminable quests and Merlyn's frequent ineptness as a magician. There are allusions to classic children's books. For example, Kay and Wart are invited to dine and are trapped by Madame Mim in her cottage in the forest, an episode which recalls Hansel and Gretel. The excessive sweets found at the castle of Queen Morgan burlesque the excessive food imagery of some children's and young adult books. As in many young people's books, friendly animals aid the hero to achieve a quest.

Sometimes the comedy is broad and modern. In the original version, a neon movie sign hangs over Morgan's door: "The Queen of Air and Darkness, Now Showing" and she is "a very beautiful lady, wearing beach pajamas and smoked glasses." Quotations from and allusions to the classic literature abound, as well as silly rhymes and parodies of popular tunes.

There are realistic hunting scenes and a fantastic battle against griffins and wyverns. Wart and Kay talk and act like modern young teenaged boys, but the adults are mostly comic stereotypes. White's clever line drawings illustrate the book.

Drastically revised for *The Once and Future King,* the Arthurian story became a tetralogy about the futility of war, rather than a domestic tragedy of incest. As a result the revised version is more somber and lacks much of the playfulness and extravagance of the original as well as White's clever drawings.

Mistress Masham's Repose resulted from his infatuation for a thirteen-year-old farm girl and his interest in Jonathan Swift's *Gulliver's Travels.* Dedicated to Amaryllis Virginia Garnett, the daughter of David Garnett in whose rural cottage White stayed for a year upon returning from Ireland and before taking up permanent residence in Alderney, this comic children's novel with a complex plot owes something to White's earlier detective novels but much more to his experiences at the Stowe estate and his enthusiasm for Gulliver's visit to the Lilliputians.

The orphaned heroine of this book proves that White could write well about women, if they were young enough. Maria, ten years old, studious, bespectacled, but impulsive and adventurous, lives in Malplaquet, a nearly ruined eighteenth-century Northamptonshire mansion, four time longer than Buckingham Palace. Her enemies are Miss Brown, her governess and cousin; and Mr. Hater, the local clergyman and her guardian. Her only friends are Mrs. Noakes, the cook and only servant; and the impecunious Professor, who lives in a cottage on the grounds. This setting allows White to crowd in all sorts of allusions to persons, literature, events, and gossip of the eighteenth and nineteenth century, things that fill his eighteenth-century social histories, *The Age of Scandal: An Excursion through a Minor Period* and *The Scandalmonger.*

The story begins when Maria, playing pirate, invades an island in the midst of an ornamental lake and discovers that Mistress Masham's Repose, a classical summer pavilion, is home to five hundred descendants of Swift's Lilliputians.

The plot has two parts. One concerns the recovery of Maria's inheritance and the second concerns her rescue of the Lilliputians from Miss Brown and Mr. Hater, who wish to sell them as curiosities to the circus or the movies. Maria and the Professor join forces to prevent this.

This novel also has minute details of farming and hunting, along with a recreation of eighteenth-century British speech. Like Merlyn in *The Sword in the Stone,* the Professor acts as the patient Rousseau-like instructor of Maria. And like White, he is also an absent-minded, scholarly pacifist, difficult to tear away from his scholarly researches and somewhat inept in practical matters.

The novel is filled with incongruous scenes such as the Professor's chopping wood with a sixpenny hatchet from Woolworth's beneath an eighteenth century marble monument to the theatre. The place names and those of the monuments on the grounds of the estate are often erudite jokes. The novel has obvious debts to both Swift's *Gulliver's Travels* and Lewis's *Alice in Wonderland.*

There are some flaws. Miss Brown's and Mr. Hater's plot to murder Maria does not ring true. The last chapter shifts in tone and perspective. Some of the language and allusions in the novel recall too closely White's eighteenth-century research notes. This is young people's literature only for the very bright. But its message of the difference between love and possession and how to become a true friend is very clear.

His publisher discovered his manuscript of *The Goshawk* after his move to Alderney and urged its publication. A fictionalized autobiographical account of how White trained a goshawk using seventeenth century methods and then lost it through carelessness, it has become a nature story for young people, at least in England, according to François Gallix. Many of the details of the three sections of this book, including the names of the goshawks Gos and Cully as well as their characterizations as insane and lunatic, appear earlier in *The Sword in the Stone.* It has an easy Attic style and is filled with exacting falconry details about jesses and swivels but also with a message about the harm in trying to own even an animal.

This book has some of the same concerns as his other books: the contrast between past and present, the inferiority of the present to the past, the evils of possession, the destruction of war, and the folly of mankind.

The Master: An Adventure Story, which continues some of the themes of his earlier books, is a curious failure. Dedicated to Robert Louis Stevenson and bearing a quotation from Shakespeare's *Tempest,* this formula adventure novel is set on the sterile island of Rockall, halfway between Russia and America. Conceived in 1941 out of White's concern for Hitler and World War II and abandoned in 1944, this story was taken up and recast in 1955 to reflect his current bêtes noires. Its situations and character types are flat, stereotyped, and dull. The story concerns the kidnapping of twelve-year-old twins, Nicky and Judy, by a 157-year-old scientist called the Master, who has invented a diabolical super vibrator to give him control of the world. The twins along with their dog Jokey are held prisoner in the caverns of Rockall by the megalomaniac but physically frail Master and his small staff of associates: a drunken Dr. Jones; weak-willed Squadron Leader Frinton; Pinkie, a tongueless black cook; Mr. Blenkinsop, a cultivated but villainous Chinaman; and a couple of anonymous mechanics. As the plot develops, the Master sets about educating Nicky to eventually rule the world that he plans to conquer and save it from the atomic bomb. The novel is full of topical references to the Cold War and political leaders, such as President Eisenhower, Sir Anthony Eden, and Premier Khrushchev. In this context, the characters' discussions over "Might is Right" and "Might for Right," vital in the Arthurian novels, sound only academic and petulant here. The Master is a perversion of White's voluble teacher figures such as Merlyn and the Professor.

White's delight in life and learning is evident in his fantasy novels. Because his works are so learned and unique in their points of view, they will probably remain sui generis in the history of young adult literature.

—Hugh T. Keenan

* * *

WHITNEY, Phyllis A(yame). American. Born in Yokohama, Japan, 9 September 1903. Educated at schools in Japan, China, the Philippines, California, and Texas; McKinley High School, Chicago, graduated 1924. Married 1) George A. Garner in 1925 (divorced 1945), one daughter; 2) Lovell F. Jahnke in 1950 (died 1973). Dance instructor, San Antonio, Texas, one year; children's book editor, Chicago *Sun,* 1942-46, and Philadelphia *Inquirer,* 1947-48; instructor in juvenile fiction writing, Medill School of Journalism, Northwestern University, Chicago, Illinois, 1945, and New York University, 1947-58. Member, Board of Directors, 1959-62, and president, 1975, Mystery Writers of America. Recipient: Mystery Writers of America Edgar Allan Poe best juvenile award, 1961, for *Mystery of the Haunted Pool,* and 1964, for *Mystery of the Hidden Hand;* Edgar Allan Poe best juvenile nominations, 1962, for *The Secret of the Tiger Eyes,* 1971, for *Mystery of the Scowling Boy,* and 1974, for *The Secret of the Missing Footprint;* Sequoyah Children's Book award, 1963, for *Mystery of the Haunted Pool;* "Today's Woman" citation, Council of Cerebral Palsy Auxiliaries of Nassau County, 1983; Grandmaster award, Mystery Writers of America, 1988, for lifetime achievement; Malice Domestic award, 1989, for lifetime achievement. Agent: c/o McIntosh and Otis Inc., 310 Madison Avenue, New York, NY 10017. Address: Rt. 1, Box 175 F, Faber, VA, 22938, U.S.A.

PUBLICATIONS FOR YOUNG ADULTS

PUBLICATIONS FOR ADULTS

Fiction

A Place for Ann, illustrated by Helen Blair. Boston, Houghton Mifflin, 1941.
A Star for Ginny, illustrated by Hilda Frommholz. Boston, Houghton Mifflin, 1942.
A Window for Julie, illustrated by Jean Anderson. Boston, Houghton Mifflin, 1943.
The Silver Inkwell, illustrated by Hilda Frommholz. Boston, Houghton Mifflin, 1945.
Willow Hill. New York, Reynal, 1947.
Ever After. Boston, Houghton Mifflin, 1948.
Mystery of the Gulls, illustrated by Janet Smalley. Philadelphia, Westminster Press, 1949.
Linda's Homecoming. Philadelphia, McKay, 1950.
The Island of Dark Woods, illustrated by Philip Wishnefsky. Philadelphia, Westminster Press, 1951; as *Mystery of the Strange Traveler,* 1967.
Love Me, Love Me Not. Boston, Houghton Mifflin, 1952.
Step to the Music. New York, Crowell, 1953.
A Long Time Coming. Philadelphia, McKay, 1954.
Mystery of the Black Diamonds, illustrated by John Gretzer. Philadelphia, Westminster Press, 1954; as *Black Diamonds,* Leicester, Brockhampton Press, 1957.
Mystery on the Isle of Skye, illustrated by Ezra Jack Keats. Philadelphia, Westminster Press, 1955.
The Fire and the Gold. New York, Crowell, 1956.
The Highest Dream. Philadelphia, McKay, 1956.
Mystery of the Green Cat, illustrated by Richard Horwitz. Philadelphia, Westminster Press, 1957.
Secret of the Samurai Sword. Philadelphia, Westminster Press, 1958.
Creole Holiday. Philadelphia, Westminster Press, 1959.
Mystery of the Haunted Pool, illustrated by H. Tom Hall. Philadelphia, Westminster Press, 1960.
Secret of the Tiger's Eye, illustrated by Richard Horwitz. Philadelphia, Westminster Press, 1961.
Mystery of the Golden Horn, illustrated by Georgeann Helms. Philadelphia, Westminster Press, 1962.
Mystery of the Hidden Hand, illustrated by H. Tom Hall. Philadelphia, Westminster Press, 1963.
Secret of the Emerald Star, illustrated by Alex Stein. Philadelphia, Westminster Press, 1964.
Mystery of the Angry Idol, illustrated by Al Fiorentino. Philadelphia, Westminster Press, 1965.
Secret of the Spotted Shell, illustrated by John Mecray. Philadelphia, Westminster Press, 1967.
Secret of Goblin Glen, illustrated by Al Fiorentino. Philadelphia, Westminster Press, 1968.
The Mystery of the Crimson Ghost. Philadelphia, Westminster Press, 1969.
Secret of the Missing Footprint, illustrated by Alex Stein. Philadelphia, Westminster Press, 1969.
The Vanishing Scarecrow. Philadelphia, Westminster Press, 1971.
Nobody Likes Trina. Philadelphia, Westminster Press, 1972.
Mystery of the Scowling Boy, illustrated by John Gretzer. Philadelphia, Westminster Press, 1973.
Secret of Haunted Mesa. Philadelphia, Westminster Press, 1975.
Secret of the Stone Face. Philadelphia, Westminster Press, 1977.

Novels

Red Is for Murder. Chicago, Ziff Davis, 1943; as *Red Carnelian,* New York, Paperback Library, 1968; London, Coronet, 1976.
The Quicksilver Pool. New York, Appleton Century Crofts, 1955; London, Coronet, 1973.
The Trembling Hills. New York, Appleton Century Crofts, 1956; London, Coronet, 1974.
Skye Cameron. New York, Appleton Century Crofts, 1957; London, Hurst and Blackett, 1959.
The Moonflower. New York, Appleton Century Crofts, 1958; as *The Mask and the Moonflower,* London, Hurst and Blackett, 1960.
Thunder Heights. New York, Appleton Century Crofts, 1960; London, Coronet, 1973.
Blue Fire. New York, Appleton Century Crofts, 1961; London, Hodder & Stoughton, 1962.
Window on the Square. New York, Appleton Century Crofts, 1962; London, Coronet, 1969.
Seven Tears for Apollo. New York, Appleton Century Crofts, 1963; London, Coronet, 1969.
Black Amber. New York, Appleton Century Crofts, 1964; London, Hale, 1965.
Sea Jade. New York, Appleton Century Crofts, 1965; London, Hale, 1966.
Columbella. New York, Doubleday, 1966; London, Hale, 1967.
Silverhill. New York, Doubleday, 1967; London, Heinemann, 1968.
Hunter's Green. New York, Doubleday, 1968; London, Heinemann, 1969.
The Winter People. New York, Doubleday, 1969; London, Heinemann, 1970.
Lost Island. New York, Doubleday, 1970; London, Heinemann, 1971.
Listen for the Whisperer. New York, Doubleday, and London, Heinemann, 1972.
Snowfire. New York, Doubleday, and London, Heinemann, 1973.
The Turquoise Mask. New York, Doubleday, 1974; London, Heinemann, 1975.
Spindrift. New York, Doubleday, and London, Heinemann, 1975.
The Golden Unicorn. New York, Doubleday, 1976; London, Heinemann, 1977.
The Stone Bull. New York, Doubleday, and London, Heinemann, 1977.
The Glass Flame. New York, Doubleday, 1978; London, Heinemann, 1979.
Domino. New York, Doubleday, 1979; London, Heinemann, 1980.
Poinciana. New York, Doubleday, 1980; London, Heinemann, 1981.
Vermilion. New York, Doubleday, 1981; London, Heinemann, 1982.
Emerald. New York, Doubleday, and London, Heinemann, 1983.
Rainsong. New York, Doubleday, and London, Heinemann, 1984.
Dream of Orchids. New York, Doubleday, and London, Hodder & Stoughton, 1985.
The Flaming Tree. New York, Doubleday, and London, Hodder & Stoughton, 1986.
Silversword. New York, Doubleday, and London, Hodder & Stoughton, 1987.
Feather on the Moon. New York, Doubleday, and London, Hodder & Stoughton, 1988.

Rainbow in the Mist. New York, Doubleday, and London, Hodder & Stoughton, 1989.
The Singing Stones. New York, Doubleday, and London, Hodder & Stoughton, 1990.
Woman without a Past. New York, Doubleday, 1991.
The Ebony Swan. New York, Doubleday, 1992.

Other

Writing Juvenile Fiction. Boston, The Writer, 1947; revised edition, 1960.
Writing Juvenile Stories and Novels: How to Write and Sell Fiction for Young People. Boston, The Writer, 1976.
Guide to Fiction Writing. Boston, The Writer, 1982; London, Poplar Press, 1984.
Writing to Win: Winning Essays Submitted to the Phyllis A. Whitney Writing Contest, 1983-1987. Patchogue. New York, Patchogue-Medford Library, 1988.

*

Manuscript Collection: Mugar Memorial Library, Boston University.

Critical Study: Entry in *Contemporary Literary Criticism,* Volume 42, Detroit, Gale, 1987, pp. 431-438.

Phyllis A. Whitney comments:

Two elements from my early life have influenced me as a writer. When I was thirteen and living in Kobe, Japan, my mother, father and I spent many quiet winter evenings reading aloud. We read a number of mysteries of that period—and I was inoculated!

Since I grew up in beautiful, interesting places in Japan, China, and the Philippines, I developed an eye for settings. Now, for each new mystery novel that I write I look for a place that speaks to my imagination and excites my inventive faculties. This process has kept me writing for all these years—since new places can never grow stale.

*   *   *

In addition to her many adult novels, most of which can be classified as romance or mystery and which are enjoyed by young adult readers, Phyllis Whitney has written numerous young adult novels and mysteries. She is also the author of works about writing for juvenile audiences: *Writing Juvenile Fiction* and *Writing Juvenile Stories and Novels: How to Write and Sell Fiction for Young People.*

Many of her novels for young people, especially those published between 1941 and 1954, appeal to girls rather than boys, as indicated in the names of girls being in the titles: *A Place for Ann* (1941), *A Star for Ginny* (1942), *A Window for Julie* (1943), *Linda's Homecoming* (1950), *Nobody Likes Trina* (1972). The novels are primarily didactic. With the exception of *The Vanishing Scarecrow,* published in 1971, all of Whitney's mysteries for young people have titles beginning with the word mystery or secret. These novels are characterized by strong adventure set against vivid backgrounds. *Secret of the Spotted Shell* is set in the Virgin Islands. Other novels are set in Turkey, Norway, Japan, Greece, South Africa, and many places in the United States.

Some of Whitney's adult fiction may also be enjoyed by female young adult readers. These novels deal with young women who try

to make their own way in the world, who encounter a series of dangerous adventures, and who eventually marry their true loves. These novels include *The Quicksilver Pool,* set on Staten Island during the Civil War; *The Trembling Hills,* a love story set at the time of the San Francisco earthquake; *Skye Cameron,* set in nineteenth-century New Orleans; *The Moonflower,* with a background in modern Japan; *Thunder Heights,* about the nineteenth-century Hudson River Valley; *Blue Fire,,* set in modern South Africa; and *Window on the Square,* set in Washington Square, New York, in the nineteenth century.

Other works written for older audiences may be appealing to younger female readers since they deal with relationships between mothers and daughters, female identity, and women trying to come to terms with their own pasts. Many of these women try to return to ancestral homes or reconcile with other women in their families. Phyllis Whitney's women are fallible, sometimes marrying the wrong man or misjudging character, but they see their wrongs and change. Novels with these themes include most notably *Columbella, Silverhill, Lost Island, Listen for the Whisperer, The Turquoise Mask,* and *The Golden Unicorn.* Whitney's writing is eloquent and charming. Those of all ages susceptible to romance and mystery are drawn to the novels.

Among those works noted as young adult novels are a sizable number including *A Place for Ann* (illustrated by Helen Blair); *A Star for Ginny* (illustrated by Hilda Frommholz); *A Window for Julie* (illustrated by Jean Anderson); *The Silver Inkwell* (also illustrated by Frommholz); *Willow Hill; Ever After; Linda's Homecoming; Love Me, Love Me Not; Step to the Music; A Long Time Coming; The Fire and The Gold; The Highest Dream; Creole Holiday;* and *Nobody Likes Trina.*

Whitney's first novel, *A Place for Ann,* brought her some success and allowed her to be self-sufficient. *Willow Hill* published in 1947 was ahead of its time in dealing with a controversial subject. It is the story of a young white girl and her high school friends. They have to deal with the integration of a housing project in their neighborhood.

Whitney's young adult mysteries are even more numerous. *The Mystery of the Gulls* involves Taffy Saunders and her adventure on Mackinac Island. Taffy's mother inherits a hotel, but someone keeps trying to scare them away from the island. Taffy decides she must be the one to solve the mystery of who is trying to close the hotel down. *The Island of Dark Woods,* later published as *Mystery of the Strange Traveller,* deals with a phantom stagecoach passenger who helps Laurie and her sister solve a mystery. *The Mystery of the Black Diamonds* involves a treasure map that an old prospector has given Angie and Mark, two youths who think the whole thing is a hoax. Their parents take them to a ghost town called Blossom, strange things start happening, and they then begin believing in and searching for the map's treasures. *The Mystery on the Isle of Skye* is about an orphan raised by her grandmother. When the grandmother falls ill, Cathy MacLeod is sent on a trip to the Isle of Skye with her uncle, aunt, and two cousins. A series of mysteries ensue and she and her cousins puzzle them out. *The Mystery of the Golden Horn* has Vicki, the young protagonist, being told by a young gypsy that a golden horn is the key to her fortune. Searching for the secret of this mysterious horn, Vicki faces many dangers. *Secret of The Emerald Star* is about Robin Ward and a house with menacing stone lions and a high iron gate. This is Devery House occupied by old Mrs. Devery, her daughter-in-law, and blind granddaughter, Stella. At first Robin feels sorry for Stella, but it soon becomes obvious to Robin that Stella's real problem is that her grandmother does not understand Stella. Robin is also troubled by Mr. Lemon who is strange and menacing. The two girls play detective and become involved in a dangerous mystery. *The Mystery of the Angry Idol* is about a summer of secrets. Jan Pendleton worries that her visit with her grandmother would be dull until she meets Neil, the boy next door, and the aloof Patrick. Soon comes the realization that a dark-bearded stranger is watching the house and watching over a fearsome-looking Chinese idol kept in great-grandmother Althea's room. The idol is stolen. Jan is not the only one trying to find out the idol's mysteries. A family secret and another treasure map play prominent roles in *Secret of Goblin Glen*. In the town of Camberhills is the mystery of the great unsolved bank robbery. The thieves' hideout was Goblin Glen, but no one has ever been able to decipher the map and find the loot. Trina Lorey, grandniece of one of the robbers, tries her hand at finding the treasure. But she is not the only one looking. She has to work fast and quietly to solve the mystery and to clear her family name.

Other juvenile mysteries include *Mystery of the Green Cat, Secret of the Samurai Sword, Mystery of the Haunted Pool, Secret of the Tiger's Eye, Mystery of the Hidden Hand, Secret of the Spotted Shell, Mystery of the Crimson Ghost, Secret of the Missing Footprint, The Vanishing Scarecrow, Mystery of the Scowling Boy, Secret of Haunted Mesa,* and *Secret of the Stone Face.* Each is intriguing, filled with characters who try to uncover secrets and solve crises; each represents her successful mystery equation.

—Lesa Dill

———————

WIESEL, Elie(zer). American. Born in Sighet, Romania, 30 September 1928; immigrated to United States, 1956, naturalized citizen, 1963. Educated at Sorbonne, University of Paris, France, 1948-51. Married Marion Erster Rose in 1969; one son and one stepdaughter. Worked variously as foreign correspondent for *Yedioth Ah'oronoth,* Tel Aviv, Israel, *L'Arche,* Paris, France, and *Jewish Daily Forward,* New York City, 1949-68; writer and lecturer, since 1964; Distinguished Professor of Judaic Studies, City College of the City University of New York, New York City, 1972-76; Andrew W. Mellon Professor in the Humanities, Boston University, Boston, Massachusetts, University Professor of Philosophy and Religious Studies since 1976. Distinguished Visiting Professor of Literature and Philosophy, Florida International University, 1982; Henry Luce Visiting Scholar in the Humanities and Social Thought, Whitney Humanities Center, Yale University, 1982-83. Member of board of overseers, Bar-Ilan University, since 1970; member of board of directors, American Associates of Ben-Gurion University of the Negev, since 1973, National Committee on American Foreign Policy, since 1983, International Rescue Committee, since 1985, Hebrew Arts School, and Humanitas; member of board of governors, Tel-Aviv University, since 1976, Haifa University, since 1977, and Oxford Centre for Postgraduate Hebrew Studies, since 1978; member of board of trustees, Yeshiva University, since 1977, and American Jewish World Service, since 1985; chairman, U.S. President's Commission on the Holocaust, 1979-80, U.S. Holocaust Memorial Council, 1980-86; member of jury, 1984 Neustadt International Prize for Literature; chairman of advisory board, World Union of Jewish Students, since 1985; co-founder of National Jew-

ish Center for Learning and Leadership; adviser, Boston University Institute for Philosophy and Religion, National Institute against Prejudice and Violence, and the International Center in New York, Inc; member of editorial boards, *Midstream Religion and Literature* (University of Notre Dame), *Sh'ma: Journal of Jewish Responsibility,* and *Hadassah;* chairman of editorial board, *Holocaust and Genocide Studies: An International Journal.* Recipient: Herzl Literary award; David Ben-Gurion award; International Kaplun Foundation award from Hebrew University of Jerusalem; American-Israeli Friendship award; Prix Rivarol, 1963, for *The Town beyond the Wall;* Ingram Merrill award, 1964; William and Janice Epstein Fiction award from Jewish Book Council, 1965, for *The Town beyond the Wall;* National Jewish Book awards, 1965, for *The Town beyond the Wall,* and 1972, for *Souls on Fire;* International Remembrance award from the World Federation of Bergen-Belsen Associations, 1965, for *The Town beyond the Wall* and all other writings; Jewish Heritage award, 1966, for excellence in literature; Prix Medicis (France), 1968, for *Le Mendiant de Jerusalem;* Prix Bordin from French Academy, 1972, and Frank and Ethel S. Cohen award from Jewish Book Council, 1973, both for *Souls on Fire;* Eleanor Roosevelt Memorial award, 1972; American Liberties Medallion from American Jewish Committee, 1972; Literary Avodah award from Jewish Teachers' Association, 1972; Martin Luther King, Jr., Medallion from City College of the City University of New York, 1973; award for Distinguished Service to American Jewry from National Federation of Jewish Men's Clubs, 1973; Faculty Distinguished Scholar award from Hofstra University, 1974; Scopus award from Hebrew University of Jerusalem, 1974; Rambam award from American Mizrachi Women, 1974; Holocaust Memorial award from New York Society of Clinical Psychologists, 1975; Jewish Heritage award from Haifa University, 1975; Spertus International award, 1976; Myrtle Wreath award from Hadassah, 1977; King Solomon award, 1977; Humanitarian award from B'rith Sholom, 1978; Joseph Prize for Human Rights from Anti-Defamation League of B'nai B'rith, 1978; Presidential Citation from New York University, 1979; Inaugural award for Literature from Israeli Bonds Prime Minister's Committee, 1979; Zalman Shazar award from the State of Israel, 1979. Prix Livre-International and Bourse Goncourt, both 1980, and Prix des Bibliothecaires, 1981, all for *Le Testament d'un poete juif assassine;* Jabotinsky Medal from State of Israel, 1980; Rabbanit Sarah Herzog award from Emunah Women of America, 1981; Jordan Davidson Humanitarian award from Florida International University, 1983; Literary Lions award from New York Public Library, 1983; fellow, Timothy Dwight College, Yale University, 1983; International Literary Prize for Peace from Royal Academy of Belgium, 1983; Le Grand Prix de la Litterature de la Ville de Paris, 1983, for *Le Cinquieme fils;* Le Grand Prix Litteraire de Festival International de Deauville, 1983; Anatoly Shcharansky Humanitarian award, 1983; Commander de la Legion d'Honneur, France, 1984, elevated to Grand Officier, 1990; Congressional Gold Medal of Achievement, 1984; Distinguished Writers award from Lincolnwood Library, 1984; Chancellor Joseph H. Lookstein award from Bar-Ilan University, 1984; Sam Levenson Memorial award from Jewish Community Relations Council, 1985; Comenius award from Moravian College, 1985; Henrietta Szold award from Hadassah, 1985; Anne Frank award, 1985; International Holocaust Remembrance award from State of Israel Bonds, 1985; Voice of Conscience award from American Jewish Congress, 1985; Distinguished Community Service award from Mutual of America, 1985; Covenant of Peace award from Synagogue Council of America, 1985; Freedom of Worship Medal from Franklin D. Roosevelt Four Freedoms Foundation, 1985; Jacob Pat award from World Congress of Jewish Culture, 1985; Humanitarian award from International League of Human Rights, 1985. Nobel Peace Prize, 1986; Distinguished Foreign-Born American award from International Center, 1986; Freedom Cup award from Women's League for Israel, 1986; Jacob Javits Humanitarian award of U.J.A. Young Leadership, 1986; Medal of Liberty award, 1986; Freedom award from International Rescue Committee, 1987; Achievement award from Artists and Writers for Peace in the Middle East, 1987; La Grande Medaille de Vermeil de la Ville de Paris, 1987; La Medaille l'Universite de Paris, 1987; La Medaille de la Chancellerie de l'Universite de Paris, 1987; Eitinger Prize from University of Oslo, 1987; Lifetime Achievement award from *Present Tense* magazine, 1987; special Christopher award, 1987; Profiles in Courage award from B'nai B'rith, 1987; Achievement award from State of Israel, 1987; Seminary Medal from Jewish Theological Seminary of America, 1987; Special award from National Committee on American Foreign Policy, 1987; Metcalf Cup and Prize for Excellence in Teaching from Boston University, 1987; Gra-Cruz da Ordem Nacional do Cruzeiro do Sul, Brazil, 1987; Centennial Medal from University of Scranton, 1987; Golda Meir Senior Humanitarian award, 1987; Hofstra University Presidential Medal, 1988; honorary fellow, Beth Hatefutsoth, 1988; Human Rights Law award from International Human Rights Law Group, 1988; Herzl Literary award; David Ben-Gurion award; International Kaplun Foundation award from Hebrew University of Jerusalem; American-Israeli Friendship award; S. Y. Agnon Gold Medal; approximately fifty honorary doctorates. Agent: Georges Borchardt, 136 East 57th St., New York, NY 10022. Address: University Professors, Boston University, 745 Commonwealth Ave., Boston, MA 02215, U.S.A.

PUBLICATIONS

Novels

L'Aube. Paris, Seuil, 1960; as *Dawn,* translated by Frances Frenaye, New York, Hill & Wang, 1961.
Le Jour. Paris, Seuil, 1961; as *The Accident,* translated by Anne Borchardt, New York, Hill & Wang, 1962.
La Ville de la chance. Paris, Seuil, 1962; as *The Town beyond the Wall,* translated by Stephen Becker, New York, Atheneum, 1964.
Les Portes de la foret. Paris, Seuil, 1964; as *The Gates of the Forest,* translated by Frances Frenaye, New York, Holt, 1966.
Le Mendiant de Jerusalem. Paris, Seuil, 1968; as *A Beggar in Jerusalem,* translated by the author and Lily Edelman, New York, Random House, 1970.
Le Serment de Kolvillag. Paris, Seuil, 1973; as *The Oath,* translated by Marion Wiesel, New York, Random House, 1973.
Le Testament d'un poete juif assassine. Paris, Seuil, 1980; as *The Testament,* translated by Marion Wiesel, New York, Simon & Schuster, 1981.
Le Cinquieme Fils. Paris, Grasset, 1983; as *The Fifth Son,* translated by Marion Wiesel, New York, Warner, 1985.
Le Crepuscule, au loin. Paris, Grasset et Fasquelle, 1987; as *Twilight,* translated by Marion Wiesel, New York, Summit, 1988.

Fiction

The Golem: The Story of a Legend as Told by Elie Wiesel, translated by Anne Borchardt. New York, Summit, 1983.

The Six Days of Destruction: Meditations toward Hope, with Albert H. Friedlander. Mahwah, New Jersey, Paulist Press, 1988.

Essays and Short Stories

Le Chant des morts. Paris, Seuil, 1966; as *Legends of Our Time,* translated by Steven Donadio, New York, Holt, 1968.
Entre deux soleils. Paris, Seuil, 1970; as *One Generation After,* translated by the author and Lily Edelman, New York, Random House, 1970.
Paroles d'etranger. Paris, Seuil, 1982.
Signes d'Exode. Paris, Grasset, 1985.
Against Silence: The Voice and Vision of Elie Wiesel, edited by Irving Abrahamson. Three volumes, New York, Holocaust Library, 1985.

Plays

Zalmen; ou, La Folie de Dieu. Paris, Seuil, 1968; as *Zalmen; or, The Madness of God,* translated by Lily Edelman and Nathan Edelman, New York, Holt, 1968.
Le proces de Shamgorod tel qu'il se deroula le 25 fevrier 1649: Piece en trois actes (first produced in Paris, 1981). Paris, Seuil, 1979; as *The Trial of God (as It Was Held on February 25, 1649, in Shamgorod): A Play in Three Acts,* translated by Marion Wiesel, New York, Random House, 1979.

Other

Un di velt hot geshvign (memoir; in Yiddish; title means "And the World Has Remained Silent"). [Buenos Aires], 1956; as *La Nuit,* Paris, Minuit, 1958; as *Night,* translated by Stella Rodway, New York, Hill & Wang, 1960.
Les Juifs du silence (originally published in Hebrew as a series of articles for newspaper *Yedioth Ah'oronoth*). Paris, Seuil, 1966; as *The Jews of Silence: A Personal Report on Soviet Jewry,* translated by Neal Kozodoy, New York, Holt, 1966.
La Nuit, L'Aube, [and] Le Jour. Paris, Seuil, 1969; as *Night, Dawn, [and] The Accident: Three Tales,* New York, Hill & Wang, 1972.
Celebration hassidique: Portraits et legendes. Paris, Seuil, 1972; as *Souls on Fire: Portraits and Legends of Hasidic Masters,* translated by Marion Wiesel, New York, Random House, 1972.
Ani maamin: A Song Lost and Found Again (cantata; first performed at Carnegie Hall, 1973), translated by Marion Wiesel, with music by Darius Milhaud. New York, Random House, 1974.
Celebration biblique: Portraits et legendes. Paris, Seuil, 1975; as *Messengers of God: Biblical Portraits and Legends,* translated by Marion Wiesel, New York, Random House, 1976.
Conversations with Elie Wiesel by Harry James Cargas. Mahwah, New Jersey, Paulist Press, 1976.
Un Juif aujourd'hui: Recits, essais, dialogues. Paris, Seuil, 1977; as *A Jew Today,* translated by Marion Wiesel, New York, Random House, 1978.
Dimensions of the Holocaust, with others. Muskogee, Oklahoma, Indiana University Press, 1978.
Four Hasidic Masters and Their Struggle against Melancholy. Indiana, University of Notre Dame Press, 1978.
Images from the Bible, illustrated by Shalom of Safed. New York, Overlook Press, 1980.
Five Biblical Portraits. Indiana, University of Notre Dame Press, 1981.

The Haggadah (cantata), music by Elizabeth Swados. New York, S. French, 1982; *The Haggadah for Passover,* illustrated by Mark Podwal, New York, Simon & Schuster, 1993.

Somewhere a Master: Further Hasidic Portraits and Legends, translated by Marion Wiesel. New York, Simon & Schuster, 1982.

Job ou Dieu dans la Tempete, with Josy Eisenberg. Paris, Grasset et Fasquelle, 1986.

L'oublie. Paris, Seuil, 1989; as *The Forgotten,* translated by Stephen Becker, New York, Summit, in press.

Evil and Exile, with Philippe-Michael de Saint-Cheron, translated by Jon Rothschild. Indiana, University of Notre Dame Press, 1990.

From the Kingdom of Memory. New York, Summit, 1990.

A Journey of Faith: A Dialogue between Elie Wiesel and John Cardinal O'Connor, with John O'Connor. New York, Donald I. Fine, 1990.

In Dialogue and Dilemma with Elie Wiesel, interviewed by David Patterson. Wakefield, New Hampshire, Longwood Academic, 1991.

Sages and Dreamers: Biblical, Talmudic, and Hasidic Portraits and Legends. New York, Summit, 1991.

Nine and One-Half Mystics: The Kabbala Today. New York, Macmillan, 1992.

*

Media Adaptations: *The Madness of God* (adapted for the stage by Marion Wiesel), Washington, D.C., 1974; *Night* (sound recording), New York, Caedmon, 1982.

Biography: Essay in *Contemporary Authors Autobiography Series,* Volume 4, Detroit, Gale, 1986, pp. 353-62; entry in *Dictionary of Literary Biography Yearbook: 1986,* Detroit, Gale, 1987, pp. 19-28; entry in *Dictionary of Literary Biography Yearbook: 1987,* Detroit, Gale, 1988, pp. 388-401; entry in *Dictionary of Literary Biography,* Volume 83: *French Novelists since 1960,* Detroit, Gale, 1989.

Bibliography: *Elie Wiesel: A Bibliography* by Molly Abramowitz, Metuchen, New Jersey, Scarecrow, 1974; *Elie Wiesel: A Small Measure of Victory* by Gene Koppel and Henry Kaufmann, Tucson, University of Arizona, 1974; *Confronting the Holocaust: The Impact of Elie Wiesel* edited by Alvin Rosenfeld and Irving Greenberg, Bloomington, Indiana University Press, 1979; *A Consuming Fire: Encounters with Elie Wiesel and the Holocaust* by John K. Roth, Louisville, Kentucky, Knox Press, 1979; *The Vision of the Void: Theological Reflections on the Works of Elie Wiesel* by Michael G. Berenbaum, Middletown, Connecticut, Wesleyan University Press, 1979; *Legacy of Night: The Literary Universe of Elie Wiesel* by Ellen S. Fine, Albany, State University of New York Press, 1982; *Elie Wiesel: Messenger to All Humanity* by Robert McAfee Brown, Indiana, University of Notre Dame Press, 1983; *Elie Wiesel: Messenger from the Holocaust* by Carol Greene, Chicago, Illinois, Children's Press, 1987.

Critical Study: Entry in *Contemporary Literary Criticism,* Detroit, Gale, Volume 3, 1975, Volume 5, 1976, Volume 11, 1979, Volume 37, 1986.

*   *   *

"How can we imagine what is beyond imagination.... How can we retell what escapes language?" This is Elie Wiesel's response to the notion of Holocaust literature. Although he is considered by many to be the world's most eloquent and prolific author of this genre, Wiesel views *Un di velt hot geshvign,* published in 1956 (later edited and republished in English as *Night*) as his only work on the subject. His other novels, *Dawn, The Accident, The Town beyond the Wall, The Gates of the Forest, A Beggar in Jerusalem, The Oath,* and *The Testament,* take place either before or after the events of the Holocaust by design. "I try not to make it tolerable," Wiesel related to author Diane Cooper-Clark in *Interviews with Contemporary Novelists.* "When I see that it becomes tolerable, I don't speak about it. That's why I have written so little about the Holocaust."

Wiesel's silence is carefully executed. Although his works do not directly address the Holocaust, they are all informed by it and they introduce issues that force the reader to come to terms with humanity's capacity for degradation and God's seeming callousness in the midst of human suffering. Wiesel's simple writing style belies his ability to engage his audience in the grand conflict he has experienced as life. In this engagement, Wiesel displays his mastery by convincing even the most skeptical reader that life is an urgent act requiring each person to examine the significance of his existence.

Drawing on his early theological training to craft his works, Wiesel incorporates traditional Jewish approaches to understanding the human dilemma. In *By Words Alone,* Sidra DeKoven Ezrahi has identified the major influences of Jewish literature in Wiesel's works. The traditional Hebrew narratives, Ezrahi asserts, provided Wiesel with a model for the fusion of legend and real experience. In this respect, Wiesel also appeals to the Hasidic tradition that places more import on eyewitness testimony than accurate documentation to establish truth. This is of particular significance with the events of the Holocaust since official records of formal plans by the Germans to eradicate those they deemed "undesirable" do not exist. Wiesel establishes through his novel *Night* and his subsequent works that the Holocaust did happen and it continues to affect its perpetrators, victims, and all of humanity.

In *Dawn,* for example, Wiesel portrays a young Holocaust survivor, Elisha, who becomes involved in the fight for freedom in Palestine after the war. The roles are reversed for Elisha as he becomes the executioner of a British soldier who killed another young Israeli. Elisha is confronted with the bitter reality that those who just experienced humanity's most cruel act further brutalize themselves as they kill others to ensure the survival of their nation. Elisha realizes in choosing to kill the British soldier, he has killed himself.

Another characteristic of Hebraic tradition is that the central conflict of the novel, which usually deals with the ramifications of God's involvement with human affairs, is left unresolved. Some have compared examples of traditional Jewish legends with what Ezrahi calls the "fragments of a violated theodicy" in Wiesel's works. Wiesel sets up the plot conflict by introducing situations that challenge the bond between God and humanity. Then, rather than neatly resolving the conflict, Wiesel leaves the reader with a myriad of unresolved questions about the essence of life and the nature of God.

The Accident clearly exemplifies Wiesel's use of this technique. After intense introspection, the protagonist realizes the "accident" that nearly killed him was really a suicide attempt—the ultimate act of rebellion against God. The act stemmed from the character's inability to resolve his concentration camp experience and the role of God in the Holocaust. Suicide became the most significant way in which the character could claim for himself what he had previously ascribed to God: the right to decide whether life is worth living. Through another round of agonizing self-examination, the character concludes that life's significance lies in questions rather than answers.

Wiesel's writings appeal to a wide range of readers from those just beginning to realize the questions of life to those well versed in the process of inquiry. The issues he addresses—identity, the breakdown of one's support network, the nature of God, human limitations, the construction of an orderly existence in the midst of chaos, man's inhumanity to man—are at the core of the human experience. To the young, Wiesel stands as a witness to the events of the Holocaust while he provides a framework for the questioning that inevitably occurs as people discover life is not as certain, concrete, and predictable as they once believed. The more experienced reader will find a challenge in the profound conflict hidden under Wiesel's deceptively simple writing style.

—Linda Ross

———

WILKINSON, Brenda. American. Born in Moultrie, Georgia, 1 January 1946. Educated at Hunter College of the City University of New York. Separated; two daughters. Poet and author. Conducts poetry readings. Recipient: National Book award nominee, 1976, for *Ludell; Ludell and Willie* was named one of the outstanding children's books of the year by the *New York Times* and a best book for young adults by the American Library Association, both 1977.

PUBLICATIONS FOR YOUNG ADULTS

Fiction

Ludell. New York, Harper, 1975.
Ludell and Willie. New York, Harper, 1976.
Ludell's New York Time. New York, Harper, 1980.
Not Separate, Not Equal. New York, Harper, 1987.
Definitely Cool. New York, Scholastic, 1993.

Nonfiction

Jesse Jackson: Still Fighting for the Dream. Morristown, New Jersey, Silver Burdett Press, 1990.

*

Biography: Essay in *Speaking for Ourselves, Too* compiled and edited by Donald R. Gallo, National Council of Teachers of English, 1993.

*   *   *

Brenda Wilkinson specializes in writing about African Americans growing up in the New South. Her first three books are auto-

biographical in nature while her fourth novel deals with more universal experiences. In every book there is a common theme of unity in the black community against the frighteningly cruel world of the whites.

Ludell, Ludell and Willie, and *Ludell's New York Time* tell the story of Ludell Wilson from age eleven to eighteen. Ludell is a fatherless child being raised by her grandmother in Waycross, Georgia, in the 1950s. *Ludell* deals mainly with her problems in a segregated school but also with her growing awareness of boys and the real world. The conversation is in authentic black dialect and the subjects discussed are those of concern to an eleven-year-old girl. Religion plays an important part. *Ludell and Willie* focuses on Ludell's growing attraction to Willie, the boy next door and the brother of her best friend, Ruthie Mae Johnson. They are truly in love but are bound to good behavior by the ironclad rules of Ludell's grandmother, Mama. Ludell matures quickly as she begins working for white people at very low wages and things come to a climax as Mama's health declines and Ludell nurses her through her final illness. Ludell's mother, Dessa, comes home from New York (where she has been living most of Ludell's life) to take care of business matters and she insists that Ludell return with her to New York, even though it means Ludell must leave high school just short of graduation. Even worse for Ludell is being separated from Willie. Reluctantly Ludell leaves Waycross for New York City. Upon her arrival in the North, *Ludell's New York Time* begins. She finishes high school and looks for work, experiencing prejudice in the North as her job search takes more time than expected. Eventually Ludell returns to Waycross and marries Willie.

Not Separate, Not Equal is the story of six African American students chosen to integrate the Pineridge, Georgia, white high school. Pineridge is a fictional town, but the real world of 1965 is portrayed accurately in the novel. Again, the heroine is a plucky teenager, in this case an orphan. Malene Freeman has been adopted by a well-to-do couple after the tragic death of her sharecropper parents. She is one of the six students picked to go to the formerly all-white Pineridge High. The usual demonstrations occur but Malene is personally targeted by a deranged white man. All six students fall victim to his scheming but are rescued in a bittersweet effort. The novel ends with the community moving toward desegregation: some black families leave town, some white families begin building a private school, yet none can escape the fact that the New South is here to stay.

Wilkinson has just the right level of sophistication in each book. *Ludell* is a rather simplistic book as it should be with an eleven-year-old heroine. Gradually the series becomes more complex as Ludell becomes more aware of the true rigors of life. She realizes that the easy-going nature of the blacks around her is an attempt to deal with the discrimination and outright hatred of the white world. However, she does not feel that her mother's escape to New York is the answer either. The forces of change have very little to do with Waycross except to make the local people more aware of their situation. Ludell has enough problems of her own; only when she moves up North does she begin to realize how the problems of all African Americans are her problems, too.

Although the "Ludell" series is more complex, *Not Separate, Not Equal* is an excellent attempt to deal with the issue of desegregation on its own. The social problems are more prominent in this book and there is not as much of the banter that makes the "Ludell" books so entertaining. *Not Separate, Not Equal* stands beside Ann Waldron's *The Integration of Mary-Larkin Thornhill* as a classic depiction of the school integration movement.

Brenda Wilkinson has done a good job altogether in capturing a recent time in American history as well as the personalities of some very believable teenagers. She also has a real feel for accurately depicting the backdrop of southern Georgia.

—Sharon Clontz Bernstein

WILLARD, Barbara (Mary). British. Born in Hove, Sussex, 12 March 1909. Educated at Convent of La Sainte Union, Southampton. Actress, novelist, and screenwriter. Recipient: Guardian award for children's fiction, 1972, for *The Sprig of Broom,* 1973, for *A Cold Wind Blowing,* and 1974, for *The Iron Lily; The Iron Lily* was also named an American Library Association notable book; Whitbread award, 1984. Agent: David Higham Associates Ltd., 5-8 Lower John Street, London, W1R 4HA. Address: Forest Edge, Nutley, Uckfield, Sussex, England.

PUBLICATIONS FOR YOUNG ADULTS

Fiction

Portrait of Philip (for adults), London, Macmillan, 1950; revised edition (for young adults), as *He Fought for His Queen,* London, Heinemann, and New York, Warne, 1954.
The House with Roots, illustrated by Robert Hodgson. London, Constable, 1959; New York, Watts, 1960.
Son of Charlemagne, illustrated by Emil Weiss. New York, Doubleday, 1959; London, Heinemann, 1960.
The Dippers and Jo, illustrated by Jean Harper. London, Hamish Hamilton, 1960.
Eight for a Secret, illustrated by Lewis Hart. London, Constable, 1960; New York, Watts, 1961.
The Penny Pony, illustrated by Juliette Palmer. London, Hamish Hamilton, 1961.
The Summer with Spike, illustrated by Anne Linton. London, Constable, 1961; New York, Watts, 1962.
If All the Swords in England, illustrated by Robert M. Sax. New York, Doubleday, and London, Burns Oates, 1961.
Stop the Train!, illustrated by Jean Harper. London, Hamish Hamilton, 1961.
Duck on a Pond, illustrated by Mary Rose Hardy. London, Constable, and New York, Watts, 1962.
Hetty, illustrated by Pamela Mara. London, Constable, 1962; New York, Harcourt, 1963.
Augustine Came to Kent, illustrated by Hans Guggenheim. New York, Doubleday, 1963; Kingswood, Surrey, World's Work, 1964.
The Battle of Wednesday Week, illustrated by Douglas Hall. London, Constable, 1963; as *Storm from the West,* New York, Harcourt, 1964.
The Dippers and the High-Flying Kite, illustrated by Maureen Eckersley. London, Hamish Hamilton, 1963.
The Suddenly Gang, illustrated by Lynette Hemmant. London, Hamish Hamilton, 1963.
A Dog and a Half, illustrated by Jane Paton. London, Hamish Hamilton, 1964; New York, Nelson, 1971.

The Pram Race, illustrated by Constance Marshall. London, Hamish Hamilton, 1964.
Three and One to Carry, illustrated by Douglas Hall. London, Constable, 1964; New York, Harcourt, 1965.
The Wild Idea, illustrated by Douglas Bissett. London, Hamish Hamilton, 1965.
Charity at Home, illustrated by Douglas Hall. London, Constable, 1965; New York, Harcourt, 1966.
Surprise Island, illustrated by Jane Paton. London, Hamish Hamilton, 1966; New York, Meredith Press, 1969.
The Richleighs of Tantamount, illustrated by C. Walter Hodges. London, Constable, 1966; New York, Harcourt, 1967.
The Grove of Green Holly, illustrated by Gareth Floyd. London, Constable, 1967; as *Flight to the Forest,* New York, Doubleday, 1967.
The Pet Club, illustrated by Lynette Hemmant. London, Hamish Hamilton, 1967.
To London! To London!, illustrated by Antony Maitland. London, Longman, and New York, Weybright & Talley, 1968.
Hurrah for Rosie!, illustrated by Gareth Floyd. London, Hutchinson, 1968.
Royal Rosie, illustrated by Gareth Floyd. London, Hutchinson, 1968.
The Family Tower. London, Constable, and New York, Harcourt, 1968.
The Toppling Towers. London, Longman, and New York, Harcourt, 1969.
The Pocket Mouse, illustrated by Mary Russon. London, Hamish Hamilton, and New York, Knopf, 1969; illustrated by M. Harford-Cross, London, MacRae, 1981.

"Mantlemass" series:

The Lark and the Laurel, illustrated by Gareth Floyd. London, Longman, and New York, Harcourt, 1970.
The Sprig of Broom, illustrated by Paul Shardlow. London, Longman, 1971; New York, Dutton, 1972.
A Cold Wind Blowing. London, Longman, 1972; New York, Dutton, 1973.
The Iron Lily. London, Longman, 1973; New York, Dutton, 1974.
Harrow and Harvest. London, Kestrel, 1974; New York, Dutton, 1975.
The Miller's Boy, illustrated by Gareth Floyd. London, Kestrel, and New York, Dutton, 1976.
The Eldest Son. London, Kestrel, 1977.
A Flight of Swans. London, Kestrel, 1980.
The Keys of Mantlemass. London, Kestrel, 1981.
Priscilla Pentecost, illustrated by Doreen Roberts. London, Hamish Hamilton, 1970.
The Reindeer Slippers, illustrated by Tessa Jordan. London, Hamish Hamilton, 1970.
The Dragon Box, illustrated by Tessa Jordan. London, Hamish Hamilton, 1972.
Jubilee!, illustrated by Hilary Abrahams. London, Heinemann, 1973.
Bridesmaid, illustrated by Jane Paton. London, Hamish Hamilton, 1976.
The Country Maid. London, Hamish Hamilton, 1978; New York, Greenwillow, 1980.
The Gardener's Grandchildren. London, Kestrel, 1978; New York, McGraw, 1979.
Summer Season. London, MacRae, 1981.

Spell Me a Witch, illustrated by Phillida Gili. London, Hamish Hamilton, 1979; New York, Harcourt, 1981.
Famous Rowena Lamont. London, Hardy, 1983.
The Queen of the Pharisees' Children. London, MacRae, 1984.
Smiley Tiger, illustrated by Laszlo Acs. London, MacRae, 1984.
Ned Only. London, MacRae, 1985.

Other

Editor, *Hullabaloo! About Naughty Boys and Girls,* illustrated by Fritz Wegner. London, Hamish Hamilton, and New York, Meredith Press, 1969.
Junior Motorist: The Driver's Apprentice, with Frances Howell, illustrated by Ionicus. London, Collins, 1969.
Chichester and Lewes, illustrated by Graham Humphreys. London, Longman, 1970.
Editor, *Happy Families,* illustrated by Krystyna Turska. London, Hamish Hamilton, and New York, Macmillan, 1974.
Translator, *Convent Cat,* by Bunshu Iguchi, illustrated by Iguchi. London, Hamish Hamilton, 1975; New York, McGraw, 1976.
Editor, *Field and Forest,* illustrated by Faith Jaques. London, Kestrel, 1975.
Translator, *The Giants' Feast,* by Max Bollinger, illustrated by Monika Laimgruber. London, Hamish Hamilton, 1975.

PUBLICATIONS FOR ADULTS

Novels

Love in Ambush, with Elizabeth Helen Devas. London, Howe, 1930.
Ballerina. London, Howe, 1932.
Candle Flame. London, Howe, 1932.
Name of Gentleman. London, Howe, 1933.
Joy Befall Thee. London, Howe, 1934.
As Far as in Me Lies. London, Nelson, 1936.
Set Piece. London, Nelson, 1938.
Personal Effects. London, Macmillan, 1939.
The Dogs Do Bark. London, Macmillan, 1948.
Celia Scarfe. New York, Appleton-Century, 1951.
Proposed and Seconded. London, Macmillan, 1951.
Echo Answers. London, Macmillan, 1952.
Winter in Disguise. London, Joseph, 1958.

Plays

Brother Ass and Brother Lion, adaptation of the story of "St. Jerome, The Lion and the Donkey" by Helen J. Waddell. London, J. Garnet Miller, 1951.
One of the Twelve (one-act play). London, French, 1954.
Fit for a King. London, J. Garnet Miller, 1955.

Radio Play: *Duck on a Pond,* from her own book, 1962.

Television Play: *Merry Go Round,* 1965.

Other

Sussex. London, Batsford, 1965; New York, Hastings House, 1966.
Editor, *"I...": An Anthology of Diarists.* London, Chatto & Windus, 1972.

Biography: Essay in *Something about the Author Autobiography Series,* Volume 5, Detroit, Gale, 1988; entry in *Fourth Book of Junior Authors and Illustrators* edited by Doris de Montreville and Elizabeth D. Crawford, New York, H.W. Wilson, 1978.

Critical Study: Entry in *Children's Literature Review,* Volume 2, Detroit, Gale, 1976.

*   *   *

After turning from adult fiction to novels for young readers, Barbara Willard has continued to write regularly and enthusiastically for them for nearly thirty years. Although her works are enormously varied, both she and many of her readers recognize the particular success of the novels inspired by English history and the Wealden area of Sussex. Through absorbing stories of young people caught up in the effects of great historical events, Willard leads the reader to an understanding of the issues involved. At the same time, her fully realized and attractive characters face personal experiences which seem contemporary.

It was in the Wealden Forest novels that Willard "found her voice." Her descriptions of the forest create a world with which the reader grows familiar, learning to recognize how the landscape has evolved over centuries. A characteristic earlier book with a contemporary setting, *The Battle of Wednesday Week* is a competent, Arthur Ransome-style holiday story. Separated from adults, young people take risks, face dangers, and learn how to coexist with resented new members of an extended family. Willard pursues these themes in later novels, but here the plot which carries them seems contrived and the dialogue stilted.

By comparison, the historical books from *The Lark and the Laurel* onward show an author who is not only writing with confidence but also with enjoyment and commitment. This novel marks the beginning of the Mantlemass sequence, the series for which Willard will be best remembered. The eight novels share the setting of the forest and Mantlemass, the manor house in which generations of the Medley and Mallory families live, and the sequence stretches from the Wars of the Roses to the Civil War in the seventeenth century.

Although the periods and settings may seem alien to contemporary young adults, they are introduced through these novels to experiences and emotions with which they can readily identify: strong parents try to force children to live out their own dreams rather than enabling them to make choices for themselves, siblings compete for parents' attention and praise, large extended families create tensions as different generations and the children of different marriages try to live peacefully in the same house, and young people discover that intense love does not necessarily lead to happiness. In each of the novels, Willard returns to the problems girls face in finding satisfying lives for themselves. Some of the young women gain independence through circumstances and become respected equals with the men with whom they live and work. Others fight against society's expectations of women and succeed against the odds. These are strong, spirited characters developed over several novels.

As a historical novelist, Willard avoids the trap of didacticism by making her characters act out relevant situations so that the reader is drawn into complex issues through involvement in their experiences. Piers Medley in *A Cold Wind Blowing* is a powerless spectator as he watches his uncle, a monk, die for his beliefs and sees the local priory destroyed. His friend becomes one of the moving spirits in the Dissolution movement, and his young wife, Isabella, dies because she is unable to come to terms with breaking the vows she made as a novice nun. In one sense, the Mantlemass characters live a timeless life sheltered in the forest; in *The Sprig of Broom,* Richard Plantagenet, the illegitimate son of Richard III, lives in the forest undiscovered by the world outside for many years. Gradually, however, as the novels progress, the sanctuary of the forest is destroyed as woodland is cut down, industry begins to develop, and strangers move in. The central families become dispersed, and the divided loyalties of civil wars are acted out in Mantlemass itself. Above all, the historical settings provide the opportunity for plots in which action is important but always authentic. Willard is an accomplished storyteller.

Although each of the Mantlemass novels stands by itself, the reader gains additional pleasure from the cumulative effect of the whole sequence. Characters are further developed, mysteries are gradually solved, the long-term effects of important events can be traced, incidents are seen from different perspectives through the use of changing viewpoints, and there is the satisfaction of following the evolution of the forest and the central families. Throughout, the novels are linked by buildings and objects which become symbols of the past by the end of the sequence.

Willard's fascination with the forest continues into later novels, such as *Famous Rowena Lamont,* in which more recent events are set against the background, the people, and the dialect of the area. As she has written, "What happier fate for any author than to live in a setting that demands to be written about?" and it is for her novels inspired by the Sussex Weald for which Barbara Willard has won several awards and been rightly praised.

—Judith Atkinson

WILLEY, Margaret. American. Born in Chicago, Illinois, 5 November 1950. Educated at Grand Valley State College, Allendale, Michigan, B.Ph., B.A. 1975; Bowling Green State University, Ohio, M.F.A. 1979. Married Richard Joanisse in 1980; one daughter. Writer. Recipient: Creative Artist Grant, Michigan Council of the Arts, 1984-85; American Library Association citations as one of the year's best books for young adults, 1983, for *The Bigger Book of Lydia,* 1986, for *Finding David Dolores,* 1988, for *If Not for You,* and 1990, for *Saving Lenny.* Address: 431 Grant, Grand Haven, MI 49417, U.S.A.

PUBLICATIONS FOR YOUNG ADULTS

Novels

The Bigger Book of Lydia. New York, Harper, 1983.
Finding David Dolores. New York, Harper, 1986.
If Not for You. New York, Harper, 1988.
Saving Lenny. New York, Bantam, 1990.
The Melinda Zone. New York, Bantam, 1993.

*   *   *

The success of Margaret Willey's books for young adults is due at least in part to her skill at presenting totally believable characters who must struggle to resolve their problems in her coming-of-age dilemmas. Hers are distinctly drawn personalities with a wide range of conflicts: problems with parents; troubles with boyfriends; breeches of loyalty between best friends; school woes; and particularly, always, the struggle to find and to be oneself. Diverse though the works and characters of this three-time ALA Best Book awardee certainly are, it is easy to recognize a common thread: the attempt of the protagonist to strike a balance in the chaotic blend of relationships that so often characterizes adolescence. It is precisely the efforts to reconcile their own needs and desires with the often urgent and sometimes demanding needs and expectations of those around them that form the central themes of Willey's writings.

The reconciliation of such competing forces has central focus in *The Melinda Zone,* a touching story which depicts the difficulties of a fifteen-year-old trying desperately to find herself while torn in an emotional tug-of-war between her parents. Caught between these two adults whose paths lead in drastically different directions, Melinda seeks to avoid having to choose between her mother and father by spending her summer instead with her aunt and uncle and the older cousin she has always idolized. The warm affectionate relationship between her caring Aunt Rita and carefree, witty Uncle Ted casts a telling shadow on the uneasy state of affairs between Melinda's own parents who have been divorced since Melinda was a baby. The problem with them, Melinda explains to her cousin, is that they spend all their time arguing "over whose fault everything is."

The only angry words in Melinda's summer home are those that pass between her cousin Sharon and Uncle Ted and Aunt Rita, but even those are not enough to prevent her from enjoying the uncustomary spirit of independence living with her uncle and aunt brings. It is to be a summer filled with—nothing, if that is what Melinda chooses. Sensing her niece's need to make her own decisions about how to spend her time, Aunt Rita allows the confused teen a season totally free of the usual pressures and demands her parents place on her.

Melinda's Michigan summer away from home and parents takes on added purpose with the growing conflict between Sharon and her own parents. Once again she is called upon to play the role she knows so well: peacemaker. But this time, someone else, not she, is at the center of the conflict. Strange, Melinda thinks, that this young woman, the one she always thought had it all, should be so unhappy, should get along so badly with clearly wonderful parents. Caught up in an unlucky relationship with a boyfriend who is much older than she, Sharon has her own "finding" of herself to do. The pain of their parent-child conflict mirrors somewhat the pain Melinda is causing by her own silence and reluctance to phone or write her mother or father.

And then there is Paul. One of Sharon's castaways, this sensitive, young boy-next-door has serious parent troubles of his own. But his perceptiveness and wit enable him to be what Melinda most needs at the moment—a friend. With Paul she can be totally at ease; with him she does not have to keep acting as if "everything is fine, everything is wonderful. Even sometimes when it isn't." In turn, Melinda is there to help Paul discover whether there is life after Sharon, and perhaps more importantly, to listen with understanding as he reveals the fact that though he lives with his parents, he is separated from them by a barrier more unyielding and unreconcilable than any Melinda has ever known.

It is Paul to whom she confides her joy at being finally free "from trying to be who my mother thinks I am when I'm with her and who my father thinks I am when I'm with him." Melinda returns to

Milwaukee with many of her problems intact, hut there is reason to believe she will not stray too far from the independence and self-identity she has found in that wonderful place, that place Paul dubbed "The Melinda Zone."

In another of Willey's works, Lydia's search for identity becomes somehow entangled in the tiny girl's obsession with size, with measurements, with detail, in *The Bigger Book of Lydia*. A confused and insecure Lydia has great difficulty in making friends and joining in activities that others relish; in a very real sense, her physical smallness does indeed make her fragile—not just physically but emotionally and socially as well. In spite of her considerable capability to help others in her family, Lydia can not help herself, at least not until Michelle arrives. Willey has created in Michelle one of her most truly unforgettable characters. The troubled teenager's shocking physical condition reflects an inner chaos. She, too, needs assistance from Lydia, but this relationship is no one-way street. Together, the two girls seek the courage to deal with a world that previously has proven too much to bear.

In *Saving Lenny,* it is Jesse who does all the giving and Lenny who does all the taking in a misguided and painful relationship. Skillfully revealed through letters and passages written from the perspectives of the key players, this story deals with the conflicts which occur as a result of Jesse's blind devotion to a love which cannot survive. She must deal not only with the doomed relationship and with her own limitations at fulfilling Lenny's needs, but also with the chasm the relationship causes between Jesse and her parents and between Jesse and her best friend.

Loyalty between friends is also a central theme in *If Not for You.* A young girl becomes so engrossed in her friendship with her best friend's older sister that the two grow painfully distant, with Bonnie increasingly ensnared in a role she is unprepared to play. The process results in Bonnie's estrangement not only from her best friend, but also from her boyfriend and from her parents, and pulls her uncomfortably deep into an unnatural relationship with a young married couple. She must learn, as does Jesse in *Saving Lenny,* that a romanticized world gone sour can be the worst kind of nightmare. Her awakening is a difficult one.

Willey's books for young adults are marked by presentation of realistic dilemmas that are both timeless and contemporary, serious yet resolvable. By shaping her characters and crafting her plots with respect for reality she manages to produce satisfying outcomes without simplistic answers or sappy, happy endings. Through a blend of self-reliance and collaboration with others, her dynamic heroines come, if not to an absolute answer, then at least to an understanding of the problem that is life.

—Jan Tyler

WILLIAMS-GARCIA, Rita. American.

PUBLICATIONS FOR YOUNG ADULTS

Fiction

Blue Tights. New York, Dutton, 1988.
Fast Talk on a Slow Track. New York, Dutton, 1991.

*   *   *

Focusing her attention on contemporary African American youth, Rita Williams-Garcia informs her fictional teenagers with her own experiences as student, as teacher, as dancer. Her two young adult novels concern black adolescents struggling for a sense of identity against the backdrop of inner city New York. In her 1988 *Blue Tights,* fifteen-year-old Joyce Collins is an outsider, desperate to belong in a school that derides her talent as a dancer and scoffs at her unballetic body. Seventeen-year-old Denzel Watson of the 1991 novel *Fast Talk on a Slow Track* is an insider, an urban success story as the valedictorian of his class on his way to his freshman year at Princeton. Both protagonists, brash and arrogant, hide behind masks. Challenged to "show their face" they adopt a bravado that poses real danger and threatens to undermine discovery of their best selves. Their self-absorption and cockiness—one the result of self-loathing; the other, of self-aggrandizing—belie the insecurity that define them. Williams-Garcia explores these two young people learning to trust themselves apart from the crowd and to develop strength of character "alone and in touch."

For Williams-Garcia this coming-of-age struggle involves confrontation with both one's family and one's peers. These two novels provide Williams-Garcia the opportunity to create dramatically different family constellations with whom the adolescents contend. Joyce has been reared mainly by her religiously fanatic aunt since her mother is often absent, herself a young teenager when Joyce was born. Williams-Garcia does not shy away from the harsh circumstances that define Joyce and her family. Aunt Em's severe treatment of Joyce stems from a horrific self-induced coat hanger abortion she suffered in her adolescence. Williams-Garcia provides less sensational, daily evidence of the grinding poverty that eats at this family. For them material possessions provide false security and love. Her mother Minnie atones to Joyce with the gift of a real leather coat. Williams-Garcia evinces that their desperation to be somebody too often gets confused with ownership of things. Minnie looks with both envy and disgust at the successful man who fathered Joyce, but now clothes his new wife and two young sons in real fur and leather. Joyce is similarly convinced that clothes serve as talisman to popularity.

No such difficulties surround Denzel's family. A product of an urban middle-class home, Denzel lives with both his parents and a younger sister in security and ease. Yet his home allows Williams-Garcia to present another model of familial interaction. More comfortable in the integrated school he attends and with the white friends he attracts, Denzel clashes with his Afrocentric father for whom black pride is the nucleus of all things. Denzel even rails against his given name Dinizulu.

With both novels, Williams-Garcia dramatizes with painful honesty the collision between class as well as race, not only in the home, but also among the teenagers at school and on the streets. Joyce "didn't like the so-called better school or her honors classes. The Jewish boys told jokes that the whole class laughed at, but that she never got at all." Once transferred out of those classes, Joyce finds "someone else to cast are-they-for-real? glances to." Her discovery of an African American dance troupe refocuses the alternately angry and hurt Joyce on her talent as a dancer—she discovers brothers and sisters prideful of their culture who rejoice in movement that speaks to that culture. Here her crude and sexually explicit language has less relevance. Although written in the third person, Williams-Garcia creates an intimate voice for Joyce that rings true whether it is in its crassness or in its sweetness.

Denzel's first-person narrative also sizzles with believable black vernacular, especially in his conversations with the street-smart kids with whom he spends a summer selling candy door-to-door. Without flinching, Williams-Garcia places the cocky Denzel, recently back from a disastrous preparatory experience at Princeton, smack up against the illiterate Mello, a confident young salesman of the streets. The clash between their lives and their cultures forms the intense core of this novel and allows Williams-Garcia another arena to explore class differences. Each boy oversteps the code that defines his particular world, and choices and decisions flow from these transgressions.

Being responsible to and for oneself may be obvious rhetoric, but Williams-Garcia provides powerful resonance to this theme through her credible characters who speak in their own idiom with refreshing honesty and occasional humor. Williams-Garcia reminds readers that observing life from the wings may be safe but being onstage defines the real action—and the real character. Concluding her novels with her protagonists on stage (at her school's ballet class demonstrating a movement for the other students and back at Princeton signing the honor statement of an examination with his given name Dinizulu), Williams-Garcia indicates her characters' willingness to move on without guile and defense. Joyce looks in the dance mirror at herself "as something wonderful opening up before her eyes" while Denzel insists he has "thrown down the mask and [is] ready to fly."

—Susan P. Bloom

WINDSOR, Patricia (Frances). Also writes as Colin Daniel. American. Born in New York City, 21 September 1938. Educated at Bennington College, and Westchester Community College; New York University, associate's degree. Married Laurence Charles Windsor, Jr., in 1959 (divorced 1978); one daughter and one son. Vice-president, Windsor-Morehead Associates, New York, 1960-63; novelist. Teacher of creative writing, Westchester, New York, 1975-78; member of faculty, Institute of Children's Literature, Redding Ridge, Connecticut, 1976—; instructor, University of Maryland Writers Institute, 1981-83, and OPEN University, Washington, D.C. Senior editor, Harper and Row, beginning 1973; editor-in-chief of *Easterner* for American Telephone and Telegraph, Washington, D.C., 1979-81. Member, Citizens' Committee on Employment, Chicago, 1963-64; Family Planning Associations, London, England, assistant director of central inquiries, 1972-73, counselor, 1974-75; correspondent, National Council of Social Service, London, 1974—; active in YWCA and North Westchester Association for Retarded Children. Recipient: *Chicago Tribune Book World* Honor Book award, 1973, Best Books for Young Adults award, American Library Association, 1973, Austrian State award for Books for Children and Youth, 1981, all for *The Summer Before; Diving for Roses* was named a notable book of 1976 by the *New York Times;* Edgar Allan Poe award, Mystery Writers of America, 1985, for *The Sandman's Eyes.* Agent: Amy Berkower, Writers House, Incorporated, 21 West 26th Street, New York, NY 10010, U.S.A.

PUBLICATIONS FOR YOUNG ADULTS

Novels

The Summer Before. New York, Harper, 1973.

Something's Waiting for You, Baker D. New York, Harper, 1974.
Home Is Where Your Feet Are Standing. New York, Harper, 1975.
Diving for Roses. New York, Harper, 1976.
Mad Martin. New York, Harper, 1976.
Killing Time. New York, Harper, 1980.
The Sandman's Eyes. New York, Delacorte, 1985.
How a Weirdo and a Ghost Can Change Your Entire Life, illustrated by Jacqueline Rogers. New York, Delacorte, 1986.
The Hero. New York, Delacorte, 1988.
The Christmas Killer. New York, Scholastic, 1991.
Two Weirdos and a Ghost. New York, Dell, 1991.
Very Weird and Moogly Christmas. New York, Dell, 1991.

Novels as Colin Daniel

Demon Tree. New York, Dell, 1983.

Short Stories

Old Coat's Cat. New York, Macmillan, 1974.
Rain. New York, Macmillan, 1976.
The Girl with the Click Click Eyes. New York, Heinemann, 1977.

*   *   *

Patricia Windsor was born in The Bronx, started college in Vermont, has worked in Maryland, and now lives in New Jersey. But the time she spent as a counselor at a social services agency in England, a job which brought her into direct contact with troubled youngsters, may have been the seminal influence behind her successful string of novels, books which deal centrally with problems confronted by today's adolescents. Her discovery of Paul Zindel's *My Darling, My Hamburger* provided Windsor with a useful model: Zindel's novel convinced her that literature for young adults need not be the treacly, escapist fare of her own youth, but could deal authentically with the dilemmas of real life. Windsor's frequently dark, brooding novels reflect her early appreciation for the science fiction and fantasy writings of Isaac Asimov and Theodore Sturgeon. Nonetheless, she consistently avoids mere escapism, seeking rather to portray the real struggles and conflicts of young protagonists who, for a variety of reasons, find themselves simultaneously isolated from and in bitter conflict with the society around them.

The Summer Before (1973), her first and most widely read novel, details young Alexandra Appleton's emotional breakdown following the death of her eccentric, life-loving boyfriend Bradley—a death for which she partially blames herself. Typical of Windsor's protagonists, Alexandra feels isolated—in this case, from her parents, who fail to understand both the nature of her attachment to Bradley and the depth of her wrenching grief following his death. Ultimately, the passage of time, the intervention of a sympathetic psychiatrist, and the promise of new personal attachments combine to nudge Alexandra in the direction of health, self-forgiveness, and the possibility of happiness.

Diving for Roses (1976) describes a similar odyssey toward personal wholeness, although Jean, that novel's young narrator, faces distinctly different challenges: the awakening of her own sexuality, a broken home, an out-of-wedlock pregnancy, and an alcoholic mother. In Jean's instance, her sense of isolation is quite justified: the small community where she lives is well aware of her mother's sickness, and the townspeople routinely shun both mother and daughter, who are caught up in an unhealthy cycle of mutual dependency. Jean has long assumed that her mother is merely "crazy," mentally deranged, but she ultimately learns the true nature of her problem from young Doctor Curtin, a man with whom the girl entertains a brief flirtation. Jean confronts her mother, who sets out on the road toward health by joining Alcoholics Anonymous. Having become comfortable with the role of caretaker, however, Jean is puzzled by the fact that she cannot wholeheartedly celebrate her mother's recovery. But when Jean becomes pregnant by her predatory boyfriend, she herself seeks help from peers at ALANON (Alcoholics Anonymous Family Groups). Finally, an infinitely more self-sufficient Jean is able to join her mother in severing the cords of shared victimization which had bound them together for so long.

In *The Hero* (1988), the specific problem faced by teenager Dale O. Fither is, ironically, a gift: he is a psychic and can foresee threats to the lives of children around him. His courageous interventions on behalf of these children win Dale (or, rather, his alter ego "Joe Dean") the reputation of a hero—an isolating, differentiating mantle which Dale desperately wants to cast off. Dale's distant, mercenary father, however, sees in Dale's abilities the potential for family fame and fortune. Soon Dale is an unwilling resident of a rural Virginia institute presided over by the sinister Dr. Airman, who, for twisted reasons of his own, has surrounded himself with a cadre of psychic youngsters. Even as he seeks to uncover the true nature of Airman's evil designs, Dale struggles to come to terms with the burdensome aspects of his own makeup which set him apart from others.

The Hero reflects many characteristics of the traditional detective story, and indeed Windsor has embraced the mystery genre with notable success. For example, in *The Sandman's Eyes* (1985), eighteen-year-old Mike Thorn returns to his small hometown after two years in a reformatory, determined to clear his name from the suspicion that he was involved in the murder of a woman whose body he had discovered. Toward that end, he must track down the real killer, but his quest leads him along unexpected paths—lost and found parents, old and new loves. And in one of Windsor's latest novel, *The Christmas Killer* (1991), Rose Potter is visited by the ghost of a murdered girl who shows her the resting places of other victims of a maniacal serial killer. Rose's twin brother is supportive and sympathetic, and her mother is able to provide the answer as to why Rose has been singled out for these macabre visitations. But no one can spare Rose from her own ultimate confrontation with the crazed murderer, that "other" with whom she shares a terrifying psychic bond.

Windsor's novels for young adults have been critically well-received. For example, *The Summer Before* was cited in 1973 as a Best Book for Young Adults by the American Library Association, and, in 1981, its German translation was honored with the Austrian State Award for Books for Youth; similarly, *The Sandman's Eyes* won the Edgar Allan Poe Award from the Mystery Writers of America in 1986 for the best juvenile mystery. And her dozen books, especially *The Summer Before,* have enjoyed the allegiance of a host of young readers, who may well identify with Windsor's tortured protagonists.

It is true that these same protagonists, especially to an adult audience, might often seem overly precocious, self-pitying, rebellious, and resolutely solipsistic. Indeed, Windsor emerges as an implicit apologist for her self-absorbed protagonists, sharing their mistrust of and reaction against such authority figures as parents, mental health professionals, the police, and organized religion. For example, in Windsor's novels (*The Christmas Killer* is a notable exception), parents are repeatedly portrayed as weak, distant, deceptive, or ineffective, and her characters frequently invent their own religious systems, having found only aridity in the established church.

Still, these twin strains of concern with the self and rebellion against authority have clearly struck resonant chords among Windsor's young readership. And *any* reader—adult or juvenile—can find much to admire in Windsor's taut, exciting plots and in the lyrical beauty of her prose style.

—William Ryland Drennan

———

WOJCIECHOWSKA, Maia (Teresa). Also writes as Maia Rodman. American. Born Warsaw, Poland, 7 August 1927; immigrated to the United States, 1942; became citizen, 1950. Educated at Sacred Heart Academy, Los Angeles; Immaculate Heart College, Hollywood, 1945-46. Married 1) Selden Rodman in 1950 (divorced 1957), two daughters; 2) Richard Larkin in 1972 (divorced 1981). Poet, translator, and writer of children's fiction. Translator for Radio Free Europe, 1949-51; assistant editor, *Retail Wholesale and Department Store Union Record,* New York City, 1953-55; copy girl, *Newsweek,* New York City, 1956; assistant editor, *RWDSU Record* (labor newspaper), New York City, 1957; assistant editor, *American Hairdresser* (trade publication), New York City, 1958-60; agent and editor, Kurt Hellmer, New York City, 1960-61; independent literary agent, 1960-61; publicity manager, Hawthorn Books, Inc., New York City, 1961-65. Professional tennis player and instructor, 1949—. Founder and president of Maia Productions, Inc., Independent Books, 1975—, and ENOUGH!!!, 1986—; Councilwoman, Township of Bergen, New Jersey, 1992. Recipient: *New York Herald Tribune* Children's Spring Book Festival Awards honor book, 1964, and John Newbery Medal, 1965, both for *Shadow of a Bull;* awarded Deutscher Jugendbuchpries, 1968; named to New Jersey Literary Hall of Fame, 1985. Agent: Gunther Stuhlmann, P.O. Box 276, Becket, MA 01223. Address: 122 North Railroad Ave., Mahwah, NJ 07430, U.S.A.

PUBLICATIONS FOR YOUNG ADULTS (AS MAIA WOJCIECHOWSKA IN THE UNITED STATES AND AS MAIA RODMAN IN THE UNITED KINGDOM)

Fiction

Shadow of a Bull, illustrated by Alvin Smith. New York, Atheneum, and London, Hamish Hamilton, 1964.
A Kingdom in a Horse. New York, Harper, 1966.
The Hollywood Kid. New York, Harper, 1967.
A Single Light. New York, Harper, 1968.
Tuned Out. New York, Harper, 1968; London, Macmillan, 1976.
Hey, What's Wrong with This One?, illustrated by Joan Sandin. New York, Harper, 1969.
Don't Play Dead Before You Have To. New York, Harper, 1970.
The Rotten Years. New York, Doubleday, 1971.
The Life and Death of a Brave Bull, illustrated by John Groth. New York, Harcourt, 1972.
Through the Broken Mirror with Alice. New York, Harcourt, 1972.

How God Got Christian into Trouble. Philadelphia, Westminster/
John Knox, 1984.
Dreams of [Golf, Wimbleton, the Superbowl]. Pebble Beach, Cali-
fornia, Pebble Beach Press Ltd., n.d.

Other

*Odyssey of Courage: The Adventure of Alvar Nunez Cabeza de
Vaca,* illustrated by Alvin Smith. New York, Atheneum, 1965;
London, Burns Oates, 1967.
Till the Break of Day: Memories, 1939-1942 (autobiographical).
New York, Harcourt, 1973.
Winter Tales from Poland, illustrated by Laszlo Kubinyi. New York,
Doubleday, 1973.

PUBLICATIONS FOR CHILDREN

Fiction

Market Day for Ti Andre, illustrated by Wilson Bigaud. New York,
Viking, 1952.

PUBLICATIONS FOR ADULTS

Fiction

The People in His Life. New York, Stein and Day, 1980.

Play

All at Sea, adaptation of a work by Slawomir Mrozek, produced in
New York, 1968.

Other

The Loved Look: International Hairstyling Guide. New York,
American Hairdresser, 1960.
Translator, *The Bridge to the Other Side,* by Monika Kotowska.
New York, Doubleday, 1970.

*

Media Adaptations: *Tuned Out* was adapted for film and released
as *Stoned: An Anti-Drug Film* by Learning Corp. of America, 1981;
A Single Light was adapted for film and released by Learning Corp.
of America, 1986; the movie rights to *The People in His Life* and
Shadow of a Bull have been optioned.

Biography: Entry in *Third Book of Junior Authors,* New York,
H.W. Wilson, 1972; entry in *More Books by More People* edited by
Lee Bennet Hopkins, Citation, 1974; essay in *Something about the
Author Autobiography Series,* Volume 1, Detroit, Gale, 1986.

Manuscript Collection: Kerlan Collection, University of Minnesota; De Grummond Collection, University of Mississippi.

Critical Study: Entry in *Children's Literature Review,* Volume 1,
Detroit, Gale, 1976; *Contemporary Literary Criticism,* Volume 26,
Detroit, Gale, 1983.

Maia Wojciechowska comments:

   After spending six years of my life on a major Catholic novel and
finding nobody interested, I am into writing sport fiction. Why?
Because only in sports can one theologically separate b.s. from the
real thing, which is pursuit of excellence. It takes dedication, hard
work, and love of what you're doing to be a winner. I am writing
about winners because the young today are being told that it's O.K.
to be a loser and that's an unacceptable lie. An antidote for what ails
us in this country is ruthless honesty.... The best thing that ever
happened to me as a writer is the great Ben Hogan liking my book
Dreams of Golf. It's better than a front page review anywhere!

*   *   *

   Well-known as poet, translator, and author of young people's
fiction, Maia Wojciechowska has been popular since the early 1960s,
mainly because she portrays her protagonists struggling to assert
themselves, something that all young people long to accomplish.
   Winner of the Newbery Medal in 1965 for *Shadow of a Bull,*
Wojciechowska makes it apparent that she once fought a bull. With
the knowledge she gleaned from studying bullfighting in the arena
and from books, she makes the story of Manolo Olivar an exciting,
danger-filled drama. Manolo is expected by the whole town of
Arcangel in Spain to become a famous, fearless bullfighter like his
father who died as he killed the bull in his greatest of all bull fights.
But, as in most of Wojciechowska's novels, the protagonist needs
to become his own true self and refuses to become what others wish
him to be. In this case, Manolo wishes to be a doctor and not a
bullfighter. But he also knows he must not disgrace his family and
his father's name. The reader cannot help feeling the agonies, the
loneliness, the frustrations of Manolo as he gathers his courage to
face not only his first bull, but also to admit to himself and to the
city of Arcangel that he wants to help and heal instead of maiming
and killing.
   Wojciechowska eloquently writes of individuals struggling to
conquer fear, to belong, and to acquire knowledge of themselves.
She makes the reader feel like he or she is part of the story and
inside the main character, no matter what the setting. Her settings
are vivid, whether in Spain or in New York's East Village. The
characters are realistic, and her dialogue generally rings true.
   A story containing a variety of lonely, lost people who are brought
together by a miraculous discovery, *A Single Light* portrays a deaf-
and-dumb girl in Spain who grows up with no one to love and no
one loving her. Her mother died when she was just a baby and her
father rejects her because he feels she is punishment for his sins.
The girl is eventually taken in by a priest, and it is at his church that
the girl discovers a beautiful, white marble statue of the Christ
Child hidden behind the altar. The girl is happy because she has
found something to love, until a Renaissance art expert from America,
so obsessed with finding the lost statue that he has no time for love
or friendship in his life, happens upon the little village and discovers the lost statue. Everything is changed in the village. Greed becomes the overwhelming conqueror of all except the girl. The story
changes from sadness to happiness as Wojciechowska cleverly
weaves this simple tale of love and understanding around a poor,
unfortunate girl with no name. It is a moving story of regeneration,
one of longing and hope for the future, of love and understanding,
themes easily recognized and remembered by readers.
   Drugs will always be a social issue that confronts young people.
Tuned Out takes place during the sixties, when LSD made its ruin-
ous entrance into so many young lives. The story portrays sixteen-

year-old Jim looking forward to his older brother Kevin coming home from college. Jim's happiness is short-lived, because he discovers that Kevin is not only smoking marijuana, but is using LSD as well. This is a typical "bad-trip from drugs" story, including laid-back hippies and the "hey, man, cool" talk, but the message is still important today. Wojciechowska tells the story so vividly and realistically, the reader experiences the pain and frustration that each of the boys feels as they learn the consequences of using drugs. One feels the anguished misery and glimpses the road leading to nowhere when drugs are involved in one's life. Even though the story takes place in the sixties, it will never be outdated so long as the drug scene never changes, and death waits around the corner for the users. Wojciechowska clearly portrays her knowledge of human nature, the weaknesses and frustrations, the doubts and needs, giving young adults something to think about as they face temptations.

The Hollywood Kid is about another troubled young person. Bryan, who has a glamorous mother, a stepfather who is a director, and a father he scarcely knows who is a teacher and a poet, attends a school in the East, out of the way of his movie actress mother. He loses his stepfather to death as the book begins, and throughout the novel he struggles with anxieties and confusion, unhappy in the world of movie stars and famous celebrities. Through the need and search for love, Wojciechowska once again conveys to young adults that even though adults are what they are and may sometimes lean on their own children for support, the realities of life must be faced and one CAN go on, learning from the shortcomings of others.

Everyone longs for a better world and a happier environment, and everyone has problems, especially preteens and teenagers, who not only have to deal with changing bodies and feelings but face the overwhelming prospect of soon becoming responsible adults. Wojciechowska effectively articulates the doubts and fears, the awkwardness and frustrations, the struggles and temptations of her characters. Sometimes her monologues tend to drag a little and the pace slows somewhat, but the appeal of her books for teenagers remains strong as they deal with the universal themes of self-realization and the need for love.

—Carol Doxey

WOLFF, Virginia Euwer. American. Born in Portland, Oregon, 25 August 1937. Educated at Smith College, Northampton, Massachusetts, A.B. 1959; Long Island University, New York, 1974-75; Warren Wilson College, Swannanoa, North Carolina. Married Art Wolff in 1959 (divorced 1976); one son and one daughter. English teacher at junior high school in Bronx, New York, 1959-60; teacher at private schools in Philadelphia, Pennsylvania, 1968-72, and New York, 1972-74; teacher of English at public high school in Hood River, Oregon, since 1976. Lecturer on techniques of fiction writing at Willamette Writers' Conference, 1977. Swimming teacher and lifeguard. Violinist with Mid-Columbia Sinfonietta. Recipient: First prize in poetry from Long Island University, 1976; awards from Oregon Teachers as Writers for poems and from *Willamette Week* for story "Pole Beans for Rent," both 1979; International Reading Association award for older readers, *Probably Still Nick Swansen*, 1989. Lives in Parkdale, Oregon.

PUBLICATIONS FOR YOUNG ADULTS

Novels

Rated PG. New York, St. Martin's, 1980.
Probably Still Nick Swansen. New York, Holt, 1988.
The Mozart Season. New York, Holt, 1991.
Make Lemonade. New York, Holt, 1993.

*

Biography: Essay in *Speaking for Ourselves, Too* compiled and edited by Donald R. Gallo, National Council of Teachers of English, 1993.

*   *   *

Virginia Euwer Wolff introduces young-adult readers to worlds of adolescence they may never have considered. Whether learning disabled or precocious, her protagonists must learn to deal with internal conflicts while trying to fit into a world that lacks accommodations for those who are not typical.

In *Probably Still Nick Swansen,* sixteen-year-old Nick attends high school in Room 19, a special class for students with learning problems. Although Wolff never supplies a precise diagnosis of Nick's condition, Shana, who had attended Room 19 before "Going Up," categorizes both of them as suffering from "minimal brain dysfunction." The label is unnecessary for readers because Wolff creates Nick's world with language. She includes notes he tries to decipher that leave out crucial words; she reveals his hesitation about asking questions for fear of looking stupid; she documents the shame and despair he experiences when he overhears adults characterize students in Room 19 as "droolers," even though Nick possesses an encyclopedic knowledge of amphibians and the uncanny ability to remember complex scientific data about them.

Nick faces two major crises during the novel. The first involves the immediate problems connected with inviting Shana to the prom, making necessary arrangements, and dealing with the embarrassment of having her stand him up the night of the dance. The second source of turmoil comes from a recurring nightmare based on the drowning of his older sister nine years earlier. Although he had loved and idolized Dianne, he had not been able to save her, and he cannot free himself from guilt over her death. His inarticulate memories of trying to force her back to life wrench the readers into his world of pain.

As Wolff provides Nick's perspective on events, she might easily have turned Shana into a villain for snubbing him. But the explanation is not so simple. Despite her move "Up" from Room 19, Shana must cope with a world that often proves too complex and parents that label her stupid. She tells Nick that she has learned where "Up" is: "It's where you flunk tests all the time, and everybody wants you to be so smart all the time, it's so much faster...." By the novel's end, Nick's growing acceptance of life's ambiguities brings a measure of peace.

Because much of the story is told from Nick's viewpoint, although not in first person, the novel is sometimes difficult to read. However, Nick shares many concerns with all adolescents, including the problems of handling well-meaning but misguided teachers and parents who offer unsolicited advice.

Suggestions from family, friends, and teachers almost overwhelm Allegra Shapiro in Wolff's novel *The Mozart Season*. An extraordinary violinist, Allegra, age twelve, is the youngest musician chosen as a contestant in the Ernest Bloch Competition held in her hometown of Portland, Oregon. Her summer is devoted to extended rehearsals of the required Mozart concerto and to the intense struggle required to fuse her own interpretation of the music with the composer's original vision.

Allegra's childhood has been dominated by music. Both her parents are professional musicians who perform in numerous concerts, give lessons, and signal the end to their disagreements by playing duets. Only Allegra's older brother does not play a musical instrument, turning instead to art as a creative outlet. Most acquaintances of Allegra's parents are also musicians. Allegra's own best friends are beautiful and talented achievers, one determined to be an architect, the other a dancer. Because the major characters possess so many talents, bridging the gap between their lives and those of the average reader seems less successful than the connections Wolff achieved previously.

The world of page turning, concerts, practice, lessons, and musical interpretation rarely appears in such detail as that provided by Wolff. Talented young adults might appreciate finding fellow artists in the pages of a novel, but the appeal seems limited. A subplot involving Allegra's need to integrate the Jewish and Gentile heritages from her ancestors remains equally intellectualized.

Wolff dares to explore the lives of adolescents who are removed from the mainstream but who must cope with the same problems of identity and self-acceptance faced by their peers. Whether her audience will be limited to a select group of readers remains unclear.

—Kathy Piehl

WOLITZER, Hilma. American. Born in Brooklyn, New York, 25 January 1930. Educated at Brooklyn Museum Art School, Brooklyn College of the City University of New York, and New School for Social Research, New York. Married Morton Wolitzer in 1952; two daughters. Writer and teacher of writing workshops. Has also worked as nursery school teacher and portrait artist at a resort. Bread Loaf Writers Conference, staff assistant, 1975 and 1976, staff member, 1977-78 and 1980-92. Visiting lecturer in writing at University of Iowa, 1978-79 and 1983, Columbia University, 1979-80, New York University, 1984, and Swarthmore College, 1985. Recipient: Bread Loaf Writers Conference scholarship, 1970; fellowships from Bread Loaf Writers Conference, 1974, Guggenheim Foundation, 1976-77, and National Endowment for the Arts, 1978; Great Lakes College Association award, 1974-75, for *Ending;* new York State English Council Excellence in Letters award, 1980; American Academy and Institute of Arts and Letters award (literature), 1981; Janet Heidinger Kafka Prize (honorable mention), University of Rochester, 1981, for *Hearts*. Agent: Amanda Urban, ICM, 40 West 57th St., New York, NY 10019. Address: 500 East 85th St., Apt. 18H, New York, NY 10028, U.S.A.

PUBLICATIONS FOR YOUNG ADULTS

Novels

Ending. New York, Morrow, 1974.

In the Flesh. New York, Morrow, 1977.
Hearts. New York, Farrar, Straus, 1980.
In the Palomar Arms. New York, Farrar, Straus, 1983.
Silver. New York, Farrar, Straus, 1988.
Introducing Shirley Braverman. New York, Farrar, Straus, 1975.
Out of Love. New York, Farrar, Straus, 1976.
Toby Lived Here. New York, Farrar, Straus, 1978.
Wish You Were Here. New York, Farrar, Straus, 1985.

Other

Contributor, *From Pop to Culture.* New York, Holt, 1970.
Contributor, *The Secret Life of Our Time,* edited by Gordon Lish. New York, Doubleday, 1973.
Contributor, *Bitches and Sad Ladies,* edited by Pat Rotter. New York, Harper Magazine Press, 1975.
Contributor, *The Bread Loaf Anthology of Contemporary Short Stories,* edited by Robert Pack and Jay Parini. Middlebury, Vermont, Bread Loaf, 1987.
Contributor, *The Bread Loaf Anthology of Contemporary American Essays,* edited by Robert Pack and Jay Parini. Middlebury, Vermont, Bread Loaf, 1989.
Contributor, *Vital Lines,* edited by John Mukand, M.D. New York, St. Martin's Press, 1990.

Screenplays: *In the Flesh* and *Ending,* an episode from the series *Family,* ABC-TV, three shows for PBS-TV, and *Single Women, Married Men* (teleplay), CBS-TV.

*

Media Adaptations: *Ending, In the Flesh,* and *Hearts* have been optioned for motion picture production.

Biography: Essay in *Speaking for Ourselves, Too* compiled and edited by Donald R. Gallo, National Council of Teachers of English, 1993.

*   *   *

Hilma Wolitzer writes with a realism that invokes both emotion and a correlation to one's own life. The autobiographical quality makes it easier for the reader to identify with the characters, the pace of the stories are brisk yet the plots are complex enough to keep the reader interested and concerned about the outcome, and an overall theme in her young adult novels is taking control of one's life for growth. A prominent story line includes a recent death in the family with which the main character is coming to terms. The end result of working through the grief process is emotional development and maturity in the main character.

In *Wish You Were Here,* Bernie Segel struggles with accepting his father's death and his mother's remarriage. The main focus is Bernie's obsession to secretly earn enough money for a plane ticket so he can go live with his paternal grandfather in Florida. Torn between missing his father and feeling guilty when he doesn't, Bernie stumbles through a series of typical adolescent problems involving relationships: strong feelings for a girl, bickering with an older sister, resentment toward his future stepfather, and clinging to memories of his relationship with his grandfather.

Bernie is strong willed. As he learns to work through the problems in his various family relationships, he reminds himself he won't be around later to enjoy the fruits of his labor and that he will actually miss each of these people he is so anxious to get away from. He realizes he must keep his plan in focus if he is to succeed.

When his plan is botched by the surprise visit of his grandfather, he is disappointed but eventually realizes running away would have solved nothing. Because his grandfather looks much older than he remembered and admits to Bernie that he, too, misses his father, Bernie realizes he is only afraid of forgetting his father altogether. He solves this new problem by deciding to follow an old Jewish custom for remembering the dead. In this way, a piece of his father can always be with him, even if the family situation must change. Since Bernie discovers the way to solve his problem and in doing so comes to understand why he came up with his original "solution" to his dilemma, the resolution of the story is not only very realistic, but satisfying.

A similar novel focuses on a female protagonist who struggles to accept not only the sudden death of her father, but to overcome the embarrassment of her present situation. In *Toby Lived Here,* twelve-year-old Toby and her six-year-old sister Anne find themselves in a foster home. Their mother has suffered an emotional breakdown after the death of their father. While worrying that such an illness may be hereditary, Toby is deceptive about the circumstances that brought the girls into foster care. Wolitzer again employs an involved plot and ardent realism to elicit empathy for Toby and to establish an understanding in the reader for emotional and mental disorders.

Though *Hearts* was written for an adult audience, it will appeal to young people because they will be able to relate to the emotionally immature main character and her thirteen-year-old stepdaughter. Linda Reismann is a twenty-six-year-old widow. Her husband dies after only six weeks of marriage, and Linda sets off across the country to deposit the malcontent Robin with relatives she's never met.

Robin resents her stepmother, and the hostility that surrounds their relationship intensifies as they travel from New Jersey to Iowa and then to California. Arrangements had been made for Robin to live with her grandfather, but when they arrive in Iowa they find he's had a stroke and will soon be placed into a nursing home. Linda, unclear of her own goals, makes an attempt to find Robin's mother. As they travel, the ice in their relationship at times melts, but at other times it begins to freeze again. Their cross-country quest becomes a learning experience as their lives converge with an array of people they meet at stops along the way. As the cloak of naivete falls from Linda's shoulders, she realizes the anger Robin displays to both Linda and her real mother is a mask for feeling abandoned. Linda realizes, too, that Robin is her only link to her deceased husband, her only family. "It was because she could not say aloud that she was *bound* to Robin, that you can become a family by the grace of accident and will, that we have a duty to console one another as best we can."

Like the other protagonists in Wolitzer's novels, Linda—and to an extent Robin—have journeyed to a closing of one part of their lives and the opening of a new part. They've both grown emotionally by accepting the death of husband and father, while at the same time they've learned to gain more control over their lives.

—Lisa A. Wroble

WREDE, Patricia C(ollins). American. Born in Chicago, Illinois, 27 March 1953. Educated at Carleton College, Northfield, Minnesota, A.B. 1974; University of Minnesota, Minneapolis, M.B.A. 1977. Married James M. Wrede in 1976 (divorced, 1992). Rate review analyst, Minnesota Hospital Association, Minneapolis, Minnesota, 1977-78; financial analyst, B. Dalton Bookseller, Minneapolis, Minnesota, 1978-80; financial analyst, 1980-81, senior financial analyst, 1981-83, senior accountant, 1983-85, Dayton-Hudson Corporation, Minneapolis, Minnesota; full-time writer, since 1985. Laubach reading tutor. Recipient: "Books for Young Adults" Recommended Reading List citation, 1984, for *Daughter of Witches,* and 1985, for *The Seven Towers;* Minnesota Book award for Fantasy and Science Fiction, 1991, and American Library Association, "Best Book for Young Adults" citation, both for *Dealing with Dragons;* ALA "Best Books" for *Searching for Dragons,* 1992; ALA "Notable" for *Searching for Dragons,* 1993. Agent: Valerie Smith, Route 44-55, RR Box 160, Modena, NY 12548. Address: 4900 West 60th St., Edina, MN 55424-1709, U.S.A.

PUBLICATIONS FOR YOUNG ADULTS

Fiction

Shadow Magic. New York, Ace Books, 1982.
Daughter of Witches. New York, Ace Books, 1983.
The Seven Towers. New York, Ace Books, 1984.
The Harp of Imach Thyssel. New York, Ace Books, 1985.
Talking to Dragons. Tempo/MagicQuest Books, 1985.
Caught in Crystal. New York, Ace Books, 1987.
Sorcery and Cecelia, with Caroline Stevermer. New York, Ace Books, 1988.
Snow White and Rose Red. New York, Tor Books, 1989.
Dealing with Dragons. San Diego, Harcourt, 1990.
Mairelon the Magician. New York, Tor Books, 1991.
Searching for Dragons. San Diego, Harcourt, 1991.
Calling on Dragons. San Diego, Jane Yolen Books, 1993.

Other

Contributor, *Liavek,* edited by Will Shetterly and Emma Bull. New York, Ace Books, 1985.
Contributor, *Liavek: The Players of Luck,* edited by Will Shetterly and Emma Bull. New York, Ace Books, 1986.
Contributor, *Spaceships and Spells,* edited by Jane Yolen. New York, Harper & Row, 1987.
Contributor, *Liavek: Spells of Binding,* edited by Will Shetterly and Emma Bull. New York, Ace Books, 1988.
Contributor, *The Unicorn Treasury,* edited by Bruce Coville. New York, Doubleday, 1988.
Contributor, *Liavek: Festival Week,* edited by Will Shetterly and Emma Bull. New York, Ace Books, 1990.
Contributor, *Tales of the Witch World 3,* edited by Andre Norton. New York, Tor Books, 1990.

*

Biography: Essay in *Authors and Artists for Young Adults,* Vol. 8, Detroit, Gale, 1991.

*   *   *

Patricia C. Wrede's "Enchanted Forest" series turns the classic fairy tale on its head, side, and every other way. Mixing true fairy-tale tradition with a wry humor, Wrede has created a world where cats talk to witches, dragons talk to princesses, and magicians talk to anyone who will listen. The four novels, *Talking to Dragons, Dealing with Dragons, Searching for Dragons,* and *Calling on Dragons,* deal with the denizens of the Enchanted Forest and the countries around it.

The wizards are the villains of the saga, and the dragons (particularly Kazul, King of the Dragons) are among the heroes—or usually heroines. Kazul is female, dragons believing that "King" is one job and "Queen" another. Each of the novels focuses on a particular character, letting familiar acquaintances become best of friends.

Wrede's strength is her ability to twist the elements of classic fairy tale into new and believable forms. The characters she creates are particularly strong. Her beautiful youngest princess of Linderwall, Cimorene, is not petite, blonde, beautiful, and somewhat brainless, but is instead tall, brunette, lovely, and intelligent. She is anything but a "proper" princess. Bored by her traditional "princess" lessons, she coerces the palace cook into teaching her cookery, the court magician into magic lessons, and the castle arms master into fencing lessons. Her father and mother put a stop to each activity as soon as they learn of it, making poor Cimorene more bored and unhappy. When informed by her exasperated parents that she must marry the handsome prince Therandil (admittedly good-looking, but also blond, brainless, and boring), Cimorene accepts the advice of the talking frog in a nearby pond and takes off for parts unknown, becoming the dragon Kazul's princess. Having a princess to cook and clean for one is a status symbol among the dragons. Cimorene is quite a good cook and a tidy housekeeper—more unprincessly traits. Wrede's first novel, chronologically, *Dealing with Dragons,* introduces the reader to Cimorene, Kazul, and the Witch Morwen.

Morwen is perhaps Wrede's finest character in the series. A less typical witch would be hard to find. She is short and slender and not at all bad-looking. She lives in an immaculate cottage in the Enchanted Forest. Like most witches she is interested in herb lore, which she uses in rather unorthodox ways. In *Talking to Dragons,* she cures both a wizard's malignant spell and a very bad burn with the same fragrant herbal remedy. She lives with her nine cats, none of which is a proper witchy black (she encounters some trouble with this in *Calling on Dragons*). Over her doorway she keeps a sign inscribed "NONE OF THIS NONSENSE, PLEASE," which sums up Morwen's attitude perfectly. The nine cats assume individual characteristics in *Calling on Dragons,* but each retains his or her unique personality. The cats are useful in Morwen's magic spells as well as being companionable.

Searching for Dragons introduces Mendanbar, King of the Enchanted Forest. Mendanbar is an intelligent young man, allergic to the pomp his majordomo insists is due his position as well as the idea of marriage with the brainless princesses that populate the surrounding countries. He possesses all the magic of the Forest and is equally adept at dealing with the head of the Council of Wizards or the surly gargoyle that hangs in his study. Wrede peppers her stories with sly references to both classic fairy tales and well-known fantasy works. Take, for example, the sales patter of Gypsy Jack, itinerant peddler and proprietor of the best magical repair shop in the realm: "What do you need? Shoes?... Ah! You want seven league boots!... Or there's a swell pair of ruby slippers that'd be perfect for the lady. I'll throw in the magic belt that goes with 'em for free."

"The Enchanted Forest Chronicles" follow Cimorene and her friends from her beginnings as a young princess to her triumph as mother of the unknown Prince of the Enchanted Forest. Since each novel follows a different character's point of view, the reader is able to empathize with all the major characters. *Talking to Dragons* focuses on Princess Cimorene, *Dealing with Dragons* on King Mendenbar, *Searching for Dragons* on Morwen, and *Calling on Dragons* on Daystar, Cimorene's son.

All four novels are highly enjoyable journeys into a world of magic. The "Enchanted Forest" is a place the reader will want to visit again and again.

—Louise J. Winters

WRIGHT, Richard (Nathaniel). American. Born near Natchez, Mississippi, 4 September 1908. Educated at a junior high school in Jackson, Mississippi. Married 1) Rose Dhima Meadman in 1938 (marriage ended); 2) Ellen Poplar in 1941, two daughters. Novelist, short story writer, poet and essayist. Worked for the Federal Writers Project, and the Federal Negro Theatre Project; clerk at U.S. Post Office in Chicago, Illinois, during 1920s. Communist Party member, 1932-44; Harlem Editor, *Daily Worker,* New York. Recipient: Prize from *Story* magazine, 1938, for *Uncle Tom's Children;* Guggenheim fellowship, 1939; Spingarn Medal from National Association for the Advancement of Colored People, 1940, for *Native Son.* Died 28 November 1960, in Paris, France.

PUBLICATIONS

Novels

Native Son. New York, Harper, and London, Gollancz, 1940.
The Outsider. New York, Harper, 1953; London, Angus & Robertson, 1954.
Savage Holiday. New York, Avon, 1954.
The Long Dream. New York, Doubleday, 1958; London, Angus & Robertson, 1960.
Lawd Today. New York, Walker, 1963; London, Blond, 1965.
The Man Who Lived Underground. Paris, Aubier-Flammarion, 1971.

Short Stories

Uncle Tom's Children: Four Novellas. New York, Harper, 1938; London, Gollancz, 1939; augmented edition; as *Uncle Tom's Children: Five Long Stories,* New York, Harper, 1940.
Eight Men. Cleveland, World, 1961.
Quintet. San Diego, California, Pyramid Books, 1961.
Farthing's Fortunes. New York, Atheneum, 1976.

Plays

Native Son (The Biography of a Young American), with Paul Green (produced New York, 1941; London, 1948). New York and London, Harper, 1941.
Daddy Goodness, adaptation of a play by Louis Sapin (produced New York, 1968).

Screenplay: *Native Son,* 1951.

Other

How Bigger Was Born: The Story of "Native Son," One of the Most Significant Novels of Our Time and How It Came to Be Written. New York, Harper, 1940.
The Negro and Parkway Community House. Chicago, privately printed, 1941.
Twelve Million Black Voices: A Folk History of the Negro in the United States. New York, Viking Press, 1941; London, Londsay Drummond, 1947.
Black Boy: A Record of Childhood and Youth. New York, Harper, and London, Gollancz, 1945.
Black Power: A Record of Reactions in a Land of Pathos. New York, Harper, 1954; London, Dobson, 1956.
Bandoeng: 1.500.000.000 hommes, translated by Helene Claireau. Paris, Calman-Levy, 1955; as *The Color Curtain: A Report on the Bandung Conference,* Cleveland, World, and London, Dobson, 1956.
Pagan Spain. New York, Harper, 1956; London, Bodley Head, 1960.
White Man, Listen! New York, Doubleday, 1957.
Letters to Joe C. Brown, edited by Thomas Knipp. Kent, Ohio, Kent State University Libraries, 1968.
What the Negro Wants. Japan, Kaitakusha, 1972.
American Hunger (autobiography). New York, Harper, 1977.
The Richard Wright Reader, edited by Ellen Wright and Michel Fabre. New York, Harper, 1978.
The Life and Work of Richard Wright, edited by David Ray and Robert M. Farnsworth. Columbia, Montana, University of Missouri, 1979.
New Essays on Native Son, edited by Keneth Kinnamon. New York, Cambridge University Press, 1990.
Works. New York, Viking, 1991.

*

Bibliographies: "A Bibliography of Richard Wright's Words" by Michael Fabre and Edward Margolies, in *New Letters 38* (Kansas City, Missouri), Winter 1971; "Richard Wright: An Essay in Bibliography" by John M. Reilly in *Resources for American Literary Study* (College Park, Maryland), Autumn 1971.

Critical Studies: *Richard Wright* by Constance Webb, New York, Putnam, 1968; *Richard Wright* by Robert Bone, Minneapolis, University of Minnesota Press, 1969; *The Art of Richard Wright* by Edward Margolies, Carbondale, Southern Illinois University Press, 1969; *The Example of Richard Wright* by Dan McCall, New York, Harcourt Brace, 1969; *Richard Wright: An Introduction to the Man and His Work* by Carl Brignano, Pittsburgh, University of Pittsburgh Press, 1970; *The Emergence of Richard Wright: A Study in Literature and Society* by Kenneth Kinnamon, Urbana, University of Illinois Press, 1972; *Twentieth Century Interpretations of "Native Son,"* edited by H.A. Baker, Englewood Cliffs, New Jersey, Prentice Hall, 1972; entry in *Contemporary Literary Criticism,* Detroit, Gale, Volume 1, 1973, Volume 3, 1975, Volume 4, 1975, Volume 9, 1978, Volume 14, 1980, Volume 21, 1982; *Richard Wright* by David Bakish, New York, Ungar, 1973; *The Unfinished Quest of Richard Wright* by Michel Fabre, translated by Isabel Barzun, New York, Morrow, 1973; *Richard Wright Impressions and Perspectives,* edited by David Ray and R.M. Farnsworth, Ann Arbor, University of Michigan Press, 1973.

*   *   *

Richard Wright's novels, autobiographies, essays, dramatic scripts, poetry, and other nonfiction draw on the poverty and segregation of his childhood in the South and early adulthood in Chicago. A politically oriented writer, Wright focuses clearly and forcefully on the brutal and dehumanizing effects of racism on the black person. His first published work, *Uncle Tom's Children,* is a collection of novellas dealing with confrontations of blacks and whites, emphasizing the dignity of man and the oppression of a black underclass. His first novel, *Lawd Today,* was not published until after his death. In a bold, naturalistic style it centers around the life of Jake Jackson, a violent, untutored man from Chicago whose mean environment offers little opportunity and little hope.

Of more interest to the young adult is Wright's powerful protest novel, *Native Son,* which introduces us to Bigger Thomas, a poor, young, black man of twenty years who accidentally murders a rich, young, white woman. A prominent theme in this book is that blacks become criminals because of their environment. Bigger's crime, though, has two effects on him—that of giving him an identity and that of consuming him with fear and guilt so that he rapidly brings about his own destruction. By the end of the story, Bigger, imprisoned and sentenced to death, realizes that his life does have meaning and that the black man is no less human than the white man. The birth of Bigger, Wright has written, occurred in his own childhood, and there was not just one Bigger, but many. This novel is a powerful indictment of racism, an indictment of the white man as the oppressor, of the black man as submissive to the oppressor. *Native Son* was the first novel by a Black American writer to achieve critical acclaim and popular success. It was later made into a stage play and twice was adapted on film.

Wright's most salient work for the young adult, and regarded by many as his masterpiece, is his autobiography, *Black Boy,* the highly readable, poignant account of Wright's childhood in the South. The book begins as he accidentally burns his house down lighting broom straws in the fireplace. Readers learn how he became a drunkard in his sixth year, when older drunks gave him drinks in the saloon; how begging for drinks became his obsession; how the older drunks paid him nickels for repeating obscenities to women. Wright's father was a night porter but left home when Wright was still of preschool age. His mother worked as a cook. Throughout the book the descriptions of his hunger, of his fantasies about food, occur over and over. By eighth grade, despite all his troubles and tragedies, Wright had a clear goal of going to the North, where everything was possible—he had read the Horatio Alger books—and becoming a writer. By the time he left the South, however, seventeen-year-old Wright knew that he was not really leaving, because his feelings already had been formed there. He was taking a part of the South to transplant in different soil, to see if it could grow differently and bloom. Wright felt if that miracle happened, he would know that the South, too, could overcome despair and violence. He headed north with the hope that life could be lived with dignity, that other persons need not be violated.

Black Boy is a violent book, describing how Wright's mother and grandmother beat him, so hard sometimes that he lost consciousness. For a time he was in an orphan home, again with too little to eat. From a religious family, Wright eventually was sent to a Seventh-day Adventist school where his teacher, also his aunt, beat him. He had several stints in public school, but his primary concern there was to prove himself, as a newcomer, by fighting fellow students. As he grew older and taller, Wright spent more time with older boys and with them developed a sense of camaraderie, strengthened by their fear and loathing of white boys. There are violent expressions of hate and hostility involving real and bloody battles. Wright describes throwing rocks, cinders, coal, sticks, and broken bottles, all the while longing for deadlier weapons. Although set in the 1920s, readers will make comparisons with the gang warfare among big-city poor of the 1990s.

The posthumously published *American Hunger* is a sequel to *Black Boy,* tracing Wright's migration to and his early years as a writer in Chicago. Wright gradually became disillusioned with race relations in the United States and moved to France, where he wrote several other lesser novels, short stories, and strident political essays.

It is *Black Boy* that most eloquently presents Wright's message of the destructive power of racism. The book is an American classic, a powerful, sad, and hopeful story of growing up in this country, as important today as when first published almost fifty years ago.

—Mary Lystad

WRIGHTSON, (Alice) Patricia. Australian. Born in Lismore, New South Wales, 21 June 1921. Educated at State Correspondence School, 1933-34; St. Catherine's College, Stanthorpe, Queensland, 1932. Married in 1943 (divorced 1953); one daughter and one son. Secretary and administrator, Bonalbo District Hospital, 1946-60, and Sydney District Nursing Association, 1960-64; assistant editor, 1964-70, and editor, 1970-75, *School Magazine,* Sydney; writer. Recipient: Australian Children's Book Council Book of the Year award, 1956, for *The Crooked Snake;* Notable Books of the Year award from American Library Association, 1963, for *The Feather Star;* Book of the Year award runner-up from Children's Book Council of Australia, and Children's Spring Book Festival award from *Book World,* both 1968, and Hans Christian Andersen Honors List award of the International Board on Books for Young People (IBBY), 1970, all for *A Racecourse for Andy;* Book of the Year Honour List award from Children's Book Council of Australia, 1974, IBBY's Honor List for text award, 1976, *Voice of Youth Advocate*'s Annual Selection of Best Science Fiction and Fantasy Titles for Young Adults, 1988, and Hans Christian Andersen Medal, all for *The Nargun and the Stars;* O.B.E. (Officer, Order of the British Empire), 1978; Book of the Year award from Children's Book Council of Australia, and *Guardian* award commendation, both 1978, IBBY's Books for Young People Honor List award, and Hans Christian Andersen Honors List award, both 1979, all for *The Ice Is Coming;* New South Wales Premier's award for Ethnic Writing, 1979, selection as one of the Children's Books of the Year by Child Study Association of America, all 1979, all for *The Dark Bright Water;* Book of the Year award high commendation from Children's Book Council of Australia, 1982, for *Behind the Wind;* Carnegie Medal Commendation, 1983, Book of the Year award from the Children's Book Council of Australia, *Boston Globe/Horn Book* award for Fiction, Hans Christian Andersen Medal, and *Ob-*

server Teenage Fiction Prize, all 1984, all for *A Little Fear;* Dromkeen Children's Literature Foundation Medal, 1984, for "a significant contribution to the appreciation and development of children's literature in Australia"; chosen to deliver sixteenth annual Arbuthnot Lecture, 1985; Golden Cat award from the Sjoestrands ForlagAB, 1986, for "a contribution to children's and young adult literature"; Hans Christian Andersen Medal, 1986, for *Moon Dark;* Lady Cutler award, 1986, New South Wales Premier's Special Occasional award, 1988. Address: Lohic, P.O. Box 91, Maclean, NSW 2463, Australia.

PUBLICATIONS FOR YOUNG ADULTS

Fiction

The Crooked Snake, illustrated by Margaret Horder. Sydney and London, Angus and Robertson, 1955.
The Bunyip Hole, illustrated by Margaret Horder. Sydney and London, Angus and Robertson, 1958.
The Rocks of Honey, illustrated by Margaret Horder. Sydney, Angus and Robertson, 1960; London, Angus and Robertson, 1961.
The Feather Star, illustrated by Noela Young. London, Hutchinson, 1962; New York, Harcourt Brace, 1963.
Down to Earth, illustrated by Margaret Horder. New York, Harcourt Brace, and London, Hutchinson, 1965.
I Own the Racecourse!, illustrated by Margaret Horder. London, Hutchinson, 1968; as *A Racecourse for Andy,* New York, Harcourt Brace, 1968.
An Older Kind of Magic, illustrated by Noela Young. London, Hutchinson, and New York, Harcourt Brace, 1972.
The Nargun and the Stars. London, Hutchinson, 1973; New York, Atheneum, 1974.
The Ice Is Coming. Richmond, Victoria, and London, Hutchinson, and New York, Atheneum, 1977.
The Dark Bright Water. Richmond, Victoria, and London, Hutchinson, and New York, Atheneum, 1979.
Night Outside, illustrated by Beth Peck. Melbourne, Rigby, 1979; New York, Atheneum, 1985.
Behind the Wind. Richmond, Victoria, and London, Hutchinson, 1981; as *Journey Behind the Wind,* New York, Atheneum, 1981.
A Little Fear. Richmond, Victoria and London, Hutchinson, and New York, McElderry, 1983.
Moon-Dark, illustrated by Noela Young. Richmond, Victoria, Hutchinson, 1987; New York, McElderry, 1988.
The Song of Wirrun. Richmond, Victoria, Century Hutchinson, 1987.
Balyet. Richmond, Victoria, and London, Hutchinson, and New York, McElderry, 1989.
The Sugar-Gum Tree, illustrated by David Cox. Ringwood, Vic., Australia, and New York, Viking, 1991.

Other

Editor, *Beneath the Sun: An Australian Collection for Children.* Sydney, Collins, 1972; London, Collins, 1973.
Editor, *Emu Stew: An Illustrated Collection of Stories and Poems for Children.* Melbourne and London, Kestrel, 1976.
The Haunted Rivers. Maclean, New South Wales, Eighth State Press, 1983.

*

Media Adaptations: *The Nargun and the Stars* (television series), ABC-TV, 1977; *I Own the Racecourse* (film), Barron Films, 1985.

Biography: Essay in *Something about the Author Autobiography Series,* Volume 4, Detroit, Gale, 1987, pp. 335-46; essay in *Authors and Artists for Young Adults,* Volume 5, Detroit, Gale, 1990, pp. 236-237.

Critical Studies: Entry in *Children's Literature Review,* Detroit, Gale, Volume 4, 1982, Volume 14, 1988; entry in *Fourth Book of Junior Authors and Illustrators,* New York, H.W. Wilson, 1978.

Manuscript Collections: Lu Rees Archives, Canberra College of Advanced Education Library, Australia; Kerlan Collection, University of Minnesota.

*   *   *

Few authors have changed the literature of their country, but Patricia Wrightson is one of them. Publication of *The Nargun and the Stars* in 1972 marked the beginning of an authentic Australian fantasy based upon the folklore of Australia's indigenous people rather than that of its European inhabitants and upon Wrightson's skill at rendering the country's ancient, distinctive landscapes. After publishing two fairly conventional holiday adventure stories, she found her own voice in *The Rocks of Honey,* a realistic novel that deals with themes she develops in her later fantasy: of the deep and long-standing attachment of Australia's Aboriginal people to their land, of the possibility of understanding between Aboriginal and European Australians based upon respect for Aboriginal culture and attachment to the land itself, and of the healing power of nature.

Wrightson's novel *The Feather Star* depicts the awakening of a fifteen-year-old girl to a sense of time and mortality. Lindy Martin realizes that she has grown beyond unreflective childhood and can choose between finding self-realization in human fellowship and in enjoyment of the natural world, and a doctrine of sin and retribution in an after-life preached by a loveless old religious crank who rails at Lindy and her friends. Wrightson also uses the symbols of a regenerating feather starfish and of the stars themselves to carry an idea central to her later work: that of the continuity of life on earth and its relationship with the life of a self-sufficient universe.

In *The Nargun and the Stars* Wrightson's discovery of the creatures of Aboriginal folklore enables her to create the fantasy she had long wished to write by allowing magic to enter believably into the Australian bushland. Further, the spirits of the land constitute a specifically Australian link between humankind and nature and provide the cause for a fantastic hero-journey and the means by which it is conducted. The huge stone figure of the Nargun is simultaneously an adversary of great power and an embodiment of the land and of an aspect of the hero's psyche; the tale of Simon Brent's learning to understand the Nargun and helping to deal with it is also a tale of his healing through acceptance of his angry loneliness after his parents' death. In the remote setting of Wongadilla, a sheep station among the ridges of the Great Dividing Range, Simon learns to trust the shrewd simplicity of two middle-aged cousins who see themselves as stewards rather than owners of the land and to feel, in moments of unity with the natural world, the transience of human life that is part of that world. Again Wrightson rejects belief in sin and retribution; the land and its ancient spirits are neither good nor evil, and Simon's symbolic experience of rebirth helps him to appreciate the isolation and mortality of all human beings and to find, in love and responsibility for others and in patient endurance, a creed by which to live.

The Song of Wirrun, a fantasy trilogy consisting of *The Ice is Coming, The Dark Bright Water,* and *Behind the Wind,* further develops the theme of self-realization through the hero-tale of Wirrun, a young Aboriginal Australian whose story encompasses an entire life in the setting of the whole continent. Wirrun journeys from late adolescence to fully initiated adulthood. He accepts his special calling as a hero, and comes to understand the darker side of his own nature in the person of his friend Ularra; he accepts the contrasexual part of himself in the person of the spirit-wife, the Yunggamurra, and endures the pain of losing her; he achieves final apotheosis after facing the figure of Wulgaru, who embodies the man-made but tormenting belief in sin and purgation. Wirrun overcomes his apparent annihilation by asserting his self-hood, and achieves the status of a culture-hero, present throughout the country, living on "behind the wind." Most of Wrightson's human characters, especially in the second and third volume of the trilogy, are Aboriginal Australians; the remainder are the Aboriginal spirits of the land. She is scrupulously careful to remain faithful to her sources and to the strongly localized nature of Aboriginal folklore, yet she seamlessly incorporates both into a narrative of high fantasy unprecedented in Australian literature for young adults, and unmatched in length, scope, and moral seriousness.

A Little Fear extends Wrightson's examination of individuation to encompass old age. Agnes Tucker has run away from the constraint of a home for the elderly to the independence of her dead brother's farm, certain that in its pastoral setting she will find peace and fulfilment. Wrightson undercuts the conventions of pastoral, however; this land has defeated settlers in the past, and in the person of the Njimbin, a small but truculent spirit, will defeat Mrs. Tucker also. The dog Hector understands the unsentimental reality of the land better than Mrs. Tucker does, and knows that the seemingly inexplicable events that she fears are symptoms of senile dementia are actually the work of the Njimbin and the creatures he controls. Mrs. Tucker's courage seems sufficient to save her, but in the suffocating storm of midges that brings the narrative to a climax she realizes that, unlike the Njimbin, she is a mortal part of a larger reality that she cannot ignore. She accepts the limitations of age, but her restored assertiveness enables her to bargain for a future that retains the greatest possible independence.

In *Moon-Dark* the dog of *A Little Fear* develops into Blue, the central character in an exploration of the effects of ecological imbalance among the animal communities in the Clarence River estuary. Wrightson uses the local Aboriginal figure of Keeting, the moon, to resolve the problem, but not without requiring self-help and cooperation among the animals. *Balyet,* the most recent of Wrightson's novels for young adults, uses an Aboriginal story of the echo to explore the theme of an adolescent girl's growth through testing social rules and the authority of elders. The ancient story and its modern re-enactment show that the old should learn that the wisest rules must change with changing circumstances, and the young that self-absorption is incompatible with maturity.

—John Murray

Y-Z

YATES, Elizabeth. American. Born in Buffalo, New York, 6 December 1905. Educated at Franklin School, Buffalo; Oaksmere, Mamaroneck, New York. Married William McGreal in 1929 (died 1963). Writer, lecturer. Staff member at writers conferences at University of New Hampshire, University of Connecticut, and Indiana University, beginning 1956; instructor at Christian Writers and Editors conferences, Green Lake, Wisconsin, beginning 1962; trustee, Peterborough Town Library. Recipient: *New York Herald Tribune* Spring Book Festival juvenile award, 1943, for *Patterns on the Wall;* Newbery honor book, 1944, for *Mountain Born;* Spring Book Festival older honor, 1950, John Newbery Medal, 1951, William Allen White Children's Book Award, 1953, all for *Amos Fortune, Free Man;* Boys' Clubs of America Gold Medal, 1953, for *A Place for Peter;* Jane Addams Children's Book Award from U.S. section of Women's International League for Peace and Freedom, 1955, for *Rainbow 'round the World: A Story of UNICEF;* Sara Josepha Hale Award, 1970. Honorary degrees: Litt.D. from Aurora College, 1965, Eastern Baptist College, 1966, University of New Hampshire, 1967, Ripon College, 1970, New England College, 1972, Rivier College, 1979, and Franklin Pierce College, 1981.

PUBLICATIONS FOR YOUNG ADULTS

Fiction

Patterns on the Wall, illustrated by Warren Chappell. New York, Knopf, 1943; as *The Journeyman,* Greenville, South Carolina, Bob Jones University Press, 1990.
A Place for Peter, illustrated by N.S. Unwin. New York, Coward, 1953.

Other

Amos Fortune, Free Man, illustrated by N.S. Unwin. New York, Aladdin, 1950.
David Livingstone. Evanston, Illinois, Row Peterson, 1952.
Prudence Crandall, Woman of Courage, illustrated by N.S. Unwin. New York, Aladdin, 1955.
Someday You'll Write. New York, Dutton, 1962.
New Hampshire. New York, Coward, 1969.

Autobiographical trilogy:

My Diary—My World. Philadelphia, Westminster, 1981.
My Widening World. Philadelphia, Westminster, 1983.
One Writer's Way. Philadelphia, Westminster, 1984.

PUBLICATIONS FOR CHILDREN

Fiction

High Holiday. London, A. & C. Black, 1938.
Hans and Frieda in the Swiss Mountains, illustrated by Nora S. Unwin. New York and London, Nelson, 1939.
Climbing Higher. London, A. & C. Black, 1939; as *Quest in the Northland,* New York, Knopf, 1940.

Haven for the Brave. New York, Knopf, 1941.
Under the Little Fir and Other Stories, illustrated by N.S. Unwin. New York, Coward, 1942.
Around the Year in Iceland, illustrated by Jon Nielsen. Boston, Heath, 1942.
Mountain Born, illustrated by N.S. Unwin. New York, Coward, 1943.
Once in the Year, illustrated by N.S. Unwin. New York, Coward, 1947.
Sam's Secret Journal, illustrated by Allan Eitzen. New York, Friendship, 1964.
Carolina's Courage, illustrated by N.S. Unwin. New York, Dutton, 1964; as *Carolina and the Indian Doll,* London, Methuen, 1965.
An Easter Story, illustrated by N.S. Unwin. New York, Dutton, 1967.
With Pipe, Paddle and Song: A Story of the French-Canadian Voyageurs, illustrated by N.S. Unwin. New York, Dutton, 1968.
Sarah Whitcher's Story, illustrated by N.S. Unwin. New York, Dutton, 1971.
We, the People, illustrated by N.S. Unwin. Taftsville, Vermont, Countryman Press, 1975.
The Seventh One, illustrated by Diana Charles. New York, Walker, 1978.
Silver Lining, illustrated by A.L. Morris. Canaan, New Hampshire, Phoenix, 1981.

Other

Joseph (Bible story), illustrated by N.S. Unwin. New York, Knopf, 1947.
The Young Traveller in the U.S.A. London, Phoenix House, 1948.
The Christmas Story, illustrated by N.S. Unwin. New York, Aladdin, 1949.
Children of the Bible, illustrated by N.S. Unwin. New York, Aladdin, 1950; London, Meiklejohn, 1951.
Rainbow 'round the World: A Story of UNICEF, illustrated by Betty Alden and Dirk Gringhuis. Indianapolis, Bobbs-Merrill, 1954.
Gifts of True Love: Based on the Old Carol "The Twelve Days of Christmas," illustrated by N.S. Unwin. Wallingford, Pennsylvania, Pendle Hill, 1958.
Skeezer, Dog with a Mission, illustrated by Joan Drescher. New York, Harvey House, 1973.

Editor

Piskey Folk: A Book of Cornish Legends, by Enys Tregarthen, photographs by husband, William McGreal. New York, John Day, 1940.
The Doll Who Came Alive, by E. Tregarthen, illustrated by N.S. Unwin. New York, John Day, 1942; London, Faber, 1944.
The White Ring, illustrated by N.S. Unwin. New York, Harcourt, 1949.
Sir Gibbie, by George MacDonald. New York, Dutton, 1963; London, Blackie, 1967.
The Lost Princess; or, The Wise Woman, by G. MacDonald. New York, Dutton, 1965.

PUBLICATIONS FOR ADULTS

Fiction

Wind of Spring. New York, Coward, 1945; London, Cassell, 1948.
Nearby. New York, Coward, 1947; London, Cassell, 1950.
Beloved Bondage. New York, Coward, 1948.
Guardian Heart. New York, Coward, 1950; London, Museum Press, 1952.
Brave Interval. New York, Coward, 1952; London, Bakers, 1953.
Hue and Cry. New York, Coward, 1953.
The Carey Girl. New York, Coward, 1956.
The Next Fine Day. New York, John Day, 1962; London, Dent, 1964.
On That Night. New York, Dutton, 1969.

Other

Pebble in a Pool: The Widening Circles of Dorothy Canfield Fisher's Life. New York, Dutton, 1958, as *The Lady from Vermont: Dorothy Canfield Fisher's Life and World.* Brattleboro, Vermont, Greene, 1971.
The Lighted Heart. New York, Dutton, 1960.
Howard Thurman: Portrait of a Practical Dreamer. New York, John Day, 1964.
Up the Golden Stair: An Approach to a Deeper Understanding of Life through Personal Sorrow. New York, Dutton, 1966.
Is There a Doctor in the Barn?: A Day in the Life of Forrest F. Tenney, D.V.M. New York, Dutton, 1966.
The Road through Sandwich Notch. Brattleboro, Vermont, Stephen Greene, 1972.
A Book of Hours. Norton, Connecticut, Vineyard Books, 1976.
Call It Zest: The Vital Ingredient after Seventy. Brattleboro, Vermont, Stephen Greene, 1977; London, Prior, 1978.
Sound Friendships: The Story of Willa and Her Hearing Ear Dog. Woodstock, Vermont, Countryman Press, 1987.

Editor

Gathered Grace: A Short Selection of George MacDonald's Poems. Cambridge, Heffer, 1938.
Your Prayers and Mine. Boston, Houghton, 1954.

*

Media Adaptations: *Amos Fortune, Free Man* was adapted as a filmstrip and record by Miller-Brody, 1969. *Skeezer, Dog with a Mission* was adapted as a television film by National Broadcasting Company (NBC), 1981. *Mountain Born* was adapted as a film by Disney Films.

Biography: Entry in *The Junior Book of Authors,* New York, H.W. Wilson, 1951; essay in *Something about the Author Autobiography Series,* Volume 6, Detroit, Gale, 1988.

Bibliography: *A Bio-Bibliography of Elizabeth Yates* by Sister Margaret L. Trudell, Nashua, New Hampshire, Rivier College, unpublished thesis, 1970.

Manuscript Collection: Special Collections, Mugar Memorial Library, Boston University.

Although Elizabeth Yates has written numerous books for adult audiences, her most abiding interest has been her young adult readers, to whom her work has introduced a range of topics from biographies and folktales to travel and writing techniques. Her books have retained their appeal to a second and third generation of these young readers; for example, forty years after its initial publication, *Amos Fortune, Free Man* continues to sell more than three thousand copies annually. Well into her eighties, Yates has continued to discuss books and writing with school groups, often driving a considerable distance to do so. In addition, when a young girl asked for advice on becoming a writer, Yates's answer was the book *Someday You'll Write,* in which she describes writing as a craft requiring patience, discipline, and hard work. She further describes her own development as a writer in her memoirs (*The Lighted Heart*) and her published diaries (*My Diary—My World, My Widening World,* and *One Writer's Way*).

Influenced by Thomas Hardy and George Eliot, Yates chronicles the lives of actual and fictional individuals whose characters determine their destiny. She has written biographies of people of strong convictions like Dorothy Canfield Fisher (*Pebble in a Pool*), David Livingston, Howard Thurman (subtitled *Portrait of a Practical Dreamer*), Amos Fortune, and Prudence Crandall, who challenged the laws of Connecticut when, in 1833, she began a private girls' school which admitted black and white students on an equal basis.

Elizabeth Yates is best known, of course, for *Amos Fortune, Free Man,* winner of the 1951 Newbery Award and Herald Tribune Spring Festival Prize, as well as the 1953 William Allen White Children's Book Award. Yates's approach to this subject is typical of her method in writing. Seeing Amos Fortune's grave in a Jaffrey (New Hampshire) cemetery, she was intrigued by the inscription and began a thorough search of the historical records. When she knew everything that the records could tell her about Amos's life and about the slave trade, her knowledge of New England history and her artist's eye for understanding and portraying people helped her fill in the gaps. As a result, the reader shares not only Amos's hopes and triumphs, but also his fears, frustrations, and errors in judgment; Amos Fortune is a complex and credible character whose actions are completely plausible.

Amos possesses the character traits Yates admires. For instance, he feels a strong sense of responsibility to lead and care for others. When he and his fellow At-mun-shi are captured by the slavers, he tries unsuccessfully to organize resistance. Equally futile is his lengthy search for his sister, but when he cannot find her and buy her freedom, he tries instead to give other helpless women at least a few last days of dignity and freedom. Repeatedly he emphasizes to younger slaves and freedmen alike, the overwhelming importance of the freedom and respect earned through developing a skill. Amos's will further demonstrates his belief in the importance of education, as he leaves a substantial bequest to the local schools.

Amos's self-respect comes from his pride in craftsmanship and his well-developed sense of honor. He will not accept manumission until he also possesses skills sufficient to earn a living for himself and his family. He therefore masters two trades, weaving and tanning, and when finally he is freed, it is because he has bought his freedom and so has fulfilled his commitment to help provide for his master's widow. A skilled weaver and tanner, he prospers because he and his wife are industrious and thrifty.

Even though Amos was a prince among the At-mun-shi, more important to him is his identity as a simple Christian. Thus he consistently displays fortitude, humility, charity, and consideration for the feelings of others. He patiently endures setbacks in gaining his long-delayed freedom, and, despite his skills and his growing wealth, he makes no retort to the infrequent instances of overt racism, nor to the many small slights and the pervasive atmosphere of insensitivity. Also, whether in the lush forests of Africa or in the hilly New England countryside, Amos retains his attitude of humble awe toward the natural world. To him, Mount Monadnock speaks a language of signs that allows him to anticipate and prepare for storms, and though he eventually forgets all At-mun-shi words except his own name, Amos continues the tribal custom of reverently kissing the earth.

Likewise, even while he is busily engaged in establishing his own home and his business, Amos continues to show concern for the welfare of others. A notable example is the Burdoo family, whose improvidence makes them foils for Amos and his family. Moses Burdoo was, like Amos, a skilled craftsman, but even when he was alive, the town frequently was called upon to help support his family, and his death has reduced his children to a kind of indentured servitude. When Amos in effect adopts Polly Burdoo and sets her brothers on the path to learning trades, he offers a kind of charity that allows the family to regain their dignity.

Several of Yates's fictional characters share Amos Fortune's attributes. For example, Peter of *Mountain Born* and *A Place for Peter* is, like Amos, a youth who grows toward maturity in a pastoral setting which instills in him an appreciation of the changing seasons and—through his caring for his pet ewe—a love for animals. Moreover, when the farmhand Benj explains to Peter that he kills the rattlesnakes only to protect the humans and the sheep and thus he asks the rattlesnakes' forgiveness before killing them, he demonstrates a reverence for nature similar to that of the At-mun-shi, who also kill only out of necessity and then burn the entrails in expiation to the spirits of their animal victims.

In *Carolina's Courage,* inspired by a century-old Indian doll given to her by a friend, Yates relates the story of young Carolina Putnam and her treasured doll Lydia-Lou. The Putnam family must leave behind most of their possessions when they leave their New Hampshire home to become homesteaders in Nebraska. The delicately beautiful china and sawdust doll is the one personal possession Carolina's father allows her to take, a major source of consolation for her during the trying journey. Just short of their destination, however, as the wagon train is delayed by the threat of hostile Indians, Carolina wanders to the banks of a nearby stream, where she meets an Indian girl with a crude doll made of buffalo hide. After playing together for a while, the two girls part, but the Indian girl insists that they exchange dolls. Remembering that she has been taught to share, Carolina reluctantly agrees and so, without being aware of it, ensures the safety of the entire party as they travel through Indian territory.

Like the Indian doll, the stencil wall designs discovered during the renovation of her home Shieling (named for a type of shelter used by shepherds on the Isle of Skye) led Yates to write the novel *Patterns on the Wall.* Fascinated by the art of stenciling, she combined her research on the subject with historical facts about the dreadful New Hampshire winter of 1816, to tell the story of Jared Austin, an artist whose talent makes him suspect among his fellow New Englanders. Blamed for the snowfalls that occur in every month that year, Jared is accused of being a devil, and he becomes an outcast, losing everything but the consolation he derives from his art. With a fortitude akin to that of Amos Fortune, however, Jared considers his troubles part of a divine plan to remind him of God's power and providential care.

Throughout her career, Yates's books have reflected her interests and her values. She has written about *Children of the Bible* and children affected by the work of UNICEF (*Rainbow 'round the World*), about those who work with animals (*Is There a Doctor in the Barn?*) and those who train animals to assist the hearing-impaired (*Sound Friendships* and *Skeezer, Dog with a Mission*). *The Lighted Heart* is an inspirational account of the modifications Yates and her husband, William McGreal, made in their lives as—with courage and fortitude worthy of her most heroic characters—they adapted to his increasing loss of sight. In *Call It Zest: The Vital Ingredient after Seventy,* Elizabeth Yates explains a lifestyle that includes service on the Boards of the New Hampshire Association for the Blind, Hearing Ear Dog Program, and White Pines College, as well as volunteer work at three nursing homes, the community hospital, and the town library. Obviously she, like Amos Fortune, has discovered that hard work for the benefit of others is the secret to a long and vigorous life.

—Charmaine Allmon Mosby

YEP, Laurence (Michael). American. Born in San Francisco, California, 14 June 1948. Educated at Marquette University, Milwaukee, 1966-68; University of California, Santa Cruz, B.A. 1970; State University of New York at Buffalo, 1970-75, Ph.D. 1975. Writer. Part-time instructor of English, Foothill College, Mountain View, California, 1975, and San Jose City College, California, 1975-76; visiting lecturer in Asian American studies, University of California, Berkeley, 1987-1989, writer-in-residence, 1990. Recipient: Book-of-the-Month-Club Writing Fellowship, 1970; *Dragonwings* was named one of the *New York Times* Outstanding Books of the Year, 1975; Newbery Medal Honor Book, American Library Association (ALA), Children's Book Award, International Reading Association, Jane Addams Children's Book Award Honor Book, Jane Addams Peace Association, and Carter G. Woodson Book Award, National Council for Social Studies, all 1976, *Boston Globe-Horn Book* Award Honor Book, 1977, Lewis Carroll Shelf Award, University of Wisconsin, 1979, selected as one of New York Public Library's Books for the Teen Age, 1980, 1981, and 1982, and Friends of Children and Literature Award, 1984, all for *Dragonwings; Child of the Owl* was named one of *School Library Journal*'s Best Books for Spring, and one of the *New York Times* Outstanding Books of the Year, both 1977; *Boston Globe-Horn Book* Award for fiction, 1977, and Jane Addams Children's Book Award, 1978, both for *Child of the Owl;* Commonwealth Club of California Silver Medal, 1979, for *Sea Glass; Dragon Steel* was selected one of Child Study Association of America's Children's Books of the Year, 1986; *Boston Globe-Horn Book* Honor Award, 1989, for *The Rainbow People.* Agent: Maureen Walters, Curtis Brown Agency, 10 Astor Place, New York, NY 10003. Address: 921 Populus Place, Sunnyvale, CA 94086, U.S.A.

PUBLICATIONS FOR YOUNG ADULTS

Fiction

Sweetwater, illustrated by Julia Noonan. New York, Harper, 1973; London, Faber, 1976.
Dragonwings. New York, Harper, 1975.

Child of the Owl. New York, Harper, 1977.
Sea Glass. New York, Harper, 1979.
Dragon of the Lost Sea. New York, Harper, 1982.
Kind Hearts and Gentle Monsters. New York, Harper, 1982.
The Mark Twain Murders. New York, Four Winds Press, 1982.
Liar, Liar. New York, Morrow, 1983.
The Serpent's Children. New York, Harper, 1984.
The Tom Sawyer Fires. New York, Morrow, 1984.
Dragon Steel. New York, Harper, 1985.
Mountain Light (sequel to *The Serpent's Children*). New York, Harper, 1985.
Shadow Lord. New York, Harper, 1985; Bath, Chivers, 1987.
The Curse of the Squirrel, illustrated by Dirk Zimmer. New York, Random House, 1987.
Lost Garden. Englewood Cliffs, New Jersey, Silver Burdett Press, 1990.
Dragon Cauldron. New York, HarperCollins, 1991.
The Star Fisher. New York, Morrow, 1991.
Tongues of Jade. New York, HarperCollins, 1991.
Dragon War. New York, HarperCollins, 1992.

Plays

Age of Wonders (produced by Asian American Theater Company, 1987).
Pay the Chinaman, and Fairy Bones (produced in San Francisco, 1987).

Other

Reteller, *The Rainbow People* (collection of Chinese-American folk tales), illustrated by David Wiesner. New York, Harper, 1989.
A Lesson Plan Book for Dragonwings. Jefferson City. Missouri, 1990.
When the Bomb Dropped: The Story of Hiroshima. New York, Random House, 1990.
Editor, *American Dragons: A Collection of Asian American Voices.* New York, HarperCollins, 1993.
Reteller, *The Shell Woman and the King,* illustrated by Yang Ming-Yi. New York, Dial, 1993.
Reteller, *Foxfire,* illustrated by Jean and Mou-sien Tseng. New York, Scholastic, 1994.

Publications for Adults

Fiction

Seademons. New York, Harper, 1977.
Monster Makers, Inc. New York, Arbor House, 1986.

*

Media Adaptations: *Dragonwings,* a filmstrip with record or cassette, Miller-Brody, 1979; *The Curse of the Squirrel,* a cassette, Random House, 1989. *Sweetwater* is available in braille and as a "talking book."

Biography: Entry in *Dictionary of Literary Biography,* Volume 52, *American Writers for Children since 1960: Fiction,* Detroit, Gale, 1986, pp. 392-98; entry in *Fifth Book of Junior Authors and Illustrators,* New York, H.W. Wilson, 1983; essay in *Authors and Artists for Young Adults,* Volume 5, Detroit, Gale, 1990; essay in

Speaking for Ourselves: Autobiographical Sketches by Notable Authors of Books for Young Adults, Volume 1, compiled and edited by Donald R. Gallo, National Council of Teachers of English, 1990.

Critical Studies: Entry in *Children's Literature Review,* Volume 3, 1978; Volume 17, 1989, Detroit, Gale; entry in *Contemporary Literary Criticism,* Volume 35, Detroit, Gale, 1985.

*   *   *

Laurence Yep is a literary bridge builder. Some of his bridges connect his readers with Chinese-American and Chinese traditions, folklore, history, thought, and experiences. Since he began publishing in 1969, Yep has authored works of folklore, science fiction, fantasy, short stories, essays, plays, realistic fiction, historical fiction, and picture books.

Employing universal themes in his work, Yep touches concerns that affect all people; finding personal and cultural identity, separating from parents, becoming independent, and coming to terms with a changing body are all masterfully handled in Yep's books for young people. He bridges the gap between the concerns of young people and their resolution by his characters. As Yep straddles the line between children's and young adult literature, his books are links between the reading of elementary school and the reading of middle, junior high school, and early high school years.

Yep frequently deals with a multidimensional, multicultural world. Explaining in his autobiography, *Lost Garden,* that he was brought up in an urban neighborhood of mixed ethnicity, where, as the neighborhood changed, he felt like an outsider in a place wherein he once felt most at home. "At a time when so many children are now proud of their ethnic heritages, I'm ashamed to say that when I was a child, I didn't want to be Chinese. It took me years to realize that I was Chinese whether I wanted to be or not. And it was something I had to learn to accept: to know it's strengths and weaknesses. It's something that is a part of me from the deepest levels of my soul to my most every day actions."

Yep utilizes Chinese-American and Chinese characters in many of his books. Moon Shadow, the young protagonist in *Dragonwings,* who was born in China, sees the United States with fresh eyes when he joins the father and the Tang men who comprise the Chinese bachelor society in San Francisco in the early 1900s. While exploring the theme of a man fulfilling a dream, Yep shows the beauty and strengths of Chinese culture, the racism and bigotry against the Chinese as it existed at the time of the story, and the strong bonds of friendships that can develop between people of different races.

Both China and the United States are used as the settings for *Serpent's Children* and *Mountain Light.* Yep begins each novel by painting a vivid portrait of the life of the rural poor from Kwangtung province in the mid-1800s. The commitment to the cause of eliminating British and Manchu rule plays a major role in shaping many characters. Seen through the eyes of Cassia, the female narrator and Squeaky Lau, the male narrator, the novel deals with issues of tradition: foot binding, the role of women in society, belonging and acceptance, etc. Taking a stand and sacrificing for beliefs are sensitively handled in these books as well. Both books contrast life in China with the life of some characters in the United States.

In contrast to Yep's historical fiction, *Child of the Owl, Sea Glass,* and *Star Fisher* have a modern American setting and feature Chinese-American protagonists, between twelve and fifteen, who undertake personal journeys to discover their individuality. To some degree autobiographical, two of the these novels feature strong female voices. *American Dragons* is also set in contemporary America, but instead of a single voice, it contains many. Consisting of a variety of poems, short stories, and an excerpt from a play, gathered by Yep but written by a variety of authors with Asian roots, this timely collection of personal and often moving narratives examines questions of personal, cultural, and sexual identity, and looks at intergenerational and cultural problems.

The Rainbow People and *Tongues of Jade* supply readers with two additional collections of stories. With a single David Wiesner, black and white illustration at the beginning of each story, both books consist of simple yet powerful folktales with roots in the traditional folklore of China's Kwangtung province. The author used old Chinese myths as background material when he wrote *Dragon of the Lost Sea, Dragon Steel, Dragon Cauldron,* and *Dragon War,* interconnected fantasy novels that trace the adventures of Shimmer, the dragon princess, who forges friendships and interdependencies as she tries to restore her lost home.

Yep writes for outsiders, or those who don't fit in. For Yep this can mean being overweight, not being athletic, not being the perfect child—dilemmas faced by many young adults or at least ones they can relate to on. Streetwise Casey, in *Child of the Owl,* begrudgingly leaves behind the only life she has ever known, living on-the-edge with her father, a compulsive gambler who is suddenly hospitalized, and goes to live with her elderly grandmother. Casey learns, changes, and grows as she discovers more about her heritage. Overweight Craig in *Sea Glass* feels as if he is a constant disappointment to his athletic parents, but through experiences and the friendship he develops with his uncle, he gains the strength and wisdom to accept who he is. Craig learns that his "Chineseness" separates him because of the bigotry of some, but his humanity and inner strengths connect him with others. Joan Lee and her family in *Star Fisher* encounter both bigotry and kindness in West Virginia. They adapt to new traditions like baking apple pies and find the courage to begin again, blending the new with the old.

In *Sweetwater,* Yep uses the genre of science fiction to explore differences between groups sharing the same planet with indigenous people. Thirteen-year-old Tyree's love of music enables him to form a strong bond with the aliens and discover his family roots as well. Yep contrasts the inhabitants of another future civilization and how its people deal with differences in *Seademons.* On still another planet, Yep uses a somewhat older protagonist seeking to find his place in his own society in *Shadow Lord,* the twenty-second novel of the "Star Trek" series.

Yep sensitively develops complex characters who wrestle with self-understanding, and struggle to develop new relationships with family members and peers. All share concerns about where they fit into society. Charley and Chris, two teens who on the surface are vastly different, come to care for each after an initial confrontation in *Kind Hearts and Gentle Monsters. Liar, Liar* generates excitement and tension when a fatal car crash occurs and questions of murder begin to be asked. Suspense builds as Sean, the sixteen-year-old protagonist, confronts the killer and overcomes his panic to save himself.

In *The Mark Twain Murders* and *The Tom Sawyer Fires,* Yep mixes fact and fiction to re-create San Francisco in the late Civil War years when Samuel Clemens, a.k.a. Mark Twain, worked as a newspaper reporter and when Tom Sawyer, an actual city firefighter, became a local hero. A fifteen year old, the Duke of Baywater, narrates both books. After his mother's death and the murder of his brutal stepfather, the teen maintains his illusions regarding the royal identity of his real father as he helps to solve crimes and thwart confederate plots. The teen discovers that heroic actions matter even when they are kept secret and a title attached to a name does little to establish identity, taking action means much more.

Yep's books ask questions about growing up. In *Sea Glass,* the father queries, "So it doesn't matter to you if you win or lose?" Craig, the son, replies with the question, "How do you measure success anyway?" His characters offer advice on living. Cassia in *Mountain Light* says, "Stand tall when you go home. Don't let anyone shrink to a clown." By including both young and old people with much to learn, young and old who feel they already know it all, elders as mentors, Yep gives a sense of authenticity to his multidimensional characters.

Writing fiction, folklore and his autobiography, Yep illustrates that there is no stereotypical Chinese-American, Chinese, or Asian family and/or character. Rather than appealing to one specific group, his work has qualities that have universal appeal. The insights Yep gained as an outsider flavor his writings. Bridging different cultures, readers are able to enjoy the stories Yep weaves, while looking through a window to greater understandings of the worlds of differences and similarities that co-exist in life. Vivid images, complex characters, and well-plotted action linger on the pages of Yep's novels.

—Karen Ferris Morgan

YOLEN, Jane (Hyatt). American. Born in New York City, 11 February 1939. Educated at Staples High School, Westport, Connecticut, graduated 1956; Smith College, Northampton, Massachusetts, B.A. 1960; New School for Social Research, New York; University of Massachusetts, Amherst, 1975-76, M.Ed. 1976. Married David W. Stemple in 1962; one daughter and two sons. Staff member, *This Week* magazine and *Saturday Review,* New York, 1960-61; assistant editor, Gold Medal Books, New York, 1961-62; associate editor, Rutledge Books, New York, 1962-63; assistant editor, Alfred A. Knopf Juvenile Books, New York, 1963-65; Lecturer in Education, Smith College, 1979-84. Columnist (*Children's Bookfare*), *Daily Hampshire Gazette,* Northampton, Massachusetts, 1972-80. Massachusetts delegate, Democratic National Convention, Miami, 1972. Member of the Board of Directors, Society of Children's Book Writers since 1974, and Children's Literature Association, 1977-79; President, Science-Fiction Writers of America, 1986-88. Editor in chief, Jane Yolen Books, imprint of Harcourt Brace, since 1988. Recipient: Boys' Club of America Junior Book award, 1968, for *The Minstrel and the Mountain;* Lewis Carroll Shelf award, 1968, for *The Emperor and the Kite,* and 1973, for *The Girl Who Loved the Wind; The Emperor and the Kite* was selected one of the *New York Times's* Best Books of the Year and as a Caldecott Honor Book, both 1968; *World on a String: The Story of Kites* was named an ALA Notable Book, 1968; Chandler Book Talk Reward of Merit, 1970; *The Girl Who Loved the Wind* was selected for the Children's Book Showcase of the Children's Book Council, 1973, and *The Little Spotted Fish,* 1976; Society of Children's Book Writers Golden Kite award, 1974, ALA Notable Book and National Book award nomination, both 1975, all for *The Girl Who Cried Flowers and Other Tales;* Golden Kite Honor Book, 1975, for *The Transfigured Hart,* and 1976, for *The Moon Ribbon and Other Tales;* Christopher Medal, 1978, for *The Seeing Stick;*

Children's Choice from the International Reading Association and the Children's Book Council, 1980, for *Mice on Ice,* and 1983, for *Dragon's Blood;* Parents' Choice award from the Parents' Choice Foundation, 1982, for *Dragon's Blood,* 1984, for *The Stone Silenus,* and 1989, for *Piggins* and *The Three Bears Rhyme Book; The Gift of Sarah Barker* was selected one of *School Library Journal*'s Best Books for Young Adults, 1982, and *Heart's Blood,* 1985; Garden State Children's Book award from the New Jersey Library Association, 1983, for *Commander Toad in Space;* CRABerry award from Acton Public Library, Maryland, 1983, for *Dragon's Blood; Heart's Blood* was selected one of ALA's Best Books for Young Adults, 1984; Daedelus award, 1986, for "a body of work—fantasy and short fiction"; *The Lullaby Songbook* and *The Sleeping Beauty* were each selected one of Child Study Association of America's Children's Books of the Year, 1987; Caldecott Medal, 1988, for *Owl Moon;* World Fantasy award, 1988, for *Favorite Folktales from around the World;* Kerlan award for "singular achievements in the creation of children's literature," 1988; Parents' Choice Silver Seal award, Jewish Book Council award, and Association of Jewish Libraries award, all 1988, Judy Lopez Honor Book and Nebula award finalist, both 1989, all for *The Devil's Arithmetic;* Golden Sower award from the Nebraska Library Association, 1989, for *Piggins;* thirteen of Yolen's books have been selected by the Junior Literary Guild. LL.D.: College of Our Lady of the Elms, Chicopee, Massachusetts, 1980; Regina Medal, Catholic Library Association, 1992, for body of work; Smith College Medal, 1992, Distinguished Alumna Mythopoeic Society award, 1993, for *Briar Rose,* 1993; Rhysling award, for best science fiction/fantasy poem for *Will,* 1993; Young Adult Best Books, American Library Association, *Briar Rose;* Charlotte award, New York State Reading Council, for *Piggins,* 1991. Agent: Marilyn Marlow, Curtis Brown, 10 Astor Place, New York, NY 10003. Address: 31 School Street, Box 27, Hatfield, MA 01038, U.S.A.

PUBLICATIONS FOR YOUNG ADULTS

Fiction

Simple Gifts: The Story of the Shakers, illustrated by Betty Fraser. New York, Viking Press, 1976.
The Gift of Sarah Barker. New York, Viking Press, 1981.
Dragon's Blood. New York, Delacorte Press, 1982; London, MacRae, 1983.
Neptune Rising: Songs and Tales of the Undersea Folk, illustrated by David Wiesner. New York, Philomel, 1982.
Children of the Wolf. New York, Viking Kestrel, 1984.
Heart's Blood. New York, Delacorte Press, and London, MacRae, 1984.
The Stone Silenus. New York, Philomel, 1984.
A Sending of Dragons, illustrated by Tom McKeveny. New York, Delacorte Press, and London, MacRae, 1987.
The Devil's Arithmetic. New York, Viking Kestrel, 1988.
Vampires. New York, Harper, 1991.
Briar Rose. New York, Tor, 1992.
Here There Be Dragons, illustrated by David Wilgus. San Diego, Harcourt Brace, forthcoming.

Other

Editor, *Zoo 2000: Twelve Stories of Science Fiction and Fantasy Beasts.* New York, Seabury Press, 1973; London, Gollancz, 1975.

Editor, *Shape Shifters: Fantasy and Science Fiction Tales about Humans Who Can Change Their Shapes.* New York, Seabury Press, 1978.
Editor, with Martin H. Greenberg and Charles G. Waugh, *Dragons and Dreams: A Collection of New Fantasy and Science Fiction Stories.* New York, Harper, 1986.
Editor, with Martin H. Greenberg and Charles G. Waugh, *Spaceships and Spells.* New York, Harper, 1987.
Editor, with Martin H. Greenberg, *Werewolves.* New York, Harper, 1988.
The Faery Flag: Stories and Poems of Fantasy and the Supernatural. New York, Orchard, 1989.
Editor, with Martin H. Greenberg, *Things That Go Bump in the Night.* New York, Harper, 1989.
Editor, *2040 A.D.* New York, Delacorte, 1990.
A Letter from Phoenix Farm, photographs by Jason Stemple. Katonah, New York, Owen, 1992.

PUBLICATIONS FOR CHILDREN

Fiction

The Witch Who Wasn't, illustrated by Arnold Roth. New York, Macmillan, and London, Collier Macmillan, 1964.
Gwinellen, The Princess Who Could Not Sleep, illustrated by Ed Renfro. New York, Macmillan, 1965.
Trust a City Kid, with Anne Huston, illustrated by J.C. Kocsis. New York, Lothrop, 1966; London, Dent, 1967.
Isabel's Noel, illustrated by Arnold Roth. New York, Funk and Wagnalls, 1967.
The Emperor and the Kite, illustrated by Ed Young. Cleveland, World, 1967; London, Macdonald, 1969.
The Minstrel and the Mountain, illustrated by Anne Rockwell. Cleveland, World, and Edinburgh, Oliver and Boyd, 1968.
Greyling: A Picture Story from the Islands of Shetland, illustrated by William Stobbs. Cleveland, World, 1968; London, Bodley Head, 1969.
The Longest Name on the Block, illustrated by Peter Madden. New York, Funk and Wagnalls, 1968.
The Wizard of Washington Square, illustrated by Ray Cruz. New York, World, 1969.
The Inway Investigators; or, The Mystery at McCracken's Place, illustrated by Allan Eitzen. New York, Seabury Press, 1969.
The Seventh Mandarin, illustrated by Ed Young. New York, Seabury Press, and London, Macmillan, 1970.
Hobo Toad and the Motorcycle Gang, illustrated by Emily McCully. New York, World, 1970.
The Bird of Time, illustrated by Mercer Mayer. New York, Crowell, 1971.
The Girl Who Loved the Wind, illustrated by Ed Young. New York, Crowell, 1972; London, Collins, 1973.
The Girl Who Cried Flowers and Other Tales, illustrated by David Palladini. New York, Crowell, 1974.
Rainbow Rider, illustrated by Michael Foreman. New York, Crowell, 1974; London, Collins, 1975.
The Adventures of Eeka Mouse, illustrated by Myra Gibson McKee. Middletown, Connecticut, Xerox, 1974.
The Boy Who Had Wings, illustrated by Helga Aichinger. New York, Crowell, 1974.

The Magic Three of Solatia, illustrated by Julia Noonan. New York, Crowell, 1974.

The Little Spotted Fish, illustrated by Friso Henstra. New York, Seabury Press, 1975.

The Transfigured Hart, illustrated by Donna Diamond. New York, Crowell, 1975.

The Moon Ribbon and Other Tales, illustrated by David Palladini. New York, Crowell, 1976; London, Dent, 1977.

Milkweed Days, photographs by Gabriel Amadeus Cooney. New York, Crowell, 1976.

The Sultan's Perfect Tree, illustrated by Barbara Garrison. New York, Parents' Magazine Press, 1977.

The Seeing Stick, illustrated by Remy Charlip and Demetra Marsalis. New York, Crowell, 1977.

The Hundredth Dove and Other Tales, illustrated by David Palladini. New York, Crowell, 1977; London, Dent, 1979.

The Giants' Farm, illustrated by Tomie de Paola. New York, Seabury Press, 1977.

Hannah Dreaming, photographs by Alan Epstein. Springfield, Massachusetts, Springfield Museum of Fine Arts, 1977.

The Mermaid's Three Wisdoms, illustrated by Laura Rader. New York, Collins World, 1978.

No Bath Tonight, illustrated by Nancy Winslow Parker. New York, Crowell, 1978.

The Simple Prince, illustrated by Jack Kent. New York, Parents' Magazine Press, 1978.

Spider Jane, illustrated by Stefen Bernath. New York, Coward McCann, 1978.

Dream Weaver and Other Tales, illustrated by Michael Hague. New York, Collins, 1979.

The Giants Go Camping, illustrated by Tomie de Paola. New York, Seabury Press, 1979.

Spider Jane on the Move, illustrated by Stefen Bernath. New York, Coward McCann, 1980.

Mice on Ice, illustrated by Lawrence Di Fiori. New York, Dutton, 1980.

Commander Toad in Space, illustrated by Bruce Degen. New York, Coward McCann, 1980.

The Robot and Rebecca: The Mystery of the Code-Carrying Kids, illustrated by Catherine Deeter. New York, Random House, 1980.

Shirlick Holmes and the Case of the Wandering Wardrobe, illustrated by Anthony Rao. New York, Coward McCann, 1981.

Uncle Lemon's Spring, illustrated by Glen Rounds. New York, Dutton, 1981.

The Boy Who Spoke Chimp, illustrated by David Wiesner. New York, Knopf, 1981.

Brothers of the Wind, illustrated by Barbara Berger. New York, Philomel, 1981.

The Acorn Quest, illustrated by Susanna Natti. New York, Crowell, 1981.

The Robot and Rebecca and the Missing Owser, illustrated by Lady McCrady. New York, Knopf, 1981.

Sleeping Ugly, illustrated by Diane Stanley. New York, Coward McCann, 1981.

Commander Toad and the Planet of the Grapes, illustrated by Bruce Degen. New York, Coward McCann, 1982.

Commander Toad and the Big Black Hole, illustrated by Bruce Degen. New York, Coward McCann, 1983.

Commander Toad and the Dis-Asteroid, illustrated by Bruce Degen. New York, Coward McCann, 1985.

Commander Toad and the Intergalactic Spy, illustrated by Bruce Degen. New York, Coward McCann, 1986.

Piggins, illustrated by Jane Dyer. San Diego, Harcourt Brace, 1987; London, Piccadilly Press, 1988.

Owl Moon, illustrated by John Schoenherr. New York, Philomel, 1987.

Commander Toad and the Space Pirates, illustrated by Bruce Degen. New York, Putnam, 1987.

Picnic with Piggins, illustrated by Jane Dyer. San Diego, Harcourt Brace, 1988.

Piggins and the Royal Wedding. San Diego, Harcourt Brace, 1989.

Dove Isabeau. San Diego, Harcourt Brace, 1989.

Dream Wever. New York, Putnam, 1989.

Baby Bear's Bedtime Book, illustrated by Jane Dyer. San Diego, Harcourt Brace, 1990.

Sky Dogs, illustrated by Barry Moser. San Diego, Harcourt Brace, 1990.

Tam Lin, illustrated by Charles Mikolaycak. San Diego, Harcourt Brace, 1990.

The Dragon's Boy. New York, Harper, 1990.

Elfabet: An ABC of Elves. Boston, Little Brown, 1990.

Letting Swift River Go. Boston, Little Brown, 1990.

All Those Secrets of the World, illustrated by Leslie Baker. Boston, Little Brown, 1991.

Wizard's Hall. San Diego, Harcourt Brace, 1991.

Eeny, Meeny, Miney Mole, illustrated by Kathryn Brown. San Diego, Harcourt Brace, 1992.

Encounter, illustrated by David Shannon. San Diego, Harcourt Brace, 1992.

Honkers, illustrated by Leslie Baker. Boston, Little Brown, 1993.

Mouse's Birthday, illustrated by Bruce Degen. New York, Putnam, 1993.

The Girl in the Golden Bower, illustrated by Jane Dyer. Boston, Little Brown, 1994.

Beneath the Ghost Moon, illustrated by Laurel Molk. Boston, Little Brown, forthcoming.

Grandad Bill's Song, illustrated by Melissa Bay Mathis. New York, Philomel, forthcoming.

Little Mouse and Elephant: A Tale from Turkey (retelling), illustrated by John Segal. New York, Harper, forthcoming.

The Musicians of Bremen: A Tale from Germany (retelling), illustrated by John Segal. New York, Harper, forthcoming.

The Traveler's Rose, illustrated by Leo and Diane Dillon. New York, Philomel, forthcoming.

Plays

Robin Hood, music by Barbara Green (produced Boston, 1967).

Poetry

See This Little Line?, illustrated by Kathleen Elgin. New York, McKay, 1963.

It All Depends, illustrated by Don Bolognese. New York, Funk and Wagnalls, 1969.

An Invitation to the Butterfly Ball: A Counting Rhyme, illustrated by Jane Breskin Zalben. New York, Parents' Magazine Press, 1976; Kingswood, Surrey, World's Work, 1978.

All in the Woodland Early: An ABC Book, music by the author, illustrated by Jane Breskin Zalben. Cleveland, Collins, 1979.

How Beastly! A Menagerie of Nonsense Poems, illustrated by James Marshall. New York, Collins, 1980.

Dragon Night and Other Lullabies, illustrated by Demi. New York, Methuen, 1980; London, Methuen, 1981.

Ring of Earth: A Child's Book of Seasons, illustrated by John Wallner. San Diego, Harcourt Brace, 1986.

The Three Bears Rhyme Book, illustrated by Jane Dyer. San Diego, Harcourt Brace, 1987.

Best Witches. New York, Putnam, 1989.

Bird Watch, illustrated by Ted Lewin. New York, Philomel, 1990.

Dinosaur Dances, illustrated by Bruce Degen. New York, Putnam, 1990.

Raining Cats and Dogs, illustrated by Janet Street. San Diego, Harcourt Brace, 1993.

Welcome to the Greenhouse: A Story of the Tropical Rainforest, illustrated by Laura Regan. New York, Putnam, 1993.

What Rhymes With Moon?, illustrated by Ruth Tietjen Councell. New York, Philomel, 1993.

Sacred Places, illustrated by David Shannon. San Diego, Harcourt Brace, forthcoming.

Other

Pirates in Petticoats, illustrated by Leonard Vosburgh. New York, McKay, 1963.

World on a String: The Story of Kites. Cleveland, World, 1968.

Editor, *The Fireside Song Book of Birds and Beasts,* music by Barbara Green, illustrated by Peter Parnall. New York, Simon and Schuster, 1972.

Friend: The Story of George Fox and the Quakers. New York, Seabury Press, 1972.

The Wizard Islands, illustrated by Robert Quackenbush. New York, Crowell, 1973.

Ring Out! A Book of Bells, illustrated by Richard Cuffari. New York, Seabury Press, 1974; London, Evans, 1978.

Editor, *Rounds about Rounds,* music by Barbara Green, illustrated by Gail Gibbons. New York, Watts, 1977; London, Watts, 1978.

Editor, *The Lullaby Songbook,* music arranged by Adam Stemple, illustrated by Charles Mikolaycak. San Diego, Harcourt Brace, 1986.

The Sleeping Beauty (retelling), illustrated by Ruth Sanderson. New York, Knopf, 1986.

The Lap-Time Song and Play Book, musical arrangements by Adam Stemple, illustrated by Margot Tomes. San Diego, Harcourt Brace, 1989.

Publisher, *Appleblossom.* San Diego, Harcourt Brace, 1991.

Hark!, A Christmas Sampler, original music and arrangements by Adam Stemple, illustrated by Tomie de Paola. New York, Putnam, 1991.

Publisher, *The Jewel of Life.* San Diego, Harcourt Brace, 1991.

Publisher, *The Patchwork Lady.* San Diego, Harcourt Brace, 1991.

Publisher, *The Red Ball.* San Diego, Harcourt Brace, 1991.

Editor, *Street Rhymes around the World,* illustrated by seventeen international artists. Honesdale, Pennsylvania, Wordsong, 1992.

PUBLICATIONS FOR ADULTS

Fiction

The Lady and the Merman, illustrated by Barry Moser. Easthampton, Massachusetts, Pennyroyal Press, 1977.

Cards of Grief. New York, Ace, 1984; London, Futura, 1986.

Sister Light, Sister Dark. New York, Tor, 1988.

White Jenna. New York, Tor, 1989.

Short Stories

Tales of Wonder. New York, Schocken, 1983; London, Futura, 1987.

Dragonfield and Other Stories. New York, Ace, 1985.

Merlin's Booke. New York, Steeldragon Press, 1986.

Nonfiction

Writing Books for Children. Boston, The Writer, 1973; revised edition, 1983.

Touch Magic: Fantasy, Faerie, and Folklore in the Literature of Childhood. New York, Philomel, 1981.

Guide to Writing for Children. Boston, The Writer, 1989.

Other

Contributor, *Dragons of Light,* edited by Orson Scott Card. New York, Ace, 1981.

Contributor, *Elsewhere,* edited by Terri Windling and Mark Alan Arnold. New York, Ace, 2 vols., 1981-82.

Contributor, *Hecate's Cauldron,* edited by Susan Schwartz. New York, DAW, 1982.

Contributor, *Heroic Visions,* edited by Jessica Amanda Salmonson. New York, Ace, 1983.

Contributor, *Faery!,* edited by Terri Windling. New York, Ace, 1985.

Contributor, *Liavek,* edited by Will Shetterly and Emma Bull. New York, Ace, 1985.

Contributor, *Moonsinger's Friends,* edited by Schwartz. Bluejay, 1985.

Contributor, *Imaginary Lands,* edited by Robin McKinley. New York, Greenwillow, 1985.

Contributor, *Don't Bet on the Prince: Contemporary Feminist Fairy Tales in North America and England,* by Jack Zipes. New York, Methuen, 1986.

Editor, *Favorite Folktales from around the World.* New York, Pantheon, 1986.

Contributor, *Liavek: Players of Luck,* edited by Will Shetterly and Emma Bull. New York, Ace, 1986.

Contributor, *Liavek: Wizard's Row,* edited by Will Shetterly and Emma Bull. New York, Ace, 1987.

Contributor, *Visions,* by Donald R. Gallo. New York, Delacorte, 1987.

Contributor, *Liavek: Spells of Binding,* edited by Will Shetterly and Emma Bull. New York, Ace, 1988.

Contributor, *Invitation to Camelot,* by Parke Godwin. New York, Ace, 1988.

Contributor, *The Unicorn Treasury,* by Bruce Coville. New York, Doubleday, 1988.

Editor, *Xanadu.* New York, Tor, 1993.

Editor, *Camelot.* New York, Philomel, forthcoming.

*

Media Adaptations: *The Seventh Mandarin* (film), Xerox Films, 1973; *The Emperor and the Kite* (filmstrip with cassette), Listening Library, 1976; *The Bird of Time* (play, produced Northampton, Massachusetts, 1982); *The Girl Who Cried Flowers and Other Tales* (cassette), Weston Woods, 1983; *Dragon's Blood* (television movie), CBS Storybreak, 1985; *Commander Toad in Space* (cassette), Listening Library, 1986; *Touch Magic...Pass It On* (cassette), Weston Woods, 1987; *Owl Moon* (filmstrip with cassette), Weston Woods, 1988; *Piggins and Picnic with Piggins* (cassette), Caedmon, 1988; *Commander Toad* (half hour movie), Churchill Films, 1993. Author of *Merlin and the Dragons,* Light Year Entertainment, 1991.

Biography: Entry in *Dictionary of Literary Biography,* Volume 52, Detroit, Gale, 1986; essay in *Something about the Author Autobiography Series,* Volume 4, Detroit, Gale, 1987; essay in *Speaking for Ourselves: Autobiographical Sketches by Notable Authors of Books for Young Adults,* Volume 1, compiled and edited by Donald R. Gallo, National Council of Teachers of English, 1990.

Manuscript Collection: Kerlan Collection, University of Minnesota, Minneapolis.

Critical Study: Entry in *Children's Literature Review,* Volume 4, Detroit, Gale, 1982.

Jane Yolen comments:
I am a storyteller. I never feel more alive than when I am sitting at my desk in front of my typewriter and stories simply leak out of my fingertips onto the keyboard. I don't know where they come from, but once the first draft is out there, the hard work really begins: the shaping, pounding, kneading, pummeling the thing into shape.

Of course the story is never quite as wonderful at the end as one hopes at the beginning. As Edith Wharton said: "I dream of an eagle, I give birth to a hummingbird." That's why we writers keep on writing, looking for that great soaring eagle, forgetting that the hummingbird is also beautiful. And it flies.

*   *   *

Jane Yolen is an American author of 130 books in a variety of genres. She is best known, however, for her books of fantasy, written in the style of folk and fairy tales. Her books have won major state and national awards and have been translated into ten languages. Because of her versatility, wit, and use of language, she is a perfect author for young adults.

Several of Yolen's books in the fairy tale genre have adult themes and are meant for older readers. Although her books are inspired by folk literature, they are not retellings but her own creations. Young adult readers learn that fairy tales and fantasy can teach them about themselves, the nature of love, and their places in the world. *Neptune Rising: Songs and Tales of the Undersea Folk* and *The Faery Flag: Stories and Poems of Fantasy and the Supernatural* are collections of original stories written primarily in the form of fairy tales. *Neptune Rising* contains original stories and poems about "sea folks." The stories, usually about love between these creatures and humans, teach that there is pain and danger in seeking out and loving those belonging in a different element.

The Faery Flag also contains original stories and poems about a variety of topics. In one humorous tale, three old wolves tell their side of the stories in which they were depicted as the villains. Two poems in this book are reflections by female characters from famous fairy tales, "Beauty and the Beast: an Anniversary" and "The Golden Stair."

For the reader between eleven and twelve years of age, there are *The Wizard's Hall,* a novel about a reluctant hero and *The Dragon's Boy,* Yolen's imaginative retelling of King Arthur's boyhood.

The pit dragon trilogy, *Dragon's Blood, Heart's Blood,* and *A Sending of Dragons,* are three fantasy novels set on the distant planet Austar, in the future. In this series, the reader watches the psychological, moral, and spiritual development of Jakkin as he moves from slavery to freedom, from boyhood to manhood, and from responsibility only for himself to taking on responsibility for others. In the first book, Jakkin is working as a bond servant in the nursery for fighting dragons. He steals a dragon hatchling for himself so that he can attain freedom. In books two and three, Jakkin rescues Akki, the girl he loves, first from a dangerous group of rebels and then from a society in which robot-like people live underground and sacrifice dragons to remain alive. The planet Austar is a complete fantasy world. In it Yolen develops a complete life cycle for dragons, making them familiar animals to the reader. These books are exciting adventure stories in which the characters reach maturity.

Two of Yolen's books of realistic, modern fiction for young adults are about the Holocaust. Each of these relies on an element of fantasy to teach about the importance of the past.

The Devil's Arithmetic, describes life inside a concentration camp. Hannah is suddenly and mystically transported from her safe home in New York to a small Jewish village in Poland at the beginning of the Holocaust, but then she's captured by the Nazis and sent to a concentration camp. In it, Hannah dies a hero. When Hannah returns to the present, she understands the importance of keeping the past alive.

Briar Rose, although recommended for adults, would be interesting to high-school students. The death of her grandmother leads Becca to seek information about her grandmother's past. This search ends at the site of an internment camp in Poland. Becca begins to understand her grandmother's unique life, told in the metaphor of Sleeping Beauty. The elements of the fairy tale are metaphorically intertwined with Becca's grandmother's experiences; briars are the barbed wire; the sleep is her transportation in a death truck; and, the kiss was the CPR administered to her.

A third book of realistic fiction, *The Stone Silenus* uses fantasy to maintain tension. Melissa is obsessed with her father after his suicide, constantly focusing on things he said, wrote, and did. When she meets a young man who looks and sounds similar to her father, she thinks he may be her father who has returned.

The Gift of Sarah Barker and *Children of the Wolf* are two novels of historical fiction. *The Gift of Sarah Barker,* set in a Shaker Community during the middle 1800s, tells a story of the growing love between two adolescents. Because the Shakers profess celibacy, the two try to keep their relationship a secret. Again, characteristics of fairy tales infuse themselves within the story. The two adolescents are young innocents, the girl's mother represents the "cruel" parent, while the kind and supporting mother of the sect is comparable to a godmother.

Children of the Wolf, based on actual newspaper accounts, is an imaginative recreation of the attempt of a missionary to raise two children who have lived with wolves. Although it would seem, that the two feral children should be the center to the story, the story is told from the point of view of the missionary, Mohandas, who comes to understand his own gift for love, compassion, and ability to care for others.

It is this self-realization and reliance that defines Yolen's work, whether it be fiction or nonfiction.

—Etta Miller

ZALBEN, Jane Breskin. American. Born in New York City, 21 April 1950. Educated at Queens College of the City University of New York, B.A. 1971; Pratt Institute Graphic Center, graduate study in lithography, 1971-72. Married Steven Zalben in 1969; two sons. Painter, etcher, lithographer, and illustrator; designer and author of children's books. Dial Press, New York, assistant to art director of children's book department, 1971-72; Thomas Y. Crowell Co., New York, free-lance book designer, 1972; Holt, Rinehart & Winston, Inc., New York, free-lance book designer, since 1976; art director, Charles Scribner's Sons, until 1976. Taught college at the School of Visual Arts, Manhattan, for eighteen years. Currently lectures about writing and illustration. Address: 70 South Road, Sands Point, New York, 11050, U.S.A.

PUBLICATIONS FOR YOUNG ADULTS

Fiction

Maybe It Will Rain Tomorrow. New York, Farrar, Straus, 1982.
Here's Looking at You, Kid. New York, Farrar, Straus, 1984.
Water from the Moon. New York, Farrar, Straus, 1987.
Earth to Andrew O. Blechman, illustrated by the author. New York, Farrar, Straus, 1989.
The Fortuneteller in 5B. New York, Holt, 1991.

PUBLICATIONS FOR CHILDREN

Fiction (illustrated by the author)

Cecilia's Older Brother. New York, Macmillan, 1973.
Lyle and Humus. New York, Macmillan, 1974.
Basil and Hillary. New York, Macmillan, 1975.
Penny and the Captain. New York, Philomel Books, 1978.
Norton's Nighttime. New York, Philomel Books, 1979.
Will You Count the Stars without Me? New York, Farrar, Straus, 1979.
Oliver's and Allison's Week. New York, Farrar, Straus, 1980.
A Perfect Nose for Ralph. New York, Philomel Books, 1980.
Oh, Simple! New York, Farrar, Straus, 1981.
Porcupine's Christmas Blues. New York, Philomel Books, 1982.
Beni's First Chanukah. New York, Holt, 1988.
Happy Passover, Rosie. New York, Holt, 1990.
Leo & Blossom's Sukkah. New York, Holt, 1990.
Beni's Little Library. New York, Holt, 1991.
Goldie's Purim. New York, Holt, 1991.
Buster Gets Braces. New York, Holt, 1992.
Happy New Year, Beni. New York, Holt, 1993.

*

Illustrator: *Jeremiah Knucklebones* by Jan Wahl, 1974; *An Invitation to the Butterfly Ball* by Jane H. Yolen, 1976; *The Walrus and the Carpenter* by Lewis Carroll, 1986; *Starlight & Moonshine: Poetry of the Supernatural* by William Shakespeare, 1987; *All in the Woodland Early: An ABC Book* by Jane Yolen, 1991; *Inner Chimes: Poems on Poetry* edited by Bobbye S. Goldstein, 1992; *Lewis Carroll's Jabberwocky* by Lewis Carroll, 1992.

*   *   *

Jane Breskin Zalben sets her first-person narratives for young adults in the complex, sprawling world of New York City and its suburbs, an urban environment providing her middle-class characters with ready access to such pleasures as art museums, Chinese food, music lessons, and foreign films. Within this setting, however, they must learn to cope with the same misunderstandings and misinterpretations in relations with family and friends common to adolescents in any surroundings.

Just as New York City provides a context for Zalben's writing, so do the observances and traditions related to Judaism form strands in her novels. While *The Fortuneteller in 5B* includes the strongest Jewish element of any of her works, Jewish backgrounds of her characters are apparent in *Earth to Andrew O. Blechman,* especially in preparations for a bar mitzvah; in *Water from the Moon,* in which Nicole's family exchanges Hanukkah gifts; and in her first novel, in which Jonathan and his family are Jewish.

In many ways, her first novel for young adults, *Maybe It Will Rain Tomorrow,* remains her most powerful. Sixteen-year-old Beth Corey must come to terms with her mother's suicide. Confused and abandoned, she moves in with her father, his second wife, Linda, and their baby daughter. However, Beth has never reconciled herself to her father's seeking a divorce and blames him and Linda for causing the grief that drove her mother to kill herself. At the same time she blames herself for not preventing the suicide and feels angry and guilty. "Wasn't I a good enough reason for Mom to stay around?" she asks her aunt.

Feeling like an intruder in her new home, she refuses to contribute to the family welfare, clashing with Linda in particular. Beth's search for a new relationship leads to her involvement with Jonathan, a handsome, talented, flute player in her music-theory class. Jonathan takes music lessons in New York City, and Beth joins his informal musical group that performs sidewalk concerts.

Like all Zalben's adolescents, Beth is frankly interested in sex and places a high value on physical attractiveness. Her sexual involvement with Jonathan is handled matter-of-factly. Yet, when he tells her he plans to spend the summer working at a resort in the Catskills to earn money for music lessons, Beth feels betrayed again. "I slept with you because I trusted you," she tells him. "Trust means a great deal to me and I feel our trust has been broken."

A tentative reconciliation through letters ends after Beth visits him at the resort and realizes that Jonathan's involvement with her had been more casual than she had understood. Yet, by the novel's end, Beth takes the first steps toward recognizing the aspects of her mother's life and personality that contributed to her decision to commit suicide. She also makes initial efforts to fit in with her new family.

In *Here's Looking at You Kid,* the narrator is a young man. Seventeen-year-old Eric Fine must find his place in the Long Island neighborhood to which his family has moved recently. His first friendship develops after he meets Enid Tannenbaum at a Bergman film. Sharing a love for movies, they plan to collaborate on a screenplay, but Eric is diverted by gorgeous Kimberley Wright, who dates him while her boyfriend is gone during spring vacation. Even though Eric suspects that Kimberley is using him and realizes his attraction to her hurts Enid, Eric cannot resist.

Eric's perception about his own feelings may be more insightful than the average adolescent's, but Zalben convinces readers of his intelligence and ability to analyze his responses to people. He muses, "...if I could put Enid's mind in Kimberley's body, I'd have it made—or would I?" His acceptance into the New York University film program suggests a possible future in which he explores such questions through movies he creates.

Zalben returns to a female narrator in *Water from the Moon*. Nicole Bernstein has successful, happily married parents, a supportive best friend, and economic security. Her longing for romance leads her to magnify the interest an intern in her father's advertising company expresses in her. She convinces herself that the five-year age difference between her and Joshua Brent, the twenty-one-year-old New York University senior makes no difference. The revelation of his interest in a woman his own age hurts Nicole deeply. Meanwhile, Nicole's longing for adventure leads to a friendship with Tanya Rubano, a fellow art student. Nicole's efforts to secure promises of intense and abiding friendship are rebuffed by Tanya, who cannot afford to make strong emotional attachments—her mother has never outgrown her hippie lifestyle and moves from city to city in search of old friends and new experiences.

Nicole's extreme disappointment over Joshua's and Tanya's unwillingness to make commitments to her seems strange, especially when contrasted with the losses suffered by Beth in Zalben's first novel. The tension between Nicole's brother, Robby, and their father forms a subplot, but the origin of their conflict remains unexplained except for a brief reference to the seeming inevitability of father-son, mother-daughter clashes. In sum, *Water from the Moon* represents a less substantial and emotionally involving novel than its predecessors.

Zalben's latest novels are directed at readers in a lower age range. In *Earth to Andrew O. Blechman*, Andrew agrees to help tutor Lou Pearlstein, his upstairs neighbor, in preparation for a long-delayed bar mitzvah. In return, Lou, a vaudeville veteran, teaches aspiring comedian Andrew some of his jokes. Andrew's grandmother lives in the basement of the same brownstone, and her developing romance with Lou culminates in an engagement announcement at Lou's bar mitzvah. A parallel plot concerns Andrew's rivalry with another boy at school.

In *The Fortuneteller in 5B*, a sequel of sorts, Madame Van Dam has moved into the brownstone. She occupies the apartment vacated by Lou, who has moved in with Andrew's grandmother after their wedding. Alexandria Pilaf tells about her discovery of Van Dam's past. Alexandria and her friend Jenny's speculations that the elderly woman is a vampire are eventually replaced with the truth: Van Dam's parents and sister, along with many other Gypsies, had died in Nazi concentration camps. The knowledge that Madame Van Dam has survived such horror helps Alexandria work through her loss of her father, who has died of cancer.

Readers will be particularly impacted by the author's note in *The Fortuneteller in 5B* describing the concentration camp at Terezin, where thousands of children were sent during World War II. Most died in Auschwitz. Zalben notes that hundreds of Christians, such as Van Dam's relatives, died at the hands of Nazis as well.

—Kathy Piehl

ZINDEL, Paul. American. Born in Staten Island, New York, 15 May 1936. Educated at Port Richmond High School, Staten Island; Wagner College, New York, B.S. in chemistry 1958, M.Sc. 1959. Married Bonnie Hildebrand in 1973; one son, one daughter. Technical writer, Allied Chemical, New York, 1958-59; chemistry teacher,

Tottenville High School, Staten Island, New York, 1959-69; playwright and author of children's books, since 1969. Playwright-in-residence, Alley Theatre, Houston, Texas, 1967. Recipient: Recipient: Ford Foundation grant, 1967, for drama; Child Study Association of America named *The Pigman* a Children's Book of the Year, 1968; *Boston Globe-Horn Book* award for text in *The Pigman*, 1969; *New York Times* Outstanding Children's Book of the Year citations for *My Darling, My Hamburger*, 1969, *I Never Loved Your Mind*, 1970, *Pardon Me, You're Stepping on My Eyeball!*, 1976, *The Undertaker's Gone Bananas*, 1978 and *The Pigman's Legacy*, 1980; the *Village Voice* Obie award for the Best American Play, the New York Drama Critics Vernon Rice Drama Desk award for the Most Promising Playwright, and New York Drama Critics Circle award for Best American Play of the Year, all 1970; Pulitzer Prize in Drama and New York Critics award, both 1971, for *The Effect of Gamma Rays on Man-in-the-Moon Marigolds*; Honorary Doctorate of Humanities from Wagner College, 1971; American Library Association's Best Young Adult Books citations, for *The Effect of Gamma Rays on Man-in-the-Moon Marigolds*, 1971, *Pigman*, 1975, *Pardon Me, You're Stepping on My Eyeball!*, 1976, *Confessions of a Teenage Baboon*, 1977, *The Pigman's Legacy*, 1980, and *To Take a Dare*, 1982; *Media & Methods* Maxi award, 1973, for *The Pigman;* New York Public Library "books for the teen age" citations for *Confessions of a Teenage Baboon*, 1980, *The Effect of Gamma Rays on Man-in-the-Moon Marigolds*, 1980, 1981 and 1982, *A Star for the Latecomer*, 1981 and *The Pigman's Legacy*, 1981 and 1982. Agent: Curtis Brown, Ltd., 10 Astor Place, New York, NY 10003.

PUBLICATIONS FOR YOUNG ADULTS

Fiction

The Pigman. New York, Harper, 1968; London, Bodley Head, 1969.
My Darling, My Hamburger. New York, Harper, 1969; London, Bodley Head, 1970.
I Never Loved Your Mind. New York, Harper, 1970; London, Bodley Head, 1971.
The Effect of Gamma Rays on Man-in-the-Moon Marigolds, illustrated by Dong Kingman. New York, Harper, 1971.
Pardon Me, You're Stepping on My Eyeball! New York, Harper, and London, Bodley Head, 1976.
Confessions of a Teenage Baboon. New York, Harper, 1977; London, Bodley Head, 1978.
The Undertaker's Gone Bananas. New York, Harper, 1978; London, Bodley Head, 1979.
The Pigman's Legacy. Mew York, Harper, and London, Bodley Head, 1980.
A Star for the Latecomer, with wife, Bonnie Zindel. New York, Harper, and London, Bodley Head, 1980.
The Girl Who Wanted a Boy. New York, Harper, and London, Bodley Head, 1981.
To Take a Dare, with Crescent Dragonwagon. New York, Harper, 1982.
Harry and Hortense at Hormone High. New York, Harper, 1984; London, Bodley Head, 1985.
The Amazing and Death-Defying Diary of Eugene Dingman. New York, Harper, and London, Bodley Head, 1987.
A Begonia for Miss Applebaum. New York, Harper, and London, Bodley Head, 1989.

The Pigman & Me. New York, HarperCollins, 1992.
David & Della. New York, HarperCollins, 1993.

PUBLICATIONS FOR CHILDREN

Fiction

I Love My Mother, illustrated by John Melo. New York, Harper, 1975.

PUBLICATIONS FOR ADULTS

Fiction

When Darkness Falls. New York, Bantam, 1984.

Plays

Dimensions of Peacocks (produced New York, 1959).
Euthanasia and the Endless Hearts (produced New York, 1960).
A Dream of Swallows (produced Off-Broadway, 1962).
And Miss Reardon Drinks a Little (produced Los Angeles, 1967; produced on Broadway, 1971). New York, Dramatists Play Service, 1971.
The Secret Affairs of Mildred Wild (produced New York City, 1972). New York, Dramatists Play Service, 1973.
Let Me Hear You Whisper. New York, Dramatists Play Service, 1973.
The Ladies Should Be in Bed (produced New York, 1978). With *Let Me Hear You Whisper,* New York, Dramatists Play Service, 1973; *Let Me Hear You Whisper,* illustrated by Stephen Gammell, published separately, New York, Harper, 1974.
Ladies at the Alamo (also director; produced New York, 1975). New York, Dramatists Play Service, 1977.
A Destiny on Half Moon Street (produced Coconut Grove, Florida, 1985).
Amulets against the Dragon Forces. New York, Circle Repertory Company, 1989.

Screenplays: *Up the Sandbox,* 1972; *Mame,* 1974; *Maria's Lovers,* with others, 1984; *Runaway Train,* with Djordje Milicevic and Edward Bunker, 1985.

Television Plays: *Let Me Hear You Whisper,* 1966; *The Effect of Gamma Rays on Man-in-the-Moon Marigolds,* 1966; *Alice in Wonderland,* 1985; *Babes in Toyland,* with Leslie Briscusse, 1986.

*

Theatrical Activities:
Director: **Play**—*Ladies at the Alamo,* New York, 1975.

Media Adaptations: *The Effect of Gamma Rays on Man-in-the-Moon Marigolds* (play), produced in Houston, Texas, at Alley Theatre, 1964, produced Off-Broadway at Mercer-O'Casey Theatre, April 7, 1970; *Let Me Hear You Whisper* (television movie), NET-TV, 1966; *The Pigman* (cassette; filmstrip with cassette), Miller-Brody/Random House, 1978; *My Darling, My Hamburger* (cassette; filmstrip with cassette), Current Affairs and Mark Twain Media, 1978.

Biography: Essay in *The Marble in the Water: Essays on Contemporary Writers of Fiction for Children and Young Adults* by David Rees, Boston, Massachusetts, Horn Book, 1980; entry in *Dictionary of Literary Biography; Twentieth-Century American Dramatists,* Volume 7, Detroit, Gale, 1981; *Fifth Book of Junior Authors and Illustrators,* New York, Wilson, 1983; essay in *Speaking for Ourselves: Autobiographical Sketches by Notable Authors of Books for Young Adults,* Volume 1, compiled and edited by Donald R. Gallo, National Council of Teachers of English, 1990.

Manuscript Collection: Boston University.

Critical Studies: Entry in *Children's Literature Review,* Volume 3, Detroit, Gale, 1978; *Presenting Paul Zindel* by Jack Jacob Forman, Boston, Twayne, 1988.

*   *   *

The first thing one remembers about Paul Zindel's young adult novels are the incongruous, often nonsensical titles—*My Darling, My Hamburger; Pardon Me, You're Stepping on My Eyeball; The Undertaker's Gone Bananas.* Then there are the bizarre-sounding names of even more bizarre characters—Paranoid Pete; Schizoid Susie; Edna Shinglebox; Chris Phlegm; Joan Hybred. The stories with these strange titles and odd characters are an amalgam of usually mixed-up, well-meaning teenagers interacting with one another to resolve personal problems in a world peopled with irresponsible single parents, foolish teachers, cruel cops, and other adults of whom the most sane and least destructive could be characterized as innocuous. Zindel's novels are made to order for young adults because they confirm and flesh out two of the most widely-held beliefs of adolescents: that they are superior to adults and live more honest lives than adults do. It's not that Zindel himself shares these beliefs, but because he thinks that many teenagers do, he creates a world of exaggeration and caricature that appeals to the young adult sensibility.

Most of Zindel's young adult fiction is narrated by teen protagonists whose literary voices are snappy and colloquial ("My mother and father never touch each other, which makes me wonder how on earth I was ever born."); the teen characters often communicate using what Zindel refers to as "transitional pictures"—letters written in cursive, graffiti, lists, and doodling. Even in his autobiographical portrait *The Pigman and Me,* Zindel writes messages to his readers in cursive to gain their attention. The plots put parents in the background, who then seem to emerge only to harass or stifle the teen heroes and heroines. The interpersonal relationships of Zindel's fictional teenagers are largely of three kinds: boy-girl; teenager-senior adult; and son/daughter-single parent.

Above all, Zindel's fiction is written to teach lessons to his readers—lessons that Zindel himself and his protagonists have learned. The most important lesson for Zindel is self-worth. Before one can reach out to relate to and help others, one must have a sense of one's own worth. It is a lesson that Zindel didn't learn until he was an adult. His father left home for another woman when Zindel was two years old, and his itinerant nurse-mother dragged him and his older sister from one dwelling to another, often moving every year. When he was fifteen, he spent a lonely year-and-a-half in a sanitorium recovering from tuberculosis. Only after he won the

Pulitzer Prize in 1971 for the autobiographical play *The Effect of Gamma Rays on Man-in-the-Moon Marigolds* did Zindel feel comfortable with his own sense of self-worth.

Zindel's first young adult novel, *The Pigman,* which many feel is his best work, was a ground-breaking event because—along with S.E. Hinton's *The Outsiders*—it transformed what had been called the teen "junior novel" from a predictable, stereotyped story about high school sports and dances to one about complex teenage protagonists dealing with real concerns: broken families, peer pressure, drug use, sexuality, runaways, and ethnic and racial differences. *The Pigman* and *The Pigman's Legacy* (the sequel written thirteen years later) feature John and Lorraine, two teenagers alienated from their parents and school who learn the twin lessons of self-worth and taking responsibility for their actions. In the first book, the two young teens meet and grow close to Mr. Pignati (they call him The Pigman because of his treasured collection of marble pigs), an old man who has not accepted his wife's death. They also gain a sense of self-worth and grow fond of one another because of their genuine friendship with the old man. But in a rash moment, they betray his trust by throwing a party in his house while he is recovering in the hospital from a heart attack. The party gets out of hand, and the collection of marble pigs is destroyed. Broken by this breach of trust, The Pigman suffers a fatal heart attack soon after—and John and Lorraine are left questioning their complicity in his death. In the sequel, the two teenagers—still guilty about their friend's death two years later—go to the abandoned house and find a homeless and sick old man living there. Plagued by the memories of their experience with The Pigman, they bring the tramp food and just before his death go on a gambling spree with him to Atlantic City.

In one way or another Zindel's other novels are concerned with building self-confidence. *My Darling, My Hamburger* focuses on the contrast between two sets of boyfriend-girlfriend relationships and how the attitudes and actions of parents affect the sexual responsibility of these teens; the boy and girl whose parents show love, tolerance, and understanding act responsibly while the other pair, afflicted by low self-esteem and alienated from their parents, act irresponsibly. *Pardon Me, You're Stepping on My Eyeball* is about fifteen-year-old Marsh Mellow, who can't accept his father's death and can't cope with his mother's alcoholism and emotional abuse of him. In a special education class, he meets Edna Shinglebox whose parents pull her in two directions: she's pushed into doing things she doesn't want to do and is overprotected from doing what she wants to do. Together, these two misfits face an even crazier world. After surviving a series of wild and unbelievable events, they eventually confront the reality of their lives and earn hard-

won esteem. Similarly, in *The Confessions of a Teenage Baboon,* a teenager overcomes his mother's mental abuse to forge a positive self-identity and declare independence from her emotional control.

Zindel also would like his readers to appreciate life by learning how to cope with death. He portrays teen protagonists who deal with death directly in the two "Pigman" books, *Confessions of a Teenage Baboon, Harry and Hortense at Hormone High,* and *A Begonia for Miss Applebaum,* in which two of the science teacher's students celebrate life with Miss Applebaum as she is dying of cancer. In these stories—and especially in the lighter novel *The Undertaker's Gone Bananas*—Zindel looks at death "not as a foe, but as an inevitable adventure." It is a part of life which should be accepted and not feared.

Zindel's humor permeates even the most serious of his novels. His humor is exaggerated, farcical, mocking, and sometimes slapstick. In *Harry and Hortense at Hormone High,* Harry says of his mother: "When my mother prepares meat loaf, she looks like a woman trying to beat an abalone." Marsh Mellow in *Pardon Me* says the food in the school cafeteria is served on a plate "that looked like it was the final resting place for a stuffed rodent." The humor is not subtle, and adults may think it is juvenile and derogatory, but that's precisely why teen readers like it and why Zindel uses it.

Zindel's later writing *(The Girl Who Wanted a Boy, The Amazing and Death-Defying Diary of Eugene Dingman, Harry and Hortense at Hormone High* especially) is more contrived than his earlier work, although *A Begonia for Miss Applebaum* is genuinely touching in places. His most recent book is a memoir entitled *The Pigman and Me,* a book that describes the real people on whom he modelled many of his fictional characters throughout his career. Because his characters are drawn from his life and because his stories are driven by lessons he has learned from his life, it is not surprising that many of his novels are derivative of one another. Yet Zindel feels that his books have something to teach his readers. "If you haven't croaked before finishing the book," Zindel writes to his teen readers in *The Pigman and Me,* "then you'll understand how I survived being a teenager and you'll know this important secret." How Zindel survived his adolescence is how his characters survive; the author hopes that "this important secret" will help his readers deal with their own lives.

—Jack Forman

TITLE
INDEX

The following list includes the titles of all fiction, nonfiction, drama, and poetry for young adults cited in the main entries; selected works edited, such as anthologies and collections for young adults, are also listed. Titles of series listed in the main entries are included, along with the date of the earliest published title in the series. Plays adapted by authors from their own works of the same name are not listed individually. The name in parenthesis is meant to direct the reader to the appropriate entry where fuller information is given.

A for Ami (N. Mazer), 1988
A, My Name Is Ami (N. Mazer), 1986
Ab to Zogg: A Lexicon for Science-Fiction and Fantasy Readers (Merriam), 1977
Abba Abba (Burgess), 1977
Abbess of Crewe (Spark), 1973
Abby, My Love (Irwin), 1985
A.B.C. Murders: A New Poirot Mystery (Christie), 1936
ABC's of Ecology (Asimov), 1972
ABC's of Space (Asimov), 1969
ABC's of the Earth (Asimov), 1971
ABC's of the Ocean (Asimov), 1970
About Michael Jackson (Haskins), 1985
About the B'nai Bagels (Konigsburg), 1969
About the Crusades (Treece), 1966
Abraham: A Biography (Kamm), 1948
Absent in the Spring (Christie), 1944
Abysmal Brute (London), 1913
Abyss (Card), 1989
Accent on April (Cavanna), 1960
Acceptable Time (L'Engle), 1988
Acceptance Speech (Gipson), 1960
Accident (Colman), 1980
Accident (Wiesel), 1962
Accidental Tourist (Tyler), 1985
Ace Hole, Midge Detective (Spiegelman), 1974
Acorn-Planter: A California Forest Play... (London), 1916
Across Five Aprils (Hunt), 1964
Across Five Summers (Card), 1971
Across the Barricades (Lingard), 1972
Across the Fruited Plain (Means), 1940
Across the Plains, with Other Memories and Essays (Stevenson), 1892
Across the Sea of Stars (Clarke), 1959
Acts of King Arthur and His Noble Knights: From the Winchester Manuscripts of Thomas Malory and Other Sources (Steinbeck), 1976
Acts of Love (Daly), 1986
Ad Feminam (Bach, editor), 1989
Adam Clayton Powell: Portrait of a Marching Black (Haskins), 1974
Adam of the Road (Vining), 1942
Adding a Dimension: Seventeen Essays on the History of Science (Asimov), 1964
Additional Dialogue: Letters of Dalton Trumbo, 1942-1962 (Trumbo), 1970
Adelaide Ghost (Garfield), 1977
Adella Mary in Old New Mexico (Means), 1939
Admiral Guinea (Stevenson), 1884
Adonis and the Alphabet, and Other Essays (Huxley), 1956
Adrift (Baillie), 1983
Adulthood Rites (Butler), 1988

Adventure (London), 1911
Adventure in Granada (Myers), 1985
Adventure of Sherlock Holmes (A. Doyle), 1892
Adventure of the Christmas Pudding, and Selection of Entrees (Christie), 1960
Adventure of the Solitary Cyclist (A. Doyle), 1991
Adventures and Brave Deeds of the Ship's Cat on the Spanish Maine: Together with the Most Lamentable Losse of the Alcestis and Triumphant Firing of the Port of Chagres (Adams), 1977
Adventures of Ali Baba Bernstein (Hurwitz), 1985
Adventures of Captain Grief (London), 1954
Adventures of Colonel Sellers (Twain), 1965
Adventures of Dick Varley (Serraillier), 1954
Adventures of Gerard (A. Doyle), 1903
Adventures of Huckleberry Finn, Tom Sawyer's Comrade (Twain), 1884
Adventures of Johnny May (Branscum), 1984
Adventures of Pirates and Sea-Rovers (Pyle), 1908
Adventures of the Speckled Band and Other Stories (A. Doyle), 1991
Adventures of Thomas Jefferson Snodgrass (Twain), 1928
Adventures of Tom Sawyer (Twain), 1876
Adventures of Tommy (H. Wells), 1929
Affectionately Eve (Sinclair), 1961
African Literature (Gordimer), 1972
African Treasury: Articles, Essays, Stories, Poems by Black Africans (L. Hughes), 1960
After All, They're Only Cats (Moyes), 1973
After Dark (Rubinstein, editor), 1988
After Democracy: Addresses and Papers on the Present World Situation (H. Wells), 1932
After Many a Summer (Huxley), 1939
After the Bomb (Miklowitz), 1985
After the Bomb: Week One (Miklowitz), 1987
After the Dancing Days (Rostkowski), 1986
After the Fireworks (Huxley), n.d
After the First Death (Cormier), 1979
After the Funeral (Christie), 1953
After the Goat Man (Byars), 1974
After the Last Race (Koontz), 1974
After the Rain (N. Mazer), 1987
After the Tempest (Trease), 1938
After the Wedding (Colman), 1975
After Thursday (Ure), 1985
Afterlives: Stories about Life after Death (Sargent, editor), 1986
Aftershock (Thiele), 1952
Afterthoughts in Eden (Asher), 1975
Against All Opposition: Black Explorers in America (Haskins), 1992
Against Silence: The Voice and Vision of Elie Wiesel (Wiesel), 1985
Against the Fall of Night (Clarke), 1953
Against the Odds (R. Klein), 1989

At the Sign of the Dog and Rocket (Mark), 1985
At the Sign of the Two Heroes (Meigs), 1920
At the Sound of the Beep (Sachs), 1990
At the Top of My Voice and Other Poems (Holman), 1970
Atlas Shrugged (Rand), 1957
Atom: Journey across the Subatomic Cosmos (Asimov), 1991
Atrocious Two (Greenwald), 1978
Attack on the King (Stine), 1986
August 22nd (Sinclair), 1965
Augustine Came to Kent (Willard), 1963
Aunt Augusta's Elephant (Trease), 1991
Aunt Bedelia's Cats (Dillon), 1958
Aunt Flora (Coatsworth), 1953
Aunt Jo's Scrap-Bag (Alcott), 1872-1882
Aunt Kipp (Alcott), 1868
Aunt Maria (D. Jones), 1991
Aurora: Beyond Equality (McIntyre, editor), 1976
Author Considers His Resources (Bradbury), 1979
Authorized Murder: A Puzzle in Four Days and Sixty Scenes (Asimov), 1976
Autobiographical Notes (Baldwin), 1953
Autobiography (Christie), 1977
Autobiography of Miss Jane Pittman (Gaines), 1971
Autobiography of Rosa Parks (Haskins), 1990
Autobiography of Upton Sinclair (Sinclair), 1962
Autocracy of Mr. Parham: His Remarkable Adventures in This Changing World (H. Wells), 1930
Autograph Letters, Original Mss., Books, Portraits and Curios from the Library of the Late R.L. Stevenson (Stevenson), 1914-16
Autumn People (Bradbury), 1965
Autumn Song (T. Hughes), 1971
Autumn Street (Lowry), 1980
Awakening Land (C. Richter), 1966
Away Goes Sally (Coatsworth), 1934
Away Is a Strange Place to Be (Hoover), 1990
Axe-Age, Wolf-Age: A Selection from the Norse Myths (Crossley-Holland), 1985
Ayn Rand Column: A Collection of Her Weekly Newspaper Articles (Rand), 1991
Azazel (Asimov), 1988

B, My Name Is Bunny (N. Mazer), 1987
Babe Didrikson: Athlete of the Century (Knudson), 1985
Babe Ruth and Hank Aaron: The Home Run Kings (Haskins), 1974
Babes in the Darkling Wood (H. Wells), 1940
Baby Project (Ellis), 1986
Baby Sister (Sachs), 1986
Baby Sitting Is a Dangerous Job (Roberts), 1985
Baby-Sitter (Stine), 1989
Baby-Sitter II (Stine), 1991
Babyface (N. Mazer), 1990
Babylon (Paton Walsh), 1982
Bachelors (Spark), 1960
Bachman Books: Four Early Novels (King), 1985
Back Home (Magorian), 1984
Back to Before (Slepian), 1993
Back to Class (Glenn), 1988
Back to the Stone Age (Burroughs), 1937
Back-yard War (Fisk), 1990

Backlash (Fisk), 1988
Backup Goalie (D. Hughes), 1992
Bad Blood (Ashley), 1988
Bad Boys (Cisneros), 1980
Bad Penny (A. Jones), 1990
Bad Place (Koontz), 1990
Badger on the Barge and Other Stories (Howker), 1984
Badlands of Hark (Stine), 1985
Bag of Moonshine (Garner), 1986
Baily's Bones (Kelleher), 1988
Baker Street Dozen (A. Doyle), 1989
Baker's Dozen: A Collection of Stories (Garfield, editor), 1973
Baker's Dozen: Thirteen Short Fantasy Novels (Asimov, editor), 1984
Ballad of Kon-Tiki and Other Verses (Serraillier), 1952
Ballad of Peckham Rye (Spark), 1960
Ballad of St. Simeon (Serraillier), 1970
Ballad of the Sad Cafe: The Novels and Stories of Carson McCullers (McCullers), 1951
Ballad of Two Who Flew (Asher), 1976
Ballads (Stevenson), 1890
Ballerina (Willard), 1932
Ballerina on Skates (Sherburne), 1961
Ballet Fever (Cavanna), 1978
Ballet One series (Asher), from 1989
Balook (Anthony), 1990
Balyet (Wrightson), 1989
Bananas Looks at TV (Stine), 1981
Bandit of Hell's Bend (Burroughs), 1925
Bandoeng: 1.500.000.000 hommes (Wright), 1955
Bang, You're Dead! (Treece), 1966
Bang-Bang You're Dead and Other Stories (Spark), 1982
Banjo (R.N. Peck), 1982
Banjo, the Puppy (Harnett), 1938
Banner Year (Cavanna), 1987
Banquets of the Black Widowers (Asimov), 1984
Barbara Jordan (Haskins), 1977
Barbary (McIntyre), 1986
Bardic Voices: The Lark & the Wren (Lackey), 1992
Barefoot in the Grass: The Story of Grandma Moses (Armstrong), 1970
Barn (Avi), 1994
Barney the Beard (Bunting), 1975
Barons' Hostage: A Story of Simon de Montfort (Trease), 1952
Barrie and Daughter (Caudill), 1943
Baseball Fever (Hurwitz), 1981
Baseball in April and Other Stories (Soto), 1990
Baseball Tips (D. Hughes), 1993
Basic Philosophy of Aldous Huxley (Huxley), 1984
Basket Case (R.N. Peck), 1979
Basketball Girl of the Year (Walden), 1970
Bass and Billy Martin (Phipson), 1972
Bathwater Gang (Spinelli), 1990
Bathwater Gang Gets down to Business (Spinelli), 1992
Batterpool Business (D. Jones), 1967
Battle Circle (Anthony), 1978
Battle in the Arctic Seas: The Story of Convoy PQ 17 (T. Taylor), 1976
Battle in the English Channel (T. Taylor), 1983
Battle of Gettysburg (Carter), 1990
Battle of Wednesday Week (Willard), 1963

Best Supernatural Tales of Arthur Conan Doyle (A. Doyle), 1979

Best Thing in Edinburgh: An Address to the Speculative Society of Edinburgh in March 1873 (Stevenson), 1923

Best Wedding Dress (Colman), 1960

Best Wishes (Rylant), 1992

Betrayal (Cherryh), 1989

Betsey Brown (Shange), 1985

Betty Friedan: A Voice for Women's Rights (Meltzer), 1985

Between Planets (Heinlein), 1951

Between Time and Timbuktu; or, Prometheus-5: A Space Fantasy (Vonnegut), 1972

Between Two Worlds (Lingard), 1991

Between Two Worlds (Sinclair), 1941

Beyond 1984: Remembrance of Things Future (Bradbury), 1979

Beyond Another Door (Levitin), 1977

Beyond Jupiter: The Worlds of Tomorrow (Clarke), 1972

Beyond Silence (Cameron), 1980

Beyond the Burning Lands (Christopher), 1971

Beyond the Chocolate War (Cormier), 1985

Beyond the Dark River (M. Hughes), 1979

Beyond the Divide (Lasky), 1983

Beyond the Fall of Night (Clarke), 1990

Beyond the Farthest Star (Burroughs), 1964

Beyond the Labyrinth (Rubinstein), 1988

Beyond the Mexique Bay: A Traveller's Journal (Huxley), 1934

Beyond the Mists (Benchley), 1975

Beyond the Stars (Asimov, editor), 1987

Beyond the Tomorrow Mountains (Engdahl), 1973

Beyond the Weir Bridge (Burton), 1970

Beyond Thirty (Burroughs), 1955

BFG (Dahl), 1982

Bianca (Phipson), 1988

Bicentennial Man and Other Stories (Asimov), 1976

Bicycle Man (Bunting), 1992

Big Apple Mysteries (Asimov, editor), 1983

Big Base Hit (D. Hughes), 1990

Big Bend (Gipson), 1952

Big Brass Key (Park), 1983

Big Brother Barges In (Latham), 1940

Big Cheese (Bunting), 1977

Big Egg (Mayne), 1967

Big Find (Bunting), 1978

Big Four (Christie), 1927

Big Green Umbrella (Coatsworth), 1944

Big Red Barn (Bunting), 1979

Big Rock Candy (Johnson), 1957

Big Sea (L. Hughes), 1940

Big Splash (Kendall), 1960

Big Step (Colman), 1957

Big Time (Grant), 1982

Big Wander (Hobbs), 1992

Big Wheel and the Little Wheel (Mayne), 1965

Bigger (Calvert), 1994

Bigger Book of Lydia (Willey), 1983

Biggest Thief in Town (Trumbo), 1949

Bike Repairman (Bradbury), 1978

Bilgewater (Gardam), 1976

Bill Cosby: America's Most Famous Father (Haskins), 1988

Bill of Rights: How We Got It and What It Means (Meltzer), 1990

Bill Porter: A Drama of O. Henry in Prison (Sinclair), 1925

Billy the Great (Guy), 1992

Binary (Crichton), 1972

Binding Ties (Adler), 1983

Bingo Brown and the Language of Love (Byars), 1989

Bingo Brown, Gypsy Lover (Byars), 1990

Bingo Brown's Guide to Romance (Byars), 1992

Bio of a Space Tyrant (Anthony), 1985

Bio of an Ogre: The Autobiography of Piers Anthony to Age 50 (Anthony), 1988

Bio-Futures: Science Fiction Stories about Biological Metamorphosis (Sargent, editor), 1976

Biochemistry and Human Metabolism (Asimov), 1952

Biographical Letter and Critical Opinions (Sinclair), 1922

Bird Smugglers (Phipson), 1977

Bird, The Frog, and the Light (Avi), 1994

Birds of Summer (Snyder), 1983

Birkin (Phipson), 1965

Birth and Death of the Universe (Asimov), 1975

Birth of the Republic (Carter), 1988

Birth of the United States, 1763-1816 (Asimov), 1974

Birth of the Firebringer (M. Pierce), 1985

Birthday Murder (Bennett), 1977

Bishop and the Devil (Serraillier), 1971

Bit of Give and Take (Ashley), 1984

Bittersweet (Thomas), 1973

Bittersweet Temptation (Donovan), 1979

Bizou (N. Klein), 1983

Black Americans: A History in Their Own Words, 1619-1983 (Meltzer), 1984

Black and White Two-Dimensional Planes (Shange), 1979

Black Anti-Semitism and Jewish Racism (Baldwin), 1969

Black Arrow: A Tale of the Two Roses (Stevenson), 1888

Black Banner Abroad (Trease), 1954

Black Banner Players (Trease), 1952

Black Beauty (McKinley, adapter), 1986

Black Book (Morrison, editor), 1974

Black Boy: A Record of Childhood and Youth (Wright), 1945

Black Cauldron (Alexander), 1965

Black Child (Thomas), 1981

Black Coffee (Christie), 1934

Black Diamonds (Whitney), 1957

Black Diamonds: A Search for Arctic Treasure (Houston), 1982

Black Doctor and Other Tales of Terror and Mystery (A. Doyle), 1925

Black Feeling, Black Talk (Giovanni), 1968

Black Feeling, Black Talk/Black Judgement (Giovanni), 1970

Black Folktales (Lester, reteller), 1969

Black Girl, White Girl (Moyes), 1989

Black Hair (Soto), 1985

Black Hearts in Battersea (Aiken), 1964

Black Interpreters: Notes on African Writing (Gordimer), 1973

Black Jack (Garfield), 1968

Black Judgement (Giovanni), 1968

Black Magic and Music: A Novelist's Perspective on Bangor (King), 1983

Black Magic: A Pictorial History of the Negro in American Entertainment (L. Hughes), 1967

Black Maria (D. Jones), 1991

Black Misery (L. Hughes), 1969

Black Music in America: A History through Its People (Haskins), 1987

Black Night, Red Morning (Trease), 1944

Book of Modern Stories (Burton, editor), 1959
Book of Morgaine (Cherryh), 1979
Book of Negro Humor (L. Hughes), 1966
Book of Negro Folklore (L. Hughes), 1958
Book of Old Edinburgh (Dunlop, editor), 1984
Book of Pirates (Pyle), 1891
Book of Seasons: An Anthology (Garnett, editor), 1952
Book of Shai (Cherryh, translator), 1984
Book of Sorrows (Wangerin), 1985
Book of the Dun Cow (Wangerin), 1978
Book of Three (Alexander), 1964
Books for You (Knudson), 1971
Boomerang Clue (Christie), 1935
Boomerang Kids (Okimoto), 1987
Boon, The Mind of the Race, The Wild Asses of the Devil, and The
     Last Trump (H. Wells), 1915
Border Hawk: August Bondi (Alexander), 1958
Bored with Being Bored!: How to Beat the Boredom Blahs (Stine),
     1982
Borgel (Pinkwater), 1990
Boris and Borsch (R. Klein), 1990
Born of the Sun (Cross), 1983
Born to Run (Lackey), 1992
Born to the Land: An American Portrait (Ashabranner), 1989
Borning Room (Fleischman), 1991
Borrowed Brother (Means), 1958
Boss (Baillie), 1992
Boss Cat (K. Hunter), 1971
Boss of the Pool (R. Klein), 1986
Bostock and Harris; or, The Night of the Comet (Garfield), 1979
Boston Belles (Coatsworth), 1952
Boston: A Documentary Novel of the Sacco-Vanzetti Case (Sinclair),
     1928
Bouncers (Fisk), 1964
Bound for the Rio Grande: The Mexican Struggle, 1845-1850
     (Meltzer), 1974
Boundary Riders (Phipson), 1962
Bowlful of Stars (Means), 1934
Bows against the Barons (Trease), 1934
Box, Fox, Ox and the Peacock (Bunting), 1974
Boy and the Monkey (Garfield), 1969
Boy Beneath the Sea (Clarke), 1958
Boy in the Moon (Koertge), 1990
Boy in the Off-White Hat (L. Hall), 1984
Boy Next Door (Cavanna), 1956
Boy to Remember (Walden), 1960
Boy Who Couldn't Make up His Mind (Colman), 1965
Boy Who Owned the School (Paulsen), 1990
Boy Who Reversed Himself (Sleator), 1986
Boy Who Wasn't There (Peyton), 1992
Boy with the Parrot: A Story of Guatemala (Coatsworth), 1930
Boy: Tales of Childhood (Dahl), 1984
Boyfriend (Stine), 1990
Boyhood of Grace Jones (Langton), 1972
Boys' Life of Will Rogers (Keith), 1937
Boys' Sherlock Holmes: A Selection From the Works of A. Conan
     Doyle (A. Doyle), 1961
Bozos on Patrol (Stine), 1992
Brains of Animals and Man (Freedman), 1972
Brainstorm (Myers), 1977
Brass Butterfly (Golding), 1958

Brass Check: A Study of American Journalism (Sinclair), 1919
Brass Dragon (Bradley), 1969
Brave (Lipsyte), 1991
Brave New World (Huxley), 1932
Brave New World and Brave New World Revisited (Huxley), 1960
Brave New World Revisited (Huxley), 1958
Bread and Honey (Southall), 1970
Bread Bin (Aiken), 1974
Bread Book: All about Bread and How to Make It (Meyer), 1971
Bread—and Roses: The Struggle of American Labor, 1865-1915
     (Meltzer), 1967
Breadhorse (Garner), 1975
Break Dancing (Haskins), 1985
Break in the Sun (Ashley), 1980
Break of Dark (Westall), 1982
Break with Charity: A Story about the Salem Witch Trials (Rinaldi),
     1992
Breakdowns; From Maus to Now: An Anthology of Strips
     (Spiegelman), 1977
Breakfast of Champions; or, Goodbye Blue Monday (Vonnegut),
     1973
Breaking Ice: An Anthology of Contemporary African-American
     Fiction (McMillan, editor), 1990
Breaking Up (N. Klein), 1980
Breakthroughs in Science (Asimov), 1960
Breaktime (Chambers), 1978
Breath of Fresh Air (Cavanna), 1966
Breathing Lessons (Tyler), 1988
Breathing Method (King), 1984
Breed to Come (Norton), 1972
Briar Rose (Yolen), 1992
Brickyard Summer (Janeczko), 1989
Bride (McIntyre), 1985
Bride at Eighteen (Colman), 1966
Bridesmaid (Willard), 1976
Bridge (Neville), 1988
Bridge to Terabithia (Paterson), 1977
Bridge-Builders (Sutcliff), 1959
Bridges to Cross (Janeczko), 1986
Bridle the Wind (Aiken), 1983
Brief Candles (Huxley), 1930
Brief Garland (Keith), 1971
Brier, His Book (J. Miller), 1988
Brigadier General (A. Doyle), 1906
Bright Candles (Benchley), 1974
Bright Days, Stupid Nights (H. Mazer), 1992
Bright Shadow (Avi), 1985
Bright Shadow (Thomas), 1983
Bring out the Banners (Trease), 1994
Bring to a Boil and Separate (Irwin), 1980
Britain Yesterday (Trease), 1975
British Campaign in France and Flanders (A. Doyle), 1916-20
British Folk Tales: New Versions (Crossley-Holland), 1987
British Nationalism and the League of Nations (H. Wells), 1918
Broccoli Tapes (Slepian), 1989
Broken Bridge (Pullman), 1990
Broken Cord (Dorris), 1987
Broken Date (Stine), 1991
Broken Hearts (Stine), 1993
Broken Saddle (Aldridge), 1982
Bronze Bow (Speare), 1961

Bronze Sword (Treece), 1966
Brooklyn Doesn't Rhyme (Blos), 1994
Brooklyn Story (Mathis), 1970
Brother Ass and Brother Lion (Willard), 1951
Brother, Can You Spare a Dime? The Great Depression, 1929-1933 (Meltzer), 1969
Brother Dusty-Feet (Sutcliff), 1952
Brother in the Land (Swindells), 1984
Brother Night (Kelleher), 1991
Brothers (D. Hughes), 1986
Brothers and Sisters: Modern Stories by Black Americans (Adoff, editor), 1970
Brothers of Earth (Cherryh), 1976
Brothers of No Kin and Other Stories (C. Richter), 1924
Brothers of the Heart: A Story of the Old Northwest, 1837-38 (Blos), 1985
Brothers: A Story (H. Wells), 1938
Brown Honey in Broomwheat Tea (Thomas), 1993
Brown Satchel Mystery (Cavanna), 1954
Brownie (M. Hunter), 1986
Brownsea Silver (Peyton), 1964
Brynhild (H. Wells), 1937
Bubo, the Great Horned Owl (George), 1954
Buccaneers and Marooners of America (Pyle, editor), 1891
Buddy and the Old Pro (Tunis), 1955
Buffalo Hunt (Freedman), 1988
Buffy the Vampire Slayer (Cusick), 1992
Building Blocks (Voigt), 1984
Building Blocks of the Universe (Asimov), 1957
Bull Run (Fleischman), 1993
Bullies & Me (Savitz), 1991
Bully of Library Place (Bach), 1988
Bulpington of Blup: Adventures, Poses, Stresses, Conflicts, and Disaster in a Contemporary Brain (H. Wells), 1932
Bumblebee Flies Anyway (Cormier), 1983
Bundle of Nerves: Stories of Horror, Suspense, and Fantasy (Aiken), 1976
Bunyip Hole (Wrightson), 1958
Burden (Christie), 1956
Bureaucats (Adams), 1985
Burg-O-Rama Man (Tchudi), 1984
Burger's Daughter (Gordimer), 1979
Burma Rifles: A Story of Merrill's Marauders (Bonham), 1960
Burmese Days (Orwell), 1934
Burning Bright: A Play in Story Form (Steinbeck), 1950
Burning Bright: Play in Three Acts (Steinbeck), 1951
Burning Daylight (London), 1910
Burning Glass (Johnson), 1966
Burning of Njal (Treece), 1964
Burning Questions of Bingo Brown (Byars), 1988
Burning Water (Lackey), 1989
Burning Wheel (Huxley), 1916
Burrswood, Focus of Healing (Furlong), 1978
Bury Me Deep (Pike), 1991
Bus Ride (Sachs), 1980
Busybody Nora (Hurwitz), 1976
But Do Blondes Prefer Gentlemen? (Burgess), 1986
But I Am Sara (Means), 1961
But I'll Be Back Again: An Album (Rylant), 1989
But in the Fall I'm Leaving (Rinaldi), 1985
But Jasper Came Instead (Nöstlinger), 1983

But What of Earth? (Anthony), 1976
Butty Boy (Paton Walsh), 1975
Buy Jupiter and Other Stories (Asimov), 1975
By the Highway Home (Stolz), 1971
By the Pricking of My Thumbs (Christie), 1968
By the Sword (Lackey), 1991
Byron: A Poet Dangerous to Know (Trease), 1969

C, My Name Is Cal (N. Mazer), 1990
Cabaret for Freedom (Angelou), 1960
Cadbury's Coffin (Swarthout), 1982
Calabrian Quest (Trease), 1990
Calico Captive (Speare), 1957
California Childhood: Recollections and Stories of the Golden State (Soto, editor), 1988
California Feeling (Beagle), 1969
Call (Westall), 1989
Call of Earth (Card), 1993
Call of Fife and Drum: Three Novels of the Revolution (Fast), 1987
Call of the Mountain (Meigs), 1940
Call of the Wild (London), 1903
Call to Arms (Trease), 1935
Callahan and Company (Robinson), 1987
Callahan Touch (Robinson), 1993
Callahan's Crosstime Saloon (Robinson), 1977
Callahan's Lady (Robinson), 1989
Callahan's Secret (Robinson), 1986
Callender Papers (Voigt), 1983
Callie's Castle (Park), 1974
Callie's Family (Park), 1988
Calling B for Butterfly (Lawrence), 1982
Calling on Dragons (Wrede), 1993
Callow Pit Coffer (Crossley-Holland), 1968
Came Back to Show You I Could Fly (R. Klein), 1990
Cameo Rose (Branscum), 1989
Camford Visitation (H. Wells), 1937
Camilla (L'Engle), 1965
Camilla Dickinson (L'Engle), 1951
Can Bears Predict Earthquakes? Unsolved Mysteries of Animal Behavior (Freedman), 1982
Can David Do It? (Asher), 1991
Can of Worms (Mark), 1990
Can You Sue Your Parents for Malpractice? (Danziger), 1979
Can't Hear You Listening (Irwin), 1990
Canada North (Mowat), 1967
Canary in a Cathouse (Vonnegut), 1961
Candid Reminiscences: My First Thirty Years (Sinclair), 1932
Candidate for Murder (Nixon), 1991
Candle Flame (Willard), 1932
Candle for St. Anthony (Spence), 1977
Candle in the Dark (Swindells), 1983
Candle in the Mist (Means), 1931
Candle in the Night (Swindells), 1974
Candy (R. White), 1949
Candy for King (Leeson), 1983
Cannery Row (Steinbeck), 1945
Cannily, Cannily (French), 1981
Canoeing, Kayaking, and Rafting (Paulsen), 1979
Cantaloup Crescent (Lillington), 1970
Canterbury Tales (McCaughrean, reteller), 1984
Canyons (Paulsen), 1990

Celebrated Jumping Frog of Calaveras County, and Other Sketches (Twain), 1867
Celebrations: A New Anthology of Black American Poetry (Adoff, editor), 1977
Celestial Navigation (Tyler), 1974
Celia Scarfe (Willard), 1951
Celine (Cole), 1989
Centaur Aisle (Anthony), 1982
Center: From a Troubled Past to a New Life (Meyer), 1980
Centurian (Treece), 1967
Certain Magic (Orgel), 1976
Certain Personal Matters: A Collection of Material, Mainly Autobiographical (H. Wells), 1897
Chadwick's Chimney (Thiele), 1979
Chagres: Power of the Panama Canal (Latham), 1964
Chain Letter (Pike), 1986
Chain of Fire (Naidoo), 1989
Chaining the Lady (Anthony), 1978
Challenge of the Spaceship: Previews of Tomorrow's World (Clarke), 1959
Challenge of the Sea (Clarke), 1960
Challenge of the Wolf Knight (Stine), 1985
Challenge of the Green Knight (Serraillier), 1966
Champion's Choice (Tunis), 1940
Championship Game (D. Hughes), 1990
Chance Child (Paton Walsh), 1978
Chance, Luck and Destiny (Dickinson), 1975
Change at Maythorn (Trease), 1962
Change in the Wind (Naylor), 1980
Change the Locks (French), 1993
Change! Seventy-One Glimpses of the Future (Asimov), 1981
Changed Man (Card), 1992
Changeling (Mayne), 1961
Changeling (Sutcliff), 1974
Changeling Sea (McKillip), 1988
Changeover: A Supernatural Romance (Mahy), 1984
Changes in Latitudes (Hobbs), 1988
Changes: A Trilogy (Dickinson), 1975
Chanur's Homecoming (Cherryh), 1986
Chanur's Legacy (Cherryh), 1992
Chanur's Venture (Cherryh), 1984
Chaos Mode (Anthony), 1993
Chapterhouse: Dune (Herbert), 1985
Characters and Viewpoint (Card), 1988
Charity at Home (Willard), 1965
Charity Bazaar: An Allegorical Dialogue (Stevenson), 1929
Charlie and the Chocolate Factory (Dahl), 1964
Charlie and the Great Glass Elevator (Dahl), 1972
Charlotte Sometimes (Farmer), 1969
Charmed Life (D. Jones), 1977
Chartbreak (Cross), 1986
Chartbreaker (Cross), 1987
Chase (Koontz), 1972
Chaucer and His World (Serraillier), 1967
Chaucer as a Philologist (Tolkien), 1943
Cheap Thrills (Koertge), 1976
Cheater (Stine), 1993
Cheater and Flitter Dick: A Novel (Branscum), 1983
Checking on the Moon (J. Davis), 1991
Cheerful Heart (Vining), 1959

Cheerleader (N. Klein), 1985
Cheers (Collier), 1960
Chemicals of Life: Enzymes, Vitamins, Hormones (Asimov), 1954
Chemistry and Human Health (Asimov), 1956
Chemo Kid (Lipsyte), 1992
Chernevog (Cherryh), 1990
Cherokee Bat and the Goat Guys (Block), 1991
Cherry Ann and the Dragon Horse (Coatsworth), 1955
Cherry Tree (McCaughrean, reteller and translator), 1992
Chessmen of Mars (Burroughs), 1922
Chicago Days, Hoboken Nights (Pinkwater), 1991
Chicano Girl (Colman), 1973
Chichester and Lewes (Willard), 1970
Chicken Run (Chambers), 1968
Chico of Guatemala (Cavanna), 1963
Chief (Bonham), 1971
Chief (Lipsyte), 1993
Chief Joseph: War Chief of the Nez Perce (Ashabranner), 1962
Chief's Daughter (Sutcliff), 1967
Child Abuse Help Book (Haskins), 1981
Child Life in New England, 1790-1840 (Speare), 1961
Child O'War: The True Story of a Sailor Boy in Nelson's Navy (Garfield), 1972
Child of Fire (O'Dell), 1974
Child of the Air (Chetwin), 1991
Child of the Owl (Yep), 1977
Child's Garden of Verses (Stevenson), 1885
Childhood's End (Clarke), 1953
Children (Fast), 1947
Children of Bach (Dillon), 1992
Children of Dune (Herbert), 1976
Children of Green Knowe (Boston), 1954
Children of Hastur (Bradley), 1981
Children of Morrow (Hoover), 1973
Children of the Dust (Lawrence), 1985
Children of the Fox (Paton Walsh), 1978
Children of the Frost (London), 1902
Children of the Great Spirit: A Course on the American Indian (Means), 1932
Children of the Maya: A Guatemalan Indian Odyssey (Ashabranner), 1986
Children of the Night (Lackey), 1992
Children of the Promise (Means), 1941
Children of the River (L. Crew), 1989
Children of the Storm (Koontz), 1972
Children of the Wild West (Freedman), 1983
Children of the Wolf (Yolen), 1984
Children's Book (Latham), 1933
Children's Crusade (Treece), 1958
Children's War (T. Taylor), 1971
Chile Kings (West), 1967
Chimaera's Cooper (Anthony), 1990
Chimes of Alyafaleyn (Chetwin), 1993
Chimneys of Green Knowe (Boston), 1958
China Coin (Baillie), 1992
China Past—China Future (Carter), 1994
China People (Farmer), 1960
China Quest (E. Lewis), 1937
China Year (Neville), 1991
Chinese Americans (Meltzer), 1980
Chinese Handcuffs (Crutcher), 1989

Dark Way: Stories from the Spirit World (Hamilton), 1990
Dark Wind (Hillerman), 1982
Darkangel (M. Pierce), 1982
Darkangel trilogy (M. Pierce), 1982-1990
Darkest Hour (Andrews), 1993
Darkest Hours (Carter), 1988
Darkfall (Koontz), 1984
Darkling (Peyton), 1989
Darkness Comes (Koontz), 1984
Darkness in My Soul (Koontz), 1972
Darkness Visible (Golding), 1979
Darkness Within (Fast), 1953
Darkover Landfall (Bradley), 1972
Darkover series (Bradley), from 1962
Date for Diane (Cavanna), 1946
Dateline: Troy (Fleischman), 1995
Daughter of Discontent (Colman), 1971
Daughter of Don Saturnino (O'Dell), 1979
Daughter of the Snows (London), 1902
Daughter of Witches (Wrede), 1983
Daughter's a Daughter (Christie), 1952
Daughter's Geography (Shange), 1983
Daughters of Eve (Duncan), 1979
Daughters of the Law (Asher), 1980
Daughters of the Rich (London), 1971
David (Holm), 1963
David & Della (Zindel), 1993
David and Jonathan (Voigt), 1992
David and Paula (Fast), 1982
David Balfour (Stevenson), 1893
David Glasgow Farragut: Our First Admiral (Latham), 1967
David Livingstone (Yates), 1952
David's New World: The Making of a Sportsman (Harnett), 1937
Davita's Harp (Potok), 1985
Dawn (Andrews), 1990
Dawn (Butler), 1987
Dawn (Wiesel), 1961
Dawn of Fear (Cooper), 1970
Dawn Palace: The Story of Medea (Hoover), 1988
Dawn Wind (Sutcliff), 1961
Dawnstone (Paton Walsh), 1973
Day and the Way We Met (Stolz), 1956
Day Before Christmas (Bunting), 1992
Day in the Life of Hollywood (Bradbury, editor), 1992
Day in Windsor (Huxley), 1953
Day Martin Luther King, Jr. Was Shot: A Photo History of the Civil Rights Movement (Haskins), 1992
Day No Pigs Would Die (R.N. Peck), 1972
Day of the Ness (Norton), 1975
Day of the Starwind (Hill), 1980
Day of the Unicorn (M. Hunter), 1961
Day the Senior Class Got Married (Miklowitz), 1983
Day They Came to Arrest the Book (Hentoff), 1982
Day without Wind (Mayne), 1964
Daybreak, 2250 A.D.,(Norton), 1954
Daydreams on Video (Geras), 1989
Daymaker (Halam), 1987
Days of Fear (Nixon), 1983
Days of the Rebels, 1815-1840 (Atwood), 1977
Days to Remember: A Garland of Historic Anniversaries (Trease), 1973

Daystar (Walden), 1955
Daz 4 Zoe (Swindells), 1990
D.D. Home: His Life and Mission (Doyle, editor), 1921
Deacon Brodie; or, The Double Life (Stevenson), 1880
Dead Man's Folly (Christie), 1956
Dead Man's Mirror, and Other Stories (Christie), 1937
Dead Men Don't Ski (Moyes), 1959
Dead Moon and Other Tales from East Anglia and the Fen Country (Crossley-Holland), 1982
Dead Zone (King), 1979
Deadeye Dick (Vonnegut), 1982
Deadly Game of Magic (Nixon), 1983
Deadly Gift (Bennett), 1969
Deadly Promise (Nixon), 1992
Dealing with Dragons (Wrede), 1990
Dealing; or, the Berkeley-to-Boston Forty-Brick Lost-Bag Blues (Crichton), 1971
Dean R. Koontz: A New Collection (Koontz), 1992
Dean R. Koontz: Three Complete Novels, The Servants of Twilight, Darkfall, Phantoms (Koontz), 1991
Dear Bill, Remember Me? and Other Stories (N. Mazer), 1976
Dear Bruce Springsteen (Major), 1987
Dear Fred (Peyton), 1981
Dear God: Children's Letters (Heller), 1987
Dear Lovely Death (L. Hughes), 1931
Dear Lovey Hart, I Am Desperate (Conford), 1975
Dear Mom, Get Me Out of Here! (Conford), 1992
Dear Nobody (Doherty), 1991
Dear Rebecca, Winter is Here (George), 1993
Dearest Kate (Eyerly), 1961
Death and the Dutch Uncle (Moyes), 1968
Death Comes as the End (Christie), 1944
Death Dealers (Asimov), 1958
Death Grip (Bennett), 1993
Death Has Lost Its Charm for Me (Bradbury), 1987
Death in the Air (Christie), 1935
Death in the Clouds (Christie), 1935
Death Is a Lonely Business (Bradbury), 1985
Death Is Hard to Live With: Teenagers and How They Cope with Death (Bode), 1993
Death of Sleep (McCaffrey), 1990
Death on the Agenda (Moyes), 1962
Death on the Nile (Christie), 1937
Death Ticket (Bennett), 1985
Deathman, Do Not Follow Me (Bennett), 1968
Deathwatch (R. White), 1972
Deathwing over Veynaa (Hill), 1980
Debate on Spiritualism (A. Doyle), 1922
Debutante Hill (Duncan), 1958
December Rose (Garfield), 1986
Decision at Doona (McCaffrey), 1969
Decision in Philadelphia: The Constitutional Convention of 1787 (Collier), 1986
Decline of English Murder and Other Essays (Orwell), 1965
DeDe Takes Charge! (Hurwitz), 1984
Deed for the King of Spain (Baldwin), 1974
Deenie (Blume), 1973
Deep Danger (R. White), 1952
Deep Like the Rivers: A Biography of Langston Hughes, 1902-1967 (Haskins), 1973
Deep Range (Clarke), 1957

Dragons of Darkness (Card, editor), 1981
Dragons of Light (Card, editor), 1983
Dragonsdawn (McCaffrey), 1988
Dragonsinger (McCaffrey), 1977
Dragonsong (McCaffrey), 1976
Dragonwings (Yep), 1975
Drake, the Man They Called a Pirate (Latham), 1960
Dram Road (Lawrence), 1983
Drawbridge Gate (Harnett), 1954
Drawing of Three (King), 1989
Dread Companion (Norton), 1970
Dreadful Future of Blossom Culp (R. Peck), 1983
Dream, Benjamin's Dream, Benjamin's Bicentennial Blast: Three
    Short Stories (Asimov), 1976
Dream Cage: A Comic Drama in Nine Dreams (Chambers), 1982
Dream Catcher (M. Hughes), 1986
Dream Dancer (Bunting), 1974
Dream House (Mark), 1987
Dream of Debs (London), 1912(?)
Dream of Ghosts (Bonham), 1973
Dream of Queens and Castles (Bauer), 1990
Dream Watcher (Wersba), 1968
Dream: A Novel (H. Wells), 1924
Dream-Time (Treece), 1967
Dreaming Emmett (Morrison), 1986
Dreaming of Larry (Ure), 1991
Dreamland Lake (R. Peck), 1973
Dreams and Drummers (Smith), 1978
Dreams of Victory (Conford), 1973
Dreams of [Golf, Wimbleton, the Superbowl] (Wojciechowska),
    1965
Dreamsnake (McIntyre), 1978
Dreamstone (Cherryh), 1983
Dresses of Red and Gold (R. Klein), 1993
Dribbling, Shooting, and Scoring Sometimes (Paulsen), 1976
Drift (Mayne), 1985
Drifting Snow (Houston), 1992
Driver's Seat (Spark), 1970
Drop-Out (Eyerly), 1963
Drowned Ammet (D. Jones), 1977
Drowning of Stephan Jones (Greene), 1991
Drug of Choice (Crichton), 1970
Druid of Shannara (T. Brooks), 1991
Drummer Boy (Garfield), 1969
Drummers of Jericho (Meyer), 1994
Dry Victories (Jordan), 1972
Duck on a Pond (Willard), 1962
Ducks and Drakes (Harnett), 1942
Duel in the Desert (Myers), 1986
Duet (A. Doyle), 1903
Duet, with an Occasional Chorus (A. Doyle), 1899
Duke Decides (Tunis), 1939
Duke Ellington (Collier), 1991
Dukes (R.N. Peck), 1984
Dumb Cake (Garfield), 1977
Dumb Witness (Christie), 1937
Dump Days (Spinelli), 1988
Dunc and Amos and the Red Tattoos (Paulsen), 1993
Dunc and Amos Hit the Big Top (Paulsen), 1993
Dunc and the Scam Artist (Paulsen), 1993
Dunc and the Haunted House (Paulsen), 1993

Dunc and the Flaming Ghost (Paulsen), 1992
Dunc Breaks the Record (Paulsen), 1992
Dunc Gets Tweaked (Paulsen), 1992
Dunc's Doll (Paulsen), 1992
Dunc's Dump (Paulsen), 1993
Dunc's Halloween (Paulsen), 1992
Dunc's Undercover Christmas (Paulsen), 1993
Dune (Herbert), 1965
Dune Messiah (Herbert), 1969
Duplicate (Sleator), 1988
Durango Street (Bonham), 1965
Dusky Day (Means), 1933
Dust of the Earth (V. and B. Cleaver), 1975
Dust Tracks on a Road (Hurston), 1942
Dustland (Hamilton), 1980
Dutch Are Coming (Trease), 1965
Dutch Colt (Meigs), 1952
Dutch Courage, and Other Stories (London), 1922
Dynamite Do-It-Yourself Pen Pal Kit (Stine), 1980
Dynamite's Funny Book of the Sad Facts of Life (Stine), 1980

"E" Is for Elisa (Hurwitz), 1991
E, My Name Is Emily (N. Mazer), 1991
Eagle Fur (R.N. Peck), 1978
Eagle Island (Baillie), 1989
Eagle Mask: A West Coast Indian Tale (Houston), 1966
Eagle of the Ninth (Sutcliff), 1954
Eagle's Egg (Sutcliff), 1981
Eagles Have Flown (Treece), 1954
Ealdwood (Cherryh), 1989
Ear, Nose and Throat (S. Townsend), 1989
Early Americana and Other Stories (C. Richter), 1936
Early Asimov: Or, Eleven Years of Trying (Asimov), 1972
Early Ayn Rand: A Selection from Her Unpublished Fiction (Rand),
    1984
Early Christian Church and Modern Spiritualism (A. Doyle), 1925
Early Tales and Sketches, Volume 1: 1851-1864 (Twain), 1979
Earth Is Room Enough: Science Fiction Tales of Our Own Planet
    (Asimov), 1957
Earth-Moon (T. Hughes), 1976
Earth-Owl and Other Moon-People (T. Hughes), 1963
Earth to Andrew O. Blechman (Zalben), 1989
Earth to Matthew (Danziger), 1991
Earth Witch (Lawrence), 1981
Earth: Our Crowded Spaceship (Asimov), 1974
Earth-Father (Crossley-Holland), 1976
Earthdark (M. Hughes), 1977
Earthfasts (Mayne), 1966
Earthlight (Clarke), 1955
Earthly Possessions (Tyler), 1977
Earthly Powers (Burgess), 1980
Earthminds trilogy (Sargent), 1980-1984
Earthquake! (Miklowitz), 1977
Earthquakes: Nature in Motion (Nixon), 1981
Earthsea (Le Guin), 1977
Earthsea Trilogy (Le Guin), 1979
Earthseed (Sargent), 1983
East End at Your Feet (Dhondy), 1976
East of Eden (Steinbeck), 1952
East of Midnight (T. Lee), 1977
East of the Sun/West of the Moon (Asher), 1985

First the Egg (Moeri), 1982
First Two Lives of Lukas-Kasha (Alexander), 1978
First Wedding, Once Removed (Deaver), 1990
Fiscal Question (A. Doyle), 1905
Fisherman and the Bird (Levitin), 1982
Fishing Party (Mayne), 1960
Fit for a King (Willard), 1955
Fit of Shivers: Tales for Late at Night (Aiken), 1990
Five August Days (Burton), 1981
Five Autumn Songs for Children's Voices (T. Hughes), 1969
Five Biblical Portraits (Wiesel), 1981
Five Bushel Farm (Coatsworth), 1939
Five Fates (Herbert), 1970
Five Hundred (Dillon), 1972
555 Pointers for Beginning Actors and Directors (Latham), 1935
Five Little Pigs (Christie), 1942
Five Modern Canadian Poets (Atwood), 1970
Five Patients: The Hospital Explained (Crichton), 1970
Five Poems (Walker), 1972
Five Were Missing (Duncan), 1972
Flagship Hope: Aaron Lopez (Alexander), 1960
Flambards (Peyton), 1978
Flambards Divided (Peyton), 1981
Flambards in Summer (Peyton), 1969
Flambards Trilogy (Peyton), 1980
Flame into Being: The Life and Work of D.H. Lawrence (Burgess), 1985
Flame-Coloured Taffeta (Sutcliff), 1985
Flamers (Fisk), 1979
Flash Flood (Thiele), 1970
Flashback: The Amazing Adventures of a Film Horse (Rubinstein), 1990
Fledgling (Langton), 1980
Flesh in the Furnace (Koontz), 1972
Flight Deck (R. White), 1961
Flight of Angels (Trease), 1988
Flight of Swans (Willard), 1980
Flight to Adventure (Serraillier), 1947
Flight to the Forest (Willard), 1967
Flivver King: A Story of Ford-America (Sinclair), 1937
Floating Admiral (Christie), 1931
Floatplane Notebooks (Edgerton), 1988
Flood at Reedsmere (Burton), 1968
Flood Tide (Cherryh, editor), 1990
Floor Games (H. Wells), 1911
Flora MacDonald and Bonnie Prince Charlie (M. Hunter), 1987
Florence Nightingale (Caudill), 1953
Florina and the Wild Bird (Serraillier, translator), 1952
Flower Fables (Alcott), 1855
Flower Garden (Bunting), 1994
Flowers in the Attic (Andrews), 1979
Flowers of Anger (L. Hall), 1976
Flute in Mayferry Street (Dunlop), 1976
Flux (Card), 1992
Fly Away Home (Bunting), 1991
Fly Away Home (Nöstlinger), 1975
Fly Free (Adler), 1984
Fly Free (Phipson), 1979
Fly into Danger (Phipson), 1978
Fly on the Wall (Hillerman), 1971
Fly West (Southall), 1974

Fly, Wheels, Fly! (Savitz), 1970
Fly-by-Night (Peyton), 1968
Flyaway (L. Hall), 1987
Flying 19 (Aldridge), 1966
Flying Changes (L. Hall), 1991
Flying Machine (Bradbury), 1986
Flying Saucers (Asimov, editor), 1982
Fog (M. Lee), 1972
Fog Comes on Little Pig Feet (R. Wells), 1972
Fog Hounds, Wind Cat, Sea Mice (Aiken), 1984
Fogarty (Neville), 1969
Foghorn (Bradbury), 1977
Folk of the Air (Beagle), 1987
Folk of the Fringe (Card), 1989
Follow a Shadow (Swindells), 1989
Follow My Black Plume (Trease), 1963
Follow My Leader (Harnett), 1949
Follow the Drum (Norton), 1942
Follow the Footprints (Mayne), 1953
Following the Equator: A Journey around the World (Twain), 1897
Food and People (Huxley), 1949
Food Is Love (Asher), 1979
Food of the Gods, and How It Came to Earth (H. Wells), 1904
Fool (Garfield), 1977
Fool's Gold (Snyder), 1993
Fool's Hill (B. Hall), 1992
Foot in the Grave (Aiken), 1990
Footnote to History: Eight Years of Trouble in Samoa (Stevenson), 1892
Footprints at the Window (Naylor), 1981
Footsteps (Garfield), 1980
Footsteps on the Stairs (Adler), 1982
For Colored Girls Who Have Considered Suicide/When the Rainbow Is Enuf: A Choreopoem (Shange), 1976
For Esme—With Love and Squalor, and Other Stories (Salinger), 1953
For Love of Jody (Branscum), 1979
For Love of Evil (Anthony), 1988
For the Birds (Atwood), 1990
For the New Intellectual: The Philosophy of Ayn Rand (Rand), 1961
Forbidden Fountain of Oz (McGraw), 1980
Forbidden Paths of Thual (Kelleher), 1979
Forbidden Tower (Bradley), 1977
Forecast of the World's Affairs (H. Wells), 1925
Forehanding and Backhanding—If You're Lucky (Paulsen), 1978
Foreign Affair (J. Townsend), 1982
Foreign Policy (A. Doyle), 1893
Forerunner Foray (Norton), 1973
Forest of the Night (J. Townsend), 1974
Forever (Blume), 1975
Forever and the Earth (Bradbury), 1984
Forever Formula (Bonham), 1979
Forgotten (Wiesel), forthcoming
Forgotten Beasts of Eld (McKillip), 1974
Forgotten Girl (Colman), 1990
Forgotten Island (Coatsworth), 1942
Forgotten Village (Steinbeck), 1941
Formal Feeling (Oneal), 1982
Fort of Gold (Dillon), 1961
FortDog July (R.N. Peck), 1992

Furl of Fairy Wind (M. Hunter), 1986
Furl of Fairy Wind: Four Stories (M. Hunter), 1977
Further Adventures of the Family from One End Street (Garnett), 1956
Further Adventures of Robinson Crusoe (Treece), 1958
Further Inquiry (Kesey), 1990
Further Tales of Uncle Remus (Lester, reteller), 1990
Future Days: A Nineteenth-Century Vision of the Year 2000 (Asimov), 1986
Future in America: A Search After Realities (H. Wells), 1906
Future in Question (Asimov, editor), 1980
Future in Space (Asimov), 1993
Future on Fire (Card, editor), 1991
Futuretrack Five (Westall), 1983

Gabriel Hounds (Stewart), 1967
Gaffer Samson's Luck (Paton Walsh), 1984
Galactic Derelict (Norton), 1959
Galactic Warlord (Hill), 1979
Galápagos: A Novel (Vonnegut), 1985
Galax-Arena (Rubinstein), 1992
Galaxies (Asimov), 1968
Gambling—Who Really Wins? (Haskins), 1978
Game (London), 1905
Game of Danger (Duncan), 1962
Game of Dark (Mayne), 1971
Game of Soldiers (Needle), 1985
Gamebuster (Johnson), 1990
Games... (R. Klein), 1986
Gammage Cup (Kendall), 1959
Garden behind the Moon: A Real Story of the Moon Angel (Pyle), 1895
Garden of Broken Glass (Neville), 1975
Garden of Earthly Delights (Beagle), 1981
Garden of Rama (Clarke), 1991
Garden of Shadows (Andrews), 1987
Gardener's Grandchildren (Willard), 1978
Garland for Girls (Alcott), 1887
Gate of Ivrel (Cherryh), 1976
Gates of Bannerdale (Trease), 1956
Gates of Hell (Cherryh), 1986
Gates of Paradise (Andrews), 1989
Gates of the Forest (Wiesel), 1966
Gates to Tomorrow: An Introduction to Science Fiction (Norton, editor), 1973
Gateway (Walden), 1946
Gather Together in My Name (Angelou), 1974
Gathering (Hamilton), 1981
Gathering of Days: A New England Girl's Journal, 1830-32 (Blos), 1979
Gathering of Flowers: Stories about Being Young in America (Thomas, editor), 1990
Gathering of Gargoyles (M. Pierce), 1984
Gathering of Old Men (Gaines), 1983
Gavriel and Jemal: Two Boys of Jerusalem (Ashabranner), 1984
Gem of a Murder (Robertson), 1959
General Zapped an Angel (Fast), 1970
Generation Warriors (McCaffrey), 1991
Genetic Code (Asimov), 1963
Genetic Effects of Radiation (Asimov), 1966
Genie on the Loose (Leeson), 1984

Genie with the Light Blue Hair (Conford), 1989
Genius and the Goddess (Huxley), 1955
Gentlehands (Kerr), 1978
Gently Touch the Milkweed (L. Hall), 1970
(George) (Konigsburg), 1970
George and Red (Coatsworth), 1969
George Gissing and H.G. Wells: Their Friendship and Correspondence (H. Wells), 1961
George McGinnis: Basketball Superstar (Haskins), 1978
George Orwell: The Lost Writings (Orwell), 1988
George W. Goethals: Panama Canal Engineer (Latham), 1965
George Washington and the Birth of Our Nation (Meltzer), 1986
George Washington and the Water Witch (Fast), 1956
George's Marvellous Medicine (Dahl), 1981
Gerald's Game (King), 1992
German War (A. Doyle), 1914
Get Lost (R. Klein), 1987
Get Lost, Little Brother (Adler), 1983
Get off the Unicorn (McCaffrey), 1977
Get on Board: The Story of the Underground Railroad (Haskins), 1993
Get on out of Here, Philip Hall (Greene), 1981
Getting Born (Freedman), 1978
Getting On with It (Slepian), 1985
Getting to Know Dogs (Harnett), 1947
Ghost Abbey (Westall), 1988
Ghost after Ghost (Chambers, editor), 1982
Ghost Behind Me (Bunting), 1984
Ghost Belonged to Me (R. Peck), 1975
Ghost Brother (Adler), 1990
Ghost Carnival: Stories of Ghosts in Their Haunts (Chambers), 1977
Ghost Children (Bunting), 1989
Ghost Dance Caper (M. Hughes), 1978
Ghost Downstairs (Garfield), 1972
Ghost Eye (Bauer), 1992
Ghost from the Grand Banks (Clarke), 1990
Ghost Front (Bonham), 1968
Ghost Host (Singer), 1987
Ghost in the Tower (Westall), 1992
Ghost Messengers (Swindells), 1986
Ghost of a Chance (Clapp), 1958
Ghost of Ballyhooly (Cavanna), 1971
Ghost of Lone Cabin (Latham), 1940
Ghost of Rhodes Manor (Latham), 1939
Ghost of Summer (Bunting), 1977
Ghost of the Great River Inn (L. Hall), 1981
Ghost Paddle: A Northwest Coast Indian Tale (Houston), 1972
Ghost Ship to Ganymede (Swindells), 1980
Ghost Women (Rostkowski), 1986
Ghost Wore White (Cavanna), 1950
Ghost's Hour, Spook's Hour (Bunting), 1987
Ghostly Companions (Alcock), 1984
Ghosts (Asimov, editor), 1988
Ghosts (Chambers, editor), 1969
Ghosts (Mayne, editor), 1971
Ghosts and Journeys (Westall), 1988
Ghosts 4 (Chambers, editor), 1978
Ghosts I Have Been (R. Peck), 1977
Ghosts of Departure Point (Bunting), 1982
Ghosts of Forever (Bradbury), 1981

Handful of Thieves (Bawden), 1967
Handful of Time (Pearson), 1987
Handles (Mark), 1983
Handmaid's Tale (Atwood), 1985
Hands Off Our School! (Lingard), 1992
Hang for Treason (R.N. Peck), 1976
Hanging Judge (Stevenson), 1914
Hanging On (Koontz), 1973
Hanging On: How Animals Carry Their Young (Freedman), 1977
Happenings at North End School (Colman), 1970
Happily Ever After (Colman), 1986
Happily Ever After (Serraillier), 1963
Happy Birthday, Dear Duck (Bunting), 1988
Happy Birthday, Wanda June (Vonnegut), 1960
Happy Endings (Geras), 1986
Happy Endings Are All Alike (Scoppettone), 1978
Happy Families (Willard, editor), 1974
Happy Funeral (Bunting), 1982
Happy Little Family (Caudill), 1947
Happy Thyme (Anthony), 1993
Happy Turning: A Dream of Life (H. Wells), 1945
Hard Life of the Teenager (Collier), 1972
Hard Love (Grant), 1983
Hard Sell (Anthony), 1990
Hard Way Home (Peyton), 1962
Harlem, U.S.A.: The Story of a City within a City (Baldwin), 1976
Harmony Arms (Koertge), 1992
Harp of Fishbones and Other Stories (Aiken), 1972
Harp of Imach Thyssel (Wrede), 1985
Harper Hall of Pern (McCaffrey), 1979
Harpist in the Wind (McKillip), 1979
Harris and Me (Paulsen), 1993
Harrow and Harvest (Willard), 1974
Harry and Hortense at Hormone High (Zindel), 1984
Harry Bridges (Trumbo), 1941
Harry Truman (Miklowitz), 1975
Hart's Hope (Card), 1982
Harvest Gypsies: On the Road to the Grapes of Wrath (Steinbeck), 1988
Hasan (Anthony), 1977
Hatchet Rack Trim (Paulsen), 1989
Hatchett (Paulsen), 1987
Haunt of Ghosts (Chambers, editor), 1987
Haunted (Stine), 1991
Haunted Computer and the Android Pope (Bradbury), 1981
Haunted Earth (Koontz), 1973
Haunted Hound (R. White), 1950
Haunted Houses (Chambers), 1971
Haunted Mountain: A Story of Suspense (M. Hunter), 1972
Haunted Night (Phipson), 1970
Haunted One (Bennett), 1989
Haunted Rivers (Wrightson), 1983
Haunting of Cassie Palmer (Alcock), 1980
Haunting of Chas McGill and Other Stories (Westall), 1983
Haunting of Kildoran Abbey (Bunting), 1978
Haunting of Lamb House (Aiken), 1991
Haunting of Safekeep (Bunting), 1985
Haunting Tales from Japan (Kendall, reteller), 1985
Have Space Suit—Will Travel (Heinlein), 1958
Have You Got Your Ticket? (Serraillier), 1972
Have You Seen These? (Asimov), 1974

Have Your Own Extraterrestrial Adventure (Hill), 1983
Haveli (Staples), 1993
Havelok the Dane (Crossley-Holland), 1964
Havelok the Dane (Serraillier), 1967
Havelok the Warrior (Serraillier), 1968
Hawk That Dare Not Hunt by Day (O'Dell), 1975
Hawkeye Adventure (Irwin), 1966
Hawkeye Lore (Irwin), 1968
Hawkmistress (Bradley), 1982
Haym Salomon, Son of Liberty (Fast), 1941
Haymeadow (Paulsen), 1992
Hazel Rye (V. and B. Cleaver), 1983
He Fought for His Queen (Willard), 1954
He Landed from London (Latham), 1935
He Went with Captain Cook (Kamm), 1952
He Will Not Walk With Me (Bach), 1985
He's My Baby, Now (Eyerly), 1977
Headless Cupid (Snyder), 1971
Heads, I Win (Hermes), 1988
Healer (Dickinson), 1983
Heart Is a Lonely Hunter (McCullers), 1940
Heart of a Woman (Angelou), 1981
Heart's Blood (Yolen), 1984
Heartbeat (H. Mazer), 1989
Heartbeat (N. Mazer), 1989
Heartbreak Tennis (Walden), 1977
Hearts (Wolitzer), 1980
Hearts of Three (London), 1918
Heartsease (Dickinson), 1969
Heather, Oak, and Olive: Three Stories (Sutcliff), 1972
Heaven (Andrews), 1985
Heaven and Hell (Huxley), 1956
Heaven Cent (Anthony), 1988
Heaven Chronicles (Vinge), 1991
Heaven Makers (Herbert), 1968
Heavenly Host (Asimov), 1975
Heavy Time (Cherryh), 1991
Hebrew People: A History of the Jews from Biblical Times to the Present Day (Kamm), 1967
Hedgehog Boy (Langton), 1985
Heir of Sea and Fire (McKillip), 1977
Heirs of Hammerfell (Bradley), 1989
Helen (Fast), 1966
Helga and the White Peacock (Meigs), 1922
Helicon Home Colony (Sinclair), 1906
Hell: A Verse Drama and Photo-play (Sinclair), 1923
Hellburner (Cherryh), 1992
Hello...Wrong Number (Sachs), 1981
Hell's Edge (J. Townsend), 1963
Hell's Gate (Koontz), 1970
Hellstrom's Hive (Herbert), 1973
Help, Pink Pig! (Adler), 1990
Helping Horse (Phipson), 1974
Helter-Skelter (Moyes), 1968
Henchmans at Home (Burton), 1970
Hengest's Tale (Paton Walsh), 1966
Henry (Bawden), 1988
Henry and Emmy Tibbett series (Moyes), from 1959
Henry James and H.G. Wells: A Record of Their Friendship, Their Debate on the Art of Fiction, and Their Quarrel (H. Wells), 1958

Henry Reed, Inc. (Robertson), 1958
Henry Reed's Baby-Sitting Service (Robertson), 1966
Henry Reed's Big Show (Robertson), 1970
Henry Reed's Journey (Robertson), 1963
Henry Reed's Think Tank (Robertson), 1986
Her Blue Body Everything We Know: Earthling Poems 1965-1990
   (Walker), 1991
Her First Ball: Short Stories (Burton, editor), 1959
Her Kissin' Cousin (Clapp), 1957
Her Majesty, Grace Jones (Lackey), 1974
Heracles the Strong (Serraillier), 1970
Hercule Poirot's Casebook: Fifty Stories (Christie), 1984
Hercule Poirot's Christmas (Christie), 1938
Hercule Poirot's Early Cases (Christie), 1974
Herd of Deer (Dillon), 1969
Here Abide Monsters (Norton), 1973
Here Comes Everybody: An Introduction to James Joyce for the
   Ordinary Reader (Burgess), 1965
Here Comes Zelda Claus and Other Holiday Disasters (L. Hall),
   1989
Here There Be Dragons (Yolen), 1973
Here's Hermione, A Rosy Cole Production (Greenwald), 1991
Here's Looking at You, Kid (Zalben), 1984
Here's to the Sophomores (Petersen), 1984
Heretics of Dune (Herbert), 1984
Heritage of Hastur (Bradley), 1975
Heritage of the Star (Engdahl), 1973
Hero (Baillie), 1991
Hero (Windsor), 1988
Hero Ain't Nothin' But a Sandwich (Childress), 1973
Hero and the Crown (McKinley), 1985
Heroes and History (Sutcliff), 1965
Heroine of the Titanic: A Tale Both True and Otherwise of the Life
   of Molly Brown (Blos), 1991
Hessian (Fast), 1972
Hestia (Cherryh), 1979
Hetty (Willard), 1962
Hetty of the Grande Deluxe (Means), 1951
Hey, Big Spender! (Bonham), 1972
Hey, Dad! (B. Doyle), 1978
Hey Kid! Does She Love Me? (H. Mazer), 1985
Hey, Phantom Singlet (French), 1975
Hey, What's Wrong with This One? (Wojciechowska), 1969
H.G. Wells Calendar: A Quotation From the Works of H.G. Wells
   for Every Day in the Year (H. Wells), 1911
H.G. Wells: Early Writings in Science and Science Fiction (H. Wells),
   1975
H.G. Wells in Love: Postscript to an Experiment in Autobiography
   (H. Wells), 1984
H.G. Wells' Interview With J.V. Stalin (Marxism v. Liberalism) (H.
   Wells), 1950
H.G. Wells Papers at the University of Illinois (H. Wells), 1958
H.G. Wells, S. de Madariaga, J. Middleton Murry, C.E.M. Joad on
   the New World Order (H. Wells), 1940
H.G. Wells Science Fiction Treasury (H. Wells), 1987
H.G. Wells's Literary Criticism (H. Wells), 1980
Hi Johnny (M. Hunter), 1963
Hi-Ran-Ho: A Picture Book of Verse (Chambers, editor), 1971
Hickory, Dickory, Death (Christie), 1955
Hickory, Dickory, Dock (Christie), 1955
Hidden Louisa May Alcott: A Collection of her Unknown Thrillers
   (Alcott), 1984

Hidden Ones (Halam), 1988
Hidden Shrine (Myers), 1985
Hidden Treasure (J. Townsend), 1988
Hidden Treasure (Trease), 1989
Hidden Turnings: A Collection of Stories through Time and Space
   (D. Jones, editor), 1989
Hide and Seek (Coatsworth), 1956
Hide till Daytime (Phipson), 1977
Hideaway (Koontz), 1992
Hideaway (McGraw), 1983
Hideout (Bunting), 1991
Hiding (N. Klein), 1976
Hiding Place (Robertson), 1965
Higbee's Halloween (R.N. Peck), 1990
High Cost of Living (Sinclair), 1919
High Crimes and Misdemeanors (Greenberg), 1979
High Deeds of Finn MacCool (Sutcliff), 1967
High King (Alexander), 1968
High Pavement Blues (Ashley), 1983
High School Dirty Poems (Koertge), 1991
High Tide for Labrador (Bunting), 1975
High Trail to Danger (Nixon), 1991
High Way Home (Fisk), 1973
High White Wall (Sherburne), 1957
High Wizardry (Duane), 1990
Highest Dream (Whitney), 1956
Highpockets (Tunis), 1948
Hiking and Backpacking (Paulsen), 1978
Hilda Wade (A. Doyle), 1900
Hill 568 (E. White), 1991
Hill of Adventure (Meigs), 1922
Hill Road (Mayne), 1969
Hillerman Country: A Journey through the Southwest with Tony
   Hillerman (Hillerman), 1991
Hillingdon Fox (Mark), 1991
Hills of Varna (Trease), 1948
Him She Loves? (Kerr), 1984
Hired Nose (Koertge), 1974
His Enemy, His Friend (Tunis), 1967
His First Best Country (J. Miller), 1987
His Last Bow: Some Reminiscences of Sherlock Holmes (A. Doyle),
   1917
His Own Where (Jordan), 1971
Hispanic Americans (Meltzer), 1982
History Is One (H. Wells), 1919
History of Helpless Harry (Avi), 1980
History of Middle-Earth (Tolkien), 1983-84
History of Mr. Polly (H. Wells), 1910
History of Physics (Asimov), 1984
History of Science Fiction from 1938 to the Present (Asimov),
   1971
History of Spiritualism (A. Doyle), 1926
Hit and Run (Phipson), 1985
Hit and Run (Stine), 1978
Hitchhiker (Stine), 1993
Hitting, Pitching, and Running Maybe (Paulsen), 1977
H.M.S. Hood vs. Bismarck: The Battleship Battle (T. Taylor),
   1982
Ho-Ming, Girl of New China (E. Lewis), 1934
Hobbit; or, There and Back Again (Tolkien), 1937
Hocus Pocus; or, What's the Hurry, Son? (Vonnegut), 1990

Holding Me Here (Conrad), 1986
Hole in the Head (Fisk), 1991
Hole in the Hill (Park), 1961
Hole in the Tree (George), 1957
Holiday at the Dew Drop Inn: A One End Street Story (Garnett), 1962
Holiday for Murder (Christie), 1947
Holiday House: The First Fifty Years (Freedman), 1985
Hollow (Christie), 1952
Hollow Hills (Stewart), 1973
Hollow Land (Gardam), 1981
Hollow: A Hercule Poirot Mystery (Christie), 1946
Holly from the Bongs: A Nativity Play (Garner), 1966
Hollywood Kid (Wojciechowska), 1967
Holy Face and Other Essays (Huxley), 1929
Holy Terror (H. Wells), 1939
Homage to Catalonia (Orwell), 1938
Homage to QWERT YUIOP: Selected Journalism 1978-1985 (Burgess), 1986
Home (Doherty), 1988
Home Again, Home Again Jiggity Jig (Scoppettone), 1969
Home before Dark (Bridgers), 1976
Home Colony: A Prospectus (Sinclair), 1906
Home Computer Handbook (Herbert), 1985
Home Course in Religion (Soto), 1991
Home Free (Lasky), 1985
Home Is Where Your Feet Are Standing (Windsor), 1975
Home Place (Gipson), 1950
Homecoming (Voigt), 1981
Homecoming of Beorhtnoth Beorhthelm's Son (Tolkien), 1954
Homecoming Saga series (Card), from 1993
Home-Front (Burch), 1992
Homesmind (Sargent), 1984
Homeward Bounders (D. Jones), 1981
Honestly, Myron (D. Hughes), 1982
Honey for the Bears (Burgess), 1963
Honey of a Chimp (N. Klein), 1980
Honeysuckle Hedge (Clapp), 1960
Honor Bound (Bonham), 1963
Honor Sands (M. Lee), 1966
Honours Physiography (H. Wells), 1893
Hooded Man (Bennett), 1992
Hook (T. Brooks), 1992
Hook a Fish, Catch a Mountain (George), 1975
Hoopdriver's Holiday (H. Wells), 1964
Hooper Haller (D. Hughes), 1981
Hoops (Myers), 1981
Hope and a Hatchet (Paulsen), 1978
Horn of Africa (Caputo), 1980
Horned Helmet (Treece), 1963
Hornet's Nest (Watson), 1967
Horror of the Heights and Other Tales of Suspense (A. Doyle), 1992
Horrors of the Haunted Museum (Stine), 1984
Horse and His Boy (C. Lewis), 1954
Horse Called Dragon (L. Hall), 1971
Horse-Fancier (Dillon), 1985
Horse Hunters (R.N. Peck), 1988
Horse Stories (Coatsworth), 1954
Horse Trader (L. Hall), 1981
Horse with Eight Hands (Phipson), 1974
Horse's Tale (Twain), 1907
Horse-Tamer (Farley), 1958
Horsemaster (Singer), 1985

Horsemen on the Hills (Trease), 1971
Horses Make a Landscape Look More Beautiful (Walker), 1984
Hospital Sketches (Alcott), 1863
Hospital Sketches [and] Camp and Fireside Stories (Alcott), 1869
Hospital Zone (Stolz), 1956
Hostage (Holm), 1980
Hostage (T. Taylor), 1987
Hostages to Fortune (Lingard), 1976
Hot and Cold Summer (Hurwitz), 1984
Hot Day (Greenwald), 1972
Hot Gates, and Other Occasional Pieces (Golding), 1965
Hot Sleep (Card), 1978
Hothouse by the East River (Spark), 1973
Hound-Dog Man (Gipson), 1949
Hound Dunnit (Asimov, editor), 1987
Hound of Death, and Other Stories (Christie), 1933
Hound of the Baskervilles (A. Doyle), 1902
Hound of Ulster (Sutcliff), 1963
Hounds of the King, with Two Radio Plays (Treece), 1965
Hounds of the King (Treece), 1955
Hour of the Wolf (Calvert), 1983
House between the Worlds (Bradley), 1980
House beyond the Meadow (Behn), 1955
House Like a Lotus (L'Engle), 1984
House Made of Dawn (Momaday), 1968
House of Dies Drear (Hamilton), 1968
House of Fear (Roberts), 1983
House of Hanover: England in the Eighteenth Century (Garfield), 1976
House of Pride and Other Tales of Hawaii (London), 1912
House of Secrets (Bawden), 1964
House of Shadows (Norton), 1984
House of Stairs (Sleator), 1974
House of Temperley (A. Doyle), 1910
House of the Swan (Coatsworth), 1948
House of the Fifers (Caudill), 1954
House of Thunder (Koontz), 1982
House of Tomorrow (G. Crew), 1988
House of Wings (Byars), 1972
House on Fairmont (Mayne), 1968
House on Mango Street (Cisneros), 1983
House on Mayferry Street (Dunlop), 1977
House on Parchment Street (McKillip), 1973
House on the Hill (Dunlop), 1987
House on the Shore (Dillon), 1955
House under the Hill (Means), 1949
House with Roots (Willard), 1959
Houseboat Summer (Coatsworth), 1942
Houses and History (Sutcliff), 1960
How a Weirdo and a Ghost Can Change Your Entire Life (Windsor), 1986
How Animals Defend Their Young (Freedman), 1978
How Animals Learn (Freedman), 1969
How Bigger Was Born: The Story of "Native Son," One of the Most Significant Novels of Our Time and How It Came to Be Written (Wright), 1940
How Birds Fly (Freedman), 1977
How Bright the Dawn (Walden), 1962
How Can You Hijack a Cave? (Petersen), 1988
How Edith McGillicuddy Met R.L.S (Steinbeck), 1943
How God Got Christian into Trouble (Wojciechowska), 1984
How Green You Are! (Doherty), 1982

Kaffir Boy in America: An Encounter with Apartheid (Mathabane), 1989

Kaffir Boy: The True Story of a Black Youth's Coming of Age in Apartheid South Africa (Mathabane), 1986

Kaleidoscopes Baroque: A Poem (Atwood), 1965

Karate Dancer (Smith), 1987

Karen Kepplewhite Is the World's Best Kisser (Bunting), 1983

Kate (Little), 1971

Kate and the Revolution (J. Townsend), 1982

Kate Rider (Burton), 1974

Katherine Dunham (Haskins), 1982

Kathleen, Please Come Home (O'Dell), 1978

Katy at Home (Serraillier), 1957

Katy at School (Serraillier), 1959

Keep Calm (Phipson), 1978

Keep Laughing (Grant), 1991

Keep the Aspidistra Flying (Orwell), 1936

Keeper (Naylor), 1986

Keeper of the City (Duane), 1989

Keeper of the Isis Light (M. Hughes), 1980

Keeping Christina (Bridgers), 1993

Keeping Henry (Bawden), 1988

Keeping Kitty's Dates (Latham), 1931

Kelly 'n' Me (Levoy), 1992

Kelly's Creek (Smith), 1975

Kelpie (Mayne), 1987

Kelpie's Pearls (M. Hunter), 1964

Kempton-Wace Letters (London), 1903

Kept in the Dark (Bawden), 1982

Kesey (Kesey), 1977

Kesey's Garage Sale (Kesey), 1973

Kestrel (Alexander), 1982

Kevin Corbett Eats Flies (Hermes), 1986

Key (Dillon), 1967

Key Out of Time (Norton), 1963

Key to Midnight (Koontz), 1979

Keys of Mantlemass (Willard), 1981

Keystone Kids (Tunis), 1943

Kick a Stone Home (Smith), 1974

Kickoff Time (D. Hughes), 1991

Kid Comes Back (Tunis), 1946

Kid from Tomkinsville (Tunis), 1940

Kidnapped (Stevenson), 1886

Kidnapping of Christina Lattimore (Nixon), 1979

Kids Having Kids: The Unwed Teenage Parent (Bode), 1980

Kids Still Having Kids: People Talk about Teen Pregnancy (Bode), 1992

Kids' Code and Cipher Book (Garden), 1981

Kids' School Lunch Bag (Bode), 1972

Kif Strike Back (Cherryh), 1985

Kill the Editor (Robinson), 1991

Killashandra (McCaffrey), 1985

Killer Diller (Edgerton), 1991

Killer Fish (Freedman), 1982

Killer in Dark Glasses (Treece), 1965

Killer Snakes (Freedman), 1982

Killing Boy (Miklowitz), 1993

Killing Freeze (L. Hall), 1988

Killing Mr. Griffin (Duncan), 1978

Killing the Kudu (Meyer), 1990

Killing Time (Windsor), 1980

Killing Tree (Bennett), 1972

Killobyte (Anthony), 1993

Kilternan Legacy (McCaffrey), 1975

Kim/Kimi (Irwin), 1987

Kimako's Story (Jordan), 1981

Kind Hearts and Gentle Monsters (Yep), 1982

Kind of Thief (Alcock), 1991

Kind of Wild Justice (Ashley), 1978

Kindness (Rylant), 1989

Kindred (Butler), 1979

King (Angelou), 1990

King at the Door (Cole), 1979

King Big-Ears (Dillon), 1961

King Coal (Sinclair), 1917

King Creature, Come (J. Townsend), 1980

King Death's Garden (Halam), 1986

King Horn (Crossley-Holland), 1965

King in the Garden (Garfield), 1984

King Kong and Other Poets (Burch), 1986

King Leopold's Soliloquy: A Defense of His Congo Rule (Twain), 1905

King Midas (Sinclair), 1901

King Nimrod's Tower (Garfield), 1982

King of Kazoo (R.N. Peck), 1976

King of the Dead (MacAvoy), 1991

King of the Sticks (Southall), 1979

King Stork (Pyle), 1973

King Who Was a King: The Book of a Film (H. Wells), 1929

King's Corsair (Trease, translator), 1954

King's Fifth (O'Dell), 1966

King's Persons (Greenberg), 1963

King's Room (Dillon), 1970

King's Things (D. Jones), 1969

Kingdom and the Cave (Aiken), 1960

Kingdom by the Sea (Westall), 1990

Kingdom in a Horse (Wojciechowska), 1966

Kingdom of the Sun (Asimov), 1960

Kingdom of the Winding Road (Meigs), 1915

Kingdom of the Wicked (Burgess), 1985

Kingdom under the Sea and Other Stories (Aiken, reteller), 1971

Kings and Queens of Scotland (Dunlop), 1984

Kings in Hell (Cherryh), 1987

Kings, Prophets, and History (Kamm), 1966

Kipps: A Monograph (H. Wells), 1905

Kirith (McKinley), 1978

Kirk's Law (R.N. Peck), 1981

Kirlian Quest (Anthony), 1978

Kiss File JC 100 (Hoy), 1988

Kiss the Clown (Adler), 1986

Kisschase (A. Jones), 1989

Kissimmee Kid (V. and B. Cleaver), 1981

Kitchen God's Wife (Tan), 1991

Kitchen Warriors (Aiken), 1983

Kite That Won the Revolution (Asimov), 1963

Kitten Stand (Coatsworth), 1945

Kitty's Class Day (Alcott), 1868

Kiviok's Magic Journey: An Eskimo Legend (Houston), 1973

Klontarf (Thiele), 1988

Knave of Dreams (Norton), 1975

Knee Deep in Ice Cream and Other Stories (Naylor), 1967

Legacy of Terror (Koontz), 1971
Legend of Tarik (Myers), 1981
Legends of Our Time (Wiesel), 1968
Legions of Hell (Cherryh), 1987
Legions of the Eagle (Treece), 1954
Lenny Kandell, Smart Aleck (Conford), 1983
Lens of the World (MacAvoy), 1990
Leonardo Touch (Eyerly), 1976
Leslie (Sherburne), 1972
Lesser Evils: Ten Quartets (Soto), 1988
Lesson before Dying (Gaines), 1993
Lesson Plan Book for Dragonwings (Yep), 1990
Lester's Turn (Slepian), 1981
Let Sleeping Vets Lie (Herriot), 1973
Let the Balloon Go (Southall), 1976
Let the Circle Be Unbroken (M. Taylor), 1981
Let's Hear It for the Queen (Childress), 1976
Letter from Phoenix Farm (Yolen), 1992
Letter to the Friends of Democracy (Steinbeck), 1940
Letters from Jack London: Containing an Unpublished Correspon-
    dence Between London and Sinclair Lewis (London), 1965
Letters from the Inside (Marsden), 1991
Letters from the Sandwich Islands Written for the Sacramento Union
    (Twain), 1937
Letters Home: Correspondence, 1950-1963 (Plath), 1975
Letters of Aldous Huxley (Huxley), 1969
Letters of Fire and Other Unsettling Stories (Geras), 1984
Letters of J.R.R. Tolkien (Tolkien), 1981
Letters of Robert Louis Stevenson to His Family and Friends
    (Stevenson), 1899
Letters to a Millionaire (Sinclair), 1939
Letters to Alicia (Steinbeck), 1965
Letters to Children (C. Lewis), 1985.
Letters to Elizabeth: A Selection of Letters from John Steinbeck to
    Elizabeth Otis (Steinbeck), 1978
Letters to Jenny (Anthony), 1993
Letters to Joe C. Brown (Wright), 1968
Letters to Judd, An American Workingman (Sinclair), 1926
Letters to My Israeli Sons: The Story of Jewish Survival (Reid
    Banks), 1979
Letters to the Press: The Unknown Conan Doyle (A. Doyle), 1986
Letting Go (L. Hall), 1987
Liar, Liar (Yep), 1983
Liars (Petersen), 1992
Libby on Wednesday (Snyder), 1990
Liberty Jail (Card), 1975
Library of the Universe (Asimov), 1988-90
Lie (Vonnegut), 1992
Lie Factory Starts (Sinclair), 1934
Life and Death of a Brave Bull (Wojciechowska), 1972
Life and Death of Martin Luther King, Jr (Haskins), 1977
Life and Energy (Asimov), 1962
Life and Time (Asimov), 1978
Life and Work of Richard Wright (Wright), 1979
Life as I Find It (Twain), 1961
Life Before Man (Atwood), 1979
Life I Really Lived (West), 1979
Life in Colonial America (Speare), 1963
Life on the Edge of the Continent: Selected Poems (Koertge), 1982
Life on the Mississippi (Twain), 1883
Life without Friends (E. White), 1987

Lifeguard (Cusick), 1988
Lifetimes Under Apartheid (Gordimer), 1986
Light (Asimov), 1970
Light beyond the Forest: The Quest for the Holy Grail (Sutcliff),
    1979
Light in the Dark: The Life of Samuel Gridley Howe (Meltzer),
    1964
Light in the Forest (C. Richter), 1953
Light Princess (McKinley, adapter), 1988
Lighthouse Island (Coatsworth), 1968
Lightning (Koontz), 1988
Lights Out (Stine), 1991
Like Mother, Like Daughter (Bauer), 1985
Likely Place (Fox), 1967
Lila the Werewolf (Beagle), 1974
Lilith Summer (Irwin), 1979
Lillie of Watts: A Birthday Discovery (Walter), 1969
Lillie of Watts Takes a Giant Step (Walter), 1971
Lillipilly Hill (Spence), 1960
Liluli (Huxley), 1919
Lily and the Lost Boy (Fox), 1987
Limbo on the Loose: A Midsummer Night's Dream (Sinclair), 1948
Limbo: Six Stories and a Play (Huxley), 1920
Limericks Too Gross (Asimov), 1978
Lincoln: A Photobiography (Freedman), 1987
Lincoln: In His Own Words (Meltzer), 1993
Lincoln University Poets (L. Hughes), 1954
Lincoln Yesterday and Today (Latham), 1933
Linda's Homecoming (Whitney), 1950
Linda's Lie (Ashley), 1982
Lindbergh the Lone Flier (Fisk), 1968
Line Drive (D. Hughes), 1990
Linger (Kerr), 1993
Linnet (Watson), 1971
Lion and the Unicorn: Socialism and the English Genius (Orwell),
    1941
Lion Cub (Dillon), 1966
Lion of Comarre, and Against the Fall of Night (Clarke), 1968
Lion, The Witch, and the Wardrobe (C. Lewis), 1950
Lion's Cub (Hoover), 1974
Lion's Paw (R. White), 1946
Lion's Whiskers (Ashabranner), 1959
Lioness Rampant (T. Pierce), 1988
Lionhearted (Savitz), 1975
Lisa, Bright and Dark (Neufeld), 1969
Listen for the Fig Tree (Mathis), 1974
Listen for the Singing (Little), 1977
Listen, Mom and Dad (Card), 1978
Listening Woman (Hillerman), 1978
Listerdale Mystery, and Other Stories (Christie), 1934
Literature and Reality (Fast), 1950
Literature and Science (Huxley), 1963
Literature of Connecticut History (Collier), 1983
Little Bit Dead (Reaver), 1992
Little Brother (Baillie), 1985
Little by Little: A Writer's Education (Little), 1987
Little Destiny (V. and B. Cleaver), 1979
Little Fear (Wrightson), 1983
Little Fingerling: A Japanese Folk Tale (M. Hughes), 1989
Little Green Spacemen (Fisk), 1974
Little Haymakers (Coatsworth), 1949

Little Hill: Poems and Pictures (Behn), 1949
Little Lady of the Big House (London), 1916
Little Little (Kerr), 1981
Little Love (Hamilton), 1984
Little Love, a Little Learning (Bawden), 1965
Little Love Song (Magorian), 1991
Little Lower Than the Angels (McCaughrean), 1987
Little Man, Little Man: A Story of Childhood (Baldwin), 1976
Little Men (West), 1954
Little Men: Life at Plumfield with Jo's Boys (Alcott), 1871
Little Mermaid (McKinley), 1989
Little Mexican and Other Stories (Huxley), 1924
Little Old Ladies in Tennis Shoes (Asher), 1989
Little Orange Book (Donovan), 1961
Little Soup's Birthday (R.N. Peck), 1991
Little Soup's Bunny (R.N. Peck), 1976
Little Soup's Hayride (R.N. Peck), 1991
Little Soup's Turkey (R.N. Peck), 1992
Little Steel (Sinclair), 1938
Little Treasury of Dinosaurs (Asimov), 1989
Little Wars: A Game for Boys From Twelve Years of Age to One Hundred and Fifty and for That More Intelligent Sort of Girls Who Like Boys' Games and Books With an Appendix on Kriegspiel (H. Wells), 1913
Little Wilson and Big God, Being the First Part of the Confessions of Anthony Burgess (Burgess), 1986
Little Women or, Meg, Jo, Beth and Amy (Alcott), 1868-69
Littlest House (Coatsworth), 1940
Live and Let Die (Fleming), 1954
Live Forest (Dillon), 1948
Lives of Christopher Chant (D. Jones), 1988
Living by the Word: Selected Writings, 1973-1987 (Walker), 1988
Living Fire (Fisk), 1987
Living in Imperial Rome (Dillon), 1974
Living in the Future (Asimov, editor), 1985
Living River (Asimov), 1959
Living Stage (Thiele), 1970
Living through History: The Edwardian Era (Trease), 1986
Living up the Street: Narrative Recollections (Soto), 1985
Livingstone's Companions (Gordimer), 1971
Lizard Music (Pinkwater), 1976
Llana of Gathol (Burroughs), 1948
Lo Chau of Hong Kong (Cavanna), 1963
Load of Unicorn (Harnett), 1959
Loads of Codes and Secret Ciphers (Janeczko), 1981
Local News (Soto), 1993
Lock and Key: The Secret of Locking Things Up, In, and Out (Tchudi), 1993
Locked in Time (Duncan), 1985
Log from the "Sea of Cortez": The Narrative Portion of the Book, "Sea of Cortez," (Steinbeck), 1951
Log Jam (M. Hughes), 1987
Loitering with Intent (Spark), 1981
London: A Concise History (Trease), 1975
London's Essays of Revolt (London), 1926
Lonely Hearts Club (R. Klein), 1987
Lonely Maria (Coatsworth), 1960
Loners (Garden), 1972
Lonesome Sorrel (Robertson), 1952
Long after Ecclesiates (Bradbury), 1985
Long after Midnight (Bradbury), 1976

Long Black Coat (Bennett), 1973
Long Claws: An Arctic Adventure (Houston), 1981
Long Day Wanes (Burgess), 1965
Long Dream (Wright), 1958
Long Journey Home: Stories from Black History (Lester), 1972
Long Live the Queen (E. White), 1989
Long Night (Mayne), 1957
Long Night Watch (Southall), 1983
Long Sleep (Koontz), 1975
Long Struggle: The Story of American Labor (Haskins), 1976
Long Time between Kisses (Scoppettone), 1982
Long Time Coming (Whitney), 1954
Long Tom and the Dead Hand (Crossley-Holland), 1992
Long Valley (Steinbeck), 1938
Long Voyage (Christopher), 1960
Long Walk (King), 1979
Long Way Down (R. White), 1977
Long Way from Home (Wartski), 1980
Long Way from Verona (Gardam), 1971
Look at Cars (Fisk), 1959
Look at Newspapers (Fisk), 1962
Look through My Window (Little), 1970
Look! What a Wonder! (Thomas), 1976
Looking at Poetry (Thiele, editor), 1960
Looking at the Moon (Pearson), 1991
Looking for Trouble (Marsden), 1993
Looking for Your Name (Janeczko, editor), 1993
Looking On (Miles), 1978
Lord Baden-Powell of the Boy Scouts (Fast), 1941
Lord Edgware Dies (Christie), 1933
Lord God Made Them All (Herriot), 1981
Lord of the Flies (Golding), 1954
Lord of the Rings trilogy (Tolkien), 1954-55
Lord of Thunder (Norton), 1962
Los Angeles (Bradbury), 1984
Losers and Winners (F. Miller), 1986
Losers in Space (Stine), 1991
Losers Weepers (Needle), 1981
Lost and Found: Four Stories (Garnett), 1974
Lost Boy (Fox), 1988
Lost Boys (Card), 1992
Lost Continent (Burgess), 1963
Lost Face (London), 1910
Lost Garden (Yep), 1990
Lost Island (Dillon), 1952
Lost on Venus (Burroughs), 1935
Lost Road and Other Writings: Language and Legend before The Lord of the Rings (Tolkien), 1987
Lost Star (Hoover), 1979
Lost World (A. Doyle), 1912
Lost Worlds of 2001 (Clarke), 1972
Lothian Run (M. Hunter), 1970
Lots and Lots of Candy (Meyer), 1976
Lottery Rose (Hunt), 1976
Lotus Caves (Christopher), 1969
Lou in the Limelight (K. Hunter), 1981
Loud, Resounding Sea (Bonham), 1963
Louis Armstrong: An American Success Story (Collier), 1985
Louisa M. Alcott's Proverb Stories (Alcott), 1868
Louisa May Alcott: Her Life, Letters and Journals (Alcott), 1889
Louisa May Alcott's Fairy Tales and Fantasy Stories (Alcott), 1992

Love Affair (Bradbury), 1983
Love All (Chambers, editor), 1988
Love and Mr. Lewisham: The Story of a Very Young Couple (H. Wells), 1900
Love and Society (Sinclair), 1922
Love Bombers (Miklowitz), 1980
Love by Any Other Name (Foley), 1983
Love, Death, and the Ladies' Drill Team (West), 1955
Love in Ambush (Willard), 1930
Love in Black and White: The Triumph of Love over Prejudice and Taboo (Mathabane), 1992
Love Is a Missing Person (Kerr), 1975
Love Is One of the Choices (N. Klein), 1978
Love Is the Crooked Thing (Wersba), 1987
Love, Laurie (Cavanna), 1953
Love Life: Stories (Mason), 1989
Love Me, Love Me Not (Whitney), 1952
Love of Life, and Other Stories (London), 1906
Love, or a Season (Stolz), 1964
Love Song for Joyce (Duncan), 1958
Love Space Demands: A Continuing Saga (Shange), 1991
Love Story, Take Three (Miklowitz), 1986
Love's Pilgrimage (Sinclair), 1911
Loveland (Swarthout), 1968
Loves Music, Loves to Dance (Clark), 1991
Loving Someone Else (Conford), 1991
Loving You, Loving Me (Chambers, editor), 1980
Low Tide (Mayne), 1993
Lucho of Peru (Cavanna), 1961
Lucie Babbidge's House (Cassedy), 1989
Lucifer Wilkins (Garfield), 1973
Luck and Pluck (Swarthout), 1973
Luck of Pokey Bloom (Conford), 1975
Luck of Texas McCoy (Meyer), 1984
Lucky Bag: Classic Irish Children's Stories (Dillon, editor), 1985
Lucky Breaks Loose (D. Hughes), 1990
Lucky Fights Back (D. Hughes), 1991
Lucky the Detective (D. Hughes), 1992
Lucky's Crash Landing (D. Hughes), 1990
Lucky's Gold Mine (D. Hughes), 1990
Lucky's Mud Festival (D. Hughes), 1991
Lucky's Tricks (D. Hughes), 1992
Lucy (Kincaid), 1990
Ludell (Wilkinson), 1975
Ludell and Willie (Wilkinson), 1976
Ludell's New York Time (Wilkinson), 1980
Luke and Angela (Nöstlinger), 1979
Lulu's Library (Alcott), 1886-89
Lump in the Middle (Adler), 1989
Lyddie (Paterson), 1991
Lydia (Fast), 1964
Lydia, Queen of Palestine (Orlev), 1993
Lying Days (Gordimer), 1953
Lyonnesse: Poems (Plath), 1971
Lythande (Bradley), 1986

Macaire (Stevenson), 1885
Machine-Gunners (Westall), 1975
Machineries of Joy (Bradbury), 1964
Machines That Think (Asimov, editor), 1984
MacLeod Place (Armstrong), 1972

Mad Detective (Lillington), 1992
Mad King (Burroughs), 1926
Mad Martin (Windsor), 1976
Mad Max: Beyond the Thunderdome (Vinge), 1985
Madam, Will You Talk? (Stewart), 1955
Madrigals for the Space Age (Bradbury), 1972
"Magic": A Biography of Earvin Johnson (Haskins), 1981
Magic and the Night River (Bunting), 1978
Magic at Wychwood (Watson), 1970
Magic Book (Roberts), 1986
Magic Bookshelf (Clapp), 1966
Magic Door (Fast), 1979
Magic Finger (Dahl), 1966
Magic Johnson Story (Haskins), 1988
Magic Kingdom for Sale—Sold (T. Brooks), 1986
Magic of the Glits (Adler), 1979
Magic of Xanth (Anthony), 1981
Magic Stone (Farmer), 1964
Magic's Pawn (Lackey), 1989
Magic's Price (Lackey), 1990
Magic's Promise (Lackey), 1990
Magical Adventures of Pretty Pearl (Hamilton), 1983
Magical Worlds of Fantasy (Asimov, editor), 1983-84
Magician (Baillie), 1953
Magician's Nephew (C. Lewis), 1955
Magicians of Caprona (D. Jones), 1980
Magnolia (Thomas), 1977
Magpie Island (Thiele), 1974
Mairelon the Magician (Wrede), 1991
Major Andre: Brave Enemy (Duncan), 1969
Make Lemonade (Wolff), 1993
Make Like a Tree and Leave (Danziger), 1990
Make Way for Sam Houston! (Fritz), 1986
Makers (Kelleher), 1986
Making Good (Serraillier), 1955
Making It Happen (Naylor), 1970
Making Movies: Student Films to Features (Colman), 1969
Making Music (Fisk), 1966
Making Music for Money (Collier), 1976
Making of a Moon: The Story of the Earth Satellite Program (Clarke), 1957
Making of Fingers Finnigan (Doherty), 1983
Making of Man: The Story of Our Ancient Ancestors (Collier), 1974
Making Sense: Animal Perception and Communication (B. Brooks), 1993
Making the Team (D. Hughes), 1990
Malaria Ross (Kamm), 1963
Malaya and Singapore (Kamm), 1963
Malayan Trilogy (Burgess), 1964
Malaysian Stories (Burgess, editor), 1969
Malcolm X (Adoff), 1970
Maldonado Miracle (T. Taylor), 1973
Male and Female under Eighteen: Frank Comments from Young People about Their Sex Roles Today (Merriam, editor), 1973
Mall (Cusick), 1992
Mama (McMillan), 1987
Mama, Let's Dance (Hermes), 1991
Mama's Going to Buy You a Mockingbird (Little), 1984
Mammonart: An Essay in Economic Interpretation (Sinclair), 1925
Mammoth Book of Classic Science Fiction: Short Novels of the 1930's (Asimov, editor), 1988

Michael, Brother of Jerry (London), 1917
Mickey the Mighty (Latham), 1937
Micky Darlin' (Kelleher), 1992
Microcosmic Tales: 100 Wondrous Science Fiction Short-Short Stories (Asimov, editor), 1980
Middle English Vocabulary (Tolkien), 1922
Middle Sister (Duncan), 1960
Midnight (Koontz), 1989
Midnight Fox (Byars), 1968
Midnight Hour Encores (B. Brooks), 1986
Midnight Is a Place (Aiken), 1974
Midnight Thief (Serraillier), 1963
Midnight Whispers (Andrews), 1992
Midshipman Lee (R. White), 1938
Midshipman Lee of the Naval Academy (R. White), 1954
Midsummer Magic (Dillon), 1950
Midsummer Night's Death (Peyton), 1978
Mikado (Lillington, reteller), 1988
Milk, Butter, and Cheese: The Story of Dairy Products (Meyer), 1974
Millennium: A Comedy of the Year 2000 (Sinclair), 1924
Miller's Boy (Willard), 1976
Millie (Fast), 1973
Millie Willenheimer and the Chestnut Corporation (D. Hughes), 1983
Millie's Boy (R.N. Peck), 1973
Million Dollar Month (Plath), 1971
Million-Miler: The Story of an Air Pilot (Tunis), 1942
Millions of Lisa (A. Jones), 1990
Mills of God (Armstrong), 1973
Mimosa Tree (V. and B. Cleaver), 1970
Mind and Body (Sinclair), 1921
Mind at the End of Its Tether (H. Wells), 1945
Mind at the End of Its Tether, and The Happy Turning (H. Wells), 1945
Mind of My Mind (Butler), 1977
Mindbenders (Fisk), 1987
Minden Curse (Roberts), 1978
Mindkiller (Robinson), 1982
Miniature Cathedral and Other Poems (Wangerin), 1986
Miniature Mysteries: 100 Malicious Little Mystery Stories (Asimov, editor), 1981
Minnipins (Kendall), 1960
Minpins (Dahl), 1991
Minstrel and the Dragon Pup (Sutcliff), 1993
Mirage (Fast), 1965
Miranda Going Home (Spence), 1985
Miriam's Well (Ruby), 1993
Mirror Crack'd from Side to Side (Christie), 1962
Mirror for the Sky (West), 1948
Mirror, Mirror (Garfield), 1976
Mirror of Her Own (Guy), 1981
Misadventures of John Nicholson: A Christmas Story (Stevenson), 1887
Misery (King), 1987
Mismatched Summer (Adler), 1991
Miss Amanda Snap (Greenwald), 1972
Miss Marple, the Complete Short Stories (Christie), 1985
Miss Marple's Final Cases, and Two Other Stories (Christie), 1979
Miss Patch's Learn-to-Sew Book (Meyer), 1969
Missing (Stine), 1990

Missing Angel Juan (Block), 1993
Missing Book-Keeper (Robertson), 1969
Missing Brother (Robertson), 1950
Missing from Home (Trease), 1936
Missing Gator of Gumbo Limbo: An Ecological Mystery (George), 1992
Missing in Manhattan (Clark), 1986
Missing May (Rylant), 1992
Missing Persons League (Bonham), 1975
Missing Pieces (Asher), 1984
Missing, Presumed Dead (Robertson), 1961
Mississippi Challenge (Walter), 1992
Mississippi Pilot (Twain), 1877
Mist over Athelney (Trease), 1958
Mister Corbett's Ghost, and Other Stories (Garfield), 1969
Mistress Malapert (Watson), 1955
Mistress Masham's Repose (T. White), 1946
Mists of Avalon (Bradley), 1983
Mixed-Marriage Daughter (Colman), 1968
Miz Lil and the Chronicles of Grace (Wangerin), 1988
Moccasin Trail (McGraw), 1952
Mock Revolt (V. and B. Cleaver), 1971
Model Village (Fisk), 1990
Modern Aladdin; or, The Wonderful Adventures of Oliver Munier (Pyle), 1892
Modern China (Carter), 1986
Modern Electronics (Carter), 1986
Modern Mephistopheles (Alcott), 1877
Modern Mephistopheles [and] A Whisper in the Dark (Alcott), 1889
Modern Russian and English Revolutionaries: A Frank Exchange of Ideas Between Commander Lev Uspensky, Soviet Writer, and H.G. Wells (H. Wells), 1942
Modern Utopia (H. Wells), 1905
Mojo and the Russians (Myers), 1977
Moksha: Writings on Psychedelics and the Visionary Experience 1931-1963 (Huxley), 1977
Mole and Beverley Miller (A. Jones), 1987
Mollie Make-Believe (Bach), 1974
Molly by Any Other Name (Okimoto), 1990
Mom, the Wolf Man and Me (N. Klein), 1972
Moment in History: The First Ten Years of the Peace Corps (Ashabranner), 1971
Mona Lisa Overdrive (Gibson), 1988
Monasteries and Monks (Harnett), 1963
Monday Voices (Greenberg), 1965
Money Creek Mare (Calvert), 1981
Money Machine (Robertson), 1969
Money Room (McGraw), 1981
Money Writes! (Sinclair), 1927
Moneychangers (Sinclair), 1908
Monitor and the Merrimack: Battle of the Ironclads (Carter), 1993
Monkey in the Middle (Bunting), 1984
Monkey Sonatas (Card), 1993
Monmouth: A Tragedy (Stevenson), 1928
Monster (Pike), 1992
Monster Garden (Alcock), 1988
Monster Maker (Fisk), 1979
Monster Men (Burroughs), 1929
Monsters (Asimov, editor), 1988
Monsters and the Critics and Other Essays (Tolkien), 1983

Mr. Corbett's Ghost (Garfield), 1968
Mr. Little (R.N. Peck), 1979
Mr. Monkey and the Gotcha Bird (Myers), 1984
Mr. Parker Pyne, Detective (Christie), 1934
Mr. Pride's Umbrella (Bunting), 1980
Mr. Pringle and the Prince (Phipson), 1979
Mr. Tucket (Paulsen), 1969
Mr. Whittier (Vining), 1974
Mrs. Darling's Daughter (Colman), 1962
Mrs. Fish, Ape, and Me, the Dump Queen (N. Mazer), 1980
Mrs. Frisby and the Rats of NIMH (O'Brien), 1971
Mrs. McGinty's Dead (Christie), 1952
Mrs. Portree's Pony (L. Hall), 1986
Much Ado about Aldo (Hurwitz), 1978
Mucker (Burroughs), 1921
Mudcake Princess (Clapp), 1979
Mudlarks (Harnett), 1941
Mukhtar's Children (Watson), 1968
Mulberry Music (Orgel), 1971
Mule Bone: A Comedy of Negro Life in Three Acts (Hurston), 1931
Mules and Men (Hurston), 1935
Mummies of Guanajuato (Bradbury), 1978
Mummy: Or Ramses the Damned (Rice), 1989
Murder à la Mode (Moyes), 1963
Murder After Hours (Christie), 1954
Murder at Dunsinane (Serraillier), 1967
Murder at Hazelmoor (Christie), 1931
Murder at the ABA: A Puzzle in Four Days and Sixty Scenes (Asimov), 1976
Murder at the Gallop (Christie), 1963
Murder at the Spaniel Show (L. Hall), 1988
Murder at the Vicarage (Christie), 1930
Murder by 3's (Moyes), 1965
Murder Fantastical (Moyes), 1967
Murder for Christmas (Christie), 1939
Murder in a Pig's Eye (L. Hall), 1990
Murder in Mesopotamia (Christie), 1936
Murder in Retrospect (Christie), 1942
Murder in the Calais Coach (Christie), 1934
Murder in the Dark: Short Fictions and Prose Poems (Atwood), 1983
Murder in the News, and Other Stories (Christie), 1937
Murder in Three Acts (Christie), 1934
Murder Is Announced (Christie), 1950
Murder Is Easy (Christie), 1939
Murder of Hound Dog Bates: A Novel (Branscum), 1982
Murder of Roger Ackroyd (Christie), 1926
Murder on Board (Christie), 1974
Murder on the Nile (Christie), 1948
Murder on the Aisle: The 1987 Mystery Writers of America Anthology (Clark, editor), 1987
Murder on the Links (Christie), 1923
Murder on the Menu (Asimov, editor), 1984
Murder on the Orient Express (Christie), 1934
Murder She Said (Christie), 1961
Murder with Mirrors (Christie), 1952
Murderer (Holman), 1978
Muscles! (Knudson), 1983
Music at Night and Other Essays (Huxley), 1931
Music of Summer (Guy), 1992

Music of What Happens: Poems That Tell Stories (Janeczko, editor), 1988
Mute (Anthony), 1981
Mutiny of the Elsinore (London), 1914
My Animals (Armstrong), 1973
My Black Me: A Beginning Book of Black Poetry (Adoff, editor), 1974
My Brother Is Special (Wartski), 1979
My Brother Michael (Stewart), 1960
My Brother Sam Is Dead (Collier), 1974
My Crooked Family (Collier), 1991
My Daniel (Conrad), 1989
My Darling, My Hamburger (Zindel), 1969
My Darling Villain (Reid Banks), 1977
My Debut as a Literary Person, with Other Essays and Stories (Twain), 1906
My Diary—My World (Yates), 1981
My Discovery of America (Mowat), 1985
My Dreams Ride High (Walden), 1963
My Enemy, My Ally (Duane), 1984
My Fabulous New Life (Greenwald), 1993
My Father's Son: Memories of War and Peace (Mowat), 1992
My Favorite Mystery [Suspense] Stories (Daly, editor), 1966-68
My Favorite Stories (Daly, editor), 1948
My Friend, My Love (Colman), 1983
My Friend the Murderer and Other Mysteries and Adventures (A. Doyle), 1893
My Friend's Got This Problem, Mr. Candler (Glenn), 1991
My Girl (Hermes), 1991
My Glorious Brothers (Fast), 1948
My House (Giovanni), 1972
My Life as a Body (N. Klein), 1987
My Lifetime in Letters (Sinclair), 1960
My Mate Shofiq (Needle), 1978
My Mother Is Not Married to My Father (Okimoto), 1979
My Name Is Asher Lev (Potok), 1972
My Name is Nobody (Wartski), 1988
My Name Is Not Angelica (O'Dell), 1989
My Name Is Paula Popowich! (M. Hughes), 1983
My Pretty Pony (King), 1989
My Proud Beauty (Lillington), 1963
My Side of the Mountain (George), 1959
My Sister Mike (Walden), 1956
My Sister Sif (Park), 1986
My Sister, the Vampire (Garden), 1992
My Son's Story (Gordimer), 1990
My Summer Vacation (Koertge), 1975
My Sweet Audrina (Andrews), 1982
My Sweet Untraceable You (Scoppettone), 1994
My Wicked, Wicked Ways (Cisneros), 1987
My Widening World (Yates), 1983
My World's the Stage (Walden), 1964
Mysteries and Adventures (A. Doyle), 1889
Mysterious Affair at Styles (Christie), 1920
Mysterious Disappearance of Leon (I Mean Noel) (Raskin), 1972
Mysterious Key, and What It Opened (Alcott), 1867
Mysterious Mr. Quin (Christie), 1930
Mysterious Mr. Ross (Alcock), 1987
Mysterious Stranger: A Romance (Twain), 1916
Mysterious World of Marcus Leadbeater (Southall), 1990
Mystery at Love's Creek (Cavanna), 1965

New Look at the Old Testament (Kamm), 1965
New Machiavelli (H. Wells), 1911
New Mexico (Hillerman), 1974
New Mexico, Rio Grande, and Other Essays (Hillerman), 1992
New Moon (Meigs), 1924
New Negro Poets: U.S (L. Hughes), 1964
New Neighbors for Nora (Hurwitz), 1979
New Pilgrims' Progress (Twain), 1870
New Poems and Variant Readings (Stevenson), 1918
New Revelation; or, What Is Spiritualism? (A. Doyle), 1918
New Rights of Man (H. Wells), 1942
New Russia: Eight Talks Broadcast, with H.R. Knickerbocker, Sir
    John Russell, Sir Bernard Pares, Margaret S. Miller, B. Mouat-
    Jones, Stafford Talbot, and Frank Owen (H. Wells), 1931
New Shoes for Sylvia (Hurwitz), 1993
New Song (L. Hughes), 1938
New Teaching of History, with a Reply to Some Recent Criticisms
    of "The Outline of History." (H. Wells), 1921
New Woman (Boissard), 1982
New Women of Wonder: Recent Science Fiction Stories by Women
    about Women (Sargent, editor), 1978
New World or No World (Herbert, editor), 1970
New World Order, Whether It Is Attainable, How It Can Be At-
    tained, and What Sort of World a World at Peace Will Have to Be
    (H. Wells), 1940
New Worlds for Old (H. Wells), 1908
New York (Burgess), 1976
Newfound (J. Miller), 1989
Newly Discovered Long Story "An Old Song" and a Previously
    Unpublished Short Story "Edifying Letters of the Rutherford
    Family," (Stevenson), 1982
Next America (Adoff, editor), 1953
Next Millennium (Asimov), 1990
Next-Door Neighbours (Ellis), 1989
Nicholas and the Woolpack (Harnett), 1953
Nicholas Factor (Myers), 1983
Night (Wiesel), 1960
Night Chills (Koontz), 1976
Night Cry (Naylor), 1984
Night, Dawn, [and] The Accident: Three Tales (Wiesel), 1972
Night Fall (Aiken), 1969
Night Ferry to Death (Moyes), 1985
Night Fires (Lingard), 1993
Night Gift (McKillip), 1976
Night Journey (Lasky), 1981
Night Journeys (Avi), 1979
Night Kites (Kerr), 1986
Night Mare (Anthony), 1983
Night of January 16th (Rand), 1936
Night of Masks (Norton), 1964
Night of Power (Robinson), 1985
Night of the Comet: A Comedy of Courtship Featuring Bostock
    and Harris (Garfield), 1979
Night of the Bozos (Slepian), 1983
Night of the Aurochs (Trumbo), 1979
Night of the Whale (Spinelli), 1985
Night Outside (Wrightson), 1979
Night School (Swindells), 1989
Night Shift (King), 1978
Night Swimmers (Byars), 1980
Night the White Deer Died (Paulsen), 1978

Night Tree (Bunting), 1991
Night's Daughter (Bradley), 1985
Night-Born... (London), 1913
Nightbirds on Nantucket (Aiken), 1966
Nightfall (Asimov), 1990
Nightfall and Other Stories (Asimov), 1969
Nightfall One and Nightfall Two (Asimov), 1969
Nightfall: Twenty SF Stories (Asimov), 1971
Nightjohn (Paulsen), 1993
Nightmare (Roberts), 1989
Nightmare Journey (Koontz), 1975
Nightmares and Dreamscapes (King), 1993
Nightmares in the Sky: Gargoyles and Grotesques (King), 1988
Nightpool (Murphy), 1985
NIK: Now I Know (Chambers), 1988
Nilda (Mohr), 1973
Nine and One-Half Mystics: The Kabbala Today (Wiesel), 1992
Nine Billion Names of God: The Best Short Stories of Arthur C.
    Clarke (Clarke), 1967
Nine Coaches Waiting (Stewart), 1958
Nine Radio Plays (Latham), 1940
Nine Stories (Salinger), 1953
Nine Tomorrows: Tales of the Near Future (Asimov), 1959
Niner (Johnson), 1994
1936...Peace? (Huxley), 1936
1984 (Orwell), 1949
1984: Spring: A Choice of Futures (Clarke), 1984
1985 (Burgess), 1978
Ninety-Nine Novels: The Best in English since 1939: A Personal
    Choice (Burgess), 1984
Nitty Gritty (Bonham), 1968
Nixon Poems (Merriam), 1970
No Applause, Please (Singer), 1977
No Beat of Drum (Burton), 1966
No Boats on Bannermere (Trease), 1949
No Easy Circle (Naylor), 1972
No Escape (Phipson), 1979
No Horn at Midnight (Trease), 1938
No Kidding (B. Brooks), 1989
No Laughing Matter (Heller), 1986
No Man's Land (R. White), 1969
No Mentor But Myself: A Collection of Articles, Essays, Re-
    views, and Letters on Writings and Writers (London), 1979
No Monsters in the Closet (Roberts), 1983
No More Saturday Nights (N. Klein), 1988
No Name in the Street (Baldwin), 1972
No Nap (Bunting), 1989
No Night Without Stars (Norton), 1975
No Pasoran! (They Shall Not Pass): A Story of the Battle of Madrid
    (Sinclair), 1937
No Place Like: Selected Stories (Gordimer), 1978
No Promises in the Wind (Hunt), 1970
No Reck'ning Made (Greenberg), 1993
No Strangers Here (Kamm), 1968
No Such Country: A Book of Antipodean Hours (G. Crew), 1991
No Such Things...? (Bunting), 1976
No-Return Trail (Levitin), 1978
Noah's Castle (J. Townsend), 1975
Nobel Lecture (Golding), 1984
Noble Gasses (Asimov), 1966
Nobody Else Can Walk It for You (Petersen), 1982

Rapunzel (Rogasky, reteller), 1982
Rascal: A Memoir of a Better Era (North), 1963
Rascals from Haskell's Gym (Bonham), 1977
Rated PG (Wolff), 1980
Rattle Bag: An Anthology of Poetry (T. Hughes, editor), 1982
Rattlesnakes (Freedman), 1984
Ravensgill (Mayne), 1970
Raw (Spiegelman), 1990
Raw—Number Three: High Culture for Low Brows (Spiegelman), 1991
Rawhide Knot and Other Stories (C. Richter), 1978
Ray Bradbury: Selected Stories (Bradbury), 1975
Ray Charles (Mathis), 1973
Re Joyce (Burgess), 1965
Re:Creation (Giovanni), 1970
Reach for a Star (Means), 1957
Reach for Tomorrow (Clarke), 1956
Read Yourself Raw: Comix Anthology for Damned Intellectuals (Spiegelman), 1987
Reading, Writing, Region: A Checklist and Purchase Guide for School and Community Libraries (J. Miller), 1984
Ready or Not (Stolz), 1953
Real Book about Franklin D. Roosevelt (Merriam), 1952
Real Estate Careers (Haskins), 1978
Real Live Dinosaur and other Stories (Lillington), 1990
Real Me (Miles), 1974
Real Plato Jones (Bawden), 1993
Real-Life Rape (Bode), 1990
Really Weird Summer (McGraw), 1977
Realm of Algebra (Asimov), 1961
Realm of Measure (Asimov), 1960
Realm of Numbers (Asimov), 1959
Reap the Whirlwind (Cherryh), 1989
Reap the Whirlwind (Lackey), 1989
Rear-View Mirrors (Fleischman), 1986
Reasonable Man's Peace (H. Wells), 1917
Rebel (Burton), 1971
Rebel on a Rock (Bawden), 1978
Rebel Spurs (Norton), 1962
Rebellion Town: Williamsburg, 1776 (T. Taylor), 1973
Rebels of the Heavenly Kingdom (Paterson), 1983
Rebirth (Cherryh), 1989
Rebuilding Coventry: A Tale of Two Cities (S. Townsend), 1988
Recollection Creek (Gipson), 1955
Reconstruction of the Fabian Society (H. Wells), 1906
Records of a Family of Engineers (Stevenson), 1912
Red Comet (Trease), 1936
Red Dog, Blue Fly: Football Poems (Mathis), 1991
Red Fox Running (Bunting), 1993
Red Hart Magic (Norton), 1976
Red Heels and Roses (Clapp), 1961
Red King (Kelleher), 1990
Red One (London), 1918
Red Planet (Heinlein), 1949
Red Pony (Steinbeck), 1937
Red Prophet (Card), 1988
Red Queen, White Queen (Treece), 1958
Red Room (H. Wells), 1896
Red Settlement (Treece), 1960
Red Shift (Garner), 1973
Red Towers of Granada (Trease), 1966

Red-Headed League (A. Doyle), 1989
Rediscovery (Bradley), 1993
Rediscovery: A Novel of Darkover (Lackey), 1993
Redwall (Jacques), 1987
Reefs of Taprobane: Underwater Adventures Around Ceylon (Clarke), 1957
Reflections in a Golden Eye (McCullers), 1941
Reflections of South Africa (Gordimer), 1986
Refuge (M. Hughes), 1989
Refuge (Vinge), 1993
Refugees (A. Doyle), 1893
Regatta Mystery, and Other Stories (Christie), 1939
Regiment (Mowat), 1955
Reindeer Slippers (Willard), 1970
Rejected of Men: A Story of To-day (Pyle), 1903
Relativity of Wrong: Essays on the Solar System and Beyond (Asimov), 1988
Religions (Haskins), 1971
Religions of the World (Haskins), 1991
Reliving the Passion: Meditations on the Suffering, Death, and Resurrection of Jesus as Recorded in Mark (Wangerin), 1992
Reluctant God (Service), 1988
Remarkable Andrew (Trumbo), 1941
Remarkable Journey of Prince Jen (Alexander), 1991
Remember Me (Pike), 1989
Remember Me to Harold Square (Danziger), 1987
Remember the Days: A Short History of the Jewish American (Meltzer), 1974
Remember Who You Are: Stories about Being Jewish (Hautzig), 1990
Remembered Death (Christie), 1945
Remembering the Good Times (R. Peck), 1985
Remove Protective Coating a Little at a Time (Donovan), 1973
Rendezvous with Rama (Clarke), 1973
Renegades of Pern (McCaffrey), 1989
Report on Planet Three and Other Speculations (Clarke), 1972
Report to the Principal's Office (Spinelli), 1991
Reportage, the San Francisco Quake: Two Accounts (London), 1968
Representing Super Doll (R. Peck), 1974
Rescue the Earth (Mowat), 1990
Rescue: The Story of How Gentiles Saved Jews in the Holocaust (Meltzer), 1988
Rescue! (Kelleher), 1985
Rescued Heart (Johnson), 1961
Research Magnificent (H. Wells), 1915
Resettling (Lingard), 1975
Reshaping Man's Heritage: Biology in the Service of Man (H. Wells), 1944
Resistance: Profiles in Nonviolence (Haskins), 1970
Rest of the Robots (Asimov), 1964
Restless Ghost: Three Stories by Leon Garfield (Garfield), 1969
Restoree (McCaffrey), 1967
Retold African Myths (Tate), 1992
Retreat to Glory: The Story of Sam Houston (Latham), 1965
Retrospect: An Omnibus of His Fiction and Non-Fiction Over Three Decades (Huxley), 1933
Return (Levitin), 1987
Return of Lanny Budd (Sinclair), 1953
Return of Robinson Crusoe (Treece), 1958
Return of Sherlock Holmes (A. Doyle), 1905
Return of Tarzan (Burroughs), 1915

Return of the King (Tolkien), 1955
Return of the Shadow: The History of The Lord of the Rings, Part 1 (Tolkien), 1988
Return to Bitter Creek (Smith), 1986
Return to Earth (Hoover), 1980
Return to Freedom (Kamm), 1962
Return to Oz (Vinge), 1985
Return to South Town (Graham), 1976
Return to the Ebro (Doherty), 1985
Reunion (Lingard), 1977
Revenge of the Incredible Dr. Rancid and His Youthful Assistant, Jeffrey (Conford), 1980
Revolt at Ratcliffe's Rags (Cross), 1980
Revolting Rhymes (Dahl), 1982
Revolution (London), 1909
Revolution! (Garfield), 1989
Revolution, and Other Essays (London), 1910
Revolution in the Congo (E. Cleaver), 1971
Revolution: Stories and Essays (London), 1979
Revolutionaries: Agents of Change (Haskins), 1971
Revolutionary Petunias and Other Poems (Walker), 1973
Rhyme Stew (Dahl), 1990
Rhymes about Ourselves (Chute), 1932
Rhymes about the City (Chute), 1946
Rhymes about the Country (Chute), 1941
Rhymes about Us (Chute), 1974
Rice without Rain (Ho), 1990
Rich and Famous Like My Mom (Colman), 1988
Rich and Famous: The Further Adventures of George Stable (Collier), 1975
Rich Uncle (Robertson), 1963
Richard Adams's Favorite Animal Stories (Adams, editor), 1981
Richard Wright Reader (Wright), 1978
Richleighs of Tantamount (Willard), 1966
Richthofen the Red Baron (Fisk), 1968
Riddle and the Rune (Chetwin), 1987
Riddle Book (Crossley-Holland, editor), 1982
Riddle in Red (Cavanna), 1948
Riddle of Stars (McKillip), 1979
Riddle-Master of Hed (McKillip), 1976
Ride a Dark Horse (L. Hall), 1987
Ride into Morning: The Story of Tempe Wick (Rinaldi), 1991
Ride Proud, Rebel! (Norton), 1961
Ride the Green Dragon (Norton), 1985
Ride to Danger (Treece), 1959
Ride When You're Ready (Bunting), 1974
Ride with Huey the Engineer (J. Miller, editor), 1988
Riders of the Storm (Burton), 1972
Ridin' the Moon in Texas: Word Paintings (Shange), 1987
Riding, Roping, and Bulldogging—Almost (Paulsen), 1977
Riff Remember (L. Hall), 1973
Rifles for Watie (Keith), 1957
Right to an Answer (Burgess), 1960
Right to Remain Silent (Meltzer), 1972
Right-Hand Man (Peyton), 1977
Righteous Revenge of Artemis Bonner (Myers), 1992
Rightful Owner (J. Miller, editor), 1989
Rights of Man; or, What Are We Fighting For? (H. Wells), 1940
Rim of the Morning: Six Stories (Thiele), 1966
Rimrunners (Cherryh), 1989
Rinehart Lifts (Knudson), 1980

Rinehart Shouts (Knudson), 1987
Ring (Anthony), 1968
Ring for the Sorcerer (Park), 1967
Ring of Death (Hoy), 1990
Ring of Endless Light (L'Engle), 1980
Ring of Fear (McCaffrey), 1971
Ring of Fire (Murphy), 1977
Ring Out, Bow Bells! (Harnett), 1953
Ring-Rise, Ring-Set (M. Hughes), 1982
Rings of Ice (Anthony), 1974
Rio Grande (Hillerman), 1975
Rio Grande Stories (Meyer), 1993
Rip-Roaring Russell (Hurwitz), 1983
Rising Sun (Crichton), 1992
Risk n' Roses (Slepian), 1990
Risking Love (Orgel), 1985
Rita Hayworth and Shawshank Redemption: A Story from "Different Seasons" (King), 1983
Rita the Weekend Rat (Levitin), 1971
Rites of Passage (Golding), 1980
Rites of Passage (Greenberg), 1971
River (Paulsen), 1991
River at Green Knowe (Boston), 1959
River at Her Feet (Sherburne), 1965
River Murray Mary (Thiele), 1979
River Rats, Inc (George), 1979
River Runners: A Tale of Hardship and Bravery (Houston), 1979
Riverman (Baillie), 1986
R.L.S. Teuila (Stevenson), 1899
R.L.S.: Stevenson's Letters to Charles Baxter (Stevenson), 1956
Road (London), 1907
Road Ahead (Lowry), 1988
Road Goes Ever On: A Song Cycle (Tolkien), 1967
Road of Dreams (Christie), 1925
Road to Camlann: The Death of King Arthur (Sutcliff), 1981
Road to Canterbury (Serraillier), 1979
Road to Christmas (Park), 1962
Road to Damietta (O'Dell), 1985
Road to Dunmore (Dillon), 1966
Road to Infinity (Asimov), 1979
Road to Memphis (M. Taylor), 1990
Road to Miklagard (Treece), 1957
Road to Nowhere (Pike), 1993
Road to Wigan Pier (Orwell), 1937
Road under the Sea (Park), 1962
Roadside Valentine (Adler), 1983
Roadwork: A Novel of the First Energy Crisis (King), 1981
Roald Dahl's Book of Ghost Stories (Dahl, editor), 1983
Roanoke: A Novel of the Lost Colony (Levitin), 1973
Rob's Place (J. Townsend), 1987
Robber Bride (Atwood), 1993
Robbers (Bawden), 1979
Robbie and the Leap Year Blues (N. Klein), 1981
Robert Louis Stevenson: Hitherto Unpublished Prose Writings (Stevenson), 1921
Robin and His Merry Men (Serraillier), 1969
Robin and the Wren (Serraillier), 1974
Robin in the Greenwood (Serraillier), 1967
Robinsheugh (Dunlop), 1975
Robinson (Spark), 1958
Robodad (Carter), 1990

Serpent's Reach (Cherryh), 1980
Serpent's Silver (Anthony), 1988
Serpent's Tooth (Swindells), 1988
Servants of Twilight (Koontz), 1988
Set Piece (Willard), 1938
Seth and Me and Rebel Make Three (Eyerly), 1983
Setting the Stage (Thiele), 1969
Settlement of the Trouble Between Mr. Thring and Mr. Wells: A Footnote to the Problem of the Troublesome Collaborator (H. Wells), 1930
Seven (McCullers), 1954
Seven Cardinal Virtues of Science Fiction (Asimov, editor), 1981
Seven Days to a Brand New Me (Conford), 1982
Seven Deadly Sins of Science Fiction (Asimov, editor), 1980
Seven Dials Mystery (Christie), 1929
Seven from the Stars (Bradley), 1962
Seven Good Years and Other Stories (Hautzig, translator and adapter), 1984
Seven Kings of England (Trease), 1955
Seven Queens of England (Trease), 1953
Seven Sovereign Queens (Trease), 1968
Seven Spells to Sunday (Norton), 1979
Seven Stages (Trease), 1964
Seven Stories (H. Wells), 1953
Seven Strange & Ghostly Tales (Jacques), 1991
Seven Towers (Wrede), 1984
Seven Treasure Hunts (Byars), 1991
Seventeen against the Dealer (Voigt), 1989
Seventeen Seconds (Southall), 1973
Seventeenth Summer (Daly), 1942
Seventeenth Swap (McGraw), 1986
Seventeenth-Street Gang (Neville), 1966
Seventh Pebble (Spence), 1980
Seventh Raven (Dickinson), 1981
Seventh Son (Card), 1987
Seventh Windmill Book of One-Act Plays (Lillington), 1972
Several Kinds of Silence (Singer), 1988
Sex Education (J. Davis), 1988
Sex Object (Koertge), 1979
Shabanu: Daughter of the Wind (Staples), 1989
Shade of the Tree (Anthony), 1986
Shades of Dark: Ghost Stories (Chambers, editor), 1984
Shadow (Phipson), 1989
Shadow and Act (Ellison), 1964
Shadow Guests (Aiken), 1980
Shadow Hawk (Norton), 1960
Shadow in the North (Pullman), 1988
Shadow in the Plate (Pullman), 1987
Shadow like a Leopard (Levoy), 1981
Shadow Lord (Yep), 1985
Shadow Magic (Wrede), 1982
Shadow Man (Grant), 1992
Shadow of a Bull (Wojciechowska), 1964
Shadow of a Star (Sherburne), 1959
Shadow of Spain, and Other Plays (Trease), 1953
Shadow of the Hawk (Trease), 1949
Shadow of the Red Moon (Myers), 1987
Shadow of Vesuvius (Dillon), 1977
Shadow on Devil's Peak (Walden), 1961
Shadow on the Hills (Thiele), 1977
Shadow over Wide Rain (Means), 1942

Shadow Shark (Thiele), 1988
Shadow under the Sea (Trease), 1990
Shadowfires (Koontz), 1987
Shadowmaker (Nixon), 1994
Shadows (L. Hall), 1977
Shadows in the Water (Lasky), 1992
Shadows Offstage (Bennett), 1974
Shadows on Little Reef Bay (Adler), 1985
Shadows on the Wall (Naylor), 1980
Shadrach's Crossing (Avi), 1983
Shake Up (D. Hughes), 1993
Shaker, Why Don't You Sing? (Angelou), 1983
Shakespeare (Burgess), 1970
Shakespeare and His Stage (Chute), 1953
Shakespeare in Harlem (L. Hughes), 1942
Shaky Island (Park), 1962
Shape of Things to Come: The Ultimate Revolution (H. Wells), 1933
Shape Shifters: Fantasy and Science Fiction Tales about Humans Who Can Change Their Shapes (Yolen, editor), 1978
Shaping of England (Asimov), 1969
Shaping of France (Asimov), 1972
Shaping of Middle-Earth: The Quenta, the Ambarkanta, and the Annals (Tolkien), 1986
Shaping of North America from Earliest Times to 1763 (Asimov), 1973
Shardik (Adams), 1974
Sharelle (Neufeld), 1983
Sharing Susan (Bunting), 1991
Shark beneath the Reef (George), 1989
Sharks (Freedman), 1985
Sharks in the Shadows (Thiele), 1988
Sharra's Exile (Bradley), 1981
Shatterbelt (Thiele), 1987
Shattered (Koontz), 1973
Shattered Chain (Bradley), 1976
She's My Girl! (Cavanna), 1949
Sheila's Dying (Carter), 1987
Shell Lady's Daughter (Adler), 1983
Shell Woman and the King (Yep, reteller), 1993
Shelter from the Wind (Bauer), 1976
Shelter on Blue Barns Road (Adler), 1981
Shepherd Moon: A Novel of the Future (Hoover), 1984
Shepherd Watches, a Shepherd Sings (T. Taylor), 1977
Sherlock Holmes (A. Doyle), 1899
Sherlock Holmes: A Definitive Text (A. Doyle), 1957
Sherlock Holmes Illustrated Omnibus (A. Doyle), 1978
Sherlock Holmes Letters (A. Doyle), 1986
Sherlock Holmes: Selected Stories (A. Doyle), 1951
Sherlock Holmes: The Published Apocrypha (A. Doyle), 1980
Sherlock Holmes Through Time and Space (Asimov, editor), 1984
Sherlock Holmes: Two Complete Adventures (A. Doyle), 1989
Shield Ring (Sutcliff), 1956
Shifting Sands (Sutcliff), 1977
Shiloh and Other Stories (Mason), 1982
Shine (Paton Walsh), 1988
Shining (King), 1977
Shining Company (Sutcliff), 1990
Ship to Rome (Trease), 1972
Ship Who Sang (McCaffrey), 1969
Ship Who Searched (McCaffrey), 1992

Some Year for Ellie (Rylant), 1986
Someday a Tree (Bunting), 1993
Someday I'll Laugh about This (L. Crew), 1990
Someday You'll Write (Yates), 1962
Someone Is Hiding on Alcatraz Island (Bunting), 1984
Someone to Love Me (Eyerly), 1987
Someone to Love (N. Mazer), 1983
Someone's Mother Is Missing (H. Mazer), 1990
Something beyond Paradise (Slepian), 1987
Something for Kitty Genovese (Scoppettone), 1971
Something Happened (Heller), 1974
Something in Common and Other Stories (L. Hughes), 1963
Something Left to Lose (Brancato), 1976
Something out of Nothing (Colman), 1968
Something Out There (Gordimer), 1984
Something to Do (Alcott), 1873
Something Upstairs: A Tale of Ghosts (Avi), 1988
Something Wicked This Way Comes (Bradbury), 1962
Something's Waiting for You, Baker D (Windsor), 1974
Something-Special Horse (L. Hall), 1985
Sometimes a Great Notion (Kesey), 1964
Sometimes I Don't Love My Mother (Colman), 1977
Sometimes I Think I Hear My Name (Avi), 1982
Somewhere a Master: Further Hasidic Portraits and Legends (Wiesel), 1982
Somewhere in the Darkness (Myers), 1992
Son of Charlemagne (Willard), 1959
Son of Someone Famous (Kerr), 1974
Son of Tarzan (Burroughs), 1917
Son of the Black Stallion (Farley), 1947
Son of the Sun (London), 1912
Son of the Valley (Tunis), 1949
Son of the Wolf: Tales of the Far North (London), 1900
Song for a Dark Queen (Sutcliff), 1978
Song for a Tattered Flag (Trease), 1992
Song in My Head and Other Poems (Holman), 1985
Song in the Sky (Thomas), 1976
Song of Sixpence (Asher), 1976
Song of Solomon (Morrison), 1977
Song of the Forest (Dillon), 1955
Song of the Gargoyle (Snyder), 1991
Song of Wirrun (Wrightson), 1987
Songmaster (Card), 1980
Songs for the Philologists (Tolkien), 1936
Songs of Action (A. Doyle), 1898
Songs of Distant Earth (Clarke), 1986
Songs of Muad'Dib: The Poetry of Frank Herbert (Herbert), 1992
Songs of Our Nation (Sinclair), 1941
Songs of the Dream People: Chants and Images from the Indians and Eskimos of North America (Houston, editor), 1972
Songs of the Road (A. Doyle), 1911
Songs of Travel and Other Verses (Stevenson), 1896
Sons from Afar (Voigt), 1987
Sorceress and the Cygnet (McKillip), 1991
Sorcery and Cecelia (Wrede), 1988
Sos the Rope (Anthony), 1968
Soul Brothers and Sister Lou (K. Hunter), 1968
Soul Catcher (Herbert), 1972
Soul of a Bishop: A Novel—With Just a Little Love in It—About Conscience and Religion and the Real Troubles of Life (H. Wells), 1917

Soul of the City (Cherryh), 1986
Soul of the Silver Dog (L. Hall), 1992
Soul on Fire (E. Cleaver), 1978
Soul on Ice (E. Cleaver), 1968
Souls on Fire: Portraits and Legends of Hasidic Masters (Wiesel), 1972
Soulscript: Afro-American Poetry (Jordan, editor), 1970
Soumchi (Farmer, translator), 1980
Sound of Chariots (M. Hunter), 1972
Sound of Coaches (Garfield), 1974
Sound of Strings (Keith), 1992
Sound to Remember (Levitin), 1979
Sounder (Armstrong), 1969
Soup (R.N. Peck), 1974
Soup and Me (R.N. Peck), 1975
Soup for President (R.N. Peck), 1978
Soup in Love (R.N. Peck), 1992
Soup in the Saddle (R.N. Peck), 1983
Soup on Fire (R.N. Peck), 1987
Soup on Ice (R.N. Peck), 1985
Soup on Wheels (R.N. Peck), 1981
Soup's Drum (R.N. Peck), 1980
Soup's Goat (R.N. Peck), 1984
Soup's Hoop (R.N. Peck), 1990
Soup's Uncle (R.N. Peck), 1988
Sour Land (Armstrong), 1971
Source of Magic (Anthony), 1979
South African Writing Today (Gordimer, editor), 1967
South Moon Under (Rawlings), 1933
South of the Angels (West), 1960
South Sea Tales (London), 1911
South Town (Graham), 1958
Southern Mountain Speech (J. Miller, editor), 1992
Soviet Science Fiction (Asimov, editor), 1962
Space Cadet (Heinlein), 1948
Space Challenge: The Story of Guion Bluford, an Authorized Biography (Haskins), 1984
Space Cops: High Moon (Duane), 1992
Space Cops: Kill Station (Duane), 1992
Space Cops: Mindblast (Duane), 1991
Space Demons (Rubinstein), 1986
Space Dictionary (Asimov), 1970
Space Dictionary (Asimov), 1971
Space Dreamers (Clarke), 1969
Space Family Stone (Heinlein), 1969
Space Hostages (Fisk), 1967
Space Mail 1 (Asimov, editor), 1980
Space Mail 2 (Asimov, editor), 1982
Space Station Seventh Grade (Spinelli), 1982
Space Trap (M. Hughes), 1983
Spaceburger (Pinkwater), 1993
Spaceships and Spells (Yolen, editor), 1987
Spain and Peace (Fast), 1952
Spanish Hoof (R.N. Peck), 1985
Spanish Letters (M. Hunter), 1964
Spanish Roundabout (Daly), 1960
Spanish Smile (O'Dell), 1982
Spanish-American War: Imperial Ambitions (Carter), 1992
Sparkles for Bright Eyes (Alcott), 1879
Sparkling Cyanide (Christie), 1945
Spartacus (Fast), 1951

Speaker for the Dead (Card), 1986

Specially Wonderful Day (Clapp), 1972

Speckled Band: An Adventure of Sherlock Holmes (A. Doyle), 1912

Spectre (Nixon), 1982

Speculations (Asimov, editor), 1982

Speeches for Doctor Frankenstein (Atwood), 1966

Speed (Knudson), 1983

Speedway Contender (Bonham), 1964

Spell for Chameleon (Anthony), 1977

Spell Is Cast (Cameron), 1964

Spell Me a Witch (Willard), 1979

Spell #7: A Geechee Quick Magic Trance Manual (Shange), 1979

Spell of New Mexico (Hillerman, editor), 1976

Spell Sword (Bradley), 1974

Spellbound (Pike), 1989

Spellcoats (D. Jones), 1979

Spellhorn (Doherty), 1989

Spence + Lila (Mason), 1988

Sphere (Crichton), 1987

Spice Island Mystery (Cavanna), 1969

Spider's Web (Christie), 1957

Spinning-Wheel Stories (Alcott), 1884

Spiral Stair (Aiken), 1979

Spire (Golding), 1964

Spirit House (Sleator), 1991

Spirit River (M. Hughes), 1988

Spiritualism and Rationalism (A. Doyle), 1920

Spiritualism: Some Straight Questions and Direct Answers (A. Doyle), 1922

Spirtualist's Reader (Doyle, editor), 1924

Spitball Gang (Paulsen), 1980

Splintered Sword (Treece), 1965

Split Infinity (Anthony), 1980

Split Sisters (Adler), 1986

Spock's World (Duane), 1988

Spokesman's Secretary, Being the Letters of Mame to Mom (Sinclair), 1926

Spook Birds (Bunting), 1981

Sport for the Fun of It (Tunis), 1940

Sport of Nature (Gordimer), 1987

Sporting Blood: Selections From Jack London's Greatest Sports Writing (London), 1981

Sporting Chance: Stories of Winning and Losing (Chambers, editor), 1985

Sports and Games (Keith), 1941

Sports Great Magic Johnson (Haskins), 1989

$port$, Heroics, and Hysterics (Tunis), 1928

Sports Poetry (Knudson), 1971

Spreading Fires (Knowles), 1974

Sprig of Broom (Willard), 1971

Spring Begins in March (Little), 1966

Spring Comes Riding (Cavanna), 1950

Spring Comes to the Ocean (George), 1966

Spring Harvest (Tolkien, editor), 1918

Spring, Summer, Autumn, Winter (T. Hughes), 1974

Spring-Heeled Jack (Pullman), 1989

Springboard to Summer (Bunting), 1975

Springtime and Harvest: A Romance (Sinclair), 1901

Spud Tackett and the Angel of Doom (Branscum), 1983

Spunk: The Selected Stories of Zora Neale Hurston (Hurston), 1985

Spurs for Suzanna (Cavanna), 1947

Spy (Sinclair), 1919

Spy Called Michel-E (Walden), 1967

Spy Catchers (Trease), 1976

Spy on Danger Island (Walden), 1965

Spy Who Loved Me (Fleming), 1962

Spy Who Talked Too Much (Walden), 1968

Spy with Five Faces (Walden), 1966

Spycase Built for Two (Walden), 1969

Square Root of Wonderful (McCullers), 1958

Squib (Bawden), 1971

St. Francis of Assisi (Bawden), 1983

St. Ives; Being the Adventures of a French Prisoner in England (Stevenson), 1897

St. Patrick's Day in the Morning (Bunting), 1980

Stable of Fear (Bunting), 1974

Stakes Are High (Ashabranner, editor), 1954

Stalin-Wells Talk: The Verbatim Record, and A Discussion (H. Wells), 1934

Stalker (Nixon), 1985

Stalkers: All New Tales of Terror and Suspense (Koontz), 1989

Stamp Twice for Murder (Cavanna), 1981

Stand (King), 1978

Stand Down (E. White), 1992

Stand to Horse (Norton), 1956

Standing Tall, Looking Good (Miklowitz), 1991

Star (H. Wells), 1913

Star Baby (Nixon), 1989

Star Beast (Heinlein), 1954

Star Begotten: A Biological Fantasia (H. Wells), 1937

Star Born (Norton), 1957

Star Crusade (Cherryh, translator), 1980

Star Fisher (Yep), 1991

Star for Ginny (Whitney), 1942

Star for the Latecomer (Zindel), 1980

Star Gate (Norton), 1958

Star Guard (Norton), 1955

Star Invaders (King), 1964

Star Ka'at (Norton), 1976

Star Ka'at World (Norton), 1978

Star Ka'ats and the Plant People (Norton), 1979

Star Ka'ats and the Winged Warriors (Norton), 1981

Star Lord (Lawrence), 1978

Star Man's Son, 2250 A.D. (Norton), 1952

Star of Danger (Bradley), 1965

Star Over Bethlehem, and Other Stories (Christie), 1965

Star Quest (Koontz), 1968

Star Rangers (Norton), 1953

Star Rover (London), 1915,

Star Trek II: The Wrath of Khan (McIntyre), 1982

Star Trek III: The Search for Spock (McIntyre), 1984

Star Trek IV: The Voyage Home (McIntyre), 1986

Starblood (Koontz), 1972

Starbodies (Knudson), 1978

Stardance (Robinson), 1979

Stardust Otel (Janeczko), 1993

Starfarers (McIntyre), 1989

Stark Munro Letters (A. Doyle), 1895

Stark Naked: A Paranomastic Odyssey (Juster), 1969

Starman Jones (Heinlein), 1953

Starring Sally J. Freedman As Herself (Blume), 1977

Stranger at Green Knowe (Boston), 1961
Stranger Came Ashore: A Story of Suspense (M. Hunter), 1975
Stranger in the House (Sherburne), 1963
Stranger Is Watching (Clark), 1978
Stranger with My Face (Duncan), 1981
Stranger, You and I (Calvert), 1987
Strangers (Koontz), 1986
Strangers in Africa (Ashabranner), 1963
Strangers in the House (Lingard), 1981
Streams to the River, River to the Sea: A Novel of Sacagawea (O'Dell), 1986
Street (Aiken), 1978
Street Gangs: Yesterday and Today (Haskins), 1974
Strength and Health (Sinclair), 1910
Strength of the Strong (London), 1911
Strictly for Laughs (Conford), 1985
Strike Deep (Koontz), 1974
String of Chances (Naylor), 1982
Strings: A Gathering of Family Poems (Janeczko, compiler), 1984
Stringybark Summer (O'Neill), 1985
Striped Ships (McGraw), 1991
Stroke of Luck (D. Hughes), 1991
Stronghold (M. Hunter), 1974
Stuck (Scoppettone), 1972
Student Almoner (Kamm), 1955
Study in Scarlet (A. Doyle), 1888
Sub (Petersen), 1993
Subatomic Monster: Essays on Science (Asimov), 1985
Subnuclear Zoo: New Discoveries in High Energy Physics (Engdahl), 1977
Successful Treatment of Stuttering (Irwin), 1980
Such Divinity (Trease), 1939
Such Nice Kids (Bunting), 1990
Such Nice People (Scoppettone), 1980
Such, Such Were the Joys (Orwell), 1953
Sudden Fame (Colman), 1966
Sudden Silence (Bunting), 1988
Sudden Star (Sargent), 1979
Sudden Wild Magic (D. Jones), 1992
Suddenly (Colman), 1987
Suddenly Gang (Willard), 1963
Suddenly Super Rich (Miklowitz), 1989
Sugar Blue (V. and B. Cleaver), 1984
Sugar Isn't Everything (Roberts), 1987
Sugar Ray Leonard (Haskins), 1982
Sugar-Gum Tree (Wrightson), 1991
Sula (Morrison), 1973
Summer after the Funeral (Gardam), 1973
Summer Before (Windsor), 1973
Summer Begins (Asher), 1980
Summer Birds (Farmer), 1962
Summer Girls, Love Boys, and Other Short Stories (N. Mazer), 1982
Summer Home (Grant), 1981
Summer I Learned about Life (Meyer), 1983
Summer in Between (Spence), 1959
Summer Life (Soto), 1990
Summer of Fear (Duncan), 1976
Summer of My German Soldier (Greene), 1973
Summer of the Falcon (George), 1962
Summer of the Swans (Byars), 1970

Summer People (J. Townsend), 1972
Summer Queen (Vinge), 1991
Summer Rules (Lipsyte), 1981
Summer Season (Willard), 1981
Summer Smith Begins (Asher), 1986
Summer to Die (Lowry), 1977
Summer Visitors (Mayne), 1961
Summer Wheels (Bunting), 1992
Summer with Spike (Willard), 1961
Summerboy (Lipsyte), 1982
Summering (Greenberg), 1966
Summer's End (Savitz), 1984
Summer's Lease (Sachs), 1979
Summoned to Tourney (Lackey), 1992
Sun (Asimov), 1972
Sun Goes Free (Serraillier), 1977
Sun Horse, Moon Horse (Sutcliff), 1977
Sun, Moon, Star (Vonnegut), 1980
Sun on the Stubble (Thiele), 1961
Sun Shines Bright (Asimov), 1981
Sunburn (Stine), 1993
Sunday Father (Neufeld), 1975
Sunday, Sunday (Asher), 1981
Sunfall (Cherryh, editor), 1981
Sunken Sailor (Moyes), 1961
Sunningdale Mystery (Christie), 1933
Sunnycove (Walden), 1948
Supercomputers (Carter), 1985
Superduper Teddy (Hurwitz), 1980
Superfudge (Blume), 1980
Supergirl (N. Mazer), 1984
Superluminal (McIntyre), 1983
Supernatural Tales of Sir Arthur Conan Doyle (A. Doyle), 1988
Superstar Team (D. Hughes), 1991
Support Your Local Wizard (Duane), 1990
Suppose You Met a Witch (Serraillier), 1973
Supreme Prize and Other Poems (Trease), 1926
Surfacing (Atwood), 1972
Surfer and the City Girl (Cavanna), 1981
Surfing Country (Bunting), 1974
Surprise Island (Willard), 1966
Surprise Party (Stine), 1990
Surprise! Surprise!: A Collection of Mystery Stories with Unexpected Endings (Christie), 1965
Surrender (R. White), 1966
Surrogate Sister (Bunting), 1984
Surrounded (Koontz), 1974
Survey Ship (Bradley), 1980
Survival: A Thematic Guide to Canadian Literature (Atwood), 1972
Survivor (Butler), 1978
Survivor (R. White), 1964
Survivors (Bradley), 1979
Susan Cornish (Caudill), 1955
Susanna Siegelbaum Gives up Guys (Foley), 1991
Sussex (Willard), 1965
Susy's Scoundrel (Keith), 1974
Swag of Stories: Australian Stories (Garfield, editor), 1977
Swallows (Mayne), 1972
Swarm in May (Mayne), 1955
Sweat and the Gold (Savitz), 1984
Sweeney's Adventure (Krumgold), 1942

Sweet and Sour: Tales from China (Kendall), 1978
Sweet as a Pickle and Clean as a Pig (McCullers), 1964
Sweet Bells Jangled out of Tune (Brancato), 1980
Sweet Flypaper of Life (L. Hughes), 1955
Sweet Friday Island (T. Taylor), 1984
Sweet Illusions (Myers), 1987
Sweet Thursday (Steinbeck), 1954
Sweet Whispers, Brother Rush (Hamilton), 1982
Sweetly Sings the Donkey (V. and B. Cleaver), 1985
Sweets from a Stranger and Other Science Fiction Stories (Fisk), 1982
Sweetwater (Yep), 1973
Swift Rivers (Meigs), 1932
Swiftly Tilting Planet (L'Engle), 1978
Swimmer (Savitz), 1986
Swing in the Summerhouse (Langton), 1967
Switch on the Night (Bradbury), 1955
Switcharound (Lowry), 1985
Switching Tracks (D. Hughes), 1982
Switherby Pilgrims (Spence), 1967
Sword and the Circle: King Arthur and the Knights of the Round Table (Sutcliff), 1981
Sword in Sheath (Norton), 1949
Sword in the Stone (T. White), 1938
Sword Is Drawn (Norton), 1944
Sword of Aldones (Bradley), 1962
Sword of Shannara (T. Brooks), 1977
Sword of the Spirits (Christopher), 1972
Sword of the Spirits Trilogy (Christopher), 1980
Sword of the Wilderness (Coatsworth), 1936
Swords from the North (Treece), 1967
Swords of Mars (Burroughs), 1936
Sycamore Year (M. Lee), 1974
Sylvia (Fast), 1960
Sylvia (Sinclair), 1913
Sylvia Game (Alcock), 1982
Sylvia Plath's Selected Poems (Plath), 1985
Sylvia's Marriage (Sinclair), 1914
Symposium (Spark), 1990
Synthetic Men of Mars (Burroughs), 1940

Tacey Cromwell (C. Richter), 1942
Tackling, Running, and Kicking—Now and Again (Paulsen), 1977
Take a Call, Topsy! (Cavanna), 1947
Take a Chance, Gramps! (Okimoto), 1990
Take Care of My Girl (Hermes), 1992
Take My Word for It (Marsden), 1992
Taken at the Flood (Christie), 1948
Taken Girl (Vining), 1972
Takeover (Spark), 1976
Taking Care of Terrific (Lowry), 1983
Taking Root: Jewish Immigrants in America (Meltzer), 1974
Taking Sides (N. Klein), 1974
Taking Sides (Soto), 1991
Taking Terri Mueller (N. Mazer), 1981
Taking the Ferry Home (Conrad), 1988
Tale of a One-Way Street and Other Stories (Aiken), 1978
Tale of Sunlight (Soto), 1978
Tale of Taliesin (Crossley-Holland), 1992
Tale of Tawny and Dingo (Armstrong), 1979
Tale of the Body Thief (Rice), 1992

Tale of the Monster Horse (Serraillier), 1950
Tale of Three Landlubbers (Serraillier), 1970
Tale of Time City (D. Jones), 1987
Tale of Two Cities (Kamm, editor), 1973
Talent Is Not Enough: Mollie Hunter on Writing for Children (M. Hunter), 1976
Tales and Essays (Stevenson), 1950
Tales and Fantasies (Stevenson), 1905
Tales for a Winter's Night (A. Doyle), 1989
Tales from Europe (Crossley-Holland), 1991
Tales from Planet Earth (Clarke), 1989
Tales from the House Behind: Fables, Personal Reminiscences, and Short Stories (Frank), 1962
Tales from the Jungle Book (McKinley, adapter), 1985
Tales from the Mabinogion (Crossley-Holland), 1984
Tales from the White Hart (Clarke), 1957
Tales of a Dead King (Myers), 1983
Tales of a Fourth Grade Nothing (Blume), 1972
Tales of Adventure and Medical Life (A. Doyle), 1922
Tales of Alvin Maker series (Card), from 1987
Tales of Long Ago (A. Doyle), 1922
Tales of Myrtle the Turtle (Robertson), 1974
Tales of Space and Time (H. Wells), 1899
Tales of St. Columba (Dunlop), 1992
Tales of Ten Worlds (Clarke), 1962
Tales of Terror and Mystery (A. Doyle), 1922
Tales of the Black Widowers (Asimov), 1974
Tales of the Early World (T. Hughes), 1988
Tales of the Fish Patrol (London), 1905
Tales of the Gauchos (Coatsworth, editor), 1946
Tales of the Occult (Asimov, editor), 1989
Tales of the Ring and Camp (A. Doyle), 1922
Tales of the Unexpected [of Life and Adventure, of Wonder] (H. Wells), 1922-23
Tales of Three Planets (Burroughs), 1964
Tales of Uncle Remus: The Adventures of Brer Rabbit (Lester, reteller), 1987
Tales out of School: A Survey of Children's Fiction (Trease), 1949
Talisman (King), 1984
Talismans for Children (Atwood), 1965
Talismans of Shannara (T. Brooks), 1993
Talk: Conversations with William Golding (Golding), 1970
Talking Car (Fisk), 1988
Talking Earth (George), 1983
Talking God (Hillerman), 1989
Talking Mysteries: A Conversation with Tony Hillerman (Hillerman), 1991
Talking to Dragons (Wrede), 1985
Tall Hunter (Fast), 1942
Tamarack Tree (Clapp), 1986
Tambourines to Glory (L. Hughes), 1958
Taming the Star Runner (Hinton), 1988
Tanar of Pellucidar (Burroughs), 1930
Tangle Box (T. Brooks), 1994
Tangle Garden (Vining), 1928
Tangled Butterfly (Bauer), 1980
Tangled Waters (Means), 1935
Tangled Webb (McGraw), 1993
Tantalizing Locked Room Mysteries (Asimov, editor), 1982
Tar Baby (Morrison), 1981
Tara Finds the Door to Happiness (Means), 1926

Taran Wanderer (Alexander), 1967
Taronga (Kelleher), 1986
Tarot (Anthony), 1987
Tarzan and the Ant Men (Burroughs), 1924
Tarzan and the Castaways (Burroughs), 1964
Tarzan and the City of Gold (Burroughs), 1933
Tarzan and the Forbidden City (Burroughs), 1938
Tarzan and the Foreign Legion (Burroughs), 1947
Tarzan and the Golden Lion (Burroughs), 1923
Tarzan and the Jewels of Opar (Burroughs), 1918
Tarzan and the Leopard Men (Burroughs), 1935
Tarzan and the Lion-Men (Burroughs), 1934
Tarzan and the Lost Empire (Burroughs), 1929
Tarzan and the Madman (Burroughs), 1964
Tarzan and the Tarzan Twins, with Jad-Bal-Ja, the Golden Lion
     (Burroughs), 1936
Tarzan at the Earth's Core (Burroughs), 1930
Tarzan, Lord of the Jungle (Burroughs), 1928
Tarzan of the Apes (Burroughs), 1914
Tarzan the Invincible (Burroughs), 1931
Tarzan the Magnificent (Burroughs), 1939
Tarzan the Terrible (Burroughs), 1921
Tarzan the Triumphant (Burroughs), 1931
Tarzan the Untamed (Burroughs), 1920
Tarzan Twins (Burroughs), 1927
Tarzan's Quest (Burroughs), 1936
Taste of Blackberries (Smith), 1973
Taste of Freedom: Three Stories from Black History (Lester), 1983
Taste of Sangria (Robertson), 1968
Taste of Smoke (Bauer), 1993
Tattooed Potato and Other Clues (Raskin), 1975
Tavi of the South Seas (Cavanna), 1965
T-Backs, T-Shirts, COAT and Suit (Konigsburg), 1993
Tea with the Black Dragon (MacAvoy), 1983
Teacher's Guide: Science Fiction (Bradbury), 1968
Teacher's Pet (Cusick), 1990
Teacher's Pet (Hurwitz), 1988
Teacup Full of Roses (Mathis), 1972
Team (Peyton), 1975
Technology and the Frontiers of Knowledge (Clarke), 1973
Teddy Bear Habit
Teddy Teabury's Fabulous Fact (Asher), 1985
Teddy Teabury's Peanutty Problems (Asher), 1987
Teen-Age Alcoholism (Haskins), 1976
Teenagers Who Made History (Freedman), 1961
Teeth of the Gale (Aiken), 1988
Teetoncey (T. Taylor), 1974
Teetoncey and Ben O'Neal (T. Taylor), 1975
Tehanu: The Last Book of Earthsea (Le Guin), 1990
Telempath (Robinson), 1976
Tell Me How Long the Train's Been Gone (Baldwin), 1968
Tell Me If the Lovers Are Losers (Voigt), 1982
Tell Me No Lies (Colman), 1978
Tell My Horse (Hurston), 1938
Telling the World (Sinclair), 1939
Telly Is Watching You (Fisk), 1989
Temple of My Familiar (Walker), 1989
Ten Little Indians (Christie), 1965
Ten Little Niggers (Christie), 1939
Ten Mile Treasure (Norton), 1981
Ten Thousand Desert Swords (Ashabranner), 1960

Ten Tiny Fingers, Nine Tiny Toes (S. Townsend), 1991
Ten-Cent Island (Park), 1968
Tenth [and Eleventh] Ghost Book (Chambers, editor), 1975-76
Teresita of the Valley (Means), 1943
Term Paper (Rinaldi), 1980
Terminal Man (Crichton), 1972
Terrible Churnadryne (Cameron), 1959
Terrible Fisk Machine (D. Jones), 1970
Terrible Things (Bunting), 1980
Territorial Rights (Spark), 1979
Terror in Russia?: Two Views (Sinclair), 1938
Terrorists (Meltzer), 1983
Terry on the Fence (Ashley), 1975
Testament (Wiesel), 1981
Tex (Hinton), 1979
Text and Pretexts: An Anthology with Commentaries (Huxley, edi-
     tor), 1932
Text-Book of Biology (H. Wells), 1892-1893
Textbook of Americanism (Rand), 1946
T.H. Huxley as a Man of Letters (Huxley), 1932
Thaddeus Stevens and the Fight for Negro Rights (Meltzer), 1967
Thank You, Dr. Martin Luther King, Jr! (Tate), 1990
Thanksgiving for All (Latham), 1932
Thanksgiving Programs for the Lower Grades (Latham), 1937
That Ghost, That Bride of Time: Excerpts from a Play-in-Progress
     (Bradbury), 1976
That Girl Andy (Means), 1962
That Julia Redfern (Cameron), 1982
That Son of Richard III: A Birth Announcement (Bradbury), 1974
That Was Then, This Is Now (Hinton), 1971
That's My Baby (N. Klein), 1988
That's the Way It Is, Amigo (Colman), 1975
Theft: A Play in Four Acts (London), 1910
Their Blood Is Strong (Steinbeck), 1938
Their Eyes Were Watching God (Hurston), 1937
Theirs Be the Guilt: A Novel of the War between the States (Sinclair),
     1959
Them That Glitter and Them That Don't (Greene), 1983
Themes and Variations (Huxley), 1950
Then Again, Maybe I Won't (Blume), 1971
Then Is All Love? It Is, It Is! (Bradbury), 1981
Thendara House (Bradley), 1983
Theo Zephyr (D. Hughes), 1987
There Is a Tide (Christie), 1948
There's a Bat in Bunk Five (Danziger), 1980
There's a Girl in My Hammerlock (Spinelli), 1991
There's Always Danny (Ure), 1988
There's an End of May (Lillington), 1975
There's No Escape (Serraillier), 1950
There's Something on the Roof! (Fisk), 1966
Therese of Lisieux (Furlong), 1987
They Call Me Carpenter: A Tale of the Second Coming (Sinclair),
     1922
They Came to Baghdad (Christie), 1951
They Do It with Mirrors (Christie), 1952
They Do Things Differently There (Mark), 1985
They Lived with the Dinosaurs (Freedman), 1980
They Never Came Home (Duncan), 1969
They Served the People (Kamm), 1954
They Walk in the Night (Coatsworth), 1969
They Wrote in English (Burgess), 1988

2061: Odyssey Three (Clarke), 1988
2010: Odyssey Two (Clarke), 1982
Two Thousand Years of Space Travel (Freedman), 1963
Two to Conquer (Bradley), 1980
Two Towers (Tolkien), 1954
Two Truths in My Pocket (Ruby), 1982
Two Valleys (Fast), 1933
Two Weirdos and a Ghost (Windsor), 1991
Two's Company (Cavanna), 1951
Two-Fisted Painters Action Adventure (Spiegelman), 1980
Two-Headed Poems (Atwood), 1978
Tyger Voyage (Adams), 1976
Tyler, Wilkin, and Skee (Burch), 1963
Tyrannosaurus Prescription and One Hundred Other Essays
    (Asimov), 1989

Ugliest Boy (Branscum), 1978
Ugly Little Boy (Asimov), 1992
Ugly Little Boy/The Widget, the Wadget, and Boff (Asimov), 1989
Unabridged Jack London (London), 1981
Unaccompanied Sonata and Other Stories (Card), 1981
Unbroken Web (Adams), 1980
Uncharted Stars (Norton), 1969
Uncle Bernac: A Memory of Empire (A. Doyle), 1897
Uncle Daniel and the Raccoon (K. Hunter), 1972
Uncle Gustav's Ghosts (Thiele), 1974
Uncle in the Attic (Needle), 1987
Uncle Matt's Mountain (Park), 1962
Uncle Tom's Children: Four Novellas (Wright), 1938
Uncle Tom's Children: Five Long Stories (Wright), 1940
Uncle Vampire (Grant), 1993
Uncollected Poems (Plath), 1965
Uncollected Stars (Anthony, editor), 1986
Uncollected Stories (A. Doyle), 1982
Unconquered (Rand), 1940
Under Alien Stars (Service), 1990
Under Black Banner (Trease), 1950
Under Dog, and Other Stories (Christie), 1929
Under Pressure (Herbert), 1974
Under the Autumn Garden (Mark), 1977
Under the Lilacs (Alcott), 1878
Under the North Star (T. Hughes), 1981
Under the Orange Grove (Dillon), 1968
Under the Sun and Over the Moon (Crossley-Holland), 1989
Undercover Secret (Thiele), 1982
Underground Alley (Mayne), 1958
Underground Creatures (Mayne), 1983
Underground Lifestyles Handbook (Koontz), 1970
Underground Man (Meltzer), 1972
Understanding Physics (Asimov), 1966
Understanding the Floatplane (Edgerton), 1987
Undertaker's Gone Bananas (Zindel), 1978
Underwoods (Stevenson), 1887
Undying Fire: A Contemporary Novel (H. Wells), 1919
Unearthing Suite (Atwood), 1983
Uneasy Money (Brancato), 1986
Unexpected Guest (Christie), 1958
Unfinished Portrait (Christie), 1934
Unfinished Portrait of Jessica (R. Peck), 1991
Unfinished Tales of Númenór and Middle-Earth (Tolkien), 1980
Unicorn Dream (Hill), 1992

Unicorn Point (Anthony), 1989
Union Club Mysteries (Asimov), 1983
United on Vacation (Hoy), 1989
Universe Ahead: Stories of the Future (Engdahl, editor), 1975
Universe: From Flat Earth to Quasar (Asimov), 1966
Unleaving (Paton Walsh), 1976
Unseen World (Asimov), 1970
Unsleeping Sword (Trease), 1934
Until We Reach the Valley (Irwin), 1979
Unvanquished (Fast), 1942
Unwed Mother (Miklowitz), 1977
Up a Road Slowly (Hunt), 1966
Up and Down Spring (Hurwitz), 1993
Up and Down the River (Caudill), 1951
Up and Over (Smith), 1976
Up Country (Carter), 1989
Up from Jericho Tel (Konigsburg), 1986
Up Hill and Down: Stories (Coatsworth), 1947
Up in Seth's Room (N. Mazer), 1979
Up in the Tree (Atwood), 1978
Up Periscope (R. White), 1956
Up the Chimney Down (Aiken), 1984
Up to Bat (D. Hughes), 1991
Up to Low (B. Doyle), 1982
Uphill All the Way (L. Hall), 1984
Ups and Downs of Carl Davis III (Guy), 1989
Upton Sinclair Anthology (Sinclair), 1934
Upton Sinclair: Biographical and Critical Opinions (Sinclair), 1917
Upton Sinclair: Four Unpublished Letters (Sinclair), 1984
Upton Sinclair on "Comrade" Kautsky (Sinclair), 1931
Upton Sinclair on the Soviet Union (Sinclair), 1938
Upton Sinclair Presents William Fox (Sinclair), 1933
Upton Sinclair's Last Will and Testament (Sinclair), 1934
Urgent Copy: Literary Studies (Burgess), 1968
Urn Burial (Westall), 1987
Us and Uncle Fraud (Lowry), 1984
Us Maltbys (Means), 1966
Utopia 14 (Vonnegut), 1954

Vacant Country (H. Wells), 1899
Vagabundos (Bonham), 1969
Vailima Letters: Robert Louis Stevenson to Sidney Colvin, 1890-
    1894 (Stevenson), 1895
Vainglory (McCaughrean), 1991
Vale of the Vole (Anthony), 1987
Valentine (Garfield), 1977
Valentine Bears (Bunting), 1983
Valentine Rosy (Greenwald), 1984
Valerie Valentine Is Missing (Walden), 1971
Valley Between (Thiele), 1981
Valley of Broken Cherry Trees (Namioka), 1980
Valley of Deer (Dunlop), 1989
Valley of Fear (A. Doyle), 1914
Valley of Spiders (H. Wells), 1964
Valley of the Moon (London), 1913
Vampire (Cusick), 1991
Vampire Chronicles (Rice), 1989
Vampire Chronicles series (Rice), from 1976
Vampire Lestat (Rice), 1985
Vampires (Garden), 1973
Vampires (Yolen), 1991

Woods at the End of Autumn Street (Lowry), 1987
Woodsong (Paulsen), 1990
Wool (Cavanna), 1972
Wool-Pack (Harnett), 1951
Word of Warning (A. Doyle), 1928
Word or Two with You: New Rhymes for Young Readers (Merriam), 1981
Word Power in 5 Easy Lessons: A Simplified Approach to Excellence in Grammar, Punctuation, Sentence Structure, Spelling and Penmanship (Armstrong), 1969
Word to Caesar (Trease), 1956
Wordhoard: Anglo-Saxon Stories (Crossley-Holland), 1969
Wordhoard: Anglo-Saxon Stories (Paton Walsh), 1969
Words and Music (Mayne), 1963
Words and Their Meanings (Huxley), 1940
Words by Heart (Sebestyen), 1979
Words from Exodus (Asimov), 1963
Words from History (Asimov), 1968
Words from the Myths (Asimov), 1961
Words in Genesis (Asimov), 1962
Words of Science and the History behind Them (Asimov), 1959
Words on the Map (Asimov), 1962
Work and Turn (Spiegelman), 1979
Work, Wealth, and Happiness of Mankind (H. Wells), 1931
Work: A Story of Experience (Alcott), 1873
Working Days: The Journals of the Grapes of Wrath (Steinbeck), 1989
Works (H. Wells), 1924
Works (H. Wells), 1926-27
Works (Wright), 1991
World Almanac: The Complete 1868 Original and Selections from 25, 50, and 100 Years Ago (Foley, editor), 1992
World Brain (H. Wells), 1938
World Eater (Swindells), 1981
World, Its Debts, and the Rich Men (H. Wells), 1922
World Minus Zero: An SF Anthology (Chambers, editor), 1971
World of Aldous Huxley: An Omnibus of His Fiction and Non-Fiction over Three Decades (Huxley), 1947
World of Carbon (Asimov), 1958
World of Ellen March (Eyerly), 1964
World of Farley Mowat: A Selection (Mowat), 1980
World of Light: A Comedy in Three Acts (Huxley), 1931
World of Nitrogen (Asimov), 1958
World of Our Fathers: The Jews of Eastern Europe (Meltzer), 1974
World of Ray Bradbury (Bradbury), 1964
World of Strangers (Gordimer), 1958
World of William Clissold: A Novel at a New Angle (H. Wells), 1926
World Series (Tunis), 1941
World Set Free: A Story of Mankind (H. Wells), 1914
World to Win, 1940-1942 (Sinclair), 1946
World Upside Down (Mayne), 1954
World Wreckers (Bradley), 1971
World's End (Sinclair), 1940
World's End (Vinge), 1984
Worlds beyond Dune: The Best of Frank Herbert (Herbert), 1987
Worlds of Anne McCaffrey (McCaffrey), 1981
Worlds of Frank Herbert (Herbert), 1970
Worlds within Worlds: The Story of Nuclear Energy (Asimov), 1972
Worm and the Ring (Burgess), 1961

Worm Charmers (Fisk), 1989
Worms of Kukumlima (Pinkwater), 1981
Worthing Chronicle (Card), 1983
Worthing Saga (Card), 1990
Would You Settle for Improbable? (Petersen), 1981
Wounded Sky (Duane), 1983
Wounded Wolf (George), 1978
Wraiths of Time (Norton), 1976
Wreath for a Bridal (Plath), 1970
Wreck of the Saginaw (Robertson), 1954
Wrecker (Stevenson), 1892
Wright Brothers: How They Invented the Airplane (Freedman), 1991
Wrinkle in Time (L'Engle), 1962
Write On Rosy!: A Young Author in Crisis (Greenwald), 1988
Writer's Experience (Ellison), 1964
Writer's Prospect—III: Censorship and Spoken Literature (Huxley), 1956
Writing in Reality (Tchudi), 1978
Writing on the Hearth (Harnett), 1971
Writing on the Wall (Garfield), 1982
Writing on the Wall (Reid Banks), 1981
Writing Popular Fiction (Koontz), 1973
Writing to Survive: The Private Notebooks of Conrad Richter (C. Richter), 1988
Writing Young Adult Novels (Irwin), 1988
Wrong Box (Stevenson), 1889
Wulf (Crossley-Holland), 1988
Wyndcliffe (Lawrence), 1974
Wyrms (Card), 1987

X Factor (Norton), 1965
X Stands for Unknown (Asimov), 1984
Xanadu Manuscript (J. Townsend), 1977
Xenocide (Card), 1991
Xenogenesis series (Butler), from 1987

Yang the Youngest and his Terrible Ear (Namioka), 1992
Yankee at the Court of King Arthur (Twain), 1889
Yankee Privateer (Norton), 1955
Yarn: The Things It Makes and How to Make Them (Meyer), 1972
Yaxley's Cat (Westall), 1991
Yea! Wildcats! (Tunis), 1944
Year and a Day (Furlong), 1990
Year and a Day (Mayne), 1976
Year King (Farmer), 1977
Year of Prophesying (H. Wells), 1924
Year of Sweet Senior Insanity (Levitin), 1982
Year of the Currawong (Spence), 1965
Year of the Gopher (Naylor), 1987
Year of the Jeep (Robertson), 1968
Year of the Lucy (McCaffrey), 1986
Yearling (Rawlings), 1938
Yellow Aeroplane (Mayne), 1968
Yellow Blue Jay (Hurwitz), 1986
Yellow-Jacket Jock (Thiele), 1969
Yellow Raft in Blue Water (Dorris), 1987
Yellow Warning (Cavanna), 1951
Yesterday (Geras), 1992
Yesterday's Daughter (Calvert), 1986
Yesterday's Island (Bunting), 1979

CONTRIBUTORS

AGEE, Hugh. Professor of English Education, University of Georgia, Athens; Past President of the Assembly on Literature for Adolescents (ALAN) of NCTE. Contributor of articles and reviews to *ALAN Review* and other publications. **Essays:** Robbie Branscum; Robert Burch; Gary Paulsen; Robert Newton Peck; Ann Rinaldi.

ALBERGHENE, Janice M. Associate Professor of English, Fitchburg State College, Massachusetts. Author of numerous articles on children's literature, including "Moralists, But with No Pretense," 1988, "Humor in Children's Literature," 1988, and "Artful Memory: Jean Fritz, Autobiography and the Child Reader," 1989. Past President of the Children's Literature Association. **Essays:** M.E. Kerr; Daniel Manus Pinkwater.

ANTCZAK, Janice. Professor, Brookdale Community College, Lincroft, New Jersey. Author of *Science Fiction: The Mythos of a New Romance,* published by Neal-Schuman, 1985, and an essay on Pamela Sargent for *Twentieth-Century Children's Writers.* **Essays:** Jay Bennett; Pamela Sargent.

APSELOFF, Marilyn F. Associate Professor of English, Kent State University, Ohio. Author of *Virginia Hamilton: Ohio Explorer in the World of Imagination,* 1978; *Nonsense Literature for Children: From Aesop to Seuss* (with Celia Catlett Anderson), 1989, *They Wrote for Children Too: An Annotated Bibliography of Children's Literature in Education,* and of essays in *World Book Encyclopedia, Illinois English Bulletin, Children's Literature in Education,* and other periodicals. **Essay:** Joan Blos.

ATKINSON, Judith. Head of English Department, Wolfreton School. Author of numerous articles on English teaching, including contributions to *Developing Response to Fiction,* 1983, and *Teaching Literature for Examinations,* 1986. **Essays:** Jill Paton Walsh; Barbara Willard.

BARKER, Keith. Librarian, Westhill College, Birmingham; review editor, *School Librarian;* former editor, *Youth Library Review;* Vice Chair, Youth Libraries Group of the U.K. Library Association. Author of *In the Realms of Gold,* 1986, *Bridging the Gap,* and monographs on Gillian Cross and Dick King-Smith; contributor, *Twentieth-Century Children's Writers.* **Essays:** Farrukh Dhondy; Monica Furlong; Christine Nostlinger; Phillip Pullman; Rosemary Wells.

BARON, Henry J. Department of English, Calvin College, Grand Rapids, Michigan. **Essays:** Lorenz Graham; Stephen Tchudi.

BARROW, Craig W. Instructor, Department of English, University of Tennessee at Chattanooga. Author of articles about science fiction, contemporary fiction, drama in performance, and issues in humanities; author of *Montage in James Joyce's Ulysses.* Contributor to *Beacham's Guide to Literature for Young Adults.* **Essays:** Ernest J. Gaines; William Golding.

BELVISO, Melanie. Freelance writer. **Essays:** Lynn Hall; R.R. Knudson; Anne McCaffrey; Spider Robinson.

BENSON, Linda G. Instructor in English, Southwest Missouri State University, Montana; doctorate student, Illinois State University. **Essays:** Octavia Butler; Vonda N. McIntyre.

BERNSTEIN, Sharon Clontz. Librarian for the Blind and Physically Handicapped, South Georgia Regional Library, Valdosta, Georgia. **Essays:** Kristin Hunter; Lois Ruby; Pamela F. Service; Maureen Crane Wartski; Brenda Wilkinson.

BLOOM, Susan P. Director and Assistant Professor, Center for the Study of Children's Literature, Simmons College, Boston. **Essays:** Russell Freedman; Milton Meltzer; Rita Williams-Garcia.

BRADLEY, Patricia L. Instructor in English, Western Kentucky University, Bowling Green. **Essays:** Paula Danziger; Irene Hunt.

BUCHANAN, Bill. Librarian, Ramsey Library, University of North Carolina, Asheville. **Essays:** Margaret Mahy; Jean Davies Okimoto.

BUTTS, Dennis. Freelance writer and critic; editor, *Henty Society Bulletin.* Former Principal Lecturer in English, Bulmershe College of Higher Education, Reading, Berkshire. Author of *Living Words* (with John Merrick), 1966, and *R.L. Stevenson,* 1966. Editor of *Pergamon Poets 8,* 1970, *Good Writers for Young Readers: Critical Essays,* 1977, and *The Secret Garden,* 1987. **Essay:** Robert Louis Stevenson.

CART, Michael. Former director of California Public Library, Beverly Hills; now full-time writer and critic of young adult literature. **Essays:** Bruce Brooks; John Donovan.

CHANCE, Rosemary. Middle school librarian; instructor of children's and young adult literature, Department of Library Science, Sam Houston State University, Texas; member of Young Adult Library Services Association of the American Library Association. **Essays:** Willo Davis Roberts; Jerry Spinelli.

CHAPMAN, Edgar L. Ph.D. in English literature; author of numerous articles on science fiction including an essay on T.H. White for *Twentieth-Century Science Fiction Writers;* contributor to *Beacham's Guide to Literature for Young Adults.* **Essays:** Edgar Rice Burroughs; Aldous Huxley.

CHASTON, Joel D. Instructor in young adult literature, Southwest Missouri State University, Montana; coauthor of *Growing into Theme Study* and articles on young adult writers; contributor to several journals and reference volumes, including *Beacham's Guide to Literature for Young Adults* and *Dictionary of Literary Biography.* **Essays:** S.E. Hinton; Mollie Hunter; Ellen Raskin.

CHAUVETTE, Cathy. Reviewer, *School Library Journal,* "Adult Books for YAs"; coauthor "Easy Talking;" contributor to "Up for Discussion," "How Do You Manage," and *Twentieth-Century Science Fiction Writers.* **Essays:** Marion Zimmer Bradley; R.A. MacAvoy.

CLINE, Ruth K.J. Coauthor of a column in the *ALAN Review;* author of *Focus on Families,* 1990, a resource book for young adults; currently revising a text on young adult literature with Bill McBride. **Essay:** Will Hobbs.

COLLINS, Carol Jones. Librarian, Montclair Kimberley Academy, New Jersey; author of article "A Tool for Change: Young Adult Literature in the Lives of Young Adult African Americans," in *Library Trends.* **Essay:** Jim Haskins.

CREANY, Anne Drolett. Assistant Professor of Education, Clarion University of Pennsylvania. **Essays:** Marion Dane Bauer; Walter Farley; Virginia Hamilton; Mary Stolz.

CREW, Hilary S. Ph.D. candidate, School of Communications, Information, and Library Studies, Rutgers University, New Brunswick, New Jersey. Author of "Blossom Culp and Her Ilk: The Independent Female in Richard Peck's Young Adult Fiction" in *Top of the News,* 1987, and "From Labyrinth to Celestial City: Setting and Portrayal of the Female Adolescent in Science Fiction" in *Youth Services in Libraries,* 1988; contributor, *Twentieth-Century Children's Writers.* **Essays:** Robin McKinley; Richard Peck.

DAVIS, Hazel K. Instructor, Ohio University, Athens; Past President of ALAN. Author of essays in *Beacham's Guide to Literature for Young Adults* and teaching guides for Bantam on *Animal Farm* and *A Midsummer Night's Dream.* **Essays:** Jenny Davis; William Sleator; Zilpha Keatley Snyder.

DAVIS, J. Madison. Professor of Journalism and head of the professional writing program at the University of Oklahoma. Author of *The Murder of Frau Schütz; Red Knight;* author of numerous works of nonfiction; lectures internationally. **Essays:** Ralph Ellison; Harold Keith.

DILL, Lesa. Assistant Professor of English, Western Kentucky University, Bowling Green; Ph.D. in English and linguistics. **Essays:** Richard Adams; V.C. Andrews; Piers Anthony; Isaac Asimov; Peter Beagle; Phyllis A. Whitney.

DINGLEY, Robert. Senior Lecturer in English, University of New England, Australia. Contributor to *Dictionary of Literary Biography Series, The Victorian Fantasists, Makers of Nineteenth-Century Culture* and other reference guides. **Essays:** Agatha Christie; Sue Townsend.

DISHNOW, Ruth E. District librarian, School District of Rib Lake, Wisconsin; President, Wisconsin Association of School Librarians; Member, ALA Best Books for Young Adults Committee. **Essay:** Tamora Pierce.

DOXEY, Carol. Librarian, South Georgia Regional Library, Valdosta. Former librarian, Estherville Public Library, Iowa. **Essays:** C.S. Adler; Sandy Asher; June Foley; Betty Miles; P.J. Petersen; Marilyn Sachs; Harriet May Savitz; Marilyn Singer; Jan Slepian; Amelia Elizabeth Walden; Maia Wojciechowska.

DRENNAN, William Ryland. Associate Professor of English, University of Wisconsin Center-Baraboo/Sauk County. Contributor to *Beacham's Guide to Literature for Young Adults.* **Essay:** Patricia Windsor.

DUKE, Charles R. Dean, College of Education and Human Services, Clarion University, Pennsylvania; reviewer, *ALAN Review;* coeditor of *Poets' Perspectives;* editor of *Exercise Exchange;* director of Penn Rivers Writing Project, an affiliate of the National Writing Project. **Essays:** Maureen Daly; Conrad Richter.

DUNLOP, Eileen. Writer of novels for children and young adults, including *The Maze Stone, Clementina, The House on the Hill, The Valley of Deer, Finn's Island,* and *Green Willow's Secret.* Former

headmistress, Preparatory School of Dollar Academy. **Essays:** Josephine Kamm; Joan Lingard; Geraldine McCaughrean.

EAGLEN, Audrey. Order Department Manager, Cuyahoga County Public Library, Cleveland; Assistant Professor, Kent State University, Kent, Ohio; contributing editor, *Collection Building;* columnist, *School Library Journal;* reviewer, *New York Times Book Review* and other journals. Author of *Buying Books: A Practical Guide for Librarians,* 1989. **Essays:** Anonymous (*Go Ask Alice*); Francesca Lia Block; Judy Blume; Lois Duncan; Norma Klein; Barbara Wersba.

EDWARDS, Edna Earl. Instructor, West Georgia College, Carrollton; reviewer, *ALAN Review;* author of two young adult biographies for Salem Press. **Essays:** Robin F. Brancato; Gloria Miklowitz.

ELLEMAN, Barbara. Editor, Children's Books Section, American Library Association *Booklist,* Chicago. Contributor, *Twentieth-Century Children's Writers.* **Essay:** Nancy Bond.

ENO, Laurie Ann. Graduate student, Center for the Study of Children's Literature, Simmons College. **Essay:** Rosa Guy.

ERICSON, Bonnie O. Associate Professor of English Education, California State University, Northridge. Former high school teacher; active in National Council of Teachers of English, the California Association of Teachers of English, and ALAN/NCTE; reviewer, *ALAN Review;* wrote a column in *California English* for five years. **Essays:** Christopher Crutcher; Hadley Irwin.

ESSELMAN, Mary D. Instructor and coordinator of writing program, Georgetown University, Washington, D.C. Contributor, *Beacham's Guide to Literature for Young Adults.* **Essays:** Sandra Cisneros; Terry McMillan.

EVANS, Gwyneth. Instructor, Malaspina University College, Vancouver Island, British Columbia. Contributor to *Canadian Children's Literature;* author of numerous articles on children's literature, including five entries just completed for the *Dictionary of Literary Biography* volumes on English children's writers. **Essays:** John Christopher; Kit Pearson; K.M. Peyton; Geoffrey Trease.

EVANS, Ron. Professor of English and former Dean of Arts and Sciences, University of West Florida, Pensacola: author of three monographs, numerous journal articles, and three books. **Essays:** Ken Kesey; J.D. Salinger; Kurt Vonnegut.

FORMAN, Jack. Reference/bibliographic services librarian, Mesa College Library, San Diego; book reviewer for *Library Journal, School Library Journal,* and *Journal of Youth Services in Libraries.* Author of *Presenting Paul Zindel,* 1988, and of several articles on children's literature. **Essays:** Robert Lipsyte; Nicholasa Mohr; Walter Dean Myers; Chaim Potok; Paul Zindel.

FULLER, Lawrence B. Instructor, Bloomsburg University, Pennsylvania; contributor, *Beacham's Guide to Literature for Young Adults.* **Essays:** Phil Caputo; Sandra Scoppettone.

GARRETT, Linda. High school librarian; Ph.D. candidate, Texas Woman's University, Denton; author of two articles for *Masterplots* series and a book of media center skills for Neal-Schuman Press. **Essays:** Jean Fritz; Kathryn Lasky.

GIBSON, Lois Rauch. Professor of English and Chair of the Department of Language and Literature at Coker College, Hartsville, South Carolina. **Essay:** Mark Mathabane.

GLEASON, Virginia L. Children's librarian, Springfield-Greene County Public Library, Missouri. Author of a children's book review column for ten years for Gannett Press's Pennywhistle Press. **Essays:** James Houston; Theodore Taylor.

GOULD, Karen J. Freelance writer. **Essays:** C.J. Cherryh; Ayn Rand; Joan D. Vinge.

GREENLAW, M. Jean. Recipient of Arbuthnot Award, for outstanding teaching of children's literature. Professor of Education, University of North Texas, Denton; book review editor, *New Advocate;* Chair of the NCTE Poetry Award Committee. Author of *Storybook Classrooms: Using Children's Literature in the Learning Center-Primary Grades* (with Karla H. Wendelin), 1984, and *Educating the Gifted: A Sourcebook* (with Margaret E. McIntosh), 1988. **Essays:** H.M. Hoover; Carolyn Meyer; Zibby Oneal; Meredith Ann Pierce; Ouida Sebestyen.

GRONER, Marlene San Miguel. Department of Humanities, State University of New York, College, Farmingdale. Coauthor, *A Blueprint for Writers,* 1992; contributor, *Beacham's Guide to Literature for Young Adults.* **Essay:** Robert Heinlein.

GUTTENBERG, Laurie Schwartz. Instructor, State University of New York, College at Farmingdale and College at Old Westbury. **Essays:** Jeannette Eyerly; Howard Fast; Joanne Greenberg; Betty Cavanna.

HAGEN, Lyman B. Professor of English, Arkansas State University; author of books and articles on a wide range of American writers; contributor, *Beacham's Guide to Literature for Young Adults.* **Essay:** Maya Angelou.

HAMLEY, Dennis. University instructor, Hertfordshire; school librarian; reviewer, *The School Librarian* and *Times Educational Supplement;* organizes the *Lending Our Minds Out* residential creative writing courses for children. Author of children's books, including *Hare's Choice, Badger's Fate, Tigger and Friends,* and *The War and Freddy.* **Essays:** Nicholas Fisk; Robert Leeson; Robert Swindells.

HANNIGAN, Jane Anne. Professor Emerita, Columbia University, New York; editor, *The Best of Library Literature.* Author and editor of numerous articles and books; contributor, *Twentieth-Century Children's Writers.* **Essays:** Annette Curtis Klause; Sonia Levitin.

HELLER, Terry. Department of English, Coe College, Cedar Rapids, Iowa. Contributor, *Beacham's Guide to Literature for Young Adults, Dictionary of Literary Biography,* and Salem Press publications; author of *The Turn of the Screw: Bewildered Vision.* **Essays:** Orson Scott Card; Frank Herbert.

HIGGINS, James E. Professor of Education, Queens College, City University of New York. Author of *Beyond Words: Mystical Fancy in Children's Literature,* 1970; contributor, *Twentieth-Century Children's Writers.* **Essay:** Mark Twain.

HILL, Elbert R. Professor of children's and adolescent literature, Southeastern Oklahoma State University, Durant. Contributor, *Beacham's Guide to Literature for Young Adults.* **Essay:** Leon Garfield.

HILL, Patricia. Elementary school teacher, Vancouver, British Columbia; graduate student, Children's Literature, Center for the Study of Children's Literature, Simmons College, Boston; intern for the managing editor, *Horn Book* Magazine; member, Children's Literature Roundtable, Vancouver, and Canadian Children's Book Center. **Essays:** Brian Doyle; Sarah Ellis; Elizabeth George Speare.

HIMMEL, Maryclare O'Donnell. Graduate, Center for the Study of Children's Literature, Simmons College, Boston. Contributor, *Sixth Book of Junior Authors and Illustrators* and *A Reader's Companion to Twentieth Century Children's Literature;* editor for children's books, *Boston Globe.* **Essays:** Eve Bunting; Sheila Greenwald.

HOLLINDALE, Peter. Instructor in English, York University, England; author of *Choosing Books for Children,* 1974, *Ideology and the Children's Book,* 1988, and several articles on children's literature and drama; contributor, *Twentieth-Century Children's Writers.* **Essays:** Jan Needle; Mary Stewart.

HUNT, Caroline C. Department of English, College of Charleston, South Carolina. Contributor of numerous articles to various publications, including *Beacham's Guide to Literature for Young Adults* and *Dictionary of Literary Biography.* **Essays:** Vivien Alcock; Cynthia Harnett; Michelle Magorian.

ISKANDER, Sylvia Patterson. Professor of English, University of Southwestern Louisiana, Lafayette; guest editor, *Children's Literature Quarterly,* 1989. Author of *Rousseau's Emile and Early Children's Literature,* 1971, and of the entry on Isaac Bashevis Singer in *Dictionary of Literary Biography,* and other articles on children's literature, including "Arabic Adventurers and American Investigators: Cultural Values in Adolescent Detective Fiction" for *Children's Literature;* contributor, *Twentieth-Century Children's Writers.* **Essay:** Robert Cormier; Cynthia Voigt.

JENKINSON, David Professor and Associate Dean, Faculty of Education, University of Manitoba, Winnipeg; columnist, "Portraits," *Emergency Librarian.* Author of essays in *Profiles* and *Meeting the Challenge,* and contributor to *The Junior Encyclopedia of Canada* and *Twentieth-Century Children's Writers.* **Essay:** Kevin Major.

JOHN, Judith Gero. Assistant Professor of Literature, Southwest Missouri State University, Springfield. Author of several articles; contributor, *Dictionary of Literary Biography.* **Essays:** Dean Hughes; John Rowe Townsend.

JOHNSON, Deidre. Assistant Professor, West Chester University, Pennsylvania. Editor of *Stratemeyer Pseudonyms and Series Books: An Annotated Bibliography of Stratemeyer and Stratemeyer Syndicate Publications,* 1983; author of numerous essays on series books and children's literature; contributor, *Twentieth-Century Children's Writers.* **Essays:** Ellen Conford; Keith Robertson.

JOHNSTON, Susanne L. Former lecturer in English, University of Wisconsin, Stout, Menominee, Wisconsin. Reviewer, *ALAN Re-*

view; coauthor (with Elizabeth Poe) of *Focus on Relationships,* forthcoming. **Essays:** Jean Craighead George; Chap Reaver.

JONES, Patrick. Manager, Tecumseh Branch, Allen County Public Library, Fort Wayne, Indiana. **Essays:** Christopher Pike; R.L. Stine.

KAMM, Antony. Author, editor, and critic; part-time lecturer, Department of English Studies, University of Stirling. Former Chairman, Children's Book Group, Publishers Association, and Children's Book Circle. Author of *Books and the Teacher* (with Boswell Taylor), 1966, *Choosing Books for Younger Children,* 1977, and of information books for children. Editor of *Scottish Traditional Rhymes* (with Eileen Dunlop), 1985, *An Irish Childhood* (with A.N. Jeffares), 1987, and *A Jewish Childhood* (with A.N. Jeffares), 1988; contributor, *Twentieth-Century Children's Writers.* **Essays:** Anne Frank; Rosemary Sutcliff; Henry Treece.

KAYWELL, Joan F. Instructor, University of South Florida, Tampa. Former teacher of high school English, Kathleen High School, Lakeland, Florida. Member, Board of Directors for ALAN; member, Advisory Board for NCTE's Achievement Awards in Writing and the NCATE/NCTE Folio Review Committee; and Executive Secretary for the Florida Council of Teachers of English (FCTE). Contributor to numerous journals, including *ALAN Review;* author, *Adolescent Literature as a Complement to the Classics* and *Adolescents At Risk: Fiction and Nonfiction for Young Adults, Parents, and Professionals.* **Essay:** Bette Greene.

KEENAN, Hugh T. Professor of English, Georgia State University, Atlanta. Author of articles on Old English, Middle English, and medieval literature; essays on James Marshall, Doris B. Smith, Molesworth, Robert Burch, and Joel Chandler Harris. Editor of *Papers by Medievalists,* 1971, *Narrative Theory and Children's Literature, Typology and English Medieval Literature,* 1992, "Narrative Theory and Children's Literature" issue of *Studies in the Literary Imagination,* 1985, and *Joel Chandler Harris: The Author in His Time and Ours,* 1986; contributor, *Twentieth-Century Children's Writers.* **Essays:** Shirley Rousseau Murphy; Doris Buchanan Smith; T.H. White.

KENNEY, Donald J. Academic Librarian, Assistant to the University Librarian, Virginia Polytechnic Institute and State University; former middle school librarian; coeditor, American Library Association's *Journal of Youth Services in Libraries (JOY);* editor, "Library Connection" column, *ALAN Review;* former coeditor of the "Young Adult Literature" column in the *English Journal.* Contributor of articles on young adult literature, library literacy, and reference service to various journals. **Essays:** Frank Bonham; Katherine Paterson.

KIES, Cosette. Chair and Professor, Department of Library and Information Studies, Northern Illinois University. Author of numerous articles and books, including *Supernatural Fiction for Teens,* 1992, *Presenting Young Adult Horror Fiction,* 1992, and *Presenting Lois Duncan,* 1994. **Essay:** Richie Tankersley Cusick.

KINGMAN, Lee. Director, *Horn Book,* Boston; former assistant and juvenile editor, Houghton Mifflin, Boston; book editor, poster and calendar designer. Contributor, *Twentieth-Century Children's Writers;* author of numerous books for children and adults. **Essays:** Esther Forbes; Florence Crannell Means; Howard Pyle.

LAFFERTY, Fiona. Freelance editor and writer. Former editor of *British Book News Children's Books;* children's books editor of *The Daily Telegraph;* advisor to *Good Book Guide* and compiler of the annual *Good Book Guide to Children's Books;* contributor, *Twentieth-Century Children's Writers.* **Essays:** Kenneth Lillington; Judith O'Neill.

LAWRENCE, Keith. Assistant Professor, American Literature, Brigham Young University, Provo, Utah. **Essays:** Eloise Jarvis McGraw; Toni Morrison; Farley Mowat; Lensey Namioka; Amy Tan; Jessamyn West; Robb White.

LENTZ, Kate. Graduate student, Center for the Study of Children's Literature, Simmons College, Boston. **Essays:** Ann Head; Linda Hoy; Hans Peter Richter.

LENTZ, Parish. Middle school teacher, Providence Country Day School, Rhode Island. **Essay:** Glendon Swarthout.

LESESNE, Teri S. University instructor of children's and young adult literature. Contributor of reviews to various journals. **Essays:** Terry Davis; Mel Glenn.

LEWIS, Leon. Professor of English, Appalachian State University, Boone. Author of contemporary poetry and film, and *Henry Miller: The Major Writings,* 1986; contributor, *Beacham's Guide to Literature for Young Adults.* **Essays:** Langston Hughes; June Jordan.

LIVINGSTON, Myra Cohn. Senior Extension Instructor, University of California, Los Angeles; lecturer on poetry; former creative-writing instructor for children, Dallas Public Library; instructor, Los Angeles County Museum of Art, Beverly Hills Public Library, and University of California Elementary School, Los Angeles; former instructor and poet-in-residence, Beverly Hills Unified School District. Contributor, *Twentieth-Century Children's Writers;* author of fiction and poetry for children and adults. **Essays:** Arnold Adoff; Harry Behn; Paul Janeczko; Eve Merriam.

LOWE-EVANS, Mary. Instructor, University of West Florida, Pensacola. Author of *Crimes against Fecundity: Joyce and Population Control,* 1989 and *Frankenstein: Mary Shelley's Wedding Guest,* 1993. **Essays:** Margaret Atwood; Anthony Burgess; Eilis Dillon; Nadine Gordimer; Sylvia Plath.

LOWERY-MOORE, Hollis. Chair of Language, Literacy, and Special Populations, Sam Houston State University, Huntsville; teacher of middle and secondary school reading. Contributor to several journals, including *Exercise Exchange* and the *ALAN Review.* **Essays:** Janet Bode; Madeleine L'Engle; Louise Moeri; Cynthia Rylant.

LYSTAD, Mary. Research Sociologist, National Institute of Mental Health, Washington, D.C. Author of *As They See It: Changing Values of College Youth,* 1973, *Violence at Home,* 1974, *A Child's World as Seen in His Stories and Drawings,* 1974, *From Dr. Mather to Dr. Seuss: 200 Years of American Books for Children,* 1980, *At Home in America,* 1984, and several books for children, including *Millicent the Monster,* 1968, and *The Halloween Parade,* 1973; contributor, *Twentieth-Century Children's Writers.* **Essays:** Joan Aiken; William Armstrong; Olive Ann Burns; Betsy C. Byars; Eleanor Cameron; Rebecca Caudill; Bill and Vera Cleaver; Bruce Clements; Hila Colman; Clyde Edgerton; Nikki Giovanni; E.L. Konigsburg;

Elizabeth Foreman Lewis; Sharon Bell Mathis; Harry Mazer; Norma Fox Mazer; Emily Neville; Joan Lowery Nixon; Scott O'Dell; John Tunis; Alice Walker; Richard Wright.

MAPPIN, Alf. Editor of three Australian journals about children's literature: *Magpies, The Literature Base,* and *Papers: Explorations into Children's Literature.* **Essay:** Allan Baillie.

McEWEN, Fred. Professor of English, Waynesburg College, Pennsylvania. Author of numerous articles; contributor, *Beacham's Guide to Literature for Young Adults.* **Essays:** John Knowles; Jack London; Upton Sinclair; H.G. Wells.

McKINNEY, Caroline S. High school teacher. Contributor of articles on young adult literature to *English Journal, ALAN Review, Beacham's Guide to Literature for Young Adults,* and Instructor's *Middle Years.* **Essays:** Pam Conrad; Frances A. Miller; Joyce Carol Thomas; Ellen Emerson White.

MERCIER, Cathryn M. Associate Director and Assistant Professor, Center for the Study of Children's Literature, Simmons College, Boston; former Chair, *Boston Globe-Horn Book* Award and member, 1994 Caldecott Committee. Author of *Presenting Zibby Oneal* (with Susan Bloom) and reviews for *Five Oaks.* **Essays:** Brock Cole; Amy Ehrlich; Paula Fox; Cynthia D. Grant.

MILLER, Etta. Instructor, Curriculum & Instruction, Texas Christian University, Fort Worth; teacher of reading methods courses that incorporate the use of children's literature as the center of a focused unit; developed drama strategies for helping students respond to literature. Contributor, *Beacham's Guide to Literature for Young Adults.* **Essays:** Jean Little; Jane Yolen.

MILLICHAP, Joseph R. Professor of English, Western Kentucky University, Bowling Green. Author of four books and more than fifty articles on American literature; contributor, *Beacham's Guide to Literature for Young Adults.* **Essays:** Carson McCullers; Margaret Mitchell; John Steinbeck.

MOE, Christian H. Professor of Theatre, Southern Illinois University, Carbondale; member of the Advisory Board, Institute of Outdoor Drama; director of Playwrights' Program, Association for Theater in Higher Education; associate member, Dramatists' Guild. Author of *Creating Historical Drama* (with George McCalmon), 1965, and of an essay on D.H. Lawrence as playwright, and, with Cameron Garbutt, of several plays for children. Joint editor of *The William and Mary Theatre: A Chronicle,* 1968, "Bibliography of Theatrical Craftsmanship" (published annually in several journals), 1971-80, and *Six New Plays for Children,* 1971; contributor, *Twentieth-Century Children's Writers.* **Essays:** Nathaniel Benchley; Marjorie Kinnan Rawlings.

MORGAN, Karen Ferris. Ph.D. candidate; freelance writer. **Essays:** Michael Dorris; Jamaica Kincaid; Art Spiegelman; Laurence Yep.

MORTON, Gerald W. Department of English, Auburn University, Montgomery. Contributor, *Beacham's Guide to Literature for Young Adults.* **Essays:** James Herriot; Sterling North.

MOSBY, Charmaine Allmon. Professor of English, Western Kentucky University, Bowling Green. Contributor, *Beacham's*

Guide to Literature for Young Adults. **Essays:** Monica Hughes; Bobbie Ann Mason; N. Scott Momaday; Patricia Moyes; Anne Rice; Anne Tyler; Elizabeth Yates.

MOSLEY, Mattie J. Associate Professor of Library Science, Louisiana State University, Shreveport. Member, ALA, Louisiana Association of School Library; contributor, *Beacham's Guide to Literature for Young Adults, Masterplots II,* and *Louisiana Library Bulletin.* **Essay:** Elizabeth Gray Vining.

MURRAY, John. English Department Head, Australian Catholic University, Strathfield. Author of articles on Patricia Wrightson and Rudyard Kipling; reviewer of Australian children's literature. **Essays:** John Marsden; Patricia Wrightson.

NELSON, Claudia. Assistant Professor of English, Southwest Texas State University. Author of *Boys Will Be Girls: The Feminine Ethic and British Children's Fiction, 1857-1917* (Rutgers UP) and of assorted articles on children's literature. Forthcoming books include an anthology of essays on the social history of girlhood in Britain and America, coedited with Lynne Vallone, and a study of images of fatherhood in Victorian periodicals. **Essays:** Sylvia Louise Engdahl; Sally Watson.

NELSON, Harold. Professor of English and Literature, Minot State University, North Dakota; director of the Northern Plains Writing Project, and North Dakota State coordinator for the National Writing Project. Contributor, *Beacham's Guide to Literature for Young Adults* and *Masterplots.* **Essays:** Stephen King; Julius Lester.

NEWBERY, Linda. English teacher; reviewer, *School Librarian* and *Books for Keeps.* Author of young adult fiction, including *Run with the Hare, Hard and Fast,* and a trilogy set during World War I and in Ireland: *Some Other War, The Kind Ghosts,* and *The Weaving of the Green.* **Essay:** Jean Ure.

NIEUWENHUIZEN, Agnes. Freelance writer. **Essay:** Gillian Rubinstein.

NILSEN, Alleen Pace. Professor of English and assistant vice president of Academic Affairs, Arizona State University, Tempe. Author of *Presenting M.E. Kerr,* 1986, and *Literature of Today's Young Adults* (with Ken Donelson), 1989, and of numerous articles in *School Library Journal, College English, English Journal,* and *Language Arts;* contributor, *Twentieth-Century Children's Writers.* **Essay:** Alice Childress.

PATON WALSH, Jill. English teacher, Enfield Girls Grammar School, Middlesex; Whittall lecturer, Library of Congress, Washington, D.C. Contributor, *Twentieth-Century Children's Writers;* author of several books for children and adults. **Essays:** Nina Bawden; L.M. Boston; Penelope Farmer; Ursula K. Le Guin.

PAUSACKER, Jenny. Freelance writer of plays, educational kits, short stories and novels. Author of two novels for young adults, *What Are Ya?* and *Can You Keep a Secret?,* and her junior novel, *Fast Forward.* **Essay:** Ivan Southall.

PEARSON, Kit. Author of six children's books: *The Daring Game,* 1986, *A Handful of Time,* 1987, *The Sky Is Falling,* 1989, *The*

Singing Basket, 1990, *Looking at the Moon,* 1991, and *The Lights Go on Again,* 1993. Contributor, *Twentieth-Century Children's Writers.* **Essay:** Sylvia Cassedy.

PFLIEGER, Pat. Assistant Professor of English, West Chester University, Pennsylvania. Author of *A Reference Guide to Modern Fantasy for Children,* 1984, *Beverly Cleary,* 1991, and a forthcoming picture book for young children, *The Fog's Net.* **Essay:** Jane Langton.

PIEHL, Kathy. Assistant Professor and Reference Librarian, Mankato State University, Minnesota. Contributor of articles on children's and young adult books in *Children's Literature in Education, New Advocate, Children's Literature Association Quarterly, English Journal, Journal of Youth Services in Libraries, Voice of Advocates,* and other journals. Member, Phoenix Award Committee of the Children's Literature Association; contributor, *Children's Literature Abstracts, Dictionary of Literary Biography,* and *Twentieth-Century Romance & Historical Writers.* **Essays:** Patricia Calvert; Gillian Cross; Julie Reece Deaver; Jan Mark; Barbara Rogasky; Margaret Rostkowski; Virginia Euwer Wolff; Jane Breskin Zalben.

PINNEY, Reba. Professor of Education, Ohio University, Athens. Author of various journal articles and reviews. **Essays:** Marchette Chute; Esther Hautzig; Anne Holm.

POE, Elizabeth A. Associate Professor of English, Radford University, Virginia. Editor, *Signal.* Past President, Assembly on Literature for Adolescents of NCTE (ALAN), former book review editor, *ALAN Review,* former chair, Colorado Blue Spruce Young Adult Book Award Committee. Author of *Focus on Sexuality, Focus on Relationships,* and journal articles. **Essay:** Alden R. Carter.

PRICE, Catherine. Associate Professor, Department of Secondary Education, Valdosta State College, Georgia; former school media specialist. **Essay:** Paul Fleischman.

PROTHEROUGH, Robert. Teacher; senior lecturer. Author of seven books for teachers and lecturers, numerous articles; editor, *English in Education;* reviewer for many journals, including *Times Educational Supplement* and *School Librarian.* **Essays:** Bernard Ashley; Aidan Chambers; Peter Dickinson; Alan Garner; William Mayne; George Orwell; Robert Westall.

RANSON, Nicholas. Associate Professor of English, University of Akron; published poet and regular contributor to the *Henry Society Bulletin;* coeditor, *Ideological Approaches to Shakespeare,* 1992. **Essays:** Arthur Conan Doyle; Eve Garnett; Ted Hughes.

RAY, Sheila. Editor, *School Librarian;* retired librarian and library school lecturer in literature and librarianship for young people. Author of *Children's Fiction: A Handbook for Librarians,* 1972; *The Blyton Phenomenon,* 1982; and *Library Service to Schools,* 3rd edition, 1982; contributor of reviews and articles to several periodicals, including *Children's Literature Abstracts.* **Essays:** Eileen Dunlop; Adèle Geras.

REED, Arthea J.S. Professor and Chair, Educational Department, University of North Carolina, Asheville; reviewer, *ALAN Review.* Author of *Reaching Adolescents: The Young Adult Book and the School,* 1985; *Comics to Classics: A Parent's Guide to Books for Teens and Preteens, Teacher's Guides to the Signet Classic Steinbeck Novellas,* and numerous articles in the field of young adult literature. **Essay:** Christopher and James Lincoln Collier.

REISS, John. Instructor, Department of English, Western Kentucky University, Bowling Green. **Essay:** Jim Wayne Miller.

RICH, Susan. Graduate student, Center of the Study of Children's Literature, Simmons College, Boston. Intern, *Horn Book;* member, The Canadian Children's Book Centre. **Essays:** Nancy Garden; Norton Juster.

ROBERTS, Garyn G. Assistant Professor, Department of American Thought and Language, Michigan State University. Author and editor of several books on American literary and cultural topics, including *Dick Tracy and American Culture: Morality and Mythology, Text and Context;* recently published the article "Humor and the Apocalypse: Jack London's *The Scarlet Plague*" in *THALIA: A Journal of Literary Humor.* **Essay:** Ray Bradbury.

ROSS, Linda. Freelance writer. **Essays:** Tanith Lee; Stephen Levenkron; C.S. Lewis; Dalton Trumbo; Elie Wiesel.

RUTHERFORD, Leonie Margaret. Instructor, Department of English and Communication Studies, University of New England, Australia. Contributor, *Dictionary of Literary Biography;* wrote articles about eighteenth-century British literature, Australian literature, historical and textual bibliography, and children's literature. Member, The Association for the Study of Australian Literture (ASAL), Centre for Australian Language and Literature Studies (CALLS), Bibliographical Society of Australia and New Zealand (BSANZ). **Essays:** Jane Gardam; Robin Klein.

RUTLEDGE, Walker. Instructor in English, Western Kentucky University, Bowling Green; Director, English Honors Program. **Essays:** Eldridge Cleaver; Roald Dahl; Joseph Heller.

SAXBY, Maurice. Former English department head, lecturer, and teacher, Kuring-gai College, now University of Technology, Sydney, Australia; developed Australia's first master's program in children's literature; first national president and lifetime member of the Children's Book Council of Australia. Served as judge for the Hans Christian Andersen awards and the Australian Children's Book of the Year awards. Author of several reference works on Australian young people's literature, including *A History of Australian Children's Literature, 1841-1941; A History of Australian Children's Literature, 1941-1970;* and *The Proof of the Puddin': Australian Children's Literature, 1970-1990.* Contributor to various journals and reference works. **Essays:** Gary Crew; Simon French; Joan Phipson.

SCHMIDT, Gary D. Chairman, Department of English, Calvin College, Grand Rapids, Michigan. Reviewer for *ALAN Review.* Author of *Robert McCloskey,* 1989, *Hugh Lofting,* 1992, and *Katherine Paterson,* forthcoming. Coeditor of *The Voice of the Narrator in Children's Literature,* 1988, and *Sitting at the Feet of the Past: Retelling the North American Folktale,* 1992. **Essays:** Patricia Clapp; Minfong Ho; Felice Holman; Jean Lee Latham; Myron Levoy; Beverly Naidoo; Uri Orlev.

SEITER, Richard D. Associate Professor of English, Central Michigan University, Mount Pleasant. Author of articles on Eleanor

Cameron, Roald Dahl, Ezra J. Keats, Robert C. O'Brien, and Henry Treece. **Essay:** Jane Leslie Conly; Robert C. O'Brien.

SHELTON, Pamela L. Columnist and freelance writer. **Essay:** Gary Soto.

SHUTE, Carolyn. Graduate, Center of the Study of Children's Literature, Simmons College, Boston; Content Research Editor, Houghton Mifflin. Instructor in children's literature, University of Prince Edward Island, Charlottetown, and Northern Essex Community College, Massachusetts; reviewer, *Horn Book* Guide; contributor, "Bookviews." **Essays:** Berlie Doherty; Ron Koertge; Mildred Pitts Walter.

SMITH, Karen Patricia. Assistant Professor, Graduate School of Library and Information Studies, Queens College, Flushing; board member, Children's Literature Association. Author of *The English Psychological Fantasy Novel: A Bequest of Time,* 1985, and *Claiming a Place in the University: The Portrayal of Minorities in Seven Works by Andre Norton,* 1986; editor, with Rod McGillis, of *Special Section on Black Children's Literature* in *Children's Literature Association Quarterly,* 1988, contributor of articles and essays to several journals, including *Children's Literature Association Quarterly, Wilson Library Bulletin; School Library Journal, Journal of Youth Services in Libraries,* and *Library Trends.* **Essays:** Susan Cooper; Mildred D. Taylor.

SNYDER, Mary. Graduate student in Library and Information Science, Texas Woman's University. Director of Texas Women's University Children's Library. Instructor in Children's Literature. Teacher at the elementary and secondary levels and secondary school librarian. **Essay:** Brent Ashabranner.

SPENCER, Albert F. Assistant Professor of Education, University of Nevada, Las Vegas. Author of articles on education and book reviewer for the *Library Journal.* **Essays:** Nat Hentoff; Zoa Sherburne.

STAHL, John D. Associate Professor of English, Virginia State University and Polytechnic, Blacksburg. Author of articles in *Children's Literature, Children's Literature Association Quarterly;* contributor, *Twentieth-Century Children's Writers.* **Essays:** Katie Letcher Lyle, Phyllis Reynolds Naylor; Doris Orgel.

STERN, Madeleine B. Freelance writer; partner in Leona Rostenberg and Madeleine Stern Rare Books, New York. Author of *Imprints on History: Book Publishers and American Frontiers,* 1956, *We the Women: Career Firsts of Nineteenth-Century America,* 1963, *Heads and Headlines: The Phrenological Fowlers,* 1791, *Books and Book People in 19th-Century America,* 1978, *Between Boards: New Thoughts on Old Books* (with Leona Rostenberg), 1978, *Antiquarian Bookselling in the United States: A History from the Origins to the 1940s,* 1985, *Old and Rare: Forty Years in the Book Business* (with Leona Rostenberg), 1988, and of biographies of Margaret Fuller, Louisa May Alcott, Mrs. Frank Leslie, Isabel Barrows, and Stephen Pearl Andrews. Editor of *Women on the Move,* 1972, *The Victoria Woodhull Reader,* 1974, *Publishers for Mass Entertainment in 19th-Century America,* 1980, *Phrenological Dictionary of 19th-Century Americans,* 1982, and *Critical Essays on Louisa May Alcott,* 1984, and of *Louisa's Wonder Book,* 1975, *Behind a Mask: The Unknown Thrillers of Louisa May Alcott,* 1975,

Plots and Counterplots: More Unknown Thrillers, 1976, *A Modern Mephistopheles and Taming a Tartar,* 1987, and *A Double Life: Newly Discovered Thrillers of Louisa May Alcott,* 1988, all by Louisa May Alcott; associate editor of *Selected Letters of Louisa May Alcott,* 1988, and *The Journals of Louisa May Alcott,* 1989. **Essay:** Louisa May Alcott.

STONE, Michael. Visiting fellow and former senior lecturer, University of Wallongong. Author of several articles on James Aldridge's novels; editor, *Children's Literature and Modern Literary Theory,* 1991, and *Children's Literature: Finding an Australian Voice,* 1993. **Essays:** James Aldridge; Eleanor Spence.

STRICKLAND, Robbie W. Associate Professor of Secondary Education, Valdosta State College, Georgia; coordinator of an annual conference on young adult literature. Contributor, *ALAN Review.* **Essays:** Avi; Sue Ellen Bridgers.

SUKRAW, Tracy J. Freelance writer; reviewer of books for children and young adults; author of articles for *Episcopal Times.* **Essays:** Janine Boissard; William Gibson; Fred Gipson; Barbara Hall; Lynne Reid Banks; Muriel Spark; Walter Wangerin, Jr.

SUTHERLAND, Zena. Professor Emerita, University of Chicago Graduate Library School; associate editor, *Bulletin of the Center for Children's Books.* Author of *History in Children's Books,* 1967, *The Best in Children's Books,* 1973 (revised 1980, 1986), *Burning Bright,* 1979, *Close to the Sun,* 1979, *Barnboken i USA* with Fred Erisman), 1986, and, with M. Cunningham, *Across the World, From Sea to Shining Sea, Over the Moon, Promises to Keep, Slide down the Sky, Arbuthnot Anthology* (with May Hill Arbuthnot), 4th edition 1976, *The Arbuthnot Lectures 1970-1979,* 1980, *Children in Libraries,* 1981, and *The Scott Foresman Anthology of Children's Literature* (with Myra Cohn Livingston), 1984. **Essay:** Cornelia Lynde Meigs.

THOMAS, Gillian. Associate Professor of English, Saint Mary's University, Halifax, Nova Scotia. Author of *Harriet Martineau,* 1985, and of numerous articles and reviews on 19th-century fiction and children's literature. **Essay:** Joseph Krumgold.

TOWNSEND, John Rowe. Part-time children's books editor, *Guardian,* Manchester and London; visiting lecturer, University of Pennsylvania, Philadelphia, and University of Washington, Seattle; May Hill Arbuthnot lecturer, Atlanta; Anne Carroll Moore lecturer, New York Public Library; Whittall lecturer, Library of Congress, Washington, D.C.; faculty member, Simmons College, Boston. Contributor, *Twentieth-Century Children's Writers;* author of books for children and adults. **Essay:** Janni Howker.

TYLER, Jan. Instructor of English and German, Black River Technical College, Pocahontas, Arkansas; freelance writer of feature articles; President, Pocahontas School Board, Arkansas. Author of children's book, *Holly Lolly;* author of booklet of original skits used by and for teens in drug awareness/self esteem programs. **Essay:** Margaret Willey.

TYRKUS, Michael J. Freelance writer and filmmaker. Graduate student in English, University of Toledo, Ohio; assistant editor, Gale Research Inc., Detroit. **Essays:** Arthur C. Clarke; Michael Crichton.

VALENTIC, Suzanne M. Freelance writer and critic. **Essays:** James Baldwin; Linda Crew; Zora Neale Hurston; Suzanne Fisher Staples.

VANDERGRIFT, Kay E. Associate Professor, School of Communication, Information and Library Studies, Rutgers University, New Brunswick, New Jersey; children's book reviewer for *School Library Journal*. Author of *Child and Story: The Literary Connection,* 1980, and *Children's Literature: Theory, Research and Teaching,* 1989. **Essay:** Ntozake Shange.

WALSH, Karen E. Graduate student, Center for the Study of Children's Literature, Simmons College, Boston. Intern, *Horn Book* magazine. **Essays:** Ian Fleming; Patricia Hermes.

WHITE, Donna R. Assistant Professor of English, Clemson University, South Carolina. Editor of *Books for Children,* a review service of Clemson University English Department. Member, Modern Language Association Children's Division and Children's Literature Association. **Essays:** Lloyd Alexander; Grace Chetwin; Kevin Crossley-Holland; Carol Kendall; Patricia McKillip; Andre Norton.

WHITE, Kerry. Freelance writer and bibliographer. Author of *Australian Children's Books: A Bibliography,* 1992, *Australian Children's Fiction: The Subject Guide,* 1993, numerous articles and reviews on Australian writing, and a forthcoming book on children's poetry collections. **Essays:** Victor Kelleher; Ruth Park; Colin Thiele.

WHITEHEAD, Frank. Reader in English and Education, University of Sheffield, 1973-81; editor, *Use of English,* 1969-75. Author of *The Disappearing Dais,* 1966, *Creative Experiment,* 1970, and *Children and Their Books* (with others), 1977. **Essays:** Hester Burton; A.E. Johnson.

WIGAN, Angela. Freelance writer. **Essay:** Elizabeth Coatsworth.

WILSON, Linda. Coeditor of *Journal of Youth Services in Libraries (JOY).* Contributing annotator to *Books for You,* a publication of the National Council of Teachers of English. **Essays:** Alice Bach; Mildred Lee.

WINTERS, Louise J. Freelance writer. **Essays:** Terry Brooks; Tony Hillerman; Brian Jacques; Mercedes Lackey; Patricia Wrede.

WROBLE, Lisa A. Freelance writer and author of fiction and nonfiction for children and nonfiction for adults. Contributor to *Dictionary of Literary Biography.* Member of Society of Children's Book Writers and Illustrators and the Children's Literature Association. **Essays:** Mary Higgins Clark; Johanna Hurwitz; Dean R. Koontz; John Neufeld; Ian Serraillier; Hilma Wolitzer.

YATES, Jessica. Former librarian, the School of St. David and St. Katharine, Hornsey, London. Freelance writer; reviewer for *School Librarian, Times Educational Supplement,* the British Science Fiction Association, and the Tolkien Society. Author of *Tudors and Stuarts: An Annotated Bibliography of Children's Fiction,* 1977, the text for *A Middle-earth Album,* 1979, *Teenager to Young Adult: Recent Paperback Fiction for 13 to 19 Years,* 1986, and editor of *Dragons and Warrior Daughters: Fantasy Stories by Women Writers,* 1989. Author of articles on children's literature and librarianship in *Children's Literature in Education, Children's Book Bulletin, Books for Keeps, Times Educational Supplement,* and *School Librarian.* **Essays:** Diane Duane; Ann Halam; Douglas Hill; Allan Frewin Jones; Diana Wynne Jones; Louise Lawrence; J.R.R. Tolkien.

ZAIDMAN, Laura M. Professor of English, University of South Carolina, Sumter. Contributor to *Dictionary of Literary Biography,* and of articles in other journals. Editor of *British Children's Writers, 1880-1914,* volume of *Dictionary of Literary Biography.* Guest coeditor, with Lois Rauch Gibson, of *Children's Literature Association Quarterly,* winter 1991 issue. **Essays:** Harper Lee; Lois Lowry; Eleanora Tate.

ISBN 1-55862-202-0